STARTING OUT WITH

Visual Basic® 2008 UPDATE

Fourth Edition

Tony Gaddis

Haywood Community College

Kip Irvine

Florida International University

Addison-Wesley

Boston San Francisco New York
London Toronto Sydney Tokyo Singapore Madrid
Mexico City Munich Paris Cape Town Hong Kong Montreal

Editor in Chief: Michael Hirsch
Acquisition Editor: Matt Goldstein
Editorial Assistant: Sarah Milmore
Senior Production Supervisor: Marilyn Lloyd
Text Designer: Joyce Cosentino Wells
Cover Designer: Elena Sidorova
Online Product Manager: Bethany Tidd
Senior Media Buyer: Ginny Michaud
Marketing Manager: Erin Davis
Senior Manufacturing Buyer: Carol Melville
Production Services: Gillian Hall, The Aardvark Group

The interior of this book was composed in QuarkXPress 6.52. The main type face used in the text is Sabon. The display font is Stone Sans.

Library of Congress Cataloging-in-Publication Data
Gaddis, Tony.
Starting out with Visual Basic 2008 / Tony Gaddis, Kip Irvine. -- Updated 4th ed.
p. cm.
ISBN 978-0-13-607695-7
1. Microsoft Visual BASIC. 2. BASIC (Computer program language) I. Irvine, Kip R., 1951- II. Title.
QA76.73.B3G327 2010
005.2'762--dc22 2008055546

Addison-Wesley
is an imprint of

www.pearsonhighered.com

ISBN 13: 9780136076957
ISBN 10: 0136076955
2 3 4 5 6 7 8 9 10—EB—12 11 10 09

Locations of VideoNotes

http://www.aw.com/gaddis/vb

Contents in Brief

Contents

Preface

Welcome to *Starting Out with Visual Basic 2008 Update, Fourth Edition*. This book is intended for use in an introductory programming course. It is designed for students who have no prior programming background, but even experienced students will benefit from its depth of detail and the chapters covering databases, Web applications, and other advanced topics. The book is written in clear, easy-to-understand language and covers all the necessary topics of an introductory programming course. The text is rich in concise, practical, and real-world example programs, so the student not only learns how to use the various controls, constructs, and features of Visual Basic, but also learns why and when to use them.

Changes in the Fourth Edition

In addition to updating the book for use with Visual Basic 2008, the following pedagogical changes and quality improvements were made:

- The book has been extensively tested to ensure the highest level of quality and to eliminate errors.
- Many of the more complex tutorials have been simplified so students get actively involved in them at a quicker pace.
- The material on variables and data types in Chapter 3 has been simplified and reorganized so the student first learns about the most commonly used data types before being exposed to any of the more advanced data types.
- The section on Formatting Numbers for Output in Chapter 3 has been revised. The student now learns how to use the `ToString` method with a format string, rather than the `Format` functions that were discussed in the previous edition. This new approach greatly simplifies the process of formatting a value for output, and is used consistently throughout the rest of the book.
- The `TryParse` method is introduced in Chapter 4 as a reliable tool for converting TextBox input to other data types, and validating user input.
- Chapter 10, Working with Databases, has been revised to provide more detailed explanations and additional tutorials. The examples and tutorials now work with SQL server databases, which are directly supported by Visual Basic.

New to the Updated Fourth Edition

This special updated version of the Fourth Edition contains the following additional material:

- **Overview of LINQ**—An overview of Language Integrated Query (LINQ) has been added to Chapter 10.
- **Online VideoNotes**—An extensive series of online VideoNotes have been developed to accompany this text. Throughout the book, VideoNote icons alert the student to videos covering specific topics. Additionally, one Programming Challenge at the end of each chapter now has an accompanying video note explaining how to develop the problem's solution. The videos are available at `www.aw.com/gaddisvb`.
- **Additional Programming Problems**—Additional programming problems have been added to many of the chapters.

Visual Basic 2008 Express Edition

The book is bundled with Microsoft's Visual Basic 2008 Express Edition—a streamlined product that captures the best elements of Visual Studio in an ideal format for learning programming. The Express edition offers an impressive set of tools for developing and debugging Windows applications, including those that work with databases and use SQL.

A Look at Visual Basic: Past and Present

The first version of Visual Basic was introduced in 1991. Prior to its introduction, writing a GUI interface for an application was no small task. Typically, it required hundreds of lines of C code for even the simplest *Hello World* program. Additionally, an understanding of graphics, memory, and complex system calls were often necessary. Visual Basic was revolutionary because it significantly simplified this process. With Visual Basic, a programmer could visually design an application's user interface. Visual Basic would then generate the code necessary to display and operate the interface. This allowed the programmer to spend less time writing GUI code and more time writing code to perform meaningful tasks.

The evolution of Visual Basic from version 1 to version 6 followed a natural progression. Each new release was an improved version of the previous release, providing additional features and enhancements. Visual Basic versions offered backward compatibility, where code written in an older version was compatible with a newer version of the Visual Basic development environment.

In 2002, Microsoft released a new object-oriented software platform known as .NET. The .NET platform consists of several layers of software that sit above the operating system and provide a secure, managed environment in which programs can execute. In addition to providing a managed environment for applications to run, .NET also provided new technologies for creating Internet-based programs and programs that provide ser-vices over the Web. Along with the introduction of the .NET platform, Microsoft introduced a new version of Visual Basic known as VB .NET 2002, which allowed programmers to write desktop applications or Web applications for the .NET platform.

VB .NET was not merely a new and improved version of VB 6, however. VB .NET was a totally new programming environment, and the Visual Basic language was dramatically revised. The changes were substantial enough that programs written in earlier versions of Visual Basic were not compatible with VB .NET. Microsoft provided a utility that could be used to convert older Visual Basic applications to the new VB .NET syntax, but the results were not always perfect. Although this was frustrating for some Visual Basic developers, Microsoft reasoned the changes were necessary to ensure that Visual Basic continued to evolve as a modern, professional programming environment.

In 2003, Microsoft released VB .NET 2003, which was a minor update. VB .NET 2003 provided support for PDAs and handheld computers, and offered better compiler performance. The next version of VB was known as Visual Basic 2005. It introduced many new language features, several new controls, and many new tools for writing, editing, and debugging code.

This book is written for the most recent version of Visual Basic, which is known as Visual Basic 2008. This version of Visual Basic includes several enhancements that make Visual Basic even more powerful as a professional programming system. Many of the new features are beyond the scope of this book, so we do not cover them all. The following list summarizes some of the most significant new features of VB 2008:

- Local variable type inference
- Extension methods for existing data types

- Additional capabilities for object initialization
- Anonymous data types
- XML support
- LINQ support (Language Integrated Query)
- Lambda expressions and expression trees
- Support for partial methods
- Nullable data types
- Ternary `If` operator
- Friend assemblies
- Relaxed delegate binding

Organization of the Text

The text teaches Visual Basic 2008 step-by-step. Each chapter covers a major set of programming topics, introduces controls and GUI elements, and builds knowledge as the student progresses through the book. Although the chapters can be easily taught in their existing sequence, there is some flexibility. The following diagram suggests possible sequences of instruction.

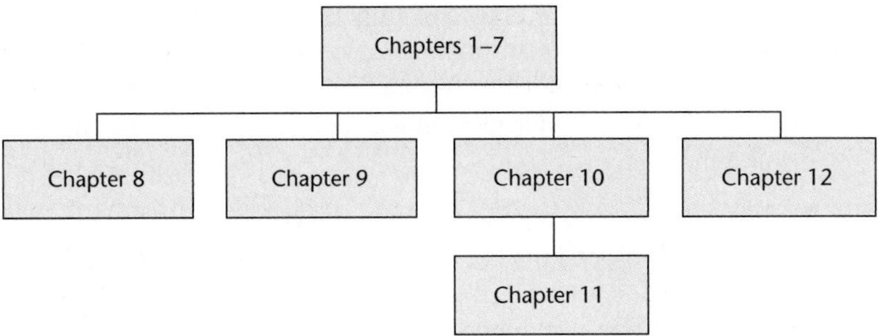

Chapters 1 through 7 cover the fundamentals of program design, flow control, modular programming, and the most important Visual Basic controls. The instructor may then continue in any order with Chapters 8, 9, 10, or 12. Part of Chapter 11 relies on database concepts, so it should be covered after Chapter 10.

Brief Overview of Each Chapter

Chapter 1: Introduction to Programming and Visual Basic. This chapter provides an introduction to programming, the programming process, and Visual Basic. Object-oriented programming and the event-driven model are explained. The components of programs, such as keywords, variables, operators, and punctuation are covered, and tools such as flowcharts and pseudocode are presented. The student gets started using the Visual Basic environment in a hands-on tutorial.

Chapter 2: Creating Applications with Visual Basic. The student starts by creating a simple application that displays a graphic image. In the tutorials that follow, the student adds controls, modifies properties, and enables the application to respond to events. An introduction to the *Visual Basic Help* system, with a tutorial on debugging, is given.

Chapter 3: Variables and Calculations. Variables, constants, and the Visual Basic data types are introduced. The student learns to gather input and create simple arithmetic statements. The intricacies of GUI design are introduced as the student learns about grouping controls with group boxes, assigning keyboard access keys, and setting the tab order. The student is introduced to exceptions and learns to write simple exception handlers. Debugging techniques for locating logic errors are covered.

Chapter 4: Making Decisions and Working with Strings. The student learns about relational operators and how to control the flow of a program with the `If...Then`, `If...Then...Else`, and `If...Then...ElseIf` statements. Logical operators are introduced, and the `Select Case` statement is covered. Important applications of these constructs are discussed, such as testing numeric values, strings, and determining if a value lies within a range. Several string-handling functions and string methods are introduced. Class-level variables, message boxes, radio buttons, and check boxes are introduced.

Chapter 5: Lists, Loops, Validation, and More. This chapter begins by showing the student how to use input boxes as a quick and simple way to gather input. Next, list boxes and combo boxes are introduced. The chapter covers repetition control structures: the `Do While`, `Do Until`, and `For...Next` loops. Counters, accumulators, running totals, and other application-related topics are discussed. Finally, the student learns about the CausesValidation property, the Validating event, the Validated event, and how these are used to perform input validation.

Chapter 6: Procedures and Functions. The student learns how and why to modularize programs with general procedures and functions. Arguments, parameters, and return values are discussed. Debugging techniques for stepping into and over procedures are introduced.

Chapter 7: Multiple Forms, Standard Modules, and Menus. This chapter shows how to add multiple forms to a project and how to create a standard module to hold procedures and functions that are not associated with a specific form. It covers creating a menu system, with commands and submenus that the user may select from.

Chapter 8: Arrays, Timers, and More. This chapter discusses both single dimension and multidimensional variable arrays. Many array programming techniques are presented, such as summing all the elements in an array, summing all the rows or columns in a two-dimensional array, searching an array for a specific value, sorting arrays, and using parallel arrays. The Enabled property, timer controls, splash screens, and control anchoring and docking are covered, as well as programming techniques for generating random numbers.

Chapter 9: Files, Printing, and Structures. This chapter begins by discussing how to save data to sequential text files and then read the data back into an application. The OpenFileDialog, SaveFileDialog, FontDialog, and ColorDialog controls are introduced. The PrintDocument control is discussed, with a special focus on printing reports. The chapter shows the student how to create user-defined data types with structures.

Chapter 10: Working with Databases. This chapter introduces basic database concepts. The student learns how to display a database table in a DataGridView control and write applications that display, sort, and update database data. The Structured Query Language (SQL) is introduced. An application that shows how to display database data in list boxes, text boxes, labels, and combo box is presented. The chapter concludes with an overview of Language Integrated Query (LINQ).

Chapter 11: Developing Web Applications. This chapter shows the student how to create ASP.NET applications that run on Web Browsers such as Internet Explorer, Netscape, and Mozilla Firefox. Using Microsoft Visual Web Developer 2008, the student learns how to use Web server controls and Web forms to build interactive, database-driven Web applications.

Chapter 12: Classes, Collections, and Scrollable Controls. This chapter introduces classes as a tool for creating abstract data types. The process of analyzing a problem and determining its classes is discussed, and techniques for creating objects, properties, and methods are introduced. Collections are presented as structures for holding groups of objects. The *Object Browser*, which allows the student to see information about the classes, properties, methods, and events available to a project, is also covered. The chapter shows the student how to construct horizontal and vertical scroll bars and track bar controls. The chapter concludes by introducing inheritance, and shows how to create a class that is based on an existing class.

Appendix A: User Interface Design Guidelines. Discusses how to design user interfaces that are simple, without distracting features, and that conform to Microsoft Windows standards.

Appendix B: Converting Mathematical Expressions to Programming Statements. Shows the student how to convert a mathematical expression into a Visual Basic programming statement.

Appendix C: Answers to Checkpoints. Students may test their progress by comparing their answers to Checkpoints with the answers provided. The answers to all Checkpoints are included.

Appendix D: Glossary. Provides a glossary of the key terms presented in the text.

The following appendixes are located on the Student CD-ROM:

Appendix E: Visual Basic 2008 Function and Method Reference. Provides a reference for all the intrinsic functions and methods that are covered in the text. The exceptions that may be caused by these functions and methods are also listed.

Appendix F: Binary and Random-Access Files. Describes programming techniques for creating and working with binary and random-access data files.

The following appendix is available on the Companion Website for this book at `http://www.aw.com/gaddisvb`

Appendix G: Answers to Odd-Numbered Review Questions. Provides another tool that students can use to gauge their progress.

Features of the Text

Concept Statements. Each major section of the text starts with a concept statement. This statement concisely summarizes the meaning of the section.

Tutorials. Each chapter has several hands-on tutorials that reinforce the chapter's topics. Many of these tutorials involve the student in writing applications that can be applied to real-world problems.

VideoNotes. A series of online videos, developed specifically for this book, are available for viewing at `www.aw.com/gaddisvb`. Icons appear throughout the text alerting the student to videos about specific topics.

Checkpoints. Checkpoints are questions placed at intervals throughout each chapter. They are designed to query the student's knowledge immediately after learning a new topic. Answers to all the Checkpoints are provided in Appendix C.

Notes. Notes are short explanations of interesting or often misunderstood points relevant to the topic being discussed.

Tips. Tips advise the student on the best techniques for approaching different programming problems and appear regularly throughout the text.

Warnings. Warnings caution the student about certain Visual Basic 2008 features, programming techniques, or practices that can lead to malfunctioning programs or lost data.

Review Questions and Exercises. In the tradition of all Gaddis texts, each chapter presents a thorough and diverse set of review questions and exercises. These include traditional fill-in-the-blank, true or false, multiple choice, and short answer questions. There are also unique tools for assessing a student's knowledge. For example, *Find the*

Error questions ask the student to identify syntax or logic errors in brief code segments. *Algorithm Workbench* questions ask the student to design code segments to satisfy a given problem. There are also *What Do You Think?* questions that require the student to think critically and contemplate the topics presented in the chapter. The answers to the odd-numbered review questions appear in Appendix G, which can be found on the Companion Website for this book at `http://www.aw.com/gaddisvb`.

Programming Challenges. Each chapter offers a pool of programming exercises designed to solidify the student's knowledge of the topics at hand. In most cases, the assignments present real-world problems to be solved. When applicable, these exercises also include input validation rules.

Supplements

Student

The following supplementary material is bundled with the book:

- A Student CD-ROM containing the source code and files required for the chapter tutorials. The CD-ROM also contains Appendix E, *Visual Basic 2008 Function and Method Reference*, and Appendix F, *Binary and Random-Access Files*.
- Microsoft Visual Basic 2008 Express Edition

Instructor

The following supplements are available to qualified instructors:

- Answers to all Review Questions in the text
- Solutions for all Programming Challenges in the text
- PowerPoint presentation slides for every chapter
- Test bank
- Test generation software that allows instructors to create customized tests

For information on how to access these supplements, visit the Pearson Education Instructor Resource Center at `http://www.pearsonhighered.com/irc` or send e-mail to computing@aw.com.

Web Resources

Self-assessment quizzes, PowerPoint slides, source code files, glossary flashcards, and answers to odd-numbered review questions are available on the Companion Website for *Starting Out with Visual Basic 2008* at `http://www.aw.com/gaddisvb`.

Acknowledgments

There were many helping hands in the development and publication of this text. The authors would like to thank the following faculty reviewers for their helpful suggestions and expertise during the production of the manuscript:

Robert M. Benavides, *Collin County Community College*
Nancy Burns. *Professor of Computer Science, Chipola College*
Mara Casado, *Associate Professor at Manatee College*
Dr. Robert Coil, *Cincinnati State Technical and Community College*
Carol A. DesJardins, *St. Clair County Community College*
Jean Evans, *Brevard Community College*
Pierre M. Fiorini, PhD, *University of Southern Maine*
Arlene Flerchinger, *Chattanooga State Technical Community College*
Larry Fudella, *Erie Community College*
Gail M. Gehrig, *Florida Community College at Jacksonville*
Iskandar Hack, *Indiana University—Purdue University at Fort Wayne*
Phil Larschan, *Tulsa Community College*
Joo Eng Lee-Partridge, *Central Connecticut State University*
Gary Marrer, *Glendale Community College*

George McOuat, *Hawaii Pacific University*
Sylvia Miner, *Florida International University*
Robert Nields, *Cincinnati State Technical and Community College*
Gregory M. Ogle
Rembert N. Parker, *Anderson University*
Gurmukh Singh, *SUNY at Fredonia*
Elaine Yale Weltz, *Seattle Pacific University*
Floyd Jay Winters, *Program Director, Computer Science, Manatee Community College*
Sheri L. York, *Ball State University*

Reviewers of the Previous Editions

Ronald Bass, *Austin Community College*
Ronald Beauchemin, *Springfield Technical Community College*
Zachory T. Beers, *Microsoft Corporation*
Bob Benavides, *Collin County Community College District*
Skip Bottom, *J. Sargeant Reynolds Community College*
Harold Broberg, *Indiana Purdue University*
Joni Catanzaro, *Louisiana State University*
Robert Coil, *Cincinnati State Community and Technical College*
William J. Dorin, *Indiana University*
Arlene Flerchinger, *Chattanooga State Technical Community College*
Lawrence Fudella, *Erie Community College*
Jayanta Ghosh, *Florida Community College*
David M. Himes, *Oklahoma State University, Okmulgee*
Greg Hodge, *Northwestern Michigan College*
Corinne Hoisington, *Central Virginia Community College*
May-Chuen Hsieh, *Southwest Tennessee Community College*
Lee A. Hunt, *Collin County Community College*
Art Lee, *Lord Fairfax Community College*
Norman McNeal, *Dakota County Technical College*
Gary Marrer, *Glendale Community College*
Billy Morgan, *Holmes Community College*
Joan P. Mosey, *Point Park College*
Robert Nields, *Cincinnati State Community and Technical College*
Merrill B. Parker, *Chattanooga State Technical Community College*
Carol M. Peterson, *South Plains Community College*
Anita Philipp, *Oklahoma City Community College*
T. N. Rajashekhara, *Camden County College*
Mark Reis, *University of Virginia*
Angeline Surber, *Mesa Community College*
Robert L. Terrell, *Walters State Community College*
Margaret Warrick, *Allan Hancock College*
Catherine Wyman, *DeVry Institute, Phoenix*

The authors would like to thank their families for their tremendous support throughout this project. We would also like to thank everyone at Addison-Wesley who was part of our production and marketing team. We are fortunate to have Matt Goldstein as our editor, guiding us through the delicate process of developing the book. We are also fortunate to have on our team Erin Davis, Sarah Milmore, Marilyn Lloyd, Bethany Tidd, Gillian Hall, Kathleen Cantwell, Holly McLean-Aldis, Joyce Cosentino Wells, and Elena Sidorova. You are all great people to work with!

About the Authors

Tony Gaddis is the principal author of the *Starting Out with* series of textbooks. Tony has nearly two decades of experience teaching computer science courses, primarily at Haywood Community College in North Carolina. He is a highly acclaimed instructor who was previously selected as North Carolina's Community College *Teacher of the Year*, and has received the *Teaching Excellence* award from the National Institute for Staff and Organizational Development. Besides Visual Basic books, the *Starting Out with* series includes introductory books on programming logic and design, Alice, the C++ programming language, Java™, Python, and Microsoft® C#®, all published by Addison-Wesley.

Kip Irvine holds M.S. (computer science) and D.M.A. (music composition) degrees from the University of Miami. He was formerly on the faculty at Miami-Dade Community College, and is presently a member of the School of Computing and Information Sciences at Florida International University. His published textbooks include *COBOL for the IBM Personal Computer*, *Assembly Language for Intel-Based Computers*, *C++ and Object-Oriented Programming*, and *Advanced Visual Basic .NET*.

CHAPTER 1

Introduction to Programming and Visual Basic

TOPICS

Microsoft Visual Basic is a powerful software development system for creating applications that run in Windows XP and Windows Vista. With Visual Basic, you can do the following:

- Create applications with graphical windows, dialog boxes, and menus
- Create applications that work with databases
- Create Web applications and applications that use Internet technologies
- Create applications that display graphics

Visual Basic is a favorite tool among professional programmers. Its combination of visual design tools and BASIC programming language make it intuitive, allowing developers to create powerful real-world applications in a relatively short time.

Before plunging into learning Visual Basic, we will review the fundamentals of computer hardware and software, and then build an understanding of how a Visual Basic application is organized.

1.1 Computer Systems: Hardware and Software

CONCEPT: Computer systems consist of similar hardware devices and hardware components. This section provides an overview of computer hardware and software organization.

Hardware

The term **hardware** refers to a computer's physical components. A computer, as we generally think of it, is not an individual device, but rather a system of devices. Like the instruments in a symphony orchestra, each device plays its own part. A typical computer system consists of the following major components:

1. The central processing unit (CPU)
2. Main memory
3. Secondary storage devices
4. Input devices
5. Output devices

The organization of a computer system is shown in Figure 1-1.

Figure 1-1 The organization of a computer system

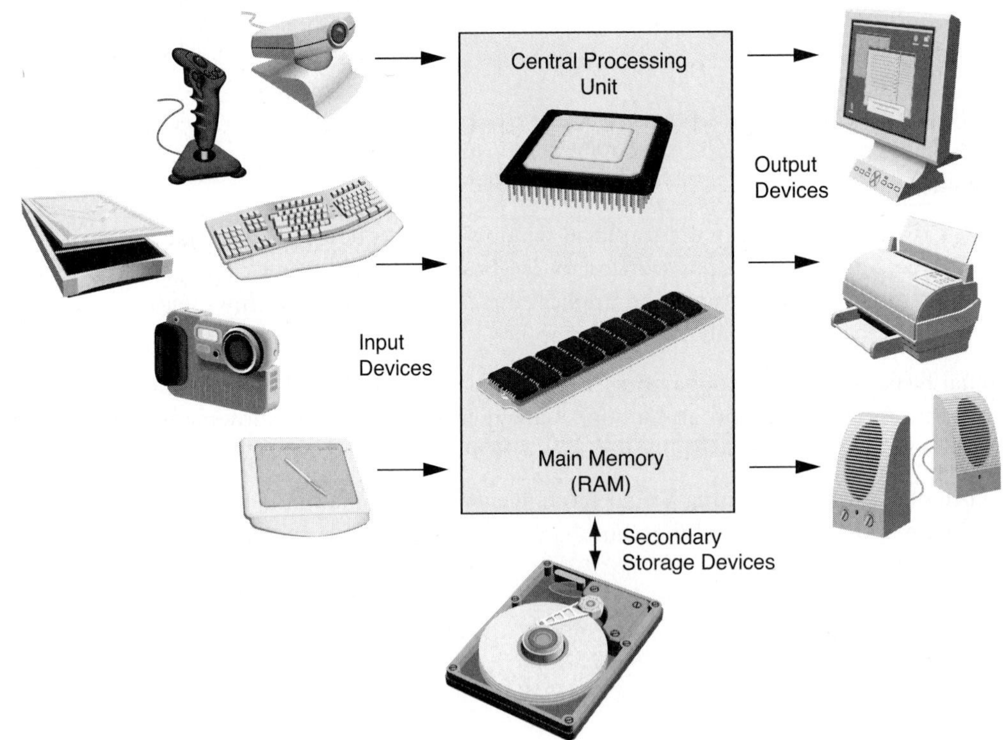

1. The CPU

When a computer is performing the tasks that a program tells it to do, we say that the computer is running or executing the program. The **central processing unit**, or **CPU**, is the part of a computer that actually runs programs. The CPU is the most important component in a computer because without it, the computer could not run software.

A **program** is a set of instructions that a computer's CPU follows to perform a task. The program's instructions are stored in the computer's memory, and the CPU's job is to fetch those instructions, one by one, and carry out the operations that they command. In memory, the instructions are stored as a series of **binary numbers**. A binary number is a sequence of 1s and 0s, such as

```
11011011
```

This number has no apparent meaning to people, but to the computer it might be an instruction to multiply two numbers or read another value from memory.

2. Main Memory

You can think of main memory as the computer's work area. This is where the computer stores a program while the program is running, as well as the data that the program is working with. For example, suppose you are using a word processing program to write an essay for one of your classes. While you do this, both the word processing program and the essay are stored in main memory.

Main memory is commonly known as **random-access memory**, or **RAM**. It is called this because the CPU is able to quickly access data stored at any random location in RAM. RAM is usually a volatile type of memory that is used only for temporary storage while a program is running. When the computer is turned off, the contents of RAM are erased. Inside your computer, RAM is stored in microchips.

3. Secondary Storage

The most common type of secondary storage device is the **disk drive**. A disk drive stores data by magnetically encoding it onto a circular disk. Most computers have a disk drive mounted inside their case. External disk drives, which connect to one of the computer's communication ports, are also available. External disk drives can be used to create backup copies of important data or to move data to another computer.

In addition to external disk drives, many types of devices have been created for copying data, and for moving it to other computers. For many years floppy disk drives were popular. A floppy disk drive records data onto a small floppy disk, which can be removed from the drive. The use of floppy disk drives has declined dramatically in recent years, in favor of superior devices such as USB drives. USB drives are small devices that plug into the computer's USB (universal serial bus) port, and appear to the system as a disk drive. USB drives, which use flash memory to store data, are inexpensive, reliable, and small enough to be carried in your pocket.

Optical devices such as the CD (compact disc) and the DVD (digital versatile disc) are also popular for data storage. Data is not recorded magnetically on an optical disc, but is encoded as a series of pits on the disc surface. CD and DVD drives use a laser to detect the pits and thus read the encoded data. Optical discs hold large amounts of data, and because recordable CD and DVD drives are now commonplace, they are good mediums for creating backup copies of data.

4. Input Devices

Input is any data the computer collects from the outside world. The device that collects the data and sends it to the computer is called an **input device**. Common input devices are the keyboard, mouse, scanner, and digital camera. Disk drives and CD drives can also be considered input devices because programs and data are retrieved from them and loaded into the computer's memory.

5. Output Devices

Output is any data the computer sends to the outside world. It might be a sales report, a list of names, a graphic image, or a sound. The data is sent to an **output device**, which formats and presents it. Common output devices are monitors and printers. Disk drives and CD recorders can also be considered output devices because the CPU sends data to them in order to be saved.

Software

Software refers to the programs that run on a computer. There are two general categories of software: operating systems and application software. An **operating system** or **OS** is a set of programs that manages the computer's hardware devices and controls their processes. Windows XP, Windows Vista, Mac OSX, and Linux are all operating systems.

Application software refers to programs that make the computer useful to the user. These programs, which are generally called applications, solve specific problems or perform general operations that satisfy the needs of the user. Word processing, spreadsheet, and database packages are all examples of application software. As you work through this book, you will develop application software using Visual Basic.

Checkpoint

1.1 List the five major hardware components of a computer system.

1.2 What is main memory? What is its purpose?

1.3 Explain why computers have both main memory and secondary storage.

1.4 What are the two general categories of software?

1.2 Programs and Programming Languages

CONCEPT: A program is a set of instructions a computer follows in order to perform a task. A programming language is a special language used to write computer programs.

What Is a Program?

Computers are designed to follow instructions. A computer program is a set of instructions that enables the computer to solve a problem or perform a task. For example, suppose we want the computer to calculate someone's gross pay—a *Wage Calculator* application. Figure 1-2 shows a list of things the computer should do.

Collectively, the instructions in Figure 1-2 are called an **algorithm**. An algorithm is a set of well-defined steps for performing a task or solving a problem. Notice these steps are sequentially ordered. Step 1 should be performed before Step 2, and so on. It is important that these instructions are performed in their proper sequence.

Figure 1-2 Program steps—*Wage Calculator* application

1. Display a message on the screen: *How many hours did you work?*
2. Allow the user to enter the number of hours worked.
3. Once the user enters a number, store it in memory.
4. Display a message on the screen: *How much do you get paid per hour?*
5. Allow the user to enter an hourly pay rate.
6. Once the user enters a number, store it in memory.
7. Once both the number of hours worked and the hourly pay rate are entered, multiply the two numbers and store the result in memory as the amount earned.
8. Display a message on the screen that shows the amount of money earned. The message must include the result of the calculation performed in Step 7.

States and Transitions

It is helpful to think of a running computer program as a combination of states and transitions. Each state is represented by a snapshot (like a picture) of the computer's memory. Using the *Wage Calculator* application example from Figure 1-2, the following is a memory snapshot taken when the program starts:

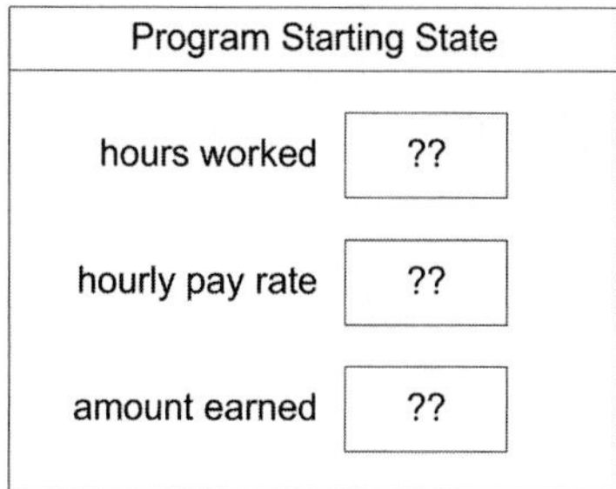

In Step 3, the number of hours worked by the user is stored in memory. Suppose the user enters the value 20. A new program state is created:

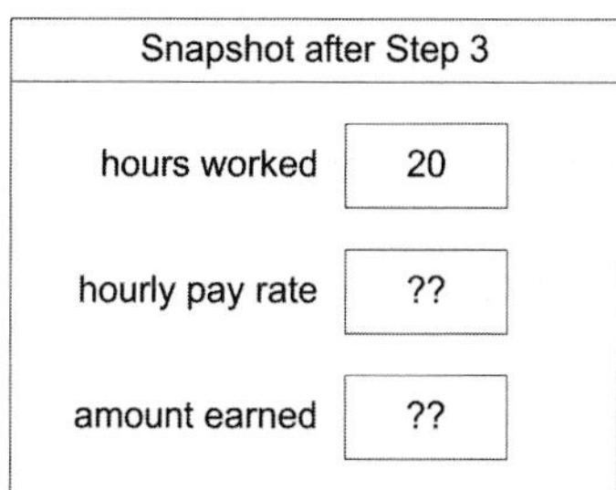

In Step 6, the hourly pay rate entered by the user is stored in memory. Suppose the user enters the value 25. The following memory snapshot shows the new program state:

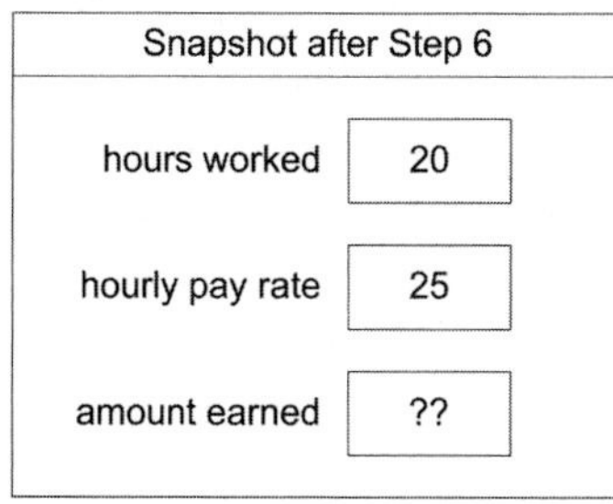

In Step 7, the application calculates the amount of money earned, saving it in a variable. The following memory snapshot shows the new program state:

Snapshot after Step 7	
hours worked	20
hourly pay rate	25
amount earned	500

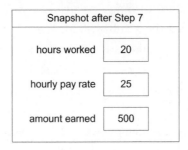

The memory snapshot produced by Step 7 represents the final program state.

Programming Languages

In order for a computer to perform instructions such as the wage calculator algorithm, the steps must be converted to a format the computer can process. As mentioned earlier, a program is stored in memory as a series of binary numbers. These numbers are known as **machine language instructions**. The CPU only processes instructions written in machine language. Our *Wage Calculator* application might look like the following at the moment when it is executed by the computer:

`1010110111010100011110000110111010001111000111001101010111 0` etc.

The CPU interprets these binary or machine language numbers as commands. As you might imagine, the process of encoding an algorithm in machine language is tedious and difficult. Programming languages, which use words instead of numbers, were invented to ease this task. Programmers can write their applications in programming language statements, and then use special software called a **compiler** to convert the program into machine language. Names of some popular recent programming languages are shown in Table 1-1. This list is only a small sample—there are thousands of programming languages.

Visual Basic is more than just a programming language. It is a programming environment, with tools for creating screen elements and programming language statements. Although Visual Basic, as a whole, is radically different from the original BASIC programming language, its programming statements are similar.

Table 1-1 Popular programming languages

Language	Description
Visual Basic, C#	Popular programming languages for building Windows and Web applications. Use a graphical user interface.
C, C++	Powerful advanced programmng languages that emphasize flexibility and fast running times. C++ is also object-oriented.
Java	Flexible and powerful programming language that runs on many different computer systems. Often used to teach object-oriented programming.
Python	Simple, yet powerful programming language used for graphics and small applications.
PHP	Programming language used for creating interactive Web sites.
JavaScript	Scripting language used in Web applications that provides rich user interfaces for Web browsers.

Procedural and Object-Oriented Programming

There are primarily two methods of programming used today: procedural programming and object-oriented programming.

Procedural Programming

The earliest programming languages were procedural. Procedural programming means that a program is made of one or more procedures. A **procedure** is a set of programming language statements that are executed by the computer. The statements might gather input from the user, manipulate information stored in the computer's memory, perform calculations, or any other operation necessary to complete its task. The wage calculator algorithm shown in Figure 1-2 can be thought of as a procedure. If the algorithm's eight steps are performed in order, one after the other, it will succeed in calculating and displaying the user's gross pay.

Procedural programming was the standard when users were interacting with text-based computer terminals. For example, Figure 1-3 shows the screen of an older MS-DOS computer running a program that performs the wage calculator algorithm. The user has entered the numbers shown in bold.

Object-Oriented Programming

Object-oriented programming or OOP is an industry standard model for designing and coding programs. When designing applications, designers use real-world objects to express patterns, called classes in software. An example is a student registration application, in which we would choose students, transcripts, and accounts as possible classes. The program we write would create objects, or instances of these classes.

Classes contain attributes, expressed as variables. For example, a class named Account would probably contain attributes such as balance, account ID, and payment history. In Visual Basic, classes are used to describe the objects that appear on the screen. When a program runs, these objects are created and displayed.

Figure 1-3 *Wage Calculator* application

```
How many hours did you work? 10
How much are you paid per hour? 15
You have earned $150.00
C>_
```

Graphical User Interface

In text-based environments using procedural programs, the user responds to the program. Modern operating systems, such as the Windows family, use a **graphical user interface**, or GUI (pronounced *gooey*). Although GUIs have made programs friendlier and easier to interact with, they have not simplified the task of programming. GUIs require on-screen elements such as windows, dialog boxes, buttons, and menus. The program must handle the user's interactions with these on-screen elements, in any order the user might choose to select them. No longer does the user respond to a program—now the program responds to a user.

GUIs have helped influence the shift from procedural programming to object-oriented programming. Whereas procedural programming is centered on creating procedures, object-oriented programming is centered on creating **objects**. An object is a programming element that contains data and actions. The data contained in an object is known as its **attributes.** In Visual Basic, an object's attributes are called **properties.** The actions that an object performs are known as the object's **methods.** The object is, conceptually, a self-contained unit consisting of data (properties) and actions (methods).

Perhaps the best way to understand objects is to experience a program that uses them. The following steps guide you through the process of running a demonstration program located on the Student CD. The program was created with Visual Basic.

Required Software Setup

To use this book, you must install two pieces of software:

- **Microsoft Visual Studio 2008** or **Visual Basic 2008 Express.** From now on, we will drop the "2008" from both names. If you will be covering Chapter 11, you will also need **Visual Web Developer 2008 Express.**
- **The student sample program files**, located on the CD-ROM packaged with this book.

VideoNote

Forms, Controls, and Properties

Installing the Sample Program Files

The Student CD included with this book contains sample program files that are required in many of the tutorials. Before you can use these files you must copy them from the Student CD to your computer's hard drive. If you are working in a college computer lab, it is possible that the sample program files have already been copied to the computers in the lab. If this is the case, your professor will tell you where they are located. In Tutorial 1-1, you will execute the *Wage Calculator* application.

Tutorial 1-1:

Running the *Wage Calculator* application

Assuming you have installed Visual Studio or Visual Basic Express and the sample programs from the Student CD on your computer, you're ready to begin Tutorial 1-1.

Step 1: In Windows, double-click the *My Computer* icon or the *Windows Explorer* icon.

Step 2: In Windows, navigate to the folder on your computer containing the student sample programs. Then navigate to the *Chap1\Wage Calculator\bin* folder. Double-click the file *Wage Calculator.exe* (the *.exe* filename extension may not be visible). The program's window should display.

The window shown in Figure 1-4 can be thought of as an object. In Visual Basic terminology, this window object is known as a **Form object**. The form also contains numerous other objects. As shown in Figure 1-5, it has four Label objects, two TextBox objects, and two Button objects. In Visual Basic, these objects are known as **controls**.

The appearance of a screen object, such as a form or other control, is determined by the object's properties. For example, each of the Label controls has a property known as Text. The value stored in the **Text property** becomes the text displayed by the label. For instance, the Text property of the topmost label on the form is set to the value *Number of Hours Worked*. Beneath it is another Label control, whose Text property is set to

Figure 1-4 *Wage Calculator* screen

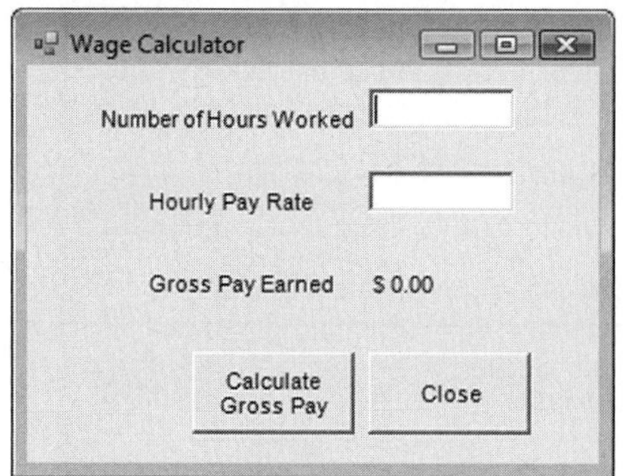

Figure 1-5 Types of controls

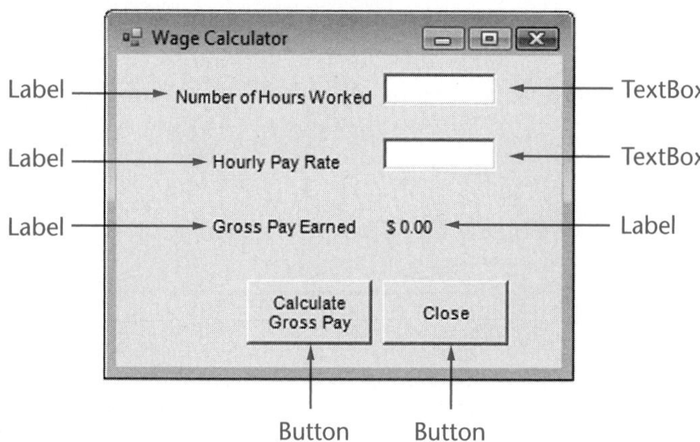

Hourly Pay Rate. The Button controls also have a Text property. The Text property of the leftmost button is set to *Calculate Gross Pay*, and the rightmost button has its Text property set to *Close*. Even the window, or form, has a Text property, which determines the text displayed in the window's title bar. *Wage Calculator* is the value stored in this form's Text property. Part of the process of creating a Visual Basic application is deciding what values to store in each object's properties.

VideoNote

Event-Driven Programming

Event-Driven Programming

Programs that operate in a GUI environment must be **event-driven**. An event is an action that takes place within a program, such as the clicking of a control. All Visual Basic controls are capable of detecting various events. For example, a Button control can detect when it has been clicked and a TextBox control can detect when its contents have changed.

Names are assigned to all of the events that can be detected. For instance, when the user clicks a Button control, a `Click` event occurs. When the contents of a TextBox control changes, a `TextChanged` event occurs. If you wish for a control to respond to a specific event, you must write a special type of method known as an **event procedure**. An event procedure is a method that is executed when a specific event occurs. If an event occurs, and there is no event procedure to respond to that event, the event is ignored.

Part of the Visual Basic programming process is designing and writing event procedures. Tutorial 1-2 demonstrates an event procedure using the *Wage Calculator* application you executed in Tutorial 1-1.

Tutorial 1-2:
Running an application that demonstrates event procedures

Step 1: With the *Wage Calculator* application from Tutorial 1-1 still running, enter the value **10** in the first TextBox control. This is the number of hours worked.

Step 2: Press the Tab key. Notice that the cursor moves to the next TextBox control. Enter the value **15**. This is the hourly pay rate. The window should look like that shown in Figure 1-6.

Step 3: Click the *Calculate Gross Pay* button. Notice that in response to the mouse click, the application multiplies the values you entered in the TextBox controls and displays the result in a Label control. This action is performed by an event procedure that responds to the button being clicked. The window should look like that shown in Figure 1-7.

Figure 1-6 Text boxes filled in on the *Wage Calculator* form

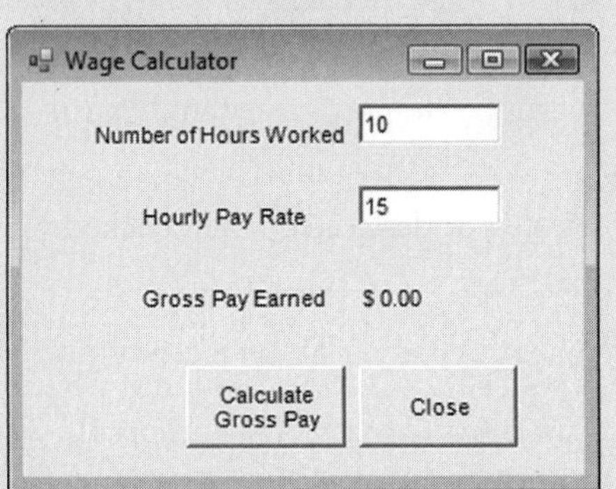

Figure 1-7 Gross pay calculated

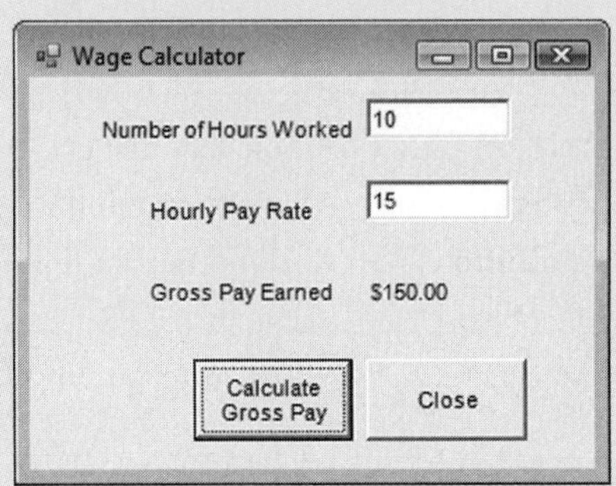

Step 4: Next, click the *Close* button. The application responds to this event by terminating. This is because an event procedure closes the application when the button is clicked.

This simple application demonstrates the essence of object-oriented, event-driven programming. In the next section, we examine the controls and event procedures more closely.

1.3 More about Controls and Programming

CONCEPT: As a Visual Basic programmer, you must design and create the two major components of an application: the GUI elements (forms and other controls) and the programming statements that respond to and/or perform actions (event procedures).

While creating a Visual Basic application, you will spend much of your time doing three things: creating the GUI elements that make up the application's user interface, setting the properties of the GUI elements, and writing programming language statements that respond to events and perform other operations. In this section, we take a closer look at these aspects of Visual Basic programming.

Visual Basic Controls

In the previous section, you saw examples of several GUI elements, or controls. Visual Basic provides a wide assortment of controls for gathering input, displaying information, selecting values, showing graphics, and more. Table 1-2 lists some of the commonly used controls.

Table 1-2 Visual Basic controls

Control Type	Description
CheckBox	A box that is checked or unchecked when clicked with the mouse
ComboBox	A control that is the combination of a ListBox and a TextBox
Button	A rectangular button-shaped object that performs an action when clicked with the mouse
Form	A window, onto which other controls may be placed
GroupBox	A rectangular border that functions as a container for other controls
HScrollBar	A horizontal scroll bar that, when moved with the mouse, increases or decreases a value
Label	A box that displays text that cannot be changed or entered by the user
ListBox	A box containing a list of items
RadioButton	A round button that is either selected or deselected when clicked with the mouse
PictureBox	A control that displays a graphic image
TextBox	A rectangular area in which the user can enter text, or the program can display text
VScrollBar	A vertical scroll bar that, when moved with the mouse, increases or decreases a value

If you have any experience using Microsoft Windows, you are already familiar with most of the controls listed in Table 1-2. The Student CD contains a simple demonstration program in Tutorial 1-3 that shows you how a few of them work.

Tutorial 1-3:
Running an application that demonstrates various controls

Step 1: In Windows, navigate to the location where the sample program files have been copied from the Student CD.

Step 2: Navigate to the the *Chap1\Controls Tour\bin* folder.

Step 3: Double-click the file *Program2.exe.*

Step 4: Once the program loads and executes, the window shown in Figure 1-8 should appear on the screen.

Step 5: The program presents several Visual Basic controls. Experiment with each one, noticing the following actions, which are performed by event procedures:

- When you click the small down arrow (▾) in the ComboBox control, you see a list of pets. When you select one, the name of the pet appears below the combo box.
- When you click the CheckBox control, its text changes to indicate that the check box is checked or unchecked.
- When you click an item in the ListBox control, the name of that item appears below the list box.
- When you select one of the RadioButton controls, the text below them changes to indicate which one you selected. You may only select one at a time.

Figure 1-8 Control demonstration screen

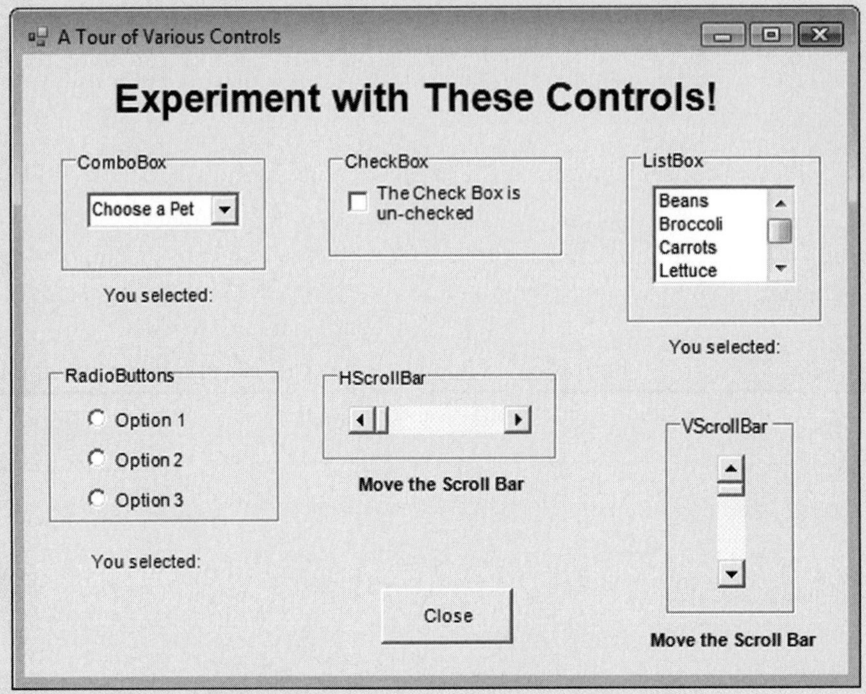

- You move the horizontal scroll bar (HScrollBar) and the vertical scroll bar (VScrollBar) by doing the following:
  - Clicking either of the small arrows at each end of the bar
  - Clicking inside the bar on either side of the slider
  - Clicking on the slider and while holding down the mouse button, moving the mouse to the right or left for the horizontal scroll bar, or up or down for the vertical scroll bar.

  When you move either of the scroll bars, the text below it changes to a number. Moving the scroll bar in one direction increases the number, and moving it in the other direction decreases the number.

Step 6: Click the *Close* button to end the application.

The Name Property

The appearance of a control is determined by its properties. Some properties, however, establish nonvisual characteristics. An example is the control's **Name property**. When the programmer wishes to manipulate or access a control in a programming statement, he or she must refer to the control by its name.

When you create a control in Visual Basic, it automatically receives a default name. The first Label control created in an application receives the default name `Label1`. The second Label control created receives the default name `Label2`, and the default names continue in this fashion. The first TextBox control created in an application is automatically named `TextBox1`. As you can imagine, the names for each subsequent TextBox control are `TextBox2`, `TextBox3`, and so on. You can change the control's default name to something more descriptive.

Table 1-3 lists all the controls, by name, in the *Wage Calculator* application (Section 1.2), and Figure 1-9 shows where each is located.

Table 1-3 *Wage Calculator* controls

Control Name	Control Type	Description
`Label1`	Label	Displays the message *Number of Hours Worked*
`Label2`	Label	Displays the message *Hourly Pay Rate*
`Label3`	Label	Displays the message *Gross Pay Earned*
`txtHoursWorked`	TextBox	Allows the user to enter the number of hours worked
`txtPayRate`	TextBox	Allows the user to enter the hourly pay rate
`lblGrossPay`	Label	Displays the gross pay, after the `btnCalcGrossPay` button has been clicked
`btnCalcGrossPay`	Button	When clicked, multiplies the number of hours worked by the hourly pay rate
`btnClose`	Button	When clicked, terminates the application

Figure 1-9 *Wage Calculator* controls

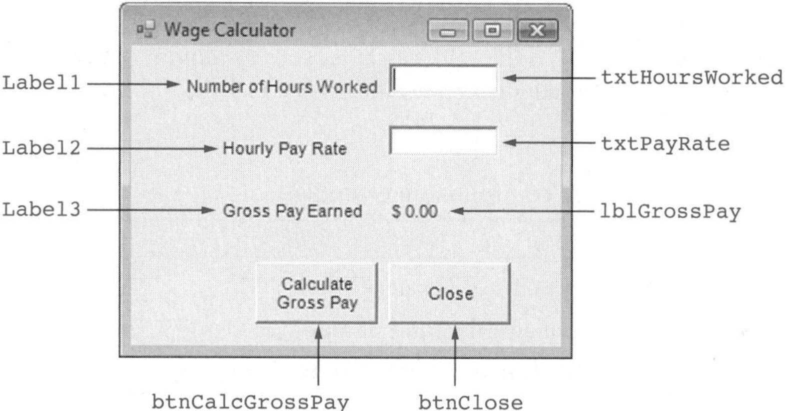

Control Naming Rules and Conventions

Three controls shown in Figure 1-9 (`Label1`, `Label2`, and `Label3`), still have their default names. The other five controls have programmer-defined names because those controls play an active role in the application's event procedures, and their names appear in the application's programming statements. Any control that activates programming statements or whose name appears in a programming statement should have a descriptive, programmer-defined name.

NOTE: Some programmers prefer to give all the controls in their application meaningful names, including ones that do not activate programming statements or whose names do not appear in programming statements.

Although you have a great deal of flexibility in naming controls, there are some standard rules. First, control names must start with a letter. The remaining characters may be letters, digits, or underscore characters only. You cannot use spaces, special symbols, or punctuation characters in a control name. In addition to the mandatory rules, there are three general guidelines to follow when naming controls:

1. The first three letters of the name should be a lowercase prefix indicating the control's type. In the *Wage Calculator* application, programmer-defined names use the following standard three-letter prefixes:

   - `lbl` indicates a Label control.
   - `txt` indicates a TextBox control.
   - `btn` indicates a Button control.

   There are standard prefixes for other controls as well. They are discussed in Chapter 2.
2. The first letter after the prefix should be uppercase. In addition, if the name consists of multiple words, the first letter of each word should be capitalized. This makes the name more readable. For example, `txtHoursWorked` is easier to read than `txthoursworked`.
3. The part of the control name that appears after the three-letter prefix should describe the control's purpose in the application. This makes the control name very helpful to anyone reading the application's programming statements. For example, it is evident that the `btnCalcGrossPay` control is a button that calculates the gross pay.

These guidelines are not mandatory rules, but they are standard conventions that programmers follow. You should use these guidelines when naming the controls in your applications as well. Table 1-4 describes several fictitious controls and suggests appropriate programmer-defined names for them.

Table 1-4 Programmer-defined control name examples

Control Description	Suggested Name
A text box in which the user enters his or her age	`txtAge`
A button that, when clicked, calculates the total of an order	`btnCalcTotal`
A label that is used to display the distance from one city to another	`lblDistance`
A text box in which the user enters his or her last name	`txtLastName`
A button that, when clicked, adds a series of numbers	`btnAddNumbers`

1.5 What is an algorithm?

1.6 Why were computer programming languages invented?

1.7 What are the two methods of programming used today?

1.8 What does event-driven mean?

1.9 Describe the difference between a property and a method.

1.10 Why should the programmer change the name of a control from its default name?

1.11 If a control has the programmer-defined name `txtRadius`, what type of control is it?

1.12 What is the default name given to the first TextBox control created in an application?

1.13 Is `txtFirst+LastName` an acceptable control name? Why or why not?

Programming an Application

Let's look at some source code from the *Wage Calculator* application you saw in Tutorial 1-3. The code shown here is part of the event procedure that executes when the user clicks the *Calculate* button. The line numbers that appear to the left of the statements are not part of the code, but they will help us provide a description of each statement.

```
1:    Dim dblHoursWorked As Double
2:    Dim dblPayRate As Double
3:    Dim dblGrossPay As Double
4:    dblHoursWorked = txtHoursWorked.Text
5:    dblPayRate = txtPayRate.Text
6:    dblGrossPay = dblHoursWorked * dblPayRate
7:    lblGrossPay.Text = dblGrossPay.ToString("c")
```

- Lines 1, 2, and 3 declare variables to hold the hours worked, pay rate, and gross pay.
- Line 4 copies the contents of the TextBox control named `txtHoursWorked` into the `dblHoursWorked` variable. Each TextBox control has a Text property that holds the contents of the TextBox at runtime. By *contents*, we mean the text typed by the user.
- Line 5 copies the contents of the TextBox named `txtPayRate` into the `dblPayRate` variable.
- Line 6 calculates the employee's gross pay by multiplying the hours worked by the hourly pay rate. The calculated value is stored in the variable named `dblGrossPay`.
- Line 7 converts the number in the `dblGrossPay` variable into a string with currency format, such as $500.00 and copies the string to the Label control named `lblGrossPay`.

Table 1-5 refers to the fundamental elements in a Visual Basic program.

Table 1-5 Visual Basic language elements

Language Element	Description
Keywords	Words that have a special meaning in a programming language. Keywords may only be used for their intended purpose. Some examples in Visual Basic are `Private`, `Sub`, `Dim`, and `End`.
Programmer-defined names	Words or names defined by the programmer.
Operators	Operators perform operations on one or more **operands**. An operand is usually a piece of data, such as a number. Examples of operators include +, –, *, and /.
Remarks	Also known as **comments**, remarks are notes that explain the purpose of statements or sections of code. Although remarks are part of an application's code, they are ignored by the compiler. They are intended for the programmer or others who might read the application's code.
Syntax	Rules that must be followed when constructing a method. Syntax dictates how keywords, operators, and programmer-defined names may be used.

Keywords

There are two keywords in line 1: `Dim` and `Double`. They are repeated in lines 2 and 3. Each of these words has a special meaning in Visual Basic and can only be used for its intended purpose. As you will see, a programmer is allowed to make up his or her own names for certain things in a program. Keywords, however, are reserved and cannot be used for anything other than their designated purpose. Part of learning a programming language is learning what the keywords are, what they mean, and how to use them.

Programmer-Defined Names (Identifiers)

The word `dblGrossPay`, which appears in lines 6 and 7, is a programmer-defined name, or **identifier**. It is not part of the Visual Basic language, but rather a name made up by the programmer to identify a variable. Variables are named memory locations that hold data while a program is running.

Operators

In line 6 the following statement appears:

```
dblGrossPay = dblHoursWorked * dblPayRate
```

The = and * symbols are operators, which perform operations on pieces of data known as operands. The * operator multiplies two operands, and the = operator stores a value in a variable or a property.

Comments (Remarks)

Comments, or remarks, help the reader of a program understand the purpose of program statements. Sometimes you (the programmer) will have to reread and understand your own code. Comments are a great way to remind you of what you were thinking when you created the program. The following are examples of comments:

```
'Convert the values in the text box to numbers,
'and calculate the gross pay.
```

A comment must begin with either an apostrophe (`'`) or the `REM` keyword. When a program runs, the computer ignores comments.

You should always add descriptive comments to your code. The extra time it takes is well spent. Someday you may have to modify or maintain code written by another programmer and you will appreciate the time spent to comment the code!

Syntax

Each statement shown in the sample code is written according to the rules of Visual Basic. The rules, known collectively as **language syntax**, define the correct way to use keywords, operators, and programmer-defined names. If a programming statement violates the Visual Basic syntax, the application will not run until it is corrected.

1.4 The Programming Process

CONCEPT: **The programming process consists of several steps, which include designing, creating, testing, and debugging activities.**

Imagine building a bridge without a plan. How could it be any easier to create a complex computer program without designing its appearance and behavior? In this section, we introduce some of the most important knowledge you will gain from this book—how to begin creating a computer application. Regardless of which programming language you use in the future, good program design principles always apply.

Steps for Developing a Visual Basic Application

1. Clearly define what the application is to do.
2. Visualize the application running on the computer and design its user interface.
3. Make a list of the controls needed.
4. Define the values of each control's relevant properties.
5. Make a list of methods needed for each control.
6. Create a flowchart or pseudocode version of each method.
7. Check the flowchart or pseudocode for errors.
8. Start Visual Basic and create the forms and other controls identified in Step 3.
9. Write the code for the event procedures and other methods created in Step 6.
10. Attempt to run the application. Correct any syntax errors found and repeat this step as many times as necessary.
11. Once all syntax errors are corrected, run the program with test data for input. Correct any runtime errors. Repeat this step as many times as necessary.

These steps emphasize the importance of planning. Just as there are good ways and bad ways to paint a house, there are good ways and bad ways to write a program. A good program always begins with planning.

With the *Wage Calculator* application as our example, let's look at each of these steps in greater detail.

1. Clearly define what the application is to do.

This step requires that you identify the purpose of the application, the information to be input, the processing to take place, and the desired output. For example, the requirements for the *Wage Calculator* application are as follows:

Purpose:	To calculate the user's gross pay
Input:	Number of hours worked, hourly pay rate
Process:	Multiply number of hours worked by hourly pay rate. The result is the user's gross pay
Output:	Display a message indicating the user's gross pay

2. Visualize the application running on the computer and design its user interface.

Before you create an application on the computer, first you should create it in your mind. Step 2 is the visualization of the program. Try to imagine what the computer screen will look like while the application is running. Then, sketch the form or forms in the application. For instance, Figure 1-10 shows a sketch of the form presented by the *Wage Calculator* application.

Figure 1-10 Sketch of the *Wage Calculator* form

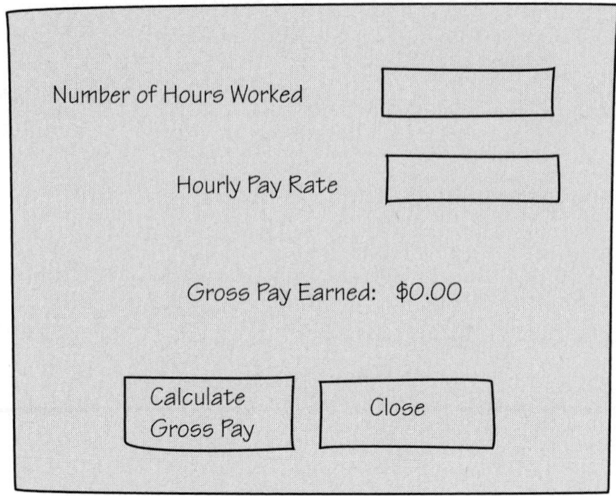

3. Make a list of the controls needed.

The next step is to list all the controls needed. You should assign names to all controls that will be accessed or manipulated in the application code, and provide a brief description of each control. Table 1-6 lists the controls in the *Wage Calculator* application.

4. Define the values of each control's relevant properties.

Other than Name, Text is the only control property modified in the *Wage Calculator* application. Table 1-7 lists the value of each control's Text property.

Table 1-6 *Wage Calculator* controls

Control Type	Control Name	Description
Form	(Default)	A small form that will serve as the window onto which the other controls will be placed
Label	(Default)	Displays the message *Number of Hours Worked*
Label	(Default)	Displays the message *Hourly Pay Rate*
Label	(Default)	Displays the message *Gross Pay Earned*
TextBox	`txtHoursWorked`	Allows the user to enter the number of hours worked
TextBox	`txtPayRate`	Allows the user to enter the hourly pay rate
Label	`lblGrossPay`	Displays the gross pay, after the `btnCalcGrossPay` button has been clicked
Button	`btnCalcGrossPay`	When clicked, multiplies the number of hours worked by the hourly pay rate; stores the result in a variable and displays it in the `lblGrossPay` label
Button	`btnClose`	When clicked, terminates the application

Table 1-7 *Wage Calculator* control values

Control Type	Control Name	Text
Form	(Default)	"Wage Calculator"
Label	(Default)	"Number of Hours Worked"
Label	(Default)	"Hourly Pay Rate"
Label	(Default)	"Gross Pay Earned"
Label	lblGrossPay	"$0.00"
TextBox	txtHoursWorked	""
TextBox	txtPayRate	""
Button	btnCalcGrossPay	"Calculate Gross Pay"
Button	btnClose	"Close"

5. Make a list of methods needed for each control.

Next, you should list the event procedures and other methods you will write. There are only two event procedures in the *Wage Calculator* application. Table 1-8 lists and describes them. Notice the Visual Basic names for the event procedures. `btnCalcGrossPay_Click` is the name of the procedure invoked when the `btnCalcGrossPay` button is clicked and `btnClose_Click` is the event procedure that executes when the `btnClose` button is clicked.

Table 1-8 *Wage Calculator* event procedures

Method	Description
btnCalcGrossPay_Click	Multiplies the number of hours worked by the hourly pay rate; these values are entered into the txtHoursWorked and txtPayRate TextBox controls and the result is stored in the lblGrossPay.Text property
btnClose_Click	Terminates the application

6. Create a flowchart or pseudocode version of each method.

A **flowchart** is a diagram that graphically depicts the flow of a method. It uses boxes and other symbols to represent each step. Figure 1-11 shows a flowchart for the `btnCalcGrossPay_Click` event procedure.

There are two types of boxes in the flowchart shown in Figure 1-11: ovals and rectangles. The flowchart begins with an oval labeled *Start* and ends with an oval labeled *End*. The rectangles represent a computational process or other operation. Notice that the symbols are connected with arrows that indicate the direction of the program flow.

Many programmers prefer to use pseudocode instead of flowcharts. **Pseudocode** is a cross between human language and a programming language. Although the computer can't understand pseudocode, programmers often find it helpful to plan an algorithm in a language that's almost a programming language but still very readable by humans. The following is a pseudocode version of the `btnCalcGrossPay_Click` event procedure:

Store Number of Hours Worked × Hourly Pay Rate in dblGrossPay.
Copy dblGrossPay in lblGrossPay.Text.

Figure 1-11 Flowchart for `btnCalcGrossPay_Click` event procedure

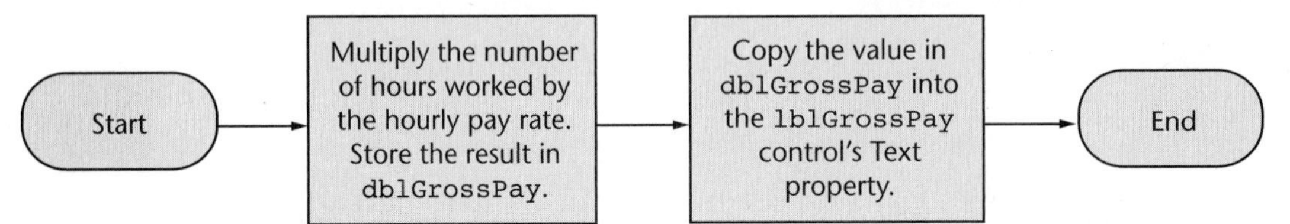

7. Check the code for errors.

In this phase the programmer reads the flowcharts and/or pseudocode from the beginning and steps through each operation, pretending that he or she is the computer. The programmer jots down the current contents of variables and properties that change and sketches what the screen looks like after each output operation. By checking each step, a programmer can locate and correct many errors.

8. Start Visual Studio and create the forms and other controls identified in Step 3.

This step is the first actual work done on the computer. Here, the programmer uses Visual Studio to create the application's user interface and arrange the controls on each form.

9. Write the code for the event procedures and other methods created in Step 6.

This is the second step performed on the computer. The event procedures and other methods may be converted into code and entered into the computer using Visual Studio.

10. Attempt to run the application. Correct any syntax errors found and repeat this step as many times as necessary.

If you have entered code with syntax errors or typing mistakes, this step will uncover them. A **syntax error** is the incorrect use of a programming language element, such as a keyword, operator, or programmer-defined name. Correct your mistakes and repeat this step until the program runs.

11. Once all syntax errors are corrected, run the program with test data for input. Correct any runtime errors. Repeat this step as many times as necessary.

Runtime errors (errors found while running the program) are mistakes that do not prevent an application from executing but cause it to produce incorrect results. For example, a mistake in a mathematical formula is a common type of **runtime error**. When runtime errors are found in a program, they must be corrected and the program retested. This step must be repeated until the program reliably produces satisfactory results.

1.14 What four items should be identified when defining what a program is to do?

1.15 Describe the importance of good planning in the process of creating a Visual Basic application.

1.16 What does it mean to visualize a program running? What is the value of such an activity?

1.17 What is a flowchart?

1.18 What is pseudocode?

1.19 What is a runtime error?

1.20 What is the purpose of testing a program with sample data or input?

1.21 How much testing should you perform on a new program?

1.5 Visual Studio and Visual Basic Express (the Visual Basic Environment)

CONCEPT: Visual Studio and Visual Basic Express consist of tools that you use to build Visual Basic applications. The first step in using Visual Basic is learning about these tools.

NOTE: The programs in this book can be written using either Microsoft Visual Studio or Microsoft Visual Basic Express. There are only minor differences between the two products. In cases where they work identically, we will refer to them as **Visual Studio**.

In Chapter 2 you will build your first Visual Basic application. First, you need to know how to start Visual Studio and understand its major components. Visual Studio is an **integrated development environment** (IDE) that provides the necessary tools for creating, testing, and debugging software. Visual Studio can be used to create applications not only with Visual Basic, but also with other languages such as Visual C++ and C#. Tutorial 1-4 guides you through the Visual Studio startup process and gives you a hands-on tour of its tools for creating Visual Basic applications.

Tutorial 1-4:
Starting Visual Studio

The following steps guide you through the Visual Studio startup process.

Step 1: Click the *Start* button and open the *All Programs* menu (or *Programs* menu for earlier versions of MS Windows). Ask your classroom instructor for the location in the menu of either Visual Studio 2008 or Visual Basic 2008 Express—whichever one your class will be using.

TIP: If you are using Visual Studio rather than Visual Basic Express, the first time you run the software, you may see a window entitled *Choose Default Environment Settings*. Select *Visual Basic Development Settings* from the list and click the *Start Visual Studio* button. (You can always change the settings later as the window explains.)

Step 2: Next, you should see the *Start Page*, as shown in Figure 1-12. Your screen may not appear exactly as shown in the figure, because some of the information shown here comes from the Web. Later in this chapter, we will show you how to control the appearance of Visual Studio.

Figure 1-12 Visual Studio *Start Page*

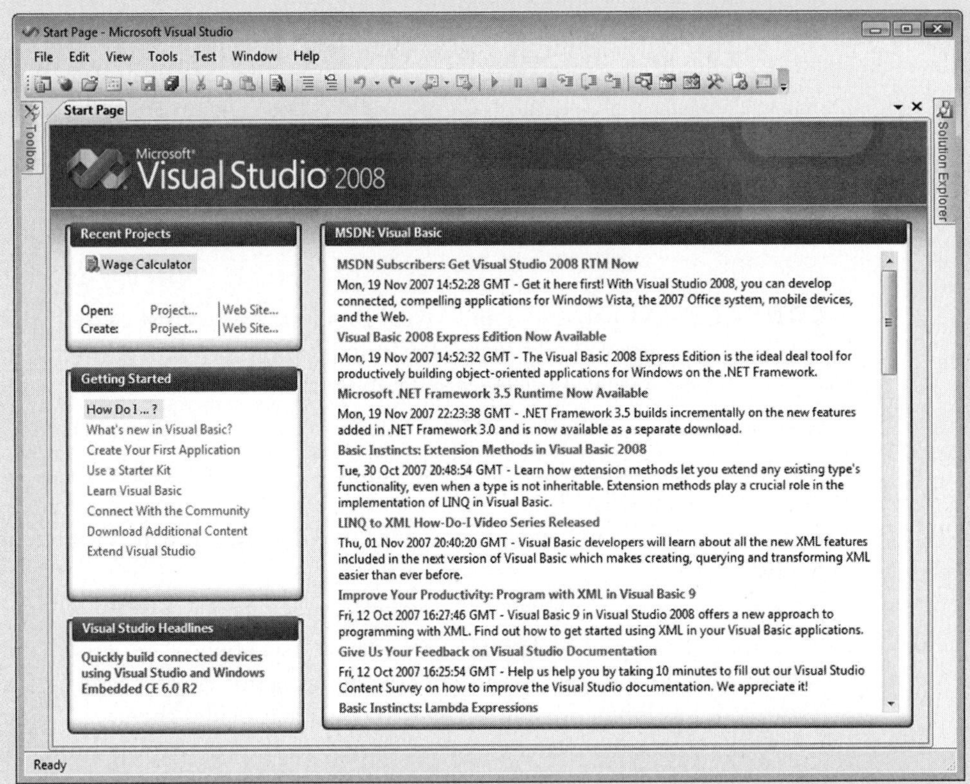

TIP: If you do not see the *Start Page* shown in Figure 1-12, click *View* in the menu bar, click *Other Windows*, and then click *Start Page*.

Step 3: Visual Studio allows you to set certain defaults for Visual Basic programming. In the menu bar, click *Tools* and then click *Options* (Figure 1-13). If you are using Visual Basic Express, you will not see the *Device Tools* option.

Step 4: In the *Options* dialog, under *Projects and Solutions*, select *General* (Figure 1-14). To the right of the Visual Studio projects location edit box, click the *Browse* button [...]. Select a new location to save your programming projects (you may be assigned a location by your instructor).

Figure 1-13 Visual Studio *Options* dialog

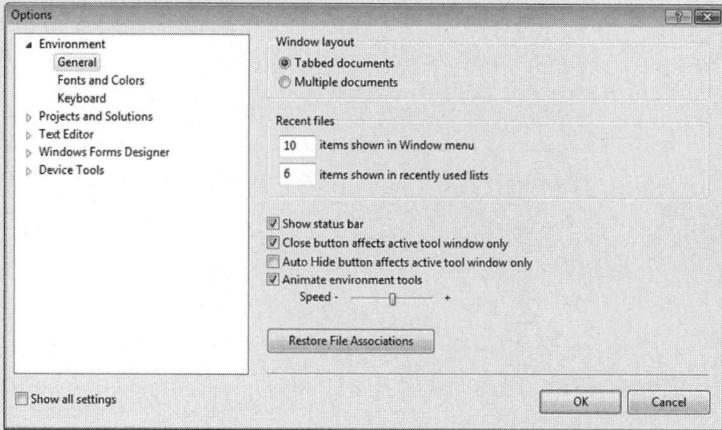

Figure 1-14 Setting the Visual Studio projects location

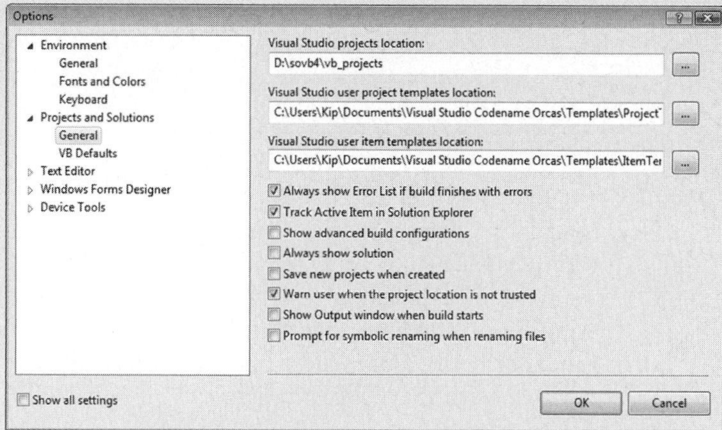

Step 5: Still in the *Options* dialog, under *Projects and Solutions*, select *VB Defaults* (Figure 1-15). Set *Option Strict* to *On* and set *Option Infer* to *Off*. (We will explain what these options mean in Chapter 3.) Click *OK* to close the dialog.

Figure 1-15 Setting *VB Defaults* in the *Options* dialog

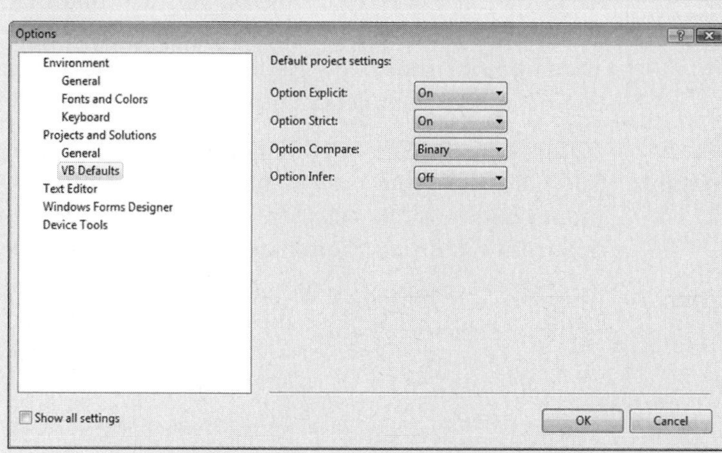

Step 6: Each application you create with Visual Studio is called a **project.** Now you will start a new project. In the menu bar, click *File*, then click *New Project.* The ***New Project* dialog box** shown in Figure 1-16 appears. (Visual Basic Express shows fewer templates than Visual Studio.)

Figure 1-16 *New Project* dialog box

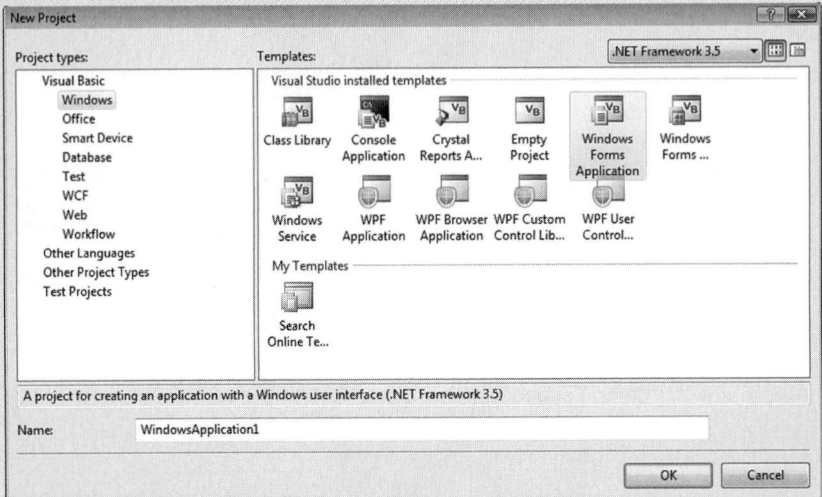

Step 7: The left pane, labeled *Project types*, lists the different programming languages available in Visual Studio. (Visual Basic Express shows only the right pane, with a smaller number of templates.) The right pane, labeled *Templates*, lists the types of applications you can create in the selected language. If you are using Visual Studio, select *Windows* under *Visual Basic* in the *Project types* pane. For both Visual Studio and Visual Basic Express, select *Windows Forms Application* in the *Templates* pane.

Step 8: The *Name* text box is where you enter the name of your project. Visual Studio automatically fills this box with a default name. In Figure 1-16 the default name is *WindowsApplication1*. Change the project name to `Tutorial 1-4` and click the *OK* button.

NOTE: A project consists of numerous files. When you begin a new project, Visual Studio stores the files in a folder with the same name as the project. As you create additional projects, you will find that default names such as *WindowsApplication1* do not help you remember what each project does. Therefore, you should always change the name of a new project to something that describes the project's purpose.

Step 9: Select *Save All* from the *File* menu. The *Location* text box shows where the project folder will be created on your system. If you wish to change the location, click the *Browse* button and select the desired drive and folder.

Step 10: Click the *Save* button. You should now see the Visual Studio window similar to the one shown in Figure 1-17.

NOTE: Visual Studio is customizable. Your screen might not appear exactly as shown in Figure 1-17. As you continue through this chapter, you will learn how to arrange the screen elements in different ways.

Figure 1-17 Visual Studio environment with a new project open

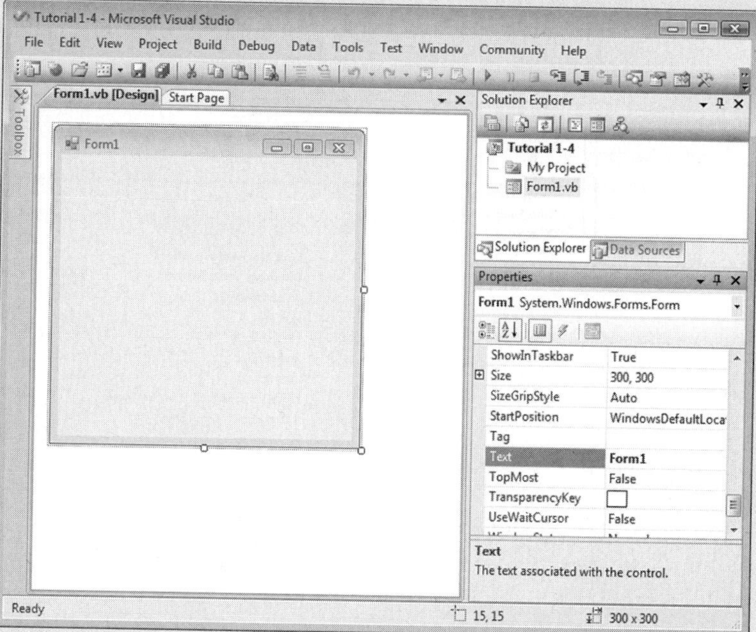

Step 11: Now you will set some of the Visual Studio options so your screens and code will appear as the examples shown in this book. Click *Tools* on the menu bar. On the *Tools* menu, click *Options . . .* The **Options dialog box** appears. In the left pane click *Text Editor*, and then click *Basic*, as shown in Figure 1-18. (If you are using Visual Basic 2008 Express, simply click *Text Editor Basic*.) Be sure all options are checked.

Figure 1-18 *VB Specific* text editor options

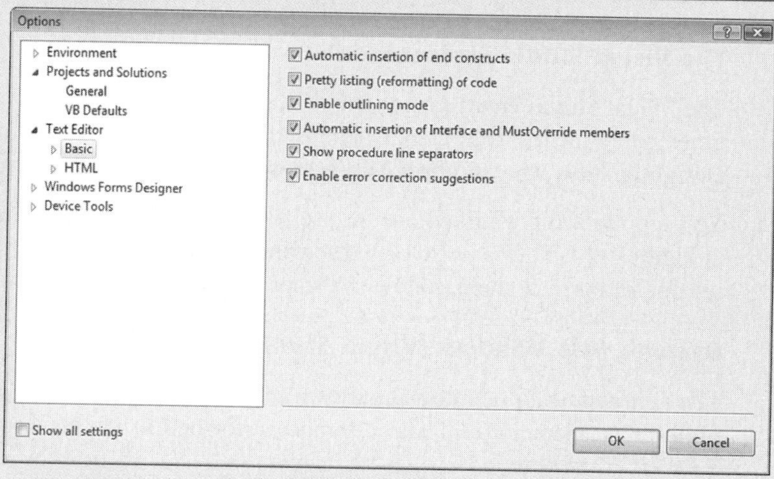

Step 12: Scroll down the left pane and select *Windows Forms Designer*. Make sure your settings match those shown in Figure 1-19. Specifically, *GridSize* should be set to *8, 8*, *ShowGrid* should be set to *True*, and *SnapToGrid* should be set to *True*. These settings control the grid you use to design forms.

TIP: To change the *GridSize* setting, click the area where the current setting is displayed, erase it, and enter `8, 8` as the new setting. To change either the *ShowGrid* or *SnapToGrid* settings, click the area where the current setting is displayed, then click the down arrow button (▾) that appears. Select *True* from the menu that drops down.

Figure 1-19 *Windows Forms Designer* settings

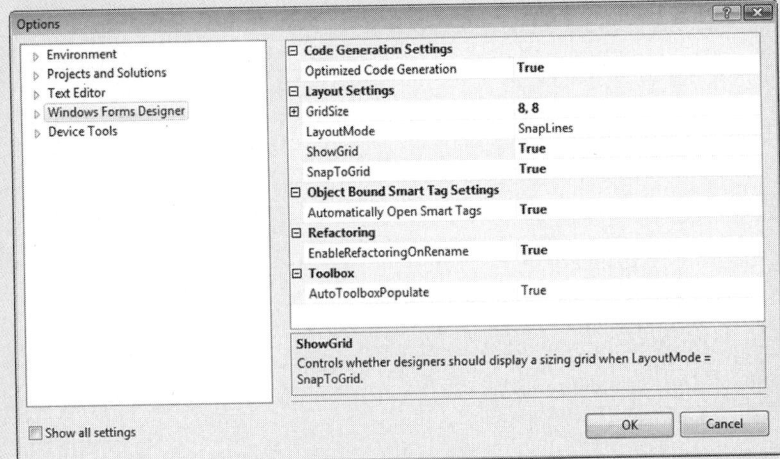

NOTE: The options you set in Steps 10 through 13 will remain set until you or someone else changes them. If you are working in a shared computer lab and you find that your screens and/or the appearance of your code does not match the examples shown in this book, you will probably need to reset these options.

Step 13: Click *OK* to close the dialog box.

The Visual Studio Environment

The Visual Studio environment (for Visual Basic) consists of a number of windows and other components. Figure 1-20 shows the locations of the following components: the ***Design*** window, the ***Solution Explorer*** window, and the ***Properties*** window.

You can move the windows around, so they may not appear in the exact locations shown in Figure 1-20. You can also close the windows so they do not appear at all. If you do not see one or more of them, follow the steps in Tutorial 1-5 to make them visible.

Dynamic Help Window (Visual Studio Only)

The ***Dynamic Help*** window, as shown in Figure 1-21 gives you a list of help topics that provide excellent tutorial and reference information about Visual Basic. It is available only in Visual Studio. Display the *Dynamic Help* window by selecting *Dynamic Help* from the menu bar's *Help* menu.

Figure 1-20 The *Design* window, *Solution Explorer* window, and *Properties* window

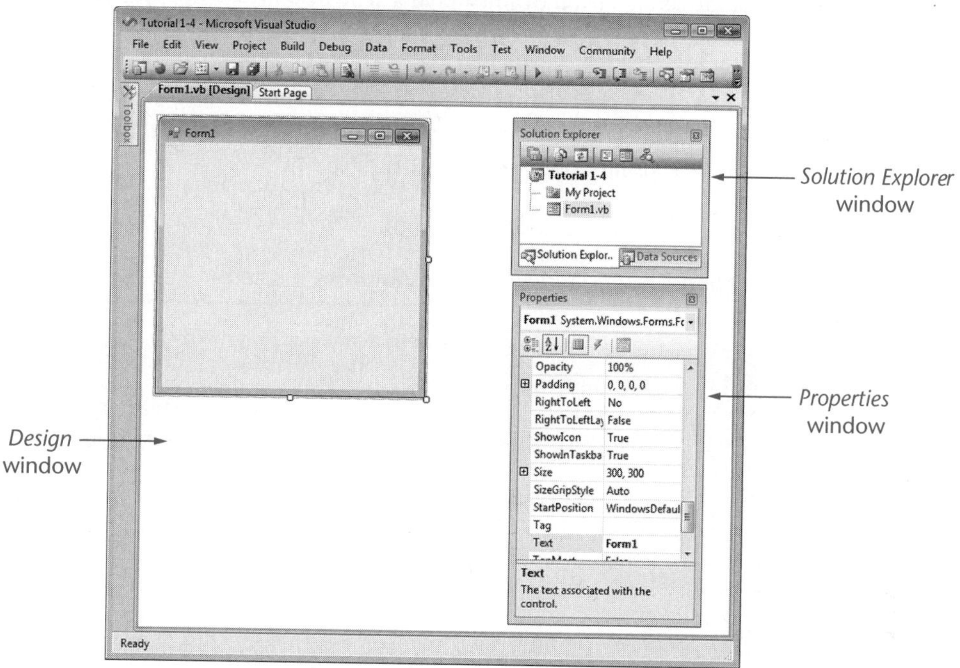

Figure 1-21 The *Dynamic Help* window

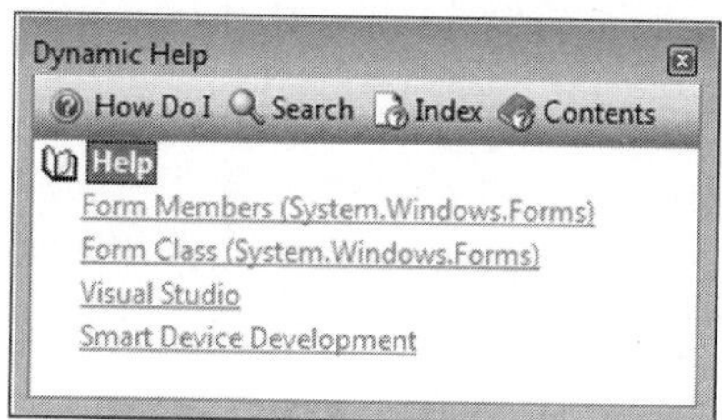

Tutorial 1-5:
Opening the *Design*, *Solution Explorer*, *Dynamic Help*, and *Properties* windows in Visual Studio

Step 1: (This tutorial is for Visual Studio users only.) If you do not see the *Design* window, click *View* on the menu bar. On the *View* menu, click *Designer*. You can also press Shift+F7 on the keyboard.

Step 2: If you do not see the *Solution Explorer* window, click *View* on the menu bar. On the *View* menu, click *Solution Explorer*. You can also press Ctrl+Alt+L on the keyboard.

Step 3: If you do not see the *Dynamic Help* window or the *Dynamic Help* window tab, click *Help* on the menu bar. On the *Help* menu, click *Dynamic Help*.

Step 4: If you do not see the *Properties* window, click *View* on the menu bar. On the *View* menu, click *Properties*. You can also press F4 on the keyboard.

Hidden Windows

Many windows in Visual Studio have a feature known as *Auto Hide*. When *Auto Hide* is turned on, the window is displayed only as a tab along one of the edges of the *Visual Studio* window. This feature gives you more room to view your application's forms and code. Figure 1-22 shows how the *Solution Explorer* and *Properties* windows appear when their *Auto Hide* feature is turned on. Notice the tabs that read *Solution Explorer* and *Properties* along the right edge of the screen.

Figure 1-22 The *Solution Explorer* and *Properties* windows hidden

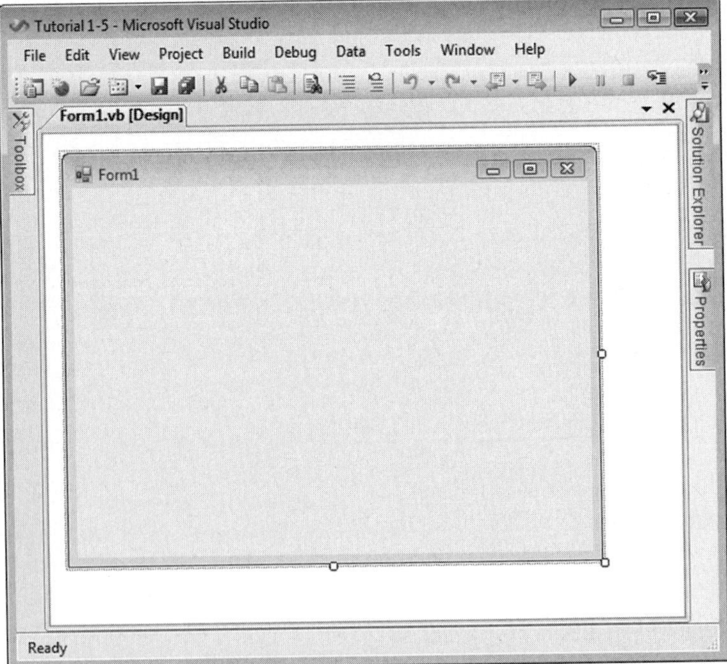

To display a hidden window, hover the mouse pointer over its tab, which pulls the window back into view. If you want the window to remain in view for a time, click its tab. The window will remain displayed until you click outside of it.

- To set a window to *Auto Hide*, right-click its caption bar and select *Auto Hide*.
- To remove the *Auto Hide* feature from a window, click its tab to display it; then right-click its caption bar and deselect *Auto Hide*.

(Alternatively, you can click the little pushpin icon on the window's caption bar to turn *Auto Hide* on and off.)

Docked and Floating Windows

Figure 1-17 shows the *Solution Explorer* and *Properties* windows when they are **docked**, which means they are attached to each other or to one of the edges of the *Visual Studio* window. Alternatively, the windows can be **floating**. You can control whether a window is **docked (dockable)** or floating as follows:

- To change a window from dockable to floating, right-click its caption bar and select *Floating*.

- To change a window from floating to dockable, right-click its caption bar and select *Dockable*.

When you click and drag one of these windows by its title bar, you move it out of the docked position, and the window becomes floating. Double-clicking the window's title bar produces the same effect. Figure 1-23 shows these windows floating.

To dock a floating window, double-click its title bar or drag it to one of the edges of the main window. You may use whichever style you prefer—docked or floating. When windows are floating, they behave as normal windows. You may move or resize them to suit your preference.

Figure 1-23 *Solution Explorer* and *Properties* windows floating

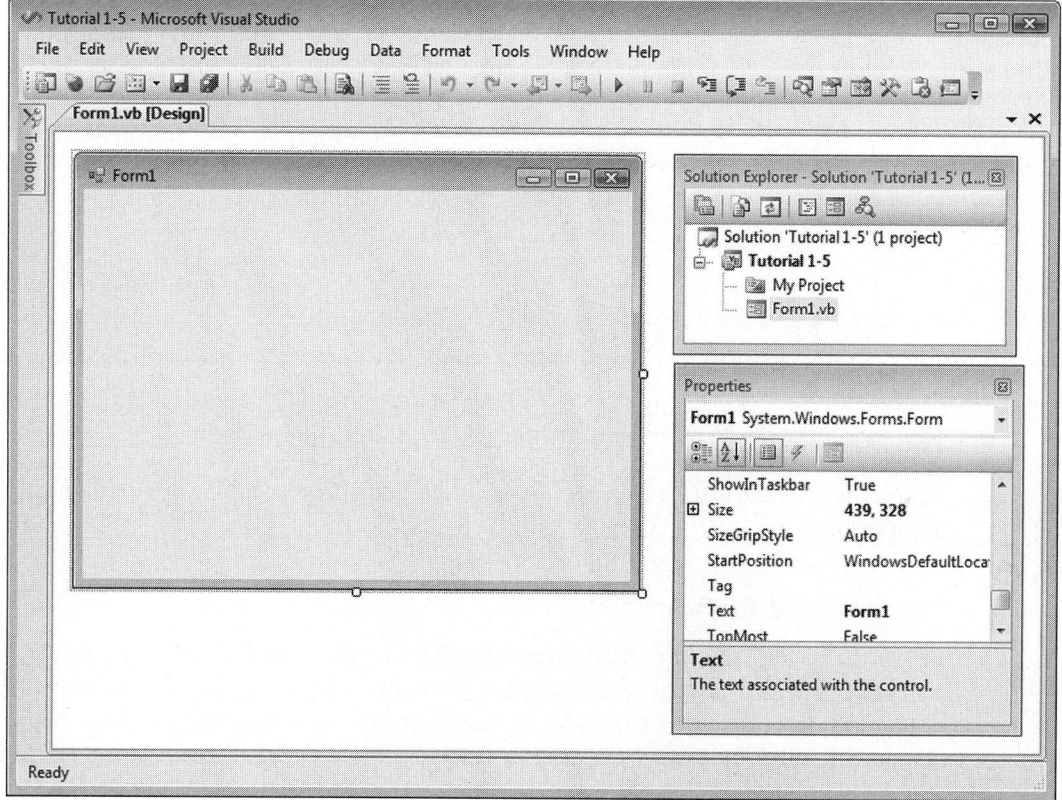

TIP: A window cannot float if its *Auto Hide* feature is turned on.

Now you have the Visual Basic environment set up properly to work with the projects in this book. Next, we will look at the individual elements.

The Title Bar

The title bar indicates the name of the project you are currently working on. The title bar shown in Figure 1-24 shows the name Tutorial 1-5. Visual Studio is currently in **Design mode**, the mode in which you design and build an application. Chapter 2 covers **Run mode** (runtime), the mode in which you run and test an application. **Break mode** is when an application is suspended for debugging purposes.

Figure 1-24 Visual Studio in Design mode

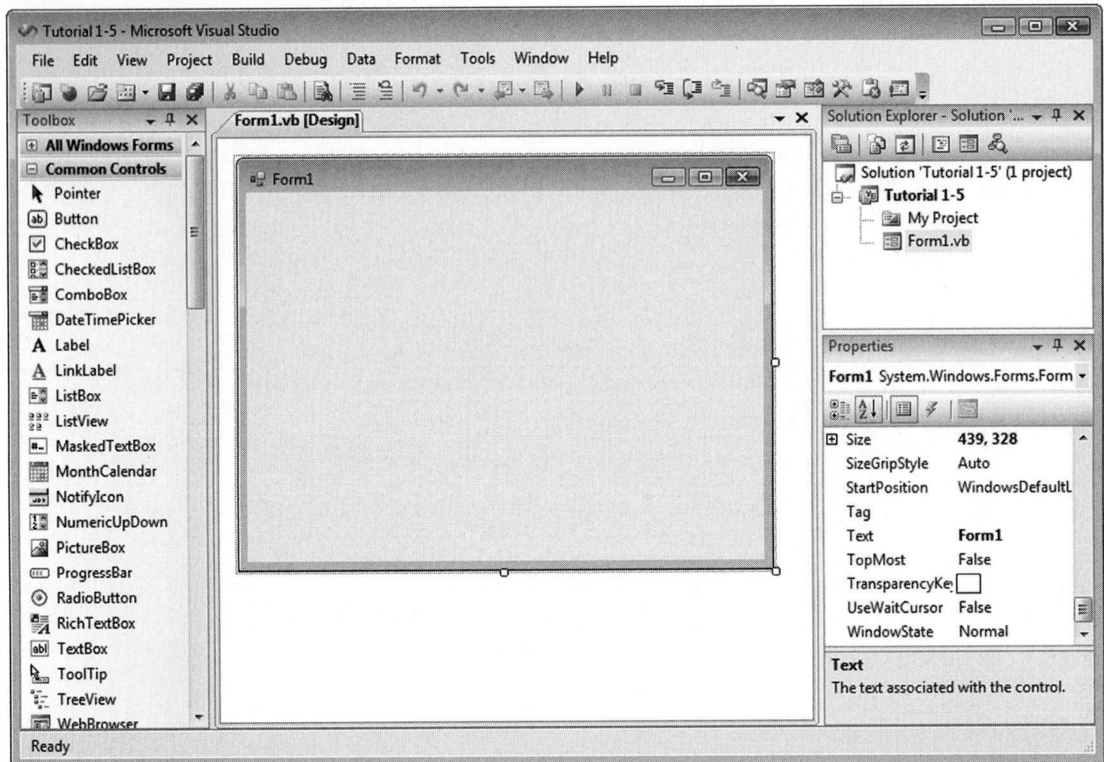

The Menu Bar

Below the title bar is the menu bar, from which you access menus when building an application.

The Standard Toolbar

Below the menu bar is the standard toolbar. The **standard toolbar** contains buttons that execute frequently used commands. All commands executed by the toolbar may also be executed from a menu, but the standard toolbar gives you quicker access to them. The standard toolbar buttons open windows with a single click. Figure 1-25 identifies the standard toolbar buttons and Table 1-9 gives a brief description of each.

Figure 1-25 Visual Basic standard toolbar buttons

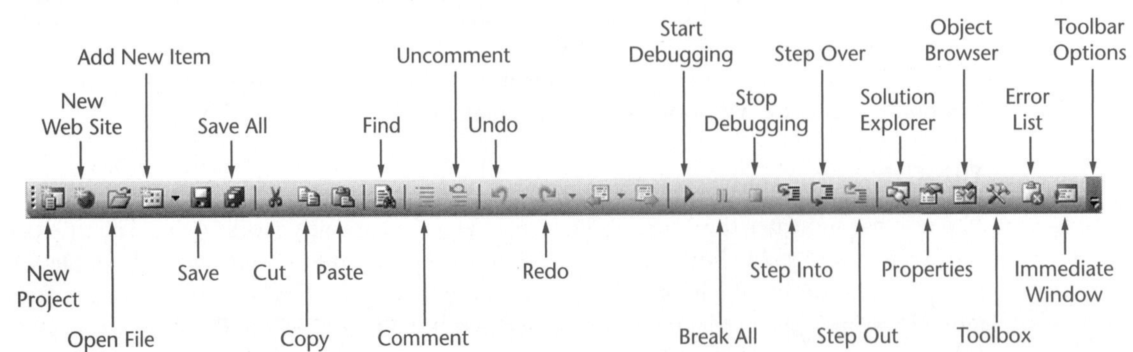

Table 1-9 Visual Basic toolbar buttons

Toolbar Button	Description
New Project	Starts a new project
New Web Site	Creates a new Web site (used in Web Forms applications)
Open File	Opens an existing file
Add New Item	Adds a new item such as a form to the current project. This button has a drop-down list (shown by the downward pointing arrow) that lets you select from several types of items.
Save *filename*	Saves the file named by *filename*
Save All	Saves all of the files in the current project
Cut	Cuts the selected item to the clipboard
Copy	Copies the selected item to the clipboard
Paste	Pastes the contents of the clipboard
Find	Searches for text in your application code
Comment	Comments out the selected lines
Uncomment	Uncomments the selected lines
Undo	Undoes the most recent operation
Redo	Redoes the most recently undone operation
Start Debugging	Starts debugging (running) your program
Break All	Pauses execution of your program
Stop Debugging	Stops debugging (running) your program
Step Into	Traces (steps) into the code in a procedure
Step Over	Executes the next statement without tracing into procedure calls
Step Out	Exits the current procedure while still debugging
Solution Explorer	Opens the *Solution Explorer* window
Properties	Opens the *Properties* window
Object Browser	Opens the *Object Browser* window
Toolbox	Opens the *Toolbox* window, displaying, for example, visual controls you can place on Windows forms
Error List	Displays a list of most recent errors generated by the Visual Basic compiler
Immediate Window	Opens the *Immediate* window, which is used for debugging
Toolbar Options	Lets you add buttons to or remove buttons from the toolbar

NOTE: As with most Windows applications, menu items and buttons cannot be used when they are grayed out.

The *Toolbox* Window

Figure 1-26 shows the *Toolbox* **window**, with all groups (tabs) closed. The *Toolbox* contains buttons and icons that let you build rich visual interfaces in Windows desktop applications. You have already seen some of the tools in tutorials in the earlier part of this chapter.

The *Toolbox* window is divided into sections, which are accessible by clicking on named tabs. Clicking a tab displays the entries in the group. Figure 1-27 shows the *Toolbox* window after the user has clicked the *Common Controls* tab. The controls in this group include Buttons, Labels, TextBoxes, and other common controls. Not all of the *Toolbox* items can be displayed at once, so scroll arrows are provided.

TIP: The *Toolbox* window is only activated when a form is open in Design mode.

Using ToolTips

A **ToolTip** is a small rectangular box that pops up when you hover the mouse over a button on the toolbar or in the *Toolbox* for a few seconds. The box contains a short description of the button's purpose. Figure 1-28 shows the ToolTip that appears when the cursor is left sitting on the *Save All* button. Use a ToolTip whenever you cannot remember a particular button's function.

Figure 1-26 The *Toolbox* window, with all tabs closed

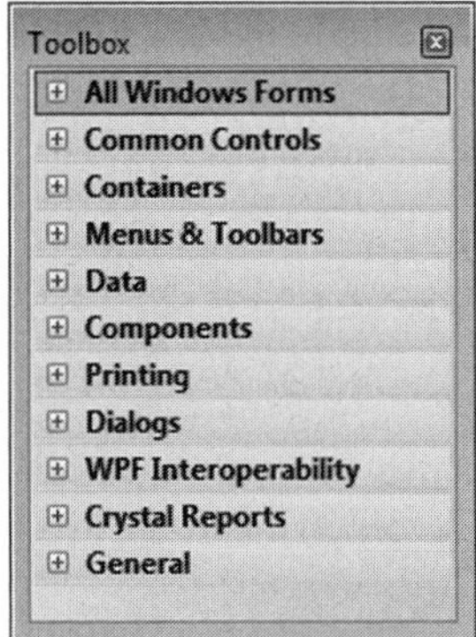

Figure 1-27 The *Toolbox* window, showing *Common Controls*

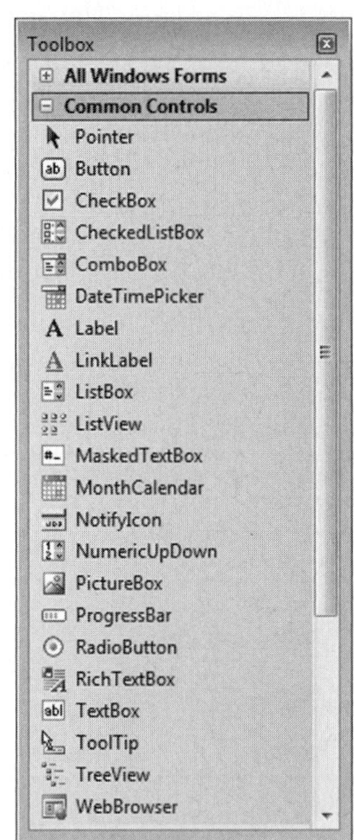

Figure 1-28 *Save All* ToolTip

Tutorial 1-6 introduces you to Visual Studio.

Tutorial 1-6: Getting familiar with Visual Studio

If Visual Studio is not running on your computer, follow the steps in Tutorial 1-4. This exercise will give you practice working with elements of the Visual Basic environment.

Step 1: Make sure *Auto Hide* is turned off for the *Solution Explorer* and *Properties* windows. If your *Solution Explorer* and *Properties* windows are in the docked position, double-click each of their title bars to undock them. (If they are already floating, skip to Step 2.)

Step 2: Practice moving the windows around on the screen by clicking and dragging their title bars.

Step 3: Double-click the title bars of each of the windows to move them back to their docked positions.

Step 4: The *Solution Explorer*, *Properties* window, *Dynamic Help* window, and *Toolbox* each have a *Close* button in their upper right corner. Close each of these windows by clicking their *Close* buttons (*Dynamic Help* does not appear in Visual Basic Express).

Step 5: Do you remember which buttons on the toolbar restore the *Solution Explorer*, *Properties* window, and *Toolbox*? If not, move your mouse cursor over any button on the toolbar, and leave it there until the ToolTip appears. Repeat this procedure on different buttons until you find the ones whose ToolTips read *Solution Explorer*, *Properties Window*, and *Toolbox*.

Step 6: Click the appropriate buttons on the toolbar to restore the *Solution Explorer*, *Properties*, and *Toolbox* windows.

Step 7: Exit Visual Studio by clicking *File* on the menu bar, then clicking *Exit* on the *File* menu. You may see a dialog box asking you if you wish to save changes to a number of items. Because we are just experimenting with the Visual Basic environment, click *No*.

In this section, you learned to start Visual Studio, interact with Visual Studio, and identify many on-screen tools and components. In Chapter 2, you will start building your first application.

Checkpoint

1.22 Briefly describe the purpose of the *Solution Explorer* window.

1.23 Briefly describe the purpose of the *Properties* window.

1.24 Briefly describe the purpose of the *Dynamic Help* window.

1.25 Briefly describe the purpose of the standard toolbar.

1.26 What is Design mode? What is Run mode? What is Break mode?

1.27 What is the difference between the toolbar and the *Toolbox*?

1.28 What is a ToolTip?

Summary

1.1 Computer Systems: Hardware and Software

- The major hardware components of a computer are the central processing unit (CPU), main memory, secondary storage devices, input devices, and output devices. Computer programs are stored in machine language, as a series of binary numbers.
- Main memory holds the instructions for programs that are running and data programs are working with. RAM is usually volatile, used only for temporary storage.
- The two general categories of software are operating systems and application software.

1.2 Programs and Programming Languages

- The two primary methods of programming in use today are procedural and object-oriented.
- The advent of graphical user interfaces (GUIs) has influenced the shift from procedural programming to object-oriented.
- There are several types of controls available in Visual Basic. Applications in this chapter contained forms, Labels, TextBoxes, Buttons, CheckBoxes, RadioButtons, ListBoxes, ComboBoxes, and scroll bars.
- The appearance of a screen object, such as a form or other control, is determined by the object's properties.
- An event-driven program is one that responds to events or actions that take place while the program is running.

1.3 More about Controls and Programming

- All controls have a name. Programmers manipulate or access a control in a programming statement by referring to the control by its name. When the programmer creates a control in Visual Basic, it automatically receives a default name.
- Any control whose name appears in a programming statement should have a descriptive, programmer-defined name. Although programmers have a great deal of flexibility in naming controls, they should follow some standard guidelines.
- The fundamental language elements of an event procedure or other method are keywords, programmer-defined names, operators, remarks, and syntax.

1.4 The Programming Process

- This section outlines the steps for designing and creating a Visual Basic application.

1.5 Visual Studio and Visual Basic Express (the Visual Basic Environment)

- The Visual Basic environment, which is part of Visual Studio, consists of tools used to build Visual Basic applications.
- Visual Basic can be used to create many different types of applications.

Key Terms

algorithm
application software
attributes
binary number
Break mode
button
central processing unit (CPU)
CheckBox

ComboBox
comments
compiler
controls
Design mode
Design window
disk drive
docked (dockable) windows
Dynamic Help window
event-driven
event procedure
floating window
flowchart
Form object
graphical user interface (GUI)
GroupBox
hardware
HScrollBar
identifier
input
input device
integrated development environment (IDE)
keywords
Label
language syntax
ListBox
machine language instructions
main memory
methods
Name property
New Project dialog box
object-oriented programming (OOP)
objects
operands
operating system (OS)
operators
Options dialog box
output
output device
PictureBox
procedural programming
procedure
program
programmer-defined name
programming languages
project
properties
Properties window
pseudocode
RadioButton
random-access memory (RAM)
remarks
Run mode
runtime error
secondary storage
software
Solution Explorer window
standard toolbar
syntax
syntax error
Text property
TextBox
Toolbox window
ToolTip
VScrollBar

Review Questions and Exercises

Fill-in-the-Blank

1. The job of the ______________________ is to fetch instructions, carry out the operations commanded by the instructions, and produce some outcome or resultant information.
2. A(n) ______________________ is an example of a secondary storage device.
3. The two general categories of software are ______________________ and ______________________.
4. A program is a set of ______________________.
5. Since computers can't be programmed in natural human language, algorithms must be written in a(n) ______________________ language.
6. ______________________ is the only language computers really process.

7. Words that have special meaning in a programming language are called ______________________.

8. Words or names defined by the programmer are called ______________________.

9. ______________________ are characters or symbols that perform operations on one or more operands.

10. A(n) ______________________ is part of an application's code but is ignored by the compiler. It is intended for documentation purposes only.

11. The rules that must be followed when constructing a program are called ______________________.

12. ______________________ is information a program gathers from the outside world.

13. ______________________ is information a program sends to the outside world.

14. A(n) ______________________ is a set of well-defined steps for performing a task or solving a problem.

15. A(n) ______________________ is a diagram that graphically illustrates the flow of a program.

16. ______________________ is a cross between human language and a programming language.

17. To set the Visual Basic environment options, click the *Options . . .* command, which is found on the ______________________ menu.

18. If you do not see the *Solution Explorer* or *Properties* windows in Visual Studio, you may use the ______________________ menu to bring them up.

19. A(n) ______________________ is a container for holding a project.

20. A(n) ______________________ is a group of files that make up a software application.

21. The ______________________ window allows you to navigate among the files in your project.

22. The ______________________ window shows most of the currently selected object's properties and those properties' values.

23. When windows are ______________________, it means they are attached to each other or to one of the edges of the Visual Studio main window.

24. To dock a floating window, ______________________ its title bar or drag it to one of the edges of the main window.

25. Visual Studio's ______________________ window indicates the name of the project you are working on while you are in Design mode.

26. All commands executed by the ______________________ may also be executed from a menu.

27. The ______________________ window contains your application's form. This is where you design your application's user interface by placing controls on the form that appears when your application executes.

28. You use the ______________________ to place controls on an application's form. It contains buttons for the commonly used Visual Basic controls.

29. The ______________________ window displays help topics that are relevant to the operation you are currently performing in Visual Basic.

30. A(n) ______________________ is a small box that is displayed when you hold the mouse cursor over a button on the toolbar or in the *Toolbox* for a few seconds.

Short Answer

1. What is the difference between main memory and secondary storage?
2. What is the difference between operating system software and application software?
3. Briefly describe what procedural programming means.
4. Briefly describe what object-oriented programming means.
5. Briefly describe what an event-driven program is.
6. Why has the advent of graphical user interfaces (GUIs) influenced the shift from procedural programming to object-oriented/event-driven programming?
7. From what you have read in this chapter, describe the difference between a Label control and a TextBox control. When is it appropriate to use one or the other?
8. When creating a VB application, you will spend much of your time doing what three things?
9. What is a form?
10. Summarize the mandatory rules that you must follow when naming a control.
11. What is a keyword?
12. What is the purpose of inserting comments in a program?
13. What is language syntax?
14. What is a syntax error?
15. What is a runtime error?
16. What is an operator?
17. What is a flowchart?
18. What is pseudocode?
19. What default name will VB give to the first Label control that you place on a form? What default name will VB assign to the first TextBox control that you place on a form?
20. What property determines the text that is displayed by a Label control?
21. What is *Auto Hide*? How do you turn *Auto Hide* on or off?
22. What is the *Toolbox* window in Visual Studio?
23. What is the standard toolbar in Visual Studio?
24. What is a tooltip?
25. If you do not see the *Solution Explorer* window in Visual Studio, how do you display it?
26. If you do not see the *Properties* window in Visual Studio, how do you display it?

27. How do you display the *Dynamic Help* window in Visual Studio?
28. What mode is Visual Basic in while you are designing and building an application?
29. What mode is Visual Basic in while you are running an application?
30. What mode is Visual Basic in while an application is suspended for debugging?
31. Figure 1-29 shows the Visual Basic IDE. What are the names of the four areas that are indicated in the figure?

Figure 1-29 The Visual Basic IDE

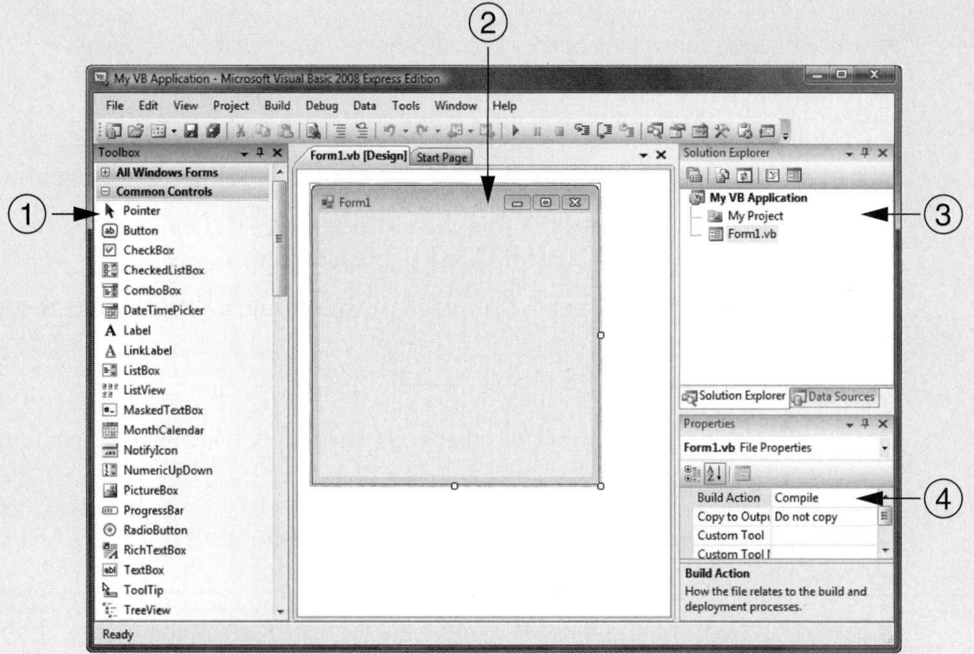

What Do You Think?

1. Are each of the following control names legal or illegal? If a name is illegal, indicate why.
   a. `txtUserName`
   b. `2001sales`
   c. `lblUser Age`
   d. `txtName/Address`
   e. `btnCalcSubtotal`
2. What type of control does each of the following prefixes usually indicate?
   a. `btn`
   b. `lbl`
   c. `txt`
3. For each of the following controls, make up a legal name that conforms to the standard control name convention described in this chapter.
   a. A TextBox control in which the user enters his or her last name
   b. A Button control that, when clicked, calculates an annual interest rate
   c. A Label control used to display the total of an order
   d. A Button control that clears all the input fields on a form

4. The following control names appear in a Visual Basic application used in a retail store. Indicate what type of control each is and guess its purpose.
   a. `txtPriceEach`
   b. `txtQuantity`
   c. `txtTaxRate`
   d. `btnCalcSale`
   e. `lblSubTotal`
   f. `lblTotal`

Programming Challenges

1. **Carpet Size**

   You have been asked to create an application for a carpet sales and installation business. The application should allow the user to enter the length and width of a room and calculate the room's area in square feet. The formula for this calculation is

   $$Area = Length \times Width$$

   In this exercise, you will gain practice using Steps 1 through 6 of the programming process described in Section 1.5:

   1. Clearly define what the application is to do.
   2. Visualize the application running on the computer and design its user interface.
   3. Make a list of the controls needed.
   4. Define the values of each control's properties.
   5. Make a list of methods needed for each control.
   6. Create a flowchart or pseudocode version of each method.

   Step 1: Describe the following characteristics of this application:

   Purpose
   Input
   Process
   Output

   Step 2: Draw a sketch of the application's form and place all the controls that are needed.

   Step 3: Make a list of the controls you included in your sketch. List the control type and the name of each control.

   Step 4: List the value of the Text property for each control, as needed. (Remember, some controls do not have a Text property.)

   Step 5: List each method needed. Give the name of each method and describe what each method does.

   Step 6: For each method you listed in Step 5, draw a flowchart or write pseudocode.

2. **Available Credit**

   A retail store gives each of its customers a maximum amount of credit. A customer's available credit is determined by subtracting the amount of credit used by the customer from the customer's maximum amount of credit. As you did in Programming Challenge 1, perform Steps 1 through 6 of the programming process to design an application that determines a customer's available credit.

VideoNote
Solving the Sales Tax Problem

3. **Sales Tax**

   Perform Steps 1 through 6 of the programming process to design an application that gets from the user the amount of a retail sale and the sales tax rate. The application should calculate the amount of the sales tax and the total of the sale.

4. **Account Balance**

   Perform Steps 1 through 6 of the programming process to design an application that gets from the user the starting balance of a savings account, the total dollar amount of the deposits made to the account, and the total dollar amount of withdrawals made from the account. The application should calculate the account balance.

CHAPTER

2 Creating Applications with Visual Basic

TOPICS

In this chapter you will develop your first application, which displays a map and written directions to the Highlander Hotel. This application uses a form with labels, a PictureBox control, and buttons. You will write your first event procedures (also known as event handlers) in Visual Basic code and then you will learn to use the Label control's AutoSize, BorderStyle, and TextAlign properties. You will be introduced to clickable images, dynamic help, context-sensitive help, and the debugging process.

2.1 Focus on Problem Solving: Building the *Directions* Application

CONCEPT: In this section you create your first Visual Basic application: a window that displays a map and road directions to a hotel. In the process you learn how to place controls on a form and manipulate various properties.

The desk clerks at the historic Highlander Hotel frequently receive calls from guests requesting driving directions. Some desk clerks are not familiar with the street numbers or exits, and inadvertently give unclear or incorrect directions. The hotel manager has asked you to create an application that displays a map to the hotel. The desk clerks can refer to the application when giving directions to customers over the phone. We will use the following steps to create the application:

1. Clearly define what the application is to do.
2. Visualize the application running on the computer and design its user interface.
3. Make a list of the controls needed.
4. Define the values of each control's relevant properties.
5. Start Visual Basic and create the forms and other controls.

Now we will take a closer look at each of these steps.

1. Clearly define what the application is to do.

Purpose: Display a map to the Highlander Hotel
Input: None
Process: Display a form
Output: Display on the form a graphic image showing a map

2. Visualize the application running on the computer and design its user interface.

Before you create an application on the computer, first you should create it in your mind. This step is the visualization of the program. Try to imagine what the computer screen will look like while the application is running. Then draw a sketch of the form or forms in the application. Figure 2-1 shows a sketch of the *Directions* form presented by this application.

Figure 2-1 Sketch of *Directions* form

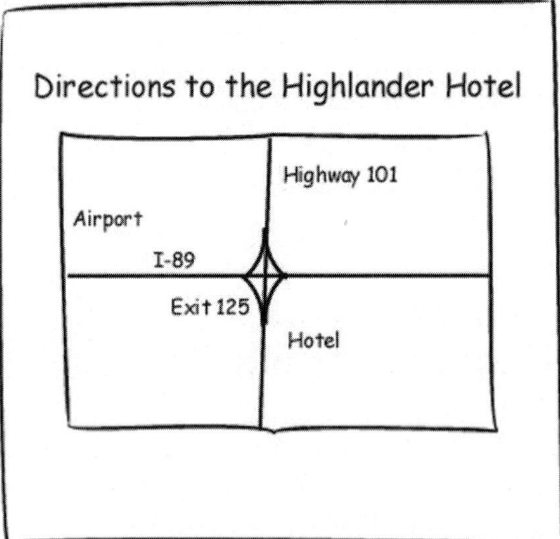

3. Make a list of the controls needed.

In this step you list all the needed controls. You should assign names to all the controls that will be accessed or manipulated in the application code and provide a brief description of each control. Our application only needs three controls, listed in Table 2-1. Because none of the controls are used in code, we will keep their default names.

Table 2-1 *Directions* application controls

Control Type	Control Name	Description
Form	(Default Name: *Form1*)	A small form that will serve as the window onto which the other controls will be placed
Label	(Default Name: *Label1*)	Displays the message *Directions to the Highlander Hotel*
PictureBox	(Default Name: *PictureBox1*)	Displays the graphic image showing the map to the hotel

4. Define the values of each control's relevant properties.

Each control's property settings are listed in Table 2-2.

Table 2-2 *Directions* application control properties

Property	Value
Form	
Name	*Form1*
Text	*Directions*
Label	
Name	*Label1*
Text	*Directions to the Highlander Hotel*
TextAlign	*MiddleCenter*
Font	Microsoft sans serif, bold, 16 point
PictureBox	
Name	*PictureBox1*
Image	*HotelMap.jpg*
SizeMode	*StretchImage*

Notice that in addition to the Name and Text properties, we are setting the TextAlign and Font properties of the Label control. The **TextAlign property** determines how the text is aligned within the label. We will discuss this property in detail later.

In addition to its Name property, we are setting the PictureBox control's Image and SizeMode properties. The Image property lists the name of the file containing the graphic image. We will use *HotelMap.jpg*, which is located in the student sample programs folder named *Chap2*. The **SizeMode property** is set to *StretchImage*, which allows us to resize the image. If the image is too small, we can enlarge it (stretch it). If it is too large, we can shrink it.

5. Start Visual Basic and create the forms and other controls.

Now you are ready to construct the application's form. Tutorial 2-1 gets you started.

Tutorial 2-1:
Beginning the *Directions* application

In this tutorial you begin the *Directions* application. You will create the application's form and use the *Properties* window to set the form's Text property.

VideoNote

Starting a Project

Step 1: Start Visual Studio (or Visual Basic Express), as you did in Chapter 1. Select one of the following ways to execute the *New Project* command:

- Click *File* on the menu bar and then click *New Project . . .*
- Click the *New Project* icon, the first icon on the left side of the Visual Studio toolbar

The *New Project* window will appear. If you are using Visual Studio, in the *Project types* pane, select *Windows* under *Visual Basic*. Select the *Windows Forms Application* icon in the *Templates* pane. Each project has a name. The default project name, such as *WindowsApplication1*, appears in the *Name* text box. Replace this name with `Directions`. Click the *OK* button to close the window.

> **NOTE:** Your project will be saved in the location specified in the *Tools→ Options* menu, in the category named *Projects and Solutions*. The *Visual Studio projects location* text box contains a directory name, which you can change.

Step 2: The Visual Basic environment should be open with a blank form named *Form1* in the *Design* window, as shown in Figure 2-2. Click the form to select it.

Step 3: Look at the *Properties* window. It should appear as shown in Figure 2-3.

Figure 2-2 *Form1* displayed in the *Design* window

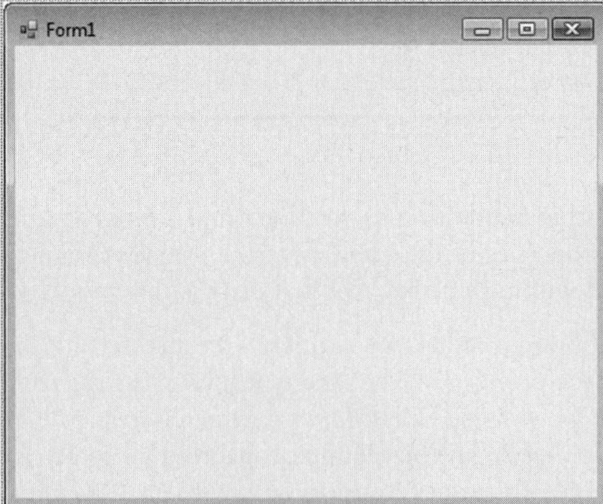

Because you have selected *Form1*, the *Properties* window displays the properties for the *Form1* object. The drop-down list box at the top of the window shows the name of the selected object, *Form1*. Below that, the object's properties are displayed in two columns. The left column lists each property's name and the right column shows each property's value. Below the list of properties is a brief description of the currently selected property.

> **TIP:** The *Properties* window has two buttons near the top that control the order of names in the window. The first sorts by category and the second sorts alphabetically. We will use the alphabetical sort in our examples.

The Text property is highlighted, which means it is currently selected. A form's Text property holds the text displayed in the form's title bar. It is initially set to the same value as the form name, so this form's Text property equals *Form1*. Follow the instructions in Steps 4 and 5 to change the Text property to *Directions*.

Step 4: Double-click the word *Form1* inside the Text property.

Step 5: Delete the word *Form1* and type **`Directions`** in its place. Press the Enter key. Notice that the word *Directions* now appears in the form's title bar.

Step 6: Although you changed the form's Text property, you did not change its name. Scroll the *Properties* window up to the top of the list of properties, as shown in Figure 2-4. The Name property is still set to the default value, *Form1*.

Figure 2-3 *Properties* window showing *Form1*

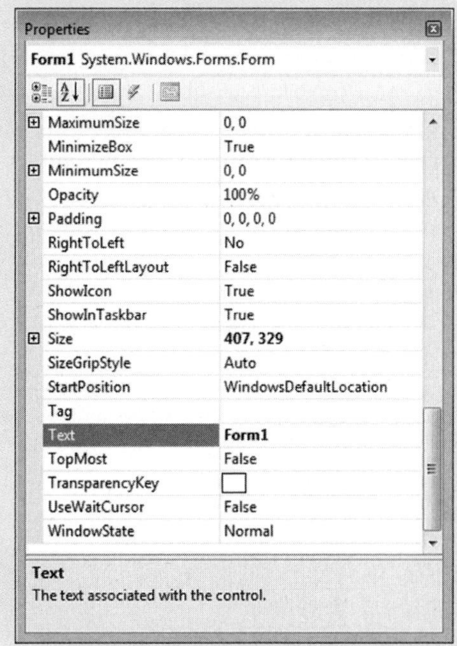

Figure 2-4 *Properties* window scrolled to top

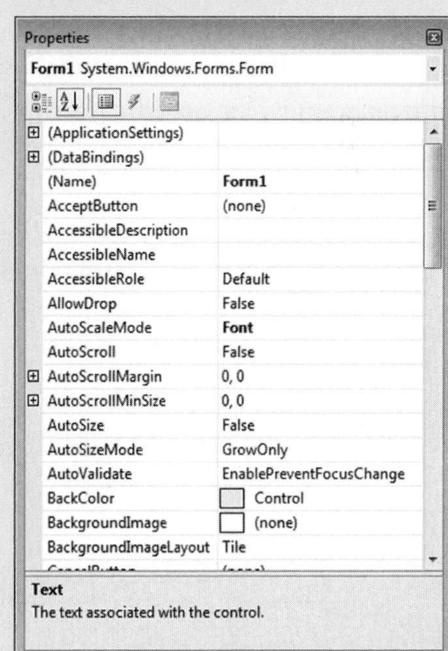

The next step is to add a Label control to the form. Tutorial 2-2 guides you through the process.

Tutorial 2-2: Adding a Label control to the *Directions* application

VideoNote
Using Label Controls

Step 1: Now you are ready to add the Label control to the form. Make sure the *Common Controls* tab is open in the *Toolbox* window, as shown in Figure 2-5, and double-click the *Label* control icon. The label appears on the form with a dotted line around it and a small white square in its upper left corner, as shown in Figure 2-6. The dotted-line rectangle is called a **bounding box**—it marks the tightest rectangle that contains all parts of the control.

Figure 2-5 Label control tool

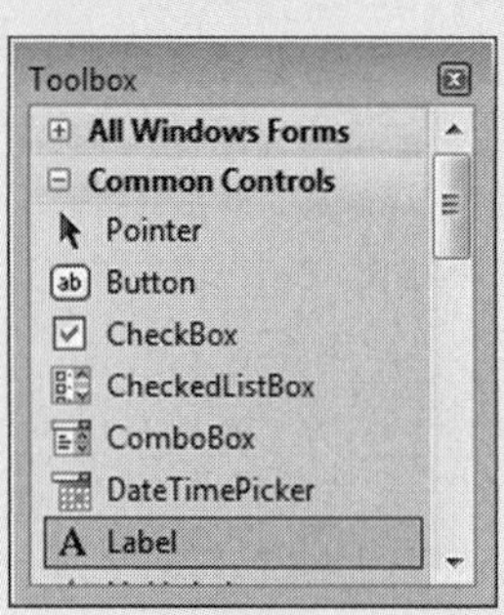

Figure 2-6 Label control on form

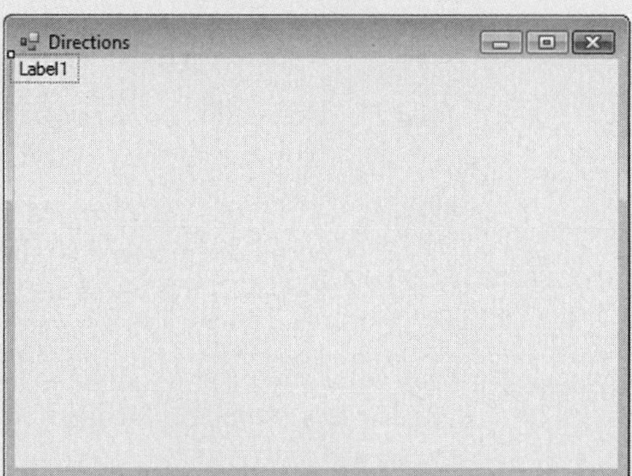

Step 2: Look at the *Properties* window. Because the label you just placed on the form is currently selected, the *Properties* window shows its properties (see Figure 2-7). The Text property is set, by default, to *Label1*. Double-click this value to select it, and replace its value by typing `Directions to the Highlander Hotel` in its place. Press the [Enter] key. When you have typed the new text into the Text property, the form appears, as shown in Figure 2-8. The label resizes itself to fit the contents of the Text property.

Figure 2-7 *Properties* window

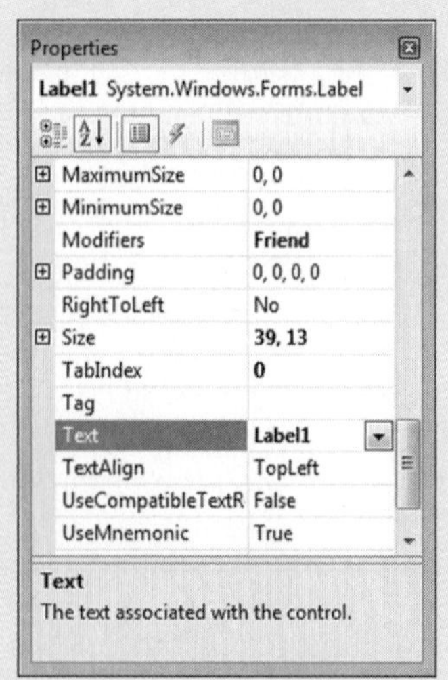

Figure 2-8 Label with new text property value

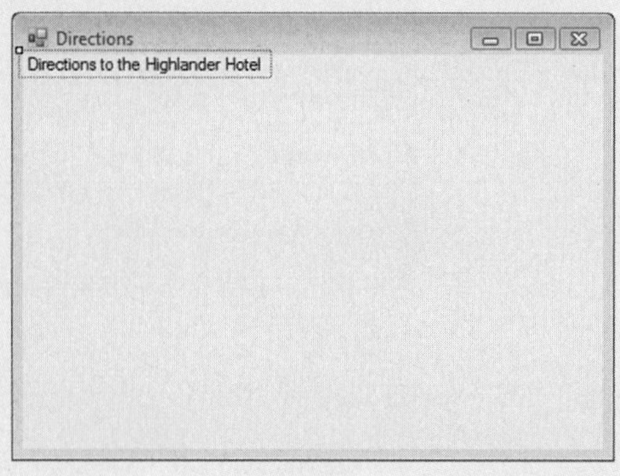

Step 3: Next, you will move the label to a new location on the form. Move the mouse over the label on the form, hold down the left mouse button, and drag the label to the top middle area of the form, as shown in Figure 2-9. From now on, we will refer to this type of operation as *dragging the control.*

Step 4: The AutoSize property of a label, which is *True* by default, makes the label automatically adjust its size depending on the contents of the Text property. Set the label's AutoSize property to *False* by double-clicking the AutoSize property. Figure 2-10 shows how square handles appear around the label. For practice, use the mouse to drag the handles and change the label's size.

Figure 2-9 After moving the Label control

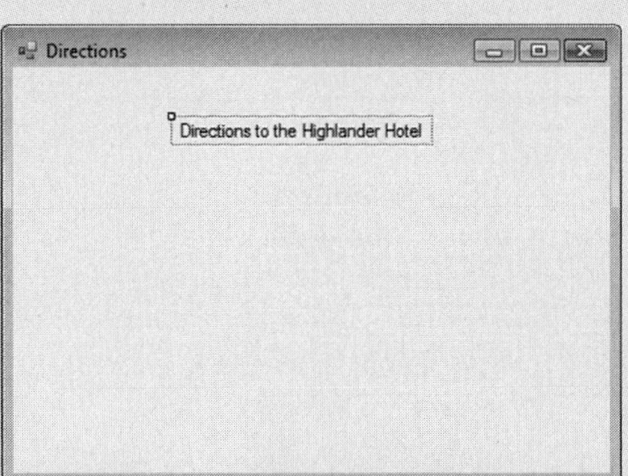

Figure 2-10 Label control, with AutoSize = *False*

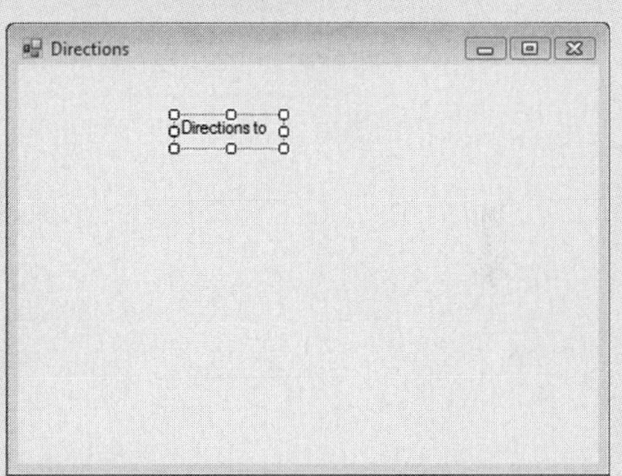

By default, a label's text is aligned with the top and left edges of the label's bounding box. The position of the text within a label's bounding box is controlled by the TextAlign property, which may be set to any of the following values: *TopLeft*, *TopCenter*, *TopRight*, *MiddleLeft*, *MiddleCenter*, *MiddleRight*, *BottomLeft*, *BottomCenter*, or *BottomRight*. Figure 2-11 shows nine Label controls, each with a different TextAlign value.

Figure 2-11 Text alignments

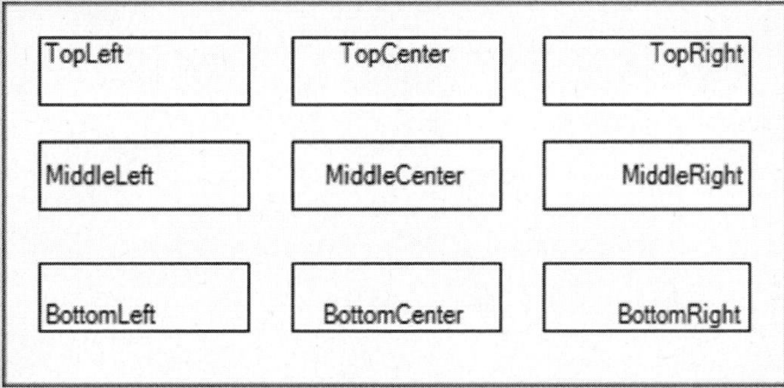

Tutorial 2-3 takes you through the process of aligning the label's text.

Tutorial 2-3:
Setting the Label's TextAlign property

Step 1: With the Label selected, look at the *Properties* window. Notice that the value of the TextAlign property is *TopLeft*.

Step 2: Click the *TextAlign* property. Notice that a down-arrow button ( ) appears next to the property value. Click the arrow and a small dialog box with nine buttons appears. Each of the buttons represents a TextAlign value, as shown in Figure 2-12.

Step 3: Click the *MiddleCenter* button. The label's text is now centered in the middle of the label's bounding box, as shown in Figure 2-13.

Figure 2-12 *TextAlign* drop-down dialog box

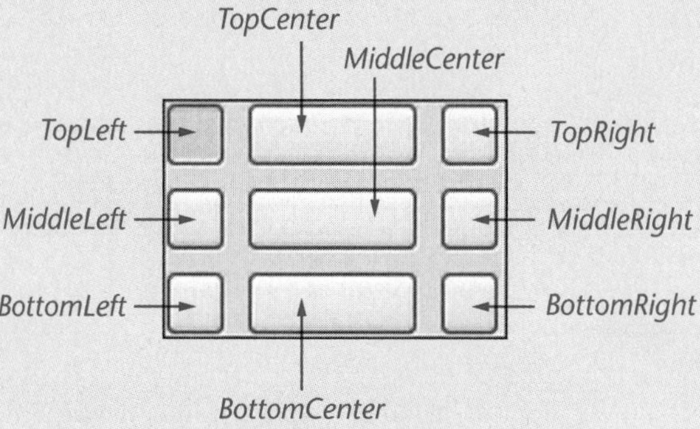

Figure 2-13 Label text centered

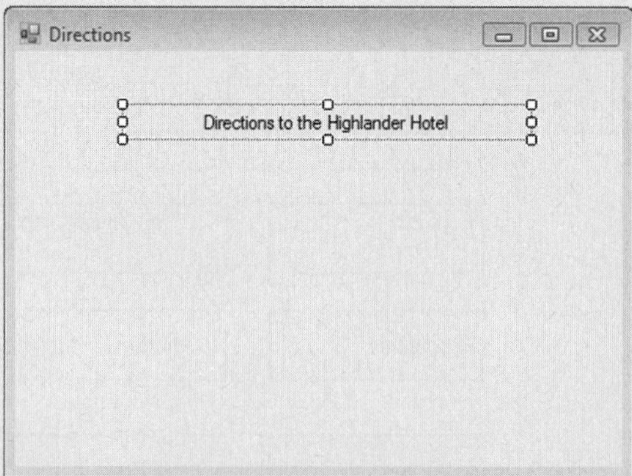

In the planning phase, we indicated that the label's text should be displayed in a 16-point bold Microsoft sans serif font. These characteristics are controlled by the label's Font property. The **Font property** allows you to set the font, font style, and size of the label's text. Tutorial 2-4 shows you how to change the font size and style of labels.

Tutorial 2-4:
Changing the Label's font size and style

Step 1: With the Label selected, click the *Font* property in the *Properties* window. Notice that an ellipsis button (…) appears. When you click the ellipsis button, the *Font* dialog box appears, as shown in Figure 2-14.

Figure 2-14 *Font* dialog box

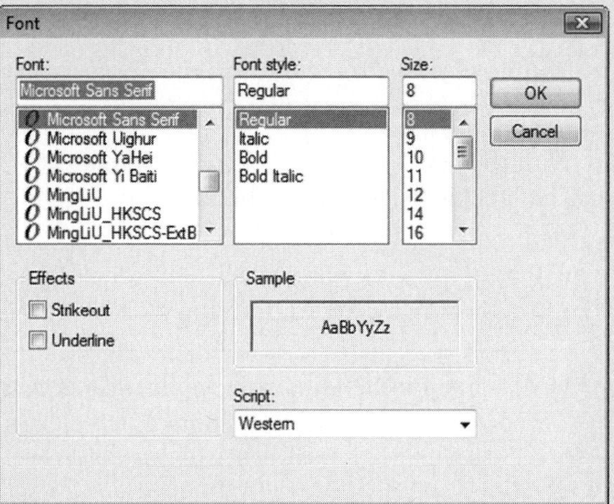

Step 2: *Microsoft Sans Serif* is already the selected font. Click *Bold* under *Font style*, and select *16* under *Size*. Notice that the text displayed in the *Sample* box changes to reflect your selections. Click the *OK* button.

The text displayed by the label is now in 16-point bold Microsoft sans serif. Unfortunately, not all the text can be seen because it is too large for the Label control. You must enlarge both the form and the Label control so all of the label text is visible.

Step 3: Select the form by clicking anywhere on it, except on the Label control. You will know you have selected the form when the **sizing handles** appear around it and the form's properties appear in the *Properties* window.

Step 4: Use the form's sizing handles to widen the form, and then select the label and enlarge it so it appears similar to the one shown in Figure 2-15.

Figure 2-15 Resized form showing all text

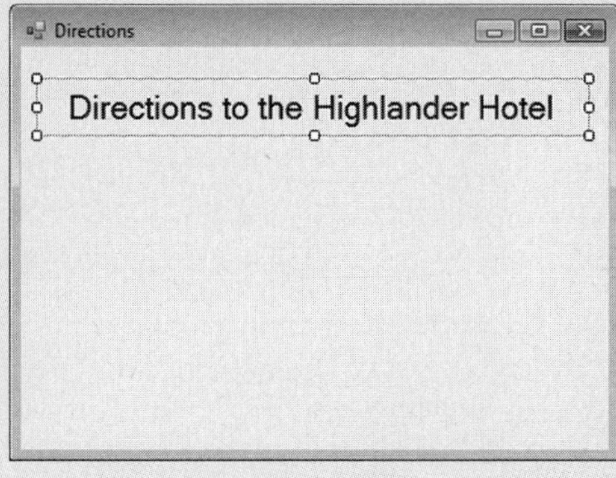

To delete a control, select it and press the Delete key on the keyboard. In Tutorial 2-5 you add another Label control to the form (one that you will not need) and then you delete it.

Tutorial 2-5:
Deleting a control

Step 1: Double-click the *Label* tool in the *Toolbox*. Another Label control appears on the form.

Step 2: With the new Label control still selected, press the Delete key on the keyboard. The label is deleted from the form.

TIP: If you accidentally delete a control you can restore it with the *Undo* button ( ) on the standard toolbar.

The last step in building this application is to insert the street map. In Tutorial 2-6 you insert a **PictureBox control**, which can be used to display an image.

Tutorial 2-6:
Inserting a PictureBox control

Step 1: Double-click the *PictureBox* tool in the *Toolbox*. An empty PictureBox control appears on the form. Move the control to a position approximately in the center of the form, as shown in Figure 2-16.

Figure 2-16 PictureBox control placed

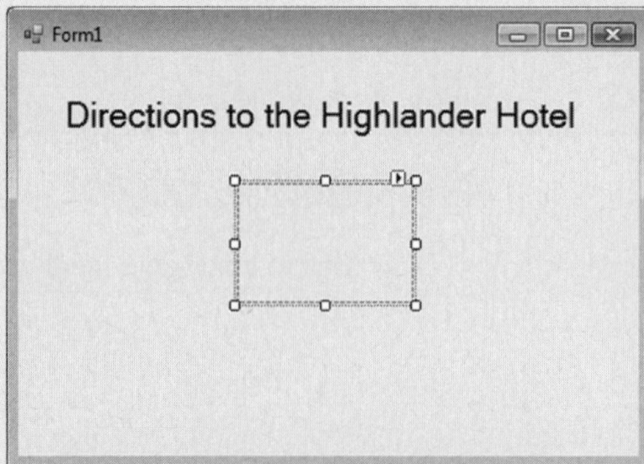

Step 2: The PictureBox control displays an image in a variety of ways, depending on the setting of the SizeMode property. Set the SizeMode property to *StretchImage*. This will make the image stretch or shrink so it fits within the bounding box of the PictureBox control.

The Image property is currently set to *(none)*, indicating that no image is loaded into the PictureBox control. Our next task is to load an image that was copied to your computer from the Student CD.

Step 3: Click the PictureBox's Image property and notice that a *Browse* button (...) appears next to the property value. Click the button to display the *Select Resource* dialog box, as shown in Figure 2-17. Select *Local resource* and click the *Import* button. When the *Open* dialog box appears, navigate to the file named *HotelMap.jpg* in the student sample programs directory, in the *Chap2* folder. After you click the *OK* button, the graphic shown in Figure 2-18 should appear in the PictureBox control.

Step 4: Because the SizeMode property is set to *StretchImage*, the image expands to fit the size of the PictureBox control. Use the control sizing handles to enlarge the image so its details are clearly visible (see Figure 2-19).

TIP: You may want to enlarge the form again to make more room for the image.

NOTE: You have now seen that properties are set in the *Properties* window in one of three ways:

- Typing a value for the property
- Selecting a value for the property from a drop-down list by clicking the down-arrow button ( )
- Establishing a value for the property with a dialog box, which appears when the *Browse* button (...) is clicked

Figure 2-17 Using the *Select Resource* dialog box to insert an image

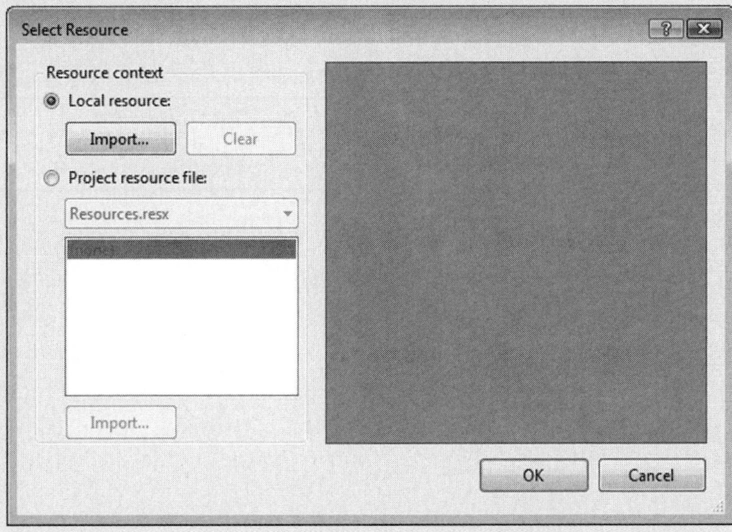

Figure 2-18 PictureBox control with image in place

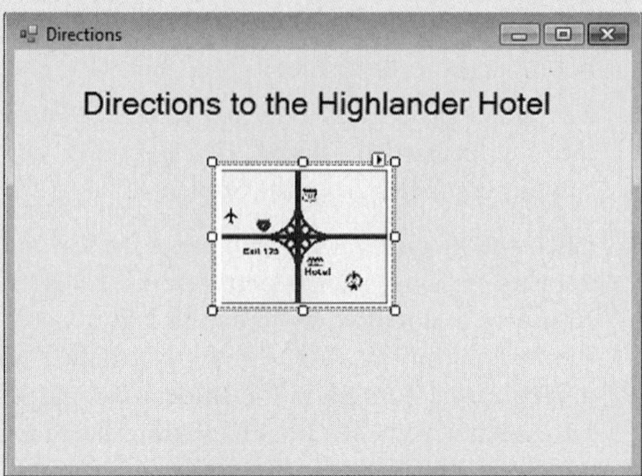

Figure 2-19 *HotelMap.jpg* enlarged

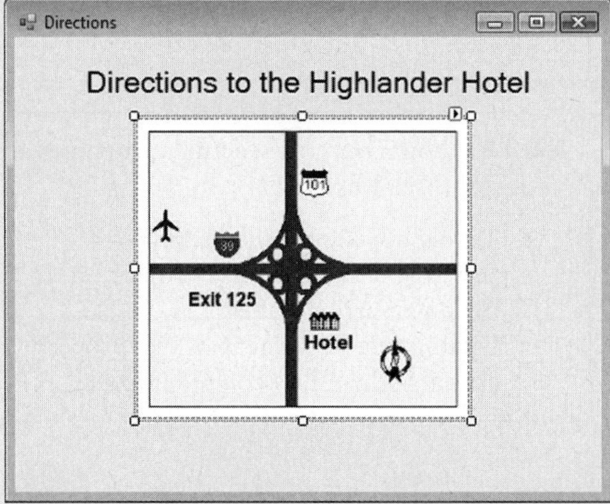

Now it's time to save the changes that you've made to your project. Tutorial 2-7 describes three different ways to save a project.

Tutorial 2-7:
Saving and running the application

Step 1: You may use any of the following methods to save a project (application).

- Click *File* on the menu bar, then click *Save All* on the *File* menu
- Press Ctrl+Shift+S on the keyboard
- Click the *Save All* button on the standard toolbar

Use one of these methods to save your project. You will see the dialog window shown in Figure 2-20. If you wish, you can click the *Browse* button to change the diectory in which your application will be saved.

Now you will run the application. It doesn't have any event procedures, so it will only display the PictureBox and Label. There are three ways to run an application in Visual Studio:

- Click the *Start Debugging* button (▶) on the toolbar
- Click *Debug* on the menu bar, then click *Start Debugging* on the *Debug* menu
- Press the F5 key

Figure 2-20 Confirming the *Name, Location,* and *New Solution Name* when saving a project

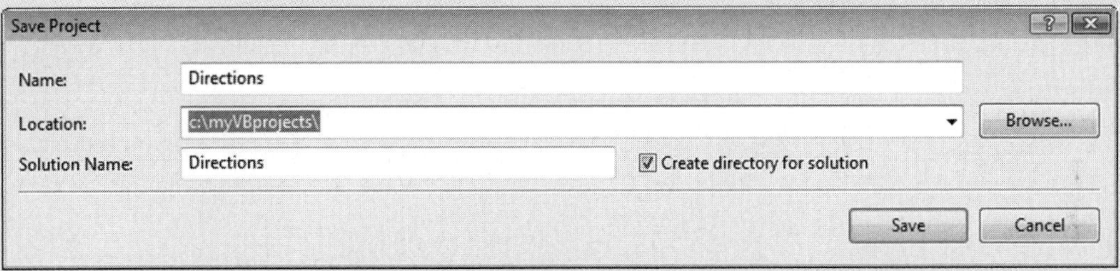

Step 2: Run the application using one of the ways listed above. After a short delay, you will see the application's form display, as shown in Figure 2-21. We say that the program is now in Run mode.

Figure 2-21 Running the *Directions* application

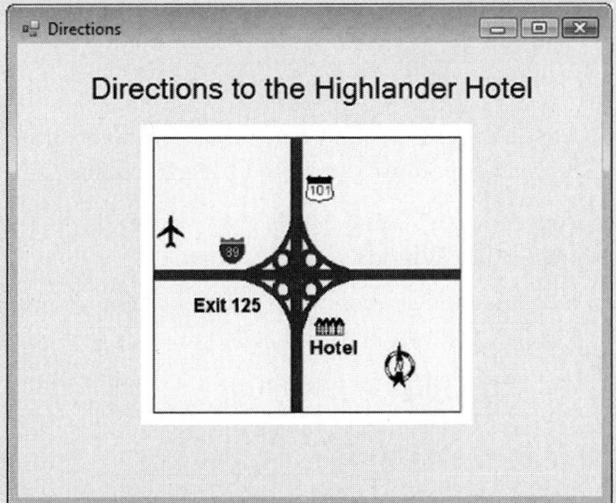

TIP: Save your work often to prevent the accidental loss of changes you have made to your project.

Step 3: Now you will stop the application (end its execution). Select one of the following actions:

- Click the *Close* button (☒) on the application window
- Click *Debug* on the menu bar, then click *Stop Debugging* on the *Debug* menu

The application will stop and Visual Studio will return to Design mode.

Closing a Project

To close the current project, click *File* on the menu bar, and then click *Close Project*. If you have made changes to the project since the last time you saved it, you will see a dialog box asking you if you want to save your changes (see Figure 2-22).

Figure 2-22 Closing a project, confirming *Save* or *Discard*

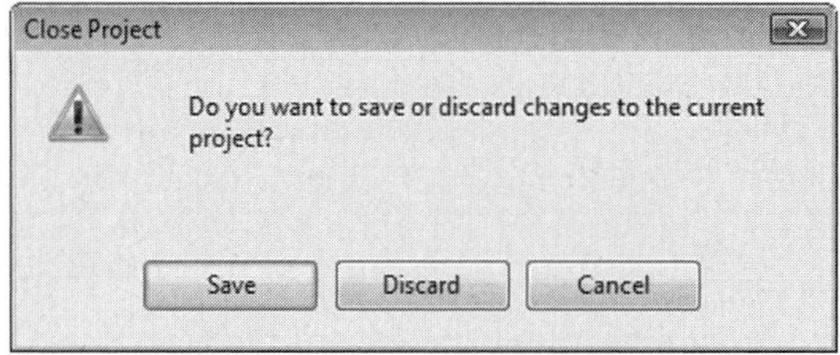

Tutorial 2-8 explains how to close your Visual Basic project.

Tutorial 2-8:
Closing a Visual Basic project

Step 1: To close a Visual Basic project, click *File* on the menu bar, then click *Close Project*. If you are prompted to save changes, do so.

Step 2: You can exit Visual Studio (or Visual Basic Express) the same way you exit most other Windows applications:

- Click the *File* menu and then click the *Exit* command
- Click the *Close* button (☒) on the right edge of the title bar

Use one of these methods to exit Visual Studio.

2.1 You want to change what is displayed in a form's title bar. Which of its properties do you change?

2.2 How do you insert a Label control onto a form?

2.3 What is the purpose of a control's sizing handles?

2.4 What are the possible values for a label's TextAlign property?

2.5 How do you delete a control?

2.6 What happens when you set a PictureBox control's SizeMode property to *StretchImage*?

2.7 What is the name of the dotted-line rectangle surrounding the Label control when looking at a form in Design mode?

How Solutions and Projects Are Organized on the Disk

A **solution** is a container that holds Visual Basic projects (see Figure 2-23). A project must belong to a solution. When you create a new project, Visual Studio automatically creates a solution with the same name as the project, and inserts the project in the solution. For example, when you created the *Directions* project, a solution named *Directions* was created, and the project was inserted in the *Directions* solution. In Visual Basic Express, the solution name is always the same name as the project.

Tutorial 1-4 showed that Visual Studio (or Visual Basic Express) uses a default location for saving projects and solutions. It creates a folder at this location, using the name of the solution (which is also the name of the project). Several files, and some other folders, are created and stored in this folder.

When you created the *Directions* project and the solution containing it, Visual Studio created a folder named *Directions* at the location specified in the *Save Project* dialog box. All files related to the project were stored in this folder (see Figure 2-24). The **solution file** is named *Directions.sln*. Inside the solution folder is a project folder (also named *Directions*). The contents of this folder are shown in Figure 2-25. The file named *Directions.vbproj* is called the **project file.**

Figure 2-23 Relationship between a solution and its projects

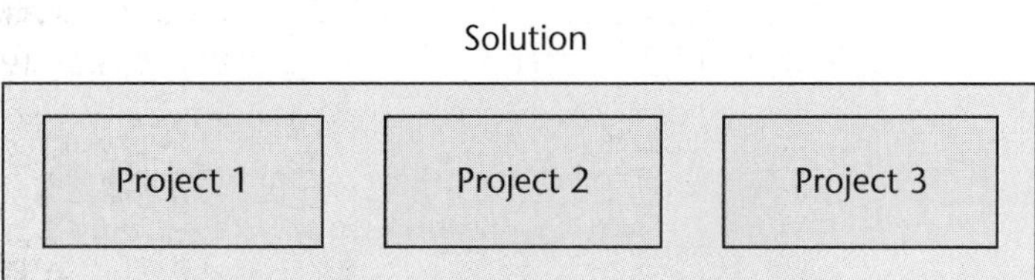

Figure 2-24 *Directions* solution folder

Name	Size	Type
Directions		File Folder
Directions.sln	1 KB	Microsoft Visual Studio Solution
Directions.suo	8 KB	Visual Studio Solution User Options

Figure 2-25 Inside the *Directions* project folder

Name	Size	Type
bin		File Folder
My Project		File Folder
obj		File Folder
Directions.vbproj	5 KB	Visual Basic Project file
Directions.vbproj.user	1 KB	Visual Studio Project User Options file
Form1.Designer.vb	3 KB	Visual Basic Source file
Form1.resx	6 KB	.NET Managed Resources File
Form1.vb	1 KB	Visual Basic Source file

Opening Existing Projects

There are three ways to open an existing project:

- Click the project name in the *Recent Projects* panel of the *Start Page*, as shown in Figure 2-26. The project should open immediately; if it doesn't, you may have moved the project to a different directory, deleted the project, or its files may have become corrupted.
- Click the *Open Project* button and browse for the project name. In Visual Studio, you will see the *Open Project* dialog box, as shown in Figure 2-27. Select the solution file (extension *.sln*) and click the *Open* button.
- Click *File* in the menu bar and then click *Open Project* in the *File* menu. Browse for the project using the *Open Project* dialog box, select the solution file, and click the *Open* button.

Tutorial 2-9 guides you through the steps of opening an existing project.

Figure 2-26 List of recent projects on the *Start Page*

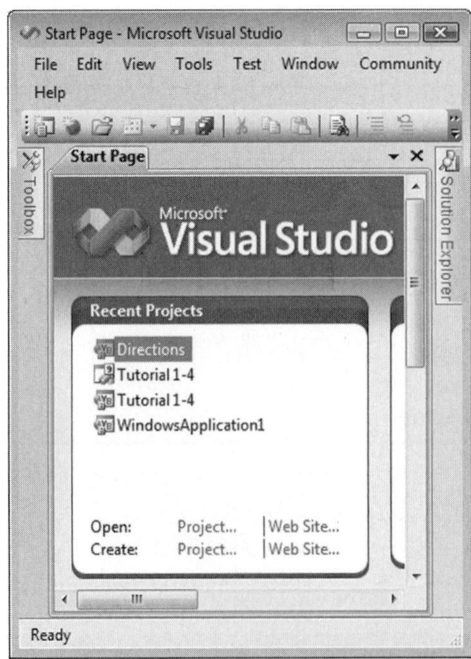

Figure 2-27 *Open Project* dialog box with *Directions* solution folder open

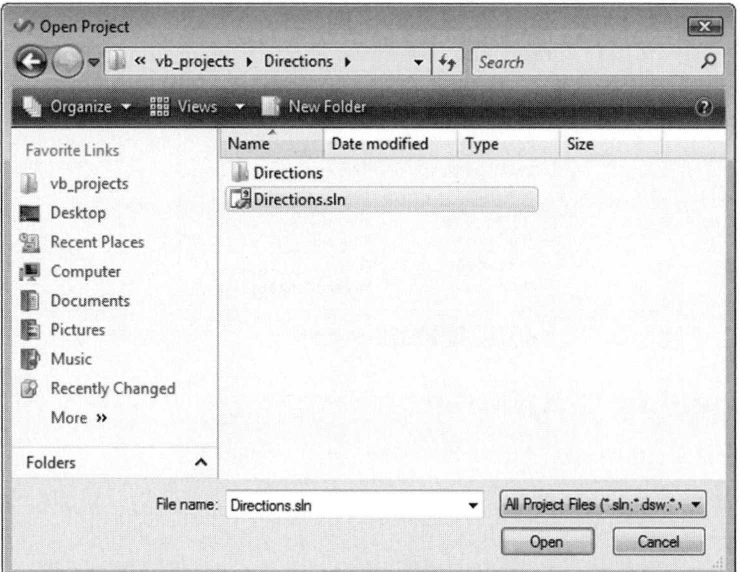

Tutorial 2-9:
Opening an existing project

This tutorial assumes that the *Directions* project is saved to your disk and Visual Studio is not currently running.

Step 1: Start Visual Studio or Visual Basic Express. From the *Start Page*, open the *Directions* project by clicking its name in the *Recent Projects* panel. Another way to open the *Directions* project is to click *File* on the menu bar, and then click *Open Project*. This also causes the *Open Project* dialog box to appear. Browse to and open the *Directions* folder, select the *Directions.sln* file, and click the *Open* button.

Step 2: After performing one of these actions, the *Directions* project should be open and you should see the form with the map to the hotel displayed in the *Design* window. If you do not see the form displayed, look in the *Solution Explorer* window and double-click the name *Form1.vb*.

(Leave the project open because you will use it in Tutorial 2-10.)

More about the *Properties* Window

In this section you will learn about the *Properties* window's **object box** and its *Alphabetical* and *Categorized* buttons. Figure 2-28 shows the location of the object box. The *Alphabetical* and *Categorized* buttons appear just below the object box, on a small toolbar. Figure 2-29 shows the location of the buttons on this toolbar.

Figure 2-28 Object box

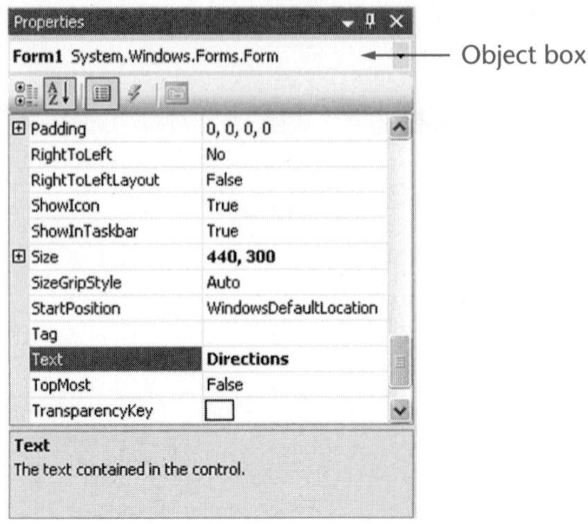

Figure 2-29 *Categorized* and *Alphabetical* buttons

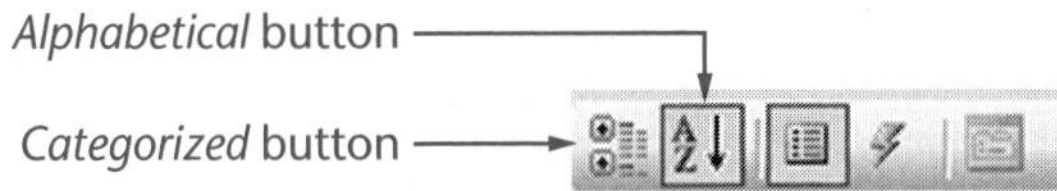

In addition to clicking objects in the *Design* window, you can also use the object box on the *Properties* window to select any object in the project. The object box provides a drop-down list of the objects in the project.

The *Categorized* and *Alphabetical* buttons affect the way properties are displayed in the *Properties* window. When the ***Alphabetical* button** is selected, the properties are displayed in alphabetical order. When the ***Categorized* button** is selected, related properties are displayed together in groups. For example, in categorized view, a Label control's **BackColor property** and **BorderStyle property** are displayed within the *Appearance* group. Figure 2-30 shows examples of the *Properties* window in each view.

Figure 2-30 *Properties* window in alphabetical and categorized views

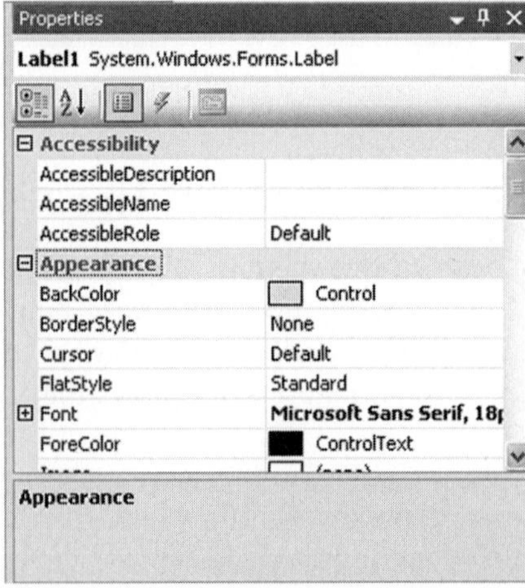

A few of the properties, including the Name property, are enclosed in parentheses. Because these properties are used so often, VB designers enclosed them in parentheses to make them appear at the top of the alphabetical list. In Tutorial 2-10 you practice using these components of the *Properties* window.

Tutorial 2-10:

Using the Object box, *Alphabetical* button, and *Categorized* button

Step 1: With the *Directions* project loaded, click the down-arrow button ( ) that appears at the right edge of the object box. You should see the names of the *Form1*, *Label1*, and *PictureBox1* controls.

Step 2: Click the name *Label1* in the list. *Label1* is now selected in the *Design* window. Repeat this procedure, selecting the *PictureBox1* control and the *Form1* control. As you select these objects, notice that they become selected in the *Design* window.

Step 3: Select the *Label1* control and click the *Categorized* button. Scroll through the list of properties displayed in the *Properties* window. Notice there are several categories of properties.

2.8 Describe three ways to open an existing project.

2.9 What are the two viewing modes for the *Properties* window? How do you select either of these modes? What is the difference between the two?

2.10 Open the *Directions* project. In the *Properties* window, arrange *Form1*'s properties in categorized order. Under what category does the Text property appear? Under what category does the Name property appear?

2.11 How can you select an object using only the *Properties* window?

2.2 Focus on Problem Solving: Responding to Events

CONCEPT: An application responds to events, such as mouse clicks and keyboard input, by executing code known as *event procedures* or *event handlers*. In this section, you write event procedures for the directions application.

VideoNote
Responding to Events

The manager of the Highlander Hotel reports that the *Directions* application has been quite helpful to the desk clerks. Some clerks, however, requested that the application be modified to display written directions as well as the map. Some also requested a more obvious way to exit the application, other than clicking the standard Windows *Close* button, located on the application's title bar.

You decide to add a button to the application form that, when clicked, causes the written directions to appear. In addition, you decide to add an *Exit* button that causes the application to stop when clicked.

Figure 2-31 shows the modified sketch of the form presented by this application.

Figure 2-31 Modified *Directions* application sketch

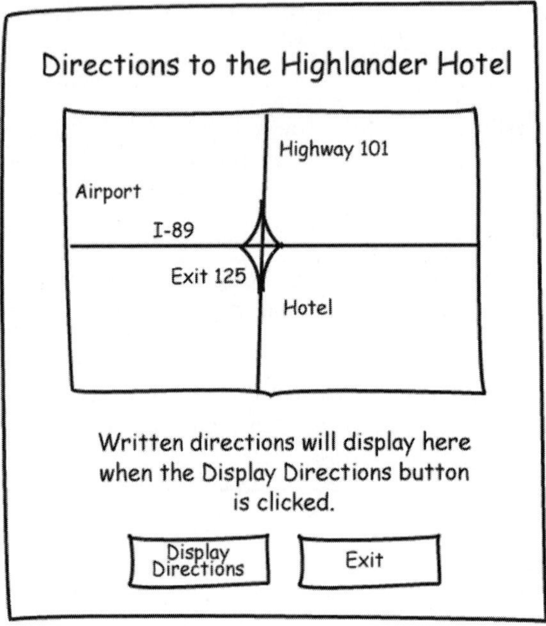

Table 2-3 lists the controls that will be added to the application. Because the Label control will be accessed in code and the buttons will have code associated with them, you will assign them names.

Table 2-3 Controls to be added to *Directions* application

Control Type	Control Name	Description
Label	`lblDirections`	Displays written directions to the hotel
Button	`btnDisplayDirections`	When clicked, causes the `lblDirections` control's text to appear on the form
Button	`btnExit`	Stops the application when clicked

VideoNote
The Name Property

Property settings for all controls are listed in Table 2-4. The table mentions a new property, Visible, used with the `lblDirections` control. Visible is a **Boolean property**, which means it can only hold one of two values: *True* or *False*. When a control's **Visible property** is set to *True*, the control can be seen on the form. A control is hidden, however, when its Visible property is set to *False*. In this application, we want the `lblDirections` control to be hidden until the user clicks the `btnDisplayDirections` button, so we initially set its Visible property to *False*.

Table 2-4 *Directions* application control properties

Property	Value
Label	
Name	`lblDirections`
Text	*Traveling on I-89, take Exit 125 onto Highway 101 South. The hotel is on the left, just past the I-89 intersection. Traveling on Highway 101 North, the hotel is on the right, just before the I-89 intersection.*
Visible	*False*
Button	
Name	`btnDisplayDirections`
Text	*Display Directions*
Button	
Name	`btnExit`
Text	*Exit*

Only two event procedures (event handlers) are needed in the *Directions* application, as shown in Table 2-5. `btnDisplayDirections_Click` is the name of the procedure that is invoked when the `btnDisplayDirections` button is clicked, and `btnExit_Click` is the event procedure that executes when the `btnExit` button is clicked.

Table 2-5 *Directions* application event procedures

Method	Description
`btnDisplayDirections_Click`	Causes the `lblDirections` control to become visible on the form; this is accomplished by setting the Label's Visible property to *True*
`btnExit_Click`	Terminates the application

Figure 2-32 shows a flowchart for the `btnDisplayDirections_Click` event procedure. Figure 2-33 shows a flowchart for the `btnExit_Click` event procedure.

Figure 2-32 Flowchart for `btnDisplayDirections_Click`

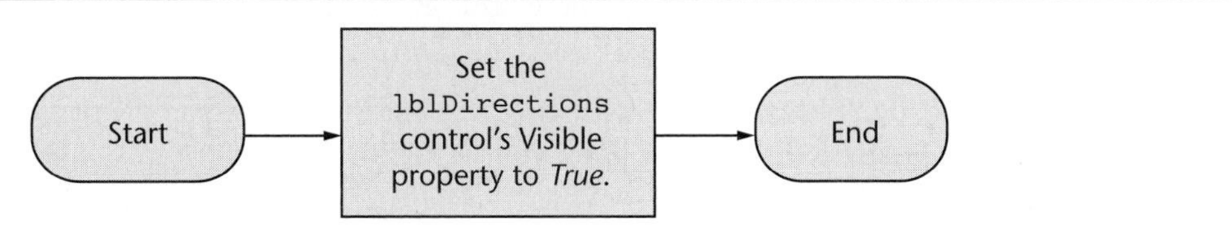

Figure 2-33 Flowchart for `btnExit_Click`

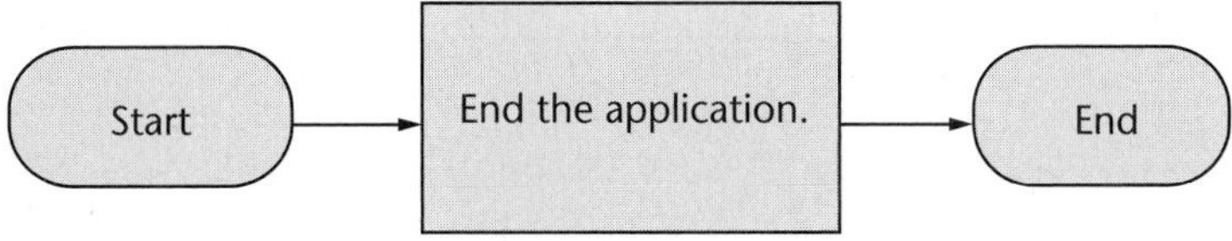

Now that you have seen flowcharts for the event procedures, let's look at the actual code you will write. The code for the `btnDisplayDirections_Click` event procedure is as follows:

```
Private Sub btnDisplayDirections_Click(ByVal sender As System.Object, _
  ByVal e As System.EventArgs) Handles btnDisplayDirections.Click

  ' Make the directions visible
  lblDirections.Visible = True
End Sub
```

NOTE: The first two lines of code shown here will initially appear as one long line in the Visual Studio editor. Our example shows how to break the long line into two lines.

Event procedures are a type of Sub procedure. The word *Sub* is an abbreviation for the general term *subroutine*. This event procedure begins with the keywords `Private Sub` and ends with the keywords `End Sub`. Among other things, the first line of the event procedure (printed as two lines) identifies the control it belongs to and the event it responds to. This is illustrated in Figure 2-34.

Figure 2-34 Parts of the first line of an event procedure

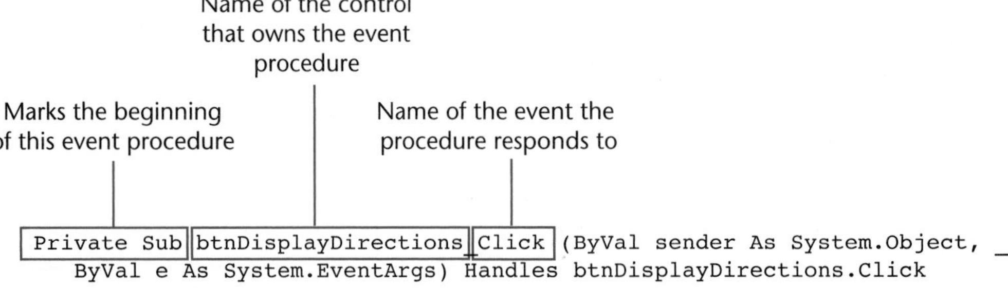

In Figure 2-34, the name of the control owning the procedure appears after the words `Private Sub`. An underscore character separates the name of the owning control from the name of the event the procedure responds to (`Click`). Therefore, the lines in the figure indicate the beginning of a method belonging to the `btnDisplayDirections` control. The method responds to the `Click` event, by executing when the user clicks the button.

For now, don't be concerned with anything else that appears in the first two lines of code. As you progress through the book you will learn more about it.

The next line reads

```
' Make the directions visible
```

The apostrophe (`'`) marks the beginning of a comment. Recall from Chapter 1 that a *comment* is a note of explanation intended for people (including yourself) reading a program's source code. Comments are part of the program but do not affect the program's execution. The comment *Make the directions visible* explains in ordinary terms what action the next line of code performs. A person reading the code doesn't have to guess what it does.

Always use descriptive comments in your code that explain how and why you are performing tasks. Imagine creating a large and complex application. Once you have tested and debugged it, you give it to its user and move on to the next project. Ten months later, the user asks you to make a modification (or worse, to track down and fix an elusive bug). As you look through several hundred lines of code, you are astonished to discover that some of it makes no sense! If only you had left notes to yourself explaining the different parts of the program. Writing comments takes time, but it almost always saves time later.

The next line in our sample code reads:

```
lblDirections.Visible = True
```

This is an **assignment statement.** The equal sign, known as the **assignment operator,** copies the value on its right side into the item on its left. The item to the left of the operator is `lblDirections.Visible`. It identifies the Visible property of the `lblDirections` control. The standard notation for referring to a control's properties in code is: `ControlName.PropertyName`. The value to the right of the equal sign, `True`, is copied into the `lblDirections.Visible` property. The effect of this statement is that the `lblDirections` control becomes visible on the form.

TIP: In an assignment statement, the name of the item receiving the value must be on the left side of the = operator. The following statement, for example, is wrong:

```
True = lblDirections.Visible            'Error
```

Statements between the first and last lines of the `btnDisplayDirections` procedure are indented. Although it is not required, it is a common practice to indent the lines inside a procedure so they are visually set apart. In this book, we are careful to use correct indentation. Many programmers prefer to leave a blank line before the `End Sub` statement, for readability. While we do not follow the convention, partly to save printing space, we think it is an excellent idea.

`btnExit_Click` Procedure

Next, let's look at the `btnExit_Click` event procedure:

```
Private Sub btnExit_Click(ByVal sender As System.Object, _
    ByVal e As System.EventArgs) Handles btnExit.Click

   'End the application by closing the window
   Me.Close()
End Sub
```

This procedure contains only one executable statement: `Me.Close()`, which closes the main window (*Form1*) and ends the program. The `Me` object is used to identify the current Form object (*Form1*). When the form closes, the application ends. In Tutorial 2-11 you add the controls required to complete this part of the application.

Tutorial 2-11:
Placing the `lblDirections`, `btnDisplayDirections`, and `btnExit` controls in the *Directions* application

Step 1: Start Visual Studio and open the *Directions* project. View the *Form1* form, in Design mode. If it is not visible, double-click its name in *Solution Explorer*.

Step 2: You will place the new controls at the bottom of the form, below the graphic. Because the form is too small to accommodate them, you will need to enlarge it. Drag the bottom edge of the form down until it looks something like the one shown in Figure 2-35. (Don't worry about the exact size of the form. You can adjust it again later.)

Figure 2-35 *Directions* application with enlarged form

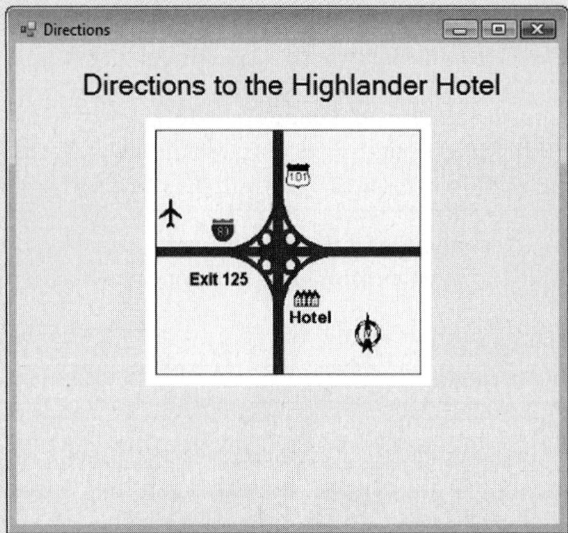

Step 3: Create a new Label control on the form and move it to a location below the image.

Step 4: Make sure the new Label control is selected and set its AutoSize property to *False*.

Step 5: Resize the Label control and position it so it appears similar to the *Label2* control shown in Figure 2-36.

Step 6: Change the Label control's Name property to `lblDirections`.

Step 7: You are about to enter the following text into the label's Text property:

```
Traveling on I-89, take Exit 125 onto Highway 101 South.
The hotel is on the left, just past the I-89 intersection.
Traveling on Highway 101 North, the hotel is on the right,
just before the I-89 intersection.
```

Select the label's Text property, and then click the down-arrow button (⌄):

When the editing box appears, as shown in Figure 2-37, type the hotel directions shown above. Type all the text on a single line before pressing the Enter key. When you are finished, click the mouse in a different property, and the text you typed will be saved.

TIP: The editing box you just used permits you to press the Enter key at the end of individual lines.

Step 8: Make sure the Label control's TextAlign property is set to *TopLeft*. The form should now appear similar to the one shown in Figure 2-38.

Step 9: Double-click the label's Visible property to set it to *False*.

Figure 2-36 Positioning a Label control

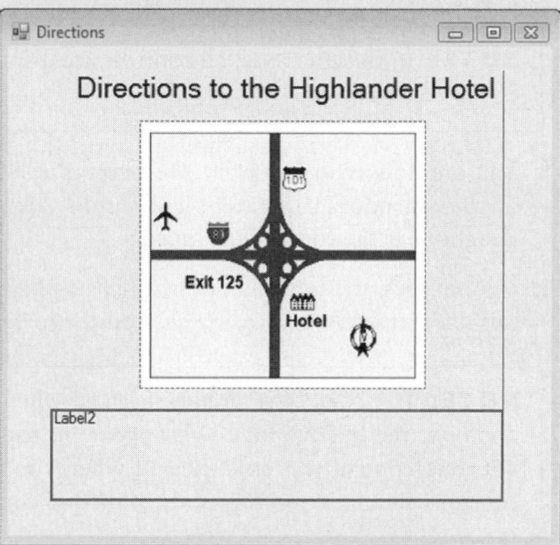

Figure 2-37 Editing box for the label's Text property

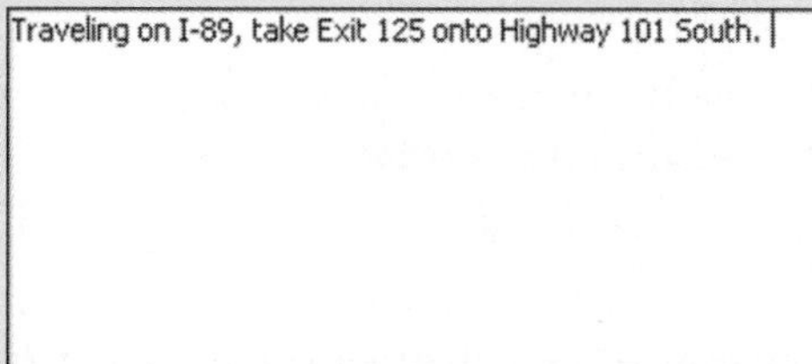

Figure 2-38 Label with directions text entered

> **NOTE:** In Design mode, all controls are displayed, even if their Visible property is set to *False*.

Step 10: You are now ready to place the buttons. Double-click the button tool in the *Toolbox* window. A default-sized button named `Button1` appears on the form. Drag it near the form's bottom edge.

Step 11: Double-click the button tool in the *Toolbox* window again. Another button, this one named `Button2`, appears on the form.

> **NOTE:** If a control is already selected when you double-click a tool in the *Toolbox*, the new control will appear on top of the selected control. If the `Button1` control was still selected when you created `Button2`, the `Button2` control will appear on top of the `Button1` control.

Drag the `Button2` control to the bottom edge of the form and place it to the right of the `Button1` control. Arrange the two buttons, as shown in Figure 2-39.

Step 12: Select the `Button1` button.

Step 13: In the *Properties* window, change the button's Name to **`btnDisplayDirections`**.

Step 14: Change the Text property to **`Display Directions`**. Because the button is not large enough to accommodate the text, use the button's sizing handles to increase its height, as shown in Figure 2-40.

Step 15: Select the `Button2` button.

Step 16: In the *Properties* window, change the button's name to **`btnExit`** and change the button's Text property to **`Exit`**.

Step 17: Resize the `btnExit` button so its size is the same as the `btnDisplay-Directions` button. Your form should now resemble the one shown in Figure 2-41.

Figure 2-39 Buttons in place

Figure 2-40 Button with increased height

Display Directions

Figure 2-41 Buttons placed

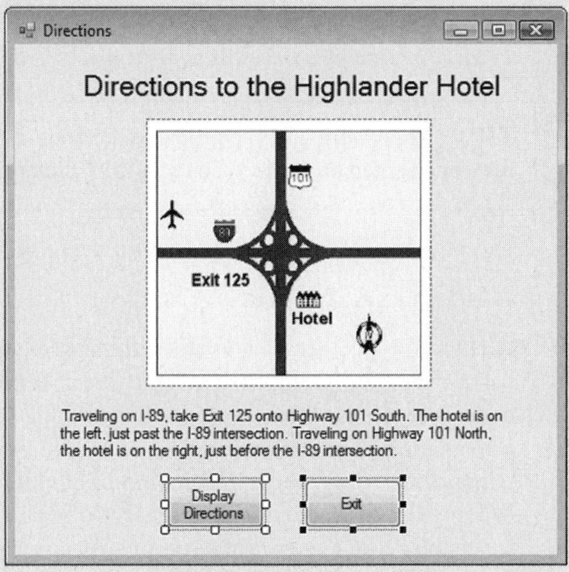

In Tutorial 2-12 you write the event procedures for the buttons.

Tutorial 2-12:
Writing event procedures for the *Directions* application

Step 1: Double-click the *Display Directions* button (`btnDisplayDirections`). The ***Code* window** opens, as shown in Figure 2-42.

NOTE: The *Code* window is a text-editing window in which you write code. Notice that a code template appears for the `btnDisplayDirections_Click` event procedure. The template consists of the first and last lines of the procedure. You must add the code that appears between these two lines.

Figure 2-42 *Code* window showing the event handler for the `btnDisplayDirections` button

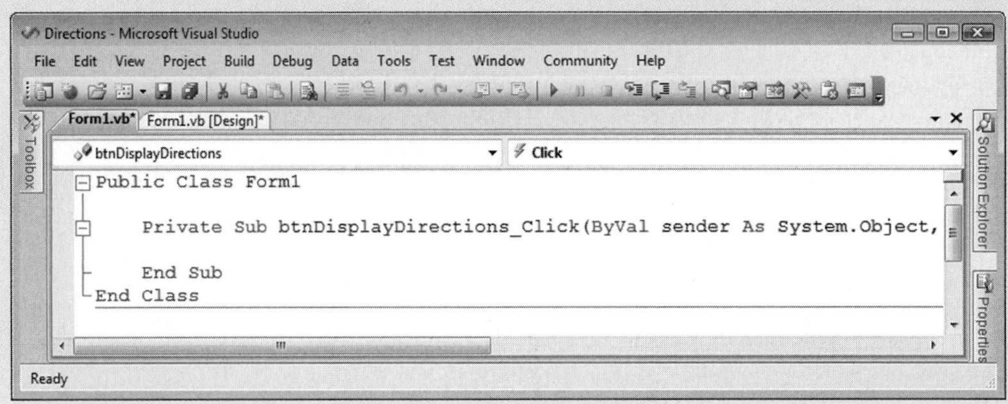

Step 2: Type the following code between the first and last lines of the `btnDisplayDirections_Click` procedure:

```
' Make the directions visible.
lblDirections.Visible = True
```

TIP: Make sure you type the code exactly as it appears here. Otherwise, you may encounter an error when you run the application.

Did you notice that as you entered the second line,

`lblDirections.Visible = True`,

when you typed the period the scrollable list appeared (see Figure 2-43)? This list is called an **IntelliSense** auto list box. It provides help and some automatic code completion while you are developing an application. The list displays information that may be used to complete part of a statement. It contains the name of every property and method belonging to the `lblDirections` object. When you type the letter *V*, the selector bar in the list box automatically moves to Visible. You can continue typing, or you can press the Tab key or Spacebar to select *Visible* from the list. You may then continue typing.

Another **auto list box** appears when you type the = operator, showing two values: *False* and *True* (see Figure 2-44). *False* and *True* are the only valid values you can assign to the Visible property. Either continue typing or let the auto list box help you select the code to insert.

TIP: If you did not see the auto list box, then that feature has been disabled. To enable it, click *Tools* on the menu bar, then click *Options . . .* Click the *Show all settings* option, then select *Text Editor*, *Basic*, and *General* (see Figure 2-45). Verify that the *Auto list members* option is checked.

Figure 2-43 Auto list box

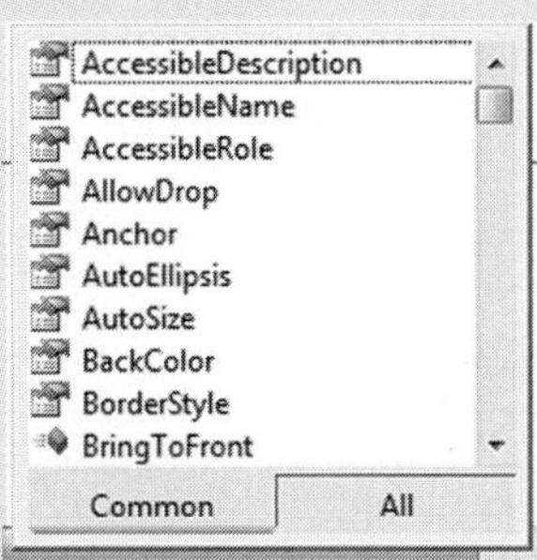

Figure 2-44 Selecting between *False* and *True*

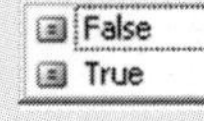

Figure 2-45 Controlling the general editor settings for Visual Basic

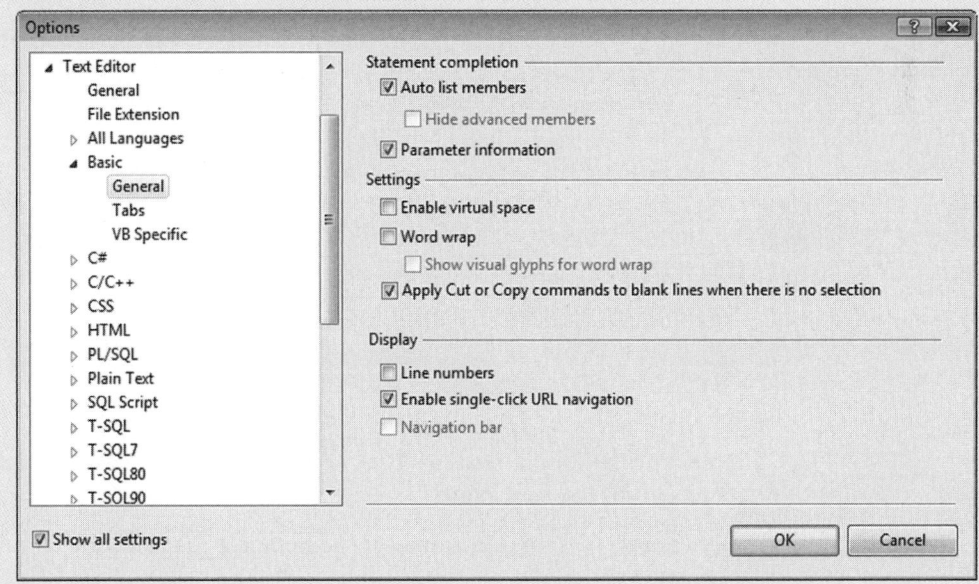

Step 3: Now you will switch back to the *Design* window. There are four different ways to do this. Use one of these techniques to open the *Design* window.

- Notice at the top of the *Code* window the two tabs shown in Figure 2-46. You can open the *Design* window by clicking the *Form1.vb [Design]* tab, and then you can open the *Code* window again by clicking the *Form1.vb* tab.

- You can click *View* on the menu bar, and then click *Designer* on the *View* menu.
- You can use the *Solution Explorer* window. Click the *View Designer* button ( ) to switch to the *Design* window, and click the *View Code* button ( ) to switch back to the *Code* window.
- You can also press Shift+F7 on the keyboard.

Figure 2-46 Design and code tabs

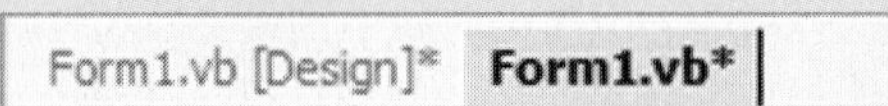

Step 4: Now you must write the event procedure for the other button. On the form, double-click the *Exit* button. The *Code* window reappears, as shown in Figure 2-47.

Figure 2-47 *Code* window, ready for *Exit* button code

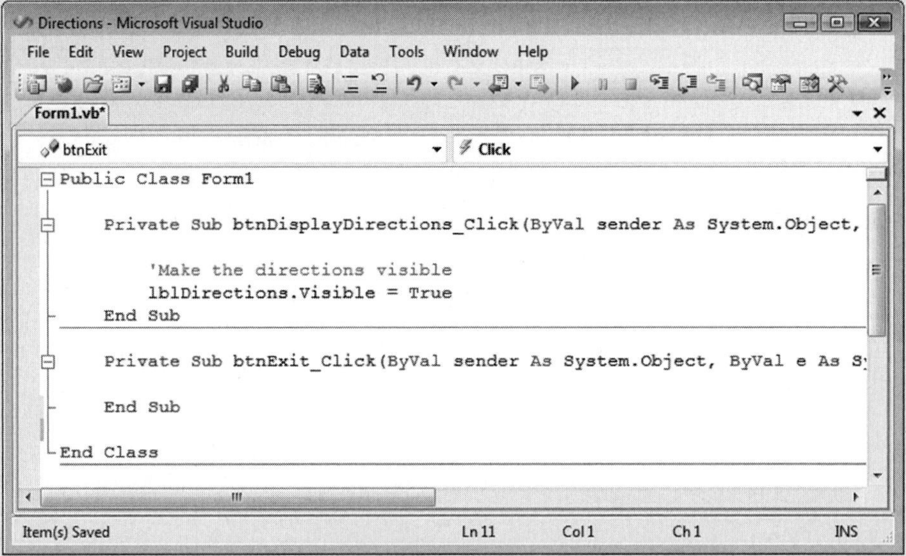

Notice that Visual Studio has now provided a **code template** for the `btnExit_Click` procedure.

Step 5: Between the first and last lines of the `btnExit_Click` code template, type the following code:

```
' End the application by closing the window.
Me.Close()
```

The *Code* window should now look like the one shown in Figure 2-48.

Step 6: Use the *Save All* command on the *File* menu to save the project.

Step 7: Click the *Start* button (▶) on the Visual Studio toolbar. The application begins executing, as shown in Figure 2-49. Notice that the `lblDirections` label is not visible.

Figure 2-48 *Code* window with `btnExit_Click` procedure completed

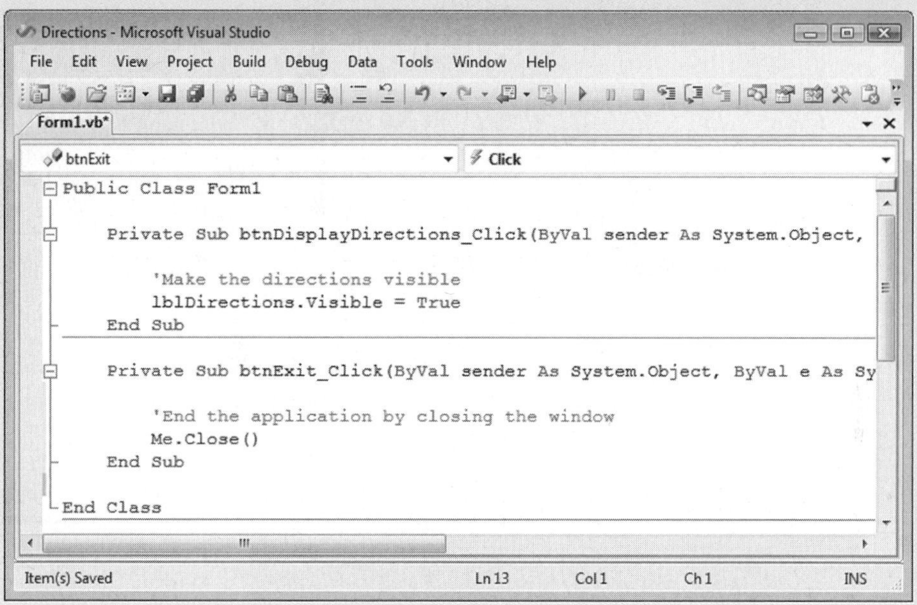

Figure 2-49 *Directions* application at startup

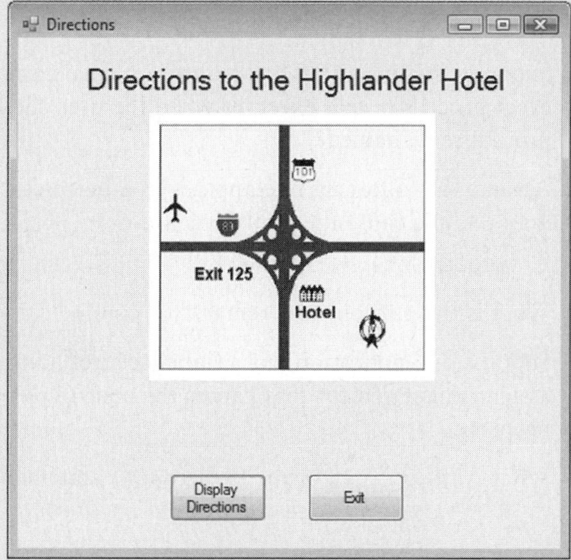

Step 8: Click the *Display Directions* button. The written directions appear on the form, as shown in Figure 2-50.

Figure 2-50 *Directions* application with text displayed

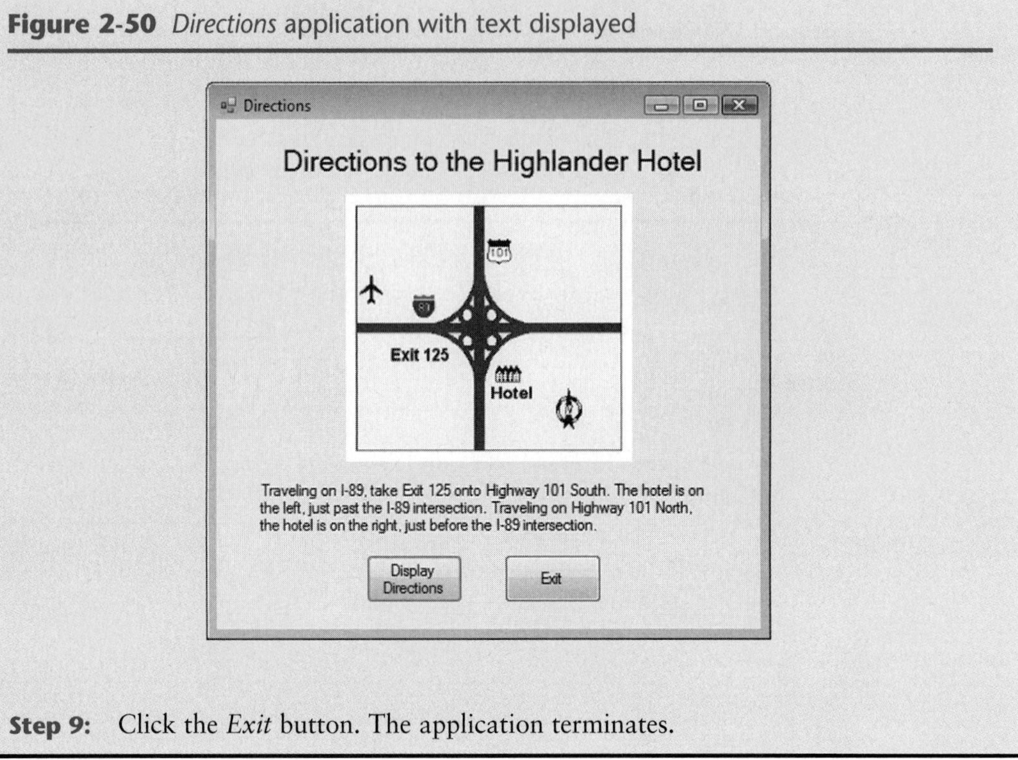

Step 9: Click the *Exit* button. The application terminates.

Checkpoint

2.12 How do you decide if you will keep a control's default name or assign it a name?

2.13 What is a Boolean property?

2.14 Suppose an application has a button named `btnShowName`. The button has an event procedure that executes when the user clicks it. What would the event procedure be named?

2.15 Assume the following line appears in a button's `Click` event procedure. What does the line cause the application to do?

```
' Display the word "Hello"
```

2.16 What is the purpose of a remark (or comment)?

2.17 Suppose an application has a Label control named `lblSecretAnswer`. Write an assignment statement that causes the control to be hidden. (*Hint*: Use the Visible property.)

2.18 What is the purpose of the `Me.Close()` statement?

Changing Text Colors

You have already learned that the font style and size of text on a control can be easily changed through the *Properties* window. You can also change the text background and foreground color with the BackColor and ForeColor properties. Tutorial 2-13 walks you through the process.

Tutorial 2-13:
Changing the text colors

Step 1: With the *Directions* project loaded, open the *Design* window.

Step 2: Select the *Label1* control. This is the Label control whose Text property reads *Directions to the Highlander Hotel.*

Step 3: In the *Properties* window, look for the BackColor property. This is the property that establishes the background color for the label text. Click the property value. A down-arrow button (▾) appears.

Step 4: Click the down-arrow button (▾). A drop-down list of colors appears, as shown in Figure 2-51.

The drop-down list has three tabs: *Custom*, *Web*, and *System*. The *System* tab lists colors defined in the current Windows configuration. The *Web* tab lists colors displayed with consistency in Web browsers. The *Custom* tab displays a color palette, as shown in Figure 2-52.

Select a color from one of the tabs. Notice that the label text background changes to the color you selected.

Figure 2-51 BackColor drop-down list

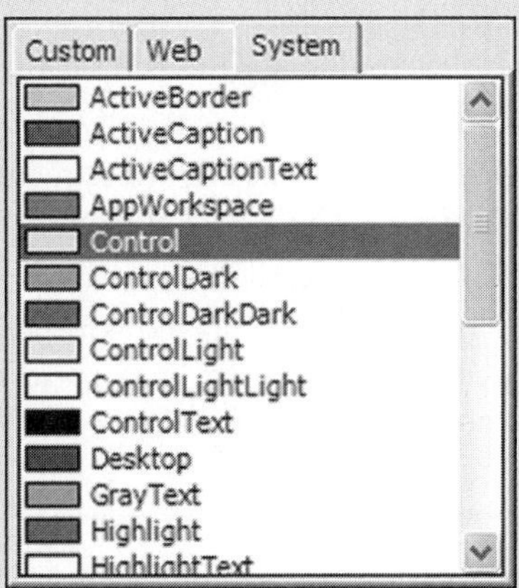

Figure 2-52 Custom color palette

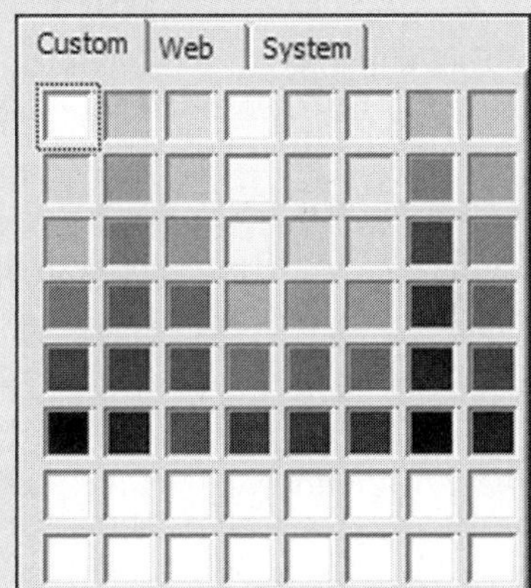

Step 5: Now look for the **ForeColor property** in the *Properties* window. When you click it, a down-arrow button (▾) appears.

Step 6: Click the down-arrow button (▾) and notice the same drop-down list as you saw in Step 4. Once again, select a color from one of the tabs. Notice that the label's text foreground color changes to the color you selected.

Step 7: Start the application to test the new colors. After you close the application, save your project.

Setting the FormBorderStyle Property and Locking Controls

The FormBorderStyle Property

Sometimes you want to prevent the user from resizing, minimizing, or maximizing a window, or from closing a window using its *Close* button (▣). You can control all of these actions by selecting an appropriate value for the form's **FormBorderStyle property**. Table 2-6 shows a list of the possible values for the FormBorderStyle property.

Table 2-6 Values for FormBorderStyle

Value	Description
Fixed3D	Displays a 3D border. The form's size is fixed and displayed with *Minimize*, *Maximize*, and *Close* buttons on its title bar. Although the form may be maximized and minimized, it may not be resized by its edges or corners.
FixedDialog	This type of border shows *Minimize*, *Maximize*, and *Close* buttons on its title bar. Although the form may be maximized and minimized, it may not be resized by its edges or corners.
FixedSingle	The form's size is fixed and uses a border that is a single line. The form is displayed with *Minimize*, *Maximize*, and *Close* buttons on its title bar. Although the form may be maximized and minimized, it may not be resized by its edges or corners.
FixedToolWindow	Intended for use with floating toolbars. Only shows the title bar with a *Close* button. May not be resized.
None	The form is displayed with no border at all. Subsequently, there is no title bar, and no *Minimize*, *Maximize*, and *Close* buttons. The form may not be resized.
Sizable	This is the default value. The form is displayed with *Minimize*, *Maximize*, and *Close* buttons on its title bar. The form may be resized, but the controls on the form do not change position.
SizableToolWindow	Like *FixedToolWindow*, but resizable.

Locking Controls

Once you have placed all the controls in their proper positions on a form, it is usually a good idea to lock them. When you lock the controls on a form, they cannot be accidentally moved at design time. They must be unlocked before they can be moved.

To lock all the controls on a form, place the cursor over an empty spot on the form and right-click. A small menu pops up. One of the selections on the menu is *Lock Controls*.

In Tutorial 2-14 we modify the value of the form's FormBorderStyle property so the user cannot minimize, maximize, or resize the window. We will also lock the controls on the form.

Tutorial 2-14:
Setting the FormBorderStyle property and locking the controls in the *Directions* application

Step 1: Select the *Directions* form and find the FormBorderStyle property in the *Properties* window.

Step 2: Click the FormBorderStyle property. A down-arrow button ( ) appears. Click the down-arrow button ( ) to see a list of values.

Step 3: Click *FixedSingle*.

Step 4: Start the application and test the new border style. Notice that you can move the window, but you cannot resize it by its edges or its corners.

Step 5: Click the *Exit* button to end the application.

Step 6: Now you will lock the controls. Place the cursor over an empty spot on the form and right-click. A small menu pops up.

Step 7: Click the *Lock Controls* command.

Step 8: Select any control on the form and try to move it. Because the controls are locked, you cannot move them.

Step 9: Save the project.

WARNING: Be careful. Locked controls can still be deleted.

When you are ready to move the controls, just right-click over an empty spot on the form and select the *Lock Controls* command again. This toggles (reverses) the locked state of the controls.

Printing Your Code

To print a project's code, open the *Code* window, click *File* on the menu bar, and then click the *Print* command on the *File* menu.

Checkpoint

2.19 Which function key displays the *Code* window?

2.20 What three color categories are available when you edit a control's BackColor property?

2.21 What happens when you modify a Label control's BackColor property?

2.22 What happens when you modify a Label control's ForeColor property?

2.23 What property do you set in order to prevent a form from being resized when the application is running?

2.24 What happens when you lock the controls on a form?

2.25 How do you lock the controls on a form?

2.26 How do you unlock the controls on a form?

2.3 Modifying the Text Property with Code

CONCEPT: Quite often, you will need to change a control's Text property with code. This is done with an assignment statement.

While building the directions application, you learned that an assignment statement copies a value into a property while the application is running. Recall that the following statement sets the `lblDirections` control's Visible property to *True*.

```
lblDirections.Visible = True
```

You use the same technique to change the value of a control's Text property. For example, assume an application has a Label control named `lblMessage`. The following statement copies the sentence *Programming is fun!* to the control's Text property.

```
lblMessage.Text = "Programming is fun!"
```

Once the statement executes, the message displayed by the `lblMessage` control changes to

```
Programming is fun!
```

The quotation marks in the statement are not part of the message. They simply mark the beginning and end of the set of characters assigned to the property. In programming terms, a group of characters inside a set of quotation marks is called a **string literal**. You'll learn more about string literals in Chapter 3.

We usually display messages on a form by setting the value of a Label control's Text property. In Tutorial 2-15 you open and examine an application on the Student CD that demonstrates this technique.

Tutorial 2-15:
Examining an application that displays messages

Step 1: Start Visual Studio and open the *KiloConverter* project from the student sample programs folder named *Chap2\KiloConverter*.

Step 2: Open the *Design* window, which displays *Form1*, as shown in Figure 2-53.

Step 3: Click the *Start* button (▸) to run the application.

Step 4: Once the application is running, click the *Inches* button. The form displays the number of inches equivalent to a kilometer, as shown in Figure 2-54.

Step 5: Experiment with the other buttons and observe the messages that are displayed when each is clicked.

Step 6: Click the *Exit* button to exit the application. Let's examine the application code. Figure 2-55 shows the *KiloConverter* application form with its controls labeled.

The buttons `btnInches`, `btnFeet`, `btnYards`, and `btnMiles` each change the `lblMessage` Text property when clicked. Use the following step to view the *KiloConverter* event procedures.

Figure 2-53 *Kilometer Converter* form

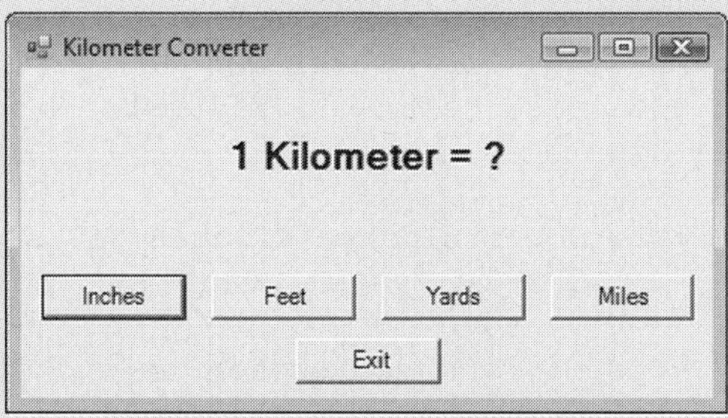

Figure 2-54 One kilometer converted to inches

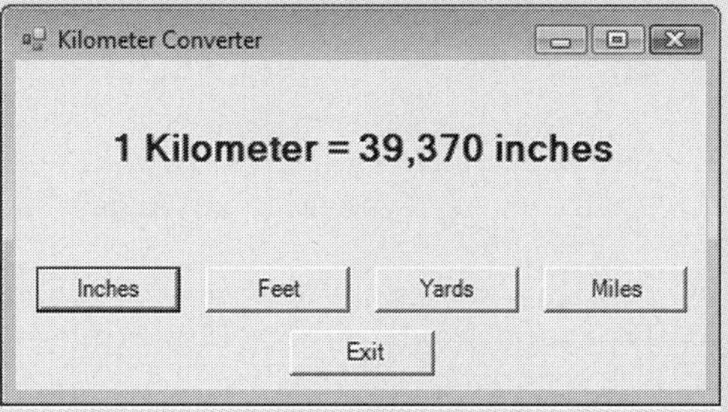

Figure 2-55 *KiloConverter* application controls

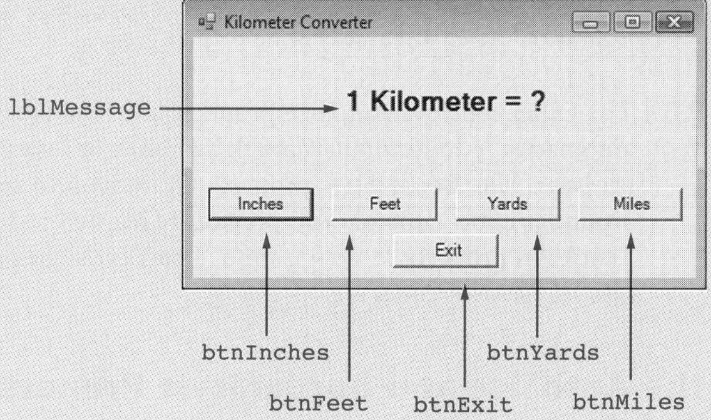

Step 7: Click the *View Code* button (☰) in the *Solution Explorer* window. The *Code* window appears. The window shows the following event procedure code:

```
Private Sub btnExit_Click(ByVal sender As System.Object, _
    ByVal e As System.EventArgs) Handles btnExit.Click

  ' End the application.
  Me.Close()
End Sub
```

```
Private Sub btnFeet_Click(ByVal sender As System.Object, _
    ByVal e As System.EventArgs) Handles btnFeet.Click

  ' Display the conversion to feet.
  lblMessage.Text = "1 Kilometer = 3,281 feet"
End Sub

Private Sub btnInches_Click(ByVal sender As System.Object, _
    ByVal e As System.EventArgs) Handles btnInches.Click

  ' Display the conversion to inches.
  lblMessage.Text = "1 Kilometer = 39,370 inches"
End Sub

Private Sub btnMiles_Click(ByVal sender As System.Object, _
    ByVal e As System.EventArgs) Handles btnMiles.Click

  ' Display the conversion to miles.
  lblMessage.Text = "1 Kilometer = 0.6214 miles"
End Sub

Private Sub btnYards_Click(ByVal sender As System.Object, _
    ByVal e As System.EventArgs) Handles btnYards.Click

  ' Display the conversion to yards.
  lblMessage.Text = "1 Kilometer = 1,093.6 yards"
End Sub
```

2.4 The AutoSize, BorderStyle, and TextAlign Properties

CONCEPT: The Label control's AutoSize property allows a label to change size automatically to accommodate the amount of text in its Text property. The BorderStyle property allows you to set a border around a Label control. You previously learned to set the TextAlign property at design time. The TextAlign property can also be set with code.

Using the AutoSize and BorderStyle Properties in a Label Control

The Label control has two additional properties, AutoSize and BorderStyle, which give you greater control over the label's appearance.

The AutoSize Property

The **AutoSize property** is a Boolean property, which is set to *True* by default. When AutoSize is set to *False*, the bounding box of the Label control remains, at runtime, the size that it was given at design time. If the text copied into the label's Text property is too large to fit in the control's bounding box, the text is only partially displayed. When a label's AutoSize property is set to *True*, however, the label's bounding box will automatically resize to accommodate the text in the label's Text property.

The BorderStyle Property

The Label control's BorderStyle property may have one of three values: *None*, *FixedSingle*, and *Fixed3D*. The property is set to *None* by default, which means the label will have no border. If BorderStyle is set to *FixedSingle*, the label will be outlined with a border that is a single pixel wide. If BorderStyle is set to *Fixed3D*, the label will have a recessed 3D appearance. Figure 2-56 shows an example of two Label controls: one with BorderStyle set to *FixedSingle* and the other with BorderStyle set to *Fixed3D*.

Quite often you will want to display output, such as the results of a calculation, in a Label control with a border. You will see many example applications in this book that use this approach.

Figure 2-56 *FixedSingle* and *Fixed3D* BorderStyle examples

Changing a Label's TextAlign Property with Code

The Label control's TextAlign property establishes the alignment, or justification of the control's displayed text. It can equal one of the following values: *TopLeft*, *TopCenter*, *TopRight*, *MiddleLeft*, *MiddleCenter*, *MiddleRight*, *BottomLeft*, *BottomCenter*, or *BottomRight*. At design time, you establish the TextAlign property's value with the *Properties* window. You can also set the property with code at runtime. You do this by using an assignment statement to store one of the following values in the property:

```
ContentAlignment.TopLeft
ContentAlignment.TopCenter
ContentAlignment.TopRight
ContentAlignment.MiddleLeft
ContentAlignment.MiddleCenter
ContentAlignment.MiddleRight
ContentAlignment.BottomLeft
ContentAlignment.BottomCenter
ContentAlignment.BottomRight
```

For example, assume an application uses a Label control named `lblReportTitle`. The following statement aligns the control's text with the middle and center of the control's bounding box.

```
lblReportTitle.TextAlign = ContentAlignment.MiddleCenter
```

TIP: When you write an assignment statement that stores a value in the TextAlign property, an auto list box appears showing all the valid values.

2.27 Suppose an application has a Label control named `lblTemperature`. Write a code statement that causes the label's Text property to display the message *48 degrees*.

2.28 What results when a Label control's AutoSize property is set to *False*? When it is set to *True*?

2.29 What are the possible values for the Label control's BorderStyle property, and what result does each value produce?

2.30 Suppose an application has a Label control named `lblName`. Write the programming statements described by the following:

- A statement that aligns the label's text in the top right.
- A statement that aligns the label's text in the bottom left.
- A statement that aligns the label's text in the top center.

2.5 Clickable Images

CONCEPT: Controls other than buttons have `Click` event procedures. In this section, you learn to create PictureBox controls that respond to mouse clicks.

In this chapter, you learned that buttons have `Click` event procedures. A `Click` event procedure is executed when the user clicks the button. Other controls, such as PictureBoxes and labels, may also have `Click` event procedures. In Tutorial 2-16 you write `Click` event procedures for a group of PictureBox controls.

Tutorial 2-16:
Writing `Click` event procedures for PictureBox controls

Step 1: Open the *Flags* project from the student sample programs folder named *Chap2\Flags*.

Step 2: Open the *Design* window and look at *Form1*. Figure 2-57 shows the form and the names of the controls on the form.

Step 3: Select the `lblMessage` control and set its TextAlign property to *MiddleCenter*, and its Font property to *Microsoft sans serif, bold, 10 points*.

Step 4: Change the form's Text property to **`Flags`**.

Step 5: `PictureBox1` shows the flag of the United States. Rename this control **`picUSA`**.

Step 6: `PictureBox2` shows the flag of Canada. Rename this control **`picCanada`**.

Step 7: `PictureBox3` shows the flag of the United Kingdom. Rename this control **`picUK`**.

Step 8: `PictureBox4` shows the flag of Australia. Rename this control **`picAustralia`**.

Step 9: `PictureBox5` shows the flag of Brazil. Rename this control **`picBrazil`**.

Step 10: `PictureBox6` shows the flag of Italy. Rename this control **`picItaly`**.

Step 11: Double-click the `picUSA` control. The *Code* window appears with a code template for the `picUSA_Click` procedure. Write the following code shown here in color, which copies the string `"United States of America"` into the `lblMessage` Text property.

```
Private Sub picUSA_Click(ByVal sender As System.Object, _
    ByVal e As System.EventArgs) Handles picUSA.Click

  ' Display the country name
  lblMessage.Text = "United States of America"
End Sub
```

Figure 2-57 *Form1* of the *Flags* project

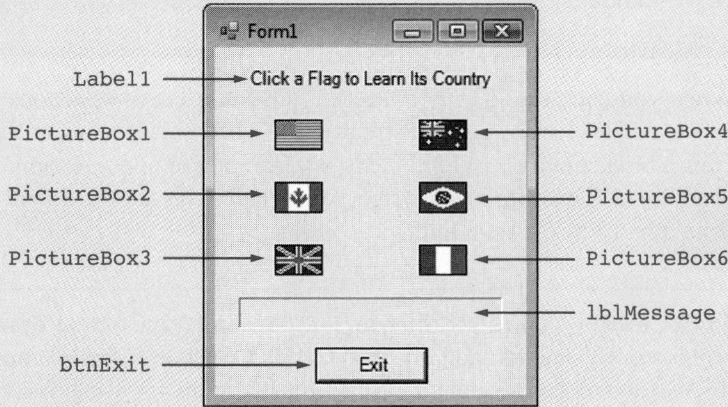

Step 12: Repeat the process outlined in Step 11 for each of the other PictureBox controls. The `Click` procedure for each PictureBox control should copy the name of its flag's country into the `lblMessage.Text` property.

Step 13: Save the application.

Step 14: Run the application. When you click any of the flags, you should see the name of the flag's country appear in the `lblMessage` Label control. For example, when you click the flag of Australia, the form should appear similar to the one shown in Figure 2-58.

Figure 2-58 *Flags* application identifying flag of Australia

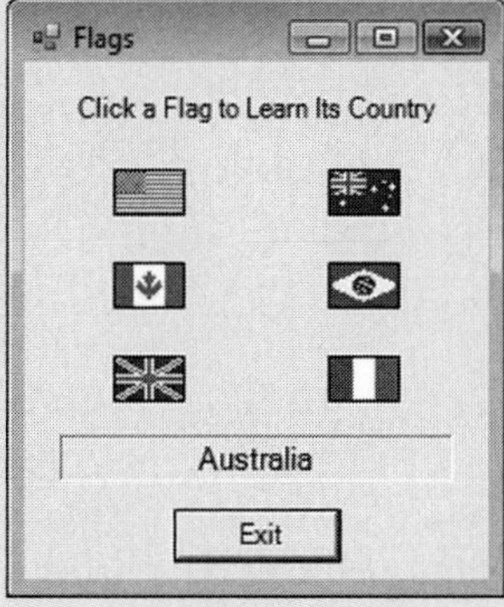

Step 15: Exit the application.

2.6 Using Visual Studio Help

Microsoft Document Explorer

When you click the Visual Studio *Help* menu, a list of selections shown in Figure 2-59 appears. The Help system is also called the Microsoft Document Explorer. Table 2-7 contains a brief summary of each menu selection in the upper section of the *Help* menu. The contents of the entire Help system are dynamic because it downloads new information from Microsoft over the Internet.

TIP: When it comes to displaying Help information, Visual Basic Express is very different from Visual Studio. To avoid confusion between the two products, the following discussion will focus only on Visual Studio. If you are using Visual Basic Express, note that many help functions discussed here are directly accessible from the *Help* menu. Also, when you need help on a control or keyword in Visual Basic Express, you can press the F1 function key to view relevant help information.

Figure 2-59 Upper section of the Visual Studio *Help* menu

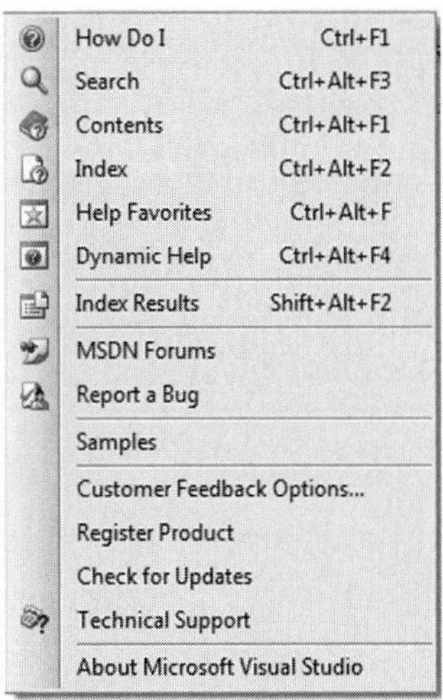

Table 2-7 Microsoft Document Explorer options

How Do I	Contains a list of task-based topics related to Visual Basic programming and application development. The list is divided into categories, each of which is a hyperlink that takes you to a help page with lots of specific tasks.
Search	Lets you search the full text of help topics for words or phrases.
Contents	Displays a top-level table of contents for the help library.
Index	Lets you search for topics using predefined keywords. As you type a keyword, Document Explorer automatically moves to the right position in the list of topics.
Help Favorites	When you view individual help topics, you can bookmark them and add them to your list of favorite help topics. Then when you click *Help Favorites*, you can see your list of bookmarks.
Dynamic Help	Provides links to information found in local help, based on the task you are trying to accomplish in Visual Studio. Not available in Visual Basic Express.

The *How Do I* selection contains a long list of topics that changes often as new entries are added by Microsoft. You might think of these as short tutorials on Windows and Web development.

A help *Search* lets you search for words and phrases within the complete text of Help topics. You can use three types of filters to narrow or widen the search:

- *Language*—programming languages such as Visual Basic, C#, or C++
- *Technology*—select from Windows Forms, Web forms, and other types of applications
- *Content Type*—narrow the search to include only specific types of information

A help *Search* example is shown in Figure 2-60. We have completed a search for help relating to the *Button* topic. The following filters are set: Language = *Visual Basic*, Technology = *Windows Forms*, and Content Type = *All*. In the *Content Type* category, you click on individual check boxes to select different types of content to be searched. The search results are displayed in the lower part of the window, containing both text and hyperlinks. If you click on any of the headings or links, you are taken to help pages that display complete information.

Figure 2-60 Using the *Search* window in Visual Studio Help

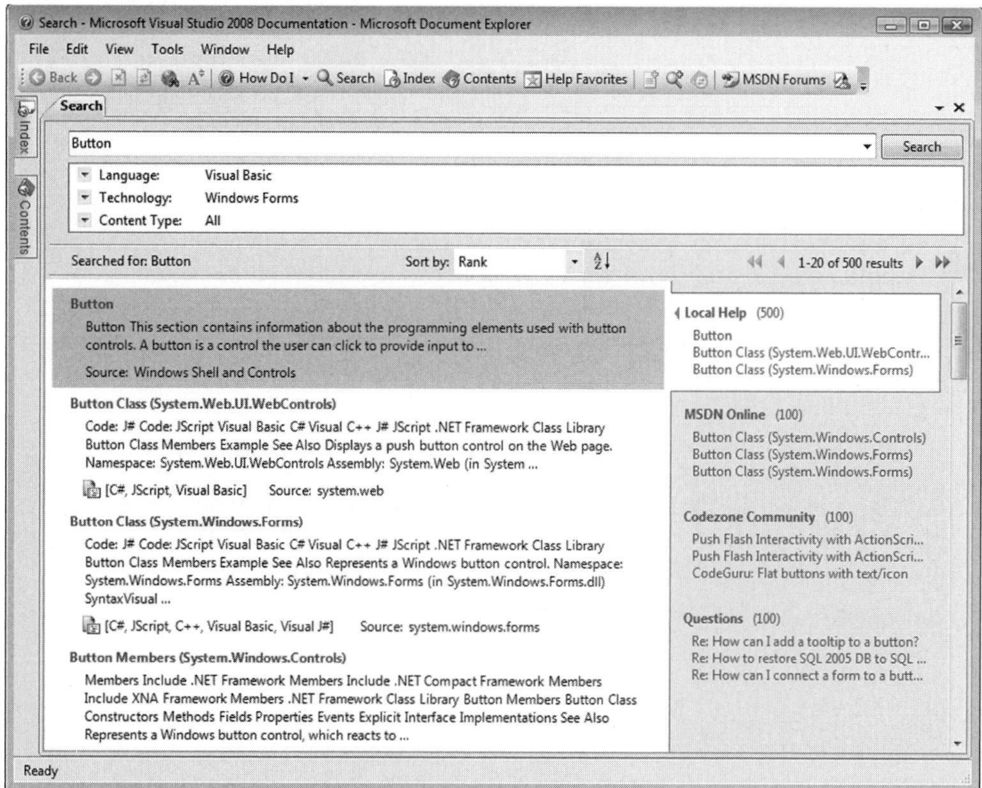

A help *Contents* example for Visual Studio is shown in Figure 2-61. The first topic, *Development Tools and Languages*, includes reference information about Visual Basic. You can expand any high-level topic by clicking the + to the left of the topic name. (This list does not contain the same items in Visual Basic Express.)

An *Index* lookup is shown in Figure 2-62, where we have typed the *Button* keyword. The list of topics shows all index entries using that keyword. When you click on any of these entries, the text window in the right-hand pane shows detailed information about the selected topic.

Figure 2-61 Help *Contents*

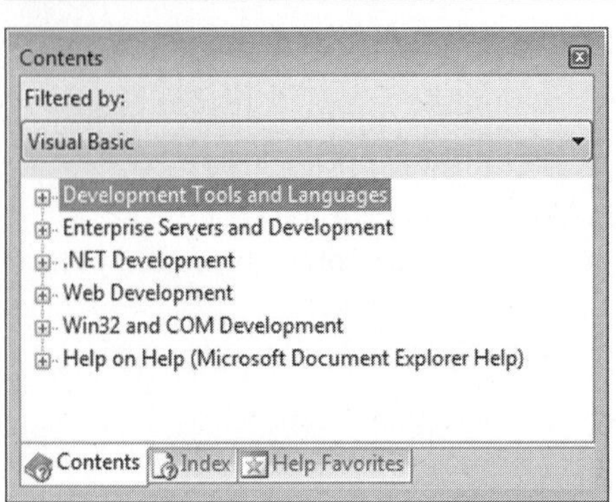

Figure 2-62 Searching the *Index* for the *Button* keyword

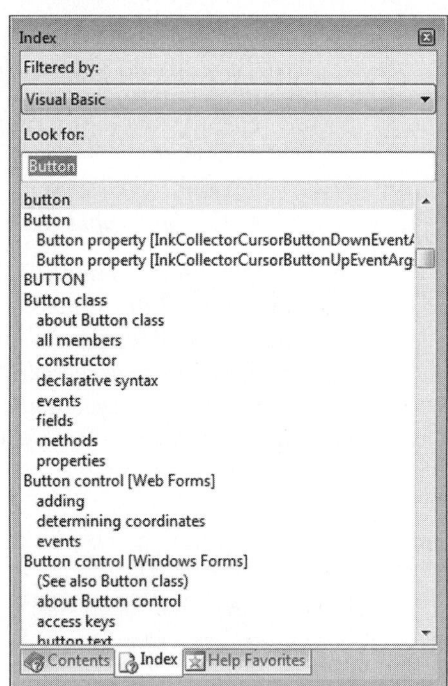

Dynamic Help adapts its list of topics to the task you are trying to accomplish in Visual Studio. Figure 2-63 shows the list of help topics after the user selected a form in *Design* view before activating *Dynamic Help*. The first two topics in the displayed list relate to forms. The last two topics, *Visual Studio*, and *Smart Device Development*, appear in every *Dynamic Help* window, regardless of the current task.

Figure 2-63 *Dynamic Help* activated after the user selected a form in Design view

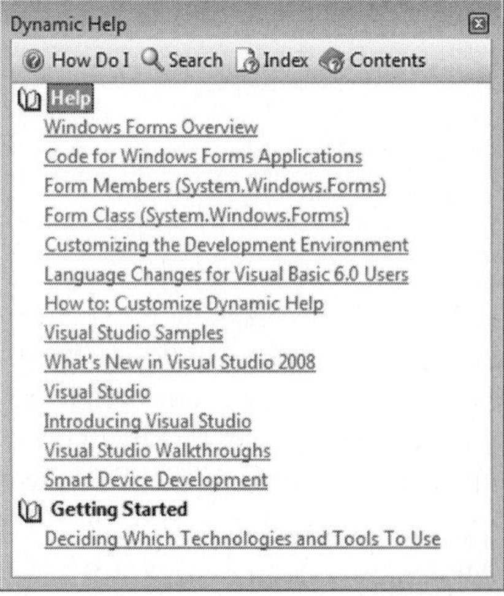

Context-Sensitive Help (F1 key)

Finally, an easy way to display help on a single topic is to press the F1 key. This is called **context-sensitive help**. In Figure 2-65, the user selected a Button control on a form and then pressed F1. The *Help* window explains all about the Button control. If more than one help topic is found, you can select from a drop-down list labeled *F1 Options* in the upper left corner of the *Help* window's text area. Look for it in Figure 2-64.

Figure 2-64 Displaying a single topic after pressing the F1 key

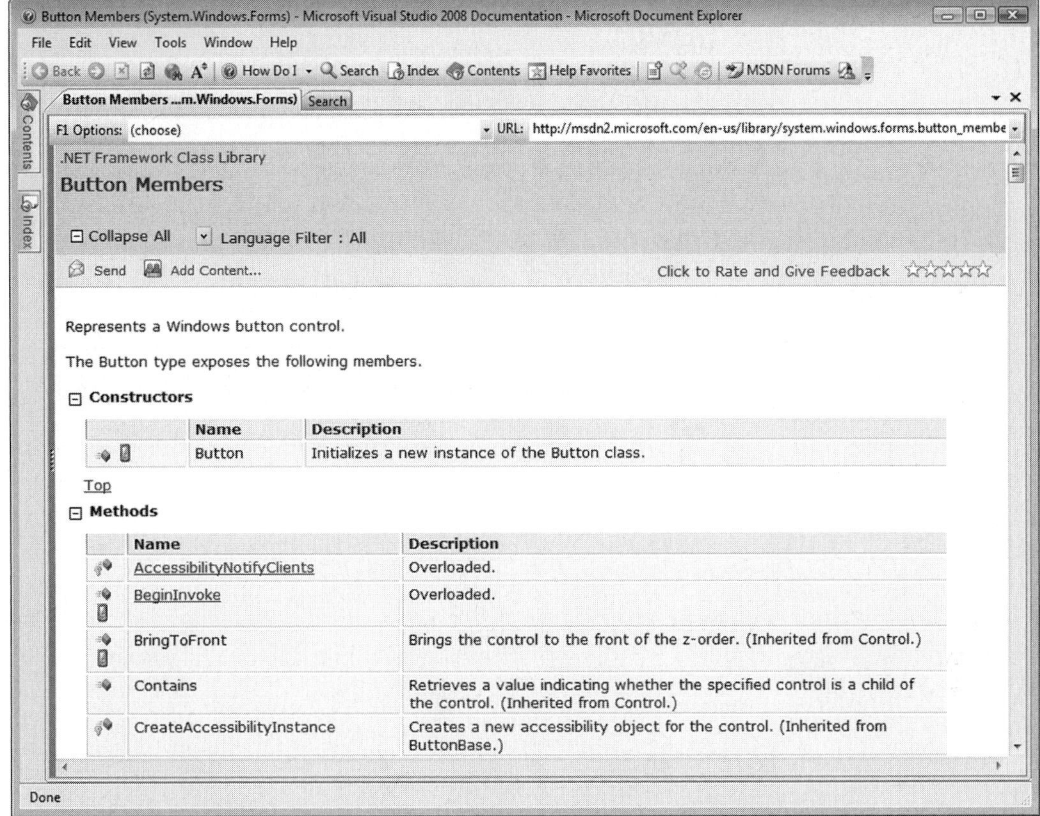

In Tutorial 2-17, you will use *Dynamic Help* in Visual Studio.

Tutorial 2-17:
Using *Dynamic Help* in Visual Studio

Step 1: Start Visual Studio and load the *Directions* project. Make sure the *Design* window is open.

Step 2: Select *Dynamic Help* from the *Help* menu. The *Dynamic Help* window should open.

Step 3: In the *Design* window, select one of the Label controls on the form. Notice that the content of the *Dynamic Help* window changes. It should look similar to Figure 2-65, showing topics relating to Label controls. *(The exact list of topics may be different in your window because Microsoft updates its Help Web site regularly.)*

Figure 2-65 *Dynamic Help* activated after the user selects a Label control

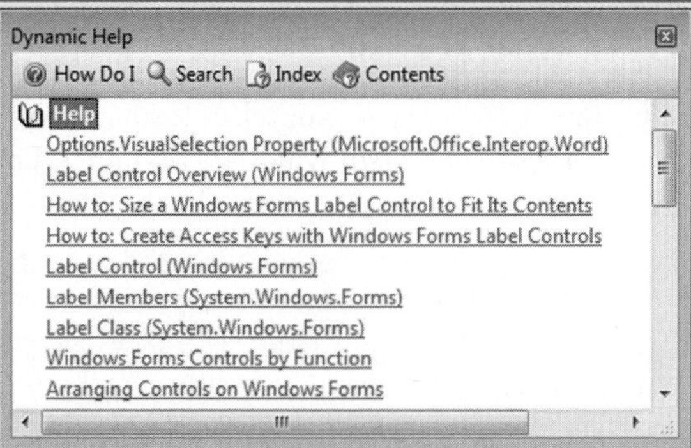

Step 4: Click the *Label Members* help topic, which should cause the *Help* window shown in Figure 2-66 to display. This window provides help on all the properties and methods of the Label control.

Figure 2-66 Displaying the *Label Members* Help topic

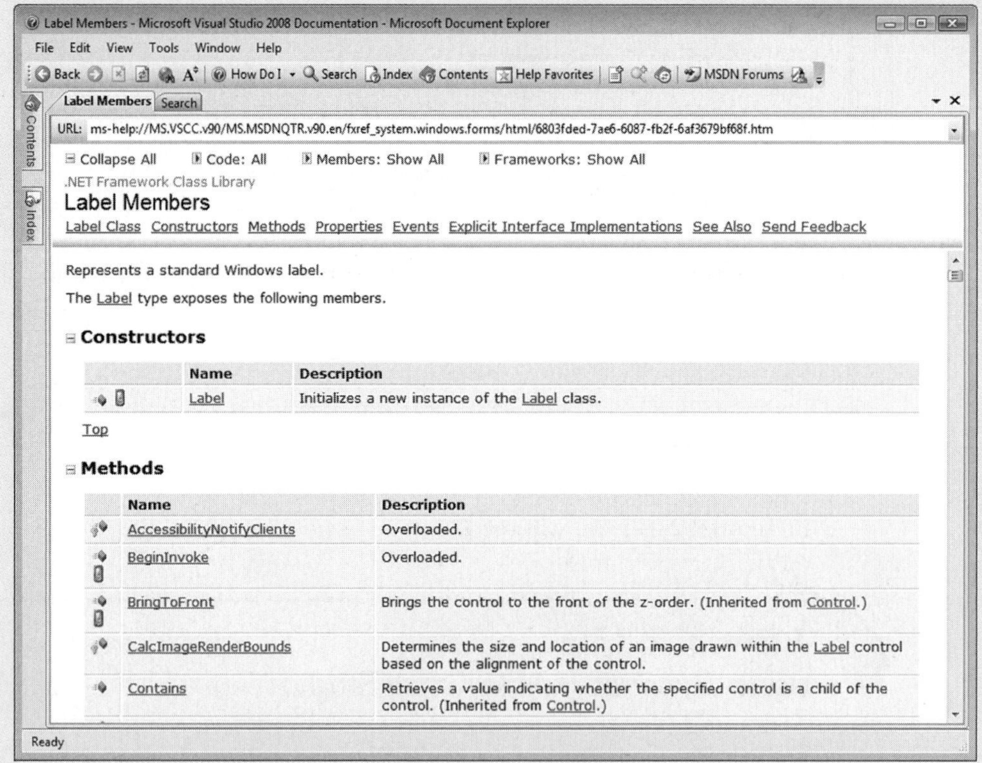

Step 5: Click the *Close* button ( ) in the upper right corner of the *Label Members* Help window.

Step 6: Look at the *Dynamic Help* window again. Figure 2-67 shows the locations of the *Contents*, *Index*, and *Search* buttons. When any of these buttons are clicked, another Help window with additional functionality appears in the same location as the *Solution Explorer*. The **Contents button** displays a table of contents in which related topics are organized into groups. The ***Index* button** displays a searchable alphabetized index of all the help topics. The ***Search* button** allows you to search for help using keywords.

Figure 2-67 *Dynamic Help* window buttons

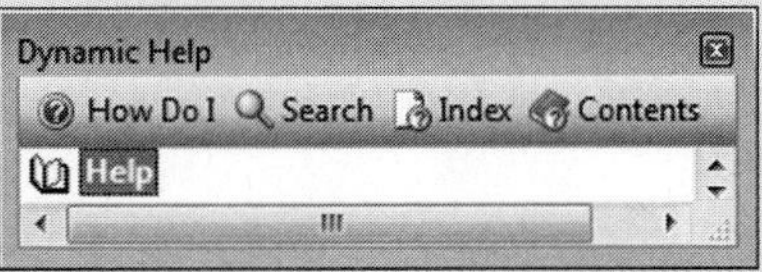

Step 7: In the *Dynamic Help* window's toolbar, click the *Search* button. The *Search* window should appear. There are so many topics in the MSDN help system that you need to narrow down your search using the following criteria: Language, Technology, and Content Type.

- In the Language list, select only *Visual Basic.*
- In the Technology list, select only *Windows Forms.*
- In the Content Type list, select only *Documentation & Articles.*

Enter *Label.Text* into the input text line and click the *Search* button. Figure 2-68 shows a sample of the type of help information you should see. *(The exact list of topics may be different in your window because Microsoft updates its Help Web site regularly.)*

Figure 2-68 Searching for the Label.Text property

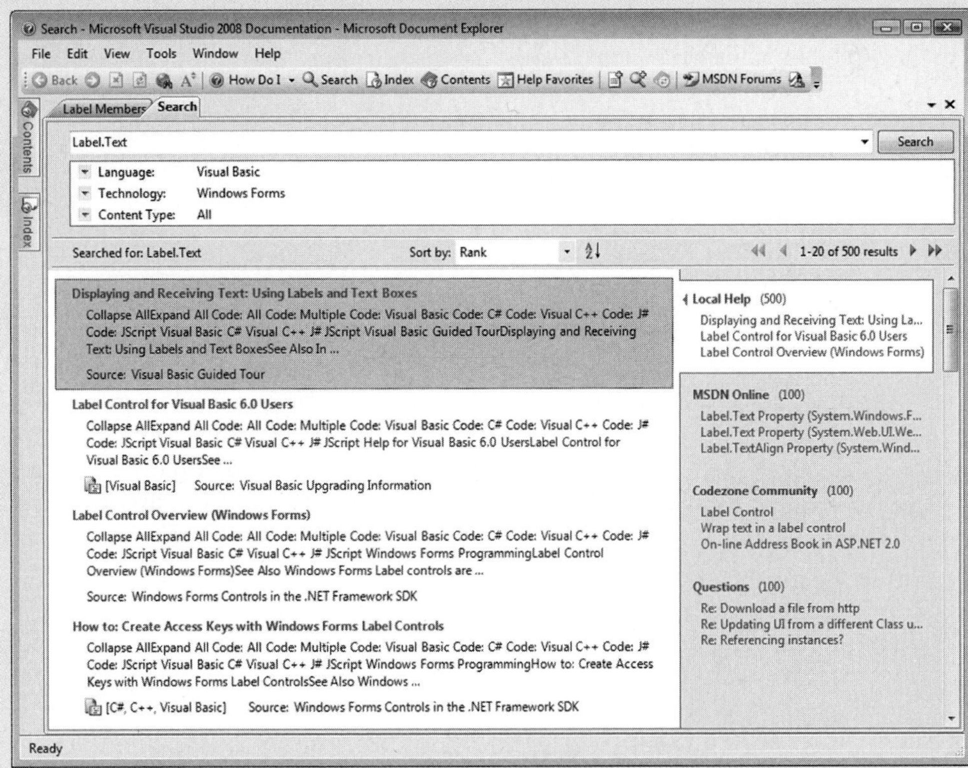

Step 8: You may find it helpful to keep a list of favorite help topics you can find quickly in the future. For example, right-click the help topic you selected in Step 7. The context menu, as shown in Figure 2-69 lets you add this topic to your list of Help Favorites. Add several help topics to your Help Favorites. When you are done, close the *Search* window.

Figure 2-69 Adding a help topic to your Help Favorites

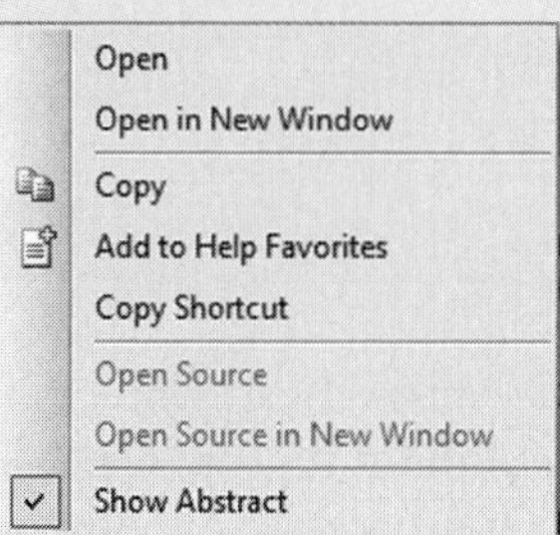

Step 9: In the *Dynamic Help* window, click the *Index* button. The Index lookup panel appears in the left side of the *Search* window. Set the *Filtered by* selection to *Visual Basic.*

Step 10: Type *Label control* into the box near the top labeled as *Look for:* (see Figure 2-70). Notice how Label control appears in different contexts. When you select the entry relating to Windows Forms, the help topic's text should appear.

Figure 2-70 Using the *Index* window

Step 11: Click the *Help Favorites* tab at the bottom of the *Search* window, as shown in Figure 2-71. You will see a list of help topics you previously added to your Help Favorites. This list is saved when you exit Visual Studio.

Step 12: Close the project.

Figure 2-71 *Help Favorites* window

2.7 Debugging Your Application

CONCEPT: At some point, most applications contain bugs (errors) that prevent the application from operating properly. In this section, you learn fundamental debugging techniques.

Visual Basic reports errors in your project as soon as it finds them. In general, there are two types of errors: compile errors and runtime errors.

Compile errors are syntax errors, such as misspelled keywords or the incorrect use of operators or punctuation. Visual Basic checks each line of code for compile errors as soon as you enter it. When a compile error is found, it is underlined with a jagged blue line. A description of the error is also displayed in the *Error List* window. You display it by clicking *View* on the menu bar, and then selecting *Error List*.

Runtime errors are errors found while an application is running. They are not syntax errors but result if there is an attempt to perform an operation that Visual Basic cannot execute.

Tutorial 2-18 demonstrates how Visual Basic reports compile errors.

Tutorial 2-18:
Locating a compile error in Design mode

Step 1: Open the *Directions* project and open the *Code* window.

Step 2: You will modify the `btnExit_Click` procedure so it contains a syntax error. Position the text editing cursor at the end of the line that reads `Me.Close()`.

Step 3: Type a period at the end of the line and press [Enter]. Notice that the statement is now underlined with a jagged blue line, as shown in Figure 2-72.

Figure 2-72 Error underlined

```
Private Sub btnExit_Click(ByVal sender As System.Object, ByVal

    'End the application by closing the window
    Me.Close().
End Sub
```

Step 4: Look at the *Error List* window, which should appear similar to Figure 2-73. It shows an error message indicating that the statement is not valid.

Figure 2-73 *Error List* window with error message

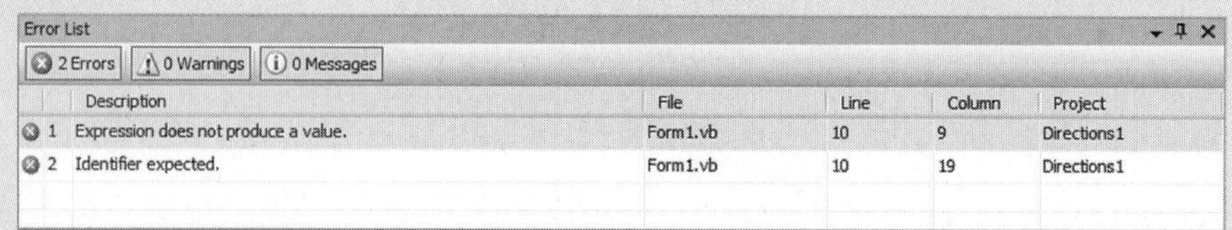

Error List

2 Errors | 0 Warnings | 0 Messages

	Description	File	Line	Column	Project
1	Expression does not produce a value.	Form1.vb	10	9	Directions1
2	Identifier expected.	Form1.vb	10	19	Directions1

Step 5: The *Error List* window also helps you find the statement that contains the error. If you do not see it, select *Error List* from the *View* menu. Double-click the error message in the *Error List* window. Notice that the erroneous statement is highlighted in the *Code* window.

TIP: Sometimes you will see an error message you do not fully understand. When this happens, look at the highlighted area of the line containing the error and try to determine the problem. When you figure out what caused the error, consider how it relates to the error message.

Step 6: Erase the period to correct the error.

Checkpoint

2.31 In Visual Studio, if the *Dynamic Help* window is not visible, how do you display it?

2.32 Describe two ways to display a searchable alphabetized index of help topics.

2.33 How do you cause the *Contents*, *Index*, and *Search* windows to display only help topics related to Visual Basic?

2.34 What is context-sensitive help?

2.35 What are the two general types of errors in a Visual Basic project?

Summary

2.1 Focus on Problem Solving: Building the *Directions* Application

- The *Properties* window is used at design time to set control property values. The PictureBox control's SizeMode property determines how the control will place and size its image.
- Small squares (sizing handles) are used to enlarge or shrink the control. Once you place a control on a form, you can move it by clicking and dragging. To delete a control, select it and then press the Delete key.
- To run an application click the *Start Debugging* button on the toolbar, click the *Start Debugging* command on the *Debug* menu, or press the F5 key. To end a running application, click the *Stop Debugging* command on the *Debug* menu or click the *Close* button on the application window.
- When you create a new project, Visual Studio automatically creates a solution with the same name as the project, and adds the project to the solution. The solution and the project are stored on the disk in a folder with the same name as the solution. The solution file ends with the *.sln* extension and the project file ends with the *.vbproj* extension.
- To open an existing project, click its name on the *Start Page*, click the *Open Project* button on the toolbar, or click *File* on the menu bar, then click *Open Project*.
- The *Properties* window's object box provides a drop-down list of the objects in the project. The *Alphabetical* button causes the properties to be listed alphabetically. The *Categorized* button causes related properties to be displayed in groups.

2.2 Focus on Problem Solving: Responding to Events

- The apostrophe (`'`) marks the beginning of a comment in code. A comment is a note of explanation that is ignored by Visual Basic.
- The `Me.Close()` statement causes the current form to close. If the current form is the application's startup form, the application ends.
- To display the *Code* window, you click the *View Code* button on the *Solution Explorer* window, click *View* on the menu bar, then *Code*, or press the F7 key on the keyboard.
- The color of a label's text is changed with the BackColor and ForeColor properties.
- Once you have placed all the controls in their proper positions on a form, it is a good idea to lock them.

2.3 Modifying the Text Property with Code

- You may change a control's Text property with code. An assignment statement copies a value into the property at runtime.

2.4 The AutoSize, BorderStyle, and TextAlign Properties

- You can set the TextAlign property with code at runtime by using an assignment statement to store a valid value in the property.

2.5 Clickable Images

- Buttons are not the only controls with `Click` event procedures. Other controls, such as PictureBoxes and Labels, also have `Click` event procedures.

2.6 Using Visual Studio Help

- In Visual Studio (but not Visual Basic Express), the *Dynamic Help* window displays a list of help topics that changes as you perform operations. The window also has buttons to view the help contents, view the index, and search for a help topic. The same commands are available in the *Help* menu of Visual Basic Express.
- In Visual Basic Express, you can select a control or keyword and press the F1 key to view immediate help.

2.7 Debugging Your Application

- Visual Basic checks each line of code for syntax errors as soon as you enter it. When a compile error is found, it is underlined with a jagged blue line.
- Runtime errors occur while an application is running. They are not syntax errors, but result if there is an attempt to perform an operation that Visual Basic cannot execute.

Key Terms

Alphabetical button
assignment operator
assignment statement
auto list box
AutoSize property
BackColor property
Boolean property
BorderStyle property
bounding box
Categorized button
code template
Code window
compile errors
Contents button
context-sensitive help
Font property
ForeColor property
FormBorderStyle property
Index button
IntelliSense
object box
PictureBox control
project file
runtime errors
Search button
SizeMode property
sizing handles
solution (container)
solution file
string literal
TextAlign property
Visible property

Review Questions and Exercises

Fill-in-the-Blank

1. The ______________________ property determines how a Label control's text is aligned.
2. A PictureBox control's ______________________ property lists the name of the file containing the graphic image.
3. A PictureBox control's ______________________ property determines how the graphic image will be positioned and scaled to fit the control's bounding box.
4. When set to ______________________, the TextAlign property causes text to appear in the bottom right area of a Label control.
5. The contents of a form's Text property is displayed on the form's ______________________.
6. Anytime you select an existing control, ______________________ appear, which you use to resize the control.

7. A control's ______________________ is a transparent rectangular area that defines the control's size.

8. A Label control's ______________________ property establishes the font, style, and size of the label's displayed text.

9. To delete a control during design time, select it and press the ______________________ key.

10. The ______________________ control is used to display graphic images.

11. The SizeMode property is set to ______________________ by default.

12. When the ______________________ button is selected on the *Solution Explorer* window, it opens the *Code* window.

13. Clicking the ______________________ button in the *Properties* window causes related properties to be listed in groups.

14. Visible is a ______________________ property, which means it can only hold one of two values: *True* or *False*.

15. An apostrophe (') in code marks the beginning of a ______________________.

16. The equal sign (=) is known as the ______________________ operator. It copies the value on its right into the item on its left.

17. In an assignment statement, the name of the item receiving the value must be on the ______________________ side of the = operator.

18. Visual Basic automatically provides a code ______________________, which is the first and last lines of an event procedure.

19. The ______________________ statement causes the application to end.

20. The ______________________ property establishes the background color for a Label control's text.

21. The ______________________ property establishes the color of the type for a Label control's text.

22. The ______________________ property allows you to prevent the user from resizing, minimizing, or maximizing a form, or closing a form using its *Close* button.

23. When you ______________________ the controls on a form, they cannot be accidentally moved at design time.

24. You display text in a form's title bar by setting the value of the form's ______________________ property.

25. You commonly display messages on a form by setting the value of a Label control's ______________________ property.

26. The ______________________ property causes the Label control to resize automatically to accommodate the amount of text in the Text property.

27. ______________________ is a help screen displayed for the currently selected item.

28. ______________________ errors are errors found while an application is running.

True or False

Indicate whether the following statements are true or false.

1. T F: Sizing handles appear around the control that is currently selected.
2. T F: The PictureBox control has an ImageStretch property.
3. T F: The Visible property is Boolean.
4. T F: A control is hidden at design time if its Visible property is set to *False*.
5. T F: You can delete a locked control.
6. T F: A control is accessed in code by its Text property.
7. T F: The TextAlign property causes a control to be aligned with other controls on the same form.
8. T F: Text is frequently the first property that the programmer changes, so it is listed in parentheses in the *Properties* window. This causes it to be displayed at the top of the alphabetized list of properties.
9. T F: Resizing handles are positioned along the edges of a control's bounding box.
10. T F: A label's text is *MiddleCenter* aligned by default.
11. T F: You can run an application in the Visual Studio environment by pressing the F5 key.
12. T F: The first line of an event procedure identifies its name and event it handles.
13. T F: You should be very cautious about, and even avoid, placing comments in your code.
14. T F: In an assignment statement, the name of the item receiving the value must be on the right side of the = operator.
15. T F: You can bring up the *Code* window by pressing the F7 key when the *Design* window is visible.
16. T F: The BackColor property establishes the color of a Label control's text.
17. T F: A form's BorderStyle property can be used to prevent the user from resizing, minimizing, or maximizing a window, or closing the window using its *Close* button.
18. T F: When you lock the controls on a form, the user must enter a password before the application will run.
19. T F: You cannot modify a control's Text property with code.
20. T F: The *Properties* window only shows a control's properties that may be changed at design time.
21. T F: The AutoSize property is set to *True* by default.
22. T F: PictureBox controls have a `Click` event procedure.
23. T F: Context-sensitive help is a help screen displayed for the currently selected item.
24. T F: You access context-sensitive help by pressing the F1 key.

Short Answer

1. Explain the difference between an object's Text and its Name.
2. List three ways to run an application within the Visual Studio environment.
3. List three ways to display the *Code* window.
4. Why is the code between the first and last lines of an event procedure usually indented?
5. How do you make a PictureBox control respond to mouse clicks?

What Do You Think?

1. Why, in the *Properties* window, do you change some properties with a drop-down list or a dialog box, while you change others by typing a value?
2. Why is it a good idea to equip a form with a button that terminates the application, if the form already has a standard Windows *Close* button in the upper right corner?
3. What is the benefit of creating PictureBox controls that respond to mouse clicks?

Find the Error

1. Open the *Error1* project from the student sample programs folder named *\Chap2\Error1*. Run the application. When Visual Basic reports an error, find and fix the error.
2. Open the *Error2* project from the student sample programs folder named *\Chap2\Error2*. Run the application. When Visual Basic reports an error, find and fix the error.

Programming Challenges

1. **Welcome Screen Modification**

   For this exercise, you will modify an application that displays a welcome screen for the First Gaddis Bank. After starting Visual Studio, open the *First Gaddis* project from the student sample programs folder named *Chap2\First Gaddis*. Figure 2-74 shows the application's form.

Figure 2-74 *First Gaddis* welcome screen, *Form1*

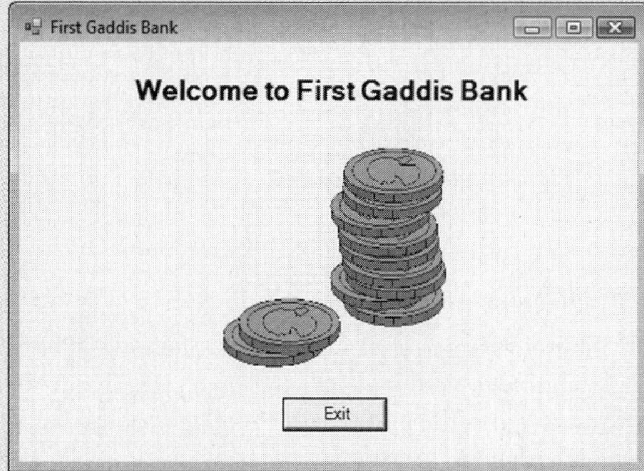

Make the following modifications to the application:

a. Change the form's title bar text to read *First Gaddis Bank*.
b. Change the label's Font property to *Microsoft sans serif, bold, 14.25 point*.
c. Change the label's text alignment to middle center.
d. Change the button's name to `btnExit`.
e. Change the button's text to read *Exit*.
f. Change the label's background color to a shade of light blue, or another color of your choice.
g. Change the form's background color to the same color you chose for the label.
h. Write a `Click` event procedure for the button that closes the application window.

VideoNote
The Name and Address Problem

2. **Name and Address**

Create an application that displays your name and address when a button is clicked. The application's form should appear as shown in Figure 2-75 when it first runs. Once the *Show Info* button is clicked, the form should appear similar to the one shown in Figure 2-76.

Figure 2-75 Intitial *Name and Address* form

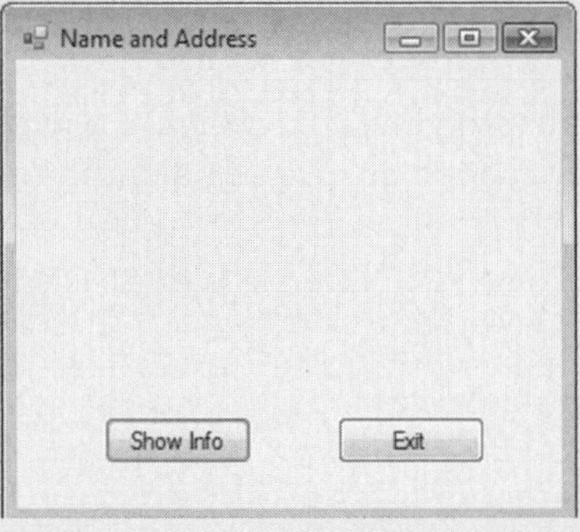

Figure 2-76 *Name and Address* form after *Show Info* button is clicked

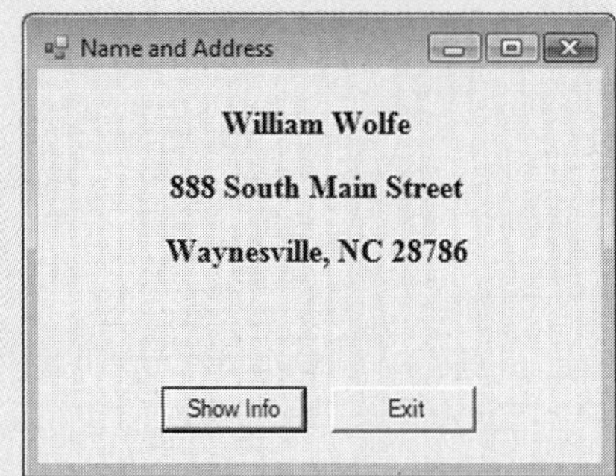

Here are the detailed property specifications:

a. The button that displays the name and address should be named `btnShowInfo`. Its text should read *Show Info*.
b. The button that closes the application should be named `btnExit`. Its text should read *Exit*.
c. The form should have three Label controls. The first will hold your name, the second will hold your street address, and the third will hold your city, state, and ZIP code. The labels should be named `lblName`, `lblStreet`, and `lblCityStateZip`, respectively. The labels' Font property should be set to *Times New Roman, bold, 12 point*. The labels' TextAlign property should be set to *MiddleCenter*.
d. The form's title bar should read *Name and Address*.

3. **Math Tutor Application**

You are to create a *Math Tutor* application. The application should display a simple math problem in a Label control. The form should have a button that displays the answer to the math problem in a second label, when clicked. It should also have a button that closes the application. Figure 2-77 shows an example of the application's form before the button is clicked to display the answer. Figure 2-78 shows the

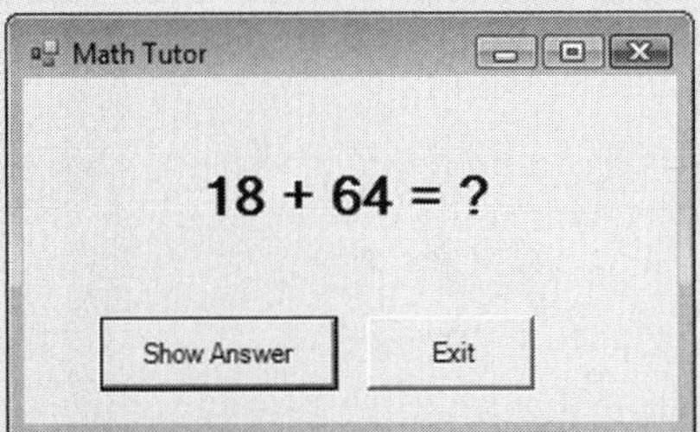

Figure 2-77 Initial *Math Tutor* application

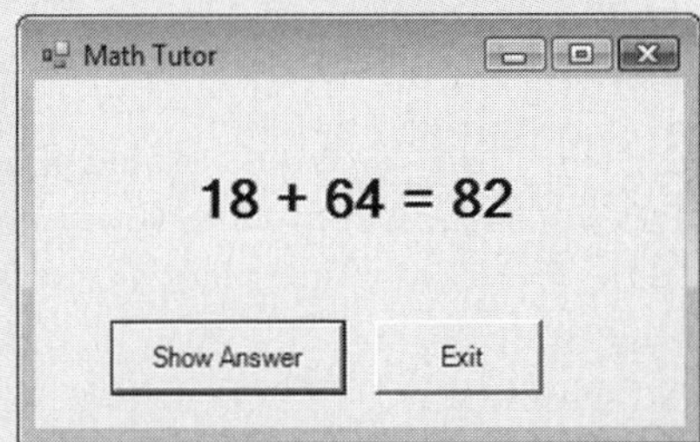

Figure 2-78 *Math Tutor* application after *Show Answer* button is clicked

form after the *Show Answer* button is clicked. Here are the detailed property specifications:

a. The button that displays the answer should be named `btnShowAnswer`. Its Text property should read *Show Answer*.

b. The button that closes the application should be named `btnExit`. Its Text property should read *Exit*.

c. The label that displays the answer to the math problem should be named `lblAnswer`.

d. The form's title bar should read *Math Tutor*.

Design Your Own Forms

4. **State Abbreviations**

The following table shows lists of six states and their official abbreviations.

State	Abbreviation
Virginia	VA
North Carolina	NC
South Carolina	SC
Georgia	GA
Alabama	AL
Florida	FL

Create an application that allows the user to select a state, and then displays that state's official abbreviation. The form should have six buttons, one for each state. When the user clicks a button, the application displays the state's abbreviation in a Label control.

5. **Latin Translator**

Look at the following list of Latin words and their meanings.

Latin	English
sinister	left
dexter	right
medium	center

Create an application that translates the Latin words to English. The form should have three buttons, one for each Latin word. When the user clicks a button, the application should display the English translation in a Label control. When the user clicks the *sinister* button, the translation should appear with middle left alignment. When the user clicks the *dexter* button, the translation should appear with middle right alignment. When the user clicks the *medium* button, the translation should appear with middle center alignment.

6. Clickable Image

Create an application with a PictureBox control. For the Image property, use one of Visual Basic's graphics files. If Visual Studio is installed, graphics files may be stored in the following file on your hard drive: *C:\Program Files\Microsoft Visual Studio 9.0\Common7\VS2008ImageLibrary\1033\VS2008ImageLibrary.zip*. In this file, you will find several folders of graphics files. Explore them and select a file you want to use. If you are using Visual Basic Express, you can obtain graphic files from the Internet or from your instructor.

Once you have selected a graphic file, place a Label control on the form. Then, write code in the PictureBox control's `Click` event procedure that displays the name of your school in the Label control.

7. Joke and Punch line

A joke typically has two parts: a setup and a punch line. For example, this might be the setup for a joke:

> *How many programmers does it take to change a light bulb?*

And this is the punch line:

> *None. That's a hardware problem.*

Think of your favorite joke and identify its setup and punch line. Then, create an application that has a Label and two buttons on a form. One of the buttons should read "Setup" and the other button should read "Punch line." When the *Setup* button is clicked, display the joke's setup in the Label. When the *Punch line* button is clicked, display the joke's punch line in the Label.

CHAPTER

3 Variables and Calculations

TOPICS

This chapter covers the use of text boxes to gather input from users. It also discusses the use of variables, named constants, type conversion functions, and mathematical calculations. You will be introduced to the GroupBox control as a way to organize controls on an application's form. The *Format* menu commands, which allow you to align, size, and center controls are also discussed. You will learn about the form's `Load` procedure, which automatically executes when a form is loaded into memory, and debugging techniques for locating logic errors.

3.1 Gathering Text Input

CONCEPT: In this section, we use the TextBox control to gather input the user has typed on the keyboard. We also alter a form's tab order and assign keyboard access keys to controls.

The programs you have written and examined so far perform operations without requiring information from the user. In reality, most programs ask the user to enter values. For example, a program that calculates payroll for a small business might ask the user to enter the name of the employee, the hours worked, and the hourly pay rate. The program then uses this information to print the employee's paycheck.

A **text box** is a rectangular area on a form that accepts keyboard input. As the user types, the characters are stored in the text box. In Visual Basic, you create a text box with a **TextBox control**. Tutorial 3-1 examines an application that uses a TextBox control.

Tutorial 3-1:
Using a TextBox control

Step 1: Open the *Greetings* project from the student sample programs folder named *Chap3\Greetings*.

Step 2: Click the *Start* button (▸) to run the application. The application's form appears, as shown in Figure 3-1. The TextBox control is the white rectangular area beneath the label that reads *Enter Your Name*.

Notice that the TextBox control shows a blinking text cursor, indicating it is ready to receive keyboard input.

Step 3: Type your name. As you enter characters on the keyboard, they appear in the TextBox control.

Step 4: Click the *Show Greeting* button. The message *Hello* followed by the name you entered, appears in a label below the TextBox control. The form now appears similar to the one shown in Figure 3-2.

Step 5: Click inside the TextBox control and use the [Delete] and/or [Backspace] key to erase the name you entered. Enter another name, and then click the *Show Greeting* button. Notice that the greeting message changes accordingly.

Step 6: Click the *Exit* button to exit the application. You have returned to Design mode.

Step 7: Look at the application's form in the *Design* window. Figure 3-3 shows the form with its controls.

Notice that the name of the TextBox control starts with `txt`, which is the standard prefix for TextBox controls. Like the Label control, the TextBox control has a Text property. However, the Label control's Text property is only for displaying information—the user cannot directly alter its contents. The TextBox

Figure 3-1 *Greetings* project initial form

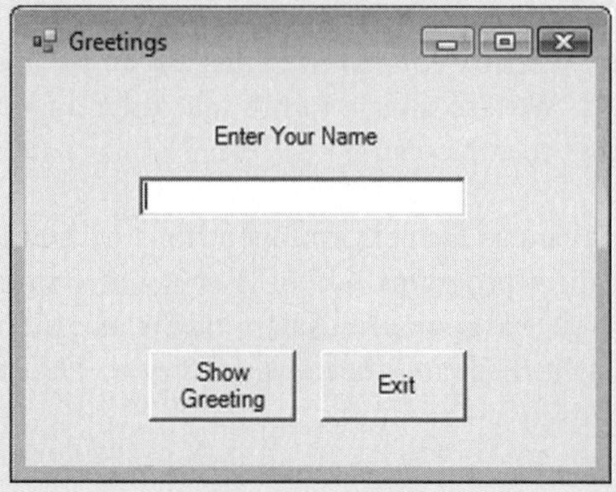

Figure 3-2 *Greetings* project completed form

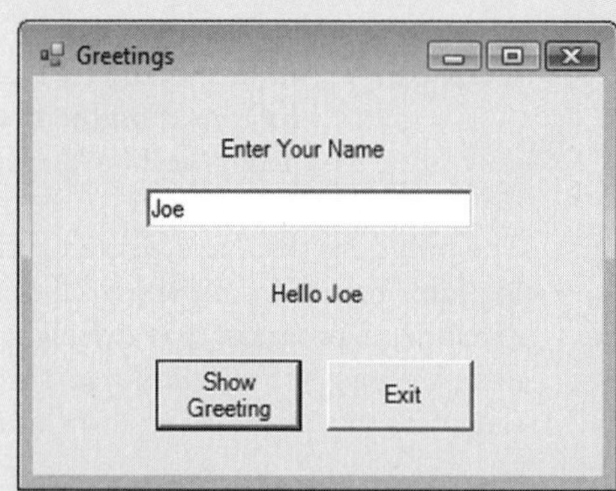

control's Text property is for input purposes. The user can alter it by typing characters into the TextBox control. Whatever the user types into the TextBox control is stored, as a string, in its Text property.

Figure 3-3 *Greetings* project form with controls labeled

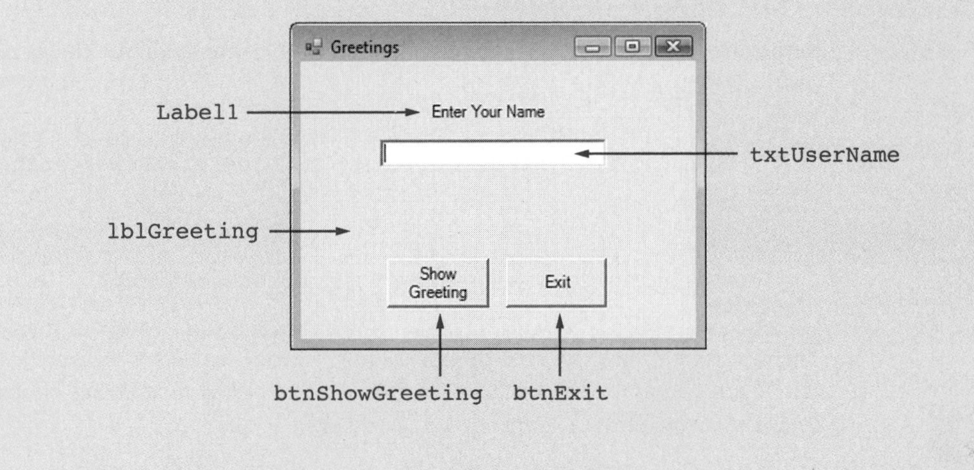

Using the Text Property in Code

You access a TextBox control's Text property in code the same way you access other properties. For example, assume an application has a Label control named `lblInfo` and a TextBox control named `txtInput`. The following assignment statement copies the contents of the TextBox control's Text property into the Label control's Text property.

```
lblInfo.Text = txtInput.Text
```

Clear a Text Box

Recall from the discussion on object-oriented programming in Chapter 1 that an object contains methods, which are actions the object performs. To execute an object's method, write a statement that calls the method. The general format of such a statement is

```
Object.Method
```

Object is the name of the object and *`Method`* is the name of the method that is being called.

A *`TextBox`* control is an object, and has a variety of methods that perform operations on the text box or its contents. One of these methods is `Clear`, which clears the contents of the text box's Text property. The general format of the `Clear` method is

```
TextBoxName.Clear()
```

`TextBoxName` is the name of the TextBox control. Here is an example:

```
txtInput.Clear()
```

When this statement executes, the Text property of `txtInput` is cleared and the text box appears empty on the screen.

You can also clear a text box by assigning the predefined constant `String.Empty` to its Text property. Here is an example:

```
txtInput.Text = String.Empty
```

Once this statement executes, the Text property of `txtInput` is cleared and the text box appears empty on the screen.

String Concatenation

Returning to the *Greetings* application, let's look at the code for the `btnShowGreeting` control's `Click` event:

```
Private Sub btnShowGreeting_Click(ByVal sender As System.Object, _
        ByVal e As System.EventArgs) Handles btnShowGreeting.Click

   ' Display a customized greeting to the user
   ' in the lblGreeting control
   lblGreeting.Text = "Hello " & txtUserName.Text
End Sub
```

The assignment statement in this procedure introduces a new operator: the ampersand (`&`). When the ampersand is used in this way, it performs a **string concatenation**. This means that one string is appended to another.

The `&` operator creates a string that is a combination of the string on its left and the string on its right. Specifically, it appends the string on its right to the string on its left. For example, assume an application uses a Label control named `lblMessage`. The following statement copies the string "Good morning Charlie" into the control's Text property:

```
lblMessage.Text = "Good morning " & "Charlie"
```

In our *Greetings* application, if the user types *Becky* into the `txtUserName` control, the control's Text property is set to *Becky*. So the statement

```
lblGreeting.Text = "Hello " & txtUserName.Text
```

assigns the string `"Hello Becky"` to `lblGreeting`'s Text property.

Look again at the assignment statement. Notice there is a space in the string literal after the word *Hello*. This prevents the two strings being concatenated from running together.

In a few moments, it will be your turn to create an application using TextBox controls and string concatenation. Tutorial 3-2 leads you through the process.

Aligning Controls in Design Mode

Visual Studio provides a convenient way to align controls on forms. When you drag a control to a position on a form that aligns with another control, guide lines automatically appear. In Figure 3-4, for example, a TextBox has been placed below an existing TextBox. The blue guide lines tell us the two controls are aligned vertically. If either control is dragged sideways, the guide lines disappear.

In Figure 3-5, two TextBox controls are aligned horizontally, indicated by lavender guide lines. In Figure 3-6, guide lines appear for simultaneous vertical and horizontal alignment. All in all, this feature of Visual Studio takes the guesswork out of aligning controls, saving you a lot of time. Tutorial 3-2 shows you how to build the *Date String* application.

Figure 3-4 Vertical guide lines align two TextBox controls

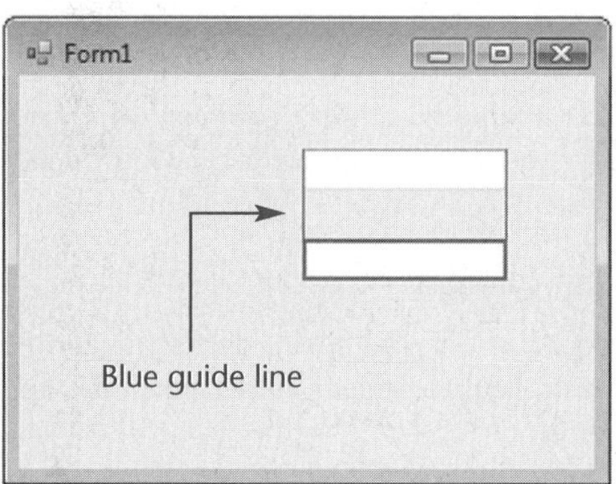

Figure 3-5 Horizontal guide lines align two TextBox controls

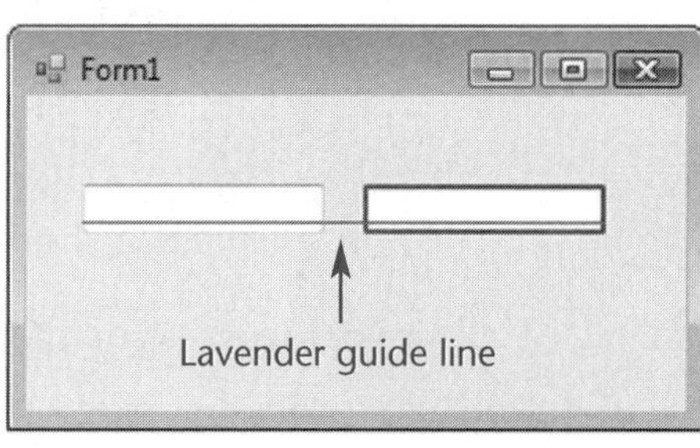

Figure 3-6 Horizontal and vertical guide lines can be used together

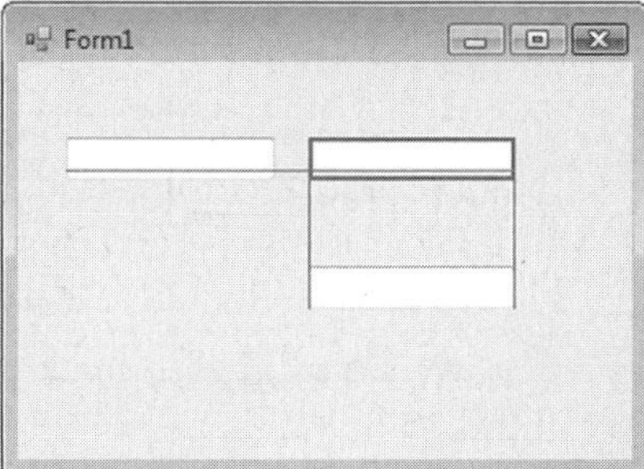

Tutorial 3-2:
Building the *Date String* application

You will create an application that lets the user enter the following information about today's date:

- The day of the week
- The name of the month
- The numeric day of the month
- The year

When the user enters the information and clicks a button, the application displays a date string such as Friday, December 5, 2008.

Step 1: Start Visual Studio and start a new Windows application named *Date String*.

Step 2: Create the form shown in Figure 3-7, using the following instructions:

- You insert TextBox controls by double-clicking the TextBox tool in the ToolBox. When a TextBox control is created, it will be given a default name. As with other controls, you can change a TextBox control's name by modifying its Name property.

- Give each control the name indicated in the figure. The labels that display *Enter the day of the week:*, *Enter the month:*, *Enter the day of the month:*, and *Enter the year:* will not be referred to in code, so they may keep their default names.
- Set the `lblDateString` label's AutoSize property to False, it's BorderStyle property to *Fixed3D*, and its TextAlign property to *MiddleCenter*. Resize the label as shown in Figure 3-7, and delete the contents of the label's Text property.
- Set the form's Text property to *Date String*.

As you place TextBox control on your form, delete the contents of their Text properties. This will cause them to appear empty when the application runs.

Figure 3-7 *Date String* form

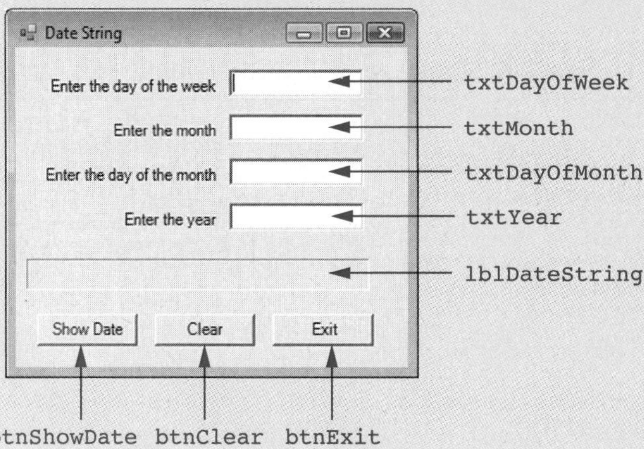

Step 3: Next, you will write code for the `btnShowDate` button's `Click` event procedure. Double-click the button to create the code template, and then enter the lines shown in bold:

```
Private Sub btnShowDate_Click(ByVal sender As System.Object, _
        ByVal e As System.EventArgs) Handles btnShowDate.Click

    ' Concatenate the input and build the date string.
    lblDateString.Text = txtDayOfWeek.Text & ", " _
        & txtMonth.Text & " " _
        & txtDayOfMonth.Text & ", " _
        & txtYear.Text
End Sub
```

This example introduces a new programming technique: breaking up long lines of code with the line-continuation character. The **line-continuation character** is actually two characters: a space, followed by an underscore or underline character.

Quite often, you will find yourself writing statements that are too long to fit entirely inside the *Code* window. Your code will be hard to read if you have to scroll the *Code* window to the right to view long statements. The line-continuation character allows you to break a long statement into several lines.

Here are some rules to remember about the line-continuation character:

- A space must immediately precede the underscore character.
- You cannot break up a word, quoted string, or name using the line-continuation character.
- You cannot separate an object name from its property or method name.
- You cannot put a comment at the end of a line after the line-continuation character. The line-continuation character must be the last thing you type on a line.

TIP: Another way to deal with long code lines is to reduce the font size used in the *Code* window by clicking *Tools* on the menu bar, and then clicking the *Options . . .* command. On the *Options* dialog box, click the arrow next to *Environment* in the left pane, and then click *Fonts and Colors*. Then you may select the desired font and size.

Step 4: The `btnClear` button allows the user to start over with a form that is empty of previous values. The `btnClear_Click` event procedure clears the contents of all the TextBox controls and the `lblDateString` label. To accomplish this, the procedure calls each TextBox control's `Clear` method, and assigns the special value `String.Empty` to `lblDateString`'s Text property. (The value `String.Empty` represents an empty string. Assigning `String.Empty` to a label's Text property clears the value displayed by the label.) Enter the following bold code into the `btnClear_Click` event procedure:

```
Private Sub btnClear_Click(ByVal sender As System.Object, _
    ByVal e As System.EventArgs) Handles btnClear.Click

  ' Clear the Text Boxes and lblDateString
  txtDayOfWeek.Clear()
  txtMonth.Clear()
  txtDayOfMonth.Clear()
  txtYear.Clear()
  lblDateString.Text = String.Empty
End Sub
```

Step 5: Enter the following code (shown in bold), which terminates the application, into the `btnExit_Click` event procedure:

```
Private Sub btnExit_Click(ByVal sender As System.Object, _
    ByVal e As System.EventArgs) Handles btnExit.Click

  ' End the application by closing the form.
  Me.Close()
End Sub
```

Step 6: Save the project.

Step 7: Click the *Start* button (▶) to run the application. With the application running, enter the requested information into the TextBox controls and click the *Show Date* button. Your form should appear similar to the one shown in Figure 3-8.

Figure 3-8 Running the *Date String* application

Step 8: Click the *Clear* button to test it, and then enter new values into the TextBox controls. Click the *Show Date* button.

Step 9: Click the *Exit* button to exit the application.

The `Focus` Method

When an application is running and a form is displayed, one of the form's controls always has the **focus**. The control having the focus is the one that receives the user's keyboard input or mouse clicks. For example, when a TextBox control has the focus, it receives the characters that the user enters on the keyboard. When a button has the focus, pressing the Enter key executes the button's `Click` event procedure.

You can tell which control has the focus by looking at the form at runtime. When a TextBox control has the focus, a blinking text cursor appears inside it, or the text inside the TextBox control appears highlighted. When a button, radio button, or check box has the focus, a thin dotted line appears around the control.

NOTE: Only controls capable of receiving some sort of input, such as text boxes and buttons, may have the focus.

Often, you want to make sure a particular control has the focus. Consider the *Date String* application, for example. When the *Clear* button is clicked, the focus should return to the `txtDayOfWeek` TextBox control. This would make it unnecessary for the user to click the TextBox control in order to start entering another set of information.

In code, you move the focus to a control by calling the **`Focus` method**. The method's general syntax is:

```
ControlName.Focus()
```

where *`ControlName`* is the name of the control. For instance, you move the focus to the `txtDayOfWeek` TextBox control with the statement `txtDayOfWeek.Focus()`. After the statement executes, the `txtDayOfWeek` control will have the focus. In Tutorial 3-3, you add this statement to the *Clear* button's `Click` event procedure so `txtDayOfWeek` has the focus after the TextBox controls and the `lblDateString` label are cleared.

Tutorial 3-3:
Using the `Focus` method

Step 1: Open the *Date String* project that you created in Tutorial 3-2.

Step 2: Open the *Code* window and add the statements shown in bold to the `btnClear_Click` event procedure.

```
Private Sub btnClear_Click(ByVal sender As System.Object, _
    ByVal e As System.EventArgs) Handles btnClear.Click

  ' Clear the Text Boxes and lblDateString
  txtDayOfWeek.Clear()
  txtMonth.Clear()
  txtDayOfMonth.Clear()
  txtYear.Clear()
  lblDateString.Text = ""
  ' Return the focus to txtDayOfWeek
  txtDayOfWeek.Focus()
End Sub
```

Step 3: Run the application. Enter some information into the TextBox controls, and then click the *Clear* button. The focus should return to the `txtDayOfWeek` TextBox control.

Step 4: Save the project.

Controlling a Form's Tab Order with the TabIndex Property

In Windows applications, pressing the Tab key changes the focus from one control to another. The order in which controls receive the focus is called the **tab order**. When you place controls on a form in Visual Basic, the tab order will be the same sequence in which you created the controls. In many cases this is the tab order you want, but sometimes you rearrange controls on a form, delete controls, and add new ones. These modifications often lead to a disorganized tab order, which can confuse and irritate the users of your application. Users want to tab smoothly from one control to the next, in a logical sequence.

You can modify the tab order by changing a control's TabIndex property. The **TabIndex property** contains a numeric value, which indicates the control's position in the tab order. When you create a control, Visual Basic automatically assigns a value to its TabIndex property. The first control you create on a form will have a TabIndex of 0, the second will have a TabIndex of 1, and so on. The control with a TabIndex of 0 will be the first control in the tab order. The next control in the tab order will be the one with a TabIndex of 1. The tab order continues in this sequence.

You may change the tab order of a form's controls by selecting them, one-by-one, and changing their TabIndex property in the *Properties* window. An easier method, however, is to click *View* on the menu bar, and then click *Tab Order*. This causes the form to be displayed in **tab order selection mode**. In this mode, each control's existing TabIndex value is displayed on the form. Then you establish a new tab order by clicking the controls in the order you want. When you are finished, exit tab order selection mode by pressing the Esc key. Tutorial 3-4 shows you how to change the tab order.

Tutorial 3-4:
Changing the tab order

In this tutorial, you rearrange the controls in the *Date String* application, and then change the tab order to accommodate the controls' new positions.

Step 1: Open the *Date String* project that you created in Tutorials 3-2 and 3-4.

Step 2: Open the application's form in the *Design* window. Rearrange the controls to match Figure 3-9. (You might want to enlarge the form temporarily so you have room to move some of the controls around. Don't forget to move the labels that correspond to the TextBox controls.)

Figure 3-9 *Date String* form

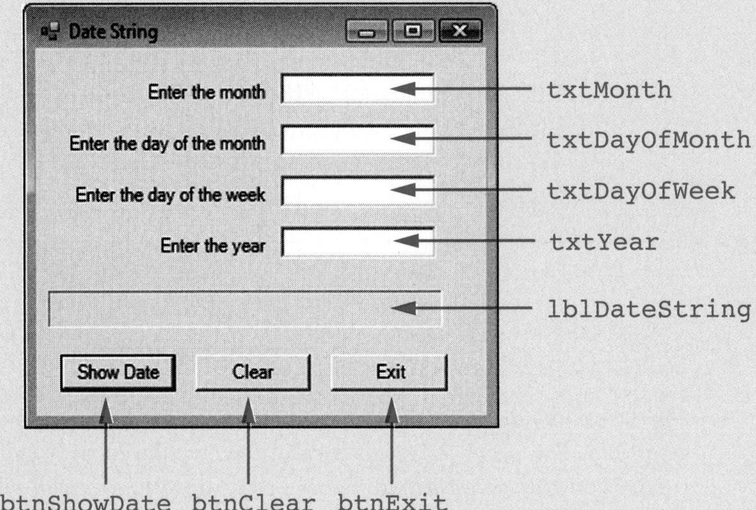

Step 3: Run the application and notice which control has the focus. Press the Tab key several times and observe the tab order.

Step 4: Stop the application and return to Design mode.

Step 5: Click *View* on the menu bar, and then click *Tab Order*. The form should switch to tab order selection mode, as shown in Figure 3-10. The numbers displayed in the upper left corner of each control are the existing TabIndex values.

> **NOTE:** Your existing TabIndex values may be different from those shown in Figure 3-10.

Step 6: Click the following controls in the order they are listed here: `txtMonth`, `txtDayOfMonth`, `txtDayOfWeek`, `txtYear`, `btnShowDate`, `btnClear`, `btnExit`.

Figure 3-10 Form in tab order selection mode

Step 7: The controls you clicked should now have the following TabIndex values displayed:

```
txtMonth:       0
txtDayOfMonth:  1
txtDayOfWeek:   2
txtYear:        3
btnShowDate:    4
btnClear:       5
btnExit:        6
```

NOTE: The Label controls cannot receive the focus, so do not be concerned with the TabIndex values displayed for them.

Step 8: Press the [Esc] key to exit tab order selection mode.

Step 9: Don't forget to change the `btnClear_Click` event procedure so `txtMonth` gets the focus when the form is cleared. The code for the procedure is as follows, with the modified lines in bold:

```
Private Sub btnClear_Click(ByVal sender As System.Object, _
        ByVal e As System.EventArgs) Handles btnClear.Click

    ' Clear the Text Boxes and lblDateString
    txtDayOfWeek.Clear()
    txtMonth.Clear()
    txtDayOfMonth.Clear()
    txtYear.Clear()
    lblDateString.Text = ""
    ' Return the focus to txtMonth
    txtMonth.Focus()
End Sub
```

Step 10: Run the application and test the new tab order.

Step 11: End the application and save the project.

Here are a few last notes about the TabIndex property:

- If you do not want a control to receive the focus when the user presses the Tab key, set its **TabStop property** to *False*.
- An error will occur if you assign a negative value to the TabIndex property in code.
- A control whose Visible property is set to *False* or whose Enabled property is set to *False* cannot receive the focus.
- GroupBox and Label controls have a TabIndex property, but they are skipped in the tab order.

Assigning Keyboard Access Keys to Buttons

An **access key**, also known as a **mnemonic**, is a key pressed in combination with the Alt key to access a control such as a button quickly. When you assign an access key to a button, the user can trigger a `Click` event either by clicking the button with the mouse or by using the access key. Users who are quick with the keyboard prefer to use access keys instead of the mouse.

You assign an access key to a button through its Text property. For example, assume an application has a button whose Text property is set to *Exit*. You wish to assign the access key Alt+X to the button, so the user may trigger the button's `Click` event by pressing Alt+X on the keyboard. To make the assignment, place an ampersand (`&`) before the letter *x* in the button's Text property: `E&xit`. Figure 3-11 shows how the Text property appears in the *Property* window.

Although the ampersand is part of the button's Text property, it is not displayed on the button. With the ampersand in front of the letter *x*, the letter will appear underlined as shown in Figure 3-12. This indicates that the button may be clicked by pressing Alt+X on the keyboard.

Figure 3-11 Text property `E&xit`

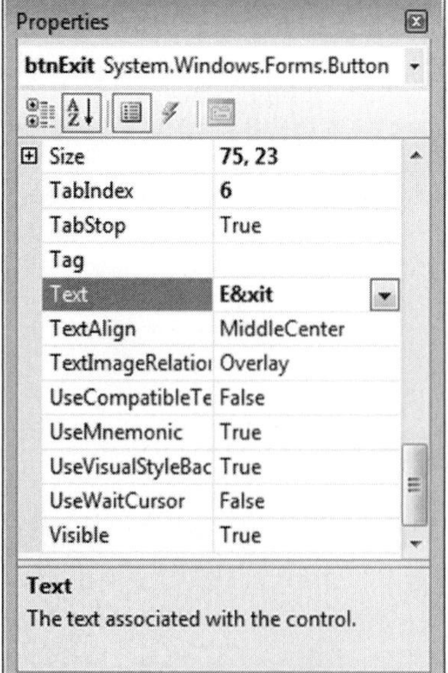

Figure 3-12 Button with `E&xit` text

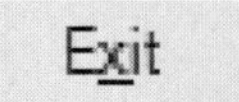

NOTE: Access keys do not distinguish between uppercase and lowercase characters. There is no difference between Alt+*X* and Alt+*x*.

Suppose we had stored the value `&Exit` in the button's Text property. The ampersand is in front of the letter *E*, so [Alt]+[E] becomes the access key. The button will appear as shown in Figure 3-13.

Assigning the Same Access Key to Multiple Buttons

Be careful not to assign the same access key to two or more buttons on the same form. If two or more buttons share the same access key, a `Click` event is triggered for the first button created when the user presses the access key.

Displaying the & Character on a Button

If you want to display an ampersand character on a button use two ampersands (`&&`) in the Text property. Using two ampersands causes a single ampersand to display and does not define an access key. For example, if a button has the Text property `Beans && Cream` the button will appear as shown in Figure 3-14.

Figure 3-13 Button with `&Exit` text

Exit

Figure 3-14 Button with text `Beans && Cream`

Beans & Cream

Accept Buttons and Cancel Buttons

An **accept button** is a button on a form that is clicked when the user presses the [Enter] key. A **cancel button** is a button on a form that is clicked when the user presses the [Esc] key. Forms have two properties, AcceptButton and CancelButton, which allow you to designate an accept button and a cancel button. When you select these properties in the *Properties* window, a down-arrow button (▼) appears, which allows you to display a drop-down list. The list contains the names of all the buttons on the form. You select the button that you want to designate as the accept button or cancel button.

Any button that is frequently clicked should probably be selected as the accept button. This will allow keyboard users to access the button quickly and easily. *Exit* or *Cancel* buttons are likely candidates to become cancel buttons. In Tutorial 3-5, you set access keys, accept, and cancel buttons.

Tutorial 3-5:
Setting access keys, accept, and cancel buttons

In this tutorial, you assign access keys to the buttons in the *Date String* application, and set accept and cancel buttons.

Step 1: Open the *Date String* project that you have worked on in Tutorials 3-2 through 3-4.

Step 2: Open the application's form in the *Design* window.

Step 3: Select the *Show Date* button (`btnShowDate`) and change its text to read *Show &Date*. This assigns [Alt]+[D] as the button's access key.

Step 4: Select the *Clear* button (`btnClear`) and change its text to read *Clea&r*. This assigns Alt+R as the button's access key.

Step 5: Select the *Exit* button (`btnExit`) and change its text to read *E&xit*. This assigns Alt+X as the button's access key.

Step 6: Select the form, and then select the AcceptButton property in the *Properties* window. Click the down-arrow button (▾) to display the drop-down list of buttons. Select `btnShowDate` from the list.

Step 7: With the form still selected, select the CancelButton property in the *Properties* window. Click the down-arrow button (▾) to display the drop-down list of buttons. Select `btnExit` from the list.

Step 8: Run the application and test the buttons' new settings. Notice that when you press the Enter key, the *Show Date String* button's `Click` procedure is executed; when you press the Esc key, the application exits.

NOTE: When the application executes, the access keys you assigned to the buttons are not displayed as underlined characters until you press the Alt key.

Step 9: Save the project.

Checkpoint

3.1 What TextBox control property holds text entered by the user?

3.2 Assume an application has a label named `lblMessage` and a TextBox control named `txtInput`. Write the statement that takes text the user entered into the TextBox control and assigns it to the label's Text property.

3.3 If the following statement is executed, what will the `lblGreeting` control display?

```
lblGreeting.Text = "Hello " & "Jonathon, " & "how are you?"
```

3.4 What is the line-continuation character, and what does it do?

3.5 What is meant when it is said that a control has the focus?

3.6 Write a statement that gives the focus to the `txtLastName` control.

3.7 What is meant by tab order?

3.8 How does the TabIndex property affect the tab order?

3.9 How does Visual Basic normally assign the tab order?

3.10 What happens when a control's TabStop property is set to *False*?

3.11 Assume a button's Text property is set to the text *Show &Map*. What effect does the & character have?

3.12 What is an accept button? What is a cancel button? How do you establish these buttons on a form?

3.2 Variables and Data Types

CONCEPT: Variables hold information that may be manipulated, used to manipulate other information, or remembered for later use.

VideoNote

Introduction to Variables

A **variable** is a storage location in computer memory that holds data while a program is running. It is called a variable because the data it holds can be changed by statements in the program.

In this chapter, you have seen programs that store data in properties belonging to Visual Basic controls. Although control properties are useful, you must store data in variables when performing calculations. Generally speaking, you can do a number of things with variables:

- Copy and store values entered by the user so the values can be manipulated
- Perform arithmetic on numeric values
- Test values to determine that they meet some criterion
- Temporarily hold and manipulate the value of a control property
- Remember information for later use in a program

Think of a variable as a name that represents a location in the computer's random-access memory (RAM). When a value is stored in a variable, it is actually stored in RAM. You use the assignment operator (=) to store a value in a variable, just as you do with a control property. For example, suppose a program uses a variable named `intLength`. The following statement stores the value 112 in that variable:

```
intLength = 112
```

When this statement executes, the value 112 is stored in the memory location the name `intLength` represents. As another example, assume the following statement appears in a program that uses a variable named `strGreeting` and a TextBox control named `txtName`:

```
strGreeting = "Good morning " & txtName.Text
```

Suppose the user has already entered Holly into the `txtName` TextBox control. When the statement executes, the variable `strGreeting` is assigned the string `"Good morning Holly"`.

Declaring Variables

A **variable declaration** is a statement that creates a variable in memory when a program executes. The declaration indicates the name you wish to give the variable and the type of information the variable will hold. Here is the general form of a variable declaration:

```
Dim VariableName As DataType
```

Here is an example of a variable declaration:

```
Dim intLength As Integer
```

Let's look at each part of this statement, and its purpose:

- The `Dim` keyword tells Visual Basic that a variable is being declared.
- `intLength` is the name of the variable.
- `As Integer` indicates the variable's data type. We know it will be used to hold integer numbers.

You can declare multiple variables with one `Dim` statement, as shown in the following statement. It declares three variables, all holding integers:

```
Dim intLength, intWidth, intHeight As Integer
```

Assigning Values to Variables

A value is put into a variable with an assignment statement. For example, the following statement assigns the value 20 to the variable `intUnitsSold`:

```
intUnitsSold = 20
```

The = operator is called the assignment operator. A variable name must always appear on the left side of the assignment operator. For example, the following would be incorrect:

```
20 = intUnitsSold
```

On the right side of the operator, you can put a literal, another variable, or a mathematical expression that matches the variables type. In the following, the contents of the variable on the right side of the = sign is copied into the variable on the left side:

```
intUnitsSold = intUnitsOnHand
```

Suppose `intUnitsOnHand` already equals 20. Then Figure 3-15 shows how the value 20 is copied into the memory location represented by `intUnitsSold`.

Figure 3-15 Assigning `intUnitsOnHand` to `intUnitsSold`

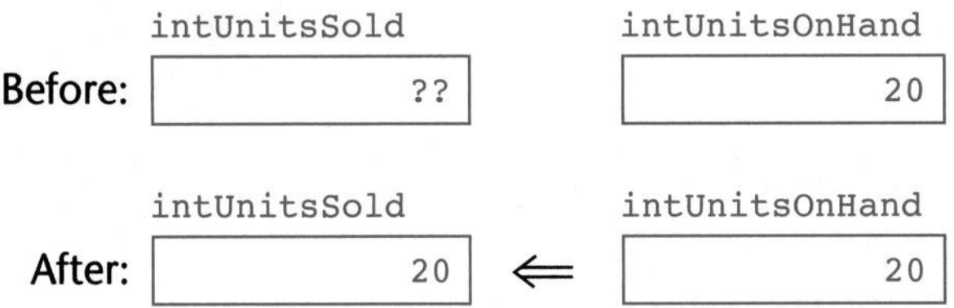

The assignment operator only changes the left operand. The right operand (or expression) does not change value. Sometimes your program will contain a series of statements that pass a value from one variable to the next. When the following statements execute, all three variables will contain the same value, 50:

```
Dim intA, intB, intC As Integer
intA = 50
intB = intA
intC = intB
```

A variable can hold only one value at a time. If you assign a new value to the variable, the new value replaces the variable's previous contents. There is no way to "undo" this operation. For example:

```
Dim intA, intB As Integer
intA = 50
intA = 99
```

After the second assignment statement, `intA` equals 99. The value 50 no longer exists in memory.

Integer Data Types

Integer data types hold integer values such as –5, 26, 12345, and 0. The following code example shows examples of the different integer types available in Visual Basic:

```
Dim bytInches As Byte
Dim shrtFeet as Short
Dim intMiles As Integer
Dim lngNationalDebt As Long

bytInches = 26
shrtFeet = 32767
intMiles = 2100432877
lngNationalDebt = 4000000000001
```

We usually use a three– or four–letter prefix when naming each variable. The prefix is not required, but it helps you to remember a variable's type. Table 3-1 lists the Visual Basic integer data types, showing their naming prefixes and descriptions. Unsigned integers can only hold positive values (zero is considered positive). Signed integers can hold both positive and negative values.

Table 3-1 Integer data types

Type	Naming Prefix	Description
Byte	`byt`	Holds an unsigned integer value in the range 0 to 255
Short	`shrt`	Holds a signed integer in the range –32,768 to +32,767
Integer	`int`	Holds a signed integer in the range –2,147,483,648 to 2,147,483,647
Long	`lng`	Holds a signed integer in the range –9,223,372,036,854,775,808 to 9,223,372,036,854,775,807

Each type has a different storage size and range of possible values it can hold. Most of the time, you will use the Integer data type for integer-type values. Its name is easy to remember, and Integer values are efficiently processed by the computer.

Integer Literals

When you write an integer literal in your program code, Visual Basic assumes the literal is type Integer if the value fits within the allowed range for the Integer data type. A value larger than that will be assumed to be type Long. On rare occasions, if you may want to override the literal's default type, append a special character to the end of the number:

I Integer literal
L Long integer literal
S Short integer literal

In the following code example, an integer literal uses the L character to identify it as type Long:

```
Dim lngCounter As Long
lngCounter = 10000L
```

In the following, an integer literal uses the S character to identify it as type Short:

```
Dim shrtFeet as Short
shrtFeet = 1234S
```

TIP: You cannot embed commas in numeric literals. The following, for example, causes an error: `intMiles = 32,767`

Floating-Point Data Types

Values that have fractional parts and use a decimal point must be stored in one of Visual Basic's floating-point data types. Table 3-2 lists the floating-point data types, showing their naming prefixes and descriptions.

Table 3-2 Floating-point data types

Type	Naming Prefix	Description
Single	`sng`	Holds a signed single precision real number with 7 significant digits, in the range of approximately plus or minus 1.0×10^{38}
Double	`dbl`	Holds a signed double precision real number with 15 significant digits, in the range of approximately plus or minus 1.0×10^{308}
Decimal	`dec`	Decimal real number, 29 significant digits. Its range (with no decimal places) is +/–79,228,162,514,264,337,593,543,950,335

Significant Digits

The significant digits measurement for each floating-point data type is important for certain kinds of calculations. Suppose you were simulating a chemical reaction and needed to calculate the number of calories produced. You might produce a number such as 1.234567824724. If you used a variable of type Single, only the first seven digits would be kept in computer memory, and the remaining digits would be lost. The last digit would be rounded upward, producing 1.234568. This loss of precision happens because the computer uses a limited amount of storage for floating-point numbers. If you did the same chemical reaction calculation using a variable of type Double, the entire result would be safely held in the number, with no loss of precision.

The Decimal data type is used in financial calculations when you need a great deal of precision. This data type helps prevent rounding errors from creeping into repeated calculations.

The following code demonstrates each floating-point data type:

```
Dim sngTemperature As Single
Dim dblWindSpeed As Double
Dim decBankBalance As Decimal

sngTemperature = 98.6
dblWindSpeed = 35.373659262
decBankBalance = 1234567890.1234567890123456789D
```

Notice that the last line requires a `D` suffix on the number to identify it as a Decimal literal. Otherwise, Visual Basic would assume that the number was type Double.

Floating-Point Literals

Floating-point literals can be written in either fixed-point or scientific notation. The number 47281.97, for example, would be written in scientific notation as 4.728197×10^4. Visual Basic requires the letter E just before the exponent in scientific notation. So, our sample number would be written in Visual Basic like this:

```
4.728197E+4
```

The + sign after the E is optional. Here is an example of a value having a negative exponent:

```
4.623476E-2
```

Scientific notation is particularly useful for very large numbers. Instead of writing a value such as 12340000000000000000000000000000.0, for example, it is easier to write 1.234E+31.

Boolean Data Type

A Boolean type variable can only hold one of two possible values: *True* or *False*. The values True and False are built-in Visual Basic keywords. The word Boolean is named after George Boole, a famous mathematician of the nineteenth century. (His Boolean algebra is the basis for all modern computer arithmetic.)

We use Boolean variables to hold information that is either true or false. The standard naming prefix for Boolean variables is `bln`. Here is an example:

```
Dim blnIsRegistered As Boolean
blnIsRegistered = True
```

We will begin using Boolean variables in Chapter 4.

Char Data Type

Variables of the Char data type can hold a single Unicode character. Unicode characters are the set of values that can represent a large number of international characters in different languages. To assign a character literal to a Char variable, enclose the character in double quotations marks, followed by a lowercase "c". The standard naming prefix for Char variables is `chr`. The following is an example:

```
Dim chrLetter As Char
chrLetter = "A"c
```

String Data Type

A variable of type String can hold between zero and about 2 billion characters. The characters are stored in sequence. A string literal, as you have seen earlier, is always enclosed in quotation marks. In the following code, a string variable is assigned various string literals:

```
Dim strName As String
strName = "Jose Gonzalez"
```

The standard naming prefix for String variables is `str`.

An empty string literal can be coded as `""` or by the special identifier named `String.Empty`:

```
strName = ""
strName = String.Empty
```

Date Data Type

A variable of type Date can hold date and time information. Date variables are assigned a prefix of `dat` or `dtm`. You can assign a date literal to a Date variable, as shown here:

```
Dim dtmBirth As Date
dtmBirth = #5/1/2009#
```

Notice that the Date literal is enclosed in # symbols. A variety of date and time formats are permitted. All of the following Date literals are valid:

```
#12/10/2009#
#8:45:00 PM#
#10/20/2009 6:30:00 AM#
```

A Date literal can contain a date, a time, or both. When specifying a time, if you omit AM or PM, the hours value is assumed to be based on a 24-hour clock. If you supply a date without the time, the time portion of the variable defaults to 12:00 AM.

In Tutorial 3-6, you will assign text to a variable.

Tutorial 3-6:
Assigning text to a variable

In this tutorial, you will modify a program that assigns the contents of text boxes to a string variable.

Step 1: Open the *Variable Demo* project from the student sample programs folder named *Chap3\Variable Demo*.

Step 2: View the *Form1* form in the *Design* window, as shown in Figure 3-16.

Step 3: Double-click the *Show Name* button, which opens the *Code* window. Type the following lines, shown in bold:

```
Private Sub btnShowName_Click(ByVal sender As System.Object, _
        ByVal e As System.EventArgs) Handles btnShowName.Click

    ' Declare a string variable to hold the full name.
    Dim strFullName As String

    ' Combine the first and last names
    ' and copy the result to lblFullName
    strFullName = txtFirstName.Text & " " & txtLastName.Text
    lblFullName.Text = strFullName
End Sub
```

Figure 3-16 *Variable Demo* application, *Form1*

Step 4: In the *Design* window, double-click the *Clear* button and insert the following lines in the *Code* window (shown in bold):

```
Private Sub btnClear_Click(ByVal sender As System.Object, _
        ByVal e As System.EventArgs) Handles btnClear.Click
```

```
   ' Clear TextBox controls and the Label
   txtFirstName.Clear()
   txtLastName.Clear()
   lblFullName.Text = String.Empty

   ' Set focus to first TextBox control
   txtFirstName.Focus()
End Sub
```

Step 5: In the *Design* window, double-click the *Exit* button and insert the following lines in the *Code* window (shown in bold):

```
Private Sub btnExit_Click(ByVal sender As System.Object, _
      ByVal e As System.EventArgs) Handles btnExit.Click

   ' Close the application window
   Me.Close()
End Sub
```

Step 6: Save the project.

Step 7: Run the program, type in a name, and click the *Show Name* button. The output should look similar to that shown in Figure 3-17.

Figure 3-17 *Variable Demo* application, running

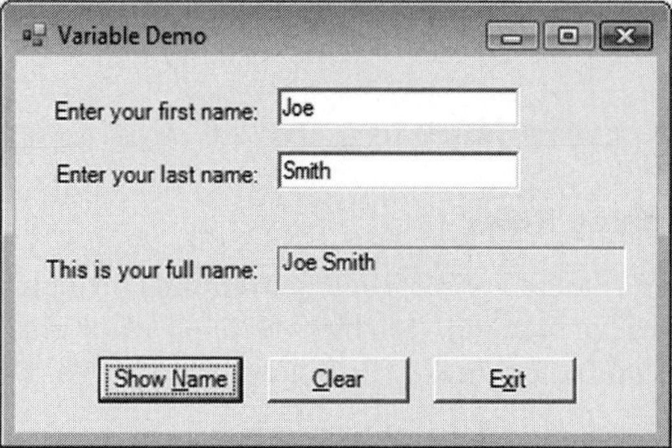

TIP: **Code outlining** is a Visual Studio tool that lets you expand and collapse sections of code. As your programs get longer, it is helpful to collapse procedures you have already written. Then you can concentrate on new sections of code. For example, Figure 3-18a shows the `btnShowName_Click` procedure from the *Variable Demo* application. A minus sign (–) appears next to its heading, and a horizontal line separates it from the next procedure.

If we click the minus sign next to an expanded procedure, it collapses into a single line showing its name (Figure 3-18b). You can modify outlining options by right-clicking in the *Code* window and selecting *Outlining*.

Figure 3-18a Expanded `btnShowName_Click` procedure

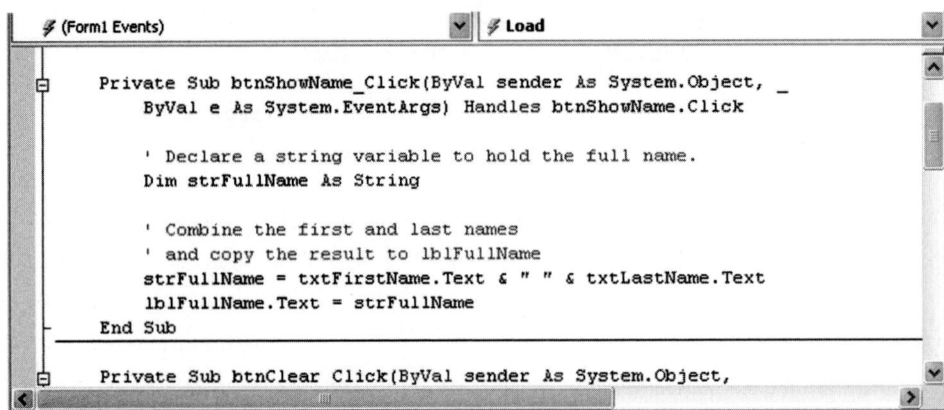

Figure 3-18b Collapsed `btnShowName_Click` procedure

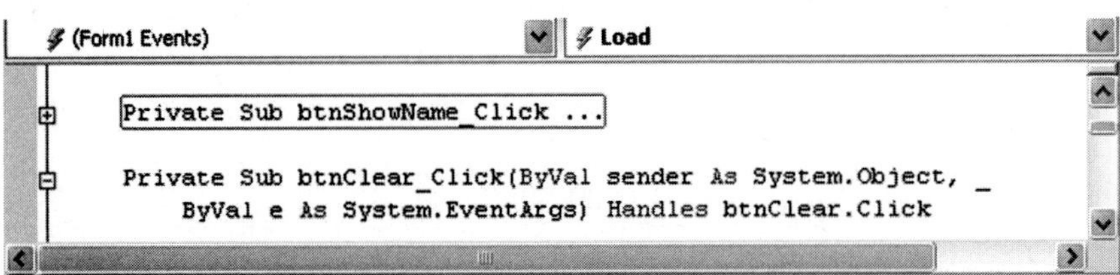

Variable Naming Rules and Conventions

Naming Rules

Just as there are rules and conventions for naming controls, there are rules and conventions for naming variables. Naming rules must be followed because they are part of Visual Basic syntax. The following are Visual Basic's naming rules for variables:

- The first character must be a letter or an underscore character.
- After the first character, you may use letters, numeric digits, and underscore characters.
- Variable names cannot contain spaces or periods.
- Variable names cannot be Visual Basic keywords. For example, words such as `Dim`, `Sub`, and `Private` are predefined in Visual Basic, and their use as variables would confuse the compiler.

Naming Conventions

Naming conventions are guidelines based on recommendations of professional designers, programmers, and educators. If you follow a consistent naming convention, your program source code will be easier to read and understand. In this book, we use a convention in which a three-letter prefix is used in variable names to identify their data type. Table 3-3 lists the variable naming prefixes that we use in this book.

Aside from the variable's prefix, we follow a common capitalization style used in most programming textbooks. After the variable's type prefix, the next letter should be capitalized. Subsequent characters should be lowercase, except the first letter of each word. All variables listed in Table 3-3 follow this rule.

Table 3-3 Recommended prefixes for variable names

Variable Type	Prefix	Examples
Boolean	`bln`	`blnContinue`, `blnHasRows`
Byte	`byt`	`bytInput`, `bytCharVal`
Char	`chr`	`chrSelection`, `chrMiddleInitial`
Date, DateTime	`dat` or `dtm`	`datWhenPublished`, `dtmBirthDate`
Decimal	`dec`	`decWeeklySalary`, `decGrossPay`
Double	`dbl`	`dblAirVelocity`, `dblPlanetMass`
Integer	`int`	`intCount`, `intDaysInPayPeriod`
Long	`lng`	`lngElapsedSeconds`
Object	`obj`	`objStudent`, `objPayroll`
Short	`shrt`	`shrtCount`
Single	`sng`	`sngTaxRate`, `sngGradeAverage`
String	`str`	`strLastName`, `strAddress`

TIP: *Be descriptive!* All nontrivial variables should have descriptive names. Avoid short names such as *gp*, *n*, *ldp*, *G5*, and so on. No one reading program code understands short, cryptic variable names. In fact, if you happen to read one of your old programs a few months after writing it, you will depend on descriptive variables to help you remember the meaning of your code.

Variable Declarations and the IntelliSense Feature

When you are entering a variable declaration, Visual Studio's IntelliSense feature helps you fill in the data type. Suppose you begin to type a variable declaration such as the following:

```
Dim decPayRate As
```

If you press the Spacebar at this point, a list box appears with all the possible data types in alphabetical order, as shown in Figure 3-19. When the list box appears, type the first few letters of the data type name, and the box will highlight the data type that matches what you have typed. For example, after you type *dec* the Decimal data type will be highlighted. Press the Tab key to select the highlighted data type.

TIP: You can use the arrow keys or the mouse with the list box's scroll bar to scroll through the list. Once you see the desired data type, double-click it with the mouse.

Figure 3-19 IntelliSense list box

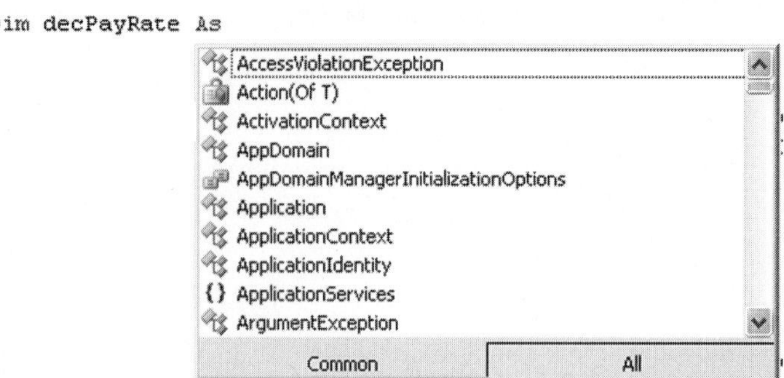

Default Values and Initialization

When a variable is first created it is assigned a default value. Variables with a numeric data type (such as Byte, Decimal, Double, Integer, Long, and Single) are assigned the value 0. Boolean variables are initially assigned the value False, and Date variables are assigned the value 12:00:00 AM, January 1 of year 1. String variables are automatically assigned a special value called `Nothing`.

You may also specify a starting value in the `Dim` statement. This is called **initialization.** Here is an example:

```
Dim intUnitsSold As Integer = 12
```

This statement declares `intUnitsSold` as an integer and assigns it the starting value 12. Here are other examples:

```
Dim strLastName As String = "Johnson"
Dim blnIsFinished As Boolean = True
Dim decGrossPay As Decimal = 2500
Dim chrMiddleInitial As Char = "E"c
```

Forgetting to initialize variables can lead to program errors. Unless you are certain a variable will be assigned a value before being used in an operation, always initialize it. This principle is particularly true with string variables. Performing an operation on an uninitialized string variable often results in a runtime error, causing the program to halt execution because the value `Nothing` is invalid for many operations. To prevent such errors, always initialize string variables or make sure they are assigned a value before being used in other operations. A good practice is to initialize string variables with an empty string, as shown in the following statement:

```
Dim strName As String = String.Empty
```

Checkpoint

3.13 What is a variable?

3.14 Show an example of a variable declaration.

3.15 Which of the following variable names are written with the convention used in this book?

a. `decintrestrate`
b. `InterestRateDecimal`
c. `decInterestRate`

3.16 Indicate whether each of the following is a legal variable name. If it is not, explain why.

a. `count`
b. `rate*Pay`
c. `deposit.amount`
d. `down_payment`

3.17 What default value is assigned to each of the following variables?

a. Integer
b. Single
c. Boolean
d. Byte
e. Date

3.18 Write a Date literal for the following date and time: 5:35:00 PM on February 20, 2008.

3.19 *Bonus question*: Find out which famous Microsoft programmer was launched into space in early 2007. Was this programmer connected in any way to Visual Basic?

Performing Calculations

CONCEPT: Visual Basic has powerful arithmetic operators that perform calculations with numeric variables and literals.

VideoNote Problem Solving with Variables

There are two basic types of operators in Visual Basic: unary and binary. These reflect the number of operands an operator requires. A **unary operator** requires only a single operand. The negation operator, for example, causes a number to be negative:

```
-5
```

It can be applied to a variable. The following line negates the value in `intCount`:

```
-intCount
```

A **binary operator** works with two operands. The addition operator (+) is binary because it uses two operands. The following mathematical expression adds the values of two numbers:

```
5 + 10
```

The following adds the values of two variables:

```
intA + intB
```

Table 3-4 lists the binary arithmetic operators in Visual Basic. Addition, subtraction, multiplication, division, and exponentiation can be performed on both integer and floating-point data types. Only two operations (integer division and modulus) must be performed on integer types.

Table 3-4 Arithmetic operators in Visual Basic

Operator	Operation
+	Addition
–	Subtraction
*	Multiplication
/	Floating-point division
\	Integer division
MOD	Modulus (remainder from integer division)
^	Exponentiation (x^y = x^y)

Addition

The addition operator (+) adds two values, producing a sum. The values can be literals or variables. The following are examples of valid addition expressions:

```
intA + 10
```

```
20 + intB
```

The question is, what happens to the result? Ordinarily, it is assigned to a variable, using the assignment operator. In the following statement, `intC` is assigned the sum of the values from `intA` and `intB`:

```
intC = intA + intB
```

This operation happens in two steps. First, the addition takes place. Second, the sum is assigned to the variable on the left side of the = sign.

The following example adds the contents of two Double variables that hold rainfall measurements for the months of March and April:

```
dblCombined = dblMarchRain + dblAprilRain
```

Subtraction

The subtraction operator (–) subtracts the right-hand operand from the left-hand operand. In the following, the variable `intC` will contain the difference between `intA` and `intB`:

```
intC = intA – intB
```

Alternatively, the difference might be assigned back to the variable `intA`:

```
intA = intA – intB
```

The following statement uses Decimal variables. It subtracts an employee's tax amount from his or her gross pay, producing the employee's net pay:

```
decNetPay = decGrossPay – decTax
```

Addition and Subtraction in Applications

How can addition and subtraction statements be useful in an application? Suppose a college registration program needs to add the credits completed by a student during two semesters (Fall and Spring). First, the variables would be declared:

```
Dim intFallCredits, intSpringCredits, intTotalCredits As Integer
```

Then the application would assign values to `intSpringCredits` and `intFallCredits`, perhaps by asking for their input from the user. Finally, the program would calculate the total credits for the year:

```
intTotalCredits = intFallCredits + intSpringCredits
```

Multiplication

The multiplication operator (*) multiplies the right-hand operand by the left-hand operand. In the following statement, the variable `intC` is assigned the product of multiplying `intA` and `intB`:

```
intC = intA * intB
```

The following statement uses Decimal variables to multiply an item's price by the sales tax rate, producing a sales tax amount:

```
decTaxAmount = decItemPrice * decTaxRate
```

Floating-Point Division

The floating-point division operator (/) divides one floating-point value by another. The result, called the quotient, is also a floating-point number. For example, the following statement divides the total points earned by a basketball team by the number of players, producing the average points per player:

```
dblAverage = dblTotalPoints / dblNumPlayers
```

If you try to divide by zero, the program will stop and produce an error message. Suppose `dblNumPlayers` were equal to zero. Then the message dialog shown in Figure 3-20 would appear when the program ran.

Figure 3-20 Error generated because of division by zero

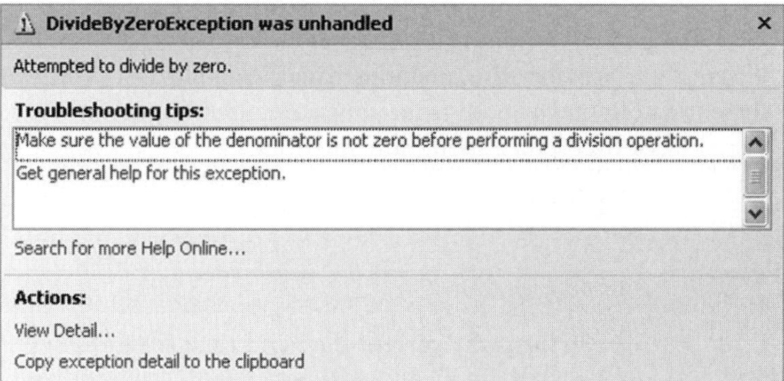

Integer Division

The integer division operator (\) divides one integer by another, producing an integer result. For example, suppose we know the number of minutes it will take to finish a job, and we want to calculate the number of hours that are contained in that many minutes. The following statement uses integer division to divide the `intMinutes` variable by 60, giving the number of hours as a result:

```
intHours = intMinutes \ 60
```

Integer division does not save any fractional part of the quotient. The following statement, for example, produces the integer 3:

```
intQuotient = 10 \ 3
```

Modulus

The modulus operator (`MOD`) performs integer division and returns only the remainder. The following statement assigns 2 to the variable named `intRemainder`:

```
intRemainder = 17 MOD 3
```

Note that 17 divided by 3 equals 5, with a remainder of 2. Suppose a job is completed in 174 minutes, and we want to express this value in both hours and minutes. First, we can use integer division to calculate the hours (2):

```
intTotalMinutes = 174
intHours = intTotalMinutes \ 60
```

Next, we use the `MOD` operator to calculate the remaining minutes (54):

```
intMinutes = intTotalMinutes Mod 60
```

Now we know that the job was completed in 2 hours, 54 minutes.

Exponentiation

Exponentiation calculates a variable *x* taken to the power of *y* when written in the form *x* ^ *y*. The value it returns is of type Double. For example, the following statement assigns 25.0 to `dblResult`:

```
dblResult = 5.0 ^ 2.0
```

You can use integers as operands, but the result will still be a Double:

```
dblResult = intX ^ intY
```

Negative and fractional exponents are permitted.

Getting the Current Date and Time

Your computer system has an internal clock that calculates the current date and time. Visual Basic provides the functions listed in Table 3-5, which allow you to retrieve the current date, time, or both from your computer. Functions are commands recognized by Visual Basic that return useful information.

Table 3-5 Date and time functions

Function	Description
`Now`	Returns the current date and time from the system
`TimeOfDay`	Returns the current time from the system, without the date
`Today`	Returns the current date from the system, without the time

The following code demonstrates how to use the `Now` function:

```
Dim dtmSystemDate As Date
dtmSystemDate = Now
```

After the code executes, `dtmSystemDate` will contain the current date and time, as reported by the system. The `TimeOfDay` function retrieves only the current time from the system, demonstrated by the following statement.

```
dtmSystemTime = TimeOfDay
```

After the statement executes, `dtmSystemTime` will contain the current time, but not the current date. Instead, it will contain the date January 1 of year 1. The `Today` function retrieves only the current date from the system, demonstrated by the following statement:

```
dtmSystemDate = Today
```

After the statement executes, `dtmSystemDate` will contain the current date, but will not contain the current time. Instead, it will contain the time 00:00:00.

TIP: Later in this chapter you will see how to use the `ToString` method to display only the date value or time value inside a Date variable.

Variable Scope

Every variable has a scope and a lifetime. A variable's **scope** refers to the part of a program where the variable is visible and may be accessed by programming statements. There are three types of variable scope:

- A variable declared inside a procedure is called a *local variable*. This type of variable is only visible from its declaring statement to the end of the same procedure. When the procedure ends, the variable is destroyed.
- If a variable is declared inside a class, but outside of any procedure, it is called a *class-level variable*.
- If a variable is declared outside of any class or procedure, it is called a *global variable*.

Declaring Variables Before They Are Used

The first rule of scope is that a variable cannot be used before it is declared. Visual Basic executes statements in a procedure in sequential order, from the first statement to the last. If a programming statement attempts to use a variable before it has been declared, an error occurs. For example, in the following code sequence line 3 generates an error because `dblAverage` has not been declared yet:

```
1:   Dim dblTotal As Double = 500.0
2:   Dim dblCount As Double = 10.2
3:   dblAverage = dblTotal / dblCount          ' ERROR
4:   Dim dblAverage As Double
```

If we just reverse the statements in lines 3 and 4, the program compiles correctly:

```
1:   Dim dblTotal As Double = 500.0
2:   Dim dblCount As Double = 10.2
3:   Dim dblAverage As Double
4:   dblAverage = dblTotal / dblCount          ' OK
```

Using a Variable That Is Not in the Current Scope

Another rule of scope is that a variable declared inside a procedure is visible only to statements inside the same procedure. For example, suppose an application has the following two event procedures. The variable `intValue` is declared in the `btnButtonOne_Click` procedure. An error results when a statement in the `btnButtonTwo_Click` procedure attempts to access the `intValue` variable:

```
Private Sub btnButtonOne_Click(ByVal sender As System.Object, _
      ByVal e As System.EventArgs) Handles ButtonOne.Click

    ' Declare an Integer variable named intValue.
    Dim intValue As Integer
```

```
        ' Assign a value to the variable.
        intValue = 25
    End Sub

    Private Sub btnButtonTwo_Click(ByVal sender As System.Object, _
            ByVal e As System.EventArgs) Handles ButtonTwo.Click

        ' Attempt to assign a value to the
        ' intValue variable. This will cause an error!
        intValue = 32
    End Sub
```

What if we declared `intValue` again in the `btnButtonTwo` procedure? Then the program would compile, and we would have created two different variables having the same name. Each has its own scope, separate from the other:

```
    Private Sub btnButtonOne_Click(ByVal sender As System.Object, _
            ByVal e As System.EventArgs) Handles ButtonOne.Click

        ' Declare an Integer variable named intValue.
        Dim intValue As Integer
        ' Assign a value to the variable.
        intValue = 25
    End Sub

    Private Sub btnButtonTwo_Click(ByVal sender As System.Object, _
            ByVal e As System.EventArgs) Handles ButtonTwo.Click

        ' Declare an Integer variable named intValue.
        Dim intValue As Integer
        ' Assign a value to the variable.
        intValue = 32
    End Sub
```

Variables having the same name are completely separate from each other if they are declared in different procedures.

Using the Same Variable Name Twice in the Same Scope

Another scope rule says that you cannot declare two variables by the same name within the same scope. The following example violates the rule:

```
    Private Sub btnButtonOne_Click(ByVal sender As System.Object, _
            ByVal e As System.EventArgs) Handles ButtonOne.Click

        Dim intValue As Integer
        intValue = 25

        Dim intValue As Integer     ' Error!
        intValue = 32
    End Sub
```

Combined Assignment Operators

Quite often, programs have assignment statements in the following form:

```
intNumber = intNumber + 1
```

On the right-hand side of the assignment operator, 1 is added to `intNumber`. The result is then assigned to `intNumber`, replacing the value that was previously stored there. Similarly, the following statement subtracts 5 from `intNumber`.

```
intNumber = intNumber - 5
```

Table 3-6 shows examples of similar statements. Assume that the variable `x` is set to 6 prior to each statement's execution.

Table 3-6 Assignment statements (Assume x = 6 prior to each statement's execution)

Statement	Operation Performed	Value of x after the Statement Executes
`x = x + 4`	Adds 4 to x	10
`x = x - 3`	Subtracts 3 from x	3
`x = x * 10`	Multiplies x by 10	60
`x = x / 2`	Divides x by 2	3

Assignment operations are common in programming. For convenience, Visual Basic offers a special set of operators designed specifically for these jobs. Table 3-7 shows the **combined assignment operators**, or **compound operators**.

Table 3-7 Combined assignment operators

Operator	Example Usage	Equivalent To
`+=`	`x += 2`	`x = x + 2`
`-=`	`x -= 5`	`x = x - 5`
`*=`	`x *= 10`	`x = x * 10`
`/=`	`x /= y`	`x = x / y`
`\=`	`x \= y`	`x = x \ y`
`&=`	`strName &= lastName`	`strName = strName & lastName`

Operator Precedence

It is possible to build **mathematical expressions** with several operators. The following statement assigns the sum of 17, `x`, 21, and `y` to the variable `intAnswer`.

```
intAnswer = 17 + x + 21 + y
```

Some expressions are not that straightforward, however. Consider the following statement:

```
dblOutcome = 12 + 6 / 3
```

What value will be stored in `dblOutcome`? If the addition takes place before the division, then `dblOutcome` will be assigned 6. If the division takes place first, `dblOutcome` will be assigned 14. The correct answer is 14 because the division operator has higher **precedence** than the addition operator.

Mathematical expressions are evaluated from left to right. When two operators share an operand, the operator with the highest precedence executes first. Multiplication and division have higher precedence than addition and subtraction, so `12 + 6 / 3` works like this:

- 6 is divided by 3, yielding a result of 2.
- 12 is added to 2, yielding a result of 14.

It can be diagrammed as shown in Figure 3-21.

Figure 3-21 dblOutcome = 12 + 6 / 3

```
dblOutcome = 12  +  6  /  3
                    └──┬──┘
                       ▼
dblOutcome = 12  +     2
             └────┬────┘
                  ▼
dblOutcome =      14
```

The precedence of the arithmetic operators, from highest to lowest, is as follows:

1. Exponentiation (the ^ operator)
2. Multiplication and division (the * and / operators)
3. Integer division (the \ operator)
4. Modulus (the MOD operator)
5. Addition and subtraction (the + and – operators)

The multiplication and division operators have the same precedence. This is also true of the addition and subtraction operators. When two operators with the same precedence share an operand, the operator on the left executes before the operator on the right.

Table 3-8 shows some example mathematical expressions with their values.

Table 3-8 Mathematical expressions and their values

Expression	Value
`5 + 2 * 4`	13
`2^3 * 4 + 3`	35
`10 / 2 - 3`	2
`8 + 12 * 2 - 4`	28
`6 - 3 * 2 + 7 - 1`	6

Grouping with Parentheses

Parts of a mathematical expression may be grouped with parentheses to force some operations to be performed before others. In the following statement, the sum of *x*, *y*, and *z* is divided by 3. The result is assigned to `dblAverage`.

```
dblAverage = (x + y + z) / 3
```

Without the parentheses, however, *z* would be divided by 3, and the result added to the sum of *x* and *y*. Table 3-9 shows more expressions and their values.

Table 3-9 Additional mathematical expressions and their values

Expression	Value
`(5 + 2) * 4`	28
`10 / (5 - 3)`	5
`8 + 12 * (6 - 2)`	56
`(6 - 3) * (2 + 7) / 3`	9

More about Mathematical Operations: Converting Mathematical Expressions to Programming Statements

In algebra, the mathematical expression $2xy$ describes the value 2 times x times y. Visual Basic, however, requires an operator for any mathematical operation. Table 3-10 shows some mathematical expressions that perform multiplication and the equivalent Visual Basic expressions.

Table 3-10 Visual Basic equivalents of mathematical expressions

Mathematical Expression	Operation	Visual Basic Equivalent
$6B$	6 times B	`6 * B`
(3)(12)	3 times 12	`3 * 12`
$4xy$	4 times x times y	`4 * x * y`

Checkpoint

3.20 What value will be stored in `dblResult` after each of the following statements executes?

a. `dblResult = 6 + 3 * 5`
b. `dblResult = 12 / 2 - 4`
c. `dblResult = 2 + 7 * 3 - 6`
d. `dblResult = (2 + 4) * 3`
e. `dblResult = 10 \ 3`
f. `dblResult = 6 ^ 2`

3.21 What value will be stored in `intResult` after each statement executes?

a. `intResult = 10 MOD 3`
b. `intResult = 47 MOD 15`

3.22 Write a statement that assigns the current time of day to the variable `dtmThisTime`.

3.23 Write a statement that assigns the current date and time to a variable named `dtmCurrent`.

3.24 Explain the meaning of the term scope when applied to variables.

3.25 What will be the final value of `dblResult` in the following sequence?

```
Dim dblResult As Double = 3.5
dblResult += 1.2
```

3.26 What will be the final value of `dblResult` in the following sequence?

```
Dim dblResult As Double = 3.5
dblResult *= 2.0
```

3.4 Mixing Different Data Types

Implicit Type Conversion

When you assign a value of one data type to a variable of another data type, Visual Basic attempts to convert the value being assigned to the data type of the receiving variable.

This is known as an **implicit type conversion**. Suppose we want to assign the integer 5 to a variable of type Single named `sngNumber`:

```
Dim sngNumber As Single = 5
```

When the statement executes, the integer 5 is automatically converted into a single-precision real number, which is then stored in `sngNumber`. This conversion is a **widening conversion** because no data is lost.

Narrowing Conversions

If you assign a real number to an integer variable, Visual Basic attempts to perform a **narrowing conversion**. Often, some data is lost. For example, the following statement assigns 12.2 to an integer variable:

```
Dim intCount As Integer = 12.2          'intCount = 12
```

Assuming for the moment that Visual Basic is configured to accept this type of conversion, the 12.2 is rounded downward to 12. Similarly, the next statement rounds upward to the nearest integer when the fractional part of the number is .5 or greater:

```
Dim intCount As Integer = 12.5          'intCount = 13
```

Another narrowing conversion occurs when assigning a Double value to a variable of type Single. Both hold floating-point values, but Double permits more significant digits:

```
Dim dblOne As Double = 1.2342376
Dim sngTwo As Single = dblOne           'sngTwo = 1.234238
```

The value stored in `sngTwo` is rounded up to 1.234238 because variables of type Single can only hold seven significant digits.

Converting Strings to Numbers

Under some circumstances, Visual Basic will try to convert string values to numbers. In the following statement, `"12.2"` is a string containing a numeric expression:

```
Dim strTemp As String = "12.2"
```

The string "12.2" is a string of characters in a numeric-like format that cannot be used for calculations. When the following statements execute, the string "12.2" is converted to the number 12.2:

```
Dim sngTemperature As Single
sngTemperature = "12.2"
```

If we assign the string "12.2" to an Integer variable, the result is rounded downward to 12:

```
Dim intCount As Integer
intCount = "12.2"
```

A similar effect occurs when the user enters a number into a TextBox control. Usually we want to assign the contents of the TextBox's Text property to a numeric variable. The Text property by definition holds strings, so its contents are implicitly converted to a number when we assign it to a numeric variable, as shown here:

```
intCount = txtCount.Text
```

Figure 13-22 shows an example of the steps that occur when the user's input into a TextBox is assigned to a numeric variable.

Figure 3-22 Implicit conversion of TextBox into a numeric variable

1. The user enters this value into `txtCount`: "26"
2. An assignment statement in an event procedure executes: `intCount = txtCount.Text`
3. The contents of the Text property is converted to a numeric value: 26

Option Strict

Visual Basic has a configuration option named ***Option Strict*** that determines whether certain implicit conversions are legal. If you set *Option Strict* to *On*, only widening conversions are permitted (such as Integer to Single). Figure 3-23 shows how implicit conversion between numeric types must be in a left-to-right direction in the diagram. A Decimal value can be assigned to a variable of type Single, an Integer can be assigned to a variable of type Double, and so on. If, on the other hand, *Option Strict* is set to *Off*, all types of numeric conversions are permitted, with possible loss of data.

To set *Option Strict* for a single project, right-click the project name in the *Solution Explorer* window, select *Properties*, and then select the *Compile* tab, as shown in Figure 3-24. From the *Option Strict* drop-down list, you can select *On* or *Off*.

We recommend setting *Option Strict* to *On*, so Visual Basic can catch errors that result when you accidentally assign a value of the wrong type to a variable. When set to *On*, *Option Strict* forces you to use a conversion function, making your intentions clear. This approach helps to avoid runtime errors.

Figure 3-23 Conversions permitted with *Option Strict On*

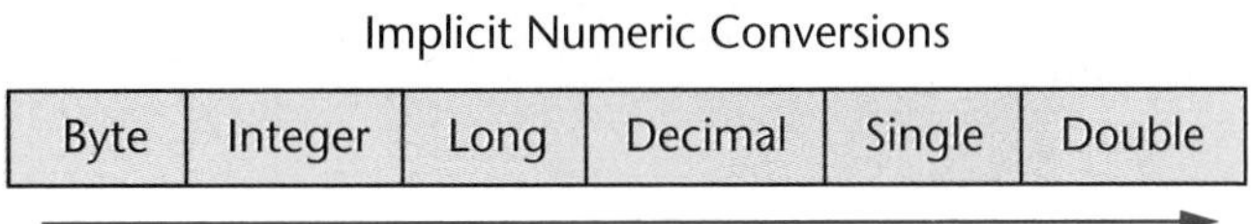

Figure 3-24 *Project Properties* window

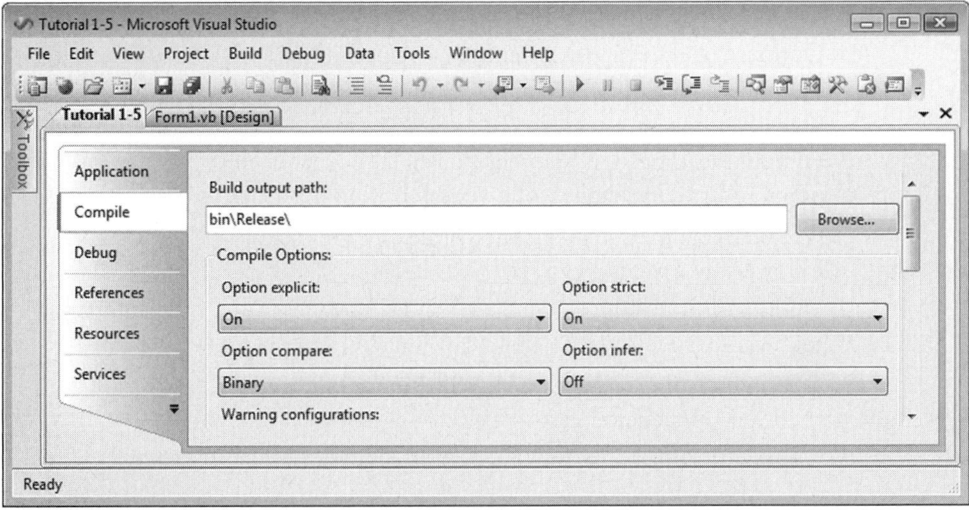

Type Conversion Runtime Errors

The following statement does not compile with *Option Strict* set to *On*:

```
Dim intCount As Integer = "abc123"
```

But if *Option Strict* has been set to *Off*, a program containing this statement will compile without errors. Then, when the program executes, it will stop when it reaches this statement because the string "abc123" contains characters that prevent the string from being converted to a number. The program will generate a runtime error message. Recall from Chapter 2 that runtime errors are errors that occur while the application is running. The type of error in this case is also known as a **type conversion error** or **type mismatch error.**

Runtime errors are harder to catch than syntax errors because they occur while a program is running. Particularly in programs where the user has a number of choices (mouse clicks, keyboard input, menus, and so on), it is very difficult for a programmer to predict when runtime errors might occur. Nevertheless, there are certain conversion functions shown in the next section that reduce the chance of this type of mishap.

TIP: Can the best-trained programmers avoid runtime errors? To discover the answer to that question, spend some time using commercial Web sites and notice all the little things that go wrong. Software reliability is particularly hard to guarantee when users have lots of choices.

Literals

Literals (constants) have specific types in Visual Basic. Table 3-11 lists the more common types. Many literals use a suffix character (*C*, *D*, @, *R*, *I*, *L*, *F*, *S*, !) to identify their type.

Table 3-11 Representing literals (constants) in Visual Basic

Type	Description	Example
Boolean	Keywords *True* and *False*	`True`
Byte	Sequence of decimal digits between 0 and 255	`200`
Char	Single letter enclosed in double quotes followed by the lowercase letter *C*	`"A"c`
Date	Date and/or time representation enclosed in # symbols	`#1/20/05 3:15 PM#`
Decimal	Optional leading sign, sequence of decimal digits, optional decimal point and trailing digits, followed by the letter *D* or @	`+32.0D` `64@`
Double	Optional leading sign, sequence of digits with a decimal point and trailing digits, followed by optional letter *R*	`3.5` `3.5R`
Integer	Optional leading sign, sequence of decimal digits, followed by optional letter *I*	`-3054I` `+26I`
Long	Optional leading sign, sequence of decimal digits, followed by the letter *L*	`40000000L`
Short	Optional leading sign, sequence of decimal digits, followed by the letter *S*	`12345S`
Single	Optional leading sign, sequence of digits with a decimal point and trailing digits, followed by the letter *F* or !	`26.4F` `26.4!`
String	Sequence of characters surrounded by double quotes	`"ABC"` `"234"`

It's important to know literal types because you often assign literal values to variables. If the receiving variable in an assignment statement has a different type from the literal, an implied conversion takes place. If *Option Strict* is *On*, some conversions are automatic and others generate errors. You need to understand why.

Most of the time, you will be inclined to use no suffix with numeric literals. As long as the receiving variable's data type is compatible with the literal's data type, you have no problem:

```
Dim lngCount As Long = 25              'Integer assigned to Long
Dim dblSalary As Double = 2500.0       'Double assigned to Double
```

In the following example, however, we're trying to assign a Double to a Decimal, which is not permitted when *Option Strict* is *On*:

```
Dim decPayRate As Decimal = 35.5       'Double to Decimal (?)
```

If you know how to create numeric literals, all you have to do is append a *D* to the number. The following is valid:

```
Dim decPayRate As Decimal = 35.5D
```

Named Constants

You have seen several programs and examples where numbers and strings are expressed as literal values. For example, the following statement contains the literal numeric value 0.129:

```
dblPayment = dblPrincipal * 0.129
```

Suppose this statement appears in a banking program that calculates loan information.

In such a program, two potential problems arise. First, it is not clearly evident to anyone other than the original programmer what the number 0.129 is. It appears to be an interest rate, but in some situations there are other fees associated with loan payments. How can you determine the purpose of this statement without painstakingly checking the rest of the program?

The second problem occurs if this number is used in other calculations throughout the program and must be changed periodically. Assuming the number is an interest rate, if the rate changes from 12.9% to 13.2% the programmer will have to search through the source code for every occurrence of the number.

Both of these problems can be addressed by using named constants. A **named constant** is like a variable whose content is read-only, and cannot be changed by a programming statement while the program is running. The following is the general form of a named constant declaration:

```
Const ConstantName As DataType = Value
```

Here is an example of a named constant declaration:

```
Const dblINTEREST_RATE As Double = 0.129
```

It looks like a regular variable declaration except for the following differences:

- The word `Const` is used instead of `Dim`.
- An initialization value is required.
- By convention, all letters after the prefix are capitals.
- Words in the name are separated by the underscore character.

The keyword `Const` indicates that you are declaring a named constant instead of a variable. The value given after the = sign is the value of the constant throughout the program's execution.

A value must be assigned when a named constant is declared or an error will result. An error will also result if any statements in the program attempt to change the contents of a named constant.

One advantage of using named constants is that they help make programs self-documenting. The statement

```
dblPayment = dblPrincipal * 0.129
```

can be changed to read

```
dblPayment = dblPrincipal * dblINTEREST_RATE
```

A new programmer can read the second statement and know what is happening. It is evident that `dblPrincipal` is being multiplied by the interest rate.

Another advantage to using named constants is that consistent changes can easily be made to the program. Let's say the interest rate appears in a dozen different statements throughout the program. When the rate changes, the value assigned to the named constant in its declaration is the only value that needs to be modified. If the rate increases to 13.2% the declaration is changed to the following:

```
Const dblINTEREST_RATE as Double = 0.132
```

Every statement that uses `dblINTEREST_RATE` will use the new value.

It is also useful to declare named constants for common values that are difficult to remember. For example, any program that calculates the area of a circle must use the value *pi*, which is 3.14159. This value could easily be declared as a named constant, as shown in the following statement:

```
Const dblPI as Double = 3.14159
```

TIP: In this chapter, named constants are declared at the beginnings of procedures. In a later chapter we will demonstrate how named constants can also be declared at the class level.

Explicit Type Conversions

Let's assume for the current discussion that *Option Strict* is set to *On*. If you try to perform anything other than a widening conversion, your code will not compile. Visual Basic has a set of conversion functions to solve this problem.

What Is a Function?

A **function** is a named, self-contained body of code, to which you send some input (Figure 3-25). The function performs a predetermined operation and produces a single output. A well-known function in mathematics is the $y = \text{abs}(\ x\ )$ function, which finds the absolute value x and stores it in y. The only reason a function might not produce the same output all the time is that it could be affected by the values of variables elsewhere in the program.

Figure 3-25 A function receives input and produces a single output

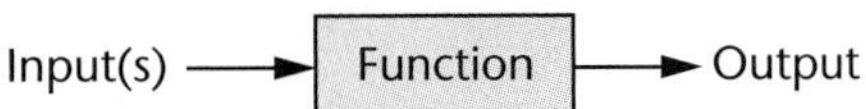

Visual Basic Conversion Functions

Table 3-12 lists the Visual Basic conversion functions that we will use most often. The input to each conversion function is an expression, which is another name for a constant, a variable, or a mathematical expression (such as 2.0 + 4.2). The following situations require a conversion function:

- When assigning a wider numeric type to a narrower numeric type. In Figure 3-23 (page 131), the arrow pointing from left to right indicates automatic conversions. Any conversion in the opposite direction requires a call to a conversion function. Examples are Long to Integer, Decimal to Long, Double to Single, and Double to Decimal.
- When converting between Boolean, Date, Object, String, and numeric types. These all represent different categories, so they require conversion functions.

Table 3-12 Commonly used type conversion functions

Function	Description
`CDate(` *expr* `)`	Converts a String expression to a Date. Input can also be a Date literal, such as `"10/14/2009 1:30 PM"`.
`CDbl(` *expr* `)`	Converts an expression to a Double. If the input expression is a String, a leading currency symbol ($) is permitted, as are commas. The decimal point is optional.
`CDec(` *expr* `)`	Converts an expression to a Decimal. If the input expression is a String, a leading currency symbol ($) is permitted, as are commas. The decimal point is optional.
`CInt(` *expr* `)`	Converts an expression to an Integer. If the input expression is a String, a leading currency symbol ($) is permitted, as are commas. The decimal point is optional, as are digits after the decimal point.
`CStr(` *expr* `)`	Converts an expression to a String. Input can be a mathematical expression, Boolean value, a date, or any numeric data type.

Details

The `CDate` function is often used when assigning the contents of a TextBox control to a Date variable. In the next example, the TextBox is named `txtBirthDay`:

```
Dim datBirthday As Date = CDate(txtBirthDay.Text)
```

The `CDbl` function is often used when assigning the contents of a TextBox control to a Double variable.

```
Dim dblSalary As Double = CDbl(txtPayRate.Text)
```

The `CDec` function is often used when assigning the contents of a TextBox control to a Decimal variable.

```
Dim decPayRate As Decimal = CDec(txtPayRate.Text)
```

Also, `CDec` is required when assigning a Double value to a Decimal:

```
Dim dblPayRate As Double
Dim decPayRate As Decimal = CDec(dblPayRate)
```

You cannot directly assign a numeric literal to a Decimal because literals are assumed to be of type Double. Instead, you must either use the `CDec` function to convert the literal, or append a `D` suffix character to the literal. The following examples are correct:

```
Dim decPayRate As Decimal = CDec(26.50)
Dim decPayRate2 As Decimal = 26.50D
```

The `CInt` function is required when assigning any floating-point type to an integer:

```
Dim dblWeight As Double = 3.5
Dim intWeight As Integer = CInt(dblWeight)
```

The `CInt` function is also required when assigning a TextBox control to an integer:

```
Dim intWeight As Integer = CInt(txtWeight.Text)
```

If You Want to Know More: `CInt` and Rounding

The `CInt` function converts an expression to an Integer. If the input value contains digits after the decimal point, a special type of rounding occurs, called *banker's rounding*. Here's how it works:

- If the digit after the decimal point is less than 5, the digits after the decimal point are removed from the number. We say the number is *truncated.*
- If the digit after the decimal point is a 5, the number is rounded toward the nearest even integer.
- If the digit after the decimal point is greater than 5 and the number is positive, it is rounded to the next highest integer.
- If the digit after the decimal point is greater than 5 and the number is negative, it is rounded to the next smallest integer.

Invalid Conversions

What happens if you call a conversion function, passing a value that cannot be converted? Here's an example:

```
Dim dblSalary As Double
dblSalary = CDbl("xyz")
```

The program stops with a runtime error, displaying the dialog box shown in Figure 3-26. The specific type of error, also known as an **exception**, is called an *InvalidCastException.* The text inside the list box consists of hyperlinks, which take you to specific *Visual Studio Help* pages. Later in this chapter, you will learn how to catch errors like this so the program won't stop.

Figure 3-26 Error displayed when trying to perform an invalid conversion from String to Double

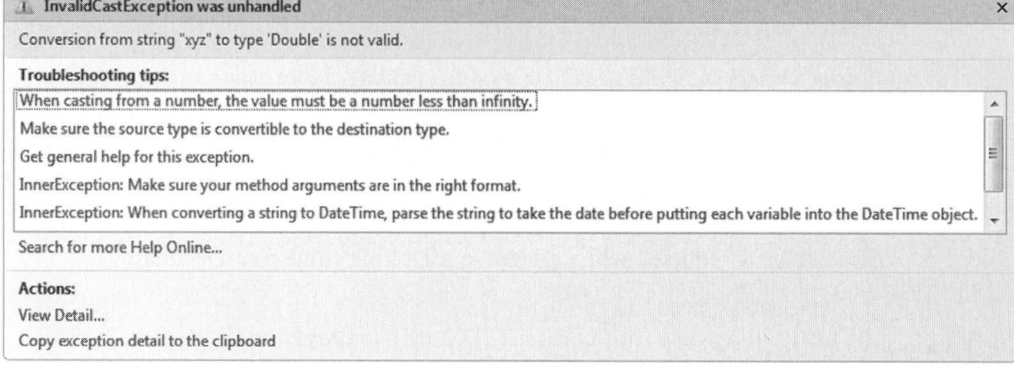

The `Val` Function (Optional Topic)

An alternative technique for converting strings to numeric values is to use the `Val` function. The `Val` function converts a string like `"34.7"` to a number such as 34.7. For example, suppose an application uses a TextBox control named `txtInput` and has the following code:

```
Dim intNumber As Integer
intNumber = txtInput.Text
```

The second statement assigns the contents of the TextBox control's Text property to an integer variable. To prevent the possibility of a type conversion error we can rewrite the statement to use the `Val` function:

```
intNumber = Val(txtInput.Text)
```

The `Val` function expects its argument to be a string. `Val` converts the string argument to a numeric value and returns the numeric value to the statement that called the function.

In Figure 3-27, the number that `Val` returns is assigned to `intNumber`. If `"45"` is stored in `txtInput`'s Text property, the `Val` function returns the number 45, which is assigned to the `intNumber` variable.

Figure 3-27 The `Val` function

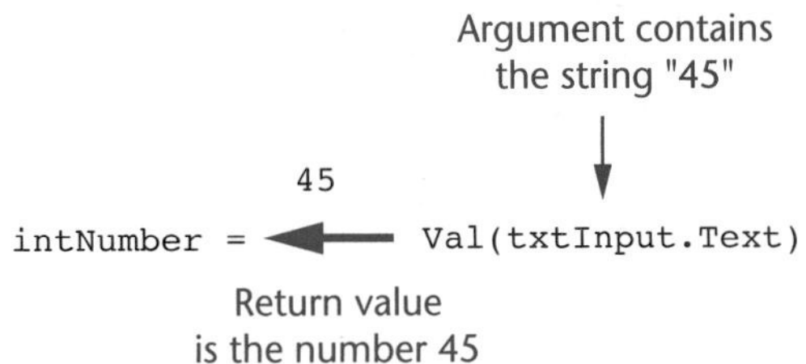

If the string passed to `Val` contains a decimal point, `Val` automatically returns a value of type Double:

```
Dim dblOne As Double = Val("10.5")
```

If the string you pass to the `Val` function cannot be converted to a number, it returns zero. In the example, suppose the user enters **`$5000`** into the text box. The function assigns a default value of zero to `dblSalary` because the $ character is not permitted:

```
Dim dblSalary As Double = Val(txtSalary.Text)
```

The `Val` function does not let you know the user made a mistake. For this reason, you usually need to write additional statements that check for a zero value and assume that a user would never purposely enter a salary of zero. Conditional statements are covered in Chapter 4.

TIP: At one time, the `Val` function was the only tool available in Visual Basic for converting strings to numbers. Because other conversion functions do a better job than `Val`, professional programmers prefer not to use it.

Tutorial 3-7:
Examining a *Simple Calculator* application

This tutorial examines an application that functions as a simple calculator. The application has two TextBox controls, into which you enter numbers. There are buttons for addition, subtraction, multiplication, division, exponentiation, integer division, and modulus. When you click one of these buttons, the application performs a math operation using the two numbers entered into the TextBox controls and displays the result in a label.

Step 1: Open the *Simple Calculator* project from the Chapter 3 sample programs folder named *Simple Calculator*.

Step 2: Click the *Start* button to run the application. The application's form appears, as shown in Figure 3-28.

Figure 3-28 *Simple Calculator* form

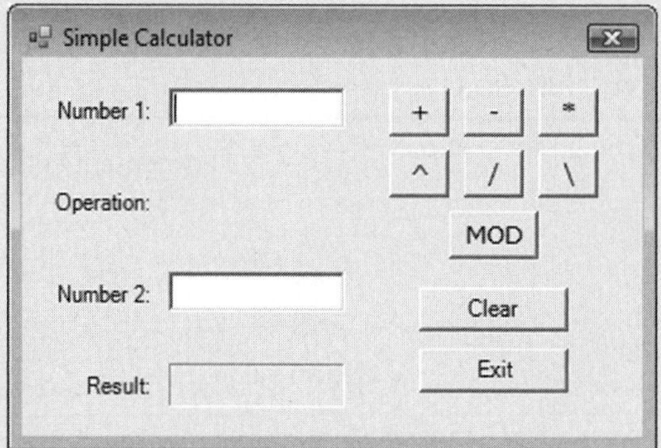

Step 3: Enter **10** into the *Number 1* TextBox control. (In the program source code, this TextBox control is named `txtNumber1`.)

Step 4: Enter **3** into the *Number 2* TextBox control. (In the program source code, this TextBox control is named `txtNumber2`.)

Step 5: Click the + button. Notice that next to the word *Operation* a large plus sign appears on the form. This indicates that an addition operation has taken place. (The plus sign is displayed in a label named `lblOperation`.) The result of 10 + 3 displays in the *Result* label, which is named `lblResult`. The form appears as shown in Figure 3-29.

Step 6: Click the – button. Notice that the `lblOperation` label changes to a minus sign and the result of 10 minus 3 displays in the `lblResult` label.

Step 7: Click the *, ^, /, \, and *MOD* buttons. Each performs a math operation using 10 and 3 as its operands and displays the result in the `lblResult` label.

Step 8: If you wish to experiment with other numbers, click the *Clear* button and continue.

Step 9: When you are finished, click the *Exit* button.

Figure 3-29 Result of 10 + 3

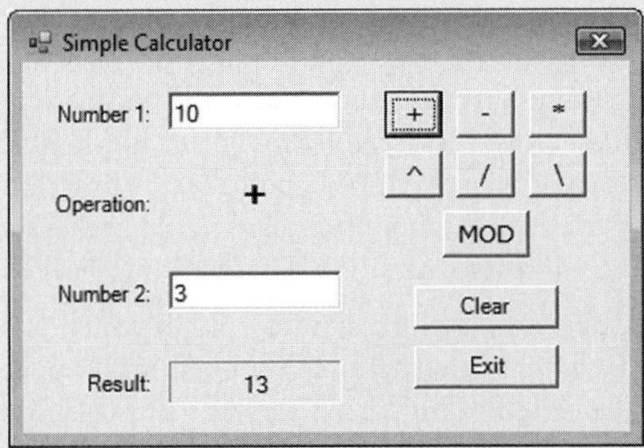

Step 10: Open *Form1* in the *Design* window, if it is not already open. Double-click the + button on the application form. This opens the *Code* window, with the text cursor positioned in the `btnPlus_Click` event procedure. The code is as follows:

```
Private Sub btnPlus_Click(ByVal sender As System.Object, _
  ByVal e As System.EventArgs) Handles btnPlus.Click

  ' Perform addition
  Dim dblResult As Double
  lblOperation.Text = "+"
  dblResult = CDbl(txtNumber1.Text) + CDbl(txtNumber2.Text)
  lblResult.Text = CStr(dblResult)
End Sub
```

Step 11: Examine the other event procedures in this application. Most of the arithmetic operator button handlers are similar, except those for the Integer division and Modulus operators. In the Integer division operator handler, for example, the result variable is an integer, and the `CInt` function converts the contents of the TextBox controls:

```
Private Sub btnIntegerDivide_Click(ByVal sender As _
    System.Object, ByVal e As System.EventArgs) _
    Handles btnIntegerDivide.Click

  ' Perform integer division
  Dim intResult As Integer
  lblOperation.Text = "\"
  intResult = CInt(txtNumber1.Text) \ CInt(txtNumber2.Text)
  lblResult.Text = CStr(intResult)
End Sub
```

If You Want to Know More: Full Set of VB Conversion Functions

Table 3-13 contains a more complete list of Visual Basic conversion functions than the one shown earlier. Although you may not use some of these functions all the time, you certainly need to know where to find them.

Table 3-13 Visual Basic type conversion functions

Function	Description
`CBool(` *expr* `)`	Converts an expression to a Boolean value. The expression must be a number, a string that represents a number, or the strings `"True"` or `"False"`. Otherwise a runtime error is generated. If the expression is nonzero, the function returns *True*. Otherwise it returns *False*. For example, `CBool(10)` and `CBool("7")` return *True*, while `CBool(0)` and `CBool("0")` return *False*. If the argument is the string `"True"`, the function returns *True*, and if the expression is the string `"False"`, the function returns *False*.
`CByte(` *expr* `)`	Converts an expression to a Byte, which can hold the values 0 through 255. If the argument is a fractional number, it is rounded. If the expression cannot be converted to a value in the range of 0–255, a runtime error is generated.
`CChar(` *expr* `)`	Converts a string expression to a Char. If the string contains more than one character, only the first character is returned. For example, `CChar("xyz")` returns the character *x*.
`CDate(` *expr* `)`	Converts an expression to a Date. String expressions must be valid Date literals. For example, `CDate("#10/14/2009 1:30 PM#")` returns a Date with the value *1:30 PM, October 14th, 2009*. If the expression cannot be converted to a Date value, a runtime error is generated.
`CDbl(` *expr* `)`	Converts a numeric or string expression to a Double. If the expression converts to a value outside the range of a Double, or is not a numeric value, a runtime error is generated.
`CDec(` *expr* `)`	Converts a numeric or string expression to a Decimal. The `CDec` function can convert strings starting with a `$` character, such as $1,200.00. Commas are also permitted. If the expression converts to a value outside the range of a Decimal, or is not a numeric value, a runtime error is generated.
`CInt(` *expr* `)`	Converts a numeric or string expression to an Integer. If the expression converts to a value outside the range of an Integer, or is not a numeric value, a runtime error is generated. Rounds to nearest integer.
`CLng(` *expr* `)`	Converts a numeric or string expression to a Long (long integer). If the expression converts to a value outside the range of a Long, or is not a numeric value, a runtime error is generated.
`CObj(` *expr* `)`	Converts an expression to an Object.
`CShort(` *expr* `)`	Converts a numeric or string expression to a Short (short integer). If the expression converts to a value outside the range of a Short, or is not a numeric value, a runtime error is generated.
`CSng(` *expr* `)`	Converts a numeric or string expression to a Single. If the expression converts to a value outside the range of a Single, or is not a numeric value, a runtime error is generated. The input expression may conatain commas, as in "1,234."
`CStr(` *expr* `)`	Converts a numeric, Boolean, Date, or string expression to a String. Input can be an arithmetic expression, a Boolean value, a date, or any numeric data type.

3.27 After the statement `dblResult = 10 \ 3` executes, what value will be stored in `dblResult`?

3.28 After each of the following statements executes, what value will be stored in `dblResult`?

a. `dblResult = 6 + 3 * 5`
b. `dblResult = 12 / 2 - 4`
c. `dblResult = 2 + 7 * 3 - 6`
d. `dblResult = (2 + 4) * 3`

3.29 What value will be stored in `dblResult` after the following statement executes?

```
dblResult = CInt("28.5")
```

3.30 Will the following statement execute or cause a runtime error?

```
dblResult = CDbl("186,478.39")
```

3.31 What is a named constant?

3.32 Assuming that `intNumber` is an integer variable, what value will each of the following statements assign to it?

a. `intNumber = 27`
b. `intNumber = CInt(12.8)`
c. `intNumber = CInt(12.0)`
d. `intNumber = (2 + 4) * 3`

3.33 When does a type conversion runtime error occur? (Assume *Option Strict* is *Off*).

3.34 Excluding the `Val()` function, which function converts the string "860.2" to value of type Double?

3.35 How would the following strings be converted by the `CDec` function?

a. `48.5000`
b. `$34.95`
c. `2,300`
d. `Twelve`

3.5 Formatting Numbers and Dates

Users of computer programs generally like to see numbers and dates displayed in an attractive, easy to read format. Numbers greater than 999, for instance, should usually be displayed with commas and decimal points. The value 123456.78 would normally be displayed as "123,456.78".

TIP: Number formatting is dependent on the locale that is used by the computer's Microsoft Windows operating system. That includes Windows XP, Windows Vista, and earlier versions of Windows. *Localization* refers to the technique of adapting your formats for various regions and countries of the world. For example, in North America a currency value is formatted as 123,456.78. In many European countries, the same value is formatted as 123.456,78. In this book, we will only display North American formats, but you can find help on using other types of formats by looking for the topic named *localization* in Visual Studio help.

`ToString` Method

All numeric and date data types in Visual Basic contain the **`ToString` method.** This method converts the contents of a variable to a string. The following code segment shows an example of the method's use.

```
Dim intNumber As Integer = 123
lblNumber.Text = intNumber.ToString()
```

In the second statement the `number` variable's `ToString` method is called. The method returns the string "123", which is assigned to the Text property of `lblNumber`.

By passing a formatting string to the `ToString` method, you can indicate what type of format you want to use when the number or date is formatted. The following statements create a string containing the number 1234.5 in Currency format:

```
Dim dblSample As Double
Dim strResult As String
dblSample = 1234.5
strResult = dblSample.ToString("c")
```

When the last statement executes, the value assigned to `strResult` is `"$1,234.50"`. Notice that an extra zero was added at the end because currency values usually have two digits to the right of the decimal point. The value `"c"` is called a format string. Table 3-14 shows the format strings used for all types of floating-point numbers (Double, Single, and Currency), assuming the user is running Windows in a North American locale. The format strings are not case sensitive, so you can code them as uppercase or lowercase letters. If you call `ToString` using an integer type (Byte, Integer, or Long), the value is formatted as if it were type Double.

Table 3-14 Standard numeric format strings

Format String	Description
`N` or `n`	Number format
`F` or `f`	Fixed-point scientific format
`E` or `e`	Exponential scientific format
`C` or `c`	Currency format
P or p	Percent format

Number Format

Number format (`n` or `N`) displays numeric values with thousands separators and a decimal point. By default, two digits display to the right of the decimal point. Negative values are displayed with a leading minus (–) sign. Example:

```
-2,345.67
```

Fixed-Point Format

Fixed-point format (`f` or `F`) displays numeric values with no thousands separator and a decimal point. By default, two digits display to the right of the decimal point. Negative values are displayed with a leading minus (–) sign. Example:

```
-2345.67
```

Exponential Format

Exponential format (`e` or `E`) displays numeric values in scientific notation. The number is normalized with a single digit to the left of the decimal point. The exponent is marked by the letter `e`, and the exponent has a leading + or – sign. By default, six digits display to the right of the decimal point, and a leading minus sign is used if the number is negative. Example:

```
-2.345670e+003
```

Currency Format

Currency format (`c` or `C`) displays a leading currency symbol (such as `$`), digits, thousands separators, and a decimal point. By default, two digits display to the right of the decimal point. Negative values are surrounded by parentheses. Example:

```
($2,345.67)
```

Percent Format

Percent format (`p` or `P`) causes the number to be multiplied by 100 and displayed with a trailing space and `%` sign. By default, two digits display to the right of the decimal point. Negative values are displayed with a leading minus (–) sign. The following example uses `–.2345`:

```
-23.45 %
```

Specifying the Precision

Each numeric format string can optionally be followed by an integer that indicates how many digits to display after the decimal point. For example, the format `n3` displays three digits after the decimal point. Table 3-15 shows a variety of numeric formatting examples, based on the North American locale.

Table 3-15 Numeric formatting examples (North American locale)

Number Value	Format String	ToString( ) Value
12.3	`n3`	12.300
12.348	`n2`	12.35
1234567.1	`n`	1,234,567.10
123456.0	`f2`	123456.00
123456.0	`e3`	1.235e+005
.234	`p`	23.40%
–1234567.8	`c`	($1,234,567.80)

Rounding

Rounding can occur when the number of digits you have specified after the decimal point in the format string is smaller than the precision of the numeric value. Suppose, for example, that the value 1.235 were displayed with a format string of `n2`. Then the displayed value would be 1.24. If the next digit after the last displayed digit is 5 or higher, the last displayed digit is rounded *away from zero*. Table 3-16 shows examples of rounding using a format string of `n2`.

Table 3-16 Rounding examples, using the `n2` display format string

Number Value	Formatted As
1.234	1.23
1.235	1.24
1.238	1.24
–1.234	–1.23
–1.235	–1.24
–1.238	–1.24

Integer Values with Leading Zeros

Integer type variables (Byte, Integer, or Long) have a special format string, `D` (or `d`), that lets you specify the minimum width for displaying the number. Leading zeros are inserted if necessary. Table 3-17 shows examples.

Table 3-17 Formatting integers, using the `D` (`d`) format string

Integer Value	Format String	Formatted As
23	D	23
23	D4	0023
1	D2	01

Formatting Dates and Times

When you call the `ToString` method using a Date or DateTime variable, you can format it as a short date, short time, long date, and so on. Table 3-18 lists the most commonly used format strings for dates and times. The following example creates a string containing `"8/10/2009"`, called the short date format.

```
Dim dtmSample As Date = "#8/10/2009#"
Dim strResult As String = dtmSample.ToString("d")
```

The following example gets the current date and formats it with a long date format.

```
Dim strToday As String = Today().ToString("D")
```

Date/time format strings are case sensitive.

Table 3-18 Common date/time formats

Format String	Description
`d`	Short date format, which shows the month, day, and year. An example is `"8/10/2009"`.
`D`	Long date format, which contains the day of the week, month, day, and year. An example is `"Monday, August 10, 2009"`.
`t`	Short time format, which shows the hours and minutes. An example is `"3:22 PM"`.
`T`	Long time format, which contains the hours, minutes, seconds, and an AM/PM indicator. An example is `"3:22:00 PM"`.
F	Full (long) date and time. An example is `"Monday August 10, 2009 3:22:00 PM"`.

Tutorial 3-8 examines the *Format Demo* application.

Tutorial 3-8:
Examining the *Format Demo* application

Step 1: Open the *Format Demo* project from the Chapter 3 sample programs folder named *Format Demo*.

Step 2: Run the application, as shown in Figure 3-30. The five buttons on the left are used for formatting floating-point numeric values. The five buttons on the right are for formatting dates and times. The text in each button shows which format string is used when the `ToString` method is called.

Figure 3-30 *Format Demo* application

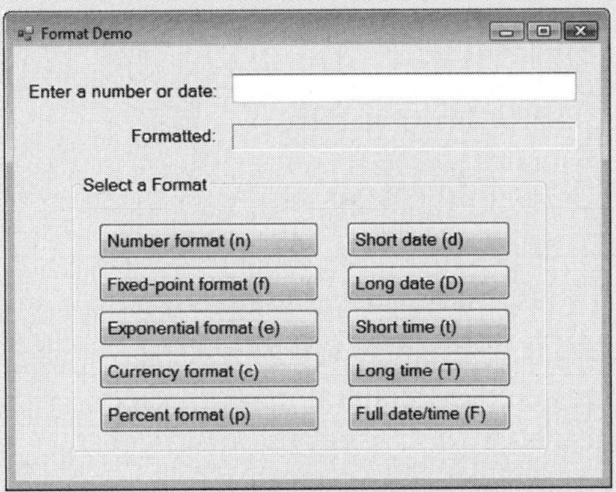

Step 3: Enter the value `67895.34926` into the TextBox control at the top of the form. Click the *Number format (n)* button. You should see the output shown in Figure 3-31.

Step 4: Click the *Fixed-point format (f)* button. Notice how the number next to the Formatted label changes its appearance.

Step 5: Click the remaining buttons on the left side. Change the value of the number in the TextBox control, and experiment with each of the format buttons on the left side.

Step 6: Enter the following date into the TextBox: *May 5, 2009 6:35 PM.*

Step 7: Click the *Short date (d)* button. You should see the date displayed as "5/5/2009".

Step 8: Click the other date and time buttons in the right-hand column. Notice all the ways the date and time can be displayed.

Step 9: Close the application window by clicking the X in the upper right corner. Open the form's code window and examine the code in each button's `Click` event handler.

Figure 3-31 Showing a Number format

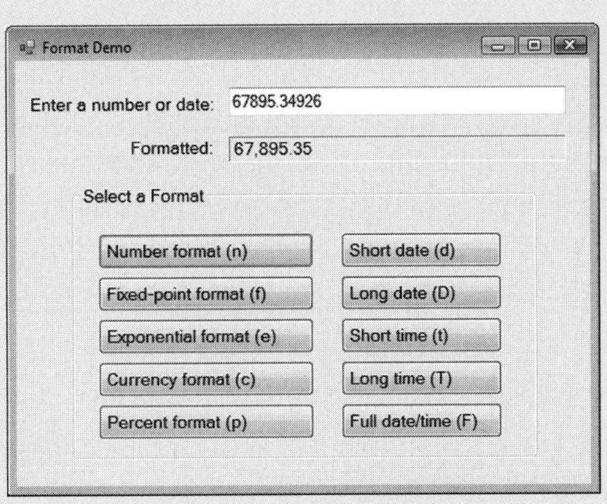

3.36 Write a statement that uses the `ToString` method to convert the contents of a variable named `dblSalary` to a Currency format.

3.37 For each of the following numeric formats, identify the format string used as the input parameter when calling the `ToString` method.

a. Currency
b. Exponential scientific
c. Number
d. Percent
e. Fixed-point

3.38 How can you make the `ToString` method display parentheses around a number in Currency format when the number is negative?

3.39 In the following table, fill in the expected values returned by the `ToString` function when specific numeric values are used with specific format strings.

Number Value	Format String	`ToString( )` Value
12.3	n4	
12.348	n1	
1234567.1	n3	
123456.0	f1	
123456.0	e3	
.234	p2	
–1234567.8	c3	

3.40 Show an example of formatting a Date variable in Long Time format when calling the `ToString` method.

3.41 Show an example of formatting a Date variable in Long Date format when calling the `ToString` method.

3.6 Exception Handling

CONCEPT: A well-engineered program should report errors and try to continue. Or, it should explain why it cannot continue, and then shut down. In this section, you learn how to recover gracefully from errors, using a technique known as exception handling.

We have seen that runtime errors can happen when an attempt to convert a string to a number fails. Often, an uninformed user will enter a value in a TextBox that doesn't conform to Visual Basic's rules for converting strings to numbers. Suppose the following code in a button's `Click` event handler assigns the contents of a TextBox to a variable:

```
Dim decSalary As Decimal
decSalary = CDec(txtSalary.Text)
```

Then, when we run the program, the user enters a nonnumeric value, as shown in Figure 3-32, resulting in the error message shown on the right. If the user had entered $4000, or $4,000, the `CDec` function would have converted the input into Decimal. But this user had a different idea about how to enter numbers.

A common way of describing a runtime error is to say that an *exception was thrown*, and the exception was *not handled*. Or, one can refer to it as an **unhandled exception**.

Failure Can Be Graceful

Exceptions can be thrown because of events outside the programmer's control. A disk file may be unreadable, for example, because of a hardware failure. The user may enter invalid data. The computer may be low on memory. Exception handling is designed to let programs recover from errors when possible. Or, if recovery is not possible, a program should fail gracefully, letting the user know why it failed. Under no circumstances should it just halt without warning. In this section we will show how you can handle exceptions.

Figure 3-32 User input causes a runtime error

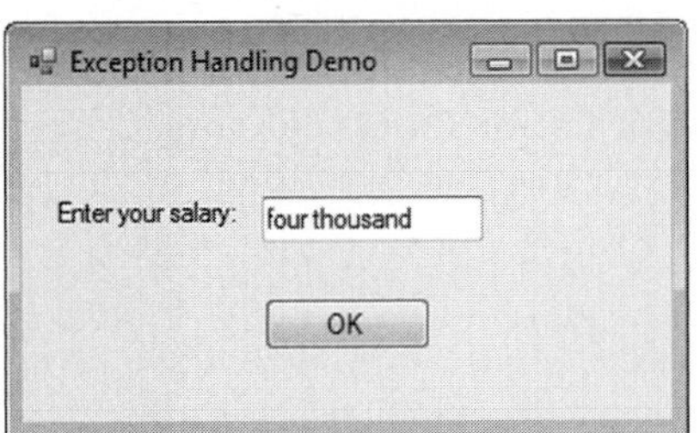

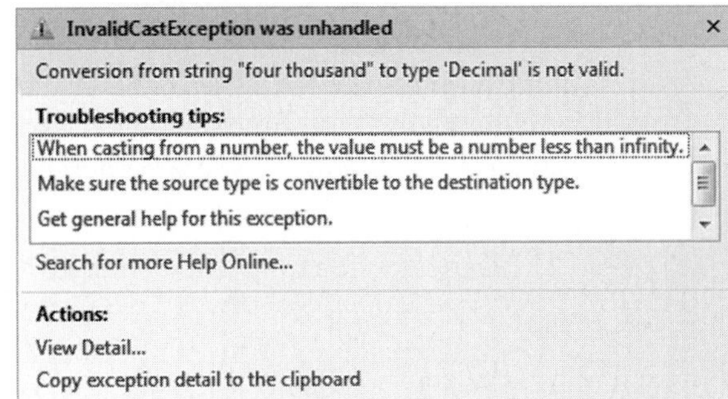

`MessageBox.Show` Function

Before we show how exceptions are handled in Visual Basic, let's look at an easy way to notify the user when an error has occurred. The `MessageBox.Show` function displays a pop-up window containing a message and an *OK* button, as shown in Figure 3-33. The user clicks the button to close the window. Here are two basic formats for `MessageBox.Show`:

```
MessageBox.Show( message )
MessageBox.Show( message, caption )
```

The following statement displays the message in Figure 3-33:

```
MessageBox.Show("Please try again, and enter a number")
```

We will return to the `MessageBox.Show` function in Chapter 4 and explain its capabilities in more detail.

Figure 3-33 Window displayed by the `MessageBox.Show` function

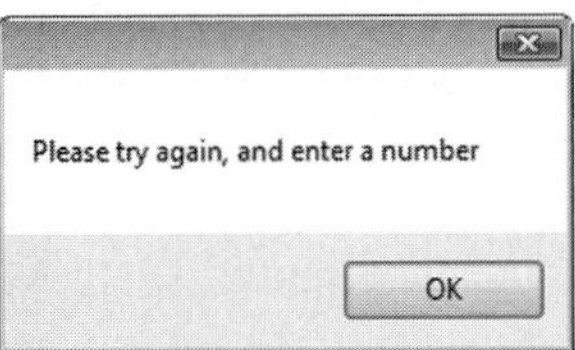

Handling Exceptions

Visual Basic, along with most modern programming languages, provides a simple mechanism for handling exceptions. It's called an **exception handler**, and uses a **`Try-Catch` block**. It begins with the `Try` keyword and statements, followed by a `Catch` clause and statements, and concludes with the keywords `End Try`. This is a simplified format of a `Try-Catch` block, leaving out some options:

```
Try
   try-statements
Catch [exception-type]
   catch-statements
End Try
```

The *`try-statements`* consists of a list of program statements you would like to execute. They represent the code that would have existed even if you were not using exception handling. The *`catch-statements`* are one or more statements you would like to execute only if an exception is thrown. The optional *`exception-type`* argument lets you name the type of exception you want to catch.

Let's use the salary input example we saw earlier. We enclose statements in the `Try` block that input the salary and display a confirmation message by calling the `MessageBox.Show` function. The `Catch` block displays a message telling the user to try again. Lines are numbered for reference:

```
1: Try
2:    Dim decSalary As Decimal
3:    decSalary = CDec(txtSalary.Text)
4:    MessageBox.Show("Your salary is " & decSalary.ToString() & " dollars")
5: Catch
6:    MessageBox.Show("Please try again, and enter a number")
7: End Try
```

If we run the program as before and enter a valid salary, the program confirms the amount, as shown in Figure 3-34. If the user enters an invalid value, line 3 throws an exception, causing the program to jump to line 6.

Figure 3-34 Valid user input, with confirmation message

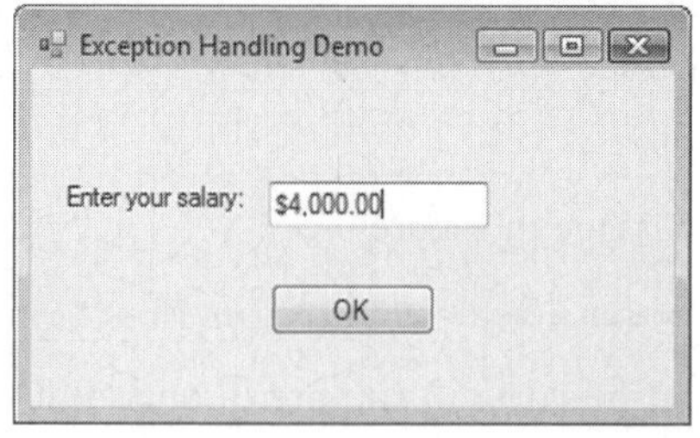

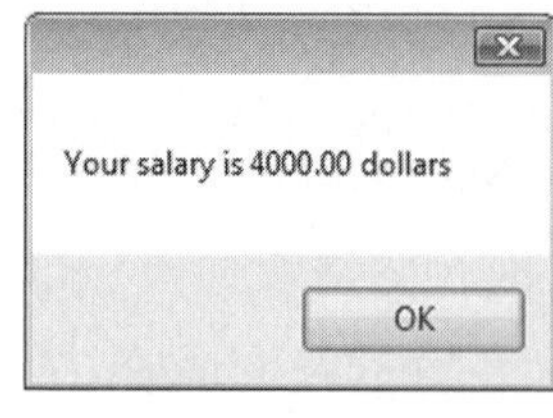

The `MessageBox.Show` function displays a helpful message, as shown in Figure 3-35. Notice that line 4 never executes when an exception is thrown. Most exception blocks have the same pattern, where some statements in a `Try` block are skipped when an exception occurs.

NOTE: In later chapters, you will see that exception handling is more often used to handle errors that cannot be anticipated by programmers. Examples are database connection errors, file input/output errors, and so on. To keep things simple in this chapter, we use exceptions to handle data conversion errors. In Chapter 4, you will learn to prevent errors by using `If` statements.

Figure 3-35 Invalid user input, causing the exception to be handled

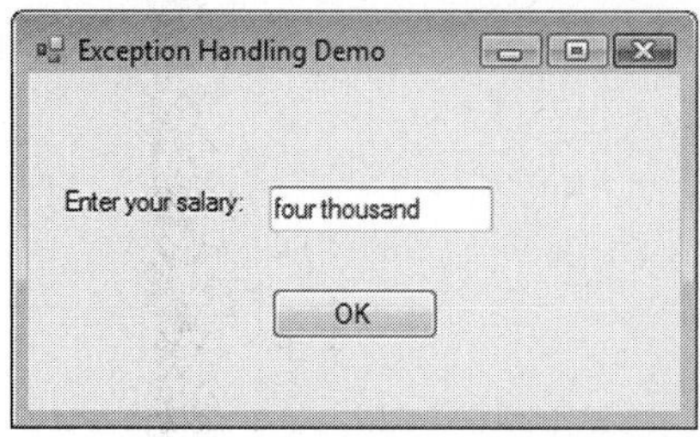

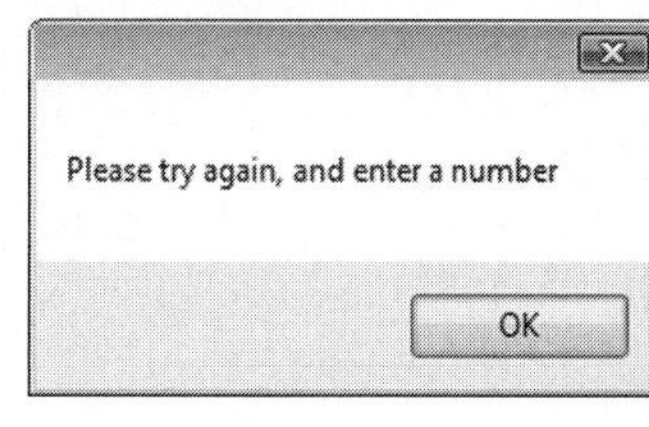

Displaying Exception Object Information

When you catch an exception, you can display the properties of the `Exception` object it returns. For example, in the `Catch` block, identified by the `Catch` keyword, we can assign an arbitrary name (`ex`) to the exception object:

```
Catch ex As Exception
```

On the next line, we can display the Message property of the `Exception` in a message box:

```
MessageBox.Show(ex.Message)
```

The user sees a standardized message generated by Visual Basic's runtime system (see Figure 3-36). Here's a more complete example that adds a title to the message box:

```
Try
  Dim decSalary As Decimal
  decSalary = CDec(txtSalary.Text)
Catch ex As Exception
  MessageBox.Show(ex.Message, "Salary input error")
End Try
```

Figure 3-36 Displaying an exception's Message property

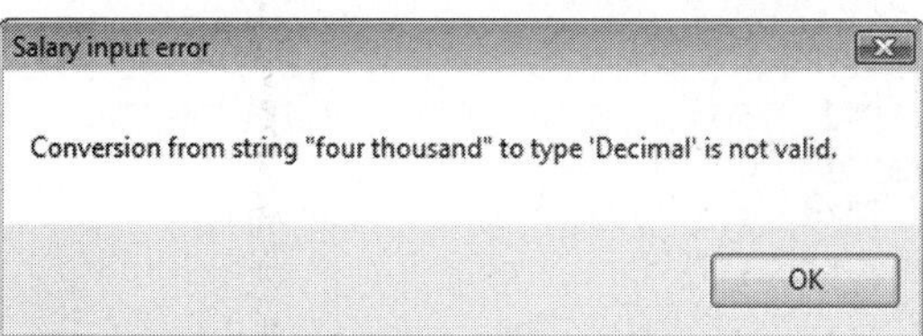

If You Want to Know More: Handling Multiple Errors

A sequence of statements in a `Try` block might throw more than one type of exception. Suppose a program inputs someone's yearly salary, the number of pay periods per year, and then divides to get the salary amount per pay period, as shown in Figure 3-37. Someone earning $50,000 with 26 pay periods per year would earn (50000 / 26) = 1923.08 per pay period. Here's the code that would do it, located in a `Try` block. Some of the lines are numbered for reference:

```
      Try
1:      Dim decAnnualSalary As Decimal
2:      Dim intPayPeriods As Integer
3:      Dim decSalary As Decimal
4:      decAnnualSalary = CDec(txtAnnualSalary.Text)
5:      intPayPeriods = CInt(txtPayPeriods.Text)
6:      decSalary = decAnnualSalary / intPayPeriods
7:      lblSalary.Text = decSalary.ToString()
      Catch
8:      MessageBox.Show("Please try again, and enter a number")
      End Try
```

Figure 3-37 The *Salary Calculation* program

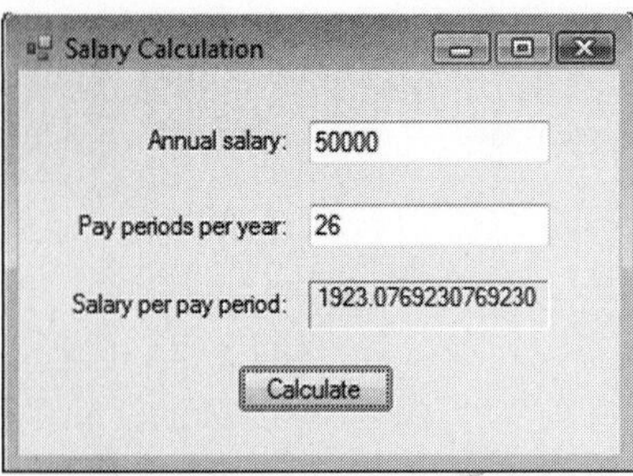

Suppose line 4 threw an exception because the user entered an illegal *annual salary*. The program would jump immediately to line 8 in the `Catch` block. Or, suppose the user entered a valid annual salary, but an invalid number for *the pay periods per year*. Then line 5 would throw an exception, and the program would immediately jump to line 8. In both cases, we can see that any remaining statements in the `Try` block are skipped when an exception is thrown.

What if the user entered a value of zero for the pay periods per year? Then a divide by zero exception would be thrown on line 6, which doesn't match the error message we show the user in line 8. That's when we could use two `Catch` blocks, one for bad number formats, and another for dividing by zero (shown in bold):

```
Try
  Dim decAnnualSalary As Decimal
  Dim intPayPeriods As Integer
  Dim decSalary As Decimal
  decAnnualSalary = CDec(txtAnnualSalary.Text)
  intPayPeriods = CInt(txtPayPeriods.Text)
  decSalary = decAnnualSalary / intPayPeriods
  lblSalary.Text = decSalary.ToString()
Catch ex As InvalidCastException
  MessageBox.Show("Please try again, and enter a number")
Catch ex As DivideByZeroException
  MessageBox.Show("Pay periods per year cannot be zero")
End Try
```

Each `Catch` block mentions a specific exception type, so the error message can focus on what the user did wrong. This is a more sophisticated way of handling exceptions, but it requires you to find out the exception type ahead of time. A simple way to achieve this is to run the program without a `Try-Catch` block and copy the name of the exception from the title bar of the runtime error dialog box, as shown in Figure 3-38. Tutorial 3-9 walks you through a salary calculation program with exception handling.

Figure 3-38 `InvalidCastException` example

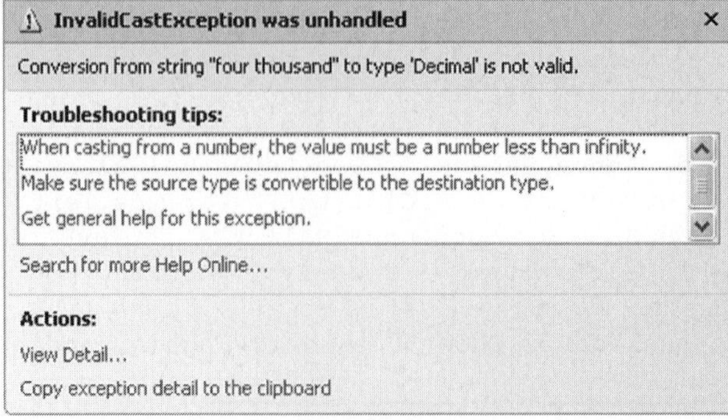

Tutorial 3-9:
Salary Calculation application with exception handling

In this tutorial, you will create an application that asks the user to input a person's annual salary and number of pay periods per year. The program calculates the amount of salary they should receive per pay period. First, you will implement the program without exception handling, test it, and note how runtime errors occur. Then, you will add exception handling to the program and test it again. Figure 3-39 shows the form layout.

Figure 3-39 The *Salary Calculation* form

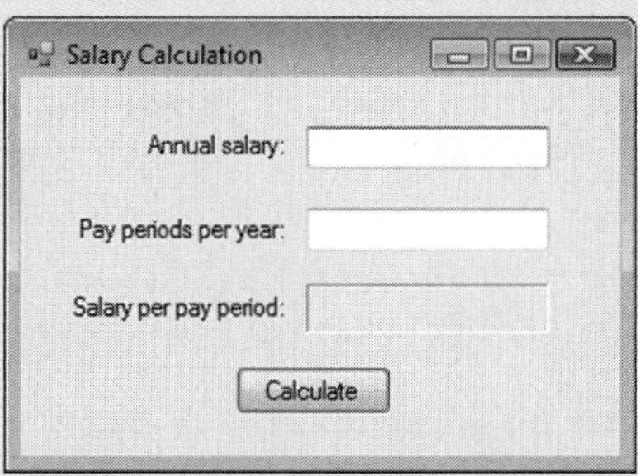

Step 1: Create a new project named *Salary Calculation.*

Step 2: Set the form's Text property to *Salary Calculation.*

Step 3: Add two TextBox controls to the form named *txtAnnualSalary* and *txtPayPeriods.*

Step 4: Add a Label control to the form just below the two text boxes named *lblSalary*. Set its BorderStyle property to *Fixed3D.*

Step 5: Add a Button control to the form named *btnCalculate* and assign *Calculate* to its Text property.

Step 6: Add appropriate labels next to the text boxes so your program's form looks like the form shown in Figure 3-39.

Step 7: Double-click the *Calculate* button to open the *Code* window. Insert the following code shown in bold into its `Click` event handler:

```
1: Private Sub btnCalculate_Click(ByVal sender As System.Object, _
2:   ByVal e As System.EventArgs) Handles bntCalculate.Click
3:
4:   Dim decAnnualSalary As Decimal ' annual salary
5:   Dim intPayPeriods As Integer   ' number of pay periods per year
6:   Dim decSalary As Decimal       ' salary per pay period
7:
8:   decAnnualSalary = CDec(txtAnnualSalary.Text)
9:   intPayPeriods = CInt(txtPayPeriods.Text)
10:  decSalary = decAnnualSalary / intPayPeriods
11:  lblSalary.Text = decSalary.ToString("c")
```

Lines 4 through 6 define the variables used in this procedure. Lines 8 and 9 copy the salary and number of pay periods from text boxes into variables. Line 10 calculates the amount of salary per pay period and line 11 assigns the result to a Label control named `lblSalary`.

Step 8: Save and run the program. Enter **75000** for the annual salary, and **26** for the pay periods per year. When you click *Calculate*, the output should be $2,884.62.

Step 9: Erase the contents of the pay periods text box and click the *Calculate* button. You should see a runtime error dialog box appear, saying *InvalidCastException* was unhandled. After reading the dialog box, click the *Stop Debugging* button on the Visual Studio toolbar. The program should return to Design mode.

Your next task will be to add exception handling to the program to prevent the type of runtime error you just saw. It is never desirable for a program to halt like this when the user enters bad data.

Step 10: Revise the code in the `btnCalculate_Click` handler method so it looks like the following:

```
Dim decAnnualSalary As Decimal ' annual salary
Dim intPayPeriods As Integer   ' number of pay periods per year
Dim decSalary As Decimal       ' salary per pay period

Try
  decAnnualSalary = CDec(txtAnnualSalary.Text)
  intPayPeriods = CInt(txtPayPeriods.Text)
Catch
  MessageBox.Show("The input fields must contain " _
    & "nonzero numeric values.", "Error")
End Try

decSalary = decAnnualSalary / intPayPeriods
lblSalary.Text = decSalary.ToString("c")
```

Step 11: Save and run the program again. Enter an annual salary of **75000**, and leave the pay periods text box blank. You should see a message box that says *The input fields must contain nonzero numeric values.* After you close the message box, however, a runtime error still appears, with the caption *DivideByZeroException was unhandled.* Click the *Stop Debugging* button on the Visual Studio toolbar to return to Design mode.

Do you see why a runtime error still happened? After the `Catch` clause in the exception handler executed, the program still attempted to divide `decAnnualSalary` by `intPayPeriods`. Because the latter equaled zero, a divide by zero error occurred. The next step will fix this problem.

Step 12: Open the *Code* window and revise the `btnCalculateClick` handler method once again. The way the code is written now, the division calculation only occurs if the pay periods value is converted to an integer without errors:

```
Dim decAnnualSalary As Decimal ' annual salary
Dim intPayPeriods As Integer   ' number of pay periods per year
Dim decSalary As Decimal       ' salary per pay period

Try
  decAnnualSalary = CDec(txtAnnualSalary.Text)
  intPayPeriods = CInt(txtPayPeriods.Text)
  decSalary = decAnnualSalary / intPayPeriods
  lblSalary.Text = decSalary.ToString("c")
Catch
  MessageBox.Show("The input fields must contain " _
    & "nonzero numeric values.", "Error")
End Try
```

Step 13: Save and run the program. Test it with valid data, as before. Test it by leaving the pay periods text box blank. The message box should alert the user, but the program should not halt.

Step 14: Click the *Stop Debugging* button to end the program, or click the *Close* icon in the upper right corner of the program's window.

3.7 Group Boxes and the Load Event Procedure

CONCEPT: In this section we discuss the GroupBox control, which is used to group other controls. We will also discuss the Load event procedure, which is executed when a form loads into memory.

Group Boxes

A group box is a rectangular border with an optional title that appears in the border's upper left corner. Other controls may be placed inside a group box. You can give forms a more organized look by grouping related controls together inside group boxes.

In Visual Basic, you use the **GroupBox control** to create a group box with an optional title. The title is stored in the GroupBox control's Text property. Figure 3-40 shows a GroupBox control. The control's Text property is set to *Personal Data*, and a group of other controls are inside the group box.

Figure 3-40 GroupBox containing other controls

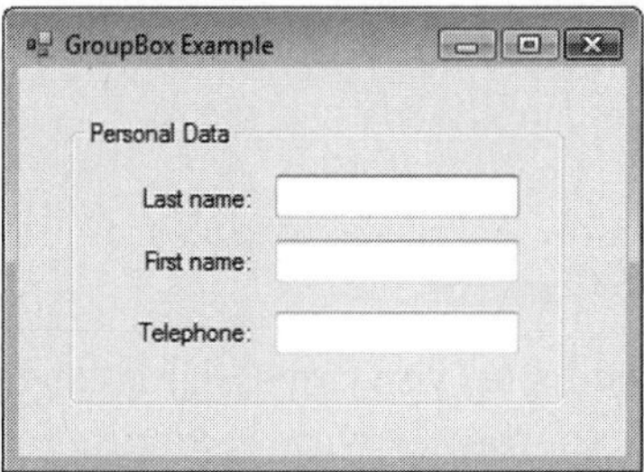

Creating a Group Box and Adding Controls to It

To create a group box, select the *GroupBox* control from the *Containers* section of the *Toolbox* window and then draw the group box at the desired size on the form. To add another control to the group box, select the GroupBox control that you placed on the form, and then double-click the desired tool in the Toolbox to place another control inside the group box.

The controls you place inside a group box become part of a group. When you move a group box, the objects inside it move as well. When you delete a group box, the objects inside it are also deleted.

Moving an Existing Control to a Group Box

If an existing control is not inside a group box, but you want to move it to the group box, follow these steps:

1. Select the control you wish to add to the group box.
2. Cut the control to the clipboard.
3. Select the group box.
4. Paste the control.

Group Box Tab Order

The value of a control's TabIndex property is handled differently when the control is placed inside a GroupBox control. GroupBox controls have their own TabIndex property and the TabIndex value of the controls inside the group box are relative to the GroupBox control's TabIndex property. For example, Figure 3-41 shows a GroupBox control displayed in tab order selection mode. As you can see, the GroupBox control's TabIndex is set to 2. The TabIndex of the controls inside the group box are displayed as 2.0, 2.1, 2.2, and so on.

NOTE: The TabIndex properties of the controls inside the group box will not appear this way in the *Properties* window. They will appear as 0, 1, 2, and so on.

Figure 3-41 Group box TabIndex values

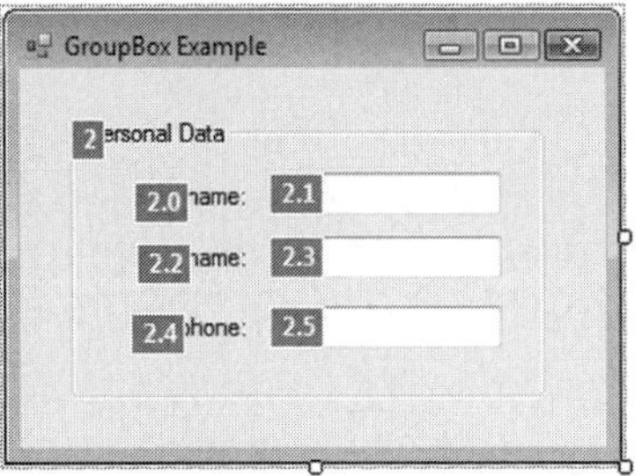

Assigning an Access Key to a GroupBox Control

Although GroupBox controls cannot receive the focus, you can assign a keyboard access key to them by preceding a character in their Text property with an ampersand (&). When the user enters the access key, the focus moves to the control with the lowest TabIndex value inside the group box.

Selecting and Moving Multiple Controls

It is possible to select multiple controls and work with them all at once. For example, you can select a group of controls and move them all to a different location on the form. You can also select a group of controls and change some of their properties.

Select multiple controls by using one of the following techniques:

- Position the cursor over an empty part of the form near the controls you wish to select. Click and drag a selection box around the controls. This is shown in Figure 3-42. When you release the mouse button, all the controls that are partially or completely enclosed in the selection box will be selected.
- Hold down the Ctrl key while clicking each control you wish to select.

After using either of these techniques, all the controls you have selected will appear with sizing handles. You may now move them, delete them, or use the *Properties* window to set many of their properties to the same value.

Figure 3-42 Selecting multiple controls by clicking and dragging the mouse

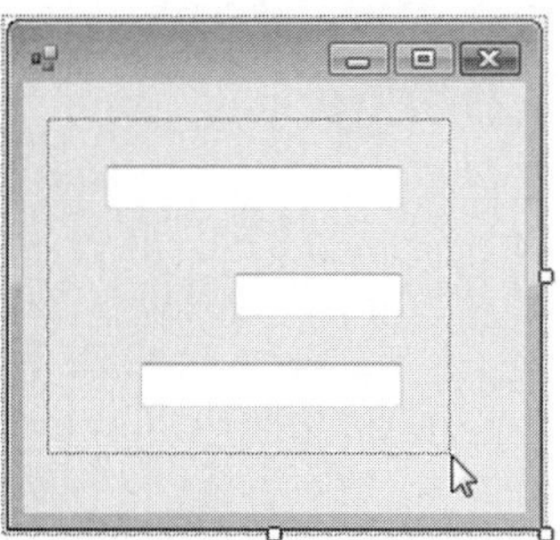

TIP: In a group of selected controls, it is easy to deselect a control that you have accidentally selected. Simply hold down the Ctrl key and click the control you wish to deselect.

The Load Event Procedure

When a form loads into memory, a Load event takes place. If you need to execute code automatically when a form is displayed, you can place the code in the form's **Load event procedure**. For example, in the next section you will develop an application that displays the current date and time on the application's form. You will accomplish this by writing code in the form's Load event procedure that retrieves the date and time from the system.

To write code in a form's Load event procedure, double-click any area of the form where there is no other control. The *Code* window will appear with an event procedure similar to the following:

```
Private Sub Form1_Load(ByVal sender As System.Object, _
  ByVal e As System.EventArgs) Handles MyBase.Load

End Sub
```

Inside the procedure, simply write the statements you wish the procedure to execute. Be sure to leave a blank line before your first line of code.

3.42 How is a group box helpful when designing a form with a large number of controls?

3.43 When placing a new control inside an existing GroupBox control, what must you do before you double-click the new control in the *ToolBox*?

3.44 How is the clipboard useful when you want to move an existing control into a group box?

3.45 How does the tab order of controls inside a group box correspond to the tab order of other controls outside the group box?

3.46 Which event procedure executes when the program's startup form displays?

3.8 Focus on Program Design and Problem Solving: Building the *Room Charge Calculator* Application

A guest staying at the Highlander Hotel may incur the following types of charges:

- Room charges, based on a per-night rate
- Room service charges
- Telephone charges
- Miscellaneous charges

The manager of the Highlander Hotel has asked you to create an application that calculates the guest's total charges. Figure 3-43 shows the application's form after the user has entered values into the text boxes and clicked the *Calculate Charges* button.

Figure 3-43 Sample output from the *Room Charge Calculator* application

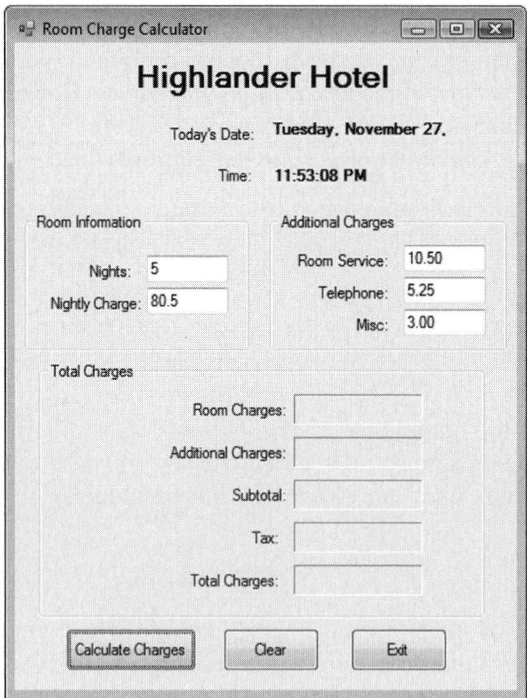

Figure 3-44 shows how the controls are arranged on the form with names. You can use this diagram when designing the form and assigning values to the Name property of each control. Notice that all Label controls appearing to the left to TextBox controls have their TextAlign property set to *MiddleRight*. This causes the labels to be right-aligned. The same is true of the labels on the lower half of the form, including *Room Charges, Additional Charges,* and so on. All those labels have their TextAlign property set to *MiddleRight*. Table 3-19, located at the end of this section, can be used as a reference.

Figure 3-44 Named controls

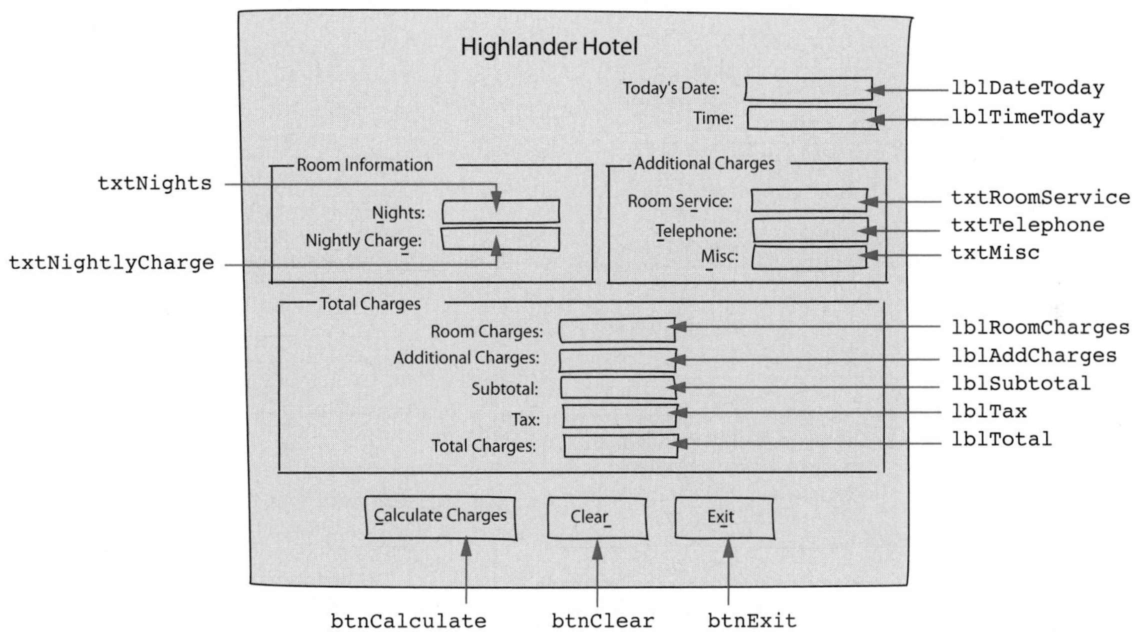

Table 3-19 lists and describes the methods (event procedures) needed for this application. Notice that a `Load` event procedure is needed for the form.

Table 3-19 Methods in the *Room Charge Calculator* application

Method	Description
`btnCalculate_Click`	Calculates the room charges, additional charges, subtotal (room charges plus additional charges), 8% tax, and the total charges. These values are copied to the Text properties of the appropriate labels.
`btnClear_Click`	Clears the TextBox controls, and the labels used to display summary charge information. This procedure also resets the values displayed in the `lblDateToday` and `lblTimeToday` labels.
`btnExit_Click`	Ends the application
`Form1_Load`	Initializes the `lblDateToday` and `lblTimeToday` labels to the current system date and time

Figure 3-45 shows the flowchart for the `btnCalculate_Click` procedure. The procedure uses the following Decimal variables:

```
decRoomCharges
decAddCharges
decSubtotal
decTax
decTotal
```

The procedure also uses a named constant, `decTAX_RATE`, to hold the tax rate.

Figure 3-45 Flowchart for `btnCalculate_Click`

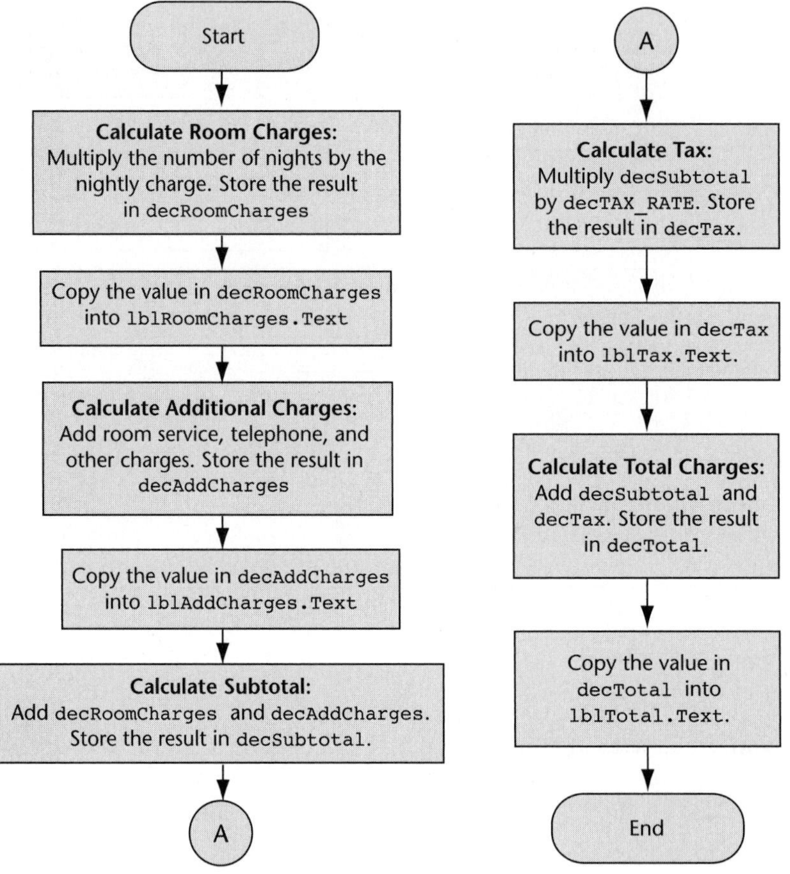

The flowchart in Figure 3-45 uses a new symbol: (A)

This is called the **connector symbol** and is used when a flowchart is broken into two or more smaller flowcharts. This is necessary when a flowchart does not fit on a single page or must be divided into sections. A connector symbol, which is a small circle with a letter or number inside it, allows you to connect two flowcharts. In the flowchart shown in Figure 3-45, the (A) connector indicates that the second flowchart segment begins where the first flowchart segment ends.

The flowcharts for the `btnClear_Click`, `btnExit_Click`, and `Form1_Load` procedures are shown in Figures 3-46, 3-47, and 3-48, respectively.

Recall that the form's `Load` procedure executes each time the form loads into memory. Tutorial 3-10 shows you how to create the *Room Charge Calculator* application.

Figure 3-46 Flowchart for `btnClear_Click`

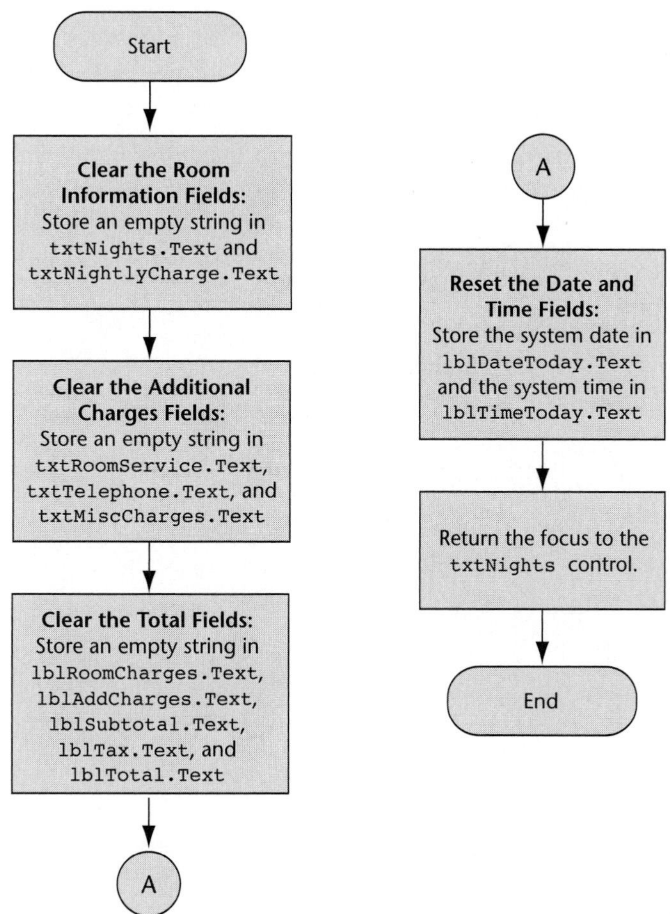

Figure 3-47 Flowchart for `btnExit_Click`

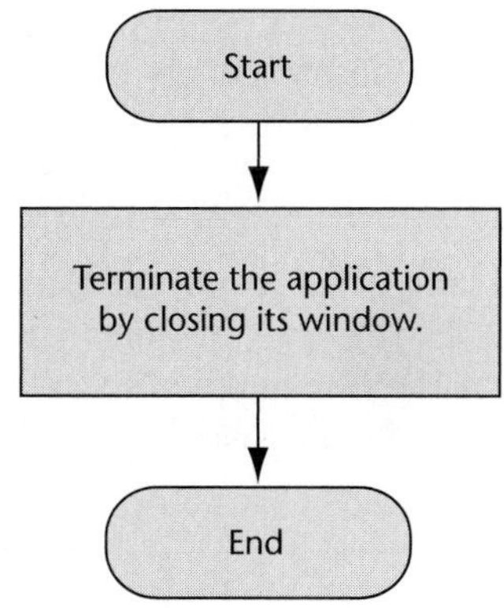

Figure 3-48 Flowchart for `Form1_Load` procedure

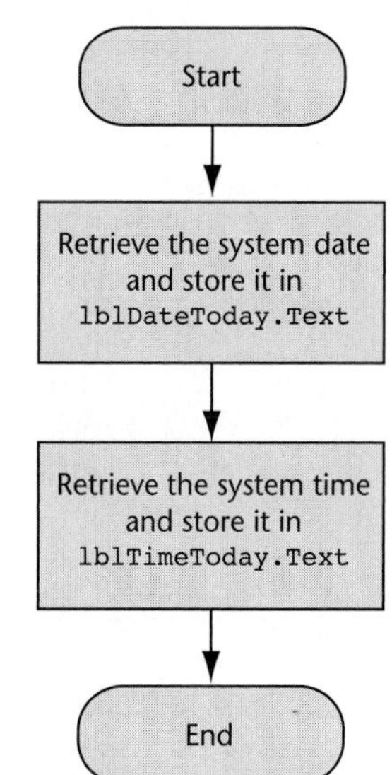

Tutorial 3-10:
Beginning the *Room Charge Calculator* application

Step 1: Create a new Windows application project named *Room Charge Calculator*.

Step 2: Figure 3-44 shows a sketch of the application's form and shows the names of the named controls. Refer to this figure as you set up the form and create the controls. Once you have completed the form, it should appear as shown in Figure 3-49.

Figure 3-49 The *Room Charge Calculator* form

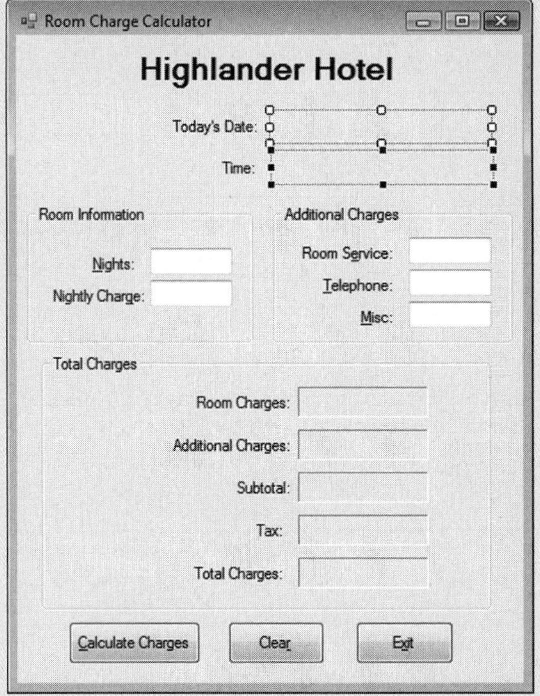

TIP: Most of the controls are contained inside group boxes. Refer to Section 3.7 for instructions on creating controls inside a group box.

TIP: The TextBox controls are all the same size, and all the Label controls that display output are the same size. If you are creating many similar instances of a control, it is easier to create the first one, set its size and properties as needed, copy it to the clipboard, and then paste it onto the form to create another one.

Step 3: Table 3-20 (on page 164) lists the relevant property settings of all the controls on the form. Refer to this table and make the necessary property settings.

Step 4: Now you will write the application's event procedures, beginning with the form's `Load` procedure. Double-click any area of the form not occupied by another control. The *Code* window should open with a code template for the

`Form1_Load` procedure. Complete the procedure by typing the following code shown in bold:

```
Private Sub Form1_Load(ByVal sender As System.Object, _
    ByVal e As System.EventArgs) Handles MyBase.Load

  ' Get today's date from the system and display it.
  lblDateToday.Text = Now.ToString("D")
  ' Get the current time from the system and display it.
  lblTimeToday.Text = Now.ToString("T")
End Sub
```

Step 5: Double-click the *Calculate Charges* button. The *Code* window should open with a code template for the `btnCalculate_Click` procedure. Complete the procedure by typing the following code shown in bold:

```
Private Sub btnCalculate_Click(ByVal sender As _
    System.Object, ByVal e As System.EventArgs) _
    Handles btnCalculate.Click

  ' Declare variables for the calculations.
  Dim decRoomCharges As Decimal    ' Room charges total
  Dim decAddCharges As Decimal     ' Additional charges
  Dim decSubtotal As Decimal       ' Subtotal
  Dim decTax As Decimal            ' Tax
  Dim decTotal As Decimal          ' Total of all charges
  Const decTAX_RATE As Decimal = 0.08D     ' Tax rate

  Try
    ' Calculate and display the room charges. Handle
    ' error if the fields are blank.
    decRoomCharges = CDec(txtNights.Text) * _
      CDec(txtNightlyCharge.Text)
    lblRoomCharges.Text = decRoomCharges.ToString("c")
  Catch
    MessageBox.Show("Nights and Nightly Charge must be numbers", _
      "Error")
  End Try

  Try
    ' Calculate and display the additional charges. Handle
    ' error if fields are blank.
    decAddCharges = CDec(txtRoomService.Text) + _
      CDec(txtTelephone.Text) + _
      CDec(txtMisc.Text)
    lblAddCharges.Text = decAddCharges.ToString("c")
  Catch
    MessageBox.Show("Room service, Telephone, and Misc. " _
        & "must be numbers", "Error")
  End Try

  ' Calculate and display the subtotal.
  decSubtotal = decRoomCharges + decAddCharges
  lblSubtotal.Text = decSubTotal.ToString("c")

  ' Calculate and display the tax.
  decTax = decSubtotal * decTAX_RATE
  lblTax.Text = decTax.ToString("c")
```

```
        ' Calculate and display the total charges.
        decTotal = decSubtotal + decTax
        lblTotal.Text = decTotal.ToString("c")
    End Sub
```

Exception handling was used in this procedure to check for missing user input. If the user forgets to enter the number of nights and the nightly charge, for example, the first `Catch` block displays a message box, as shown in Figure 3-50. Imagine how much better this is than letting the program halt unexpectedly. If the user forgets to enter amounts for room service, telephone, and miscellaneous charges, a second `Catch` block displays the message box shown in Figure 3-51.

Figure 3-50 Message box displayed by first exception handler

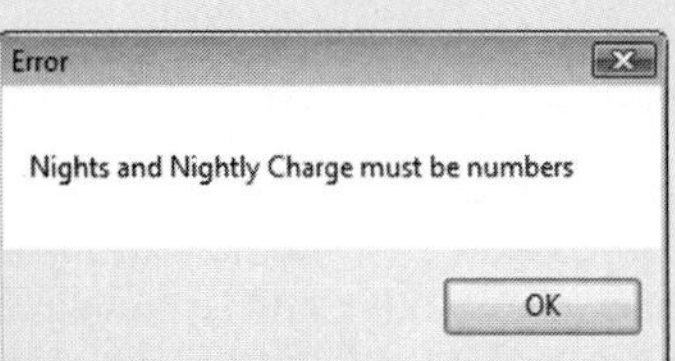

Figure 3-51 Message box displayed by second exception handler

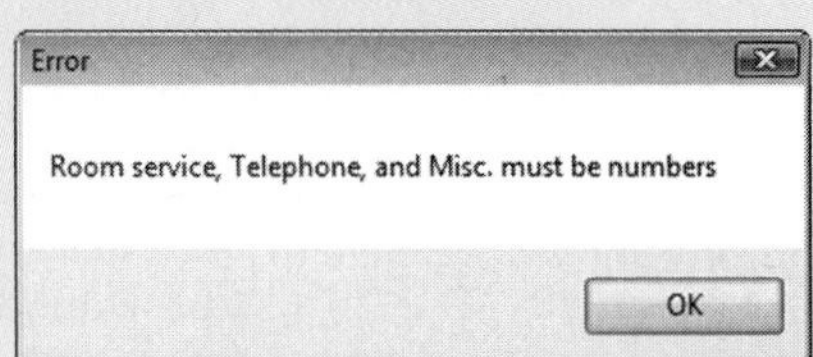

TIP: When you type the name of a built-in Visual Basic function or a method in the *Code* window, an IntelliSense box appears showing help on the function or method's arguments. If you do not want to see the IntelliSense box, press the [Esc] key when it appears.

Step 6: Open the *Design* window and double-click the *Clear* button. The *Code* window should open with a code template for the `btnClear_Click` procedure. Complete the procedure by typing the following code shown in bold.

```
Private Sub btnClear_Click(ByVal sender As System.Object, _
    ByVal e As System.EventArgs) Handles btnClear.Click

  ' Clear the room info fields.
  txtNights.Clear()
  txtNightlyCharge.Clear()
  ' Clear the additional charges fields.
  txtRoomService.Clear()
  txtTelephone.Clear()
  txtMisc.Clear()

  ' Clear the total fields.
  lblRoomCharges.Text = String.Empty
  lblAddCharges.Text = String.Empty
  lblSubtotal.Text = String.Empty
  lblTax.Text = String.Empty
  lblTotal.Text = String.Empty

  ' Get today's date from the operating system and display it.
  lblDateToday.Text = Now.ToString("D")
```

```
   ' Get the current time from the operating system and display it.
   lblTimeToday.Text = Now.ToString("T")

   ' Reset the focus to the first field.
   txtNights.Focus()
End Sub
```

Step 7: Open the *Design* window and double-click the *Exit* button. The *Code* window should open with a code template for the `btnExit_Click` procedure. Complete the procedure by typing the following code shown in bold.

```
Private Sub btnExit_Click(ByVal sender As System.Object, _
     ByVal e As System.EventArgs) Handles btnExit.Click

   ' End the application, by closing the window.
   Me.Close()
End Sub
```

Step 8: Use the *Save All* command on the *File* menu (or the *Save All* button) to save the project.

Step 9: Run the application. If there are errors, compare your code with that shown, and correct them. Once the application runs, enter test values, as shown in Figure 3-52 for the charges and confirm that it displays the correct output.

Figure 3-52 Sample output from the *Room Charge Calculator* application

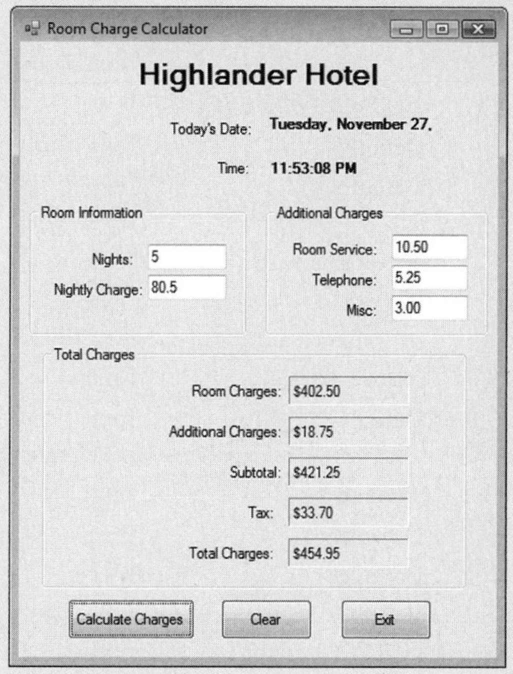

Table 3-20 lists each control, along with any relevant property values.

Table 3-20 Named controls in *Room Charge Calculator* form

Control Type	Control Name	Property	Property Value
Label	(Default)	Text: Font: TextAlign:	*Highlander Hotel* *MS sans serif, bold, 18 point* *MiddleCenter*
Label	(Default)	Text: TextAlign:	*Today's Date:* *MiddleRight*
Label	`lblDateToday`	Text: AutoSize: Font.Bold: BorderStyle: TextAlign:	(Initially cleared) *False* *True* *None* *MiddleLeft*
Label	(Default)	Text: TextAlign:	*Time:* *MiddleRight*
Label	`lblTimeToday`	Text: AutoSize: Font.Bold: BorderStyle: TextAlign:	(Initially cleared) *False* *True* *None* *MiddleLeft*
Group box	(Default)	Text:	*Room Information*
Label	(Default)	Text: TextAlign:	*&Nights:* *MiddleRight*
TextBox	`txtNights`	Text:	(Initially cleared)
Label	(Default)	Text: TextAlign:	*Nightly Char&ge:* *MiddleRight*
TextBox	`txtNightlyCharge`	Text:	(Initially cleared)
Group box	(Default)	Text:	*Additional Charges*
Label	(Default)	Text: TextAlign:	*Room Se&rvice:* *MiddleRight*
TextBox	`txtRoomService`	Text:	(Initially cleared)
Label	(Default)	Text: TextAlign:	*&Telephone:* *MiddleRight*
TextBox	`txtTelephone`	Text:	(Initially cleared)
Label	(Default)	Text: TextAlign:	*&Misc:* *MiddleRight*
TextBox	`txtMisc`	Text:	(Initially cleared)
Group box	(Default)	Text:	*Total Charges*
Label	(Default)	Text: TextAlign:	*Room Charges:* *MiddleRight*
Label	`lblRoomCharges`	Text: AutoSize: BorderStyle:	(Initially cleared) *False* *Fixed3D*
Label	(Default)	Text: TextAlign:	*Additional Charges:* *MiddleRight*
Label	`lblAddCharges`	Text: AutoSize: BorderStyle:	(Initially cleared) *False* *Fixed3D*

(*continues*)

Table 3-20 Named controls in *Room Charge Calculator* form (*continued*)

Control Type	Control Name	Property	Property Value
Label	(Default)	Text: TextAlign:	*Subtotal:* *MiddleRight*
Label	`lblSubtotal`	Text: AutoSize: BorderStyle:	(Initially cleared) *False* *Fixed3D*
Label	(Default)	Text: TextAlign:	*Tax:* *MiddleRight*
Label	`lblTax`	Text: AutoSize: BorderStyle:	(Initially cleared) *False* *Fixed3D*
Label	(Default)	Text: TextAlign:	*Total Charges:* *MiddleRight*
Label	`lblTotal`	Text: AutoSize: BorderStyle:	(Initially cleared) *False* *Fixed3D*
Button	`btnCalculate`	Text: TabIndex:	*C&alculate Charges* 2
Button	`btnClear`	Text: TabIndex:	*Clea&r* 3
Button	`btnExit`	Text: TabIndex:	*E&xit* 4

Changing Colors with Code (Optional Topic)

Chapter 2 showed how to change the foreground and background colors of a control's text by setting the ForeColor and BackColor properties in the *Design* view. In addition to using the *Properties* window, you can also store values in these properties with code. Visual Basic provides numerous values that represent colors, and can be assigned to the ForeColor and BackColor properties in code. The following are a few of the values:

```
Color.Black
Color.Blue
Color.Cyan
Color.Green
Color.Magenta
Color.Red
Color.White
Color.Yellow
```

For example, assume an application has a Label control named `lblMessage`. The following code sets the label's background color to black and foreground color to yellow:

```
lblMessage.BackColor = Color.Black
lblMessage.ForeColor = Color.Yellow
```

Visual Basic also provides values that represent default colors on your system. For example, the value `SystemColors.Control` represents the default control background color and `SystemColors.ControlText` represents the default control text color. The following statements set the `lblMessage` control's background and foreground to the default colors.

```
lblMessage.BackColor = SystemColors.Control
lblMessage.ForeColor = SystemColors.ControlText
```

In Tutorial 3-11, you will modify the *Room Charge Calculator* application so that the total charges are displayed in white characters on a blue background. This will make the total charges stand out visually from the rest of the information on the form.

Tutorial 3-11:
Changing a label's colors

In this tutorial, you will modify two of the application's event procedures: `btnCalculate_Click` and `btnClear_Click`. In the `btnCalculate_Click` procedure, you will add code that changes the `lblTotal` control's color settings just before the total charges are displayed. In the `btnClear_Click` procedure, you will add code that reverts `lblTotal`'s colors back to their normal state.

Step 1: With the *Room Charge Calculator* project open, open the *Code* window and scroll to the `btnCalculate_Click` event procedure.

Step 2: Add the following lines to the end of the `btnCalculate_Click` procedure:

```
' Change the background and foreground colors
' for the total charges.
lblTotal.BackColor = Color.Blue
lblTotal.ForeColor = Color.White
```

Step 3: Add the following bold lines to the end of the `btnClear_Click` procedure, just before the line at the end that calls the `Focus` method. The existing line is shown to help you find the right location:

```
' Reset the lblTotal control's colors.
lblTotal.BackColor = SystemColors.Control
lblTotal.ForeColor = SystemColors.ControlText

' Reset the focus to the first field.
txtNights.Focus()
```

Step 4: Save the project.

Step 5: Run and test the application. When you click the *Calculate Charges* button, the value displayed in the `lblTotal` label should appear in white text on a blue background. When you click the *Clear* button, the color of the `lblTotal` label should return to normal.

3.9 More about Debugging: Locating Logic Errors

CONCEPT: Visual Studio allows you to pause a program, and then execute statements one at a time. After each statement executes, you may examine variable contents and property values.

A **logic error** is a mistake that does not prevent an application from running, but causes the application to produce incorrect results. Mathematical mistakes, copying a value to the wrong variable, or copying the wrong value to a variable are examples of logic errors. Logic errors can be difficult to find. Fortunately, Visual Studio provides you with debugging tools that make locating logic errors easier.

Visual Studio allows you to set breakpoints in your program code. A **breakpoint** is a line you select in your source code. When the application is running and it reaches a breakpoint, the application pauses and enters Break mode. While the application is paused, you may examine variable contents and the values stored in certain control properties.

Visual Studio allows you to **single-step** through an application's code once its execution has been paused by a breakpoint. This means that the application's statements execute one at a time, under your control. After each statement executes, you can examine variable and property values. This process allows you to identify the line or lines of code causing the error. In Tutorial 3-12, you single-step through an application's code.

Tutorial 3-12:
Single-stepping through an application's code at runtime

In this tutorial, you set a breakpoint in an application's code, run it in debugging mode, and single-step through the application's code to find a logic error.

Step 1: Open the *Average Race Times* project from the student sample programs folder named *Chap3\Average Race Times*.

Step 2: Run the application. The application's form appears, as shown in Figure 3-53.

Figure 3-53 *Average Race Times* form

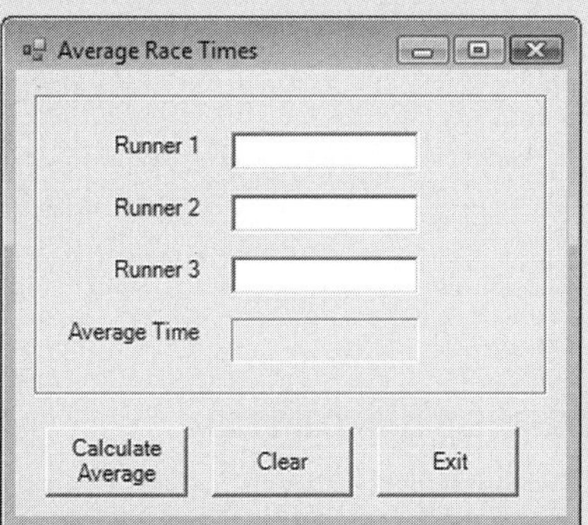

Step 3: This application allows you to enter the finishing times of three runners in a race, and then see their average time. Enter **25** as the time for all three runners.

Step 4: Click the *Calculate Average* button. The application displays the incorrect value 58.3 as the average time. (The correct value should be 25.)

Step 5: Click the *Exit* button to stop the application.

Step 6: Open the *Code* window and locate the following line of code, which appears in the `btnCalculate_Click` event procedure:

```
sngRunner1 = CSng(txtRunner1.Text)
```

This line of code is where we want to pause the execution of the application. We must make this line a breakpoint.

Step 7: Click the mouse in the left margin of the *Code* window, next to the line of code, as shown in Figure 3-54.

Figure 3-54 Click the mouse in the left margin of the *Code* window

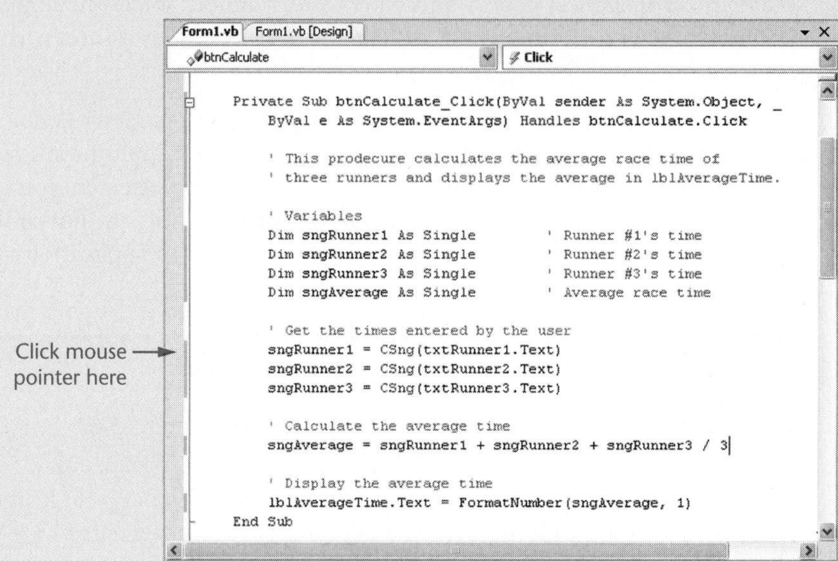
Form1.vb
Form1.vb [Design]
btnCalculate
Click
Private Sub btnCalculate_Click(ByVal sender As System.Object, _
ByVal e As System.EventArgs) Handles btnCalculate.Click
' This prodecure calculates the average race time of
' three runners and displays the average in lblAverageTime.
' Variables
Dim sngRunner1 As Single ' Runner #1's time
Dim sngRunner2 As Single ' Runner #2's time
Dim sngRunner3 As Single ' Runner #3's time
Dim sngAverage As Single ' Average race time
' Get the times entered by the user
sngRunner1 = CSng(txtRunner1.Text)
sngRunner2 = CSng(txtRunner2.Text)
sngRunner3 = CSng(txtRunner3.Text)
' Calculate the average time
sngAverage = sngRunner1 + sngRunner2 + sngRunner3 / 3
' Display the average time
lblAverageTime.Text = FormatNumber(sngAverage, 1)
End Sub
Click mouse pointer here

Step 8: Notice that a red dot appears next to the line in the left margin. This is shown in Figure 3-55.

Figure 3-55 Breakpoint code highlighted

```
Form1.vb
btnCalculate                                  Click

Private Sub btnCalculate_Click(ByVal sender As System.Object, _
    ByVal e As System.EventArgs) Handles btnCalculate.Click

    ' This prodecure calculates the average race time of
    ' three runners and displays the average in lblAverageTime.

    ' Variables
    Dim sngRunner1 As Single        ' Runner #1's time
    Dim sngRunner2 As Single        ' Runner #2's time
    Dim sngRunner3 As Single        ' Runner #3's time
    Dim sngAverage As Single        ' Average race time

    ' Get the times entered by the user
    sngRunner1 = CSng(txtRunner1.Text)
    sngRunner2 = CSng(txtRunner2.Text)
    sngRunner3 = CSng(txtRunner3.Text)

    ' Calculate the average time
    sngAverage = sngRunner1 + sngRunner2 + sngRunner3 / 3

    ' Display the average time
    lblAverageTime.Text = FormatNumber(sngAverage, 1)
End Sub
```

The dot indicates that a breakpoint has been set on this line. Another way to set a breakpoint is to move the text cursor to the line you wish to set as a breakpoint, and then press F9.

Step 9: Now that you have set the breakpoint, run the application. When the form appears, enter **25** as the time for each runner.

Step 10: Click the *Calculate Average* button. When program execution reaches the breakpoint, it goes into Break mode and the *Code* window reappears. The breakpoint line is shown with yellow highlighting and a small yellow arrow appears in the left margin, as shown in Figure 3-56.

Figure 3-56 Breakpoint during Break mode

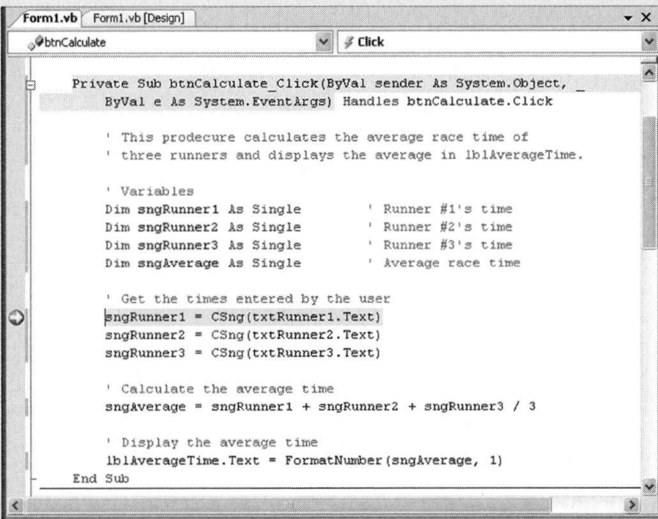
Form1.vb
Form1.vb [Design]
btnCalculate
Click
Private Sub btnCalculate_Click(ByVal sender As System.Object, _
ByVal e As System.EventArgs) Handles btnCalculate.Click
' This prodecure calculates the average race time of
' three runners and displays the average in lblAverageTime.
' Variables
Dim sngRunner1 As Single ' Runner #1's time
Dim sngRunner2 As Single ' Runner #2's time
Dim sngRunner3 As Single ' Runner #3's time
Dim sngAverage As Single ' Average race time
' Get the times entered by the user
sngRunner1 = CSng(txtRunner1.Text)
sngRunner2 = CSng(txtRunner2.Text)
sngRunner3 = CSng(txtRunner3.Text)
' Calculate the average time
sngAverage = sngRunner1 + sngRunner2 + sngRunner3 / 3
' Display the average time
lblAverageTime.Text = FormatNumber(sngAverage, 1)
End Sub

The yellow highlighting and small arrow indicate the application's current execution point. The **execution point** is the next line of code that will execute. (The line has not yet executed.)

NOTE: If the highlighting and arrow appear in a color other than yellow, the color options on your system may have been changed.

Step 11: To examine the contents of a variable or control property, hover the cursor over the variable or the property's name in the *Code* window. A small box will appear showing the variable or property's contents. For example, Figure 3-57 shows the result of hovering the mouse pointer over the expression `txtRunner1.Text` in the highlighted line. The box indicates that the property is currently set to 25.

Figure 3-57 `txtRunner1.Text` property contents revealed

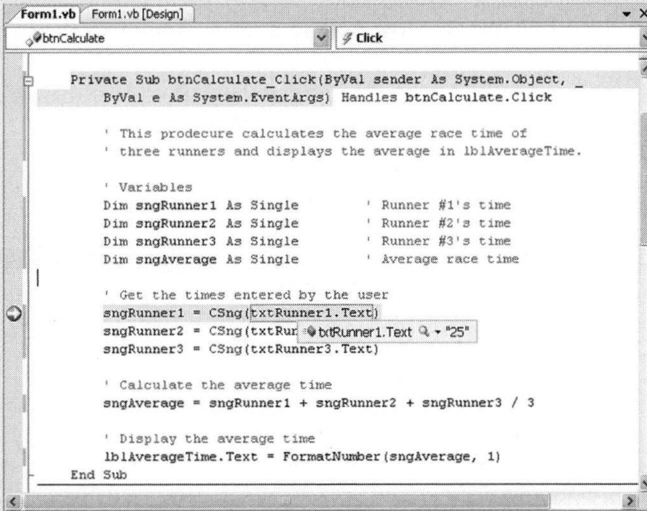
Form1.vb
Form1.vb [Design]
btnCalculate
Click
Private Sub btnCalculate_Click(ByVal sender As System.Object, _
ByVal e As System.EventArgs) Handles btnCalculate.Click
' This prodecure calculates the average race time of
' three runners and displays the average in lblAverageTime.
' Variables
Dim sngRunner1 As Single ' Runner #1's time
Dim sngRunner2 As Single ' Runner #2's time
Dim sngRunner3 As Single ' Runner #3's time
Dim sngAverage As Single ' Average race time
' Get the times entered by the user
sngRunner1 = CSng(txtRunner1.Text)
sngRunner2 = CSng(txtRur
txtRunner1.Text "25"
sngRunner3 = CSng(txtRunner3.Text)
' Calculate the average time
sngAverage = sngRunner1 + sngRunner2 + sngRunner3 / 3
' Display the average time
lblAverageTime.Text = FormatNumber(sngAverage, 1)
End Sub

Step 12: Now hover the mouse pointer over the variable name `sngRunner1`. A box appears indicating that the variable is set to 0.0. Because the highlighted statement has not yet executed, no value has been assigned to this variable.

Step 13: You may also examine the contents of variables with the *Autos*, *Locals*, and *Watch* windows. Figure 3-58 shows the *Locals* window, which normally appears near the bottom of your screen.

Figure 3-58 The *Locals* window

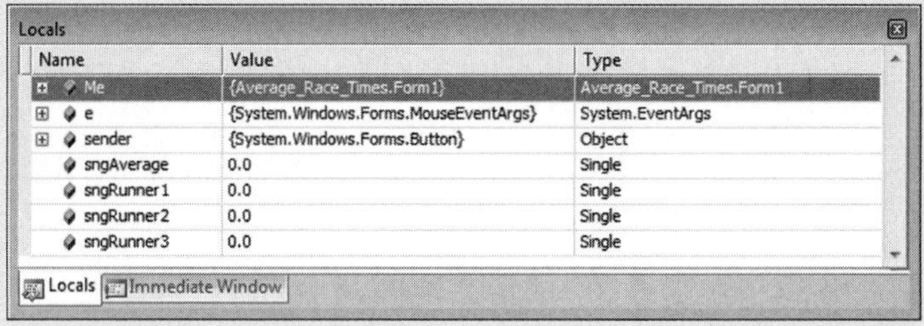

A description of each window follows:

- The ***Autos* window** (Visual Studio only) displays a list of the variables appearing in the current statement, the three statements before, and the three statements after the current statement. The current value and the data type of each variable are also displayed.
- The ***Immediate* window** allows you to type debugging commands using the keyboard. This window is generally used by advanced programmers.
- The ***Locals* window** displays a list of all the variables in the current procedure. The current value and the data type of each variable are also displayed.
- The ***Watch* window** allows you to add the names of variables you want to watch. This window displays only the variables you have added. Visual Studio lets you open multiple *Watch* windows, whereas Visual Basic Express offers only one *Watch* window.

Step 14: From the menu, select *Debug*, select *Windows*, select *Watch*, and select *Watch*. (If you're using Visual Studio, you must select one of several *Watch* windows.) A *Watch* window should appear, similar to the one shown in Figure 3-59.

Figure 3-59 *Watch 1* window displayed

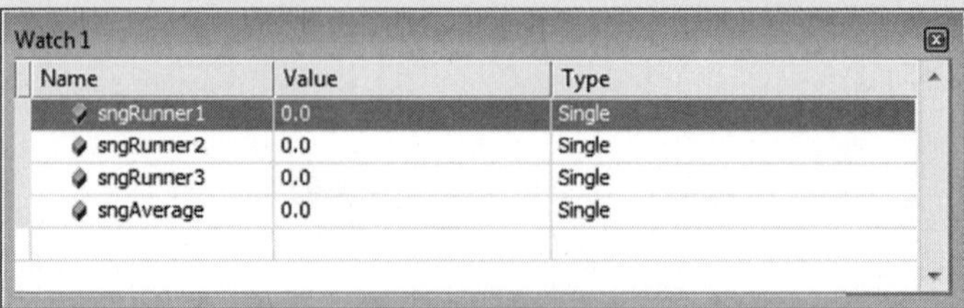

Step 15: If you do not already see the variables `sngRunner1`, `sngRunner2`, `sngRunner3`, and `sngAverage` displayed in the *Watch* window, you can add them by performing the following:

- Click the first blank line in the window.
- Type **`sngRunner1`** and press Enter.
- Type **`sngRunner2`** and press Enter.
- Type **`sngRunner3`** and press Enter.
- Type **`sngAverage`** and press Enter.

You have added the variables `sngRunner1`, `sngRunner2`, `sngRunner3`, and `sngAverage` to the *Watch* window. The variables are all equal to zero.

Step 16: Now you are ready to single-step through each statement in the event procedure. To do this, use the ***Step Into* command**. (The *Step Over* command, which is similar to *Step Into*, is covered in Chapter 6.) You activate the *Step Into* command by one of the following methods:

- Press the F8 key.
- Select *Debug* from the menu bar, and then select *Step Into* from the *Debug* menu.

NOTE: Visual Studio users: We assume your profile is set to Visual Basic Developer. If your profile is set to *Visual Studio Developer*, the *Step Into* command is executed by the F11 key instead of the F8 key.

When you activate the *Step Into* command, the highlighted statement is executed. Press the F8 key now. Look at the *Watch* window and notice that the `sngRunner1` variable is now set to 25.0. Also notice that the next line of code is now highlighted.

Step 17: Press the F8 key two more times. The variables `sngRunner1`, `sngRunner2`, and `sngRunner3` should display values of 25 in the *Watch* window.

Step 18: The following statement, which is supposed to calculate the average of the three scores, is now highlighted:

```
sngAverage = sngRunner1 + sngRunner2 + sngRunner3 / 3.0
```

After this statement executes, the average of the three numbers should display next to `sngAverage`. Press F8 to execute the statement.

Step 19: Notice that the *Watch* window now reports that `sngAverage` holds the value 58.3333321. This is not the correct value, so there must be a problem with the math statement that just executed. Can you find it? The math statement does not calculate the correct value because the division operation takes place before any of the addition operations. You must correct the statement by inserting a set of parentheses.

From the menu, select *Debug*, and then click *Stop Debugging* to halt the application. In the *Code* window, insert a set of parentheses into the math statement so it appears as follows:

```
sngAverage = (sngRunner1 + sngRunner2 + sngRunner3) / 3
```

Step 20: Next, you will clear the breakpoint so the application will not pause again when it reaches that line of code. To clear the breakpoint, use one of the following methods:

- Click the mouse on the breakpoint dot in the left margin of the *Code* window.
- Press Ctrl+Shift+F9.
- Select *Debug* from the menu bar, and then select *Delete All Breakpoints* from the *Debug* menu.

Step 21: Run the application again. Enter **25** as each runner's time, and then click the *Calculate Average* button. This time the correct average, 25.0, is displayed.

Step 22: Click the *Exit* button to stop the application.

If You Want to Know More: Debugging Commands in the Toolbar

Visual Studio provides a toolbar for debugging commands, shown in Figure 3-60.

Figure 3-60 *Debug* toolbar commands

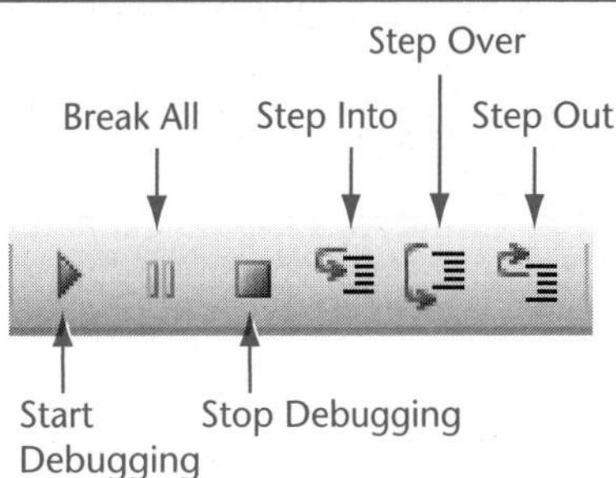

Checkpoint

3.47 What is the difference between a syntax error and a logic error?

3.48 What is a breakpoint?

3.49 What is the purpose of single-stepping through an application?

Summary

3.1 Gathering Text Input

- Words and characters typed into a TextBox control is stored in the control's Text property. The standard prefix for TextBox control names is txt.
- The & operator is used to perform string concatenation.
- The control that has the focus receives the user's keyboard input or mouse clicks. The focus is moved by calling the `Focus` method.
- The order in which controls receive the focus when the [Tab] key is pressed at runtime is called the tab order. When you place controls on a form, the tab order will be the same sequence in which you created the controls. You can modify the tab order by changing a control's TabIndex property.
- Tab order selection mode allows you to easily view the TabIndex property values of all the controls on a form.
- If you do not want a control to receive the focus when the user presses the [Tab] key, set its TabStop property to *False*.
- You assign an access key to a button by placing an ampersand (&) in its Text property. The letter that immediately follows the ampersand becomes the access key. That letter appears underlined on the button.
- Forms have two properties named AcceptButton and CancelButton. AcceptButton refers to the control that will receive a `Click` event when the user presses the [Enter] key. CancelButton refers to the control that will receive a `Click` event when the user presses the [Esc] key.

3.2 Variables and Data Types

- The assignment operator (=) is used to store a value in a variable, just as with a control property. A variable's data type determines the type of information that the variable can hold.
- Rules for naming variables are enforced by the Visual Basic compiler. Naming conventions, on the other hand, are not rigid—they are based on a standard style of programming.
- When a variable is first created in memory, Visual Basic assigns it an initial value, which depends on its data type. You may also initialize a variable, which means that you specify the variable's starting value.
- Variables of the Date (DateTime) data type can hold a date and time. You may store values in a Date variable with date literals, strings, or user input.
- Each Visual Basic data type has a method named `ToString` that returns a string representation of the variable calling the method.

3.3 Performing Calculations

- A unary operator has only one operand. An example is the negation operator (minus sign).
- A binary operator has two operands. An example is the addition operator (plus sign).
- The \ symbol identifies the integer division operator.

- The * symbol identifies the multiplication operator.
- The ^ symbol identifies the exponentiation operator.
- The `MOD` operator returns the remainder after performing integer division.
- When two operators share an operand, the operator with the highest precedence executes first. Parts of a mathematical expression may be grouped with parentheses to force some operations to be performed before others.
- A combined assignment operator combines the assignment operator with another operator.
- The `Now` function retrieves the current date and time from the computer system. The `TimeOfDay` function retrieves the current time. The `Today` function retrieves the current date.
- A variable's scope determines where a variable is visible and where it can be accessed by programming statements.
- A variable declared inside a procedure is called a local variable. This type of variable is only visible from its declaring statement to the end of the same procedure. If a variable is declared inside a class, but outside of any procedure, it is called a class-level variable. If a variable is declared outside of any class or procedure, it is called a global variable.

3.4 Mixing Different Data Types

- Implicit type conversion occurs when you assign a value of one data type to a variable of another data type. Visual Basic attempts to convert the value being assigned to the data type of the destination variable.
- A narrowing conversion occurs when a real number is assigned to one of the integer type variables. It also occurs when a larger type is assigned to a smaller type.
- A widening conversion occurs when data of a smaller type is assigned to a variable of a larger type. An example is when assigning any type of integer to a Double.
- Visual Basic attempts to convert strings to numbers, particularly when the strings contain digits. Other permitted characters are a single $, a single decimal point, a leading sign, and commas.
- The *Option Strict* statement determines whether certain implicit conversions are legal. When *Option Strict* is *On*, only widening conversions are permitted. When *Option Strict* is *Off*, both narrowing and widening conversions are permitted.
- A type conversion or type mismatch error is generated when an automatic conversion is not possible.
- An explicit type conversion is performed by one of Visual Basic's conversion functions. The conversion functions discussed in this chapter are `CDate` (convert to date), `CDbl` (convert to Double), `CDec` (convert to Decimal), `CInt` (convert to Integer), and `CStr` (convert to String).
- The `CInt` function performs a special type of rounding called bankers rounding.
- The `Val` function converts a string argument to a number.
- Visual Basic provides several type conversion functions, such as `CInt` and `CDbl`, which convert expressions to other data types.
- Tutorial 3-7 showed a simple calculator program that uses the `CInt` and `CDbl` functions.

3.5 Formatting Numbers and Dates

- Ordinarily, numeric values should be formatted when they are displayed. Formatting gives your programs a more professional appearance.
- The `ToString` method converts the contents of a variable into a string.
- You can pass a format string as an input argument to the `ToString` method. The format string can be used to configure the way a number or date is displayed.
- Number format (`n` or `N`) displays numeric values with thousands separators and a decimal point.
- Fixed-point format (`f` or `F`) displays numeric values with no thousands separator and a decimal point.
- Exponential format (`e` or `E`) displays numeric values in scientific notation. The number is normalized with a single digit to the left of the decimal point.
- Currency format (`c` or `C`) displays a leading currency symbol (such as $), digits, thousands separators, and a decimal point.
- Percent format (`p` or `P`) causes the number to be multiplied by 100 and displayed with a trailing space and % sign.
- You can use the `ToString` method to format dates and times. Several standard formats were shown in this chapter: short date, long date, short time, long time, and full date and time.

3.6 Exception Handling

- Exception handling is a structured mechanism for handling errors in Visual Basic programs.
- Exception handling begins with the `Try` keyword, followed by one or more `Catch` blocks, followed by `End Try`.
- Some types of errors are preventable by the programmer, such as dividing by zero. Other errors may be caused by user input, which is beyond the control of the programmer.
- When a program throws an exception, it generates a runtime error. An unhandled exception causes a program to terminate and display an error message.
- You can write exception handlers that catch exceptions and find ways for the program to recover. Your exception handler can also display a message to the user.
- Exception handlers can handle multiple exceptions by specifically identifying different types of exceptions with different catch blocks.

3.7 Group Boxes, Form Formatting, and the Load Event Procedure

- A GroupBox control, which is used as a container for other controls, appears as a rectangular border with an optional title. You can create the GroupBox first and then create other controls inside it. Alternatively, you can drag existing controls inside the GroupBox.
- In the *Design* window, grid lines can be used to align controls. You can select and work with multiple controls simultaneously.
- Every form has a `Load` event procedure, executed when the form loads into memory. If you need to execute code before a form is displayed, place it in the form's `Load` event handler.

3.8 Focus on Program Design and Problem Solving: Building the *Room Charge Calculator* Application

- The *Room Charge Calculator* application calculates charges for guests at an imaginary hotel. It combines many of the techniques introduced in this chapter, such as type conversion functions, formatting numbers, and formatting dates.
- Visual Basic provides numerous values that represent colors. These values may be used in code to change a control's foreground and background colors.

3.9 More about Debugging: Locating Logic Errors

- A logic error is a programming mistake that does not prevent an application from compiling, but causes the application to produce incorrect results.
- A runtime error occurs during a program's execution—it halts the program unexpectedly.
- A breakpoint is a line of code that causes a running application to pause execution and enter Break mode. While the application is paused, you may perform debugging operations such as examining variable contents and the values stored in control properties.
- Single-stepping is the debugging technique of executing an application's programming statements one at a time. After each statement executes, you can examine variable and property contents.

Key Terms

accept button
access key
Autos window
binary operator
breakpoint
cancel button
code outlining
combined assignment operators
compound operators
connector symbol
exception
execution point
exception handler
expression
focus
`Focus` method
function
GroupBox control
Immediate window
implicit type conversion
initialization
line-continuation character
`Load` event procedure
Locals window
logic error
mathematical expression
mnemonic
named constant
naming conventions
narrowing conversion
Option Strict
precedence
scope (of a variable)
single-step
Step Into command
string concatenation
tab order
tab order selection mode
TabIndex property
TabStop property
text box
TextBox control
`ToString` method
`Try-Catch` block
type conversion error
type mismatch error
variable
variable declaration
unary operator
unhandled exception
Watch window
widening conversion

Review Questions and Exercises

Fill-in-the-Blank

1. The ______________________ control allows you to capture input the user has typed on the keyboard.
2. ______________________ is the standard prefix for TextBox control names.
3. ______________________ means that one string is appended to another.
4. The ______________________ character allows you to break a long statement into two or more lines of code.
5. The ______________________ character is actually two characters: a space followed by an underscore.
6. The control that has the ______________________ is the one that receives the user's keyboard input or mouse clicks.
7. The order in which controls receive the focus is called the ______________________.
8. You can modify the tab order by changing a control's ______________________ property.
9. If you do not want a control to receive the focus when the user presses the Tab key, set its ______________________ property to *False*.
10. An access key is a key that you press in combination with the ______________________ key to access a control such as a button quickly.
11. You define a button's access key through its ______________________ property.
12. A(n) ______________________ is a storage location in the computer's memory, used for holding information while the program is running.
13. A(n) ______________________ is a statement that causes Visual Basic to create a variable in memory.
14. A variable's ______________________ determines the type of information the variable can hold.
15. A(n) ______________________ variable is declared inside a procedure.
16. A(n) ______________________ error is generated anytime a nonnumeric value that cannot be automatically converted to a numeric value is assigned to a numeric variable or property.
17. A(n) ______________________ is a specialized routine that performs a specific operation, and then returns a value.
18. The ______________________ function converts an expression to an integer.
19. The ______________________ format string, when passed to the `ToString` method, produces a number in Currency format.
20. A(n) ______________________ is information that is being passed to a function.
21. When two operators share an operand, the operator with the highest ______________________ executes first.
22. A(n) ______________________ is like a variable whose content is read-only; it cannot be changed while the program is running.
23. A(n) ______________________ appears as a rectangular border with an optional title.

24. A form's ______________________ procedure executes each time a form loads into memory.

25. A(n) ______________________ is a line of code that causes a running application to pause execution and enter Break mode.

True or False

Indicate whether the following statements are true or false.

1. T F: The TextBox control's Text property holds the text entered by the user into the TextBox control at runtime.
2. T F: You can access a TextBox control's Text property in code.
3. T F: The string concatenation operator automatically inserts a space between the joined strings.
4. T F: You cannot break up a word with the line-continuation character.
5. T F: You can put a comment at the end of a line, after the line-continuation character.
6. T F: Only controls capable of receiving input, such as TextBox controls and buttons, may have the focus.
7. T F: You can cause a control to be skipped in the tab order by setting its TabPosition property to *False*.
8. T F: An error will occur if you assign a negative value to the TabIndex property in code.
9. T F: A control whose Visible property is set to *False* still receives the focus.
10. T F: GroupBox and Label controls have a TabIndex property, but they are skipped in the tab order.
11. T F: When you assign an access key to a button, the user can trigger a `Click` event by typing Alt+ the access key character.
12. T F: A local variable may be accessed by any other procedure in the same Form file.
13. T F: When a string variable is created in memory, Visual Basic assigns it the initial value 0.
14. T F: A variable's scope is the time during which the variable exists in memory.
15. T F: A variable declared inside a procedure is only visible to statements inside the same procedure.
16. T F: The `CDbl` function converts a number to a string.
17. T F: If the `CInt` function cannot convert its argument, it causes a runtime error.
18. T F: The multiplication operator has higher precedence than the addition operator.
19. T F: A named constant's value can be changed by a programming statement, while the program is running.
20. T F: The statement `lblMessage.BackColor = Color.Green` will set `lblMessage` control's background color to green.
21. T F: You can select multiple controls simultaneously with the mouse.
22. T F: You can change the same property for multiple controls simultaneously.

23. T F: To group controls in a group box, draw the controls first, then draw the group box around them.

24. T F: While single-stepping through an application's code in Break mode, the highlighted execution point is the line of code that has already executed.

Multiple Choice

1. When the user types input into a TextBox control, in which property is it stored?
   a. Input
   b. Text
   c. Value
   d. Keyboard

2. Which character is the string concatenation operator?
   a. `&`
   b. `*`
   c. `%`
   d. `@`

3. In code, you move the focus to a control with which method?
   a. `MoveFocus`
   b. `SetFocus`
   c. `ResetFocus`
   d. `Focus`

4. Which form property allows you to specify a button to be clicked when the user presses the Enter key?
   a. DefaultButton
   b. AcceptButton
   c. CancelButton
   d. EnterButton

5. Which form property allows you to specify a button that is to be clicked when the user presses the Esc key?
   a. DefaultButton
   b. AcceptButton
   c. CancelButton
   d. EnterButton

6. You can modify a control's position in the tab order by changing which property?
   a. TabIndex
   b. TabOrder
   c. TabPosition
   d. TabStop

7. You assign an access key to a button through which property?
   a. AccessKey
   b. AccessButton
   c. Mnemonic
   d. Text

8. A group box's title is stored in which property?
   a. Title
   b. Caption
   c. Text
   d. Heading

9. You declare a named constant with which keyword?
   a. `Constant`
   b. `Const`
   c. `NamedConstant`
   d. `Dim`

10. Which of the following is the part of a program in which a variable is visible and may be accessed by programming statement?
    a. segment
    b. lifetime
    c. scope
    d. module

11. If a variable named `dblTest` contains the value 1.23456, then which of the following values will be returned by the expression `dblTest.ToString("N3")`?
    a. 1.23456
    b. 1.235
    c. 1.234
    d. +1.234

12. If the following code executes, which value is assigned to `strA`?

```
Dim dblTest As Double = 0.25
Dim strA = dblTest.ToString("p")
```

    a. `"0.25"`
    b. `"2.50"`
    c. `"25.00"`
    d. `"0.25"`

Short Answer

1. Describe the difference between the Label control's Text property and the TextBox control's Text property.
2. How do you clear the contents of a text box?
3. What is the focus when referring to a running application?
4. Write a statement that sets the focus to the `txtPassword` control.
5. How does Visual Basic automatically assign the tab order to controls?
6. How does a control's TabIndex property affect the tab order?
7. How do you assign an access key to a button?
8. How does assigning an access key to a button change the button's appearance?
9. What is the difference between the Single and Integer data types?
10. Create variable names that would be appropriate for holding each of the following information items:
    a. The number of backpacks sold this week
    b. The number of pounds of dog food in storage
    c. Today's date
    d. An item's wholesale price
    e. A customer's name
    f. The distance between two galaxies, in kilometers
    g. The number of the month (1 = January, 2 = February, and so on)

11. Why should you always make sure that a string variable is initialized or assigned a value before it is used in an operation?
12. When is a local variable destroyed?
13. How would the following strings be converted by the `CDec` function?
    a. `"22.9000"`
    b. `"1xfc47uvy"`
    c. `"$19.99"`
    d. `"0.05%"`
    e. `String.Empty`
14. Briefly describe how the `CDec` function converts a string argument to a number.
15. Complete the following table by providing the value of each mathematical expression:

Expression	Value
5 + 2 * 8	____________
20 / 5 – 2	____________
4 + 10 * 3 – 2	____________
(4 + 10) * 3 – 2	____________

16. Assuming that the variable `dblTest` contains the value 67521.584, complete the following table, showing the value returned by each function call:

Function Call	Return Value
`dblTest.ToString("d2")`	____________
`dblTest.ToString("c2")`	____________
`dblTest.ToString("e1")`	____________
`dblTest.ToString("f2")`	____________

17. Describe one way to select multiple controls in Design mode.
18. Describe three ways to set a breakpoint in an application's code.

What Do You Think?

1. Why doesn't Visual Basic automatically insert a space between strings concatenated with the `&` operator?
2. Why would you want to use the line-continuation character to cause a statement to span multiple lines?
3. Why are Label controls not capable of receiving the focus?
4. Why should the tab order of controls in your application be logical?
5. Why assign access keys to buttons?
6. What is the significance of showing an underlined character on a button?
7. Generally speaking, which button should be set as a form's default button?
8. Why can't you perform arithmetic operations on a string, such as `"28.9"`?
9. Suppose a number is used in calculations throughout a program and must be changed every few months. What benefit is there to using a named constant to represent the number?
10. How can you get your application to execute a group of statements each time a form is loaded into memory?
11. How can you place an existing control in a group box?

12. Visual Basic automatically reports syntax errors. Why doesn't it automatically report logic errors?

Find the Error

1. Load the *Chap3\ Error1\ Error1* project from the student sample programs folder. Run the application. Type **2**, **4**, and **6** into the three TextBox controls, and then click the *Show Sum* button. The application reports the sum as 246. Fix the application so it correctly displays the sum of the numbers.
2. Load the *Chap3\ Error2\ Error2* project from the student sample programs folder. The application has an error. Find the error and fix it.
3. Load the *Chap3\ Error3\ Error3* project from the student sample programs folder. The `btnCalculate_Click` procedure contains an error. Find the error and fix it.

Algorithm Workbench

1. Create a flowchart that shows the necessary steps for making the cookies in the following recipe:

   Ingredients:

   1/2 cup butter
   1 egg
   1 cup sifted all-purpose flour
   1/2 cup brown sugar
   1/2 cup sugar
   1/2 teaspoon vanilla
   1/2 teaspoon salt
   1/2 teaspoon baking soda
   1/2 cup chopped nuts
   1/2 cup semisweet chocolate chips

   Steps:

   Preheat oven to 375°.
   Cream the butter.
   Add the sugar and the brown sugar to the butter and beat until creamy.
   Beat the egg and vanilla into the mixture.
   Sift and stir the flour, salt, and baking soda into the mixture.
   Stir the nuts and chocolate chips into the mixture.
   Shape the mixture into 1/2-inch balls.
   Place the balls about one inch apart on a greased cookie sheet.
   Bake for 10 minutes.

2. A hot dog, still in its package, should be heated for 40 seconds in a microwave. Draw a flowchart showing the necessary steps to cook the hot dog.
3. The following pseudocode algorithm for the event procedure `btnCalcArea_Click` has an error. The event procedure is supposed to calculate the area of a room's floor. The area is calculated as the room's width (entered by the user into `txtWidth`), multiplied by the room's length (entered by the user into in `txtLength`). The result is displayed with the label `lblArea`. Find the error and correct the algorithm.
   a. Multiply the `intWidth` variable by the `intLength` variable and store the result in the `intArea` variable.
   b. Copy the value in `txtWidth.Text` into the `intWidth` variable.
   c. Copy the value in `txtLength.Text` into the `intLength` variable.
   d. Copy the value in the `intArea` variable into `lblArea.Text`.
4. The following steps should be followed in the event procedure `btnCalcAvailCredit_Click`, which calculates a customer's available credit. Construct a flowchart that shows these steps.

a. Copy the value in the TextBox control `txtMaxCredit` into the variable `decMaxCredit`.
b. Copy the value in the TextBox control `txtUsedCredit` into the variable `decUsedCredit`.
c. Subtract the value in `decUsedCredit` from `decMaxCredit`. Store the result in `decAvailableCredit`
d. Copy the value in `decAvailableCredit` into the label `lblAvailableCredit`.

5. Convert the flowchart you constructed in Exercise 4 into Visual Basic code.
6. Design a flowchart or pseudocode for the event procedure `btnCalcSale_Click`, which calculates the total of a retail sale. Assume the program uses `txtRetailPrice`, a TextBox control that holds the retail price of the item being purchased, and `decTAX_RATE`, a constant that holds the sales tax rate. The event procedure uses the items above to calculate the sales tax for the purchase and the total of the sale. Display the total of the sale in a label named `lblTotal`.
7. Convert the flowchart or pseudocode you constructed in Exercise 6 into Visual Basic code.

Programming Challenges

VideoNote
The Miles per Gallon Calculator Problem

1. **Miles per Gallon Calculator**

Create an application that calculates a car's gas mileage. The formula for calculating the miles that a car can travel per gallon of gas is:

$$MPG = \frac{miles}{gallons}$$

In the formula *MPG* is miles-per-gallon, *miles* is the number of miles that can be driven on a full tank of gas, and *gallons* is the number of gallons that the tank holds.

The application's form should have TextBox controls that let the user enter the number of gallons of gas the tank holds, and the number of miles the car can be driven on a full tank. When the *Calculate MPG* button is clicked, the application should display the number of miles that the car can be driven per gallon of gas. The form should also have a *Clear* button that clears the input and results, and an *Exit* button that ends the application. The application's form should appear as shown in Figure 3-61.

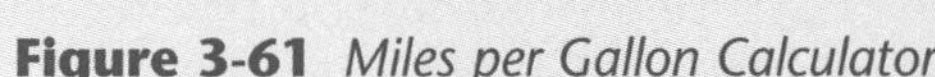

Figure 3-61 *Miles per Gallon Calculator*

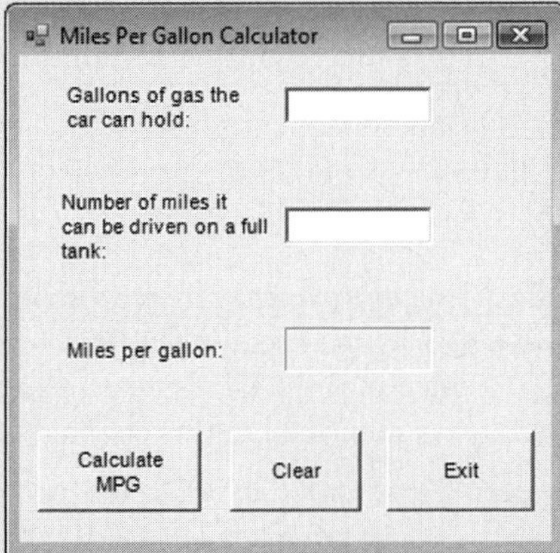

Use the following set of test data to determine if the application is calculating properly:

Gallons	Miles	Miles per Gallon
10	375	37.50
12	289	24.08
15	190	12.67

2. **Stadium Seating**

   There are three seating categories at an athletic stadium. For a baseball game, Class A seats cost $15 each, Class B seats cost $12 each, and Class C seats cost $9 each. Create an application that allows the user to enter the number of tickets sold for each class. The application should be able to display the amount of income generated from each class of ticket sales and the total revenue generated. The application's form should resemble the one shown in Figure 3-62.

Figure 3-62 *Stadium Seating* form

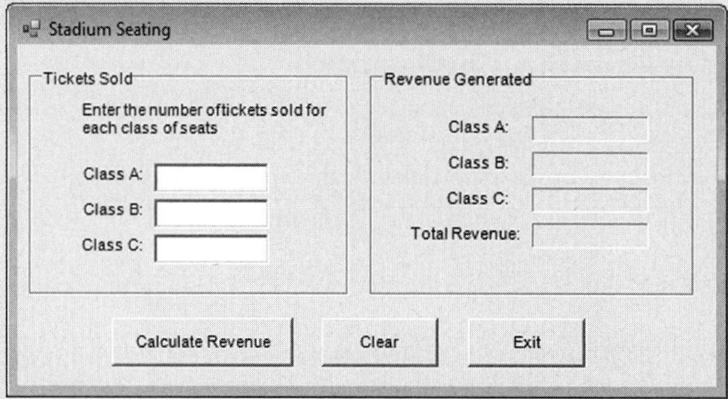

Use the following test data to determine if the application is calculating properly:

Ticket Sales	Revenue
Class A: 320	Class A: $4,800.00
Class B: 570	Class B: $6,840.00
Class C: 890	Class C: $8,010.00
	Total Revenue: $19,650.00
Class A: 500	Class A: $7,500.00
Class B: 750	Class B: $9,000.00
Class C: 1,200	Class C: $10,800.00
	Total Revenue: $27,300.00
Class A: 100	Class A: $1,500.00
Class B: 300	Class B: $3,600.00
Class C: 500	Class C: $4,500.00
	Total Revenue: $9,600.00

3. **Test Score Average**

   Create an application that allows the user to enter five test scores. It should be able to calculate and display the average score. The application's form should resemble the one shown in Figure 3-63. Notice that the labels next to each TextBox control have been assigned an access key. As described in this chapter, use a label to assign an access key indirectly to a TextBox control.

Figure 3-63 *Test Score Average* form

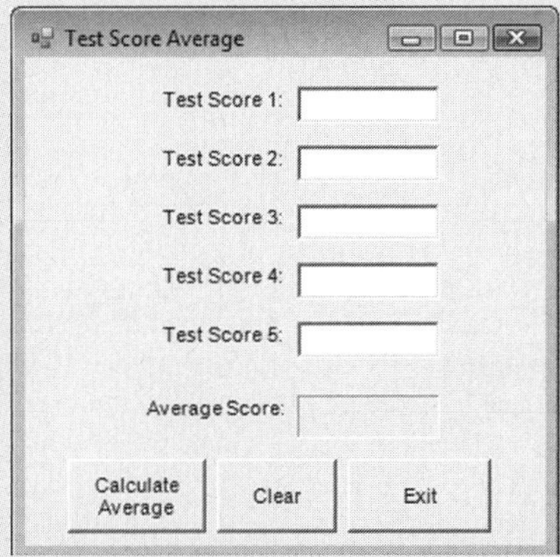

Use the following test data to determine if the application is calculating properly:

Test Scores	Averages
Test Score 1: 85 Test Score 2: 90 Test Score 3: 78 Test Score 4: 88 Test Score 5: 92	Average: 86.60
Test Score 1: 90 Test Score 2: 80 Test Score 3: 70 Test Score 4: 60 Test Score 5: 50	Average: 70.00
Test Score 1: 100 Test Score 2: 92 Test Score 3: 56 Test Score 4: 89 Test Score 5: 74	Average: 82.2

4. Theater Revenue

A movie theater only keeps a percentage of the revenue earned from ticket sales. The remainder goes to the movie company. Create an application that calculates and displays the following figures for one night's box office business at a theater:

a. *Gross revenue for adult tickets sold.* This is the amount of money taken in for all adult tickets sold.

b. *Net revenue for adult tickets sold.* This is the amount of money from adult ticket sales left over after the payment to the movie company has been deducted.

c. *Gross revenue for child tickets sold.* This is the amount of money taken in for all child tickets sold.

d. *Net revenue for child tickets sold.* This is the amount of money from child ticket sales left over after the payment to the movie company has been deducted.

e. *Total gross revenue.* This is the sum of gross revenue for adult and child tickets sold.

f. *Total net revenue.* This is the sum of net revenue for adult and child tickets sold.

The application's form should resemble the one shown in Figure 3-64.

Figure 3-64 *Theater Revenue* form

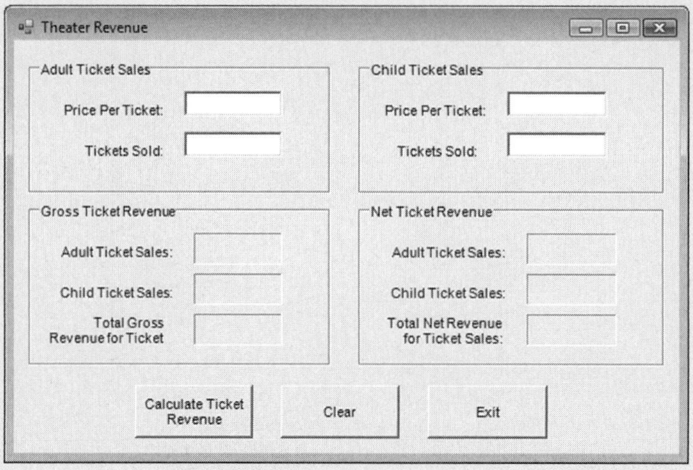

Assume the theater keeps 20% of its box office receipts. Use a named constant in your code to represent this percentage. Use the following test data to determine if the application is calculating properly:

Ticket Sales		**Revenue**	
Price per Adult Ticket:	$6.00	Gross Adult Ticket Sales:	$720.00
Adult Tickets Sold:	120	Gross Child Ticket Sales:	$288.00
Price per Child Ticket:	$4.00	Total Gross Revenue:	$1,008.00
Ticket Sales (*continued*)		**Revenue** (*continued*)	
Child Tickets Sold:	72	Net Adult Ticket Sales:	$144.00
		Net Child Ticket Sales:	$57.60
		Total Net Revenue:	$201.60

Design Your Own Forms

5. **How Many Widgets?**

The Yukon Widget Company manufactures widgets that weigh 9.2 pounds each. Create an application that calculates how many widgets are stacked on a pallet, based on the total weight of the pallet. The user should be able to enter how much the pallet weighs alone and how much it weighs with the widgets stacked on it. The user should click a button to calculate and display the number of widgets stacked on the pallet. Use the following test data to determine if the application is calculating properly:

Pallet	Pallet and Widgets	Number of Widgets
100	5,620	600
75	1,915	200
200	9,400	1,000

6. **Celsius to Fahrenheit**

Create an application that converts Celsius to Fahrenheit. The formula is $F = 1.8 * C + 32$ where F is the Fahrenheit temperature and C is the Celsius temperature. Use the following test data to determine if the application is calculating properly:

Celsius	Fahrenheit
100	212
0	32
56	132.8

7. **Currency**

Create an application that converts U.S. dollar amounts to pounds, euros, and yen. The following conversion factors are not accurate, but you can use them in your application:

1 dollar = 0.68 pound
1 dollar = 0.83 euro
1 dollar = 108.36 yen

In your code, declare named constants to represent the conversion factors for the different types of currency. For example, you might declare the conversion factor for yen as follows:

```
Const dblYEN_FACTOR As Double = 108.36
```

Use the named constants in the mathematical conversion statements. Use the following test data to determine whether the application is calculating properly:

Dollars	**Conversion Values**	
$100.00	Pounds:	68
	Euros:	83
	Yen:	10,836
$ 25.00	Pounds:	17
	Euros:	20.75
	Yen:	2,709
$ 1.00	Pounds:	0.68
	Euros:	0.83
	Yen:	108.36

8. **Monthly Sales Tax**

A retail company must file a monthly sales tax report listing the total sales for the month, and the amount of state and county sales tax collected. The state sales tax rate is 4% and the county sales tax rate is 2%. Create an application that allows the user to enter the total sales for the month. From this figure, the application should calculate and display the following:

a. The amount of county sales tax
b. The amount of state sales tax
c. The total sales tax (county plus state)

In the application's code, represent the county tax rate (0.02) and the state tax rate (0.04) as named constants. Use the named constants in the mathematical statements. Use the following test data to determine whether the application is calculating properly:

Total Sales	**Tax Amounts**	
9,500	County sales tax:	$190.00
	State sales tax:	$380.00
	Total sales tax:	$570.00
5,000	County sales tax:	$100.00
	State sales tax:	$200.00
	Total sales tax:	$300.00
15,000	County sales tax:	$300.00
	State sales tax:	$600.00
	Total sales tax:	$900.00

9. **Property Tax**

A county collects property taxes on the assessment value of property, which is 60% of the property's actual value. If an acre of land is valued at $10,000, its assessment value is $6,000. The property tax is then $0.64 for each $100 of the assessment value. The tax for the acre assessed at $6,000 will be $38.40. Create an application that displays the assessment value and property tax when a user enters the actual value of a property. Use the following test data to determine if the application is calculating properly:

Actual Property Value	Assessment and Tax	
100,000	Assessment value:	$ 60,000.00
	Property tax:	384.00
75,000	Assessment value:	45,000.00
	Property tax:	288.00
250,000	Assessment value:	150,000.00
	Property tax:	960.00

10. **Pizza Pi**

Joe's Pizza Palace needs an application to calculate the number of slices a pizza of any size can be divided into. The application should do the following:

a. Allow the user to enter the diameter of the pizza, in inches.
b. Calculate the number of slices that can be cut from a pizza that size.
c. Display a message that indicates the number of slices.

To calculate the number of slices that can be cut from the pizza, you must know the following facts:

a. Each slice should have an area of 14.125 inches.
b. To calculate the number of slices, divide the area of the pizza by 14.125.

The area of the pizza is calculated with the following formula:

$$Area = \pi r^2$$

NOTE: π is the Greek letter pi. 3.14159 can be used as its value. The variable r is the radius of the pizza. Divide the diameter by 2 to get the radius.

Use the following test data to determine if the application is calculating properly:

Diameter of Pizza	Number of Slices
22 inches	27
15 inches	13
12 inches	8

11. **Distance Traveled**

Assuming there are no accidents or delays, the distance that a car travels down the interstate can be calculated with the following formula:

$$Distance = Speed \times Time$$

Create a VB application that allows the user to enter a car's speed in miles-per-hour. When a button is clicked, the application should display the following:

- The distance the car will travel in 5 hours
- The distance the car will travel in 8 hours
- The distance the car will travel in 12 hours

12. **Tip, Tax, and Total**

Create a VB application that lets the user enter the food charge for a meal at a restaurant. When a button is clicked, it should calculate and display the amount of a 15 percent tip, 7 percent sales tax, and the total of all three amounts.

13. Body Mass Index

Create a VB application that lets the user enter his or her weight (in pounds) and height (in inches). The application should calculate the user's body mass index (BMI). The BMI is often used to determine whether a person with a sedentary lifestyle is overweight or underweight for their height. A person's BMI is calculated with the following formula:

$$BMI = weight \times 703 \,/\, height^2$$

14. How Much Insurance?

Many financial experts advise that property owners should insure their homes or buildings for at least 80 percent of the amount it would cost to replace the structure. Create a VB application that lets the user enter the replacement cost of a building and then displays the minimum amount of insurance he or she should buy for the property.

15. How Many Calories?

A bag of cookies holds 40 cookies. The calorie information on the bag claims that there are 10 "servings" in the bag and that a serving equals 300 calories. Create a VB application that lets the user enter the number of cookies they actually ate and then reports the number of total calories consumed.

16. Automobile Costs

Create a VB application that lets the user enter the monthly costs for the following expenses incurred from operating his or her automobile: loan payment, insurance, gas, oil, tires, and maintenance. The program should then display the total monthly cost of these expenses and the total annual cost of these expenses.

CHAPTER 4

Making Decisions and Working with Strings

TOPICS

In this chapter, you will learn how programs use `If...Then`, `If...Then...Else`, and `If...Then...ElseIf` statements to make decisions. You will learn how to compare values using relational operators and build complex comparisons using logical operators. You will be introduced to the `Select Case` statement, radio buttons (which allow the user to select one choice from many possible choices), and check boxes (which allow the user to make on/off or yes/no types of selections). You will learn more about message boxes, which display messages to the user, class-level variables, and the process of input validation.

4.1 The Decision Structure

CONCEPT: The decision structure allows a program's logic to have more than one path of execution.

In the programs you have written so far, statements execute sequentially. This means that statements are executed one after the other, in the order in which they appear.

You might think of sequentially executed statements as the steps you take as you walk down a road. To complete the journey, you must start at the beginning and take each step, one after the other, until you reach your destination. This is illustrated in Figure 4-1.

Figure 4-1 Sequence instruction

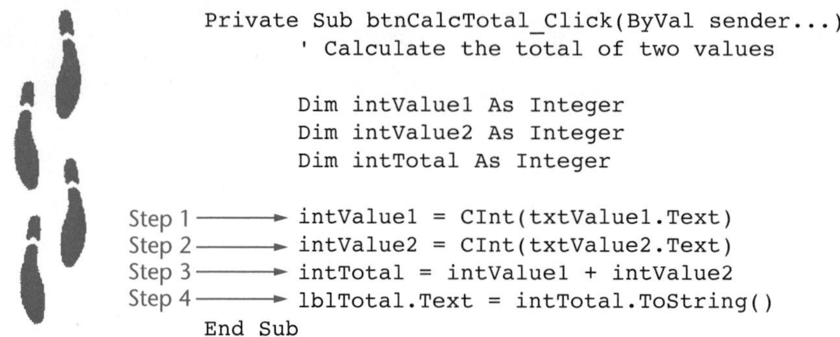

Private Sub btnCalcTotal_Click(ByVal sender...)
' Calculate the total of two values
Dim intValue1 As Integer
Dim intValue2 As Integer
Dim intTotal As Integer
Step 1
intValue1 = CInt(txtValue1.Text)
Step 2
intValue2 = CInt(txtValue2.Text)
Step 3
intTotal = intValue1 + intValue2
Step 4
lblTotal.Text = intTotal.ToString()
End Sub

This type of code is called a **sequence structure** because the statements are executed in sequence, without branching in another direction. Programs often need more than one path of execution because many algorithms require a program to execute some statements only under certain circumstances. This can be accomplished with a **decision structure**.

Decision Structures in Flowcharts and Pseudocode

In a decision structure's simplest form, an action is taken only when a condition, also known as a **Boolean expression**, equals *True*. If the condition equals *False*, the action is not performed. Figure 4-2 shows a flowchart segment for a decision structure. The diamond symbol represents a yes/no question, or a true/false condition. If the answer to the question is *yes* (or if the condition is true), the program flow follows one path. If the answer to the question is *no* (or the condition is false), the program flow follows another path.

In the flowchart, the action *Wear a coat* is performed only when it is cold outside. If it is not cold outside, the action is skipped. The action is **conditionally executed** because it is only performed when a certain condition (*cold outside*) exists. Figure 4-3 shows a more elaborate flowchart, where three actions are taken, only when it is cold outside.

Decision structures can also be expressed as pseudocode. For example, the decision structure shown in Figure 4-2 can be expressed as

If it is cold outside Then
    Wear a coat.
End If

The *End If* statement marks the end of the decision structure in pseudocode. The statements appearing between *If...Then* and *End If* are executed only when the condition that is being tested is true. In our example, "it is cold outside" is the condition. The decision structure shown in Figure 4-3, which conditionally executes three actions, can be expressed as

If it is cold outside Then
    Wear a coat.
    Wear a toboggan.
    Wear gloves.
End If

Figure 4-2 Simple decision structure flowchart

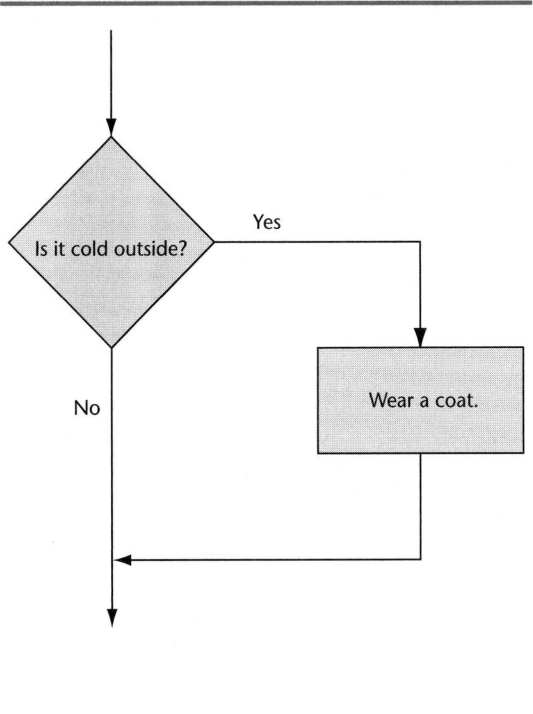

Figure 4-3 Three-action decision structure flowchart

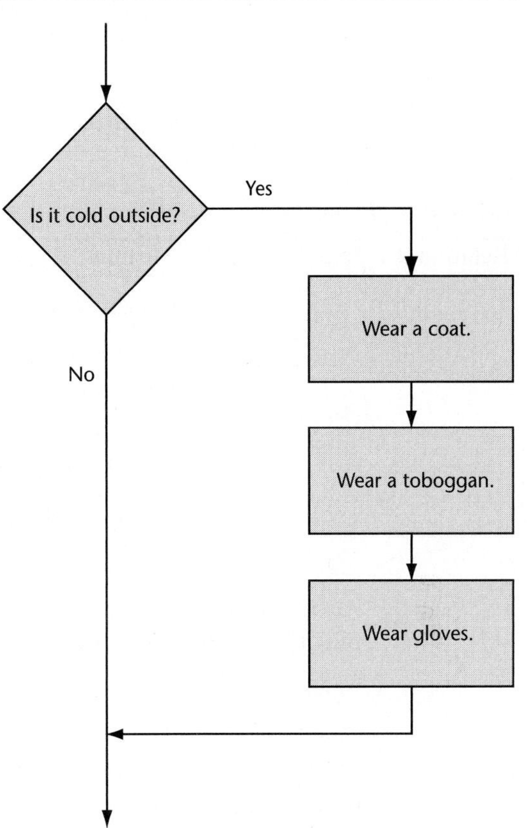

TIP: A condition is often referred to by programmers as a Boolean expression. The word "Boolean" is taken from the mathematician George Boole, who invented a system of mathematics known as Boolean algebra.

4.2 The `If...Then` Statement

CONCEPT: The `If...Then` statement causes other statements to execute only under a certain condition.

VideoNote
The `If...Then` Statement

One way to code a decision structure in Visual Basic is with the `If...Then` statement. Here is the general form of the **`If...Then`** statement.

```
If condition Then
  statement
  (more statements may follow)
End If
```

The `If...Then` statement is really very simple: if the *condition* is true, the statement or statements that appear between the `If...Then` and the `End If` are executed. Otherwise, the statements are skipped.

Using Relational Operators to Form Conditions

Typically, the condition tested by an `If...Then` statement is formed with a relational operator. A **relational operator** determines whether a specific relationship exists between two values. For example, the greater than operator (>) determines whether one value is greater than another. The equal to operator (=) determines whether two values are equal. Table 4-1 lists the Visual Basic relational operators.

Table 4-1 Visual Basic relational operators

Relational Operator	Meaning
>	Greater than
<	Less than
=	Equal to
<>	Not equal to
>=	Greater than or equal to
<=	Less than or equal to

All relational operators are binary, which means they use two operands. Here is an example of an expression using the greater than operator:

length > *width*

This expression is called a relational expression. A **relational expression** consists of a relational operator and its operands. This one is used to determine whether *length* is greater than *width*. The following expression determines whether *length* is less than *width*:

length < *width*

Table 4-2 shows examples of several relational expressions that compare the variables *x* and *y*.

TIP: A relational expression is a specific type of Boolean expression.

Table 4-2 Relational expressions

Relational Expression	Meaning
x > *y*	Is *x* greater than *y*?
x < *y*	Is *x* less than *y*?
x >= *y*	Is *x* greater than or equal to *y*?
x <= *y*	Is *x* less than or equal to *y*?
x = *y*	Is *x* equal to *y*?
x <> *y*	Is *x* not equal to *y*?

Relational expressions can only be evaluated as true or false. If *x* is greater than *y*, the expression *x* > *y* is true, while the expression *x* < *y* is false.

The = operator, when used in a relational expression, determines whether the operand on its left is equal to the operand on its right. If both operands have the same value, the expression is true. Assuming that *a* is 4, the expression *a* = 4 is true and the expression *a* = 2 is false.

There are two operators that can test more than one relationship at the same time. The >= operator determines whether the operand on its left is greater than or equal to the operand on the right. Assuming that a is 4, *b* is 6, and *c* is 4, the expressions *b* >= a and *a* >= *c* are true, and *a* >= 5 is false. When using this operator, the > symbol must precede the = symbol, with no space between them.

The <= operator determines whether the left operand is less than or equal to the right operand. Once again, assuming that *a* is 4, *b* is 6, and *c* is 4, both *a* <= *c* and *b* <= 10 are true, but *b* <= *a* is false. When using this operator, the < symbol must precede the = symbol, with no space between them.

The <> operator is the *not equal* operator. It determines whether the operand on its left is not equal to the operand on its right, which is the opposite of the = operator. As before, assuming *a* is 4, *b* is 6, and *c* is 4, both *a* <> *b* and *b* <> *c* are true because a is not equal to *b* and *b* is not equal to *c*. However, *a* <> *c* is false because *a* is equal to *c*. Values compared by a relational expression need not be exactly the same type. Suppose we compare a variable of type Single to an integer constant, as in the following:

```
sngTemperature > 40
```

In this example, the integer 40 is temporarily converted to a Single so the comparison can take place. You do not have to worry about doing this conversion. It is carried out automatically by the Visual Basic compiler. Similarly, we might want to compare a Double to a Single, as in the following:

```
dblTemperature < sngBoilingPoint
```

The value of `sngBoilingPoint` is automatically converted to type Double so the values can be compared.

Putting It All Together

The following `If...Then` statement uses the > operator to determine whether `decSales` is greater than 50000. If that condition is true, the Boolean variable `blnGetsBonus` is set to *True*.

```
If decSales > 50000 Then
  blnGetsBonus = True
End If
```

The following example conditionally executes multiple statements.

```
If decSales > 50000 Then
  blnGetsBonus = True
  decCommissionRate = 0.12
  intDaysOff = intDaysOff + 1
End If
```

Here are some specific rules to remember about the `If...Then` statement:

- The words `If` and `Then` must appear on the same line.
- Nothing other than a comment can appear after the `Then` keyword, on the same line.
- The `End If` statement must be on a line by itself. Only a comment may follow it on the same line.

Tutorial 4-1 examines an application that uses the `If...Then` statement.

Tutorial 4-1:
Examining an application that uses the `If...Then` statement

Step 1: Open the *Test Score Average 1* project from the student sample programs folder named *Chap4\Test Score Average 1*.

Step 2: Run the application. The form appears, as shown in Figure 4-4.

Step 3: Enter the following test scores in the three text boxes: **`80`**, **`90`**, **`75`**.

Step 4: Click the *Calculate Average* button. The average test score is displayed.

Step 5: Click the *Clear* button, and then enter the following test scores in the three text boxes: **`100`**, **`97`**, **`99`**.

Step 6: Click the *Calculate Average* button. This time, in addition to the average test score being displayed, a congratulatory message appears. The form appears, as shown in Figure 4-5.

Figure 4-4 *Test Score Average* form

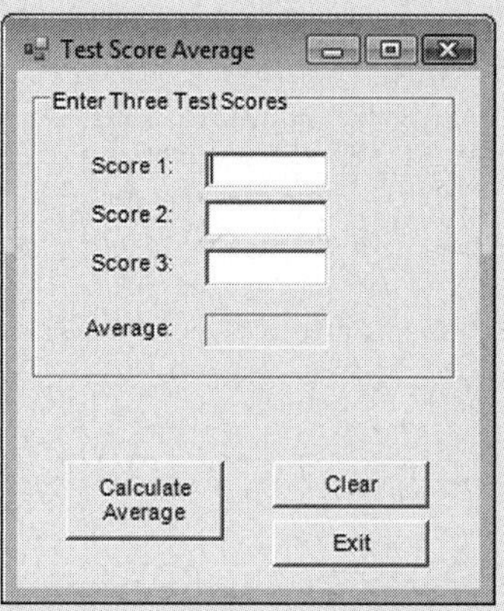

Figure 4-5 Average and message displayed

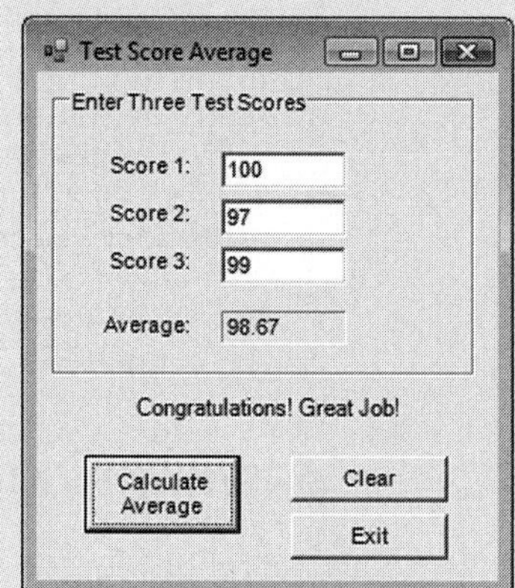

Step 7: Click the *Exit* button to terminate the application.

Step 8: Open the *Code* window and find the `btnCalculate_Click` event procedure. The code is as follows:

```
Private Sub btnCalculate_Click(ByVal eventSender As _
    System.Object, ByVal eventArgs As _
    System.EventArgs) _
    Handles btnCalculate.Click

  ' This procedure calculates and displays the
  ' average test score. If the score is high, it
  ' displays a congratulatory message.
  Dim sngScore1 As Single
  Dim sngScore2 As Single
  Dim sngScore3 As Single
  Dim sngAverage As Single

  ' Copy the scores into the variables
  sngScore1 = CSng(txtScore1.Text)
  sngScore2 = CSng(txtScore2.Text)
  sngScore3 = CSng(txtScore3.Text)
```

```
    ' Calculate and display the average
    sngAverage = (sngScore1 + sngScore2 + sngScore3) / 3
    lblAverage.Text = sngAverage.ToString("n")

    ' If the score is high, compliment the student.
    If sngAverage > 95 Then
      lblMessage.Text = "Congratulations! Great Job!"
    End If
End Sub
```

Near the end of the procedure, the following statement displays a congratulatory message if `sngAverage` contains a value greater than 95:

```
If sngAverage > 95 Then
  lblMessage.Text = "Congratulations! Great Job!"
End If
```

Programming Style and the If...Then Statement

In each `If...Then` statement we have looked at, conditionally executed statements are indented. This is not a syntax requirement, but a programming style convention. For example, compare the following statements:

```
If decSales > 50000 Then
  blnGetsBonus = True
  decCommissionRate = 0.12
  intDaysOff = intDaysOff + 1
End If
```

```
If decSales > 50000 Then
blnGetsBonus = True
decCommissionRate = 0.12
intDaysOff = intDaysOff + 1
End If
```

Both `If...Then` statements produce the same result. The first example, however, is more readable than the second because the conditionally executed statements are indented.

NOTE: Visual Basic automatically indents conditionally executed statements when you type an `If...Then` statement. If this feature has been turned off, you can turn it on by clicking *Tools* on the menu bar, then clicking *Options*. In the *Options* dialog box, perform the following:

- Click the *Show all settings* check box. Then, click *Text Editor* in the left pane, then click *Basic*, then click *Tabs*. Make sure *Smart* is selected in the dialog box under *Indenting*.
- In the left pane, click *VB Specific*. Make sure *Automatic Insertion of end constructs* and *Pretty listing (reformatting) of code* are both checked.

Using Relational Operators with Math Operators

It is possible to use a relational operator and math operators in the same expression. Here is an example:

```
If intX + intY > 20 Then
  lblMessage.Text = "It is true!"
End If
```

When a relational operator appears in the same expression as one or more math operators, the math operators always execute first. In this statement, the + operator adds `intX` and `intY`. The result is compared to 20 using the > operator. Here is another example:

```
If intX + intY > intA - intB Then
  lblMessage.Text = "It is true!"
End If
```

In this statement, the result of `intX + intY` is compared, using the > operator, to the result of `intA – intB`.

Most programmers prefer to use parentheses to clarify the order of operations. Relying on operator precedence rules is risky because the rules are hard to remember. Here is a preferred way to write the foregoing `If` statement:

```
If (intX + intY) > (intA – intB) Then
  lblMessage.Text = "It is true!"
End If
```

Using Function Calls with Relational Operators

It is possible to compare the return value of a function call with another value, using a relational operator. Here is an example:

```
If CInt(txtInput.Text) < 100 Then
  lblMessage.Text = "It is true!"
End If
```

This `If...Then` statement calls the `CInt` function to get the numeric value of `txtInput.Text`. The function's return value is compared to 100 by the < operator. If the result of `CInt(txtInput.Text)` is less than 100, the assignment statement is executed.

Using Boolean Variables as Flags

A **flag** is a Boolean variable that signals when some condition exists in the program. When the flag is set to *False*, it indicates the condition does not yet exist. When the flag is set to *True*, it means the condition does exist. Look at the following code, which uses a Boolean variable named `blnQuotaMet`.

```
If blnQuotaMet Then
  lblMessage.Text = "You have met your sales quota"
End If
```

The preceding statement assigns the string `"You have met your sales quota"` to `lblMessage.Text` if the Boolean variable equals *True*. If `blnQuotaMet` is *False*, the assignment statement is not executed. It is not necessary to use the = operator to compare the variable to *True*. The statement is equivalent to the following:

```
If blnQuotaMet = True Then
  lblMessage.Text = "You have met your sales quota"
End If
```

Checkpoint

4.1 Assuming *x* is 5, *y* is 6, and *z* is 8, indicate whether each of the following relational expressions equals *True* or *False*:

a. $x = 5$ T F
b. $7 <= (x + 2)$ T F
c. $z < 4$ T F
d. $(2 + x) <> y$ T F
e. $z <> 4$ T F
f. $x >= 6$ T F
g. $x <= (y * 2)$ T F

4.2 In the following `If` statement, assume that `blnIsInvalid` is a Boolean variable. Exactly what condition is being tested?

```
If blnIsInvalid Then
    ' Do something
End If
```

4.3 Do both of the following `If...Then` statements perform the same operation?

```
If decSales > 10000 Then
   decCommissionRate = 0.15
End If

If decSales > 10000 Then
decCommissionRate = 0.15
End If
```

4.4 Of the two `If...Then` statements shown in Checkpoint 4.3, which is preferred, and why?

4.3 The If...Then...Else Statement

CONCEPT: The `If...Then...Else` statement executes one group of statements if the condition (or Boolean expression) is true and another group of statements if the condition is false.

VideoNote
The If...Then...Else Statement

The **`If...Then...Else`** statement is an expansion of the `If...Then` statement. Here is its format:

```
If condition Then
  statement
  (more statements may follow)
Else
  statement
  (more statements may follow)
End If
```

As in an `If...Then` statement, a Boolean expression is evaluated. If the expression is true, a statement or group of statements is executed. If the expression is false, a separate group of statements is executed, as in the following.

```
If sngTemperature < 40 Then
  lblMessage.Text = "A little cold, isn't it?"
Else
  lblMessage.Text = "Nice weather we're having!"
End If
```

The `Else` statement specifies a statement or group of statements to be executed when the expression is false. In the preceding example, when the expression `sngTemperature < 40` is false, the statement appearing after `Else` is executed. The conditionally executed statement(s) in the `Else` part are indented.

The `If...Then...Else` statement follows only one of the two paths. If you think of the statements in a computer program as steps taken down a road, consider the `If...Then...Else` statement as a fork in the road. Instead of being a momentary detour, like an `If...Then` statement, the `If...Then...Else` statement causes the program execution to follow one of two exclusive paths. Figure 4-6 shows a flowchart for this type of decision structure.

Figure 4-6 Flowchart for `If...Then...Else` statement

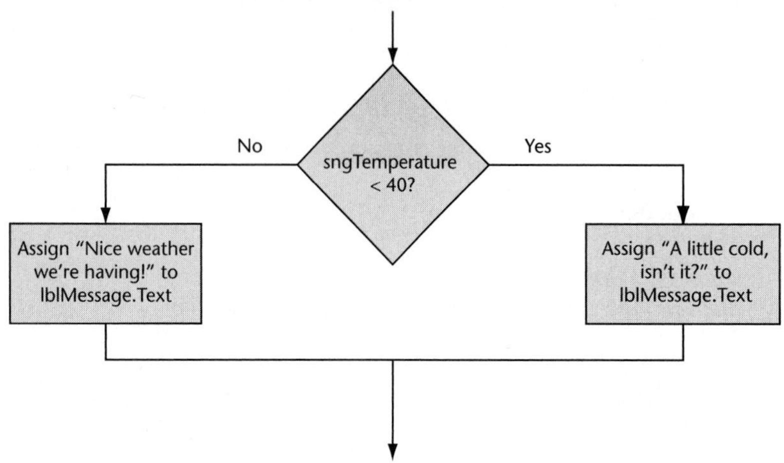

The logic shown in the flowchart in Figure 4-6 can also be expressed in pseudocode:

If sngTemperature < 40 Then
lblMessage.Text = "A little cold, isn't it?"
Else
lblMessage.Text = "Nice weather we're having!"
End If

In Tutorial 4-2 you complete an application that uses the `If...Then...Else` statement.

Tutorial 4-2: Completing an application that uses the `If...Then...Else` statement

Step 1: Open the *Test Score Average 2* project from the student sample programs folder named *Chap4\Test Score Average 2*. (This is a modification of the *Test Score Average 1* application from Tutorial 4-1.)

Step 2: Double-click the *Calculate Average* button. The *Code* window will open and show the `btnCalculate_Click` event procedure. Type the following code:

```
Private Sub btnCalculate_Click(ByVal eventSender As _
    System.Object, ByVal eventArgs As System.EventArgs) _
    Handles btnCalculate.Click

  ' This procedure calculates and displays the
  ' average test score. If the score is high, it
  ' displays a congratulatory message.
  Const sngGOOD_SCORE As Single = 95
  Dim sngScore1 As Single
  Dim sngScore2 As Single
  Dim sngScore3 As Single
  Dim sngAverage As Single
```

```
    ' Copy the scores into the variables
    Try
      sngScore1 = CSng(txtScore1.Text)
      sngScore2 = CSng(txtScore2.Text)
      sngScore3 = CSng(txtScore3.Text)
    Catch Ex As Exception
      MessageBox.Show("Test scores must be numeric","Error")
      Return
    End Try
    ' Calculate and display the average
    sngAverage = (sngScore1 + sngScore2 + sngScore3) / 3
    lblAverage.Text = sngAverage.ToString("n")

    ' If the score is high, give the student praise.
    ' Otherwise, give some encouragement.
    If sngAverage > sngGOOD_SCORE Then
      lblMessage.Text = "Congratulations! Great Job!"
    Else
      lblMessage.Text = "Keep trying!"
    End If
  End Sub
```

Step 3: Save the project.

Step 4: Run the application and input the following test scores in the three text boxes: **80, 90, 75.**

Step 5: Click the *Calculate Average* button. As shown in Figure 4-7, the average test score is displayed, and the message *Keep trying!* appears.

Figure 4-7 *Test Score Average* form with message displayed

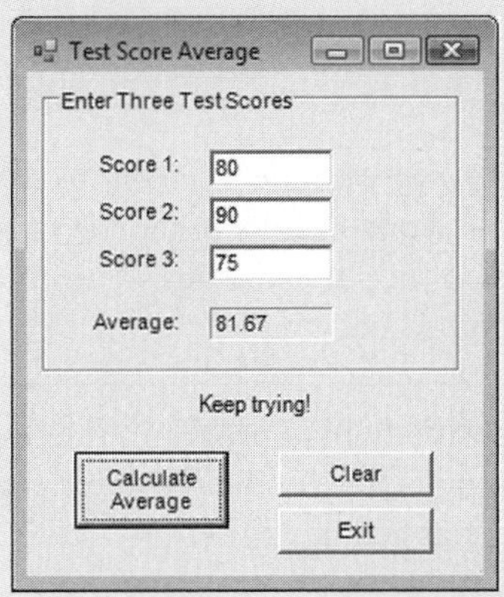

Step 6: Click the *Clear* button, and then enter the following test scores in the three text boxes: **100, 97, 99.**

Step 7: Click the *Calculate Average* button. This time, the message *Congratulations! Great job!* appears.

Step 8: Click the *Exit* button to terminate the application.

4.5 Look at each of the following code segments. What value will the `If...Then...Else` statements store in the variable `intY`?

a.
```
intX = 0
If intX < 1 Then
  intY = 99
Else
  intY = 0
End If
```

b.
```
intX = 100
If intX <= 1 Then
  intY = 99
Else
  intY = 0
End If
```

c.
```
intX = 0
If intX <> 1 Then
  intY = 99
Else
  intY = 0
End If
```

4.4 The `If...Then...ElseIf` Statement

CONCEPT: The `If...Then...ElseIf` statement is like a chain of `If...Then...Else` statements. They perform their tests, one after the other, until one of them is found to be true.

We make certain mental decisions by using sets of different but related rules. For example, we might decide which type of coat or jacket to wear by consulting the following rules:

- If it is very cold, wear a heavy coat
- Else, if it is chilly, wear a light jacket
- Else, if it is windy, wear a windbreaker
- Else, if it is hot, wear no jacket

The purpose of these rules is to decide on one type of outer garment to wear. If it is cold, the first rule dictates that a heavy coat must be worn. All the other rules are then ignored. If the first rule does not apply (if it isn't cold) the second rule is consulted. If that rule does not apply, the third rule is consulted, and so on.

TIP: When logic rules are not expressed correctly by a program, the result is called a **logic error**. The Visual Studio Debugger can help you to identify logic errors by letting you walk through the program code, one line at a time.

The way these rules are connected is very important. If they were consulted individually, we might go out of the house wearing the wrong jacket or, possibly, more than one jacket. For instance, if it is windy, the third rule says to wear a windbreaker. What if it is both windy and very cold? Will we wear a windbreaker? A heavy coat? Both? Because of the order in which the rules are consulted, the first rule will determine that a heavy coat is needed. The remaining rules will not be consulted, and we will go outside wearing the most appropriate garment.

This type of decision making is also common in programming. In Visual Basic, it is accomplished with the `If...Then...ElseIf` statement. Here is its general format:

```
If condition Then
    statement
    (more statements may follow)
ElseIf condition Then
    statement
    (more statements may follow)
(put as many ElseIf statements as necessary)
Else
    statement
    (more statements may follow)
End If
```

This construction is like a chain of `If...Then...Else` statements. The `Else` part of one statement is linked to the `If` part of another. The chain of `If...Then...Else` statements becomes one long statement. In Tutorial 4-3, you complete an application that uses the `If...Then...ElseIf` statement.

Tutorial 4-3:

Completing an application that uses the `If...Then...ElseIf` statement

In this tutorial, you will begin with the program from Tutorial 4-2 and add controls and program code that display the student's letter grade (*A*, *B*, *C*, *D*, *F*).

Step 1: Open the *Test Score Average 2* project you modified in Tutorial 4-2.

Step 2: Drag the form's border downward about one-half inch, and drag the `lblMessage` control and the three button controls downward on the form to make space for a new row of controls.

Step 3: Drag the lower border of the group box downward about one-half inch to make room for a label that will display the student's letter grade.

Step 4: Inside the group box add the new Label controls shown in Figure 4-8. When you add the label on the left, set its Text property to *Grade:*. When you add the label on the right, set its Name property to `lblGrade`, its AutoSize property to *False*, and set its BorderStyle property to *Fixed3D*.

Figure 4-8 Adding the *Grade* label inside the group box

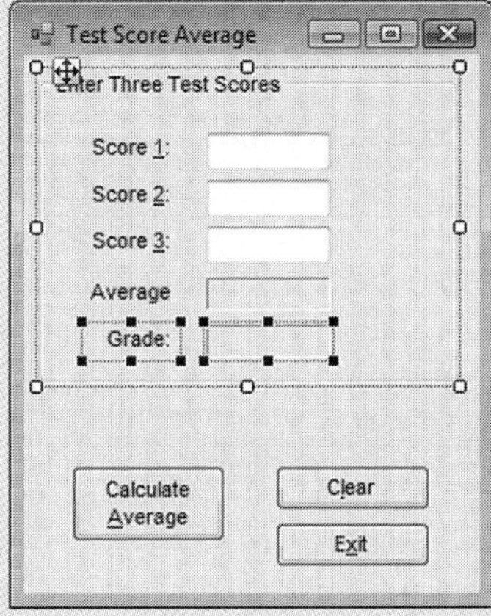

Step 5: Double-click the *Calculate Average* button. The *Code* window will open and show the `btnCalculate_Click` event procedure. Add the following code shown in bold to the procedure:

```
Private Sub btnCalculate_Click(ByVal eventSender As _
    System.Object, ByVal eventArgs As System.EventArgs) _
    Handles btnCalculate.Click

  ' This procedure calculates and displays the
  ' average test score. If the score is high, it
  ' displays a congratulatory message.
  Const sngGOOD_SCORE As Single = 95
  Dim sngScore1 As Single
  Dim sngScore2 As Single
  Dim sngScore3 As Single
  Dim sngAverage As Single

  ' Copy the scores into the variables
  Try
    sngScore1 = CSng(txtScore1.Text)
    sngScore2 = CSng(txtScore2.Text)
    sngScore3 = CSng(txtScore3.Text)
  Catch Ex As Exception
    MessageBox.Show("Test scores must be numeric","Error")
    Return
  End Try
  ' Calculate and display the average
  sngAverage = (sngScore1 + sngScore2 + sngScore3) / 3
  lblAverage.Text = sngAverage.ToString("n")

  ' Calculate and display the letter grade.
  If sngAverage < 60 Then
    lblGrade.Text = "F"
  ElseIf sngAverage < 70 Then
    lblGrade.Text = "D"
  ElseIf sngAverage < 80 Then
    lblGrade.Text = "C"
  ElseIf sngAverage < 90 Then
    lblGrade.Text = "B"
  ElseIf sngAverage <= 100 Then
    lblGrade.Text = "A"
  End If

  ' If the score is high, give the student praise.
  ' Otherwise, give some encouragement.
  If sngAverage > sngGOOD_SCORE Then
    lblMessage.Text = "Congratulations! Great Job!"
  Else
    lblMessage.Text = "Keep trying!"
  End If
End Sub
```

The `If...Then...ElseIf` statement has a number of notable characteristics. Let's analyze how it works in the *Test Score* application. First, the relational expression `average < 60` is tested:

```
If sngAverage < 60 Then
  lblGrade.Text = "F"
```

If `sngAverage` is less than 60, *F* is assigned to `lblGrade.Text`, and the rest of the `ElseIf` statements are ignored. If `sngAverage` is not less than 60, the next `ElseIf` statement executes:

```
If sngAverage < 60 Then
  lblGrade.Text = "F"
ElseIf sngAverage < 70 Then
  lblGrade.Text = "D"
```

The first `If...Then` statement filtered out all grades less than 60, so when this `ElseIf` statement executes, `sngAverage` must be 60 or greater. If `sngAverage` is less than 70, *D* is assigned to `lblGrade.Text` and the remaining `ElseIf` statements are ignored. The chain of events continues until one of the expressions is true, or the `End If` statement is encountered. Figure 4-9 uses a flowchart to describe the logic.

Figure 4-9 Flowchart for determining the student's letter grade

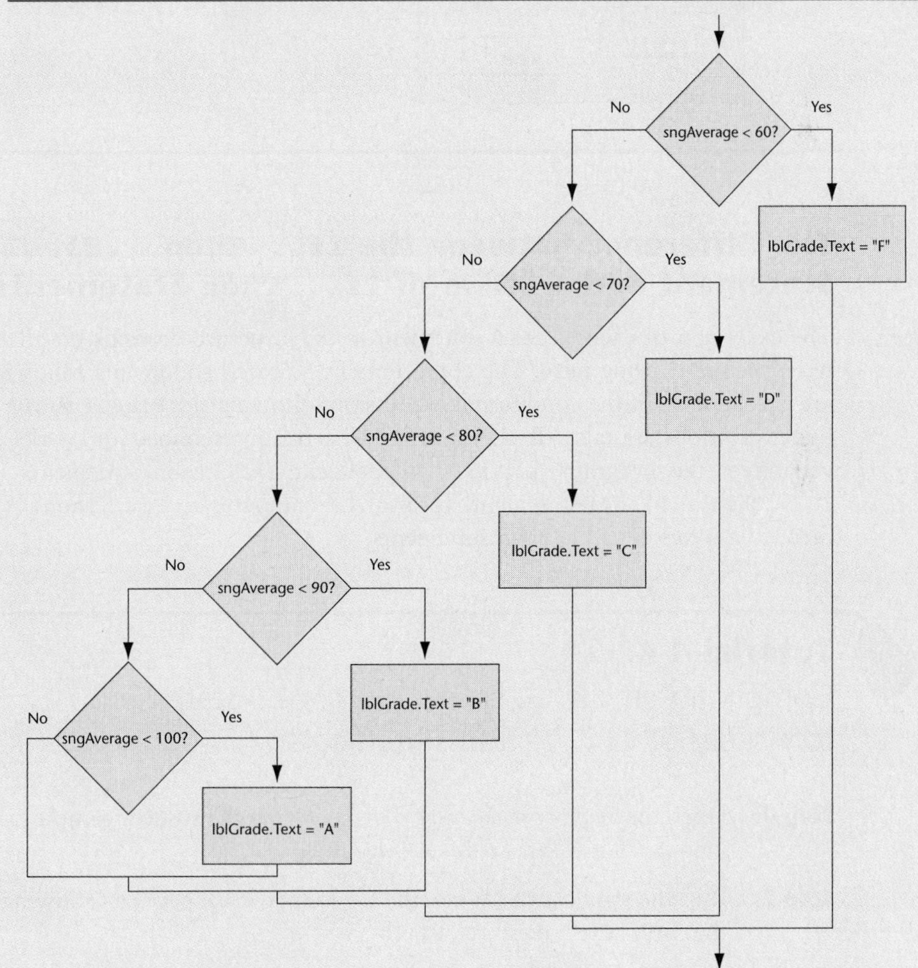

Step 6: Save the project, run the application, and input the following test scores in the text boxes: **80, 90, 75.**

Step 7: Click the *Calculate Average* button. The average test score and letter grade are displayed, along with the message *Keep trying!* (see Figure 4-10).

Step 8: Click the *Exit* button to terminate the application.

Figure 4-10 Student grade displayed

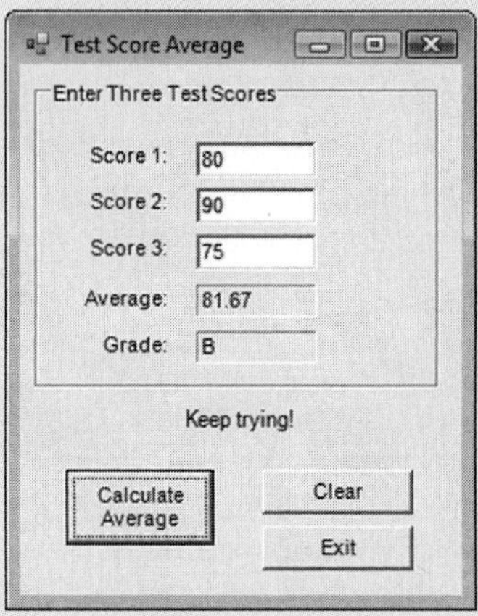

The Difference between the `If...Then...ElseIf` Statement and a Series of `If...Then` Statements

The execution of each `ElseIf` statement in the structure depends on all the conditions tested before it being false. The conditionally executed statements following an `ElseIf` are executed when the conditional expression following the `ElseIf` is true and all previous expressions are false. To demonstrate how this interconnection works, let's look at a version of the program that uses independent `If...Then` statements instead of an `If...Then...ElseIf` statement. Tutorial 4-4 compares an `If...Then...ElseIf` statement to a series of `If...Then` statements.

Tutorial 4-4:
Comparing an `If...Then...ElseIf` statement to a series of `If...Then` statements

Step 1: Open the *Test Score Average 3* project from the student sample programs folder named *Chap4\Test Score Average 3*.

Step 2: Run the application. When the form appears, enter the following test scores in the three text boxes: **40**, **40**, **40**.

Step 3: Click the *Calculate Average* button. Despite the low scores, the grade *A* is displayed. Click the *Clear* button.

Step 4: Experiment by entering more test scores and clicking the *Calculate Average* button. Notice that regardless of the scores you enter, the application always reports a grade of *A*.

Step 5: When finished, click the *Exit* button to terminate the application.

Step 6: Open the *Code* window and find the `btnCalculate_Click` event handler. Notice that instead of an `If...Then...ElseIf` statement, this procedure uses a series of `If...Then` statements to assign a letter grade. The code is as follows.

```
If sngAverage < 60 Then
  lblGrade.Text = "F"
End If
If sngAverage < 70 Then
  lblGrade.Text = "D"
End If
If sngAverage < 80 Then
  lblGrade.Text = "C"
End If
If sngAverage < 90 Then
  lblGrade.Text = "B"
End If
If sngAverage <= 100 Then
  lblGrade.Text = "A"
End If
```

In this procedure, all the `If...Then` statements execute because they are individual statements. When you ran the tutorial, you entered three scores of 40, which give an average of 40. Because this is less than 60, the first `If...Then` statement causes *F* to be assigned to `lblGrade.Text`.

```
If sngAverage < 60 Then
  lblGrade.Text = "F"
End If
```

Because the next statement is `If...Then` instead of `ElseIf`, it executes. `sngAverage` is also less than 70, therefore it causes *D* to be assigned to `lblGrade.Text`. *D* overwrites the *F* that was previously stored there.

```
If sngAverage < 60 Then
  lblGrade.Text = "F"
End If
If sngAverage < 70 Then
  lblGrade.Text = "D"
End If
```

This will continue until all the `If...Then` statements have executed. The last one will assign *A* to `lblGrade.Text`. (Most students prefer this method since *A* is the only grade it gives out!)

Using a Trailing Else

There is one minor problem with the test averaging applications shown so far: What if the user enters a test score greater than 100? The `If...Then...ElseIf` statement in the *Test Score Average 2* project handles all scores through 100, but none greater. Figure 4-11 shows the form when the user enters values greater than 100.

Figure 4-11 *Test Score Average 2* application showing values greater than 100

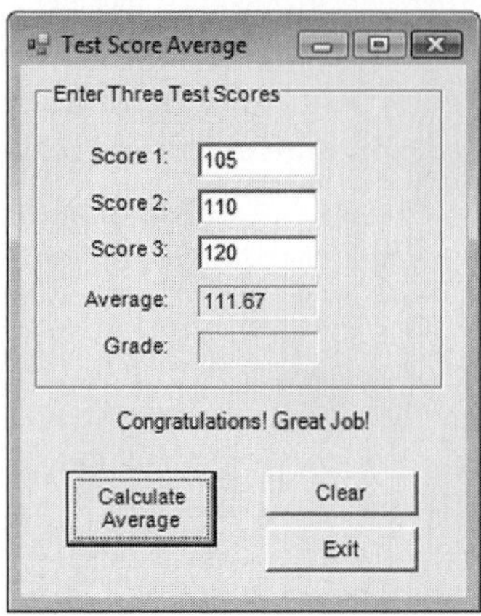

The program does not give a letter grade because there is no code to handle a score greater than 100. Assuming that any grade over 100 is invalid, we can fix the program by placing an `Else` at the end of the `If...Then...ElseIf` statement, as follows:

```
' Calculate and display the letter grade.
If sngAverage < 60 Then
  lblGrade.Text = "F"
ElseIf sngAverage < 70 Then
  lblGrade.Text = "D"
ElseIf sngAverage < 80 Then
  lblGrade.Text = "C"
ElseIf sngAverage < 90 Then
  lblGrade.Text = "B"
ElseIf sngAverage <= 100 Then
  lblGrade.Text = "A"
Else
  lblGrade.Text = "Invalid"
End If
```

The trailing `Else` catches any value that falls through the cracks. It provides a default response when the `If...Then` or none of the `ElseIf` statements finds a true condition.

TIP: When writing an `If...Then...ElseIf` statement, code the structure of the statement first, identifying all the conditions to be tested. For example, the code in our example might initially be written as follows:

```
If sngAverage < 60 Then
ElseIf sngAverage < 70 Then
ElseIf sngAverage < 80 Then
ElseIf sngAverage < 90 Then
ElseIf sngAverage <= 100 Then
Else
End If
```

This creates the framework of the statement. Next, insert the conditionally executed statements, as shown in bold in the following code:

```
If sngAverage < 60 Then
  lblGrade.Text = "F"
ElseIf sngAverage < 70 Then
  lblGrade.Text = "D"
```

```
ElseIf sngAverage < 80 Then
  lblGrade.Text = "C"
ElseIf sngAverage < 90 Then
  lblGrade.Text = "B"
ElseIf sngAverage <= 100 Then
  lblGrade.Text = "A"
Else
  lblGrade.Text = "Invalid"
End If
```

A good design approach is to decide which conditions must be tested first, and then decide what actions must be taken for each condition.

Checkpoint

4.6 The following `If...Then...ElseIf` statement has several conditions that test the variable `intX`. Assuming `intX` equals 20, how many times will the following statement compare `intX` before it finds a condition that is true?

```
If intX < 10 Then
  intY = 0
ElseIf intX < 20 Then
  intY = 1
ElseIf intX < 30 Then
  intY = 2
ElseIf intX < 40 Then
  intY = 3
Else
  intY = -1
End If
```

4.7 In the following `If...Then...ElseIf` statement, if the variable `intX` equals 5, how many times will the code assign a value to `intY`?

```
If intX < 10 Then
  intY = 0
ElseIf intX < 20 Then
  intY = 1
ElseIf intX < 30 Then
  intY = 2
ElseIf intX < 40 Then
  intY = 3
End If
```

In the following set of `If...Then` statements, if the variable `intX` equals 5, how many times will the code assign a value to `intY`?

```
If intX < 10 Then
  intY = 0
End If
If intX < 20 Then
  intY = 1
End If
If intX < 30 Then
  intY = 2
End If
If intX < 40 Then
  intY = 3
End If
```

4.5 Nested If Statements

CONCEPT: A nested **If** statement is an **If** statement in the conditionally executed code of another **If** statement. (In this section, we use the term **If** statement to refer to an **If...Then, If...Then...Else,** or **If...Then...ElseIf** statement.)

A **nested If statement** is an If statement that appears inside another If statement. In Tutorial 4-5, you will examine an application that uses nested If statements. The application determines whether a bank customer qualifies for a special loan. The customer must meet one of the following qualifications:

- Earn $30,000 per year or more and have worked in his or her current job for more than two years.
- Have worked at his or her current job for more than five years.

Tutorial 4-5:
Completing an application with a nested If statement

Step 1: Open the *Loan Qualifier* project from the student sample programs folder named *Chap4\Loan Qualifier*.

Step 2: Open *Form1* in the *Design* window. It should appear as shown in Figure 4-12.

Figure 4-12 *Loan Qualifier* application

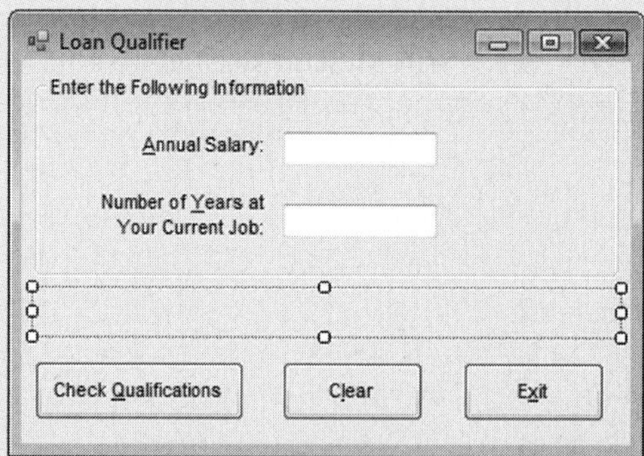

Step 3: Double-click the *Check Qualifications* button and insert the following bold statements in the btnCheckQual_Click procedure:

```
Private Sub btnCheckQual_Click(ByVal eventSender As _
    System.Object, ByVal eventArgs As System.EventArgs) _
    Handles btnCheckQual.Click

  ' Retrieve and convert the salary and years
  ' from the text boxes.
  Dim sngSalary As Single
  Dim intYearsOnJob As Integer
  Try
    sngSalary = CSng(txtSalary.Text)
    intYearsOnJob = CInt(txtYearsOnJob.Text)
```

```
Catch ex As Exception
  MessageBox.Show("Salary and Years on Job must be valid
  numbers","Error")
  Return
End Try
```

The statements declare two variables and assign them the contents of the salary and years on job text boxes.

Step 4: Next, add the following nested `If` statement to the same procedure:

```
' Determine whether the applicant qualifies
' for the special loan.
If sngSalary > 30000 Then
  If intYearsOnJob > 2 Then
    lblMessage.Text = "The applicant qualifies."
  Else
    lblMessage.Text = "The applicant does not qualify."
  End If
Else
  If intYearsOnJob > 5 Then
    lblMessage.Text = "The applicant qualifies."
  Else
    lblMessage.Text = "The applicant does not qualify."
  End If
End If
```

Step 5: Save and run the application. Enter **45000** for salary and **3** for years at current job. Click the *Check Qualifications* button. The message *The applicant qualifies* should appear on the form.

Step 6: Enter **15000** for salary and **3** for years at current job. Click the *Check Qualifications* button. The message *The applicant does not qualify* appears on the form.

Step 7: Experiment with other values. When you are finished, click the *Exit* button to terminate the application.

Examining the Nested If Statement in More Depth

In the *Loan Qualifier* project, the outermost `If` statement tests the following condition:

```
If sngSalary > 30000 Then
```

If this condition is true, the nested `If` statement shown in bold is executed:

```
If sngSalary > 30000 Then
  If intYearsOnJob > 2 Then
    lblMessage.Text = "The applicant qualifies."
  Else
    lblMessage.Text = "The applicant does not qualify."
  End If
Else
  If intYearsOnJob > 5 Then
    lblMessage.Text = "The applicant qualifies."
  Else
    lblMessage.Text = "The applicant does not qualify."
  End If
End If
```

However, if the condition `sngSalary > 30000` is not true, the `Else` part of the outermost `If` statement causes its nested `If` statement, shown in bold, to execute:

```
If sngSalary > 30000 Then
  If intYearsOnJob > 2 Then
    lblMessage.Text = "The applicant qualifies."
  Else
    lblMessage.Text = "The applicant does not qualify."
  End If
Else
  If intYearsOnJob > 5 Then
    lblMessage.Text = "The applicant qualifies."
  Else
    lblMessage.Text = "The applicant does not qualify."
  End If
End If
```

Figure 4-13 shows a flowchart for these nested `If` statements.

Figure 4-13 Flowchart of nested `If` statements

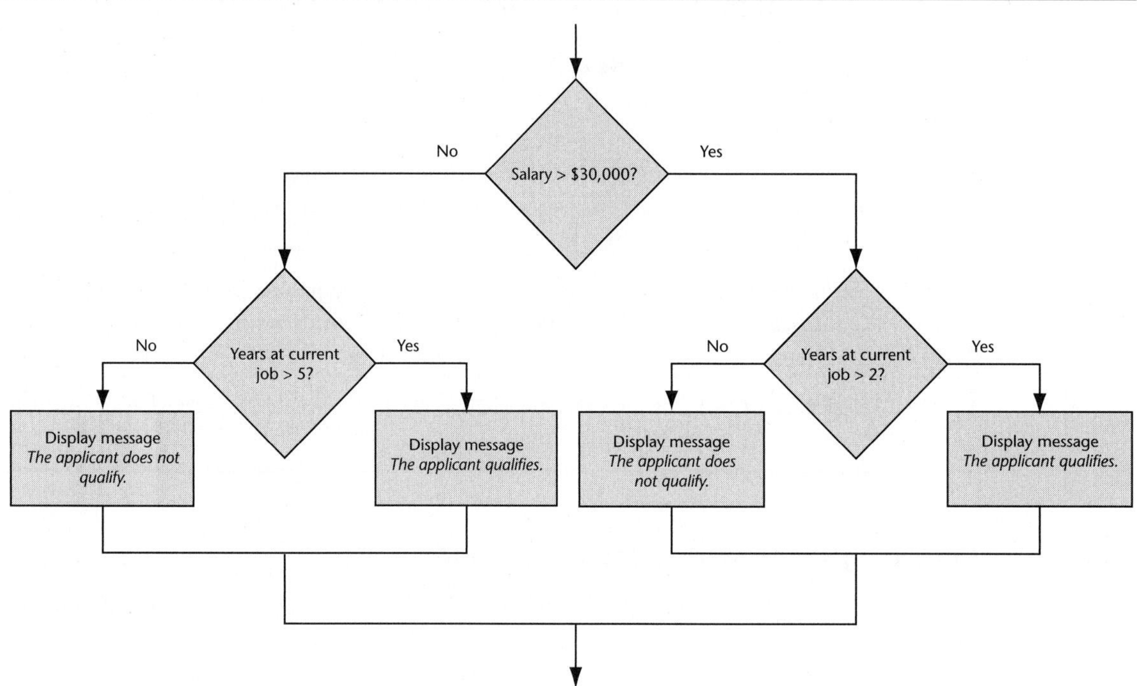

4.6 Logical Operators

CONCEPT: Logical operators combine two or more relational expressions into a single expression.

Logical operators can combine multiple Boolean expressions into a compound expression. Each individual Boolean expression might be very simple. But then, you can combine them using logical operators (also called Boolean operators) to make complex decisions. Table 4-3 lists Visual Basic's logical operators.

The And Operator

The **And operator** combines two expressions into one. Both expressions must be true for the overall expression to be true. The following If statement uses the And operator:

```
If intTemperature < 20 And intMinutes > 12 Then
  lblMessage.Text = "The temperature is in the danger zone."
End If
```

Table 4-3 Visual Basic logical operators

Operator	Effect
And	Combines two expressions into one. Both expressions must be true for the overall expression to be true.
Or	Combines two expressions into one. One or both expressions must be true for the overall expression to be true. It is only necessary for one to be true, and it does not matter which.
Xor	Combines two expressions into one. One expression (not both) must be true for the overall expression to be true. If both expressions are true, or both expressions are false, the overall expression is false.
Not	Reverses the logical value of an expression: makes a true expression false and a false expression true.

In this statement, the two relational expressions are combined into a single expression. The assignment statement is only executed if intTemperature is less than 20 and intMinutes is greater than 12. If either relational expression is false, the entire expression is false and the assignment statement is not executed.

Table 4-4 shows a truth table for the And operator. The truth table lists all the possible combinations of values that two expressions may have, followed by the resulting value returned by the And operator connecting the two conditions. As the table shows, both Expression 1 and Expression 2 must be true for the And operator to return value of *True*.

Table 4-4 Truth table for the And operator

Expression 1	Expression 2	Expression 1 **And** Expression 2
True	False	False
False	True	False
False	False	False
True	True	True

TIP: You must provide complete expressions on each side of the And operator. For example, the following is not correct because the condition on the right side of the And operator is not a complete expression:

```
intTemperature > 0 And < 100
```

The expression must be rewritten as follows:

```
intTemperature > 0 And intTemperature < 100
```

Short Circuit-Evaluation with `AndAlso`

When the `And` operator appears in a compound Boolean expression, Visual Basic evaluates both subexpressions. Consider the following example in which the first expression compares `dblX` to zero and the second expression calls a Boolean function named `CheckValue`:

```
If dblX > 0 And CheckValue(dblX) Then
  lblResult.Text = "Expression is True"
Else
  lblResult.Text = "Expression is False"
End If
```

When using the `And` operator, both subexpressions (before and after `And`) must be true for the compound expression to be true. Comparing a value to zero is fast and easy, but executing a function call can be time-consuming, depending on what's inside the function. In our example, Visual Basic calls the `CheckValue` function, regardless of the value of `dblX`. What if we could compare `dblX` to zero, and return *False* immediately if it was less than or equal to zero? Then there would be no need to call the `CheckValue` function. Such behavior is called **short-circuit evaluation.** In Visual Basic you use the **`AndAlso` operator** to achieve short-circuit evaluation. In the following example, assuming that `dblX` is less than or equal to zero, `CheckValue` is not called and *Expression is False* is displayed:

```
If dblX > 0 AndAlso CheckValue(dblX) Then
  lblResult.Text = "Expression is True"
Else
  lblResult.Text = "Expression is False"
End If
```

See the *ShortCircuit* application in the student sample programs folder named *Chap4\ShortCircuit* for an example of the `AndAlso` operator.

The `Or` Operator

The **`Or` operator** combines two expressions into one. One or both expressions must be true for the overall expression to be true. It is only necessary for one to be true, and it does not matter which. The following `If` statement uses the `Or` operator:

```
If intTemperature < 20 Or intTemperature > 100 Then
  lblMessage.Text = "The temperature is in the danger zone."
End If
```

The assignment statement will be executed if `intTemperature` is less than 20 or `intTemperature` is greater than 100. If either relational test is true, the entire expression is true and the assignment statement is executed.

Table 4-5 is a truth table for the `Or` operator.

Table 4-5 Truth table for the `Or` operator

Expression 1	Expression 2	Expression 1 `Or` Expression 2
`True`	`False`	`True`
`False`	`True`	`True`
`False`	`False`	`False`
`True`	`True`	`True`

All it takes for an `Or` expression to be true is for one of the subexpressions to be true. It doesn't matter if the other subexpression is true or false.

TIP: You must provide complete expressions on both sides of the `Or` operator. For example, the following is not correct because the condition on the right side of the `Or` operator is not a complete expression:

```
intTemperature < 0 Or > 100
```

The expression must be rewritten as follows:

```
intTemperature < 0 Or intTemperature > 100
```

Short Circuit-Evaluation with `OrElse`

When the `Or` operator appears in a compound Boolean expression, Visual Basic evaluates both expressions on the left and right side of the operator. Consider the following example, in which the first expression compares `dblX` to zero; the second calls a Boolean function named `CheckValue`:

```
If dblX = 0 Or CheckValue(dblX) Then
  lblResult.Text = "Expression is True"
End If
```

When this code executes, the expression `dblX = 0` will be tested, and then the `CheckValue` function is called. In some situations, however, it shouldn't be necessary to call the `CheckValue` function to determine the value of the compound expression. If the expression `dblX = 0` is true, then we know that the compound expression is true, so the function call can be skipped. As previously mentioned, this type of evaluation is known as short-circuit evaluation, and it can be performed with the **`OrElse` operator**.

In the following example, if `dblX` equals zero, the `CheckValue` function is not called:

```
If dblX = 0 OrElse CheckValue(dblX) Then
  lblResult.Text = "Expression is True"
End If
```

See the *ShortCircuit* application in the student sample programs folder named *Chap4/ShortCircuit* for an example of the `OrElse` operator.

The `Xor` Operator

`Xor` stands for *exclusive Or*. The **`Xor` operator** takes two expressions as operands and creates an expression that is true when one, but not both, of the subexpressions is true. The following `If` statement uses the `Xor` operator:

```
If decTotal > 1000 Xor decAverage > 120 Then
  lblMessage.Text = "You may try again."
End If
```

The assignment statement will be executed if `decTotal` is greater than 1000 or `decAverage` is greater than 120, but not both. If both relational tests are true, or neither is true, the entire expression is false. Table 4-6 shows a truth table for the `Xor` operator.

Table 4-6 Truth table for the `Xor` operator

Expression 1	Expression 2	Expression 1 `Or` Expression 2
`True`	`False`	`True`
`False`	`True`	`True`
`False`	`False`	`False`
`True`	`True`	`False`

TIP: You must provide complete expressions on both sides of the `Xor` operator. For example, the following is not correct because the condition on the right side of the `Xor` operator is not a complete expression:

```
value < 0 Xor > 100
```

The expression must be rewritten as follows:

```
value < 0 Xor value > 100
```

The `Not` Operator

The **`Not` operator** takes a Boolean expression and reverses its logical value. In other words, if the expression is true, the `Not` operator returns *False*, and if the expression is false, it returns *True*. The following `If` statement uses the `Not` operator:

```
If Not intTemperature > 100 Then
  lblMessage.Text = "You are below the maximum temperature."
End If
```

First, the expression `intTemperature > 100` is tested to be true or false. Then the `Not` operator is applied to that value. `If` the expression `intTemperature > 100` is true, the `Not` operator returns *False*. If it is false, the `Not` operator returns *True*. This example is equivalent to asking *Is intTemperature not greater than 100?* Table 4-7 shows a truth table for the `Not` operator.

Table 4-7 Truth table for the Not operator

Expression	**`Not`** Expression
`True`	`False`
`False`	`True`

Checking Numeric Ranges with Logical Operators

When your program is determining whether a number is inside a numeric range, it's best to use the `And` operator. For example, the following `If` statement checks the value in `intX` to determine whether it is in the range of 20 through 40:

```
If intX >= 20 And intX <= 40 Then
  lblMessage.Text = "The value is in the acceptable range."
End If
```

The expression in the `If` statement is true only when `intX` is greater than or equal to 20 *and* less than or equal to 40. The value in `intX` must be within the range of 20 through 40 for this expression to be true.

When your program is determining whether a number is outside a range, it's best to use the `Or` operator. The following statement determines whether `intX` is outside the range of 20 through 40:

```
If intX < 20 Or intX > 40 Then
  lblMessage.Text = "The value is outside the acceptable range."
End If
```

It is important not to get these logical operators confused. For example, the following expression cannot be true because no value exists that is both less than 20 and greater than 40.

```
If intX < 20 And intX > 40 Then
   lblMessage.Text = "The value is outside the acceptable range."
End If
```

If You Want to Know More about Using `Not`, `And`, `Or`, and `Xor` Together

It is possible to write an expression containing more than one logical operator. For example, examine the following `If` statement:

```
If intX < 0 And intY > 100 Or intZ = 50 Then
   ' Perform some statement.
End If
```

Logical operators have an order of precedence. The `Not` operator has the highest precedence, followed by the `And` operator, followed by the `Or` operator, followed by the `Xor` operator. So, in the example statement, the following expression is evaluated first:

```
intX < 0 And intY > 100
```

The result of this expression is then applied to the `Or` operator to carry out the rest of the condition. For example, if the first expression (using `And`) is true, the remainder of the condition will be tested as follows:

```
True Or intZ = 50
```

If the first expression (using `And`) is false, however, the remainder of the condition will be tested as follows:

```
False Or intZ = 50
```

Always use parentheses in logical expressions to clarify the order of evaluation. The following `If` statement confirms that the `And` operator executes before the `Or` operator:

```
If (intX < 0 And intY > 100) Or intZ = 50 Then
   ' Perform some statement.
End If
```

You can use parentheses to force one expression to be tested before others. For example, look at the following `If` statement:

```
If intX < 0 And (intY > 100 Or intZ = 50) Then
   ' Perform some statement.
End If
```

In the statement, the expression `(intY > 100 Or intZ = 50)` is tested first.

If You Want to Know More about Using Math Operators with Relational and Logical Operators

It is possible to write expressions containing math, relational, and logical operators. For example, look at the following code segment:

```
intA = 5
intB = 7
intX = 100
intY = 30
If (intX > (intA * 10)) And (intY < (intB + 20)) Then
   ' Perform some statement.
End If
```

In statements containing complex conditions, math operators execute first. After the math operators, relational operators execute. Logical operators execute last. Let's use this order to step through the evaluation of the condition shown in our sample `If` statement.

First, the math operators execute, causing the statement to become

```
If (intX > 50) And (intY < 27) Then
```

Next, the relational operators execute, causing the statement to become

```
If True And False Then
```

Since `True And False` equals *False*, the condition is false.

Checkpoint

4.8 The following truth table shows various combinations of the values *True* and *False* connected by a logical operator. Complete the table by indicating whether the result of each combination is *True* or *False*.

Logical Expression	Result
`True And False`	________
`True And True`	________
`False And True`	________
`False And False`	________
`True Or False`	________
`True Or True`	________
`False Or True`	________
`False Or False`	________
`True Xor False`	________
`True Xor True`	________
`Not True`	________
`Not False`	________

4.7 Comparing, Testing, and Working with Strings

CONCEPT: Visual Basic provides various methods in the `String` class that make it easy to work with strings. This section shows you how to use relational operators to compare strings, and discusses several intrinsic functions and string methods that perform tests and manipulations on strings.

In the preceding examples, you saw how numbers can be compared using the relational operators. You can also use relational operators to compare strings. For example, look at the following code segment, in which `strName1` and `strName2` are string variables.

```
strName1 = "Mary"
strName2 = "Mark"
If strName1 = strName2 Then
  lblMessage.Text = "The names are the same"
Else
  lblMessage.Text = "The names are NOT the same"
End If
```

The = operator tests `strName1` and `strName2` to determine whether they are equal. Since the strings `"Mary"` and `"Mark"` are not equal, the `Else` part of the `If` statement will cause the message *The names are NOT the same* to be copied to `lblMessage.Text`.

You can compare string variables with string literals as well. The following code sample uses the <> operator to determine if `strMonth` is not equal to *October*:

```
If strMonth <> "October" Then
  ' statement
End If
```

You can also use the >, <, >=, and <= operators to compare strings. Before we look at these operators, though, we must understand how characters are stored in memory.

Computers do not actually store characters, such as *A*, *B*, *C*, and so on, in memory. Instead, they store numeric codes that represent the characters. Visual Basic uses **Unicode**, which is a numbering system that represents all letters of the alphabet (lowercase and uppercase), the printable digits 0 through 9, punctuation symbols, and special characters. Each character is stored in memory as its corresponding Unicode number. When the computer is instructed to print the value on the screen, it displays the character that corresponds to the numeric code.

NOTE: Unicode is an international encoding system that is extensive enough to represent all the characters of all the world's alphabets.

In Unicode, letters are arranged alphabetically. Because *A* comes before *B*, the numeric code for the letter *A* is less than the code for the letter *B*. In the following `If` statement, the relational expression `"A" < "B"` is true.

```
If "A" < "B" Then
  ' Do something
End If
```

TIP: When comparing strings, make sure they are consistent in their use of uppercase and lowercase letters. Avoid comparing `"jones"` to `"Adams"` or `"BAKER"`, for example. The ordering of strings is affected by the choice of uppercase and lowercase letters.

When you use relational operators to compare strings, the strings are compared character-by-character. For example, look at the following code segment:

```
strName1 = "Mary"
strName2 = "Mark"
If strName1 > strName2 Then
  lblMessage.Text = "Mary is greater than Mark"
Else
  lblMessage.Text = "Mary is not greater than Mark"
End If
```

The > operator compares each character in the strings `"Mary"` and `"Mark"`, beginning with the first, or leftmost characters, as shown in Figure 4-14.

Figure 4-14 String comparison

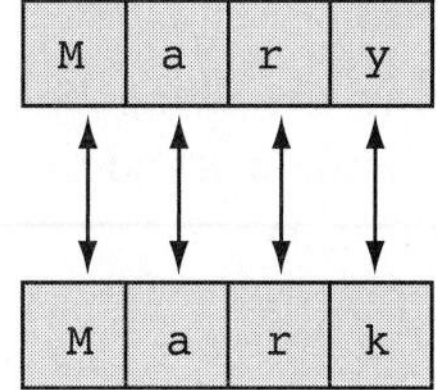

Here is how the comparison takes place:

1. The *M* in *Mary* is compared with the *M* in *Mark*. Since these are the same, the next characters are compared.

2. The *a* in *Mary* is compared with the *a* in *Mark*. Since these are the same, the next characters are compared.
3. The *r* in *Mary* is compared with the *r* in *Mark*. Since these are the same, the next characters are compared.
4. The *y* in *Mary* is compared with the *k* in *Mark*. Since these are not the same, the two strings are not equal. The character *y* is greater than *k*, so it is determined that *Mary* is greater than *Mark*.

NOTE: If one of the strings in a relational comparison is shorter in length than the other, Visual Basic treats the shorter character as if it were padded with blank spaces. For example, suppose the strings `"High"` and `"Hi"` were compared. The string `"Hi"` would be treated as if it were four characters in length, with the last two characters being spaces. Because the space character has a lower value than all other characters in Unicode, `"Hi"` would be less than `"High"`.

Testing for No Input

You can determine whether the user has entered a value into a text box by comparing the TextBox control's Text property to the predefined constant `String.Empty` as shown here:

```
If txtInput.Text = String.Empty Then
  lblMessage.Text = "Please enter a value"
Else
  ' The txtInput control contains input, so
  ' perform an operation with it here.
End If
```

The predefined constant `String.Empty` represents an **empty string**, which is a string that contains no characters.

The `If` statement copies the string *Please enter a value* to `lblMessage` if the `txtInput` control contains no input. The statements following `Else` are only executed if `txtInput` contains a value. You can use this technique to determine whether the user has provided input for a required field before performing operations on that field.

NOTE: The technique we used in the preceding `If` statement does not detect a string that contains only spaces. A space is a character, just as the letter *A* is a character. If the user types only spaces into a text box, you will have to trim away the spaces to determine if any other characters were typed. Later in this section, we will discuss functions for trimming spaces from strings.

The `ToUpper` and `ToLower` Methods

The `ToUpper` and `ToLower` methods are both members of the String class, so they may be called with any string variable or expression. The **`ToUpper` method** returns the uppercase equivalent of a string. Here is the method's general format:

```
StringExpression.ToUpper()
```

`StringExpression` can be any string variable or string expression. In the following example, `strLittleWord` and `strBigWord` are string variables:

```
strLittleWord = "Hello"
strBigWord = strLittleWord.ToUpper()
```

After the statement executes, `bigWord` will contain `"HELLO"` in uppercase letters. Notice that the original string, `"Hello"` had one uppercase letter—the initial *H*. The `ToUpper` method only converts lowercase characters. Characters that are already uppercase and characters that are not alphabet letters are not converted.

TIP: The `ToUpper` method does not modify the value of the string, but returns the string's uppercase equivalent. For example, after the statements in the previous example execute, `strLittleWord` still contains the original string `"Hello"`.

The **`ToLower` method** works just like the `ToUpper` method, except it returns a lowercase version of a string. Here is the method's general format:

```
StringExpression.ToLower()
```

In the following example, `strBigTown` and `strLittleTown` are string variables:

```
strBigTown = "NEW YORK"
strLittleTown = bigTown.ToLower()
```

After the statements execute, the variable `strLittleTown` contains the string `"new york"`. The `ToLower` method only converts uppercase characters. Characters that are already lowercase, and characters that are not alphabet letters, are not converted.

TIP: Like `ToUpper`, the `ToLower` method does not modify the original string.

You may also use the `ToUpper` and `ToLower` methods with a control's Text property. In the following example `strLastName` is a string variable:

```
strLastName = txtLastName.Text.ToUpper()
```

The `ToUpper` and `ToLower` methods are helpful in performing string comparisons. String comparisons in Visual Basic are *case sensitive*, meaning that uppercase letters are not considered the same as their lowercase counterparts. In other words, *A* is not the same as *a*. This can lead to problems when you construct `If` statements that compare strings. Tutorial 4-6 leads you through such an example.

Tutorial 4-6:
Examining an application that performs string comparisons

Step 1: Open the *Secret Word 1* project from the student sample programs folder named *Chap4\Secret Word 1*.

Step 2: Run the application. The form shown in Figure 4-15 appears.

This application asks you to enter the secret word, which might be similar to a password in some programs. The secret word is *PROSPERO*.

Step 3: Enter **`prospero`** in all lowercase letters, and click the *Ok* button. You will see the message *Wrong! That is NOT the secret word!*

Step 4: Enter **`Prospero`** with an uppercase *P*, followed by all lowercase letters. Click the *Ok* button. Once again, you see the message *Wrong! That is NOT the secret word!*

Figure 4-15 *Secret Word* form

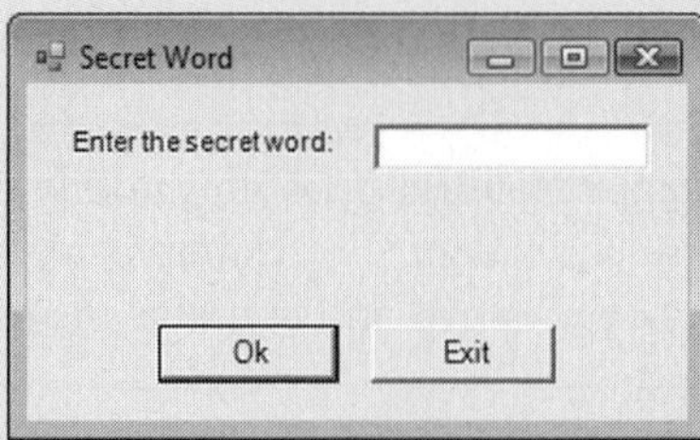

Step 5: Enter **PROSPERO** in all uppercase letters and click the *Ok* button. This time you see the message *Congratulations! That is the secret word!*

Step 6: Click the *Exit* button to close the application.

Step 7: Open the *Code* window and find the `btnOk_Click` event procedure. The code is as follows:

```
Private Sub btnOk_Click(ByVal sender As System.Object, _
  ByVal e As System.EventArgs) Handles btnOk.Click

  ' Compare the word entered with
  ' the secret word.

  If txtInput.Text = "PROSPERO" Then
    lblMessage.Text = "Congratulations! That " & _
        "is the secret word!"
  Else
    lblMessage.Text = "Wrong! That is NOT the secret word!"
  End If
End Sub
```

The `If...Then...Else` statement compares the string entered by the user to *PROSPERO* in all uppercase letters. But what if the programmer intended to accept the word without regard to case? What if *prospero* in all lowercase letters is valid as well? One solution would be to modify the `If` statement to test for all the other possible values. However, to test for all the possible combination of lowercase and uppercase letters would require a large amount of code.

A better approach is to convert the text entered by the user to all uppercase letters, and then compare the converted text to *PROSPERO*. When the user enters the word *prospero* in any combination of uppercase or lowercase characters, this test will return *True*. Modify the code by adding a call to the `ToUpper` method, as shown bold in the following code.

```
If txtInput.Text.ToUpper() = "PROSPERO" Then
  lblMessage.Text = "Congratulations! That " & _
      "is the secret word!"
Else
  lblMessage.Text = "Wrong! That is NOT the secret word!"
End If
```

Step 8: Run the application. When the form appears, Enter **prospero** in all lowercase letters and click the *Ok* button. This time you see the message *Congratulations! That is the secret word!* You can experiment with various combinations of uppercase and lowercase letters. As long as you type the word *prospero* the application will recognize it as the secret word.

Step 9: Close the project.

The `ToLower` method can also be used in Tutorial 4-6 to accomplish the same result, as shown in bold in the following code. Just make sure you compare the return value of the `ToLower` method to an all lowercase string.

```
If txtInput.Text.ToLower() = "prospero" Then
  lblMessage.Text = "Congratulations! That " & _
       "is the secret word!"
Else
  lblMessage.Text = "Wrong! That is NOT the secret word!"
End If
```

The `IsNumeric` Function

The intrinsic **`IsNumeric`** **function** accepts a string as its argument and returns *True* if the string contains a number. The function returns *False* if the string's contents cannot be recognized as a number. Here is the function's general use:

```
IsNumeric(StringExpression)
```

Here is an example:

```
Dim strNumber As String
strNumber = "576"
If IsNumeric(strNumber) Then
  lblMessage.Text = "It is a number"
Else
  lblMessage.Text = "It is NOT a number"
End If
```

In this statement, the expression `IsNumeric(strNumber)` returns *True* because the contents of `strNumber` can be recognized as a number. In the following code segment, however, the expression returns *False*:

```
strNumber = "123abc"
If IsNumeric(strNumber) Then
  lblMessage.Text = "It is a number"
Else
  lblMessage.Text = "It is NOT a number"
End If
```

When you want the user to enter numeric data, the `IsNumeric` function is useful for checking user input and confirming that it is valid.

Determining the Length of a String

The **`Length`** **property**, a member of the `String` class, returns the number of characters in a string. Here is an example:

```
Dim strName As String = "Herman"
Dim intNumChars As Integer
intNumChars = strName.Length
```

The code stores 6 in `intNumChars` because the length of the string `"Herman"` is 6.

You can also determine the length of a control's Text property, as shown in the following code:

```
If txtInput.Text.Length > 20 Then
  lblMessage.Text = "Please enter no more than 20 characters."
End If
```

There are many situations in which `Length` is useful. One example is when you must display or print a string and have only a limited amount of space.

WARNING: If you attempt to get the length of an uninitialized string variable, a runtime error occurs. You can prevent this error by initializing string variables with an empty string, as shown in the following statement:

```
Dim str As String = String.Empty
```

Optional Topic: Trimming Spaces from Strings

Sometimes it is necessary to trim leading and/or trailing spaces from a string before performing other operations on the string, such as a comparison. A **leading space** is a space that appears at the beginning, or left side, of a string. For instance, the following string has three leading spaces:

```
"   Hello"
```

A **trailing space** is a space that appears at the end, or right side, of a string, after the non-space characters. The following string has three trailing spaces:

```
"Hello   "
```

The `String` class has three methods for removing spaces: `TrimStart`, `TrimEnd`, and `Trim`. Here is the general format of each method:

```
StringExpression.TrimStart()
StringExpression.TrimEnd()
StringExpression.Trim()
```

The **`TrimStart` method** returns a copy of the string expression with all leading spaces removed. The **`TrimEnd` method** returns a copy of the string expression with all trailing spaces removed. The **`Trim` method** returns a copy of the string expression with all leading and trailing spaces removed. The following is an example:

```
strGreeting = "   Hello   "
lblMessage1.Text = strGreeting.TrimStart()
lblMessage2.Text = strGreeting.TrimEnd()
lblMessage3.Text = strGreeting.Trim()
```

In this code, the first statement assigns the string `"   Hello   "` (with three leading spaces and three trailing spaces) to the named variable, `strGreeting`. In the second statement, the `TrimStart` method is called. Its return value, `"Hello   "`, is assigned to `lblMessage1.Text`. In the third statement, the `TrimEnd` method is called. Its return value, `"   Hello"`, is assigned to `lblMessage2.Text`. In the fourth statement, the Trim method is called. Its return value, `"Hello"`, is assigned to `lblMessage3.Text`.

These methods do not modify the string variable, but return a modified copy of the variable. To actually modify the string variable you must use a statement such as the following:

```
strGreeting = strGreeting.Trim()
```

After this statement executes, the greeting variable no longer contains leading or trailing spaces.

Like the `Length` property, these methods may also be used with a control's Text property. The following is an example:

```
Dim strName As String
strName = txtName.Text.Trim()
```

The `Substring` Method

The **`Substring` method** returns a substring, or a string within a string. There are two formats:

```
StringExpression.Substring(Start)
StringExpression.Substring(Start, Length)
```

The positions of the characters in *`StringExpression`* are numbered, with the first character at position 0. In the first format shown for the method, an integer argument, *`Start`*, indicates the starting position of the string to be extracted from *`StringExpression`*. The method returns a string containing all characters from the *`Start`* position to the end of *`StringExpression`*. For example, look at the following code:

```
Dim strLastName As String
Dim strFullName As String = "George Washington"
strLastName = strFullName.Substring(7)
```

After this code executes, the variable `strLastName` will contain the string `"Washington"` because `"Washington"` begins at position 7 in `strFullName`, and continues to the end of the string.

In the second format shown for `Substring`, a second integer argument, *`Length`*, indicates the number of characters to extract, including the starting character. For example, look at the following code:

```
Dim strFirstName As String
Dim strFullName As String = "George Washington"
strFirstName = strFullName.Substring(0, 6)
```

In this code, the `Substring` method returns the six characters that begin at position 0 in `strFullName`. After the code executes, the variable `strFirstName` contains the string `"George"`.

Optional Topic: The `IndexOf` Method

The **`IndexOf` method** searches for a character or a string within a string. The method has three general formats:

```
StringExpression.IndexOf(SearchString)
StringExpression.IndexOf(SearchString, Start)
StringExpression.IndexOf(SearchString, Start, Count)
```

In the first format, *`SearchString`* is the string or character to search for within *`StringExpression`*. The method returns the character position, or index, of the first occurrence of *`SearchString`* if it is found within *`StringExpression`*. If *`SearchString`* is not found, the method returns –1. For example, look at the following code:

```
Dim strName As String = "Angelina Adams"
Dim intPosition As Integer
intPosition = strName.IndexOf("e")
```

After this code executes, the variable position equals 3 because the character *e* is found at character position 3.

NOTE: With the `IndexOf` method, the first character position is 0.

In the second format shown for `IndexOf`, a second argument, *Start*, is an integer that specifies a starting position within *`StringExpression`* for the search to begin. The following is an example:

```
Dim strName As String = "Angelina Adams"
Dim intPosition As Integer
intPosition = strName.IndexOf("A", 1)
```

After the code executes, the variable `intPosition` equals 9. The `IndexOf` method begins its search at character position 1 (the second character), so the first *A* is skipped.

NOTE: The version of the `IndexOf` method used here performs a case sensitive search. When searching for *A* it does not return the position of *a*.

In the third format shown for `IndexOf`, a third argument, *`Count`*, is an integer specifying the number of characters within *`StringExpression`* to search. Here is an example:

```
Dim strName As String = "Angelina Adams"
Dim intPosition As Integer
intPosition = strName.IndexOf("A", 1, 7)
```

After the code executes, the variable position equals –1. The `IndexOf` method searches only 7 characters, beginning at character 1. Because *A* is not found in the characters searched, the method returns –1.

WARNING: A runtime error will occur if the starting position argument passed to `IndexOf` is negative or specifies a nonexistent position. Get the length of the string before calling `IndexOf`, to ensure the index is in a valid range.

The following code shows how to use the `IndexOf` method to determine if a search string exists within a string:

```
Dim strName As String = "Angelina Adams"
If strName.IndexOf("Adams") = -1 Then
  lblMessage.Text = "Adams is not found"
End If
```

Tutorial 4-7 completes a string searching application.

Tutorial 4-7:
Completing a string searching application

In this tutorial, you will write code that implements a string searching program. You will have an opportunity to try the `IsNumeric`, `Trim`, and `IndexOf` methods. The user interface is already created, so you can concentrate on the program code that makes it work. Here are its basic features:

- A string is shown at the top of the form, as shown in Figure 4-16, containing various character patterns (*abc*, *ABC*, 00123, and so on). It uses a blue font, which appears gray on the printed page.
- The user inputs a string into the text box, indicating which substring they want to find.

- The user clicks the *Go* button, as shown in Figure 4-17.
- The program displays the position in which the substring was found. You can verify the accuracy of the result by inspecting the numbers in the scale line below the string shown in blue.
- The user can change the starting index position of the search from 0 to another value. In Figure 4-18, the user has selected index position 4 to begin searching. The next matching occurrence of *ABC* is found at index 20.
- If the user enters a nonnumeric index, an error message box pops up, as shown in Figure 4-19.

NOTE: We will be using the `Return` statement in this program, which quits (leaves) a procedure immediately. It is often used when error checking statements determine that the remaining part of the procedure should not execute. The `Exit Sub` statement can be used to carry out the same action as `Return`.

Figure 4-16 *String Finder* application, when started

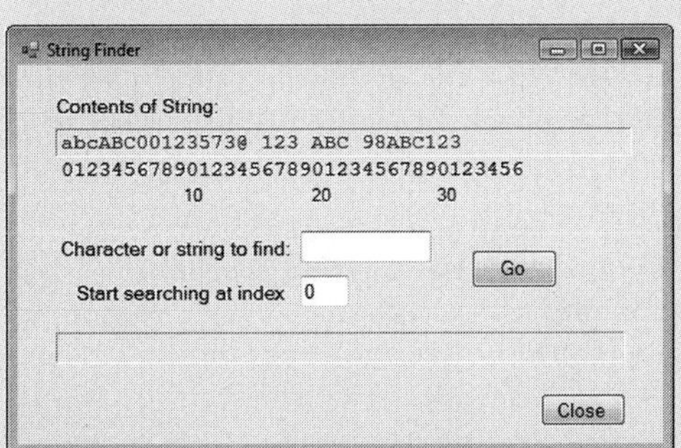

Figure 4-17 User enters substring they want to find, clicks *Go* button

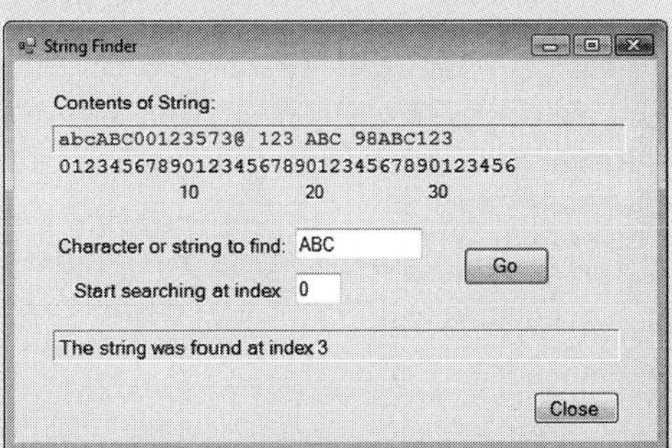

Figure 4-18 Searching for *ABC* starting at index position 4

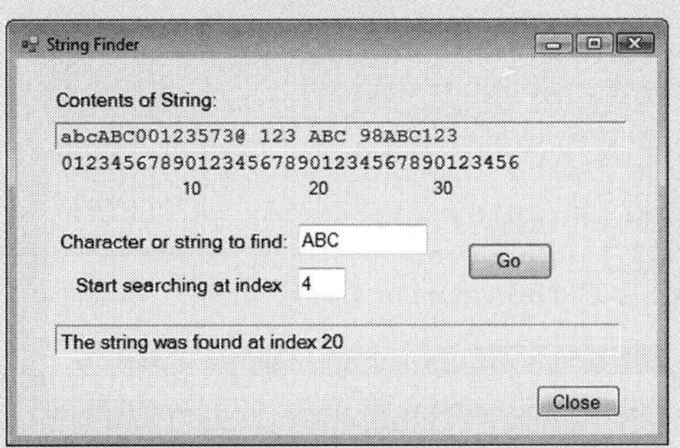

Figure 4-19 User has entered a nonnumeric index

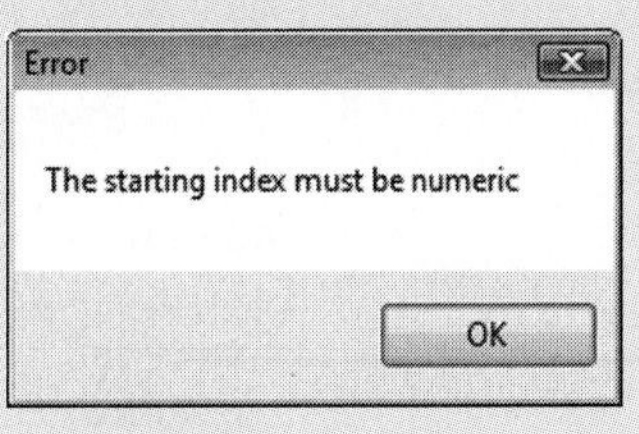

Step 1: Open the *String Finder* project from the student sample programs folder named *Chap4\String Finder*.

Step 2: Open *Form1* in Design mode. Click each control and view its name in the *Properties* window. When you begin writing code, you will want to know the control names.

Step 3: Double-click the *Go* button to open the *Code* window.

Step 4: You will be adding code to the `btnGo_Click` procedure, which handles the `Click` event for the *Go* button. Begin by adding a constant that will show the results of searching (shown in bold):

```
Private Sub btnGo_Click(ByVal sender As System.Object, _
    ByVal e As System.EventArgs) Handles btnGo.Click

  ' Value returned by IndexOf when a search fails.
  Const intNOT_FOUND As Integer = -1
```

Step 5: Next, add code to the same procedure that checks the starting index value entered by the user into the `txtStartIndex field`. If it is nonnumeric, we display an error message and exit the procedure. If it is a valid number, we assign it to the `intStart` variable:

```
  ' Make sure the starting index is numeric.
  ' Then get the starting index of the search.
  Dim intStart As Integer
  If Not IsNumeric(txtStartIndex.Text) Then
    MessageBox.Show("The starting index must be numeric", _
        "Error")
    Return
  Else
    intStart = CInt(txtStartIndex.Text)
  End If
```

Step 6: Insert the following code that checks for an empty search string. If it is blank, the procedure exits.

```
  ' Before searching, check for a possible empty string.
  ' Exit the subroutine if the string is empty.
  If txtToFind.Text.Length = 0 Then
    lblResults.Text = "There is no string to find!"
    Return
  End If
```

Step 7: Insert the following code that searches for the user's substring by calling the `IndexOf` method. It shows the results in `lblResults.Text`:

```
  ' Perform the search, returning the index of the first
  ' matching string.
  Dim intPos As Integer = lblString.Text.IndexOf _
      (txtToFind.Text, intStart)

  ' Output a message based on the search results. If the
  ' string was found, display its index position.
  If intPos = intNOT_FOUND Then
    lblResults.Text = "The string was not found"
  Else
    lblResults.Text = "The string was found at index " _
        & intPos
  End If
```

Step 8: Save and run the program. Search for the substring *ABC* starting at index 0. The program should find the string at position 3.

Step 9: Search for *ABC* starting at index 4. The program should find the string at position 20.

> **NOTE:** Some programmers dislike the use of multiple `Return` or `Exit Sub` statements because such statements create more than one exit point in a procedure. Following this rule strictly, however, can cause your code to contain complex nested `If` statements that are hard to understand and debug.

Checkpoint

4.9 Are each of the following relational expressions *True* or *False*?

a. `"ABC" > "XYZ"` ____________

b. `"AAA" = "AA"` ____________

c. `"ABC123" < "abc123"` ____________

4.10 Match the description in the right column with the method or function in the left column.

	Method	Description
_____	`IsNumeric`	a. Returns the uppercase equivalent of a string.
_____	`ToLower`	b. Returns the number of characters in a string.
_____	`ToUpper`	c. Returns a copy of a string without trailing spaces.
_____	`Length`	d. Returns a copy of a string without leading or trailing spaces.
_____	`TrimStart`	e. Searches for the first occurrence of a character or string within a string.
_____	`Substring`	f. Accepts a string as its argument and returns *True* if the string contains a number.
_____	`IndexOf`	g. Returns the lowercase equivalent of a string.
_____	`TrimEnd`	h. Extracts a string from within a string.
_____	`Trim`	i. Returns a copy of a string without leading spaces.

4.8 Focus on GUI Design: The Message Box

CONCEPT: Sometimes you need a convenient way to display a message to the user. This section discusses the `MessageBox.Show` method, which allows you to display a message in a dialog box.

A **message box** is a pop-up window that displays a message to the user. In Chapter 3 we briefly introduced the `MessageBox.Show` method, which displays a message box. In this section we will discuss the `MessageBox.Show` method in greater detail and you will learn more about its capabilities. We will discuss the following general formats of the method call:

```
MessageBox.Show(Message)
MessageBox.Show(Message, Caption)
MessageBox.Show(Message, Caption, Buttons)
MessageBox.Show(Message, Caption, Buttons, Icon)
MessageBox.Show(Message, Caption, Buttons, Icon, DefaultButton)
```

When **`MessageBox.Show`** executes, a message box (a Windows dialog box) pops up. For example, the following statement causes the message box shown in Figure 4-20 to appear:

```
MessageBox.Show("Operation complete.")
```

In the second format, *Caption* is a string to be displayed in the message box's title bar. The following statement causes the message box shown in Figure 4-21 to appear:

```
MessageBox.Show("Operation complete.", "Status")
```

Figure 4-20 Message box

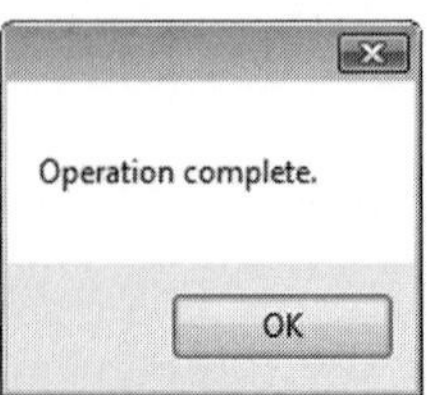

Figure 4-21 Message box with caption

In both formats, the message box has only an *OK* button. In the third format, *Buttons* is a value that specifies which buttons to display in the message box. Table 4-8 lists the available values for *Buttons* and describes each.

Table 4-8 Message box button values

Value	Description
`MessageBoxButtons.AbortRetryIgnore`	Displays *Abort*, *Retry*, and *Ignore* buttons
`MessageBoxButtons.OK`	Displays only an *OK* button
`MessageBoxButtons.OKCancel`	Displays *OK* and *Cancel* buttons
`MessageBoxButtons.RetryCancel`	Displays *Retry* and *Cancel* buttons
`MessageBoxButtons.YesNo`	Displays *Yes* and *No* buttons
`MessageBoxButtons.YesNoCancel`	Displays *Yes*, *No*, and *Cancel* buttons

For example, the following statement causes the message box shown in Figure 4-22 to appear:

```
MessageBox.Show("Do you wish to continue?", "Please Confirm", _
    MessageBoxButtons.YesNo)
```

Figure 4-22 Message box with caption and *Yes* and *No* buttons

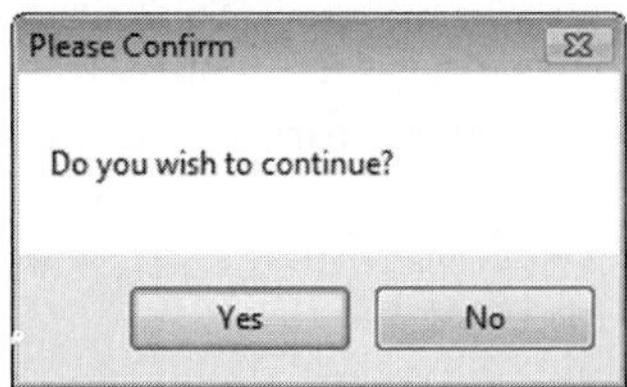

In some versions of `MessageBox.Show`, *Icon* is a value that specifies an icon to display in the message box. The available values for *Icon* are `MessageBoxIcon.Asterisk`, `MessageBoxIcon.Error`, `MessageBoxIcon.Exclamation`, `MessageBoxIcon.Hand`, `MessageBoxIcon.Information`, `MessageBoxIcon.Question`, `MessageBoxIcon.Stop`, and `MessageBoxIcon.Warning`. Figure 4-23 shows the icons matching each value. Note that some values display the same icon as others.

Figure 4-23 Message box icons

For example, the following statement causes the message box shown in Figure 4-24 to appear:

```
MessageBox.Show("Do you wish to continue?", "Please Confirm", _
    MessageBoxButtons.YesNo, MessageBoxIcon.Question)
```

Figure 4-24 Message box with caption, *Yes* and *No* buttons, and *Question* icon

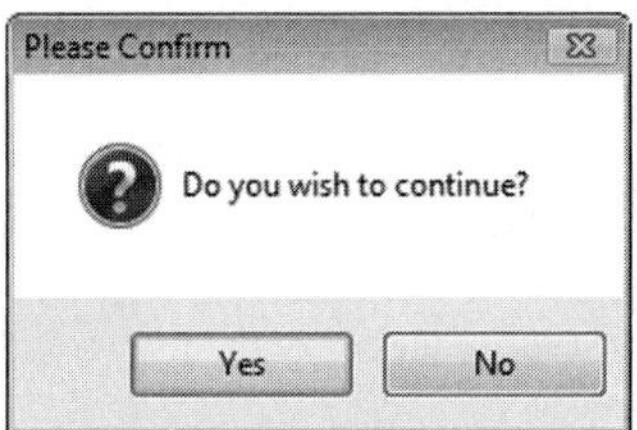

In one version of `MessageBox.Show`, the *DefaultButton* argument specifies which button to select as the default button. The default button is the button clicked when the user presses the Enter key. Table 4-9 lists the available values for this argument.

Table 4-9 *DefaultButton* values

Value	Description
`MessageBoxDefaultButton.Button1`	Selects the leftmost button on the message box as the default button
`MessageBoxDefaultButton.Button2`	Selects the second button from the left edge of the message box as the default button
`MessageBoxDefaultButton.Button3`	Selects the third button from the left edge of the message box as the default button

For example, the following statement displays a message box and selects `Button2` (the *No* button) as the default button:

```
MessageBox.Show("Do you wish to continue?", "Please Confirm", _
    MessageBoxButtons.YesNo, MessageBoxIcon.Question, _
    MessageBoxDefaultButton.Button2)
```

Determining Which Button the User Clicked

When the user clicks any button on a message box, the message box is dismissed. In code, the `MessageBox.Show` method returns an integer that indicates which button the user clicked. You can compare this value with the values listed in Table 4-10 to determine which button was clicked.

Table 4-10 `MessageBox.Show` return values

Value	Meaning
`Windows.Forms.DialogResult.Abort`	The user clicked the *Abort* button
`Windows.Forms.DialogResult.Cancel`	The user clicked the *Cancel* button
`Windows.Forms.DialogResult.Ignore`	The user clicked the *Ignore* button
`Windows.Forms.DialogResult.No`	The user clicked the *No* button
`Windows.Forms.DialogResult.OK`	The user clicked the *OK* button
`Windows.Forms.DialogResult.Retry`	The user clicked the *Retry* button
`Windows.Forms.DialogResult.Yes`	The user clicked the *Yes* button

The following code shows how an `If` statement can take actions based on which message box button the user clicked:

```
Dim intResult As Integer
intResult = MessageBox.Show("Do you wish to continue?", _
     "Please Confirm", MessageBoxButtons.YesNo)

If intResult = Windows.Forms.DialogResult.Yes Then
   ' Perform an action here
ElseIf intResult = Windows.Forms.DialogResult.No Then
   ' Perform another action here
End If
```

Using `ControlChars.CrLf` to Display Multiple Lines

If you want to display multiple lines of information in a message box, use the constant **`ControlChars.CrLf`** (`CrLf` stands for *carriage return line feed*). Concatenate it with the string you wish to display, where you wish to begin a new line (as shown in this example):

```
MessageBox.Show("This is line 1" & ControlChars.CrLf & _
     "This is line 2")
```

This statement causes the message box in Figure 4-25 to appear. When Visual Basic displays the string `"This is line 1" & ControlChars.CrLf & "This is line 2"`, it interprets `ControlChars.CrLf` as a command to begin a new line of output.

Figure 4-25 Message box displaying two lines

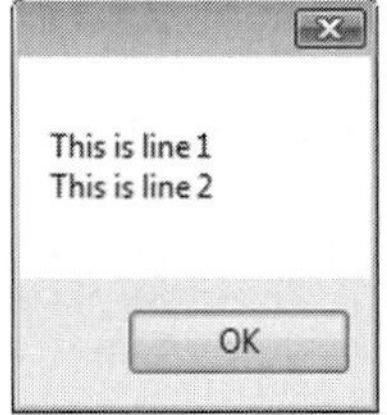

TIP: In code, you can use `ControlChars.CrLf` to create multiple lines in label text too.

Checkpoint

4.11 Match each of the message boxes in Figure 4-26 with the statement it displays.

Figure 4-26 Message boxes

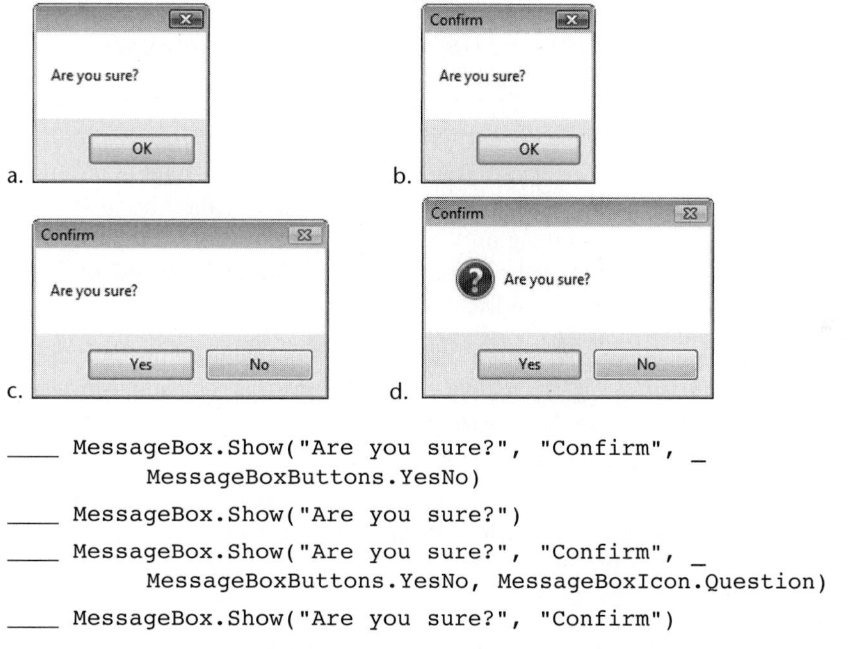


```
____ MessageBox.Show("Are you sure?", "Confirm", _
          MessageBoxButtons.YesNo)
____ MessageBox.Show("Are you sure?")
____ MessageBox.Show("Are you sure?", "Confirm", _
          MessageBoxButtons.YesNo, MessageBoxIcon.Question)
____ MessageBox.Show("Are you sure?", "Confirm")
```

4.12 What value can you compare with the `MessageBox.Show` method's return value to determine if the user has clicked the *Abort* button?

4.13 The following statement displays *William Joseph Smith* in a message box. How would you modify the statement so that *William*, *Joseph*, and *Smith* appear on three separate lines?

```
MessageBox.Show("William Joseph Smith")
```

4.9 The `Select Case` Statement

CONCEPT: In a `Select Case` statement, one of several possible actions is taken, depending on the value of an expression.

The `If...Then...ElseIf` statement allows your program to branch into one of several possible paths. It performs a series of tests and branches when one of these tests is true. The **`Select Case` statement**, which is a similar mechanism, tests the value of an expression only once, and then uses that value to determine which set of statements to branch to. Following is the general format of the `Select Case` statement. The items inside the brackets are optional.

```
Select Case TestExpression
  [Case ExpressionList
    [one or more statements]]
  [Case ExpressionList
    [one or more statements]]
  ' Case statements may be repeated
  ' as many times as necessary.
  [Case Else
    [one or more statements]]
End Select
```

The first line starts with `Select Case` and is followed by a test expression. The test expression may be any numeric or string expression that you wish to test.

Starting on the next line is a sequence of one or more `Case` statements. Each `Case` statement follows this general form:

```
Case ExpressionList
  one or more statements
```

After the word `Case` is an expression list, so-called because it may hold one or more expressions. Beginning on the next line, one or more statements appear. These statements are executed if the value of the test expression matches any of the expressions in the `Case` statement's expression list.

A `Case Else` comes after all the `Case` statements. This branch is selected if none of the `Case` expression lists match the test expression. The entire `Select Case` construct is terminated with an `End Select` statement.

WARNING: The `Case Else` section is optional. If you leave it out, however, your program will have nowhere to branch to if the test expression doesn't match any of the expressions in the `Case` expression lists.

Here is an example of the `Select Case` statement:

```
Select Case CInt(txtInput.Text)
  Case 1
    MessageBox.Show("Day 1 is Monday.")
  Case 2
    MessageBox.Show("Day 2 is Tuesday.")
  Case 3
    MessageBox.Show("Day 3 is Wednesday.")
  Case 4
    MessageBox.Show("Day 4 is Thursday.")
  Case 5
    MessageBox.Show("Day 5 is Friday.")
  Case 6
    MessageBox.Show("Day 6 is Saturday.")
  Case 7
    MessageBox.Show("Day 7 is Sunday.")
  Case Else
    MessageBox.Show("That value is invalid.")
End Select
```

Let's look at this example more closely. The test expression is `CInt(txtInput.Text)`. The `Case` statements `Case 1`, `Case 2`, `Case 3`, `Case 4`, `Case 5`, `Case 6`, and `Case 7` mark where the program is to branch to if the test expression is equal to the values 1, 2, 3, 4, 5, 6, or 7. The `Case Else` section is branched to if the test expression is not equal to any of these values.

Suppose the user has entered 3 into the `txtInput` text box, so the expression `CInt(txtInput.Text)` is equal to 3. Visual Basic compares this value with the first `Case` statement's expression list:

```
Select Case CInt(txtInput.Text)
➡ Case 1
    MessageBox.Show("Day 1 is Monday.")
```

The only value in the expression list is 1, and this is not equal to 3, so Visual Basic goes to the next `Case`:

```
Select Case CInt(txtInput.Text)
  Case 1
    MessageBox.Show "Day 1 is Monday."
➡ Case 2
    MessageBox.Show "Day 2 is Tuesday."
```

Once again, the value in the expression list does not equal 3, so Visual Basic goes to the next `Case`:

```
Select Case CInt(txtInput.Text)
  Case 1
    MessageBox.Show("Day 1 is Monday.")
  Case 2
    MessageBox.Show("Day 2 is Tuesday.")
➡ Case 3
    MessageBox.Show("Day 3 is Wednesday.")
```

This time, the value in the `Case`'s expression list matches the value of the test expression, so the `MessageBox.Show` statement on the next line executes. (If there had been multiple statements appearing between the `Case 3` and `Case 4` statements, all would have executed.) After the `MessageBox.Show` statement executes, the program jumps to the statement immediately following the `End Select` statement.

The `Select Case` Structure in Flowcharts and Pseudocode

The flowchart segment in Figure 4-27 shows the general form of a `Case` structure. The diamond represents the test expression, which is compared to a series of values. The path of execution follows the value matching the test expression. If none of the values matches a test expression, the default path is followed (`Case Else`).

As with the `If` statement, the pseudocode for the `Select Case` statement looks very similar to the actual programming statements. The following is an example:

Select Input
  Case 1
    Display Message "Day 1 is Monday."
  Case 2
    Display Message "Day 2 is Tuesday."
  Case 3
    Display Message "Day 3 is Wednesday."
  Case 4
    Display Message "Day 4 is Thursday."
  Case 5
    Display Message "Day 5 is Friday."
  Case 6
    Display Message "Day 6 is Saturday."

Case 7
Display Message "Day 7 is Sunday."
Case Else
Display Message "That value is invalid."
End Select

Figure 4-27 General form of a `Case` structure

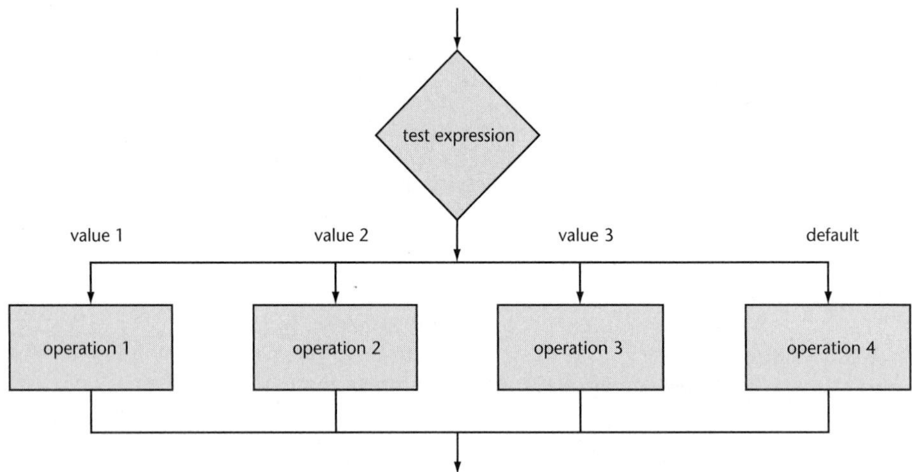

More about the Expression List

The `Case` statement's expression list can contain multiple expressions, separated by commas. For example, the first `Case` statement in the following code compares `intNumber` to 1, 3, 5, 7, and 9, and the second `Case` statement compares it to 2, 4, 6, 8, and 10. In the following code, assume that `strStatus` is a string variable:

```
Select Case intNumber
  Case 1, 3, 5, 7, 9
    strStatus = "Odd"
  Case 2, 4, 6, 8, 10
    strStatus = "Even"
  Case Else
    strStatus = "Out of Range"
End Select
```

The `Case` statement can also test string values. In the following code, assume that `strAnimal` is a string variable:

```
Select Case strAnimal
  Case "Dogs", "Cats"
    MessageBox.Show ("House Pets")
  Case "Cows", "Pigs", "Goats"
    MessageBox.Show ("Farm Animals")
  Case "Lions", "Tigers", "Bears"
    MessageBox.Show ("Oh My!")
End Select
```

You can use relational operators in the `Case` statement, as shown by the following example. The `Is` keyword represents the test expression in the relational comparison.

```
Select Case sngTemperature
  Case Is <= 75
```

```
    blnTooCold = True
  Case Is >= 100
    blnTooHot = True
  Case Else
    blnJustRight = True
End Select
```

Finally, you can determine whether the test expression falls within a range of values. This requires the `To` keyword, as shown in the following code.

```
Select Case intScore
  Case Is >= 90
    strGrade = "A"
  Case 80 To 89
    strGrade = "B"
  Case 70 To 79
    strGrade = "C"
  Case 60 To 69
    strGrade = "D"
  Case 0 To 59
    strGrade = "F"
  Case Else
    MessageBox.Show("Invalid Score")
End Select
```

The numbers used on each side of the `To` keyword are included in the range. So, the statement `Case 80 To 89` matches the values 80, 89, or any number in between.

TIP: The `To` keyword only works properly when the smaller number appears on its left and the larger number appears on its right. You can write an expression such as `10 To 0`, but it will not function properly at runtime.

Tutorial 4-8 examines a sales commission calculator application.

Tutorial 4-8:
Examining *Crazy Al's Sales Commission Calculator* application

Crazy Al's Computer Emporium is a retail seller of personal computers. The sales staff at Crazy Al's works strictly on commission. At the end of the month, each salesperson's commission is calculated according to Table 4-11.

For example, a salesperson with $16,000 in monthly sales earns a 12% commission ($1,920.00). A salesperson with $20,000 in monthly sales earns a 14% commission ($2,800.00).

Table 4-11 Sales commission rates

Sales This Month	Commission Rate
Less than $10,000	5%
$10,000 – $14,999	10%
$15,000 – $17,999	12%
$18,000 – $21,999	14%
$22,000 or more	16%

Because the staff is paid once per month, Crazy Al's allows each employee to take up to $1,500 per month in advance pay. When sales commissions are calculated, the amount of each employee's advance pay is subtracted from the commission. If any salesperson's commission is less than the amount of the advance, he or she must reimburse Crazy Al's for the difference.

Here are two examples:

- Beverly's monthly sales were $21,400, so her commission is $2,996. She took $1,500 in advance pay. At the end of the month she gets a check for $1,496.
- John's monthly sales were $12,600, so his commission is $1,260. He took $1,500 in advance pay. At the end of the month he must pay back $240 to Crazy Al's.

In this tutorial, you examine the *Crazy Al's Commission Calculator* application used to determine a salesperson's commission.

Step 1: Open the *Crazy Al* project from the student sample programs folder named *Chap4\Crazy Al*.

Step 2: Run the application. The form shown in Figure 4-28 appears.

Figure 4-28 *Crazy Al's Commission Calculator* form

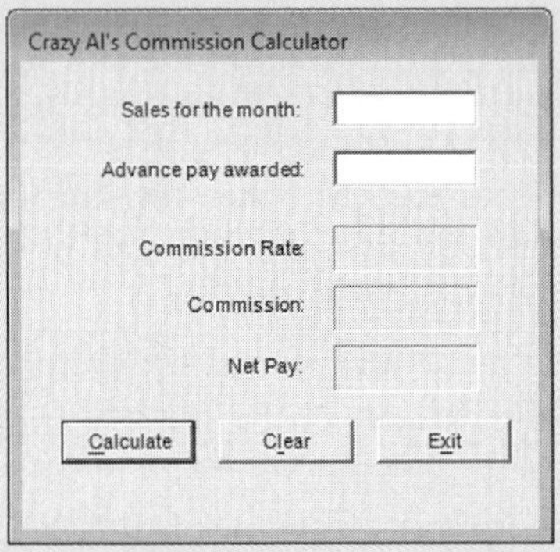

Step 3: Enter **16000** as the amount of sales for this month (first text box).

Step 4: Enter **1000** as the amount of advance pay taken (second text box). Click the *Calculate* button. You should see the commission rate, commission, and net pay information, as shown in Figure 4-29.

Step 5: Click the *Clear* button to reset the contents of the input and display fields.

Figure 4-29 Calculations filled in

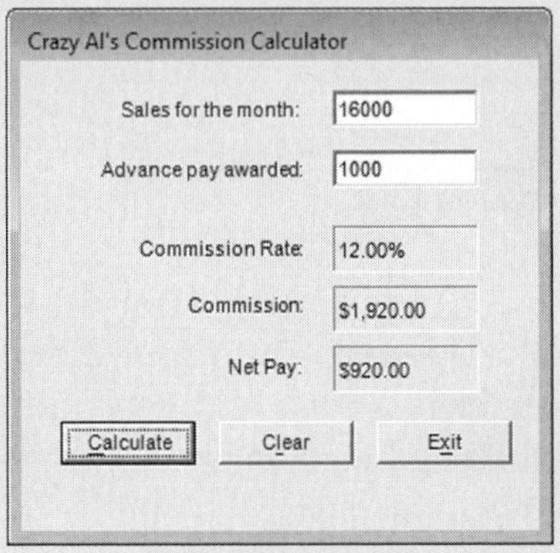

Experiment with other values for sales and advance pay.

Step 6: When you are finished, click the *Exit* button to end the application.

Step 7: Open the *Code* window and find the `btnCalculate_Click` event procedure. The code is as follows:

```
Private Sub btnCalculate_Click(ByVal eventSender As _
    System.Object, ByVal eventArgs As System.EventArgs) _
    Handles btnCalculate.Click

  Dim decSalesAmount As Decimal           ' Monthly sales amount
  Dim decAdvancePayAmount As Decimal      ' Advance pay taken
  Dim decCommissionRate As Decimal        ' Commission rate
  Dim decCommissionAmount As Decimal      ' Commission
  Dim decNetPay As Decimal                ' Net pay

  If IsNumeric(txtSalesAmount.Text) = False Then
    lblErrorMessage.Text = "Sales amount must be numeric"
    lblErrorMessage.Visible = True
    Return
  End If

  If IsNumeric(txtAdvancePayAmount.Text) = False Then
    lblErrorMessage.Text = "Advance pay amount must be numeric"
    lblErrorMessage.Visible = True
    Return
  End If

  ' Past this point, the user inputs contain decimal values.
  ' Hide the error message label and do the calculations.
  lblErrorMessage.Visible = False
  decSalesAmount = CDec(txtSalesAmount.Text)
  decAdvancePayAmount = CDec(txtAdvancePayAmount.Text)

  ' Determine the commission rate. Constants are in Decimal
  ' format.
  Select Case decSalesAmount
    Case Is < 10000
      decCommissionRate = 0.05D
    Case Is 10000 To 14999.9999
      decCommissionRate = 0.1D
    Case 15000 To 17999.9999
      decCommissionRate = 0.12D
    Case 18000 To 21999.9999
      decCommissionRate = 0.14D
    Case Is >= 22000
      decCommissionRate = 0.15D
    End Select

  ' Calculate the commission and net pay amounts.
  decCommissionAmount = decSalesAmount * decCommissionRate
  decNetPay = decCommissionAmount - decAdvancePayAmount

  ' Display the rate, commission, and net pay.
  lblCommissionRate.Text = decCommissionRate.ToString("p")
  lblCommissionAmount.Text = decCommissionAmount.ToString("c")
  lblNetPay.Text = decNetPay.ToString("c")
End Sub
```

As you can see, the `Select Case` construct has a `Case` statement for each level of sales in the commission table.

Checkpoint

4.14 Convert the following `If...Then...ElseIf` statement into a `Select Case` statement.

```
If intQuantity >= 0 And intQuantity <= 9 Then
   decDiscount = 0.1
ElseIf intQuantity >= 10 And intQuantity <= 19 Then
   decDiscount = 0.2
ElseIf intQuantity >= 20 And intQuantity <= 29 Then
   decDiscount = 0.3
ElseIf intQuantity >= 30 Then
   decDiscount = 0.4
Else
   MessageBox.Show("Invalid Data")
End If
```

4.10 Introduction to Input Validation

CONCEPT: Input validation is the process of inspecting input values and determining whether they are valid.

The accuracy of a program's output is only as good as the accuracy of its input. Therefore, it is important that your applications perform input validation on the values entered by the user. **Input validation** is the process of inspecting input values and determining whether they are valid. Now that you know how to use the `If` statement for conditional processing, you have more validation techniques at your disposal.

The `TryParse` Method

Each of the numeric classes in Visual Basic contains a method named `TryParse`. This method attempts to convert an input value to a certain numeric or date type, and returns a Boolean value that tells you if the conversion worked. For example, the `Integer.TryParse` method tries to convert an input value to Integer. It has two input parameters:

```
Integer.TryParse(valueToConvert, targetValue As Integer) As Boolean
```

The following statements attempt to convert the contents of a TextBox named `txtInput` to an integer and assign the value to `intResult`:

```
Dim intResult As Integer

If Integer.TryParse(txtInput.Text, intResult) Then
  lblResult.Text = "Success!"
Else
  lblResult.Text = "Error: an integer was not found"
End If
```

If the TextBox contains a valid integer string such as `"26"`, the variable named `intResult` is assigned the value 26. If the TextBox cannot be converted to an integer, an error message is displayed by the program.

Other classes contain `TryParse` methods, including `Short`, `Long`, `Single`, `Double`, `Decimal`, `Date`, and `Boolean`. Each has the same basic format. The following statements call `Date.TryParse` and display an error message if the conversion failed:

```
Dim dtmTemp As Date
If Not Date.TryParse("05/15/2009 8:15 PM", dtmTemp) Then
  lblResult.Text = "Not a valid date"
End If
```

Checking Multiple Values

Many applications must validate multiple user input values. You can combine calls to the `TryParse` method by using the `AndAlso` operator. The following example checks the `txtWeight` and `txtDistance` TextBox controls before copying their contents to variables:

```
If Single.TryParse(txtWeight.Text, sngWeight) _
  AndAlso Single.TryParse(txtDistance.Text, sngDistance) Then

  ' ok to use the sngWeight and sngDistance variables now
Else
  lblResult.Text = "Weight and distance must be integers"
End If
```

See the *TryParse Example* application in the Chapter 4 examples folder for a working demonstration of the `TryParse` method.

Using `If` Statements to Check Ranges of Values

In addition to checking for valid conversions, we often check input values to make sure they fall within a consistent and reasonable range. For example, consider the *Crazy Al's Commission Calculator* application. The `btnCalculate_Click` procedure gets the amount of a salesperson's sales and advance pay taken (values entered by the user) and calculates the sales commission. The following code shows part of the procedure after it has been modified to validate the user's input:

```
' Validate the input to prevent the user from
' entering negative values.
If (decSalesAmount < 0) Or (decAdvancePayAmount < 0) Then
  lblErrorMessage.Text = "Sales & advance pay must be positive"
  lblErrorMessage.Visible = True
Else
  ' Determine the commission rate.
  Select Case decSalesAmount
    Case Is < 10000
      decCommissionRate = 0.05D
    Case 10000 To 14999
      decCommissionRate = 0.1D
    Case 15000 To 17999
      decCommissionRate = 0.12D
    Case 18000 To 21999
      decCommissionRate = 0.14D
    Case Is >= 22000
      decCommissionRate = 0.15D
  End Select

  ' Calculate the commission and net pay amounts.
  decCommissionAmount = decSalesAmount * decCommissionRate
  decNetPay = decCommissionAmount - decAdvancePayAmount
```

```
    ' Display the rate, commission, and net pay.
    lblCommissionRate.Text = decCommissionRate.ToString("p")
    lblCommissionAmount.Text = decCommissionAmount.ToString("c")
    lblNetPay.Text = decNetPay.ToString("c")
  End If
```

The `If...Then...Else` statement displays an error message if `decSalesAmount` or `decAdvancePayAmount` contain negative values. The commission calculations are only performed when these variables contain nonnegative numbers.

4.11 Focus on GUI Design: Radio Buttons and Check Boxes

CONCEPT: Radio buttons appear in groups of two or more, allowing the user to select one of several options. A check box allows the user to select an item by checking a box, or delselect the item by unchecking the box.

Radio Buttons

Radio buttons are useful when you want the user to select one choice from several possible choices. Figure 4-30 shows a group of radio buttons.

A radio button may be selected or deselected. Each radio button has a small circle that appears filled-in when the radio button is selected, and appears empty when the radio button is deselected.

Visual Basic provides the **RadioButton control**, which allows you to create radio buttons. Radio buttons are normally grouped in one of the following ways:

- All radio buttons inside a group box are members of the same group.
- All radio buttons on a form not inside a group box are members of the same group.

Figure 4-31 shows two forms. The form on the left has three radio buttons that belong to the same group. The form on the right has two groups of radio buttons.

At runtime, only one radio button in a group may be selected at a time, which makes them mutually exclusive. Clicking on a radio button selects it, and automatically deselects any other radio button in the same group.

NOTE: The name *radio button* refers to the old car radios that had push buttons for selecting stations. Only one button could be pushed in at a time. When you pushed a button, it automatically popped out the currently selected button.

Figure 4-30 Radio buttons

Figure 4-31 Forms with radio buttons

Radio Button Properties

Radio buttons have a Text property, which holds the text that is displayed next to the radio button's circle. For example, the radio buttons in the leftmost form in Figure 4-31 have their Text properties set to *Coffee*, *Tea*, and *Soft Drink*.

Radio buttons have a Boolean property named Checked. The **Checked property** is set to *True* when the radio button is selected and *False* when the radio button is deselected. Their default value is *False*.

Working with Radio Buttons in Code

The standard prefix for radio button control names is `rad`. You determine if a radio button is selected by testing its Checked property. The following code shows an example. Assume that `radChoice1`, `radChoice2`, and `radChoice3` are radio buttons in the same group:

```
If radChoice1.Checked = True Then
  MessageBox.Show("You selected Choice 1")
ElseIf radChoice2.Checked = True Then
  MessageBox.Show("You selected Choice 2")
ElseIf radChoice3.Checked = True Then
  MessageBox.Show("You selected Choice 3")
End If
```

Radio Buttons have a **`CheckedChanged`** **event** that is triggered when the user selects or delelects a radio button. If you double-click a radio button in the *Design* window, a code template for the `CheckedChange` event procedure is created in the *Code* window.

Assigning a TabIndex Value and an Access Key to a Radio Button

Radio button controls have a position in the form's tab order, which may be changed with the TabIndex property. As with other controls, you can assign an access key to a radio button by placing an ampersand (`&`) in the Text property, just before the character you wish to serve as the access key. The character will appear underlined on the form. At runtime, when the user presses the Alt+*access key combination*, the focus shifts to the radio button, and the radio button is selected.

Selecting a Radio Button in Code

You can use code to select a radio button, using an assignment statement to set the desired radio button's Checked property to *True*, for example:

```
radChoice1.Checked = True
```

TIP: If you set a radio button's Checked property to *True* in Design mode (with the *Properties* window), it becomes the default radio button for that group. It is selected when the application starts up and it remains selected until the user or application code selects another radio button.

Check Boxes

A *check box* appears as a small box, labeled with a caption. An example is shown in Figure 4-32.

Figure 4-32 Check box

Visual Basic provides the **CheckBox control**, which allows you to create check boxes. Like radio buttons, check boxes may be selected or deselected at runtime. When a check box is selected, a small check mark appears inside the box. Unlike radio buttons, check boxes are not mutually exclusive. You may have one or more check boxes on a form or in a group box, and any number of them can be selected at any given time.

The standard prefix for a CheckBox control's name is `chk`. Like radio buttons, check boxes have a Checked property. When a check box is selected, or checked, its Checked property is set to *True*. When a check box is deselected, or unchecked, its Checked property is set to *False*. Here is a summary of other characteristics of the check box:

- A check box's caption is stored in the Text property.
- A check box's place in the tab order may be modified with the TabIndex property. When a check box has the focus, a thin dotted line appears around its text. You can check or uncheck it by pressing the Spacebar.
- You may assign an access key to a check box by placing an ampersand (`&`) in the Text property, just before the character that you wish to serve as the access key.
- You can use code to select or deselect a check box. Simply use an assignment statement to set the desired check box's Value property, for example:

```
chkChoice4.Checked = True
```

- You may set a check box's Checked property at design time.
- Like radio buttons, check boxes have a `CheckedChanged` event that is triggered whenever the user changes the state of the check box. If you have written a `CheckedChanged` event procedure for the check box, it will execute whenever the user checks or unchecks the check box.

In Tutorial 4-9, you examine an application that demonstrates radio buttons and check boxes.

Tutorial 4-9:
Completing an application with radio buttons and check boxes

Step 1: Open the *Radio Button Check Box Demo* project from the student sample programs folder named *Chap4\Radio Button Check Box Demo*.

Step 2: Open *Form1* in *Design* mode, as shown in Figure 4-33.

Figure 4-33 *Radio Button Check Box Demo* form

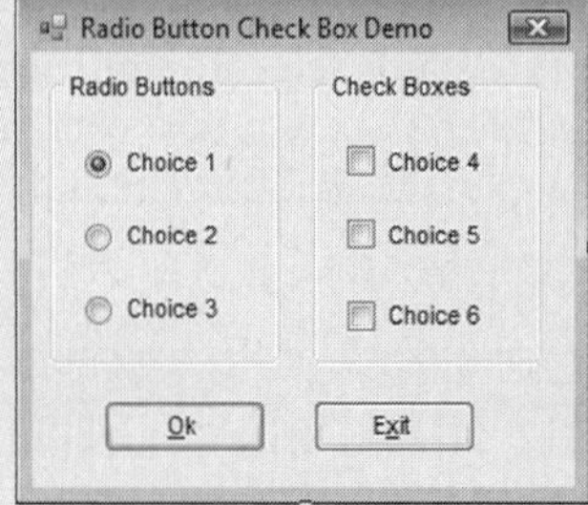

Step 3: Open the code window for *Form1*.

Step 4: Double-click the *Ok* button and insert the following code into the `btnOk_Click` event handler, which evaluates the user's radio button selection:

```
Private Sub btnOk_Click(ByVal eventSender As System.Object, _
    ByVal eventArgs As System.EventArgs) Handles btnOk.Click

  'Declare a string variable to hold a message.
  Dim strMessage As String = String.Empty

  ' The following If...ElseIf statement tests the
  ' group of radio buttons and copies the
  ' first part of the message to strMessage.

  If radChoice1.Checked = True Then
    strMessage = "You selected Choice 1"
  ElseIf radChoice2.Checked = True Then
    strMessage = "You selected Choice 2"
  ElseIf radChoice3.Checked = True Then
    strMessage = "You selected Choice 3"
  End If
```

Step 5: Continuing in the same method code area, insert the following code right after the code you inserted in Step 4:

```
  ' The following If...Then statements test the
  ' check boxes and concatenates another part
  ' of the message to strMessage.
  If chkChoice4.Checked = True Then
    strMessage &= " and Choice 4"
  End If
  If chkChoice5.Checked = True Then
    strMessage &= " and Choice 5"
  End If
  If chkChoice6.Checked = True Then
    strMessage &= " and Choice 6"
  End If

  ' Now display the message.
  MessageBox.Show(strMessage)
End Sub
```

Because the Checked property is Boolean, you can simplify statements that use it in expressions. The following expression, for example:

```
If chkChoice4.Checked Then
```

is equivalent to the longer form:

```
If chkChoice4.Checked = True Then
```

Step 6: Save the project and run the application.

Step 7: Click *Choice 3*, *Choice 4*, and *Choice 6*. You should see the message box shown in Figure 4-34. Experiment by clicking different radio buttons and check boxes. Note the results.

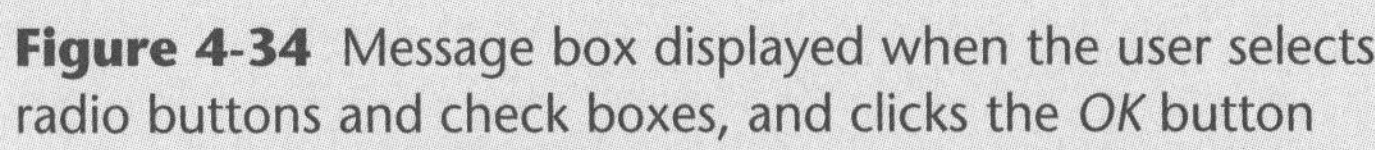

Figure 4-34 Message box displayed when the user selects radio buttons and check boxes, and clicks the *OK* button

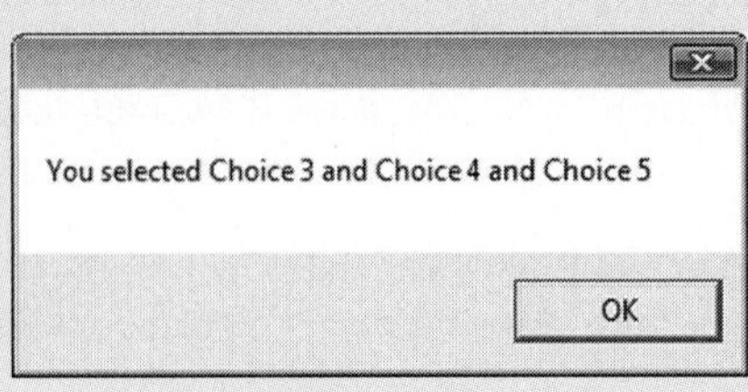

Checkpoint

4.15 In code, how do you determine whether a radio button has been selected?

4.16 If several radio buttons are placed on a form, not inside group boxes, how many of them may be selected at any given time?

4.17 In code, how do you determine whether a check box has been selected?

4.18 If several check boxes appear on a form, how many of them may be selected at any given time?

4.19 How can the user check or uncheck a check box that has the focus by using the keyboard?

4.12 Class-Level Variables

CONCEPT: Class-level variables are not local to any procedure. In a form file they are declared outside of any procedure and may be accessed by statements in any procedure in the same form.

A variable's **scope** is the area of a program in which the variable is visible. All variables you have created so far had **local scope**, meaning that each was declared and used inside a single method or procedure. Sometimes a variable needs to be created in such a way that it can be shared between two or more methods. We might declare the variable inside a class, for example, giving it **class scope** (or **module scope**).

A Visual Basic form is defined by a class, so variables declared within its code area, yet outside of any of its methods, have class scope. When we refer to a **class-level variable,** we mean a variable that has class scope. The following code example shows the difference between local scope and class scope (variable declarations shown in bold):

```
Public Class Form1

    ' Class-level variable
    Dim decTotalSalary As Decimal

    Private Sub btnAddWeekly_Click(ByVal sender As System.Object, _
        ByVal e As System.EventArgs) Handles btnAddWeekly.Click

      'Local variable
      Dim decWeeklyPay As Decimal

      decWeeklyPay = CDec(txtPay.Text)
      decTotalSalary += decWeeklyPay
```

```
14:
15:     End Sub
16:
17:     Private Sub btnShowTotal_Click(ByVal sender As System.Object, _
18:          ByVal e As System.EventArgs) Handles btnShowTotal.Click
19:        MessageBox.Show("Total salary is " & CStr(decTotalSalary))
20:
21:        ' The following statement is illegal because
22:        ' decWeeklyPay is not visible in current scope:
23:        decWeeklyPay = 0
24:     End Sub
25:
26: End Class
```

The variable `decTotalSalary` (line 4) is declared at the class level, so it is visible to all methods in the `Form1` class. We say that it has class scope. It is referenced from two different methods, on lines 13 and 19.

The variable `decWeeklyPay` (line 10) is declared inside the `btnAddWeekly_Click` method, so it has local scope. It is only visible between lines 10 and 14. Our attempt on line 23 to reference it causes a syntax error.

Overuse of Class-Level Variables

Overuse of class-level variables can lead to problems as programs become larger and more complex. While debugging a program, if you find the wrong value stored in a class-level variable, you'll have to track down every statement that accesses it to determine where the bad value is coming from. In a large program, this can be a tedious and time-consuming process.

Also, when two or more procedures modify the same variable, you must ensure that one procedure cannot upset the accuracy or correctness of another procedure by modifying a class-level variable. Class-level variables should only be used when variables must be shared between two or more class methods. In such cases, local variables are not adequate.

Checkpoint

4.20 What is the difference between a class-level variable and a local variable?

4.21 Where do you declare class-level variables?

4.13 Focus on Program Design and Problem Solving: Building the *Health Club Membership Fee Calculator* Application

CONCEPT: In this section you build the *Health Club Membership Fee Calculator* application. It will use features discussed in this chapter, including `If` statements, a `Select Case` statement, radio buttons, and check boxes.

The Bay City Health and Fitness Club charges the following monthly membership rates:

Standard adult membership:	$40/month
Child (age 12 and under):	$20/month
Student:	$25/month
Senior citizen (age 65 and over):	$30/month

The club also offers the following optional services, which increase the base monthly fee:

Yoga lessons:	add $10 to the monthly fee
Karate lessons:	add $30 to the monthly fee
Personal trainer:	add $50 to the monthly fee

Discounts are available, depending on the length of membership:

1–3 months:	No discount
4–6 months:	5% discount
7–9 months:	8% discount
10 or more months:	10% discount

The manager of the club has asked you to create a *Health Club Membership Fee Calculator* application. It should allow the user to select a membership rate, select optional services, and enter the number of months of the membership. It should calculate the member's monthly and total charges for the specified number of months. The application should also validate the number of months entered by the user. An error message should be displayed if the user enters a number less than 1 or greater than 24. (Membership fees tend to increase every two years, so there is a club policy that no membership package can be purchased for more than 24 months at a time.)

Figure 4-35 shows a sketch of the application's form. The figure also shows the name of each control with a programmer-defined name.

Figure 4-35 Sketch of the *Health Club Membership Fee Calculator* form

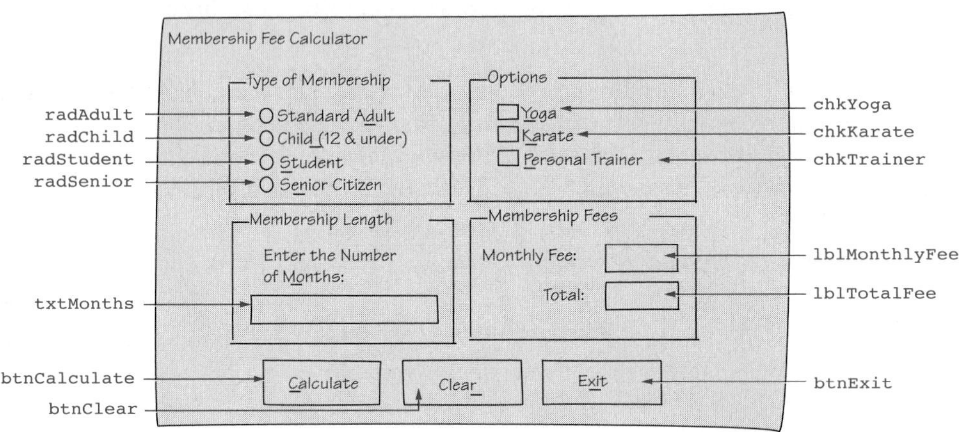

Table 4-12 lists each control, along with any relevant property settings.

Table 4-12 *Health Club Membership Fee Calculator* controls

Control Type	Control Name	Property	Property Value
Form	(Default)	Text:	*Membership Fee Calculator*
Group box	(Default)	Text:	*Type of Membership*
Radio button	`radAdult`	Text:	*Standard &Adult*
		Checked:	*True*
Radio button	`radChild`	Text:	*Chil&d (12 && under)*
Radio button	`radStudent`	Text:	*&Student*

(*continues*)

Table 4-12 *Health Club Membership Fee Calculator* controls (*continued*)

Control Type	Control Name	Property	Property Value
Radio button	`radSenior`	Text:	*S&enior Citizen*
Group box	(Default)	Text:	*Options*
Check box	`chkYoga`	Text:	*&Yoga*
Check box	`chkKarate`	Text:	*&Karate*
Check box	`chkTrainer`	Text:	*&Personal Trainer*
Group box	(Default)	Text:	*Membership Length*
Label	(Default)	Text:	*Enter the Number of &Months:*
Text box	`txtMonths`	Text:	
Group box	(Default)	Text:	*Membership Fees*
Label	(Default)	Text:	*Monthly Fee:*
Label	(Default)	Text:	*Total:*
Label	`lblMonthlyFee`	BorderStyle:	*Fixed3D*
		Text:	Initially cleared
		AutoSize:	*False*
Label	`lblTotalFee`	BorderStyle:	*Fixed3D*
		Text:	Initially cleared
		AutoSize:	*False*
Button	`btnCalculate`	Text:	*&Calculate*
Button	`btnClear`	Text:	*Clea&r*
Button	`btnExit`	Text:	*E&xit*

Table 4-13 lists and describes the event procedures (event handlers) needed for this application.

Table 4-13 *Health Club Membership Fee Calculator* event procedures

Method	Description
`btnCalculate_Click`	First, this procedure validates the number of months entered by the user. Then, if the input is valid, it calculates the monthly fees and the total fee for the time period. Charges for optional services and discounts are included. If the input is not valid, it displays an error message.
`btnClear_Click`	Clears the text box, output labels, and check boxes, and resets the radio buttons so that `radAdult` is selected.
`btnExit_Click`	Ends the application.

Figure 4-36 shows a flowchart for the `btnCalculate_Click` event procedure.

The number of months entered by the user is tested to determine whether it is valid. If the value is less than 1 or greater than 24, an error message is displayed. If the number of months is valid, the fees are calculated.

The first three processes in the calculation are (1) calculate the base monthly fee, (2) calculate and add the cost of optional services, and (3) determine the discount, if any. Each of these processes can be expanded into more detailed flowcharts. Figure 4-37 shows a more detailed view of the *calculate the base monthly fee* process.

Figure 4-36 Flowchart for `btnCalculate_Click`

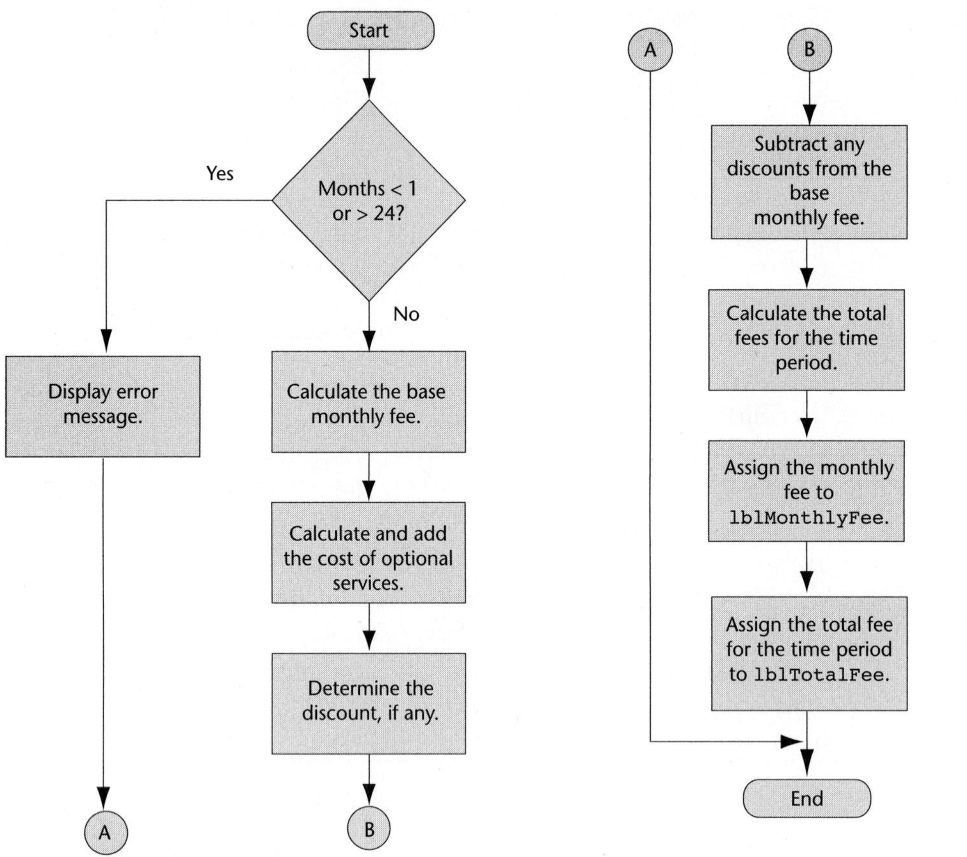

Figure 4-37 Flowchart of *calculate the base monthly fee* process

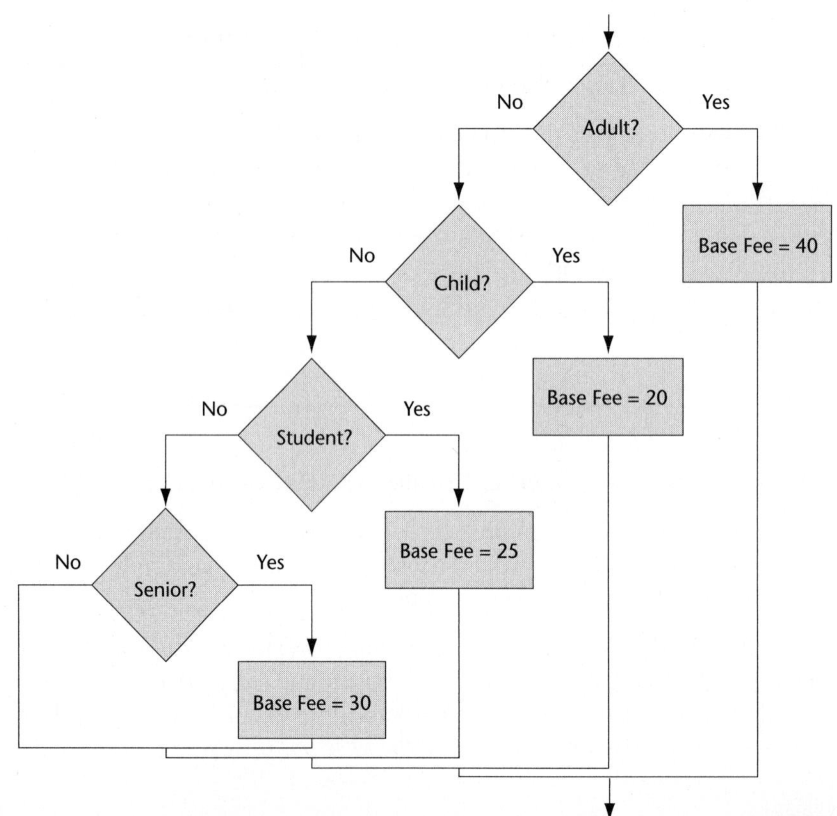

The logic in the flowchart can be expressed by the following pseudocode:

If Member is an Adult Then
Monthly Base Fee = 40
ElseIf Member is a Child Then
Montlhy Base Fee = 20
ElseIf Member is a Student Then
Monthly Base Fee = 25
ElseIf Member is a Senior Citizen Then
Monthly Base Fee = 30
End If

Figure 4-38 shows a more detailed view of the *calculate and add the cost of optional services* process.

Figure 4-38 Flowchart of *calculate and add the cost of optional services* process

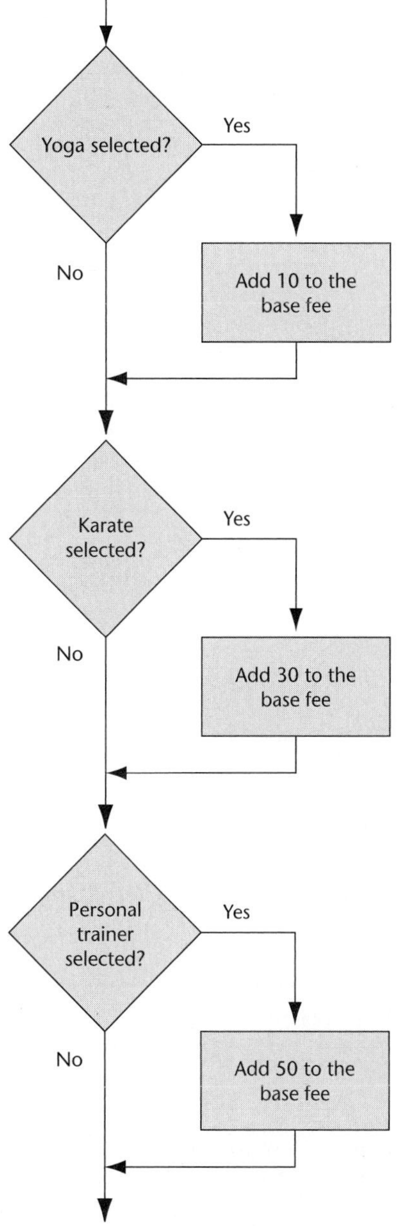

The logic in the flowchart can be expressed with the following pseudocode:

If Yoga is selected Then
Add 10 to the monthly base fee
End If
If Karate is selected Then
Add 30 to the monthly base fee
End If
If Personal Trainer is selected Then
Add 50 to the monthly base fee
End If

Figure 4-39 shows a more detailed view of the *determine the discount, if any* process.

Figure 4-39 Flowchart of *determine the discount, if any* process

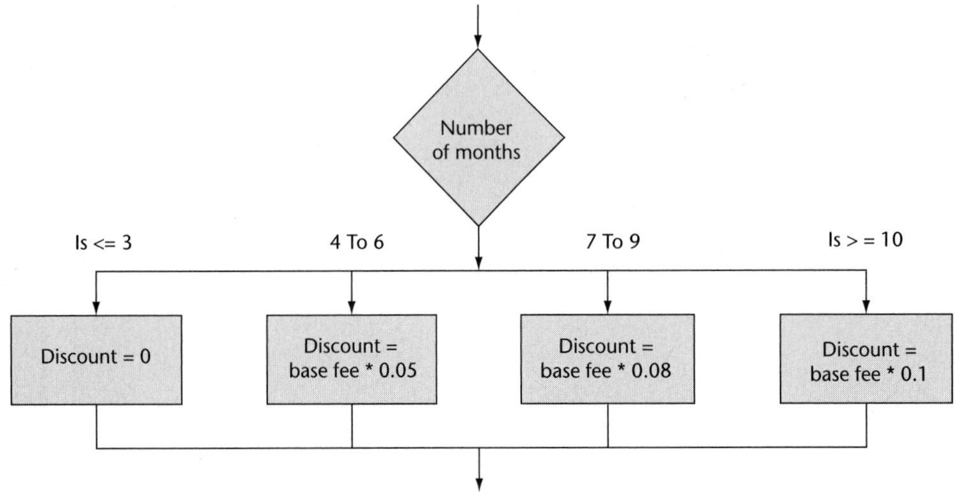

The logic in the flowchart may be expressed with the following pseudocode:

Select number of months
Case Is <= 3
Discount = 0% of monthly base fee
Case 4 To 6
Discount = 5% of monthly base fee
Case 7 To 9
Discount = 8% of monthly base fee
Case Is >= 10
Discount = 10% of monthly base fee
End Select

Tutorial 4-10 builds the *Health Club Membership Fee Calculator* application.

Tutorial 4-10:
Building the *Health Club Membership Fee Calculator* application

Step 1: Create a new Windows application project named *Health Club Membership Fee Calculator.*

Step 2: Set up the form as shown in Figure 4-40. Create the group boxes, radio buttons, and check boxes. Refer to the sketch in Figure 4-35 for the control names and Table 4-12 for the relevant property settings of each control.

Step 3: Once you have placed all the controls on the form and set their properties, you can write the application's code. First, you will write the `Dim` statements for class-level named constants used when calculating discounts. Click the *View Code* button (▤) on the *Solutions Explorer* window to open the *Code* window. Write the remarks and declarations shown on the next page. (Because these named constants are class-level, they will not be declared inside any procedure.)

Figure 4-40 *Membership Fee Calculator* form

```
Public Class Form1
  Inherits System.Windows.Forms.Form

  ' Health Club Membership Fee Calculator.
  ' This application calculates the monthly and
  ' total membership fees for the Bay City Health
  ' and Fitness Club. The base monthly fees are:
  '
  ' Standard adult membership:    $40/month
  ' Child (12 and under):         $20/month
  ' Student:                      $25/month
  ' Senior citizen (65 and over): $30/month
  '
  ' The club offers the following optional services,
  ' which increase the base monthly fee:
  '
  ' Yoga lessons:          Add $10 to the monthly fee
  ' Karate lessons:        Add $30 to the monthly fee
  ' Personal trainer:      Add $50 to the monthly fee
  '
  ' Discounts are available, depending on the length
  ' of membership. Here is a list of discounts:
  '
  ' 1 - 3 months:          No discount
  ' 4 - 6 months:          5% discount
  ' 7 - 9 months:          8% discount
  ' 10 or more months:     10% discount
```

```
' The following class-level constants are used
' to calculate discounts.
Const decDiscount4to6 As Decimal = 0.05D ' 4 to 6 months
Const decDiscount7to9 As Decimal = 0.08D ' 7 to 9 months
Const decDiscount10orMore As Decimal = 0.1D ' 10 or more mo.
```

Step 4: Open the *Design* window and double-click the *Calculate* button to create the code template for the control's `Click` event procedure. Complete the event procedure by typing the following lines (shown in bold):

```
Private Sub btnCalculate_Click(ByVal sender As _
    System.Object, ByVal e As System.EventArgs) _
    Handles btnCalculate.Click

  ' This method calculates and displays the membership fees.

  ' Declare local variables.
  Dim decBaseFee As Decimal       ' Base Monthly Fee
  Dim decDiscount As Decimal      ' Discount
  Dim decTotalFee As Decimal      ' Total Membership Fee
  Dim intMonths As Integer        ' Number of months

  ' Check the number of months and exit if it contains
  ' invalid data.
  If Not Integer.TryParse(txtMonths.Text,intMonths)Then
    MessageBox.Show("Months must be a valid integer", _
        "Input Error")
    Return
  End If

  ' Check the month range: must be 1-24.
  If (intMonths < 1) Or (intMonths > 24) Then
    MessageBox.Show("Months must be a valid integer", _
        "Input Error")
    Return
  End If
```

We use the first `If...Then` statement to prevent a runtime error if the user enters a nonnumeric value in the `txtMonths` control. The `Return` statement exits the method if an error is found because there is no point in executing any other code if there is invalid data. Similarly, the second `If...Then` statement checks the range of `intMonths` so it will always be between 1 and 24.

Step 5: Immediately after the code you just inserted, add statements that calculate the base monthly fee, based on the type of membership requested by the user. The four radio buttons (`radAdult`, `radChild`, `radStudent`, and `radSenior`) determine the base fee:

```
  ' If we reach this point, we assume the input data is valid.
  ' Calculate the base monthly fee.
  If radAdult.Checked = True Then
    decBaseFee = 40
  ElseIf radChild.Checked = True Then
    decBaseFee = 20
  ElseIf radStudent.Checked = True Then
    decBaseFee = 25
  ElseIf radSenior.Checked = True Then
    decBaseFee = 30
  End If
```

Step 6: Immediately after the code you just inserted, add statements that examine each of the check boxes (`chkYoga`, `chkKarate` , `chkTrainer`) to determine the additional services. Each will add a value to the base fee:

```
' Look for additional services.
If chkYoga.Checked = True Then
  decBaseFee += 10
End If
If chkKarate.Checked = True Then
  decBaseFee += 30
End If
If chkTrainer.Checked = True Then
  decBaseFee += 50
End If
```

Step 7: Based on the number of months, you must multiply a percentage value by the base fee to determine the amount of discount the member will receive. Insert the following code immediately following the previous code:

```
' Determine the discount, based on membership months.
Select Case intMonths
  Case Is <= 3
    decDiscount = 0
  Case 4 To 6
    decDiscount = decBaseFee * decDiscount4to6
  Case 7 To 9
    decDiscount = decBaseFee * decDiscount7to9
  Case Is >= 10
    decDiscount = decBaseFee * decDiscount10orMore
End Select
```

Step 8: Finally, subtract the discount from the base fee and calculate the total fee. Assign the base fee and monthly fee to labels. Insert the following code, finishing the `btnCalculate_Click` method:

```
  ' Adjust for discounts, calculate total fee.
  decBaseFee -= decDiscount
  decTotalFee = decBaseFee * intMonths

  ' Display the fees.
  lblMonthlyFee.Text = decBaseFee.ToString("c")
  lblTotal.Text = decTotalFee.ToString("c")
End Sub
```

Step 9: In the *Design* window, double-click the *Clear* button and insert the following code in its event handler:

```
Private Sub btnClear_Click(ByVal sender As System.Object, _
  ByVal e As System.EventArgs) Handles btnClear.Click

  ' Clear the form, reset the buttons and check boxes.
  radAdult.Checked = True
  chkYoga.Checked = False
  chkKarate.Checked = False
  chkTrainer.Checked = False
  txtMonths.Clear()
  lblMonthlyFee.Text = String.Empty
  lblTotalFee.Text = String.Empty
End Sub
```

Step 10: In the *Design* window, double-click the *Exit* button and insert the following code in its event handler:

```
Private Sub btnExit_Click(ByVal sender As System.Object, _
  ByVal e As System.EventArgs) Handles btnExit.Click

  ' End the application by closing the window.
  Me.Close()
End Sub
```

Step 11: Build the project by clicking the *Build Health Club Membership Fee Calculator* selection in the *Build* menu. Correct any syntax errors that result. Save the project.

Step 12: Run the application. If there are errors, refer to the code previously shown and correct them. If you make corrections, be sure to save the project again. Once the application runs, enter the following test data and confirm that it displays the correct output.

Type of Membership	Monthly Fee	Total
Standard adult with yoga, karate, and personal trainer for 6 months	$123.50	$741.00
Child with karate for 3 months	$50.00	$150.00
Student with yoga for 12 months	$31.50	$378.00
Senior citizen with karate and personal trainer for 8 months	$101.20	$809.60

Step 13: End the application.

Summary

4.1 The Decision Structure

- Programs often need more than one path of execution. Many algorithms require a program to execute some statements only under certain circumstances. The decision structure accomplishes this.

4.2 The `If...Then` Statement

- The `If...Then` statement can cause other statements to execute under certain conditions.
- Relational expressions can only be evaluated as *True* or *False*.
- Math operators and function calls can be used with relational operators.

4.3 The `If...Then...Else` Statement

- The `If...Then...Else` statement executes one group of statements if a condition is true and another group of statements if the condition is false.

4.4 The `If...Then...ElseIf` Statement

- The `If...Then...ElseIf` statement is like a chain of `If...Then...Else` statements that perform their tests, one after the other, until one of them is found to be true.

4.5 Nested `If` Statements

- A nested `If` statement is an `If` statement in the conditionally executed code of another `If` statement.

4.6 Logical Operators

- Logical operators connect two or more relational expressions into one (using `And`, `Or`, `AndAlso`, `OrElse`, or `Xor`), or reverse the logic of an expression (using `Not`).
- When determining whether a number is inside a numeric range, it's best to use the `And` operator.
- When determining whether a number is outside a range, it's best to use the `Or` operator.

4.7 Comparing, Testing, and Working with Strings

- Relational operators can be used to compare strings.
- An empty string is represented by two quotation marks, with no space between them.
- The intrinsic `IsNumeric` function accepts a string as its argument and returns *True* if the string contains a number. The function returns *False* if the string's contents cannot be recognized as a number.
- The `Substring` method extracts a specified number of characters from within a specified position in a string.
- The `IndexOf` method is used to search for a character or a string within a string.

4.8 Focus on GUI Design: The Message Box

- Message boxes are displayed with the `MessageBox.Show` method. The types of buttons and an icon to display in the message box can be specified.
- The return value of the `MessageBox.Show` method can be tested to determine which button the user clicked to dismiss the message box.

- The value `ControlChars.CrLf` can be concatenated with a string to produce multiple line displays.

4.9 The `Select Case` Statement

- The `Select Case` statement tests the value of an expression only once, and then uses that value to determine which set of statements to branch to.

4.10 Introduction to Input Validation

- The accuracy of a program's output depends on the accuracy of its input. It is important that applications perform input validation on the values entered by the user.

4.11 Focus on GUI Design: Radio Buttons and Check Boxes

- Radio buttons appear in groups and allow the user to select one of several possible options. Radio buttons placed inside a group box are treated as one group, separate and distinct from any other groups of radio buttons. Only one radio button in a group can be selected at any time.
- Clicking on a radio button selects it and automatically deselects any other radio button selected in the same group.
- Check boxes allow the user to select or deselect items. Check boxes are not mutually exclusive. There may be one or more check boxes on a form, and any number of them can be selected at any given time.

4.12 Class-Level Variables

- Class-Level variables are visible to all procedures (methods) in the same class.

4.13 Focus on Program Design and Problem Solving: Building the *Health Club Membership Fee Calculator* Application

- This section outlines the process of building the *Health Club Membership Fee Calculator* application using the features discussed in the chapter.

Key Terms

`And` operator
`AndAlso` operator
Boolean expression
CheckBox control
`CheckedChanged` event
Checked property
class-level variable
class scope
conditionally executed (statement)
`ControlChars.CrLf`
decision structure
empty string
flag
`If...Then`
`If...Then...Else`
`If...Then...ElseIf`
`IndexOf` method
input validation
`IsNumeric` function
leading space
Length property
local scope
logic error
logical operators
message box
`MessageBox.Show` method
module scope
nested `If` statement
`Not` operator
`Or` operator
`OrElse` operator
RadioButton control
relational expression
relational operator
scope
`Select Case` statement

sequence structure
short-circuit evaluation
`Substring` method
`ToLower` method
`ToUpper` method
trailing space
`Trim` method
`TrimEnd` method
`TrimStart` method
Unicode
`Xor` operator

Review Questions and Exercises

Fill-in-the-Blank

1. A __________ statement, when equal to *True*, can permit one or more other statementsto execute.
2. A(n) __________ operator determines if a specific relationship exists between two values.
3. Relational expressions can only be evaluated as __________ or __________.
4. A(n) __________ is a Boolean variable that signals when some condition exists in the program.
5. A non-Boolean variable or expression is considered __________ if its value is 0. If its value is anything other than 0, it is considered __________.
6. The __________ statement will execute one group of statements if the condition is true, and another group of statements if the condition is false.
7. The __________ statement is like a chain of `If...Then...Else` statements. They perform their tests, one after the other, until one of them is found to be true.
8. A __________ `If` statement is an `If` statement in the conditionally executed code of another `If` statement.
9. __________ operators connect two or more relational expressions into one or reverse the logic of an expression.
10. The __________ method returns the uppercase equivalent of a string.
11. The __________ returns a lowercase version of a string.
12. The __________ intrinsic function accepts a string as its argument and returns *True* if the string contains a number, or *False* if the string's contents cannot be recognized as a number.
13. The __________ method returns the number of characters in a string.
14. The __________ method returns a copy of a string without leading spaces.
15. The __________ method returns a copy of a string without trailing spaces.
16. The __________ method returns a copy of the string without leading or trailing spaces.
17. The __________ method extracts a specified number of characters from within a specified position in a string.
18. You can display message boxes with the __________ method.
19. The value __________ can be concatenated with a string to produce multiple line displays.

20. In a(n) __________ statement, one of several possible actions is taken, depending on the value of an expression.
21. __________ is the process of inspecting input values and determining whether they are valid.
22. ________ usually appear in groups and allow the user to select one of several possible options.
23. __________ may appear alone or in groups and allow the user to make yes/no, or on/off selections.
24. A __________ variable may be accessed by statements in any procedure in the same file as the variable's declaration.

True or False

Indicate whether the following statements are true or false.

1. T F: It is not possible to write an expression that contains more than one logical operator.
2. T F: It is not possible to write expressions that contain math, relational, and logical operators.
3. T F: You may use the relational operators to compare strings.
4. T F: Clicking on a radio button selects it, and leaves any other selected radio button in the same group selected as well.
5. T F: Radio buttons that are placed inside a group box are treated as one group, separate and distinct from any other groups of radio buttons.
6. T F: When a group of radio buttons appears on a form (outside of a group box), any number of them can be selected at any time.
7. T F: You may have one or more check boxes on a form, and any number of them can be selected at any given time.
8. T F: The `If...Then` statement is an example of a sequence structure.
9. T F: The `Dim` statement for a class-level variable appears inside a procedure.
10. T F: The `Substring` method returns a lowercase copy of a string.

Multiple Choice

1. Relational operators allow you to __________ numbers.
   a. Add
   b. Multiply
   c. Compare
   d. Average
2. This statement can cause other program statements to execute only under certain conditions.
   a. `MessageBox.Show`
   b. `Decide`
   c. `If`
   d. `Execute`

3. This is a variable, usually a Boolean, that signals when a condition exists.
   a. Relational operator
   b. Flag
   c. Arithmetic operator
   d. Float

4. This statement is like a chain of `If` statements. They perform their tests, one after the other, until one of them is found to be true.
   a. `If...Then`
   b. `If...Then...ElseIf`
   c. `Chain...If`
   d. `Relational`

5. When placed at the end of an `If...Then...ElseIf` statement, this provides default action when none of the `ElseIf` statements have true expressions.
   a. Trailing `If`
   b. Trailing `Select`
   c. Trailing `Otherwise`
   d. Trailing `Else`

6. When an `If` statement is placed within the conditionally executed code of another `If` statement, it is known as this type of statement.
   a. A nested `If`
   b. A complex `If`
   c. A compound `If`
   d. An invalid `If`

7. This operator connects two expressions into one. One or both expressions must be true for the overall expression to be true. It is only necessary for one to be true, and it does not matter which.
   a. `And`
   b. `Or`
   c. `Xor`
   d. `Not`

8. This operator connects two expressions into one. Both expressions must be true for the overall expression to be true.
   a. `And`
   b. `Or`
   c. `Xor`
   d. `Not`

9. This operator reverses the logical value of an expression. It makes a true expression false and a true expression true.
   a. `And`
   b. `Or`
   c. `Xor`
   d. `Not`

10. This operator connects two expressions into one. One, and only one, of the expressions must be true for the overall expression to be true. If both expressions are true, or if both expressions are false, the overall expression is false.
    a. `And`
    b. `Or`
    c. `Xor`
    d. `Not`

11. When determining whether a number is inside a numeric range, it's best to use this logical operator.
    a. `And`
    b. `Or`
    c. `Xor`
    d. `Not`
12. When determining whether a number is outside a range, it's best to use this logical operator.
    a. `And`
    b. `Or`
    c. `Xor`
    d. `Not`
13. In code you should test this property of a radio button or a check box to determine whether it is selected.
    a. Selected
    b. Checked
    c. On
    d. Toggle
14. This method which is part of the numeric classes, atempts to convert a value to a certain numeric or date type.
    a. `NumericConvert`
    b. `InputConvert`
    c. `TryParse`
    d. `TryConvert`
15. str is a string variable. This statement returns the length of the string stored in `str`.
    a. `Length(str)`
    b. `str.Length`
    c. `str.StringSize`
    d. `CharCount(str)`
16. Use this method to display a message box and determine which button the user clicked to dismiss the message box.
    a. `MessageBox.Show`
    b. `MessageBox.Button`
    c. `Message.Box`
    d. `MessageBox.UserClicked`

Short Answer

1. Describe the difference between the `If...Then...ElseIf` statement and a series of `If...Then` statements.
2. In an `If...Then...ElseIf` statement, what is the purpose of a trailing `Else`?
3. What is a flag and how does it work?
4. Can an `If` statement test expressions other than relational expressions? Explain.
5. Briefly describe how the `And` operator works.
6. Briefly describe how the `Or` operator works.
7. How is the `Xor` operator different from the `Or` operator?

8. How is the `AndAlso` operator different from the `And` operator?
9. How is the `OrElse` operator different from the `Or` operator?

What Do You Think?

1. Why are the relational operators called relational?
2. Answer the following questions about relational expressions with a *yes* or *no*.
   a. If it is true that $x > y$ and it is also true that $x < z$, does that mean $x < z$ is true?
   b. If it is true that $x >= y$ and it is also true that $z = x$, does that mean that $z = y$ is true?
   c. If it is true that $x <> y$ and it is also true that $x <> z$, does that mean that $z <> y$ is true?
3. Why do most programmers indent the conditionally executed statements in a decision structure?
4. Explain why you cannot convert the following `If...Then...ElseIf` statement into a `Select Case` statement.

```
If sngTemperature = 100 Then
   intX = 0
ElseIf intPopulation > 1000 Then
   intX = 1
ElseIf sngRate < .1 Then
   intX = -1
End If
```

Find the Error

1. What is syntactically incorrect in each of the following statements?

a.
```
If intX > 100
  MessageBox.Show("Invalid Data")
End If
```
b.
```
Dim str As String = "Hello"
Dim intLength As Integer
intLength = Length(str)
```
c.
```
If intZ < 10 Then
  MessageBox.Show("Invalid Data")
```
d.
```
Dim str As String = "123"
If str.IsNumeric Then
  MessageBox.Show("It is a number.")
End If
```
e.
```
Select Case intX
  Case < 0
    MessageBox.Show("Value too low.")
  Case > 100
    MessageBox.Show("Value too high.")
  Case Else
    MessageBox.Show("Value just right.")
End Select
```

Algorithm Workbench

1. Read the following instructions for cooking a pizza, and then design a flowchart with a decision structure that shows the necessary steps to cook the pizza with either thin and crispy or thick and chewy crust.

a. For thin and crispy crust, do not preheat the oven. Bake pizza at 450 degrees for 15 minutes.
b. For thick and chewy crust, preheat the oven to 400 degrees. Bake pizza for 20 minutes.

2. Write an `If` statement that assigns 0 to `intX` when `intY` is equal to 20.
3. Write an `If` statement that multiplies `decPayRate` by 1.5 when hours is greater than 40.
4. Write an `If` statement that assigns 0.2 to `decCommissionRate` when sales is greater than or equal to $10,000.00.
5. Write an `If` statement that sets the variable `intFees` to 50 when the Boolean variable `blnIsMax` equals *True*.
6. Write an `If...Then...Else` statement that assigns 1 to `intX` when `intY` is equal to 100. Otherwise it should assign 0 to `intX`.
7. The string variable `strPeople` contains a list of names, such as *Bill Jim Susan Randy Wilma* and so on. Write code that searches people for *Gene*. If *Gene* is found in `strPeople`, display a message box indicating that *Gene* was found.
8. Write an `If...Then` statement that prints the message *The number is valid* if the variable `sngSpeed` is within the range 0 through 200.
9. Write an `If...Then` statement that prints the message *The number is not valid* if the variable `sngSpeed` is outside the range 0 through 200.
10. Convert the following `If...Then...ElseIf` statement into a `Select Case` statement.

```
If intSelection = 1 Then
   MessageBox.Show("Pi times radius squared")
ElseIf intSelection = 2 Then
   MessageBox.Show("Length times width")
ElseIf intSelection = 3 Then
   MessageBox.Show("Pi times radius squared times height")
ElseIf intSelection = 4 Then
   MessageBox.Show("Well okay then, good bye!")
Else
   MessageBox.Show("Not good with numbers, eh?")
End If
```

Programming Challenges

1. **Larger and Smaller**

   Create an application that allows the user to enter two integers on a form similar to the one shown in Figure 4-41. The application should determine which value is larger than the other, or it should determine that the values are equal. Before comparing the numbers, use the `TryParse` method to verify that both inputs are valid integers. If an error is found, display an appropriate message to the user. Use a Label control to display all messages. The *Exit* button should close the window.

Figure 4-41 *Minimum/Maximum* form

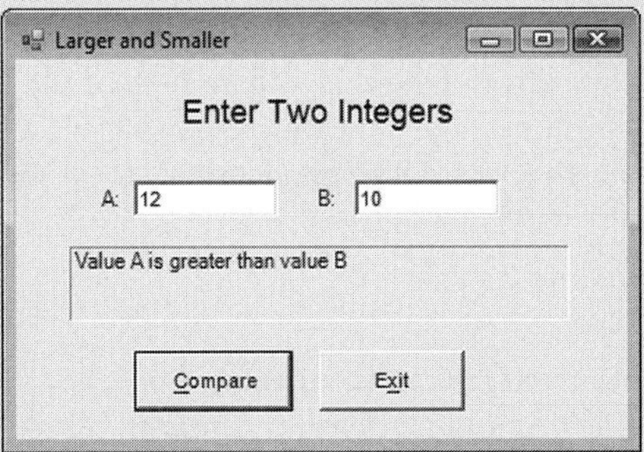

VideoNote

The Roman Numeral Converter Problem

2. **Roman Numeral Converter**

Create an application that allows the user to enter an integer between 1 and 10 into a text box on a form similar to the one shown in Figure 4-42. Use a `Select Case` statement to identify which Roman numeral is the correct translation of the integer. Display the Roman numeral in a Label control. If the user enters an invalid value, display an appropriate error message and do not attempt the conversion. Include an *Exit* button that closes the window.

Figure 4-42 *Roman Numeral Converter* form

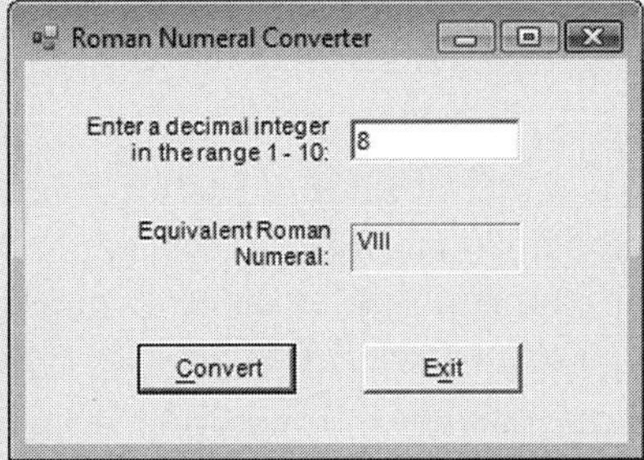

The following table lists the Roman numerals for the numbers 1 through 10.

Number	Roman Numeral
1	I
2	II
3	III
4	IV
5	V
6	VI
7	VII
8	VIII
9	IX
10	X

Input validation: Do not accept a number less than 1 or greater than 10. If the user enters a number outside this range, display an error message.

3. **Fat Percentage Calculator**

Create an application that allows the user to enter the number of calories and fat grams in a food. The application should display the percentage of the calories that come from fat. If the calories from fat are less than 30% of the total calories of the food, it should also display a message indicating the food is low in fat. (Display the message in a label or a message box.) The application's form should appear similar to the one shown in Figure 4-43.

One gram of fat has 9 Calories, so:

*Calories from fat = fat grams * 9*

The percentage of calories from fat can be calculated as:

Percentage of calories from fat = Calories from fat / total calories

Figure 4-43 *Fat Gram Calculator* form

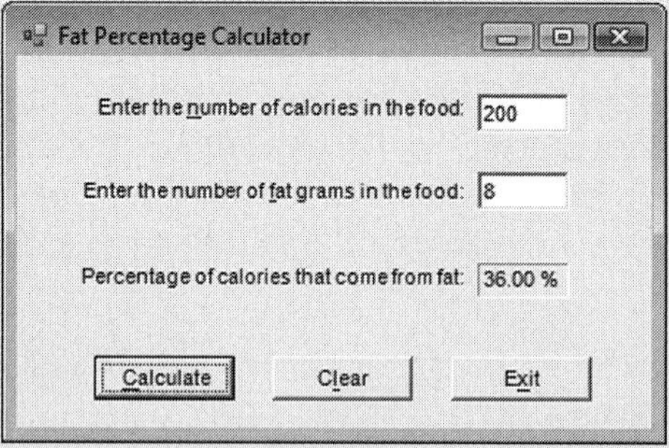

Input validation: Make sure the number of calories and fat grams are numeric, and are not less than 0. Also, the number of calories from fat cannot be greater than the total number of calories. If that happens, display an error message indicating that either the calories or fat grams were incorrectly entered.

Use the following test data to determine if the application is calculating properly:

Calories and Fat	Percentage Fat
200 calories, 8 fat grams	Percentage of calories from fat: 36%
150 calories 2 fat grams	Percentage of calories from fat: 12% (a low-fat food)
500 calories, 30 fat grams	Percentage of calories from fat: 54%

4. **Running the Race**

Create an application that allows the user to enter the names of three runners and the time it took each of them to finish a race. The application should display who came in first, second, and third place. You can assume that the two runners will never have exactly the same finishing times. The application's form should appear similar to the one shown in Figure 4-44. The *Clear* button should clear all text boxes and calculated labels. The *Exit* button should close the window. Include the following input error checking: No runner name can be blank, and finishing times must be both numeric and positive.

Use the following test data to determine if the application is calculating properly:

Names and Times	Results	
John, 87 seconds	First place:	Carol
Carol, 74 seconds	Second place:	John
Shelly, 94 seconds	Third place:	Shelly

Figure 4-44 *Race Results* form

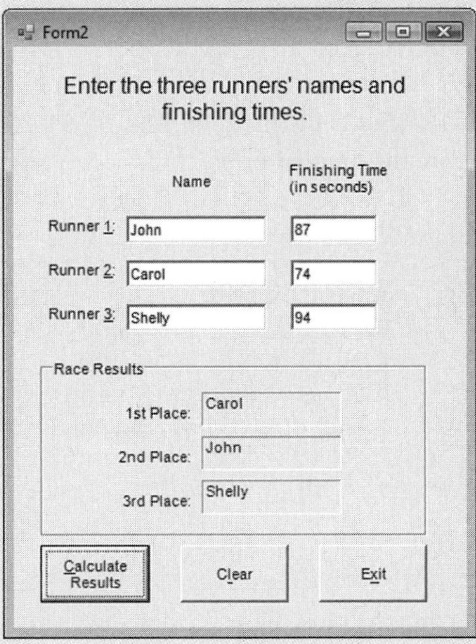

5. **Software Sales**

A software company sells three packages, Package A, Package B, and Package C, which retail for $99, $199, and $299, respectively. Quantity discounts are given according to the following table:

Quantity	Discount
10 through 19	20%
20 through 49	30%
50 through 99	40%
100 or more	50%

Create an application that allows the user to enter the number of units sold for each software package. The application's form should resemble Figure 4-45.

Figure 4-45 *Software Sales* form

Software Sales
Quantity Sold
Package A: 15
Package B: 75
Package C: 120
Package A: $1,188.00
Package B: $8,955.00
Package C: $17,940.00
Grand Total: $28,083.00
Calculate
Clear
Exit

The application should calculate and display the order amounts and the grand total in a Label control. Error checking: make sure all inputs are valid integers and not negative. The *Clear* button must clear all text boxes and calculated labels. The *Exit* button must close the window. Suggestion: use a separate `Select Case` statement for each software package. Each `Select Case` statement should list the given quantity ranges, and for each, determine the software package price.

Input validation: Make sure the number of units for each package is numeric, and is not negative.

Use the following test data to determine if the application is calculating properly:

Units Sold		Amount of Order	
Package A:	15 units	Package A:	$1,188.00
Package B:	75 units	Package B:	$8,955.00
Package C:	120 units	Package C:	$17,940.00
		Grand Total:	$28,083.00

Design Your Own Forms

6. **Bank Charges**

A bank charges $10 per month, plus the following check fees for a commercial checking account:

$0.10 each for less than 20 checks
$0.08 each for 20 through 39 checks
$0.06 each for 40 through 59 checks
$0.04 each for 60 or more checks

Create an application that allows the user to enter the number of checks written. The application should compute and display the bank's service fees for the month. All checks for the month are assigned the same charge, based on the total number of checks written during the month. Suggestion: use a Select Case statement to assign the per-check processing fee.

Input validation: Do not accept a negative value for the number of checks written. Ensure that all values are numeric. The *Clear* button must clear the text box and the label that displays the monthly service charge.

Use the following test data to determine if the application is calculating properly:

Number of Checks	Total Fees
15	$ 11.50
25	$ 12.00
45	$ 12.70
75	$ 13.00

7. **Shipping Charges**

The Fast Freight Shipping Company charges the rates listed in the following table.

Weight of the Package (in kilograms)	Shipping Rate per Mile
2 kg or less	$0.01
Over 2 kg, but not more than 6 kg	$0.015
Over 6 kg, but not more than 10 kg	$0.02
Over 10 kg, but not more than 20 kg	$0.025

Create an application that allows the user to enter the weight of the package and the distance it is to be shipped, and then displays the charges.

Input validation: Do not accept values of 0 or less for the weight of the package. Do not accept weights of more than 20 kg (this is the maximum weight the company will ship). Do not accept distances of less than 10 miles or more than 3000 miles. These are the company's minimum and maximum shipping distances. Suggestion: use the OrElse operator to combine the two range conditions that check for package weights that are too small or too large. Use exception handling to check for nonnumeric data.

Use the following test data to determine if the application is calculating properly:

Weight and Distance	Shipping Cost
1.5 Kg, 100 miles	$ 1.00
5 Kg, 200 miles	$ 3.00
8 Kg, 750 miles	$ 15.00
15 Kg, 2000 miles	$ 50.00

8. **Speed of Sound**

The following table shows the approximate speed of sound in air, water, and steel.

Medium	Speed
Air	1,100 feet per second
Water	4,900 feet per second
Steel	16,400 feet per second

Create an application that displays a set of radio buttons allowing the user to select air, water, or steel. Provide a text box to let the user enter the distance a sound wave will travel in the selected medium. Then, when the user clicks a button, the program should display the amount of time it will take. Format the output to two decimal places.

Input validation: Do not accept distances less than 0. Always check for nonnumeric data.

Use the following test data to determine if the application is calculating properly:

Medium and Distance	Speed of Sound
Air, 10,000 feet	9.09 seconds
Water, 10,000 feet	2.04 seconds
Steel, 10,000 feet	0.61 seconds

9. **Freezing and Boiling Points**

The following table lists, in degrees Fahrenheit, the freezing and boiling points of several substances. Create an application that allows the user to enter a temperature. The program should then display a list of the substances that freeze at that temperature, followed by a list of substances that will boil at the same temperature.

Substance	Freezing Point	Boiling Point
Ethyl alcohol	–173°	172°
Mercury	– 38°	676°
Oxygen	–362°	–306°
Water	32°	212°

Use the following test data and sample outputs to determine if the application is calculating properly:

Temperature	Results
– 20°	Water will freeze and oxygen will boil.
– 50°	Mercury and water will freeze and oxygen will boil.
–200°	Ethyl alcohol, mercury, and water will freeze and oxygen will boil.
–400°	Ethyl alcohol, mercury, oxygen, and water will freeze.

10. Long-Distance Calls

A long-distance provider charges the following rates for telephone calls:

Rate Category	Rate per Minute
Daytime (6:00 a.m. through 5:59 P.M.)	$0.07
Evening (6:00 p.m. through 11:59 P.M.)	$0.12
Off-Peak (12:00 a.m. through 5:59 A.M.)	$0.05

Create an application that allows the user to select a rate category (from a set of radio buttons) and enter the number of minutes of the call, then displays the charges. Include a *Clear* button that clears the input and calculated values, and an *Exit* button that closes the window. Error checking: the minutes input by the user must be numeric, and it must be greater than zero.

Use the following test data to determine if the application is calculating properly:

Rate Category and Minutes	Charge
Daytime, 20 minutes	$ 1.40
Evening, 20 minutes	$ 2.40
Off-peak, 20 minutes	$ 1.00

11. Internet Service Provider, Part 1

An Internet service provider offers three subscription packages to its customers, plus a discount for nonprofit organizations:

a. Package A: 10 hours of access for $9.95 per month. Additional hours are $2.00 per hour.
b. Package B: 20 hours of access for $14.95 per month. Additional hours are $1.00 per hour.
c. Package C: Unlimited access for $19.95 per month.
d. Nonprofit Organizations: The service provider gives all nonprofit organizations a 20% discount on all packages.

The user should select the package the customer has purchased (from a set of radio buttons) and enter the number of hours used. A check box captioned *Nonprofit Organization* should also appear on the form. The application should calculate and display the total amount due. If the user selects the *Nonprofit Organization* check box, a 20% discount should be deducted from the final charges. Implementation note: all rates, limits, and discounts must be declared using symbolic constants (using the `Const` keyword).

Input validation: The number of hours used in a month cannot exceed 744. The value must be numeric.

Use the following data to determine if the application is calculating properly:

Package and Hours	The Monthly Charge
Package A, 5 hours, nonprofit	$ 7.96
Package A, 25 hours	$39.95
Package B, 10 hours, nonprofit	$11.96
Package B, 25 hours	$19.95
Package C, 18 hours, nonprofit	$15.96
Package C, 25 hours	$19.95

12. Internet Service Provider, Part 2 (Advanced)

Make a copy of your solution program from Programming Challenge 11. Then, using the copied program, modify it so the form has a check box captioned *Display Potential Savings*. When this check box is selected, the application should also display the amount of money that Package A customers would save if they purchased Package B or C, or the amount that Package B customers would save if they purchased Package C. If there would be no savings, the message should indicate that.

Use the following test data to determine if the application is calculating properly:

Package and Hours	Total Monthly Savings
Package A, 5 hours, nonprofit	$7.96, no savings with Packages B or C
Package A, 25 hours	$39.95, save $20.00 with Package B, and save $20.00 with Package C
Package B, 10 hours, nonprofit	$11.96, no savings with Package C
Package B, 25 hours	$19.95, no savings with Package C

13. Mass and Weight

Scientists measure an object's mass in kilograms and its weight in newtons. If you know the amount of mass of an object, you can calculate its weight, in newtons, with the following formula:

$$Weight = mass \times 9.8$$

Create a VB application that lets the user enter an object's mass and calculates its weight. If the object weighs more than 1000 newtons, display a message indicating that it is too heavy. If the object weighs less than 10 newtons, display a message indicating that it is too light.

14. Book Club Points

Serendipity Booksellers has a book club that awards points to its customers based on the number of books purchased each month. The points are awarded as follows:

- If a customer purchases 0 books, he or she earns 0 points.
- If a customer purchases 1 book, he or she earns 5 points.
- If a customer purchases 2 books, he or she earns 15 points.
- If a customer purchases 3 books, he or she earns 30 points.
- If a customer purchases 4 or more books, he or she earns 60 points.

Create a VB application that lets the user enter the number of books that he or she has purchased this month and displays the number of points awarded.

15. Body Mass Index Program Enhancement

In Programming Challenge 13 in Chapter 3 you were asked to create a VB application that calculates a person's body mass index (BMI). Recall from that exercise that the BMI is often used to determine whether a person with a sedentary lifestyle is overweight or underweight for their height. A person's BMI is calculated with the following formula:

$$BMI = weight \times 703 / height^2$$

In the formula, weight is measured in pounds and height is measured in inches. Enhance the program so it displays a message indicating whether the person has optimal weight, is underweight, or is overweight. A sedentary person's weight is considered to be optimal if his or her BMI is between 18.5 and 25. If the BMI is less than 18.5, the person is considered to be underweight. If the BMI value is greater than 25, the person is considered to be overweight.

16. **Magic Dates**

    The date June 10, 1960, is special because when we write it in the following format, the month times the day equals the year.

    6/10/60

    Create a VB application that lets the user enter a month (in numeric form), a day, and a two-digit year. The program should then determine whether the month times the day is equal to the year. If so, it should display a message saying the date is magic. Otherwise it should display a message saying the date is not magic.

17. **Time Calculator**

    Create a VB application that lets the user enter a number of seconds and works as follows:

    - There are 60 seconds in a minute. If the number of seconds entered by the user is greater than or equal to 60, the program should display the number of minutes in that many seconds.
    - There are 3,600 seconds in an hour. If the number of seconds entered by the user is greater than or equal to 3,600, the program should display the number of hours in that many seconds.
    - There are 86,400 seconds in a day. If the number of seconds entered by the user is greater than or equal to 86,400, the program should display the number of days in that many seconds.

CHAPTER 5

Lists, Loops, Validation, and More

TOPICS

This chapter begins by showing you how to use input boxes, which provide a quick and simple way to ask the user to enter data. List boxes and combo boxes are also introduced. Next, you learn to write loops, which cause blocks, or sequences of programming statements to repeat. Visual Basic has three types of loops: the `Do While` loop, the `Do Until` loop, and the `For...Next` loop. This chapter shows you how to use the CausesValidation property and the `Validating` event to ensure that the user has entered acceptable input. Finally, we cover the ToolTip control, which allows you to display pop-up messages when the user moves the mouse over controls.

5.1 Input Boxes

CONCEPT: Input boxes provide a simple way to gather input without placing a text box on a form.

An **input box** is a quick and simple way to ask the user to enter data. Figure 5-1 shows an example. In the figure, an input box displays a message to the user and provides a text box for the user to enter input. The input box also has *OK* and *Cancel* buttons.

You can display input boxes with the `InputBox` function. When the function is called, an input box such as the one shown in Figure 5-1 appears on the screen. Here is the general format:

```
InputBox(Prompt [, Title] [, Default] [, Xpos] [, Ypos])
```

Figure 5-1 Input box that requests the user's name

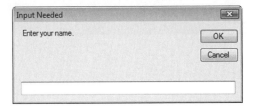

The brackets in the general format are shown around the *Title*, *Default*, *Xpos*, and *Ypos* arguments to indicate that they are optional. The first argument, *Prompt*, is a string that is displayed to the user in the input box. Normally, the string asks the user to enter a value. The optional arguments, *Title*, *Default*, *Xpos*, and *Ypos* are described as follows.

- *Title* is a string that appears in the input box's title bar. If you do not provide a value for *Title*, the name of the project appears.
- *Default* is a string to be initially displayed in the input box's text box. If you do not provide a value for *Default*, the input box's text box is left empty.
- *Xpos* and *Ypos* specify the input box's location on the screen. *Xpos* is an integer that specifies the distance of the input box's leftmost edge from the left edge of the screen. *Ypos* is an integer that specifies the distance of the topmost edge of the input box from the top of the screen. *Xpos* and *Ypos* are measured in pixels. If *Xpos* is omitted, Visual Basic centers the input box horizontally on the screen. If *Ypos* is omitted, the input box is placed near the top of the screen.

If the user clicks the input box's *OK* button or presses the Enter key, the function returns the string value from the input box's text box. If the user clicks the *Cancel* button, the function returns an empty string. To retrieve the value returned by the `InputBox` function, use the assignment operator to assign it to a variable. For example, the following statement displays the input box shown in Figure 5-2. Assume that `strUserInput` is a string variable.

```
strUserInput = InputBox("Enter your age.", "Input Needed")
```

Figure 5-2 Input box that requests the user's age

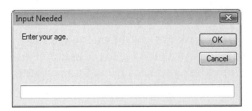

After this statement executes, the value the user entered in the input box is stored as a string in `strUserInput`. As another example, the following statement displays the input box shown in Figure 5-3.

```
strUserInput = InputBox("Enter the distance.", "Provide a Value", "150")
```

Figure 5-3 Input box with default user input

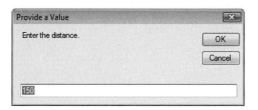

If the user clicks the *OK* button without entering a value in the text box, the input box function returns `"150"`.

NOTE: In most applications, the `InputBox` function should not be used as the primary method of input because it draws the user's attention away from the application's form. It also complicates data validation, because the box closes before validation can take place. Despite these drawbacks, it is a convenient tool for developing and testing applications.

Checkpoint

Carefully examine the input box in Figure 5-4 and complete Checkpoint items 5.1 and 5.2.

Figure 5-4 Input box that requests a number from the user

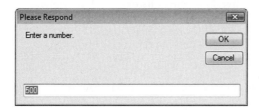

5.1 Write a statement that displays the input box at the default location on the screen.

5.2 Write a statement that displays the input box with its leftmost edge at 100 pixels from the left edge of the screen, and its topmost edge 300 pixels from the top edge of the screen.

5.2 List Boxes

CONCEPT: List boxes display a list of items and allow the user to select an item from the list.

The ListBox Control

A **ListBox control** displays a list of items and also allows the user to select one or more items from the list. (Informally, we refer to this control as a *list box*.) Figure 5-5 shows a form with two list boxes. At runtime, the user may select one of the items, causing the item to appear selected.

Figure 5-5 List box examples

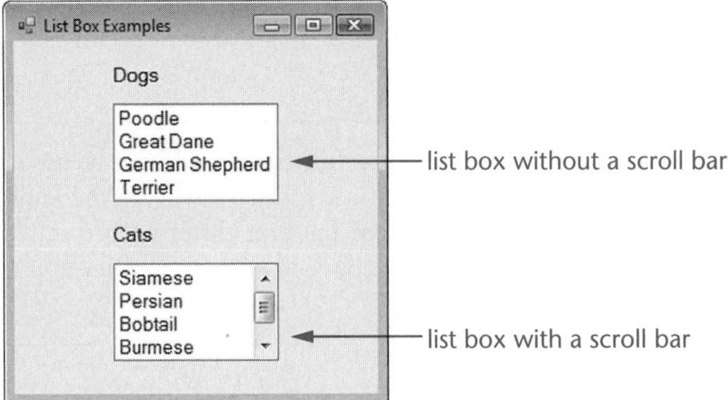

One of the list boxes in Figure 5-5 does not have a scroll bar, but the other one does. A scroll bar appears when the list box contains more items than can be displayed in the space provided. In the figure, the top list box has four items (Poodle, Great Dane, German Shepherd, and Terrier), and all items are displayed. The bottom list box shows four items (Siamese, Persian, Bobtail, and Burmese), but because it has a scroll bar, we know there are more items in the list box than those four.

Creating a ListBox Control

You create a ListBox control using either of the following methods:

- Double-click the ListBox tool in the *Toolbox* window to cause a ListBox control to appear on the form. Move the control to the desired location and resize it, if necessary.
- Click the ListBox tool in the *Toolbox* window and use the mouse to draw the ListBox control on the form with the desired location and size.

In Design mode, a ListBox control appears as a rectangle. The size of the rectangle determines the size of the list box. The standard prefix for a ListBox control's name is `lst`, where the first character is a lowercase letter L. Let's discuss some of the list box's important properties and methods.

The Items Property

The entries in a list box are stored in a property named Items. You can store values in the **Items property** (also known as the Items collection) at design time or at runtime. To store values in the Items property at design time, follow these steps:

1. Make sure the ListBox control is selected in the *Design* window.
2. In the *Properties* window, the setting for the Items property is displayed as *(Collection)*. When you select the Items property, an ellipsis button (...) appears.
3. Click the ellipsis button. The *String Collection Editor* dialog box appears, as shown in Figure 5-6.
4. Type the values that are to appear in the list box into the *String Collection Editor* dialog box. Type each value on a separate line by pressing the Enter key after each entry.
5. When you have entered all the values, click the *OK* button.

Figure 5-6 The *String Collection Editor* dialog box

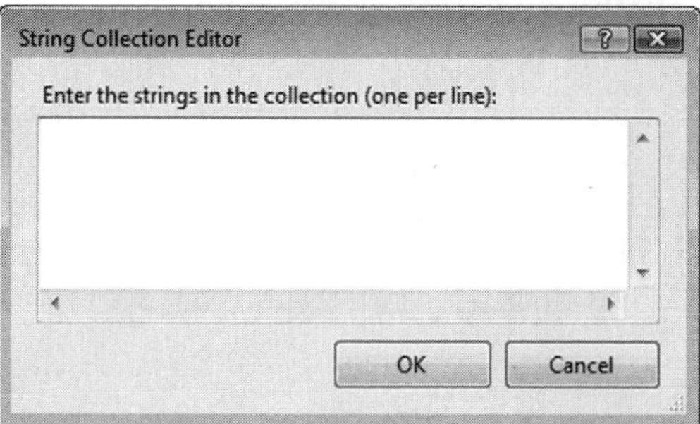

NOTE: Once you acquire the necessary skills, you will usually fill the Items collection of list boxes from external data sources (such as databases).

The Items.Count Property

You can use the **Items.Count property** to determine the number of items stored in the list box. When there are no items in the Items property, `Items.Count` equals 0. For example, assume an application has a list box named `lstEmployees`. The following `If...Then` statement displays a message box when there are no items in the list box:

```
If lstEmployees.Items.Count = 0 Then
  MessageBox.Show("There are no items in the list!")
End If
```

The following statement assigns the number of items in the list box to the variable `intNumEmployees`:

```
intNumEmployees = lstEmployees.Items.Count
```

Item Indexing

The Items property is a collection of objects, in which each has an *index*, or number. The first object in the collection has index 0, the next has index 1, and so on. The last index value is $n - 1$, where n is the number of items in the collection. When you access the Items property in code, you must supply an index, using an expression such as the following:

```
lstEmployees.Items(0)
```

If you want to assign the item to another variable, you must convert it into the appropriate type. Assuming *Option Strict* is set *On*, you can't just assign an object to any other variable type. The following statement calls `ToString` on the object so we can assign the item to a string variable.

```
strName = lstEmployees.Items(0).ToString()
```

Or, if the list box contained integers, we could assign an item to an integer variable as follows:

```
intEmployeeAge = CInt(lstEmployees.Items(0))
```

Handling Exceptions Caused by Indexes

When you use an index with the Item property, an exception is thrown if the index is out of range. Because indexes start at zero, the highest index number you can use is always one less than the collection size. You can use an exception handler to trap such an error. In the following code, assume that the variable `intIndex` contains a value that we want to use as an index. If the value in `intIndex` is out of range, the exception is handled. We display the Message property (Figure 5-7) of the exception object to give the user an idea of what went wrong.

```
Try
  strInput = lstMonths.Items(intIndex).ToString()
Catch ex As Exception
  MessageBox.Show(ex.Message)
End Try
```

Figure 5-7 Exception thrown by out of range index

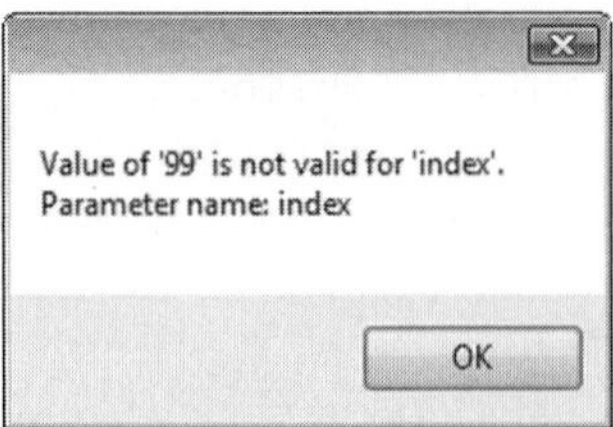

Many programmers prefer to handle indexing errors using an `If` statement. The following code is an example in which we compare the index (in a variable named `intIndex`) to the Count property of the Items collection:

```
If intIndex >= 0 And intIndex < lstMonths.Items.Count Then
  strInput = lstMonths.Items(intIndex).ToString()
Else
  MessageBox.Show("Index is out of range: " & intIndex)
End If
```

The SelectedIndex Property

When the user selects an item in a list box, the item's index is stored in the **SelectedIndex property**. If no item is selected, `SelectedIndex` is set to –1. You can use the SelectedIndex property to retrieve the selected item from the Items property. For example, assume an application has a list box named `lstLocations`. The following code segment uses an `If...Then` statement to determine whether the user has selected an item in the list box. If so, it copies the item from the Items property to the string variable `strLocation`.

```
If lstLocations.SelectedIndex <> -1 Then
  strLocation = lstLocations.Items(lstLocations.SelectedIndex).ToString()
End If
```

TIP: To prevent a runtime error, always test the SelectedIndex property to make sure it is not set to –1 before using it with the Items property to retrieve an item.

You can also use the SelectedIndex property to deselect an item by setting it to –1. For example, the following statement deselects any selected item in `lstLocations`:

```
lstLocations.SelectedIndex = -1
```

The SelectedItem Property

Whereas the SelectedIndex property contains the index of the currently selected item, the **SelectedItem property** contains the item itself. For example, suppose the list box `lstFruit` contains *Apples*, *Pears*, and *Bananas*. If the user has selected *Pears*, the following statement copies the string *Pears* to the variable `strSelectedFruit`:

```
strSelectedFruit = lstFruit.SelectedItem.ToString()
```

The Sorted Property

You can use the list box's Sorted property to cause the items in the Items property to be displayed alphabetically. This Boolean property is set to *False* by default, causing the items to be displayed in the order they were inserted into the list. When set to *True*, the items are sorted alphabetically.

The `Items.Add` Method

To store values in the Items property with code at runtime, use the **`Items.Add` method**. Here is the general format:

```
ListBox.Items.Add(Item)
```

`ListBox` is the name of the list box control. *`Item`* is the value to be added to the Items property. For example, suppose an application has a list box named `lstStudents`. The following statement adds the string `"Sharon"` to the end of the list box.

```
lstStudents.Items.Add("Sharon")
```

You can add virtually any type of values to list box, including objects. For example, the following statements add Integer, Decimal, and Date objects to list boxes.

```
Dim intNum As Integer = 5
Dim decGrossPay As Decimal = 1200.00
Dim datStartDate As Date = #12/18/2009#
lstNumbers.Items.Add(intNum)
lstWages.Items.Add(decGrossPay)
lstDates.Items.Add(datStartDate)
```

When you add an object other than a string to a list box, the text displayed in the list box is the string returned by the object's `ToString` method.

The `Items.Insert` Method

To insert an item at a specific position, you must use the `Items.Insert` method. Here is the general format of the **`Items.Insert` method**:

```
ListBox.Items.Insert(Index, Item)
```

`ListBox` is the name of the list box control. *`Index`* is an integer argument that specifies the position where *`Item`* is to be placed in the Items property. *`Item`* is the item to add to the list.

For example, suppose the list box `lstStudents` contains the following items, in the order they appear: *Bill*, *Joe*, *Geri*, and *Sharon*. Since *Bill* is the first item, its index is 0. The index for *Joe* is 1, for *Geri* is 2, and for *Sharon* is 3. Now, suppose the following statement executes.

```
lstStudents.Items.Insert(2, "Jean")
```

This statement inserts *Jean* at index 2. The string that was previously at index 2 (*Geri*) is moved to index 3, and the string previously at index 3 (*Sharon*) is moved to index 4. The items in the Items property are now *Bill*, *Joe*, *Jean*, *Geri*, and *Sharon*.

The `Items.Remove` and `Items.RemoveAt` Methods

The **`Items.Remove`** and **`Items.RemoveAt` methods** both erase one item from a list box's Items property. Here is the general format of both methods:

```
ListBox.Items.Remove(Item)
ListBox.Items.RemoveAt(Index)
```

`ListBox` is the name of the list box control. With the `Items.Remove` method, *`Item`* is the item you wish to remove. For example, the following statement erases the item *Industrial Widget* from the `lstInventory` list box.

```
lstInventory.Items.Remove("Industrial Widget")
```

If you specify an item that is not in the list box, nothing is removed.

The `Items.RemoveAt` method removes the item at a specific index. For example, the following statement removes the item at index 4 from the `lstInventory` list box:

```
lstInventory.Items.RemoveAt(4)
```

WARNING: If you specify an invalid index with the `Items.RemoveAt` method, a runtime error will occur.

The `Items.Clear` Method

The `Items.Clear` method erases all the items in the Items property. Here is the method's general format:

```
ListBox.Items.Clear()
```

For example, assume an application has a list box named `lstCars`. The following statement erases all items in the list.

```
lstCars.Items.Clear()
```

In Tutorial 5-1, you create an application with two list boxes.

Tutorial 5-1:
Creating list boxes

Step 1: Create a new Windows application project named *List Boxes*. Change the form's Text property to *List Box Demo*.

Step 2: On the form, create a list box as shown in Figure 5-8. Notice that the default name of the list box is `ListBox1`. Also notice that the name of the list box is displayed in the list box at design time. It will not appear there at runtime.

Step 3: Change the name of the list box to `lstMonths`.

Step 4: With the list box selected, click the Items property in the *Property* window. Then click the ellipsis button (...) that appears.

Step 5: The *String Collection Editor* dialog box will appear. Type the following names of the months, with one name per line: **`January`**, **`February`**, **`March`**, **`April`**, **`May`**, **`June`**, **`July`**, **`August`**, **`September`**, **`October`**, **`November`**, and **`December`**. When you are finished, the dialog box should appear as shown in Figure 5-9. Click the *OK* button to close the dialog box.

Figure 5-8 A list box

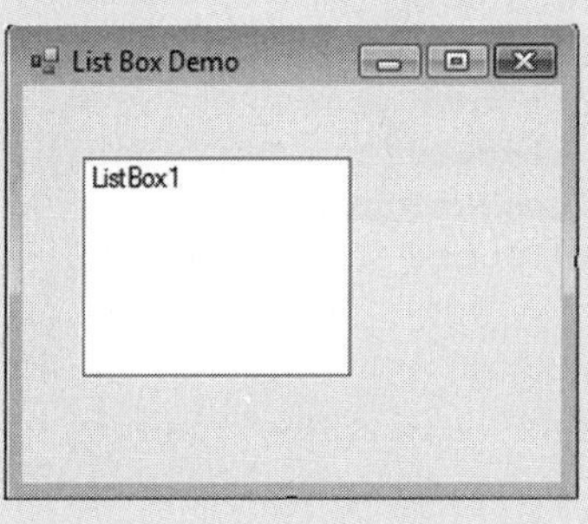

Figure 5-9 *String Collection Editor* with months filled in

Step 6: Create another list box and make it the same size as the first one. Change its name to *lstYears*. Enter the following items in its Items property: **`2006`**, **`2007`**, **`2008`**, and **`2009`**. Your form should look like the one shown in Figure 5-10.

Step 7: Create a button on the form, name it *btnOk*, and change its Text property to *OK*.

Figure 5-10 The form with two list boxes

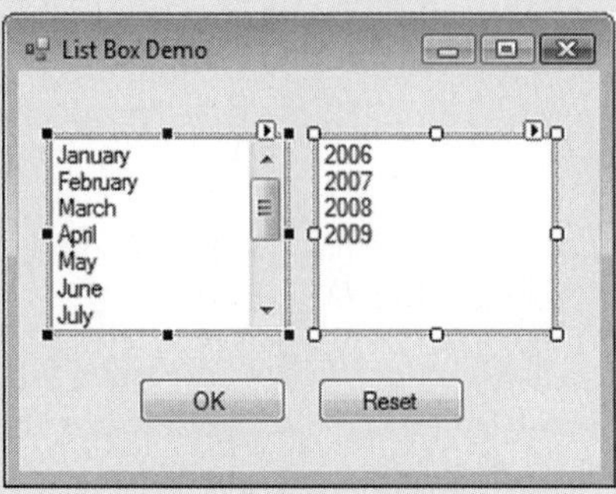

Step 8: Double-click the `btnOk` button to add a `Click` event procedure code template. Write the following code, shown in bold:

```
Private Sub btnOk_Click(ByVal sender As System.Object, _
    ByVal e As System.EventArgs) Handles btnOk.Click

  Dim strInput As String   ' Holds selected month and year

  If lstMonths.SelectedIndex = -1 Then
     ' No month is selected
     MessageBox.Show("Select a month.")
  ElseIf lstYears.SelectedIndex = -1 Then
     ' No year is selected
     MessageBox.Show("Select a year.")
  Else
     ' Get the selected month and year
     strInput = lstMonths.SelectedItem.ToString() & " " _
       & lstYears.SelectedItem.ToString()
     MessageBox.Show("You selected " & strInput)
  End If
End Sub
```

Let's take a closer look at the code. Here is the beginning of the `If...Then` statement:

```
If lstMonths.SelectedIndex = -1 Then
    ' No month is selected
    MessageBox.Show("Select a month.")
```

First, we test `lstMonths.SelectedIndex` to determine whether it is set to –1. If so, the user has not selected an item from `lstMonths`, so a message box is displayed instructing the user to do so. If the user has selected an item from `lstMonths`, the `ElseIf` portion executes.

```
ElseIf lstYears.SelectedIndex = -1 Then
   ' No year is selected
    MessageBox.Show("Select a year.")
```

This tests `lstYears.SelectedIndex` to determine whether the user has selected an item from `lstYears`. If `lstYears.SelectedIndex` equals –1, a message box instructs the user to select a year. The `Else` portion is executed if the user has selected items from both `lstMonths` and `lstYears`.

```
Else
   ' Get the selected month and year
   strInput = lstMonths.SelectedItem.ToString() & " " & _
     lstYears.SelectedItem.ToString()
   MessageBox.Show("You selected " & strInput)
End If
```

In that case, the selected items from both list boxes are concatenated and stored in the variable `strInput`. Then a message box is displayed showing the contents of `strInput`.

Step 9: Create another button on the form. Name it *btnReset* and change its text to *Reset*.

Step 10: Double-click the `btnReset` button to add a `Click` event procedure code template. Write the following code shown in bold:

```
Private Sub btnReset_Click(ByVal sender As System.Object,
     ByVal e As System.EventArgs) Handles btnReset.Click

   ' Reset the list boxes by deselecting the currently
   ' selected items
   lstMonths.SelectedIndex = -1
   lstYears.SelectedIndex = -1
End Sub
```

When this button is clicked, the SelectedIndex property of both list boxes is set to –1. This deselects any selected items.

Step 11: Run the application. Without selecting any item in either list box, click the *OK* button. A message box appears instructing you to *Select a month*.

Step 12: Select *March* in `lstMonths`, but do not select an item from `lstYears`. Click the *OK* button. This time a message box appears instructing you to *Select a year*.

Step 13: With *March* still selected in `lstMonths`, select *2009* in `lstYears`. Click the *OK* button. Now a message box appears with the message *You selected March 2009*. Click the message box's *OK* button to dismiss it.

Step 14: Click the *Reset* button. The items you previously selected in `lstMonths` and `lstYears` are deselected.

Step 15: Close the application and save it.

More about the Items Collection

The *Items collection* of a list box offers a great way to learn about Collections. In other words, what you learn about the Items collection applies to many other collections you will encounter. Table 5-1 lists the more important methods and properties of the Items collection.

You have already seen examples of `Add`, `Clear`, `Insert`, `Remove`, and `RemoveAt`. Let's look at examples of the remaining methods and properties. We assume the list box is named `lstMonths` contains the values you entered during Tutorial 5-1. In the following statement, `blnFound` equals *True*.

```
Dim blnFound As Boolean = lstMonths.Items.Contains("March")
```

Table 5-1 Methods and properties of the `ListBox.Items` collection

Method or Property	Description
`Integer` **`Add`**`(`*`item As Object`*`)`	Method: adds *`item`* to the collection, returning its index position.
`Clear``( )`	Method: removes all items in the collection. No return value.
`Boolean` **`Contains`**`(`*`value As Object`*`)`	Method: returns *True* if *`value`* is found at least once in the collection.
`Count` `As Integer`	Property: returns the number of items in the collection. Read-only, so you can read it but not change it.
`Integer` **`IndexOf`**`(`*`value As Object`*`)`	Method: returns the Integer index position of the first occurrence of *`value`* in the collection. If *`value`* is not found, the return value is –1.
`Insert``(`*`index As Integer, item As Object`*`)`	Method: insert *`item`* in the collection at position *`index`*. No return value.
`Item``(`*`index As Integer`*`) As Object`	Default property: returns the object located at position *`index`*.
`Remove``(`*`value As Object`*`)`	Method: removes *`value`* from the collection. No return value.
`RemoveAt``(`*`index As Integer`*`)`	Method: removes the item at the specified *`index`*. No return value.

In the following statement, `intIndex` equals 2 because *March* is located at index 2 in the collection.

```
intIndex = lstMonths.Items.IndexOf("March")
```

`Item` is the default property of a collection, so the following statement sets `strMonth` to *April*.

```
Dim strMonth As String = lstMonths.Items(3).ToString()
```

In the following statement, `strMonth` equals *April* because it is at index position 3 in the collection.

```
Dim strMonth As String = lstMonths.Items.Item(3).ToString()
```

Checkpoint

5.3 What is the index of the first item stored in a list box's Items property?

5.4 Which list box property holds the number of items stored in the Items property?

5.5 If a list box has 12 items stored in it, what is the index of the twelfth item?

5.6 Which list box property holds the item that has been selected from the list?

5.7 Which list box property holds the index of the item that has been selected from the list?

5.8 Assume `lstNames` is a list box with 15 items and `strSelectedName` is a string variable. Write a statement that assigns the second item to `lstNames` in `strSelectedName`.

5.3 Introduction to Loops: The Do While Loop

CONCEPT: **A loop is a repeating structure that contains a block of program statements.**

VideoNote The Do While Loop

Chapter 4 introduced decision structures, which direct the flow of a program along two or more paths. A **repetition structure**, or **loop** causes one or more statements to repeat. Visual Basic has three types of loops: the `Do While` loop, the `Do Until` loop, and the `For...Next` loop. The difference among them is how they control the repetition.

The Do While Loop

The `Do While` loop has two important parts: (1) an expression that is tested for a *True* or *False* value, and (2) a statement or group of statements that is repeated as long as the expression is true. Figure 5-11 shows a flowchart of a `Do While` loop.

Figure 5-11 Flowchart of a Do While loop

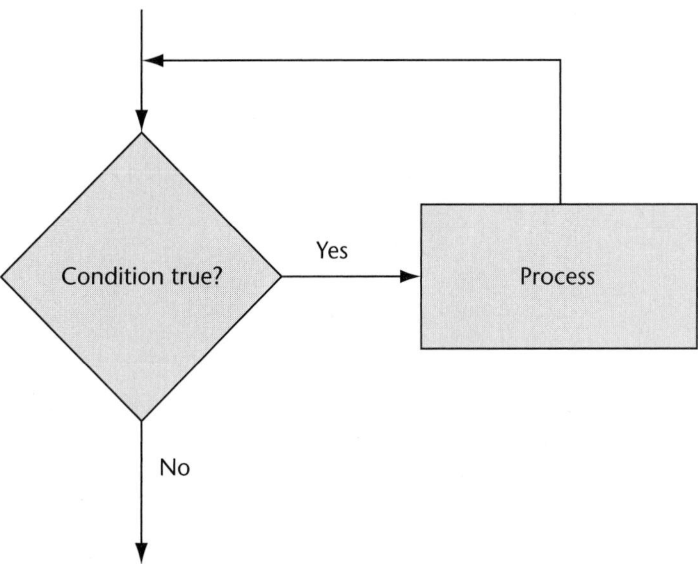

Notice the use of the diamond symbol for testing a condition. If the condition is true, the structure performs a process. Then it tests the condition again; if the condition is still true, the process is repeated. This continues as long as the condition is true when it is tested.

Here is the general format of the **Do While loop** in code:

```
Do While expression
  statement
  (more statements may follow)
Loop
```

The `Do While` statement marks the beginning of the loop, and the `Loop` statement marks the end. The statements between these are known as the *body of the loop*. When the `Loop` statement is reached, control is transferred back to `Do While` statement to test the expression again.

When the code runs, the expression in the `Do While` statement is tested. If it is true, the statements in the body of the loop are executed. (Because these statements are only executed under the condition that the expression is true, they are called **conditionally executed statements.**) This cycle repeats until the expression is false.

The `Do While` loop works like an `If` statement that executes over and over. As long as the expression is true, the conditionally executed statements will repeat. Each repetition of the loop is called an **iteration.** In Tutorial 5-2, you complete an application that demonstrates the `Do While` loop.

Tutorial 5-2:
Completing an application that uses the `Do While` loop

Step 1: Open the *Do While Demo* project from the student sample programs folder named *Chap5\Do While Demo.*

Step 2: In the *Design* window for *Form1*, double-click the *Run Demo* button to display the *Code* window.

Step 3: In the *Code* window, add the following statements (in bold) to the `Click` event handler for `btnRunDemo`:

```
Private Sub btnRunDemo_Click(ByVal sender As System.Object, _
  ByVal e As System.EventArgs) Handles btnRunDemo.Click

  ' Demonstrate the Do While loop
  Dim intCount As Integer = 0

  Do While intCount < 10
    lstOutput.Items.Add("Hello")
    intCount += 1
  Loop
End Sub
```

Let's examine this procedure. An integer variable named `intCount` is declared and initialized to the value zero. `intCount` would have been set to zero automatically anyway, but you should always initialize variables explicitly.

The `Do While` loop begins with this statement:

```
Do While intCount < 10
```

The statement tests the variable `intCount` to determine whether it is less than 10. If it is, the statements in the body of the loop are performed.

```
lstOutput.Items.Add("Hello")
intCount += 1
```

The first statement in the body of the loop adds the word *Hello* to the `lstOutput` list box. The second statement uses the += combined assignment operator to add 1 to `intCount`.

The next line reads

```
Loop
```

This marks the end of the body of the loop, so Visual Basic repeats these steps, beginning with the `Do While` statement. When the test expression `intCount < 10` is no longer true, the loop terminates and the program resumes with the line appearing immediately following the `Loop` statement.

Step 4: Save and run the application. Click the *Run Demo* button. The output should appear as shown in Figure 5-12.

Figure 5-12 Output from the *Do While Demo* application

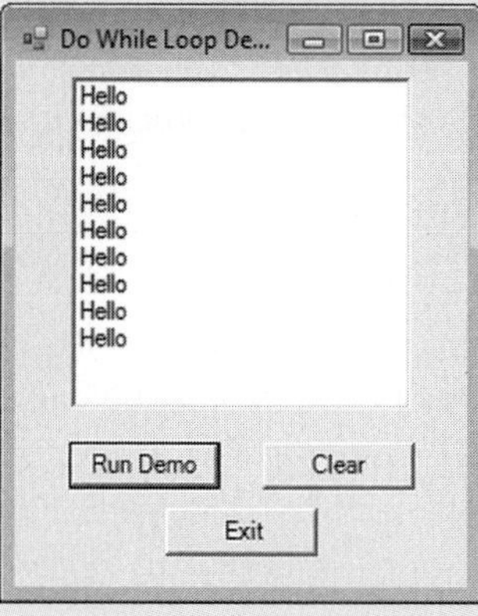

Infinite Loops

In all but rare cases, loops must contain within themselves a way to terminate. This means that something inside the loop must eventually make the test expression false. The loop in the *Do While Demo* application stops when the variable `intCount` is no longer less than 10.

If a loop does not have a way of stopping, it is called an **infinite loop**. Infinite loops keep repeating until the program is interrupted. Here is an example:

```
intCount = 0
Do While intCount < 10
  lstOutput.Items.Add("Hello")
Loop
```

This loop will execute forever because it does not contain a statement that changes `count`. Each time the test expression is evaluated, `intCount` will still be equal to 0.

Programming Style and Loops

Conditionally executed statements inside a loop body should be indented. Doing so sets them apart visually from the surrounding statements and makes it clear which statements are being repeated. For example, compare the two loops shown in the following code. The loop on the left is not properly indented, but the loop on the right is.

```
Do While intCount < 10
lstOutput.Items.Add("Hello")
intCount += 1
Loop
```

```
Do While intCount < 10
    lstOutput.Items.Add("Hello")
    intCount += 1
Loop
```

You will find that a similar style of indentation is used with the other types of loops presented in this chapter.

NOTE: As with `If...Then` statements, Visual Basic automatically indents conditionally executed statements inside a loop. If this feature has been turned off, you can turn it on by clicking *Tools* on the menu bar, and then clicking *Options*. On the *Options* dialog box, perform the following:

- Expand the *Text Editor* entry in the left pane, then expand the *Basic* entry, then click *Tabs*. Make sure *Smart* is selected.
- In the left pane, click *VB Specific*. Make sure *Pretty listing (reformatting) of code* and *Automatic insertion of end constructs* are checked.

Counters

A **counter** is a variable that is regularly incremented or decremented each time a loop iterates. To increment a variable means to add 1 to its value. To decrement a variable means to subtract 1 from its value.

The following statements increment the variable `intX`:

```
intX = intX + 1
intX += 1
```

The following statements decrement the variable `x`.

```
intX = intX – 1
intX -= 1
```

Often, a program must control or keep track of the number of iterations a loop performs. For example, the loop in the *Do While Demo* application adds *Hello* to the list box 10 times. Let's look at part of the code again.

```
Do While intCount < 10
  lstOutput.Items.Add("Hello")
  intCount += 1
Loop
```

In the code, the variable `intCount`, which starts at 0, is incremented each time through the loop. When `intCount` reaches 10, the loop stops. As a counter variable, it is regularly incremented in each iteration of the loop. In essence, `intCount` keeps track of the number of iterations the loop has performed.

TIP: `intCount` must be properly initialized. If it is initialized to 1 instead of 0, the loop will only iterate nine times.

Pretest and Posttest `Do While` Loops

A **pretest loop** evaluates its test expression before each iteration. A **posttest loop** evaluates its test expression after each iteration. The `Do While` loop may be written as either a pretest or posttest loop.

Here is the general format of the pretest `Do While` loop:

```
Do While expression
  statement
  (more statements may follow)
Loop
```

Here is the general format of the posttest Do While loop:

```
Do
   statement
   (more statements may follow)
Loop While expression
```

The following is a pretest Do While loop:

```
Do While intCount < 10
   lstOutput.Items.Add("Hello")
   intCount += 1
Loop
```

Figure 5-13 shows a flowchart for this loop.

Figure 5-13 Flowchart for pretest Do While loop

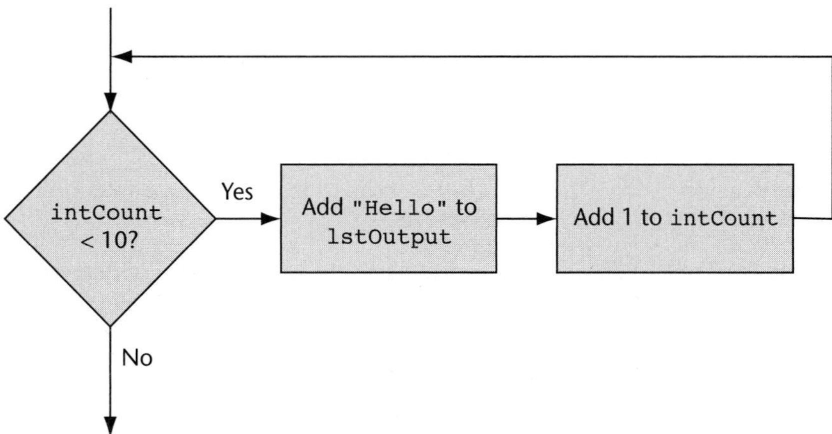

The test expression intCount < 10 is tested before each iteration of the loop. The code may be modified to create a posttest loop:

```
Do
   lstOutput.Items.Add("Hello")
   intCount += 1
Loop While intCount < 10
```

When the word *While* and the test expression are moved so that they appear after the word *Loop*, the code becomes a posttest loop. Figure 5-14 shows a flowchart for this loop. In a pretest loop, the loop is not executed if the expression evaluates to false when first tested.

A posttest loop always performs at least one iteration, even if the test expression is false from the start. For example, the following loop iterates once because the Do While loop does not evaluate the expression x < 0 until the end of the iteration:

```
Dim x As Integer
x = 1
Do
   MessageBox.Show(x.ToString)
   x += 1
Loop While x < 0
```

In Tutorial 5-3, you will modify the *Do While Demo* application to use a posttest loop.

Figure 5-14 Flowchart for posttest `Do While` loop

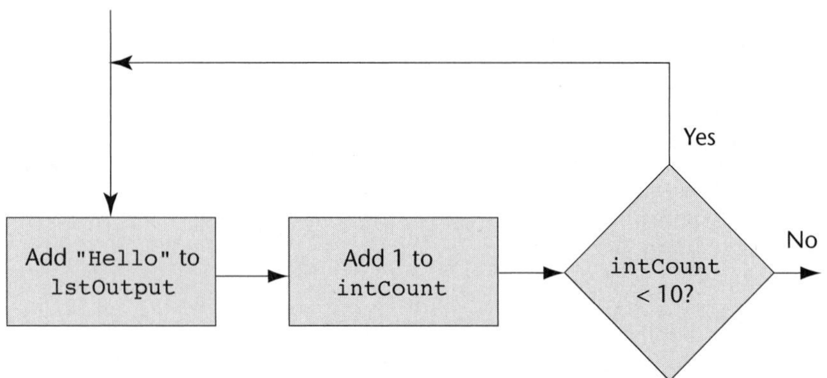

Tutorial 5-3:
Modifying the *Do While Demo* application to use a posttest loop

Step 1: Open the *Do While Demo* project from the student sample programs folder named *Chap5\Do While Demo*.

Step 2: Open the *Code* window and find the `btnRunDemo_Click` event procedure. The procedure uses a pretest `Do While` loop. Modify the loop so the procedure appears as follows. The modified lines of code are shown in bold.

```
Private Sub btnRunDemo_Click(ByVal sender As System.Object, _
  ByVal e As System.EventArgs) Handles btnRunDemo.Click

  ' Demonstrate the Do Loop While loop
  Dim intCount As Integer = 0

  Do
    lstOutput.Items.Add("Hello")
    intCount += 1
  Loop While intCount < 10
End Sub
```

Step 3: Run the application and click the *Run Demo* button. The loop should display *Hello* 10 times in the list box.

Step 4: Click the *Exit* button to end the application. In the *Code* window, modify the loop as shown here:

```
Do
  lstOutput.Items.Add("Hello")
  intCount += 1
Loop While intCount > 10
```

Although the expression `intCount > 10` is false, the statements in the body of the loop execute once.

Step 5: Run the application and click the *Run Demo* button. The loop should display *Hello* one time in the list box.

Step 6: Click the *Exit* button to end the application.

Keeping a Running Total

Some programming tasks require a running total to be kept. A **running total** is a sum of numbers that accumulates with each iteration of a loop. The variable used to keep the running total is called an **accumulator.**

The application in Tutorial 5-4 calculates a company's total sales for five days by taking daily sales figures as input and keeping a running total of them as they are gathered.

Tutorial 5-4:
Using a loop to keep a running total

In this tutorial, you will use an input box and a loop to enter five separate sales amount values. The values will be added to a total, which will be displayed. Exception handling will be used to prevent runtime errors. We show how the `Exit Do` statement can be used to exit a loop.

Step 1: Open the *Running Total* project from the student sample programs folder named *Chap5\Running Total.*

Step 2: Open *Form1* in Design mode and double-click the *Enter Sales* button.

Step 3: Double-click the *Enter Sales* button to open the *Code* window, and add the following code (shown in bold) to the button's `Click` event handler.

```
Private Sub btnEnterSales_Click(ByVal sender As System.Object, _
  ByVal e As System.EventArgs) Handles btnEnterSales.Click

  ' Get the daily sales from the user
  ' and calculate the total.

  Dim intCount As Integer     ' Loop counter
  Dim decSales As Decimal     ' To hold the daily sales
  Dim decTotal As Decimal     ' Use as an accumulator
  Dim strInput As String      ' To get the user input

  ' Store the correct starting values in the counter
  ' and the accumulator.
  intCount = 1
  decTotal = 0
  ' The following loop gets the sales for each day.
  Do While intCount <= 5
    strInput = InputBox("Enter the sales for day " & _
      intCount.ToString(), "Sales Amount Needed")
    If strInput <> String.Empty Then
      decSales = CDec(strInput)   ' Store input in sales
      decTotal += decSales        ' Add sales to total
      intCount += 1               ' Increment the counter
    End If
  Loop

  ' Display the running total.
  lblTotal.Text = decTotal.ToString("c")
End Sub
```

After the variable declarations, the procedure stores the correct starting values in the `intCount` and `decTotal` variables.

```
intCount = 1
decTotal = 0
```

It is important for these variables to be properly initialized. `intCount` determines the number of times the `Do While` loop will iterate. `decTotal` is used as an accumulator in the loop, so it must start with the value 0. If it starts with any other value, the sum of the sales figures will not be correct. The `Do While` loop uses an input box to ask for the daily sales figures. Notice the use of the following `If...Then` statement:

```
If strInput <> String.Empty Then
     decSales = CDec(strInput)      ' Store input in sales
     decTotal += decSales           ' Add sales to total
     intCount += 1                  ' Increment the counter
End If
```

If `strInput` equals an empty string, the user either clicked the *Cancel* button or did not enter a value. The `If...Then` statement processes the return value of the `InputBox` function if the user enters a value, and clicks the *OK* button or presses Enter. Inside the `If...Then` statement, the following statement converts the value entered by the user to a Decimal value and stores it in `decSales`.

```
decSales = CDec(strInput)    ' Store input in sales
```

The next statement adds the contents of `decSales` to `decTotal`.

```
decTotal += decSales         ' Add sales to total
```

`decTotal` was initialized to 0, so the first time through the loop it is set to the same value as `decSales`. In each iteration after the first, `decTotal` is increased by the amount in `decSales`. After the loop has finished, `decTotal` will contain the total of all the daily sales figures entered.

Step 4: Save and run the program. Click the *Enter Sales* button. The input box shown in Figure 5-15 asks the user to enter the sales for day 1. Enter **2000**, and click the *OK* button. (If you prefer, you may press the Enter key.)

Step 5: The application will present input boxes asking for the sales for days 2, 3, 4, and 5. Enter the following amounts:

Day 2: **1800**
Day 3: **1950**
Day 4: **2500**
Day 5: **1780**

Step 6: After you enter the sales amount for all five days, the application should display the total sales as shown in Figure 5-16.

Figure 5-15 *Sales Amount Needed* input box

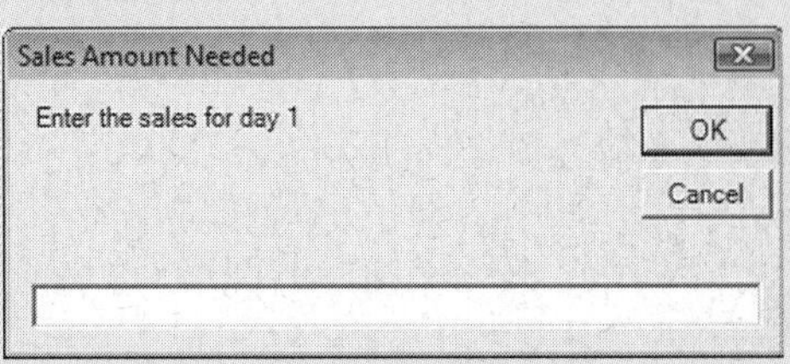

Figure 5-16 Total sales displayed

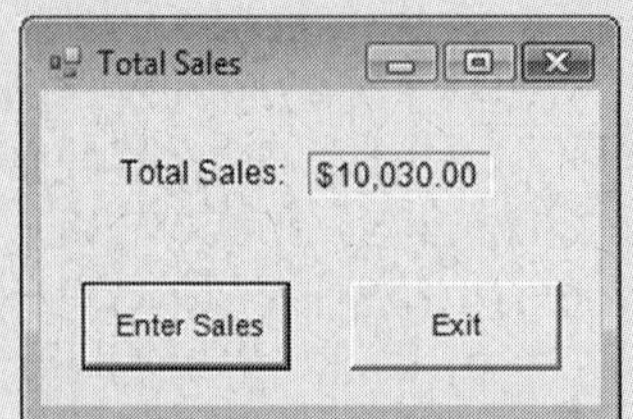

Step 7: Click the *Enter Sales* button again. When the *Sales Amount Needed* input box appears, click the *Cancel* button. Notice that the input box does not disappear, even when you click *Cancel* repeatedly.

Step 8: Click the *Stop Debugging* button on the Visual Studio toolbar, and return to the *Code* window. There is an easy way to fix the problem we just found with the *Cancel* button:

Insert an `Else` clause with an `Exit Do` statement that exits the `Do While` loop:

```
Do While intCount <= 5
   strInput = InputBox("Enter the sales for day " & _
        intCount.ToString(), "Sales Amount Needed")
   If strInput <> String.Empty Then
      decSales = CDec(strInput)       ' Store input in sales
      decTotal += decSales            ' Add sales to total
      intCount += 1                   ' Increment the counter
   Else
      Exit Do                         ' Exit the loop
   End If
Loop
```

The `Exit Do` statement is not the only way to stop, or exit a loop. You could, for example, change the value of `intCount`, forcing the loop to stop.

```
Do While intCount <= 5
   strInput = InputBox("Enter the sales for day " & _
        intCount.ToString(), "Sales Amount Needed")
   If strInput <> String.Empty Then
      decSales = CDec(strInput)       ' Store input in sales
      decTotal += decSales            ' Add sales to total
      intCount += 1                   ' Increment the counter
   Else
      intCount = 99                   ' Exit the loop
   End If
Loop
```

Whether this is more self-documenting than `Exit Do` is a matter of opinion. Consult your classroom instructor on the preferred method.

Step 9: Save and run the program again. Click the *Enter Sales* button, and then click the *Cancel* button. The program should return to the startup form (*Form1*). But we're not finished testing the program.

Step 10: Click the *Enter Sales* button, enter some random characters into the input box, and click the *OK* button. You should see the *InvalidCastException was unhandled* error message. We need to prevent this runtime error. Close the error message dialog box and then click the *Stop Debugging* button on the Visual Studio toolbar to end the program.

The call to the `CDec` function was the culprit that caused a runtime error when the user supplied bad input. Let's prevent the error with an `If...Then...Else` statement. The question is, should it be around the call to `CDec` like this?

```
If IsNumeric(strInput) Then
   decSales = CDec(strInput)          ' Store input in sales
Else
   MessageBox.Show("Please enter a valid number " _
        & "for the sales amount", "Error")
End If
```

```
decTotal += decSales                    ' Add sales to total
intCount += 1                           ' Increment the counter
```

Probably not, because if an error is detected, we don't want to execute the two statements that add to `decTotal` and `intCount`. Instead, let's put them all inside the conditional block as follows:

```
If IsNumeric(strInput) Then
  decSales = CDec(strInput)             ' Store input in sales
  decTotal += decSales                  ' Add sales to total
  intCount += 1                         ' Increment the counter
Else
    MessageBox.Show("Please enter a valid number " _
        & "for the sales amount", "Error")
End If
```

Step 11: Replace the existing `Do While` loop in the `btnEnterSales_Click` procedure with the following code. Changes are shown in bold.

```
Do While intCount <= 5
  strInput = InputBox("Enter the sales for day " & _
        intCount.ToString(), "Sales Amount Needed")
  If strInput <> String.Empty Then
    If IsNumeric(strInput) Then
      decSales = CDec(strInput)         ' Store input in sales
      decTotal += decSales              ' Add sales to total
      intCount += 1                     ' Increment the counter
    Else
      MessageBox.Show("Please enter a valid number " _
          & "for the sales amount", "Error")
    End If
  Else
    Exit Do       ' Exit the loop
  End If
Loop
```

Step 12: Save and run the program again. Experiment with entering bad input, clicking the *OK* button, the *Cancel* button, and just about anything else you can to break the program's interface.

Step 13: End the program. You're finished.

TIP: How do you end a program when it stops responding? If a program refuses to end via its own user interface, you can stop it by using the *Stop Debugging* button on the Visual Studio toolbar. This technique, unfortunately, does not help you if you're running a program's *.exe* file from the bin folder, like you did in Chapter 1. In Windows XP or Windows Vista, right-click the Windows Task bar, select *Task Manager* (Figure 5-17), select the *Applications* tab, select the program name (in our case, it's called *Total Sales*), and click the *End Task* button. This method should be used when you have no other way to end a program. *Note: Task Manager may be disabled in some school lab configurations.*

Figure 5-17 Ending a program, using *Windows Task Manager*

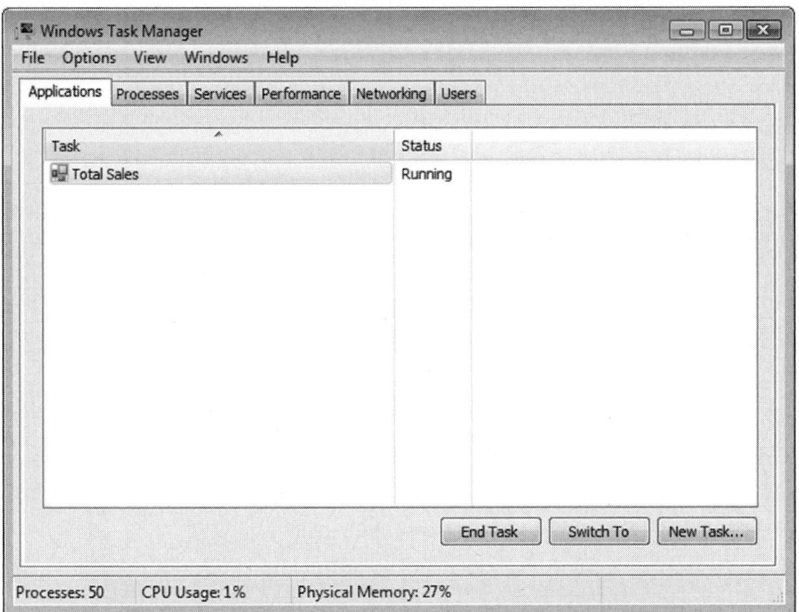

Letting the User Control the Loop

Sometimes the user must decide how many times a loop should iterate. In Tutorial 5-5, you examine a modification of a simplified version of the *Running Total* application. This version of the program asks the user how many days he or she has sales figures for. The application then uses that value to control the number of times the `Do While` loop repeats.

Tutorial 5-5:
Examining an application that uses a user-controlled loop

Step 1: Open the *User Controlled* project, from the student sample programs folder named *Chap5\User Controlled.*

Step 2: Run the application. When the form appears, click the *Enter Sales* button. The input box shown in Figure 5-18 appears.

Step 3: The input box asks you to enter the number of days you have sales figures for. Enter **3** and click the *OK* button (or press Enter).

Figure 5-18 *Number of Days Needed* input box

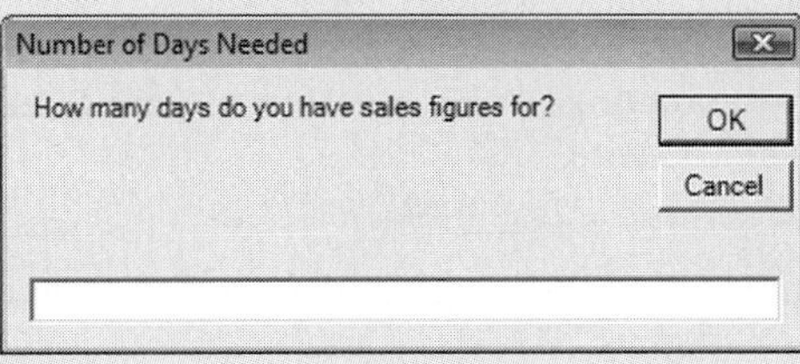

Step 4: Because you entered 3 for the number of days, the application presents three input boxes asking for the sales for days 1, 2, and 3. Enter the following values when asked:

Day 1: **1800**
Day 2: **2700**
Day 3: **2400**

Step 5: After you enter the sales figure for day 3, the application's form displays $6,900.00 as the total sales.

Step 6: Click the *Exit* button to terminate the application.

Step 7: Open the *Code* window and find the `btnEnterSales_Click` event procedure. Notice that a new variable has been added.

```
Dim intDays As Integer              ' Number of days
```

The `intDays` variable is used in the following lines which ask the user to enter the number of days for which there are sales figures. The value entered by the user is stored in days.

```
' Get the number of days from the user.
strInput = InputBox("How many days do you have sales" _
           & "figures  for?", "Number of Days Needed")
intDays = CInt(strInput)
```

Now, look at the first line of the `Do While` loop.

```
Do While intCount <= intDays
```

The loop now repeats while `intCount` is less than or equal to `intDays`. This limits the number of iterations to no more than the value entered by the user.

Checkpoint

5.9 How many times will the following code segment display the message box?

```
Dim intCount As Integer = 0
Do While intCount < 10
  MessageBox.Show("I love Visual Basic!")
Loop
```

5.10 How many times will the following code segment display the message box?

```
Dim intCount As Integer = 0
Do While intCount < 10
  MessageBox.Show("I love Visual Basic!")
  intCount += 1
Loop
```

5.11 How many times will the following code segment display the message box?

```
Dim intCount As Integer = 100
Do
  MessageBox.Show("I love Visual Basic!")
  intCount += 1
Loop While intCount < 10
```

5.12 In the following code segment, which variable is the counter and which is the accumulator?

```
Dim intA As Integer
Dim intX As Integer
```

```
Dim intY As Integer
Dim intZ As Integer
Dim strInput As String
intX = 0
intY = 0
strInput = InputBox("How many numbers do you wish to enter?")
intZ = CInt(strInput)
Do While intX < intZ
  strInput = InputBox("Enter a number.")
  intA = CInt(strInput)
  intY += intA
  intX += 1
Loop
MessageBox.Show("The sum of those numbers is " & intY.ToString())
```

5.13 The following loop adds the numbers 1 through 5 to the `lstOutput` list box. Modify the loop so that instead of starting at 1 and counting to 5, it starts at 5 and counts backward to 1.

```
Dim intCount As Integer = 1
Do While intCount <= 5
  lstOutput.Items.Add(intCount)
  intCount += 1
Loop
```

5.14 Write a `Do While` loop that uses an input box to ask the user to enter a number. The loop should keep a running total of the numbers entered and stop when the total is greater than 300.

5.15 If you want a `Do While` loop always to iterate at least once, which form should you use, pretest or posttest?

5.4 The `Do Until` and `For...Next` Loops

CONCEPT: The Do Until loop iterates until its test expression is true. The `For...Next` loop uses a counter variable and iterates a specific number of times.

The `Do Until` Loop

The `Do Until` loop repeats until its test expression is true. Here is the general format of the **`Do Until`** loop:

```
Do Until expression
  statement
  (more statements may follow)
Loop
```

Like the `Do While` loop, the `Do Until` loop may be written in pretest or posttest form. The general format shown above was for a pretest `Do Until` loop. Here is the general format of the posttest `Do Until` loop:

```
Do
  statement
  (more statements may follow)
Loop Until expression
```

In Tutorial 5-6, you examine an application that uses the `Do Until` loop. The application asks the user to enter test scores, and then displays the average of the scores.

Tutorial 5-6:
Examining an application that uses the `Do Until` loop

Step 1: Open the *Test Scores 1* project from the student sample programs folder named *Chap5\Test Scores 1*.

Step 2: Run the application. The form appears, as shown in Figure 5-19.

Step 3: Click the *Calculate Average* button. The input box shown in Figure 5-20 appears.

Figure 5-19 *Test Score Average* form

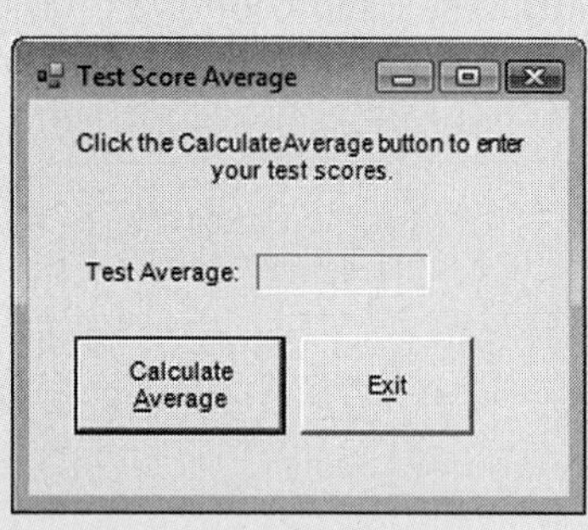

Figure 5-20 Input box

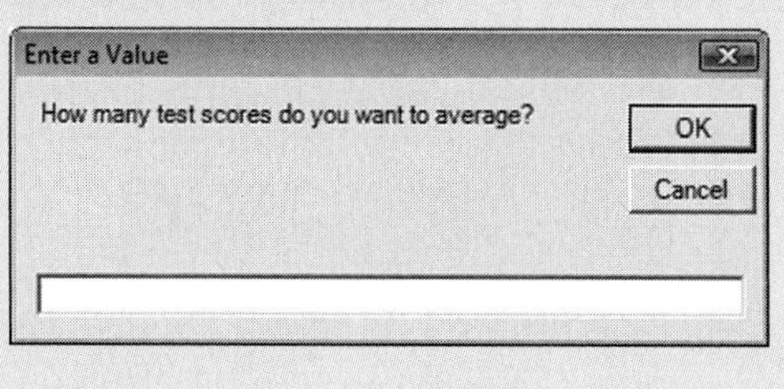

Step 4: Enter **5** for the number of test scores and click the *OK* button (or press Enter).

Step 5: Because you entered 5 for the number of test scores, the application presents five input boxes asking for scores 1, 2, 3, 4, and 5. Enter the following values when asked.

Test Score 1: **98** Test Score 3: **100** Test Score 5: **92**
Test Score 2: **87** Test Score 4: **74**

Step 6: After you enter the fifth test score, the test score average 90.2 is displayed on the application form. Click the *Exit* button to end the application.

Step 7: Open the *Code* window and look at the `btnCalcAverage_Click` event procedure. The code is as follows:

```
Private Sub btnCalcAverage_Click(ByVal sender As _
      System.Object, ByVal e As System.EventArgs) Handles _
      btnCalcAverage.Click

    ' This procedure gets the test scores, then calculates and
    ' displays the average.
    Dim sngTotal As Single          ' Holds the running total
                                    ' of test scores
    Dim intNumScores As Integer     ' The number of test scores
    Dim sngAverage As Single        ' Average of test scores
    Dim strInput As String          ' To hold user input
    Dim intCount As Integer   ' Counter variable for the loop

    ' Get the number of test scores.
    strInput = InputBox("How many test scores do you want " _
        & "to average?", "Enter a Value")
    If Not Integer.TryParse(strInput, intNumScores) Then
      Return
    End If
```

```
        ' Store the starting values in total and count.
        sngTotal = 0
        intCount = 1

        ' Get the test scores.
        Do Until intCount > intNumScores
          strInput = InputBox("Enter the value for test score " _
              & intCount.ToString, "Test Score Needed")

          sngTotal += CSng(strInput)
          intCount += 1
        Loop

        ' Calculate and display the average.
        If intNumScores > 0 Then
          sngAverage = sngTotal / intNumScores
        Else
          sngAverage = 0.0
        End If
        lblAverage.Text = sngAverage.ToString
      End Sub
```

The For...Next Loop

The `For...Next` loop is ideal for situations that require a counter because it initializes, tests, and increments a counter variable. Here is the format of the **`For...Next`** loop:

VideoNote

The `For Next` Loop

```
For CounterVariable = StartValue To EndValue [Step Increment]
  statement
  (more statements may follow)
Next [CounterVariable]
```

As usual, the brackets are not part of the syntax, but indicate the optional parts. Let's look closer at the syntax.

- *`CounterVariable`* is the variable to be used as a counter. It must be a numeric variable.
- *`StartValue`* is the value the counter variable will be initially set to. This value must be numeric.
- *`EndValue`* is the value the counter variable is tested against just prior to each iteration of the loop. This value must be numeric.
- The `Step` *`Increment`* part of the statement is optional. If it is present, *`Increment`* (which must be a numeric expression) is the amount added to the counter variable at the end of each iteration. If the `Step` *`Increment`* part of the statement is omitted, the counter variable is incremented by 1 at the end of each iteration.
- The `Next` [*`CounterVariable`*] statement marks the end of the loop and causes the counter variable to be incremented. Notice that the name of the counter variable is optional. For readability, it is recommended that you always list the name of the counter variable after the `Next` statement.

Here is an example of the `For...Next` loop:

```
For intCount = 1 To 10
  lstOutput.Items.Add("Hello")
Next intCount
```

This loop executes the `lstOutput.Items.Add("Hello")` statement 10 times. The following steps take place when the loop executes.

1. `intCount` is set to 1 (the start value).
2. `intCount` is compared to 10 (the end value). If `intCount` is less than or equal to 10, continue to Step 3. Otherwise the loop is exited.
3. The `lstOutput.Items.Add("Hello")` statement in the body of the loop is executed.
4. `intCount` is incremented by 1.
5. Go back to Step 2 and repeat this sequence.

The flowchart shown in Figure 5-21 shows loop's actions.

WARNING: It is incorrect to place a statement in the body of the `For...Next` loop that changes the counter variable's value. For example, the following loop increments `intX` twice for each iteration.

```
' Warning!
For intX = 1 To 10
  MessageBox.Show("Hello")
  intX += 1
Next intX
```

Figure 5-21 Flowchart of `For...Next` loop

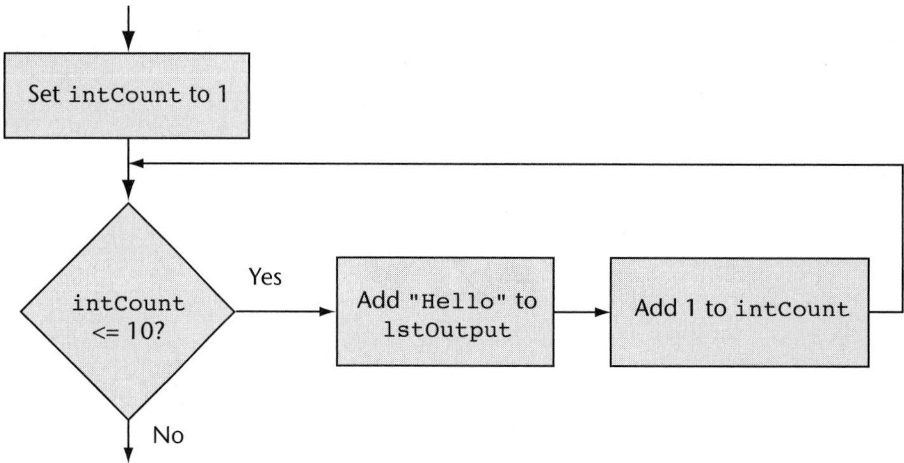

In Tutorial 5-7, you examine an application that demonstrates the `For...Next` loop.

NOTE: Because the `For...Next` loop performs its test prior to each iteration, it is a pretest loop. Unlike the `Do While` and `Do Until` loops, this is the only form the `For...Next` loop may be written in.

Tutorial 5-7:
Examining an application that uses the `For...Next` loop

Step 1: Open the *For Next Demo 1* project from the student sample programs folder named *Chap5\For Next Demo 1*.

Step 2: Run the application. The form appears as shown in Figure 5-22.

Step 3: Click the *Run Demo* button. The form now appears as shown in Figure 5-23.

Step 4: Click the *Exit* button to terminate the application.

Step 5: Open the *Code* window and find the `btnRunDemo_Click` event procedure. The code is as follows:

```
Private Sub btnRunDemo_Click(ByVal sender As System.Object, _
    ByVal e As System.EventArgs) Handles btnRunDemo.Click

  ' Demonstrate the For...Next loop.
  Dim intCount As Integer                     ' Loop counter
  Dim intSquare As Integer                    ' To hold squares
  Dim strTemp As String                       ' To hold output

  For intCount = 1 To 10
    intSquare = CInt(intCount ^ 2)
    strTemp = "The square of " & intCount.ToString() _
        & " is " & intSquare.ToString()
    lstOutput.Items.Add(strTemp)
  Next intCount
End Sub
```

Figure 5-24 illustrates the order of the steps taken by the `For...Next` loop in this program.

Figure 5-22 *For...Next Demo 1* form

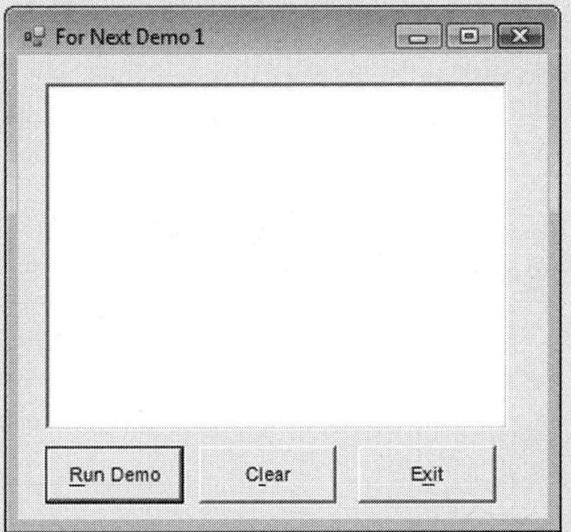

Figure 5-23 Results of `For...Next` loop

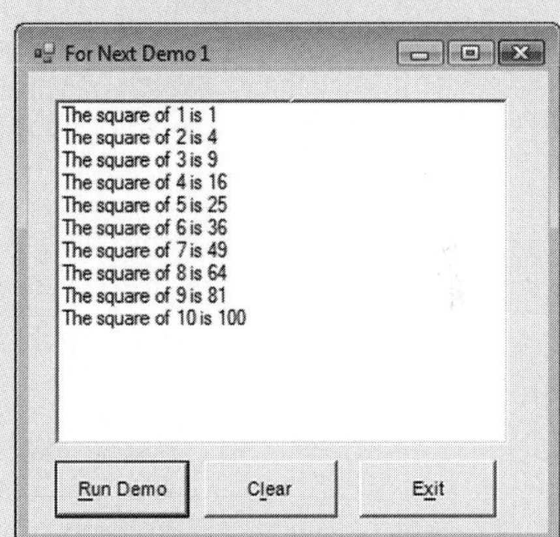

Figure 5-24 Steps in `For...Next` loop

Step 1: Initialize `intCount` to 1.

Step 2: Compare `intCount` to 10. If `intCount` is greater than 10, terminate the loop. Otherwise, go to Step 3.

```
For intCount = 1 To 10
      intSquare = CInt(intCount ^ 2)
      strTemp = "The square of " & intCount.ToString() _
          & "is" & intSquare.ToString()
      lstOutput.Items.Add(strTemp)
Next intCount
```

Step 3: Execute the body of the loop.

Step 4: Increment `intCount` by 1. Go back to Step 2.

In Tutorial 5-8, you complete a partially written application. The application will use a graphic image and a `For...Next` loop to perform a simple animation.

Tutorial 5-8:
Completing an application that uses the `For...Next` loop

Step 1: Open the *For Next Demo 2* project from the student sample programs folder named *Chap5\For Next Demo 2*.

Step 2: Open the application's form, as shown in Figure 5-25.

Figure 5-25 *For Next Demo 2* form

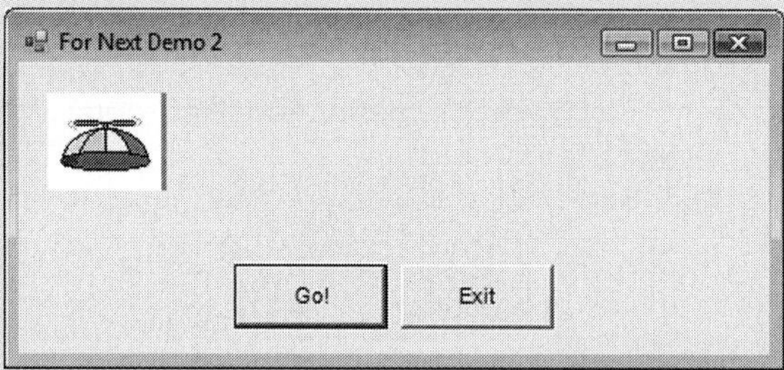

The propeller cap graphic is displayed by a PictureBox control. The PictureBox control has a Left property that specifies the distance from the left edge of the form to the left edge of the PictureBox control. (The distance is measured in pixels.) In this tutorial, you will write a `For...Next` loop that makes the image move across the form by increasing the value of the PictureBox control's Left property.

Step 3: Double-click the *Go!* button. Complete the code template for the `btnGo_Click` event procedure, as follows:

```
Private Sub btnGo_Click(ByVal sender As System.Object, _
    ByVal e As System.EventArgs) Handles btnGo.Click

  ' Run the animation
  Dim intCount As Integer
  For intCount = 16 To 328
    picPropellerCap.Left = intCount
  Next intCount
End Sub
```

Look at the first line of the `For...Next` loop:

```
For intCount = 16 To 328
```

The start value for `intCount` is 16, and its end value is 328. Inside the loop, the following statement stores the value of `intCount` in the PictureBox control's Left property:

```
picPropellerCap.Left = intCount
```

As the loop iterates, the value in the Left property grows larger, which causes the PictureBox control to move across the form.

Step 4: Run the application. Each time you click the *Go!* button, the propeller cap image should move from the form's left edge to its right edge.

Step 5: Click the *Exit* button to end the application. If you wish, open the *Code* window and experiment with different start and end values for the For...Next loop.

Specifying a Step Value

The **step value** is the value added to the counter variable at the end of each iteration of the For...Next loop. By default, the step value is 1. You can specify a different step value with the Step keyword. For example, look at the following code:

```
For intX = 0 To 100 Step 10
  MessageBox.Show("intX is now " & intX.ToString())
Next intX
```

In this loop, the starting value of intX is 0 and the ending value of intX is 100. The step value is 10, which means that 10 is added to intX at the end of each iteration. During the first iteration intX is 0, during the second iteration intX is 10, during the third iteration intX is 20, and so on.

You may also specify a negative step value if you want to decrement the counter variable. For example, look at the following loop:

```
For intX = 10 To 1 Step -1
  MessageBox.Show("intX is now " & intX.ToString())
Next intX
```

In this loop the starting value of intX is 10 and the ending value of intX is 1. The step value is –1, which means that 1 is subtracted from intX at the end of each iteration. During the first iteration intX is 10, during the second iteration intX is 9, and so on.

Summing a Series of Numbers with the For...Next Loop

The For...Next loop can be used to calculate the sum of a series of numbers, as shown in the following code:

```
Dim intX, intTotal As Integer
intTotal = 0
For intX = 1 to 100
  intTotal += intX
Next intX
MessageBox.Show("The sum of 1 through 100 is " & intTotal.ToString())
```

This code uses the variable intTotal as an accumulator, and calculates the sum of the numbers from 1 through 100. The counter variable, intX, has a starting value of 1 and an ending value of 100. During each iteration, the value of intX is added to intTotal.

You may also let the user specify how many numbers to sum, as well as the value of each number. For example, look at the following code:

```
Dim intCount, intMaxNumbers As Integer
Dim dblTotal As Double = 0
Dim dblNum As Double
Dim strInput As String
intMaxNumbers = CInt(InputBox( _
    "How many numbers do you wish to sum?"))
```

```
For intCount = 1 To intMaxNumbers
  strInput = InputBox("Enter a number")
  dblNum = CDbl(strInput)
  dblTotal += dblNum
Next intCount

MessageBox.Show("The sum of the numbers is " _
    & dblTotal.ToString())
```

This code asks the user for the number of numbers to sum. The number entered by the user is stored in `intMaxNumbers`. In the loop, the counter variable `intCount` has a starting value of 1 and an ending value of `intMaxNumbers`. This causes the loop to iterate `intMaxNumbers` times.

An input box is used in the loop to ask the user to enter a number. The value entered by the user is stored in the `dblNum` variable. The value in `dblNum` is then added to the accumulator variable, `dblTotal`.

Optional Topic: Breaking Out of a Loop

Sometimes it is necessary to stop a `Do While`, `Do Until`, or `For...Next` loop before it goes through all its iterations. You saw an example of this in Tutorial 5-4. The **`Exit Do`** and **`Exit For` statements**, when placed inside the body of a loop, stop the execution of the loop and cause the program to jump to the statement immediately following the loop.

For example, the following code is a modification of the code for summing a user-specified series of numbers shown in the previous section:

```
Dim intCount, intMaxNumbers As Integer
Dim dblTotal As Double = 0
Dim dblNum As Double
Dim strInput As String
intMaxNumbers = CInt(InputBox( _
    "How many numbers do you wish to sum?"))

For intCount = 1 To intMaxNumbers
  strInput = InputBox("Enter a number")
  If strInput = String.Empty Then
    Exit For
  Else
    dblNum = CDbl(strInput)
    dblTotal += dblNum
  End If
Next intCount

MessageBox.Show("The sum of the numbers is " _
    & dblTotal.ToString())
```

In the loop, the user is asked to enter a number in an input box. The value entered by the user is stored as a string. Recall that the `InputBox` function returns an empty string if the user clicks the *Cancel* button. An `If...Then...Else` statement tests the input variable to determine whether it contains an empty string. If so, the `Exit For` statement causes the loop to terminate.

WARNING: Use the `Exit Do` and `Exit For` statements with caution. Because they bypass the loop's normal termination, they can make your code more difficult to debug.

Deciding Which Loop to Use

Although most repetitive algorithms can be written with any of the three types of loops, each works best in different situations.

The `Do While` Loop

Use the `Do While` loop when you wish the loop to repeat as long as the test expression is true. You can write the `Do While` loop as a pretest or posttest loop. Pretest `Do While` loops are ideal when you do not want the code in the loop to execute if the test expression is false from the beginning. Posttest loops are ideal when you always want the code in the loop to execute at least once.

The `Do Until` Loop

Use the `Do Until` loop when you wish the loop to repeat until the test expression is true. You can write the `Do Until` loop as a pretest or posttest loop. Pretest `Do Until` loops are ideal when you do not want the code in the loop to execute if the test expression is true from the beginning. Posttest loops are ideal when you always want the code in the loop to execute at least once.

The `For...Next` Loop

The `For...Next` loop is a pretest loop that first initializes a counter variable to a starting value. It automatically increments the counter variable at the end of each iteration. The loop repeats as long as the counter variable is not greater than an end value. The `For...Next` loop is primarily used when the number of required iterations is known.

Checkpoint

5.16 How many times will the code inside the following loop execute? What will be displayed in the message box?

```
intX = 0
Do Until intX = 10
    intX += 2
Loop
MessageBox.Show(intX.ToString())
```

5.17 Write a `For...Next` loop that adds every fifth number, starting at zero, through 100, to the list box `lstOutput`.

5.18 Write a `For...Next` loop that repeats seven times, each time displaying an input box that asks the user to enter a number. The loop should also calculate and display the sum of the numbers entered.

5.19 Which type of loop is best to use when you know exactly how many times the loop should repeat?

5.20 Which type of loop is best to use when you want the loop to repeat as long as a condition exists?

5.21 Which type of loop is best to use when you want the loop to repeat until a condition exists?

5.5 Nested Loops

CONCEPT: A loop that is inside loop is called a nested loop.

A **nested loop** is a loop inside another loop. A clock is a good example of something that works like a nested loop. The second hand, minute hand, and hour hand all spin around the face of the clock. The hour hand, however, only makes one revolution for every 60 of the minute hand's revolutions. And it takes 60 revolutions of the second hand for the minute hand to make one revolution. This means that for every complete revolution of the hour hand, the second hand revolves 3,600 times.

The following is a code segment with a `For...Next` loop that partially simulates a digital clock. It displays the seconds from 0 through 59 in a label named `lblSeconds`.

```
For intSeconds = 0 To 59
  lblSeconds.Text = intSeconds.ToString()
Next intSeconds
```

We can add a minutes variable and another label, and nest the loop inside another loop that cycles through 60 minutes:

```
For intMinutes = 0 To 59
  lblMinutes.Text = intMinutes.ToString()
  For intSeconds = 0 To 59
    lblSeconds.Text = intSeconds.ToString()
  Next intSeconds
Next intMinutes
```

To make the simulated clock complete, another variable, label, and loop can be added to count the hours:

```
For intHours = 0 To 24
  lblHours.Text = intHours.ToString()
  For intMinutes = 0 To 59
    lblMinutes.Text = intMinutes.ToString()
    For intSeconds = 0 To 59
      lblSeconds.Text = intSeconds.ToString()
    Next intSeconds
  Next intMinutes
Next intHours
```

The innermost loop will iterate 60 times for each iteration of the middle loop. The middle loop will iterate 60 times for each iteration of the outermost loop. When the outermost loop has iterated 24 times, the middle loop will have iterated 1,440 times and the innermost loop will have iterated 86,400 times.

The simulated clock example brings up a few points about nested loops:

- An inner loop goes through all of its iterations for each iteration of an outer loop.
- Inner loops complete their iterations before outer loops do.
- To get the total number of iterations of a nested loop, multiply the number of iterations of all the loops.

5.22 What values will the following code segment add to the `lstNumbers` list box?

```
For intX = 1 to 3
    lstNumbers.Items.Add(intX)
    For intY = 1 to 2
        lstNumbers.Items.Add(intY)
    Next intY
Next intX
```

5.23 How many times will the value in `intY` be displayed in the following code segment?

```
For intX = 1 to 20
    For intY = 1 to 30
        MessageBox.Show(intY.ToString())
    Next intY
Next intX
```

5.6 Multicolumn List Boxes, Checked List Boxes, and Combo Boxes

CONCEPT: A multicolumn list box displays items in columns with a horizontal scroll bar, if necessary. A checked list box displays a check box next to each item in the list. A combo box performs many of the same functions as a list box, and it can also include a text box.

Multicolumn List Boxes

The ListBox control has a Multicolumn property that may be set to *True* or *False*. By default, it is set to *False*. When set to *True*, it causes the list box to display its list in columns. You set the size of the columns, in pixels, with the ColumnWidth property. For example, suppose a form has a list box named `lstNumbers`, as shown in Figure 5-26.

The list box's Multicolumn property is set to *True*, and its ColumnWidth property is set to *30*. The following code adds the numbers 0 through 100 to a list box:

```
For intNumber = 0 To 100
  lstNumbers.Items.Add(intNumber)
Next
```

After the code executes, the list box appears as shown in Figure 5-27.

Notice that a horizontal scroll bar automatically appears in the list box. The user may scroll through the list and select a number.

Checked List Boxes

The CheckedListBox control is a variation of the ListBox control. It supports all ListBox properties and methods discussed in Section 5.2. Each item in a CheckedListBox control, however, is displayed with a check box next to it. Figure 5-28 shows an example.

An item in a checked list box may be selected and/or checked. Only one item in a checked list box may be selected at a given time, but multiple items may be checked.

Figure 5-26 List box

Figure 5-27 List box with multicolumn display

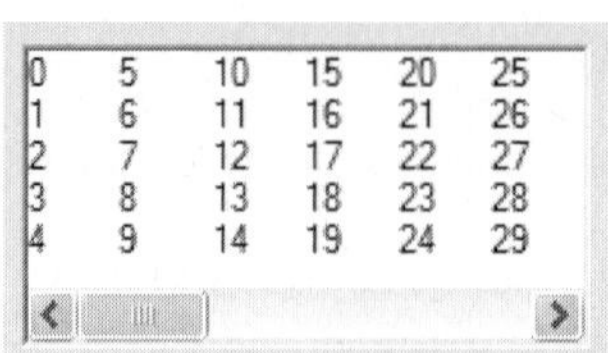

Figure 5-28 Checked list box

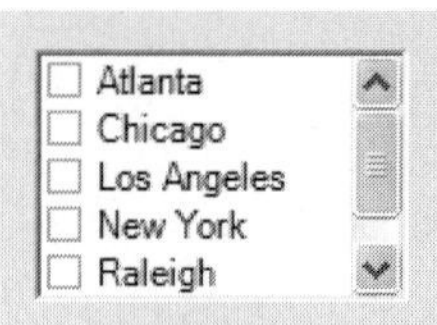

This is how the CheckOnClick property determines how items become checked:

- When set to *False*, the user clicks an item once to select it, and then clicks it again to check it (or uncheck it, if it is already checked).
- When set to *True*, the user clicks an item only once to both select it and check it (or uncheck it, if it is already checked).

The CheckOnClick property is set to *False* by default. Because this setting makes working with the control a bit complicated, you may prefer setting it to *True* for most applications.

You access the selected item in a checked list box exactly as you do with a regular list box: through the SelectedIndex and SelectedItem properties. These properties only indicate which item is selected, however, and do not report which items are checked. You access the checked items through the `GetItemChecked` method, which has the following general format:

```
CheckedListBox.GetItemChecked(Index)
```

`CheckedListBox` is the name of the CheckedListBox control. *`Index`* is the index of an item in the list. If the item is checked, the method returns *True*. Otherwise, it returns *False*. For example, assume an application has a checked list box name `clbCities`. (`clb` is the prefix for checked list boxes.) The following code counts the number of checked items:

```
Dim intIndex As Integer
Dim intCheckedCities As Integer = 0
For intIndex = 0 To clbCities.Items.Count - 1
  If clbCities.GetItemChecked(intIndex) = True Then
    intCheckedCities += 1
  End If
Next intIndex
MessageBox.Show("You checked " & intCheckedCities.ToString() & _
    " cities.")
```

As another example, assume an application uses the controls shown in Figure 5-29. The checked list box on the left is `clbCities` and the list box on the right is `lstChecked`. The *OK* button, `btnOk`, uses the following `Click` event procedure:

```
Private Sub btnOk_Click(ByVal sender As System.Object, _
    ByVal e As System.EventArgs) Handles btnOk.Click

  Dim intIndex As Integer
  For intIndex = 0 To clbCities.Items.Count - 1
    If clbCities.GetItemChecked(intIndex) = True Then
      lstChecked.Items.Add(clbCities.Items(intIndex))
    End If
  Next intIndex
End Sub
```

The `btnOk_Click` event procedure adds the items checked in the `clbCities` control to the `lstChecked` control. Figure 5-30 shows how the controls appear after the user has checked three cities and clicked the *OK* button.

Figure 5-29 Checked list box and a list box

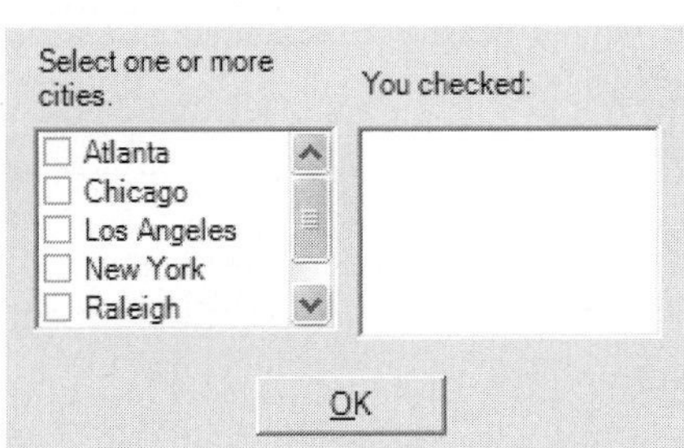

Figure 5-30 Cities checked

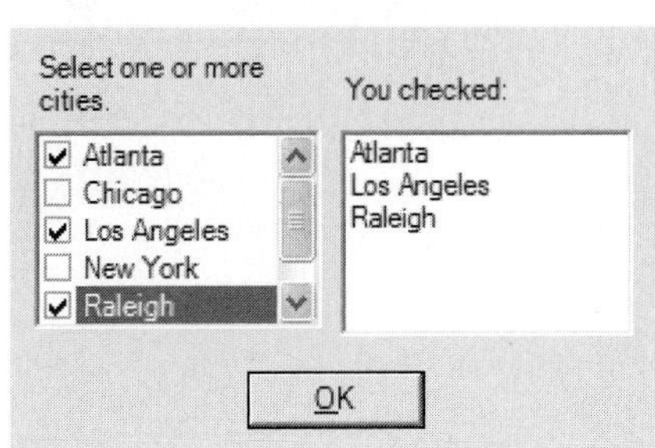

Combo Boxes

Combo boxes and list boxes are similar in the following ways:

- They both display a list of items to the user.
- They both have Items, Items.Count, SelectedIndex, SelectedItem, and Sorted properties.
- They both have `Items.Add`, `Items.Clear`, `Items.Remove`, and `Items.RemoveAt` methods.
- All of these properties and methods work the same with combo boxes and list boxes.

Additionally, a combo box has a rectangular area that functions like a text box. The user may either select an item from the combo box's list or type text into the combo box's text input area.

Like a text box, the combo box has a Text property. If the user types text into the combo box, the text is stored in the Text property. Also, when the user selects an item from the combo box's list, the item is copied to the Text property.

The standard prefix for combo box names is `cbo`.

Combo Box Styles

There are three different styles of combo boxes: the drop-down combo box, the simple combo box, and the drop-down list combo box. You select a combo box's style with its DropDownStyle property. Let's look at the differences of each style.

The Drop-Down Combo Box

This is the default setting for the combo box DropDownStyle property. At runtime, a drop-down combo box appears like the one shown in Figure 5-31.

This style of combo box behaves like either a text box or a list box. The user may either type text into the box (like a text box) or click the down arrow (▾). If the user clicks the down arrow, a list of items drops down, as shown in Figure 5-32.

Now the user may select an item from the list. When the user selects an item, it appears in the text input area at the top of the box, and is copied to the combo box's Text property.

NOTE: When typing text into the combo box, the user may enter a string that does not appear in the drop-down list.

Figure 5-31 A drop-down combo box

Figure 5-32 A list drops down when the user clicks the down arrow

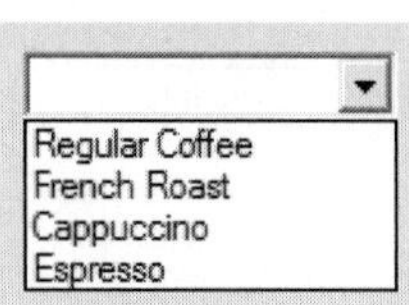

TIP: When the combo box has the focus, the user may also press Alt+↓ to drop the list down. This is also true for the drop-down list combo box.

The Simple Combo Box

With the simple style of combo box, the list of items does not drop down but is always displayed. Figure 5-33 shows an example.

As with the drop-down combo box, this style allows the user to type text directly into the combo box or select from the list. When typing, the user is not restricted to the items that appear in the list. When an item is selected from the list, it is copied to the text input area and to the combo box's Text property.

Drop-Down List Combo Box

With drop-down list combo box style, the user may not type text directly into the combo box. An item must be selected from the list. Figure 5-34 shows a drop-down list combo box.

When the user clicks the down arrow, a list of items appears, as shown in Figure 5-35.

Figure 5-33 The simple combo box

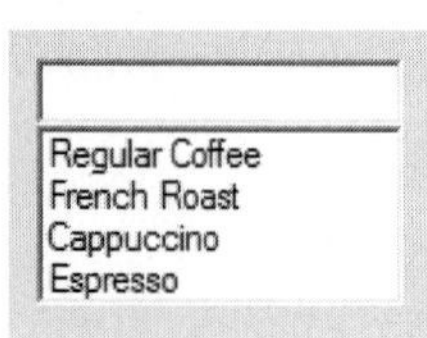

Figure 5-34 The drop-down list combo box

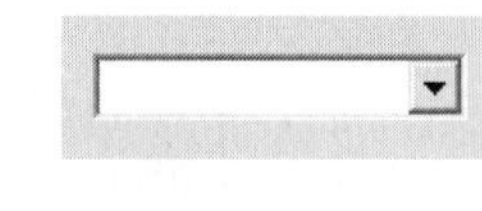

Figure 5-35 A list drops down when the user clicks the down arrow

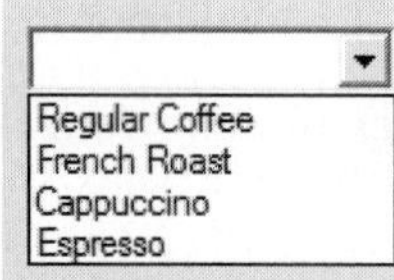

When the user selects an item from the list, it is copied to the text area at the top of the combo box and to the Text property. Because the user can only select items from the list, it is not possible to enter text that does not appear in the list.

Getting the User's Input from a Combo Box

As with the list box, you can determine which item has been selected from a combo box's list by retrieving the value in the SelectedIndex or SelectedItem properties. If the user has typed text into the combo box's text area, however, you cannot use the SelectedIndex or SelectedItem properties to get the text. The best way to get the user's input is with the Text property, which contains either the user's text input or the item selected from the list.

NOTE: The drop-down list combo box's Text property is read-only. You cannot change its value with code.

List Boxes versus Combo Boxes

The following guidelines help you decide when to use a list box and when to use a combo box.

- Use a drop-down or simple combo box when you want to provide the user a list of items to select from but do not want to limit the user's input to the items on the list.
- Use a list box or a drop-down list combo box when you want to limit the user's selection to a list of items. The drop-down list combo box generally takes less space than a list box (because the list doesn't appear until the user clicks the down arrow), so use it when you want to conserve space on the form.

In Tutorial 5-9, you create three styles of combo boxes.

Tutorial 5-9:
Creating combo boxes

In this tutorial, you will create each of the three styles of combo boxes.

Step 1: Create a new Windows application project named *Combo Box Demo.*

Step 2: Set up the form like the one shown in Figure 5-36. Draw three combo boxes: `cboCountries` (drop-down combo box), `cboPlays` (simple combo box), and `cboArtists` (drop-down list combo box).

Step 3: Enter the following items into the Items property of the `cboCountries` combo box: **`England`**, **`Ireland`**, **`Scotland`**, and **`Wales`**. Set the combo box's Sorted property to *True.*

Step 4: Enter the following items into the Items property of the `cboPlays` combo box: **`Hamlet`**, **`Much Ado about Nothing`**, **`Romeo and Juliet`**, **`A Comedy of Errors`**, and **`The Merchant of Venice`**. Set the combo box's Sorted property to *True.*

Step 5: Enter the following items into the Items property of the `cboArtists` combo box: **`Michelangelo`**, **`Raphael`**, and **`da Vinci`**.

Step 6: The `btnShow_Click` event procedure should perform the following tasks:

- Copy the selected item or typed text from the `cboCountries` combo box to the `lblCountry.Text` property.

Figure 5-36 *Combo Box Demo* form

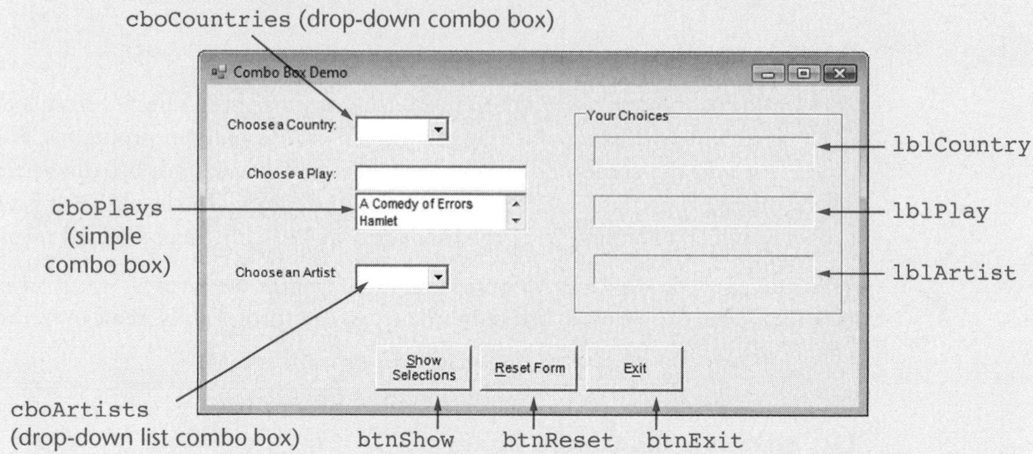

- Copy the selected item or typed text from the `cboPlays` combo box to the `lblPlay.Text` property.
- Copy the selected item from the `cboArtists` combo box to the `lblArtist.Text` property.

Enter the following code shown in bold for the `btnShow_Click` event procedure:

```
Private Sub btnShow_Click(ByVal sender As System.Object, _
      ByVal e As System.EventArgs) Handles btnShow.Click

   ' This procedure displays the combo box selections.
   lblCountry.Text = cboCountries.Text
   lblPlay.Text = cboPlays.Text
   lblArtist.Text = cboArtists.Text
End Sub
```

Step 7: The `btnReset_Click` event procedure should deselect any items that are selected in the combo boxes. As with list boxes, this is accomplished by setting the SelectedIndex property to –1. The procedure should also set the Text property of `lblCountry`, `lblPlay`, and `lblArtist` to `String.Empty`. Enter the following code for the `btnReset_Click` event procedure.

```
Private Sub btnReset_Click(ByVal sender As System.Object, _
      ByVal e As System.EventArgs) Handles btnReset.Click

   ' This procedure clears selections in the
   ' Combo Boxes and resets the labels to an empty string.
   ' Reset the combo boxes.
   cboCountries.SelectedIndex = -1
   cboCountries.Text = String.Empty
   cboPlays.SelectedIndex = -1
   cboPlays.Text = String.Empty
   cboArtists.SelectedIndex = -1
   ' Note: cboArtists.Text is read-only.

   ' Reset the labels.
   lblCountry.Text = String.Empty
   lblPlay.Text = String.Empty
   lblArtist.Text = String.Empty
End Sub
```

NOTE: If the user types characters into a combo box's text input area, those characters are not cleared by setting the SelectedIndex property to –1. You must set the Text property to `String.Empty` to accomplish that.

Step 8: The `btnExit_Click` event procedure should end the application. Write the code for that event procedure.

Step 9: Save the project and run the application. Experiment with the combo boxes by trying a combination of text input and item selection. For example, select an item from the `cboCountries` list and type text into the `cboPlays`' text input area. Click the `btnShow` button to see what you have entered.

Step 10: End the application when you are finished experimenting with it.

Checkpoint

5.24 What is the index of the first item stored in a list box or combo box's Items property?

5.25 Which list box or combo box property holds the number of items stored in the Items property?

5.26 Which list box or combo box property holds the index of the item selected from the list?

5.27 What is the difference between a drop-down and drop-down list combo box?

5.28 What is the best method of getting the user's input from a combo box?

5.29 Suppose you want to place a list box on a form, but it would take up too much space. What other control might you use?

5.7 Input Validation

CONCEPT: As long as the user of an application enters bad input, the application will produce bad output. Applications should be written to filter out bad input. We will show you how to use the `CausesValidation` property as well as the `Validating` and `Validated` events to ensure the user has entered acceptable data as input.

Perhaps the most famous saying of the computer world is "garbage in, garbage out." The integrity of an application's output is only as good as its input, so you should try to make sure garbage does not go into your applications as input. **Input validation** is the process of inspecting data given to an application by the user and determining whether it is valid. A properly designed application should give clear instructions about the kind of input that is acceptable and should not assume the user has followed those instructions. The following are a few examples of input validations performed by programs:

- Numbers are checked to ensure that they are within a range of possible values. For example, there are 168 hours in a week. It is not possible for a person to work more than 168 hours in a week.

- Values are checked for their "reasonableness." Although it might be possible for a person to work 168 hours in a week, it is not probable.
- Items selected from a menu or other sets of choices are checked to ensure that they are available options.
- Variables are checked for values that might cause problems, such as division by zero.

Most controls have a Boolean property named **CausesValidation**. Additionally, most controls are capable of triggering a `Validating` event. A control's **`Validating` event** is triggered just before the focus is shifted to another control whose CausesValidation property is set to *True*. The following scenario describes how the CausesValidation property and the `Validating` event work in harmony.

Suppose an application has two text box controls: `txtFirst` and `txtSecond`. The user has just entered a value into `txtFirst` and pressed the Tab key, which should shift the focus from `txtFirst` to `txtSecond`. But `txtSecond`'s CausesValidation property is set to *True*, so `txtFirst`'s `Validating` event is triggered before the focus shifts. The `txtFirst` control has a `Validating` event procedure, which is executed as a result of the `Validating` event being triggered. The `Validating` event procedure contains code that checks the value in `txtFirst`. If the value is invalid, the event procedure displays an error message instructing the user to reenter the data. Furthermore, the code prevents the focus from shifting if the value is not valid.

NOTE: By default, a control's CausesValidation property is set to *True*.

In Tutorial 5-10, you examine an application that demonstrates input validation.

Tutorial 5-10: Completing an application that demonstrates input validation

Step 1: Open the *Validation Demo* project from the student sample programs folder named *Chap5\Validation Demo*.

Step 2: Open the *Validation Demo* form window in Design mode. Run the program, input the values **`5`** and **`7`**, and click the *Calculate* button. The result is shown in Figure 5-37. The form instructs the user to enter two numbers in the range 1 to 10. However, the application contains no input validation code. Click the *Exit* button to end the program and return to Design mode.

Figure 5-37 *Validation Demo* form

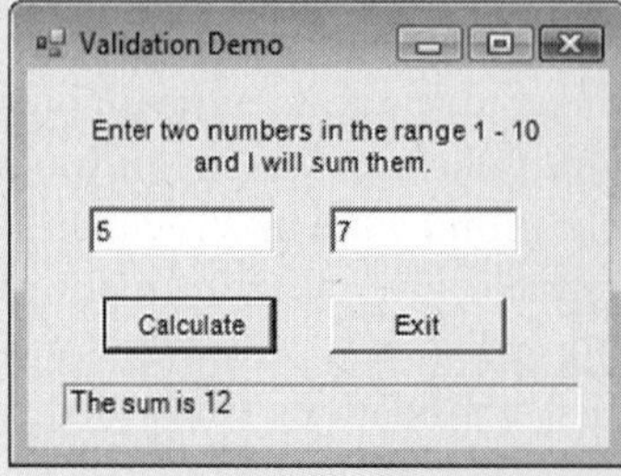

Step 3: Select the two text boxes and the two buttons, one after another. As you select each one, notice that its CausesValidation property is set to *True*. This is the CausesValidation property's default value.

Step 4: Now you will write the code for two text boxes' `Validating` event procedures. Open the *Code* window. From the class name drop-down list, select `txtNum1`, as shown in Figure 5-38.

Figure 5-38 Class name drop-down list with `txtNum1` selected

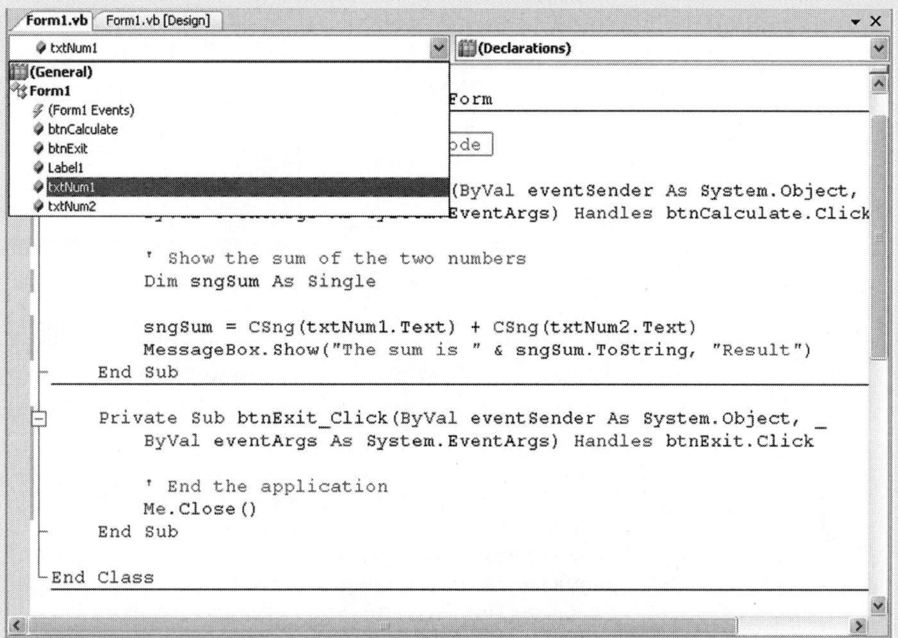

Step 5: From the method name drop-down list, select *Validating*, as shown in Figure 5-39.

Step 6: When you selected *Validating* from the method name drop-down list, Visual Studio created a code template for the `txtNum1_Validating` event procedure:

```
Private Sub txtNum1_Validating(ByVal sender As Object, _
  ByVal e As System.ComponentModel.CancelEventArgs)
  Handles txtNum1.Validating

End Sub
```

This code template is slightly different from code templates for `Click` event procedures. The difference is in the following code, which appears inside the parentheses:

```
ByVal e As System.ComponentModel.CancelEventArgs
```

This code declares an object named `e`, which is a parameter. A parameter is a special object that holds a value being passed into a procedure. This event procedure uses the `e` object as part of the input validation process.

Figure 5-39 Method name drop-down list with *Validating* selected

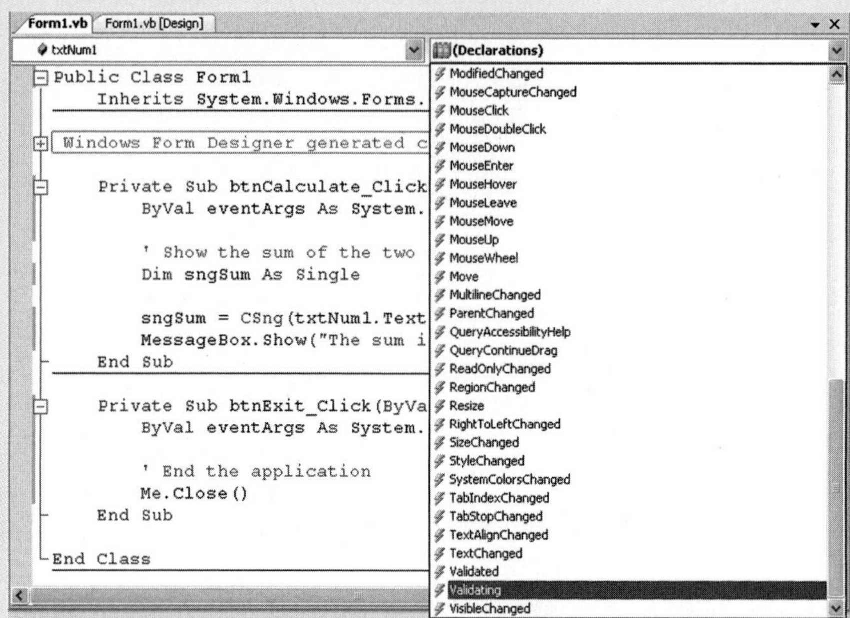

Write the following code, shown in bold, to complete the procedure.

```
Private Sub txtNum1_Validating(ByVal sender As Object, _
    ByVal e As System.ComponentModel.CancelEventArgs) _
    Handles txtNum1.Validating

  ' Validate the number entered by the user.
  If IsNumeric(txtNum1.Text) Then
    Dim sngValue As Single
    sngValue = CSng(txtNum1.Text)
    If sngValue < 1 Or sngValue > 10 Then
      ' Display an error message.
      lblMessage.BackColor = Color.Yellow
      lblMessage.Text = "Enter a value in the range 1 - 10."
      e.Cancel = True
    Else
      e.Cancel = False
    End If
  Else
    ' Display an error message.
    lblMessage.BackColor = Color.Yellow
    lblMessage.Text = "The first value must be a number."
    e.Cancel = True
  End If
End Sub
```

At runtime, this event handler executes when the focus is about to leave the `txtNum1` control and shift to a control whose CausesValidation property equals *True*. Notice the `If` statement that determines whether the value entered by the user is less than 1 or greater than 10:

```
If sngValue < 1 Or sngValue > 10 Then
  ' Display an error message.
  lblMessage.BackColor = Color.Yellow
  lblMessage.Text = "Enter a value in the range 1 - 10."
  e.Cancel = True
```

First, the lblMessage control's background color is set to yellow and an error message is assigned to its Text property. Then, by setting the e object's Cancel property to *True*, we signal that the validation failed and the input focus must remain on the textNum1 control.

Next, let's look at the Else part if the If statement, which executes if the input is valid. Setting the e object's Cancel property to *False* causes the focus to shift to the next control when the event procedure terminates:

```
Else
  e.Cancel = False
```

Step 7: Create the following Validating event handler for txtNum2. It uses the same type of error checking we saw in Step 6:

```
Private Sub txtNum2_Validating(ByVal sender As Object, _
  ByVal e As System.ComponentModel.CancelEventArgs) _
  Handles txtNum2.Validating

  ' Validate the number entered by the user.
  If IsNumeric(txtNum2.Text) Then
    Dim sngValue As Single
    sngValue = CSng(txtNum2.Text)
    If sngValue < 1 Or sngValue > 10 Then
      ' Display an error message.
      lblMessage.BackColor = Color.Yellow
      lblMessage.Text = "Enter a value in the range 1 - 10."
      e.Cancel = True
    Else
      e.Cancel = False
    End If
  Else
    ' Display an error message.
    lblMessage.BackColor = Color.Yellow
    lblMessage.Text = "The second value must be a number."
    e.Cancel = True
  End If
End Sub
```

Step 8: Save the project.

Step 9: Run the application and enter a value that is outside the range 1 through 10 for txtNum1. Press the Tab key to shift the focus to txtNum2. A message appears reporting the input error. Notice that the focus returns to the txtNum1 control. This is because the event procedure sets e.Cancel to *True* before the procedure terminates.

Step 10: Change the value in txtNum1 to a number from 1 to 10, and then press Tab to change the focus to txtNum2.

Step 11: With the focus in txtNum2, enter a number outside the range from 1 to 10. Click the *Calculate* button. Once again, a message appears reporting the input error. The focus returns to the txtNum2 control. Change the value to a number in the 1 to 10 range, and then click the *Calculate* button again. This time, the application displays the sum of the two numbers.

TIP: Closing a form containing `Validating` event handlers can be tricky. When you click the *Exit* button, for example, focus moves away from one of the text boxes and triggers a `Validation` event. If the text box that previously had the focus contained invalid data, you cannot end the program. Unfortunately, setting the *Exit* button's CausesValidation property to *False* has no effect.

Step 12: Enter a valid value in both text boxes and click the *Exit* button to close the application.

The Validated Event

After the `Validating` event has been triggered and the focus has shifted to another control, the **`Validated` event** is triggered. If you need to perform an operation on the user's input after it has been validated, such as copying it to a variable, you can write a Validated event procedure to do so.

To create a `Validated` event procedure, follow similar steps as when you create a `Validating` event procedure. First, select the name of the control in the class name drop-down list, and then select `Validated` in the method name drop-down list. A code template will be created.

Using the `SelectAll` Method to Select Text

Text boxes have a method named `SelectAll`, which you can use to make the process of correcting invalid input more convenient for the user. To understand how correcting invalid input can be inconvenient, follow the instructions in Tutorial 5-11.

Tutorial 5-11:
An example of inconvenient data input correction

Step 1: Run the *Validation Demo* project again. This time, enter a long series of digits, such as `777777777777`, in the `txtNum1` text box. Press the Tab key.

Step 2: A message appears reporting the input error. Notice that the focus returns to the `txtNum1` control.

Step 3: Press the Backspace key several times to erase the invalid number. Now you have observed the inconvenience that this application causes when the user must correct invalid input. There is no quick method of replacing long entries in the text boxes.

Step 4: Click the *Exit* button to end the application.

The **`SelectAll` method** can be used in code to automatically select the text in a text box. For example, assume that `txtName` is a text box and look at the following code:

```
txtName.SelectAll()
```

Follow the instructions in Tutorial 5-12 to modify the *Validation Demo* project so it uses the `SelectAll` method to make data correction easier.

Tutorial 5-12: Modifying the *Validation Demo* project to use the `SelectAll` method

Step 1: Open the *Validation Demo* project if it is not already open. Open the *Code* window.

Step 2: Scroll to the `txtNum1_Validating` event procedure, which is shown next. Add the following statements shown in bold:

```
Private Sub txtNum1_Validating(ByVal sender As Object, _
    ByVal e As System.ComponentModel.CancelEventArgs) _
    Handles txtNum1.Validating

  ' Validate the number entered by the user.
  If IsNumeric(txtNum1.Text) Then
    Dim sngValue As Single
    sngValue = CSng(txtNum1.Text)
    If sngValue < 1 Or sngValue > 10 Then
      ' Display an error message.
      lblMessage.BackColor = Color.Yellow
      lblMessage.Text = "Enter a value in the range 1 - 10."
      e.Cancel = True
      txtNum1.SelectAll()
    Else
      e.Cancel = False
    End If
  Else
    ' Display an error message.
    lblMessage.BackColor = Color.Yellow
    lblMessage.Text = "The first value must be a number."
    txtNum1.SelectAll()
    e.Cancel = True
  End If
End Sub
```

Step 3: Scroll to the `txtNum2_Validating` event procedure, shown here. Add the statements shown in bold.

```
Private Sub txtNum2_Validating(ByVal sender As Object, _
    ByVal e As System.ComponentModel.CancelEventArgs) _
    Handles txtNum2.Validating

  ' Validate the number entered by the user.
  If IsNumeric(txtNum2.Text) Then
    Dim sngValue As Single
    sngValue = CSng(txtNum2.Text)
    If sngValue < 1 Or sngValue > 10 Then
      ' Display an error message.
      lblMessage.BackColor = Color.Yellow
      lblMessage.Text = "Enter a value in the range 1 - 10."
      e.Cancel = True
      txtNum2.SelectAll()
    Else
      e.Cancel = False
    End If
  Else
    ' Display an error message.
    lblMessage.BackColor = Color.Yellow
```

```
            lblMessage.Text = "The first value must be a number."
            txtNum2.SelectAll()
            e.Cancel = True
        End If
    End Sub
```

Step 4: Run the application. In the `txtNum1` text box, enter a long series of digits, such as **2222222222222222**, and press the Tab key.

Step 5: A message appears reporting the input error. Notice that the focus returns to the `txtNum1` control and the series of digits is automatically selected. The code you added to `txtNum1_Validating` caused this to happen.

Step 6: Because the invalid input is already selected, you may simply type the correct number and it will automatically replace the selected value. Type a number such as **5** to see this happen.

Step 7: Repeat the process in Step 6 to confirm that the code you added to `txtNum2_Validating` works as well.

Step 8: Click the *Exit* button to end the application.

Using the `With...End With` Statement

Sometimes you must write statements that perform several operations on the same object. The following statements set several properties of the `txtName` text box:

```
txtName.Clear()
txtName.ForeColor = Color.Blue
txtName.BackColor = Color.Yellow
txtName.BorderStyle = BorderStyle.Fixed3D
```

Notice that the name `txtName` appears four times. If you use a **`With...End With`** block, you don't have to repeat the name of the `txtName` control in each statement. Here is the general format of the `With...End With` block:

```
With ObjectName
   statement
   (more statements may follow)
End With
```

Within the block, each method or property associated with *`ObjectName`* begins with a dot (`.`). Here is the equivalent code, simplified by a **`With`** block:

```
With txtName
   .Clear()
   .ForeColor = Color.Blue
   .BackColor = Color.Yellow
   .BorderStyle = BorderStyle.Fixed3D
End With
```

Checkpoint

5.30 When the focus is shifting to a control, what happens if the control's CausesValidation property is set to *True*?

5.31 When is a control's `Validating` event triggered?

5.32 By default, what value is a control's CausesValidation property set to?

5.33 Explain the purpose of the text box's `SelectAll` method.

5.34 Write code that causes the text in the `txtSerialNumber` text box to be selected.

5.35 Use the `With...End With` statement to set any three properties of a ListBox control named `lstSample`.

5.8 ToolTips

CONCEPT: ToolTips are a standard and convenient way of providing help to the users of an application. The ToolTip control allows you to assign pop-up hints to the other controls on a form.

A **ToolTip** is a small box displayed when the user holds the mouse cursor over a control. The box shows a short description of what the control does. Most Windows applications use ToolTips as a way of providing immediate and concise help to the user.

The **ToolTip control** allows you to create ToolTips for other controls on a form. Place a ToolTip control in your application just as you place other controls: double-click the ToolTip tool in the Toolbox. When you do so, a ToolTip control appears in the *Design* window, as shown in Figure 5-40.

Figure 5-40 ToolTip control

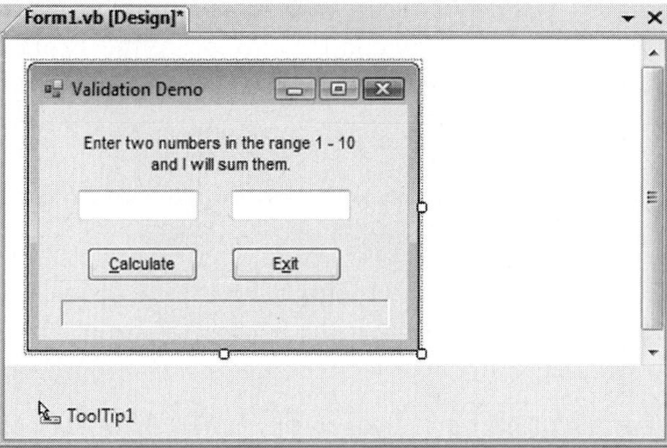

Because the ToolTip control is invisible at runtime, it does not appear on the form at design time. Instead, it appears in an area known as the component tray. The **component tray** is a resizable region at the bottom of the *Design* window that holds invisible controls.

When you add a ToolTip control to a form, a new property is added to all the other controls. The new property is named *ToolTip* on *ToolTipControl*, where *ToolTipControl* is the name of the ToolTip control. For example, suppose you add a ToolTip control to a form and keep the default name *ToolTip1*. The new property that is added to the other controls will be named *ToolTip on ToolTip1*. This new property holds the string that is displayed as the control's ToolTip.

ToolTip Properties

You can select the ToolTip control in the component tray and then examine its properties in the *Properties* window. The InitialDelay property determines the amount of time, in milliseconds, that elapses between the user pointing the mouse at a control and the

ToolTip's appearance. The default setting is 500. (One millisecond is 1/1000th of a second, so 500 milliseconds is half of a second.)

The AutoPopDelay property is also a measure of time in milliseconds. It determines how long a ToolTip remains on the screen once it is displayed. The default setting is 5000. The ReshowDelay property holds the number of milliseconds that will elapse between the displaying of different ToolTips as the user moves the mouse from control to control. The default setting is 100.

You can set these properties individually, or set them all at once with the AutomaticDelay property. When you store a value in the AutomaticDelay property, InitialDelay is set to the same value, AutoPopDelay is set to 10 times the value, and ReshowDelay is set to one-fifth the value. In Tutorial 5-13, you add ToolTips to an application.

Tutorial 5-13:
Adding ToolTips to an application

Step 1: Load the *Validation Demo* project and open the form in the *Design* window.

Step 2: Scroll down in the Toolbox until you find the ToolTip tool (ToolTip). Double-click the tool to add a ToolTip control to the component tray. Notice that the default name of the ToolTip control is *ToolTip1*.

Step 3: When you add the ToolTip1 control, Visual Basic automatically adds a new property named *ToolTip on ToolTip1* to all other controls on the form. Select the `txtNum1` text box control and locate the ToolTip on ToolTip1 property in the *Properties* window.

Step 4: Set the ToolTip on ToolTip1 property to *Enter the first number here.*

Step 5: Select the `txtNum2` property and set its ToolTip on Tooltip1 property to *Enter the second number here.*

Step 6: Set the `btnCalculate` button's ToolTip on ToolTip1 property to *Click here to add the two numbers*. Set the `btnExit` button's ToolTip on ToolTip1 property to *Click here to exit.*

Step 7: Save the project and then run it. When the form appears, hold the mouse cursor over the `txtNum1` control. The ToolTip shown in Figure 5-41 should appear.

Step 8: Experiment with the other ToolTips. When you are finished, exit the application.

Figure 5-41 ToolTip for `txtNum1` displayed

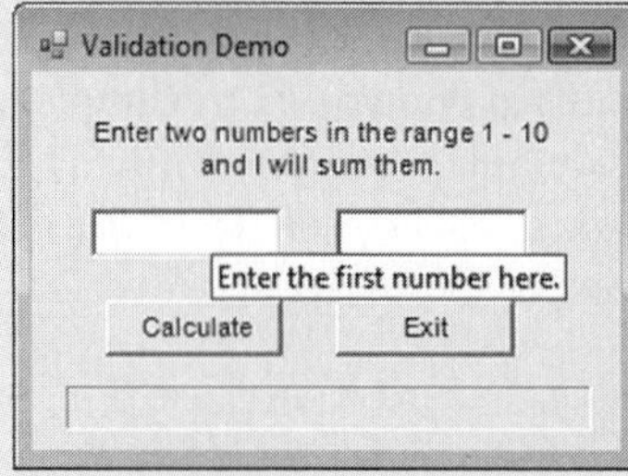

5.9 Focus on Program Design and Problem Solving: Building the *Vehicle Loan Calculator* Application

CONCEPT: In this section, you build the *Vehicle Loan Calculator* application. The application uses a loop, input validation, and ToolTips. This section also covers some of the Visual Basic intrinsic financial functions.

Visual Basic has several built-in functions for performing financial calculations. You will build a program named *Vehicle Loan Calculator*. It uses the following functions: `Pmt`, `IPmt`, and `PPmt`. Let's look at each function in detail before continuing with the case study.

The `Pmt` Function

The `Pmt` function returns the periodic payment amount for a loan. It assumes the loan has a fixed interest rate. Here is the general form of the **`Pmt` function** call:

```
Pmt(PeriodicInterestRate, NumberOfPeriods, –LoanAmount)
```

Descriptions of each argument follow:

1. *`PeriodicInterestRate`*: You usually know a loan's annual interest rate; this function, however, needs to know the loan's periodic interest rate. A loan is divided into periods, and you make a payment each period. The periodic interest rate is the rate of interest per period of the loan. For example, if you make monthly payments on a loan, the period is each month. If the annual interest rate is 9%, then the periodic interest rate is .09 divided by 12, which is .0075.
2. *`NumberOfPeriods`*: For a loan that requires monthly payments, this is the total number of months of the loan. For example, a three-year loan is given for 36 months.
3. *`LoanAmount`*: This is the amount being borrowed, which must be negative.

NOTE: The `Pmt` function can also be used to calculate payments on a savings plan. When using it for that purpose, specify the desired value of the savings as a positive number.

Here is an example of the function call:

```
dblPayment = Pmt(dblAnnInt / 12, 24, -5000)
```

In this statement, `dblAnnInt` contains the annual interest rate, 24 is the number of months of the loan, and the amount of the loan is $5,000. After the statement executes, `dblPayment` holds the fixed monthly payment amount.

The `IPmt` Function

The `IPmt` function returns the interest payment for a specific period on a loan. It assumes the loan has a fixed interest rate, with fixed monthly payments. Here is the general format of the **`IPmt` function** call:

```
IPmt(PeriodicInterestRate, Period, NumberOfPeriods, –LoanAmount)
```

Descriptions of each argument follow:

1. *PeriodicInterestRate*: As with the `Pmt` function, this function must know the periodic interest rate. (See the description of argument 1 for the `Pmt` function.)
2. *Period*: This argument specifies the period for which you wish to calculate the payment. The argument must be at least 1, and no more than the total number of periods of the loan.
3. *NumberofPeriods*: The total number of periods of the loan. (See the description of argument 2 for the `Pmt` function.)
4. *LoanAmount*: As with the `Pmt` function, the loan amount must be expressed as a negative number.

Here is an example of the function call:

```
dblInterest = IPmt(dblAnnInt / 12, 6, 24, -5000)
```

In this statement, `dblAnnInt` contains the annual interest rate, 6 is the number of the month for which you wish to calculate the payment, 24 is the number of months of the loan, and the amount of the loan is $5,000. After the statement executes, `dblInterest` holds the amount of interest paid in month 6 of the loan.

The PPmt Function

The `PPmt` function returns the principal payment for a specific period on a loan. It assumes the loan has a fixed interest rate, with fixed monthly payments. Here is the general format of the **PPmt function** call:

```
PPmt(PeriodicInterestRate, Period, NumberOfPeriods, –LoanAmount)
```

Descriptions of each argument follow:

1. *PeriodicInterestRate*: As with the `Pmt` function, this function must know the periodic interest rate. (See the description of argument 1 for the `Pmt` function.)
2. *Period*: This argument specifies the period for which you wish to calculate the payment. The argument must be at least 1, and no more than the total number of periods of the loan.
3. *NumberOfPeriods*: The total number of periods of the loan. (See the description of argument 2 for the `Pmt` function.)
4. *LoanAmount*: As with the `Pmt` function, the loan amount must be expressed as a negative number.

Here is an example of the function call:

```
dblPrincipal = PPmt(dblAnnInt / 12, 6, 24, -5000)
```

In this statement, `dblAnnInt` contains the annual interest rate, 6 is the number of the month for which you wish to calculate the payment, 24 is the number of months of the loan, and the amount of the loan is $5,000. After the statement executes, `dblPrincipal` holds the amount of principal paid in month 6 of the loan.

The Case Study

The Central Mountain Credit Union finances new and used vehicles for its members. A credit union branch manager asks you to write an application named Vehicle Loan Calculator that displays the following information for a loan:

- The monthly payment amount
- The amount of the monthly payment applied toward interest
- The amount of the monthly payment applied toward principal

The credit union currently charges 8.9% annual interest for new vehicle loans and 9.5% annual interest on used vehicle loans. The credit union does not finance a vehicle for less than 6 months or more than 48 months.

Figure 5-42 shows a sketch of the *Vehicle Loan Calculator* application's form.

Figure 5-42 Sketch of the *Vehicle Loan Calculator* form

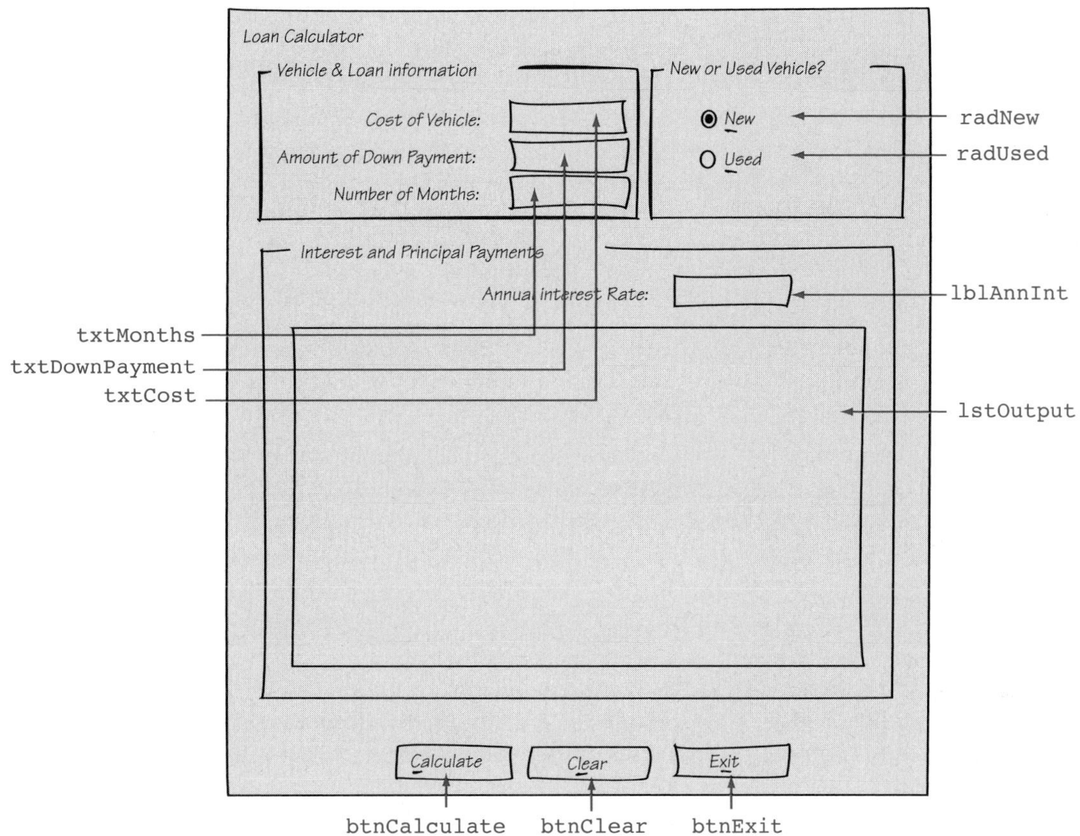

Table 5-2 lists each control, along with any relevant property settings. You will add a ToolTip control to the form.

Table 5-2 *Vehicle Loan Calculator* controls

Control Type	Control Name	Property	Property Value
Form	(Default)	Text:	*Loan Calculator*
ToolTip	(Default)		(Retain default property settings)
GroupBox	(Default)	Text: TabIndex:	*Vehicle && Loan Information* 0
Label	(Default)	Text: TabIndex:	*Cost of &Vehicle:* 0 (Relative to group box)
Text box	`txtCost`	CausesValidation: TabIndex: Text: ToolTip on ToolTip1:	*True* 1 (Relative to group box) *Enter the cost of the vehicle here.*

(*continued*)

Table 5-2 *Vehicle Loan Calculator* controls (*continued*)

Control Type	Control Name	Property	Property Value
Label	(Default)	Text:	*Amount of &Down Payment:*
Text box	`txtDownPayment`	CausesValidation: Text: ToolTip on ToolTip1:	*True* *Enter the amount of the down payment here.*
Label	(Default)	Text:	*Number of &Months:*
Text box	`txtMonths`	CausesValidation: Text: ToolTip on ToolTip1:	*True* *Enter the number of months of the loan here.*
GroupBox	(Default)	Text:	*New or Used Vehicle?*
RadioButton	`radNew`	Text: CausesValidation: ToolTip on ToolTip1:	*&New* *True* *Click here if the vehicle is new.*
RadioButton	`radUsed`	Text: CausesValidation: ToolTip on ToolTip1:	*&Used* *True* *Click here if the vehicle is used.*
GroupBox	(Default)	Text:	*Interest and Principal Payments*
Label	(Default)	Text:	*Annual Interest Rate:*
Label	`lblAnnInt`	Text: BorderStyle: AutoSize: ToolTip on ToolTip1:	 *Fixed3D* *False* *Annual interest rate*
ListBox	`lstOutput`		
Button	`btnCalculate`	Text: CausesValidation: ToolTip on ToolTip1:	*&Calculate* *True* *Click here to calculate the payment data.*
Button	`btnClear`	Text: CausesValidation: ToolTip on ToolTip1:	*C&lear* *False* *Click here to clear the form.*
Button	`btnExit`	Text: CausesValidation: ToolTip on ToolTip1:	*E&xit* *False* *Click here to exit.*

Table 5-3 lists and describes the event procedures needed in this application.

Table 5-3 *Vehicle Loan Calculator* event procedures

Method	Description
`btnCalculate_Click`	Calculates and displays a table in the list box showing interest and principal payments for the loan
`btnClear_Click`	Resets the interest rate, clears the text boxes, and clears the list box
`btnExit_Click`	Ends the application

(*continued*)

Table 5-3 *Vehicle Loan Calculator* event procedures (*continued*)

Method	Description
`radNew_CheckedChanged`	Updates the annual interest rate if the user selects a new vehicle loan
`radUsed_CheckedChanged`	Updates the annual interest rate if the user selects a used vehicle loan
`txtCost_Validating`	Validates that a numeric value has been entered `int txtCost`
`txtDownPayment_Validating`	Validates that a numeric value has been entered `int txtDownPayment`
`txtMonths_Validating`	Validates that a numeric value of 6 or greater has been entered `int txtMonths`

Figure 5-43 shows a flowchart for the `btnCalculate_Click` event handler.

Pseudocode for the `btnCalculate_Click` event handler is as follows. The actual arguments passed to the `Pmt`, `IPmt`, and `PPmt` functions are not shown.

Loan = Cost – DownPayment
Payment = Pmt()
For intCount = 0 To Months
    Interest = IPmt()
    Principal = PPmt()
    Display Month, Payment, Interest, and Principal in list box
Next intCount

Figure 5-43 Flowchart for the `btnCalculate_Click` event handler

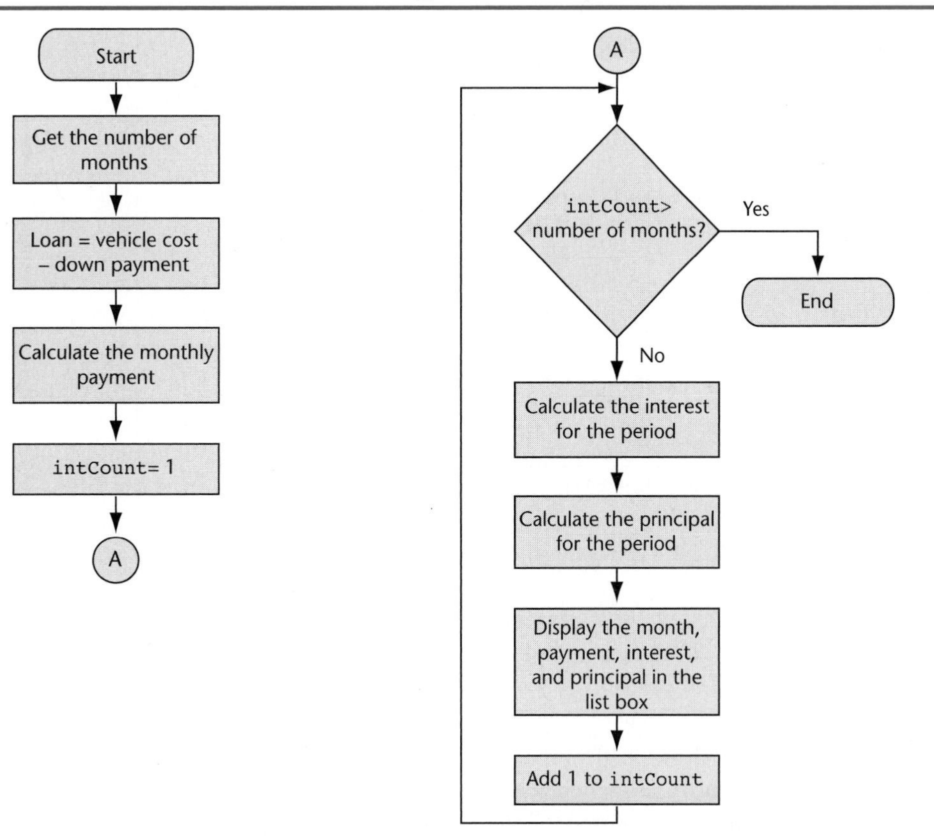

Figure 5-44 shows flowcharts for the event handlers `radNew_CheckedChanged` and `radUsed_CheckedChanged`.

These event handlers change the annual interest rate when the user clicks the `radNew` and `radUsed` radio buttons. Pseudocode for the `radNew_CheckedChanged` event handler is as follows:

If radNew is selected Then
Annual Interest Rate = 0.089
Display Annual Interest Rate in lblAnnInt
End If

Pseudocode for the `radUsed_CheckedChanged` event handler is as follows:

If radUsed is selected Then
Annual Interest Rate = 0.095
Display Annual Interest Rate in lblAnnInt
End If

Figure 5-44 Flowcharts for `radNew_CheckedChanged` and `radUsed_CheckedChanged` event handlers

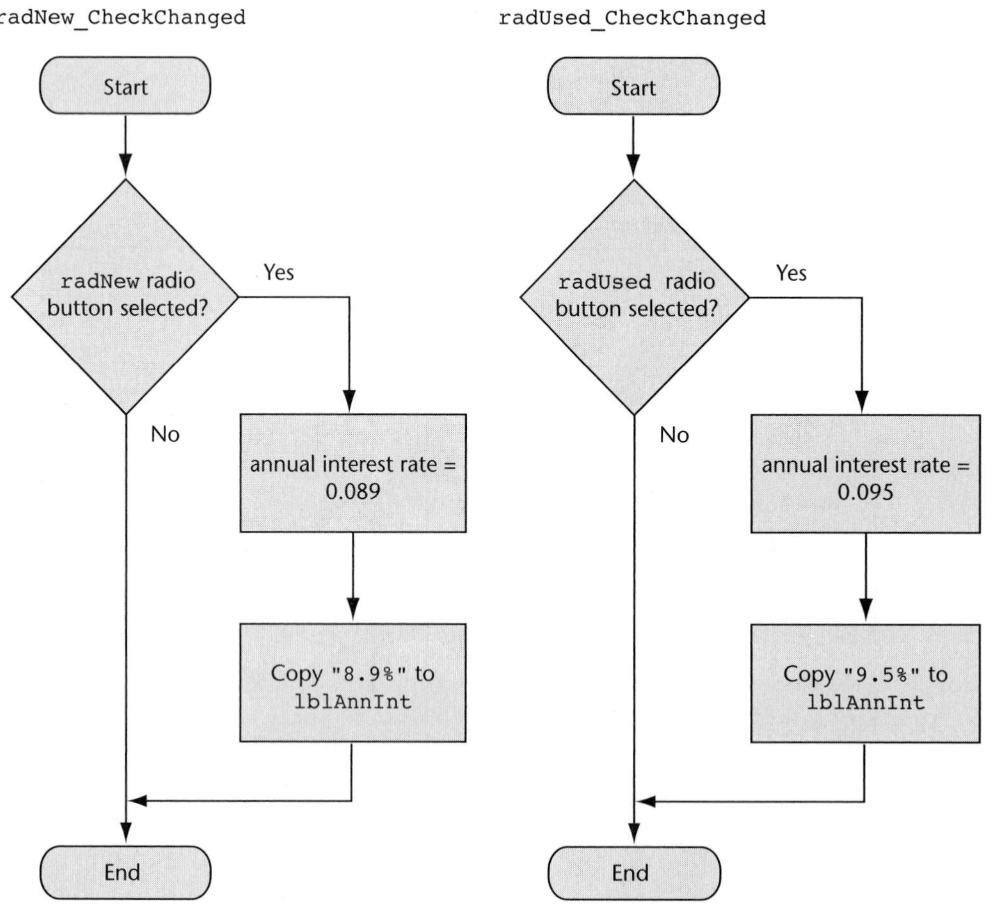

Figure 5-45 shows a flowchart for the `txtCost_Validating` event handler, which displays an error message when a nonnumeric value is entered in `txtCost`. If this happens, the value in `txtCost` is selected and the focus remains on the control.

Pseudocode for the `txtCost_Validating` event handler is as follows:

If the cost is not numeric Then
  Display "Cost must be a number."
  Select existing text in the text box.
  e.Cancel = True
Else
  e.Cancel = False
End If

Figure 5-45 Flowchart for `txtCost_Validating` event handler

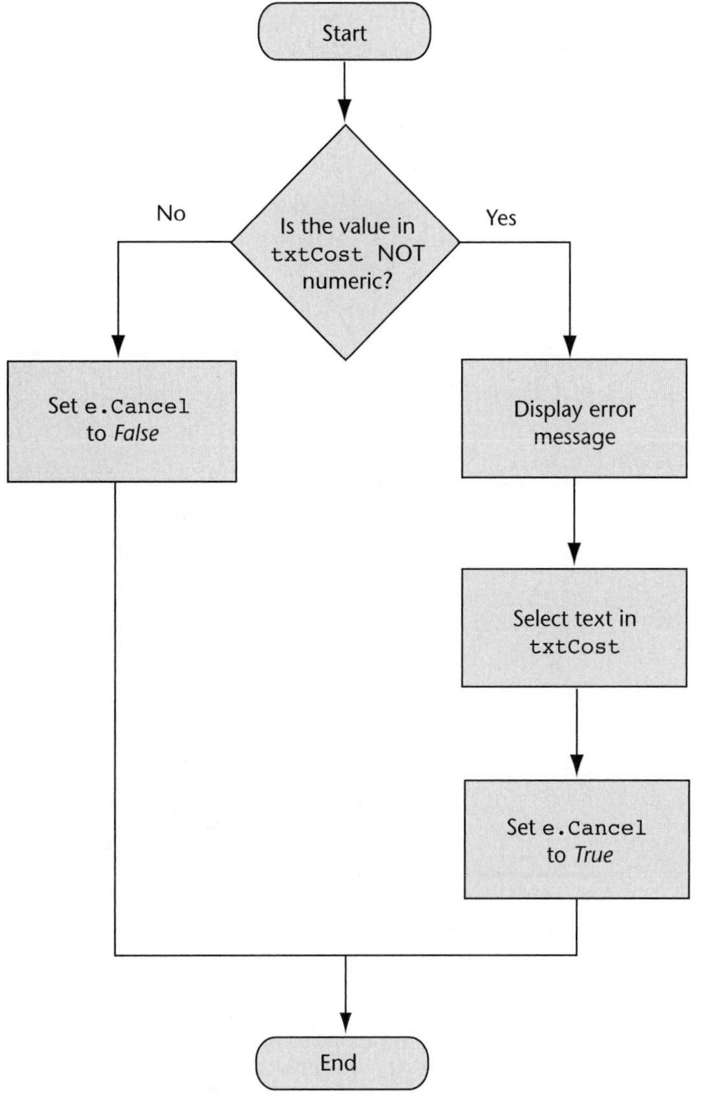

Figure 5-46 shows a flowchart for the `txtDownPayment_Validating` event procedure. This procedure displays an error message when a nonnumeric value is entered in `txtDownPayment`. If this happens, the value in `txtDownPayment` is selected, and the focus remains on the control.

Pseudocode for the `txtDownPayment_Validate` event handler is as follows:

If the down payment is not numeric Then
Display "Down payment must be a number."
Select existing text in the text box
e.Cancel = True
Else
e.Cancel = False
End If

Figure 5-46 Flowchart for `txtDownPayment_Validating` event handler

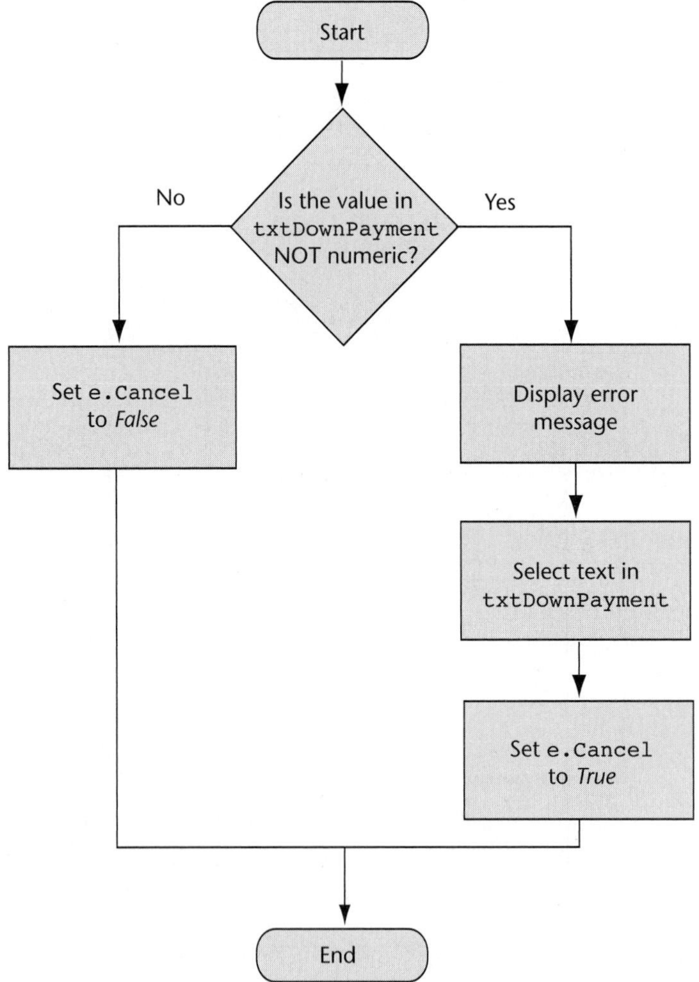

Figure 5-47 shows a flowchart for the `txtMonths_Validating` event handler. This method uses an `If...Then...ElseIf` statement to validate the value in `txtMonths`. It displays an error message when a nonnumeric value, or a value less than 6 or greater than 48, is entered in `txtMonths`. If this happens, the value in `txtCost` is selected, and the input focus remains on the control.

Pseudocode for the `txtMonths_Validating` event procedure is as follows:

If Months is not numeric Then
Display "Cost must be a number."
Select existing text in the text box
e.Cancel = True
Else If Months < 6 Or Months > 48 Then
Display "Months must be in the range 6–48."
Select existing text in the text box.
e.Cancel = True
Else
e.Cancel = False
End If

Figure 5-47 Flowchart for `txtMonth_Validating` Event Procedure

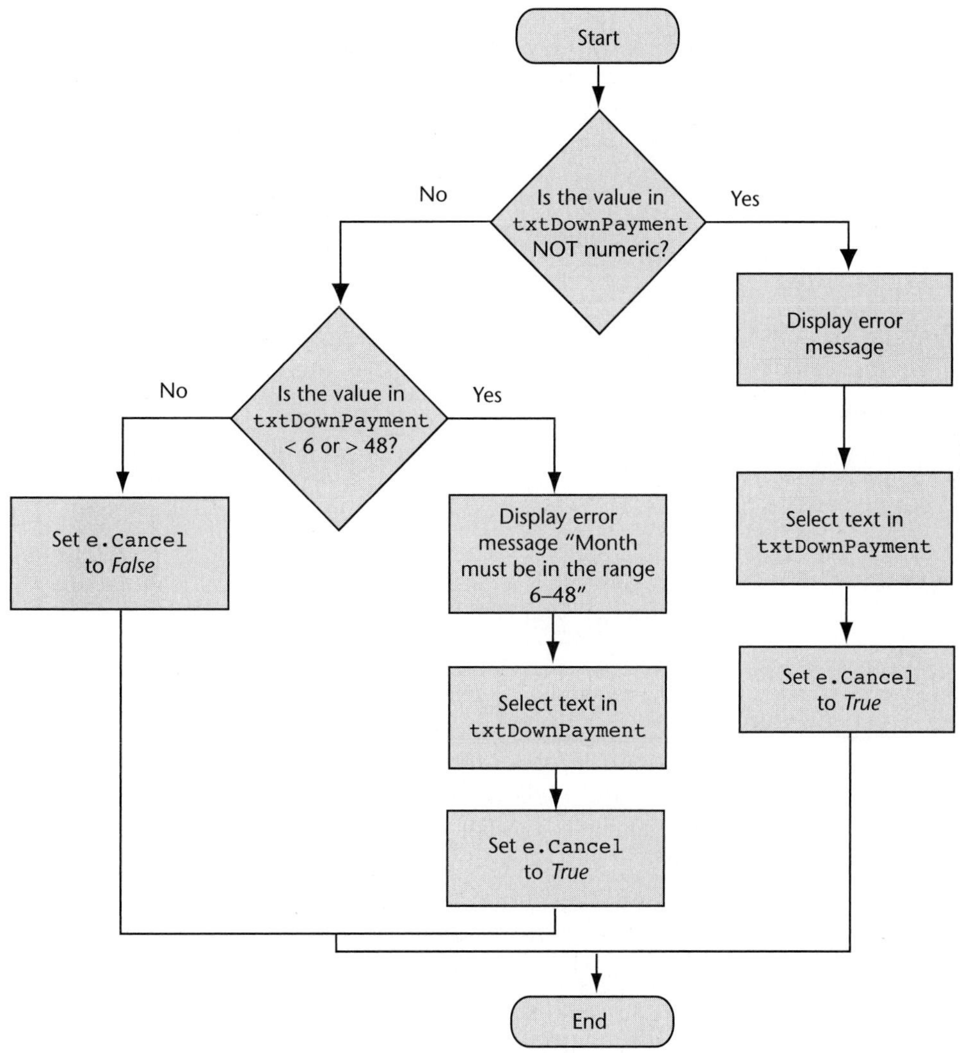

In Tutorial 5-14, you build the *Vehicle Loan Calculator* application.

Tutorial 5-14:
Building the *Vehicle Loan Calculator* application

Step 1: Create a new Windows application project named *Vehicle Loan Calculator*.

Step 2: Set up the form as shown in Figure 5-48. Refer to Figure 5-42 for the names of the programmer-defined control names, and Table 5-1 for the important property settings.

Step 3: Add a ToolTip control to the form. The ToolTip control will appear in the component tray.

Figure 5-48 *Loan Calculator* form

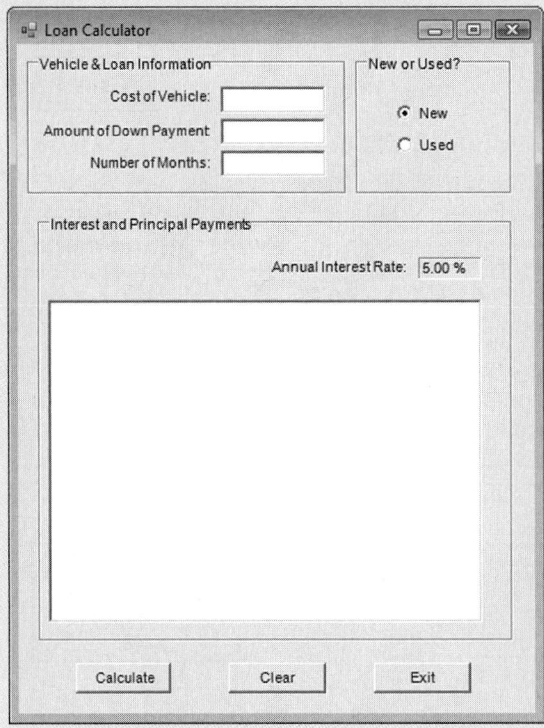

Step 4: Once you have placed all the controls on the form and set their properties, you can write the application's code. Open the *Code* window and write the following comments and class-level variable declarations. This code should not appear inside of any event procedure.

```
' Define valid month ranges.
Const intMIN_MONTHS As Integer = 6
Const intMAX_MONTHS As Integer = 48
Const sngMONTHS_YEAR As Single = 12.0 ' Months per year

' Define annual interest rates for new and used cars.
Const dblNEW_RATE As Double = 0.089   ' Interest rate, new cars
Const dblUSED_RATE As Double = 0.095 ' Interest rate, used cars

Dim dblAnnualRate As Double = dblNEW_RATE ' Annual interest rate
```

The variable, `dblAnnualRate`, which holds the annual interest rate, is declared as a class-level variable because it will be accessed by multiple procedures. It is initialized with `dblNEW_RATE` because a new vehicle loan will be selected by default.

Step 5: Create the code template for the `btnCalculate_Click` event procedure. Complete the procedure by entering the code shown in bold.

```
Private Sub btnCalculate_Click(ByVal sender As System.Object, _
        ByVal e As System.EventArgs) Handles btnCalculate.Click

    ' Calculate and display the loan payment information.

    Dim intCount As Integer   ' Counter for the loop
    Dim intMonths As Integer  ' Number of months for the loan
    Dim dblLoan As Double     ' Amount of the loan
    Dim dblPayment As Double  ' Monthly payment
    Dim dblInterest As Double   ' Interest paid for the period
    Dim dblPrincipal As Double  ' Principal paid for the period

    ' Get the number of months and calculate the loan amount
    Try
      intMonths = CInt(txtMonths.Text)
      dblLoan = CDec(txtCost.Text) - CDec(txtDownPayment.Text)
    Catch
      MessageBox.Show("Please enter numeric values")
      Return
    End Try

    ' Calculate the monthly payment
    dblPayment = Pmt(dblAnnualRate / sngMONTHS_YEAR, _
        intMonths, -dblLoan)

    ' Clear the list box.
    lstOutput.Items.Clear()

    For intCount = 1 To intMonths
      ' Holds list box output
      Dim strOut As String = String.Empty

      ' Calculate the interest for the period
      dblInterest = IPmt(dblAnnualRate / sngMONTHS_YEAR, _
          intCount, intMonths, -dblLoan)
      ' Calculate and display the principal for the period
      dblPrincipal = PPmt(dblAnnualRate / sngMONTHS_YEAR, _
          intCount, intMonths, -dblLoan)

      ' Add the month to the output string
      strOut &= "Month: " & intCount.ToString()
      ' Add the payment amount to the output string
      strOut &= "  Payment: " & dblPayment.ToString("c")
      ' Add the interest amount to the output string
      strOut &= "  Interest: " & dblInterest.ToString("c")
      ' Add the principal for the period
      strOut &= "  Principal: " & dblPrincipal.ToString("c")

      ' Add the output string to the list box
      lstOutput.Items.Add(strOut)
    Next intCount
End Sub
```

Step 6: Create the code template for the `btnClear_Click` event procedure. Complete the procedure by entering the code shown in bold.

```
Private Sub btnClear_Click(ByVal sender As System.Object, _
    ByVal e As System.EventArgs) Handles btnClear.Click
  ' Reset the interest rate, clear the text boxes
  ' and clear the list box.
  txtCost.CausesValidation = False
  txtDownPayment.CausesValidation = False
  txtMonths.CausesValidation = False
  radNew.Checked = True
  dblAnnualRate = dblNEW_RATE
  lblAnnInt.Text = dblNEW_RATE.ToString("p")
  txtCost.Clear()
  txtDownPayment.Clear()
  txtMonths.Clear()
  lstOutput.Items.Clear()
  ' Reset the focus
  txtCost.Focus()
End Sub
```

Step 7: Create the code template for the `btnExit_Click` event procedure. Complete the procedure by entering the code shown in bold.

```
Private Sub btnExit_Click(ByVal sender As System.Object, _
    ByVal e As System.EventArgs) Handles btnExit.Click

  txtCost.CausesValidation = False
  txtDownPayment.CausesValidation = False
  txtMonths.CausesValidation = False

  ' End the application
  Me.Close()
End Sub
```

Step 8: Create the code template for the `radNew_CheckedChanged` event procedure. (You can easily create the code template by opening the *Design* window and double-clicking the `radNew` control.) Complete the procedure by entering the code shown in bold.

```
Private Sub radNew_CheckedChanged(ByVal sender As
  System.Object, _
    ByVal e As System.EventArgs) Handles radNew.Checked-
  Changed

  ' If the New radio button is checked, then
  ' the user has selected a new car loan.
  If radNew.Checked = True Then
    dblAnnualRate = dblNEW_RATE
    lblAnnInt.Text = dblNEW_RATE.ToString("p")
  End If
End Sub
```

Step 9: Create the code template for the `radUsed_CheckedChanged` event procedure. Complete the procedure by entering the code shown in bold.

```
Private Sub radUsed_CheckedChanged(ByVal sender _
    As System.Object, ByVal e As System.EventArgs) _
    Handles radUsed.CheckedChanged

  ' User selected the Used Car radio button. Set
  ' the interest rate accordingly.
```

```
    If radUsed.Checked = True Then
        dblAnnualRate = dblUSED_RATE
        lblAnnInt.Text = dblUSED_RATE.ToString("p")
    End If
End Sub
```

Step 10: Create the code template for the `txtCost_Validating` event procedure. (You create the code template by opening the *Code* window, selecting `txtCost` from the class name drop-down list, and then selecting `Validating` from the method name drop-down list.) Complete the procedure by entering the code shown in bold.

```
Private Sub txtCost_Validating(ByVal sender As Object, _
    ByVal e As System.ComponentModel.CancelEventArgs) _
    Handles txtCost.Validating

    ' Validates that a number has been entered into txtCost.
    If Not IsNumeric(txtCost.Text) Then
        MessageBox.Show("Cost must be a number.", _
            "Invalid Vehicle Cost")

        ' Select the existing text in the text box.
        txtCost.SelectAll()
        ' Set e.Cancel to true so the focus will stay
        ' in this control.
        e.Cancel = True
    Else
        e.Cancel = False
    End If
End Sub
```

Step 11: Create the code template for the `txtDownPayment_Validating` event procedure. Complete the procedure by entering the code shown in bold.

```
Private Sub txtDownPayment_Validating(ByVal sender _
    As Object, ByVal e As _
    System.ComponentModel.CancelEventArgs) _
    Handles txtDownPayment.Validating

    ' Validates that a number has been entered into
    ' txtDownPayment.

    If Not IsNumeric(txtDownPayment.Text) Then
        MessageBox.Show("Down payment must be a number.", _
                "Invalid Down Payment")

        ' Select the existing text in the text box.
        txtDownPayment.SelectAll()

        ' Set e.Cancel to true so the focus will stay
        ' in this control.
        e.Cancel = True
    Else
        e.Cancel = False
    End If
End Sub
```

Step 12: Create the code template for the `txtMonths_Validating` event procedure. Complete the procedure by entering the code shown in bold.

```
Private Sub txtMonths_Validating(ByVal sender As Object, _
    ByVal e As System.ComponentModel.CancelEventArgs) _
    Handles txtMonths.Validating
```

```
    ' Validates that months is numeric
    ' and is within a valid range
    If Not IsNumeric(txtMonths.Text) Then
      MessageBox.Show("Months must be a number.", "Error")

      ' Select the existing text in the text box.
      txtMonths.SelectAll()

      ' Set e.Cancel to true so the focus will stay
      ' in this control.
      e.Cancel = True
    Else
      Dim intMonths As Integer = CInt(txtMonths.Text)

      If intMonths < intMIN_MONTHS Or _
        intMonths > intMAX_MONTHS Then

        MessageBox.Show("Months must be in the range " _
            & intMIN_MONTHS & " - " & intMAX_MONTHS, "Error")
        ' Select the existing text in the text box.
        txtMonths.SelectAll()

        ' Set e.Cancel to true so the focus will stay
        ' in this control.
        e.Cancel = True
      Else
        e.Cancel = False
      End If
    End If
  End Sub
```

Step 13: Attempt to run the application. If there are errors, compare your code and property settings with those listed to locate them.

Step 14: Save the project.

Summary

5.1 Input Boxes

- Input boxes provide a simple way to gather input from the user.

5.2 List Boxes

- A list box control displays a list of items and allows the user to select one or more items from the list.

5.3 Introduction to Loops: The `Do While` Loop

- A repetition structure, or loop, causes one or more statements to repeat. Each repetition of a loop is called an iteration.
- The `Do While` loop has an expression that is tested for *True* or *False* value and a statement or group of statements that is repeated as long as an expression is true.

5.4 The Do Until and `For...Next` Loops

- The `Do Until` loop repeats until its test expression is true.
- The `For...Next` loop initializes, tests, and increments a counter variable.
- The `Do While` and `Do Until` loops may be written as either pretest or posttest loops. The `For...Next` loop is a pretest loop.
- The `Exit Do` and `Exit For` statements, when placed inside the body of a loop, stop the execution of the loop and cause the program to jump to the statement immediately following the loop.

5.5 Nested Loops

- A loop located inside another loop is called a nested loop. It is used when a task performs a repetitive operation and each iteration of that operation is itself a repetitive operation.

5.6 Multicolumn List Boxes, Checked List Boxes, and Combo Boxes

- A multicolumn list box displays items in columns with a horizontal scroll bar, if necessary.
- A checked list box displays a check box next to each item in the list.
- There are three different styles of combo box: the drop-down combo box, the simple combo box, and the drop-down list combo box. You select a combo box's style with its DropDownStyle property.

5.7 Input Validation

- Most controls in Visual Basic have a Boolean CausesValidation property and a `Validating` event procedure. They work in harmony to provide a way of performing input validation.
- After the `Validating` event has been triggered and the focus has shifted to another control, the `Validated` event is triggered. If you need to perform an operation on the user's input after it has been validated, you can write a Validated event procedure.
- The `SelectAll` method can be used in code to automatically select the text in a text box.
- The `With...End With` statement allows you to create a `With` block. The statements inside a `With` block may perform several operations on the same object without specifying the name of the object each time.

5.8 ToolTips

- The ToolTip control allows you to create ToolTips (pop-up hints) for other controls on the same form.
- The ToolTip control is invisible at runtime; it appears in the component tray at design time.

5.9 Focus on Program Design and Problem Solving: Building the *Vehicle Loan Calculator* Application

- This section outlines the process of building the *Vehicle Loan Calculator* application using a loop, input validation, and ToolTips.
- The `Pmt` function returns the periodic payment amount for a loan. The `IPmt` function returns the required interest payment for a specific period on a loan. The `PPmt` function returns the principal payment for a specific period on a loan.

Key Terms

accumulator
CausesValidation property
combo box
component tray
conditionally executed statements
counter
`Do Until` loop
`Do While` loop
`Exit Do` statement
`Exit For` statement
`For...Next` loop
infinite loop
input box
input validation
`IPmt` function
Items property
`Items.Add` method
Items.Count property
`Items.Insert` method
`Items.Remove` method
`Items.RemoveAt` method
iteration
ListBox control
loop
nested loop
posttest loop
`Pmt` function
`PPmt` function
pretest loop
repetition structure
running total
SelectedIndex property
SelectedItem property
`SelectAll` method
step value
ToolTip
ToolTip control
`Validated` event
`Validating` event
`With` block
`With...End With` block

Review Questions and Exercises

Fill-in-the-Blank

1. A(n) ____________________ provides a simple way to gather input without placing a text box on a form.
2. A(n) ____________________ displays a list of items and allows the user to select an item from the list.
3. A ____________________ causes one or more statements to repeat.

4. If a loop does not have a way of stopping, it is called an ____________________ loop.
5. A ____________________ is a variable that is regularly incremented or decremented each time a loop iterates.
6. A ____________________ loop evaluates its test expression after each iteration.
7. Each repetition of the loop is called a(n) ____________________.
8. The ____________________ statement, when placed inside the body of a `Do While` loop, stops the execution of the loop and causes the program to jump to the statement immediately following the loop.
9. A loop that is inside another loop is called a ____________________ loop.
10. ____________________ is the process of inspecting data given as input to an application.
11. The ____________________ occurs after the `Validating` event, when the input focus shifts to another control.
12. You can use the ____________________ method to programmatically select the text in a text box.
13. The ____________________ function returns the periodic payment amount for a loan.
14. The ____________________ function returns the principal payment for a specific period on a loan.
15. The ____________________ function returns the required interest payment for a specific period on a loan.

Multiple Choice

1. You display input boxes with this function.
   a. `InBox`
   b. `Input`
   c. `InputBox`
   d. `GetInput`
2. An input box returns the value entered by the user as this.
   a. String
   b. Integer
   c. Single
   d. Boolean
3. Visual Basic automatically adds this to a list box when it contains more items than can be displayed.
   a. Larger list box
   b. Scroll bar
   c. Second form
   d. Message box
4. A list box or combo box's index numbering starts at this value.
   a. 0
   b. 1
   c. –1
   d. any value you specify

5. This property holds the index of the selected item in a list box.
   a. Index
   b. SelectedItem
   c. SelectedIndex
   d. Items.SelectedIndex
6. This method erases one item from a list box.
   a. `Erase`
   b. `Items.Remove`
   c. `Items.RemoveItem`
   d. `Clear`
7. The `Do While` statement marks the beginning of a `Do While` loop, and the `Loop` statement marks the end. The statements between these are known as one of the following.
   a. Processes of the loop
   b. Functions of the loop
   c. Substance of the loop
   d. Body of the loop
8. This type of loop evaluates its test expression before each iteration.
   a. Out-test
   b. Pretest
   c. Posttest
   d. In-test
9. One of the following is a sum of numbers that accumulates with each iteration of a loop.
   a. Counter
   b. Running total
   c. Summation function
   d. Iteration count
10. This type of loop is ideal for situations that require a counter because it is specifically designed to initialize, test, and increment a counter variable.
    a. `Do While`
    b. `Do Until`
    c. `For...Next`
    d. `Posttest Do Until`
11. You do this to get the total number of iterations of a nested loop.
    a. Add the number of iterations of all the loops
    b. Multiply the number of iterations of all the loops
    c. Average the number of iterations of all the loops
    d. Get the number of iterations of the outermost loop
12. When this ListBox control's property is set to *True*, it causes the ListBox control to display its list in multiple columns.
    a. Columns
    b. Multicolumn
    c. ColumnList
    d. TableDisplay

13. This control has a rectangular area that functions like a text box.
    a. List box
    b. Drop-down list box
    c. Combo box
    d. Input label

14. This is the standard prefix for combo box names.
    a. `cbo`
    b. `com`
    c. `cbx`
    d. `cob`

15. With this style of combo box, the list of items does not drop down, but is always displayed.
    a. Drop-down combo box
    b. Simple combo box
    c. Drop-down list combo box
    d. Simple drop-down combo list box

16. This combo box property will contain the user's text input or the item selected from the list.
    a. Input
    b. Caption
    c. List
    d. Text

17. A control's ____________________ property can be set to *True* or *False*. If it is set to *True*, the ____________________ event of the control that focus is shifting from will fire.
    a. Validating, CausesValidation
    b. CausesValidation, Validating
    c. Validated, PerformValidation
    d. PerformValidation, Validating

18. You may use this method to set the selected text in a text box.
    a. `SetSelection`
    b. `GetSelection`
    c. `SelectAll`
    d. `SelectText`

19. The statements inside this may perform several operations on the same object without specifying the name of the object each time.
    a. `Validating` procedure
    b. `With` block
    c. set of parentheses
    d. `Use Object` block

20. At design time, this container holds controls that are invisible at runtime, such as the ToolTip control.
    a. Component tray
    b. Control container
    c. Invisible control box
    d. Invisible property

True or False

Indicate whether the following statements are true or false.

1. T F: If you do not provide a value for an input box's title, an error will occur.
2. T F: If the user clicks an input box's *Cancel* button, the function returns the number –1.
3. T F: The `Items.RemoveAt` method always removes the last item in a list box (the item with the highest index value).
4. T F: Infinite loops keep repeating until the program is interrupted.
5. T F: A loop's conditionally executed statements should be indented.
6. T F: A pretest loop always performs at least one iteration, even if the test expression is false from the start.
7. T F: The `Do While` loop may be written as either a pretest or posttest loop.
8. T F: In a `For...Next` loop, the *CounterVariable* must be numeric.
9. T F: The *Step Increment* part of the `For...Next` statement is optional.
10. T F: The `For...Next` loop is a posttest loop.
11. T F: In a nested loop, the inner loop goes through all of its iterations for each iteration of an outer loop.
12. T F: To create a checked list box, you draw a regular list box and set its Checked property to *True*.
13. T F: A drop-down list combo box allows the user to either select an item from a list or type text into a text input area.
14. T F: By default, a control's CausesValidation property is set to *True*.
15. T F: The `Validated` event is triggered before the `Validating` event.

Short Answer

1. What buttons automatically appear on an input box?
2. Where is an input box positioned if you leave out the `Xpos` and `Ypos` arguments?
3. Write a statement that adds *Spinach* to the list box `lstVeggies` at index 2.
4. Write a statement that removes the item at index 12 of the combo box `cboCourses`.
5. Describe the two important parts of a `Do While` loop.
6. In general terms, describe how a `Do While` loop works.
7. Why should you indent the statements in the body of a loop?
8. Describe the difference between pretest loops and posttest loops.
9. Why are the statements in the body of a loop called conditionally executed statements?
10. What is the difference between the `Do While` loop and the `Do Until` loop?
11. Which loop should you use in situations where you wish the loop to repeat as long as the test expression is true?
12. Which type of loop should you use in situations where you wish the loop to repeat until the test expression is true?

13. Which type of loop should you use when you know the number of required iterations?
14. What feature do combo boxes have that list boxes do not have?
15. With one style of combo box the user may not type text directly into the combo box, but must select an item from the list. Which style is it?
16. With one style of combo box the Text property is read-only. Which style?
17. Describe the interaction between the CausesValidation property and the `Validating` event.
18. Why would you want to use the `SelectAll` method in a `Validating` event procedure?

What Do You Think?

1. Why is it critical that counter variables are properly initialized?
2. Why should you be careful not to place a statement in the body of a `For...Next` loop that changes the value of the loop's counter variable?
3. You need to write a loop that iterates until the user enters a specific value into an input box. Which type of loop should you choose? Why?
4. You need to write a loop that will repeat 224 times. Which type of loop will you choose? Why?
5. You need to write a loop that iterates as long as a variable has a specific value stored in it. Which type of loop will you choose? Why?
6. Why should a *Cancel* button's CausesValidation property be set to *False*?
7. You use the statement `lstNames.Items.RemoveAt(6)` to remove an item from a list box. Does the statement remove the sixth or seventh item in the list? Why?
8. What kind of control(s) do you use when you want to provide the user a list of items to select from, but do not want to limit the user's input to the items on the list?
9. What kind of control(s) do you use when you want to limit the user's selection to a list of items?

Find the Error

Identify the syntactically incorrect statements in the following:

1.
```
Loop
   intX = intX + 1
Do While intX < 100
```

2.
```
Do
    lstOutput.Items.Add("Hello")
    intX = intX + 1
While intCount < 10
```

3.
```
Loop Until intX = 99
   intX = intX + 1
Do
```

4.
```
For intX = 1
   lstOutput.Items.Add(intX)
Next intX
```

Algorithm Workbench

1. An event procedure named `btnShow_Click` must add the numbers 1 through 20 to a list box named `lstNumbers`. Design a flowchart for this event procedure.
2. Write the code that you would insert into the code template for the event procedure described in Question 1.
3. Write a `Do While` loop that uses an input box to get a number from the user. The number should be multiplied by 10 and the result stored in the variable product. The loop should iterate as long as product contains a value less than 100.
4. Write a `Do While` loop that uses input boxes to get two numbers from the user. The numbers should be added and the sum displayed message box. An input box should ask the user whether he or she wishes to perform the operation again. If so, the loop should repeat; otherwise it should terminate.
5. Write a `For...Next` loop that adds the following set of numbers to the list box `lstNumbers`.

   0, 10, 20, 30, 40, 50 . . . 1000
6. Write a loop that uses an input box to get a number from the user. The loop should iterate 10 times and keep a running total of the numbers entered.
7. Convert the following pretest `Do While` loop to a posttest `Do While` loop:

```
intX = 1
Do While intX > 0
  strInput = InputBox("Enter a number")
  intX = Clnt(strInput)
Loop
```

8. Convert the following `Do While` loop to a `Do Until` loop:

```
strInput = String.Empty
Do While strInput.ToUpper <> "Y"
  strInput = InputBox("Are you sure you want to quit?")
Loop
```

9. Convert the following `Do While` loop to a `For...Next` loop:

```
intCount = 0
Do While intCount < 50
  lstOutput.Items.Add(intCount)
  intCount += 1
Loop
```

10. Convert the following `For...Next` loop to a `Do While` loop:

```
For intX = 50 To 0 Step -1
  lstOutput.Items.Add(intX)
Next intX
```

11. Rewrite the following statements so they appear inside a `With` block:

```
txtName.Text = "(unknown)"
txtName.Font.Size = 10
txtName.BackColor = Color.Red
```

Programming Challenges

1. **Sum of Numbers**

VideoNote

The Sum of Numbers Problem

Create an application that displays a form similar to the one shown in Figure 5-49.

When the *Enter Numbers* button is clicked, the application should display the input box shown in Figure 5-50.

The input box asks the user to enter a positive integer value. Notice that the default input value is 10. When the *OK* button is clicked, the application should display a message box with the sum of all the integers from 1 through the value entered by the user, as shown in Figure 5-51.

Figure 5-49 *Sum of Numbers* form

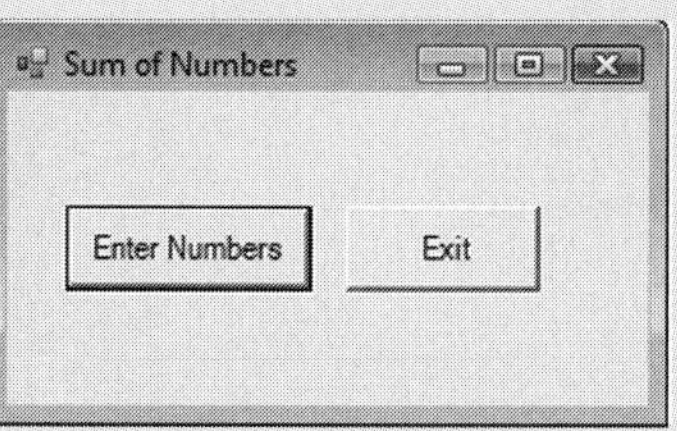

Figure 5-50 *Sum of Numbers* input box

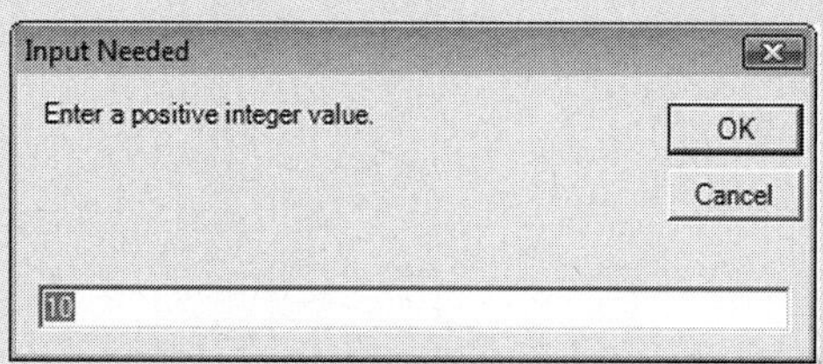

Figure 5-51 *Sum of Numbers* message box

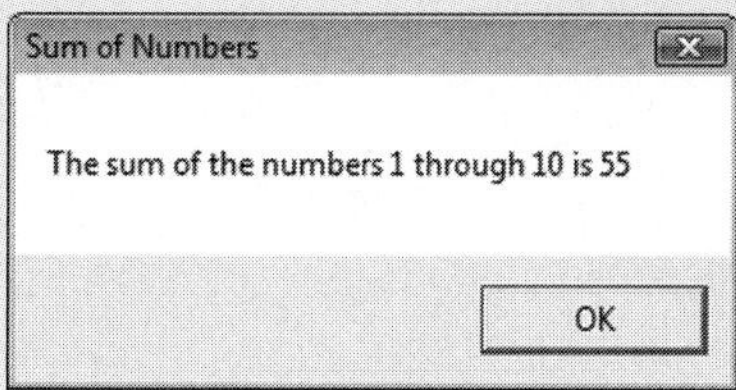

If the user enters a negative value, the application should display an error message.

Use the following test data to determine if the application is calculating properly:

Value	Sum
5	15
10	55
20	210
100	5050

2. **Distance Calculator**

If you know a vehicle's speed and the amount of time it has traveled, you can calculate the distance it has traveled as follows:

*Distance = Speed * Time*

For example, if a train travels 40 miles per hour for 3 hours, the distance traveled is 120 miles. Create an application with a form similar to the one shown in Figure 5-52.

When the user clicks the *Calculate* button, the application should display an input box asking the user for the speed of the vehicle in miles-per-hour, followed by another input box asking for the amount of time, in hours, that the vehicle has traveled. Then it should use a loop to display in a list box the distance the vehicle has traveled for each hour of that time period. Figure 5-53 shows an example of what the application's form should look like.

Figure 5-52 *Distance Calculator*

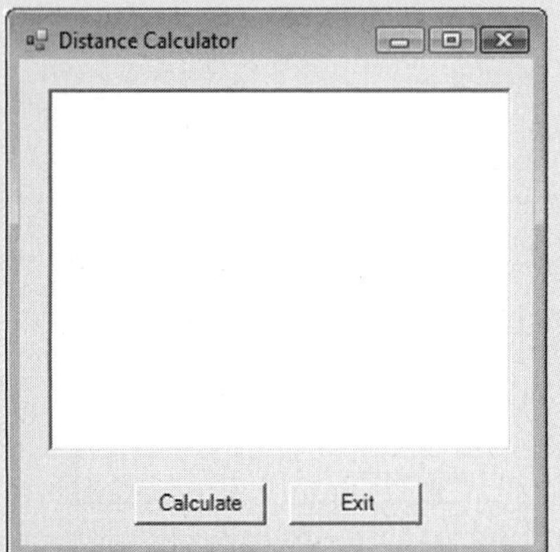

Figure 5-53 *Distance Calculator* completed

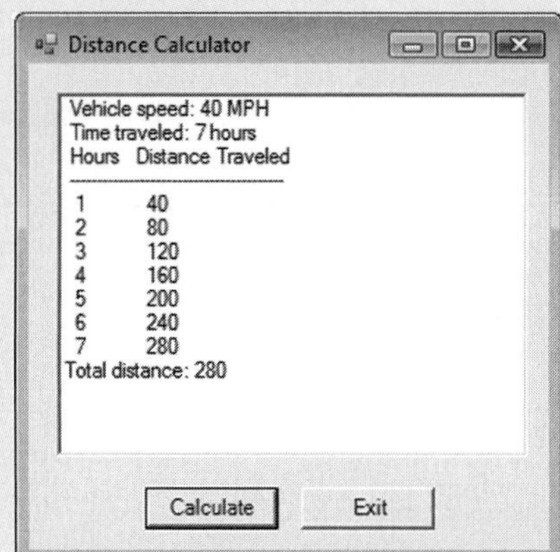

Input validation: Do not accept a value less than 1 for the vehicle's speed or the number of hours traveled.

Use the following test data to determine if the application is calculating properly.

Vehicle Speed: 60
Hours Traveled: 7

Hour	**Distance Traveled**
1	60
2	120
3	180
4	240
5	300
6	360
7	420

3. **Workshop Selector**

Table 5-4 shows a training company's workshops, the number of days of each, and their registration fees.

Table 5-4 Workshops and registration fees

Workshop	Number of Days	Registration Fee
Handling Stress	3	$595
Time Management	3	$695
Supervision Skills	3	$995
Negotiation	5	$1,295
How to Interview	1	$395

The training company conducts its workshops in the six locations shown in Table 5-5. The table also shows the lodging fees per day at each location.

Table 5-5 Training locations and lodging fees

Location	Lodging Fees per Day
Austin	$95
Chicago	$125
Dallas	$110
Orlando	$100
Phoenix	$92
Raleigh	$90

When a customer registers for a workshop, he or she must pay the registration fee plus the lodging fees for the selected location. For example, here are the charges to attend the Supervision Skills workshop in Orlando:

Registration: $995
Lodging: $100 × 3 days = $300
Total: $1,295

Design an application with a form that resembles the one shown in Figure 5-54.

Figure 5-54 *Workshop Selector* form

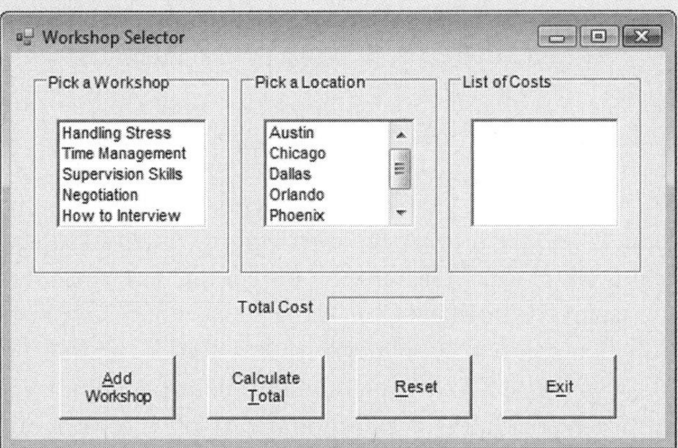

The application should allow the user to select a workshop from one list box and a location from another list box. When the user clicks the *Add Workshop* button, the application should add the total cost of the selected workshop at the selected location in the third list box. When the user clicks the *Calculate Total* button, the total cost of all the selected workshops should be calculated and displayed in the label. The *Reset* button should deselect the workshop and location from the first two list boxes, clear the third list box, and clear the total cost label.

Be sure to add appropriate ToolTips for the list boxes and the buttons.

4. **Hotel Occupancy**

The ElGrande Hotel has eight floors and 30 rooms on each floor. Create an application that calculates the occupancy rate for each floor, and the overall occupancy rate for the hotel. The occupancy rate is the percentage of rooms occupied, and may be calculated by dividing the number of rooms occupied by the number of rooms. For example, if 18 rooms on the first floor are occupied, the occupancy rate is as follows:

18 / 30 = .6 or 60%

The application's form should appear similar to the one shown in Figure 5-55.

Figure 5-55 *Hotel Occupancy* form

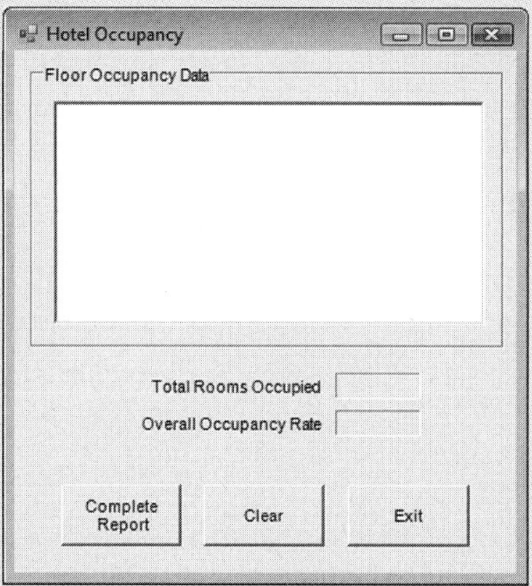

When the user clicks the *Complete Report* button, a loop should execute and iterate eight times. Each time the loop iterates, it should display an input box for one of the hotel's floors. The input box should ask the user to enter the number of rooms occupied on that floor. As the user enters a value for each floor, the loop should calculate the occupancy rate for that floor, and display the information for that floor in the list box. When the number of occupied rooms has been entered for all the floors, the application should display the total number of rooms occupied and the overall occupancy rate for the hotel. (The hotel has a total of 240 rooms.)

Figure 5-56 shows an example of the form after occupancy information has been provided for all the floors.

The *Clear* button should clear all the appropriate controls on the form. The *Exit* button should end the application. Use the values shown in Figure 5-56 to confirm that your application is performing the correct calculations. Be sure to add appropriate ToolTips for the button controls.

Input validation: Do not accept a number less than 0 or greater than 30 for the number of occupied rooms on each floor.

Figure 5-56 Completed *Hotel Occupancy* form

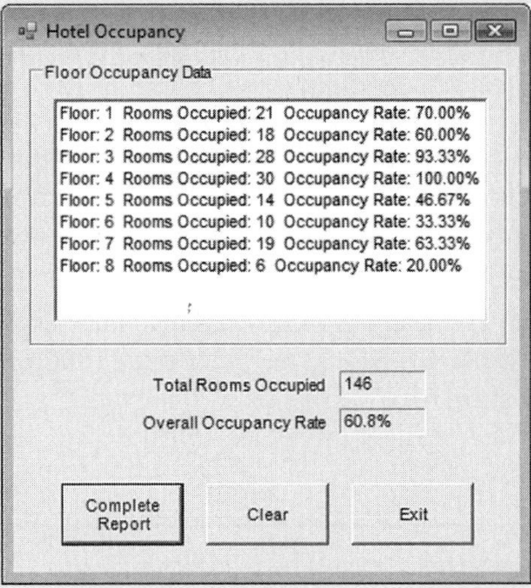

5. **Rainfall Statistics**

   Create an application that allows the user to enter each month's amount of rainfall (in inches) and calculates the total and average rainfall for a year. Figure 5-57 shows the application's form.

   Once the user has entered the amount of rainfall for each month, he or she may click the *Calculate* button to display the total and average rainfall. The *Clear* button should clear all the text boxes and labels on the form. The *Exit* button should end the application. Be sure to add appropriate ToolTips for the text boxes and the buttons.

Figure 5-57 *Rainfall Statistics* form

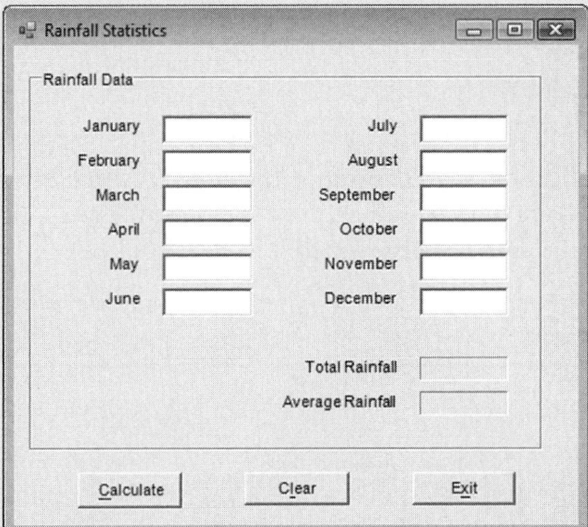

Input validation: Each text box should have a `Validating` event procedure. The event procedure should display an error message if the user has entered a nonnumeric value or a number less than 0. If either of these conditions exists, the invalid value should be selected so the user can reenter it.

6. **Bar Chart**

Create an application that prompts the user to enter today's sales for five stores. The program should then display a simple bar graph comparing each store's sales. Create each bar in the bar graph by displaying a row of asterisks (*) in a list box. Each asterisk in a bar represents $100 in sales.

Figure 5-58 shows the form with the bar chart displayed. The sales data entered was $1000 for store #1, $1200 for store #2, $1800 for store #3, $800 for store #4, and $1900 for store #5.

Figure 5-58 *Bar Chart* form

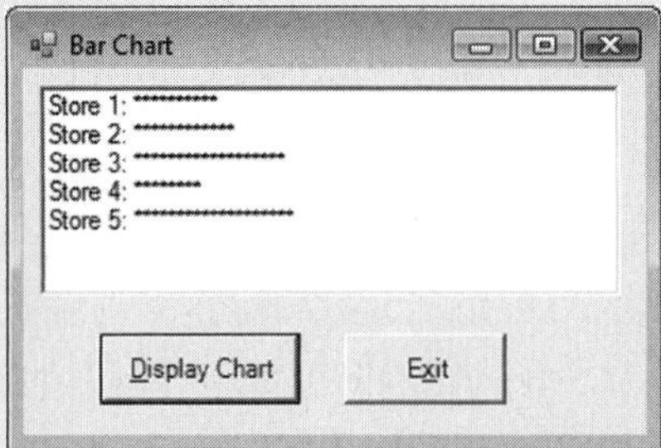

7. **Grade Report**

Create an application that allows a teacher to enter three test scores each for three students. The application should calculate each student's average test score and assign a letter grade based on the following grading scale:

Average Test Score	Letter Grade
90 or greater	A
80 through 89	B
70 through 79	C
60 through 69	D
Below 60	F

The application should prompt the user for each student's name and three test scores. Figure 5-59 shows an example of how the application's form might appear after all the data has been entered.

Figure 5-59 *Grade Report* form

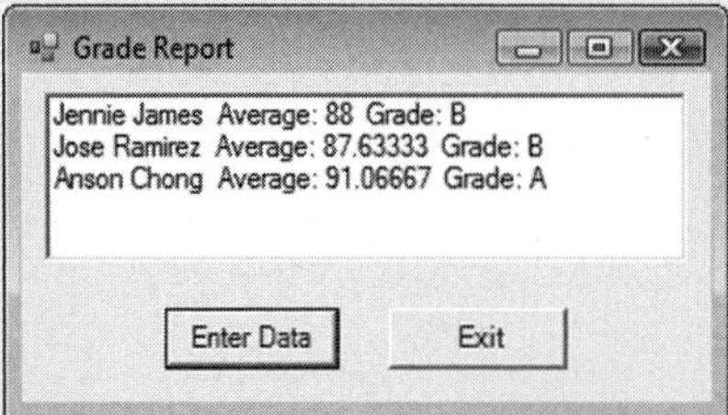

Design Your Own Forms

8. Celsius to Fahrenheit Table

In Programming Challenge 6 of Chapter 3, you created an application that converts Celsius temperatures to Fahrenheit. Recall that the formula for performing this conversion is

$$F = 1.8 * C + 32$$

In the formula, F is the Fahrenheit temperature and C is the Celsius temperature.

For this exercise, create an application that displays a table of the Celsius temperatures 0 through 20 and their Fahrenheit equivalents. The application should use a loop to display the temperatures in a list box.

9. Population

Create an application that will predict the approximate size of a population of organisms. The user should select or enter the starting number of organisms in a combo box, enter the average daily population increase (as a percentage) in a text box, and select or enter the number of days the organisms will be left to multiply in another combo box. For example, assume the user enters the following values:

Starting number of organisms: 2
Average daily increase: 30%
Number of days to multiply: 10

The application should display the following table of data.

Day	**Approximate Population**
1	2
2	2.6
3	3.38
4	4.394
5	5.7122
6	7.42586
7	9.653619
8	12.5497
9	16.31462
10	21.209

Be sure to add appropriate ToolTips for each control on the form.

Input validation: Do not accept a number less than 2 for the starting size of the population. Do not accept a negative number for the average daily population increase. Do not accept a number less than 1 for the number of days the organisms will multiply.

10. Pennies for Pay

Susan is hired for a job, and her employer agrees to pay her every day. Her employer also agrees that Susan's salary is one penny the first day, two pennies the second day, four pennies the third day, and continuing to double each day. Create an application that allows the user to select or enter into a combo box the number of days that Susan will work, and calculates the total amount of pay she will receive over that period of time.

Be sure to add appropriate ToolTips for each control on the form.

Input validation: Do not accept a number less than 1 for the number of days worked.

11. **Payroll**

    Create an application that displays payroll information. The application should allow the user to enter the following data for four employees:

    - Number of hours worked
    - Hourly pay rate
    - Percentage to be withheld for state income tax
    - Percentage to be withheld for federal income tax
    - Percentage to be withheld for FICA

    The application should calculate and display the following data for each employee in a list box:

    - Gross pay (the number of hours worked multiplied by the hourly pay rate)
    - State income tax withholdings (gross pay multiplied by state income tax percentage)
    - Federal income tax withholdings (gross pay multiplied by federal income tax percentage)
    - FICA withholdings (gross pay multiplied by FICA percentage)
    - Net pay (the gross pay minus state income tax, federal income tax, and FICA)

    When the calculations are performed, be sure to check for the following error:

    - If any employee's state income tax plus federal tax plus FICA is greater than the employee's gross pay, display an error message stating that the withholdings are too great.

    Be sure to add appropriate ToolTips for each control on the form.

12. **Ocean Levels**

    Assuming the ocean's level is currently rising at about 1.5 millimeters per year, create an application that displays the number of millimeters that the ocean will have risen each year for the next 10 years.

13. **Calories Burned**

    Running on a particular treadmill you burn 3.9 calories per minute. Create an application that uses a loop to display the number of calories burned after 10, 15, 20, 25, and 30 minutes.

14. **Budget Analysis**

    Create an application that lets the user enter the amount that he or she has budgeted for a month. A loop should then use input boxes to prompt the user for his or her expenses for the month, and keep a running total. When the loop finishes, the program should display the amount that the user is over or under budget.

15. **Speed Conversion Chart**

    Your friend Amanda, who lives in the United States, just bought an antique European sports car. The car's speedometer works in kilometers per hour. The formula for converting kilometers per hour to miles per hour is:

    $MPH = KPH * 0.6214$

    In the formula, *MPH* is the speed in miles per hour and *KPH* is the speed in kilometers per hour. Amanda is afraid she will get a speeding ticket, and has asked you to write a program that displays a list of speeds in kilometers per hour with their values converted to miles per hour. The list should display the speeds from 60 kilometers per hour through 130 kilometers per hour, in increments of 5 kilometers per hour. (In other words, it should display 60 kph, 65 kph, 70 kph, and so forth, up through 130 kph.)

CHAPTER

6 Procedures and Functions

TOPICS

There are two broad categories of procedures in Visual Basic: procedures and functions. A **procedure** is a collection of statements that performs a task. Event handlers belong to this category. A **function** is a collection of statements that performs a task and then returns a value to the part of the program that executed it. Functions that you write work like built-in functions such as `CInt` and `IsNumeric`.

This chapter discusses how to write general purpose procedures and functions. These procedures do not respond to events, but execute when they are called by statements. You will learn how to create, call, and pass arguments to these procedures as well as various techniques for debugging applications that use them.

In common object-oriented terminology, the term **method** is used to mean both procedures and functions.

6.1 Procedures

CONCEPT: You can write your own general purpose procedures that perform specific tasks. General purpose procedures are not triggered by events, but are called from statements in other procedures.

A procedure is a collection of statements that performs a task. An **event handler** or **event procedure** is a type of procedure that is executed when an event, such as a mouse click, occurs while the program is running. This section discusses general purpose procedures that are not triggered by events, but executed by statements in other procedures.

By writing your own procedures, you can **modularize** an application's code, that is, break it into small, manageable procedures. Imagine a book with a thousand pages that was not divided into chapters or sections. Finding a single topic in the book would be very difficult. Real-world applications can easily have thousands of lines of code, and unless they are modularized, they can be very difficult to modify and maintain.

Procedures can reduce the amount of duplicated code in a program. If a specific task is performed in several places, a procedure for performing that task can be written once and executed anytime it is needed.

Tutorial 6-1 walks you through an example application that uses a procedure.

Tutorial 6-1: Examining an application with a procedure

Step 1: Open the *Procedure Demo* project from the student sample programs folder named *Chap6\Procedure Demo*. The application's form is shown in Figure 6-1. The form has a list box named `lstOutput` and two buttons: `btnGo` and `btnExit`.

Figure 6-1 *Procedure Demo* form

Step 2: Open the *Code* window and find the procedure named `DisplayMessage`.

```
Sub DisplayMessage()

   ' A general procedure that displays a message.
   lstOutput.Items.Add("")
   lstOutput.Items.Add("Hello from the DisplayMessage procedure.")
   lstOutput.Items.Add("")
End Sub
```

The declaration of a procedure begins with a `Sub` statement and ends with an `End Sub` statement. The code that appears between these two statements is the body of the procedure. When the `DisplayMessage` procedure executes, it displays a blank line in the list box, followed by the string `"Hello from the DisplayMessage procedure."`, followed by another blank line.

Figure 6-2 shows the parts of the `Sub` statement.

Figure 6-2 First line of `DisplayMessage` procedure

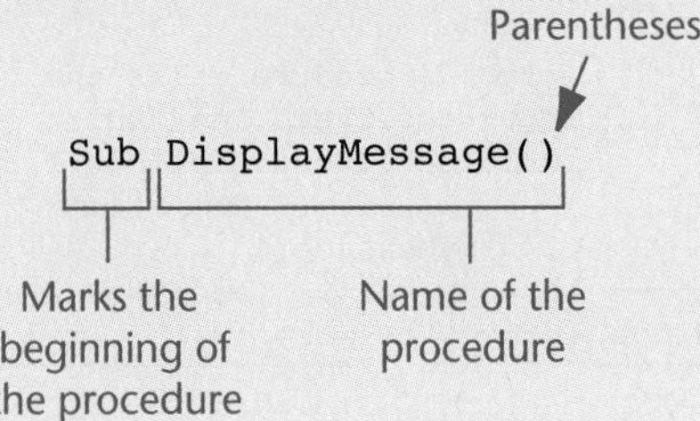

The first line of the procedure begins with the word `Sub`, followed by the name of the procedure, followed by a set of parentheses. In this procedure, the parentheses are empty. Later, you will see procedures having items inside the parentheses.

NOTE: An event handler is associated with a control, so its name is prefixed with the control's name. For example, the `btnGo` button's `Click` event procedure is named `btnGo_Click`. Since a general purpose procedure is not associated with a control, its name is not prefixed by a control name.

Step 3: General purpose procedures are not executed by an event. Instead, they must be called. Look at the following code for the `btnGo_Click` event handler. The statement printed in bold calls the `DisplayMessage` procedure.

```
Private Sub btnGo_Click(ByVal sender As System.Object, _
   ByVal e As System.EventArgs) Handles btnGo.Click

   ' This procedure calls the DisplayMessage procedure.
   lstOutput.Items.Add("Hello from the btnGo_Click procedure.")
   lstOutput.Items.Add("Now I am calling the DisplayMessage " _
        & "procedure.")

   DisplayMessage()
   lstOutput.Items.Add("Now I am back in the btnGo_Click" _
        & "procedure.")
End Sub
```

This type of statement, known as a **procedure call**, causes the procedure to execute. A procedure call is simply the name of the procedure that is to be executed. Parentheses follow the name of the procedure. You can also use the **`Call`** keyword.

```
Call DisplayMessage()
```

The `Call` keyword is optional, and is not used in this text.

When a procedure call executes, the application branches to the procedure and executes its body. When the procedure has finished, control returns to the procedure call and resumes executing at the next statement. Figure 6-3 illustrates how this application branches from the `btnGo_Click` procedure to the `DisplayMessage` procedure call, and returns to the `btnGo_Click` procedure.

Figure 6-3 Procedure call

```
Private Sub btnGo_Click(ByVal sender As System.Object, _
        ByVal e As System.EventArgs) Handles btnGo.Click

        ' This procedure calls the DisplayMessage procedure.
        lstOutput.Items.Add("Hello from the btnGo_Click procedure.")
        lstOutput.Items.Add("Now I am calling the DisplayMessage " & _
                    "procedure.")
        DisplayMessage()
        lstOutput.Items.Add("Now I am back in the btnGo_Click procedure.")
End Sub

Sub DisplayMessage()

        ' A general procedure that displays a message.
        lstOutput.Items.Add("")
        lstOutput.Items.Add("Hello from the DisplayMessage procedure.")
        lstOutput.Items.Add("")
End Sub
```


Step 4: Run the application. Click the *Go* button. The form should appear as shown in Figure 6-4.

Figure 6-4 Results of *Procedure Demo*

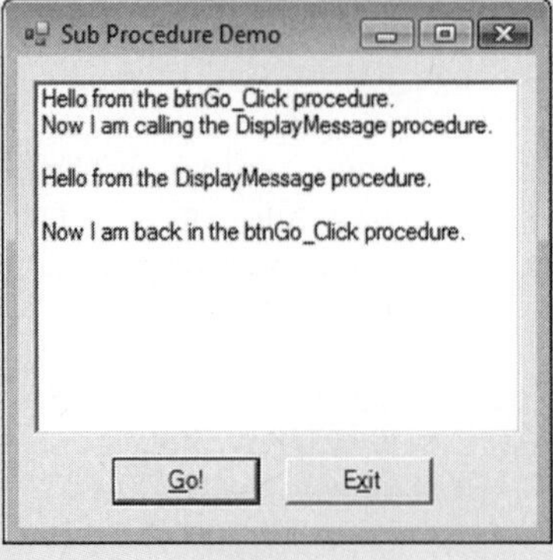

As you can see, the statements in the `btnGo_Click` event procedure executed up to the `DisplayMessage` procedure call. At that point, the application branched to the `DisplayMessage` procedure and executed all of its statements. When the `DisplayMessage` procedure finished, the application returned to the `btnGo_Click` procedure and resumed executing at the line following the `DisplayMessage` call.

Step 5: Click the *Exit* button to end the application.

Declaring a Procedure

The general format of a **procedure declaration** is as follows:

```
[AccessSpecifier] Sub ProcedureName ([ParameterList])
  [Statements]
End Sub
```

The items shown in brackets are optional. *AccessSpecifier* specifies the accessibility of the procedure. This is an important issue because some applications have more than one form. When you use the `Private` access specifier, the procedure may only be accessed by other procedures declared in the same class or form. When a procedure begins with `Public`, it may also be accessed by procedures declared in other forms. If you leave out the access specifier, it defaults to `Public`. We will begin to use access specifers in later chapters.

Following the keyword **`Sub`** is the name of the procedure. You should always give the procedure a name that reflects its purpose. You should also adopt a consistent style of using uppercase and lowercase letters. For procedure names, we use **Pascal casing**, which capitalizes the first character and the first character of each subsequent word in the procedure name. All other characters are lowercase. Using different styles of capitalization for variables and procedures lets the reader of your code know what type of entity a name belongs to.

Inside the parentheses is an optional *ParameterList*. A **parameter** is a special variable that receives a value being passed into a procedure. Later in this chapter, you will see procedures that use parameters to accept data passed into them.

The last line of a procedure declaration is the `End Sub` statement. Between the `Sub` statement and the `End Sub` statement, you write the statements that execute each time the procedure is called.

Tutorial 6-2 guides you through the process of writing procedures. In the tutorial, you add two procedures to an existing application on the student disk.

Tutorial 6-2:
Creating a procedure

The student CD contains a partially completed test averaging application that should calculate and display a grade based on three test scores. The application gives the user the following methods of determining the grade:

- Calculate the average of the three test scores and assign a letter grade.
- Drop the lowest of the three scores, calculate the average, and assign a letter grade.

Step 1: Open the *Test Average* project from the student sample programs folder named *Chap6\Test Average*.

Step 2: Open the *Design* window and examine the application's form, which is shown in Figure 6-5.

The form has three text boxes in which the user will enter three test scores. The text boxes are named `txtScore1`, `txtScore2`, and `txtScore3`. The form has the labels `lblAverage` (to display the average test score) and `lblLetterGrade` (to display the assigned letter grade). The buttons are named `btnShowGrade`, `btnDropLowest`, `btnClear`, and `btnExit`.

When the user clicks the *Show Grade* button (`btnShowGrade`), the application calculates the average of the three test scores and determines the letter grade. The average and letter grade are displayed in the appropriate labels. If the user clicks the *Show Grade/Drop Lowest Score* button (`btnDropLowest`), the application calculates the average of the two highest scores (in effect, dropping the lowest score) and determines the letter grade. The average and letter grade are displayed in the appropriate labels.

Figure 6-5 *Test Average* form

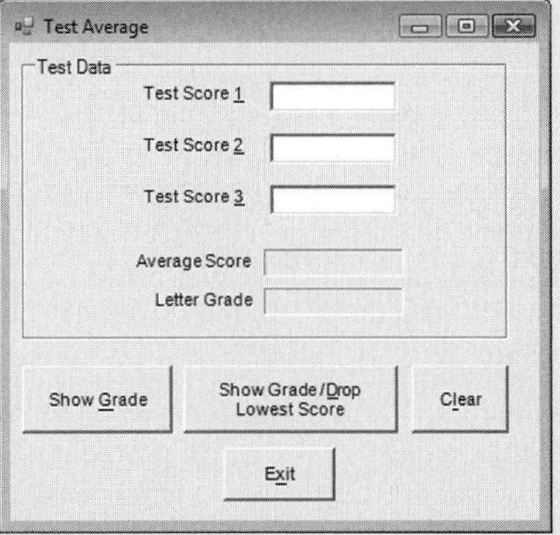

Step 3: Open the *Code* window and look at the following class-level variable declarations:

```
' Class-level variables
Dim intScore1 As Integer        ' Holds test score 1
Dim intScore2 As Integer        ' Holds test score 2
Dim intScore3 As Integer        ' Holds test score 3
Dim intAverage As Integer       ' Holds average test score
```

The application has class-level variables to hold the three test scores and the average test score. By scrolling down in the *Code* window, you can see that the following event procedures have already been written:

```
btnClear_Click
btnExit_Click
btnDropLowest_Click
btnShowGrade_Click
```

TIP: Some programmers like to prefex module-level (class-level) variable names with a prefix of *m_*. They reason that this prefix makes variables declared at the module level easily distinguishable from variables declared at the local level.

In this tutorial, you will write the following procedures:

- The `GetScores` procedure copies the values in the `txtScore1`, `txtScore2`, and `txtScore3` text boxes into the `intScore1`, `intScore2`, and `intScore3` variables, respectively.
- The `DisplayGrade` procedure displays the student's grade based on the following scale:

90 through 100	A
80 through 89	B
70 through79	C
60 through 69	D
Below 60	F

Step 4: Scroll down to the bottom of the *Code* window and find the following comment:

```
' Write the GetScores procedure here.
```

Delete the comment and in its place write the `GetScores` procedure, as follows:

```
Sub GetScores()
  ' Retrieve the test scores from text boxes
  ' and store in variables.
  intScore1 = CInt(txtScore1.Text)
  intScore2 = CInt(txtScore2.Text)
  intScore3 = CInt(txtScore3.Text)
End Sub
```

Step 5: Now you are ready to create the `DisplayGrade` procedure, which performs the following steps:

- Assigns the average test score to the `lblAverage` control's Text property.
- Determines the student's letter grade and assigns it to the `lblLetterGrade` control's Text property.

Find the following comment, which appears near the bottom of the *Code* window:

```
' Write the DisplayGrade procedure here.
```

Delete the comment and in its place write the `DisplayGrade` procedure, as follows:

```
Sub DisplayGrade()
  ' Display the intAverage score.
  lblAverage.Text = intAverage.ToString()

  ' Determine and display the letter grade.
  Select Case intAverage
    Case 90 To 100
      lblLetterGrade.Text = "A"
    Case 80 To 89
      lblLetterGrade.Text = "B"
```

```
        Case 70 To 79
            lblLetterGrade.Text = "C"
        Case 60 To 69
            lblLetterGrade.Text = "D"
        Case Else
            lblLetterGrade.Text = "F"
    End Select
End Sub
```

Step 6: Now that you have created the procedures, you can begin to place appropriate procedure calls in the existing event procedures. First, locate the `btnShowGrade_Click` event procedure. Find the line in the procedure that reads

```
' Call the GetScores procedure here.
```

Replace it with the following lines:

```
' Call the GetScores procedure
GetScores()
```

Step 7: Still in the `btnShowGrade_Click` event procedure, locate the following line:

```
' Call the DisplayGrade procedure here.
```

Replace it with the following lines:

```
' Call the DisplayGrade procedure
DisplayGrade()
```

The event procedure should now appear as the following code. The lines you added are shown in bold.

```
Private Sub btnShowGrade_Click(ByVal sender As System.Object, _
    ByVal e As System.EventArgs) Handles btnShowGrade.Click

    ' Calculate the intAverage test score and grade WITHOUT
    ' dropping the lowest score.

    ' Call the GetScores procedure.
    GetScores()

    ' Calculate the average test score.
    intAverage = CInt((intScore1 + intScore2 + intScore3) / 3)

    ' Call the DisplayGrade procedure.
    DisplayGrade()
End Sub
```

The `CInt` function call is required in this procedure because the division (/) operator produces a Double expression. We are trying to assign it to an Integer variable (`intAverage`). *Option Strict* does not allow you to automatically assign a Double expression to an Integer variable, unless you use a conversion function. A possible way to avoid the problem would be to use the Integer division (\) operator.

```
' Calculate the average test score.
intAverage = (intScore1 + intScore2 + intScore3) \ 3
```

The student whose grade was calculated might be unhappy—do you see why? Rather than rounding the score upward (which would be done by the `CInt` function), the Integer division operator truncates downward. Suppose a student's two highest scores were 86 and 73. The student's raw average would be 79.5. The following table shows the values returned by the integer division operator, compared to floating-point division (combined with the `CInt` function):

Expression	Value
`(86 + 73) \ 2`	79
`CInt(( 86 + 73 ) / 2)`	80

NOTE: Because `intAverage` is an integer variable, the `CInt` function rounds its contents to the nearest whole number.

Step 8: Locate the `btnDropLowest_Click` event procedure in the *Code* window. Find the line in the procedure that reads

```
' Call the GetScores procedure here.
```

Replace it with the following lines:

```
' Call the GetScores procedure.
GetScores()
```

Step 9: Still in the `btnDropLowest_Click` event procedure, locate the following line:

```
' Call the DisplayGrade procedure here.
```

Replace it with the following lines:

```
' Call the DisplayGrade procedure
DisplayGrade()
```

The event procedure should now appear as the following code. The lines you added are shown in bold.

```
Private Sub btnDropLowest_Click(ByVal sender As System.Object, _
    ByVal e As System.EventArgs) Handles btnDropLowest.Click

    ' Drop the lowest test score, calculate the average
    ' score, and determine the letter grade.

    ' Call the GetScores procedure.
    GetScores()

    ' Determine the lowest score (intLowest).
    Dim intLowest As Integer
    intLowest = Math.Min(intScore1, intScore2)
    intLowest = Math.Min(intLowest, intScore3)

    ' Calculate the sum of all three scores.
    Dim intTotal As Integer
    intTotal = intScore1 + intScore2 + intScore3

    ' Calculate the average, dropping the lowest score.
    intAverage = CInt((intTotal - intLowest) / 2)

    ' Call the DisplayGrade procedure.
    DisplayGrade()
End Sub
```

The code in this procedure needs some explanation. The `Math` library has a function named `Min` that returns the smaller of two numbers. When we pass it two test scores (`intScore1` and `intScore2`), the smaller of the two is assigned to `intLowest`.

```
intLowest = Math.Min(intScore1, intScore2)
```

After comparing `intLowest` to the third score, we know the lowest of the three scores.

```
intLowest = Math.Min(intLowest, intScore3)
```

First, the scores are added to produce `intTotal`. Then, the lowest score is subtracted from the total before calculating the average score (`intAverage`).

```
intTotal = intScore1 + intScore2 + intScore3
intAverage = CInt((intTotal - intLowest) / 2)
```

As explained earlier in the `btnShowGrade_Click` procedure, you must to use the the `CInt` function when assigning a Double expression to an Integer variable.

Step 10: Run the application. On the form, enter the following test scores: **90**, **92**, and **77**. Click the *Show Grade* button. If you typed everything exactly as indicated in this tutorial, the form should appear as shown in Figure 6-6.

Figure 6-6 Completed *Test Average* form after *Show Grade* button is clicked

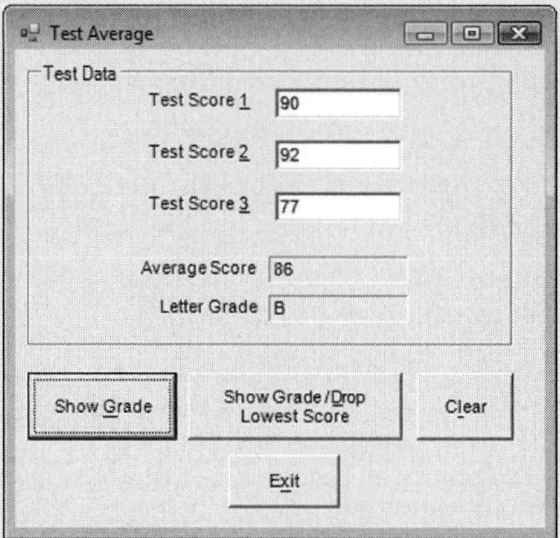

Step 11: Click the *Show Grade/Drop Low* button. The form should appear as shown in Figure 6-7.

Figure 6-7 Completed *Test Average* form after *Show Grade/Drop Low* button is clicked

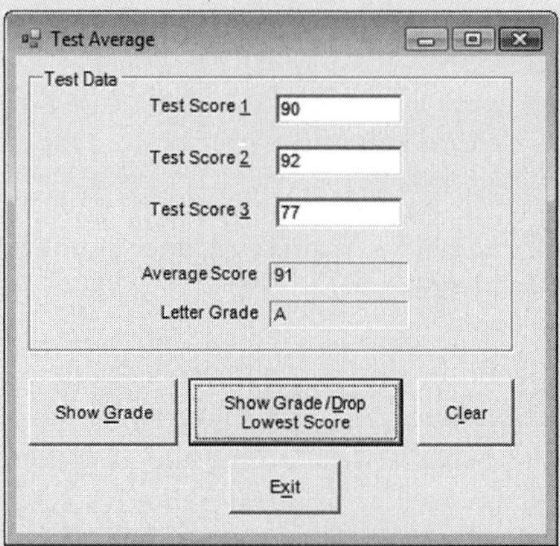

Step 12: Click the *Exit* button to end the application.

If You Want to Know More: Static Local Variables

If a procedure is called more than once in a program, the values stored in the procedure's local variables do not remain between procedure calls. This is because the local variables are destroyed when the procedure terminates, and are recreated when the procedure starts again. For example, look at the following procedure:

```
Sub ShowLocal()
  Dim intLocalNum As Integer
  MessageBox.Show(intLocalNum.ToString())
  intLocalNum = 99
End Sub
```

When this procedure is called, `intLocalNum` is automatically initialized to 0, so the message box displays 0. Although the last statement in the `ShowLocal` procedure stores 99 in `intLocalNum`, the variable is destroyed when the procedure terminates. The next time this procedure is called, `intLocalNum` is recreated and initialized to 0 again. So, each time the procedure executes, it will display 0 in the message box.

Sometimes you want a procedure to remember the value stored in a local variable between procedure calls. This can be accomplished by making the variable static. **Static local variables** are not destroyed when a procedure terminates. They exist for the lifetime of the application, although their scope is only the procedure in which they are declared.

To declare a static local variable, replace `Dim` with `Static`. Here is the general format of a **`Static`** variable declaration.

```
Static VariableName As DataType
```

For example, look at the following procedure:

```
Sub ShowStatic()
  Static intStaticNum As Integer
  MessageBox.Show(intStaticNum.ToString())
  intStaticNum += 1
End Sub
```

Notice that `intStaticNum` is declared `Static`. When the procedure is called, `intStaticNum` is automatically initialized to 0 and its value is displayed in the message box. The last statement adds 1 to `intStaticNum`. Because the variable is static, it retains its value between procedure calls. The second time the procedure is called, `intStaticNum` equals 1. Likewise, the third time the procedure is called, `intStaticNum` equals 2, and so on.

> **NOTE:** Static variables should only be used in those rare cases when a procedure must retain the value of a local variable between calls to the procedure. Also, you cannot declare a class-level variable using `Static`. Only variables declared inside a procedure may be static.

Checkpoint

6.1 Figure 6-8 shows an application's form.

The list box is named `lstOutput`. The buttons are named `btnGo` and `btnExit`. The application's procedures are as follows:

```
Private Sub btnGo_Click(ByVal sender As System.Object, _
    ByVal e As System.EventArgs) Handles btnGo.Click
```

```
    Dim intNumber As Integer

    intNumber = CInt(InputBox("Enter a number"))
    If intNumber < 10 Then
      Message1()
      Message2()
    Else
      Message2()
      Message1()
    End If
End Sub

Private Sub btnExit_Click(ByVal sender As System.Object, _
      ByVal e As System.EventArgs) Handles btnExit.Click
      'End the application
    Me.Close()
End Sub

Sub Message1()
    lstOutput.Items.Add("Able was I")
End Sub

Sub Message2()
    lstOutput.Items.Add("I saw Elba")
End Sub
```

Suppose you run this application and click the `btnGo` button. What will the application display in the list box if you enter 10 in the input box? What if you enter 5?

Figure 6-8 *Checkpoint 6.1* application form

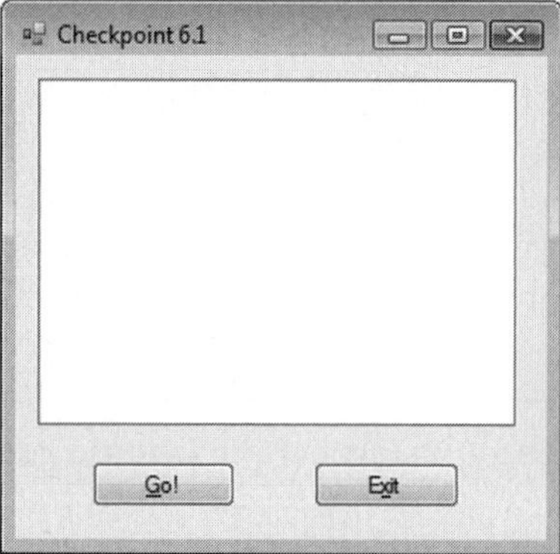

6.2 What is the difference between a regular local variable and a static local variable?

6.2 Passing Arguments to Procedures

CONCEPT: When calling a procedure, you can pass it values known as arguments.

VideoNote
Passing Arguments to Procedures

Values passed to procedures are called **arguments**. You are already familiar with how to use arguments. In the following statement, the `CInt` function is called and an argument, `txtInput.Text`, is passed to it:

```
intValue = CInt(txtInput.Text)
```

There are two ways to pass an argument to a procedure: by value or by reference. Passing an argument **by value** means that only a copy of the argument is passed to the procedure. Because the procedure has only a copy, it cannot make changes to the original argument. When an argument is passed **by reference**, however, the procedure has access to the original argument and can make changes to it.

In order for a procedure to accept an argument, it must be equipped with a parameter. A parameter is a special variable that receives an argument being passed into a procedure. Here is an example procedure that uses a parameter:

```
Sub DisplayValue(ByVal intNumber As Integer)
   ' This procedure displays a value in a message box.
   MessageBox.Show(intNumber.ToString())
End Sub
```

Notice the statement inside the parentheses in the first line of the procedure (repeated below).

```
ByVal intNumber As Integer
```

This statement declares the variable `intNumber` as an integer parameter. The **`ByVal`** keyword indicates that arguments passed into the variable are passed by value. This parameter variable enables the `DisplayValue` procedure to accept an integer argument.

> **TIP:** The declaration of a parameter looks like a regular variable declaration, except the word `ByVal` is used instead of `Dim`.

Here is an example of how you would call the procedure and pass an argument to it:

```
DisplayValue(5)
```

The argument, 5, is listed inside the parentheses. This value is passed into the procedure's parameter variable, `intNumber`. This is illustrated in Figure 6-9.

Figure 6-9 Passing 5 to `DisplayValue`

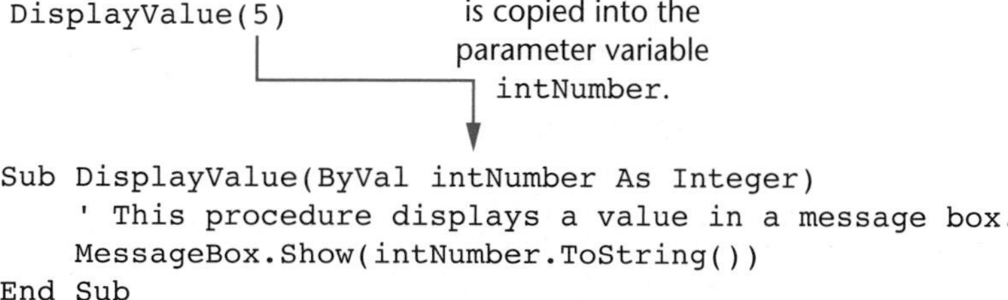

You may also pass variables and the values of expressions as arguments. For example, the following statements call the `DisplayValue` procedure, passing various arguments:

```
DisplayValue(intX)
DisplayValue(intX * 4)
DisplayValue(CInt(txtInput.Text))
```

The first statement passes the value in the variable `intX` as the argument. The second statement passes the expression `intX * 4` as the argument. The third statement passes the value returned from `CInt(txtInput.Text)` as the argument. Tutorial 6-3 guides you through an application that demonstrates argument passing.

Tutorial 6-3:
Examining an application that demonstrates passing an argument to a procedure

Step 1: Open the *Argument Demo* project from the student sample programs folder named *Chap6\Argument Demo*. The application's form is shown in Figure 6-10. The application's form has four buttons: `btnDemo1`, `btnDemo2`, `btnDemo3`, and `btnExit`.

Figure 6-10 *Argument Demo* form

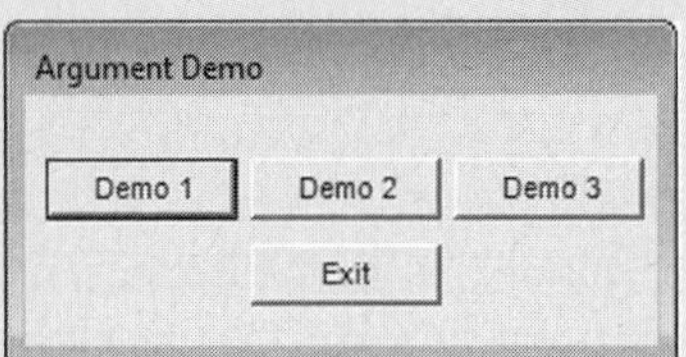

Step 2: In addition to the event procedures for each of the form's buttons, the application uses the `DisplayValue` procedure described earlier. Open the *Code* window and locate the `btnDemo1_Click` event procedure. The code is as follows:

```
Private Sub btnDemo1_Click(ByVal sender As System.Object, _
        ByVal e As System.EventArgs) Handles btnDemo1.Click

    ' This procedure passes an argument to the
    ' DisplayValue procedure.
    DisplayValue(5)
End Sub
```

This event procedure calls `DisplayValue` with 5 as the argument.

Step 3: Locate the `btnDemo2_Click` event procedure. The code is as follows:

```
Private Sub btnDemo2_Click(ByVal sender As System.Object, _
        ByVal e As System.EventArgs) Handles btnDemo2.Click

    ' This procedure calls the DisplayValue procedure
    ' several times, passing different arguments.
    DisplayValue(5)
    DisplayValue(10)
    DisplayValue(2)
    DisplayValue(16)
```

```
    ' Now, the value of an expression is passed to the
    ' DisplayValue procedure.
    DisplayValue(3 + 5)
End Sub
```

This event handler calls the `DisplayValue` procedure five times. Each procedure call is given a different argument. Notice the last procedure call:

```
DisplayValue(3 + 5)
```

This statement passes the value of an expression as the argument. When this statement executes, the value 8 is passed to `DisplayValue`.

Step 4: Locate the `btnDemo3_Click` event procedure. The code is as follows:

```
Private Sub btnDemo3_Click(ByVal sender As System.Object, _
ByVal e As System.EventArgs) Handles btnDemo3.Click

    ' This procedure uses a loop to call the DisplayValue
    ' procedure, passing a variable as the argument.
    Dim intCount As Integer
    For intCount = 1 To 10
      DisplayValue(intCount)
    Next intCount
End Sub
```

This event procedure has a local variable named `intCount`. It uses a `For...Next` loop to call the `DisplayValue` procedure ten times, each time passing the `intCount` variable as the argument.

Step 5: Run the application and click the *Demo 1* button. A message box appears displaying the value 5.

Step 6: Click the *Demo 2* button. Five successive message boxes are displayed, showing the values 5, 10, 2, 16, and 8.

Step 7: Click the *Demo 3* button. Ten successive message boxes are displayed, showing the values 1 through 10.

Step 8: Click the *Exit* button to end the application.

Passing Multiple Arguments

Often, it is useful to pass more than one argument to a procedure. For example, the following is a procedure that accepts two arguments:

```
Sub ShowSum(ByVal intNum1 As Integer, ByVal intNum2 As Integer)
   ' This procedure accepts two arguments, and displays their sum.

   Dim intSum As Integer
   intSum = intNum1 + intNum2
   MessageBox.Show("The sum is " & intSum.ToString())
End Sub
```

Assuming that `intValue1` and `intValue2` are integer variables, the following is an example call to the `ShowSum` procedure:

```
ShowSum(intValue1, intValue2)
```

When a procedure with multiple parameters is called, the arguments are assigned to the parameters in left-to-right order, as shown in Figure 6-11.

Figure 6-11 Multiple arguments passed to multiple parameters

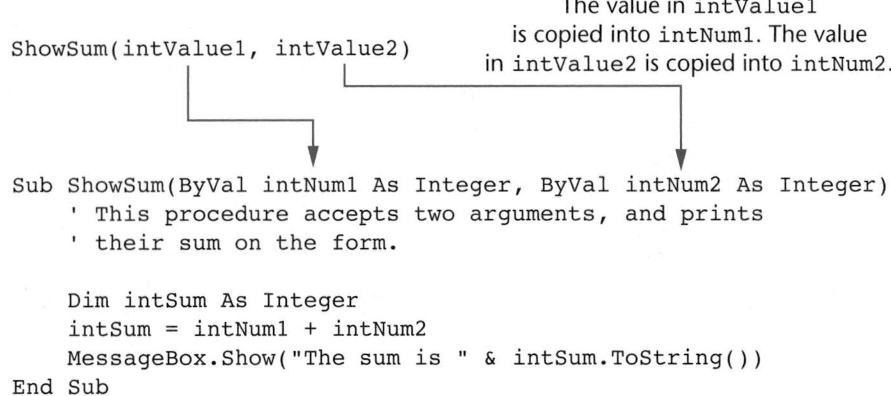
ShowSum(intValue1, intValue2)
The value in intValue1 is copied into intNum1. The value in intValue2 is copied into intNum2.

```
Sub ShowSum(ByVal intNum1 As Integer, ByVal intNum2 As Integer)
    ' This procedure accepts two arguments, and prints
    ' their sum on the form.

    Dim intSum As Integer
    intSum = intNum1 + intNum2
    MessageBox.Show("The sum is " & intSum.ToString())
End Sub
```

The following procedure call causes 5 to be assigned to the `intNum1` parameter and 10 to be assigned to `intNum2`:

```
ShowSum(5, 10)
```

However, the following procedure call causes 10 to be assigned to the `intNum1` parameter and 5 to be assigned to `intNum2`:

```
ShowSum(10, 5)
```

More about Passing Arguments by Reference

You have learned that when the `ByVal` keyword is used in the declaration of a parameter variable, an argument is passed by value to the parameter. This means that a copy of the argument is passed to the parameter variable. If the parameter's value is changed inside the procedure, it has no effect on the original argument.

When an argument is passed by reference, however, the procedure has access to the original argument. Any changes made to the parameter variable are actually performed on the original argument. Use the **`ByRef`** keyword in the declaration of a parameter variable to cause arguments to be passed by reference to the parameter. Here is an example:

```
Sub GetName(ByRef strName as String)
  ' Get the user's name
  strName = InputBox("Enter your name.")
End Sub
```

This procedure uses `ByRef` to declare the `strName` parameter. Any argument assigned to the parameter is passed by reference, and any changes made to `strName` are actually made to the argument passed into it. For example, assume the following code calls the procedure and displays the user name:

```
' Declare a string variable
Dim strUserName As String

' Get the user's name
GetName(strUserName)

' Display the user's name
MessageBox.Show("Your name is " & strUserName)
```

This code calls the `GetName` procedure and passes the string variable `strUserName`, by reference, into the `strName` parameter. The `GetName` procedure displays an input box instructing the user to enter his or her name. The user's input is stored in the `strName` variable. Because `strUserName` was passed by reference, the value stored in `strName` is actually stored in `strUserName`. When the message box is displayed, it shows the name entered by the user.

Tutorial 6-4 further demonstrates how passing an argument by reference differs from passing it by value.

Tutorial 6-4:
Working with `ByVal` and `ByRef`

In this tutorial, you examine a procedure that accepts a `ByVal` argument. Then you change `ByVal` to `ByRef`, to see how the procedure behaves differently.

Step 1: Open the *ByVal ByRef Demo* project from the student sample programs folder named *Chap6\ByVal ByRef Demo*. The application's form is shown in Figure 6-12. The form has a list box named `lstOutput` and two buttons named `btnGo` and `btnExit`.

Figure 6-12 *ByVal ByRef Demo* form

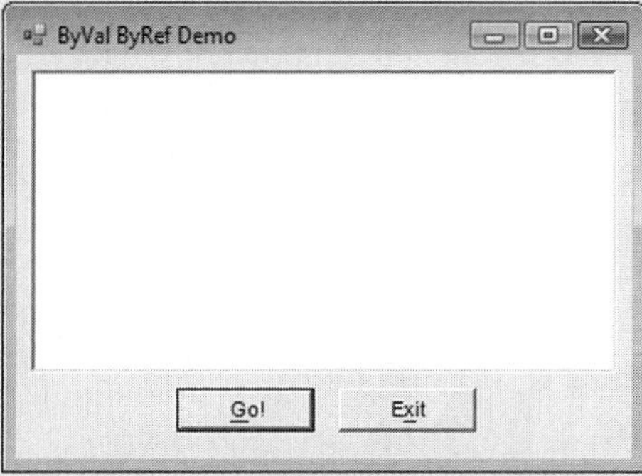

Step 2: Open the *Code* window and look at the `btnGo_Click` event procedure.

```
Private Sub btnGo_Click(ByVal sender As System.Object, _
    ByVal e As System.EventArgs) Handles btnGo.Click

  Dim intNumber As Integer = 100

  lstOutput.Items.Add("Inside btnGo_Click the value of " & _
      "intNumber is " & intNumber.ToString())
  lstOutput.Items.Add("Now I am calling ChangeArg.")

  ChangeArg(intNumber)
  lstOutput.Items.Add("Now back in btnGo_Click, the " _
      & "value of intNumber is " & intNumber.ToString())
End Sub
```

The variable `intNumber` is initialized to 100. This procedure calls the `ChangeArg` procedure and passes `intNumber` as the argument.

Step 3: Now look at the `ChangeArg` procedure. The code is as follows:

```
Sub ChangeArg(ByVal intArg As Integer)
  lstOutput.Items.Add("Inside the ChangeArg procedure, _
      I will " & "change the value of intArg.")
  intArg = 0
  lstOutput.Items.Add("intArg is now " & intArg)
End Sub
```

Notice that the parameter variable, `intArg`, is declared `ByVal`.

Step 4: Run the application and click the *Go!* button. The form should appear as shown in Figure 6-13. Although the `ChangeArg` procedure sets `intArg` to 0, the value of `intNumber` did not change. This is because the `ByVal` keyword was used in the declaration of `intArg`. (`intArg` was passed by value).

Figure 6-13 Results with argument passed by value

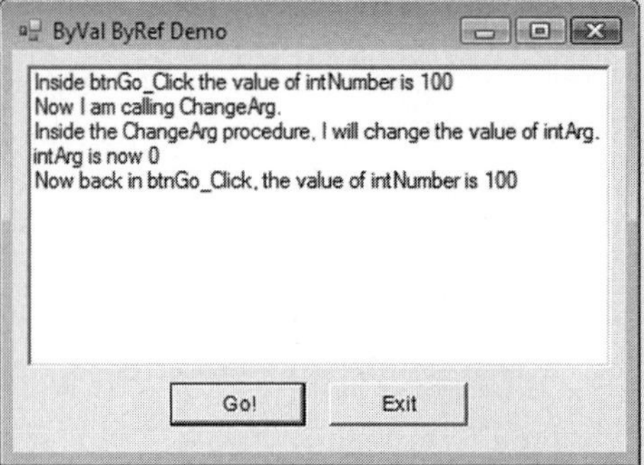
ByVal ByRef Demo
Inside btnGo_Click the value of intNumber is 100
Now I am calling ChangeArg.
Inside the ChangeArg procedure, I will change the value of intArg.
intArg is now 0
Now back in btnGo_Click, the value of intNumber is 100
Go!
Exit

Step 5: Click the *Exit* button to end the application.

Step 6: Open the *Code* window. Change `ByVal` in the `ChangeArg` procedure to `ByRef`. The first line of the procedure should now look like this:

```
Sub ChangeArg(ByRef intArg As Integer)
```

Step 7: Run the application again and click the *Go!* button. The form should appear as shown in Figure 6-14. This time, when `ChangeArg` sets `intArg` to 0, it changes the value of `intNumber` to 0. This is because the `ByRef` keyword was used in the declaration of `intArg`.

Step 8: Click the *Exit* button to end the application.

Figure 6-14 Results with argument passed by reference

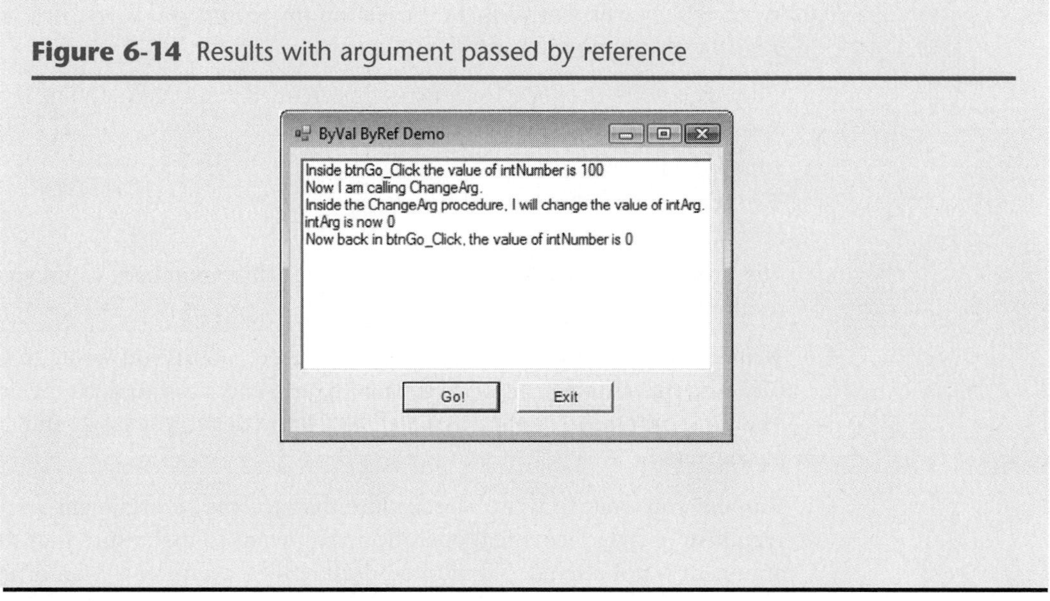
ByVal ByRef Demo
Inside btnGo_Click the value of intNumber is 100
Now I am calling ChangeArg.
Inside the ChangeArg procedure, I will change the value of intArg.
intArg is now 0
Now back in btnGo_Click, the value of intNumber is 0
Go!
Exit

NOTE: You have learned how to pass variables as arguments to procedures. You can also pass constants and expressions as arguments to procedures. Although you can pass both variable and nonvariable arguments by reference, only variable arguments can be changed by the procedure receiving the arguments. If you pass a nonvariable argument by reference to a procedure, the procedure cannot change the argument.

If You Want to Know More: Event Handler Parameters

When you create a code template for an event handler procedure, it always has two parameters. The following is an example of the first line of a button's `Click` event procedure:

```
Private Sub btnClear_Click(ByVal sender As System.Object,
  ByVal e As System.EventArgs) Handles btnClear.Click
```

The `sender` parameter references the object that triggered the event, and can be used to get information about that object. The `e` parameter contains values passed by the object that triggered the event. These values differ from one type of event to another. You do not use the `e` parameter in a `Click` event procedure, but in Chapter 5 we used it in the `Validating` event procedure. Other uses of the `e` parameter are determined by the type of event procedure being called.

Checkpoint

6.3 On paper, write the code for a procedure named `TimesTen`. The procedure must have an integer parameter variable named `intValue`. The procedure must multiply the parameter by 10 and display the result in a message box.

6.4 Write a statement that calls the `TimesTen` procedure you wrote in Checkpoint 6.3. Pass the number 25 as the argument.

6.5 On paper, write the code for a procedure named `PrintTotal`. The procedure must have the following parameters:

```
intNum1 As Integer
intNum2 As Integer
intNum3 As Integer
```

The procedure must calculate the total of the three numbers and display the result in a message box.

6.6 Write a statement that calls the `PrintTotal` procedure you wrote in Checkpoint 6.5. Pass the variables `intUnits`, `intWeight`, and `intCount` as the arguments. The three arguments will be assigned to the `intNum1`, `intNum2`, and `intNum3` parameters.

6.7 Suppose you want to write a procedure that accepts an argument, and uses the argument in a mathematical operation. You want to make sure that the original argument is not altered. Should you declare the parameter `ByRef` or `ByVal`?

6.3 Functions

CONCEPT: A function returns a value to the part of the program that called the function.

This section shows you how to write functions. Like a procedure, a function is a set of statements that perform a task when the function is called. In addition, a function returns a value that can be used in an expression.

VideoNote
Functions

In previous chapters, you called built-in Visual Basic functions many times. For instance, you used the `CInt` function to convert strings to integers. You also used the `ToString` function, which converts numbers to strings. Now you will learn to write your own functions that return values in the same way as built-in functions.

Declaring a Function

The general format of a function declaration is as follows:

```
[AccessSpecifier] Function FunctionName ([ParameterList]) _
As DataType
  [Statements]
End Function
```

A function declaration is similar to a procedure declaration. *AccessSpecifier* is optional, and specifies the accessibility of the function. As with procedures, you may use the keywords `Private`, `Public`, `Protected`, `Friend`, and `Protected Friend` as access specifiers. If you do not include an access specifier, it defaults to `Public`. Next is the keyword `Function`, followed by the name of the function. Inside the parentheses is an optional list of parameters. Following the parentheses is `As` *DataType*, where *DataType* is any data type. The data type listed in this part of the declaration is the data type of the value returned by the function.

The last line of a function declaration is the `End Function` statement. Between the `Function` statement and the `End Function` statements, are statements that execute when the function is called. Here is an example of a completed function:

```
Function Sum(ByVal sngNum1 As Single, ByVal sngNum2 As Single) _
    As Single

  Dim sngResult As Single
  sngResult = sngNum1 + sngNum2
  Return sngResult
End Function
```

This code shows a function named `Sum` that accepts two arguments, adds them, and returns their sum. (Everything you have learned about passing arguments to procedures applies to functions as well.) The `Sum` function has two parameter variables, `sngNum1` and `sngNum2`, both of the `Single` data type. Notice that the words `As Single` appear after the parentheses. This indicates that the value returned by the function will be of the `Single` data type.

Inside the function, the following lines appear:

```
Dim sngResult As Single
sngResult = sngNum1 + sngNum2
Return sngResult
```

The first line declares a local variable named `sngResult`. The second line adds the parameter variables `sngNum1` and `sngNum2` and stores the result in `sngResult`. The `Return` statement on the last line causes the function to end execution and return a value to the part of the program that called the function. The general format of the `Return` statement, when used to return a value from a function, is as follows:

```
Return Expression
```

`Expression` is the value to be returned. It can be any expression having value, such as a variable, a constant, or a mathematical expression. In this case, the `Sum` function returns the value in the `sngResult` variable. However, we could have eliminated the `sngResult` variable, and returned the expression `sngNum1 + sngNum2`, as shown in the following code:

```
Function Sum(ByVal sngNum1 As Single, ByVal sngNum2 As Single) _
    As Single
  Return sngNum1 + sngNum2
End Function
```

The data type of the `Return` statement's expression should be convertible to the function's return type. For example, if the `Sum` function returns a Single, the value of the `Return` statement's expression must be a type that automatically converts to Single. If the return value cannot be converted to the function's return data type, a runtime error occurs.

Calling a Function

Assuming that `sngTotal`, `sngValue1`, and `sngValue2` are variables of type Single, here is an example of how you might call the `Sum` function:

```
sngTotal = Sum(sngValue1, sngValue2)
```

This statement passes the variables `sngValue1` and `sngValue2` as arguments. It assigns the value returned by the `Sum` function to the variable `sngTotal`. So, if `sngValue1` is 20.0 and `sngValue2` is 40.0, the statement assigns 60.0 to `sngTotal`.

Figure 6-15 illustrates how the arguments are passed to the function and how a value is returned from the function.

Figure 6-15 Arguments passed and a value returned

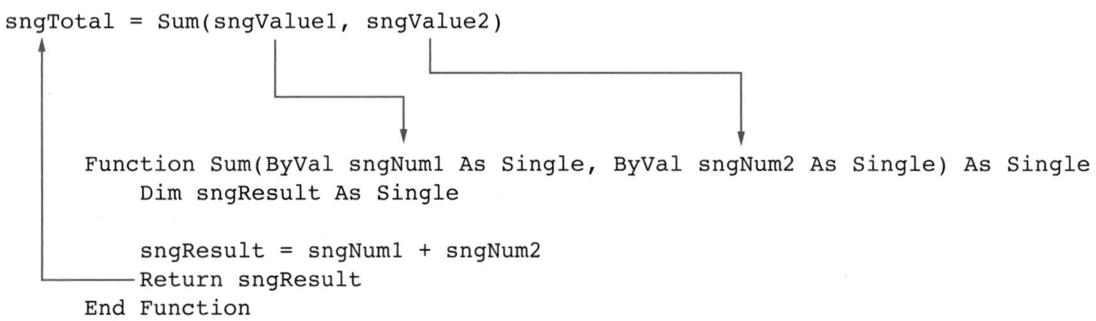

sngTotal = Sum(sngValue1, sngValue2)
Function Sum(ByVal sngNum1 As Single, ByVal sngNum2 As Single) As Single
Dim sngResult As Single
sngResult = sngNum1 + sngNum2
Return sngResult
End Function

In Tutorial 6-5, you examine an application that has several functions.

Tutorial 6-5:
Examining the *GPA Calculator* application

In this tutorial, you examine the *GPA Calculator* application, which allows a student to enter his or her grades and the number of credit hours for four courses, and then calculates the student's grade point average (GPA). The GPA is calculated in the following manner: The student receives a grade of A, B, C, D, or F for each course. Each course is then assigned a number of grade points, based on the grade. Table 6-1 shows the number of grade points assigned for each grade.

Table 6-1 Grade points assigned for each grade

Course Grade	Grade Points
A	4
B	3
C	2
D	1
F	0

Each course's grade points are multiplied by the course's credit hours, producing the course's quality points. The quality points for all the courses are then totaled and divided by the total number of credit hours. The result is the grade point average. Table 6-2 gives an example.

Table 6-2 Sample grade point average

Course Grade	Credit Hours	Grade Points	Course Quality Points
B	3	3	9
A	3	4	12
C	4	2	8
D	2	1	2
Total Credit Hours →	12	Total Quality Points →	31

GPA = Total Quality Points / Total Credit Hours
= 31 / 12
= 2.58

The *GPA Calculator* application uses functions to perform the necessary calculations.

Step 1: Open the *GPA Calculator* project from the student sample programs folder named *Chap6\GPA Calculator*. The application's form is shown in Figure 6-16.

The letter grades are entered into text boxes named `txtGrade1`, `txtGrade2`, `txtGrade3`, and `txtGrade4`. The course credit hours are entered into text boxes named `txtCreditHours1`, `txtCreditHours2`, `txtCreditHours3`, and `txtCreditHours4`. All these controls have `Validating` event procedures that ensure that the user has entered valid data.

Figure 6-16 *GPA Calculator* form

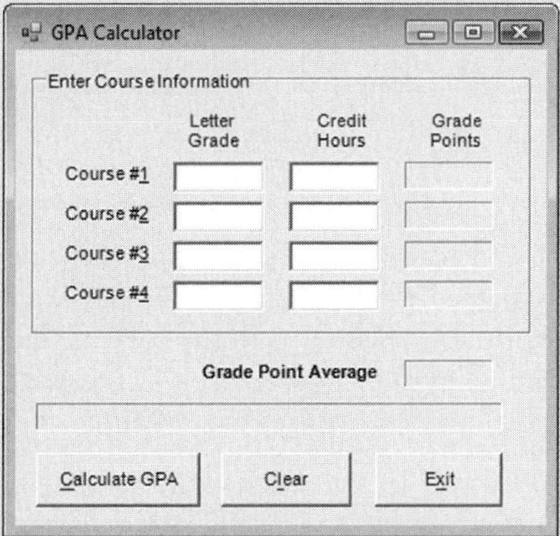

When the *Calculate GPA* button (`btnCalculate`) is clicked, the application displays the grade points for each course in the labels `lblGradePoints1`, `lblGradePoints2`, `lblGradePoints3`, and `lblGradePoints4`. The grade point average is displayed in a label named `lblGPA`.

Step 2: Open the *Code* window and look at the `btnCalculate_Click` event procedure. The code is as follows:

```
Private Sub btnCalculate_Click(ByVal sender As System.Object, _
    ByVal e As System.EventArgs) Handles btnCalculate.Click

  ' This event procedure displays the quality points for
  ' each course and the GPA.
  Dim intGradePoints As Integer
  Dim dblGradePointAvg As Double

  ' Display the quality points for course 1.
  intGradePoints = CalcGradePoints(txtGrade1.Text)
  lblGradePoints1.Text = intGradePoints.ToString()

  ' Display the quality points for course 2.
  intGradePoints = CalcGradePoints(txtGrade2.Text)
  lblGradePoints2.Text = intGradePoints.ToString()

  ' Display the quality points for course 3.
  intGradePoints = CalcGradePoints(txtGrade3.Text)
  lblGradePoints3.Text = intGradePoints.ToString()

  ' Display the quality points for course 4.
  intGradePoints = CalcGradePoints(txtGrade4.Text)
  lblGradePoints4.Text = intGradePoints.ToString()

  ' Get the grade point average and display
  ' it with 2 decimal places.
  dblGradePointAvg As Single = CalculatedGradeAverage()
  lblGPA.Text = dblGradePointAvg.ToString("n")

End Sub
```

Look at the first section of code following the variable declarations:

```
' Display the quality points for course 1.
intGradePoints = CalcGradePoints(txtGrade1.Text)
lblGradePoints1.Text = intGradePoints.ToString()
```

This code displays the grade points for course 1. The second line calls a function named `CalcGradePoints`, passing it `txtGrade1.Text`. The function's return value is assigned to the variable `intGradePoints`. The third line copies the value in `intgradePoints` to the `lblGradePoints1` label. There are similar sections of code for course 2, course 3, and course 4.

Step 3: Scroll down in the *Code* window and find the `CalcGradePoints` function. This function accepts a string argument containing a letter grade. It returns the number of grade points for that letter grade. The code for the function follows:

```
Function CalcGradePoints(ByVal strGrade As String) As Integer

  ' This function accepts a letter grade as an argument
  ' and returns the number of grade points for that grade.

  Dim intPoints As Integer

  Select Case strGrade.ToUpper()
    Case "A"
      intPoints = 4
```

```
    Case "B"
      intPoints = 3
    Case "C"
      intPoints = 2
    Case "D"
      intPoints = 1
    Case "F"
      intPoints = 0
    End Select
    ' Return the number of grade points.
    Return intPoints

End Function
```

This function uses a `Select Case` statement to determine the number of grade points, which is assigned to the `intPoints` variable. The `Return` statement returns the value of `intPoints`.

Step 4: Scroll back to the `btnCalculate_Click` event procedure. Look at the following line, which appears near the bottom of the procedure, after the grade points have been calculated and displayed for all four courses:

```
dblGradePointAvg As Double = CalculateGradeAverage()
```

The statement calls the `CalculateGradeAverage` function and assigns its return value to the `dblGradePointAvg` variable.

Step 5: Find the `CalculateGradeAverage` function.

First, it converts and assigns all the credit hours and grade points to integer variables:

```
Dim intHours1, intHours2, intHours3, intHours4 As Integer
intHours1 = CInt(txtCreditHours1.Text)
intHours2 = CInt(txtCreditHours2.Text)
intHours3 = CInt(txtCreditHours3.Text)
intHours4 = CInt(txtCreditHours4.Text)

Dim intPoints1, intPoints2, intPoints3, _
   intPoints4 As Integer
intPoints1 = CInt(lblGradePoints1.Text)
intPoints2 = CInt(lblGradePoints2.Text)
intPoints3 = CInt(lblGradePoints3.Text)
intPoints4 = CInt(lblGradePoints4.Text)
```

Next, it adds the credit hours for each course to a total named `intTotalCreditHours`.

```
' Get the total credit hours.
Dim intTotalCreditHours As Integer = _
  intHours1 + intHours2 + intHours3 + intHours4
```

Then, it multiplies each course's credit hours by its grade points. The sum of each product is added to the total quality points for all courses:

```
' Calculate the total quality points.
Dim intTotalQualityPoints As Integer = _
   (intHours1 * intPoints1) + (intHours2 * intPoints2) + _
   (intHours3 * intPoints3) + (intHours4 * intPoints4)
```

Finally, the grade point average is calculated by dividing the total quality points by the total credit hours.

```
  Return (intTotalQualityPoints / intTotalCreditHours)
End Function
```

Step 6: Scroll back to the `btnCalculate_Click` procedure and look at its last line.

```
lblGPA.Text = dblGradePointAvg.ToString("n")
```

This line formats `sngGradePointAvg` (holding the value returned from the `CalcGPA` function) and assigns it to `lblGPA.Text`.

Step 7: Run the application and enter the following values:

Course Grade	Credit Hours
B	3
A	3
C	4
D	2

Step 8: Click the *Calculate GPA* button. The form should look like the one shown in Figure 6-17.

Step 9: Click the *Exit* button to end the application.

Figure 6-17 Completed *GPA Calculator* form

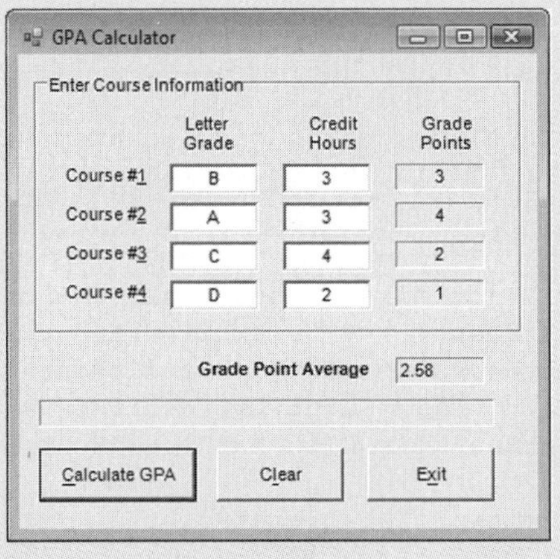

If You Want to Know More about Functions: Returning Nonnumeric Values

When writing functions, you are not limited to returning numeric values. You can return nonnumeric values, such as strings and Boolean values. For example, here is the code for a function that returns a String:

```
Function FullName(ByVal strFirst As String, ByVal strLast _
      As String) As String

   Dim strName As String
   strName = strLast & ", " & strFirst
   Return strName
End Function
```

Here is an example of a call to this function:

```
strCustomer = FullName("John", "Martin")
```

After this call, the string variable `strCustomer` will hold `"Martin, John"`.

Here is an example of a function that returns a Boolean value:

```
Function IsValid(intNum As Integer) As Boolean

  Dim blnStatus As Boolean
  If intNum >= 0 And intNum <= 100 Then
    blnStatus = True
  Else
    blnStatus = False
  End If

  Return blnStatus
End Function
```

This function returns *True* if its argument is within the range 0 to 100. Otherwise, it returns *False*. The following code segment has an `If...Then` statement with an example call to the function:

```
intValue = 20
If IsValid(intValue) Then
  MessageBox.Show("The value is within range.")
Else
  MessageBox.Show("The value is out of range.")
End If
```

When this code executes, it displays *The value is within range.* in a message box. Here is another example:

```
intValue = 200
If IsValid(intValue) Then
  MessageBox.Show("The value is within range.")
Else
  MessageBox.Show("The value is out of range.")
End If
```

When this code executes, it displays *The value is out of range.* in a message box.

Checkpoint

6.8 Look at the following function declaration and answer the questions below.

```
Function Distance(ByVal sngRate As Single, ByVal sngTime _
     As Single) As Single
```

a. What is the name of the function?
b. When you call this function, how many arguments do you pass to it?
c. What are the names of the parameter variables and what are their data types?
d. This function returns a value of what data type?

6.9 Write the first line of a function named `Days`. The function should return an integer value. It should have three integer parameters: `intYears`, `intMonths`, and `intWeeks`. All arguments should be passed by value.

6.10 Write an example function call statement for the function described in Checkpoint 6.9.

6.11 Write the first line of a function named `LightYears`. The function should return a value of the Single data type. It should have one parameter variable, `lngMiles`, of the Long data type. The parameter should be declared so that the argument is passed by value.

6.12 Write an example function call statement for the function described in Checkpoint 6.11.

6.13 Write the entire code for a function named `TimesTwo`. The function should accept an integer argument and return the value of that argument multiplied by two.

6.4 More about Debugging: Stepping Into, Over, and Out of Procedures and Functions

CONCEPT: Visual Basic debugging commands allow you to single-step through applications with procedure and function calls. The *Step Into* command allows you to single-step through a called procedure or function. The *Step Over* command allows you to execute a procedure or function call without single-stepping through its lines. The *Step Out* command allows you to execute all remaining lines of a procedure or function you are debugging.

In Chapter 3 you learned to set a breakpoint in your application's code and to single-step through the code's execution. Let's find out how to step into or step over a procedure or function and step out of a procedure or function. In Chapter 1 we showed how to configure Visual Studio to use Visual Basic keyboard settings. If you're using Visual Basic Express, the keyboard settings are set automatically.

When an application is in Break mode, the *Step Into* command causes the currently highlighted line (the execution point) to execute. If that line contains a call to a procedure or a function, the next highlighted line is the first line in that procedure or function. In other words, the *Step Into* command allows you to single-step through a procedure or function when it is called. Activate the *Step Into* command using one of the following methods:

- Press the F8 key
- Select *Debug* from the menu bar, and then select *Step Into* from the *Debug* menu
- Click the *Step Into* button ( ) on the *Debug Toolbar*, if the toolbar is visible

Like the *Step Into* command, the ***Step Over* command** causes the currently highlighted line to execute. If the line contains a procedure or function call, however, the procedure or function is executed without stepping through its statements. Activate the *Step Over* command using one of the following methods:

- Press Shift+F8
- Select *Debug* from the menu bar, and then select *Step Over* from the *Debug* menu
- Click the *Step Over* button ( ) on the *Debug Toolbar*, if the toolbar is visible

Use the ***Step Out* command** when single-stepping through a procedure or function, if you want the remainder of the procedure or function to complete execution without single-stepping. After the procedure or function has completed, the line following the procedure or function call is highlighted, and you may resume single-stepping. Activate the *Step Out* command using one of the following methods:

- Press Ctrl+Shift+F8
- Select *Debug* from the menu bar, and then select *Step Out* from the *Debug* menu
- Click the *Step Out* button ( ) on the *Debug Toolbar*, if the toolbar is visible

In Tutorial 6-6, you practice using each of these commands.

Tutorial 6-6:
Practicing the *Step Into*, *Step Over*, and *Step Out* commands

In this tutorial, you use the *GPA Calculator* application to practice single-stepping through procedures and functions.

Step 1: Open the *GPA Calculator* project from Tutorial 6-5.

Step 2: Open the *Code* window and set a breakpoint at the line in the `btnCalculate_Click` event procedure shown in Figure 6-18.

Figure 6-18 Location of breakpoint

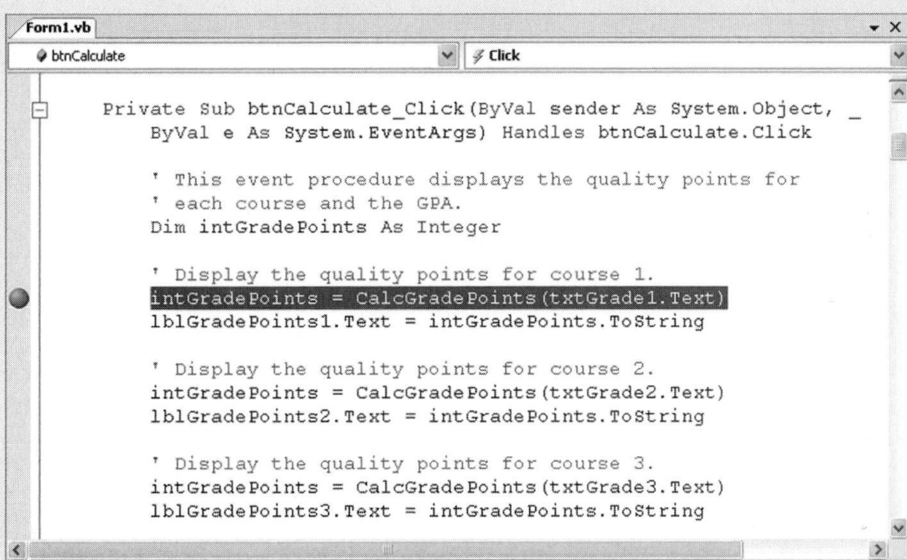

Form1.vb
btnCalculate
Click
Private Sub btnCalculate_Click(ByVal sender As System.Object, _
ByVal e As System.EventArgs) Handles btnCalculate.Click
' This event procedure displays the quality points for
' each course and the GPA.
Dim intGradePoints As Integer
' Display the quality points for course 1.
intGradePoints = CalcGradePoints(txtGrade1.Text)
lblGradePoints1.Text = intGradePoints.ToString
' Display the quality points for course 2.
intGradePoints = CalcGradePoints(txtGrade2.Text)
lblGradePoints2.Text = intGradePoints.ToString
' Display the quality points for course 3.
intGradePoints = CalcGradePoints(txtGrade3.Text)
lblGradePoints3.Text = intGradePoints.ToString

TIP: Set a breakpoint by clicking the mouse while the pointer is positioned in the left margin, next to the line of code. You can also move the text cursor to the line you wish to set as a breakpoint, and then press [F9].

Step 3: Run the application in Debug mode, and enter some grade and credit hour values on the form. (Which values you enter is unimportant, as long as they are valid.)

Step 4: Click the *Calculate GPA* button. The application enters Break mode with the breakpoint line highlighted.

Step 5: Notice that the highlighted line contains a call to the `CalcGradePoints` function. Press [F8] to execute the *Step Into* command.

Step 6: Because you pressed [F8], the first line of the `CalcGradePoints` function is highlighted next. Continue pressing the [F8] key to single-step though the `CalcGradePoints` function. When the `End Function` line is highlighted, press [F8] once more to return to the line containing the function call.

Step 7: Press the F8 key two more times. The execution point should be positioned at the line shown in Figure 6-19. Notice that this line also contains a call to the `CalcGradePoints` function.

Figure 6-19 Execution point

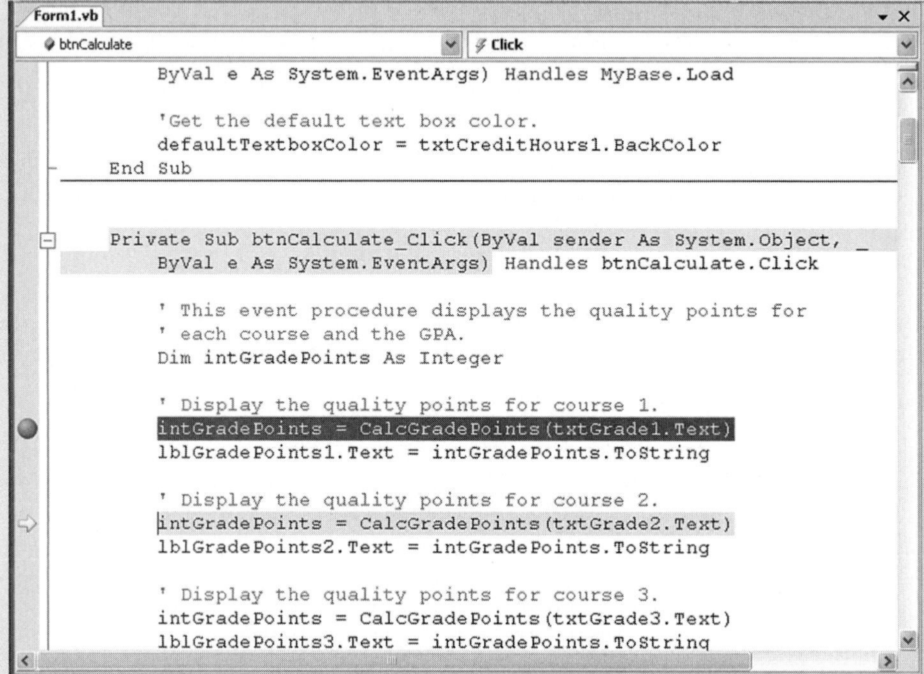
Form1.vb
btnCalculate
Click
ByVal e As System.EventArgs) Handles MyBase.Load
'Get the default text box color.
defaultTextboxColor = txtCreditHours1.BackColor
End Sub
Private Sub btnCalculate_Click(ByVal sender As System.Object, _
ByVal e As System.EventArgs) Handles btnCalculate.Click
' This event procedure displays the quality points for
' each course and the GPA.
Dim intGradePoints As Integer
' Display the quality points for course 1.
intGradePoints = CalcGradePoints(txtGrade1.Text)
lblGradePoints1.Text = intGradePoints.ToString
' Display the quality points for course 2.
intGradePoints = CalcGradePoints(txtGrade2.Text)
lblGradePoints2.Text = intGradePoints.ToString
' Display the quality points for course 3.
intGradePoints = CalcGradePoints(txtGrade3.Text)
lblGradePoints3.Text = intGradePoints.ToString

Step 8: Execute the *Step Over* command by pressing Shift+F8. The line executes the function call without single-stepping through it. The next line is now highlighted.

TIP: When the current execution point does not contain a procedure or function call, the *Step Into* and *Step Over* commands perform identically.

Step 9: Press F8 one time. The line that is now highlighted should also contain a call to the `CalcGradePoints` function. Press F8 again to step into the function.

Step 10: Because you pressed F8, the first line of the `CalcGradePoints` function should be highlighted. Press the F8 key once more to advance to the next line in the function.

Step 11: Instead of continuing to step through the function, you will now step out of the function. Now press Ctrl+Shift+F8 to execute the *Step Out* command. Single-stepping is suspended while the remaining statements in the `CalcGPA` function execute. You are returned to the `btnCalculate_Click` procedure, at the line containing the function call.

Step 12: Press F5 or click *Debug* on the menu bar and then click *Continue* to exit Break mode and resume run mode.

Step 13: Click the *Exit* button to end the application.

6.14 Suppose you are debugging an application in Break mode, and are single-stepping through a function that has been called. If you want to execute the remaining lines of the function and return to the line that called the function, what command do you use? What key(s) do you press to execute this command?

6.15 Suppose you are debugging an application in Break mode and the current execution point contains a procedure call. If you want to single-step through the procedure that is being called, what command do you use? What key(s) do you press to execute this command?

6.16 Suppose you are debugging an application in Break mode, and the current execution point contains a function call. If you want to execute the line, but not single-step through the function, what command do you use? What key(s) do you press to execute this command?

6.5 Focus on Program Design and Problem Solving: Building the *Bagel and Coffee Price Calculator* Application

CONCEPT: In this section you build the *Bagel and Coffee Price Calculator* application. It uses procedures and functions to calculate the total of a customer order.

Brandi's Bagel House has a bagel and coffee delivery service for the businesses in her neighborhood. Customers may call in and order white and whole wheat bagels with a variety of toppings. Additionally, customers may order three different types of coffee. Here is a complete price list:

Bagels:

White bagel	$1.25
Whole wheat bagel	$1.50

Toppings:

Cream cheese	$0.50
Butter	$0.25
Blueberry jam	$0.75
Raspberry jam	$0.75
Peach jelly	$0.75

Coffee:

Regular coffee	$1.25
Cappuccino	$2.00
Café au lait	$1.75

(*Note:* Delivery for coffee alone is not offered.)

Brandi, the owner, has asked you to write an application that her staff can use to record an order as it is called in. The application should display the total of the order, including 6% sales tax. Figure 6-20 shows a sketch of the application's form and identifies all the controls with programmer-defined names.

Figure 6-20 Sketch of *Brandi's Bagel House* form

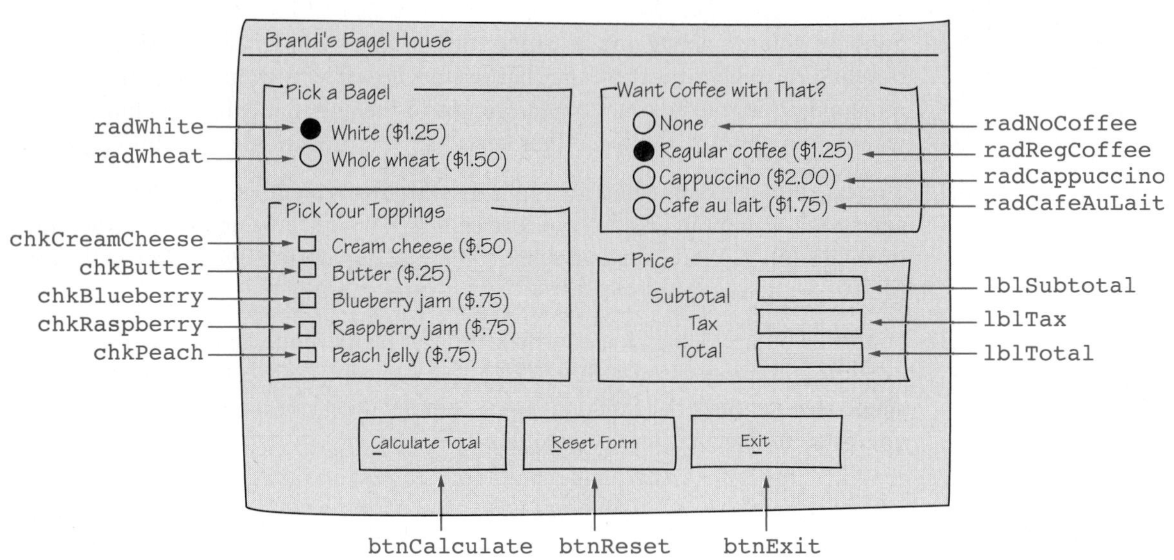

Table 6-3 lists each control, along with any relevant property settings.

Table 6-3 *Bagel and Coffee Calculator* controls

Control Type	Control Name	Property	Property Value
Form	(Default)	Text:	*Brandi's Bagel House*
ToolTip	(Default)		(Retain all default property settings.)
GroupBox	(Default)	Text:	*Pick a Bagel*
RadioButton	`radWhite`	Text: Checked: ToolTip on ToolTip1:	*White ($1.25)* *True* *Click here to choose a white bagel.*
RadioButton	`radWheat`	Text: ToolTip on ToolTip1:	*Whole Wheat ($1.50)* *Click here to choose a whole wheat bagel.*
GroupBox	(Default)	Text:	*Pick Your Toppings*
CheckBox	`chkCreamCheese`	Text: ToolTip on ToolTip1:	*Cream Cheese ($.50)* *Click here to choose cream cheese.*
CheckBox	`chkButter`	Text: ToolTip on ToolTip1:	*Butter ($.25)* *Click here to choose butter.*

(*continued*)

Table 6-3 *Bagel and Coffee Calculator* controls (*continued*)

Control Type	Control Name	Property	Property Value
CheckBox	`chkBlueberry`	Text: ToolTip on ToolTip1:	*Blueberry Jam ($.75)* *Click here to choose blueberry jam.*
CheckBox	`chkRaspBerry`	Text: ToolTip on ToolTip1:	*Raspberry Jam ($.75)* *Click here to choose raspberry jam.*
CheckBox	`chkPeach`	Text: ToolTip on ToolTip1:	*Peach Jelly ($.75)* *Click here to choose peach jelly.*
GroupBox	(Default)	Text:	*Want coffee with that?*
RadioButton	`radNoCoffee`	Text: ToolTip on ToolTip1:	None *Click here to choose no coffee.*
RadioButton	`radRegCoffee`	Text: Checked: ToolTip on ToolTip1:	*Regular Coffee ($1.25)* *True* *Click here to choose regular coffee.*
RadioButton	`radCappuccino`	Text: ToolTip on ToolTip1:	*Cappuccino ($2.00)* *Click here to choose cappuccino.*
RadioButton	`radCafeAuLait`	Text: Checked: ToolTip on ToolTip1:	*Cafe au lait ($1.75)* *False* *Click here to choose cafe au lait.*
GroupBox	(Default)	Text:	*Price*
Label	(Default)	Text:	*Subtotal*
Label	`lblSubtotal`	Text: AutoSize: BorderStyle:	 *False* *Fixed3D*
Label	(Default)	Text:	*Tax*
Label	`lblTax`	Text: AutoSize: BorderStyle:	 *False* *Fixed3D*
Label	(Default)	Text:	*Total*
Label	`lblTotal`	Text: AutoSize: BorderStyle:	 *False* *Fixed3D*
Button	`btnCalculate`	Text: ToolTip on ToolTip1:	*&Calculate Total* *Click here to calculate the total of the order.*
Button	`btnReset`	Text: ToolTip on ToolTip1:	*&Reset Form* *Click here to clear the form and start over.*
Button	`btnExit`	Text: ToolTip on ToolTip1:	*E&xit* *Click here to exit.*

Table 6-4 lists and describes the methods (event procedures, procedures, and functions) used in this application.

Table 6-4 Methods for *Bagel and Coffee Calculator*

Method	Type of Method	Description
`btnCalculate_Click`	Event procedure	Calculates and displays the total of an order. Calls the following functions: `BagelCost`, `CoffeeCost`, `ToppingCost`, and `CalcTax`.
`btnExit_Click`	Event procedure	Ends the application.
`btnReset_Click`	Event procedure	Resets the controls on the form to their initial values. Calls the following procedures: `ResetBagels`, `ResetToppings`, `ResetCoffee`, `ResetPrice`.
`BagelCost`	Function	Returns the price of the selected bagel.
`ToppingCost`	Function	Returns the total price of the selected toppings.
`CoffeeCost`	Function	Returns the price of the selected coffee.
`CalcTax`	Function	Accepts an argument, `amount`, which is the amount of a sale. Returns the amount of sales tax on that amount. The tax rate is stored in a class-level constant, `taxRate`.
`ResetBagels`	Procedure	Resets the bagel type radio buttons to their initial value.
`ResetToppings`	Procedure	Resets the topping check boxes to unchecked.
`ResetCoffee`	Procedure	Resets the coffee radio buttons to their initial values.
`ResetPrice`	Procedure	Sets the `lblSubtotal`, `lblTax`, and `lblTotal` labels to `""`.

Figure 6-21 shows a flowchart for the `btnCalculate_Click` event procedure. This procedure calculates the total of an order and displays its price. Notice that very little math is actually performed in this procedure, however. It calls the `BagelCost`, `ToppingCost`, `CoffeeCost`, and `CalcTax` functions to get the values it needs.

Notice that a new flowchart symbol, which represents a call to a procedure or function, is introduced.

Pseudocode for the `btnCalculate_Click` procedure is as follows:

subtotal = BagelCost() + ToppingCost() + CoffeeCost()
tax = CalcTax(subtotal)
total = subtotal + tax

lblSubtotal.Text = subtotal
lblTax.Text = tax
lblTotal.Text = total

Figure 6-22 shows a flowchart for the `btnReset_Click` event procedure. The purpose of this procedure is to reset all the radio buttons, check boxes, and labels on the form to their initial values. This operation has been broken into the following procedures: `ResetBagels`, `ResetToppings`, `ResetCoffee`, `ResetPrice`. When `btnReset_Click` executes, it simply calls these procedures.

Pseudocode for the `btnReset_Click` procedure is as follows:

ResetBagels()
ResetToppings()
ResetCoffee()
ResetPrice()

Figure 6-21 Flowchart for `btnCalculate_Click` event procedure

Figure 6-22 Flowchart for `btnReset_Click` event procedure

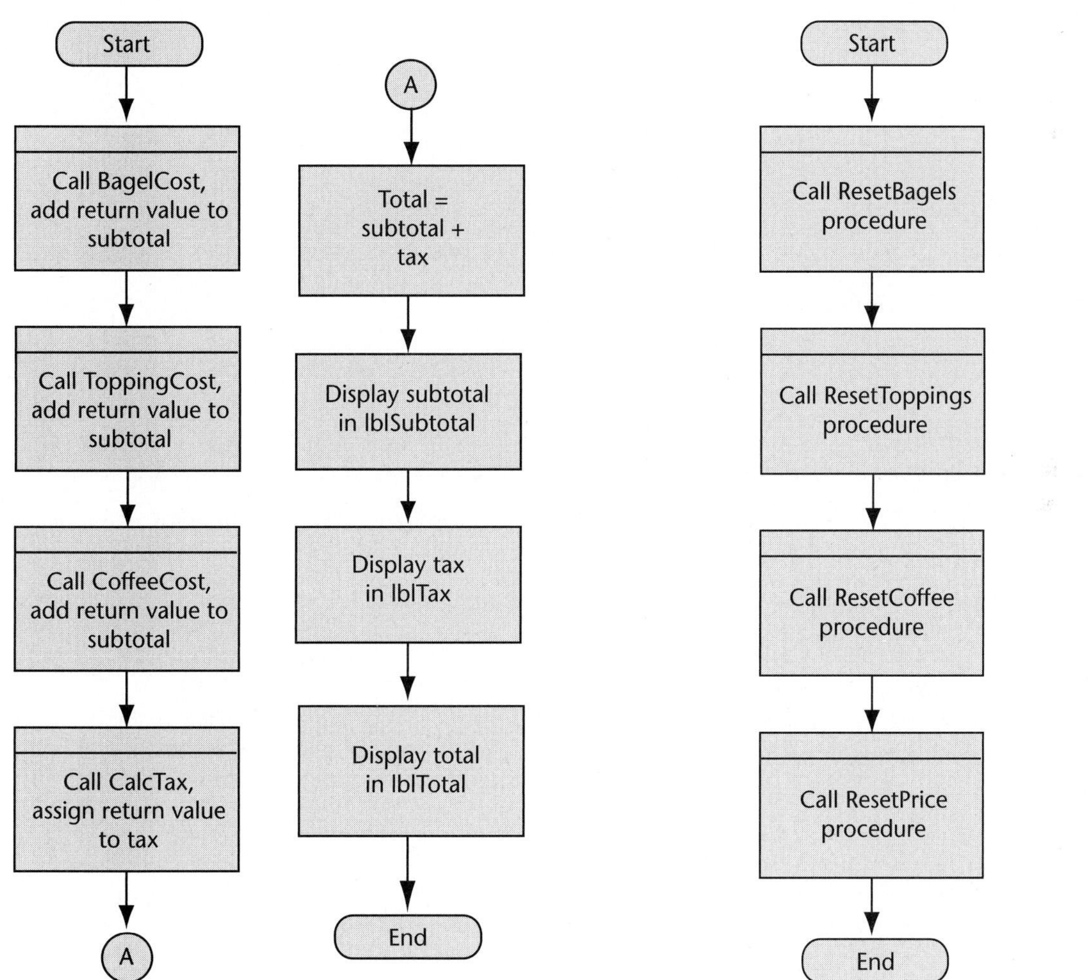

Figure 6-23 shows a flowchart for the `BagelCost` function. This function determines whether the user has selected white or whole wheat, and returns the price of that selection.

Figure 6-23 Flowchart for `BagelCost` function

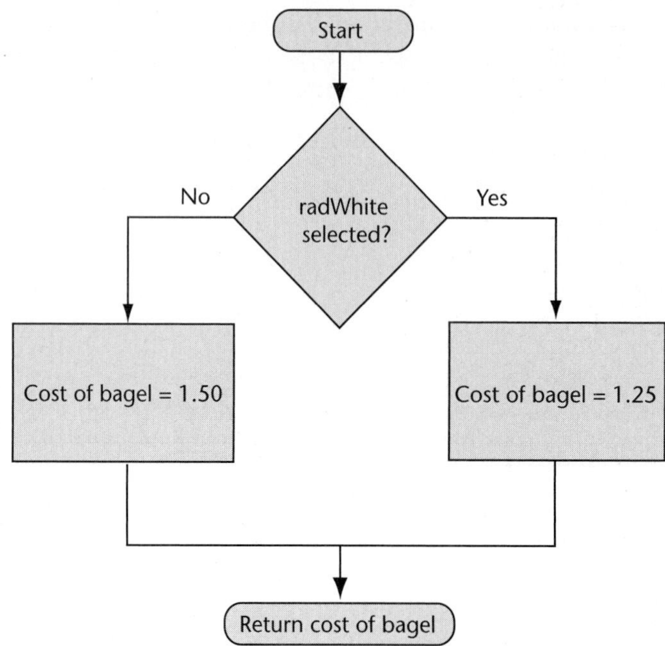

Pseudocode for the `BagelCost` function is as follows:

If radWhite Is Selected Then
   cost of bagel = 1.25
Else
   cost of bagel = 1.5
End If
Return cost of bagel

Figure 6-24 shows a flowchart for the `ToppingCost` function. This function examines the topping check boxes to determine which toppings the user has selected. The total topping price is returned.

Pseudocode for the `ToppingCost` function is as follows:

cost of topping = 0.0
If chkCreamCheese Is Selected Then
   cost of topping += 0.5
End If
If chkButter Is Selected Then
   cost of topping += 0.25
End If
If chkBlueberry Is Selected Then
   cost of topping += 0.75
End If
If chkRaspberry Is Selected Then
   cost of topping += 0.75
End If
If chkPeach Is Selected Then
   cost of topping += 0.75
End If
Return cost of topping

Figure 6-24 Flowchart for `ToppingCost` function

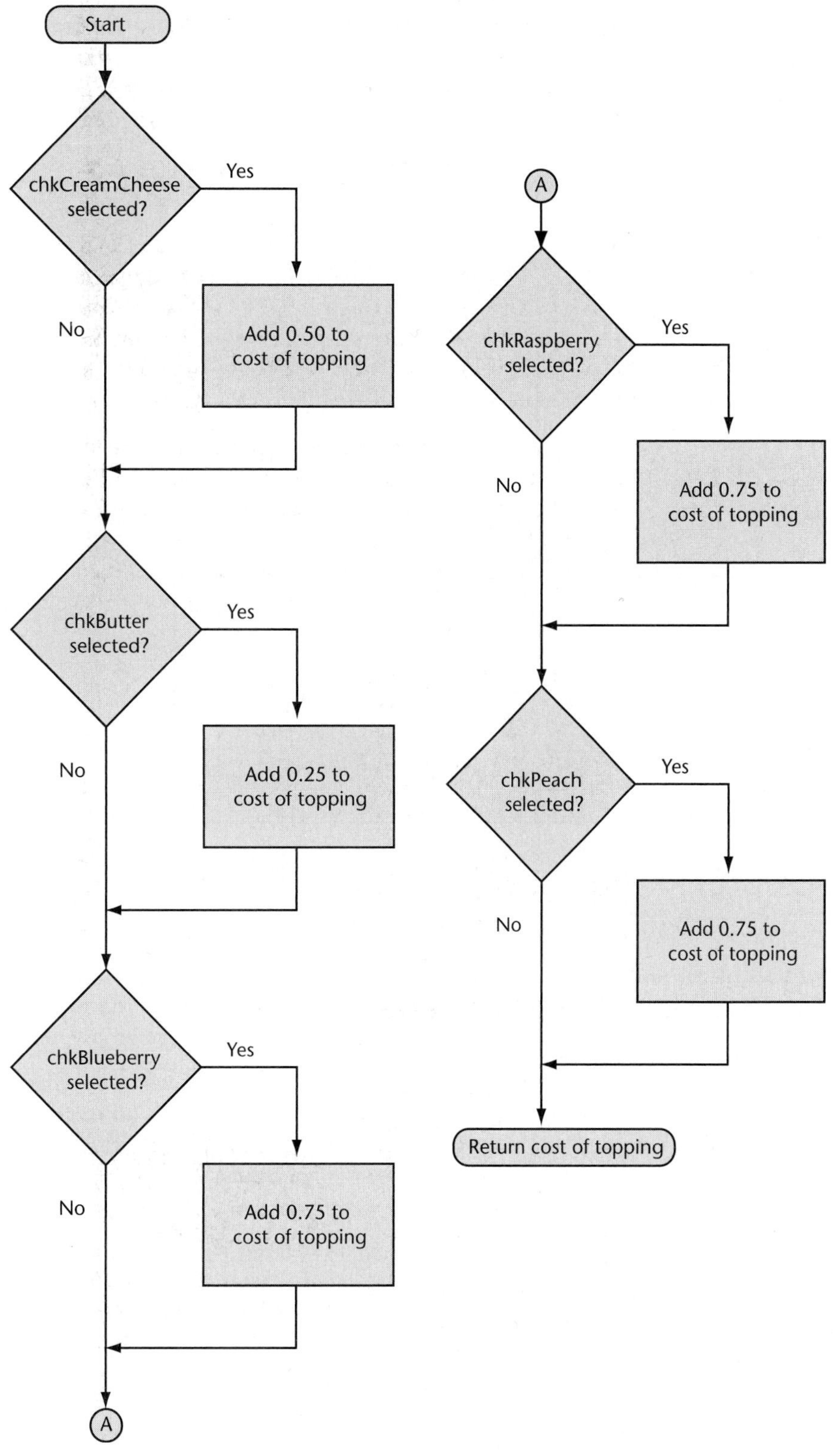

Figure 6-25 shows a flowchart for the `CoffeeCost` function. This function examines the coffee radio buttons to determine which coffee (if any) the user has selected. The price is returned.

Figure 6-25 Flowchart for `CoffeeCost` function

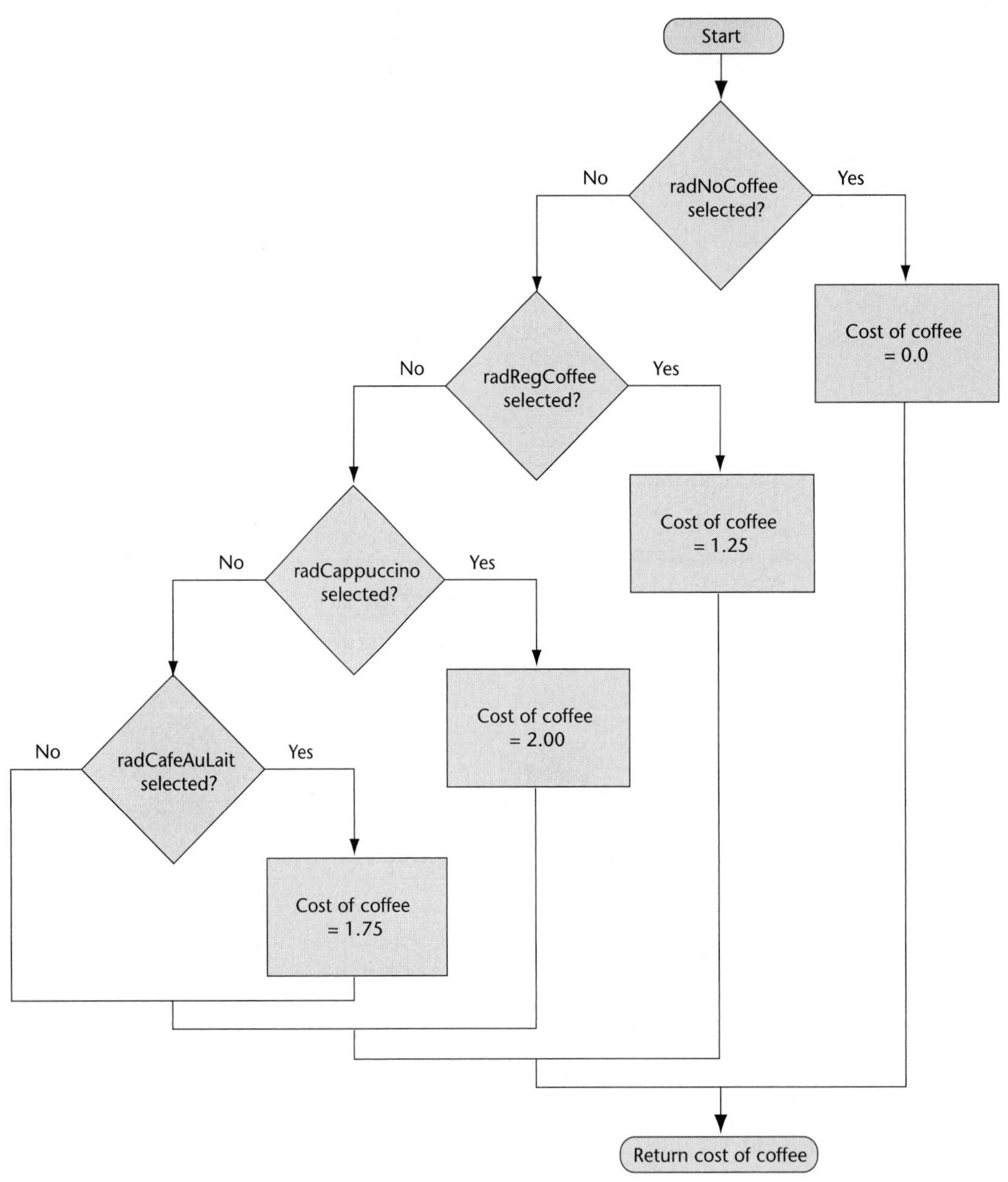

Pseudocode for the `CoffeeCost` function is as follows:

If radNoCoffee Is Selected Then
cost of coffee = 0
ElseIf radRegCoffee Is Selected Then
cost of coffee = 1.25
ElseIf radCappuccino Is Selected Then
cost of coffee = 2
ElseIf radCafeAuLait Is Selected Then
cost of coffee = 1.75
End If
Return cost of coffee

Figure 6-26 shows a flowchart for the `CalcTax` function. Note that `CalcTax` accepts an argument, which is passed into the `amount` parameter variable. The value tax rate holds the sales tax rate. The amount of sales tax is returned.

Pseudocode for the `CalcTax` function is as follows:

*sales tax = amount * taxRate*
Return sales tax

Figure 6-27 shows a flowchart for the `ResetBagels` procedure. This procedure resets the bagel radio buttons to their initial values.

Pseudocode for the `ResetBagels` procedure is as follows:

radWhite = Selected
radWheat = Deselected

Figure 6-26 Flowchart for `CalcTax` function

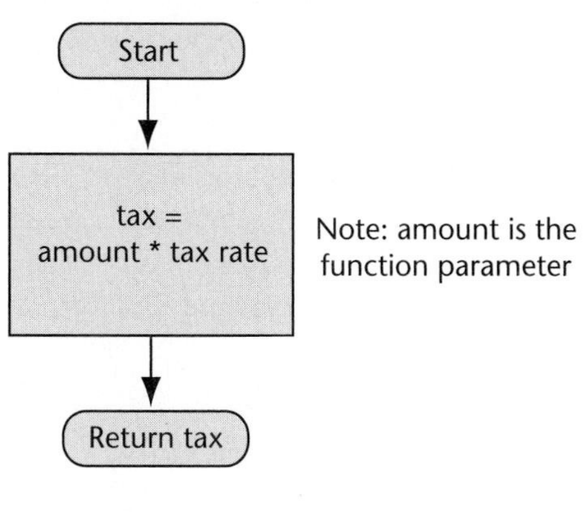

Figure 6-27 Flowchart for `ResetBagels` procedure

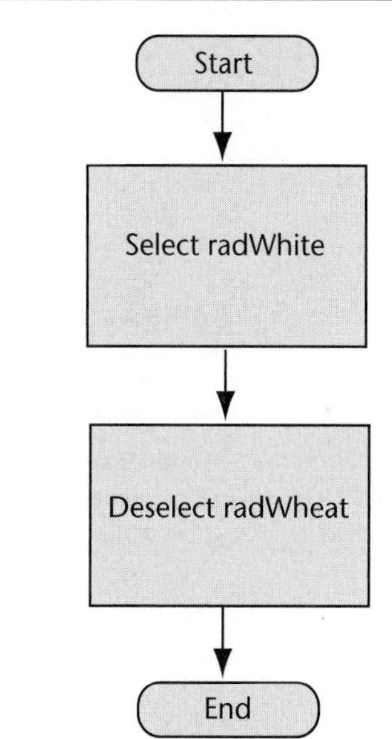

Figure 6-28 shows a flowchart for the `ResetToppings` procedure. This procedure unchecks all the topping check boxes.

Pseudocode for the `ResetToppings` procedure is as follows:

chkCreamCheese= Unchecked
chkButter = Unchecked
chkBlueberry= Unchecked
chkRaspberry= Unchecked
chkPeach = Unchecked

Figure 6-29 shows a flowchart for the `ResetCoffee` procedure. This procedure resets the coffee radio buttons to their initial values.

Figure 6-28 Flowchart for `ResetToppings` procedure

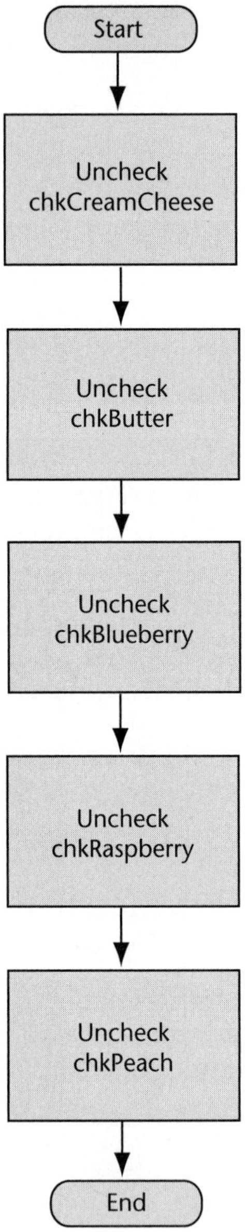

Start
Uncheck chkCreamCheese
Uncheck chkButter
Uncheck chkBlueberry
Uncheck chkRaspberry
Uncheck chkPeach
End

Figure 6-29 Flowchart for `ResetCoffee` procedure

Start
Deselect radNoCoffee
Select radRegCoffee
Deselect radCappuccino
Deselect radCafeAuLait
End

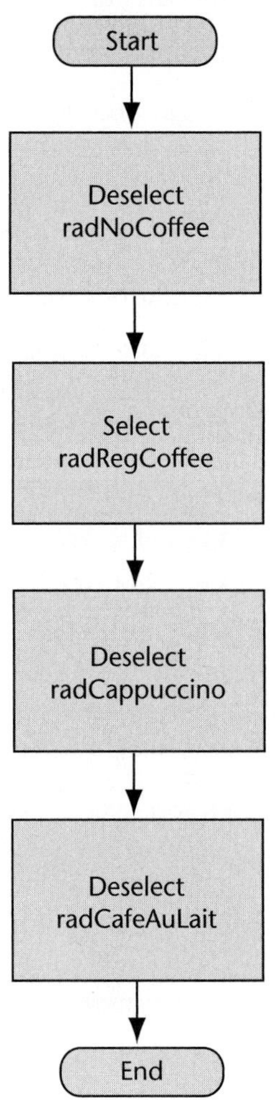

Pseudocode for the `ResetCoffee` procedure is as follows:

radNoCoffee = Deselected
radRegCoffee = Selected
radCappuccino = Deselected
radCafeAuLait = Deselected

Figure 6-30 shows a flowchart for the `ResetPrice` procedure. This procedure copies an empty string to `lblSubtotal`, `lblTax`, and `lblTotal`.

Figure 6-30 Flowchart for `ResetPrice` procedure

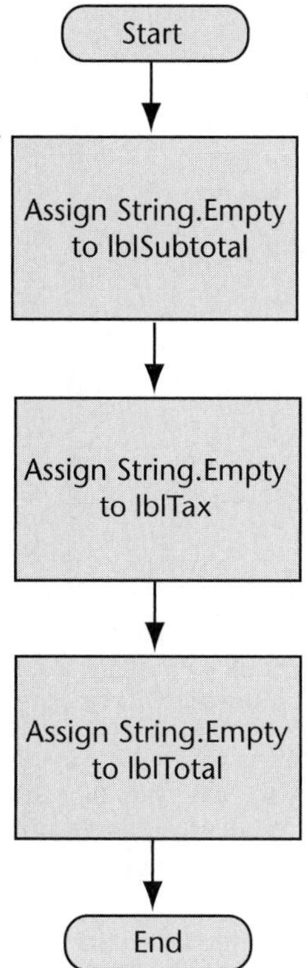

Pseudocode for the `ResetPrice` procedure is as follows:

lblSubtotal.Text = String.Empty
lblTax.Text = String.Empty
lblTotal.Text = String.Empty

In Tutorial 6-7, you build the *Bagel House* application.

Tutorial 6-7:
Building the *Bagel House* application

Step 1: Create a new Visual Basic Windows application named *Bagel House*.

Step 2: Set up the form as shown in Figure 6-31. Refer to Figure 6-20 and Table 6-3 for specific details about the controls and their properties.

Step 3: Once you have placed all the controls on the form and set their properties, you can begin writing the code. Start by opening the *Code* window and writing the following comments and class-level variable declaration:

```
' This application calculates the total order for a bagel and
' coffee at Brandi's Bagel house. The application uses
' several functions to calculate the total cost.

Const decTAX_RATE As Decimal = 0.06D      ' Sales tax rate
```

Figure 6-31 *Brandi's Bagel House* form

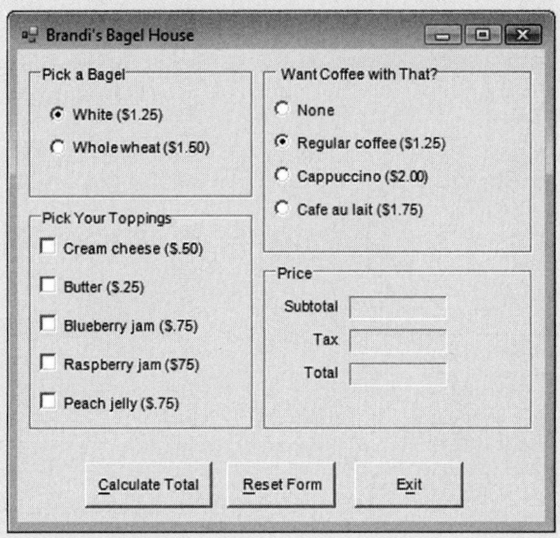

Step 4: Now write the `btnCalculate_Click`, `btnReset_Click`, and `btnExit_Click` event procedures, as follows:

```
Private Sub btnCalculate_Click(ByVal sender As System.Object, _
      ByVal e As System.EventArgs) Handles btnCalculate.Click
   ' This procedure calculates the total of an order.

   Dim decSubtotal As Decimal        ' Holds the order subtotal
   Dim decTax As Decimal             ' Holds the sales tax
   Dim decTotal As Decimal           ' Holds the order total

   decSubtotal = BagelCost() + ToppingCost() + CoffeeCost()
   decTax = CalcTax(decSubtotal)
   decTotal = decSubtotal + decTax

   lblSubtotal.Text = decSubtotal.ToString("c")
   lblTax.Text = decTax.ToString("c")
   lblTotal.Text = decTotal.ToString("c")
End Sub

Private Sub btnReset_Click(ByVal sender As System.Object, _
      ByVal e As System.EventArgs) Handles btnReset.Click
   ' This procedure resets the controls to default values.

   ResetBagels()
   ResetToppings()
   ResetCoffee()
   ResetPrice()
End Sub

Private Sub btnExit_Click(ByVal sender As System.Object, _
      ByVal e As System.EventArgs) Handles btnExit.Click

   ' End the application
   Me.Close()
End Sub
```

Step 5: Write the code for the `BagelCost` function:

```
Function BagelCost() As Decimal
  ' This function returns the cost of the bagel.

  If radWhite.Checked = True Then
    Return 1.25D
  Else
    Return 1.5D
  End If
End Function
```

Step 6: Write the code for the `ToppingCost` function:

```
Function ToppingCost() As Decimal
  ' This function returns the cost of the toppings.

  Dim decCostOfTopping As Decimal = 0

  If chkCreamCheese.Checked = True Then
    decCostOfTopping += 0.5D
  End If
  If chkButter.Checked = True Then
    decCostOfTopping += 0.25D
  End If
  If chkBlueberry.Checked = True Then
    decCostOfTopping += 0.75D
  End If
  If chkRaspberry.Checked = True Then
    decCostOfTopping += 0.75D
  End If
  If chkPeach.Checked = True Then
    decCostOfTopping += 0.75D
  End If

  Return decCostOfTopping
End Function
```

Step 7: Write the code for the `CoffeeCost` function:

```
Function CoffeeCost() As Decimal
  ' This function returns the cost of the
  ' selected coffee.

  If radNoCoffee.Checked = True Then
    Return 0
  ElseIf radRegCoffee.Checked = True Then
    Return 1.25D
  ElseIf radCappuccino.Checked = True Then
    Return 2
  ElseIf radCafeAuLait.Checked = True Then
    Return 1.75D
  End If

End Function
```

Step 8: Write the code for the `CalcTax` function.

```
Function CalcTax(ByVal decAmount As Decimal) As Decimal
   ' This function receives the sale amount. It
   ' calculates and returns the sales tax, based
   ' on the sale amount.

   Return decAmount * decTAX_RATE
End Function
```

Step 9: Write the code for the `ResetBagels`, `ResetToppings`, `ResetCoffee`, and `ResetPrice` procedures.

```
Private Sub ResetBagels()
   ' This procedure resets the bagel selection.

   radWhite.Checked = True
End Sub

Sub ResetToppings()
   ' This procedure resets the topping selection.

   chkCreamCheese.Checked = False
   chkButter.Checked = False
   chkBlueberry.Checked = False
   chkRaspberry.Checked = False
   chkPeach.Checked = False
End Sub

Sub ResetCoffee()
   ' This procedure resets the coffee selection.

   radRegCoffee.Checked = True
End Sub

Sub ResetPrice()
   ' This procedure resets the price.

   lblSubtotal.Text = String.Empty
   lblTax.Text = String.Empty
   lblTotal.Text = String.Empty
End Sub
```

Step 10: Save and run the program. If there are errors, use debugging techniques you have learned to find and correct them.

Step 11: When you're sure the application is running correctly, save it one last time.

Summary

6.1 Procedures

- The declaration for a procedure begins with a `Sub` statement and ends with an `End Sub` statement. The code that appears between these two statements is the body of the procedure.
- When a procedure call executes, the application branches to that procedure and executes its statements. When the procedure has finished, the application branches back to the procedure call and resumes executing at the next statement.
- Static local variables are not destroyed when a procedure returns. They exist for the lifetime of the application, although their scope is limited to the procedure in which they are declared.
- To declare a static local variable, substitute the word `Static` for `Dim`.

6.2 Passing Arguments to Procedures

- A parameter is a special variable that receives an argument value passed into a procedure or function. If a procedure or function has a parameter, you must supply an argument when calling the procedure or function.
- When a procedure or function with multiple parameters is called, arguments are assigned to the parameters in left-to-right order.
- There are two ways to pass an argument to a procedure: by value or reference. Passing an argument by value means that only a copy of the argument is passed to the procedure. Because the procedure has only a copy, it cannot make changes to the original argument. When an argument is passed by reference, however, the procedure has access to the original argument and can make changes to it.

6.3 Functions

- A function returns a value to the part of the program that called it. Similar to a procedure, it is a set of statements that perform a task when the function is called.
- A value from a function is returned by the `Return` statement.

6.4 More about Debugging: Stepping Into, Over, and Out of Procedures and Functions

- Visual Basic debugging commands (*Step Into*, *Step Over*, and *Step Out*) allow you to step through application code and through called procedures and function.

6.5 Focus on Program Design and Problem Solving: Building the *Bagel and Coffee Price Calculator* Application

- This section outlines the process of building the *Bagel and Coffee Price Calculator* application, with a focus on program design and problem solving.

Key Terms

arguments
by reference (pass argument)
by value (pass argument)
`ByRef`
`ByVal`
`Call` keyword
event handler
event procedure
function
method
modularize
parameter
Pascal casing
procedure
procedure call
procedure declaration
`Static`
static local variables
Step Out command
Step Over command
`Sub` (reserved word)

Review Questions and Exercises

Fill-in-the-Blank

1. A(n) ________________ is a named block of code that performs a specific task and does not return a value.
2. A(n) ________________ statement causes a procedure to be executed.
3. A(n) ________________ is a named block of statements that executes and returns a value.
4. You return a value from a function with the ________________ statement.
5. ________________ local variables are not destroyed when a procedure returns.
6. Values passed to a procedure or function are called ________________.
7. A(n) ________________ is a special variable that receives an argument passed to a procedure or function.
8. When an argument is passed by ________________ a copy of the argument is assigned to the parameter variable.
9. When an argument is passed by ________________ the procedure has access to the original argument.
10. The ________________ debugging command allows you to single-step through a called procedure or function.

Multiple Choice

1. Which of the following terms means to divide an application's code into small, manageable procedures?
   a. Break
   b. Modularize
   c. Parameterize
   d. Bind
2. Which type of statement causes a procedure to execute?
   a. Procedure declaration
   b. Access specifier
   c. Procedure call
   d. Step Into

3. What happens when a procedure finishes executing?
    a. The application branches back to the procedure call, and resumes executing at the next line
    b. The application terminates
    c. The application waits for the user to trigger the next event
    d. The application enters Break mode
4. In what way is a function different from a procedure?
    a. A procedure returns a value and a function does not
    b. A function returns a value and a procedure does not
    c. A function must be executed in response to an event
    d. There is no difference
5. What type of local variable retains its value between calls to the procedure or function in which it is declared?
    a. `Private`
    b. `Persistent`
    c. `Permanent`
    d. `Static`
6. What is an argument?
    a. A variable that a parameter is passed into
    b. A value passed to a procedure or function when it is called
    c. A local variable that retains its value between procedure calls
    d. A reason not to create a procedure or function
7. What keyword is used in a parameter declaration to specify that the argument is passed by value?
    a. `ByVal`
    b. `Val`
    c. `Value`
    d. `AsValue`
8. When an argument is passed to a procedure this way, the procedure has access to the original argument and may make changes to it.
    a. By value
    b. By address
    c. By reference
    d. By default
9. Which of the following is a debugging command that causes a procedure or function to execute without single-stepping through the procedure's or function's code?
    a. *Step Into*
    b. *Step Through*
    c. *Jump Over*
    d. *Step Over*
10. Which of the following is a debugging command that is used when you are stepping through a procedure's code and you wish to execute the remaining statements in the procedure without single-stepping through them?
    a. *Jump Out*
    b. *Step Through*
    c. *Step Out*
    d. *Step Over*

True or False

Indicate whether the following statements are true or false.

1. T F: A general purpose procedure is associated with a specific control.
2. T F: You must use the `Call` keyword to execute a procedure.
3. T F: The declaration of a parameter variable looks like a regular variable declaration, except `ByVal` or `ByRef` is used instead of `Dim`.
4. T F: You can pass more than one argument to a procedure or function.
5. T F: If you write a procedure or function with a parameter variable, you do not have to supply an argument when calling the procedure.
6. T F: If you are debugging an application in Break mode and you want to single-step through a procedure that will be called in the highlighted statement, you use the *Step Over* command.

Short Answer

1. Why do nonstatic local variables lose their values between calls to the procedure or function in which they are declared?
2. What is the difference between an argument and a parameter variable?
3. Where do you declare parameter variables?
4. If you are writing a procedure that accepts an argument and you want to make sure that the procedure cannot change the value of the argument, what do you do?
5. When a procedure or function accepts multiple arguments, does it matter what order the arguments are passed in?
6. How do you return a value from a function?

What Do You Think?

1. What advantage is there to dividing an application's code into several small procedures?
2. How would a static local variable be useful?
3. Give an example in which passing an argument by reference would be useful.
4. Suppose you want to write a procedure to perform an operation. How do you decide if the procedure should be a procedure or a function?
5. When debugging an application, why would you not want to single-step through every procedure or function?

Find the Error

Locate the errors in the following code examples:

1.
```
Sub DisplayValue(Dim intNumber As Integer)
    ' This displays a value.
    MessageBox.Show(intNumber.ToString())
End Sub
```

2. The following is a procedure:

```
Sub Greeting(ByVal strName As String)
   ' This procedure displays a greeting.
   MessageBox.Show("Hello " & strName)
End Sub
```

And the following is a call to the procedure:

```
Greeting()
```

3. The following is a function:

```
Function Product(ByVal intNum1 As Integer, ByVal intNum2 _
      As Integer) As Integer
   Dim intResult As Integer
   intResult = intNum1 * intNum2
End Function
```

4. The following is a function:

```
Sub Sum(ByVal intNum1 As Single, ByVal intNum2 As Single) _
      As Single
   Dim intResult As Single
   intResult = intNum1 + intNum2
   Return intResult
End Sub
```

Algorithm Workbench

1. The following statement calls a function named `Half` that returns a Decimal, which is half of the argument. Write the function.

```
intResult = Half(intNumber)
```

2. An application contains the following function:

```
Function Square(ByVal intValue As Integer) As Integer
   Return intValue ^ 2
End Function
```

Write a statement that passes the value 4 to this function and assigns its return value to a variable named `intResult`.

3. Write a procedure named `TimesTen` that accepts a single Integer argument. When the procedure is called, it should display the product of its argument multiplied by 10 in a message box.

4. An application contains the following procedure:

```
Sub Display(ByVal intArg1 As Integer, ByVal strArg2 As String, _
      ByVal sngArg3 As Single)
   MessageBox.Show("Here are the values: " & _
         intArg1.ToString() & " " & _
         strArg2 & " " & sngArg3.ToString())
End Sub
```

Write a statement that calls the procedure and passes it the following variables:

```
Dim strName As String
Dim intAge As Integer
Dim sngIncome As Single
```

Programming Challenges

1. Retail Price Calculator

VideoNote

The Retail Price Calculator Problem

Write an application that accepts from the user the wholesale cost of an item and its markup percentage. (For example, if an item's wholesale cost is $5 and its retail price is $10, then the markup is 100%.)

The program should contain a function named `CalculateRetail` that receives the wholesale cost and markup percentage as arguments, and returns the retail price of the item. The application's form should look something like the one shown in Figure 6-32.

When the user clicks the *Get Retail* button, the program should do the following:

- Verify that the values entered by the user for the wholesale cost and the markup percent are numeric and not negative
- Call the `CalculateRetail` function
- Display the retail cost as returned from the function

2. Hospital Charges

Create an application that calculates the total cost of a hospital stay. The application should accept the following input:

- The number of days spent in the hospital
- The amount of medication charges
- The amount of surgical charges
- The amount of lab fees
- The amount of physical rehabilitation charges

The hospital charges $350 per day. The application's form should resemble the one shown in Figure 6-33.

Figure 6-32 *Retail Price Calculator* form

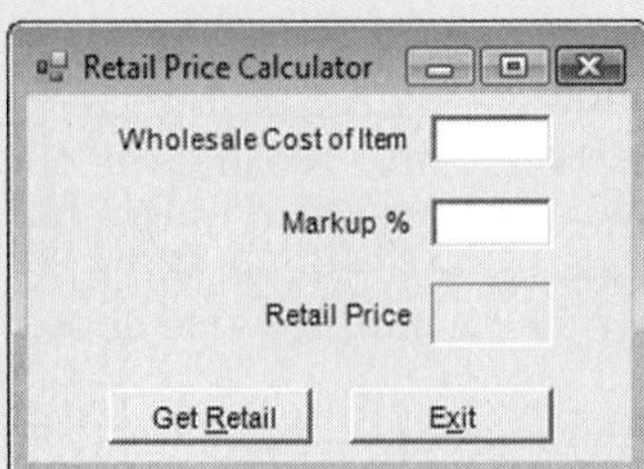

Figure 6-33 *Hospital Charges* form

Create the following functions:

`CalcStayCharges`	Calculates and returns the base charges for the hospital stay. This is computed as $350 times the number of days in the hospital.
`CalcMiscCharges`	Calculates and returns the total of the medication, surgical, lab, and physical rehabilitation charges.
`CalcTotalCharges`	Calculates and returns the total charges.

Input Validation: Do not accept a negative value for length of stay, medication charges, surgical charges, lab fees, or physical rehabilitation charges.

3. Order Status

The Middletown Wire Company sells spools of copper wiring for $100 each. The normal delivery charge is $10 per spool. Rush delivery costs $15 per spool. Create an application that displays the status of an order. The status should include the following:

- The number of spools ready to ship
- The number of spools on back order
- The shipping and handling charges
- The total amount due

The application's form should resemble the one shown in Figure 6-34.

Figure 6-34 *Order Status* form

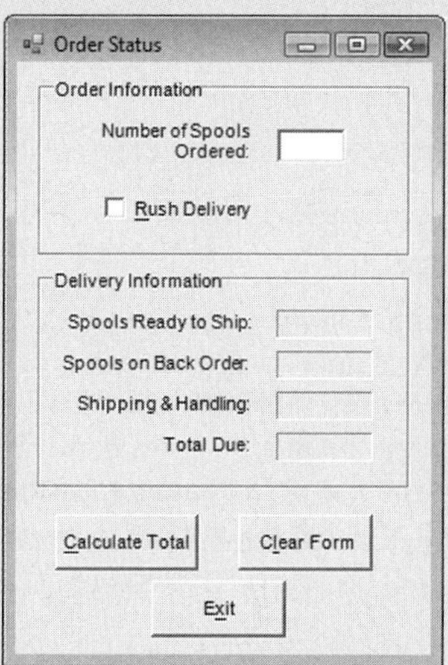

The user should enter the number of spools ordered into the text box, and check the *Rush Delivery* check box if rush delivery is desired. When the *Calculate Total* button is clicked, an input box should appear asking the user to enter the number of spools currently in stock. If the user has ordered more spools than are in stock, a portion of the order is back-ordered. For example, if the user orders 200 spools and there are only 150 spools in stock, then 150 spools are ready to ship and 50 spools are back-ordered.

The application should have the following functions, called from the *Calculate Total* button's `Click` event procedure:

`GetInStock` Displays an input box asking the user to enter the number of spools in stock. The function should return the value entered by the user.

`ReadyToShip` Accepts the following arguments: the number of spools in stock and the number of spools ordered. The function returns the number of spools ready to ship.

`BackOrdered` Accepts the following arguments: the number of spools in stock and the number of spools ordered. The function returns the number of spools on back order. If no spools are on back order, it returns 0.

`ShippingCharges` Accepts the following arguments: the number of spools ready to ship and the per-spool shipping charges. The function returns the total shipping and handling charges.

The application should have the following procedures, called from the *Clear Form* button's `Click` event procedure:

`ResetSpools` Clears the text box and the check box.

`ResetDelivery` Clears the labels that display the delivery information.

Input Validation: Do not accept orders for less than one spool.

4. **Joe's Automotive**

Joe's Automotive performs the following routine maintenance services:

- Oil change—$26.00
- Lube job—$18.00
- Radiator flush—$30.00
- Transmission flush—$80.00
- Inspection—$15.00
- Muffler replacement—$100.00
- Tire rotation—$20.00

Joe also performs other nonroutine services and charges for parts and labor ($20 per hour). Create an application that displays the total for a customer's visit to Joe's. The form should resemble the one shown in Figure 6-35. *Note*: Visual Studio lets you use an apostrophe in a project's name, but the apostrophe will prevent you from being able to run the project after it has been created.

The application should have the following functions:

`OilLubeCharges` Returns the total charges for an oil change and/or a lube job, if any.

`FlushCharges` Returns the total charges for a radiator flush and/or a transmission flush, if any.

`MiscCharges` Returns the total charges for an inspection, muffler replacement, and/or a tire rotation, if any.

`OtherCharges` Returns the total charges for other services (parts and labor), if any.

`TaxCharges` Returns the amount of sales tax, if any. Sales tax is 6%, and is only charged on parts. If the customer purchased services only, no sales tax is charged.

`TotalCharges` Returns the total charges.

Figure 6-35 *Joe's Automotive* form

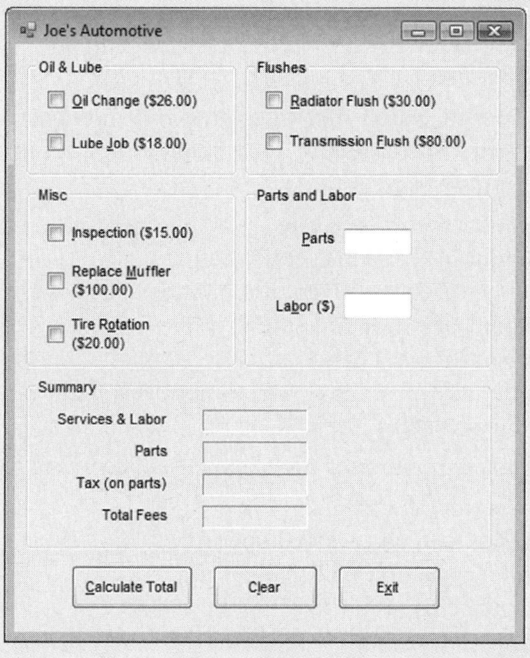

The application should have the following procedures, called when the user clicks the *Clear* button:

`ClearOilLube`	Clears the check boxes for oil change and lube job.
`ClearFlushes`	Clears the check boxes for radiator flush and transmission flush.
`ClearMisc`	Clears the check boxes for inspection, muffler replacement, and tire rotation.
`ClearOther`	Clears the text boxes for parts and labor.
`ClearFees`	Clears the labels that display the labels in the section marked *Summary*.

Input validation: Do not accept negative amounts for parts and labor charges.

Design Your Own Forms

5. **Password Verifier**

You will develop a software package that requires users to enter their passwords. Your software requires users' passwords to meet the following criteria:

- The password should be at least six characters long
- The password should contain at least one numeric digit and at least one alphabetic character

Create an application that asks the user to enter a password. The application should use a function named `IsValid` to verify that the password meets the criteria. It should display a message indicating whether the password is valid or invalid.

The `IsValid` function should accept a string as its argument and return a Boolean value. The string argument is the password to be checked. If the password is valid, the function should return *True*. Otherwise, it should return *False*.

> **TIP:** Refer to Chapter 4 for more information about working with strings.

6. **Travel Expenses**

   Create an application that calculates and displays the total travel expenses for a business trip. The user must provide the following information:

   - Number of days on the trip
   - Amount of airfare, if any
   - Amount of car rental fees, if any
   - Number of miles driven, if a private vehicle was used
   - Amount of parking fees, if any
   - Amount of taxi charges, if any
   - Conference or seminar registration fees, if any
   - Lodging charges, per night

   The company reimburses travel expenses according to the following policy:

   - $37 per day for meals
   - Parking fees, up to $10.00 per day
   - Taxi charges up to $20.00 per day
   - Lodging charges up to $95.00 per day
   - If a private vehicle is used, $0.27 per mile driven

   The application should calculate and display the following:

   - Total expenses incurred by the business person
   - The total allowable expenses for the trip
   - The excess that must be paid by the business person, if any
   - The amount saved by the business person if the expenses were under the total allowed

   The application should have the following functions:

`CalcMeals`	Calculates and returns the amount reimbursed for meals.
`CalcMileage`	Calculates and returns the amount reimbursed for mileage driven in a private vehicle.
`CalcParkingFees`	Calculates and returns the amount reimbursed for parking fees.
`CalcTaxiFees`	Calculates and returns the amount reimbursed for taxi charges.
`CalcLodging`	Calculates and returns the amount reimbursed for lodging.
`CalcTotalReimbursement`	Calculates and returns the total amount reimbursed.
`CalcUnallowed`	Calculates and returns the total amount of expenses that are not allowable, if any. These are parking fees that exceed $10.00 per day taxi charges that exceed $20.00 per day, and lodging charges that exceed $95.00 per day.
`CalcSaved`	Calculates and returns the total amount of expenses under the allowable amount, if any. For example, the allowable amount for lodging is $95.00 per day. If a business person stayed in a hotel for $85.00 per day for five days, the savings would $50.00.

   Input validation: Do not accept negative numbers for any dollar amount or for miles driven in a private vehicle. Do not accept numbers less than 1 for the number of days.

7. **Paint Job Estimator**

A painting company has determined that for every 115 square feet of wall space, one gallon of paint and eight hours of labor are required. The company charges $18.00 per hour for labor. Create an application that allows the user to enter the number of rooms to be painted and the price of the paint per gallon. The application should use input boxes to ask the user for the square feet of wall space in each room. It should then display the following information:

- The number of gallons of paint required
- The hours of labor required
- The cost of the paint
- The labor charges
- The total cost of the paint job

Input validation: Do not accept a value less than 1 for the number of rooms. Do not accept a value less than $10.00 for the price of paint. Do not accept a negative value for square footage of wall space.

8. **Falling Distance**

When an object is falling because of gravity, the following formula can be used to determine the distance the object falls in a specific time period:

$$d = \frac{1}{2} gt^2$$

The variables in the formula are as follows: d is the distance in meters, g is 9.8, and t is the amount of time in seconds that the object has been falling.

Create a VB application that allows the user to enter the amount of time that an object has fallen and then displays the distance that the object fell. The application should have a function named `FallingDistance`. The `FallingDistance` function should accept an object's falling time (in seconds) as an argument. The function should return the distance in meters that the object has fallen during that time interval.

9. **Kinetic Energy**

In physics, an object that is in motion is said to have kinetic energy. The following formula can be used to determine a moving object's kinetic energy:

$$KE = \frac{1}{2} mv^2$$

In the formula KE is the kinetic energy, m is the object's mass in kilograms, and v is the object's velocity in meters per second.

Create a VB application that allows the user to enter an object's mass and velocity and then displays the object's kinetic energy. The application should have a function named `KineticEnergy` that accepts an object's mass (in kilograms) and velocity (in meters per second) as arguments. The function should return the amount of kinetic energy that the object has.

10. **Prime Numbers**

A prime number is a number that can be evenly divided by only itself and 1. For example, the number 5 is prime because it can be evenly divided by only 1 and 5. The number 6, however, is not prime because it can be evenly divided by 1, 2, 3, and 6.

Write a Boolean function named `IsPrime` which takes an integer as an argument and returns *true* if the argument is a prime number or *false* otherwise. Use the function in an application that lets the user enter a number and then displays a message indicating whether the number is prime.

TIP: Recall that the `MOD` operator divides one number by another and returns the remainder of the division. In an expression such as `intNum1 MOD intNum2`, the `MOD` operator will return 0 if `intNum1` is evenly divisible by `intNum2`.

11. Prime Number List

This exercise assumes you have already written the `IsPrime` function in Programming Challenge 10. Create another application that uses this function to display all of the prime numbers from 1 through 100 in a list box. The program should have a loop that calls the `IsPrime` function.

CHAPTER 7

Multiple Forms, Standard Modules, and Menus

TOPICS

This chapter shows how to add multiple forms to a project and how to create a standard module to hold procedures and functions. It also covers creating a menu system, as well as context menus, with commands and submenus that the user may select from.

7.1 Multiple Forms

CONCEPT: Visual Basic projects can have multiple forms. If a form is the startup object, it is displayed when the project executes. Other forms in a project are displayed by programming statements.

The applications you have created so far display information and gather input with a single form. Visual Basic does not limit you to one form in an application. You may add other forms to create dialog boxes, display information in a separate window, and so on.

A Windows application must have a startup object. The **startup object** may be a form or a procedure named `Main`, which you will learn about later in this chapter. When a form is the startup object, it is automatically displayed when your application starts up. By default, the first form you create is the startup object. You will learn how to change the startup object later in this section.

Form Names and File Names

Each form has two names. First, the name of a form is stored in the form's Name property. Second, there is the form's file name. In this section we will discuss these names, how they relate to each other, and how they are used in a project.

The Form's Name Property

You can assign a name to a form by setting its Name property. Because applications you have created so far only use one form, you have kept the default name, *Form1*, for the application's form. When your application has multiple forms, however, you should give each one a descriptive name.

The standard prefix for form names is **`frm`**. For example, you might name a form that displays an error message `frmError`. A common name for a project's main form, the one first displayed when the application runs, is `frmMain`.

Form Files

When you create a form in Visual Basic, the code associated with the form is stored in a file with the *.vb* extension. Normally, the name of the file is the same as the name of the form. For example, assume that a project has a form named *Form1* (the form's Name property is set to *Form1*). The code for that form is stored in a file named *Form1.vb*. The *Solution Explorer* window shows an entry for each form file in a project. Figure 7-1 shows the *Solution Explorer* window with an entry for the form named *Form1.vb*.

Figure 7-1 *Solution Explorer* window with entry for *Form1.vb*

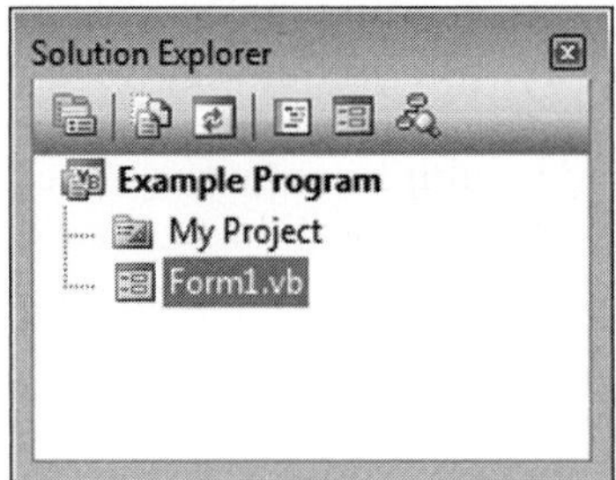

NOTE: The code stored in a form file is the same code you see when you open the form in the *Code* window.

Renaming an Existing Form File

If you change a form's file name, the form's Name property changes automatically to match the file name. If, for example, you rename the file *Form1.vb* to *frmMain.vb*, the form's Name property changes from *Form1* to `frmMain`.

On the other hand, if you change a form's Name property, the form's file name does not change automatically. To maintain consistency, you should also rename the form's file to match the name of the form. Here's how to rename a form file:

1. Right-click the form's file name in the *Solution Explorer* window.
2. A pop-up menu should appear. Select *Rename* from the pop-up menu.
3. The name of the form file should be highlighted in the *Solution Explorer* window. Type the new name for the form file. Be sure to keep the *.vb* extension.

Adding a New Form to a Project

VideoNote

Creating and Displaying a Second Form

Follow these steps to add a new form to a project:

1. Either click the *Add New Item* button ( ) on the toolbar, or click *Project* on the menu strip and click *Add Windows Form* on the *Project* menu. After performing either of these steps, the *Add New Item* dialog box, shown in Figure 7-2, should appear. Notice that in the figure, the name *Form2.vb* appears in the *Name* text box. In this example, *Form2.vb* is the default name for the new file that the form will be stored in, and *Form2* is the default name for the form.

NOTE: The default name may be different, depending on the number of forms already in the project, and whether you have renamed existing forms from their default names to other names.

Figure 7-2 *Add New Item* dialog box

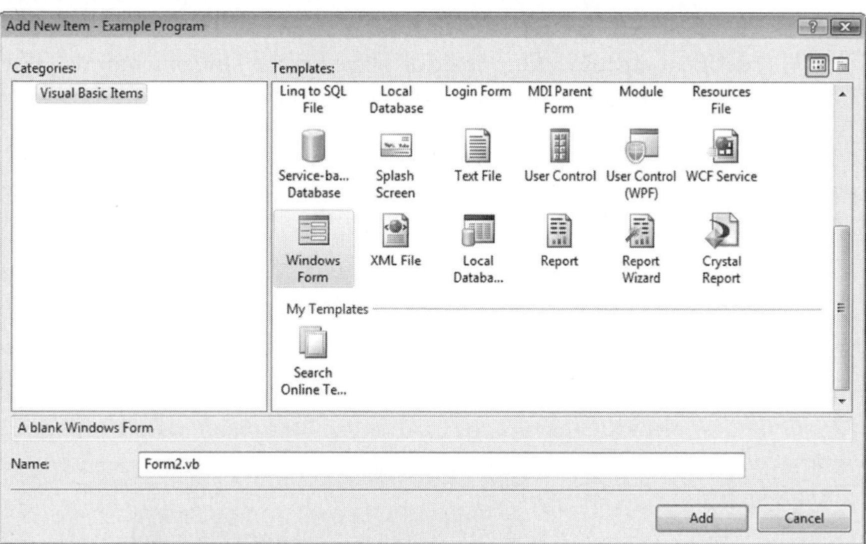

2. Under *Templates*, make sure *Windows Form* is selected.
3. Change the default name that is displayed in the *Name* text box to the name you wish to give the new form. For example, if you wish to name the new form *frmError*, enter **`frmError.vb`** in the *Name* text box.

NOTE: Be sure to keep the *.vb* extension.

4. Click the *Add* button.

After completing these steps, a new blank form is added to your project. The new form is displayed in the *Design* window and an entry for the new form appears in the *Solution Explorer* window. The *Solution Explorer* window in Figure 7-3 shows two forms: `frmError` and `frmMain`.

Figure 7-3 *Solution Explorer* window showing multiple forms

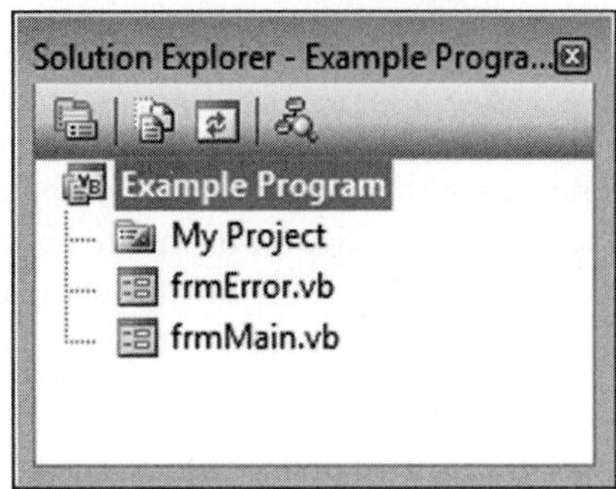

Switching between Forms and Form Code

At design time, you can easily switch to another form by double-clicking the form's entry in the *Solution Explorer* window. The form will be then displayed in the *Design* window. You can also use the tabs that appear at the top of the *Design* window to display different forms or their code. For example, look at Figure 7-4. It shows the tabs that appear for a project with two forms: `frmMain` and `frmError`. The tabs that display the *[Design]* designator cause a form to be displayed in the *Design* window. The tabs that appear without the designator cause a form's code to be displayed in the *Code* window.

Figure 7-4 *Design* window tabs

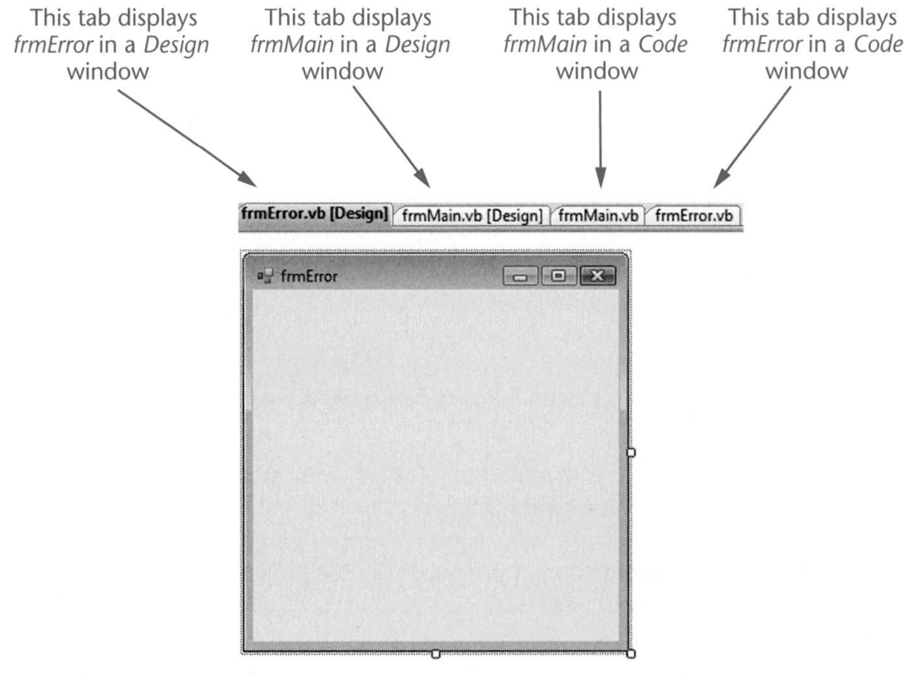

Removing a Form

If you wish to remove a form from a project and delete its file from the disk, follow these steps.

1. Right-click the form's entry in the *Solution Explorer* window.
2. On the pop-up menu, click *Delete.*

If you're using Visual Studio and you wish to remove a form from a project but you do not want to delete its file from the disk, follow one of these sets of steps. (This option is not available in Visual Basic Express.)

1. Right-click the form's entry in the *Solution Explorer* window.
2. On the pop-up menu click *Exclude From Project.*

or

1. Select the form's entry in the *Solution Explorer* window.
2. Click *Project* on the menu strip, and click *Exclude From Project.*

Changing the Startup Object to Another Form

The first form you create is, by default, the startup object. It is automatically displayed when the application runs. To make another form the startup object, follow these steps:

1. In the *Solution Explorer* window, right click the project name. Figure 7-5 shows the location of the project name in the window.

Figure 7-5 Project name in *Solution Explorer* window

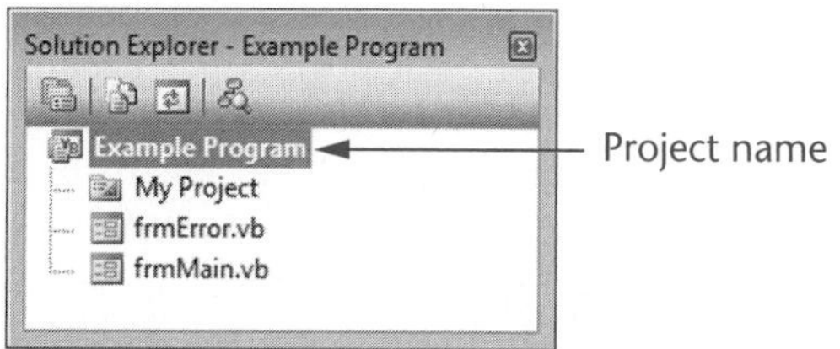

2. On the pop-up menu, click *Properties.* The project's *Property Page* should appear, as shown in Figure 7-6.
3. Make sure the Application tab is selected at the left edge of the Property Page, as shown in Figure 7-6. To change the startup form, click the down arrow (▾) in the *Startup Form* drop-down list. A list of all the forms in the project appears. Select the form that should display first when your program executes.
4. Save the project and click the Close button (×) in the upper right corner of the *Property Page.*

Figure 7-6 Project's *Property Pages* dialog box

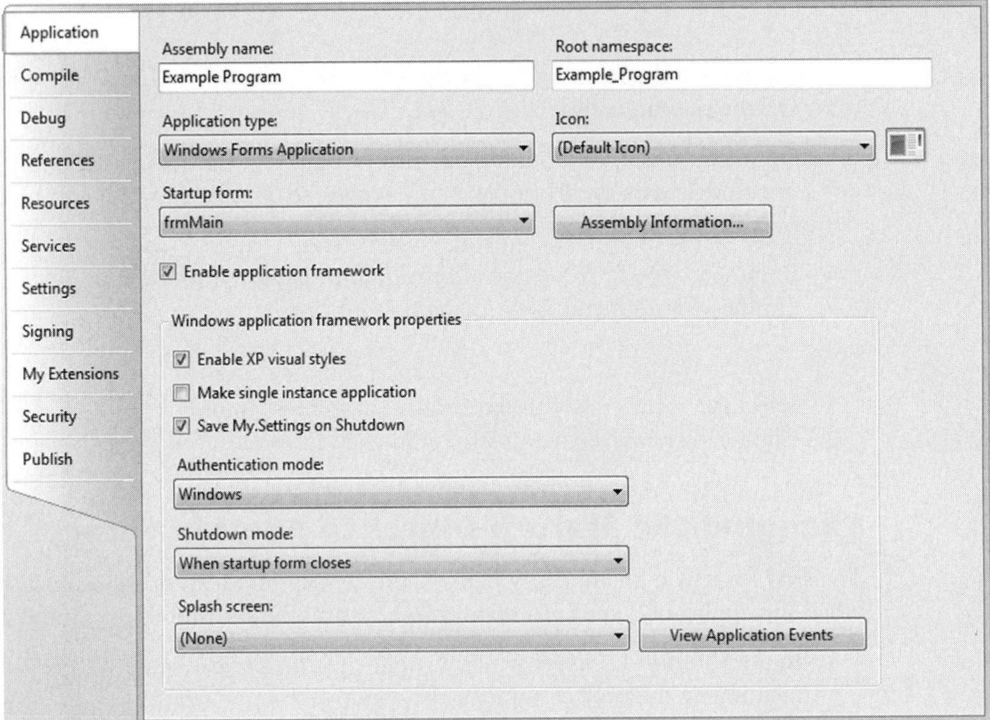

Creating an Instance of a Form

Visual Basic makes it easy to write code that displays forms. Before plunging into the details, let's briefly revisit the topic of form files. When you create a form, Visual Studio stores the code for the form in a form file. The form file contains a class declaration. A **class** is a program structure that describes an object's properties and methods. Recall that when you open a form in the *Code* window, the first and last lines of code look like the following, which mark the beginning and end of a class declaration:

```
Public Class FormName

End Class
```

`FormName` is the class name, and is based on the form's Name property. Statements appearing between these two statements belong to the form's class.

A form's class declaration by itself does not create a specific form, but is merely the description of a form. It is similar to the blueprint for a house. The blueprint itself is not a house, but is a detailed description of a house. When we use the blueprint to build an actual house, we can say we are building an instance of the house described by the blueprint. If we want, we can build several identical houses from the same blueprint. Each house is a separate instance of the house described by the blueprint. This idea is illustrated in Figure 7-7.

A form's class declaration serves a similar purpose. We can use it to create one or more instances of the form described by the class declaration, and then use the instance(s) to display the form on the screen.

Figure 7-7 Blueprints and instances of the blueprints

Blueprint that describes a house

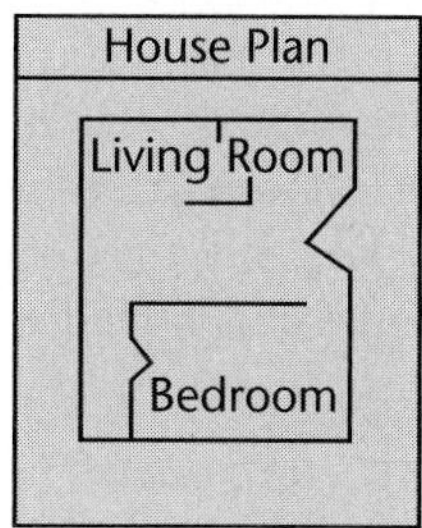

Instances of the house described by the blueprint

Displaying a Form

The first step in displaying a form is to create an instance of the form. You create an instance of a form with a `Dim` statement. The general format is as follows:

```
Dim ObjectVariable As New ClassName
```

`ObjectVariable` is the name of an object variable that references an instance of the form. An **object variable** is a variable that holds the memory address of an object and allows you to work with the object. *`ClassName`* is the form's class name. This is the same name that is stored in the form's Name property. For example, assume that you have added a form to your project and named it `frmError`. The following statement creates an instance of the form:

```
Dim errorForm As New frmError
```

Let's examine what happens as a result of this statement. First, an object variable named `errorForm` is created. This variable will reference the instance of the form. The part of the statement that reads `New frmError` causes an instance of the `frmError` form to be created in memory. Its memory address is then assigned to the `errorForm` variable. (When an object variable holds the memory address of an object, we say that it references the object.) We may now use the `errorForm` variable to perform operations with the form.

This statement does not cause the form to be displayed on the screen. It only creates an instance of the form in memory and assigns its address to the object variable. To display the form on the screen, you must use the object variable to invoke one of the form's methods.

The `ShowDialog` and `Show` Methods

A form can be either modal or modeless. When a **modal form** is displayed, no other form in the application can receive the focus until the modal form is closed. The user must close the modal form before he or she can work with any other form in the application. A **modeless form**, on the other hand, allows the user to switch focus to another form while it is displayed. The **`ShowDialog` method** causes a form to be displayed as a modal form. When this method is called, the form is displayed and it receives the focus. The general format of the method call is as follows:

```
ObjectVariable.ShowDialog()
```

`ObjectVariable` is the name of an object variable that references an instance of a form. For example, the following code creates an instance of the `frmError` form and displays it:

```
Dim errorForm As New frmError
errorForm.ShowDialog()
```

To display a modeless form, use the **`Show` method**. The general format of the `Show` method is as follows:

```
ObjectVariable.Show()
```

`ObjectVariable` is the name of an object variable that references an instance of a form. For example, the following code creates an instance of the `frmError` form and displays it as a modeless form:

```
Dim errorForm As New frmError
errorForm.Show()
```

TIP: Most of the time forms shoud be modal. It is common for a procedure to display a form, and then perform operations dependent on input gathered by the form. Therefore, you will normally use the `ShowDialog` method to display a form.

Closing a Form with the `Close` Method

Forms commonly have a button, such as *Close* or *Cancel*, which the user clicks to close the form. When the user clicks such a button, the form must call the `Close` method. The **`Close` method** closes a form and removes its visual part from memory.

The `Close` method is a member of the `System.Windows.Forms.Form` class, so, when a form closes itself, it must call its own `Close` method. This is done with the **`Me` keyword**, as shown in the following general format:

```
Me.Close()
```

In this statement, the `Me` keyword references the current instance of the form. A form executing the `Me.Close()` statement is calling its own `Close` method.

For example, assume an application has a form with a *Close* button named `btnClose`. When the user clicks the button, the form closes. The following is the code for the `btnClose_Click` event procedure:

```
Private Sub btnClose_Click(ByVal sender As System.Object, _
  ByVal e As System.EventArgs) Handles btnClose.Click

  Me.Close()
End Sub
```

The `Hide` Method

The **`Hide` method** in the Form class makes a form or control invisible, but does not remove it from memory. It has the same effect as setting the Visible property to *False*. As with the `Close` method, a form uses the `Me` keyword to call its own `Hide` method, such as `Me.Hide()`. Use the `Hide` method when, instead of closing a form, you want to remove it temporarily from the screen. After hiding a form, you may redisplay it with the `ShowDialog` or `Show` methods.

More about Modal and Modeless Forms

You have already learned that when a modal form is displayed, no other form in the application can receive the focus until the modal form is closed or hidden. There is another important aspect of modal forms. When a procedure calls the `ShowDialog` method to display a modal form, no subsequent statements in that procedure execute until the modal form is closed. This concept is illustrated in Figure 7-8.

Figure 7-8 Execution of statements after displaying a modal form

```
statement
statement
frmMessage.ShowDialog()
statement
statement
statement
```

These statements will not execute until the form referenced by **`frmMessage`** is closed.

When a procedure calls the `Show` method to display a modeless form, however, statements following the method call continue to execute after the modeless form is displayed. Visual Basic does not wait until the modeless form is closed before executing these statements. This concept is illustrated in Figure 7-9. Tutorial 7-1 demonstrates this difference between modal and modeless forms.

Figure 7-9 Execution of statements after displaying a modeless form

```
statement
statement
frmMessage.Show()
statement
statement
statement
```

These statements will execute immediately after the form referenced by **`frmMessage`** is displayed.

Tutorial 7-1:
Completing an application that displays modal and modeless forms

Step 1: Open the *Modal Modeless Demo* project from the student sample programs folder named *Chap7\Modal Modeless*.

Step 2: Look at the *Solution Explorer* window, shown in Figure 7-10. The project has two forms, `frmAnother` and `frmMain`. `frmMain` is the startup form.

Step 3: If `frmMain` is not already displayed in the *Design* window, double-click its entry in the *Solution Explorer* window. It should appear as shown in Figure 7-11.

Step 4: To look at the `frmAnother` form, double-click its entry in the *Solution Explorer* window, as shown in Figure 7-12. The *Close* button is named `btnClose`.

Figure 7-10 *Solution Explorer* window showing two forms

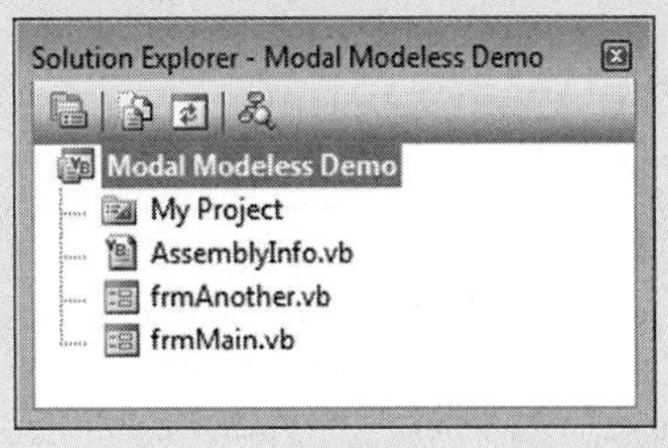

Figure 7-11 `frmMain` form

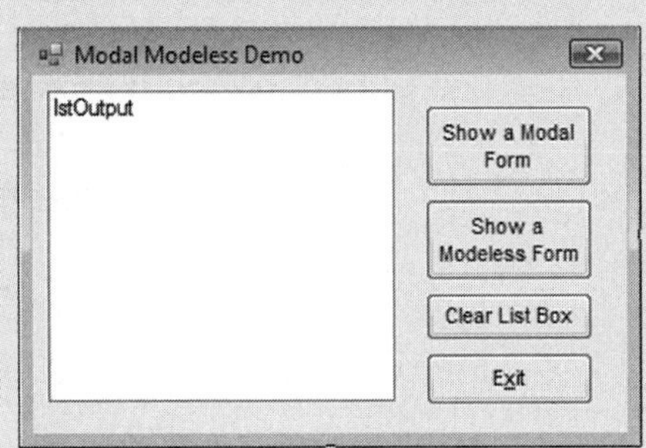

Figure 7-12 `frmAnother` form

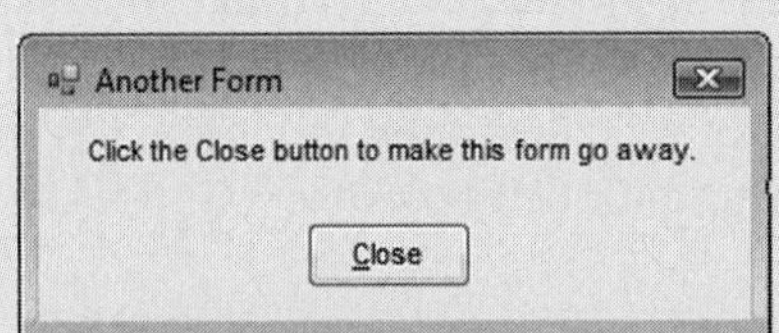

Step 5: Open the *Code* window to view the code for the `frmAnother` form. Look at the `btnClose_Click` event procedure. Its code is as follows:

```
Private Sub btnClose_Click(ByVal sender As System.Object, _
    ByVal e As System.EventArgs) Handles btnClose.Click

  ' Close the form
  Me.Close()
End Sub
```

Step 6: When this procedure executes, it closes the form. Open `frmMain` in the *Design* window and double-click the *Show a Modal Form* button. When the *Code* window appears, type the following statements in the `btnShowModal_Click` event handler:

```
Private Sub btnShowModal_Click(ByVal sender As System.Object, _
      ByVal e As System.EventArgs) Handles btnShowModal.Click

   Dim intCount As Integer                  ' Counter
   Dim anotherForm As New frmAnother        ' Form instance

   ' Show the other form in modal style.
   anotherForm.ShowDialog()

   ' Display some numbers in the list box on the main form.
   ' Because the other form is displayed in modal style, this
   ' code will not execute until the user closes the other form.
   For intCount = 1 To 10
     lstOutput.Items.Add(intCount.ToString())
   Next intCount
End Sub
```

The following statement in this procedure creates an instance of the `frmAnother` form and assigns its address to an object variable named `anotherForm`.

```
Dim anotherForm As New frmAnother        ' Form instance
```

Using the `anotherForm` variable, the `ShowDialog` method is called to display the form in modal style.

```
' Show the other form in modal style.
anotherForm.ShowDialog()
```

After the `ShowDialog` method is called, this procedure has a `For...Next` loop that displays the numbers 1 through 10 in the `lstOutput` list box. Because the `frmAnother` form is displayed in modal style, the `For...Next` loop will not execute until the user closes `frmAnother`.

Step 7: Next, create the `btnShowModeless_Click` event procedure. Its code is as follows:

```
Private Sub btnShowModeless_Click(ByVal sender As System.Object, _
      ByVal e As System.EventArgs) Handles btnShowModeless.Click

   Dim intCount As Integer                  ' Counter
   Dim anotherForm As New frmAnother        ' Form instance

   ' Show the other form in modeless style.
   anotherForm.Show()

   ' Display some numbers in the list box
   ' on the main form. Because the other form
   ' is displayed in modeless style, this code
   ' will execute while the other form is on
   ' the screen.
   For intCount = 1 To 10
     lstOutput.Items.Add(intCount.ToString())
   Next intCount
End Sub
```

The `btnShowModeless_Click` event procedure basically performs the same operation as the `btnShowModal_Click` procedure: It displays the `frmAnother` form and displays the numbers 1 through 10 in the `lstOutput` list box. The only difference is that `frmAnother` is displayed in modeless style, using the `Show` method. Therefore, the `For...Next` loop executes immediately after the `frmAnother` form is displayed. The program does not wait for the user to close the `frmAnother` form before executing the loop.

Step 8: Run the application. On the main form, click the *Show a Modal Form* button. The `frmAnother` form is displayed. Figure 7-13 shows the forms, positioned so you can see both of them. Notice that the `For...Next` loop has not executed because you do not see the numbers 1 through 10 printed on the main form.

Figure 7-13 `frmMain` form and the modal `frmAnother` form

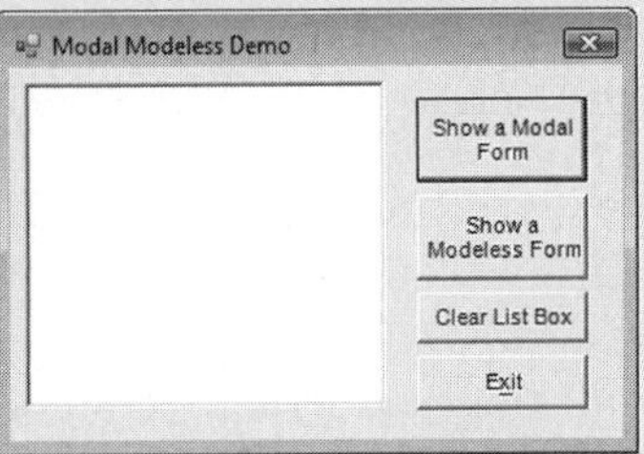

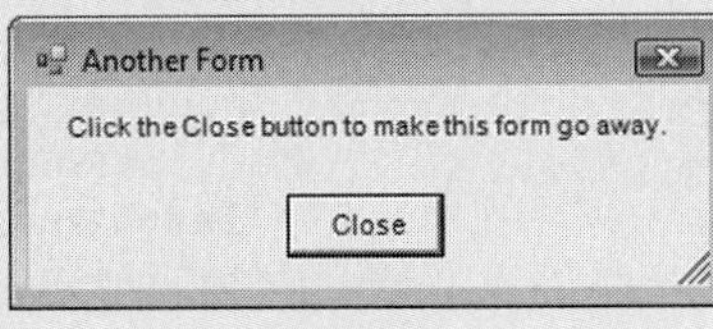

Step 9: Click the *Close* button on `frmAnother` to close the form. Now look at the `frmMain` form. As shown in Figure 7-14, the `For...Next` loop executes as soon as `frmAnother` is closed.

Figure 7-14 `frmMain` after the modal `frmAnother` form is closed

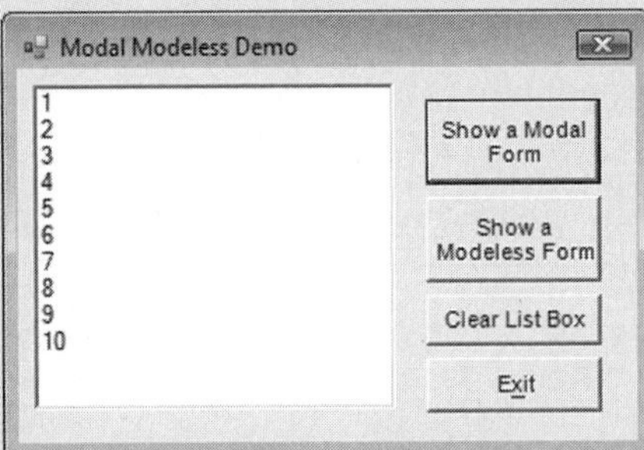

Step 10: Click the *Clear List Box* button to clear the numbers from the list box.

Step 11: Click the *Show a Modeless Form* button to display `frmAnother` in modeless style. As shown in Figure 7-15, notice that the `For...Next` loop executes immediately after the form is displayed; it does not wait for you to click the `frmAnother` *Close* button.

Figure 7-15 `frmMain` form and the modeless `frmAnother` form

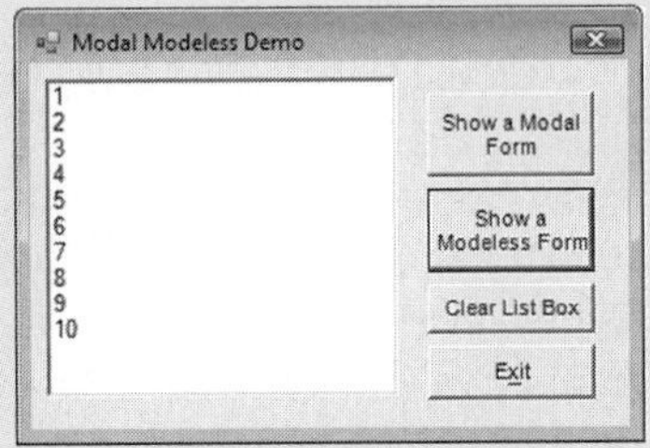

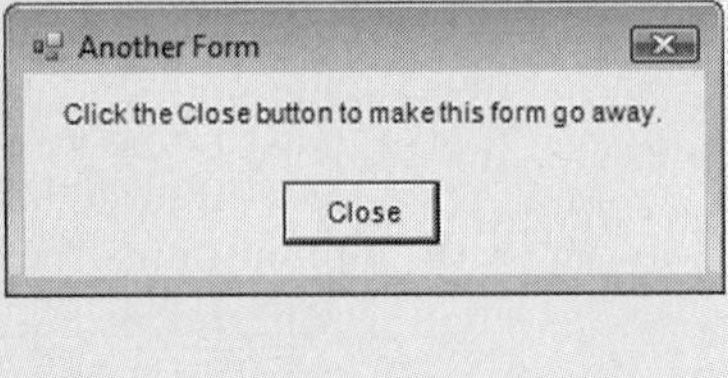

Step 12: Click the `frmAnother` *Close* button to close the form.

Step 13: Click the main form's *Exit* button to end the application.

The `Load`, `Activated`, `FormClosing`, and `FormClosed` Events

There are several events associated with forms. In this section we will discuss the `Load`, `Activated`, `FormClosing`, and `FormClosed` events.

The `Load` Event

The `Load` event was introduced in Chapter 3, but a quick review is in order. Just before a form is displayed, a `Load` event occurs. If you need to execute code automatically just before a form is displayed, you can create a `Load` event handler, executed in response to the `Load` event. To write code in a form's `Load` event handler, double-click any area of the form where there is no other control. The *Code* window appears with a code template similar to the following:

```
Private Sub frmMain_Load(ByVal sender As System.Object, _
  ByVal e As System.EventArgs) Handles MyBase.Load

End Sub
```

Complete the template with the statements you wish the procedure to execute.

The `Activated` Event

A form's `Activated` event occurs when the user switches the focus to the form from another form or application. Here are two examples of how the `Activated` event occurs:

- Application A and application B are both running, and a form in application A has the focus. The user clicks application B's form. When this happens, the `Activated` event occurs for application B's form.
- Suppose an application has a main form and a second form, and the second form is displayed in modeless style. Then each time the user clicks a form that does not have the focus, an `Activated` event occurs for that form.

The `Activated` event occurs when a form is initially displayed, following the `Load` event. If you need to execute code in any of these situations, you can create an `Activated` event handler, executed in response to the `Activated` event. To create an **`Activated` event handler**, follow these steps:

1. In the *Code* window click the class name drop-down list, and select *(formname Events)*, where *formname* is the name of the form. An example is shown in Figure 7-16.

Figure 7-16 Select *(frmMain Events)* in the class name drop-down list

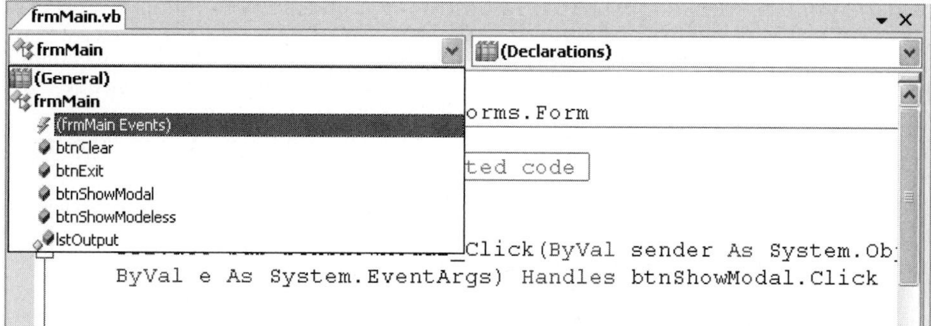

2. From the method name drop-down list, select *Activated*, as shown in Figure 7-17.

Figure 7-17 Select *Activated* in the method name drop-down list

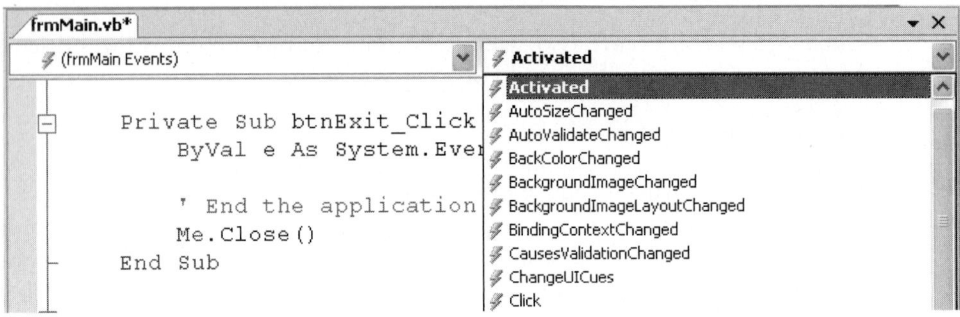

After completing these steps, a code template for the `Activated` event handler is created in the *Code* window.

The `FormClosing` Event

The `FormClosing` event occurs when a form is in the process of closing, but before it has closed. It might be in response to the `Close` method being executed, the user pressing the [Alt]+[F4] keys, or the user clicking the standard Windows *Close* button (☒) in the form's corner. To execute code in response to a form closing, such as asking the user if he or she really wants to close the form, create a **`FormClosing` event handler**. Here are the required steps:

1. In the *Code* window, click the class name drop-down list and select *(formname Events)*, where *formname* is the name of the form.
2. In the method name drop-down list, select *FormClosing*.

After completing these steps, a code template for the `FormClosing` event handler is created in the *Code* window. An example follows:

```
Private Sub frmMain_FormClosing(ByVal sender As Object, _
    ByVal e As System.ComponentModel.FormClosingEventArgs) _
    Handles Me.FormClosing

End Sub
```

One of the procedure parameters is named `e`. It has a Boolean property named *Cancel*. If you set `e.Cancel` to *True*, the form will not close. Code showing an example of this technique follows:

```
Private Sub frmMain_FormClosing(ByVal sender As Object, _
    ByVal e As System.ComponentModel.FormClosingEventArgs) _
    Handles Me.FormClosing

  If MessageBox.Show("Are you Sure?", "Confirm", _
      MessageBoxButtons.YesNo) = Windows.Forms.DialogResult.Yes Then
    e.Cancel = False           ' Continue to close the form.
  Else
    e.Cancel = True            ' Do not close the form.
  End If
End Sub
```

The `FormClosed` Event

The `FormClosed` event occurs after a form has closed. If you need to execute code immediately after a form has closed, create a **`FormClosed` event handler** by following these steps:

1. Open the *Code* window and click the class name drop-down list. In the drop-down list select *(formname Events)*, where *formname* is the name of the form.
2. Click the method name drop-down list. In the drop-down list select *FormClosed*.

After completing these steps, a code template for the `FormClosed` event handler will be created in the *Code* window.

TIP: You cannot prevent a form from closing with the `FormClosed` event procedure. You must use the `FormClosing` event handler to prevent a form from closing.

When you use the `Me.Close()` method to close an application's startup form, the application fires the `FormClosing` and `FormClosed` events.

Accessing Objects on a Different Form

When you write a statement to access a control, Visual Basic assumes the control is in the same form as the statement accessing it. For example, consider a project with a form named `frmMain`. In one of the form's procedures, the following statement appears:

```
lblName.Text = strName
```

It is assumed that `lblName` is a control on `frmMain`.

You can write code to access objects on a different form. You must fully qualify the name of the object by preceding it with the object variable name. Here is an example of such a statement, assuming that `sngAverage` is a variable declared in the current form or procedure:

```
Dim resultsForm As New frmResults
resultsForm.lblAverage.Text = sngAverage.ToString()
```

In this statement, Visual Basic knows that `lblAverage` is on the form referenced by `resultsForm`. Here is another example. Suppose an application has two forms: `frmMain` and `frmGreeting`. A procedure in the `frmMain` form contains the following code:

```
Dim greetingForm As New frmGreeting
greetingForm.lblMessage.Text = "Hello!"
greetingForm.ShowDialog()
```

The second statement stores a value in the `lblMessage` control, located on the form referenced by `greetingForm`. The third statement displays the form.

Class-Level Variables in a Form

Although a form's class-level variables are accessible to all statements in the form file, they are not accessible by default to statements outside the form file. For example, assume a project has a form named `frmAmounts`, which has the following class-level variable declaration:

```
Dim sngTotal As Single           ' Class-level variable
```

The same project has another form that uses the following statements:

```
Dim amountsForm As New frmAmounts
amountsForm.sngTotal = 100
```

Although the assignment statement has fully qualified the name of `sngTotal` by preceding it with the object variable name, the statement still cannot access it because class-level variables are private by default. The statement will cause an error when the project is compiled.

It is possible to make a class-level variable available to methods outside the class. This is done using the **Public** keyword. Here is an example:

```
Public sngTotal As Single        ' Class-level variable
```

Although class-level variables are automatically declared private by the Dim statement, you should explicitly declare them private with the **Private** keyword. Here is an example:

```
Private sngTotal As Single
```

NOTE: From this point forward, class-level variables will be declared Private unless a strong reason exists to do otherwise. By explicitly declaring private class-level variables with the Private keyword, you make your source code more self-documenting. Furthermore, programmers rarely make class variables public, because doing so would violate an important principle of object-oriented programming called *encapsulation*.

Using Private and Public Procedures in a Form

Recall from Chapter 6 that the declaration of a procedure or function may begin with an optional access specifier, such as Public or Private. When a procedure declaration begins with Private, the procedure may only be executed by statements in the same form. When a procedure begins with Public, it may also be executed by statements that are outside the form. If you do not provide an access specifier, the procedure defaults to Public. In projects that use multiple forms, you should always make the procedures in a form private unless you specifically want statements outside the form to execute the procedure. Tutorial 7-2 demonstrates how to complete an application with multiple forms.

Tutorial 7-2:
Completing an application with multiple forms

In this tutorial, you complete the *Schedule Builder* application, which allows a student to select from a list of courses and professors to build a class schedule. The application uses two forms.

Step 1: Open the *Schedule Builder* project from the student samples folder named *Chap7\Schedule Builder*.

Step 2: Looking at the *Solution Explorer* window, you will see the application has two forms: frmMain and frmSchedule. Open frmMain in the *Design* window. The form is shown in Figure 7-18 with the names of its controls labeled.

Table 7-1 gives a brief description of each control's purpose.

Step 3: Open the frmSchedule form in the *Design* window. The form is shown in Figure 7-19 with the names of its controls labeled.

The form has a set of Label controls named lblCourse1, lblCourse2, and so on, and another set of Label controls named lblProfessor1, lblProfessor2, and so on. When the btnShow button on frmMain is clicked, values are copied to these controls, as shown in Table 7-2.

Figure 7-18 `frmMain` form

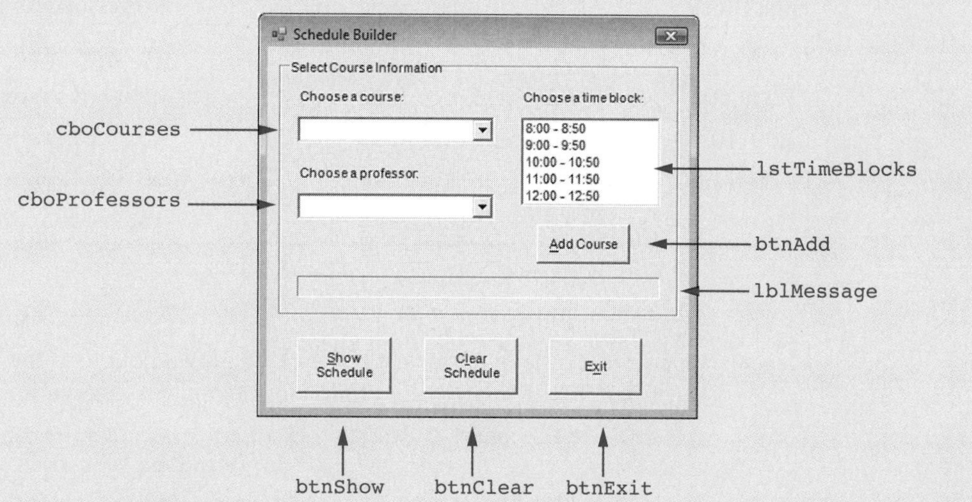

Table 7-1 *Schedule Builder* controls

Control	Purpose
`cboCourses`	A combo box with a list of courses to choose from
`cboProfessors`	A combo box with a list of professors to choose from
`lblMessage`	A Label control that displays a message when a new course has been added to the schedule
`lstTimeBlocks`	A list box with five time blocks to choose from
`btnAdd`	Adds the course selected in `cboCourses` and the professor selected in `cboProfessor` to the student's schedule for the time block chosen in `lstTimeBlocks`
`btnShow`	Displays an instance of the `frmSchedule` form showing the student's schedule
`btnClear`	Clears all the courses, professors, and time blocks from the student's schedule
`btnExit`	Ends the application

Figure 7-19 `frmSchedule` form

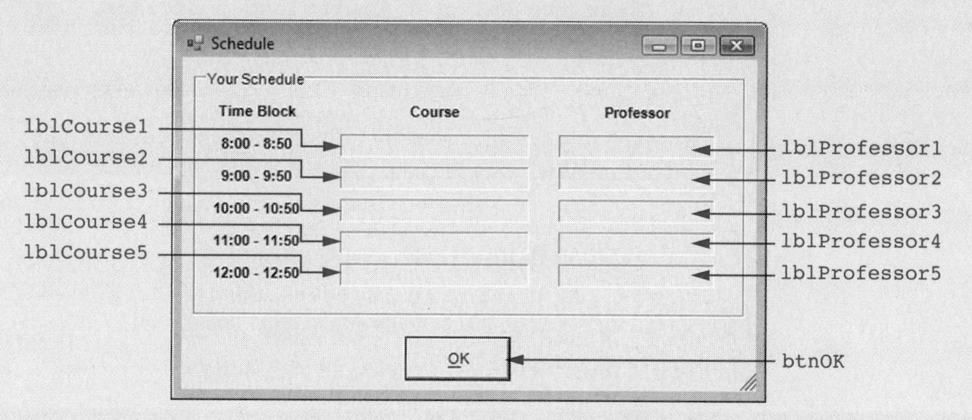

Table 7-2 How time blocks, course labels, and professor labels correspond

Time Block	Course Stored In	Professor Stored In
8:00–8:50	lblCourse1	lblProfessor1
9:00–9:50	lblCourse2	lblProfessor2
10:00–10:50	lblCourse3	lblProfessor3
11:00–11:50	lblCourse4	lblProfessor4
12:00–12:50	lblCourse5	lblProfessor5

The `btnOk` button closes the form.

Step 4: Open the `frmMain` form in the *Code* window. Complete the `btnAdd_Click` event handler by inserting the following statements (shown in bold):

```
Private Sub btnAdd_Click(ByVal sender As System.Object, _
    ByVal e As System.EventArgs) Handles btnAdd.Click

  ' This procedure adds the selected course
  ' to the schedule, which is kept in the
  ' class-level variables.
  ' Determine the time block selected and then add
  ' the course and professor.
  Select Case lstTimeBlocks.SelectedItem.ToString()
    Case "8:00 - 8:50"
      strCourse1 = cboCourses.Text
      strProfessor1 = cboProfessors.Text
    Case "9:00 - 9:50"
      strCourse2 = cboCourses.Text
      strProfessor2 = cboProfessors.Text
    Case "10:00 - 10:50"
      strCourse3 = cboCourses.Text
      strProfessor3 = cboProfessors.Text
    Case "11:00 - 11:50"
      strCourse4 = cboCourses.Text
      strProfessor4 = cboProfessors.Text
    Case "12:00 - 12:50"
      strCourse5 = cboCourses.Text
      strProfessor5 = cboProfessors.Text
  End Select
  ' Let the user know the course has been added.
  lblMessage.Text = "Course added for the " _
        & lstTimeBlocks.SelectedItem.ToString() _
        & " time block."
  ' Clear the selected course and professor.
  cboCourses.Text = String.Empty
  cboProfessors.Text = String.Empty
End Sub
```

The `btnAdd_Click` procedure uses a `Select Case` statement to determine which time block was selected. Then it copies the course and professor selected in `cboCourses` and `cboProfessors` to the proper class-level variables.

Step 5: Look at the `btnShow_Click` event procedure, as follows:

```
Private Sub btnShow_Click(ByVal sender As System.Object, _
    ByVal e As System.EventArgs) Handles btnShow.Click

  ' This procedure displays the schedule on an
  ' instance of the frmSchedule form.
```

```
    Dim scheduleForm As New frmSchedule

    ' Copy the course and professor for the
    ' 8:00 - 8:50 time block to scheduleForm.
    scheduleForm.lblCourse1.Text = strCourse1
    scheduleForm.lblProfessor1.Text = strProfessor1

    ' Copy the course and professor for the
    ' 9:00 - 9:50 time block to scheduleForm.
    scheduleForm.lblCourse2.Text = strCourse2
    scheduleForm.lblProfessor2.Text = strProfessor2

    ' Copy the course and professor for the
    ' 10:00 - 10:50 time block to scheduleForm.
    scheduleForm.lblCourse3.Text = strCourse3
    scheduleForm.lblProfessor3.Text = strProfessor3

    ' Copy the course and professor for the
    ' 11:00 - 11:50 time block to scheduleForm.
    scheduleForm.lblCourse4.Text = strCourse4
    scheduleForm.lblProfessor4.Text = strProfessor4

    ' Copy the course and professor for the
    ' 12:00 - 12:50 time block to scheduleForm.
    scheduleForm.lblCourse5.Text = strCourse5
    scheduleForm.lblProfessor5.Text = strProfessor5

    ' Display the schedule form.
    scheduleForm.ShowDialog()
End Sub
```

This procedure creates an instance of the `frmSchedule` form, copies the course and professor names stored in the class-level variables into the appropriate Label controls on the form, and then displays the form.

Step 6: Look at the `btnClear_Click` procedure. The code follows:

```
Private Sub btnClear_Click(ByVal sender As System.Object, _
    ByVal e As System.EventArgs) Handles btnClear.Click

    ' This procedure clears the items in the schedule.
    ' Clear the course names.
    strCourse1 = String.Empty
    strCourse2 = String.Empty
    strCourse3 = String.Empty
    strCourse4 = String.Empty
    strCourse5 = String.Empty
    ' Clear the professor names.
    strProfessor1 = String.Empty
    strProfessor2 = String.Empty
    strProfessor3 = String.Empty
    strProfessor4 = String.Empty
    strProfessor5 = String.Empty
    ' Reset the list box and combo boxes.
    lstTimeBlocks.SelectedIndex = -1
    cboCourses.Text = String.Empty
    cboProfessors.Text = String.Empty
End Sub
```

The procedure copies an empty string to each of the class-level variables, deselects any selected value in `lstTimeBlocks`, and clears the Text properties of `cboCourses` and `cboProfessors`.

Step 7: Complete the `btnExit_Click` and the `frmMain_FormClosing` event procedures by inserting the following statements:

```
Private Sub btnExit_Click(ByVal sender As System.Object, _
  ByVal e As System.EventArgs) Handles btnExit.Click

  ' End the application with the Close method.
  ' This allows the FormClosing event procedure to execute.
  Me.Close()
End Sub

Private Sub frmMain_FormClosing(ByVal sender As Object, _
    ByVal e As System.ComponentModel.FormClosingEventArgs) _
    Handles Me.FormClosing

  ' Confirm that the user wants to quit.
  If MessageBox.Show("Are you sure you want to quit?", _
      "Confirm", MessageBoxButtons.YesNo) _
      = Windows.Forms.DialogResult.No Then
    e.Cancel = True   ' Do not permit the window to close
  Else
    e.Cancel = False  ' Permit the window to close
  End If
End Sub
```

The `btnExit_Click` event procedure calls `Me.Close()` to close the form. Because `frmMain` is the startup object, the application ends. The `frmMain_FormClosing` event procedure displays a message box asking the user to confirm that he or she wishes to quit.

Step 8: Run the application. Select the 8:00–8:50 time block in the list box and select a course and professor from the combo boxes. Click the *Add Course* button to add the selections to the schedule. Repeat this process for the remaining time blocks. Notice that the program does not perform any error checking, so the user can omit the professor name when scheduling a course.

Step 9: After selecting a course and professor for each of the time blocks, click the *Show Schedule* button. The `frmSchedule` form, similar to the one shown in Figure 7-20, should be displayed with the courses and professors you selected.

Figure 7-20 *Schedule* form

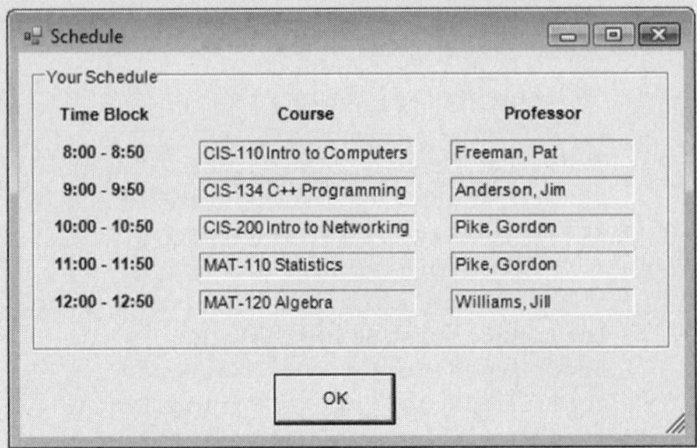

Step 10: Click the *OK* button to close the form.

Step 11: On the main form, click the *Exit* button. This calls the `Me.Close()` method, which causes the form's `FormClosing` event procedure to execute. A message box appears asking *Are you sure you want to quit?* Click the *Yes* button.

Using a Form in More Than One Project

Once you create a form, you do not have to recreate it to use it in another project. After a form has been saved to a file, it may be used in other projects. Follow these steps to add an existing form to a project:

1. With the receiving project open in Visual Studio, click *Project* on the menu strip, and then click *Add Existing Item.*
2. The *Add Existing Item* dialog box appears. Use the dialog box to locate the form file that you want to add to the project. (Remember that form files end with a *.vb* extension.) When you locate the file, select it and click the *Open* button. A copy of the form is now added to the project.

Checkpoint

7.1 How do you cause a form to be displayed automatically when your application executes?

7.2 What is the standard prefix for form names?

7.3 Describe the process of adding a new form to a project.

7.4 In Visual Studio only, describe the process of excluding a form from a project.

7.5 What is a form file? What file extension does a form file have?

7.6 What is the difference between a modal form and a modeless form?

7.7 Suppose a project has an object variable named `resultsForm`, which references an instance of a form. Write the statement that uses the `resultsForm` variable to display the form in modal style.

7.8 Write a statement that displays the form referenced by `resultsForm` in modeless style.

7.9 In which event handler do you write code if you want it to execute when the user switches to a form from another form or from another application?

7.10 Suppose a project has a form named `frmInfo` with a label named `lblCustomer`. The following declaration statement appears in `frmMain`:

```
Dim infoForm As New frmInfo
```

The `infoForm` variable references an instance of `frmInfo`. Write a statement that uses the `infoForm` variable to copy *Jim Jones* to the `lblCustomer` Label control on the `frmInfo` form.

7.11 What is the `Me` keyword used for?

7.12 Suppose you want to declare a class-level variable of the Single data type named `sngAverage` in a form. Assuming you want code in other forms to access it, write the variable declaration.

7.2 Standard Modules

CONCEPT: A standard module contains code—declarations and procedures—that are used by other files in a project.

This section shows you how to create standard modules. A **standard module** is a file containing variable declarations, procedures, and functions. Standard modules are not associated with a class or form and contain no event procedures. Like forms, standard modules are saved on disk as files that end with the *.vb* extension.

Standard modules are useful for organizing code in projects that have multiple forms. Procedures, functions, and variables used by more than one form can be stored in a standard module.

Module Names and Module Files

The content of a standard module begins with a `Module` statement and ends with an `End Module` statement. The general format follows:

```
Module ModuleName
  [Module Contents]
End Module
```

`ModuleName` is the name of the standard module. This can be any valid identifier. If you have only one standard module in your project you should give it a name that clearly relates it to the project. For example, if a project is named *Order Entry*, then its standard module might be named `OrderEntryModule`. It is possible to have multiple standard modules in a project. For example, you might have one standard module containing math procedures and another standard module containing procedures for retrieving information from a database. If your project has multiple standard modules, give each standard module a name that describes its purpose.

When you create a standard module, its code is stored in a file that is named with the *.vb* extension. Normally, the name of the file is the same as the name of the module. Therefore, a module named `OrderEntryModule` should be saved to the file *OrderEntryModule.vb*.

Adding a Standard Module

Follow these steps to add a standard module to a project.

1. Click the *Add New Item* button ( ) on the toolbar, or click *Project* on the menu strip, and then click *Add Module*. The *Add New Item* dialog box shown in Figure 7-21 should appear. Notice that in the figure, the name *Module1.vb* appears in the Name text box. In this example, *Module1.vb* is the default name for the file that the module will be stored in and *Module1* is the default name for the module.

NOTE: The default name may be different, depending on the number of modules already in the project.

2. Under *Templates*, select *Module*.
3. Change the default name that is displayed in the *Name* text box to the name you wish to give the new module file. For example, if you wish to name the new module `ExampleEntryModule`, enter *ExampleEntryModule.vb* in the *Name* text box.
4. Click the *Add* button.

NOTE: When you rename the module file, keep the *.vb* extension.

A new, empty module will be added to your project. The module is displayed in the *Code* window, and an entry for the new module appears in the *Solution Explorer* window. The *Solution Explorer* window in Figure 7-22 shows two forms and one module: `frmError`, `frmMain`, and `ExampleProjectModule`.

Figure 7-21 *Add New Item* dialog box

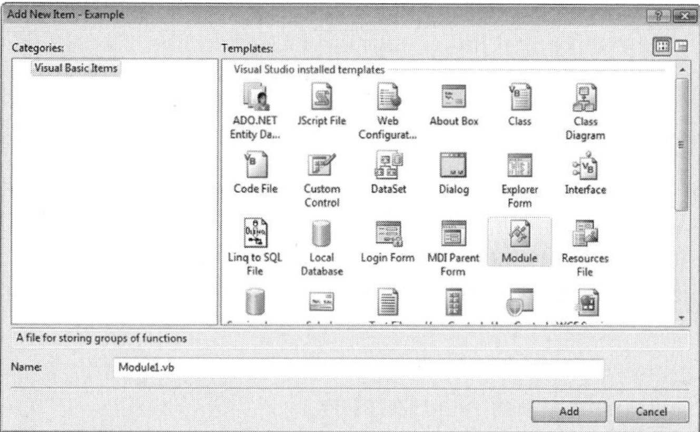

Figure 7-22 *Solution Explorer* window showing two forms and one module

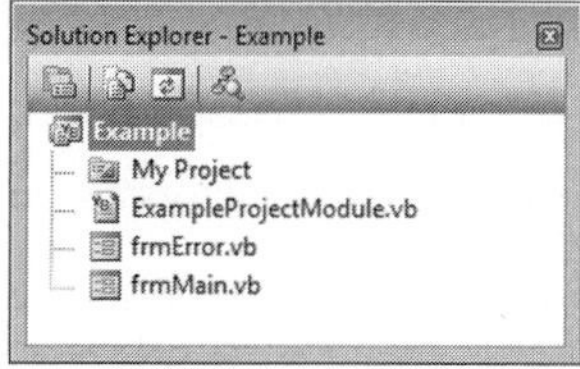

Once you have added a standard module to your project, add the code for procedures and functions to it, just as you would add code to a form.

Using `Private` and `Public` Procedures in a Module

When a procedure declaration in a module begins with `Private`, the procedure can only be accessed by statements in the same module. When a procedure declaration in a module begins with `Public`, it may be accessed by statements outside the module. If you do not provide an access specifier, a procedure becomes `Public`. For example, the following functions appear in the same module:

```
Private Function CalcArea(ByVal sngLength As Single, _
  ByVal sngWidth As Single) As Single

  ' Calculates and returns the area of a rectangle.
  Return sngLength * sngWidth
End Function

Public Function GetArea() As Single

  ' Asks the user for a rectangle's length and width,
  ' and then returns the area.
  Dim sngLength, sngWidth, sngArea As Single
  sngLength = CSng(InputBox("Enter the length of the rectangle."))
  sngWidth = CSng(InputBox("Enter the width of the rectangle."))
  sngArea = calcArea(sngLength, sngWidth)
  Return sngArea
End Function
```

The first function, `CalcArea`, is private. It can only be called from statements in the same module as the function. The second function, `GetArea`, is public. It can be called from statements outside the module. Notice that the `GetArea` function calls the `CalcArea` function. Note that the `CalcArea` function does not check for invalid input.

Module-Level Variables

A variable declared inside a module, but not inside a procedure or function, is called a **module-level variable**. The same rules about the scope of class-level variables in a form apply to module-level variables in a standard module.

- A module-level variable in a standard module is accessible to any procedure or function in the standard module.
- If a module-level variable is declared with the `Dim` or `Private` keywords, the variable is not accessible to statements outside the module. Such a variable has **module scope**.
- If a module-level variable is declared with the `Public` keyword (or no access qualifier at all), it is accessible to statements outside the standard module.

A module-level variable declared `Public` is also known as a **global variable** because it can be accessed globally, by any statement in the application.

TIP: Many programmers prefix the names of global variables with the characters `g_`. This documents the variable's scope. For example, a global Decimal variable that holds the tax rate might be named `g_decTaxRate`.

TIP: Although global variables provide an easy way to share data among procedures, forms, and modules, they should be used with caution. While debugging an application, if you find that the wrong value is being stored in a global variable, you will have to track down every statement that accesses it to determine where the bad value is coming from. Also, when two or more procedures modify the same variable, you must be careful that one procedure's actions do not upset the correctness of another procedure.

Tutorial 7-3 examines an application that uses a standard module.

Tutorial 7-3:
Examining an application that uses a standard module

In this tutorial, you examine the *Ticket Sales* application, which calculates the prices of tickets for performances in the concert hall. The hall has three sections of seats for the general public. Section A tickets cost $20 each, section B tickets cost $15 each, and section C tickets cost $10 each. There is also a student section where tickets cost $7 each. This application has three forms and a standard module. Validation event handlers are used to ensure that integer values are entered by the user.

Step 1: Open the *Ticket Sales* project from the student sample programs folder named *Chap7\Ticket Sales*.

Step 2: Look at the *Solution Explorer* window. The project has three forms: `frmMain`, `frmGeneral`, and `frmStudent`. The project also has a standard module named `TicketSalesModule`. Open `frmMain` in the *Design* window. The form is shown in Figure 7-23 with the names of its button controls labeled.

The `btnGeneral` button displays an instance of the `frmGeneral` form, which processes ticket sales to the general public. The `btnStudent` button displays an instance of the `frmStudent` form, which processes student ticket sales. The `btnExit` button ends the application.

Figure 7-23 *University Concert Hall* main form

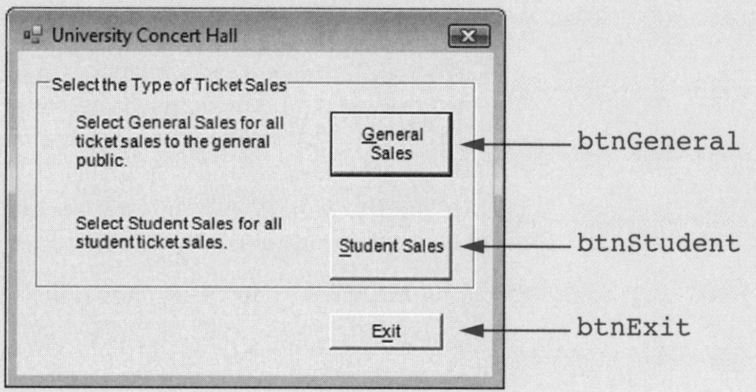

Step 3: Open the `frmGeneral` form, which is shown in Figure 7-24 with the names of its controls labeled.

Figure 7-24 *Public Ticket Sales* form

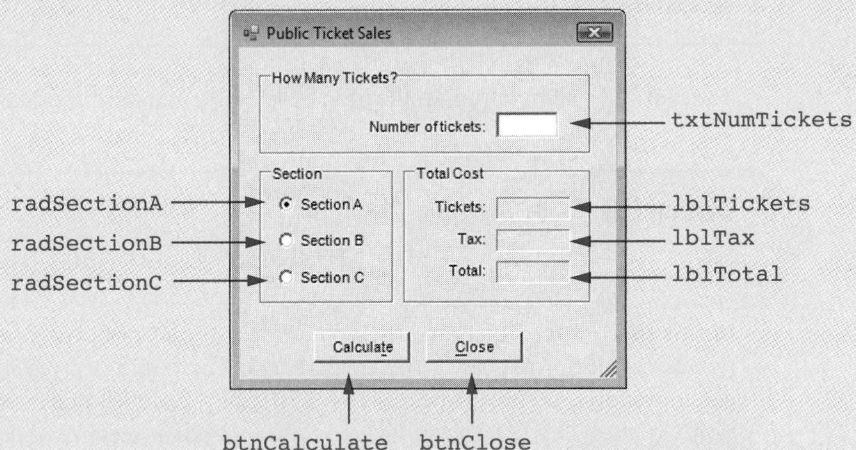

Step 4: Open the *Code* window and look at the `btnCalcuate_Click` even handler:

```
Private Sub btnCalculate_Click(ByVal sender As System.Object, _
    ByVal e As System.EventArgs) Handles btnCalculate.Click

    ' Calculate and display the ticket costs.
    Dim intNumTickets As Integer  ' Number of tickets purchased
    Dim decTicketCost As Decimal  ' Ticket price
    Dim decSalesTax As Decimal    ' Sales tax
    Dim decTotal As Decimal       ' Total cost

    ' Calculate the cost.
    intNumTickets = CInt(txtNumTickets.Text)
    decTicketCost = intNumTickets * PriceEachTicket()
    decSalesTax = CalcTax(decTicketCost)
    decTotal = decTicketCost + decSalesTax

    ' Display the cost.
    lblTickets.Text = decTicketCost.ToString("c")
    lblTax.Text = decSalesTax.ToString("c")
    lblTotal.Text = decTotal.ToString("c")
  End Sub
```

The line marked in bold calls the `CalcTax` function, which returns the amount of sales tax on the argument passed to it.

Step 5: Open the `frmStudent` form, as shown in Figure 7-25 (with the names of its controls labeled).

Step 6: Open the *Code* window and look at the `btnCalculate_Click` event procedure:

```
Private Sub btnCalculate_Click(ByVal sender _
    As System.Object, ByVal e As System.EventArgs) _
    Handles btnCalculate.Click
```

Figure 7-25 *Student Ticket Sales* form

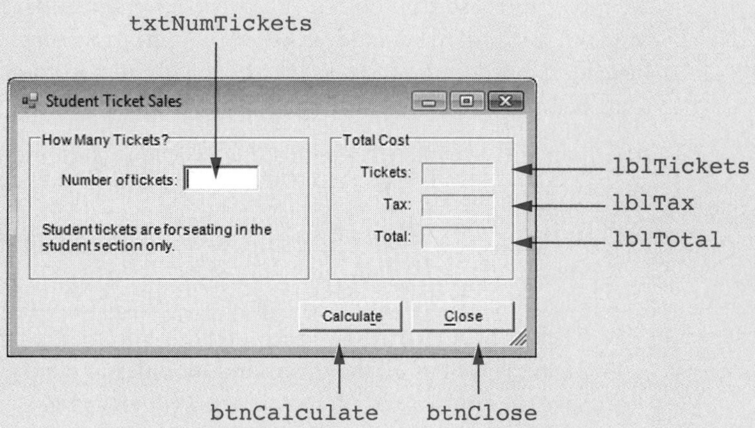


```
        ' Calculate and display the ticket costs.
        Dim intNumTickets As Integer  ' Number of tickets purchased
        Dim decTicketCost As Decimal  ' Ticket price
        Dim decSalesTax As Decimal    ' Sales tax
        Dim decTotal As Decimal       ' Total cost

        ' Calculate the cost.
        intNumTickets = CInt(txtNumTickets.Text)
        decTicketCost = intNumTickets * decSTUDENT_PRICE
        decSalesTax = CalcTax(decTicketCost)
        decTotal = decTicketCost + decSalesTax

        ' Display the cost.
        lblTickets.Text = decTicketCost.ToString("c")
        lblTax.Text = decSalesTax.ToString("c")
        lblTotal.Text = decTotal.ToString("c")
    End Sub
```

The line marked in bold calls the `CalcTax` function. Because `CalcTax` is called by statements in both forms, it is stored in a standard module.

Step 7: In the *Solution* window, open the standard module by double-clicking the entry for *TicketSalesModule.vb*. The module's contents are shown here:

```
Module TicketSalesModule
   ' This module contains the CalcTax function.

   Const decTAXRATE As Decimal = 0.06D        ' Sales Tax Rate

   Public Function CalcTax(ByVal cost As Decimal) As Decimal
      ' This function calculates and returns the
      ' sales tax on ticket sales. The ticket cost is
      ' passed as an argument.
      Return cost * decTAXRATE
   End Function

End Module
```

Step 8: Run the application and test various values on the `frmGeneral` form and the `frmStudent` form. When you have finished, close the application.

Creating an Application with No Startup Form

Visual Basic allows you to designate either a form or a public procedure called **Main** as an application's startup object. If a procedure named Main is the startup object, it must reside in a standard module. When the application runs, no form is initially displayed. Instead, the procedure Main is executed. This allows your application to perform operations before the user sees a form displayed on the screen.

After you have created a Main procedure, follow these steps to designate it as the startup object:

1. In the *Solution Explorer* window, right click the project's entry.
2. On the pop-up menu, click *Properties*. The project's *Property Page* should appear.
3. Clear the *Enable application framework* check box.
4. Click the down arrow in the *Startup Object* drop-down list. A list containing *Sub Main*, as well as all the forms and modules in the project appears. Select *Sub Main*.
5. Save the project and then close the *Property Page*.

When you run the application, the procedure Main executes. Because you have designated Main as the startup object, Visual Basic will not display a form automatically. Instead, you must write code in Main that displays a form. For example, imagine an application that has a form named frmMain and a procedure named CalcInitValues. The CalcInitValues procedure calculates some initial values and displays them on frmMain. Here is a Main procedure that calls CalcInitValues and then displays frmMain:

```
Public Sub Main()
   ' This procedure calculates the startup values
   ' for the main form.
   Dim mainForm as New frmMain    ' Declare an instance of frmMain
   CalcInitValues()               ' Call CalcInitValues.
   mainform.ShowDialog()          ' Display frmMain.
End Sub
```

Main can also be written as a function that returns an integer indicating the program's completion status. Typically, a return value of zero represents successful completion, and other values represent error codes.

Using a Standard Module in More Than One Project

It is possible to use a standard module in more than one project. For example, suppose you have created a project with a standard module that contains several commonly used math functions. Later, you find yourself working on a new project that needs many of the same functions. Instead of rewriting the functions, you can simply add the standard module to the new project.

Follow these steps to add an existing standard module to a project.

1. Click *Project* on the menu bar, and then click *Add Existing Item*.
2. The *Add Existing Item* dialog box appears. Use the dialog box to locate the module file you want to add to the project. When you locate the file, select it and click the *Open* button. The module is now added to the project.

7.13 What do standard modules contain?

7.14 With what file extension are standard modules saved?

7.15 Describe the steps you take to add a new standard module to a project.

7.16 An application's project file is named *Customers*. The application has one standard module. What name would you give the standard module?

7.17 Suppose you want to designate a procedure as an application's startup object. What name must the procedure have?

7.3 Menus

CONCEPT: Visual Basic allows you to create a system of drop-down menus for any form in your application. You use the menu designer to create a menu system.

VideoNote
Creating a Menu

In the applications you have studied so far, the user performs tasks by clicking command buttons. When an application has several operations for the user to choose from, a menu system is more commonly used than command buttons. A **menu system** is a collection of commands organized in one or more drop-down menus. The **menu designer** allows you to visually create a custom menu system for any form in an application.

Before you learn how to use the menu designer, you must learn about the typical components of a menu system. Look at the Example Menu System shown in Figure 7-26.

Figure 7-26 Example Menu System

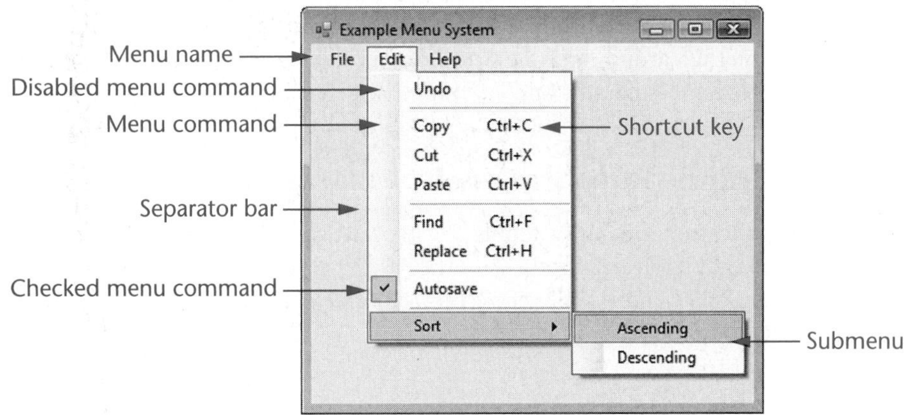

The menu system in the figure consists of the following items.

- **Menu names**—Each drop-down menu has a name. The menu names are listed on a menu strip that appears just below the form's title bar. The menu names in Figure 7-26 are *File*, *Edit*, and *Help*. The user may activate a menu by clicking the menu name. In the figure, the Edit menu has been activated. Menu items may also be assigned access keys (such as F for File, E for Edit, and H for Help). The user may also activate a menu by entering Alt + its access key.
- **Menu command**—Menus have commands. The user selects a command by clicking it, entering its access key, or entering its shortcut key.
- **Shortcut key**—A **shortcut key** is a key or combination of keys that cause a menu command to execute. Shortcut keys are shown on a menu to the right of their corresponding commands. For example, in Figure 7-26, Ctrl+C is the shortcut key for the *Copy* command. Here is the primary difference between a shortcut key and an access key: a menu command's access key only works while the menu is open, but a shortcut key may be executed at any time while the form is active.
- **Disabled menu command**—You can cause a menu command to be disabled when you do not want the user to select it. A disabled menu command appears in dim lettering (grayed out) and cannot be selected. In Figure 7-26, the *Undo* command is disabled.
- **Checked menu command**—A checked menu command is usually one that turns an option on or off. A check mark appears to the left of the command, indicating the option is turned on. When no check mark appears to the left of the command, the option is turned off. The user toggles a checked menu command each time he or she selects it. In Figure 7-26, *Autosave* is a checked menu command.
- **Submenu**—Some of the commands on a menu are actually the names of submenus. You can tell when a command is the name of a submenu because a right arrow (▸) appears to its right. Activating the name of a submenu causes the submenu to appear. For example, in Figure 7-26, clicking the *Sort* command causes a submenu to appear.
- **Separator bar**—A **separator bar** is a horizontal bar used to separate groups of commands on a menu. In Figure 7-26, separator bars are used to separate the *Copy*, *Cut*, and *Paste* commands into one group, the *Find and Replace* commands into another group, and the *Sort* command in a box by itself. Separator bars are only used as visual aids and cannot be selected by the user.

The MenuStrip Control

An application's menu system is constructed with a **MenuStrip control**. When your form is displayed in Design mode, find the *Menus & Toolbars* section of the *Toolbox* window (Figure 7-27) and double-click the *MenuStrip* icon. A MenuStrip control will appear in the component tray at the bottom of the *Design* window, with a default name of `MenuStrip1`.

When the MenuStrip control is selected, you will see the words *Type Here* displayed in a strip at the top of the form. We will informally call this the menu designer, a tool that allows you to visually edit the contents of the menu. You simply click inside this strip and type the names of the items that you want to appear in the menu. Figure 7-28 shows an example where a *File* menu has been added. As shown in the figure, you can assign an access key to a menu name by typing an ampersand (&) before the character that is to become the access key.

Each time you add an item to a menu in the menu designer, you create a **ToolStripMenuItem object**. When you select a ToolStripMenuItem object, you see its properties listed in the *Properties* window. The text that you typed for the item in the Menu Designer will appear in the object's Text property.

ToolStripMenuItem objects are given default names (stored in their Name properties) when they are created, but it is recommended that you change these names to reflect each item's position in the menu system hierarchy. For example, look at the menu system sketch in Figure 7-29. Table 7-3 lists the recommended names of this menu system's ToolStripMenuItem objects, along with the contents of their Text properties.

Figure 7-27 *Menus & Toolbars* section of the *Toolbox*

Figure 7-28 Inserting text into a menu item

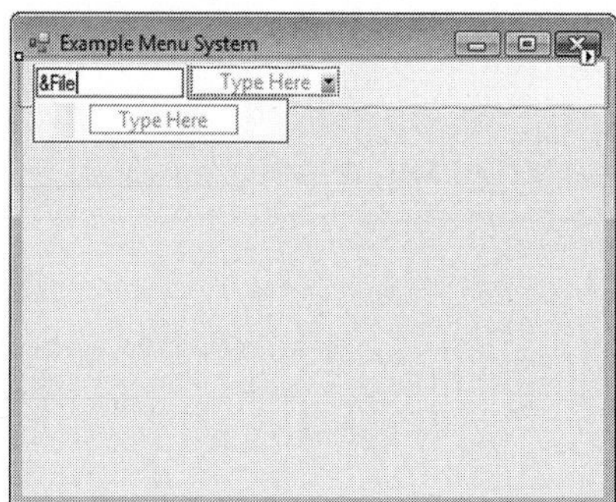

Figure 7-29 Example menu system sketch

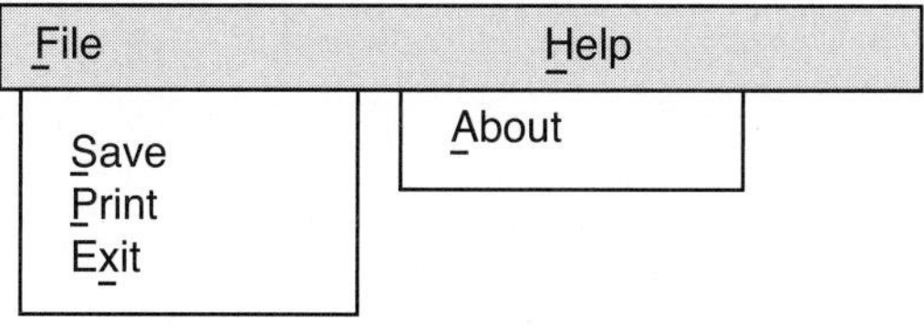

Table 7-3 ToolStripMenuItem objects and their Text properties

ToolStripMenuItem Name	Text Property
`mnuFile`	&File
`mnuFileSave`	&Save
`mnuFilePrint`	&Print
`mnuFileExit`	E&xit
`mnuHelp`	&Help
`mnuHelpAbout`	&About

The menu item names listed in Table 7-3 indicate where in the menu hierarchy each control belongs. The names of objects corresponding to commands on the *File* menu all begin with `mnuFile`. For example, the *Save* command on the *File* menu is named `mnuFileSave`. Likewise, the object for the *About* command on the *Help* menu is named `mnuHelpAbout`.

ToolStripMenuItem objects also respond to events. You can make a menu functional by writing `Click` event procedures for its objects.

How to Use the Menu Designer

Once you have placed a MenuStrip control in a form's component tray, you can use the menu designer to create menu items. Start the menu designer by selecting the MenuStrip control. Figure 7-30 shows a form with a MenuStrip control selected in the component tray, and the menu designer started. The designer appears on the form in the location that the menu system will appear.

Notice in Figure 7-30 that the words *Type Here* appear in a small box in the menu designer. This marks the position of the first menu item. A ToolStripMenuItem object is automatically created when you type text into the box. The text you type is stored in the item's Text property, and is displayed on the menu strip. Figure 7-31 shows the menu designer after the word *File* has been typed as the text for the first menu item.

Figure 7-30 MenuStrip control selected and menu designer started

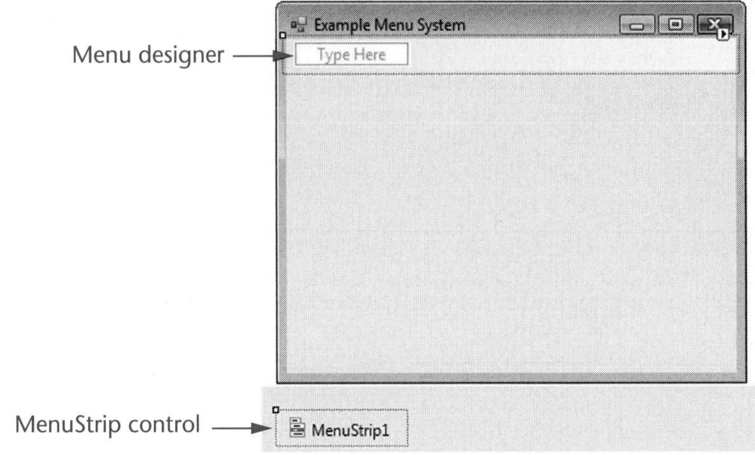

Figure 7-31 MenuStrip object with *File* as its text

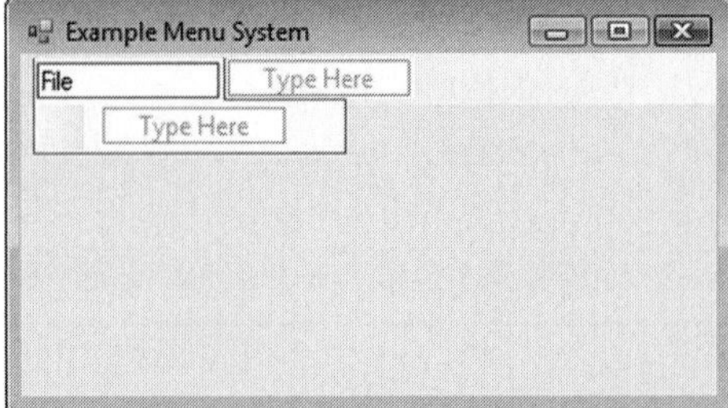

Notice that the menu designer now shows two new *Type Here* boxes, one below and one to the right of the first object. Press the ↓ key to move down, and the → key to move to the right.

In the *Type Here* boxes, enter the text that you wish your menu system to display. Figure 7-32 shows the menu designer with a more complete menu system. The menu system has a *File*, *Edit*, and *Help* menu. The *Edit* menu is displayed.

Figure 7-32 Menu designer with many items

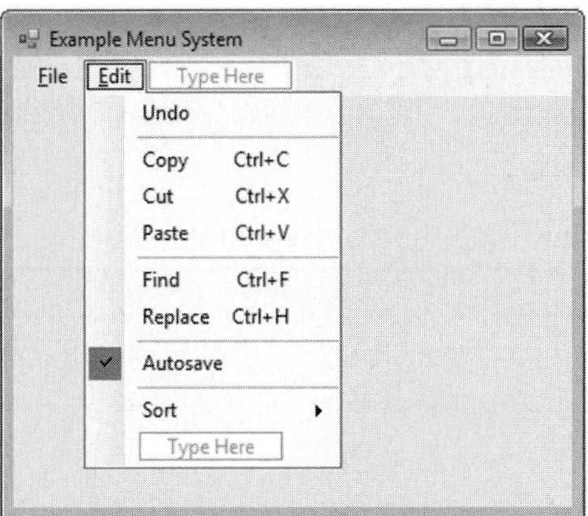

ToolStripMenuItem Object Names

The menu designer assigns default names to the ToolStripMenuItem objects as you create them. You can change a menu item object's name by changing its Name property in the *Properties* window. In Figure 7-33, the *Properties* window shows the properties of a ToolStripMenuItem object. Notice that the Name property has been changed to `mnuEditCopy`.

Figure 7-33 *Properties* window showing a ToolStripMenuItem object's properties

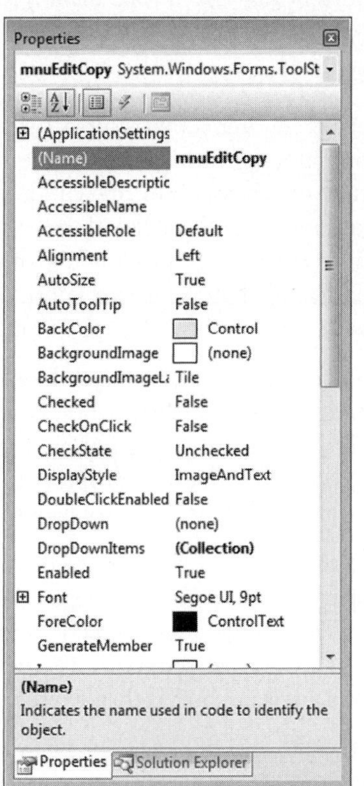

Menu items use a hierarchical naming scheme. For example, the names of all entries under the *File* menu will begin with *mnuFile*. Entries in the *Edit* menu will begin with *mnuEdit*. Individual items within these menus will dictate the remaining part of the name. For example, the *Exit* item in the *File* menu is usually named *mnuFileExit*. The *Copy* item in the *Edit* menu is usually named *mnuEditCopy*.

Shortcut Keys

As previously stated, a shortcut key is a key or combination of keys that cause a menu command to execute. Table 7-4 lists some commonly used shortcut keys in Windows applications.

Table 7-4 Some commonly used shortcut keys in Windows applications

Shortcut Key	Command
Ctrl+S	Save
Ctrl+P	Print
Ctrl+C	Copy
Ctrl+X	Cut
Ctrl+V or Shift+Insert	Paste

Shortcut keys are shown on a menu to the right of their corresponding commands. To create a shortcut key for a menu item, click the down arrow that appears next to the **ShortcutKeys property** in the *Properties* window. A dialog appears with a drop-down list of all the available shortcut keys. The dialog also allows you to select the Ctrl, Shift, or Alt key (or any combination of these). For example, if you want to assign Ctrl+S as a shortcut key, you would select the S key in the drop-down list and place a check next to Ctrl.

You must also make sure that the **ShowShortcut property** is set to *True*. When set to *False*, the item's shortcut key will not be displayed.

Checked Menu Items

Some programs have menu items that simply turn a feature on or off. For example, suppose you are creating an application that functions as an alarm clock, and you want the user to be able to turn the alarm on or off with a menu item. A common approach would be to have a checked menu item for the alarm. When a check mark appears next to the menu item, it indicates that the alarm is on. When the check mark is not displayed next to the menu item, it indicates that the alarm is off. When the user clicks the menu item, it toggles its state between on and off. This type of menu item is called a checked menu item.

To give a menu item the ability to become checked or unchecked when it is clicked by the user, you set the item's **CheckOnClick property** to *True*. You can then set the **Checked property** to either *True* or *False* to specify how the item should initially appear when the application runs. If you set the Checked property to *True*, the item will appear with a check mark next to it. If you set the Checked property to *False*, no check mark will be shown.

In code you can use the Checked property to determine whether a menu item is checked. If the Checked property is set to *True*, it means the item is checked. If the Checked property is set to *False*, it means the item is unchecked. The following code shows an example. This code tests the Checked property of a menu item named `mnuSettingsAlarm`. If the item is checked, a message box is displayed.

```
If mnuSettingsAlarm.Checked = True Then
  MessageBox.Show("WAKE UP!")
End If
```

Disabled Menu Items

A disabled menu item appears dimmed, or *grayed out*, and may not be selected by the user. You may disable a menu item by setting its Enabled property to *False*. For example, applications that provide *Cut*, *Copy*, and *Paste* commands usually disable the *Paste* command until something is cut or copied. So, the *Paste* menu item's Enabled property can be set to False at design time (in the *Properties* window), and then set to *True* in code after the *Cut* or *Copy* commands have been used. Assuming that the *Paste* menu item is named `mnuEditPaste`, the following code enables it:

```
mnuEditPaste.Enabled = True
```

Separator Bars

You can insert a separator bar into a menu in either of the following ways:

- Right-click an existing menu item. On the pop-up menu that appears, select *Insert*, and then select *Separator*. A separator bar will be inserted above the menu item.
- Type a hyphen (-) as a menu item's Text property.

Submenus

When a menu item is selected in the menu designer, a *Type Here* box is displayed to its right. Figure 7-34 shows an example. This box allows you to create a submenu item. When you create a submenu, a right arrow (▸) will automatically be displayed next to the menu item that is the parent of the submenu.

Figure 7-34 Creating a submenu

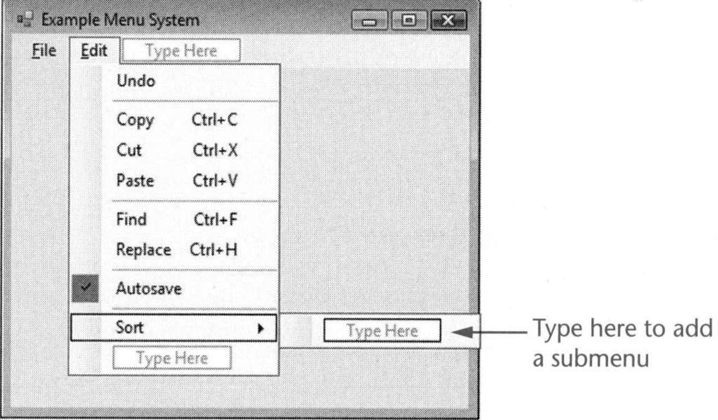

Inserting Menu Items in an Existing Menu

If you need to insert a new menu item above an existing menu item, start the menu designer by selecting the existing name, and then right-click the existing menu item. On the pop-up menu that appears, select *Insert*, and then select *MenuItem*. A new menu item will be inserted above the existing menu item.

If you need to insert a new menu item at the bottom of an existing menu, start the menu designer and simply select the desired menu or submenu. A *Type Here* box automatically appears at the bottom.

Deleting Menu Items

To delete a menu item, start the menu designer and perform one of the following procedures:

- Right-click the menu item you wish to delete. On the pop-up menu, select *Delete*.
- Select the menu item you wish to delete, and then press the Delete key.

Rearranging Menu Items

You can move a menu item by clicking and dragging. Simply select it in the menu designer and drag it to the desired location.

ToolStripMenuItem `Click` Event

You do not have to write code to display a menu or a submenu. When the user clicks a menu item that displays a menu or a submenu, Visual Basic automatically causes the menu or submenu to appear.

If a menu item does not have a menu or submenu to display, you make it functional by providing a `Click` event procedure for it. For example, assume a menu system has a *File* menu with an *Exit* command, which causes the application to end. The menu item for the *Exit* command is named `mnuFileExit`. Here is the code for the object's `Click` event procedure:

```
Private Sub mnuFileExit_Click(ByVal sender As System.Object, _
      ByVal e As System.EventArgs) Handles mnuFileExit.Click

   ' End the application
   Me.Close()
End Sub
```

To write a `Click` event procedure for a menu item, start the menu designer, then double-click the desired menu item. A code template for the `Click` event procedure will be created.

Standard Menu Items

Although all applications do not have identical menu systems, it is standard for most applications to have the following menu items:

- A *File* menu as the leftmost item on the menu strip, with the access key Alt+F.
- An *Exit* command on the *File* menu, with the access key Alt+X and optionally the shortcut key Alt+Q. This command ends the application.
- A *Help* menu as the rightmost item on the menu strip, with the access key Alt+H.
- An *About* command on the *Help* menu, with the access key Alt+A. This command displays an *About* box.

You should always add these items to your menu systems because most Windows users expect to see them. You should also assign shortcut keys to the most commonly used commands. Study the menu system in an application such as Microsoft Word or Microsoft Excel to become familiar with a typical menu design.

In Tutorial 7-4, you learn to use the menu designer by building a simple menu system.

Tutorial 7-4:
Building a menu

In this tutorial, you create an application that demonstrates how a label appears in different colors. You build a menu system that allows the user to select a color, which is then applied to a Label control. Figure 7-35 shows a sketch of the menu system.

Figure 7-35 Sketch of menu system

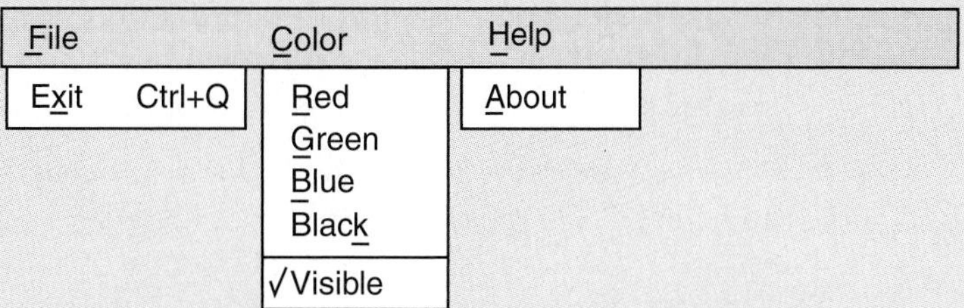

Step 1: Create a new Windows application project named *Menu Demo*.

Step 2: Change the form's Text property to **`Menu Demo`**. Place a label named **`lblMessage`** on the form and set its *Text* property to *Hello World!*, as shown in Figure 7-36.

Step 3: Double-click the *MenuStrip* tool in the *Toolbox* to add a MenuStrip control to the form.

The control, which appears in the component tray, should be selected. If it is not, select it. The menu designer should now be running, as shown in Figure 7-37.

Step 4: First, you will create the *File* menu item. In the *Type Here* box, type **`&File`**. Press the Enter key to create the object. The text *File* should now appear on the menu strip.

Figure 7-36 *Menu Demo* form

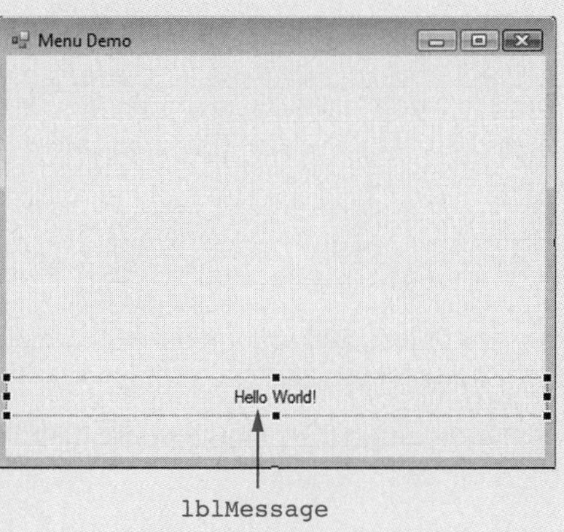

Figure 7-37 Form with menu designer running

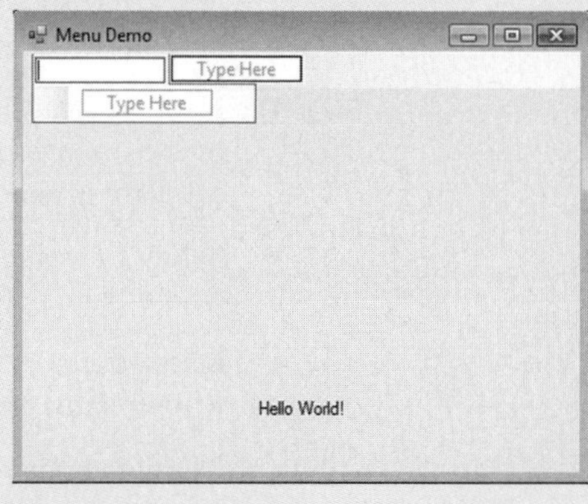

Step 5: Set the Name property for the menu item you just created. Use the mouse or the ↑ key to select the word *File* on the menu. The menu item's properties should be displayed in the *Properties* window. Change the Name property to **mnuFile**.

Step 6: Next, you must create the *Exit* menu item on the *File* menu. Use the mouse or the ↓ key to select the *Type Here* box below the *File* menu item. Type **E&xit** and press Enter to create the object. The text *Exit* should now appear on the *File* menu, as shown in Figure 7-38.

Step 7: Next, you must set the properties for the menu item you just created. Use the mouse or the ↑ key to select the word *Exit*. The menu item's properties should be displayed in the *Properties* window. Change the Name property to **mnuFileExit**. In the ShortcutKeys property select Ctrl+Q.

Step 8: Now you are ready to add the *Color* menu item. In the *Type Here* box shown in Figure 7-39 type **&Color** and press Enter.

Figure 7-38 *Exit* menu item created

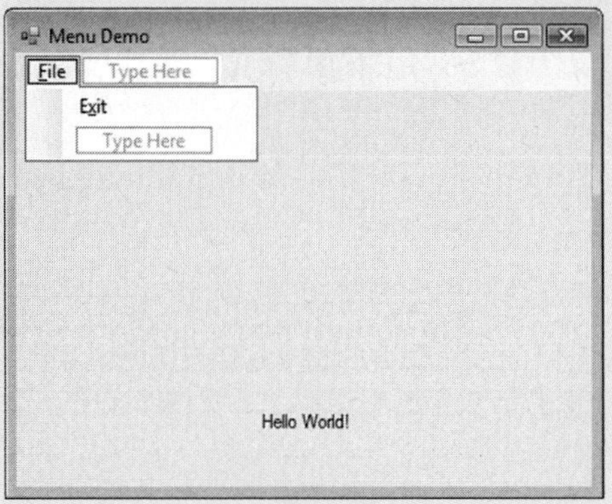

Figure 7-39 Where to type `&Color`

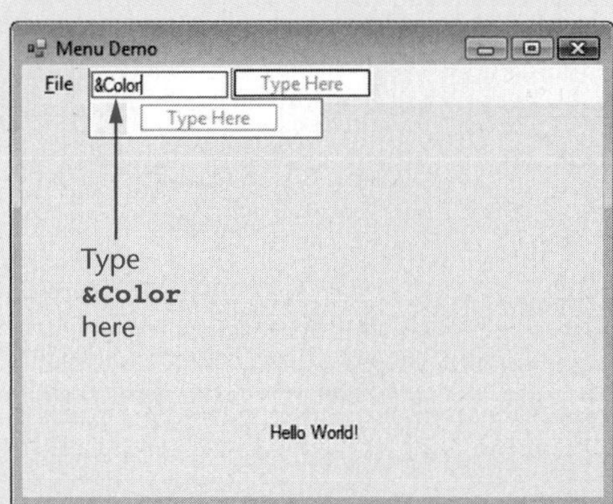

Step 9: Set the Name property for the menu item you just created. Use the mouse or the keyboard ↑ key to select the word *Color* on the menu. The menu item's properties should be displayed in the *Properties* window. Change the Name property to **mnuColor**.

Step 10: Next, you must add the first four menu items to the *Color* menu. Below the `mnuColor` menu item, add an object whose Text reads **&Red** and whose Name property is **mnuColorRed**.

Below the `mnuColorRed` object, add an object whose Text reads **&Green** and whose Name property is **mnuColorGreen**.

Below the `mnuColorGreen` object, add an object whose Text reads **&Blue** and whose Name property is **mnuColorBlue**.

Below the `mnuColorBlue` object, add an object whose Text reads **Blac&k** and whose Name property is **mnuColorBlack**.

Step 11: The menu sketch shown in Figure 7-35 (displayed earlier) shows a separator bar just below the word *Black* on the *Color* menu. Create the separator bar by typing a hyphen (-) in the *Type Here* box below the `mnuColorBlack` object.

Step 12: Below the separator bar, add an object whose Text reads **`Visible`** and whose Name property is **`mnuColorVisible`**. This object's CheckOnClick and Checked properties should both be set to *True*. The *Color* menu should now appear as shown in Figure 7-40.

Step 13: To the right of the *Color* menu item, add the *Help* menu item with the text **`&Help`** and the name **`mnuHelp`**.

Step 14: Below the word *Help*, add a menu item with the text **`&About`** and the name **`mnuHelpAbout`**. When finished, the *Help* menu should appear as shown in Figure 7-41.

Figure 7-40 Completed *Color* menu

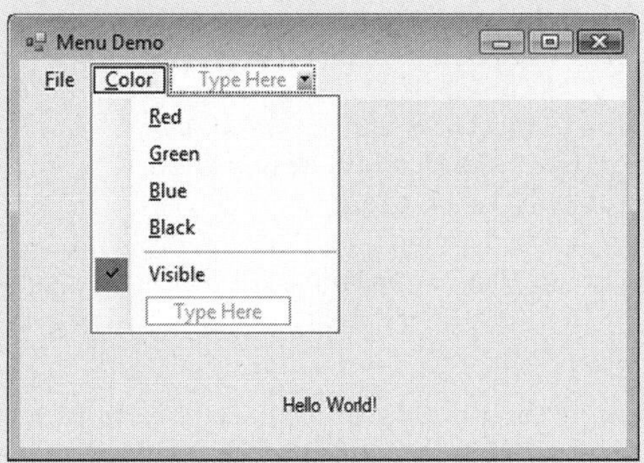

Figure 7-41 Completed *Help* menu

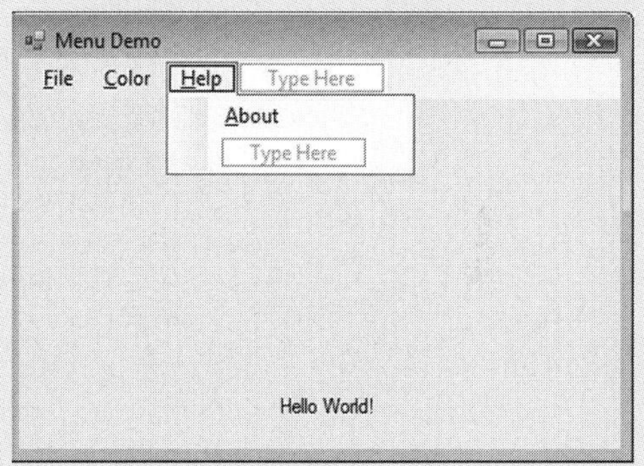

Step 15: Now you will write the `Click` event procedures for the appropriate menu items, starting with `mnuFileExit`. In the menu designer, double-click the word *Exit*, which is on the *File* menu. The *Code* window opens with a code template for the `mnuFileExit_Click` event procedure. Complete the procedure by typing the code shown in bold, as follows:

```
Private Sub mnuFileExit_Click(ByVal sender As System.Object, _
        ByVal e As System.EventArgs) Handles mnuFileExit.Click

    ' End the application
    Me.Close()
End Sub
```

Step 16: Follow this same procedure to write the event procedures for the commands on the *Color* menu. The code for the event procedures is as follows:

```
Private Sub mnuColorRed_Click(ByVal sender As System.Object, _
        ByVal e As System.EventArgs) Handles mnuColorRed.Click

    ' Set the label's foreground color to red
    lblMessage.ForeColor = Color.Red
End Sub

Private Sub mnuColorGreen_Click(ByVal sender As System.Object, _
        ByVal e As System.EventArgs) Handles mnuColorGreen.Click

    ' Set the label's foreground color to green
    lblMessage.ForeColor = Color.Green
End Sub
```

```
Private Sub mnuColorBlue_Click(ByVal sender As System.Object, _
    ByVal e As System.EventArgs) Handles mnuColorBlue.Click

  ' Set the label's foreground color to blue
  lblMessage.ForeColor = Color.Blue
End Sub

Private Sub mnuColorBlack_Click(ByVal sender _
    As System.Object, ByVal e As System.EventArgs) _
    Handles mnuColorBlack.Click

  ' Set the label's foreground color to black
  lblMessage.ForeColor = Color.Black
End Sub

Private Sub mnuColorVisible_Click(ByVal sender As _
    System.Object, ByVal e As System.EventArgs) _
    Handles mnuColorVisible.Click

    ' Make the label visible or invisible
    If mnuColorVisible.Checked = True Then
       lblMessage.Visible = True
    Else
       lblMessage.Visible = False
    End If
End Sub
```

Let's take a closer look at the `mnuColorVisible_Click` procedure. This procedure tests the `mnuColorVisible` object's Checked property to determine whether the menu item is checked. If it is checked, the user wants to make the label visible so the `lblMessage.Visible` property is set to *True*. Otherwise, the `lblMessage.Visible` property is set to *False*.

Step 17: The *Help* menu has one item: *About*. Most applications have this command, which displays a dialog box known as an *About* box. An ***About* box** usually shows some brief information about the application. Write the following code for the `mnuHelpAbout` menu item's `Click` event procedure:

```
Private Sub mnuHelpAbout_Click(ByVal sender As System.Object, _
    ByVal e As System.EventArgs) Handles mnuHelpAbout.Click

  ' Display a simple About window.
  MessageBox.Show("Menu System Demo" & vbCrLf & _
      "Designed for Starting Out with Visual Basic", _
      "About Menu Demo")
End Sub
```

Step 18: Save the project and run it. Try selecting different colors to see how they make the label appear. Also test the *Visible* command and the *About* command. When finished, type Ctrl+Q to exit the application.

Context Menus

A **context menu,** or pop-up menu, is displayed when the user right-clicks a form or control. To create a context menu, you must add a ContextMenuStrip control to a form. You do this just as you add other controls: double-click the *ContextMenuStrip* tool in the *Toolbox* window. A ContextMenuStrip control is then created in the form's component tray. The first such control will have the default name `ContextMenuStrip1`, the second will have the default name `ContextMenuStrip2`, and so on.

Once you have added a ContextMenuStrip control to a form, you select it and then add items to it with the menu designer, just as you do with a regular menu. After you have built the context menu, you add `Click` event procedures for its menu items. Then, you associate the context menu with a control by setting the control's ContextMenuStrip property to the name of the ContextMenuStrip control. At runtime, the context menu will pop up when the user right-clicks the control. For example, Figure 7-42 shows a context menu displayed when the user right-clicks a Label control.

Figure 7-42 *Context* menu

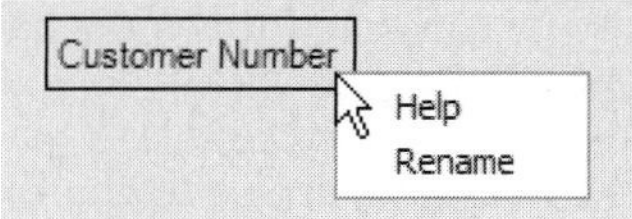

Checkpoint

7.18 Briefly describe each of the following menu system components:
  a. Menu name
  b. Menu command
  c. Disabled menu command
  d. Checked menu command
  e. Shortcut key
  f. Submenu
  g. Separator bar

7.19 What is the difference between a menu item's access key and its shortcut key?

7.20 What prefix do we use for ToolStripMenuItem objects?

7.21 Suppose an application has a *File* menu with the following commands: *Save*, *Save As*, *Print*, and *Exit*. What name would you give each of the controls?

7.22 How do you assign an access key to a menu item?

7.23 What happens if you set a ToolStripMenuItem object's CheckOnClick property to *True*?

7.24 How do you disable a menu control in code?

7.25 How do you determine whether a check mark appears next to a menu item in code?

7.26 What event procedure executes when the user clicks on a menu item?

7.27 How does the user display a context menu?

7.28 How do you associate a context menu with a control?

7.4 Focus on Problem Solving: Building the *High Adventure Travel Agency Price Quote* Application

CONCEPT: In this section you build an application for the High Adventure Travel Agency. The application uses multiple forms, a standard module, and a menu system.

The High Adventure Travel Agency offers three vacation packages for thrill-seeking customers. The rates and options vary for each package. You've been asked to create an application to calculate and itemize the charges for each package.

- **Scuba Bahama:** A weeklong cruise to the Bahamas with three days of scuba diving. Those with advanced experience may dive right in, while beginners should choose to take optional, but very affordable lessons. Rates:
  Base Charge: $1,000 per person
  Scuba Instruction: $300 per person
- **Sky Dive Colorado:** Four thrilling days with expert sky diving instructors in Colorado Springs, Colorado. For lodging, guests may choose either the Wilderness Lodge or the Luxury Inn. Sky diving instruction is included for all members of the party. Rates:
  Base Charge $800 per person
  Lodging at Wilderness Lodge $80/day per person
  Lodging at Luxury Inn $150/day per person
- **Barron Cliff Spelunk:** Seven days spent hiking and exploring caves in the Barron Cliff Wilderness Area, Tennessee. Camping equipment rental is available. Rates:
  Base Charge $700 per person
  Equipment Rental $50/day per person

  A 10% discount is given on the total charges for any package for a party of five or more.

The application will have four forms: `frmMain`, `frmScuba`, `frmSkyDive`, and `frmSpelunk`. A standard module will also be used.

The *HighAdventure.vb* Module

The standard module declares module-level variables and functions, some of which are accessible to code in the other modules. These variables are listed in Table 7-5. The variables that have global scope (accessible to all statements in the project) have the `g_` prefix.

Table 7-5 Module-level constants and variables

Constant/Variable Name	Description
`intMIN_DISCOUNT`	Private constant that specifies the minimum number of people required in a party before a discount is applied
`decDISCOUNT_RATE`	Private constant containing the discount rate for groups over a certain size (specified by `intMIN_DISCOUNT`)
`decDEPOSIT_RATE`	Private constant containing the percentage of the total package price that must be deposited
`g_strPackage`	Global string variable holding the name of the currently selected vacation package

(continued)

Table 7-5 *(continued)*

Constant/Variable Name	Description
`g_intPartyMembers`	Global integer variable indicating the number of people in the party
`g_decSubtotal`	Global decimal variable that holds the cost subtotal (before discount) of the vacation package

Table 7-6 describes the functions in the *HighAdventure.vb* module.

Table 7-6 Functions in the *HighAdventure.vb* module

Function Name	Description
`IsPositive`	This function accepts a string argument and returns *True* if the string contains a positive numeric value. Otherwise it returns *False*. It is used for input data validation.
`CalcDiscount`	This function returns the discount, if any, on a package. It accepts two arguments. The first argument is the number of party members and the second argument is the subtotal of the package.
`CalcDeposit`	This function returns the amount of the required deposit. It accepts one argument, the total of the package charges.

The `frmMain` Form

Figure 7-43 shows a sketch of `frmMain` with the form's controls labeled.

Figure 7-43 Sketch of `frmMain` form

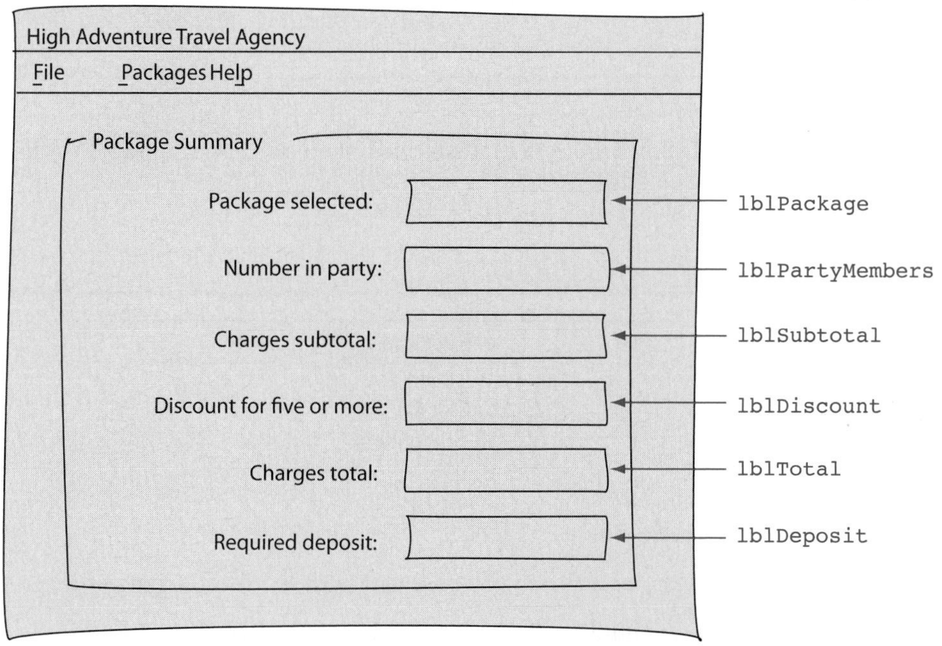

Table 7-7 lists each of the form's controls (excluding the menu item objects) along with relevant property settings. All of the Label controls having Fixed3D border styles also have AutoSize set to *False*.

Table 7-7 `frmMain` controls and property settings

Control Type	Control Name	Property	Property Value
Form	`frmMain`	Text:	*High Adventure Travel Agency*
GroupBox	(Default)	Text:	*Package Summary*
Label	(Default)	Text:	*Package selected:*
Label	`lblPackage`	Text: BorderStyle: AutoSize:	 *Fixed3D* *False*
Label	(Default)	Text:	*Number in party:*
Label	`lblPartyMembers`	Text: BorderStyle: AutoSize:	 *Fixed3D* *False*
Label	(Default)	Text:	*Charges subtotal:*
Label	`lblSubtotal`	Text: BorderStyle: AutoSize:	 *Fixed3D* *False*
Label	(Default)	Text:	*Discount for 5 or more:*
Label	`lblDiscount`	Text: BorderStyle: AutoSize:	 *Fixed3D* *False*
Label	(Default)	Text:	*Charges subtotal:*
Label	`lblTotal`	Text: BorderStyle: AutoSize:	 *Fixed3D* *False*
Label	(Default)	Text:	*Required deposit:*
Label	`lblDeposit`	Text: BorderStyle: AutoSize:	 *Fixed3D* *False*

Figure 7-44 shows a sketch of the menu system on `frmMain`. Table 7-8 lists the menu controls and their shortcut keys.

Figure 7-44 Menu system on `frmMain`

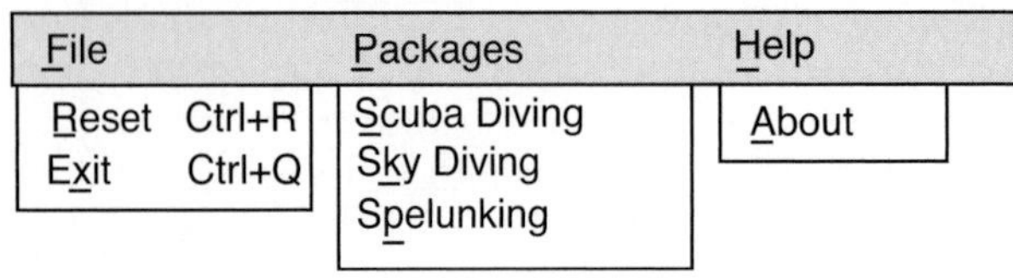

The `frmScuba` Form

Figure 7-45 shows a sketch of `frmScuba` with the form's controls labeled.

Table 7-9 lists and describes the methods in `frmMain`.

Table 7-8 `frmMain` MenuItem objects and shortcut keys

Name	Text	Shortcut Key
`mnuFile`	&File	(none)
`mnuFileReset`	&Reset	Ctrl+R
`mnuFileExit`	E&xit	Ctrl+Q
`mnuPackages`	&Packages	(none)
`mnuPackagesScubaDiving`	&Scuba Diving	(none)
`mnuPackagesSkyDiving`	S&ky Diving	(none)
`mnuPackagesSpelunking`	S&pelunking	(none)
`mnuHelp`	&Help	(none)
`mnuHelpAbout`	&About	(none)

Table 7-9 `frmMain` methods

Method	Description
`mnuFileExit_Click`	Ends the application
`mnuFileReset_Click`	Clears the `lblPackage`, `lblPartyMembers`, `lblSubtotal`, `lblDiscount`, `lblTotal`, and `lblDeposit` labels
`mnuPackagesScubaDiving_Click`	Displays the `frmScuba` form
`mnuPackagesSkyDiving_Click`	Displays the `frmSkyDive` form
`mnuPackagesSpelunking_Click`	Displays the `frmSpelunk` form
`mnuHelpAbout_Click`	Displays an *About* box
`DisplayCharges`	Calculates and displays the discount, total charges, and required deposit for the selected package

Figure 7-45 Sketch of `frmScuba` form

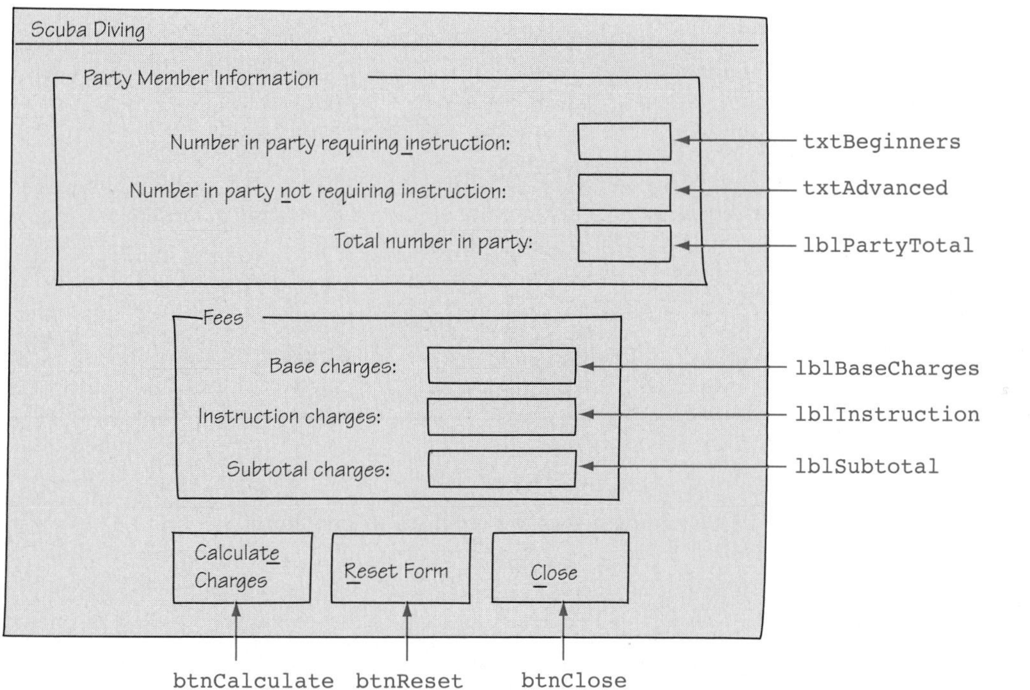

Table 7-10 lists each of the form's controls along with relevant property settings.

Table 7-10 `frmScuba` controls and property settings

Control Type	Control Name	Property	Property Value
Form	`frmScuba`	Text:	*Scuba Diving*
		GroupBox (Default) Text:	*Party Member Information*
Label	(Default)	Text:	*Number in party requiring &instruction:*
Text box	`txtBeginners`	CausesValidation: Text:	*True*
Label	(Default)	Text:	*Number in party ¬ requiring instruction:*
TextBox	`txtAdvanced`	CausesValidation: Text:	*True*
Label	(Default)	Text:	*Total number in party:*
Label	`lblPartyTotal`	Text: BorderStyle: Autosize:	 *Fixed3D* *False*
GroupBox	(Default)	Text:	*Fees*
Label	(Default)	Text:	*Base charges:*
Label	`lblBaseCharges`	Text: BorderStyle: TextAlign: AutoSize:	 *Fixed3D* *Middle Right* *False*
Label	(Default)	Text:	*Instruction charges:*
Label	`lblInstruction`	Text: BorderStyle: TextAlign: AutoSize:	 *Fixed3D* *Middle Right* *False*
Label	(Default)	Text:	*Subtotal charges:*
Label	`lblSubtotal`	Text: BorderStyle: TextAlign: AutoSize:	 *Fixed3D* *Middle Right* *False*
Button	`btnCalculate`	Text: CausesValidation:	*Calcula&te Charges* *True*
Button	`btnReset`	Text: CausesValidation:	*&Reset Form* *False*
Button	`btnClose`	Text: CausesValidation:	*&Close* *False*

Table 7-11 lists and describes the methods in `frmScuba`.

Table 7-11 `frmScuba` methods

Method	Description
`btnCalculate_Click`	Calculates and displays the total charge information for the scuba package.
`btnClose_Click`	Closes the form.
`btnReset_Click`	Clears the `txtBeginners` and `txtAdvanced` text boxes, and the `lblPartyTotal`, `lblBaseCharges`, `lblInstruction`, and `lblSubtotal` labels. Three global variables declared in the *HighAdventure.vb* module are cleared. `g_strPackage` is set to an empty string; `g_decSubtotal` and `g_intPartyMembers` are set to zero.
`txtAdvanced_Validating`	Validates that the `txtAdvanced` text box contains a positive number. If not, the user is prompted to re-enter a value for the text box. This procedure calls the `IsPositive` function, declared in the *HighAdventure.vb* module.
`txtBeginners_Validating`	Validates that the `txtBeginners` text box contains a positive number. If not, the user is prompted to re-enter a value for the text box. This procedure calls the `IsPositiveNumber` function, declared in the standard module.

The `frmSkyDive` Form

Figure 7-46 shows a sketch of `frmSkyDive` with the form's controls labeled.

Figure 7-46 Sketch of `frmSkyDive` form

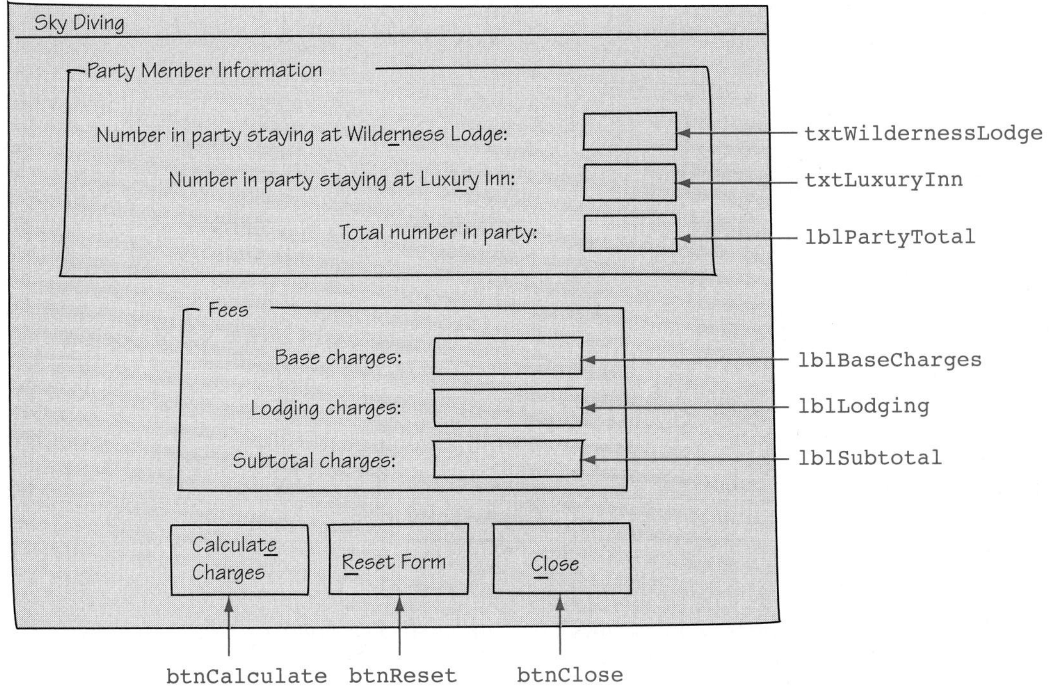

Table 7-12 lists each of the form's controls along with relevant property settings.

Table 7-12 `frmSkyDive` controls and property settings

Control Type	Control Name	Property	Property Value
Form	`frmSkyDive`	Text:	*Sky Diving*
GroupBox	(Default)	Text:	*Party Member Information*
Label	(Default)	Text:	*Number in party staying at &Wilderness Lodge:*
TextBox	`txtWildernessLodge`	CausesValidation: Text:	*True*
Label	(Default)	Text:	*Number in party staying at &Luxury Inn:*
TextBox	`txtLuxuryInn`	CausesValidation: Text:	*True*
Label	(Default)	Text:	*Total number in party:*
Label	`lblPartyTotal`	Text: BorderStyle: AutoSize:	 *Fixed3D* *False*
GroupBox	(Default)	Text:	*Fees*
Label	(Default)	Text:	*Base charges:*
Label	`lblBaseCharges`	Text: BorderStyle: TextAlign: AutoSize:	 *Fixed3D* *MiddleRight* *False*
Label	(Default)	Text:	*Lodging charges:*
Label	`lblLodging`	Text: BorderStyle: TextAlign: AutoSize:	 *Fixed3D* *MiddleRight* *False*
Label	(Default)	Text:	*Subtotal charges:*
Label	`lblSubtotal`	Text: BorderStyle: TextAlign: AutoSize:	 *Fixed3D* *MiddleRight* *False*
Button	`btnCalculate`	Text: CausesValidation:	*Calcula&te* *True*
Button	`btnReset`	Text: CausesValidation:	*&Reset Form* *False*
Button	`btnClose`	Text: CausesValidation:	*&Close* *False*

Table 7-13 lists and describes the methods in `frmSkyDive`.

Table 7-13 `frmSkyDive` methods

Method	Description
`btnCalculate_Click`	Calculates and displays the total charge information for the sky diving package.
`btnClose_Click`	Closes the form.
`btnReset_Click`	Clears the `txtWildernessLodge` and `txtLuxuryInn` text boxes, and the `lblPartyTotal`, `lblBaseCharges`, `lblLodging`, and `lblSubtotal` labels. Three global variables declared in the *HighAdventure.vb* module are cleared. `g_strPackage` is set to an empty string; `g_intPartyMembers` and `g_decSubtotal` are set to zero.
`txtLuxuryInn_Validating`	Validates that the `txtLuxuryInn` text box contains a positive number. If not, the user is prompted to re-enter a value for the text box. This procedure calls the `IsPositive` function, declared in the *HighAdventure.vb* module.
`txtWildernessLodge_Validating`	Validates that the `txtWildernessLodge` text box contains a positive number. If not, the user is prompted to re-enter a value for the text box. This procedure calls the `IsPositiveNumber` function, declared in the *HighAdventure.vb* module.

The `frmSpelunk` Form

Figure 7-47 shows a sketch of `frmSpelunk` with the form's controls labeled.

Figure 7-47 Sketch of `frmSpelunk` form

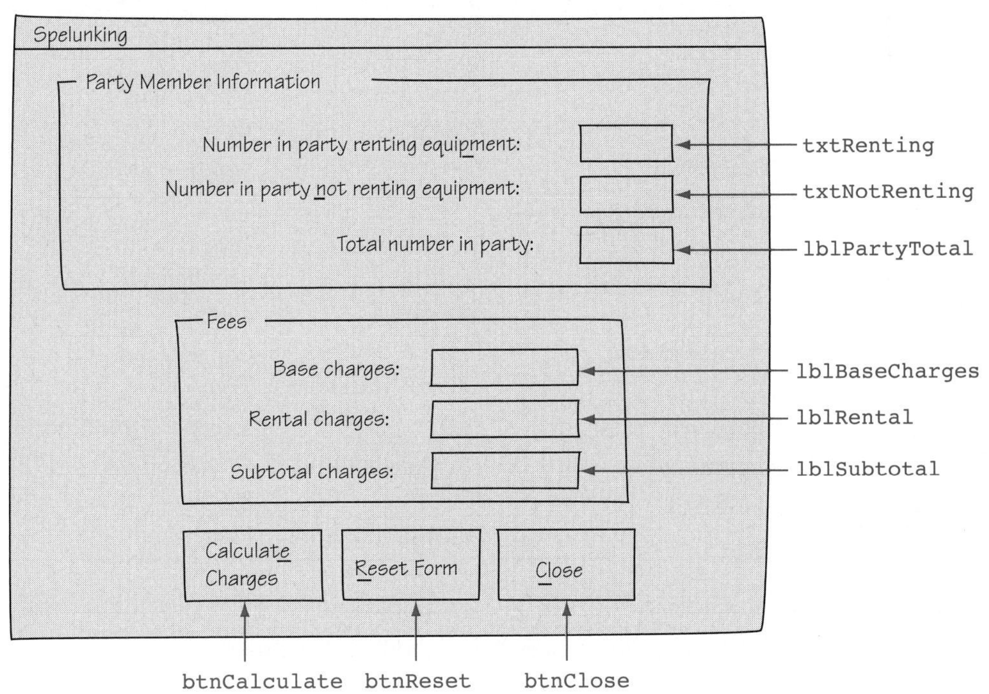

Table 7-14 lists each of the form's controls along with relevant property settings.

Table 7-14 `frmSpelunk` controls and property settings

Control Type	Control Name	Property	Property Value
Form	`frmSpelunk`	Text:	*Spelunking*
GroupBox	(Default)	Text:	*Party Member Information*
Label	(Default)	Text:	*Number in party renting &equipment:*
TextBox	`txtRenting`	CausesValidation: Text:	*True*
Label	(Default)	Text:	*Number in party ¬ renting equipment:*
TextBox	`txtNotRenting`	CausesValidation: Text:	*True*
Label	(Default)	Text:	*Total number in party:*
Label	`lblPartyTotal`	Text: BorderStyle: AutoSize:	 *Fixed3D* *False*
GroupBox	(Default)	Text:	*Fees*
Label	(Default)	Text:	*Base charges:*
Label	`lblBaseCharges`	Text: BorderStyle: TextAlign: AutoSize:	 *Fixed3D* *MiddleRight* *False*
Label	(Default)	Text:	*Rental charges:*
Label	`lblRental`	Text: BorderStyle: TextAlign: AutoSize:	 *Fixed3D* *Middle Right* *False*
Label	(Default)	Text:	*Subtotal charges:*
Label	`lblSubtotal`	Text: BorderStyle: TextAlign: AutoSize:	 *Fixed3D* *MiddleRight* *False*
Button	`btnCalculate`	Text: CausesValidation:	*Calcula&te* *True*
Button	`btnReset`	Text: CausesValidation:	*&Reset Form* *False*
Button	`btnClose`	Text: CausesValidation:	*&Close* *False*

Table 7-15 lists and describes the methods in `frmSpelunk`.

Table 7-15 `frmSpelunk` methods

Method	Description
`btnCalculate_Click`	Calculates and displays the total charge information for the spelunking package.
`btnClose_Click`	Closes the form.
`btnReset_Click`	Clears the `txtRenting` and `txtNotRenting` text boxes, and the `lblPartyTotal`, `lblBaseCharges`, `lblLodging`, and `lblSubtotal` labels. Three global variables declared in the *HighAdventure.vb* module are cleared: `g_strPackage` is set to an empty string; `g_intPartyMembers` and `g_decSubtotal` are set to zero.
`txtRenting_Validating`	Validates that the `txtRenting` text box contains a positive number. If not, the user is prompted to re-enter a value for the text box. This procedure calls the `IsPositive` function, declared in the *HighAdventure.vb* module.
`txtNotRenting_Validating`	Validates that the `txtNotRenting` text box contains a positive number. If not, the user is prompted to re-enter a value for the text box. This procedure calls the `IsPositive` function, declared in the *HighAdvenute.vb* module.

In Tutorial 7-5, you build the *High Adventure Travel Agency Price Quote* application.

Tutorial 7-5: Building the *High Adventure Travel Agency Price Quote* application

Step 1: Create a new Windows application project named *High Adventure*. When a project such as this uses multiple forms, it is convenient to set *Option Strict On* in the *Project Properties* window. Otherwise, you must insert the `Option Strict On` statement at the beginning of every form. Do the following:

- Right-click the *High Adventure* project name in the *Solution Explorer* window and select *Properties* from the pop-up menu.
- Click the *Compile* tab along the left side of the window (Figure 7-48).
- In the *Option Strict* selection box, select *On*.
- Close the *Project Properties* window.

Step 2: Add a standard module named *HighAdventure.vb* to the project, which will hold the functions described in Table 7-6. Write the following code:

```
Module HighAdventure

    ' Code module for the High Adventure Travel Agency
    ' vacation price quote package.

    ' Percentage of a package required for a deposit.
    Private Const decDEPOSIT_RATE As Decimal = 0.5D

    ' Minimum number of people in a party required before
    ' discount is applied.
    Private Const intMIN_DISCOUNT As Integer = 5
    Private Const decDISCOUNT_RATE As Decimal = 0.1D
```

Figure 7-48 Setting compile options in the project *Properties* window

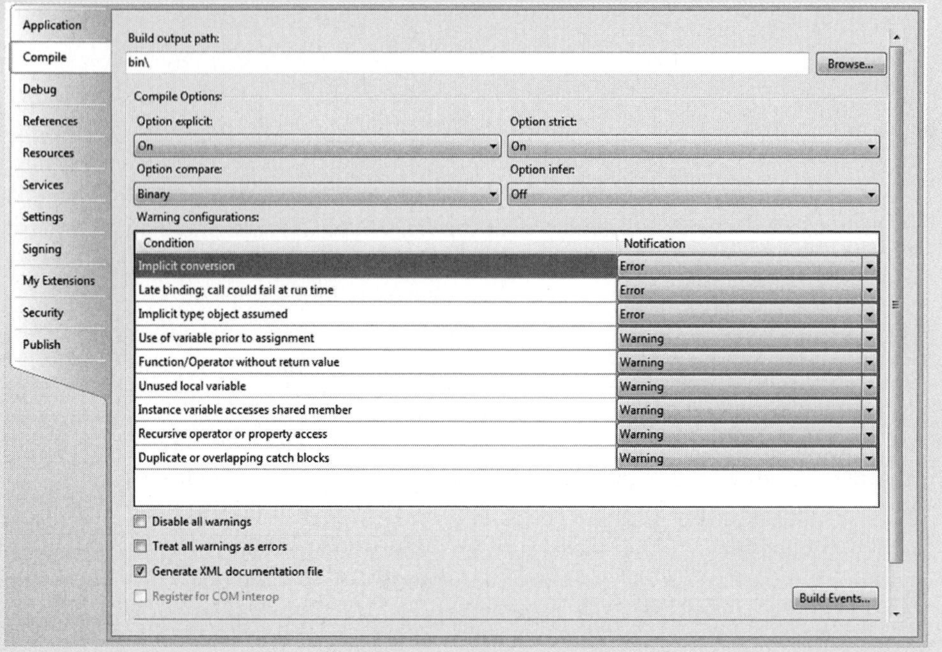
Application
Compile
Debug
References
Resources
Services
Settings
Signing
My Extensions
Security
Publish
Build output path:
bin\
Browse...
Compile Options:
Option explicit:
On
Option strict:
On
Option compare:
Binary
Option infer:
Off
Warning configurations:
Condition
Notification
Implicit conversion
Error
Late binding; call could fail at run time
Error
Implicit type; object assumed
Error
Use of variable prior to assignment
Warning
Function/Operator without return value
Warning
Unused local variable
Warning
Instance variable accesses shared member
Warning
Recursive operator or property access
Warning
Duplicate or overlapping catch blocks
Warning
Disable all warnings
Treat all warnings as errors
Generate XML documentation file
Register for COM interop
Build Events...

```
' Declare global variables.
Public g_strPackage As String           ' Name of package
Public g_intPartyMembers As Integer     ' Number in party
Public g_decSubtotal As Decimal         ' Subtotal of charges

Public Function CalcDiscount(ByVal intNumPeople As Integer, _
    ByVal decSubtotal As Decimal) As Decimal

  ' This function returns the discount, if any, on a package.
  ' The first parameter is the number of people in the
  ' travel party, and the second is the package subtotal.

  If intNumPeople >= intMIN_DISCOUNT Then
    Return decSubtotal * decDISCOUNT_RATE
  Else
    Return 0
  End If
End Function

Public Function CalcDeposit(ByVal decPackageCharges As _
    Decimal) As Decimal

  ' This function returns the amount of the required deposit.
  Return decPackageCharges * decDEPOSIT_RATE
End Function

Public Function IsPositive(ByVal strArg As String) _
    As Boolean

  ' This function accepts a string argument and returns
  ' True if the string contains a positive numeric value.
  ' Otherwise it returns False.
```

```
        If IsNumeric(strArg) Then
            If CDbl(strArg) >= 0 Then
                Return True
            End If
        End If
        Return False
    End Function
End Module
```

Step 3: Name the initial form `frmMain`. Set up the form as shown in Figure 7-49. Refer to Figure 7-43 and Table 7-7 for the control names and their property settings. Set the tab indexes for input controls in a manner that you find to be logical. Chapter 3 explains how to set tab indexes.

Step 4: Add a MenuStrip control to the form. Refer to Figure 7-44 for the menu's layout, and to Table 7-8 for the ToolStripMenuItem object properties. Figure 7-50 shows how `frmMain` should appear after you have added the menu system.

Figure 7-49 `frmMain`

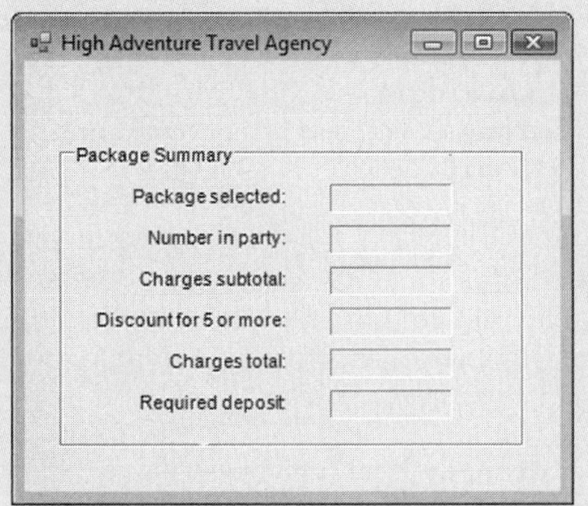

Figure 7-50 `frmMain` with the menu control in place

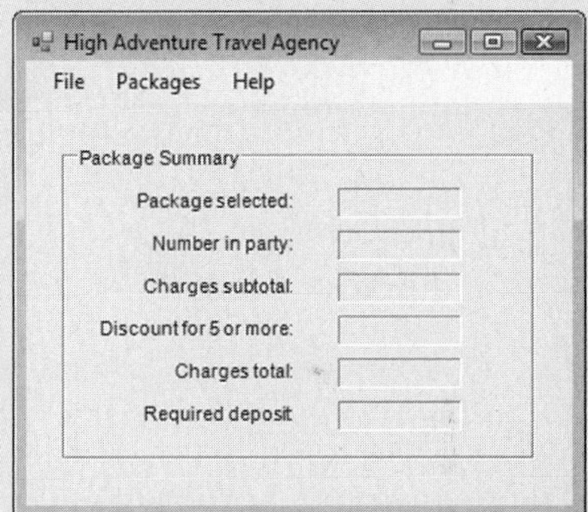

Step 5: Write the procedures for the `frmMain` form, which follows. The code consists of event procedures for the menu controls and a procedure named `DisplayCharges`.

```
Private Sub mnuFileReset_Click(ByVal sender As _
        System.Object, ByVal e As System.EventArgs) _
        Handles mnuFileReset.Click
        ' Reset the form.
        lblPackage.Text = String.Empty
        lblPartyMembers.Text = String.Empty
        lblSubtotal.Text = String.Empty
        lblDiscount.Text = String.Empty
        lblTotal.Text = String.Empty
        lblDeposit.Text = String.Empty
        ' Reset the global variables.
        g_strPackage = String.Empty
        g_intPartyMembers = 0
        g_decSubtotal = 0
    End Sub
```

```
Private Sub mnuPackagesScubaDiving_Click(ByVal sender As _
  System.Object, ByVal e As System.EventArgs) _
  Handles mnuPackagesScubaDiving.Click

  ' Calculate and display the charges for a
  ' scuba diving package.
  Dim scubaForm As New frmScuba()

  ' Display the scuba package form.
  scubaForm.ShowDialog()
  ' Display the charges less any discount and
  ' the required deposit.
  DisplayCharges()
End Sub

Private Sub mnuPackagesSkyDiving_Click(ByVal sender As _
    System.Object, ByVal e As System.EventArgs) _
    Handles mnuPackagesSkyDiving.Click

  ' Calculate and display the charges for a
  ' sky diving package.
  Dim skyDivingForm As New frmSkyDive()

  ' Display the sky diving package form.
  skyDivingForm.ShowDialog()
  ' Display the charges less any discount and
  ' the required deposit.
  DisplayCharges()
End Sub

Private Sub mnuPackagesSpelunking_Click(ByVal sender As _
    System.Object, ByVal e As System.EventArgs) _
    Handles mnuPackagesSpelunking.Click

  ' Calculate and display the charges.
  Dim spelunkForm As New frmSpelunk()

  ' Display the spelunking package form.
  spelunkForm.ShowDialog()
  ' Display charges less discount and deposit.
  DisplayCharges()
End Sub

Private Sub mnuHelpAbout_Click(ByVal sender As _
    System.Object, ByVal e As System.EventArgs) _
    Handles mnuHelpAbout.Click

  ' Display an About box.
  MessageBox.Show("Price Quote System for " & _
      "High Adventure Travel Agency", "About")

End Sub

Private Sub DisplayCharges()
  ' This procedure calculates and displays the amount
  ' of the discount (if any), the total charges less any
  ' discount, and the required deposit.
```

```
        Dim decDiscount As Decimal      ' Package discount
        Dim decTotal As Decimal         ' Total charges
        Dim decDeposit As Decimal       ' Required deposit

        ' Calculate the discount, if any.
        decDiscount = CalcDiscount(g_intPartyMembers, g_decSubtotal)

        ' Calculate the total charges, less discount.
        decTotal = g_decSubtotal - decDiscount

        ' Calculate the required deposit.
        decDeposit = CalcDeposit(decTotal)

        ' Display the data.
        lblPackage.Text = g_strPackage

        lblPartyMembers.Text = g_intPartyMembers.ToString()
        lblSubtotal.Text = g_decSubtotal.ToString("c")
        lblDiscount.Text = decDiscount.ToString("c")
        lblTotal.Text = decTotal.ToString("c")
        lblDeposit.Text = decDeposit.ToString("c")
    End Sub

    Private Sub mnuFileExit_Click(ByVal sender As _
        System.Object, ByVal e As System.EventArgs) _
        Handles mnuFileExit.Click

        ' End the application
        Me.Close()
    End Sub
```

Let's take a closer look at the event handlers that display the other forms. For example, look at `mnuPackagesScubaDiving_Click`. First, the procedure creates an instance of the `frmScuba` form and displays it in modal style.

```
Dim scubaForm As New frmScuba()

' Display the scuba package form.
scubaForm.ShowDialog()
```

When the user closes the `frmScuba` form, `DisplayCharges` is called. `DisplayCharges` is located in the `frmMain` module because it works specifically with controls on the `frmMain` form. `DisplayCharges` calculates and displays the amount of the discount (if any), the total charges less any discount, and the required deposit. The event handlers that display the other forms work in the same way.

Step 6: Add a new form to the project and name it `frmScuba`. Set up the form as shown in Figure 7-51. Refer to Figure 7-45 and Table 7-10 for the control names and their property settings. Set the tab indexes for input field in an order that seems logical. As often happens when translating a rough sketch to a finished product, the *Calculate Charges* button now displays its text on a single line. The same will be true of this button on the sky diving and spelunking forms.

Figure 7-51 `frmScuba` form

Scuba Diving
Party Member Information
Number in party requiring instruction:
Number in party not requiring instruction:
Total number in party:
Fees
Base charges:
Instruction charges:
Subtotal charges:
Calculate Charges | Reset Form | Close

Step 7: Write the class-level declarations and procedures for the `frmScuba` form, as follows:

```
' This form calculates the charges (before any discount)
' for a scuba diving package.

 ' Declare class-level constants.
 Const decScubaRate As Decimal = 1000     ' Base rate
 Const decScubaInstruct As Decimal = 300 ' Instruction rate

 Private Sub btnCalculate_Click(ByVal sender As _
    System.Object, ByVal e As System.EventArgs) _
    Handles btnCalculate.Click

   ' Calculate and display total charge information.
   Dim intNumBeginners As Integer        ' Number of beginners
   Dim intNumAdvanced As Integer         ' Number of divers
   Dim decBaseCharges As Decimal         ' Base charges
   Dim decInstructionCharges As Decimal' Instruction charges

   ' Get the number of beginners and advanced divers.
   intNumBeginners = CInt(txtBeginners.Text)
   intNumAdvanced = CInt(txtAdvanced.Text)

   ' Calculate number in party.
   g_intPartyMembers = intNumBeginners + intNumAdvanced

   ' Calculate base charges.
   decBaseCharges = decScubaRate * g_intPartyMembers
   ' Calculate instruction charges.
   decInstructionCharges = intNumBeginners * _
      decScubaInstruct
   ' Calculate total charges.
   g_decSubtotal = decBaseCharges + decInstructionCharges

   ' Display data on this form.
   lblPartyTotal.Text = g_intPartyMembers.ToString()
   lblBaseCharges.Text = decBaseCharges.ToString("c")
   lblInstruction.Text = decInstructionCharges.ToString("c")
   lblSubtotal.Text = g_decSubtotal.ToString("c")
```

```
        ' Set the name of the package.
        g_strPackage = "Scuba diving"
    End Sub

    Private Sub btnReset_Click(ByVal sender As System.Object, _
          ByVal e As System.EventArgs) Handles btnReset.Click

        ' Reset the fields on the form.
        txtBeginners.Clear()
        txtAdvanced.Clear()
        lblPartyTotal.Text = String.Empty
        lblBaseCharges.Text = String.Empty
        lblInstruction.Text = String.Empty
        lblSubtotal.Text = String.Empty

        ' Reset the global variables.
        g_strPackage = String.Empty
        g_intPartyMembers = 0
        g_decSubtotal = 0

        ' Reset the focus.
        txtBeginners.Focus()
    End Sub

    Private Sub txtAdvanced_Validating(ByVal sender As Object, _
          ByVal e As System.ComponentModel.CancelEventArgs) _
          Handles txtAdvanced.Validating

        ' txtAdvanced must contain a positive numeric value.
        If Not IsPositive(txtAdvanced.Text) Then
            ' Display error message.
            MessageBox.Show("Please enter a positive numeric " _
                 & "value.", "Error")

            ' Select contents of txtAdvanced and set the focus.
            txtAdvanced.SelectAll()
            txtAdvanced.Focus()
            e.Cancel = True
        Else
            e.Cancel = False
        End If
    End Sub

    Private Sub txtBeginners_Validating(ByVal sender As Object, _
          ByVal e As System.ComponentModel.CancelEventArgs) _
          Handles txtBeginners.Validating

        ' txtBeginners must contain a positive numeric value.
        If Not IsPositive(txtBeginners.Text) Then
            ' Display error message.
            MessageBox.Show("Please enter a positive numeric " & _
                 "value.", "Error")
            ' Select contents of txtBeginners and set the focus.
            txtBeginners.SelectAll()
            txtBeginners.Focus()
            e.Cancel = True
        Else
            e.Cancel = False
```

```
        End If
    End Sub

    Private Sub btnClose_Click(ByVal sender As System.Object, _
          ByVal e As System.EventArgs) Handles btnClose.Click

        ' Close this form
        Me.Close()
    End Sub
```

Step 8: Add a new form to the project. Name the form `frmSkyDive`. Set up the form as shown in Figure 7-52. Refer to Figure 7-46 and Table 7-12 for the control names and their property settings. Set the tab indexes for input fields in an order that seems logical.

Figure 7-52 `frmSkyDive` form

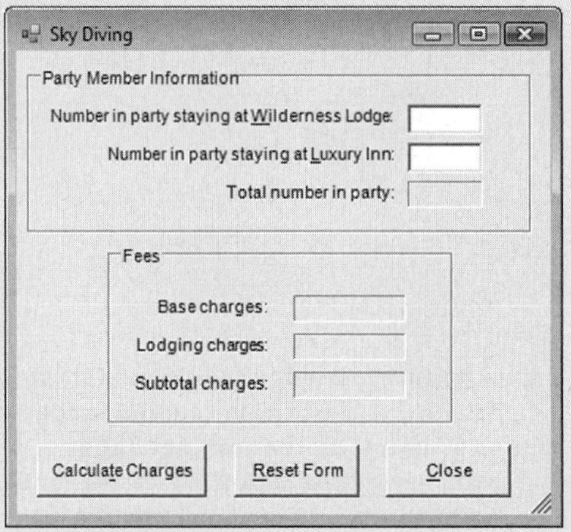

Step 9: Write the class-level declarations and procedures for the `frmSkyDive` form, as follows:

```
' This form calculates the charges (before any discount)
' for a sky diving package. Declare class-level constants.

    ' Base rate
    Const decSKY_DIVE_RATE As Decimal = 800
    ' Wilderness Lodge daily rate
    Const decLODGE_RATE As Decimal = 80
    ' Luxury Inn daily rate
    Const decLUXURY_INN_RATE As Decimal = 150

    Private Sub btnCalculate_Click(ByVal sender As System.Object, _
          ByVal e As System.EventArgs) Handles btnCalculate.Click
        ' Calculate and display total charge information.
        Dim intLodgeCount As Integer          ' Wilderness Lodge
        Dim intLuxuryInnCount As Integer      ' Luxury Inn
        Dim decBaseCharges As Decimal         ' Base charges
        Dim decLodgingCharges As Decimal      ' Lodging charges

        ' Get the numbers staying at each location.
        intLodgeCount = CInt(txtWildernessLodge.Text)
        intLuxuryInnCount = CInt(txtLuxuryInn.Text)
```

```
    ' Calculate number of people in the party.
    g_intPartyMembers = intLodgeCount + intLuxuryInnCount

    ' Calculate base charges.
    decBaseCharges = decSKY_DIVE_RATE * g_intPartyMembers

    ' Calculate lodging charges.
    decLodgingCharges = (intLodgeCount * decLODGE_RATE) _
        + (intLuxuryInnCount * decLUXURY_INN_RATE)
    ' Calculate total charges.
    g_decSubtotal = decBaseCharges + decLodgingCharges

    ' Display data on this form.
    lblPartyTotal.Text = g_intPartyMembers.ToString()
    lblBaseCharges.Text = decBaseCharges.ToString("c")
    lblLodging.Text = decLodgingCharges.ToString("c")
    lblSubtotal.Text = g_decSubtotal.ToString("c")

    ' Set the name of the package.
    g_strPackage = "Sky diving"
End Sub

Private Sub btnReset_Click(ByVal sender As System.Object, _
    ByVal e As System.EventArgs) Handles btnReset.Click

    ' Reset the fields on the form.
    txtWildernessLodge.Clear()
    txtLuxuryInn.Clear()
    lblPartyTotal.Text = String.Empty
    lblBaseCharges.Text = String.Empty
    lblLodging.Text = String.Empty
    lblSubtotal.Text = String.Empty

    ' Reset global variables.
    g_strPackage = String.Empty
    g_intPartyMembers = 0
    g_decSubtotal = 0

    ' Reset the focus.
    txtWildernessLodge.Focus()
End Sub

Private Sub txtLuxuryInn_Validating(ByVal sender As Object, _
    ByVal e As System.ComponentModel.CancelEventArgs) _
    Handles txtLuxuryInn.Validating

    ' txtLuxuryInn must contain a positive numeric value.
    If Not IsPositive(txtLuxuryInn.Text) Then
        ' Display error message.
        MessageBox.Show("Please enter a positive numeric " & _
            "value.", "Error")

        ' Select contents of txtLuxuryInn and set the focus.
        txtLuxuryInn.SelectAll()
        txtLuxuryInn.Focus()
        e.Cancel = True
    Else
        e.Cancel = False
    End If
End Sub
```

```
Private Sub txtWildernessLodge_Validating(ByVal sender As _
  Object, ByVal e As System.ComponentModel.CancelEventArgs) _
  Handles txtWildernessLodge.Validating

  ' txtWildernessLodge must contain a positive
  ' numeric value.
  If Not IsPositive(txtWildernessLodge.Text) Then
    ' Display error message.
    MessageBox.Show("Please enter a positive numeric " & _
        "value.", "Error")

    ' Select contents of txtWildernessLodge and set the focus.
    txtWildernessLodge.SelectAll()
    txtWildernessLodge.Focus()
    e.Cancel = True
  Else
    e.Cancel = False
  End If
End Sub

Private Sub btnClose_Click(ByVal sender As System.Object, _
    ByVal e As System.EventArgs) Handles btnClose.Click

  ' Close this form
  Me.Close()
End Sub
```

Step 10: Add a new form to the project. Name the form `frmSpelunk`. Set up the form as shown in Figure 7-53. Refer to Figure 7-47 and Table 7-14 for the control names and their property settings. Set the tab indexes for input fields in an order that seems logical.

Figure 7-53 `frmSpelunk` form

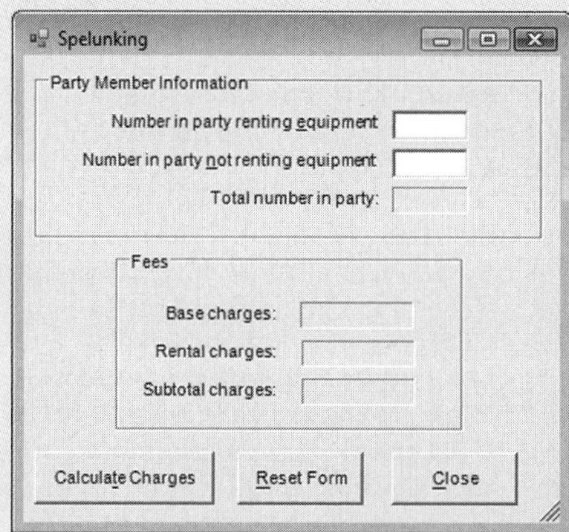

Step 11: Write the class-level variable declarations and procedures for the `frmSpelunk` form, as follows:

```
' This form calculates the charges (before any discount)
' for a spelunking package.
```

```
' Declare class-level constants.
Const decSPELUNK_RATE As Decimal = 700 ' Base rate
Const decRENTAL_RATE As Decimal = 50   ' Equip rental rate
Private Sub btnCalculate_Click(ByVal sender As System.Object, _
    ByVal e As System.EventArgs) Handles btnCalculate.Click

  ' Calculate and display total charge information.
  Dim intRenting As Integer     ' Number renting equipment
  Dim intNotRenting As Integer  ' Number not renting
  Dim decBaseCharges As Decimal        ' Base charges
  Dim decRentalCharges As Decimal      ' Rental charges

  ' Get the number renting and not renting.
  intRenting = CInt(txtRenting.Text)
  intNotRenting = CInt(txtNotRenting.Text)

  ' Calculate number in party.
  g_intPartyMembers = intRenting + intNotRenting

  ' Calculate base charges.
  decBaseCharges = decSPELUNK_RATE * g_intPartyMembers

  ' Calculate rental charges.
  decRentalCharges = intRenting * decRENTAL_RATE

  ' Calculate total charges.
  g_decSubtotal = decBaseCharges + decRentalCharges

  ' Display data on this form.
  lblPartyTotal.Text = g_intPartyMembers.ToString()
  lblBaseCharges.Text = decBaseCharges.ToString("c")
  lblRental.Text = decRentalCharges.ToString("c")
  lblSubtotal.Text = g_decSubtotal.ToString("c")

  ' Set the name of the package.
  g_strPackage = "Spelunking"
End Sub

Private Sub btnReset_Click(ByVal sender As System.Object, _
    ByVal e As System.EventArgs) Handles btnReset.Click

  ' Reset the fields on the form.
  txtRenting.Clear()
  txtNotRenting.Clear()
  lblPartyTotal.Text = String.Empty
  lblBaseCharges.Text = String.Empty
  lblRental.Text = String.Empty
  lblSubtotal.Text = String.Empty

  ' Reset global variables.
  g_strPackage = String.Empty
  g_intPartyMembers = 0
  g_decSubtotal = 0

  ' Reset the focus
  txtRenting.Focus()
End Sub

Private Sub txtNotRenting_Validating(ByVal sender As Object, _
    ByVal e As System.ComponentModel.CancelEventArgs) _
    Handles txtNotRenting.Validating
```

```
        ' txtNotRenting must contain a positive
        ' numeric value.
        If Not IsPositive(txtNotRenting.Text) Then
           ' Display error message.
           MessageBox.Show("Please enter a positive numeric " & _
                "value.", "Error")

           ' Select contents of txtNotRenting and set the focus.
           txtNotRenting.SelectAll()
           txtNotRenting.Focus()
           e.Cancel = True
        Else
           e.Cancel = False
        End If
     End Sub

     Private Sub txtRenting_Validating(ByVal sender As Object, _
           ByVal e As System.ComponentModel.CancelEventArgs) _
           Handles txtRenting.Validating

        ' txtRenting must contain a positive
        ' numeric value.
        If Not IsPositive(txtRenting.Text) Then
           ' Display error message.
           MessageBox.Show("Please enter a positive numeric " & _
                "value.", "Error")
           ' Select contents of txtBeginners and set the focus.
           txtRenting.SelectAll()
           txtRenting.Focus()
           e.Cancel = True
        Else
           e.Cancel = False
        End If
     End Sub

     Private Sub btnClose_Click(ByVal sender As System.Object, _
           ByVal e As System.EventArgs) Handles btnClose.Click

        ' Close this form
        Me.Close()
     End Sub
```

Step 12: Save the project.

Step 13: Run the application. If there are errors, refer to the code listings shown earlier to debug the application.

Summary

7.1 Multiple Forms

- Visual Basic projects can have multiple forms; one form is the startup object, displayed when the project executes. Other forms are displayed by programming statements.
- When you create a form, the code for that form is stored in a file ending with a *.vb* extension. Normally, the name of the file is the same as the name of the form. The form file contains the form class declaration, which is code that describes the form's properties and methods.
- The Project's *Property Page* dialog box allows you to designate a project's startup object.
- Before displaying a form, you must create an instance of the form. Then, you must call a method (`Show` or `ShowDialog`) to display the form. The `Show` method displays a form in modeless style. The `ShowDialog` method displays a form in modal style.
- When a modal form is displayed, no other form in the application can receive the focus until the modal form is closed. No other statements in the procedure that displayed the modal form will execute until the modal form is closed.
- A form's `Close` method removes it from the screen and from memory. A form typically uses the `Me` keyword to call its own `Close` method, as in `Me.Close()`.
- The `Load` event occurs just before a form is displayed for the first time. A form's `Activated` event occurs when the user switches to the form from another form or another application. The `FormClosing` event occurs when a form is in the process of closing, but before it has closed. The `FormClosed` event is triggered after a form has closed. You may write event handlers that execute in response to any of these events.
- Code from one form can reference objects on a different form. You must fully qualify the name of the object by preceding it with the form name, followed by a period.
- To make a form's class-level variable available to statements outside the form, declare it with the `Public` keyword. Although class-level variables are automatically declared private by the `Dim` statement, you should explicitly declare them private with the `Private` keyword.
- After a form has been saved to a form file, it may be used in other projects.

7.2 Standard Modules

- A standard module contains code—declarations and procedures—that is used by other files in a project. Standard modules are not associated with a form and contain no event procedures.
- You can designate a procedure named `Main` as an application's startup object. `Main` must reside in a standard module. When the application runs, no form is initially displayed. Instead, the procedure `Main` is executed.
- A variable declared inside a module (between the `Module` and the `End Module` statements), but not inside a procedure or function, is a module-level variable. A module-level variable declared `Public` is also known as a global variable because it can be accessed globally by any statement in the application.
- You can use the same standard module in more than one project.

7.3 Menus

- The MenuStrip control lets you create a system of drop-down menus on any form. You place a MenuStrip control on the form and then use the menu designer to create a menu system.

- An application's menu system is constructed from ToolStripMenuItem objects. When you create menu items, you name them with the `mnu` prefix.
- If you do not want the user to be able to select a menu item, set the item's Enabled property to *False* (either in Design mode or in runtime code). When a menu control's CheckOnClick property is set to *True*, it will have the ability to become checked or unchecked when clicked. When a menu control's Checked property equals *True*, a check mark appears on the menu next to the control's text.
- You make a ToolStripMenuItem object respond to clicks by providing it with a `Click` event handler.

7.4 Focus on Problem Solving: *Building the High Adventure Travel Agency Price Quote* Application

- This section outlines the process of building the *High Adventure Travel Agency Price Quote* application using multiple forms, a standard module, and a menu system.

Key Terms

About box
`Activated` event handler
Checked property
CheckOnClick property
class
`Close` method
context menu
`FormClosed` event handler
`FormClosing` event handler
`frm`
global scope
global variable
`Hide` method
`Main` (procedure)
`Me` keyword
menu designer
menu system
MenuStrip control
modal form
modeless form
module-level variable
module scope
object variable
`Private` keyword
`Public` keyword
separator bar
shortcut key
ShortcutKeys property
`Show` method
`ShowDialog` method
ShowShortcut property
standard module
startup object
ToolStripMenuItem objects

Review Questions and Exercises

Fill-in-the-Blank

1. If a form is the _______________, it is displayed first when the project executes.
2. When a _______________ form is displayed, no other form in the application can receive the focus until the form is closed.
3. A _______________ is a variable that holds the memory address of an object and allows you to work with the object.
4. The _______________ method removes a form from the screen but does not remove it from memory.
5. The _______________ method removes a form from the screen and releases the memory it is using.
6. The _______________ method displays a form in modal style.

7. The ______________ method displays a form in modeless style.
8. Standard modules contain no ______________ procedures.
9. When a procedure declaration in a form file begins with ______________, the procedure may only be accessed by statements in the same form.
10. To make a class-level variable available to statements outside the module, you declare it with the ______________ keyword.
11. A module-level variable declared `Public` is also known as a ______________ variable.
12. You can designate a procedure named ______________ as an application's startup object.
13. You can disable a menu control in code by setting its ______________ property to *False*.
14. When a menu item's ______________ property equals *True*, a check mark appears on the menu next to the item's text.
15. A ______________ is a pop-up menu that is displayed when the user right-clicks a form or control.

Multiple Choice

1. Which of the following is the standard prefix for form names?
   a. `fr`
   b. `frm`
   c. `for`
   d. `fm`
2. When this form is displayed, no other form in the application can receive the focus until the form is closed.
   a. Modal
   b. Modeless
   c. Startup
   d. Unloaded
3. When this form is displayed using a method call, statements following the method call continue to execute after the form is displayed.
   a. Modal
   b. Modeless
   c. Startup
   d. Unloaded
4. What does the `Hide` method do?
   a. Removes a form from the screen and removes it from memory
   b. Removes a form from the screen but does not remove it from memory
   c. Positions one form behind another one
   d. Removes a form from memory but does not remove it from the screen
5. This method removes the visual part of a form from memory, making the form invisible.
   a. `Remove`
   b. `Delete`
   c. `Close`
   d. `Hide`

6. If `g_intTotal` is a class-level variable, one of the following declaration statements makes it accessible to statements outside the class or module.
   a. `Dim g_intTotal As Integer`
   b. `Public g_intTotal As Integer`
   c. `Global g_intTotal As Integer`
   d. `Private g_intTotal As Integer`
7. Just before a form is initially displayed, this event occurs.
   a. `InitialDisplay`
   b. `Load`
   c. `Display`
   d. `Create`
8. This event occurs when the user switches to the form from another form or another application.
   a. `Activated`
   b. `Load`
   c. `Switch`
   d. `Close`
9. This event occurs as a form is in the process of closing, but before it has closed.
   a. `FormClosed`
   b. `StartClose`
   c. `ShutingDown`
   d. `FormClosing`
10. This event occurs after a form has closed.
    a. `FormClosed`
    b. `EndClose`
    c. `ShutDown`
    d. `FormClosing`
11. A form uses this statement to call its own `Close` method.
    a. `Form.Close()`
    b. `Me.Close()`
    c. `Close(Me)`
    d. `ThisForm.Close()`
12. If a procedure or variable is used by more than one form, where should it be declared?
    a. Standard module
    b. Form file
    c. Multiprocess module
    d. Project module
13. If you designate the procedure `Main` as the startup object, where must it reside?
    a. In the form that is also designated as the startup object
    b. In the form's `Load` event procedure
    c. In a standard module
    d. In the `frmMain` form

14. If an application's menu system has a *Cut* command on the *Edit* menu, what should the menu control for the command be named?
    a. `mnuCut`
    b. `mnuEdit`
    c. `mnuCutEdit`
    d. `mnuEditCut`

15. A menu command's ______________ only works while the menu is open, while a(n) ______________ may be executed at any time while the form is active.
    a. Shortcut key, access key
    b. Access key, shortcut key
    c. Function key, control key
    d. Alternate key, control key

16. Which of the following statements disables the `mnuFilePrint` object?
    a `mnuFilePrint.Disabled = True`
    b. `mnuFilePrint.Enabled = False`
    c. `mnuFilePrint.Available = False`
    d. `Disable mnuFilePrint`

True or False

Indicate whether the following statements are true or false.

1. T F: By default, the first form you create is the startup object.
2. T F: The `Show` method displays a form in modeless style.
3. T F: Although the `Hide` method removes a form from the screen, it does not remove it from memory.
4. T F: If you have code that you want to execute every time a form displays, the form's `Load` event procedure is the best place to write it.
5. T F: The `Activated` event only executes once—when the form is initially displayed.
6. T F: The `FormClosing` event executes before a form has completely closed.
7. T F: It is not possible to access a control on another form in code.
8. T F: A menu command's shortcut key only works while the menu is open.
9. T F: If a menu control does not display a menu or submenu, you make it functional by providing a `Click` event handler for it.
10. T F: A context menu displays when the user double-clicks a control.

Short Answer

1. Describe the process of adding a new form to a project.
2. Describe the process of removing a form from a project, but not deleting the form file.
3. Describe the process of removing a form from a project, and deleting the form file.
4. Describe the process of changing the startup object to another form.
5. What does the statement `Me.Close()` do?

6. What is the difference between the `Load` event and the `Activated` event?
7. Suppose you want to execute code when a form is about to close, but has not fully closed. Where should you place the code?
8. Suppose you want to execute code when a form has fully closed. Where should you place the code?
9. Suppose you wish to make a form's class-level variable available to statements outside the file containing the class declaration. How should you declare the variable?
10. Describe the steps for adding a standard module to a project.
11. If you wish to execute code when an application starts, before the user sees a form displayed on the screen, what must you do?
12. What is the difference between a menu control's access key and its shortcut key?
13. How do you create a checked menu item?
14. In code, how do you determine whether a check mark appears next to a menu item?
15. What is a disabled menu item? How do you make a menu item disabled?

What Do You Think?

1. If you want to display multiple forms on the screen at one time and be able to interact with any of them at any time, do you display them as modal or modeless forms?
2. You want to write code that removes a form from the screen, but you still want to access controls on the form in code. How do you accomplish this?
3. Suppose a form is named `frmStatus`, and it has a Label control named `lblArrivalGate`. Write a statement that stores the string `"D West"` in the label's Text property from another form.
4. Suppose you have written a function, named `CircleArea`, which returns the area of a circle. You call the function from numerous procedures in different form modules. Should you store the function in a form or a standard module?
5. Suppose you have written a Boolean function named `InRange`, which determines whether a value is within a range of numbers. You only call the function from code in one form. Should you store the function in the form module or a standard module?
6. Suppose you have written a procedure in a standard module named `Main` and designated it as the project's startup object. You also have a form that is to be displayed once `Main` has executed. If, when you run the application, the form does not appear on the screen, what is the most likely cause?
7. The following statements create three instances of the form `frmBannerAd`. Will all three of the forms be displayed at the same time? Why or why not?

```
Dim adForm1 As New frmBannerAd()
Dim adForm2 As New frmBannerAd()
Dim adForm3 As New frmBannerAd()
adForm1.Show()
adForm2.Show()
adForm3.Show()
```

Find the Error

What is wrong with the following statements?

1. `Hide Me`

2. *Class-level declaration in frmResults*
   ```
   Dim intNumber as Integer
   ```
   Statements in another form
   ```
   Dim resultsForm as New frmResults()
   resultsForm.intNumber = 100
   ```

3. ```
   Dim errorForm as frmError
   errorForm.ShowDialog()
   ```

4. ```
   Dim messageForm as New frmMessage
   frmMessage.ShowDialog()
   ```

5. ```
   ' Module declaration
   Module
   ```
   Statements inside the module
   ```
   End Module
   ```

Algorithm Workbench

1. An application has three forms: `frmFirst`, `frmSecond`, and `frmThird`. The `frmSecond` form has a public class-level integer variable named `intReading`. The `frmThird` form has a text box named `txtInput`. The following statements exist in the `frmFirst` form:
   ```
   Dim secondForm As New frmSecond()
   Dim thirdForm As New frmThird()
   ```
   Assume that the user has entered a value into the `txtInput` control on the `frmThird` form. Write a statement that executes after these statements and stores the value entered in `txtInput` into the `intReading` variable (in the `frmSecond` form).

2. Here is the code template for a form's `FormClosing` event procedure:
   ```
   Private Sub frmMain_FormClosing(ByVal sender As Object, _
         ByVal e As System.ComponentModel.FormClosingEventArgs) _
         Handles Me.FormClosing
   End Sub
   ```
   Suppose you only want the form to close if the user knows the secret word, which is *water*. Write statements in this procedure to ask the user to enter the secret word. If the user enters the correct secret word, the form should close. Otherwise, the form should not close. (Perform a case-insensitive test for the secret word.)

Programming Challenges

1. **Conference Registration System**

   Create an application that calculates the registration fees for a conference. The general conference registration fee is $895 per person. There is also an optional opening night dinner with a keynote address for $30 per person. Additionally, the optional preconference workshops listed in Table 7-16 are available.
   ```

Table 7-16 Optional preconference workshops

Workshop	Fee
Introduction to E-commerce	$295
The Future of the Web	$295
Advanced Visual Basic	$395
Network Security	$395

The application should have two forms. The main form should appear similar to the one shown in Figure 7-54.

Figure 7-54 *Conference Registration System* main form

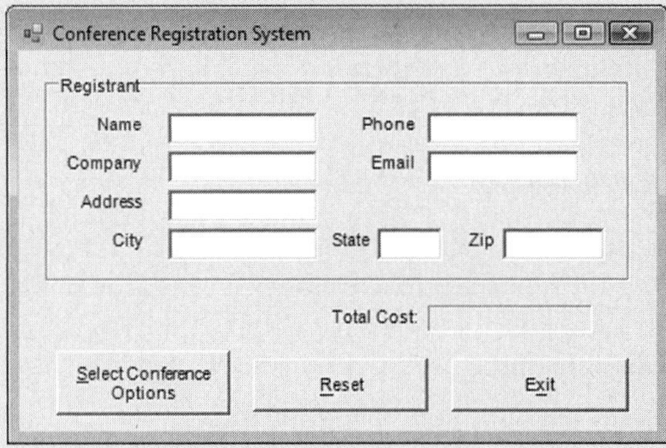

When the user clicks the *Select Conference Options* button, the form shown in Figure 7-55 should appear.

The *Conference Options* form allows the user to select the regular conference registration, the optional opening night dinner, and an optional preconference workshop. (The user cannot register for the optional events, however, without selecting the conference registration of $895.) When the *Close* button is clicked, this form should be removed from the screen and the total registration fee should appear on the main form.

Figure 7-55 *Conference Options* form

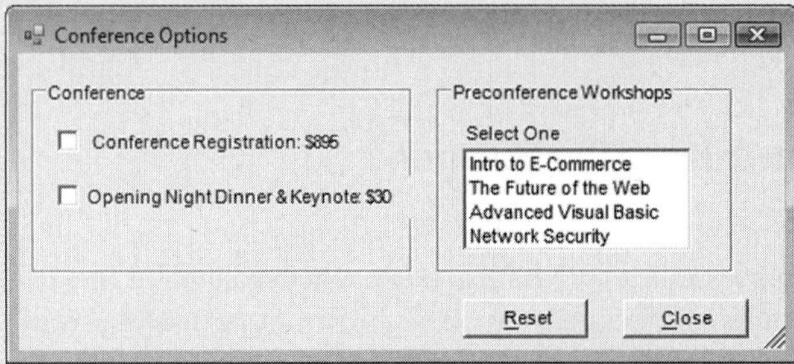

2. **Shopping Cart System**

Design an application that works as a shopping cart system. The user should be able to add any of the following items to his or her shopping cart:

Print Books (books on paper):

I Did It Your Way	$11.95
The History of Scotland	$14.50
Learn Calculus in One Day	$29.95
Feel the Stress	$18.50

Audio Books (books on tape):

Learn Calculus in One Day	$29.95
The History of Scotland	$14.50
The Science of Body Language	$12.95
Relaxation Techniques	$11.50

The application's main form should appear similar to the one shown in Figure 7-56.

Figure 7-56 *Shopping Cart* main form

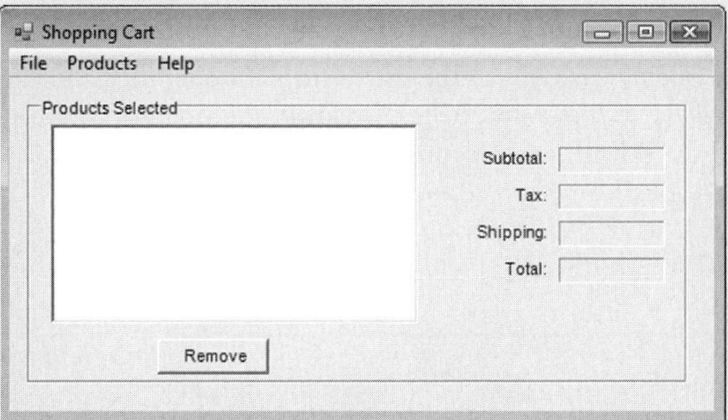

The list box shows all items in the shopping cart. There is a 6% sales tax on the total cost of the items in the shopping cart. Also, for each item in the shopping cart there is a $2.00 shipping charge. To remove an item from the shopping cart, the user selects it in the list box and clicks the *Remove* button. The subtotal, tax, shipping, and total fields should be adjusted accordingly. The main form's menu system is sketched in Figure 7-57.

Figure 7-57 *Shopping Cart* menu system

File	Products	Help
Reset Ctrl+R	Print Books	About
Exit Ctrl+Q	Audio Books	

When the user selects *Reset* from the *File* menu, all items in the shopping cart should be removed, and the subtotal, tax, shipping, and total fields should be cleared. When the user selects *Exit* from the *File* menu, the application should end. When the user selects *About* from the *Help* menu, a simple *About* box should appear. When the user selects *Print Books* from the *Products* menu, the form in Figure 7-58 should appear.

Figure 7-58 *Print Books* form

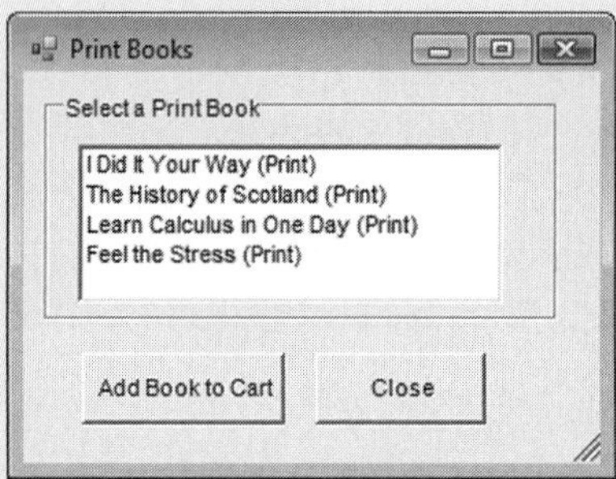

To add one of the items in the list to the shopping cart, the user selects it and clicks the *Add Book to Cart* button. To cancel the operation, the user simply clicks the *Close* button without selecting a book. On the main form, when the user selects *Audio Books* from the *Products* menu, the form in Figure 7-59 should appear.

Figure 7-59 *Audio Books* form

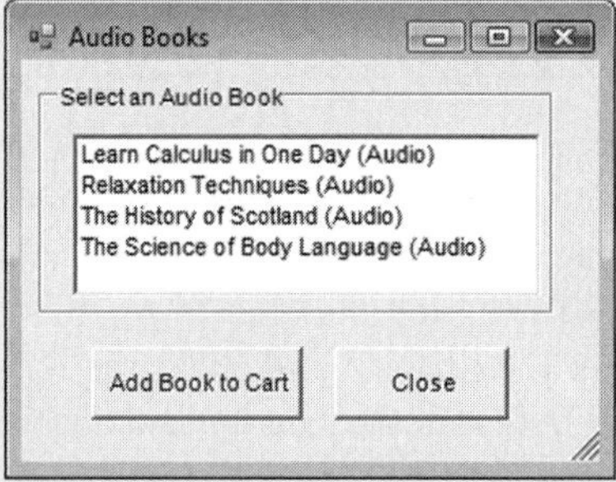

To add one of the items in the list to the shopping cart, the user selects it and clicks the *Add Book to Cart* button. To cancel the operation, the user simply clicks the *Close* button without selecting a book.

3. **Cell Phone Packages**

   Cell Solutions, a cell phone provider, sells the following packages:

300 minutes per month	$45.00 per month
800 minutes per month	$65.00 per month
1,500 minutes per month	$99.00 per month

Customers may also select the following options:

Voicemail	$ 5.00 per month
Text messaging	$10.00 per month

The provider sells the following phones:

Model 100:	$29.95
Model 110:	$49.95
Model 200:	$99.95

(A 6% sales tax applies to the sale of a phone.)

Additionally, the provider offers individual plans and family plans. With the Individual plan, the customer gets one phone. With the Family plan, the customer gets as many phones of the same model as he or she desires, and all the phones share the same minutes. Voicemail and text messaging fees are charged for each phone purchased under the Family plan.

Create an application that calculates a customer's plan cost. The application's main form should look similar to the one shown in Figure 7-60.

Figure 7-60 *Cell Phone Packages* form

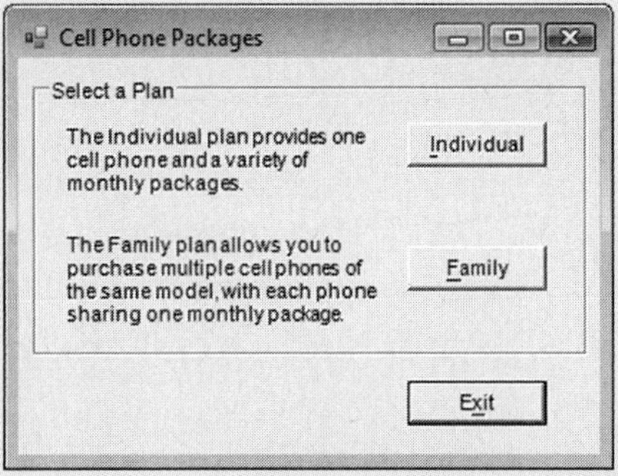

When the user clicks the *Individual* button, the form shown in Figure 7-61 should appear.

(If the Visual Studio graphics files are installed on your system, the icon displayed in the image control can be found in one of the subfolders of *Program Files\Microsoft Visual Studio 9.0\Common7* folder. If there are no graphics files in that location on your computer, substitute any graphic of your choice, or leave the image control off of the form.)

The user selects the phone model, options, and package. When the *Calculate* button is clicked, the charges are calculated and displayed.

When the user clicks the *Family* button on the main form, the form shown in Figure 7-62 should appear.

The user enters the number of phones, selects the phone model, options, and package. When the *Calculate* button is clicked, the charges are calculated and displayed.

Figure 7-61 *Individual Plan* form

Figure 7-62 *Family Plan* form

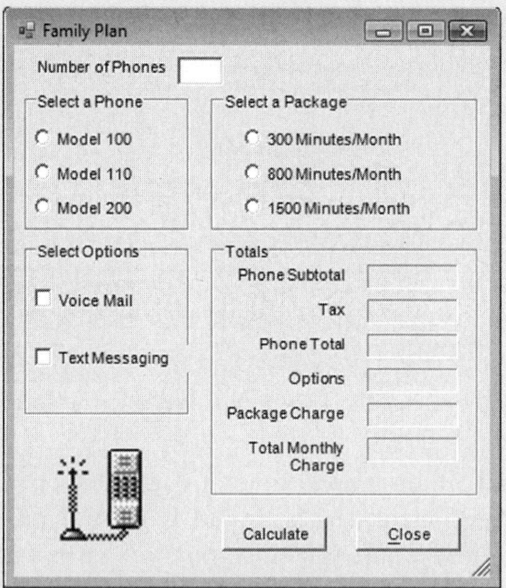

Design Your Own Forms

4. **Dorm and Meal Plan Calculator**

A university has the following dormitories:

Allen Hall	$1,500 per semester
Pike Hall	$1,600 per semester
Farthing Hall	$1,200 per semester
University Suites	$1,800 per semester

The university also offers the following meal plans:

7 meals per week	$ 560 per semester
14 meals per week	$1,095 per semester
Unlimited meals	$1,500 per semester

Create an application with two forms. The startup form holds the names of the dormitories and the other holds the meal plans. When the user selects a dormitory and meal plan, the application should show the total charges for the semester on the startup form.

5. **Shade Designer**

A custom window shade designer charges a base fee of $50 per shade. Additionally, charges are added for certain styles, sizes, and colors as follows:

Styles:

Regular shades	Add $0
Folding shades	Add $10
Roman shades	Add $15

Sizes:

25 inches wide	Add $0
27 inches wide	Add $2
32 inches wide	Add $4
40 inches wide	Add $6

Colors:

Natural	Add $5
Blue	Add $0
Teal	Add $0
Red	Add $0
Green	Add $0

Create an application that allows the user to select the style, size, color, and number of shades from list boxes or combo boxes. If a combo box is used, set its DropDownStyle property in such a way that new items cannot be added to the customer list by the user. The total charges should be displayed on a second form.

6. **Skateboard Designer**

The Skate Shop sells the following skateboard products.

Decks:

The Master Thrasher	$60
The Dictator of Grind	$45
The Street King	$50

Truck assemblies:

7.75 axle	$35
8 axle	$40
8.5 axle	$45

Wheel sets:

51 mm	$20
55 mm	$22
58 mm	$24
61 mm	$28

Additionally, the Skate Shop sells the following miscellaneous products and services:

Grip tape	$10
Bearings	$30
Riser pads	$ 2
Nuts & bolts kit	$ 3
Assembly	$10

Create an application that allows the user to select one deck from a form, one truck assembly from a form, and one wheel set from a form. The application should also have a form that allows the user to select any miscellaneous product, using check boxes. The application should display the subtotal, the amount of sales tax (at 6%), and the total of the order. Do not apply sales tax to assembly.

VideoNote The Astronomy Helper Problem

7. **Astronomy Helper**

Create an application that displays the following data about the planets of the solar system. (For your information, the distances are shown in AUs, or astronomical units. 1 AU equals approximately 93 million miles. In your application simply display the distances as they are shown here, in AUs.)

Mercury

Type	Terrestrial
Average distance from the sun	0.387 AU
Mass	3.31×10^{23} kg
Surface temperature	–173°C to 430°C

Venus

Type	Terrestrial
Average distance from the sun	0.7233 AU
Mass	4.87×10^{24} kg
Surface temperature	472°C

Earth

Type	Terrestrial
Average distance from the sun	1 AU
Mass	5.967×10^{24} kg
Surface temperature	–50°C to 50°C

Mars

Type	Terrestrial
Average distance from the sun	1.5237 AU
Mass	0.6424×10^{24} kg
Surface temperature	–140°C to 20°C

Jupiter

Type	Jovian
Average distance from the sun	5.2028 AU
Mass	1.899×10^{27} kg
Temperature at cloud tops	–110°C

Saturn

Type	Jovian
Average distance from the sun	9.5388 AU
Mass	5.69×10^{26} kg
Temperature at cloud tops	–180°C

Uranus

Type	Jovian
Average distance from the sun	19.18 AU
Mass	8.69×10^{25} kg
Temperature above cloud tops	–220°C

Neptune

Type	Jovian
Average distance from the sun	30.0611 AU
Mass	1.03×10^{26} kg
Temperature at cloud tops	–216°C

Pluto

Type	Low density
Average distance from the sun	39.44 AU
Mass	1.2×10^{22} kg
Surface temperature	–230°C

The application should have a separate form for each planet. On the main form, create a menu system that allows the user to select the planet he or she wishes to know more about.

CHAPTER

8 Arrays, Timers, and More

TOPICS

This chapter discusses arrays, which are like groups of variables that allow you to store sets of data. A single-dimensional array is useful for storing and working with a single set of data, while a multidimensional array can be used to store and work with multiple sets of data. This chapter presents many array programming techniques, such as summing and averaging the elements in an array, summing all columns in a two-dimensional array, searching an array for a specific value, and using parallel arrays. The Enabled, Anchor, and Dock properties, Timer controls, and splash screens are covered, as well as programming techniques for generating random numbers.

8.1 Arrays

CONCEPT: An array is like a group of variables with one name. You store and work with values in an array by using a subscript.

Sometimes it is necessary for an application to store multiple values of the same type. Often it is better to create an array than several individual variables. An **array** is a like group of variables that have a single name. All of the values stored within an array are called **elements**, and all are of the same data type. You access the individual elements in an array through a subscript. A **subscript**, also known as an **index**, is a number that identifies a specific element within an array.

Subscript numbering begins at 0, so the subscript of the first element in an array is 0 and the subscript of the last element in an array is one less than the total number of elements. For example, consider an array of seven integers. The subscript of the first element in the array is 0 and the subscript of the last element in the array is 6.

Declaring an Array

You declare an array much like you declare a regular variable. Here is the general format of an array declaration:

```
Dim ArrayName (upperSubscript) As DataType
```

Let's take a closer look at the syntax.

- `ArrayName` is the name of the array.
- `UpperSubscript` is the value of the array's highest subscript. This must be a positive integer or an Integer variable containing a positive number.
- `DataType` is a Visual Basic data type.

Let's look at some examples.

```
Dim intHours(6) As Integer
```

This statement declares `intHours` as an array of integers. The number inside the parentheses, `6`, indicates that the array's highest subscript is 6. Figure 8-1 shows that this array consists of seven elements with the subscripts 0 through 6. The figure shows that numeric array elements are initialized to the value 0.

Figure 8-1 `intHours` array

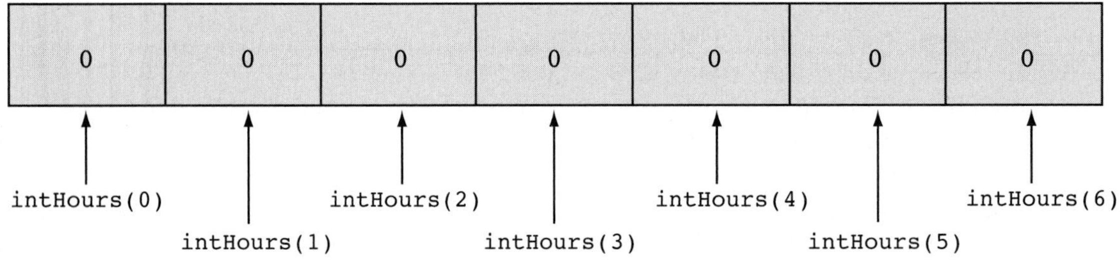

NOTE: Like regular string variables, string array elements equal the special value `Nothing`, which indicates that they have not been initialized. Before doing any work with the elements of a string array, you must store values in them, even if the values are empty strings. Later you will see how to initialize arrays at the same time they are declared.

The following is another example of an array declaration:

```
Dim decPay(4) As Decimal
```

This statement declares `decPay` as an array of five Decimal values, as shown in Figure 8-2, with subscripts 0 through 4. The following example uses the contents of an Integer variable to determine the array size:

```
Dim intSize As Integer = 4
Dim decPay(intSize) As Decimal
```

Figure 8-2 `decPay` array

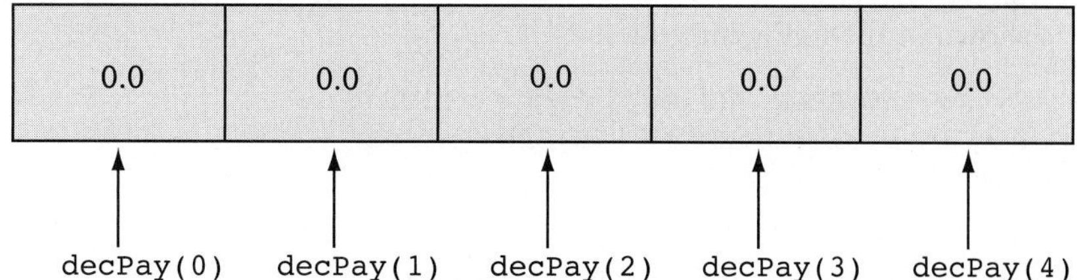

Implicit Array Sizing and Initialization

You can implicitly size an array by omitting the upper subscript in the declaration and providing an initialization list. An array initialization list is a set of numbers enclosed in a set of braces, with the numbers separated by commas. The following is an example of an array declaration that uses an initialization list:

```
Dim intNumbers() As Integer = {  2, 4, 6, 8, 10, 12 }
```

This statement declares `intNumbers` as an array of integers. The numbers 2, 4, 6, 8, 10, and 12 are stored in the array. The value 2 will be stored in element zero, 4 will be stored in element one, and so on. Notice that no upper subscript is provided inside the parentheses. The array is large enough to hold the values in the initialization list. In this example, the array has six elements, as shown in Figure 8-3.

Figure 8-3 `intNumbers` array

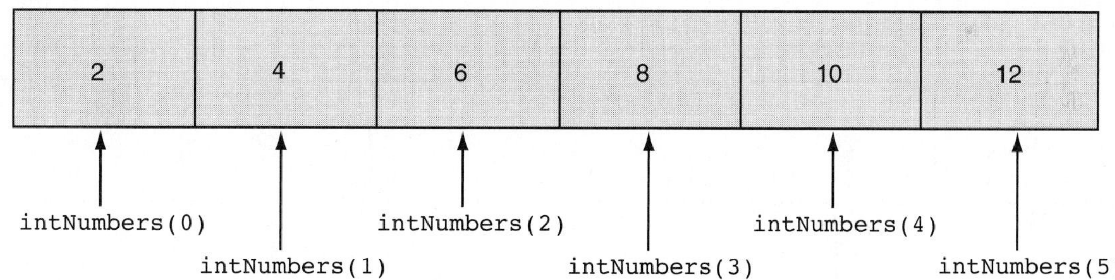

The following code declares an implicitly sized array of strings.

```
Dim strFriends() As String = { "Joe", "Geri", "Bill", "Rose" }
```

You can initialize an array with empty strings, as shown here.

```
Dim strFriends() As String = { "", "", "", "" }
```

It is a good idea to initialize a string array, particularly if there is a chance that your program will access its elements before any data has been stored there. Performing an operation on a string array element results in a runtime error if no data has been stored in the element.

NOTE: You cannot provide both an initialization list and an upper subscript in an array declaration.

Using Named Constants as Subscripts in Array Declarations

Programmers often use a named constant as the upper subscript in an array declaration, as shown in the following code:

```
Const intUPPER_SUB As Integer = 100
Dim intArray(intUPPER_SUB) As Integer
```

Working with Array Elements

You can store a value in an array element with an assignment statement. On the left of the = operator, use the name of the array with the subscript of the element you wish to assign. For example, suppose `intNumbers` is an array of integers with subscripts 0 through 5. The following statements store values in each element of the array:

```
intNumbers(0) = 100
intNumbers(1) = 200
intNumbers(2) = 300
intNumbers(3) = 400
intNumbers(4) = 500
intNumbers(5) = 600
```

TIP: The expression `intNumbers(0)` is pronounced *intNumbers sub zero.*

Figure 8-4 shows the values assigned to the elements of the array after these statements execute.

Figure 8-4 `intNumbers` array with assigned values

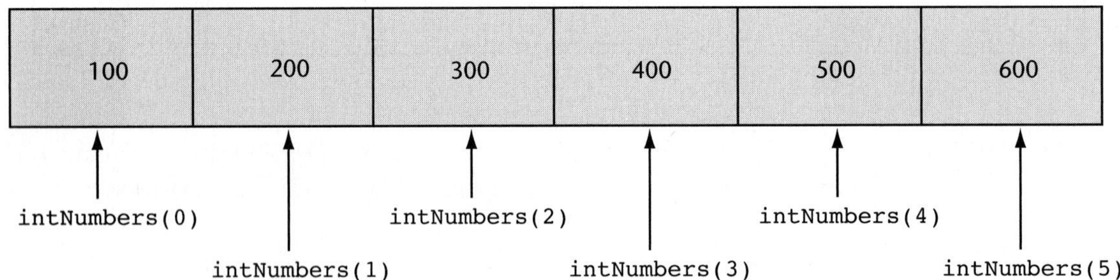

Working with array elements is no different from working with other variables. For example, the following statement multiplies `intHours(3)` by the variable `decRate` and stores the result in `decPay`:

```
decPay = intHours(3) * decRate
```

The following statement adds 1 to `intTallies(0)`:

```
intTallies(0) += 1
```

And the following statement displays `decPay(5)` in a message box:

```
MessageBox.Show(decPay(5).ToString())
```

Accessing Array Elements with a Loop

VideoNote

Accessing Array Elements with a Loop

You can assign an integer to a variable and then use the variable as a subscript. This makes it possible to use a loop to cycle through an entire array, performing the same operation on each element. This can be helpful if you want to process the elements in a large array because writing individual statements would require a lot of typing.

For example, assume `intSeries` is an array of 10 integers with subscripts 0 through 9. The following `For...Next` loop stores the value 100 in each of its elements, beginning at subscript 0:

```
Dim intCount As Integer
For intCount = 0 To 9
  intSeries(intCount) = 100
Next intCount
```

The variable `intCount`, used as the loop counter, takes on the values 0 through 9 as the loop repeats. The first time through the loop, `intCount` equals 0, so the statement `intSeries(intCount) = 100` assigns `100` to `intSeries(0)`. The second time the loop executes, the statement stores 100 in `intSeries(1)`, and so on.

Another example using the same array follows, this time using a `Do While` loop:

```
Dim intCount As Integer = 0
Do While intCount < 10
  intSeries(intCount) = 100
  intCount += 1
Loop
```

The next example shows a `For...Next` loop that gets numbers from the user and stores them in the array.

```
Dim intCount As Integer
For intCount = 0 To 9
  intSeries(intCount) = CInt(InputBox("Enter a number."))
Next intCount
```

We mentioned earlier that it is a good idea to initialize a string array if there is a chance that the program will access its elements before data has been stored there. It might be cumbersome, however, to provide a separate initializer for each array element. Instead, you can use a loop to initialize the array's elements. For example, the following code stores an empty string in each element of `strNames`, a 1000-element array of strings:

```
Dim intCount As Integer
For intCount = 0 To 999
  strNames(intCount) = String.Empty
Next intCount
```

Array Bounds Checking

The Visual Basic runtime system performs **array bounds checking**, meaning that it does not allow a statement to use a subscript outside the range of valid subscripts for an array. For example, in the following declaration, the array named `intValues` has a subscript range of 0 through 10:

```
Dim intValues(10) As Integer
```

If a statement uses a subscript that is less than 0 or greater than 10 with this array, the program will throw an exception (also known as a runtime error).

The compiler does not display an error message at design time when you write a statement that uses an invalid subscript. For example, the loop in the following code uses out-of-range subscripts:

```
Dim intValues(10) As Integer
Dim intIndex As Integer
For intIndex = 0 To 20
  intValues( intIndex) = 99
Next intIndex
```

At runtime, this loop executes until `intIndex` equals 11. At that point, when the assignment statement tries to use `intIndex` as a subscript, an exception is thrown, as shown in Figure 8-5. When this dialog box appears, click the *Break* button to enter Debug mode, or the *Continue* button to stop the application.

Figure 8-5 Dialog box reporting index outside the bounds of the array

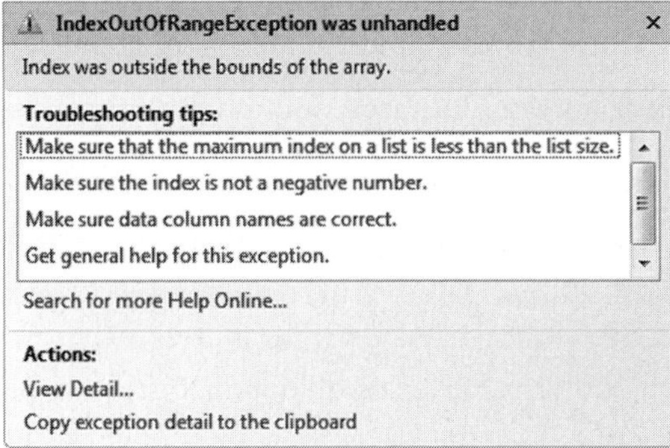

Accessing Array Elements with a `For Each` Loop

You can use a **`For Each`** loop to examine all the elements of an array, one by one. The loop can read the array elements, but it cannot modify their values. The `For Each` loop has the following general form:

`For Each` *variableName* **`As`** *type* **`In`** *arrayname*

`Next`

You can use any identifier for the variable name. The variable's *type* must match the array type. The first time the loop executes, *variableName* contains the value of the first array element. Each time the loop repeats, *variableName* contains the value of the next element.

TIP: All of the code in this section can be found in the project named *ForEach Example* in the Chapter 8 examples folder.

Integer Array Example

Let us assume that the following array is declared at the class level in a Windows form:

```
Private intArray() As Integer = {10, 20, 90, -20, 30, 75, 40, 50, 60}
```

The following `For Each` loop displays all of the array values in a ListBox control named `lstShow`:

```
For Each intVal As Integer In intArray
   lstShow.Items.Add(intVal)
Next
```

Each time the first line executes, the next value in the array is assigned to `intVal`. An example program that uses this technique is shown in Figure 8-6.

Figure 8-6 Running the `ForEach` Example program

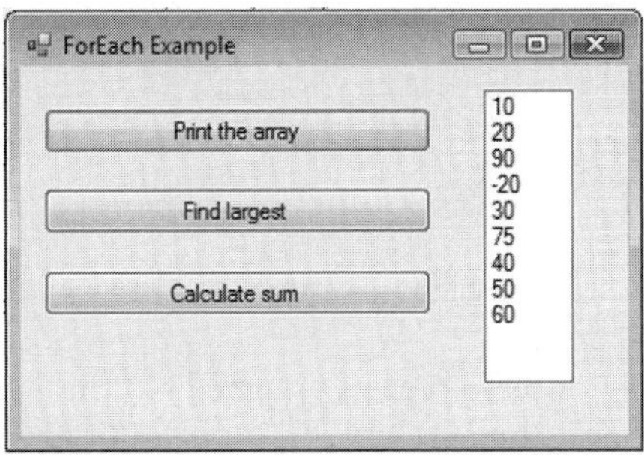

Calculating the Sum of an Array

VideoNote

Calculating the Sum of an Array's Elements

The following statements loop through the same array and calculate the sum of its elements:

```
Dim intSum As Integer = 0
For Each intVal As Integer In intArray
   intSum += intVal
Next
```

Let's use a table to show the values of `intVal` and `intSum` as we step through each line of this code. We will use line numbers for reference, and a bold typeface is used to show variables that change value:

Line		`intVal`	`intSum`
1	`Dim intSum As Integer = 0`	??	**0**
2	`For Each intVal As Integer In intArray`	**10**	0
3	`   intSum += intVal`	10	**10**
4	`Next`	10	10

This is how you read the table: When line 1 executes, the `intSum` variable holds the value 0, and the `intVal` variable is undefined. When line 2 executes, the value 10 is stored in the `intVal` variable. (Notice that `intSum` is unchanged in line 2. It still holds the value 0.) When line 3 executes, the value 10 is stored in the `intSum` variable, and `intVal` is unchanged. When the `Next` statement in line 4 executes, the loop starts over again at line 2.

During the next iteration of the loop, the second array value (20) is assigned to `intVal` in line 2. In line 3, `intSum` equals 10 + 20:

Line		intVal	intSum
2	`For Each intVal As Integer In intArray`	20	10
3	`    intSum += intVal`	20	**30**
4	`Next`	20	30

The third time through the loop, `intVal` is assigned 90 in line 2. When it is added to `intSum` in line 3, the resulting value is 120:

Line		intVal	intSum
2	`For Each intVal As Integer In intArray`	**90**	30
3	`    intSum += intVal`	90	**120**
4	`Next`	90	120

The fourth time through the loop, `intVal` is assigned –20 in line 2. When it is added to `intSum` in line 3, the resulting value is 100:

Line		intVal	intSum
2	`For Each intVal As Integer In intArray`	**–20**	120
3	`    intSum += intVal`	–20	**100**
4	`Next`	–20	100

The loop repeats until the last value in the array is added to `intSum`.

Finding the Largest Value in an Array

Sometimes you may want to examine the values in an array to find the largest value, smallest value, or even a specific value. A `For Each` loop can be combined with an `If` statement to do this. In the following example, we search for the array element with the largest value:

```
1:  Dim intLargest As Integer = intArray(0)
2:  For Each intVal As Integer In intArray
3:    If intVal > intLargest Then
4:       intLargest = intVal
5:    End If
6:  Next
```

As with the previous example, let's use a table to step through the code and see the values that will be stored in each variable. The following table shows values assigned to the variables when the loop executes for the first time:

Line		intVal	intLargest	intVal > intLargest?
1	`Dim intLargest As Integer = intArray(0)`	??	**10**	
2	`For Each intVal As Integer In intArray`	**10**	10	
3	`    If intVal > intLargest Then`	10	10	False
4	`        intLargest = intVal`			
5	`    End If`			
6	`Next`	10	10	

When the `If...Then` statement in line 3 executes, `intVal` is *not* greater than `intLargest`, so line 4 is not executed. When the `Next` statement in line 6 executes, the loop starts over at line 2.

When line 2 executes for the second time, the second number in the array (20) is assigned to `intVal`. In line 3, `intVal` is greater than `intLargest`, so line 4 executes and assigns `intVal` (20) to `intLargest`:

Line		intVal	intLargest	intVal > intLargest?
2	`For Each intVal As Integer In intArray`	20	10	
3	`If intVal > intLargest Then`	20	10	True
4	`intLargest = intVal`	20	**20**	
5	`End If`	20	20	
6	`Next`	20	20	

Then the loop executes a third time, and line 2 assigns 90 (the third array element) to `intValue`. In line 3, `intVal` is greater than `intLargest`, so line 4 assigns the larger value to `intLargest`:

Line		intVal	intLargest	intVal > intLargest?
2	`For Each intVal As Integer In intArray`	90	20	
3	`If intVal > intLargest Then`	90	20	True
4	`intLargest = intVal`	90	**90**	
5	`End If`	90	90	
6	`Next`	90	90	

The loop continues its repetitions, assigning each of the array elements to `intVal`. As it turns out, no other value in the array is greater than 90, so line 4 never executes again. When the loop finishes, `intLargest` contains the value 90 and we know that it is the largest value in the array.

Finding an Item in a ListBox

A `For Each` loop can easily process the items in a collection. Suppose we would like to search for a city name in the `Items` collection of a ListBox control named `lstCities`. We will assume that the user has entered a city name into a TextBox control named `txtCity`. Figure 8-7 shows an example of the program at runtime. Here are the statements that execute the search:

```
For Each strCity As String In lstCities.Items
   If strCity = txtCity.Text Then
      lblResult.Text = "The city was found!"
   End If
Next
```

Figure 8-7 Searching for a city name in a ListBox control

In Tutorial 8-1, you complete an application using an array.

Tutorial 8-1:
Completing an application that uses an array

JJ's House of Pizza has six employees, each paid $6 per hour. In this tutorial, you complete an application that stores the number of hours worked by each employee in an array. The application uses the values in the array to calculate each employee's gross pay.

Step 1: Open the *Simple Payroll* project located in the student sample programs folder named *Chap8\Simple Payroll*. Figure 8-8 shows the user interface.

Figure 8-8 *Simple Payroll* form

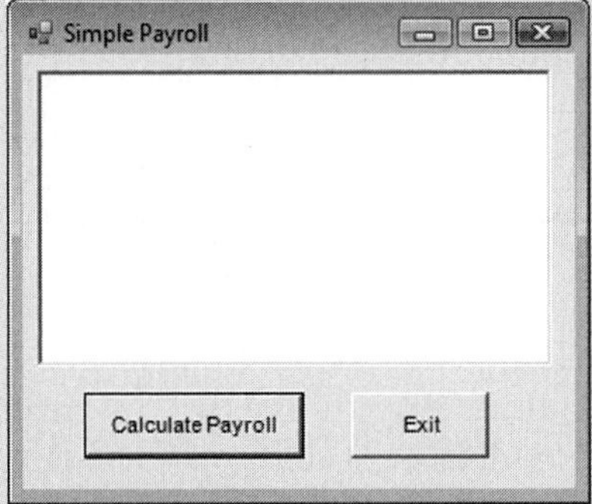

Step 2: Double-click the *Calculate Payroll* button to open its `Click` handler in the *Code* window. Take a look at the following class-level constants, which define the standard hourly pay rate, and the maximum index to be used with the array of employees:

```
' This application demonstrates an array.
Const decHOURLY_PAY_RATE As Decimal = 6
Const intMAX_EMPLOYEES As Integer = 5
```

There will be six employees in the array, with subscripts ranging from 0 to 5. The `intMAX_EMPLOYEES` constant will be useful in two cases: when declaring the array of employees, and when controlling the number of times a loop must repeat when processing the array.

Step 3: Add the following statements, shown in bold, to the `btnCalcPay_Click` event handler:

```
Private Sub btnCalcPay_Click(ByVal sender As System.Object, _
    ByVal e As System.EventArgs) Handles btnCalcPay.Click

  ' Calculate and display the gross pay earned by
  ' the employees.
  Dim intHours(intMAX_EMPLOYEES) As Integer
  Dim intCount As Integer          ' Loop counter
  Dim intEmpHours As Integer       ' Employee hours
  Dim decEmpPay As Decimal         ' Employee gross pay

  ' Get the hours worked by the employees.
  For intCount = 0 To intMAX_EMPLOYEES
    Do While Integer.TryParse(InputBox("Enter the hours worked by " _
        & " employee number " & (intCount+1).ToString(), _
        "Need Hours Worked"),intEmpHours) = False

      MessageBox.Show("Please enter an integer for hours " _
          & "worked")
    Loop
    intHours(intCount) = intEmpHours
  Next intCount

  ' Calculate and display each employee's gross pay.
  lstOutput.Items.Clear()
  For intCount = 0 To intMAX_EMPLOYEES
    decEmpPay = intHours(intCount) * decHOURLY_PAY_RATE
    lstOutput.Items.Add("Employee " & _
        (intCount + 1).ToString() & " earned " & _
        decEmpPay.ToString("c"))
  Next intCount
End Sub
```

Let's look at the code in this procedure more closely. The first variable in the procedure is an array that holds the hours worked for each employee:

```
Dim intHours(intMAX_EMPLOYEES) As Integer
```

We also declare a loop counter, a variable to hold the hours worked for a single employee, and a variable to hold the gross pay for one employee.

```
Dim intCount As Integer          ' Loop counter
Dim intEmpHours As Integer       ' Employee hours
Dim decEmpPay As Decimal         ' Employee gross pay
```

A loop asks the user to enter the number of hours each employee has worked. The value is stored at the appropriate position in the array.

```
For intCount = 0 To intMAX_EMPLOYEES
  Do While Integer.TryParse(InputBox("Enter the hours worked by" _
    & "employee number" & (intCount+1).ToString(),_
    "Need Hours Worked"),intEmpHours) = False

    MessageBox.Show("Please enter an integer for hours" _
      & "worked")
  Loop
    intHours(intCount)=intEmpHours
  NextintCount
```

Also, an inner loop calls the `TryParse` method to convert the user's input into an integer. If an invalid string is entered by the user, the inner loop displays an error message and repeats so the user can try again.

Last of all, a loop iterates through the array, calculates each employee's pay, and adds it to a list box named `lstOutput`:

```
lstOutput.Items.Clear()
For intCount = 0 To intMAX_EMPLOYEES
  decEmpPay = intHours(intCount) * decHOURLY_PAY_RATE
  lstOutput.Items.Add("Employee " & _
    (intCount + 1).ToString() & " earned " & _
    decEmpPay.ToString("c"))
Next intCount
```

Step 4: Close the *Code* window, save the project, and run the application.

Step 5: Click the *Calculate Payroll* button. A series of input boxes should appear, asking you to enter the number of hours worked for employees 1 through 6. Enter the following values in order:

Employee 1	**10**
Employee 2	**40**
Employee 3	**20**
Employee 4	**15**
Employee 5	**10**
Employee 6	**30**

After you enter the hours for employee 6, the form should appear, as shown in Figure 8-9.

Step 6: Click the *Exit* button to end the program.

Figure 8-9 *Simple Payroll* application, after entering hours for all employees

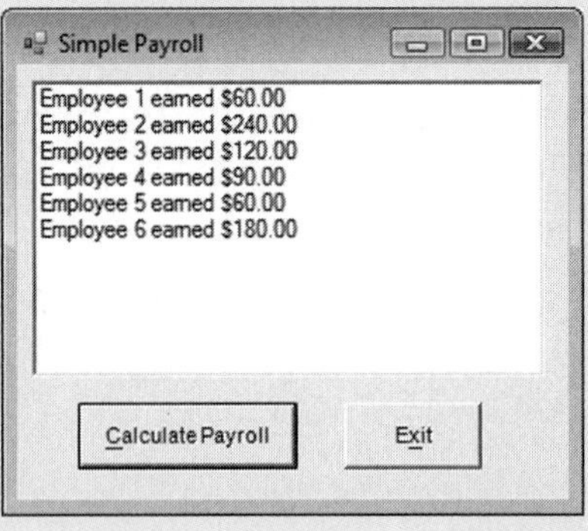

Checkpoint

8.1 Write declaration statements for the following arrays:

a. `intEmpNums`, an array of 100 integers

b. `decPayRate`, an array of 24 Decimal variables

c. `intMiles`, an array of integers initialized to the values 10, 20, 30, 40, and 50

d. `strNames`, an array of strings with an upper subscript of 12

e. `strDivisions`, an array of strings initialized to the values `"North"`, `"South"`, `"East"`, and `"West"`.

8.2 Identify the error in the following declaration:

```
Dim intNumberSet(4) As Integer = {  25, 37, 45, 60 }
```

8.3 Look at the following array declarations and indicate the number of elements in each array:

a. `Dim dblNums(100) As Double`
b. `Dim intValues() As Integer = {  99, 99, 99 }`
c. `Dim intArray(0) As Integer`

8.4 What is array bounds checking?

8.5 Assume that a procedure has the following array declaration:

```
Dim intPoints(25) As Integer
```

Write a `For...Next` loop that displays each of the array's elements in message boxes.

8.6 Rewrite your answer to Checkpoint 8.5, using a `For...Each` loop.

8.7 What values are displayed in the message boxes by the following statements? (Use a calculator if necessary.)

```
Const sngRATE As Single = 0.1
Dim intBalance(3) As Integer
Dim intCount As Integer
Dim sngResult As Single
intBalance(0) = 100
intBalance(1) = 250
intBalance(2) = 325
intBalance(3) = 500
For intCount = 0 To 3
  sngResult = intBalance(intCount) * sngRATE
  MessageBox.Show(sngResult.ToString())
Next intCount
```

8.2 More about Array Processing

CONCEPT: There are many uses for arrays, and many programming techniques can be applied to them. You can total values and search for data. Related information may be stored in multiple parallel arrays. In addition, arrays can be resized at runtime.

Determining the Number of Elements in an Array

Arrays have a Length property that holds the number of elements in the array. For example, assume the following declaration:

```
Dim intValues(25) As Integer
```

The `intValues` array has a total of 26 elements, with an upper subscript of 25. The array's Length property returns the value 26. The following is an example of code that uses the Length property:

```
For intCount = 0 to (intValues.Length – 1)
  MessageBox.Show(intValues(intCount).ToString())
Next intCount
```

The code uses the expression `intValues.Length – 1` as the loop's upper limit, because the value in the Length property is 1 greater than the array's upper subscript.

As you will learn later, the size of an array can change while an application is running. Use the Length property to get the current value of an array's size.

How to Total the Values in a Numeric Array

To total the values in a numeric array, use a loop with an accumulator variable. The loop adds the value in each array element to the accumulator. For example, assume the following array declaration exists in an application, and values have been stored in the array:

```
Dim intUnits(24) As Integer
```

The following loop adds each array element to the `intTotal` variable:

```
Dim intTotal As Integer = 0
Dim intCount As Integer
For intCount = 0 To (intUnits.Length – 1)
  intTotal += intUnits(intCount)
Next intCount
```

NOTE: The first statement in the last example sets `intTotal` to 0. Recall from Chapter 5 that an accumulator variable must be set to 0 before it is used to keep a running total or the sum will not be correct. Although Visual Basic automatically initializes numeric variables to 0, this statement emphasizes that `intTotal` must equal 0 before the loop starts.

Calculating the Average Value in a Numeric Array

The first step in calculating the average value in an array is to sum the values. The second step is to divide the sum by the number of elements in the array. Assume the following declaration exists in an application, and values have been stored in the array:

```
Dim intUnits(24) As Integer
```

The following loop calculates the average value in the `intUnits` array. The average is stored in the `dblAverage` variable.

```
Dim intTotal As Integer = 0
Dim dblAverage As Double
Dim intCount As Integer
For intCount = 0 To (intUnits.Length - 1)
  intTotal += intUnits(intCount)
Next intCount
' Use floating-point division to compute the average.
dblAverage = intTotal / intUnits.Length
```

The statement that calculates the average (`dblAverage`) must be placed after the end of the loop. It should only execute once.

Finding the Highest and Lowest Values in an Integer Array

Earlier in this chapter, when explaining `For Each` loops, we showed you how to find the largest value in an array. Let's look at a similar example that uses a `For Next` loop and accesses each array element using a subscript. Assume that the following array declaration exists in an application, and that values have been stored in the array:

```
Dim intNumbers(24) As Integer
Dim intCount As Integer
Dim intHighest As Integer = intNumbers(0)
For intCount = 1 To (intNumbers.Length - 1)
  If intNumbers(intCount) > intHighest Then
    intHighest = intNumbers(intCount)
  End If
Next intCount
```

The code begins by copying the value in the first array element to the variable `intHighest`. Next, the loop compares all remaining array elements, beginning at subscript 1, to `intHighest`. Each time it finds a value in the array greater than `intHighest`, the value is copied into `intHighest`. When the loop finishes, `intHighest` equals the largest value in the array.

Lowest Value

The following code, which finds the lowest value in the array, is nearly identical to the code for finding the highest value. When the loop finishes, `intLowest` equals the smallest value in the array.

```
Dim intNumbers(24) As Integer
Dim intCount As Integer
Dim intLowest As Integer = intNumbers(0)

For intCount = 1 To (intNumbers.Length - 1)
  If intNumbers(intCount) < intLowest Then
    intLowest = intNumbers(intCount)
  End If
Next intCount
```

Copying One Array's Contents to Another

Assume that an application has the following statements:

```
Dim intOldValues(2) As Integer
Dim intNewValues(2) As Integer
intOldValues(0) = 10
intOldValues(1) = 100
intOldValues(2) = 200
```

Suppose we want to copy the contents of the `intOldValues` array to the `intNewValues` array. We might be tempted to use a single assignment statement, such as the following:

```
intNewValues = intOldValues
```

Although this statement compiles, it does not copy the `intOldValues` array to the `intNewValues` array. Instead it causes the names `intNewValues` and `intOldValues` to reference the same array in memory.

Arrays in Visual Basic are object variables. Recall from Chapter 7 that an object variable is a variable that holds a reference to an object. When you use the assignment operator to assign one array to another, the two array variables end up referencing to the same array. For example, after the statement `intNewValues = intOldValues` executes, the `intNewValues` variable refers to the same array as the `intOldValues` variable. This situation is illustrated in Figure 8-10.

The danger of assigning `intNewValues` to `intOldValues` is that we are no longer working with two arrays, but one. If we were to change the value of any element in the `intNewValues` array, we would automatically be changing the same element of the `intOldValues` array. This action would probably be accidental, resulting in a program bug.

Rather than using a single assignment statement to copy an array, we would have to use a loop to copy the individual elements from `intOldValues` to `intNewValues`, as shown in the following code:

```
For intCount = 0 To (intOldValues.Length-1)
  intNewValues(intCount) = intOldValues(intCount)
Next intCount
```

This loop copies `intOldValue`'s elements to the `intNewValues` array. When finished, two separate arrays exist.

Figure 8-10 State of the arrays before and after the assignment statement

Initial state of the arrays

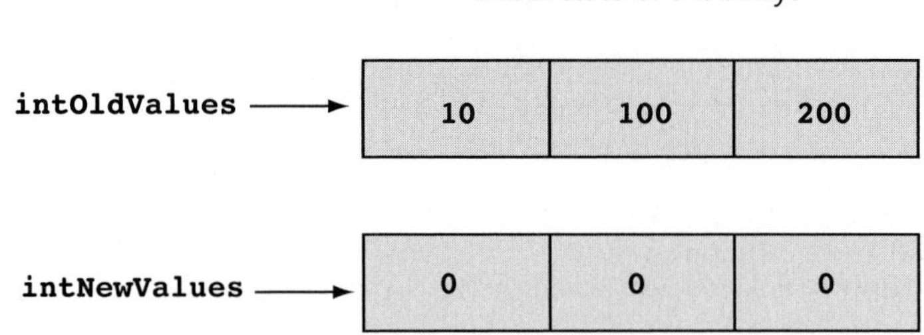

State of the arrays after the statement
`intNewValues = intOldValues` executes

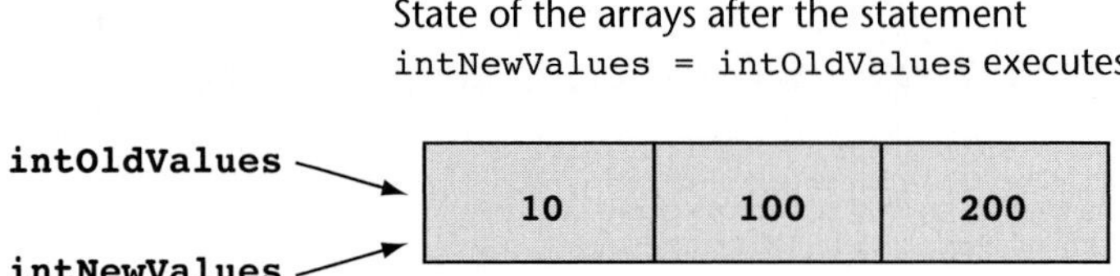

Parallel Arrays

Sometimes it is useful to store related data in two or more related arrays, also known as parallel arrays. For example, assume an application has the following array declarations:

```
Dim strNames(4) As String
Dim strAddresses(4) As String
```

The `strNames` array stores the names of five people, and the `strAddresses` array stores the addresses of the same five people. The information for one person is stored in the same relative location in each array. For instance, the first person's name is stored at `strNames(0)`, and the same person's address is stored at `strAddresses(0)`, as shown in Figure 8-11.

To access the information, use the same subscript with both arrays. For example, the following loop displays each person's name and address in a list box named `lstPeople`:

```
For intCount = 0 To 4
  lstPeople.Items.Add( "Name: " & strNames(intCount) & _
    " Address: " & strAddresses(intCount))
Next intCount
```

Figure 8-11 `strNames` and `strAddresses` parallel arrays

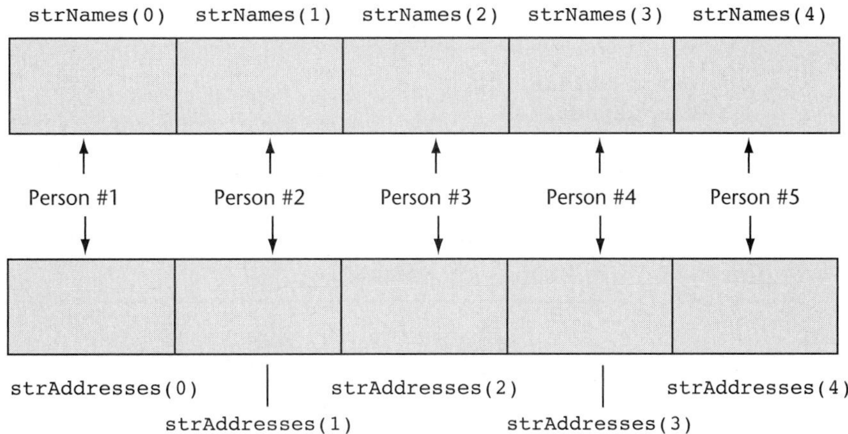

The arrays `strNames` and `strAddresses` are examples of parallel arrays. **Parallel arrays** are two or more arrays that hold related data. The related elements in each array are accessed with a common subscript. Parallel arrays are especially useful when the related data are of unlike types. For example, an application could store the names and ages of five people in the following arrays:

```
Dim strNames(5) As String
Dim intAges(5) As Integer
```

Tutorial 8-2 examines an application that uses parallel arrays to store names and working hours.

Tutorial 8-2:
Examining an application that uses parallel arrays

In this tutorial, you examine a new version of the *Simple Payroll* application in Tutorial 8-1. The new version, called *Pizza Payroll*, uses parallel arrays.

Step 1: Open the *Pizza Payroll* project from the student sample programs folder named *Chap8\Pizza Payroll.*

Step 2: Run the application. The form shown in Figure 8-12 appears.

Figure 8-12 *Pizza Payroll* form

Step 3: Click the *Calculate* button. The application uses input boxes to ask for the names of two employees and the number of hours each has worked. Enter the following names and hours worked:

Jason Martin, 10
Tim Jaynes, 40

Step 4: After entering the data for the last employee, the form should look like the one shown in Figure 8-13.

Figure 8-13 *Pizza Payroll* form completed

Step 5: Click the *Exit* button to end the application.

Step 6: Open the *Code* window and view the class-level declarations section:

```
' Class-level Constants.
  Const intNUMBER_OF_EMPLOYEES As Integer = 2
  Const intMAX_EMPLOYEE As Integer = intNUMBER_OF_EMPLOYEES - 1
  Const decHOURLY_PAY_RATE As Decimal = 6D

  ' Class-level variables.
  Private strNames(intMAX_EMPLOYEE) As String ' Employee names
  Private intHours(intMAX_EMPLOYEE) As Integer ' Hours worked
  Private decGrossPay(intMAX_EMPLOYEE) As Decimal ' Gross pay
  Private decTotalGrossPay As Decimal    ' Total gross pay
  Private intTotalHours As Integer       ' Total hours worked
```

The `decHOURLY_PAY_RATE` constant holds the hourly pay rate for each employee. The arrays, `strNames`, `intHours` and `decGrossPay`, are used as parallel arrays in the following manner: The first employee's name is stored in `strNames(0)`, hours worked are stored in `intHours(0)`and gross pay is stored in `decGrossPay(0)`. The same relationship holds for all employees. The `decTotalGrossPay` variable holds the total gross pay for all employees, and `intTotalHours` holds the total hours worked by all employees.

Step 7: Look at the code for the `btnCalculate_Click` event handler, which calls the `GetData`, `CalcPay`, and `DisplayPayrollData` methods.

```
Private Sub btnCalculate_Click(ByVal sender As System.Object, _
      ByVal e As System.EventArgs) Handles btnCalculate.Click

   GetData()
   CalcPay()
```

```
  DisplayPayrollData()
End Sub
```

The `GetData` method, called by the `Click` event handler, uses a loop to ask the user for the names and hours worked by each employee. The names are stored in the `strNames` array, and the hours are stored in the `intHours` array.

```
Sub GetData()
  ' Get the names of the employees and the
  ' hours worked by each.
  Dim intCount As Integer  ' Loop counter

  For intCount = 0 To intMAX_EMPLOYEE
    strNames(intCount) = InputBox( _
        "Enter the name of employee " _
        & "number " & (intCount + 1).ToString(), _
        "Employee Name")

    intHours(intCount) = GetEmployeeHours(strNames(intCount))
    Next intCount
  End Sub
```

Following is the `GetEmployeeHours` function. It displays an input box asking the user to enter the hours worked. A call to the `TryParse` function attempts to convert the user's input to an integer. If the conversion of successful, the hours value is returned by the function. If the conversion fails, a message box asks the user to enter an integer, and the loop repeats.

```
Function GetEmployeeHours(ByVal strName As String) As Integer

  ' Ask the user to enter the hours worked by a single
  ' employee. If the value is not a valid integer, display
  ' an error message and use a loop to ask again.
  Dim intHours As Integer
  Dim blnFinished As Boolean = False
  Do Until blnFinished
    blnFinished = Integer.TryParse(InputBox( _
      "Enter the hours worked by " _
      & strName, "Hours Worked"), intHours)

    If Not blnFinished Then
      MessageBox.Show("Please enter an integer", "Error")
    End If
  Loop
  Return intHours
End Function
```

Look at the `CalcPay` procedure, also called by the `Click` event handler. The loop calculates each employee's gross pay, inserts it in the `decGrossPay` array, adds it to the total named `decTotalGrossPay`, and adds the hours worked to the total number of hours for all employees:

```
Sub CalcPay()
  ' This procedure calculates and displays each
  ' employee's gross pay.

  Dim intCount As Integer  ' Loop counter
  Dim decGross As Decimal  ' Gross pay

  ' Calculate the gross pay for each person, the total
  ' of all gross pay values, and the total hours worked.
```

```
    For intCount = 0 To intMAX_EMPLOYEE
      decGross = intHours(intCount) * decHOURLY_PAY_RATE
      decGrossPay(intCount) = decGross
      decTotalGrossPay += decGross
      intTotalHours += intHours(intCount)
    Next
End Sub
```

Finally, `DisplayPayrollData` is called by the `Click` event handler. It uses a loop to insert each employee's name, hours, and gross pay into a list box named `lstPayData`.

```
Sub DisplayPayrollData()
  ' Displays the payroll data for each employee
  ' and the total gross pay and total hours worked.

  ' Display each employee's data.
  Dim intCount As Integer

  For intCount = 0 To intMAX_EMPLOYEE
    lstPayData.Items.Add("Name: " & strNames(intCount) _
        & "  Hours: " & intHours(intCount) & "  Gross Pay: " _
        & decGrossPay(intCount).ToString("c"))
  Next intCount

  ' Display total gross pay and total hours for all employees.
  lblTotalPayroll.Text = decTotalGrossPay.ToString("c")
  lblLaborHours.Text = intTotalHours.ToString()
End Sub
```

Parallel Relationships between Arrays, List Boxes, and Combo Boxes

Items stored in a list box or a combo box have a built-in index. The index of the first item is 0, the index of the second item is 1, and so on. Because this indexing scheme corresponds with the way array subscripts are used, it is easy to create parallel relationships between list boxes, combo boxes, and arrays.

For example, assume that an application has a list box named `lstPeople`. The following statements store three names in the list box:

```
lstPeople.Items.Add("Jean James")
lstPeople.Items.Add("Kevin Smith")
lstPeople.Items.Add("Joe Harrison")
```

When these statements execute, `"Jean James"` is stored at index 0, `"Kevin Smith"` is stored at index 1, and `"Joe Harrison"` is stored at index 2. Also assume the application has an array of strings named `strPhoneNumbers`. This array holds the phone numbers of the three people whose names are stored in the list box. The following statements store phone numbers in the array:

```
strPhoneNumbers(0) = "555-2987"
strPhoneNumbers(1) = "555-5656"
strPhoneNumbers(2) = "555-8897"
```

The phone number stored at element 0 (`"555-2987"`) belongs to the person whose name is stored at index 0 in the list box (`"Jean James"`). Likewise, the phone number stored at element 1 belongs to the person whose name is stored at index 1 in the list box, and so on. When the user selects a name from the list box, the following statement displays the person's phone number:

```
MessageBox.Show(strPhoneNumbers(lstPeople.SelectedIndex))
```

The SelectedIndex property holds the index of the selected item in the list box. This statement uses the index as a subscript in the `strPhoneNumbers` array.

It is possible however, for the SelectedIndex property to hold a value outside the bounds of the parallel array. When no item is selected, the SelectedIndex property holds –1. The following code provides error checking:

```
With lstPeople
  If .SelectedIndex > -1 And _
      .SelectedIndex < strPhoneNumbers.Length Then
    MessageBox.Show(strPhoneNumbers(.SelectedIndex))
  Else
    MessageBox.Show("That is not a valid selection.")
  End If
End With
```

Searching Arrays

Applications not only store and process information stored in arrays, but often search arrays for specific items. The most basic method of searching an array is the **sequential search**. It uses a loop to examine the elements in an array, one after the other, starting with the first. It compares each element with the value being searched for, and stops when the value is found or the end of the array is reached. If the value being searched for is not in the array, the algorithm unsuccessfully searches to the end of the array.

The pseudocode for a sequential search is as follows:

```
found = False
subscript = 0
Do While found is False and subscript < array's length
  If array(subscript) = searchValue Then
    found = True
    position = subscript
  End If
  subscript += 1
End While
```

In the pseudocode, `found` is a Boolean variable, `position` and `subscript` are integers, `array` is an array of any type, and `searchValue` is the value being searched for. When the search is complete, if the `found` variable equals *False*, the search value was not found. If `found` equals *True*, `position` contains the subscript of the array element containing the search value.

For example, suppose an application stores test scores in a single precision array named `scores`. The following pseudocode searches the array for an element containing 100:

```
' Search for a 100 in the array.
found = False
intCount = 0
Do While Not found And intCount < scores.Length
  If scores(intCount) = 100 Then
    found = True
    position = intCount
```

```
    End If
    intCount += 1
Loop

' Was 100 found in the array?
If found Then
    MessageBox.Show("Congratulations! You made a 100 on test " & _
        (position + 1), "Test Results")
Else
    MessageBox.Show("You didn't score a 100, but keep trying!", "Test Results")
End If
```

Sorting an Array

Programmers often want to sort, or arrange the elements of an array in **ascending order**, which means its values are arranged from lowest to highest. The lowest value is stored in the first element, and the highest value is stored in the last element. To sort an array in ascending order, use the `Array.Sort` method. The general format is as follows:

```
Array.Sort(ArrayName)
```

ArrayName is the name of the array you wish to sort. For example, assume that the following declaration exists in an application:

```
Dim intNumbers() As Integer = { 7, 12, 1, 6, 3 }
```

The following statement will sort the array in ascending order:

```
Array.Sort(intNumbers)
```

After the statement executes, the array values are in the following order: 1, 3, 6, 7, 12.

When you pass an array of strings to the `Array.Sort` method, the array is sorted in ascending order according to the Unicode encoding scheme, which we discussed in Chapter 3. Generally, the sort occurs in alphabetic order. But to be more specific about the order, numeric digits are first, uppercase letters are second, and lowercase letters are last. For example, assume the following declaration:

```
Dim strNames() As String = { "dan", "Kim", "Adam", "Bill" }
```

The following statement sorts the array in ascending order:

```
Array.Sort(strNames)
```

After the statement executes, the values in the array appear in this order: `"Adam"`, `"Bill"`, `"Kim"`, `"dan"`.

Dynamically Sizing Arrays

You can change the number of elements in an array at runtime, using the `ReDim` statement. The general format of the `ReDim` statement is as follows:

```
ReDim [Preserve] Arrayname (UpperSubscript)
```

The word `Preserve` is optional. If it is used, any existing values in the array are preserved. If `Preserve` is not used, existing values in the array are destroyed. *Arrayname* is the name of the array being resized. *UpperSubscript* is the new upper subscript and must be a positive whole number. If you resize an array and make it smaller than it was, elements at the end of the array are lost.

For example, the following statement resizes strNames so that 25 is the upper subscript:

```
ReDim Preserve strNames(25)
```

After this statement executes, strNames has 26 elements. Because the Preserve keyword is used, any values originally stored in strNames will still be there.

When you do not know at design time the number of elements you will need in an array, you can declare an array without a size, and use the ReDim statement later to give it a size. For example, suppose you want to write a test-averaging application that averages any number of tests. You can initially declare the array with no size, as follows:

```
Dim sngScores() As Single
```

Currently, sngScores equals Nothing, but is capable of referencing an array of Single values. Later, when the application has determined the number of test scores, a ReDim statement will give the array a size. The following code shows an example of such an operation:

```
intNumScores = CInt(InputBox("Enter the number of test sngScores."))
If intNumScores > 0 Then
  ReDim sngScores(intNumScores - 1)
Else
  MessageBox.Show("You must enter 1 or greater.")
End If
```

This code asks the user to enter the number of test scores. If the user enters a value greater than 0, the ReDim statement sizes the array with intNumScores – 1 as the upper subscript. (Because the subscripts begin at 0, the upper subscript is intNumScores – 1.)

Checkpoint

8.8 Suppose intValues is an array of 100 integers. Write a For...Next loop that totals all the values stored in the array.

8.9 Suppose intPoints is an array of integers, but you do not know the size of the array. Write code that calculates the average of the values in the array.

8.10 Suppose strSerialNumbers is an array of strings. Write a single statement that sorts the array in ascending order.

8.11 What is displayed by the message boxes in the following code segment? (You may need to use a calculator.)

```
Dim intTimes(4) As Integer
Dim intSpeeds(4) As Integer
Dim intDists(4) As Integer
intSpeeds(0) = 18
intSpeeds(1) = 4
intSpeeds(2) = 27
intSpeeds(3) = 52
intSpeeds(4) = 100
Dim intCount As Integer
For intCount = 0 To 4
  intTimes(intCount) = intCount
Next intCount
For intCount = 0 To 4
  intDists(intCount) = intTimes(intCount) * intSpeeds(intCount)
Next intCount
For intCount = 0 To 4
  MessageBox.Show(intTimes(intCount)& " " & intSpeeds(intCount) _
      & " " & intDists(intCount))
Next intCount
```

8.12 Assume that `decSales` is an array of 20 Decimal values. Write a statement that resizes the array to 50 elements. If the array has existing values, they should be preserved.

8.13 Assume that `intValidNumbers` is an array of integers. Write code that searches the array for the value 247. If the value is found, display a message indicating its position in the array. If the value is not found, display a message indicating so.

8.3 Procedures and Functions That Work with Arrays

CONCEPT: You can pass arrays as arguments to procedures and functions. You can return an array from a function. These capabilities allow you to write procedures and functions that perform general operations with arrays.

Passing Arrays as Arguments

Quite often you will want to write procedures or functions that process the data in arrays. For example, procedures can be written to store data in an array, display an array's contents, and sum or average the values in an array. Usually such procedures accept an array as an argument.

The following procedure accepts an integer array as an argument and displays the sum of the array's elements:

```
Sub DisplaySum(ByVal intArray() As Integer)
  ' Displays the sum of the elements in the
  ' argument array.

  Dim intTotal As Integer = 0     ' Accumulator
  Dim intCount As Integer         ' Loop counter
  For intCount = 0 To (intArray.Length - 1)
    intTotal += intArray(intCount)
  Next intCount
  MessageBox.Show("The total is " & intTotal.ToString())
End Sub
```

The parameter variable is declared as an array with no upper subscript specified inside the parentheses. The parameter is an object variable that references an array that is passed as an argument. To call the procedure, pass the name of an array, as shown in the following code:

```
Dim intNumbers() As Integer = {  2, 4, 7, 9, 8, 12, 10 }
DisplaySum(intNumbers)
```

When this code executes, the `DisplaySum` procedure is called and the `intNumbers` array is passed as an argument. The procedure calculates and displays the sum of the elements in `intNumbers`.

Passing Arrays by Value and by Reference

Array parameters can be declared `ByVal` or `ByRef`. Be aware, however, that the `ByVal` keyword does not restrict a procedure from accessing and modifying the argument array's elements. For example, look at the following `SetToZero` procedure:

```
Sub SetToZero(ByVal intArray() As Integer)
  ' Set all the elements of the array argument to zero.

  Dim intCount As Integer
  For intCount = 0 To intArray.Length - 1
    intArray(intCount) = 0
  Next intCount
End Sub
```

This procedure accepts an integer array as its argument and sets each element of the array to 0. Suppose we call the procedure, as shown in the following code:

```
Dim intNumbers() As Integer = {  1, 2, 3, 4, 5 }
SetToZero(intNumbers)
```

After the procedure executes, the `intNumbers` array will contain the values 0, 0, 0, 0, and 0.

Although the `ByVal` keyword does not restrict a procedure from accessing and modifying the elements of an array argument, it does prevent an array argument from being assigned to another array. For example, the following procedure accepts an array as its argument, and then assigns the parameter to another array:

```
Sub ResetValues(ByVal intArray() As Integer)
  ' Assign the array argument to a
  ' new array. Does this work?
  Dim newArray() As Integer = { 0, 0, 0, 0, 0}
  intArray = newArray
End Sub
```

Suppose we call the procedure, as shown in the following code:

```
Dim intNumbers() As Integer = {  1, 2, 3, 4, 5 }
ResetValues(intNumbers)
```

After the procedure executes, the `intNumbers` array still contains the values 1, 2, 3, 4, and 5. If the parameter array had been declared with the `ByRef` keyword, however, the assignment would have affected the argument, and the `intNumbers` array would contain the values 0, 0, 0, 0, and 0 after the procedure executed.

Returning an Array from a Function

You can return an array from a function. For example, the following function prompts the user to enter four names. The names are then returned in an array.

```
Function GetNames() As String()
  ' Get four names from the user
  ' and return them as an array
  ' of strings.
  Dim strNames(3) As String
  Dim strInput As String
  Dim intCount As Integer

  For intCount = 0 To 3
    strInput = InputBox("Enter name " & (intCount + 1).ToString())
    strNames(intCount) = strInput
  Next
  Return strNames
End Function
```

The function has a return type of `String()`, indicating that it returns an array of strings.

The return value can be assigned to any array of strings. The following code shows the function's return value being assigned to `strCustomers`:

```
Dim strCustomers() As String
strCustomers = GetNames()
```

After the code executes, the `strCustomers` array contains the names entered by the user.

An array returned from a function must be assigned to an array of the same type. For example, if a function returns an array of integers, its return value can only be assigned to an array of integers. In Tutorial 8-3, you examine an application containing several functions that work with arrays.

Tutorial 8-3:
Examining an application with functions and with arrays

In this tutorial, you examine the *Sales Data* application, which asks the user for sales figures for a series of days. It calculates and displays the total sales, average sales, highest amount of sales for a given day, and lowest amount of sales for a given day.

Step 1: Open the *Sales Data* project from the student sample programs folder named *Chap8\Sales Data*. The program's main form is shown in Figure 8-14. The *Calculate Sales Data* button is named `btnCalculate`.

Figure 8-14 *Sales Data* form

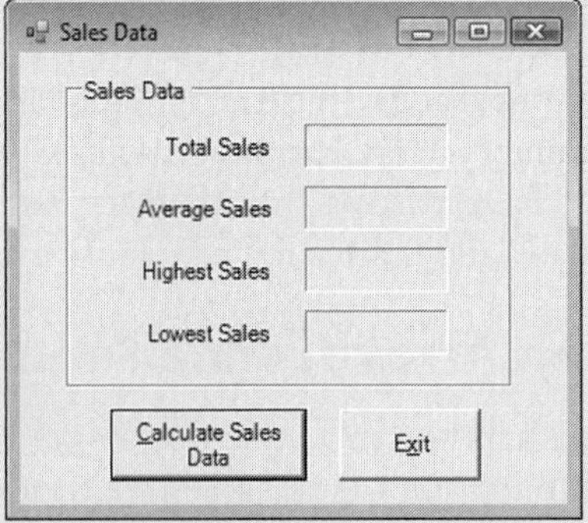

Step 2: Open the *Code* window and look for the `GetSalesData` function. The parameter `decSales` is an empty Decimal array that must be filled in by this function, using data input by the user. The `decSalesData` array temporarily holds the data until the function returns to its caller.

```
Function GetSalesData(ByRef decSales() As Decimal) As Boolean
   ' Prompts the user for sales figures and stores the
   ' values in an array. Returns True if the procedure
   ' was successful, otherwise returns False.

    Dim decSalesData() As Decimal    ' Sales data array
    Dim intNumDays As Integer = 0    ' Number of days
    Dim intCount As Integer          ' Loop counter
    Dim blnSuccess As Boolean   ' Indicates success or failure
```

A `TryParse` statement converts the value the user entered to the number of days. If an error is found, there is no purpose in going any further in this function, so it returns right away.

```
Dim strNumDays As String = InputBox("For how many days do you " _
   & "have sales?")

If Not Integer.TryParse(strNumDays, intNumDays) Then
  MessageBox.Show("You entered a nonnumeric value", _
    "Error")
  Return False
End If
```

Assuming the number of days is greater than zero, we resize the array so it can hold the sales data.

```
If intNumDays > 0 Then
  ' Resize the array to the correct number of days.
  ReDim decSalesData(intNumDays - 1)
```

A loop inputs the daily sales from the user. The message prompting the user contains a counter (`intCount`) identifying which day the sales are for, as shown in Figure 8-15.

```
' Input each day's sales from the user.
  For intCount = 0 To (intNumDays - 1)
    Dim blnValid As Boolean
    Do
      blnValid = Decimal.TryParse(InputBox(_
        "Enter the sales for " & _
        "day " & (intCount + 1).ToString,_
        decSalesData(intCount))
      If Not blnValid Then
        MessageBox.Show("Please enter a valid number")
      End If
    Loop Until blnValid
  Next intCount
```

Finally, the `decSalesData` array is assigned to the function parameter (named `decSales`) and the `blnSuccess` Boolean variable is set to *True*, indicating that the sales data was entered correctly by the user:

```
    ' Assign the array to the parameter variable.
    decSales = decSalesData
    blnSuccess = True
  Else
    MessageBox.Show("You must enter at least one day " _
        & "of sales.")
    blnSuccess = False
  End If
  Return blnSuccess
End Function
```

Figure 8-15 User input for *Sales Data*

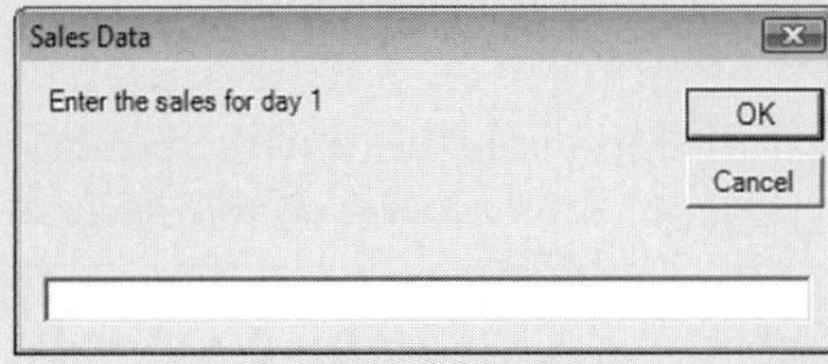

Step 3: Locate the `GetTotal` function, which receives a Decimal array and returns the total of all its elements.

```
Function GetTotal(ByVal decValues() As Decimal) As Decimal

   ' Calculate and return the total of the
   ' values in the array argument.

   Dim decTotal As Decimal = 0      ' Accumulator
   Dim intCount As Integer          ' Loop counter

   For intCount = 0 To (decValues.Length - 1)
      decTotal += decValues(intCount)
   Next
   Return decTotal
End Function
```

Step 4: Locate the `GetAverage` function, which returns the average of all elements in a Decimal array.

```
Function GetAverage(ByVal decValues() As Decimal) As Decimal
   ' Calculate and return the average of the
   ' values in the array argument.

   Return GetTotal(decValues) / decValues.Length
End Function
```

Step 5: Locate the `GetHighest` and `GetLowest` functions, which return the largest, and smallest values, respectively, in a Decimal array.

```
Function GetHighest(ByVal decValues() As Decimal) As Decimal

   ' Returns the largest value in a Decimal array.
   Dim intCount As Integer                       ' Loop counter
   Dim decHighest As Decimal = decValues(0)      ' Largest value

   For intCount = 1 To (decValues.Length - 1)
      If decValues(intCount) > decHighest Then
         decHighest = decValues(intCount)
      End If
   Next intCount
   Return decHighest
End Function

Function GetLowest(ByVal decValues() As Decimal) As Decimal

   ' Returns the smallest value in a Decimal array.
   Dim decCount As Integer                    ' Loop counter
   Dim decLowest As Decimal = decValues(0) ' Smallest value

   For decCount = 1 To (decValues.Length - 1)
      If decValues(decCount) < decLowest Then
         decLowest = decValues(decCount)
      End If
   Next decCount
   Return decLowest
End Function
```

Step 6: Near the top of the file, find the `btnCalculate_Click` event handler. Look at the event handler's local variable declarations. The `decSales` array holds sales for each day; `decTotal` holds the total sales for all days; `decAverage` holds the average sales for all days; `decHighest` holds the highest sales earned in a single day; and `decLowest` holds the lowest sales earned in a single day.

```
Private Sub btnCalculate_Click(ByVal sender As System.Object, _
    ByVal e As System.EventArgs) Handles btnCalculate.Click

  Dim decSales() As Decimal = Nothing     ' Sales array
  Dim decTotal As Decimal                 ' Total sales
  Dim decAverage As Decimal               ' Average sales
  Dim decHighest As Decimal               ' Highest sales
  Dim decLowest As Decimal                ' Lowest sales
```

Next, the event handler calls the `GetSalesData` function, passing it the `decSales` array.

```
  If GetSalesData(decSales) Then
    ' Calculate total, average, highest, and lowest sales
    decTotal = GetTotal(decSales)
    decAverage = GetAverage(decSales)
    decHighest = GetHighest(decSales)
    decLowest = GetLowest(decSales)

    ' Display the results.
    lblTotal.Text = decTotal.ToString("c")
    lblAverage.Text = decAverage.ToString("c")
    lblHighest.Text = decHighest.ToString("c")
    lblLowest.Text = decLowest.ToString("c")
  End If
End Sub
```

Step 7: Run the application, click the *Calculate Sales Data* button, and enter the following input for number of days and sales:

Number of days **5**
Sales for day 1 **1357.89**
Sales for day 2 **1564.25**
Sales for day 3 **927.12**
Sales for day 4 **1032.69**
Sales for day 5 **1468.27**

Step 8: The form should display the sales data shown in Figure 8-16.

Step 9: Exit the application.

Figure 8-16 *Sales Data* form completed

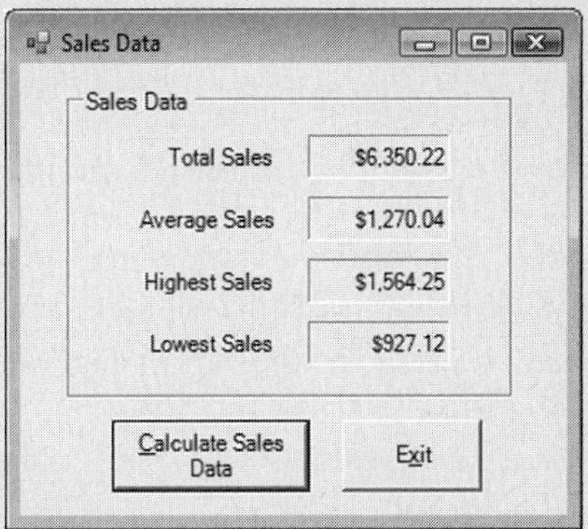

8.4 Multidimensional Arrays

CONCEPT: **You may create arrays with more than two dimensions to hold complex sets of data.**

Two-Dimensional Arrays

The arrays presented so far have had only one subscript. An array with one subscript is called a **one-dimensional array**, and is useful for storing and working with a single set of data. Sometimes, though, it is necessary to work with multiple sets of data. For example, in a grade-averaging program, a teacher might record all of one student's test scores in an array. If the teacher has 30 students, that means there must be 30 arrays to record the scores for the entire class. Instead of declaring 30 individual arrays, it would be better to declare a two-dimensional array.

A **two-dimensional array** is like an array of arrays. It can be used to hold multiple sets of values. Think of a two-dimensional array as having rows and columns of elements, as shown in Figure 8-17. This figure shows an array having three rows (numbered 0, 1, and 2) and four columns (numbered 0, 1, 2, and 3). There are a total of 12 elements in the array.

Figure 8-17 Rows and columns

	Column 0	Column 1	Column 2	Column 3
Row 0				
Row 1				
Row 2				

To declare a two-dimensional array, two sets of upper subscripts are required, the first for the rows and the second for the columns. The general format of a two-dimensional array declaration is as follows:

```
Dim ArrayName (UpperRow,Uppercolumn) As DataType
```

Let's take a closer look at the syntax.

- `ArrayName` is the name of the array.
- `UpperRow` is the value of the array's highest row subscript. This must be a positive integer.
- `UpperColumn` is the value of the array's highest column subscript. This must be a positive integer.
- `DataType` is a Visual Basic data type.

An example declaration of a two-dimensional array with three rows and four columns follows, and is shown in Figure 8-18. The highest row subscript is 2 and the highest column subscript is 3.

```
Dim sngScores(2, 3) As Single
```

Figure 8-18 Declaration of a two-dimensional array

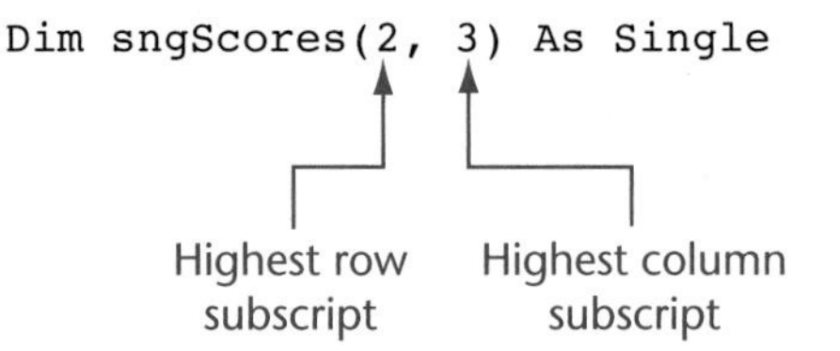

When data in a two-dimensional array is processed, each element has two subscripts, the first for its row and the second for its column. Using the `sngScores` array as an example, the elements in row 0 are referenced as follows:

```
sngScores(0, 0)
sngScores(0, 1)
sngScores(0, 2)
sngScores(0, 3)
```

The elements in row 1 are referenced as follows:

```
sngScores(1, 0)
sngScores(1, 1)
sngScores(1, 2)
sngScores(1, 3)
```

The elements in row 2 are referenced as follows:

```
sngScores(2, 0)
sngScores(2, 1)
sngScores(2, 2)
sngScores(2, 3)
```

Figure 8-19 illustrates the array with the subscripts shown for each element.

Figure 8-19 Subscripts for each element of the `sngScores` array

	Column 0	Column 1	Column 2	Column 3
Row 0	sngScores(0, 0)	sngScores(0, 1)	sngScores(0, 2)	sngScores(0, 3)
Row 1	sngScores(1, 0)	sngScores(1, 1)	sngScores(1, 2)	sngScores(1, 3)
Row 2	sngScores(2, 0)	sngScores(2, 1)	sngScores(2, 2)	sngScores(2, 3)

To access one of the elements in a two-dimensional array, you must use two subscripts. For example, the following statement stores the number 95 in `sngScores(2, 1)`:

```
sngScores(2, 1) = 95
```

Programs often use nested loops to process two-dimensional arrays. For example, the following code prompts the user to enter a score, once for each element in the array:

```
For intRow = 0 To 2
  For intCol = 0 To 3
    intNum = Cint(InputBox("Enter a score."))
    sngScores(intRow, intCol) = intNum
  Next intCol
Next intRow
```

And the following code displays all the elements in the `sngScores` array:

```
For intRow = 0 To 2
  For intCol = 0 To 3
    lstOutput.Items.Add(sngScores(intRow, intCol).ToString())
  Next intCol
Next intRow
```

In Tutorial 8-4, you complete an application that stores sales figures in a two-dimensional array. The application sums the values in each row of the two-dimensional array and sums the values in the entire array.

Tutorial 8-4:
Completing an application that sums the rows of a two-dimensional array

In a company with three divisions, each division keeps its total sales for each quarter. This application uses an array with three rows (one for each division) and four columns (one for each quarter) to store the company's sales data. The *Division Sales* form is shown in Figure 8-20.

Figure 8-20 *Division Sales* form

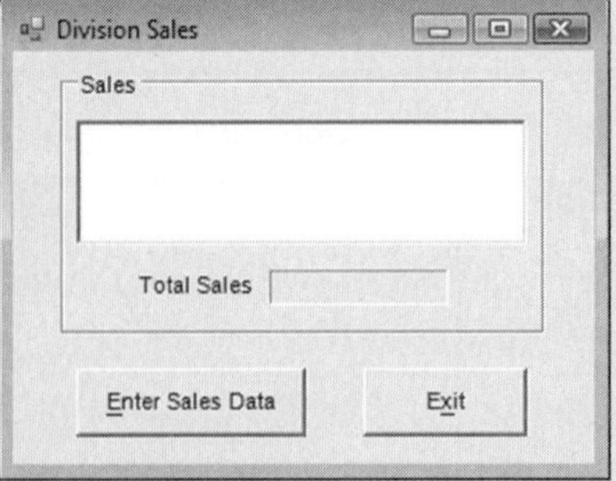

Step 1: Open the *Division Sales* project from the sample student programs folder named *Chap8\Division Sales*.

Step 2: Open the *Code* window and look at the class-level declarations of constants that define the maximum subscripts for `decSales`, a two-dimensional Decimal array.

```
' Define constants for array and loop counter limits.
Const intDIVISION_MAX As Integer = 2
Const intQUARTER_MAX As Integer = 3

' Two-dimensional sales array.
Dim decSales(intDIVISION_MAX, intQUARTER_MAX) As Decimal
```

The `decSales` array has three rows (one for each division) and four columns (one for each quarter) to store the company's sales data. The row subscripts are 0, 1, and 2, and the column subscripts are 0, 1, 2, and 3. Figure 8-21 illustrates how the quarterly sales figures are stored in the array.

Step 3: Find the `btnEnterData_Click` event handler and insert the following statements shown in bold. We will explain their purpose along the way.

```
Private Sub btnEnterData_Click(ByVal sender As System.Object, _
    ByVal e As System.EventArgs) Handles btnEnterData.Click

  ' This procedure gathers quarterly sales figures for
  ' three divisions. The totals for each division and
  ' the total sales of all divisions are displayed.

  Dim intDivision As Integer                  ' Outer loop counter
  Dim intQuarter As Integer                   ' Loop counter
  Dim decDivisionTotal As Decimal = 0         ' Division total
  Dim decCorpTotal As Decimal = 0             ' Corporate total
  Dim strSales, strMsg As String
```

Figure 8-21 Division and quarter data in the `decSales` array

	Column 0 (quarter 1)	Column 1 (quarter 2)	Column 2 (quarter 3)	Column 3 (quarter 4)
Row 0 (division 1)	decSales(0, 0) Holds data for division 1, quarter 1	decSales(0, 1) Holds data for division 1, quarter 2	decSales(0, 2) Holds data for division 1, quarter 3	decSales(0, 3) Holds data for division 1, quarter 4
Row 1 (division 2)	decSales(1, 0) Holds data for division 2, quarter 1	decSales(1, 1) Holds data for division 2, quarter 2	decSales(1, 2) Holds data for division 2, quarter 3	decSales(1, 3) Holds data for division 2, quarter 4
Row 2 (division 3)	decSales(2, 0) Holds data for division 3, quarter 1	decSales(2, 1) Holds data for division 3, quarter 2	decSales(2, 2) Holds data for division 3, quarter 3	decSales(2, 3) Holds data for division 3, quarter 4

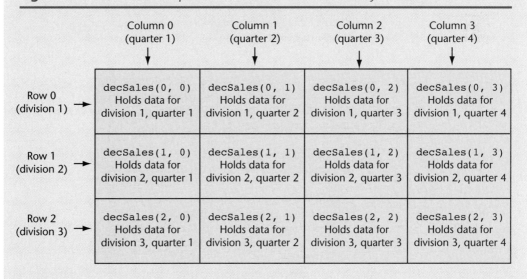

The following nested loop requests sales data from the user. The outer loop repeats once for each division of the company. The first inner loop repeats once for each quarter of the year. Another inner loop uses a `Try-Catch` block to handle input errors made by the user.

```
For intDivision = 0 To intDIVISION_MAX
  For intQuarter = 0 To intQUARTER_MAX

    ' Create a prompting message for the user.
    strMsg = "Enter sales for division " & _
        (intDivision + 1).ToString() & ", quarter " & _
        (intQuarter + 1).ToString()

    Dim blnValueOk As Boolean = False

    Do While blnValueOk = False
      ' Display the input box, using the message.
      strSales = InputBox(strMsg, "Input Sales Data")
      Try
        ' Save the sales in the array.
        decSales(intDivision, intQuarter) = CDec(strSales)
        blnValueOk = True
      Catch ex As Exception
        MessageBox.Show("That value was nonnumeric. " _
            & "Please try again.", "Error")
      End Try
    Loop
  Next intQuarter
Next intDivision
```

When the user accidentally enters a nonnumeric value for sales, the `CDec` function call throws an exception. Our `Catch` clause handles the error by displaying a MessageBox and asking the user to try again. That is why the `While` loop repeats until the user enters a valid value.

The next loop calculates and displays the sales totals for divisions. The inner loop adds sales for each quarter, producing total sales for each division.

```
For intDivision = 0 To intDIVISION_MAX
  ' Initialize the division accumulator.
  decDivisionTotal = 0

  ' Total the division sales.
  For intQuarter = 0 To intQUARTER_MAX
    ' Add dept sales to division sales.
    decDivisionTotal += decSales(intDivision, intQuarter)
  Next intQuarter

  ' Update the corporate total.
  decCorpTotal += decDivisionTotal

  ' Display the division total.
  lstOutput.Items.Add("Division " & _
    (intDivision + 1).ToString() & _
    ": " & decDivisionTotal.ToString("c"))
Next intDivision
```

Finally, we display the company total (total sales for all divisions) as follows:

```
  lblTotalSales.Text = decCorpTotal.ToString("c")
End Sub
```

Step 4: Save the project and run the application. Your output should appear similar to that shown in Figure 8-22, using your own numeric values.

Figure 8-22 Completed *Division Sales* form

Implicit Sizing and Initialization of Two-Dimensional Arrays

As with a one-dimensional array, you may provide an initialization list for a two-dimensional array. Recall that when you provide an initialization list for an array, you cannot provide the upper subscript numbers. When initializing a two-dimensional array, you must provide the comma to indicate the number of dimensions. The following is an example of a two-dimensional array declaration with an initialization list:

```
Dim intNumbers(,) As Integer = { { 1, 2, 3} , _
                                 { 4, 5, 6} , _
                                 { 7, 8, 9} }
```

Initialization values for each row are enclosed in their own set of braces. In this example, the initialization values for row 0 are `{ 1, 2, 3}`, the initialization values for row 1 are `{ 4, 5, 6}`, and the initialization values for row 2 are `{ 7, 8, 9}`. So, this statement declares an array with three rows and three columns. The same statement could also be written as follows:

```
Dim intNumbers(,) As Integer = { { 1, 2, 3} , _
                                 { 4, 5, 6} , _
                                 { 7, 8, 9} }
```

In either case, the values are assigned to the `intNumbers` array in the following manner:

```
intNumbers(0, 0) is set to 1
intNumbers(0, 1) is set to 2
intNumbers(0, 2) is set to 3

intNumbers(1, 0) is set to 4
intNumbers(1, 1) is set to 5
intNumbers(1, 2) is set to 6

intNumbers(2, 0) is set to 7
intNumbers(2, 1) is set to 8
intNumbers(2, 2) is set to 9
```

Summing the Columns of a Two-Dimensional Array

You can use nested loops to sum the columns in a two-dimensional array. The following code sums each column of an array named `intValues`, which has five rows and three columns. The outer loop controls the column subscript and the inner loop controls the row subscript. The variable `intTotal` accumulates the sum of each column.

```
' Sum the columns.
For intCol = 0 To 2
   ' Initialize the accumulator.
   intTotal = 0
   ' Sum all rows within this column.
   For intRow = 0 To 4
      intTotal += intValues(intRow, intCol)
   Next intRow
   ' Display the sum of the column.
   MessageBox.Show("Sum of column " & intCol.ToString() & _
         " is " & intTotal.ToString())
Next intCol
```

Three-Dimensional Arrays and Beyond

You can create arrays with up to 32 dimensions. The following is an example of a three-dimensional array declaration:

```
Dim decSeats(9, 11, 14) As Decimal
```

This array can be thought of as 10 sets of 12 rows, with each row containing 15 columns. This array might be used to store the prices of seats in an auditorium, in which there are 15 seats in a row, 12 rows in a section, and 10 sections in the room.

Figure 8-23 represents a three-dimensional array as pages of two-dimensional arrays.

Figure 8-23 A three-dimensional array

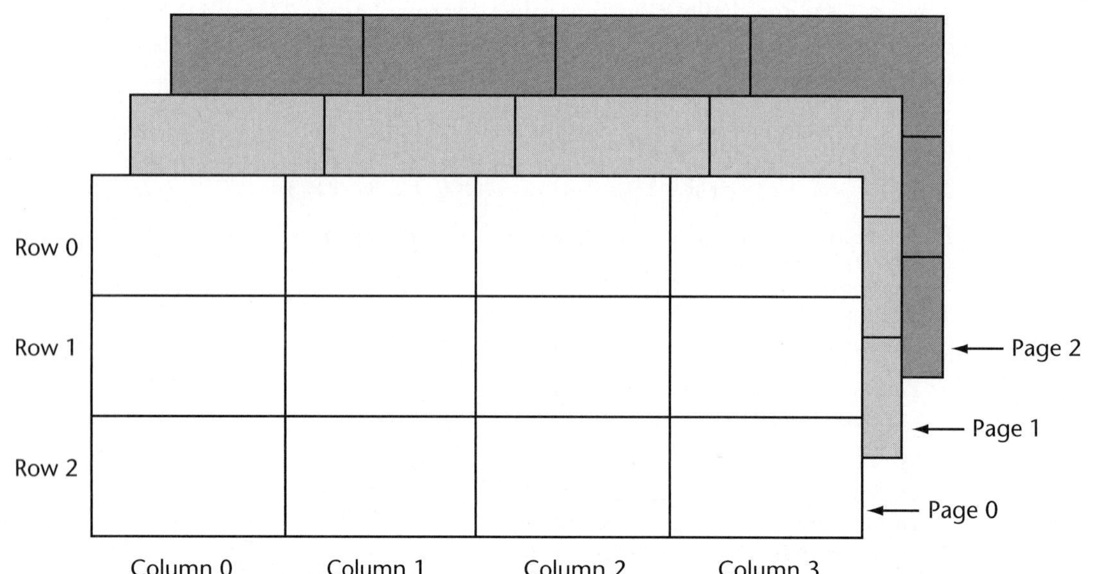

Arrays with more than three dimensions are difficult to visualize but can be useful in some programming applications. For example, in a factory warehouse where cases of widgets are stacked on pallets, an array of four dimensions can store a part number for each widget. The four subscripts of each element can represent the pallet number, case number, row number, and column number of each widget. Similarly, an array with five dimensions could be used if there were multiple warehouses.

Checkpoint

8.14 Declare a two-dimensional array of integers named `intGrades`. It should have 30 rows and 10 columns.

8.15 How many elements are in the following array?

```
Dim decSales(5, 3) As Decimal
```

8.16 Write a statement that assigns 56893.12 to the first column of the first row of the `decSales` array declared in Checkpoint 8.15.

8.17 Write a statement that displays in a message box the contents of the last column of the last row of the array `decSales` declared in Checkpoint 8.15.

8.18 Declare a two-dimensional Integer array named `intSettings` large enough to hold the following table of numbers:

```
12    24    32    21    42
14    67    87    65    90
19     1    24    12     8
```

8.19 How many rows and columns does the array declared in the following statement have?

```
Dim intMatrix(,) As Integer = { { 2, 4, 7, 0, 3} , _
    { 6, 5, 12, 8, 6} , { 9, 0, 14, 6, 0} , _
    { 16, 7, 9, 13, 10} }
```

8.20 A movie rental store keeps DVDs on 50 racks with 10 shelves each. Each shelf holds 25 DVDs. Declare a three-dimensional array of strings large enough to represent the store's storage system. Each element of the array holds a movie title.

8.5 Focus on GUI Design: The Enabled Property, Timer Control, and Splash Screens

CONCEPT: You can disable controls by setting their Enabled property to *False*. The Timer control allows your application to execute a procedure at regular time intervals. Splash screens are forms that appear while an application is initializing.

The Enabled Property

Most controls have a Boolean property named Enabled. When a control's **Enabled property** is set to *False*, it is considered disabled, which means it cannot receive the focus and cannot respond to events generated by the user. Additionally, many controls appear dimmed, or grayed out, when their Enabled property is set to *False*. For example, Figure 8-24 shows a form with labels, a text box, a group box, radio buttons, a list box, and buttons. All of these controls have their Enabled property set to *False*.

Figure 8-24 Controls with Enabled property set to *False*

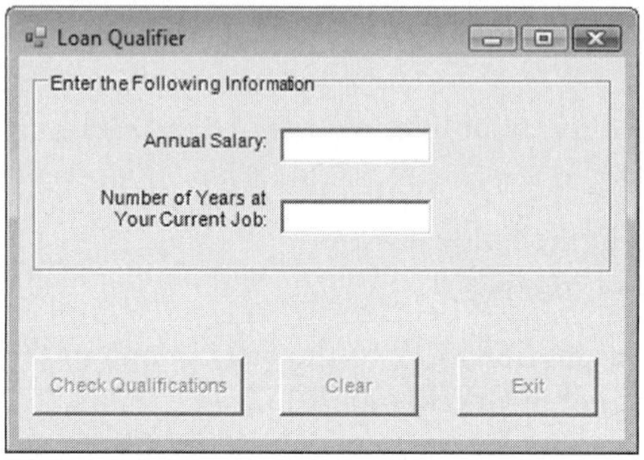

By default, a control's Enabled property is set to *True*. If you change a control's Enabled property to *False* at design time, the control is initially disabled when the application runs.

You can also change the Enabled property's value with code at runtime. For example, assume an application has a radio button named `radBlue`. The following statement disables the control:

```
radBlue.Enabled = False
```

Sometimes you do not want the user to access controls. For example, consider an application that calculates the price of two different models of a new car. One model comes only in red, yellow, and black, while the other model comes only in white, green, and orange. As soon as the user selects a model, the application can disable colors not available for that model.

The Timer Control

The **Timer control** allows an application to automatically execute code at regular time intervals. It is useful when you want an application to perform an operation at certain times or after an amount of time has passed. For example, a Timer control can perform simple animation by moving a graphic image across the screen, or it can cause a form to be hidden after a certain amount of time.

Double-click the Timer tool in the toolbox to place a Timer control on a form. (The Timer control is in the *Components* section of the toolbox.) Because the Timer control is invisible at runtime, it appears in the component tray at design time. The standard prefix for a Timer control's name is `tmr`.

Timer Events

When you place a Timer control on a form, it responds to `Tick` events as the application is running. A `Tick` event is generated at regular time intervals. If the control has a `Tick` event procedure, it is executed each time a `Tick` event occurs. Therefore, the code that you write in the `Tick` event procedure executes at regular intervals.

To create a `Tick` event procedure code template, double-click a Timer control that has been placed in the form's component tray.

Timer Control Properties

The Timer control has two important properties: Enabled and Interval. When the Enabled property is set to *True*, the Timer control responds to `Tick` events. When the Enabled property is set to *False*, the Timer control does not respond to `Tick` events (code in the control's `Tick` event procedure does not execute).

The **Interval property** can be set to a value of 1 or greater. The value stored in the Interval property is the number of milliseconds that elapse between timer events. A millisecond is a thousandth of a second, so setting the Interval property to 1000 causes a timer event to occur every second.

In Tutorial 8-5, you examine an application that demonstrates a Timer control.

Tutorial 8-5:
The *Timer Demo*

Step 1: Open the *Timer Demo* project from the sample student programs folder named *Chap8\Timer Demo*. The application's form is shown in Figure 8-25. Notice that the Timer control appears as a stopwatch in the component tray.

Figure 8-25 *Timer Demo* form

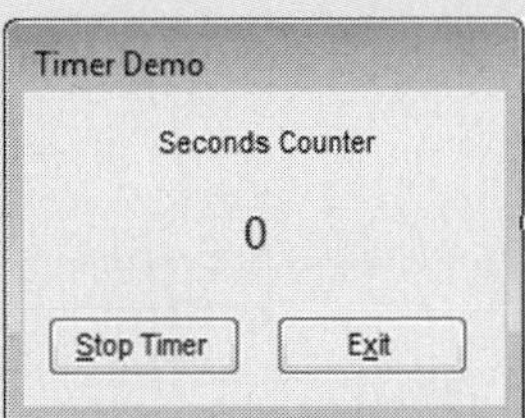

Step 2: Run the application. The form shown in Figure 8-26 appears.

Figure 8-26 *Timer Demo* application running

Step 3: The number appearing under the *Seconds Counter* label is initially set to 0, but it increments every second. After a few seconds, click the *Stop Timer* button to halt the timer.

Step 4: When you click the *Stop Timer* button, the button's text changes to *Start Timer*. Click the button again to start the timer.

Step 5: After a few seconds, click the *Exit* button to end the application.

Step 6: With the *Design* window open, select the Timer control.

Step 7: With the Timer control selected, look at the *Properties* window. The name of the control is `tmrSeconds`. Its Enabled property is initially set to *True*, and its Interval property is set to *1000*.

Step 8: Open the *Code* window and notice that a class-level variable named `intSeconds` is declared.

Step 9: Look at the `tmrSeconds_Tick` event procedure. The code is as follows:

```
Private Sub tmrSeconds_Tick(ByVal eventSender As System.Object, _
  ByVal eventArgs As System.EventArgs) Handles tmrSeconds.Tick

  ' Update the seconds display by one second.
  intSeconds += 1
  lblCounter.Text = intSeconds.ToString()
End Sub
```

Each time the `tmrSeconds_Tick` event procedure executes, it adds 1 to `intSeconds` and then copies its value to the `lblCounter` label. Because the Timer control's Interval property is set to *1000*, this event procedure executes every second (unless the Timer control's Enabled property equals *False*).

Step 10: The button that stops and starts the timer is named `btnToggleTimer`. Look at the `btnToggleTimer_Click` event procedure. The code is as follows:

```
Private Sub btnToggleTimer_Click(ByVal sender As System.Object, _
    ByVal e As System.EventArgs) Handles btnToggleTimer.Click

  ' Toggle the timer.
  If tmrSeconds.Enabled = True Then
    tmrSeconds.Enabled = False
    btnToggleTimer.Text = "&Start Timer"
  Else
    tmrSeconds.Enabled = True
    btnToggleTimer.Text = "&Stop Timer"
  End If
End Sub
```

If `tmrSeconds.Enabled` equals *True*, the code sets it to *False* and changes the button's text to *&Start Timer*. Otherwise, it sets the property to *True* and changes the button's text to *&Stop Timer*.

Splash Screens

A **splash screen** is a form displayed while an application is initializing, or loading into memory. Splash screens usually show company logos and assure the user that an application is in the process of starting up. Most major applications, such as Microsoft Word, Excel, and others display splash screens.

Forms have a **TopMost property**, which may be set to *True* or *False*. When set to *True*, it causes the form to always be displayed on top of other forms that do not have this property set to *True*. By default this property is set to *False*. Splash screens should always appear on top of the other forms in an application, so set this property to *True* for any form that will be a splash screen. Splash screens should also be displayed in modeless style (with the `Show` method) so the application can load while the splash screen is displayed.

A splash screen should automatically disappear after a short time period. You can place a Timer control on a splash screen form, set its Interval property to the desired time interval, and then code a `Tick` event procedure to close the form. Tutorial 8-6 leads you through the process of creating a splash screen.

Tutorial 8-6:
Creating a splash screen

Step 1: Create a new Windows application project named *Splash Demo*.

Step 2: Name the application's form `frmMain` and place the following controls on it:

- A label on the form with the text *This is the main form.*
- An *Exit* button that ends the application.

Your form should appear similar to the one shown in Figure 8-27.

Step 3: Add another form with the name `frmSplash` to the project. Set the form's FormBorderStyle property to *FixedToolWindow*. A window with this type of border may not be resized, minimized, or maximized.

Figure 8-27 Splash *Demo Main* form

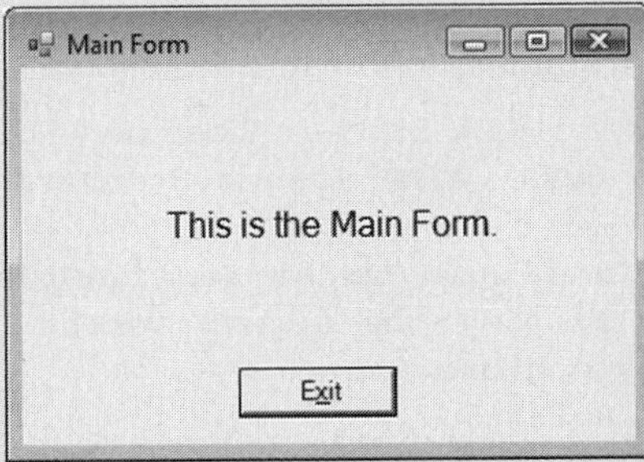

Step 4: Add the labels and Picture Box control shown in Figure 8-28 to the `frmSplash` form. Set the Picture Box control's SizeMode property to *StretchImage*. The graphic image that is shown in the figure can be replaced with any *.gif* or *.jpg* file you find on the Web (respect copyright notices, of course). Set the form's Text property to *Loading* and change the form's BackColor property to a light color.

Figure 8-28 Splash screen form

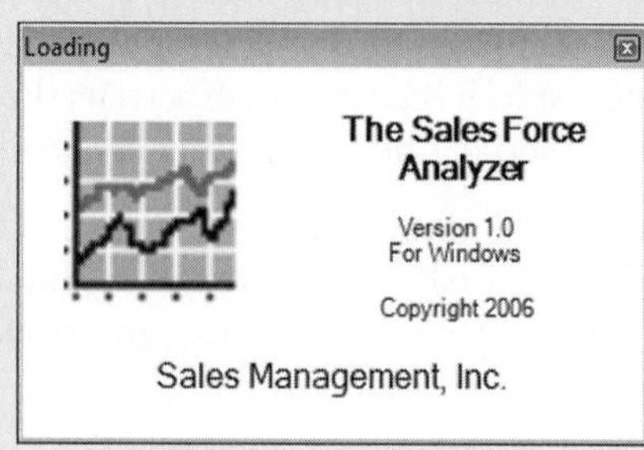

Step 5: Set the form's TopMost property to *True* to ensure that the form is always displayed on top of the other forms on the screen.

Step 6: Place a Timer control on the form. Name the Timer **tmrTimer**, set its Interval property to *5000*, and set its Enabled property to *True*.

Step 7: Double-click the `tmrTimer` control to insert a code template for its Tick event procedure. Complete the event procedure so it appears as the following code:

```
Private Sub tmrTimer_Tick(ByVal sender As System.Object, _
    ByVal e As System.EventArgs) Handles tmrTimer.Tick

  ' Close the form
  Me.Close()
End Sub
```

Step 8: Set `frmMain` as the project's startup form. (Right-click the project's entry in the *Solution Explorer* window, and then select *Properties* from the pop-up menu.)

Step 9: You will write code in the `frmMain` form's `Load` event procedure to display the splash screen. Double-click the `frmMain` form in the *Design* window to create a code template for the `Load` event procedure. Complete the event procedure by writing the following code shown in bold:

```
Private Sub frmMain_Load(ByVal sender As System.Object, _
    ByVal e As System.EventArgs) Handles MyBase.Load

  Dim splashForm As New frmSplash()
  ' Display the splash screen
  splashForm.Show()
End Sub
```

Step 10: Save and run the project. The splash screen should appear as shown in Figure 8-29, with your own graphic image appearing on the form.

Figure 8-29 Splash screen

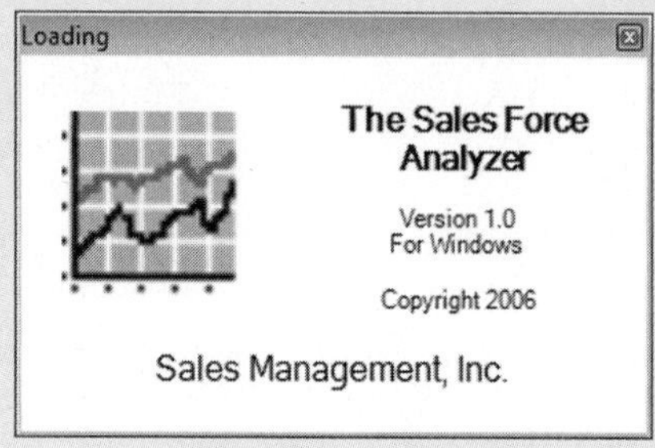

Step 11: The Timer control should unload the splash screen form after five seconds.

Step 12: On the main form, click the *Exit* button to end the application.

8.6 Focus on GUI Design: Anchoring and Docking Controls

CONCEPT: Controls have two properties, Anchor and Dock, which allow you to control the control's position on the form when the form is resized at runtime.

The Anchor Property

By default, when a user resizes a form at runtime, the positions of controls on the form do not change with respect to the top and left edges of the form. For example, in Figure 8-30, the image on the left shows the form before the user resizes it and the image on the right shows the form after the user resizes it.

Figure 8-30 A form before and after the user resizes it

Before resizing

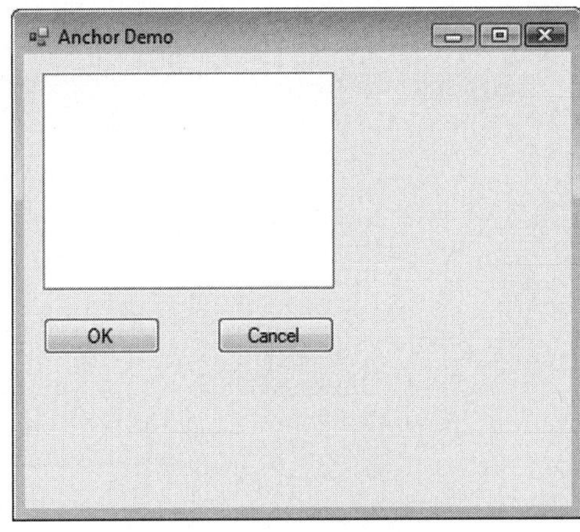

After resizing

When the user resizes the form, the positions of the list box and buttons do not change. Controls have an **Anchor property,** which allows you to anchor the control to one or more edges of a form. When a control is anchored to a form's edge, the distance between the control's edge and the form's edge remains constant when the form is resized at runtime.

When you click the Anchor property in the *Properties* window, the pop-up window shown in Figure 8-31 appears. Notice that the top and left bars are selected, indicating that the control is anchored to the top and left edges of the form. This is the Anchor property's default setting. To change the Anchor property's setting, select the bars that correspond to the edges of the form you wish to anchor the control to. For example, Figure 8-32 shows how the Anchor property appears when the control is anchored to the bottom and right edges.

Figure 8-31 Anchor property selected

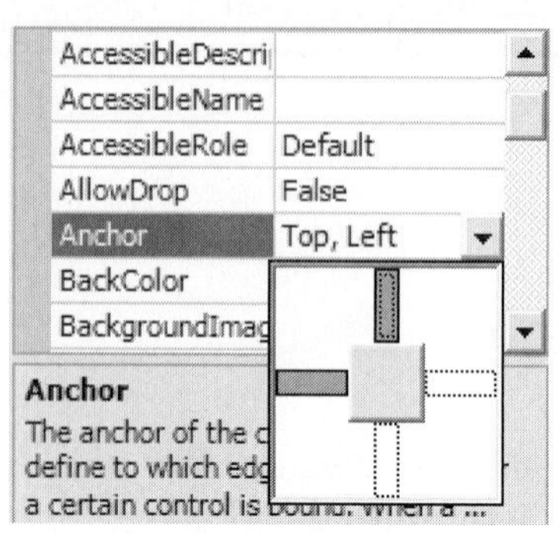

Figure 8-32 Anchor property set to the bottom and right edges

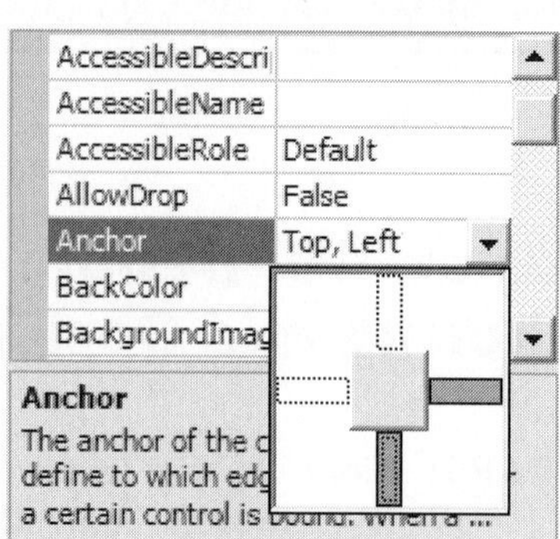

Figure 8-33 shows a form before and after it is resized. This time, the button controls are anchored to the bottom and right edges of the form and the list box is anchored to the top and left edges.

It is possible to anchor a control to opposing sides, such the top and the bottom, or the left and the right. This approach causes the control to be resized when the form is resized. For example, look at Figure 8-34. The PictureBox control is anchored to all four edges of the form, and its SizeMode property is set to *StretchImage*. When the form is resized, the PictureBox control is resized.

Figure 8-33 Buttons anchored to the bottom and right edges of the form

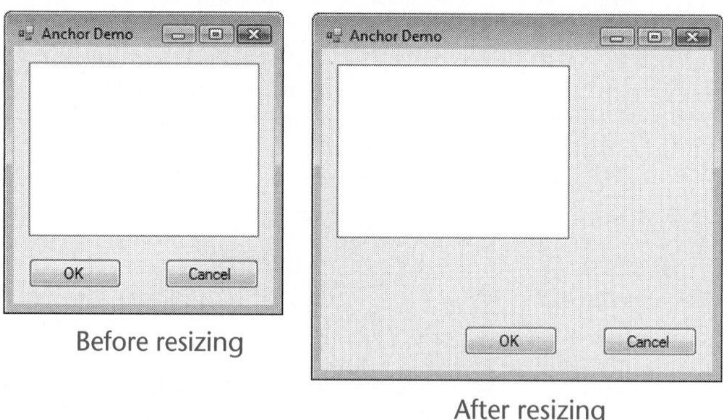

Figure 8-34 PictureBox control anchored to all four edges of the form

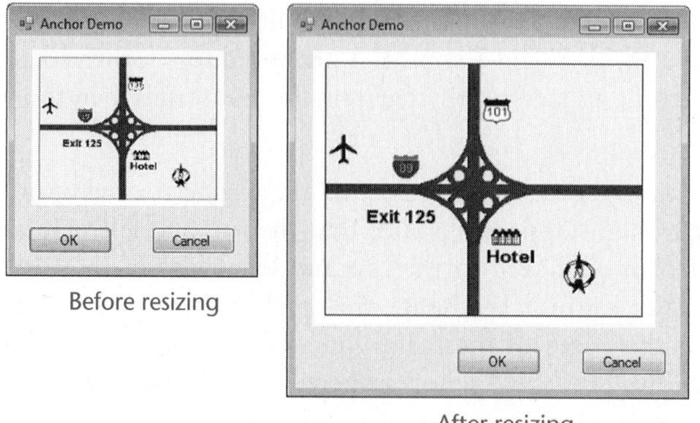

The Dock Property

When a control is docked, it is positioned directly against one of the edges of a form. Additionally, the length or width of a docked control is changed to match the length or width of the form's edge. For example, the form in Figure 8-35 has four docked buttons. A button is docked to each of the form's edges.

Figure 8-35 Form with docked buttons

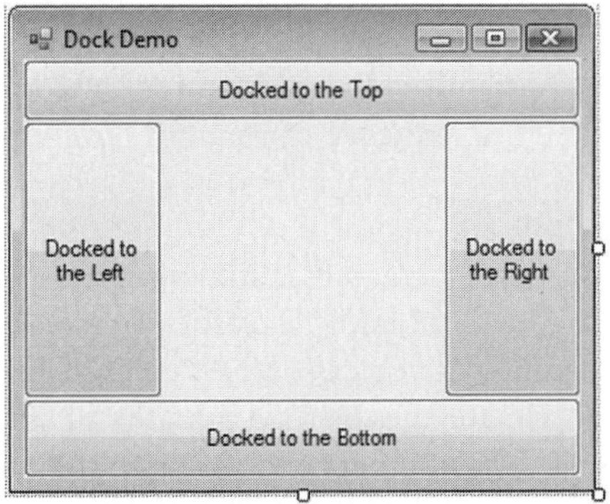

Buttons are automatically sized to fill up the edge to which they are docked. Use the **Dock property** to dock a control against a form's edge. In the *Properties* window, the pop-up window shown in Figure 8-36 appears. The figure illustrates how each button in the pop-up window affects the control. The square button in the center causes the control to fill the entire form.

Figure 8-36 Dock property selected

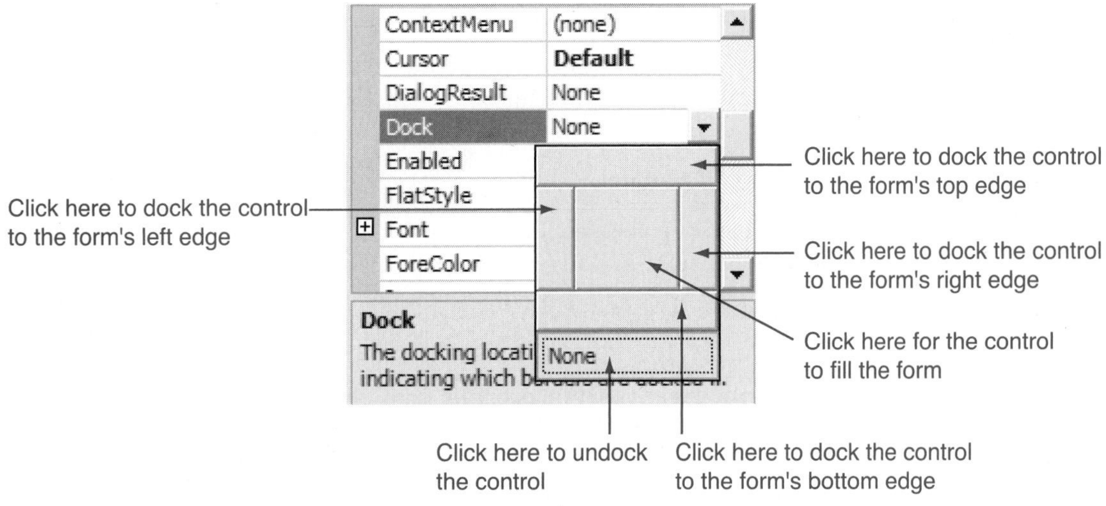

Checkpoint

8.21 Suppose a form has check box controls named `chkFreePizza` and `chkFreeCola`, and a radio button control named `radLifeTimeMember`. Write code that enables the checkboxes if the radio button is selected.

8.22 If you want a Timer control to execute its `Tick` event procedure every half second, what value do you store in its Interval property?

8.23 How do you make sure that a form is always displayed on top of other forms?

8.24 What is the purpose of the Anchor property?

8.25 What is the purpose of the Dock property?

8.7 Random Numbers

CONCEPT: Visual Basic provides tools to generate random numbers and initialize the sequence of random numbers with a random seed value.

Computer applications such as games and simulations often create what appear to be random events. A program simulating a traffic intersection, for example, might generate random numbers of simulated vehicles. Based on information provided during the simulation, planners can estimate the average amount of time drivers spend waiting at the stoplight. Similarly, random numbers can simulate the movements of stock prices, using various rules about how stock prices change.

Computers generate pseudo-random numbers using carefully crafted formulas based on years of research. The number sequences appear to be random, when in fact it's impossible to generate random numbers with digital circuits that work consistently every time. (Unless you have an old computer—then it might fail from time to time, generating truly random results.)

Pseudo-random numbers only seem to be random. Random number formulas start with a number called a seed. Visual Basic, for example, uses a **random seed value** based on the time of day, down to hundredths of a second. The seed provides initial input to the formula that generates the next number in the series.

The **`Random`** **class** provides methods and properties that make generating random numbers fairly easy. You must create an instance of `Random`, usually at the class or module level.

```
Private rand As New Random
```

By passing no parameter to the `Random` constructor, VB assumes you want to use the default random number seed. You may, if you want, pass a specific seed value:

```
Private rand As New Random(25)
```

When you provide a seed, the sequence of pseudo-random numbers created by the Random object is the same every time the program runs. That may be desirable when running specific tests and validations, but decidedly boring if the program is a computer game or simulation.

The **`Random.Next`** method returns the next integer in the series (generated by the formula). If you call it with no arguments, the returned integer is somewhere between 0 and 2,147,483,647. The following is an example, using the `rand` variable we declared earlier:

```
Dim intNum As Integer = rand.Next()
```

Alternatively, you can provide an upper limit to the generated number's range. In the following statement, the value assigned to `intNum` is somewhere between 0 and 99:

```
intNum = rand.Next(100)
```

The random integer's range does not have to begin at zero. You can add or subtract a value to shift the numeric range upward or downward. The following statement assigns a random integer to `intNum` between –50 and +49:

```
intNum = rand.Next(100) - 50
```

NextDouble

The `Random` class has a method named **`Random.NextDouble`** that returns a random floating point number between 0.0 and 1.0 (not including 1.0). Let's use the same `rand` object we declared earlier.

```
Dim dblNum As Double = rand.NextDouble()
```

If you want the random number to fall within a larger range, multiply it by a scaling factor. The following statement assigns a double between 0.0 and 500.0 to `dblNum`:

```
dblNum = rand.NextDouble() * 500.0
```

The following statement generates a random double between 100.0 and 600.0:

```
dblNum = (rand.NextDouble() * 500.0) + 100.0
```

NextBytes

The `Random` class method named `NextBytes` fills an array of Byte with random integers. Let's use the same `rand` object we declared earlier.

```
Dim byteArray(50) As Byte
rand.NextBytes(byteArray)
```

Tutorial 8-7 examines the *CatchMe* application.

Tutorial 8-7:
Examining the *CatchMe* application

In this tutorial, you will examine and run an application that displays a button. When the user tries to click the button, it moves to a new randomly chosen location. The `MouseEnter` event is used to detect when the user has moved the mouse over a control.

There are a few button and form properties that will prove useful. The current form is identified by the keyword `Me`. The width of a form, in pixels, is controlled by its `Width` property. The same is true for all controls, including buttons. The position of a button within a form is controlled by its `Top` and `Left` properties. Vertical pixel coordinates start at 0 at the top of a form, and grow in a downward direction, as shown in Figure 8-37.

Step 1: Open the *CatchMe* project from the student sample programs folder named *Chap8\CatchMe*. The form should look similar to the one shown in Figure 8-38.

Step 2: Run the program and try to click the mouse on the *Click Me* button. Notice how the caption and mouse position change. How successful were you in catching and clicking the button?

Figure 8-37 Pixel coordinates in a Visual Basic form

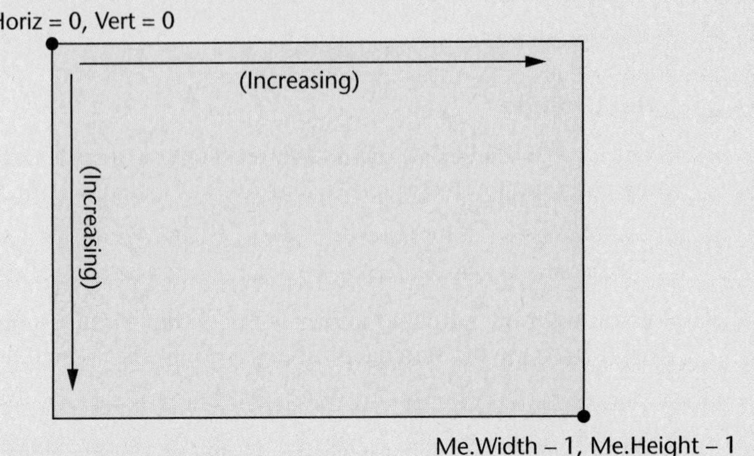

Figure 8-38 *CatchMe* application

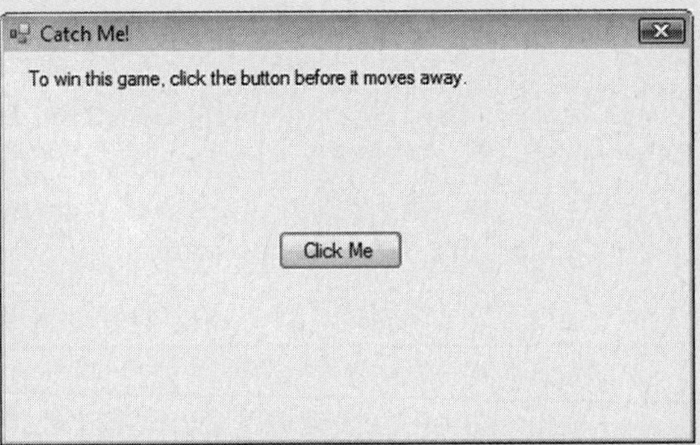

If you are not able to click the button and close the window, click the close box in the upper right corner to stop the program. Clever users might figure out that the best way to beat the game is to resize the window at runtime, so the button has nowhere to go. But we've prevented that by changing the FormBorderStyle property to FixedSingle so the window cannot be resized.

Step 3: Open the *Code* window and find two module level variables: `strCaption`, an array of strings that provide different captions for the button, and `rand`, a Random object used to generate random button coordinates.

```
' Alternative captions for the button.
Private strCaption As String() = {"Click here", _
    "Try harder!", "Try again", "Not even close", _
    "Where are you?", "I'm over here!", "Slow, aren't you?"}

  ' Random number generator object.
  Private rand As New Random()
```

Step 4: Look at the `btnCatch_Click` event handler that executes if the user manages to catch the button.

```
Private Sub btnCatch_Click(ByVal sender As System.Object, _
    ByVal e As System.EventArgs) Handles btnCatch.Click
```

```
    MessageBox.Show("You got me!", "", MessageBoxButtons.OK, _
        MessageBoxIcon.Exclamation)
    Me.Close()
End Sub
```

Step 5: Let's inspect the `btnCatch_MouseEnter` event hander details. The first two statements generate an array subscript between 0 and 1 minus the length of the `strCaption` array. The subscript is used to retrieve a new caption for the button.

```
Private Sub btnCatch_MouseEnter(ByVal sender As Object, _
    ByVal e As System.EventArgs) Handles btnCatch.MouseEnter

    ' Randomly choose a caption.
    Dim intIndex As Integer = rand.Next(strCaption.Length)
    btnCatch.Text = strCaption(intIndex)
```

Next, we want to change the button's horizontal position by setting its `Left` property. If we subtract the button's width (`btnCatch.Width`) from the form width (`Me.Width`), the resulting value makes a good maximum range for a random integer.

```
    ' Move to a new horizontal position.
    btnCatch.Left = rand.Next(Me.Width - btnCatch.Width)
```

Finally, we will change the button's vertical position by setting its `Top` property. If we subtract the button's height (`btnCatch.Height`) from the form height (`Me.Height`), the resulting value makes a good maximum range for a random integer.

```
    ' Move to a new vertical position.
    btnCatch.Top = rand.Next(Me.Height - btnCatch.Height - 30)
```

The additional value of 30 is subtracted before generating the random range, to allow for the height of the form's caption bar.

You can have a lot of fun demonstrating this program to unsuspecting users. You may want to customize it further by randomly changing the button size, border style, background color, or even the form height and width each time the button moves. How about creating multiple buttons?

Checkpoint

8.26 Describe the purpose of the `Random` class.

8.27 What happens if the same seed value is used each time a sequence of random numbers is generated?

8.28 If you do not specify a seed value when creating a Random object, what value does Visual Basic use as the seed value?

8.29 Describe the random number returned by the `Random.Next` method.

8.30 What is the purpose of the `Random.NextDouble` method?

8.31 Write a statement that assigns a random integer in the range of 1 through 100 to the variable `intRandomNumber`.

8.32 Write a statement that assigns a random integer in the range of 100 through 400 to the variable `intRandomNumber`.

8.8 Focus on Problem Solving: Building the *Demetris Leadership Center* Application

CONCEPT: **In this section you build an application that uses data stored in parallel arrays.**

The Demetris Leadership Center (DLC) publishes the books, videos, and CDs listed in Table 8-1.

Table 8-1 Demetris Leadership Center products

Product Title	Product Description	Product Number	Unit Price
Six Steps to Leadership	Book	914	$12.95
Six Steps to Leadership	CD	915	$14.95
The Road to Excellence	Video	916	$18.95
Seven Lessons of Quality	Book	917	$16.95
Seven Lessons of Quality	CD	918	$21.95
Seven Lessons of Quality	Video	919	$31.95
Teams are Made, Not Born	Book	920	$14.95
Leadership for the Future	Book	921	$14.95
Leadership for the Future	CD	922	$16.95

Suppose the vice president of sales has asked you to write a sales reporting program that does the following:

- Prompts the user for the units sold of each product
- Displays a sales report showing detailed sales data for each product and the total revenue from all products sold

The application will have a main form named `frmMain` and a splash screen form named `frmSplash`.

The `frmMain` Form

Figure 8-39 shows a sketch of `frmMain` with the form's controls labeled.

Table 8-2 lists each of the form's controls (excluding the menu controls) along with relevant property settings.

Figure 8-39 Sketch of `frmMain` form

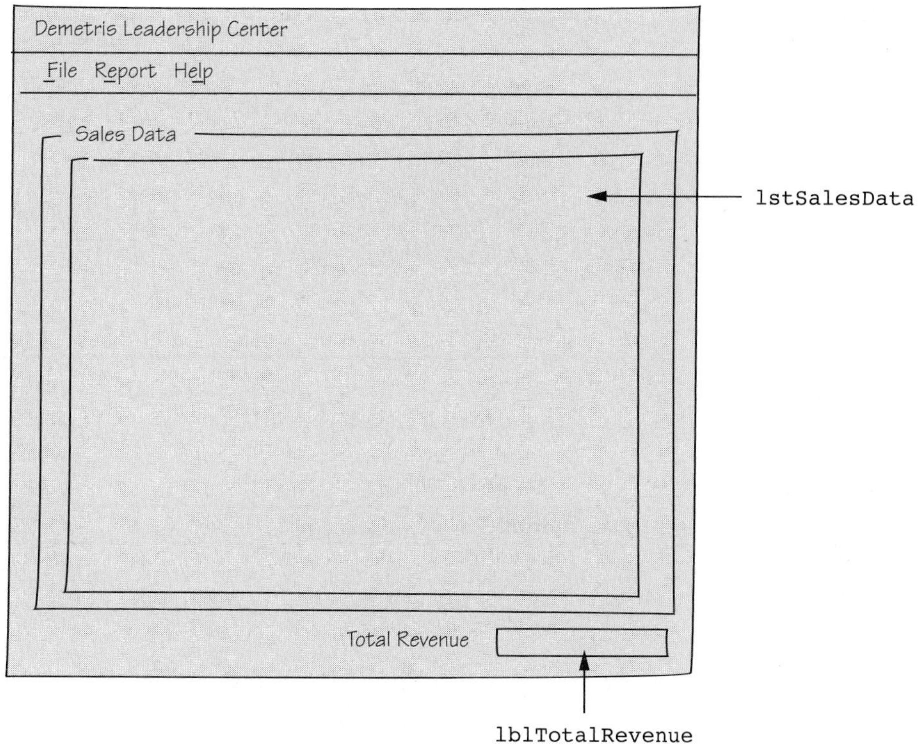

Table 8-2 `frmMain` controls and property settings

Control Type	Control Name	Property	Property Value
Form	`frmMain`	Text:	*Demetris Leadership Center*
GroupBox	(Default)	Text:	*Sales Data*
Label	(Default)	Text:	*Total Revenue*
Label	`lblTotalRevenue`	Text: BorderStyle:	 *Fixed3D*
ListBox	`lstSalesData`		
MenuStrip	(Default)		See Table 8-3 for details

Figure 8-40 shows a sketch of the menu system on `frmMain`.

Figure 8-40 Menu system on `frmMain`

File	Report	Help
Exit Ctrl+Q	Enter Sales Data Ctrl+E Display Sales Report Ctrl+D	About

Table 8-3 lists the menu item object names, text, and shortcut keys.

Table 8-3 `frmMain` menu item names, text properties, and shortcut keys

Menu Item Name	Text	Shortcut Key
`mnuFile`	&File	
`mnuFileExit`	E&xit	Ctrl+Q
`mnuReport`	&Report	
`mnuReportData`	&Enter Sales Data	Ctrl+E
`mnuReportDisplay`	&Display Sales Report	Ctrl+D
`mnuHelp`	&Help	
`mnuHelpAbout`	&About	

Table 8-4 describes the form's class-level declarations.

Table 8-4 Class-level declarations in `frmMain`

Name	Description
`intMAX_SUBSCRIPT`	A constant, set to 8, holding the upper subscript of the class-level arrays, and the upper limit of counters used in loops that process information in the arrays
`strProdNames`	An array of strings; this array holds the names of the DLC products
`strDesc`	An array of strings; this array holds the descriptions of the DLC products
`intProdNums`	An array of integers; this array holds the product numbers of the DLC products
`decPrices`	An array of Decimal variables; this array holds the prices of the DLC products
`intUnitsSold`	An array of integers; this array holds the number of units sold for each of the DLC products

The five arrays are parallel arrays, meaning that the same subscript can be used to access data relating to the same sale item. Table 8-5 lists and describes the methods in `frmMain`.

Table 8-5 `frmMain` methods

Method	Description
`InitArrays`	Procedure; copies the names, descriptions, product numbers, and unit prices of the DLC products to the class-level arrays
`mnuFileExit_Click`	Ends the application
`mnuReportData_Click`	Prompts the user for sales data
`mnuReportDisplay_Click`	Calculates and displays the revenue for each product and the total revenue
`mnuHelpAbout_Click`	Displays an *About* box
`frmMain_Load`	Displays the splash screen and calls the `InitArrays` procedure

The `frmSplash` Form

This application will display a splash screen from the main form's `Load` event procedure. Figure 8-41 shows a sketch of the splash screen form, `frmSplash`.

Figure 8-41 `frmSplash` form

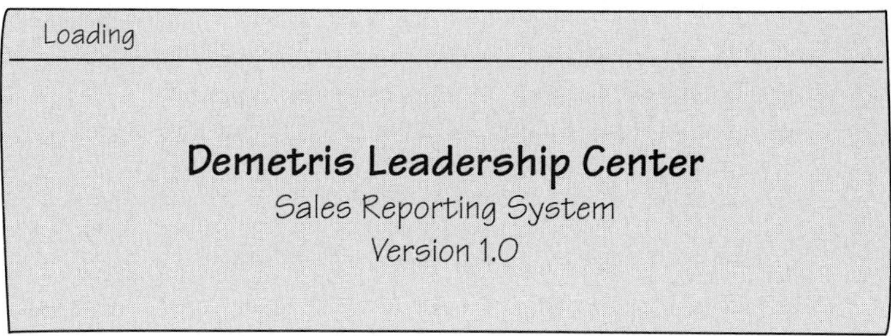

The splash screen will have a Timer control that automatically closes the form after five seconds. It will be displayed in modeless style. While it is on the screen, the `InitArrays` procedure will execute.

In Tutorial 8-8, you build the *Demetris Leadership Center Sales Reporting* application.

Tutorial 8-8:
Building the *Demetris Leadership Center Sales Reporting* application

Step 1: Create a new Windows application project named *Demetris Sales*.

Step 2: Name the initial form `frmMain`. Set up the form as shown in Figure 8-42.

Figure 8-42 `frmMain` form

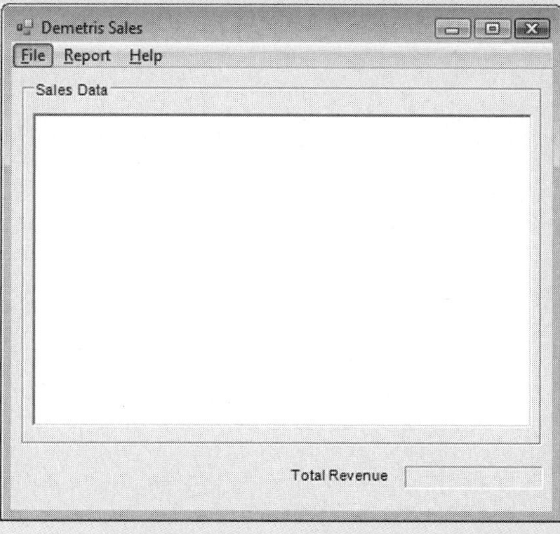

Refer to Table 8-2 for the control names and their property settings, and to Figure 8-39 for the locations of the controls in the control arrays. Refer to Figure 8-40 for the menu layout and to Table 8-3 for the menu item properties. Be sure to select `frmMain` as the startup object.

Step 3: Write the following class-level declarations in the `frmMain` form's code:

```
' Class-level declarations
Const intMAX_SUBSCRIPT As Integer = 8   ' Array upper subscript
Dim strProdNames(intMAX_SUBSCRIPT) As String  ' Product names
Dim strDesc(intMAX_SUBSCRIPT) As String       ' Descriptions
Dim intProdNums(intMAX_SUBSCRIPT) As Integer  ' Product numbers
Dim decPrices(intMAX_SUBSCRIPT) As Decimal    ' Unit prices
Dim intUnitsSold(intMAX_SUBSCRIPT) As Integer ' Units sold
```

Step 4: Create the `frmMain_Load` event procedure:

```
Private Sub frmMain_Load(ByVal sender As System.Object, _
    ByVal e As System.EventArgs) Handles MyBase.Load

  ' Create an instance of the splash screen.
  Dim splashForm As New frmSplash()
  ' Display the splash screen in modeless style.
  splashForm.Show()
  ' Initialize the arrays with product data.
  InitArrays()
End Sub
```

Step 5: Create the following procedures in `frmMain`:

```
Private Sub InitArrays()
  ' Initialize the arrays.
  ' First product
  strProdNames(0) = "Six Steps to Leadership"
  strDesc(0) = "Book"
  intProdNums(0) = 914
  decPrices(0) = 12.95D

  ' Second product
  strProdNames(1) = "Six Steps to Leadership"
  strDesc(1) = "CD"
  intProdNums(1) = 915
  decPrices(1) = 14.95D

  ' Third product
  strProdNames(2) = "The Road to Excellence"
  strDesc(2) = "Video"
  intProdNums(2) = 916
  decPrices(2) = 18.95D

  ' Fourth product
  strProdNames(3) = "Seven Lessons of Quality"
  strDesc(3) = "Book"
  intProdNums(3) = 917
  decPrices(3) = 16.95D

  ' Fifth product
  strProdNames(4) = "Seven Lessons of Quality"
  strDesc(4) = "CD"
  intProdNums(4) = 918
  decPrices(4) = 21.95D
```

```
        ' Sixth product
        strProdNames(5) = "Seven Lessons of Quality"
        strDesc(5) = "Video"
        intProdNums(5) = 919
        decPrices(5) = 31.95D

        ' Seventh product
        strProdNames(6) = "Teams Are Made, Not Born"
        strDesc(6) = "Book"
        intProdNums(6) = 920
        decPrices(6) = 14.95D

        ' Eighth product
        strProdNames(7) = "Leadership for the Future"
        strDesc(7) = "Book"
        intProdNums(7) = 921
        decPrices(7) = 14.95D

        ' Ninth product
        strProdNames(8) = "Leadership for the Future"
        strDesc(8) = "CD"
        intProdNums(8) = 922
        decPrices(8) = 16.95D
    End Sub

    Private Sub mnuReportData_Click(ByVal sender As _
          System.Object, ByVal e As System.EventArgs) _
          Handles mnuReportData.Click

        ' Prompt the user for sales data.
        Dim intCount As Integer   ' Loop counter

        ' Get unit sales for each product.
        For intCount = 0 To intMAX_SUBSCRIPT
          Do While Integer.TryParse(InputBox( _
            "Enter units sold of product number " _
            & intProdNums(intCount), _
            "Enter Sales Data"), intUnitsSold(intCount)) = False

            MessageBox.Show("Please enter an integer")
          Loop
        Next intCount
    End Sub

    Private Sub mnuReportDisplay_Click(ByVal sender _
          As System.Object, ByVal e As System.EventArgs) _
          Handles mnuReportDisplay.Click

        ' Calculates and displays the revenue for each
        ' product, as well as the total revenue.
        Dim intCount As Integer
        Dim decRevenue As Decimal
        Dim decTotalRevenue As Decimal

        ' Display the sales report header.
        lstSalesData.Items.Add("SALES REPORT")
        lstSalesData.Items.Add("____________")

        ' Display sales data for each product.
        For intCount = 0 To intMAX_SUBSCRIPT
```

```
            ' Calculate product revenue.
            decRevenue = intUnitsSold(intCount) * decPrices(intCount)
            ' Display the product data.
            lstSalesData.Items.Add("Product Number: " _
                & intProdNums(intCount))
            lstSalesData.Items.Add("Name: " & strProdNames(intCount))
            lstSalesData.Items.Add("Description: " & _
                strDesc(intCount))
            lstSalesData.Items.Add("Unit Price: " _
                & decPrices(intCount).ToString("c"))
            lstSalesData.Items.Add("Units Sold: " _
                & intUnitsSold(intCount))
            lstSalesData.Items.Add("Product Revenue: " _
                & decRevenue.ToString("c"))
            lstSalesData.Items.Add(String.Empty)
            ' Accumulate revenue.
            decTotalRevenue = decTotalRevenue + decRevenue
        Next intCount
        ' Display total revenue.
        lblTotalRevenue.Text = decTotalRevenue.ToString("c")
    End Sub

    Private Sub mnuHelpAbout_Click(ByVal sender As System.Object, _
        ByVal e As System.EventArgs) Handles mnuHelpAbout.Click

        ' Display an About box.
        MessageBox.Show("Displays a sales report for DLC.", "About")
    End Sub

    Private Sub mnuFileExit_Click(ByVal sender As System.Object, _
        ByVal e As System.EventArgs) Handles mnuFileExit.Click

        Me.Close()
    End Sub
```

Step 6: Add the splash screen form to the project, and name the form `frmSplash`. Set the form's FormBorderStyle property to *FixedToolWindow*, and set its TopMost property to *True*. Set the form's Text property to *Loading*. Select a light color for the form's BackColor property. The form should appear similar to the one shown in Figure 8-43.

Figure 8-43 `frmSplash` form

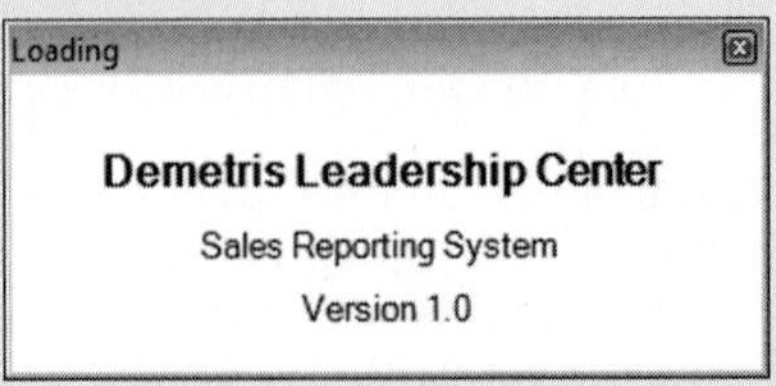

Step 7: Add a Timer control named `tmrTimer` to the `frmSplash` form. Set the control's Interval property to *5000*, and set its Enabled property to *True*.

Step 8: Write the following `Tick` event procedure for the `tmrTimer` control:

```
Private Sub tmrTimer_Tick(ByVal sender As System.Object, _
  ByVal e As System.EventArgs) Handles tmrTimer.Tick

  ' Close the splash screen
  Me.Close()
End Sub
```

Step 9: Save the project.

Step 10: Run the application. The splash screen should appear, and then automatically close after five seconds.

Step 11: When the main form appears, click the *Report* menu, and then click *Enter Sales Data*. You will be prompted with input boxes to enter the units sold for each of the DLC products. Enter the following units sold values:

Product number 914	**140**	Product number 919	**142**
Product number 915	**85**	Product number 920	**109**
Product number 916	**129**	Product number 921	**65**
Product number 917	**67**	Product number 922	**43**
Product number 918	**94**		

Step 12: Click the *Report* menu, and then click *Display Sales Report*. Your form should now appear similar to the one shown in Figure 8-44. Scroll through the sales data displayed in the list box.

Figure 8-44 Main form completed

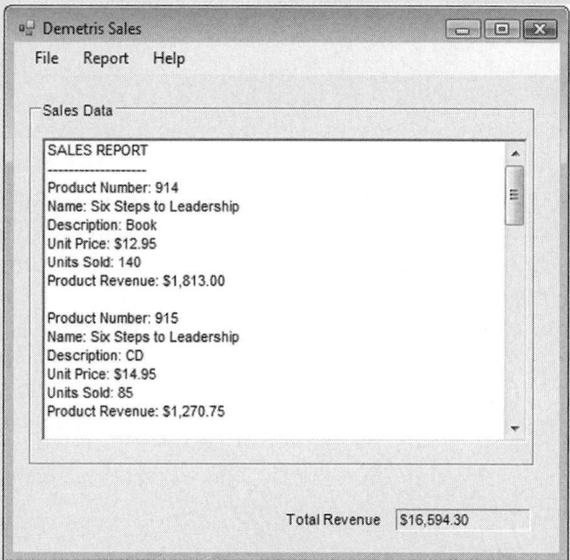

Step 13: Exit the application.

Summary

8.1 Arrays

- An array is a like group of variables with a single name. The variables within an array are called elements and are of the same data type.
- Individual variables in an array are accessed through a subscript, which is a number that pinpoints a specific element within an array. Subscript numbering begins at zero. When you declare an array you can specify the upper subscript.
- You can implicitly size an array by omitting the upper subscript in the declaration statement and providing an initialization list. An array initialization list is a set of numbers enclosed in a set of braces, with the numbers separated by commas.
- Array elements are processed the same as regular variables, but when working with array elements, you must provide a subscript.
- You can store a subscript number in a variable and then use the variable as a subscript. You can use a loop to cycle through an entire array, performing the same operation on each element.
- Visual Basic performs array bounds checking at runtime; it does not allow a statement to use a subscript outside the range of subscripts for an array.
- The `For Each` statement is a special loop designed specifically to access values from arrays and array-like structures.

8.2 More about Array Processing

- Arrays have a Length property that holds the number of elements in the array.
- To sum the numbers stored in an array, use a loop with an accumulator variable that adds all the elements. To average the numbers stored in an array, first sum all the values, and then divide the sum by the number of elements.
- To copy the values in one array to another, use a loop to copy the individual elements.
- You can create a parallel relationship between list boxes, combo boxes, and arrays.
- The sequential search algorithm uses a loop to examine the elements in an array. It compares each element with the value being searched for, and stops when the value is found or the end of the array is encountered. If the value being searched for is not in the array, the algorithm will unsuccessfully search to the end of the array.
- The `Array.Sort` method sorts the elements of an array in ascending order, which means the lowest value is stored in the first element and the highest value is stored in the last element.
- You can change the number of elements in an array at runtime with the `ReDim` statement.

8.3 Procedures and Functions That Work with Arrays

- Procedures and functions may be written to accept arrays as arguments. Functions may also be written to return arrays.

8.4 Multidimensional Arrays

- A single-dimensional array has one subscript, and is useful for storing and working with a single set of data. Two-dimensional arrays can hold multiple sets of values. Think of a two-dimensional array as having rows and columns of elements.
- To declare a two-dimensional array, two sets of upper subscripts are required: the first one for the rows and the second one for the columns. A two-dimensional array may be implicitly sized by omitting the upper subscripts from the declaration and providing an initialization list.

- When data in a two-dimensional array is processed, each element has two subscripts: one for its row and one for its column. Nested loops can be used to sum the rows or columns of a two-dimensional numeric array.
- The `For Each...Next` loop can be used to sum all the values in a numeric two-dimensional array.
- Visual Basic allows arrays of up to 32 dimensions.

8.5 Focus on GUI Design: The Enabled Property, Timer Control, and Splash Screens

- When a control's Enabled property is set to *False*, it is considered disabled, which means it cannot receive the focus, cannot respond to events generated by the user, and appears dimmed or grayed out on the form.
- The Timer control is invisible at runtime. At design time it appears in the component tray. The standard prefix for a Timer control's name is `tmr`.
- The Timer control responds to `Tick` events. When a `Tick` event occurs, the `Tick` event procedure is executed.
- When the Timer control's Enabled property is set to *True*, the Timer control responds to `Tick` events. When the Enabled property is set to *False*, the Timer control does not respond to `Tick` events and the code in the `Tick` event procedure does not execute.
- The Timer control's Interval property can be set to a positive nonzero value that is the number of milliseconds to elapse between `Tick` events.
- Splash screens usually show logos and ensure the user that a slowly loading application is in the process of starting up.

8.6 Focus on GUI Design: Anchoring and Docking Controls

- When a control is anchored to a form's edge, the distance between the control's edge and the form's edge remains constant, even when the user resizes the form.
- When a control is docked, it is positioned directly against one of the edges of a form. Additionally, the length or width of a docked control is changed to match the length or width of the form's edge.

8.7 Random Numbers

- The `Random` class contains methods that generate random sequences of numbers.
- The `Random.Next` method returns the next random integer in a series. The `Random.NextDouble` method returns a random value between 0.0 and 1.0.

8.8 Focus on Problem Solving: Building the *Demetris Leadership Center* Application

- This section outlines the process of building the *Demetris Leadership Center* application, which processes data used in parallel arrays.

Key Terms

Anchor property
array
array bounds checking
ascending order
Dock property
elements
Enabled property
`For Each` loop
index
Interval property

one-dimension array
parallel arrays
`Random` class
`Random.Next`
`Random.NextDouble`
random seed value
sequential search
splash screen
subscript
Timer control
TopMost property
two-dimensional array

Review Questions and Exercises

Fill-in-the-Blank

1. You access the individual variables in an array through a(n) ________________, which is a number that indentifies a specific element within an array.
2. The ________________ loop is a special loop designed specifically to access values from arrays and array-like structures.
3. ________________ arrays are two or more arrays that hold related data. The related elements in each array are accessed with a common subscript.
4. The ________________ algorithm uses a loop to examine the elements in an array sequentially, starting with the first one.
5. The ________________ statement resizes an array at runtime.
6. The ________________ property holds the number of elements in an array.
7. Declaring a two-dimensional array requires two sets of ________________.
8. When a control's ________________ property is set to *False*, it is considered disabled.
9. The ________________ property causes the distance between a control's edge and the form's edge to remain constant, even when the form is resized.
10. The ________________ property causes a control to be positioned directly against one of the form's edges.
11. The ________________ control allows an application to automatically execute code at regularly timed intervals.
12. The Timer control's ________________ property specifies the number of milliseconds between timer events.
13. A(n) ________________ is a window that is displayed while an application is loading.
14. The ________________ class has methods that can generate a sequence of random numbers.
15. The ________________ method generates a random integer.

Multiple Choice

1. Which of the following describes the variables within an array?
   a. Boxes
   b. Elements
   c. Subvariables
   d. Intersections

2. Which of the following identifies a specific element within an array?
   a. Element specifier
   b. Determinator
   c. Locator
   d. Subscript
3. Which of the following is the lower subscript of an array?
   a. `1`
   b. `{ }`
   c. `0`
   d. `-1`
4. When does array bounds checking occur?
   a. Runtime
   b. Design time
   c. Break time
   d. All of the above
5. Which of the following properties determines the number of elements in an array?
   a. Size
   b. Elements
   c. Length
   d. NumberElements
6. To access related data in a set of parallel arrays, how should you access the elements in the arrays?
   a. Using the same array name
   b. Using the same subscript
   c. Using the index –1
   d. Using the `GetParallelData` function
7. Which statement resizes the `intNumbers` array to 20 elements?
   a. `ReDim intNumbers(19)`
   b. `ReDim intNumbers(20)`
   c. `Resize intNumbers() To 19`
   d. `Resize intNumbers() To 20`
8. Which statement resizes the `intNumbers` array and does not erase the values already stored in the array?
   a. `ReDim intNumbers(99)`
   b. `ReDim Preserve intNumbers(99)`
   c. `Preserve intNumbers(99)`
   d. `ReSize Preserve intNumbers(99)`
9. Which of the following is an apt analogy for two-dimensional array elements?
   a. Feet and inches
   b. Books and pages
   c. Lines and statements
   d. Rows and columns
10. Which statement disables the control `lblResult`?
    a. `lblResult.Disabled = True`
    b. `Disable lblResult`
    c. `lblResult.Enabled = False`
    d. `lblResult.Dimmed = True`

11. The Timer control Interval property may be set to what type of value?
    a. 0 or greater
    b. A fractional number
    c. A negative number
    d. 1 or greater
12. Which of the following properties can you use to cause a control to fill an entire form?
    a. Fill
    b. Dock
    c. Anchor
    d. Stretch
13. Which of the following statements initializes the sequence of random numbers with a seed value?
    a. `InitRandom(10)`
    b. `Rnd(30)`
    c. `Seed(5)`
    d. `new Random(25)`
14. Which of the following properties causes a form to be displayed on top of all the other currently displayed forms?
    a. TopMost
    b. Top
    c. OnTop
    d. Front

True or False

Indicate whether the following statements are true or false.

1. T F: The upper subscript of an array must be a positive whole number.
2. T F: Numeric array elements are automatically initialized to –1.
3. T F: You may not use a named constant as a subscript in an array declaration.
4. T F: Visual Basic allows you to use a variable as a subscript when processing an array with a loop.
5. T F: You get an error message at design time when you write code that attempts to access an element outside the bounds of an array.
6. T F: The value stored in an array's Length property is the same as the array's upper subscript.
7. T F: You should use a loop to copy the values of one array to another array.
8. T F: Parallel arrays are useful when working with related data of unlike types.
9. T F: The `ReDim` statement may be used with any array.
10. T F: The value stored in the Timer control's Interval property specifies an interval in seconds.
11. T F: It is possible to anchor a control to a form's opposing edges.
12. T F: When a control is docked to a form's edge, the width or height of the control is adjusted to match the size of the form's edge.

Short Answer

1. Write code that declares a string array with three elements, and then stores your first, middle, and last names in the array's elements.

2. What values are displayed by the following code?

```
Dim intValues(4) As Integer
Dim intCount As Integer
For intCount = 0 To 4
   intValues(intCount) = intCount + 1
Next intCount
For intCount = 0 To 4
   MessageBox.Show(intValues(intCount).ToString())
Next intCount
```

3. The following code segment declares a 20-element array of integers called `intFish`. When completed, the code should ask how many fish were caught by fisherman 1 through 20 and store this information in the array. Complete the program.

```
Private Sub btnFishCatchArray_Click()
   Dim intFish(19) As Integer
   '
   ' You must finish this program. It should ask how
   ' many fish were caught by fisherman 1 - 20 and
   ' store this information in the intFish array.
End Sub
```

4. What output is generated by the following code segment? (You may need to use a calculator.)

```
Const sngRATE As Single = 0.1
Dim decBalance(4) As Decimal
Dim decDue As Decimal
Dim intCount As Integer
decBalance(0) = 100
decBalance(1) = 250
decBalance(2) = 325
decBalance(3) = 500
decBalance(4) = 1100
For intCount = 0 To 4
   decDue = decBalance(intCount) * sngRATE
   MessageBox.Show(decDue.ToString())
Next intCount
```

5. Write a statement that assigns 145 to the first column of the first row of the array declared in the following statement:

```
Dim intNumberArray(9, 11) As Integer
```

6. Write a statement that assigns 18 to the last column of the last row of the array declared in Question 5.

7. Assuming that an application uses a Timer control named `tmrClock`, write a statement that stops the timer from responding to timer events.

8. Where does the `Random` class get its seed value if you do not provide one?

What Do You Think?

1. The following code totals the values in two Integer arrays: `intNumberArray1` and `intNumberArray2`. Both arrays have 25 elements. Will the code print the correct sum of values for both arrays? Why or why not?

```
Dim intTotal As Integer = 0    ' Accumulator
For intCount = 0 To 24
    intTotal += intNumberArray1(intCount)
Next intCount
MessageBox.Show("Total for intNumberArray1 is " _
        & intTotal.ToString())
For intCount = 0 To 24
    intTotal += intNumberArray2(intCount)
Next intCount
MessageBox.Show("Total for intNumberArray2 is " _
        & intTotal.ToString())
```

2. How many elements are in the following array?

```
Dim sngSales(5, 3) As Single
```

3. How many elements are in the following array?

```
Dim sngValues(3, 3) As Single
```

4. If you are writing an application that must perform a lot of startup operations, would you choose to display the splash screen as a modal or modeless form? Why?
5. Suppose an application uses a Timer control named `tmrControl`. Write a programming statement that sets the time between timer events at three seconds.
6. Why is a computer's system time a good source of random seed values?

Find the Error

1.
```
Dim intReadings(-99) As Integer
```

2.
```
Dim intTable(10) As Integer    ' Stores 11 values
Dim i As Integer
Dim intMaxNum As Integer = 11
For i = 0 To intMaxNum
    intTable(i) = CInt(InputBox("Enter the next value:"))
Next i
```

3.
```
Dim intValues(3) = {  2, 4, 6 }
```

4.
```
' tmrTimer is a Timer control
tmrTimer.Interval = 0
```

Algorithm Workbench

1. Assume `strNames` is a string array with 20 elements. Write a `For Each... Next` loop that prints each element of the array.
2. Suppose you need to store information about 12 countries. Declare two arrays that may be used in parallel to store the names of the countries and their populations.

3. Write a loop that uses the arrays you declared in Question 2 to print each country's name and population.

4. The arrays `intNumberArray1` and `intNumberArray2` have 100 elements. Write code that copies the values in `intNumberArray1` to `intNumberArray2`.

5. Write the code for a sequential search that determines whether the value –1 is stored in the array named `intValues`. The code should print a message indicating whether the value was found.

6. Suppose an application stores the following data about employees:
   - Name, stored in a list box named `lstNames`
   - Employee number, stored in an array of strings named `strEmpNums`

   There is a parallel relationship between the list box and the array. Assume that the user has selected an employee's name from the list box. Write code that displays (in a message box) the employee number for the selected employee.

7. Declare a two-dimensional array of integers named `intGrades`. It should have 30 rows and 10 columns.

8. Assume that `sngValues` is a two-dimensional array of single precision numbers with 10 rows and 20 columns. Write a `For Each` statement that sums all the elements in the array and stores the sum in the variable `sngTotal`.

9. Write nested code using `For...Next` loops that performs the same operation requested in Question 8.

10. Suppose an application uses a two-dimensional array named `intDays`. Write code that sums each row in the array and displays the result.

    ```
    Dim intDays(29, 5) As Integer
    ```

11. Write code that sums each column in the array in Question 10.

12. Write code that uses a `For Each` statement to sum all of the elements in the array in Question 10.

13. Write a code that assigns a random integer in the range of 1 through 50 to the variable `intNum`.

14. Write a code that assigns a random integer in the range of –100 through 500 to the variable `intNum`.

Programming Challenges

1. **Largest/Smallest Array Values**

   Create an application that lets the user enter 10 values into an array. The application should display the largest and smallest values stored in the array. Figure 8-45 shows an example of the application's form after all 10 values have been entered, with the largest and smallest values displayed.

Figure 8-45 *Largest/Smallest Array Values* form

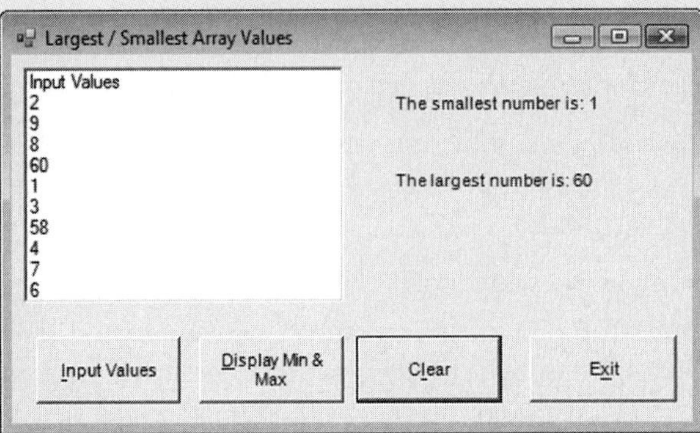

2. **Rainfall Statistics**

   Create an application that lets the user enter the rainfall for each of 12 months into an array. The application should calculate and display the following statistics: total rainfall for the year, the average monthly rainfall, and the months with the highest and lowest amounts of rainfall. Figure 8-46 shows an example of the application's form after each month's rainfall amount has been entered and the statistics have been displayed.

Figure 8-46 *Rainfall Statistics* form

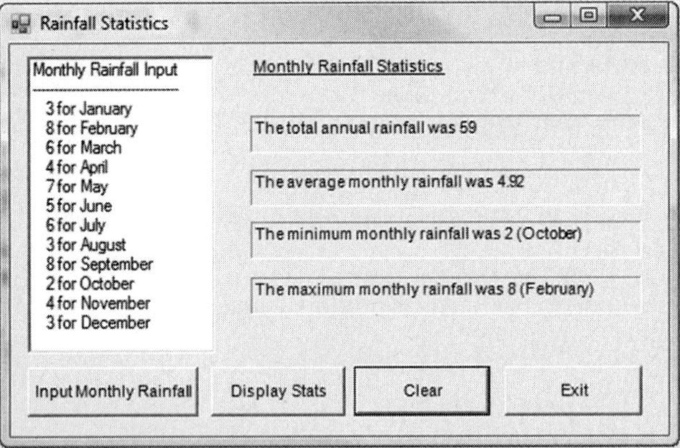

3. **Random Sentences**

   Create an application that produces random sentences as output. Create five arrays of strings, one each for nouns, adjectives, verbs, prepositions, and articles. Each array should hold several words of that part of speech. For example, the `strArticles` array could hold the strings `"the"` and `"a"`; the `strNouns` array could hold `"Martian"`, `"baby"`, `"skunk"`, `"computer"`, and `"mosquito"`; the `strPrepositions` array could hold `"around"`, `"through"`, `"under"`, `"over"`, and `"by"`; and so on.

The application should generate sentences by randomly choosing eight words (randomly generating eight array indices) from these arrays, always constructing sentences by using the parts of speech in the following order: article, adjective, noun, verb, preposition, article, adjective, noun.

For example, a sentence might be "The shiny computer flew over a huge mosquito." In this example, "The" and "a" were randomly chosen from the articles array, "shiny" and "huge" from the adjectives array, "computer" and "mosquito" from the nouns array, "flew" from the verbs array, and "over" from the prepositions array. Be careful to produce sentences that have the proper spacing, uppercase and lowercase letters, and a period at the end.

Design your form with buttons to display the next sentence, to clear all sentences currently displayed, and to close the application. Display your sentences, one per line, in a list box. Allow enough room to display at least 10 sentences. Figure 8-47 shows an example of the form using a list box. The figure shows the form with three sentences generated.

Figure 8-47 *Random Sentences* form

4. **Driver's License Exam**

The local Registry of Motor Vehicles office has asked you to create an application that grades the written portion of the driver's license exam. The exam has 20 multiple choice questions. Here are the correct answers to the questions:

1.	B	6.	A	11.	B	16.	C
2.	D	7.	B	12.	C	17.	C
3.	A	8.	A	13.	D	18.	B
4.	A	9.	C	14.	A	19.	D
5.	C	10.	D	15.	D	20.	A

Your application should store the correct answers in an array. A form, such as the one shown in Figure 8-48, should allow the user to enter answers for each question.

When the user clicks the *Score Exam* button, the application should display another form showing whether each question was answered correctly or incorrectly, and whether the student passed or failed the exam. A student must correctly answer 15 of the 20 questions to pass the exam.

Input validation: Only accept the letters A, B, C, or D as answers.

Figure 8-48 *Driver's License Exam* form

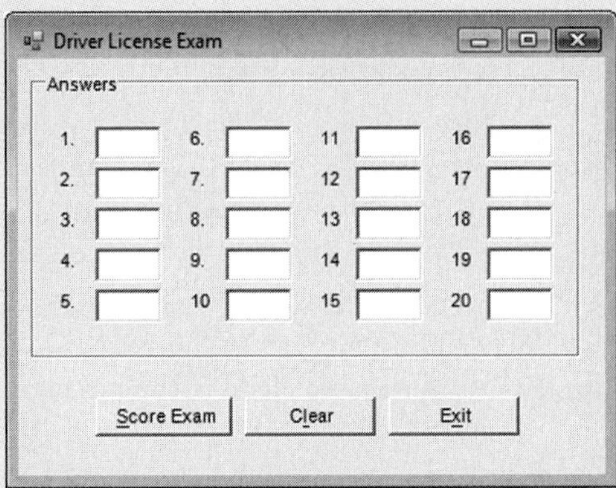

5. **PIN Verifier**

The National Commerce Bank has hired you to create an application that verifies a customer personal identification number (PIN). A valid PIN is a seven-digit number that meets the following specifications:

Digit 1: Must be in the range of 7 through 9
Digit 2: Must be in the range of 5 through 7
Digit 3: Must be in the range of 0 through 4
Digit 4: Must be in the range of 0 through 9
Digit 5: Must be in the range of 6 through 9
Digit 6: Must be in the range of 3 through 6
Digit 7: Must be in the range of 4 through 8

Notice that each digit must fall into a range of numbers. Your application should have two arrays: `intMinimum` and `intMaximum`. The `intMinimum` array should hold the minimum values for each digit, and the `intMaximum` array should hold the maximum values for each digit.

The application should allow the user to enter seven digits on a form similar to the one shown in Figure 8-49. When the *Verify* button is clicked, the application should use the `intMinimum` and `intMaximum` arrays to verify that the numbers fall into acceptable ranges.

Figure 8-49 *PIN Verifier* form

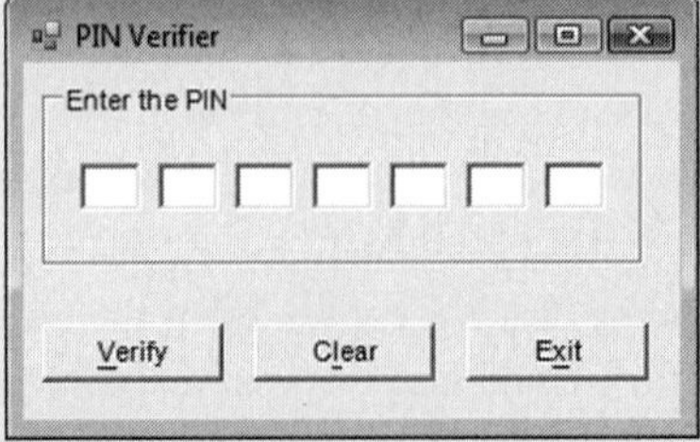

Design Your Own Forms

6. **Employee Directory**

Create an employee directory application that shows employee names in a list box on the main form. When the user selects a name from the list box, the application should display the employee's ID number, department name, and telephone number on a separate form.

The application should store all employee ID numbers, department names, and telephone numbers in separate arrays. The arrays and the list box should have a parallel relationship.

7. **Grade Book**

Suppose a teacher has five students who have taken four tests. The teacher uses the following grading scale to assign a letter grade to a student, based on the average of his or her four test scores.

Test Score	Letter Grade
90–100	A
80–89	B
70–79	C
60–69	D
0–59	F

Create an application that uses an array of strings to hold the five student names, an array of five strings to hold each student's letter grades, and five arrays of four single precision numbers to hold each student's set of test scores.

Equip the application with a menu or a set of buttons that allows the application to perform the following:

- Display a form that allows the user to enter or change the student names and their test scores.
- Calculate and display each student's average test score and a letter grade based on the average.

The application should display a splash screen when it executes.

Input validation: Do not accept test scores less than zero or greater than 100.

8. **Grade Book Modification**

Modify the *Grade Book* application in Programming Challenge 7 so it drops each student's lowest score when determining the test score averages and letter grades.

9. **Charge Account Validation**

Create an application that allows the user to enter a charge account number. The application should determine whether the number is valid by comparing it to the numbers in the following list:

5658845	4520125	7895122	8777541	8451277	1302850
8080152	4562555	5552012	5050552	7825877	1250255
1005231	6545231	3852085	7576651	7881200	4581002

The list of numbers should be stored in an array. A sequential search should be used to locate the number entered by the user. If the user enters a number that is in the array, the program should display a message indicating the number is valid. If the user enters a number that is not in the array, the program should display a message indicating the number is invalid.

The Lottery Application

10. **Lottery Application**

Create an application that simulates a lottery. The application should have an array of five integers and should generate a random number in the range 0 through 9 for each element in the array. The array is permitted to contain duplicate values. The user should then enter five digits, which the application will compare to the numbers in the array. A form should be displayed showing how many of the digits matched. If all of the digits match, display a form proclaiming the user as a grand prize winner.

11. **Soccer Team Score Application**

Suppose a soccer team needs an application to record the number of points scored by its players during a game. Create an application that asks how many players the team has, and then asks for the names of each player. The program should declare an array of strings large enough to hold the player names, and declare an array of integers large enough to hold the number of points scored by each player. The application should have a menu system or buttons that perform the following:

- Display a form allowing the user to enter the players' names.
- Display a form that can be used during a game to record the points scored by each player.
- Display the total points scored by each player and by the team.

The application should display a splash screen when it executes.

Input validation: Do not accept negative numbers as points.

12. **Number Analysis Program**

Create an application that lets the user enter 10 numbers. The program should store the numbers in an array and then display the following data:

- The lowest number in the array
- The highest number in the array
- The total of the numbers in the array
- The average of the numbers in the array

13. **Phone Number Lookup**

Create an application that has two parallel arrays: a `String` array named `strPeople` that is initialized with the names of 7 of your friends and a `String` array named `strPhoneNumbers` that is initialized with your friends' phone numbers. The program should allow the user to enter a person's name (or part of a person's name). It should then search for that person in the `strPeople` array. If the person is found, it should get that person's phone number from the `strPhoneNumbers` array and display it. If the person is not found in the `strPeople` array, the program should display a message indicating this.

14. **Rock, Paper, Scissors Game**

Create an application that lets the user play the game of "Rock, Paper, Scissors" against the computer. The program should work as follows:

(1) When the program begins, a random number in the range of 1 through 3 is generated. If the number is 1, then the computer has chosen rock. If the number is 2, then the computer has chosen paper. If the number is 3, then the computer has chosen scissors. (Don't display the computer's choice yet.)

(2) The user clicks a button to select his or her choice of rock, paper, or scissors.

(3) The computer's choice is displayed.

(4) A winner is selected according to the following rules:

- If one player chooses rock and the other player chooses scissors, then rock wins. (Rock smashes scissors.)

- If one player chooses scissors and the other player chooses paper, then scissors wins. (Scissors cuts paper.)
- If one player chooses paper and the other player chooses rock, then paper wins. (Paper covers rock.)
- If both players make the same choice, the game must be played again to determine the winner.

CHAPTER 9 Files, Printing, and Structures

TOPICS

This chapter shows you how to save data to sequential text files and then read the data back into an application. You will learn how to use the OpenFileDialog, SaveFileDialog, ColorDialog, and FontDialog controls. You can use these to equip your application with standard Windows dialog boxes for opening and saving files and for selecting colors and fonts. We discuss the PrintDocument control and how to print reports from your application. Finally, you learn how to package units of data together into structures.

9.1 Using Files

CONCEPT: A file is a collection of data stored on a computer disk. Information can be saved in a file and later reused.

Applications you have created so far require you to re-enter data each time the program runs because the data kept in controls and variables is stored in RAM, and disappears once the program stops running. To retain data between the times it runs, an application must have a way of saving the data.

Data is saved in a **file**, on a computer disk. Once saved, the data remains after the program stops running, and can be retrieved and used at a later time. In this chapter, you write applications that create files to save data. These applications do not rely on the user to re-enter data each time the application runs.

The Process of Using a File

The following steps must be taken when a file is used by an application:

1. The file must be opened. If the file does not yet exist, opening it means creating it.
2. Data is written to the file or read from the file.
3. When the application is finished using the file, the file is closed.

When a Visual Basic application is actively working with data, the data is located in memory, usually in variables and/or control properties. When data is written to a file, it is copied from the variables or control properties, as shown in Figure 9-1.

Figure 9-1 Writing data to a file

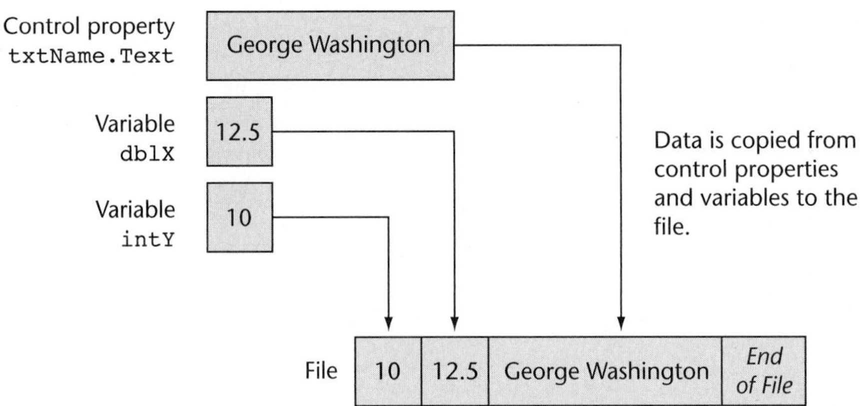

When data is read from a file, it is copied from the file into variables and/or control properties, as shown in Figure 9-2.

Figure 9-2 Reading data from a file

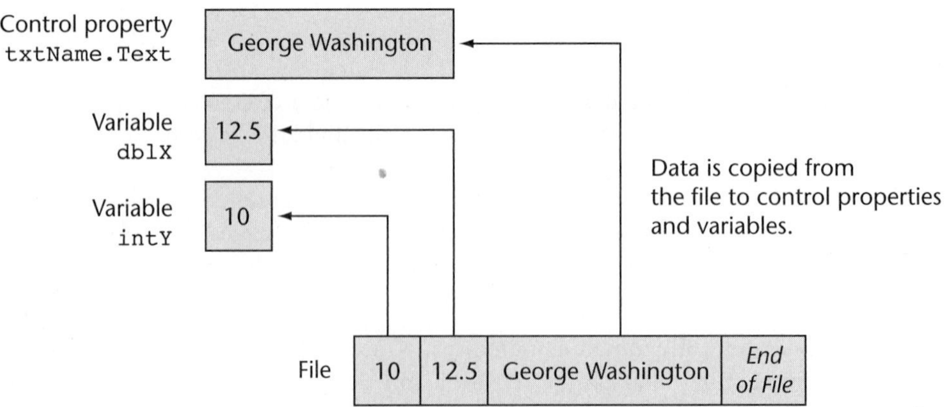

The terms input file and output file are often used. An **input file** is a file from which a program reads data. It is called an input file because the data stored in it serves as input to the program. An **output file** is a file into which a program writes data. It is called an output file because the program stores output in the file.

There are two types of files: text and binary. A **text file** contains plain text and may be opened in a text editor such as Windows Notepad. Data in **binary files** is stored as pure binary data; the content cannot be viewed with a text editor.

There are also two methods of accessing files: sequential-access and random-access. A **sequential-access file** is like a stream of data that must be read from its beginning to its end. To read an item stored in the middle or at the end of a sequential-access file, an application must read all the items in the file before it.

Data in a **random-access file** may be accessed in any order. An application can jump to any item in a random-access file without first reading the preceding items. The difference between sequential-access and random-access files is like the difference between a cassette tape and a CD. When listening to a CD, you don't need to listen to or fast-forward over unwanted songs. You simply jump to the track that you want to listen to.

Because most Visual Basic programmers prefer to use databases rather than random-access or binary files, we only discuss sequential-access text files in this chapter. Binary and random-access files are discussed in Appendix E, located on the student CD.

Writing to Files with `StreamWriter` Objects

VideoNote

Writing Data to a File

There are two basic ways to open a text file so you can write data to it: You can create a new file, or you can open an existing file so data can be appended to it. The actual writing to the file is performed by a **`StreamWriter` object**. There are two required steps:

1. Declare a `StreamWriter` variable.
2. Call either the `File.CreateText` or **`File.AppendText` method**. If you want to create a new file, call `File.CreateText` and assign its return value to the StreamWriter variable. Or, to append to an existing text file, call `File.AppendText` and assign its return value to the `StreamWriter` variable.

Before using `StreamWriter` objects, you must insert the following `Imports` statement at the top of your form's code file. This will make the **`StreamWriter` classes** available to your program:

```
Imports System.IO
```

> **NOTE:** It is possible to omit the `Imports System.IO` statement, but then every reference to the `StreamWriter` class must use its fully qualified name, which is `System.IO.StreamWriter`.

Creating a Text File

First, we will show you how to create a new text file. Begin by declaring a `StreamWriter` variable, using the following general format:

```
Dim ObjectVar As StreamWriter
```

`ObjectVar` is the name of the object variable. You may use `Private` or `Public` in place of `Dim` if you are declaring the object variable at the class-level or module-level. Here's an example:

```
Dim phoneFile As StreamWriter
```

Next, call the `CreateText` method from the `File` class, passing it the name of a file. For example:

```
phoneFile = File.CreateText("phonelist.txt")
```

Notice how the return value from `CreateText` is assigned to the `StreamWriter` variable named `phoneFile`. (The fully qualified name of the `CreateText` method is `System.IO.File.CreateText`.)

The filename that you pass to the `CreateText` method can optionally contain a complete path, such as *c:\data\vbfiles\phonelist.txt*. If you use only a filename with no path, Visual Basic assumes that the file will be created in your project's *\bin* folder.

Opening an Existing File and Appending Data to It

If a text file already exists, you may want to add more data to the end of the file. This is called *appending* to the file. First, you declare a `StreamWriter` variable:

```
Dim phoneFile As StreamWriter
```

Then you call the `File.AppendText` method, passing it the name of an existing file. For example:

```
phoneFile = File.AppendText("phonelist.txt")
```

Any data written to the file will be written to the end of the file's existing contents.

WARNING: It is possible to move an application's executable file to a location other than the project's *bin* directory. Doing so changes the default location where the files are created.

Writing Data to a File

The **`WriteLine` method** of the `StreamWriter` class writes a line of data to a file. The following is the general format of the method:

```
ObjectVar.WriteLine(Data)
```

`ObjectVar` is the name of a `StreamWriter` object variable. *`Data`* represents constants or variables whose contents will be written to the file. The `WriteLine` method writes the data to the file and then writes a newline character immediately after the data. A **newline character** is an invisible character that separates text by breaking it into another line when displayed on the screen.

NOTE: The newline character is actually stored as two characters: a carriage return (character code 13) and a linefeed character (character code 10).

To further understand how the `WriteLine` method works, let's look at an example. Assume that an application opens a file and writes three students' first names and their scores to the file with the following code:

```
Dim studentFile As StreamWriter
studentFile = File.CreateText("StudentData.txt")
studentFile.WriteLine("Jim")
studentFile.WriteLine(95)
studentFile.WriteLine("Karen")
studentFile.WriteLine(98)
studentFile.WriteLine("Bob")
studentFile.WriteLine(82)
```

You can visualize the data being written to the file in the following manner:

```
Jim<newline>95<newline>Karen<newline>98<newline>Bob<newline>82<newline>
```

The newline characters are represented here as *<newline>*. You do not actually see the newline characters, but when the file is opened in a text editor such as Notepad, its contents appear as shown in Figure 9-3. As you can see from the figure, each newline character causes the data that follows it to be displayed on a new line.

TIP: Each time the `WriteLine` method executes, it writes a separate line of text to the file.

In addition to separating the contents of a file into lines, the newline character also serves as a delimiter. A **delimiter** is an item that separates other items. When you write data to a file using `WriteLine`, newline characters are the delimiters. Later, you will see that data must be separated in order for it to be read from the file.

Figure 9-3 File contents displayed in Notepad

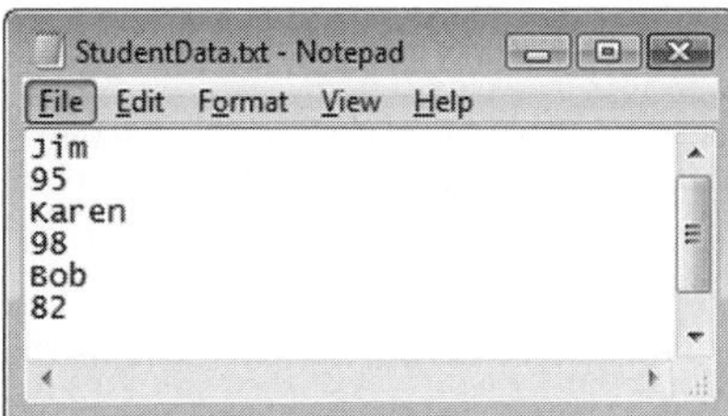

Writing a Blank Line to a File

The `WriteLine` method can write a blank line to a file by calling the method without an argument.

```
textFile.WriteLine()
```

The `Write` Method

The **`Write` method**, a member of the `StreamWriter` class, writes an item of data to a file without writing a newline character. The general format is as follows:

```
ObjectVar.Write(Data)
```

`ObjectVar` is the name of a `StreamWriter` object variable. *`Data`* represents the contents of a constant or variable that is to be written to the file. This method can be used to write data to a file without terminating the line with a newline character. For example, assume an application has a `StreamWriter` object variable named `outputFile`, as well as the following variables:

```
Dim strName As String = "Jeffrey Smith"
Dim intId As Integer = 47895
Dim strPhone As String = "555-7864"
```

The contents of all three variables are written to a single line in the file:

```
outputFile.Write(strName)
outputFile.Write(" ")
outputFile.Write(intId)
outputFile.Write(" ")
outputFile.WriteLine(strPhone)
```

The first statement writes the `strName` variable to the file. The second statement writes a space character (`" "`), the third statement writes the `intId` variable, and the fourth statement writes another space. The last statement uses the `WriteLine` method to write the phone number, followed by a newline character. Here is a sample of the output:

```
Jeffrey Smith 47895 555-7864
```

Closing a File

The opposite of opening a file is closing it. The `StreamWriter` class has a method named `Close` that closes a file. The following is the method's general format:

```
ObjectVar.Close()
```

`ObjectVar` is a `StreamWriter` object variable. After the method executes, the file that was referenced by `ObjectVar` is closed. For example, `salesFile` is an object variable that references a `StreamWriter` object. The following statement closes the file associated with `salesFile`.

```
salesFile.Close()
```

To avoid losing data, your application should always close files after it is finished using them. Computers typically create one or more buffers (memory areas) when a file is opened. When an application writes data to a file, that data is first written to the **buffer**. When the buffer is filled, all data stored there is written to the file. This technique improves the system's performance because writing data to memory is faster than writing it to a disk. The **`Close` method** writes any unsaved information remaining in the file buffer and releases memory allocated by the `StreamWriter` object.

NOTE: Once a file is closed, you must reopen it before performing any operations on it.

In Tutorial 9-1, you examine an application that writes data about three fictional persons to a file.

Tutorial 9-1:
Completing an application that writes data to a file

Step 1: Open the *File WriteLine* demo project from the student sample programs folder named *Chap9\File WriteLine Demo*. The application form is shown in Figure 9-4.

Figure 9-4 *File WriteLine Demo* form

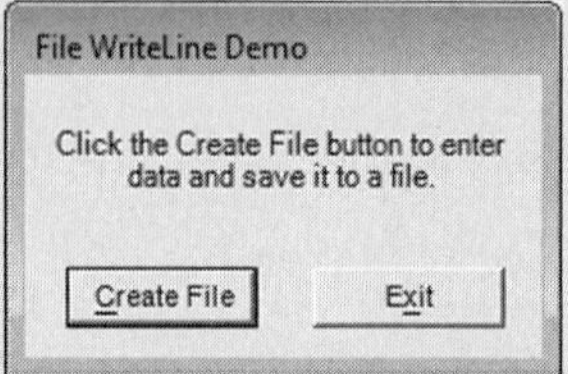

Step 2: Open the *Code* window and find the `btnCreateFile_Click` event handler. Insert the following code:

```
Private Sub btnCreateFile_Click(ByVal sender As System.Object, _
    ByVal e As System.EventArgs) Handles btnCreateFile.Click

  ' This procedure prompts the user for data and
  ' saves it to a file.

  Dim strFilename As String              ' File name
  Dim strFriend As String                ' Name of a friend
  Dim intAge As Integer                  ' To hold an age
  Dim strAddress As String               ' To hold an address
  Dim intCount As Integer                ' Loop counter
  Dim friendFile As StreamWriter         ' Object variable
  ' Get the file name from the user.
  strFilename = InputBox("Enter the filename.", _
      "Filename Needed")

  ' Open the file.
  friendFile = File.CreateText(strFilename)

  ' Get the data for three friends and write it
  ' to the file.
  For intCount = 1 To intNUM_FRIENDS
    ' Get the data.
    MessageBox.Show("Get ready to enter data for friend " & _
        intCount.ToString())
    strFriend = InputBox("Enter your friend's name.")
    Integer.TryParse(InputBox("Enter your friend's age."),intAge)
    strAddress = InputBox("Enter your friend's address.")

    ' Write the data to the file.
    friendFile.WriteLine(strFriend)
    friendFile.WriteLine(intAge)
    friendFile.WriteLine(strAddress)
  Next

  ' Close the file.
  friendFile.Close()
End Sub
```

This procedure asks the user to enter a name for the file that will be created. The name is stored in the `strFilename` variable, and used in the following statement, which opens the file:

```
friendFile = File.CreateText(strFilename)
```

The `For...Next` loop performs three iterations, each time prompting the user to enter the name, age, and address of a friend. The user's input is stored in the variables `strFriend`, `intAge`, and `strAddress`. Once the data is entered, it is written to the file with the following statements:

```
friendFile.WriteLine(strFriend)
friendFile.WriteLine(intAge)
friendFile.WriteLine(strAddress)
```

The file is then closed.

Step 3: Run the application and click the *Create File* button. When prompted to enter the filename, provide the path of a disk location that can be written to. For example, *C:\Temp\MyFriends.txt* will create the file *MyFriends.txt* in the *C:\Temp* folder. Enter a path and filename and make a note of it because you will use the same file later in this tutorial and again in Tutorial 9-2.

NOTE: If you are working in a school computer lab, you may be restricted to saving files only at certain disk locations. Ask your instructor or lab manager for these locations.

Step 4: Enter the following names, ages, and addresses as you are prompted for this data. After you have entered the data for the third friend, the application returns to the main form. Click the *Exit* button.

	Name	Age	Address
Friend 1	`Jim Weaver`	`30`	`P. O. Box 124`
Friend 2	`Mary Duncan`	`24`	`47 Elm Street`
Friend 3	`Karen Warren`	`28`	`24 Love Lane`

Step 5: In Windows, use either Windows Explorer or *My Computer* to locate the file that was created when you ran the application. Double-click the file's name to open it in the Notepad text editor. The contents of the file should appear as shown in Figure 9-5.

Figure 9-5 Contents of the file displayed in Notepad

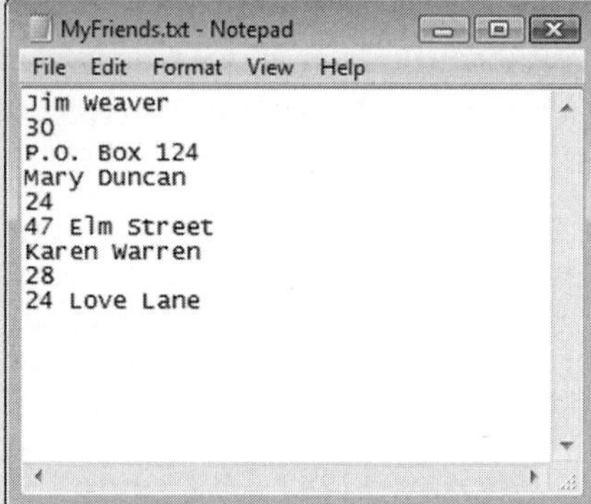

As you can see, each record is written to a separate line in the file because a newline character separates each record.

Step 6: Close the *Notepad* window that displays the text file.

Appending a File

When we **append** a file, we write new data immediately following existing data in the file. If an existing file is opened with the `AppendText` method, data written to the file is appended to the file's existing data. If the file does not exist, it is created.

For example, assume the file *MyFriends.txt* exists and contains the following data, from Tutorial 9-1:

Jim Weaver
30
P. O. Box 124
Mary Duncan
24

47 Elm Street
Karen Warren
28
24 Love Lane

The following statments open the file in append mode and write additional data to the file:

```
' Declare an object variable
Dim friendFile As StreamWriter
' Open the file.
friendFile = File.AppendText("MyFriends.txt")
' Write the data.
friendFile.WriteLine("Bill Johnson")
friendFile.WriteLine(30)
friendFile.WriteLine("36 Oak Street")
' Close the file.
friendFile.Close()
```

After this code executes, the *MyFriends.txt* file will contain the following data:

Jim Weaver
30
P. O. Box 124
Mary Duncan
24
47 Elm Street
Karen Warren
28
24 Love Lane
Bill Johnson
30
36 Oak Street

Reading Files with `StreamReader` Objects

To read data from a sequential text file, use a **`StreamReader` object**. A `StreamReader` object is an instance of the **`StreamReader` class**, which provides methods for reading data from a file. The process of creating a `StreamReader` object is similar to that of creating a `StreamWriter` object, which we discussed in the previous section. First, you declare an object variable with a declaration statement in the following general format:

VideoNote
Reading Data from a File

```
Dim ObjectVar As StreamReader
```

`ObjectVar` is the name of the object variable. As with other variables, you may use the `Private` or `Public` access specifier if you are declaring the object variable at the class level or module level.

You must create an instance of the `StreamReader` object and store its address in the object variable with the **`File.OpenText` method**. The method's general format is as follows:

```
File.OpenText(Filename)
```

`Filename` is a string or a string variable specifying the path and/or name of the file to open. This method opens the file specified by *`Filename`* and returns the address of a `StreamReader` object that may be used to write data to the file. If the file does not exist, a runtime error occurs.

The following are examples:

```
Dim customerFile As StreamReader
customerFile = File.OpenText("customers.txt")
```

The first statement creates an object variable named `customerFile`. The second statement opens the file *customers.txt* and returns the address of a `StreamReader` object that may be used to read data from the file. The address of the `StreamReader` object is assigned to the `customerFile` variable.

As in the case of the `StreamWriter` class, you need to write the following `Imports` statement at the top of your code file:

```
Imports System.IO
```

Reading Data from a File

The **`ReadLine` method** in the `StreamReader` class reads a line of data from a file. The general format of the method is as follows:

```
ObjectVar.ReadLine()
```

`ObjectVar` is the name of a `StreamReader` object variable. The method reads a line from the file associated with *`ObjectVar`* and returns the data as a string. For example, assume that `customerFile` is a `StreamReader` object variable and `strCustomerName` is a string variable. The following statement reads a line from the file and stores it in the variable:

```
strCustomerName = customerFile.ReadLine()
```

Data is read in a forward-only direction. When the file is opened, its **read position,** the position of the next item to be read, is set to the first item in the file. As data is read, the read position advances through the file. For example, consider the file named *Quotation.txt*, as shown in Figure 9-6. As you can see from the figure, the file has three lines of text. Suppose a program opens the file with the following code:

```
Dim textFile As StreamReader
textFile = File.OpenText("Quotation.txt")
```

Figure 9-6 Text file with three lines

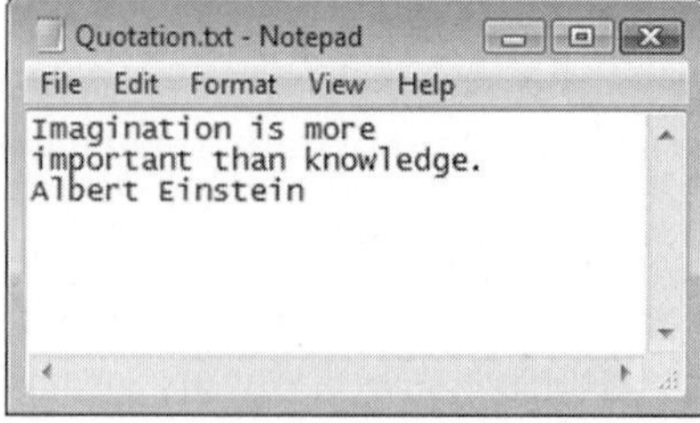
Quotation.txt - Notepad
File Edit Format View Help
Imagination is more
important than knowledge.
Albert Einstein

When this code opens the file, its read position is at the beginning of the first line, as illustrated in Figure 9-7.

Figure 9-7 Initial read position

Read position ——► Imagination is more
important than knowledge.
Albert Einstein

The following statement reads a line from the file, beginning at the current read position:

```
strInput = textFile.ReadLine()
```

After the statement executes, the input variable contains the string `"Imagination is more"`. The input file contains an invisible end-of-line marker at the end of each line. The `ReadLine` statement skips over the first end-of-line marker after reading the first line, and positions the read pointer at the beginning of the second line. Figure 9-8 illustrates the concepts.

Figure 9-8 Read position after first line is read

Imagination is more
Read position
important than knowledge.
Albert Einstein

If the `ReadLine` method is called again, the second line is read from the file and the file's read position is advanced to the third line. After all lines have been read, the read position will be at the end of the file.

Closing the File

Close an open `StreamReader` object by calling the `Close` method. The general format is as follows:

```
ObjectVar.Close()
```

Determining Whether a File Exists

The `File.OpenText` method causes a runtime error if the file it is trying to open does not exist. To prevent an error, you can call the **`File.Exists` method** to determine whether a file exists before you attempt to open it. The general format of the method is as follows:

```
File.Exists(Filename)
```

`Filename` is the name of a file, which may include the path. The method returns *True* if the file exists or *False* if the file does not exist. The following code shows an example of how to use the method to determine if a file exists prior to trying to open the file:

```
If File.Exists(strFilename) Then
   ' Open the file.
   inputFile = File.OpenText(strFilename)
Else
   MessageBox.Show(strFilename & " does not exist.")
End If
```

In Tutorial 9-2, you complete an application that uses the `ReadLine` statement to read the file you created in Tutorial 9-1.

Tutorial 9-2:
Completing an application that reads a file

Step 1: Open the *File ReadLine Demo* project from the student sample programs folder named *Chap9\File ReadLine Demo*. The form is shown in Figure 9-9.

Figure 9-9 *File ReadLine Demo* form

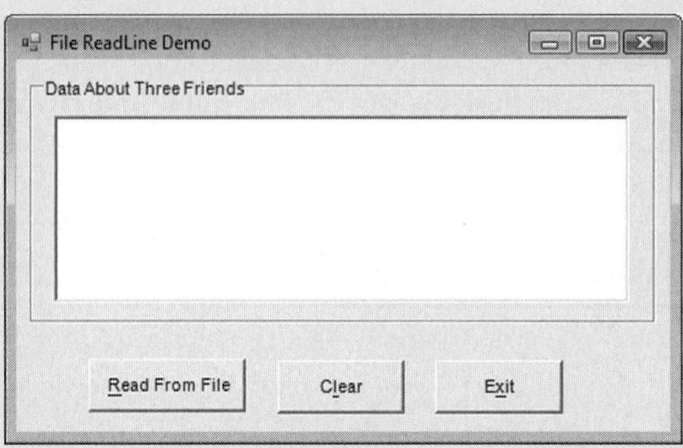

Step 2: In the design view, double-click the *Read From File* button. Insert the following code in the button's `Click` event handler:

```
Private Sub btnRead_Click(ByVal sender As System.Object, _
      ByVal e As System.EventArgs) Handles btnRead.Click

   ' This procedure reads data about friends from a file.
   Dim friendFile As StreamReader  ' Object variable
   Dim strFilename As String       ' File name
   Dim strFriendName As String     ' To hold a name
   Dim intAge As Integer           ' To hold an age
   Dim strAddress As String        ' To hold an address
   Dim intCount As Integer         ' Loop counter

   ' Get the filename from the user.
   strFilename = InputBox("Enter the file name.", _
        "Input Needed")

   ' Check to see if the file exists.
   If File.Exists(strFilename) Then
      ' Open the file.
      friendFile = File.OpenText(strFilename)

      ' Read the data.
      For intCount = 1 To intNUM_FRIENDS
         ' Read a record from the file.
         strFriendName = friendFile.ReadLine()
         intAge = CInt(friendFile.ReadLine())
         strAddress = friendFile.ReadLine()
         ' Display the data in the list box.
         lstFriends.Items.Add("Friend Number " & _
             intCount.ToString())
         lstFriends.Items.Add("Name: " & strFriendName)
         lstFriends.Items.Add("Age : " & intAge.ToString())
         lstFriends.Items.Add("Address: " & strAddress)
         lstFriends.Items.Add("") ' Add a blank line
      Next intCount

      ' Close the file.
      friendFile.Close()
   Else
      MessageBox.Show("That file does not exist.")
```

```
  End If
End Sub
```

Let's look at some details. The user is asked for the name of the file to read, which they type into an input box, as shown in Figure 9-10.

```
  strFilename = InputBox("Enter the file name.", _
     "Input Needed")
```

The procedure calls the `File.Exists` method to verify that the file exists; if it does, the `File.OpenText` method opens the file for input.

```
  If File.Exists(strFilename) Then
    ' Open the file.
    friendFile = File.OpenText(strFilename)
```

A loop begins reading the file, line by line. The `intNUM_FRIENDS` constant determines how many records will be read from the file. A record, you may recall, is the term used for information in the file corresponding to a single person. The `ReadLine` method is called three times—once for the person's name, once for the age, and once for the address.

```
For intCount = 1 To intNUM_FRIENDS
  ' Read a record from the file.
  strFriendName = friendFile.ReadLine()
  intAge = CInt(friendFile.ReadLine())
  strAddress = friendFile.ReadLine()
```

The name, age, and address are given attractive labels, and inserted into the Items collection of the `lstFriends` ListBox control.

```
' Display the data in the list box.
lstFriends.Items.Add("Friend Number " & intCount.ToString())
lstFriends.Items.Add("Name: " & strFriendName)
lstFriends.Items.Add("Age : " & intAge.ToString())
lstFriends.Items.Add("Address: " & strAddress)
lstFriends.Items.Add("")          ' Add a blank line
```

The `Else` clause at the end of the handler procedure displays a message box if the program was unable to find the file whose name was entered by the user. Perhaps the file is located in some other directory, or it was misnamed.

```
Else
  MessageBox.Show("That file does not exist.")
```

Figure 9-10 Prompting the user for the name of the file

Step 3: Run the application and click the *Read From File* button. An input box will appear asking for the filename. Enter the path and filename that you used to create the file in Step 3 of Tutorial 9-1. When you click the *OK* button on the input box, the data is read from the file and displayed in the list box, as shown in Figure 9-11. If you did not type the path and filename exactly as you did in

Tutorial 9-1, you will see a message box indicating the file was not found. In that case, click the *Read From File* button again, this time entering the correct path and filename.

Step 4: Click the *Exit* button to end the application.

Figure 9-11 *File ReadLine Demo* form completed

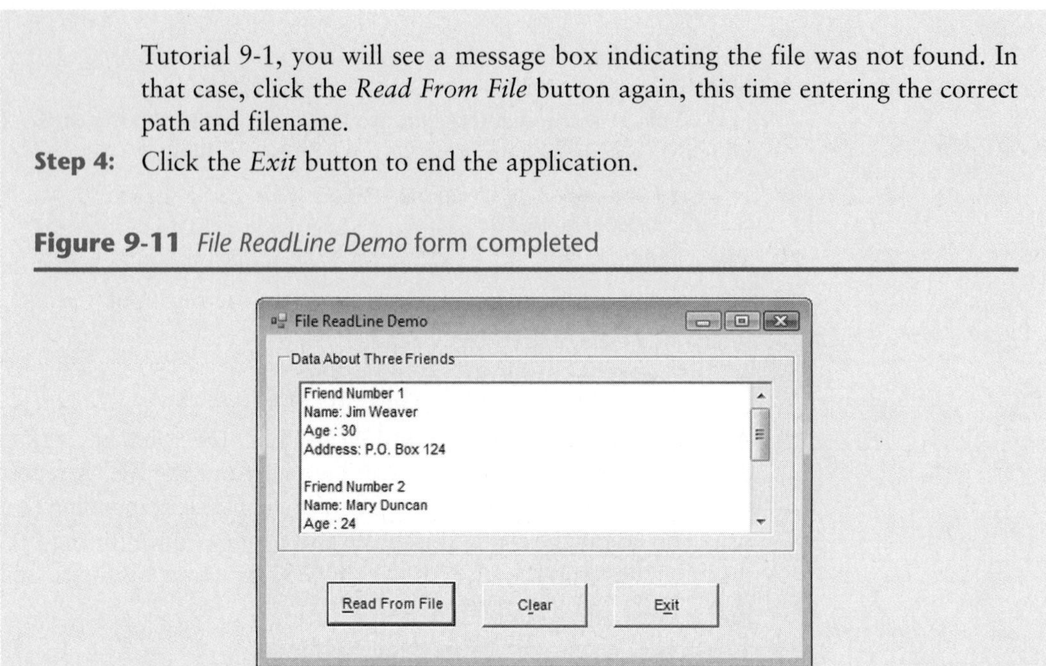

Using `vbTab` to align Display Items

The predefined `vbTab` constant moves the print position forward to the next even multiple of 8. You can use it to align columns in displayed or printed output more effectively. The following is a simple example, displayed in a list box, of a reference line followed by three lines displaying tabs and characters:

```
With ListBox1.Items
   .Add("012345678901234567890")
   .Add("X" & vbTab & "X")
   .Add("XXXXXXXXXXXX" & vbTab & "X")
   .Add(vbTab & vbTab & "X")
End With
```

In the output in Figure 9-12, the tab in line two moves the print position forward to column 8 before displaying the letter *X*. (Print positions are numbered starting at 0.) In lines three and four, the print position moves to column 16 before displaying the final letter *X*.

Figure 9-12 Demonstrating tabs in a list box

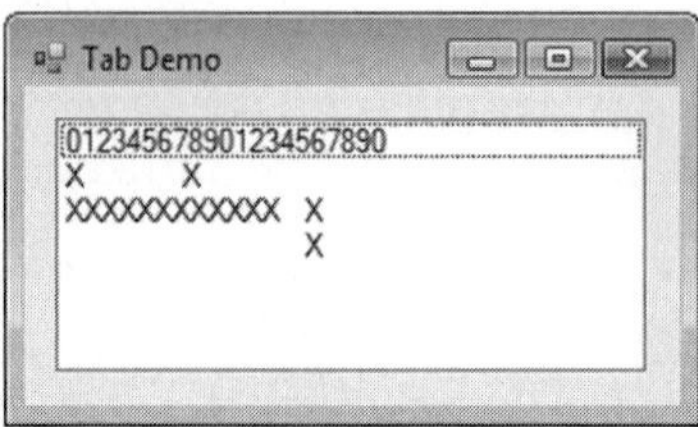

Briefly returning to the *ReadLine Demo* application from Tutorial 9-2, a slightly better way to display the person information is to insert tabs between the labels and names in the list box. Here is the appropriately modified code from the loop inside the `btnRead_Click` event handler:

```
' Display the data in the list box.
lstFriends.Items.Add("Friend Number " & vbTab _
  & intCount.ToString())
lstFriends.Items.Add("Name: " & vbTab & vbTab & strFriendName)
lstFriends.Items.Add("Age : " & vbTab & vbTab & intAge.ToString())
lstFriends.Items.Add("Address: " & vbTab & strAddress)
lstFriends.Items.Add("")                    ' Add a blank line
```

The resulting output from this code appears in Figure 9-13.

Figure 9-13 *ReadLine Demo,* using tabs in the list box

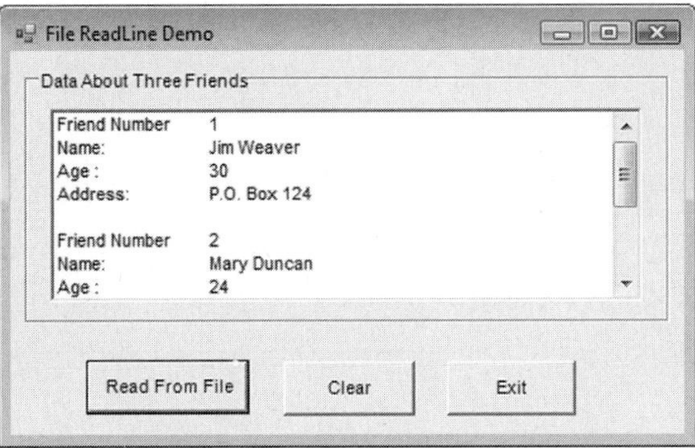

Detecting the End of a File

The File *ReadLine* Demo application in Tutorial 9-2 reads exactly three records because it knows how many records are stored in the file. In many cases, however, the amount of data in a file is unknown. When this is the case, use the **`Peek` method** to determine when the end of the file has been reached. The general format of the `Peek` method is as follows:

`ObjectVar.Peek`

`ObjectVar` is an object variable referencing a `StreamReader` object. This method looks ahead in the file, without moving the current read position, and returns the next character that will be read. If the current read position is at the end of the file (where there are no more characters to read), the method returns –1. The following is an example of a `Do While` loop that uses the `Peek` method to determine when the end of the *Scores.txt* file has been reached. The loop reads all the lines from the file and adds them to the `lstResults` list box.

```
Dim scoresFile As StreamReader
Dim strInput As String
scoresFile = File.OpenText("Scores.txt")
Do Until scoresFile.Peek = -1
  strInput = scoresFile.ReadLine()
  lstResults.Items.Add(strInput)
Loop
scoresFile.Close()
```

Tutorial 9-3 examines an application that detects the end of a file.

Tutorial 9-3: Examining an application that detects the end of a file

Step 1: Open the *File Demo* project from the student sample program folder named *Chap9\File Demo*. Run the application. The form is shown in Figure 9-14.

Figure 9-14 *File Demo* form

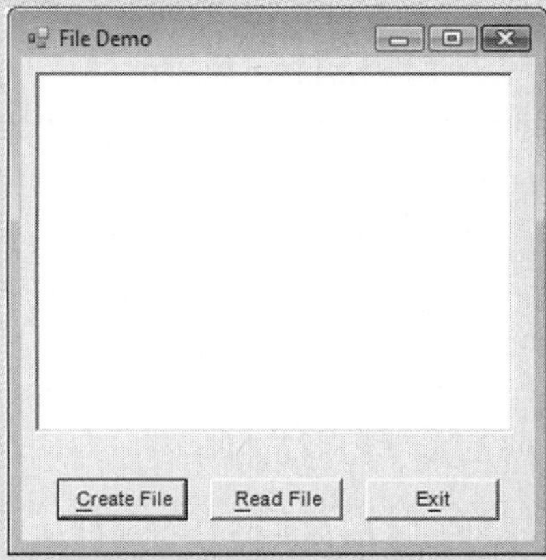

Step 2: Click the *Create File* button. An input box appears and asks: *How many numbers do you want to enter?* Enter **5** and press [Enter].

Step 3: Because you indicated you want to enter five numbers, the application will prompt you five times with an input box to enter a number. Enter the following numbers: **2**, **4**, **6**, **8**, and **10**. The application writes these numbers to a file.

Step 4: After you have entered the last number, click the *Read File* button. The application reads the numbers from the file and prints them on the form, as shown in Figure 9-15.

Figure 9-15 *File Demo* form with numbers displayed

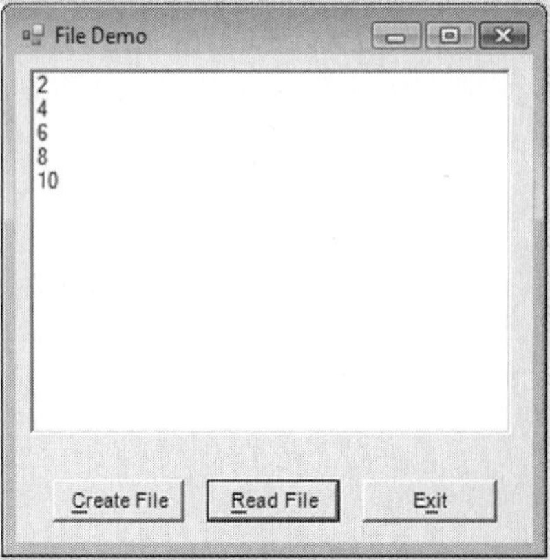

Step 5: Click the *Exit* button to end the application.

Step 6: Open the *Code* window and look at the `btnCreate_Click` event procedure. The code is as follows:

```
Private Sub btnCreate_Click(ByVal sender As System.Object, _
        ByVal e As System.EventArgs) Handles btnCreate.Click

    ' This procedure creates the file and stores
    ' the numbers entered by the user.

    Dim outputFile As StreamWriter
    Dim intMaxNumbers As Integer     ' The number of values
    Dim intCount As Integer          ' Loop counter
    Dim intNumber As Integer         ' User input

    ' Get the number of numbers from the user.
    intMaxNumbers = CInt(InputBox("How many numbers " _
         & "do you want to enter?"))
    ' Create the file.
    outputFile = File.CreateText(strFILENAME)

    ' Get the numbers and write them to the file.
    For intCount = 1 To intMaxNumbers
        Integer.TryParse(InputBox("Enter an integer.", intNumber)
        outputFile.WriteLine(intNumber)
    Next intCount

        ' Close the file.
        outputFile.Close()
    End Sub
```

First, the user is asked how many numbers will be entered, and the value is stored in `intMaxNumbers`. Next, the file is created and a loop prompts the user to enter a series of numbers, writing each one to the file. After the loop completes, the file is closed.

Step 7: Now look at the `btnRead_Click` event procedure.

```
Private Sub btnRead_Click(ByVal sender As System.Object, _
        ByVal e As System.EventArgs) Handles btnRead.Click

    ' This procedure opens the file, reads all the values
    ' from the file, and adds them to the list box.

    Dim inputFile As StreamReader

    If File.Exists(strFILENAME) Then
        inputFile = File.OpenText(strFILENAME)
        lstOutput.Items.Clear()
        Do Until inputFile.Peek = -1
            lstOutput.Items.Add(inputFile.ReadLine())
        Loop
        inputFile.Close()
    Else
        MessageBox.Show("File not found: " & strFILENAME, _
            "Error")
    End If
End Sub
```

This procedure uses the `File.Exists` method to determine that the

Numbers.txt file exists. If so, the file is opened, the list box is cleared, and the following loop executes:

```
Do Until inputFile.Peek = -1
  lstOutput.Items.Add(inputFile.ReadLine())
Loop
```

This loop repeats until the `Peek` method returns –1, indicating the end of the file has been reached. In each iteration, a line is read from the file and added to the list box. Because the loop repeats until the end of the file, it can read any number of items from the file.

Other `StreamReader` Methods

The `StreamReader` class also provides the `Read` and `ReadToEnd` methods, which we briefly discuss. The general format of the `Read` method is as follows:

```
ObjectVar.Read
```

`ObjectVar` is the name of a `StreamReader` object variable. The **`Read` method** reads only the next character from a file and returns in integer code for the character. To convert the character code to a character, use the **`Chr` function**, as shown in the following code:

```
Dim textFile As StreamReader
Dim strInput As String = String.Empty
textFile = File.OpenText("names.txt")
Do While textFile.Peek <> -1
  strInput &= Chr(textFile.Read)
Loop
textFile.Close()
```

This code opens the *names.txt* file. The `Do While` loop, which repeats until it reaches the end of the file, executes the following statement:

```
strInput &= Chr(textFile.Read)
```

This statement gets the character code for the next character in the file, converts it to a character with the `Chr` function, and concatenates that character to the string variable `strInput`. When the loop has finished, the string variable `strInput` contains the entire contents of the file names.txt.

The general format of the `ReadToEnd` method is as follows:

```
ObjectVar.ReadToEnd
```

`ObjectVar` is the name of a `StreamReader` object variable. The **`ReadToEnd` method** reads and returns the entire contents of a file, beginning at the current read position. The following is an example:

```
Dim textFile As StreamReader
Dim strInput As String
textFile = File.OpenText("names.txt")
strInput = textFile.ReadToEnd()
textFile.Close()
```

The statement `strInput = textFile.ReadToEnd()` reads the file's contents and stores it in the variable `strInput`.

Working with Arrays and Files

Saving the contents of an array to a file is easy. Use a loop to step through each element of the array, writing its contents to the file. For example, assume an application has the following array declaration:

```
Dim intValues(9) As Integer
```

The following code opens a file named *Values.txt* and writes the contents of each element of the `values` array to the file:

```
Dim outputFile as StreamWriter
outputFile = File.CreateText("values.txt")
For intCount = 0 To (intValues.Length – 1)
  outputFile.WriteLine(intValues(intCount))
Next intCount
outputFile.Close()
```

Reading the contents of a file into an array is equally straightforward. The following code opens the *Values.txt* file and reads its contents into the elements of the `intValues` array:

```
Dim inputFile as StreamReader
inputFile = File.OpenText("values.txt")
For intCount = 0 To (intValues.Length – 1)
  intValues(intCount) = CInt(inputFile.ReadLine())
Next intCount
inputFile.Close()
```

NOTE: This code does not check for the end of file, so it assumes the file contains enough values to fill the array. Also, the program will halt if the file contains a value that cannot be converted to an integer.

Checkpoint

9.1 What are the three steps in the process of using a file?

9.2 What type of object variable must you create to open a file for writing? For reading?

9.3 Write a statement that creates the file *Test.txt* so that you may write data to it. If the file already exists, its contents should be erased.

9.4 Write a statement that writes the contents of the variable `x` to a line in the file you opened in Checkpoint 9.3.

9.5 Write a statement that opens the file *Test.txt* for reading.

9.6 Write a statement that reads a line from the file you opened in Checkpoint 9.5, into the variable `x`.

9.7 How do you determine that a file already exists?

9.8 When reading a file, how does a program know it has reached end of the file?

9.2 The OpenFileDialog, SaveFileDialog, FontDialog, and ColorDialog Controls

CONCEPT: Visual Basic provides dialog controls that equip your applications with standard Windows dialog boxes for operations such as opening files, saving files, and selecting fonts and colors.

The OpenFileDialog and SaveFileDialog Controls

So far, the applications in this chapter that open a file either specify the filename as part of the code or require the user to enter the path and filename. Most Windows users, however, are accustomed to using a dialog box to browse their disk for a file to open or for a location to save a file. You can use the OpenFileDialog and SaveFileDialog controls to equip applications with standard dialog boxes used by most Windows applications.

The OpenFileDialog Control

The **OpenFileDialog control** displays a standard Windows *Open* dialog box, as shown in Figure 9-16, running under Windows Vista. The ***Open* dialog box** is useful in applications that work with files. It gives users the ability to browse for a file to open, instead of typing a long path and filename.

Figure 9-16 Windows Vista *Open* dialog box

Adding the OpenFileDialog Control to Your Project

To place an OpenFileDialog control on a form, double-click the *OpenFileDialog* tool under the *Dialogs* tab in the *Toolbox* window. Because the control is invisible at runtime, it appears in the component tray at design time. We will use the prefix `ofd` when naming the control.

Displaying an Open Dialog Box

Display an *Open* dialog box by calling the OpenFileDialog control's `ShowDialog` method. The following is the method's general format:

```
ControlName.ShowDialog()
```

`ControlName` is the name of the OpenFileDialog control. For example, assuming `ofdOpenFile` is the name of an OpenFileDialog control, the following statement calls its `ShowDialog` method:

```
ofdOpenFile.ShowDialog()
```

`ShowDialog` returns `Windows.Forms.DialogResult.OK` or `Windows.Forms.DialogResult.Cancel`, indicating which button, *OK* or *Cancel*, the user clicked to close the dialog box. When the user selects a file with the *Open* dialog box, the file's path and name are stored in the control's **Filename property**.

The following code displays an *Open* dialog box and determines whether the user has selected a file. If so, the filename is displayed as follows:

```
If ofdOpenFile.ShowDialog() = Windows.Forms.DialogResult.OK Then
  MessageBox.Show(ofdOpenFile.FileName)
Else
  MessageBox.Show("You selected no file.")
End If
```

The Filter Property

The *Open* dialog box has a *Files of type* list box, which displays a filter that specifies the type of files visible in the dialog box. Filters typically use the wildcard character (`*`) followed by a file extension. For example, the `*.txt` filter specifies that only files ending in .txt (text files) are to be displayed. The `*.doc` filter specifies that only files ending in `.doc` (Microsoft Word files) are to be displayed. The `*.*` filter allows all files to be displayed.

The dialog box in Figure 9-17 shows a list box with `*.txt` and `*.*` filters.

Figure 9-17 *Open* dialog box with `*.txt` and `*.*` filters

Use the **Filter property** to set the filters in the *Files of type* list box. This property can be set in the *Properties* window at design time, or by code at runtime. When storing a value in the Filter property, store a string containing a description of the filter and the filter itself. The description and the filter are separated with the pipe (|) symbol. For example, assuming an application has an OpenFileDialog control named `ofdOpenFile`, the following statement sets the Filter property for text files:

```
ofdOpenFile.Filter = "Text files (*.txt)|*.txt"
```

The part of the string appearing before the pipe symbol is a description of the filter, and is displayed in the *Files of type* list box. The part of the string appearing after the pipe symbol is the actual filter. In our example, the description of the filter is `Text files (*.txt)` and the filter is `*.txt`.

The pipe symbol is also used to separate multiple filters. For example, the following statement stores two filters in `ofdOpenFile.Filter`: `*.txt` and `*.*`:

```
ofdOpenFile.Filter = "Text files (*.txt)|*.txt|All Files (*.*)|*.*"
```

The description of the first filter is `Text files (*.txt)`, and the filter is `*.txt`. The description of the second filter is `All files (*.*)`, and the filter is `*.*`.

The InitialDirectory Property

By default, the *Open* dialog box displays the current directory (or folder). You can specify another directory to be initially displayed by storing its path in the **InitialDirectory property**. For example, the following code stores the path *C:\Data* in `ofdOpenFile.InitialDirectory` before displaying an *Open* dialog box:

```
ofdOpenFile.InitialDirectory = "C:\Data"
ofdOpenFile.ShowDialog()
```

When the *Open* dialog box is displayed, it shows the contents of the directory *C:\Data*.

The Title Property

By default, the *Open* dialog box displays the string `"Open"` in its title bar. You can change this by storing a string in the control's **Title property**, which displays in the dialog box's title bar.

Using the *Open* Dialog Box to Open a File

The following code assumes `ofdOpenFile` is the name of an OpenFileDialog control. It demonstrates how to set the Filter, InitialDirectory, and Title properties, display the *Open* dialog box, retrieve the filename entered by the user, and open the file.

```
' Configure the Open dialog box and display it.
With ofdOpenFile
   .Filter = "Text files (*.txt)|*.txt|All files (*.*)|*.*"
   .InitialDirectory = "C:\Data"
   .Title = "Select a File to Open"
   If .ShowDialog() = Windows.Forms.DialogResult.OK Then
     inputFile = File.OpenText(.Filename)
   End If
End With
```

The SaveFileDialog Control

The **SaveFileDialog control** displays a standard Windows *Save As* dialog box. Figure 9-18 shows such a dialog box as it appears in Windows Vista.

The ***Save As* dialog** box is useful in applications that work with files. It gives users the ability to browse their disks and to choose a location and name for the file.

The SaveFileDialog control has much in common with the OpenFileDialog control. Double-click the *SaveFileDialog* tool in the toolbox to place the control on a form. Because the control is invisible at runtime, it appears in the component tray at design time. We will use the prefix `sfd` when naming the control.

Display a *Save As* dialog box by calling the SaveFileDialog control's `ShowDialog` method. The following is the method's general format:

```
ControlName.ShowDialog()
```

`ControlName` is the name of the SaveFileDialog control. For example, assuming `sfdSaveFile` is the name of a SaveFileDialog control, the following statement calls its `ShowDialog` method:

```
sfdSaveFile.ShowDialog()
```

This method returns one of the values `Windows.Forms.DialogResult.OK` or `Windows.Forms.DialogResult.Cancel` indicating which button, *OK* or *Cancel*, the user clicked to dismiss the dialog box.

Figure 9-18 Windows Vista *Save As* dialog box

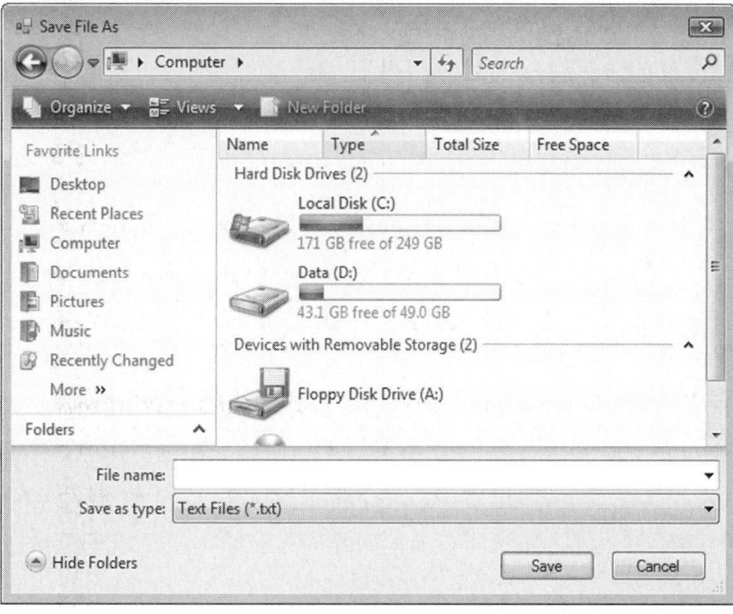

The Filename property holds the name of the file selected or entered by the user. The Filter, InitialDirectory, and Title properties work with the *Save As* dialog box the same way they do with the *Open* dialog box. The following code assumes that `sfdSaveFile` is the name of a common dialog control. It demonstrates how to set the Filter, InitialDirectory, and Title properties, display the *Save As* dialog box, retrieve the filename entered by the user, and open the file.

```
' Configure the Save As dialog box and display it.
With sfdSaveFile
  .Filter = "Text files (*.txt)|*.txt|All files (*.*)|*.*"
```

```
    .InitialDirectory = "C:\Data"
    .Title = "Save File As"
    ' If the user selected a file, open it for output.
    If .ShowDialog() = Windows.Forms.DialogResult.OK Then
      outputFile = System.IO.File.OpenText(.Filename)
    End If
  End With
```

In Tutorial 9-4, you gain experience using the OpenFileDialog and SaveFileDialog controls by creating a simple text editor application. You will also learn about the TextBox control's MultiLine property, WordWrap property, and `TextChanged` event.

Tutorial 9-4:
Creating a simple text editor application

In this tutorial, you will create a simple text editing application that allows you to create documents, save them, and open existing documents. The application will use a Multiline TextBox control to hold the document text. It will also use the menu system shown in Figure 9-19.

Figure 9-19 Simple Text Editor menu system

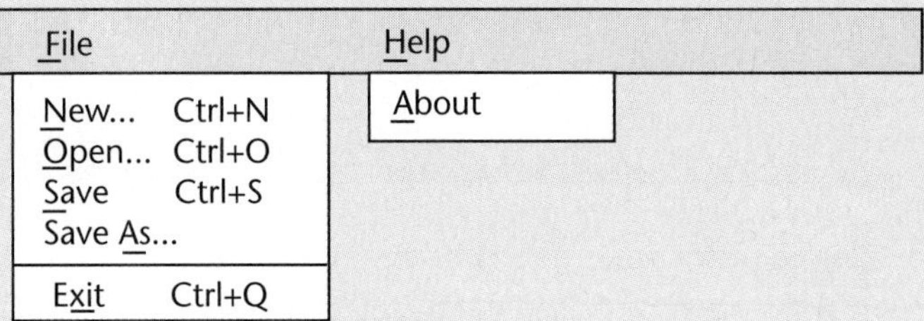

Table 9-1 lists the required menu items, showing the contents of their Text and ShortcutKeys properties.

Table 9-1 Menu items and their Text and ShortcutKeys properties

Menu Item Name	Text Property	ShortcutKeys Property
`mnuFile`	&File	(None)
`mnuFileNew`	&New...	Ctrl+N
`mnuFileOpen`	&Open...	Ctrl+O
`mnuFileSave`	&Save	(None)
`mnuFileSaveAs`	Save &As	Ctrl+S
`mnuFileExit`	E&xit	Ctrl+Q
`mnuHelp`	&Help	(None)
`mnuHelpAbout`	&About	(None)

Some of the menu item Text property values end with an ellipsis (. . .). It is a standard Windows convention for a menu item's text to end with an ellipsis if the menu item displays a dialog box.

Step 1: Create a new Windows application project named *Simple Text Editor*.

Step 2: Set the form's Name property to *frmMain* and change its filename in the *Solutions Explorer* window to *frmMain.vb*.

Step 3: Set the form's Text property to *Simple Text Editor*. Create a MenuStrip control on the form and add the menu items listed in Table 9-1. Set their Text and ShortcutKeys properties to the values shown in the table. The form should appear similar to the one shown in Figure 9-20.

Figure 9-20 Initial *Simple Text Editor* form

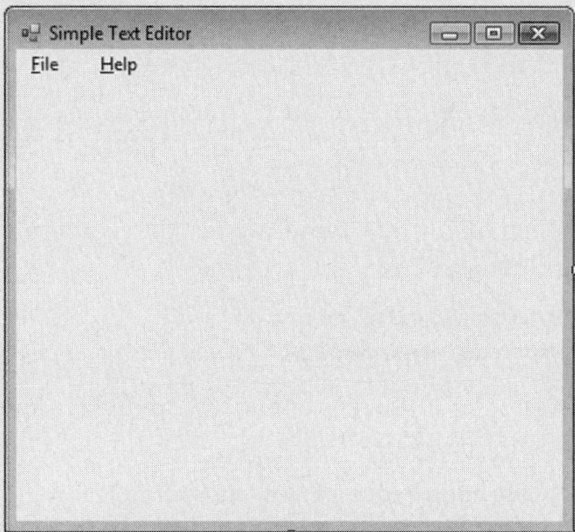

Step 4: Add a TextBox control to the form named `txtDocument` and clear the contents of its Text property. TextBox controls have a Boolean property named **Multi-Line**, which equals *False* by default. When this property equals *True*, the height of the TextBox control can be enlarged and its text can span multiple lines. Set the MultiLine property of the `txtDocument` control to *True*. TextBox controls also have a WordWrap property that, when set to *True*, causes long text lines to wrap around to the following line. By default, WordWrap equals *True*.

Step 5: Enlarge the size of the `txtDocument` control so it fills most of the form, as shown in Figure 9-21.

Step 6: Set the `txtDocument` control's Anchor property to *Top*, *Bottom*, *Left*, *Right*. This will cause the TextBox control to resize automatically if the user resizes the form.

Step 7: Add OpenFileDialog and SaveFileDialog controls to the form. (You will find these controls under the *Dialogs* tab in the Toolbox.) Name the OpenFileDialog control **`ofdOpenFile`**. Name the SaveFileDialog control **`sfdSaveFile`**.

Step 8: Set the Title property of the `ofdOpenFile` control to *Open File*. Set the Title property of the `sfdSaveFile` control to *Save File As*. Set the Filter property of both controls to *Text Files (*.txt) | *.txt*.

Figure 9-21 *Simple Text Editor* form with text box enlarged

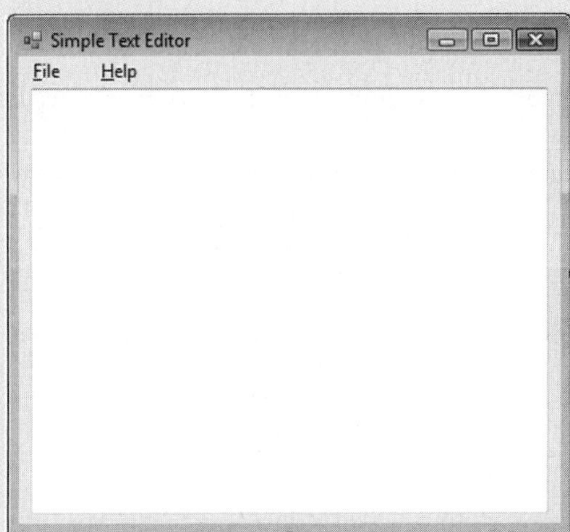

Step 9: Open the *Code* window. At the very top of the *Code* window, insert the following lines:

```
Option Strict On
Imports System.IO
```

Write the following comments and class-level declarations:

```
' Class-level variables
' The document file name.
Dim strDocumentName As String = String.Empty
' blnIsChanged equals True when the document has
' been changed since it was last saved. It equals
' False when the document has not been changed
' since it was last saved.
Dim blnIsChanged As Boolean = False
```

The `strDocumentName` variable will hold the filename under which the text box's contents are saved. When `blnIsChanged` equals *True*, it indicates that the contents of the text box have been changed since it was last saved. When this is the case, the user should be warned.

Step 10: When a TextBox control's Text property changes, a `TextChanged` event is triggered. In this step, you will write a `TextChanged` event procedure for the `txtDocument` control that sets `blnIsChanged` to *True*. With the *Code* window still open, select `txtDocument` in the class name drop-down list box, and select `TextChanged` in the method name drop-down list box. When the code template for the `txtDocument_TextChanged` event handler appears, add the following code shown in bold:

```
Private Sub txtDocument_TextChanged(ByVal sender As Object, _
        ByVal e As System.EventArgs) _
        Handles txtDocument.TextChanged

    ' Update the isChanged variable to indicate that
    ' the text has changed.
    blnIsChanged = True
End Sub
```

Step 11: Now you will write the following procedures: `ClearDocument`, `Open Document`, `SaveDocument`, and `SaveAs`. The `ClearDocument` procedure clears the `txtDocument` control's Text property, sets `strDocumentName` to an empty string, and sets `blnIsChanged` to *False*. The `OpenDocument` procedure displays an *Open* dialog box, opens the file selected by the user, and reads its contents into the text box. The `SaveDocument` procedure saves the contents of the text box to the file specified by the `strDocumentName` variable. The `SaveAs` procedure saves the contents of the text box to the file selected by the user in the *Save As* dialog box. The code for these procedures follows:

```
Sub ClearDocument()
  ' Clear the contents of the text box.
  txtDocument.Clear()
  ' Clear the document name.
  strDocumentName = String.Empty
  ' Set blnIsChanged to False.
  blnIsChanged = False
End Sub

Sub OpenDocument()
  ' Use the OpenFileDialog control to get
  ' a file name.
  Dim inputFile As StreamReader
  If ofdOpenFile.ShowDialog = Windows.Forms.DialogResult.OK Then
    strDocumentName = ofdOpenFile.FileName
    inputFile = File.OpenText(strDocumentName)
    txtDocument.Text = inputFile.ReadToEnd()
    inputFile.Close()
  End If
End Sub

Sub SaveDocument()
  ' Save the current document under the name
  ' stored in documentName.
  Dim outputFile As StreamWriter
  outputFile = File.CreateText(strDocumentName)
  outputFile.Write(txtDocument.Text)
  outputFile.Close()
  ' Update the blnIsChanged variable.
  blnIsChanged = False
End Sub

Sub SaveAs()
  If sfdSaveFile.ShowDialog = Windows.Forms.DialogResult.OK Then
    strDocumentName = sfdSaveFile.FileName
    SaveDocument()
  End If
End Sub
```

Step 12: Write `Click` event handlers for the items appearing in the *File* menu.

```
Private Sub mnuFileNew_Click(ByVal sender As System.Object, _
    ByVal e As System.EventArgs) Handles mnuFileNew.Click

  ' Begin a new document.
  If blnIsChanged = True Then
    ' Document has been changed and is not saved
    If MessageBox.Show("The current document is not saved. " _
        & "Are you sure?", "Confirm", _
        MessageBoxButtons.YesNo) = _
        Windows.Forms.DialogResult.Yes Then
      ClearDocument()
    End If
  Else
    ' Document has not changed
    ClearDocument()
  End If
End Sub

Private Sub mnuFileOpen_Click(ByVal sender As System.Object, _
    ByVal e As System.EventArgs) Handles mnuFileOpen.Click

  ' Open an existing text file.
  If blnIsChanged = True Then
    ' Document has been changed and is not saved
    If MessageBox.Show("The current document is not saved. " _
        & "Do you wish to discard your changes?", "Confirm", _
        MessageBoxButtons.YesNo) = _
        Windows.Forms.DialogResult.Yes Then
      ClearDocument()
      OpenDocument()
    End If
  Else
    ' Document has not changed
    ClearDocument()
    OpenDocument()
  End If
End Sub

Private Sub mnuFileSave_Click(ByVal sender As System.Object, _
    ByVal e As System.EventArgs) Handles mnuFileSave.Click

  ' Save the current document under its existing name.
  If strDocumentName = String.Empty Then
    ' The document has not been saved, so
    ' use Save As dialog box.
    If sfdSaveFile.ShowDialog = _
        Windows.Forms.DialogResult.OK Then
      strDocumentName = sfdSaveFile.FileName
      SaveDocument()
    End If
  Else
    SaveDocument()
  End If
End Sub
```

```
Private Sub mnuFileSaveAs_Click(ByVal sender As System.Object, _
    ByVal e As System.EventArgs) Handles mnuFileSaveAs.Click

  ' Save the current document under a new name.
  If sfdSaveFile.ShowDialog = _
      Windows.Forms.DialogResult.OK Then
    strDocumentName = sfdSaveFile.FileName
    SaveDocument()
  End If
End Sub

Private Sub mnuFileExit_Click(ByVal sender As System.Object, _
    ByVal e As System.EventArgs) Handles mnuFileExit.Click

  ' End the application with the Close method so the
  ' Closing event will trigger.
  Me.Close()
End Sub
```

Step 13: Write a `Click` event handler for the *About* menu item on the *Help* menu. The code follows:

```
Private Sub mnuHelpAbout_Click(ByVal sender As System.Object, _
    ByVal e As System.EventArgs) Handles mnuHelpAbout.Click

  ' Display an about box.
  MessageBox.Show("Simple Text Editor version 1.0")
End Sub
```

Step 14: We want to warn the user if he or she attempts to exit the application without saving the contents of the text box, so a `frmMain_FormClosing` event handler must be written. In the class name drop-down list box, select *frmMain Events*. In the method name drop-down list box, select *FormClosing*. When the code template for the `frmMain_FormClosing` event handler appears, complete the event procedure by entering the following code, shown in bold:

```
Private Sub frmMain_FormClosing(ByVal sender As Object, _
  ByVal e As System.ComponentModel.FormClosingEventArgs) _
  Handles MyBase.FormClosing

  ' If the document has not been changed, confirm
  ' before exiting.
  If blnIsChanged = True Then
    If MessageBox.Show("The current document is not saved. " _
        & "Are you sure you want to exit?", "Confirm", _
        MessageBoxButtons.YesNo) = _
        Windows.Forms.DialogResult.Yes Then
      e.Cancel = False
    Else
      e.Cancel = True
    End If
  End If
End Sub
```

Step 15: Save and run the application. If you entered all the code correctly, you should see the form shown in Figure 9-22.

Figure 9-22 *Simple Text Editor* form

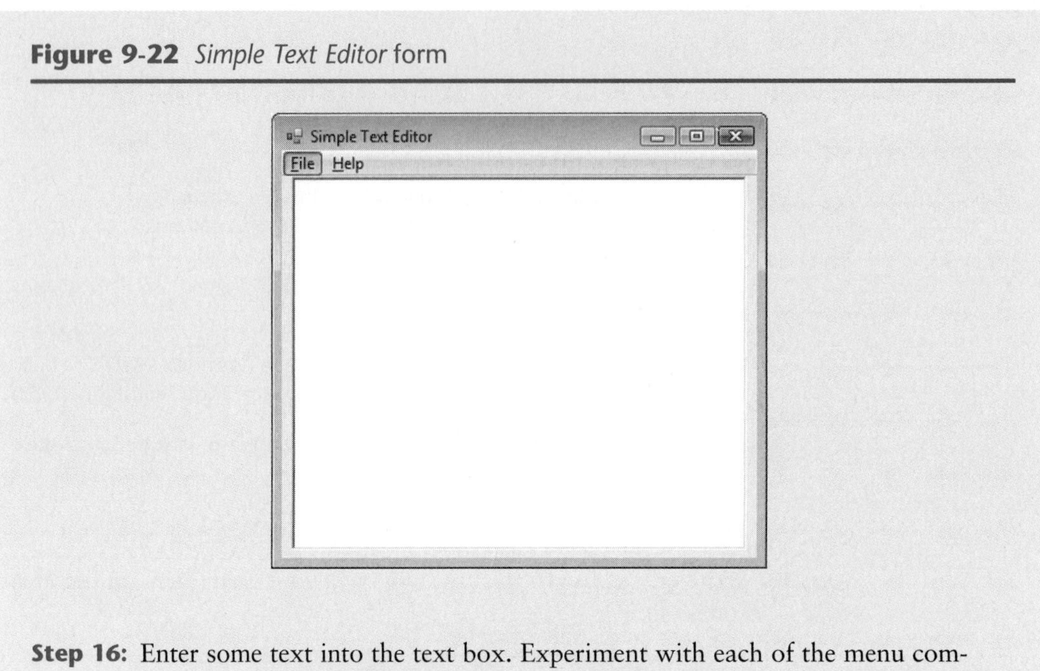

Step 16: Enter some text into the text box. Experiment with each of the menu commands to see if the application operates correctly. When you are finished, exit.

The ColorDialog and FontDialog Controls

The ColorDialog Control

The **ColorDialog control** displays a standard Windows ***Color* dialog box**. Figure 9-23 shows a default *Color* dialog box, on the left. When the user clicks the *Define Custom Colors* button, the dialog box expands to become the fully open *Color* dialog box shown on the right.

Double-click the *ColorDialog* tool in the *Dialogs* section of the toolbox to place the control on a form. Because the control is invisible at runtime, it appears in the component tray at design time. We will use the prefix `cd` when naming the control.

Figure 9-23 Windows *Color* dialog box

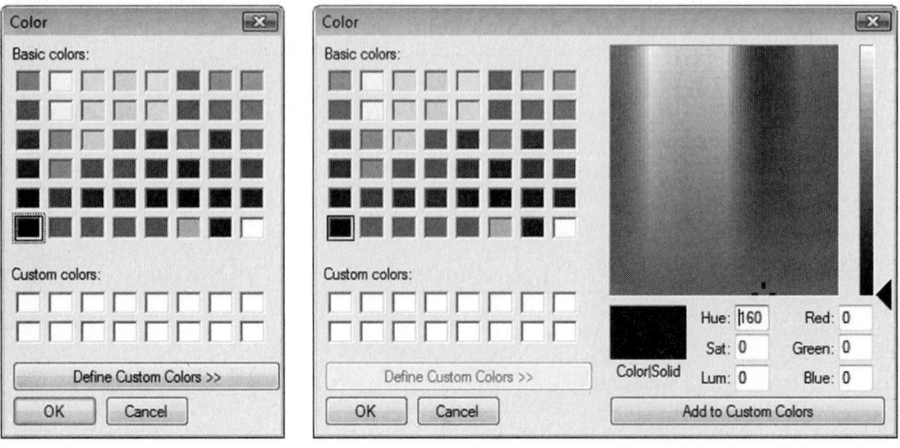

Color dialog box

Fully open *Color* dialog box

Display a *Color* dialog box by calling its `ShowDialog` method. For example, assuming `cdColor` is the name of a ColorDialog control, the following statement calls its `ShowDialog` method:

```
cdColor.ShowDialog()
```

This method returns one of the values, `Windows.Forms.DialogResult.OK` or `Windows.Forms.DialogResult.Cancel`, indicating which button, *OK* or *Cancel*, the user clicked to dismiss the dialog box. The Color property will hold a value representing the color selected by the user. This value can be used with control properties that designate color, such as ForeColor and BackColor. For example, the following code displays the *Color* dialog box and then sets the color of the text displayed by the `lblMessage` label to that selected by the user:

```
If cdColor.ShowDialog() = Windows.Forms.DialogResult.OK Then
  lblMessage.ForeColor = cdColor.Color
End If
```

By default, black is initially selected when the *Color* dialog box is displayed. If you wish to set the initially selected color, you must set the Color property to the desired color value. For example, the following code sets the initially selected color to blue:

```
cdColor.Color = Color.Blue
If cdColor.ShowDialog() = Windows.Forms.DialogResult.OK Then
  lblMessage.ForeColor = cdColor.Color
End If
```

The following code sets the initially selected color to the color of the `lblMessage` label before displaying the dialog box:

```
cdColor.Color = lblMessage.ForeColor
If cdColor.ShowDialog() = Windows.Forms.DialogResult.OK Then
  lblMessage.ForeColor = cdColor.Color
End If
```

The FontDialog Control

The **FontDialog control** displays a standard Windows ***Font* dialog box**. Figure 9-24 shows the default *Font* dialog box on the left, and a *Font* dialog box with a *Color* drop-down list on the right.

Figure 9-24 Windows *Font* dialog box

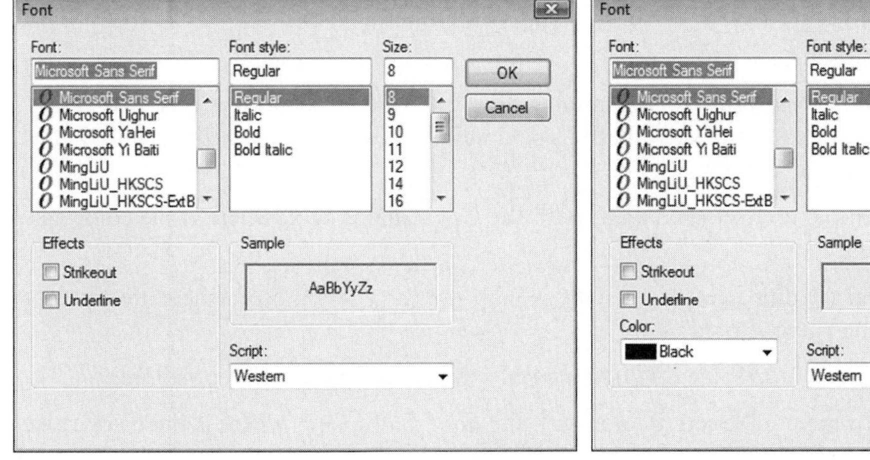

Default *Font* dialog box

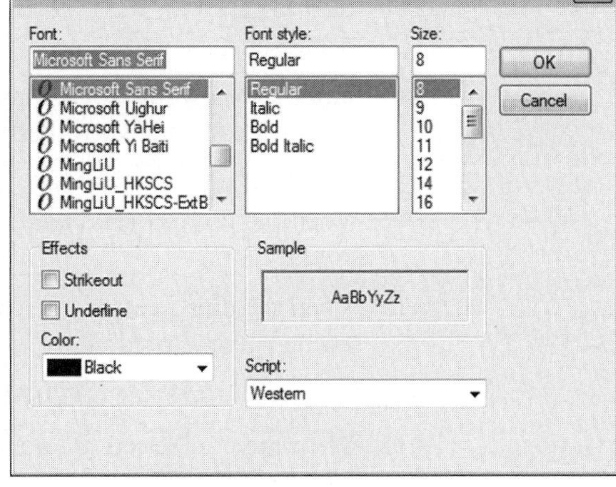

Font dialog box with color choices displayed

Double-click the *FontDialog* tool in the *Dialogs* section of the toolbox to place the control on a form. Because the control is invisible at runtime, it appears in the component tray at design time. We will use the prefix `fd` when naming the control.

You display a *Font* dialog box by calling the FontDialog control's `ShowDialog` method. For example, assuming `fdFont` is the name of a FontDialog control, the following statement calls its `ShowDialog` method:

```
fdFont.ShowDialog()
```

By default, the *Font* dialog box does not allow the user to select a color. Color is controlled by the FontDialog control's ShowColor property, which can be set to *True* or *False*. When set to *True*, the *Font* dialog box appears with a *Color* drop-down list, shown on the right in Figure 9-24.

The `ShowDialog` method returns one of the values `Windows.Forms.DialogResult.OK` or `Windows.Forms.DialogResult.Cancel` indicating which button, *OK* or *Cancel*, the user clicked to dismiss the dialog box. The Font property will hold a value representing the font settings selected by the user. The Color property will hold a value representing the color selected by the user. For example, the following code displays the *Font* dialog box and then sets the `lblMessage` control's font to that selected by the user.

```
If fdFont.ShowDialog() = Windows.Forms.DialogResult.OK Then
  lblTest.Font = fdFont.Font
End If
```

The following code displays a *Font* dialog box with a drop-down list of colors. It then sets the `lblMessage` control's font and color to the values selected by the user.

```
fdFont.ShowColor = True
If fdFont.ShowDialog() = Windows.Forms.DialogResult.OK Then
  lblTest.Font = fdFont.Font
  lblTest.ForeColor = fdFont.Color
End If
```

Checkpoint

9.9 Why is it a good idea to use the *Open* and *Save As* dialog boxes in applications that work with files?

9.10 What is the purpose of the following OpenFileDialog and SaveFileDialog properties?

Filter
InitialDirectory
Title
Filename

9.11 Suppose you want an *Open* dialog box to have the following filters: text files (**.txt*), Microsoft Word files (**.doc*), and all files (*.*). What string would you store in the Filter property?

9.12 When the user selects a color with the *Color* dialog box, where is the color value stored?

9.13 When the user selects font settings with the *Font* dialog box, where are the font setting values stored?

9.14 How do you display a *Font* dialog box with a drop-down list of colors?

9.15 When the user selects a color with the *Font* dialog box, where is the color value stored?

The PrintDocument Control

CONCEPT: **The PrintDocument control allows you to print data to the printer.**

The **PrintDocument control** gives your application the ability to print output on the printer. Double-click the *PrintDocument* tool in the Printing section of the *Toolbox* window to place a PrintDocument control on a form. Because the control is invisible at runtime, it appears in the component tray at design time. We will use the prefix `pd` when naming the control.

The `Print` Method and the `PrintPage` Event

The PrintDocument control has a **`Print` method** that starts the printing process. The method's general format is as follows:

```
PrintDocumentControl.Print()
```

When the `Print` method is called, it triggers a `PrintPage` event. You must write code in the `PrintPage` event handler to initiate the actual printing. To create a `PrintPage` event handler code template, double-click the PrintDocument control in the component tray. The following is an example:

```
Private Sub pdPrint_PrintPage(ByVal sender As System.Object, _
     ByVal e As System.Drawing.Printing.PrintPageEventArgs) _
     Handles pdPrint.PrintPage
End Sub
```

Inside the **`PrintPage` event handler**, you can write code that sends text to the printer using a specified font and color, at a specified location. We will use the following general format to call the `e.Graphics.DrawString` method:

```
e.Graphics.DrawString(String, New Font(FontName, Size, _
     Style), Brushes.Black, HPos, VPos)
```

`String` is the string to be printed. *`FontName`* is a string holding the name of the font to use. *`Size`* is the size of the font in points. *`Style`* is the font style. Valid values are `FontStyle.Bold`, `FontStyle.Italic`, `FontStyle.Regular`, `FontStyle.Strikeout`, and `FontStyle.Underline`. *`HPos`* is the horizontal position of the output. This is the distance of the output, in points, from the left margin of the paper. *`VPos`* is the vertical position of the output. This is the distance of the output, in points, from the top margin of the paper. The `Brushes.Black` argument specifies that output should be printed in black.

The following `PrintPage` event handler prints the contents of a TextBox control, `txtInput`, in a regular 12 point Times New Roman font. The horizontal and vertical coordinates of the output are 10 and 10.

```
Private Sub pdPrint_PrintPage(ByVal sender As System.Object, _
     ByVal e As System.Drawing.Printing.PrintPageEventArgs) _
     Handles pdPrint.PrintPage

   e.Graphics.DrawString(txtInput.Text, New Font("Times New Roman", _
       12, FontStyle.Regular), Brushes.Black, 10, 10)
End Sub
```

The following `PrintPage` event handler prints the string `"Sales Report"` in a bold 18 point Courier font. The horizontal and vertical coordinates of the output are 150 and 80.

```
Private Sub pdPrint_PrintPage(ByVal sender As System.Object, _
    ByVal e As System.Drawing.Printing.PrintPageEventArgs) _
    Handles pdPrint.PrintPage

  e.Graphics.DrawString("Sales Report", New Font("Courier", 18, _
      FontStyle.Bold), Brushes.Black, 150, 80)
End Sub
```

The following `PrintPage` event handler prints the contents of a file. `strFilename` is a string variable containing the name of the file whose contents are to be printed.

```
Private Sub pdPrint_PrintPage(ByVal sender As System.Object, _
    ByVal e As System.Drawing.Printing.PrintPageEventArgs) _
    Handles pdPrint.PrintPage

  Dim inputFile As StreamReader
  Dim intX As Integer = 10
  Dim intY As Integer = 10
  inputFile = File.OpenText(strFilename)
  Do While inputFile.Peek <> -1
    e.Graphics.DrawString(inputFile.ReadLine, New Font("Courier", _
        10, FontStyle.Regular), Brushes.Black, intX, intY)
    intY += 12
  Loop
  inputFile.Close()
End Sub
```

The variables `intX` and `intY` specify the horizontal and vertical positions of each line of printed output. The statement `intY += 12` inside the loop increases the vertical distance of each line by 12 points from the top of the page. The output is printed in a 10 point font, so there are 2 points of space between each line.

In Tutorial 9-5, you will modify the *Simple Text Editor* application you created in Tutorial 9-4 by adding a *Print* command to the *File* menu.

Tutorial 9-5:
Adding printing capabilities to the *Simple Text Editor* application

Step 1: Open the *Simple Text Editor* project you created in Tutorial 9-4.

Step 2: Add a Print menu item to the *File* menu, as shown in Figure 9-25. Name the `ToolStripMenuItem` object `mnuFilePrint`. Set its Text to *&Print* and its ShortcutKeys property to *Ctrl+P*. Place separator bars above and below the item.

Step 3: Add a PrintDocument control to the form. (The PrintDocument control is under the *Printing* tab in the Toolbox.) Name the control *pdPrint*.

Step 4: Double-click the `pdPrint` control to create a code template for the `pdPrint_PrintPage` event procedure. Complete the event procedure by entering the following code shown in bold:

```
Private Sub pdPrint_PrintPage(ByVal sender As System.Object, _
    ByVal e As System.Drawing.Printing.PrintPageEventArgs) _
    Handles pdPrint.PrintPage

  ' Print the contents of the text box.
  e.Graphics.DrawString(txtDocument.Text, _
    New Font("MS Sans Serif", 12, _
    FontStyle.Regular), Brushes.Black, 10, 10)
End Sub
```

Figure 9-25 Print menu item and separator bars added

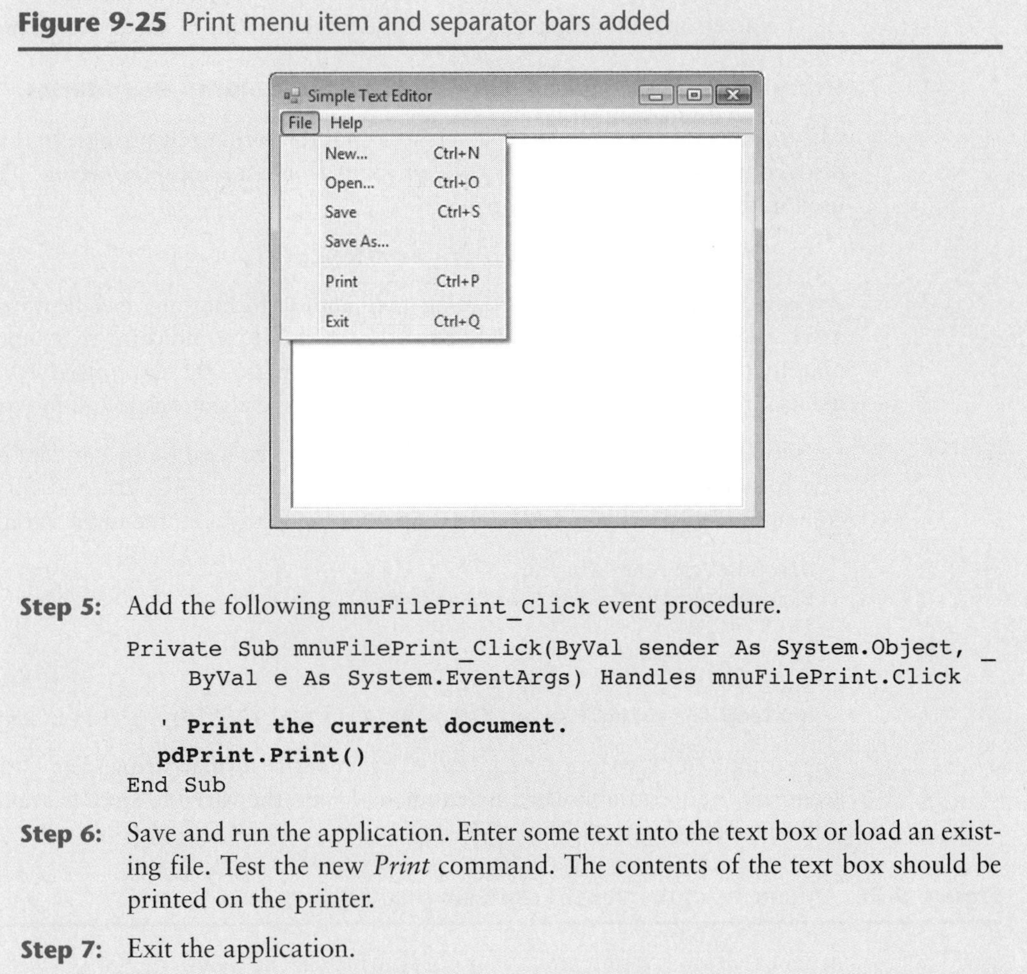

Step 5: Add the following `mnuFilePrint_Click` event procedure.

```
Private Sub mnuFilePrint_Click(ByVal sender As System.Object, _
    ByVal e As System.EventArgs) Handles mnuFilePrint.Click

  ' Print the current document.
  pdPrint.Print()
End Sub
```

Step 6: Save and run the application. Enter some text into the text box or load an existing file. Test the new *Print* command. The contents of the text box should be printed on the printer.

Step 7: Exit the application.

Formatted Reports with `String.Format`

Reports typically contain the following sections:

- A **report header**, printed first, contains the name of the report, the date and time the report was printed, and other general information about the data in the report.
- The **report body** contains the report's data and is often formatted in columns.
- An optional **report footer** contains the sum of one or more columns of data.

Printing Reports with Columnar Data

Report data is typically printed in column format, with each column having an appropriate heading. To properly align printed data in columns, you can use a monospaced font to ensure that all characters occupy the same amount of space, and use the `String.Format` method to format the data into columns. Let's take a closer look at each of these topics.

Monospaced Fonts

Most printers normally use proportionally spaced fonts such as MS sans serif. In a proportionally spaced font, the amount of space occupied by a character depends on the width of the character. For example, the letters *m* and *w* occupy more space than the letters *i* and *j*. Using proportionally spaced fonts, you may have trouble aligning data properly in columns. To remedy the problem, you can select a monospaced font such as Courier New. All characters in a monospaced font use the same amount of space on the printed page.

Using `String.Format` to Align Data along Column Boundaries

The `String.Format` method is a versatile tool for formatting strings. In this section, we discuss how to use the method to align data along column boundaries. The method is used in the following general format:

```
String.Format(FormatString, Arg0, Arg1 [,...])
```

`FormatString` is a string containing text and/or formatting specifications. *`Arg0`* and *`Arg1`* are values to be formatted. The `[,...]` notation indicates that more arguments may follow. The method returns a string that contains the data provided by the arguments *`Arg0`*, *`Arg1`*, and so on, formatted with the specifications found in *`FormatString`*.

Let's look at an example of how *`FormatString`* can be used to format data into columns. The following code produces a string with the numbers 10, 20, and 30 aligned into columns of ten characters wide each. The resulting string is stored in the variable `strTemp`.

```
Dim strTemp As String
Dim intX, intY, intZ As Integer
intX = 10
intY = 20
intZ = 30
strTemp = String.Format("{0, 10} {1, 10} {2, 10} ", intX, intY, intZ)
```

The string `"{0, 10} {1, 10} {2, 10} "` is the format string. The variable `intX` is argument 0, the variable `intY` is argument 1, and the variable `intZ` is argument 2. This is illustrated in Figure 9-26.

Figure 9-26 Arguments of the `String.Format` method

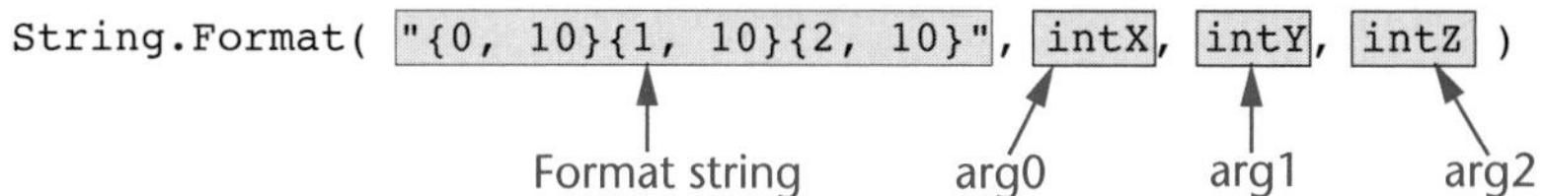

The contents of the format string specify how the data is to be formatted. In our example, the string has three sets of numbers inside curly braces. The first set is `{0, 10}`. This specifies that argument `0` (the variable `intX`) is to be placed in a column ten spaces wide. The second set is `{1, 10}`. This specifies that argument `1` (the variable `intY`) is to be placed in a column ten spaces wide. The third set, `{2, 10}`, specifies that argument `2` (the variable `intZ`) is to be placed in a column ten spaces wide. Figure 9-27 labels all these parts. There are no spaces between the sets.

Figure 9-27 Format specifications

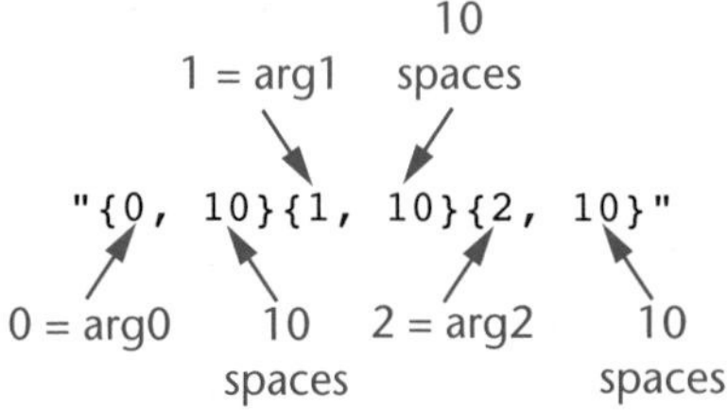

After the last statement in the previous code executes, the variable `strTemp` contains the string `"        10        20        30"`. The numbers are placed in columns of ten spaces each, as illustrated in Figure 9-28. In our example, the numbers are right justified inside the columns. If you use a negative value for a column width in the format string, the column is left justified. For example, using the variables `intX`, `intY`, and `intZ` from the previous code example, the method call

```
String.Format("{0, -10} {1, -10} {2, -10} ", intX, intY, intZ)
```

produces the string `"10        20        30        "`.

Let's examine a code sample that prints a sales report with a header, two columns of data, and a footer. The data is printed from the following parallel arrays:

```
Dim strNames As String() = {"John Smith", "Jill McKenzie", _
                            "Karen Suttles", "Jason Mabry", _
                            "Susan Parsons"}
Dim decSales As Decimal() = {2500.0, 3400.0, 4200.0, _
                             2200.0, 3100.0}
```

Figure 9-28 Column widths

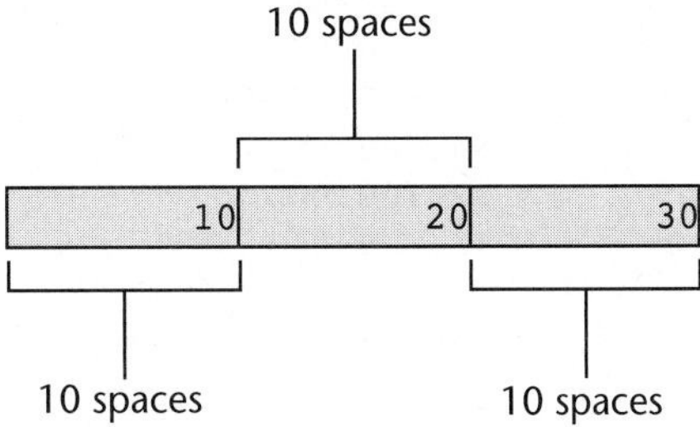

The `strNames` array contains five salespeople's names and the `decSales` array contains each salesperson's sales. The `For...Next` loop in the following event handler prints each line of data and uses an accumulator, `decTotal`, to sum the sales amounts. The contents of `decTotal` are printed in the footer to show the total sales.

```
Private Sub pdPrint_PrintPage(ByVal sender As System.Object, _
  ByVal e As System.Drawing.Printing.PrintPageEventArgs) _
  Handles pdPrint.PrintPage

  Dim intCount As Integer         ' Loop counter
  Dim decTotal As Decimal = 0     ' Accumulator
  Dim intVertPosition As Integer ' Vertical printing position

  ' Print the report header.
  e.Graphics.DrawString("Sales Report", New Font("Courier New", 12, _
      FontStyle.Bold), Brushes.Black, 150, 10)
  e.Graphics.DrawString("Date and Time: " & Now.ToString(), _
      New Font("Courier New", 12, FontStyle.Bold), _
      Brushes.Black, 10, 38)

  ' Print the column headings.
  e.Graphics.DrawString(String.Format("{ 0, 20} { 1, 20} ", _
      "NAME", "SALES"), New Font("Courier New", 12, _
      FontStyle.Bold), Brushes.Black, 10, 66)
```

```
    ' Print the body of the report.
    intVertPosition = 82
    For intCount = 0 To 4
      e.Graphics.DrawString(String.Format("{ 0, 20} { 1, 20} ", _
        strNames(intCount), decSales(intCount).ToString("c")), _
        New Font("Courier New", 12, _
        FontStyle.Regular), Brushes.Black, 10, _
        intVertPosition)
      decTotal += decSales(intCount)
      intVertPosition += 14
    Next intCount

    ' Print the report footer.
    e.Graphics.DrawString("Total Sales: " & decTotal.ToString("c"), _
        New Font("Courier New", 12, FontStyle.Bold), _
        Brushes.Black, 150, 165)
End Sub
```

The report printed by this code appears similar to the following:

```
                Sales Report

Date and Time: 10/14/2009 11:12:34 AM

                Name           Sales
          John Smith       $2,500.00
        Jill McKenzie      $3,400.00
        Karen Suttles      $4,200.00
          Jason Mabry      $2,200.00
        Susan Parsons      $3,100.00

          Total Sales: $15,400.00
```

Checkpoint

9.16 How do you trigger a PrinterDocument control's `PrintPage` event?

9.17 Assume an application has a PrintDocument control named `pdPrint`. Write a statement in the control's PrintPage event handler that prints your first and last name in an 18 point bold MS sans serif font. Print your name at 100 points from the page's left margin and 20 points from the page's top margin.

9.18 Name the three sections most reports have.

9.19 What is the difference between a proportionally spaced font and a monospaced font?

9.20 Assume that an application has a PrintDocument control named *pdPrint*. Write a statement in the control's PrintPage event procedure that prints the contents of the variables `a` and `b` in a 12 point regular Courier New font. The contents of `a` should be printed in a column 12 characters wide, and the contents of `b` should be printed in a column 8 characters wide. Print the data 10 points from the page's left margin and 50 points from the page's top margin.

9.21 Rewrite the answer you wrote to Checkpoint 9.20 so the contents of the variable `a` are left justified.

9.4 Structures

CONCEPT: Visual Basic allows you to create your own data types, into which you may group multiple data fields.

So far you have created applications that keep data in individual variables. If you need to group items, you can create arrays. Arrays, however, require elements to be of the same data type. Sometimes a relationship exists between items of different types. For example, a payroll system might use the variables shown in the following declaration statements:

```
Dim intEmpNumber As Integer       ' Employee number
Dim strFirstName As String        ' Employee's first name
Dim strLastName As String         ' Employee's last name
Dim sngHours As Single            ' Number of hours worked
Dim decPayRate As Decimal         ' Hourly pay rate
Dim decGrossPay As Decimal        ' Gross pay
```

All these variables are related because they can hold data about the same employee. The `Dim` statements, however, create separate variables and do not establish relationships.

Instead of creating separate variables that hold related data, you can group the related data. A **structure** is a data type you can create that contains one or more variables known as fields. The fields can be of different data types. Once a structure has been created, variables of the structure may be declared.

You create a structure at the class- or module-level with the **`Structure`** statement:

```
[AccessSpecifier] Structure StructureName
  FieldDeclarations
End Structure
```

`AccessSpecifier` is shown in brackets, indicating that it is optional. If you use the `Public` access specifier, the structure is accessible to statements outside the class or module. If you use the `Private` access specifier, the structure is accessible only to statements in the same class or module. *`StructureName`* is the name of the structure. *`FieldDeclarations`* is one or more declarations of fields, as regular `Dim` statements. The following is an example:

```
Structure EmpPayData
  Dim intEmpNumber As Integer
  Dim strFirstName As String
  Dim strLastName As String
  Dim sngHours As Single
  Dim decPayRate As Decimal
  Dim decGrossPay As Decimal
End Structure
```

This statement declares a structure named `EmpPayData`, having six fields.

TIP: Structure names and class names should begin with uppercase letters. This serves as a visual reminder that the structure or class name is not a variable name.

> **TIP:** If you want a structure to be available to multiple forms in a project, place the `Structure` statement, with the `Public` access specifier, in a standard module.

The `Structure` statement does not create a variable—it creates a new data type by telling Visual Basic what the data type contains. You declare variables of a structure using `Dim` statements, just as you would with any other data type. For example, the following statement declares a variable called `deptHead` as an `EmpPayData` variable:

```
Dim deptHead As EmpPayData
```

The `deptHead` variable can store six values because the `EmpPayData` data type is made of six fields, as illustrated in Figure 9-29.

Access the fields with the dot operator. For example, the following statements assign values to all six fields of the `deptHead` variable.

```
deptHead.intEmpNumber = 1101
deptHead.strFirstName = "Joanne"
deptHead.strLastName = "Smith"
deptHead.sngHours = 40
deptHead.decPayRate = 25
deptHead.decGrossPay = CDec(deptHead.sngHours) * _
     deptHead.decPayRate
```

Figure 9-29 `deptHead` variable

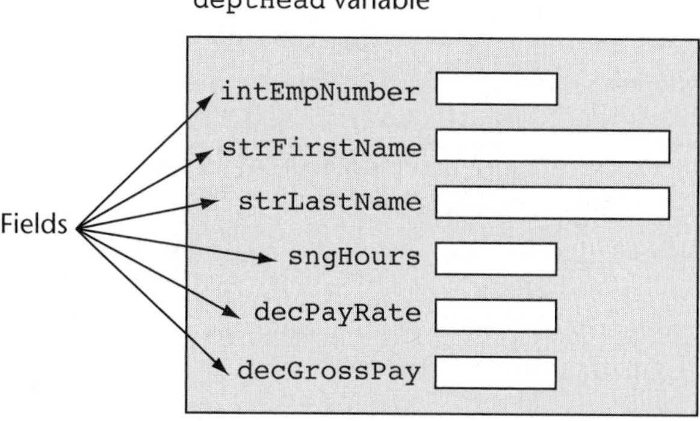

The following statement adds the `intEmpNumber` field to the `lstEmployeeList` list box:

```
lstEmployeeList.Items.Add(deptHead.intEmpNumber)
```

You can optionally use the `With` statement to simplify access to structure fields:

```
With deptHead
   .intEmpNumber = 1101
   .strFirstName = "Joanne"
   .strLastName = "Smith"
   .sngHours = 40
   .decPayRate = 25
   .decGrossPay = CDec(.sngHours) * .decPayRate
End With
```

Passing Structure Variables to Procedures and Functions

You may pass structure variables to procedures and functions. For example, the following procedure declares an `EmpPayData` parameter, passed by reference:

```
Sub CalcPay(ByRef employee As EmpPayData)
   ' This procedure accepts an EmpPayData variable
   ' as its argument. The employee's gross pay
   ' is calculated and stored in the grossPay
   ' field.
   With employee
      .decGrossPay = .sngHours * .decPayRate
   End With
End Sub
```

Arrays as Structure Members

Structures can contain array fields, but the arrays cannot be assigned initial sizes. An example is shown in the following statement:

```
Structure StudentRecord
   Dim strName As String
   Dim sngTestScores() As Single
End Structure
```

After declaring a structure variable, you can use the `ReDim` statement to establish a size for the array. Then you access the array elements with a subscript, as shown in the following example:

```
Dim student As StudentRecord
ReDim student.sngTestScores(4)
student.strName = "Mary McBride"
student.sngTestScores(0) = 89
student.sngTestScores(1) = 92
student.sngTestScores(2) = 84
student.sngTestScores(3) = 96
student.sngTestScores(4) = 91
```

Arrays of Structures

You may also declare an array of structures. For example, the following statement declares `employees` as an array of 10 `EmpPayData` variables:

```
Dim employees(9) As EmpPayData
```

To access the individual elements in the array, use a subscript as shown in the following statement:

```
employees(0).intEmpNumber = 1101
```

When working with an array of structure variables in which the structure contains an array field, use the `ReDim` statement to establish a size for the array field of each element. For example, the `StudentRecord` discussed in the previous section has a field named `sngTestScores`, which is an array of five numbers. Suppose an application declares an array of `StudentRecord` variables as follows:

```
Dim students(9) As StudentRecord
```

A loop, such as the following, can be used to set a size for each `testScores` array:

```
For intIndex = 0 To 9
  ReDim students(intIndex).testScores(4)
Next intIndex
```

You can use the array fields once they have been given a size. For example, the following statement stores 95 in `sngTestScores(0)` inside `students(5)`:

```
students(5).sngTestScores(0) = 95
```

Tutorial 9-6 examines an application that uses a structure.

Tutorial 9-6:
Examining an application with a structure

In this tutorial, you examine a modified version of the *File WriteLine Demo* project from Tutorial 9-1. This version of the project uses a structure to store the friend data.

Step 1: Open the *Structure File WriteLine Demo* project from the student sample programs folder named *Chap9\Structure File WriteLine Demo.*

Step 2: Open the *Code* window. The following statements declare the `FriendInfo` structure:

```
' Declare a structure to hold friend information.
Structure FriendInfo
  Dim strName As String                    ' To hold a name
  Dim intAge As Integer                    ' To hold an age
  Dim strAddress As String                 ' To hold an address
End Structure
```

Step 3: Look at the `btnCreateFile_Click` event handler. The procedure uses the structure variable `myFriend` to hold the names, ages, and addresses entered by the user. The `WriteLine` statement writes the contents of the structure variable's fields to the file.

```
Private Sub btnCreateFile_Click(ByVal sender As System.Object, _
    ByVal e As System.EventArgs) Handles btnCreateFile.Click

  ' This procedure prompts the user for data and
  ' saves it to a file.
  Dim strFilename As String       ' File name
  Dim intCount As Integer         ' Loop counter
  Dim myFriend As FriendInfo      ' Structure variable
  Dim friendFile As StreamWriter  ' Object variable

  ' Get the file name from the user.
  strFilename = InputBox("Enter the filename.", _
      "Filename Needed")

  ' Open the file.
  friendFile = File.CreateText(strFilename)

  ' Get the data for three friends and write it
  ' to the file.
  For intCount = 1 To intNUM_FRIENDS
```

```
        ' Get the data.
        MessageBox.Show("Get ready to enter data for friend " & _
            intCount.ToString())
        myFriend.strName = InputBox("Enter your friend's name.")
        myFriend.intAge = CInt(InputBox("Enter your friend's _
            age."))
        myFriend.strAddress = InputBox("Enter your friend's _
            address.")

        ' Write the data to the file.
        friendFile.WriteLine(myFriend.strName)
        friendFile.WriteLine(myFriend.intAge)
        friendFile.WriteLine(myFriend.strAddress)
      Next intCount

      ' Close the file.
      friendFile.Close()
    End Sub
```

Step 4: Run the application and, as you did in Tutorial 9-1, click the *Save Data to File* button. Enter a filename and data for three of your friends. The procedure saves the data.

Step 5: Exit the application.

Checkpoint

9.22 Write a statement that declares a structure named `Movie`. The structure should have fields to hold the following data about a movie.

The name of the movie
The director of the movie
The producer of the movie
The year the movie was released

9.23 Write a statement that declares a variable of the `Movie` structure that you created in Checkpoint 9.22.

9.24 Write statements that store the following data in the variable you declared in Checkpoint 9.23. (Do not use the `With` statement.)

The name of the movie: *Wheels of Fury*
The director of the movie: *Arlen McGoo*
The producer of the movie: *Vincent Van Dough*
The year the movie was released: *2008*

9.25 Rewrite the statements you wrote in Checkpoint 9.24 using the `With` statement.

9.5 Focus on Problem Solving: Modifying the *Demetris Leadership Center* Application

In Chapter 8, you created a sales reporting application for the Demetris Leadership Center. The application prompts the user to enter the number of units sold of each product and displays a sales report showing the revenue from each product and the total revenue from all products sold. In this section, you modify the application as follows:

- Replace the parallel arrays with a single array of structure variables
- Add commands to save the units sold to a file, and retrieve previously saved data
- Add a command to print the sales report

The Structure

In the original version of this application, we used parallel arrays to hold the product names, descriptions, product numbers, prices, and units sold. In this exercise, you will replace the arrays with the following structure and array declarations:

```
Structure ProductData
   Dim strName As String          ' Product name
   Dim strDesc As String          ' Description
   Dim intProdNum As Integer      ' Product number
   Dim decPrice As Decimal        ' Unit price
   Dim intUnitsSold As Integer    ' Units sold
End Structure
' Array upper subscript
Const intMAX_SUBSCRIPT As Integer = 8
' Array of ProductData
Dim products(intMAX_SUBSCRIPT) As ProductData
```

The New Menu Items

The application's *File* menu currently has one item: *Exit*. You will add the following four new items to the *File* menu: *Open File*, *Save As*, *Clear Sales Figures*, and *Print Sales Report*. The menu with the new items inserted is shown in Figure 9-30. Notice that three separator bars are also added.

Figure 9-30 File menu with new items

Open File...	Ctrl+O
Save As...	Ctrl+S
Clear Sales Figures	Ctrl+C
Print Sales Report	Ctrl+P
Exit	Ctrl+Q

Table 9-2 lists the new menu controls with their Text and Shortcut keys.

Table 9-2 New menu controls

Name	Text	Shortcut Key
mnuFileOpen	&Open File	Ctrl+O
mnuFileSaveAs	&Save As	Ctrl+S
mnuFileClear	C&lear Sales Figures	Ctrl+C
mnuFilePrint	&Print Sales Report	Ctrl+P

You will also add the procedures described in Table 9-3 to the `frmMain` module.

Table 9-3 New procedures for `frmMain`

Method	Description
`mnuFileOpen_Click`	Uses an OpenFileDialog control to display an Open dialog box. The filename selected by the user passed to the `ReadFile` procedure.
`mnuFileSaveSaveAs_Click`	Uses a SaveFileDialog control to display a Save As dialog box. The user selects or enters a filename, which is passed to the `SaveFile` procedure.
`mnuFileClear_Click`	Sets the `intUnitsSold` field of each element of the `products` array to 0, clears the contents of the `lstSalesData` list box, and clears the contents of the `lblTotalRevenue` control.
`mnuFilePrint_Click`	Uses the `PrintDocument` control to print a sales report that shows the revenue of each product and the total revenue.
`ReadFile`	Accepts a filename as its argument. The file is opened and its contents are read into the `intUnitsSold` fields of the structure variables in the `products` array.
`SaveFile`	Accepts a filename as its argument. The file is opened and the contents of the `intUnitsSold` fields of the elements in the `products` array are written to it.

In Tutorial 9-7, you modify the *Demetris Leadership Center Sales Reporting* application.

Tutorial 9-7:
Modifying the *Demetris Leadership Center Sales Reporting* application

Step 1: Open the *Demetris Leadership Center Sales Reporting* application you created in Tutorial 8-8 in Chapter 8.

Step 2: Add the following controls to the `frmMain` form:

- An OpenFileDialog control named `ofdOpenFile`.
- A SaveFileDialog control named `sfdSaveFile`.
- A PrintDocument control named `pdPrint`.

Step 3: The current version of this application has the following class-level array declarations:

```
Dim strProdNames(intMAX_SUBSCRIPT) As String  ' Product names
Dim strDesc(intMAX_SUBSCRIPT) As String       ' Descriptions
Dim intProdNums(intMAX_SUBSCRIPT) As Integer  ' Product numbers
Dim decPrices(intMAX_SUBSCRIPT) As Decimal    ' Unit prices
Dim intUnitsSold(intMAX_SUBSCRIPT) As Integer ' Units sold
```

Replace the foregoing lines with the following statements that declare a `ProductData` structure and create an array of `ProductData`, named `products`:

```
Structure ProductData
   Dim strName As String                      ' Product name
   Dim strDesc As String                      ' Description
   Dim intProdNum As Integer                  ' Product number
   Dim decPrice As Decimal                    ' Unit price
   Dim intUnitsSold As Integer                ' Units sold
End Structure

' Array of ProductData
Dim products(intMAX_SUBSCRIPT) As ProductData
```

Step 4: The `InitArrays` procedure initializes the parallel arrays. Modify it to initialize the product array instead. The new code follows:

```
Private Sub InitArrays()
   ' Initialize the arrays.
   ' First product
   products(0).strName = "Six Steps to Leadership"
   products(0).strDesc = "Book"
   products(0).intProdNum = 914
   products(0).decPrice = 12.95D

   ' Second product
   products(1).strName = "Six Steps to Leadership"
   products(1).strDesc = "CD"
   products(1).intProdNum = 915
   products(1).decPrice = 14.95D

   ' Third product
   products(2).strName = "The Road to Excellence"
   products(2).strDesc = "Video"
   products(2).intProdNum = 916
   products(2).decPrice = 18.95D

   ' Fourth product
   products(3).strName = "Seven Lessons of Quality"
   products(3).strDesc = "Book"
   products(3).intProdNum = 917
   products(3).decPrice = 16.95D

   ' Fifth product
   products(4).strName = "Seven Lessons of Quality"
   products(4).strDesc = "CD"
   products(4).intProdNum = 918
   products(4).decPrice = 21.95D

   ' Sixth product
   products(5).strName = "Seven Lessons of Quality"
   products(5).strDesc = "Video"
```

```
    products(5).intProdNum = 919D
    products(5).decPrice = 31.95

    ' Seventh product
    products(6).strName = "Teams Are Made, Not Born"
    products(6).strDesc = "Book"
    products(6).intProdNum = 920
    products(6).decPrice = 14.95D

    ' Eighth product
    products(7).strName = "Leadership for the Future"
    products(7).strDesc = "Book"
    products(7).intProdNum = 921
    products(7).decPrice = 14.95D

    ' Ninth product
    products(8).strName = "Leadership for the Future"
    products(8).strDesc = "CD"
    products(8).intProdNum = 922
    products(8).decPrice = 16.95D
End Sub
```

Step 5: Modify the `mnuReportData_Click` event procedure so it stores the user's input in the `products` array. The procedure follows, with the modified code shown in bold:

```
Private Sub mnuReportData_Click(ByVal sender As System.Object, _
    ByVal e As System.EventArgs) Handles mnuReportData.Click

    ' Prompt the user for sales data
    Dim intCount As Integer                         ' Loop counter

    ' Get unit sales for each product
    For intCount = 0 To intMAX_SUBSCRIPT

        Dim strTemp As String = InputBox( _
          "Enter units sold of product number " _
          & products(intCount).intProdNum, "Enter Sales Data")

        Integer.TryParse(strTemp, products(intCount).intUnitsSold)

    Next intCount
End Sub
```

Step 6: Modify the `mnuReportDisplay_Click` event procedure so it displays data in the `products` array. The procedure follows, with the modified code shown in bold:

```
Private Sub mnuReportDisplay_Click(ByVal sender As _
    System.Object, ByVal e As System.EventArgs) Handles _
    mnuReportDisplay.Click

    ' Calculates and displays the revenue for each
    ' product and the total revenue.
    Dim intCount As Integer
    Dim decRevenue As Decimal
    Dim decTotalRevenue As Decimal

    ' Display the sales report header.
    lstSalesData.Items.Add("SALES REPORT")
    lstSalesData.Items.Add("-----------")
    ' Display sales data for each product.
    For intCount = 0 To intMAX_SUBSCRIPT
```

```
        ' Calculate product revenue.
        decRevenue = products(intCount).intUnitsSold _
          * products(intCount).decPrice
        ' Display the product data.
        lstSalesData.Items.Add("Product Number: " _
          & products(intCount).intProdNum)
        lstSalesData.Items.Add("Name: " _
          & products(intCount).strName)
        lstSalesData.Items.Add("Description: " _
          & products(intCount).strDesc)
        lstSalesData.Items.Add("Unit Price: " _
          & products(intCount).decPrice.ToString("c"))
        lstSalesData.Items.Add("Units Sold: " _
          & products(intCount).intUnitsSold.ToString())
        lstSalesData.Items.Add("Product Revenue: " _
          & decRevenue.ToString("c"))
        lstSalesData.Items.Add(String.Empty)
        ' Accumulate revenue.
        decTotalRevenue = decTotalRevenue + decRevenue
    Next intCount

    ' Display total revenue.
    lblTotalRevenue.Text = decTotalRevenue.ToString("c")
End Sub
```

Step 7: In the *Design* window, select the MenuStrip control and add the menu items listed in Table 9-2 to the *File* menu. Refer to Figure 9-30 for each control's position.

Step 8: Add the `mnuFileOpen_Click` and `mnuFileSaveAs_Click` event procedures. The code follows:

```
Private Sub mnuFileOpen_Click(ByVal sender As System.Object, _
      ByVal e As System.EventArgs) Handles mnuFileOpen.Click

    ' Let the user select a file to open. Pass the
    ' selected filename to the ReadFile procedure.
    With ofdOpenFile
        .Filter = "Text Files (*.txt)|*.txt|All Files (*.*)|*.*"
        .Title = "Select a File to Open"
        If .ShowDialog = Windows.Forms.DialogResult.OK Then
            If .FileName <> String.Empty Then
                ReadFile(.FileName)
            Else
                MessageBox.Show("No file selected.", "Error")
            End If
        End If
    End With
End Sub

Private Sub mnuFileSaveAs_Click(ByVal sender As _
        System.Object, ByVal e As System.EventArgs) _
        Handles mnuFileSaveAs.Click

    ' Let the user select or enter a file name to save the
    ' data to. Pass the file name to the SaveFile procedure.

    With sfdSaveFile
        .Filter = "Text Files (*.txt)|*.txt|All Files (*.*)|*.*"
        .Title = "Save File As"
```

```
        If .ShowDialog = Windows.Forms.DialogResult.OK Then
            If .FileName <> String.Empty Then
                SaveFile(.FileName)
            Else
                MessageBox.Show("File not saved.", "Error")
            End If
        End If
    End With
End Sub
```

Step 9: Add the `mnuFileClear_Click` event procedure. The code follows:

```
Private Sub mnuFileClear_Click(ByVal sender As System.Object, _
        ByVal e As System.EventArgs) Handles mnuFileClear.Click

    ' Clear sales data from the list box and total revenue
    ' label, and sets each product's unitSold field to zero.

    Dim intCount As Integer   ' loop counter
    ' Clear the list box.
    lstSalesData.Items.Clear()
    ' Clear the total revenue label.
    lblTotalRevenue.Text = String.Empty

    ' Clear the unitsSold array.
    For intCount = 0 To intMAX_SUBSCRIPT
        products(intCount).intUnitsSold = 0
    Next
End Sub
```

Step 10: Add the `mnuFilePrint_Click` event procedure. The code follows:

```
Private Sub mnuFilePrint_Click(ByVal sender As System.Object, _
        ByVal e As System.EventArgs) Handles mnuFilePrint.Click

    ' Call the Print method to start printing.
    pdPrint.Print()
End Sub
```

Step 11: In the *Design* window, double-click the `pdPrint` control to create a code template for the `pdPrint_PrintPage` event procedure. Complete the procedure as follows:

```
Private Sub pdPrint_PrintPage(ByVal sender As System.Object, _
        ByVal e As System.Drawing.Printing.PrintPageEventArgs) _
        Handles pdPrint.PrintPage

    ' This procedure prints the sales report.
    Dim intCount As Integer          ' Loop counter
    Dim decRevenue As Decimal
    Dim decTotalRevenue As Decimal
    Dim intVertPos As Integer
    Dim strFormat As String = "{0,-27}{1,15}{2,10}{3,8}{4,12}{5,10}"

    ' Print the report header.
    e.Graphics.DrawString("Demetris Leadership Center " _
        & "Sales Report", New Font("Courier New", 10, _
        FontStyle.Bold), Brushes.Black, 150, 10)
    e.Graphics.DrawString("Date and Time: " & Now.ToString(), _
        New Font("Courier New", 10, FontStyle.Bold), _
        Brushes.Black, 10, 38)
```

```
    ' Print the column headings.
    e.Graphics.DrawString(String.Format(strFormat, "Product", _
        "Desc", "Prod Num", "Price", "Units Sold", _
        "Revenue"), New Font("Courier New", 10, _
      FontStyle.Bold), Brushes.Black, 10, 66)

    ' Set the vertical position for the first item.
    intVertPos = 96

    ' Print sales data for each product.
    For intCount = 0 To intMAX_SUBSCRIPT
      ' Calculate the unit revenue.
      decRevenue = products(intCount).intUnitsSold _
        * products(intCount).decPrice
      ' Accumulate the total decRevenue.
      decTotalRevenue += decRevenue
      ' Print the unit data.
      e.Graphics.DrawString(String.Format(strFormat, _
          products(intCount).strName, _
          products(intCount).strDesc, _
          products(intCount).intProdNum, _
          products(intCount).decPrice.ToString("c"), _
          products(intCount).intUnitsSold, _
          decRevenue.ToString("c"), _
          New Font("Courier New", 10, FontStyle.Regular), _
          Brushes.Black, 10, intVertPos)
      intVertPos += 14
    Next intCount

    ' Print the report footer.
    intVertPos += 14
  ' leave a blank line
    e.Graphics.DrawString("Total Revenue: " & _
        decTotalRevenue.ToString("c"), _
        New Font("Courier New", 10, _
        FontStyle.Bold), Brushes.Black, 150, intVertPos)
End Sub
```

Step 12: The `ReadFile` procedure opens the input file identified by the `strFilename` parameter. In its `Do While` loop, it uses an `If` statement to call the `TryParse` method when reading the `intUnitsSold` values. If the user has selected the wrong input file, or the file data is not in the correct order, a message box will inform the user and exit the loop. Without this type of error checking, the program could stop with a runtime error if the data in the input file is incorrect. Here is the `ReadFile` procedure:

```
Sub ReadFile(ByVal strFilename As String)

    ' Read the contents of the specified file
    ' into the unitsSold array.
    Dim inputFile As System.IO.StreamReader
    Dim intCount As Integer = 0        ' Loop counter

    ' Open the file.
    inputFile = System.IO.File.OpenText(strFilename)
    ' Read the data.
    Do While (inputFile.Peek <> -1) And _
         (intCount <= intMAX_SUBSCRIPT)
```

```
        If Integer.TryParse(inputFile.ReadLine, _
          products(intCount).intUnitsSold) = False Then
          MessageBox.Show("The data file appears to be", _
            in the wrong format", strFilename)
          Exit Do
        End If
        intCount += 1
      Loop
      ' Close the file.
      inputFile.Close()
    End Sub
```

Here is the `SaveFile` procedure:

```
Sub SaveFile(ByVal strFilename As String)

  ' Save the contents of the unitsSold array.
  Dim outputFile As System.IO.StreamWriter
  Dim intCount As Integer   ' Loop counter

  ' Open the file.
  outputFile = System.IO.File.CreateText(strFilename)
  ' Save the data.
  For intCount = 0 To intMAX_SUBSCRIPT
    outputFile.WriteLine(products(intCount).intUnitsSold)
  Next
  ' Close the file.
  outputFile.Close()
End Sub
```

Step 13: Save the project.

Step 14: Run the application. The splash screen should appear. It should automatically close after five seconds.

Step 15: When the main form appears, click the *Report* menu, and then click *Enter Sales Data*. You will be prompted with input boxes to enter the units sold for each of the DLC products. Enter the following values:

Product number 914:	**140**
Product number 915:	**85**
Product number 916:	**129**
Product number 917:	**67**
Product number 918:	**94**
Product number 919:	**142**
Product number 920:	**109**
Product number 921:	**65**
Product number 922:	**43**

Step 16: Click the *Report* menu, and then click *Display Sales Report*. The form should now show the revenue for each product and the total revenue, as shown in Figure 9-31.

Step 17: Click the *File* menu, and then click *Save As*. The *Save As* dialog box should appear. In the *File name* text box enter **`SalesData.txt`**, then click the *Save* button. This saves the units sold numbers to the file SalesData.txt.

Step 18: On the main form, click *File* on the menu strip, and then click *Clear Sales Figures* on the *File* menu. The units sold and revenue for each product, as well as the total revenue, should clear.

Step 19: Click the *File* menu, and then click *Open File*. The *Open* dialog box should appear Select the *SalesData.txt* file and click the *Open* button.

Step 20: Click the *Report* menu, and then click *Display Sales Report*. The form should now show the revenue for each product and the total revenue.

Figure 9-31 Form with sales data shown

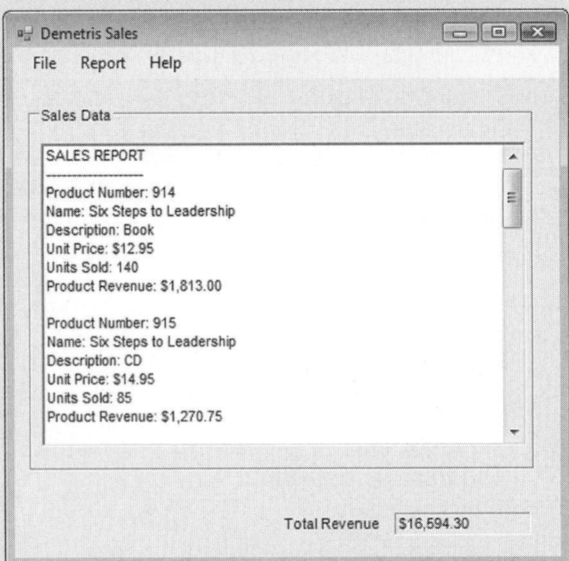

Step 21: Click the *File* menu, and then click *Print Sales Report*. The application should print a report on your printer like the following:

Demetris Leadership Center Sales Report

Date and Time: 9/26/2009 11:32:19 AM

Product	**Desc**	**Prod Num**	**Price**	**Units Sold**	**Revenue**
Six Steps to Leadership	Book	914	$12.95	140	$1,813.00
Six Steps to Leadership	CD	915	$14.95	85	$1,270.75
The Road to Excellence	Video	916	$18.95	129	$2,444.55
Seven Lessons of Quality	Book	917	$16.95	67	$1,135.65
Seven Lessons of Quality	CD	918	$21.95	94	$2,063.30
Seven Lessons of Quality	Video	919	$31.95	142	$4,536.90
Teams Are Made, Not Born	Book	920	$14.95	109	$1,629.55
Leadership for the Future	Book	921	$14.95	65	$971.75
Leadership for the Future	CD	922	$16.95	43	$728.85

Step 22: Exit the application.

Summary

9.1 Using Files

- Data is saved in a file, which is stored on a computer's disk.
- For an application to use a file, the file must be opened (which creates the file if it does not exist), data is either written to the file or read from the file, and the file is closed.
- There are two types of files: text and binary. There are two methods of accessing data in files: sequential-access and random-access.
- When a sequential file is opened, its read position is set to the first item in the file. As data is read, the read position advances through the file.
- The contents of an array are saved to a file using a loop that steps through each element of the array, writing its contents to the file.
- By specifying a namespace with the Imports statement, you can refer to names in that namespace without fully qualifying them.
- The `File.CreateText` method creates a new file or replaces an existing one. The `File.AppendText` method opens a file so more data can be appended to the end of the file. The `File.OpenText` method opens a file for reading.

9.2 The OpenFileDialog, SaveFileDialog, FontDialog, and ColorDialog Controls

- The OpenFileDialog control displays a standard Windows *Open* dialog box. The SaveFileDialog control displays a standard Windows *Save As* dialog box. The ColorDialog control displays a standard Windows *Color* dialog box. The FontDialog control displays a standard Windows *Font* dialog box.

9.3 The PrintDocument Control

- The PrintDocument control allows your application to print output. You write the code that handles the printing in the `PrintPage` event procedure. You trigger a `PrintPage` event by calling the `Print` method. You use the `e.Graphics.DrawString` method to send output to the printer.
- Reports typically have a header, body, and footer.
- To align printed data properly in columns, you must use a monospaced font to ensure that all characters occupy the same amount of space; you use the `String.Format` method to format the data into columns.

9.4 Structures

- A structure is a defined data type that you create, which contains one or more variables known as fields. Fields can be of different data types. You can create a structure with the `Structure` statement. Once you have defined a structure, you may declare instances of it.

9.5 Focus on Problem Solving: Modifying the *Demetris Leadership Center* Application

- This section outlines the process of modifying the *Demetris Leadership Center* application. Originally, it used parallel arrays, and was modified to use a structure.

Key Terms

append
binary files
buffer
`Chr` function
`Close` method
Color dialog box
ColorDialog control
delimiter
file
`File.AppendText` method
`File.Exists` method
`File.OpenText` method
Filename property
Filter property
Font dialog box
FontDialog control
InitialDirectory property
input file
MultiLine property
newline character
Open dialog box
OpenFileDialog control
output file
`Peek` method
`Print` method
PrintDocument control
`PrintPage` event handler
random-access file
`Read` method
read position
`ReadLine` method
`ReadToEnd` method
report body
report footer
report header
Save As dialog box
SaveFileDialog control
sequential-access file
`StreamReader` class
`StreamReader` object
`StreamWriter` class
`StreamWriter` object
structure
`Structure` statement
text file
Title property
`Write` method
`WriteLine` method

Review Questions and Exercises

Fill-in-the-Blank

1. Before a file can be used, it must be ________________.
2. When a file is opened, a ________________ is created, which is a small holding section of memory that data is first written to.
3. When it is finished using a file, an application should always ________________ it.
4. To write data to a sequential file, use a ________________ object.
5. To read data from a sequential file, use a ________________ object.
6. The ________________ method writes a line to a file.
7. The ________________ method reads a line from a file.
8. The ________________ character is a delimiter that marks the end of a line in a file.
9. The ________________ control allows you to print data directly to the printer.
10. You write code that handles printing in the ________________ event procedure.

11. All of the characters printed with a ________________ font occupy the same amount of space.
12. The ________________ control displays an *Open* dialog box for selecting or entering a filename.
13. The ________________ control displays a *Save As* dialog box for selecting or entering a file.
14. The ________________ control displays a *Color* dialog box for selecting a color.
15. The ________________ control displays a *Font* dialog box for selecting a font.
16. A(n) ________________ is a data type that you create, containing one or more variables, which are known as fields.

Multiple Choice

1. Which two types of files are discussed in this chapter?
   a. Real and integer
   b. Microsoft Access and Microsoft Word
   c. Text and binary
   d. Encrypted and decrypted
2. You use this type of object to write data to a file.
   a. `FileWriter`
   b. `OuputFile`
   c. `File`
   d. `StreamWriter`
3. You use this type of object to read data from a file.
   a. `FileReader`
   b. `StreamReader`
   c. `File`
   d. `Inputfile`
4. This method creates a file if it does not exist, and erases the contents of the file if it already exists.
   a. `File.OpenText`
   b. `File.AppendText`
   c. `File.CreateText`
   d. `File.OpenNew`
5. This method creates a file if it does not exist. If it already exists, data written to it will be added to the end of its existing contents.
   a. `File.OpenText`
   b. `File.AppendText`
   c. `File.CreateText`
   d. `File.OpenNew`
6. This statement writes a line of data to a file, terminating it with a newline character.
   a. `WriteLine`
   b. `SaveLine`
   c. `StoreLine`
   d. `Write`

7. This statement writes an item of data to a file, and does not terminate it with a newline character.
   a. `WriteItem`
   b. `SaveItem`
   c. `StoreItem`
   d. `Write`
8. This statement reads a line from a file.
   a. `Read`
   b. `ReadLine`
   c. `GetLine`
   d. `Input`
9. You use this method to detect when the end of a file has been reached.
   a. `End`
   b. `Peek`
   c. `LastItem`
   d. `FileEnd`
10. You use this method to determine if a file exists.
    a. `System.File.Exists`
    b. `IO.Exists`
    c. `File.Exists`
    d. `Exists.File`
11. Assuming that `ofdOpen` is an OpenFileDialog control, the following statement displays the dialog box.
    a. `ofdOpen.Display()`
    b. `Show(ofdOpen)`
    c. `ofdOpen.OpenDialog()`
    d. `ofdOpen.ShowDialog()`
12. This property determines the types of files displayed in an *Open* or a *Save As* dialog box.
    a. FileTypes
    b. Filter
    c. Types
    d. FileDisplay
13. This property determines the directory, or folder first displayed in an *Open* or *Save As* dialog box.
    a. InitialDirectory
    b. InitialFolder
    c. Location
    d. Path
14. When the user selects a file with an *Open* or *Save As* dialog box, the file's path and name are stored in this property.
    a. Filename
    b. PathName
    c. File
    d. Item

15. When a PrintDocument control's `Print` method executes, it triggers this event.
    a. `StartPrint`
    b. `PrintPage`
    c. `PagePrint`
    d. `SendPage`

16. Inside the appropriate PrintDocument event procedure, you use this method to actually send output to the printer.
    a. `e.Graphics.DrawString`
    b. `e.PrintText`
    c. `e.Graphics.SendOutput`
    d. `Print`

17. You can use this method to align data into columns.
    a. `Align`
    b. `Format.Align`
    c. `Format.Column`
    d. `String.Format`

18. This statement allows you to create a data type that contains one or more variables, known as fields.
    a. `UserDefined`
    b. `DataType`
    c. `Structure`
    d. `Fields`

True or False

Indicate whether the following statements are true or false.

1. T F: A file must be opened before it can be used.
2. T F: An input file is a file that a program can write data to.
3. T F: To read a record stored in the middle or at the end of a sequential-access file, an application must read all records in the file before it.
4. T F: The `File.CreateText` method creates a `StreamReader` object and returns a reference to the object.
5. T F: If you specify only a filename when opening a file, Visual Basic will assume the file's location to be the same folder from which the application is running.
6. T F: In addition to separating the contents of a file into lines, the newline character also serves as a delimiter.
7. T F: If you call the `WriteLine` method with no argument, it writes a blank line to the file.
8. T F: A file's read position is set to the end of the file when a file is first opened.
9. T F: The `Peek` method causes the read position to advance by one character.
10. T F: The Title property holds the name of the file the user selected with an *Open* or *Save As* dialog box.
11. T F: You can specify the font to use when sending output to the printer.

12. T F: You must use a proportionally spaced font when aligning data in columns.
13. T F: A structure may hold variables of different data types.
14. T F: `Structure` statements can appear inside a procedure or function.
15. T F: Structures may not contain arrays.
16. T F: You may declare an array of structure variables.

Short Answer

1. What are the three steps that must be taken when a file is used by an application?
2. What happens when you close a file with the `Close` method?
3. What is a file's read position? Where is the read position when a file is first opened for reading?
4. What is the difference between the `WriteLine` method and the `Write` method?
5. What happens when you use the `File.OpenText` method to open a file that does not exist?
6. What has happened when the `Peek` method returns –1?
7. What does the `ReadLine` method return when it reads a blank line?
8. What does the `Read` method return?
9. What is the difference between the `Print` method and the `PagePrint` event procedure?
10. Where must `Structure` statements appear?

What Do You Think?

1. How do you think a file buffer increases system performance?
2. Why should you call the `Peek` method before calling the `ReadLine` method?
3. You are using the `ReadLine` method to read data from a file. After each line is read, it is added to a list box. What error can potentially occur, and how do you prevent it?
4. An application has the forms `frmMain` and `frmGetData`, and the module `MainModule`. You want a structure to be available only to procedures in the `MainModule` module. Where do you place the `Structure` statement, and which access specifier do you use: `Public` or `Private`?
5. Suppose an application properly aligns the contents of a report into columns using the `String.Format` method. But, when the same report is printed on paper, the columns do not align as they should. What is the most likely cause of the problem?

Find the Error

What is wrong with the following code?

1.
```
Dim myFile As System.IO.StreamReader
myFile = File.CreateText("names.txt")
```

2.
```
If Not System.Exists(strFilename) Then
    MessageBox.Show(strFilename & " does not exist.")
End If
```

3.
```
Do Until myFile.Peek = ""
    strInput = myFile.ReadLine()
    lstResults.Items.Add(strInput)
Loop
```

4. (Assume that `ofdOpen` is an OpenFileDialog control.)

```
ofdOpen.Filter = "Text files (*.txt)&*.txt"
```

5. (Assume that `pdPrint` is a PrintDocument control.)

```
Private Sub pdPrint_PrintPage(ByVal sender As System.Object, _
    ByVal e As System.Drawing.Printing.PrintPageEventArgs) _
    Handles pdPrint.PrintPage
    pdPrint.Print("Hello World!", New Font("Times New Roman", _
        12, FontStyle.Regular), Brushes.Black, 10, 10)
End Sub
```

6. The following `Structure` statement appears in a form:

```
Structure PersonInfo
    Dim strName As String
    Dim intAge As Integer
    Dim strPhone As String
End Structure
```

The following statement appears in the same form:

```
PersonInfo.strName = "Jill Smith"
```

Algorithm Workbench

1. Suppose a file named *DiskInfo.txt* already exists, and you wish to add data to the data already in the file. Write the statements necessary to open the file.

2. Suppose you wish to create a new file named *NewFile.txt* and write data to it. Write the statements necessary to open the file.

3. Assuming an application uses a list box named `lstInventory`, write code that writes the contents of the list box to the file *Inventory.txt*.

4. Assuming an application has an array of integers named `intNumbers`, write code that writes the contents of the array to the file *numbers.txt*.

5. Write a `Structure` statement that creates a structure to hold the following data about a savings account. The structure should be declared in a standard module and be available to all modules in the project.

```
Account number (String)
Account balance (Decimal)
Interest rate (Single)
Average monthly balance (Decimal)
```

6. Assume that `CustomerData` is a structure. The following statement declares `customers` as an array of ten `CustomerData` variables:

```
Dim customers(9) As CustomerData
```

Write a statement that stores `"Jones"` in the `strLastName` field of the `customers(7)`.

7. Using the variables: `strProductName`, `intProductNum`, and `decProductPrice`, write a `String.Format` statement that returns a string with `strProductName`'s value in a column of ten spaces, `intProductNum`'s value in a column of eight spaces, and `decProductPrice`'s value in a column of six spaces.

8. Assume an application uses an OpenFileDialog control named `ofdOpen`. Write statements that display an *Open* dialog box with the initial directory *C:\Becky\Images* and use the following filters: *JPEG images (*.jpg)* and *GIF images (*.gif)*.

Programming Challenges

1. **Employee Data, Part 1**

   Create an application that allows the user to enter the following employee data: First Name, Middle Name, Last Name, Employee Number, Department, Telephone Number, Telephone Extension, and E-mail Address. The valid selections for department are Accounting, Administration, Marketing, MIS, and Sales. Once the data is entered, the user should be able to save it to a file. Figure 9-32 shows an example of the application's form. The form shown in Figure 9-32 has a combo box for selecting the department; a *Save Record* button, which writes the record to a file; a *Clear* button, which clears the text boxes; and an *Exit* button. Write code in the `Form_Load` procedure that allows the user to enter the name of the file.

Figure 9-32 *Employee Data* form for saving employee records

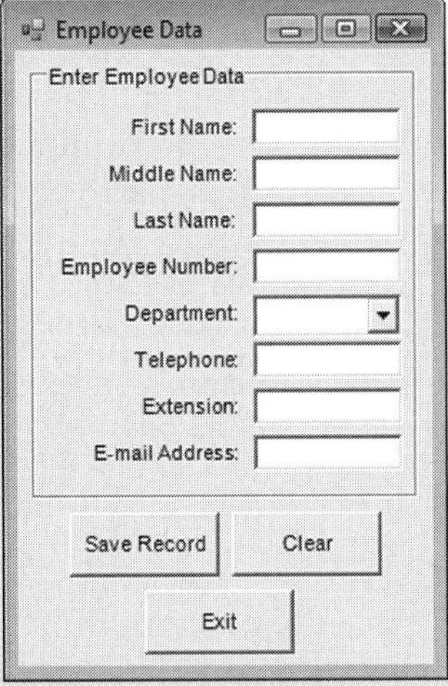

2. **Employee Data, Part 2**

   Create an application that reads the records stored in the file created by Programming Challenge 1.

   Write code in the form's `Load` procedure that allows the user to enter the name of the file, and opens the file. The form shown in Figure 9-33 has a *Next Record* button, which reads a record from the file and displays its fields; a *Clear* button, which clears the labels; and an *Exit* button. When the user clicks the *Next Record* button, the application should read the next record from the file and display it. When the end of the file is encountered, a message should be displayed.

Figure 9-33 *Employee Data* form for reading employee records

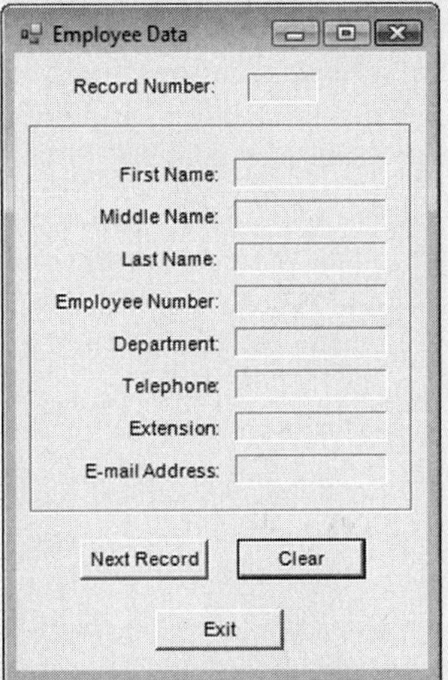

3. **Student Test Scores**

A teacher has six students and wants you to create an application that stores their grade data in a file and prints a grade report. The application should have a structure that stores the following student data: Name (a string), Test Scores (an array of five singles), and Average (a single). Because the teacher has six students, the application should use an array of six structure variables.

The application should allow the user to enter data for each student, and calculate the average test score.

Figure 9-34 shows an example form.

Figure 9-34 *Student Test Scores* form

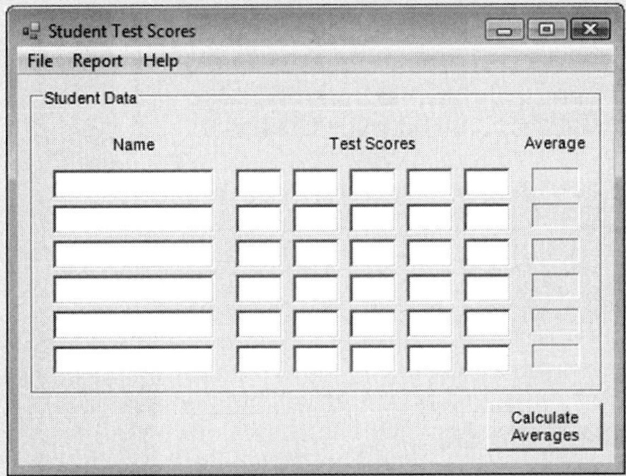

The user should be able to save the data to a file, read the data from the file, and print a report showing each student's test scores and average score. The form shown in Figure 9-34 uses a menu system. You may use buttons instead if you prefer.

Input validation: Do not accept test scores less than zero or greater than 100.

4. **Video Collection**

   Create an application that stores data about your DVD collection in a file. The application should have a structure to hold the following fields: Video Name, Year Produced, Running Time, and Rating. The application should allow the user to save the data to a file, search the file for a video by name, and print a report listing all the video records in the file. Figure 9-35 shows an example form.

Figure 9-35 *Video Collection* form

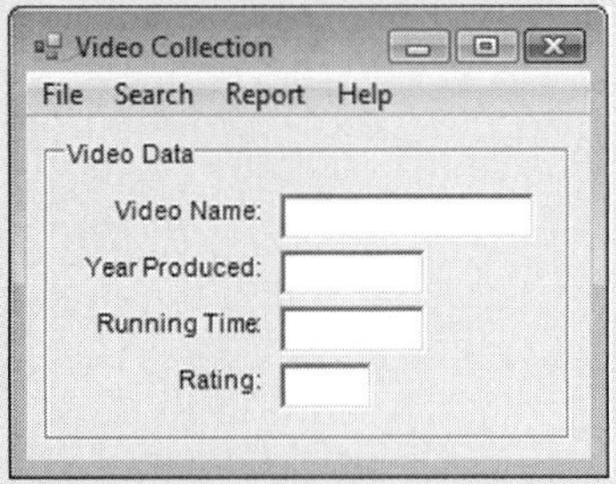

Design Your Own Forms

VideoNote
The Random Number File Generator Problem

5. **Random Number File Generator**

   Create an application that generates a series of 100 random numbers in the range of 1 through 1,000. Save the series of numbers in a file.

6. **Number Analysis**

   Create an application that reads the numbers from the file your application created for Programming Challenge 5. (If you have not completed that assignment, use the file named *NumberSet.txt* in the *Chap9* folder on the student disk. It contains a series of 100 real numbers.) Your application should perform the following:

   - Display the total of the numbers
   - Display the average of the numbers
   - Display the highest number in the file
   - Display the lowest number in the file

7. **Font and Color Tester**

   Create an application that tests the way different fonts and color combinations appear. The application should display some text in a label, and have a menu with the items *Select Font* and *Select Color*.

   The *Select Font* menu item should display a *Font* dialog box with a *Color* drop-down list. The application should change the text displayed in the label to the font and color selected in the dialog box.

   The *Select Color* menu item should display a *Color* dialog box. The application should change the background color of the label to the color selected in the dialog box.

8. **Simple Text Editor Modification**

   Modify the *Simple Text Editor* application that you created in this chapter by adding a *View* menu to the menu system. The *View* menu should have two items: *Font* and *Color*.

The *Font* menu item should display a *Font* dialog box with a *Color* drop-down list. The application should change the text displayed in the text box to the font and color selected in the dialog box.

The *Color* menu item should display a *Color* dialog box. The application should change the background color of the text box to the color selected in the dialog box.

9. Image Viewer

You can load an image into a PictureBox control at runtime by calling the `Image.FromFile` method. For example, assume that `picImage` is a PictureBox control and `filename` is a variable containing the name of a graphic file. The following statement loads the graphic file into the PictureBox control:

```
picImage.Image = Image.FromFile(filename)
```

Create an application that has a PictureBox control on a form. The PictureBox control should be configured so it fills the entire area of the form and resizes when the user resizes the form.

The application should have a *File* menu with an *Open* command. The *Open* command should display an *Open* dialog box, displaying files of the following graphic types:

- Bitmaps (**.bmp*)
- JPEG images (**.jpg*)
- GIF images (**.gif*)

When the user selects a file with the *Open* dialog box, the application should display the image in the PictureBox control.

10. Employee Data, Part 3

Create an application that performs the following operations with the employee file created by the application in Programming Challenge 1:

- Uses an *Open* dialog box to allow the user to select the file
- Allows the user to enter a new employee record and then saves the record to the file
- Allows the user to enter an employee number and searches for a record containing that employee number. If the record is found, the record is displayed.
- Displays all records, one after the other
- Prints an employee record

Equip your application with either a menu system or a set of buttons to perform these operations.

11. Customer Accounts

Create an application that uses a structure to store the following data about a customer account: Last Name, First Name, Customer Number, Address, City, State, ZIP Code, Telephone Number, Account Balance, and Date of Last Payment. The application should allow the user to save customer account records to the file, search the file for a customer by last name or customer number, and print a report listing all the customer records in the file.

Input validation: When entering a new record, make sure the user enters data for all fields. Do not accept negative numbers for the account balance.

12. Rainfall Statistics File

In Programming Challenge 2 of Chapter 8, you created an application that allows the user to enter the amount of rainfall for each month and then displays rainfall statistics. Modify the application so it can save the monthly rainfall amounts entered by the user to a file and read the monthly rainfall amounts from a file.

13. Charge Account Number File

In Programming Challenge 9 of Chapter 8, you created an application that allows the user to enter a charge account number. The program determines whether the account number is valid by comparing it to numbers in an array. Modify the application so it compares the number to the numbers in a file. Create the file using Notepad or another text editor.

CHAPTER 10 Working with Databases

TOPICS

Most businesses store their company data in databases. In this chapter you will learn basic database concepts, and how to write Visual Basic applications that interact with databases. You will learn how to use a DataGridView control to display the data in a database. You will also learn how to sort and update database data. We will finish with an application that displays database data in list boxes, text boxes, labels, and combo boxes.

10.1 Database Management Systems

CONCEPT: Visual Basic applications use database management systems to make large amounts of data available to programs.

In Chapter 9 you learned how to perform input and output operations using simple text files. If an application needs to store only a small amount of data, those types of files work well. When a large amount of data must be stored and manipulated, however, they are not practical. Many businesses keep hundreds of thousands, or even millions of data items in files. When a text file contains this much data, simple operations such as searching, inserting, and deleting become slow, inefficient, and cumbersome.

When developing applications that work with a large amount of data, most developers prefer to use a database management system. A **database management system (DBMS)** is software that is specifically designed to store, retrieve, and manipulate large amounts of data in an organized and efficient manner. Once the data is stored using the database management system, applications may be written in Visual Basic or other languages to communicate with the DBMS. Rather than retrieving or manipulating the data directly, a Visual Basic application can send instructions to the DBMS. The DBMS carries out those instructions and sends the results back to the Visual Basic application. Figure 10-1 illustrates this.

Figure 10-1 A Visual Basic application interacts with a DBMS, which manipulates data

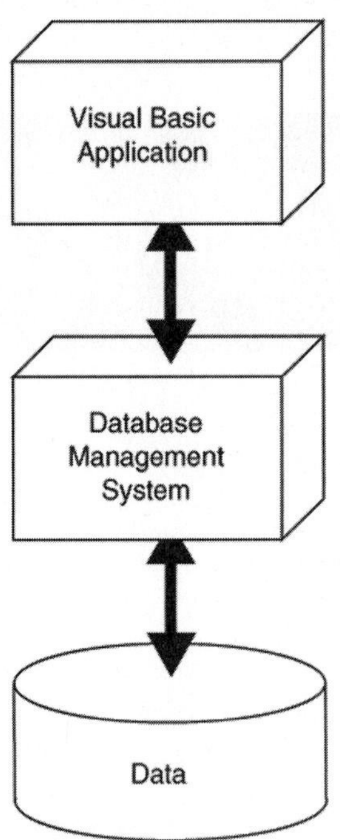

Although Figure 10-1 is greatly simplified, it illustrates the layered nature of an application that works with a database management system. The topmost layer of software, which in this case is written in Visual Basic, interacts with the user. It also sends instructions to the next layer of software, the DBMS. The DBMS works directly with the data, and sends the results of operations back to the application.

For example, suppose a company keeps all of its product records in a database. The company has a Visual Basic application that allows the user to search for information on any product by entering its product ID number. The Visual Basic application instructs the DBMS to retrieve the record for the product with the specified product ID number. The DBMS retrieves the product record and sends the data back to the Visual Basic application. The Visual Basic application displays the data to the user.

The advantage of this layered approach to software development is that the Visual Basic programmer does not need know about the physical structure of the data. He or she only needs to know how to interact with the DBMS. The DBMS handles the actual reading, writing, and searching of data.

Visual Basic is capable of interacting with many DBMSs. Some of the more popular DBMSs are Microsoft SQL Server, Oracle, DB2, and MySQL. In this chapter we will use Microsoft SQL Server Express, which is installed with Visual Basic.

10.2 Database Concepts

CONCEPT: A database is a collection of one or more tables, each containing data related to a particular topic.

A **database** is a collection of one or more tables, each containing data related to a particular topic. A **table** is a logical grouping of related information. A database might, for example, have a table containing information about employees. Another table might list information about weekly sales. Another table might contain a list of the items in a store's inventory. Let's look at a database table named *Departments*, shown in Table 10-1, which contains information about departments within a company. Each row of the table corresponds to a single department. The sample table contains the ID number, name, and number of employees in each department.

Table 10-1 *Departments* table

dept_id	dept_name	num_employees
1	Human Resources	10
2	Accounting	5
3	Computer Support	30
4	Research & Development	15

Each database record appears as a row in the table. In the *Departments* table, shown in Table 10-1, the first row contains 1, Human Resources, 10. When discussing a table, we refer to the columns by name. The columns in Table 10-1 are named dept_id, dept_name, and num_employees. Table columns are also called **fields**. Each table has a **design**, which specifies each column's name, data type, and field size and/or range of valid values. Table 10-2 contains the design of our sample *Departments* table.

Table 10-2 *Departments* table design

Field	Type	Range/Size
dept_id	Integer	–32,768 to +32,767
dept_name	String	30 characters
num_employees	Integer	–32,768 to +32,767

The *dept_id* column is called a **primary key** because it uniquely identifies each department. No two departments can ever have the same department ID. Primary keys can be either numbers or strings, but numeric values are processed by the database software more efficiently. In this table, the primary key is one column. Sometimes a primary key will consist of two or more combined columns, creating what is called a composite key.

SQL Server Column Types

When you use Visual Basic to read a database, your program copies values from a database table into program variables. Therefore, it is important to select variable types that match the type of data in the table. Table 10-3 compares SQL Server column types to Visual Basic data types. The varchar and nvarchar types permit variable-length strings. The n parameter specifies the longest string that can be stored in the column.

Table 10-3 Comparing SQL Server column types to Visual Basic types

SQL type(s)	Usage	Visual Basic Type
bit	True/false values	Boolean
datetime, smalldatetime	Dates and times	Date, DateTime
decimal, money	Financial values in which precision is important	Decimal
float	Real-number values	Double
image	Pictures, Word documents, Excel files, PDF files	Array of Byte
int	Integer values	Integer
nvarchar(n)	Variable-length strings containing 16-bit Unicode characters	String
smallint	Integers between –32,768 and +32,767	Short
text	Strings longer than 8,000 characters	String
varchar(n)	Variable-length strings containing ANSI (8-bit) characters	String

Choosing Column Names

A **database schema** is the design of tables, columns, and relationships between tables for the database. Let's look at some of the elements that belong to a schema, beginning with tables. Suppose you want to create a database to keep track of club members. First, you should choose meaningful names for each column.

Let's assume you want to store each member's first and last names, phone number, e-mail address, date joined, number of meetings attended, and a column indicating whether the person is an officer. Table 10-4 contains a possible design. Choosing the lengths of varchar columns involves some guesswork because you don't want to cut off any of the values stored in these columns. Disk space is relatively inexpensive, so it's usually better to make the columns a little larger than they need to be.

In most cases, you should never embed spaces in column names. If you do that, all references to the column name in database queries must be surrounded by brackets, as in [Last Name]. As an alternative use an underscore character between words, as in Last_Name.

Table 10-4 *Members* table sample design

Column Name	Type	Remarks
Member_ID	int	Primary key
First_Name	varchar(40)	
Last_Name	varchar(40)	
Phone	varchar(30)	
Email	varchar(50)	
Date_Joined	smalldatetime	Date only, no time values
Meetings_Attended	smallint	
Officer	bit	True/False values

Avoiding Redundancy by Using Linked Tables

Most well-designed databases keep redundant data to a minimum. It might be tempting when designing a table of employees, for example, to include the complete name of the department in which an employee works. A few sample rows are shown in Table 10-5. There are problems with this approach. We can imagine that the same department name appears many times within the *Employees* table, leading to wasted storage space. Also, someone typing in employee data might easily misspell a department name. Finally, if the company decides to rename a department, it would be necessary to find and correct every occurrence of the department name in the *Employees* table (and possibly other tables).

Table 10-5 *Employees* table with department names

Emp_Id	First_Name	Last_Name	Department
001234	Ignacio	Fleta	Accounting
002000	Christian	Martin	Computer Support
002122	Orville	Gibson	Human Resources
003000	Jose	Ramirez	Research & Development
003400	Ben	Smith	Accounting
003780	Allison	Chong	Computer Support

Rather than inserting a department name in each employee record, a good designer would store a department ID number in each row of the *Employees* table, as shown in Table 10-6. A data entry clerk would require less time to input a numeric department ID, and there would be less chance of a typing error. One would then create a separate table named *Departments*, containing all department names and IDs, as shown in Table 10-7. When looking up the name of an employee's department, we can use the department ID in the *Employees* table to find the same ID in the *Departments* table. The department name will be in the same table row. Relational databases make it easy to create links (called relationships) between tables such as *Employees* and *Departments*.

Table 10-6 *Employees* table with department ID numbers

Emp_Id	First_Name	Last_Name	Dept_Id
001234	Ignacio	Fleta	2
002000	Christian	Martin	3
002122	Orville	Gibson	1
003000	Jose	Ramirez	4
003400	Ben	Smith	2
003780	Allison	Chong	3

Table 10-7 *Departments* table

Dept_Id	Dept_Name	Dept_Size
1	Human Resources	10
2	Accounting	5
3	Computer Support	30
4	Research & Development	15

One-to-Many Relationship

Databases are usually designed around a **relational model**, meaning that relations exist between tables. A **relation** is a link or relationship that relies on a common field value to join rows from two different tables. In the relationship diagram shown in Figure 10-2, *dept_id* is the common field that links the *Departments* and *Employees* tables. The primary key field is always shown in bold.

In the *Departments* table, *dept_id* is the primary key. In the *Employees* table, *dept_id* is called a **foreign key**. A foreign key is a column in one table that references a primary key in another table. There can be multiple occurrences of a foreign key in a table. Along the line connecting the two tables, the 1 and ∞ symbols indicate a **one-to-many relationship**. A particular *dept_id* (such as 4) occurs only once in the *Departments* table, but it can appear many times (or not at all) in the *Employees* table. At first, we will work with only one table at a time. Later, we will show how to pull information from two related tables.

Figure 10-2 One-to-many relationship between *Departments* and *Employees*

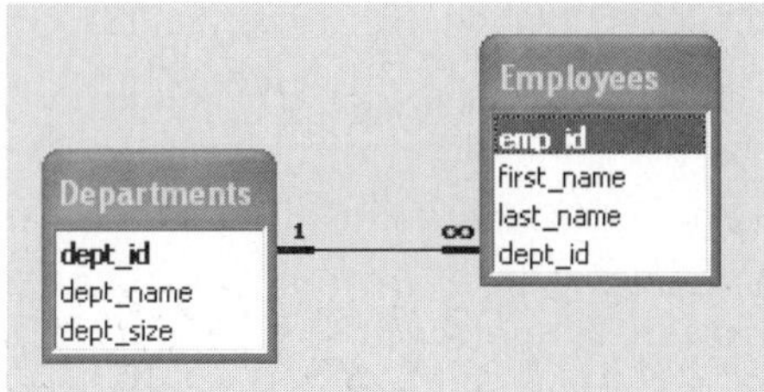

Checkpoint

10.1 How is a table different from a database?

10.2 In a table of employees, what column would make a good primary key?

10.3 Which Visual Basic data type is equivalent to the *bit* column type in Microsoft SQL Server?

10.4 Why would we not want to spell out the name of each person's department in a table of employees?

10.5 How is a foreign key different from a primary key?

10.3 DataGridView Control

CONCEPT: The DataGridView control allows you to display a database table in a grid. The grid can be used at runtime to sort and edit the contents of the table.

VideoNote The DataGridView Control

Visual Basic provides easy to use tools for displaying database tables in Windows forms and Web forms. In this chapter, we will show how to display data on a Windows form, and in Chapter 11, we will demonstrate Web forms.

Visual Basic uses a technique called **data binding** to link database tables to controls on your program's forms. Special controls, called **components**, provide the linking mechanism. When you decide to link a control to a database, a software tool named a **wizard** guides you through the process. Wizards are quite common in Microsoft Windows and many other applications such as Microsoft Word, so you have probably used one before.

We will use the following data-related components:

- **Data source.** A **data source** is usually a database, but can include text files, Excel spreadsheets, XML data, or Web services. Our data sources will be Microsoft SQL Server database files.
- **Binding source.** A **binding source** connects data bound controls to a dataset.
- **Table adapter.** A **table adapter** pulls data from one or more database tables and passes it to your program. It can select some or all table rows, add new rows, delete rows, and modify existing rows. It uses an industry standard language named **Structured Query Language** (**SQL**), which is recognized by nearly all databases.
- **Dataset.** A **dataset** is an in-memory copy of the data pulled from database tables. The table adapter does the pulling, and it copies the data to the dataset. Your program can modify rows in the dataset, add new rows, and delete rows. None of your changes are permanent, unless you tell the table adapter to write the changes back to the database. Datasets can get data from more than one data source, and from more than one table adapter.

Figure 10-3 shows the relationship between the data source, binding source, table adapter, dataset, and application. Data from a data source travels all the way to the dataset and application. The dataset's contents can be modified and viewed by the application. Updates to the dataset can be written back to the data source. In Tutorial 10-1, you show a database table in a **DataGridView control**.

Figure 10-3 Data flow from the data source to an application

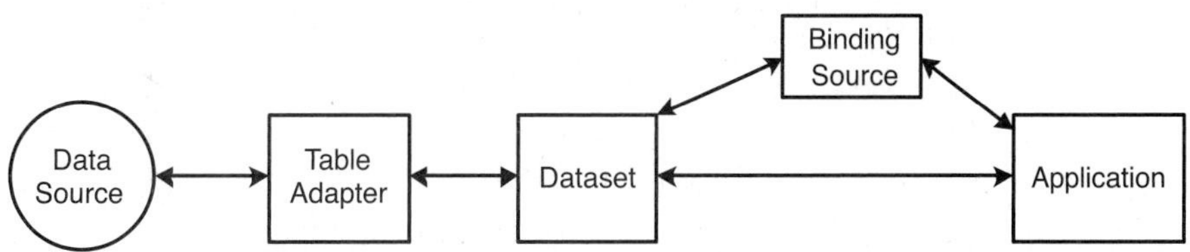

Tutorial 10-1:
Showing a database table in a DataGridView control

This tutorial leads you through the steps to display the contents of a database table in a DataGridView control. You will see all rows and columns of the data. You will see how easy it is for users of your program to sort on any column, delete rows, and insert new rows. The steps in this tutorial are designed to be carried out in Visual Studio.

The *SalesStaff* table, located in the SQL Server database named *Company*, represents information collected about sales employees. Its design is shown in Table 10-8, and some sample rows are shown in Table 10-9.

Before you begin this tutorial, make sure the *Company.mdf* file is located in the student sample programs folder named *Chap10*.

TIP: If you encounter difficulties connecting to SQL Server database files in a computer lab, your network administrator may have to adjust the computer's permission settings for Visual Studio.

Table 10-8 *SalesStaff* table design

Column Name	Type
ID	int(primary key)
Last_Name	varchar(40)
First_Name	varchar(40)
Full_Time	bit
Hire_Date	smalldatetime
Salary	decimal

Table 10-9 Sample rows in the *SalesStaff* table

ID	Last_Name	First_Name	Full_Time	Hire_Date	Salary
104	Adams	Adrian	True	05/20/1996	$35,007.00
114	Franklin	Fay	True	08/22/1995	$56,001.00
115	Franklin	Adiel	False	04/20/1986	$41,000.00
120	Baker	Barbara	True	04/22/1993	$32,000.00
135	Ferriere	Henri	True	01/01/1990	$57,000.00
292	Hasegawa	Danny	False	05/20/1997	$45,000.00
302	Easterbrook	Erin	False	07/09/1994	$22,000.00
305	Kawananakoa	Sam	True	10/20/1987	$42,000.00
396	Zabaleta	Maria	True	11/01/1985	$29,000.00
404	Del Terzo	Daniel	True	07/09/1994	$37,500.00
407	Greenwood	Charles	False	04/20/1996	$23,432.00

Step 1: Create a new Windows application project named *SalesStaff 1*.

Step 2: Set the Text property of *Form1* to *Company SalesStaff Table.*

Step 3: Save your project by selecting *Save All* from the File menu.

Step 4: Drag a DataGridView control from the *Data* section of the *Toolbox* window onto the form, so it covers the entire form. Click the small arrow (called a smart tag) pointing to the right in the upper right corner of the DataGridView. You should see a small pop-up window named *DataGridView Tasks*, as shown in Figure 10-4.

Step 5: Click the drop-down arrow next to *Choose Data Source.* In the dialog box that appears (see Figure 10-5), click *Add Project Data Source.*

Step 6: When the *Data Source Configuration Wizard* displays (see Figure 10-6), select the *Database* icon and click the *Next* button.

Figure 10-4 *DataGridView Tasks* window

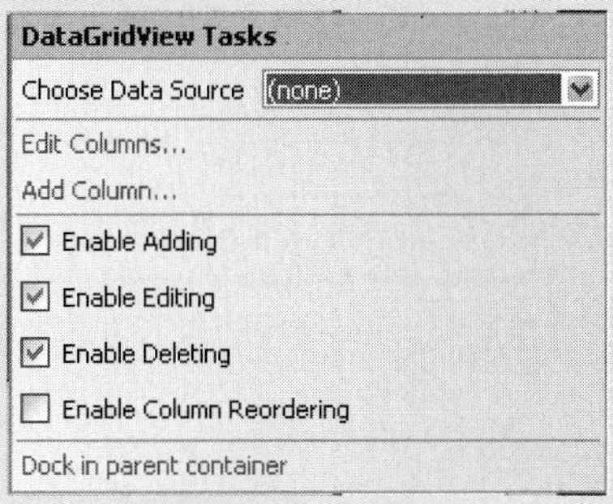

DataGridView Tasks

Choose Data Source (none)

Edit Columns...

Add Column...

☑ Enable Adding

☑ Enable Editing

☑ Enable Deleting

☐ Enable Column Reordering

Dock in parent container

Figure 10-5 Choosing a Data Source, Step 1

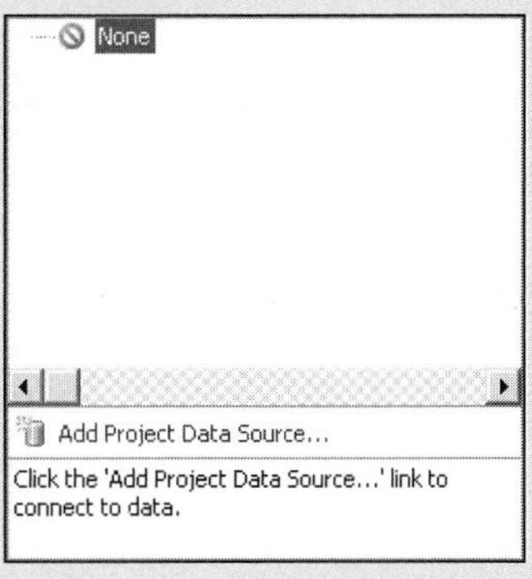

Figure 10-6 *Data Source Configuration Wizard*

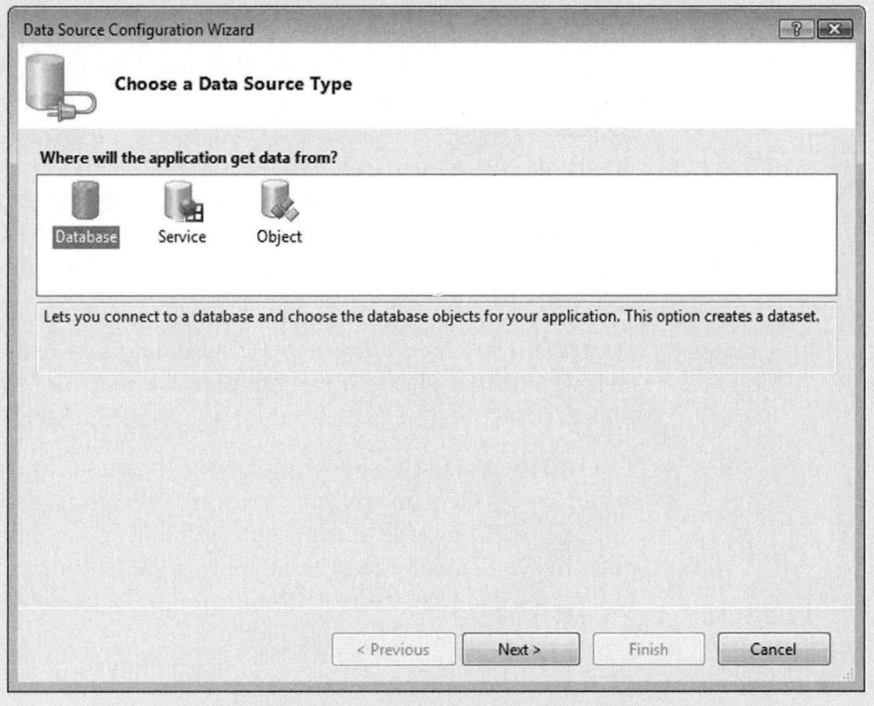

Step 7: Next, the wizard asks you to choose your data connection. If you had created data connections before, you could select one from the drop-down list. Because this is your first data connection, click the *New Connection* button, as shown in Figure 10-7.

Figure 10-7 Choose your data connection

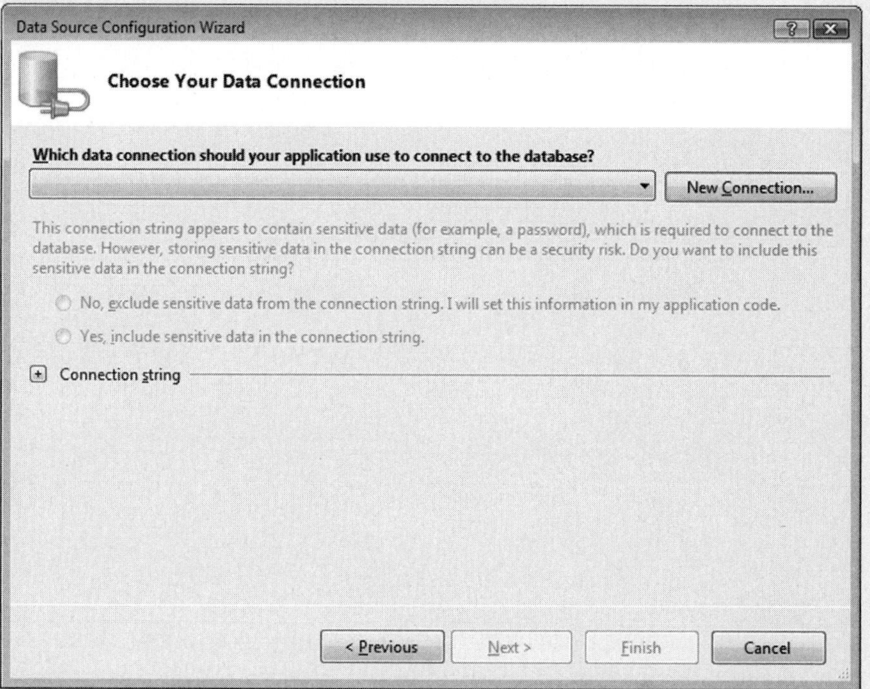

Step 8: The *Add Connection* window appears next. The controls in the window may appear different from the figure, depending on which type of data source is currently selected. The Data Source entry must be set to *Microsoft SQL Server Database File*, as shown in Figure 10-8. If it is not currently set to this, click the *Change...* button. The *Change Data Source* dialog box will appear. Select *Microsoft SQL Server Database File* and click *OK*. Back in the *Add Connection* window, click the *Browse* button and locate the *Company.mdf* database in the student sample programs folder named *Chap10*, as shown in Figure 10-9. (Your database file name field will show a complete path. We have removed the path from the example in the figure.)

Step 9: Click the *Test Connection* button. Assuming the *Test connection succeeded* message displays, click the *OK* button twice to return to the wizard, and then click the *Next* button. If the test did not succeed, check your entries.

Step 10: You will see a message similar to the one shown in Figure 10-10, asking if you want to copy the database file to the project directory. By answering *Yes*, you will be more easily able to copy your program and its database to another computer. When you hand in programming projects, for example, it is a good idea to have the database stored with the project. Click the *Yes* button to continue.

Figure 10-8 *Add Connection* window

Figure 10-9 Selecting the *Company.mdf* database file

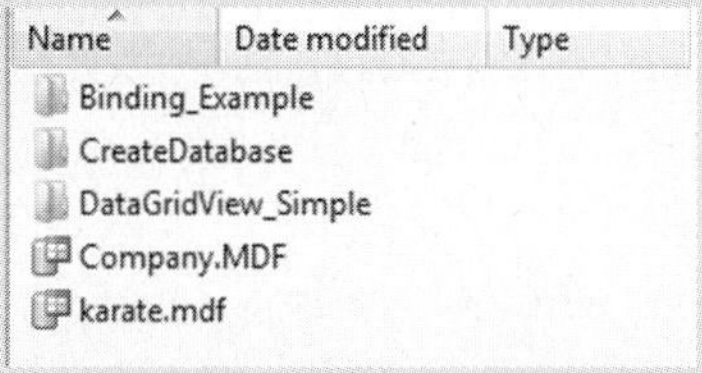

Figure 10-10 Option to copy the database file to your project

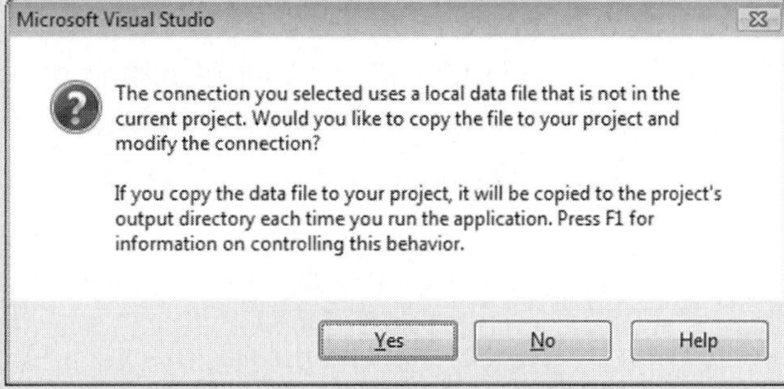

Step 11: You are given the option of saving the connection string to the application configuration file, as shown in Figure 10-11. Leave the option checked, and click the *Next* button to continue.

Figure 10-11 Saving the connection string to the configuration file

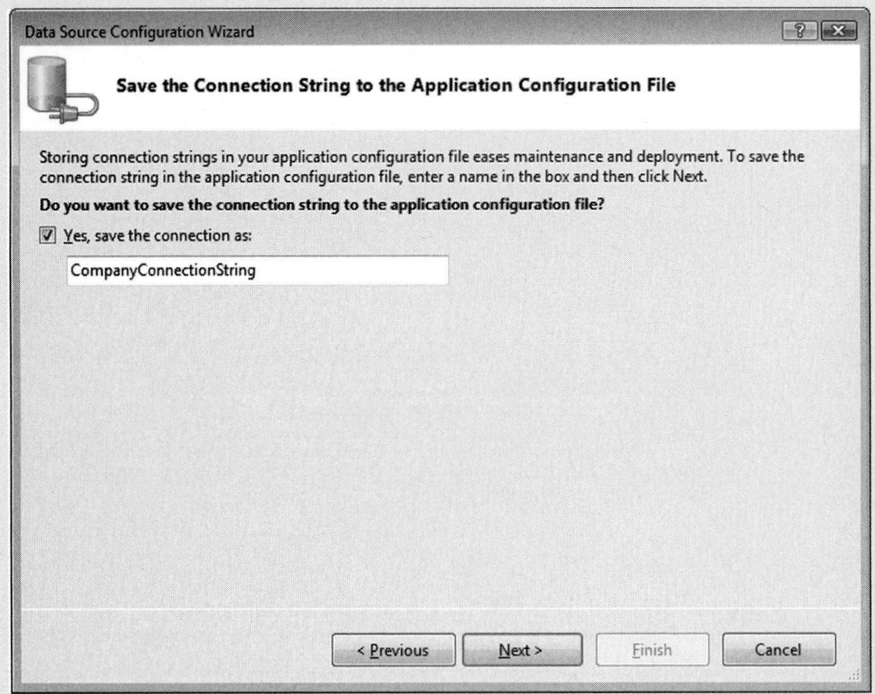

Step 12: Next, you are asked to select which database objects you want to include in your dataset. Expand the entry under Tables, place a check mark next to *SalesStaff*, and change the dataset name to *SalesStaffDataSet*, as shown in Figure 10-12. Click the *Finish* button to complete the wizard.

Step 13: Now you should see column headings in the DataGridView control (Figure 10-13) that match the *SalesStaff* columns: *ID*, *Last_Name*, *First_Name*, *Full_Time*, *Hire_Date*, and *Salary*. If necessary, widen the form and the DataGridView control.

Step 14: Select the DataGridView control and set its Anchor property to *Top*, *Bottom*, *Left*, *Right*.

Step 15: Save and run the application. You should see all the rows of the *SalesStaff* table, as shown in Figure 10-14.

In Tutorial 10-2, you will sort and update the *SalesStaff* table.

Figure 10-12 Choosing the *SalesStaff* table

Data Source Configuration Wizard

Choose Your Database Objects

Which database objects do you want in your dataset?

- Tables
  - Departments
  - Employees
  - Sales
  - SalesStaff
- Views
- Stored Procedures
- Functions

DataSet name:

SalesStaffDataSet

< Previous | Next > | Finish | Cancel

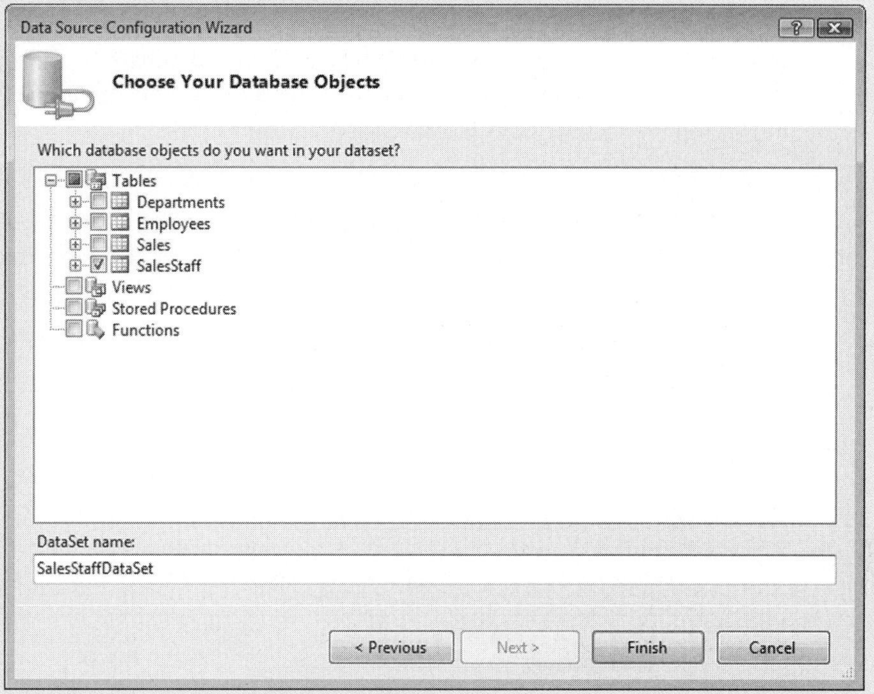

Figure 10-13 Column headings in the DataGridView control

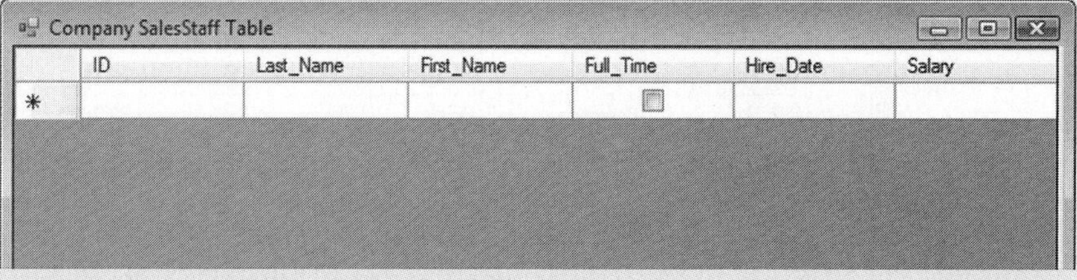

Figure 10-14 Running the application, displaying the *SalesStaff* table

Company SalesStaff Table

ID	Last_Name	First_Name	Full_Time	Hire_Date	Salary
104	Adams	Adrian	☑	5/20/1996	35007
114	Franklin	Fay	☑	8/22/1995	56001
115	Franklin	Adiel	☐	4/20/1986	41000
120	Baker	Barbara	☑	4/22/1993	32000
135	Ferriere	Henri	☑	1/1/1990	57000
292	Hasegawa	Danny	☐	5/20/1997	45000
302	Easterbrook	Erin	☐	7/9/1994	22000
305	Kawananakoa	Sam	☑	10/20/1987	42000
396	Zabaleta	Maria	☑	11/1/1985	29000
404	Del Terzo	Daniel	☑	7/9/1994	37500
407	Greenwood	Charles	☐	4/20/1996	23432
426	Locksley	Robert	☐	3/1/1992	18300

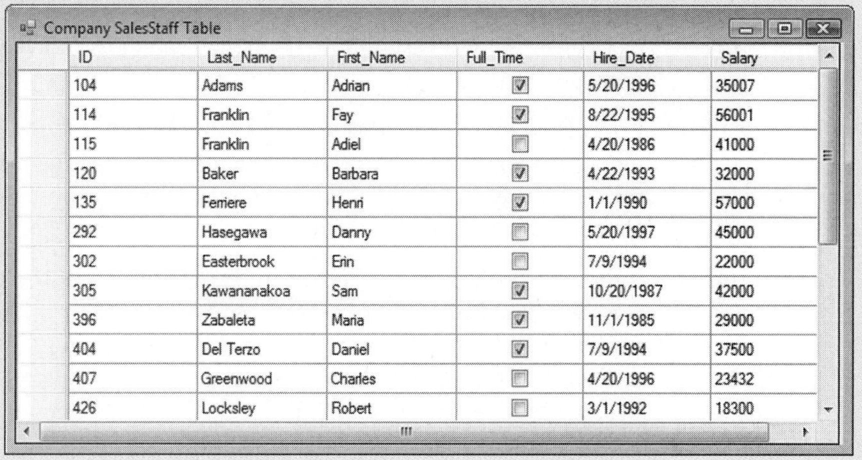

Tutorial 10-2:
Sorting and updating the *SalesStaff* table

In the previous tutorial, you learned how to add a database to a project and display a database table in a DataGridView control. Let's extend the application so you can learn more about the capabilities of DataGridView controls.

Step 1: Open the *SalesStaff* 1 project you created in Tutorial 10-1.

Step 2: Run the application. The *Full_Time* column holds True and False values—such columns are designed as type *bit* in the SQL Server database. The DataGridView control always displays *bit* values in a CheckBox control.

Step 3: Currently, the rows are listed in ascending order by ID number. Click the *Last_Name* column heading and watch the grid sort the rows in ascending order by last name (see Figure 10-15).

Figure 10-15 Sorting on the *Last_Name* column

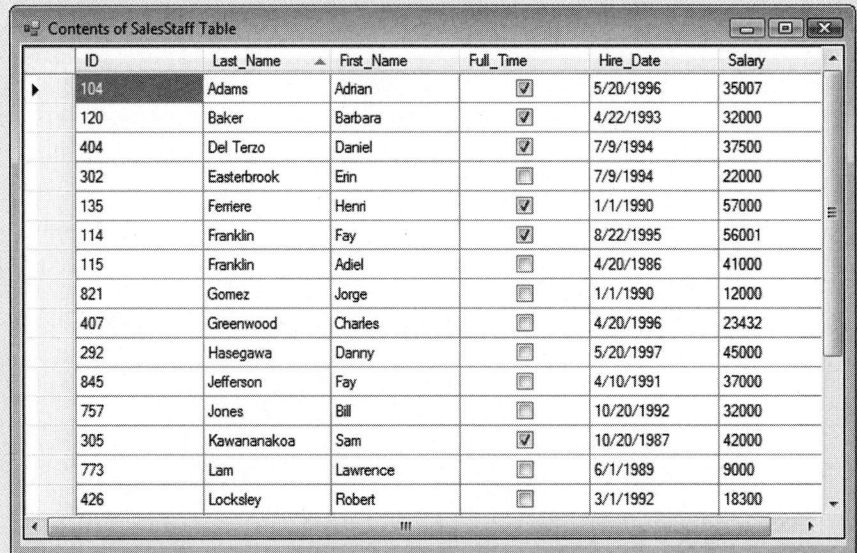

ID	Last_Name	First_Name	Full_Time	Hire_Date	Salary
104	Adams	Adrian	☑	5/20/1996	35007
120	Baker	Barbara	☑	4/22/1993	32000
404	Del Terzo	Daniel	☑	7/9/1994	37500
302	Easterbrook	Erin	☐	7/9/1994	22000
135	Ferriere	Henri	☑	1/1/1990	57000
114	Franklin	Fay	☑	8/22/1995	56001
115	Franklin	Adiel	☐	4/20/1986	41000
821	Gomez	Jorge	☐	1/1/1990	12000
407	Greenwood	Charles	☐	4/20/1996	23432
292	Hasegawa	Danny	☐	5/20/1997	45000
845	Jefferson	Fay	☐	4/10/1991	37000
757	Jones	Bill	☐	10/20/1992	32000
305	Kawananakoa	Sam	☑	10/20/1987	42000
773	Lam	Lawrence	☐	6/1/1989	9000
426	Locksley	Robert	☐	3/1/1992	18300

Step 4: Click the *Last_Name* column again and watch the rows sort in reverse on the same column.

Step 5: Place the mouse over the border between two column headings. When the mouse cursor changes to a horizontal arrow, press the mouse button and drag the border to the right or left. Doing this gives the user the opportunity to change the width of a column.

Step 6: Deleting rows: Click the button to the left of one of the grid rows. The entire row will be selected (highlighted), as shown in Figure 10-16. Press [Delete] and watch the row disappear. The row has been removed from the in-memory dataset, but not the database. Remember which row you deleted, because you will rerun the program soon and verify that the deleted row has been restored.

Figure 10-16 Selecting a DataGridView row

Contents of SalesStaff Table

ID	Last_Name	First_Name	Full_Time	Hire_Date	Salary
104	Adams	Adrian	☑	5/20/1996	35007
120	Baker	Barbara	☑	4/22/1993	32000
404	Del Terzo	Daniel	☑	7/9/1994	37500
302	Easterbrook	Erin	☐	7/9/1994	22000
135	Ferriere	Henri	☑	1/1/1990	57000
114	Franklin	Fay	☑	8/22/1995	56001
115	Franklin	Adiel	☐	4/20/1986	41000
821	Gomez	Jorge	☐	1/1/1990	12000
407	Greenwood	Charles	☐	4/20/1996	23432
292	Hasegawa	Danny	☐	5/20/1997	45000
845	Jefferson	Fay	☐	4/10/1991	37000
757	Jones	Bill	☐	10/20/1992	32000
305	Kawananakoa	Sam	☑	10/20/1987	42000
773	Lam	Lawrence	☐	6/1/1989	9000
426	Locksley	Robert	☐	3/1/1992	18300

Step 7: Inserting rows: Scroll to the bottom row of the grid and enter the following information in the empty cells: *847, Jackson, Adelle, (check Full-time), 6/1/2005, 65000*. A partial sample is shown in Figure 10-17. Press Enter to save your changes. Sort the grid on the *Last_Name* column and look for the row you inserted.

Figure 10-17 Adding a new row to a DataGridView control

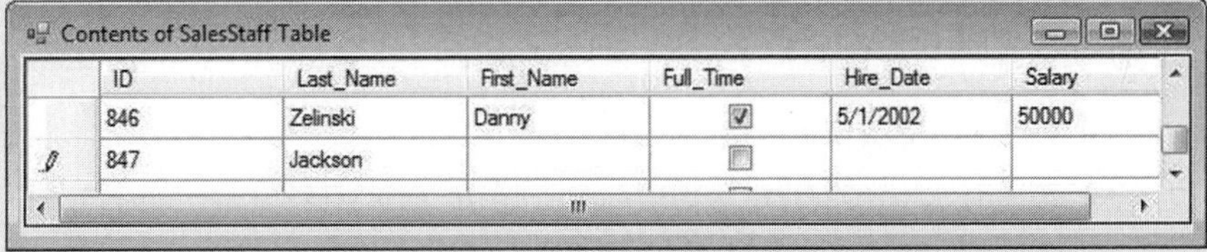

Step 8: Stop the program. Rerun the program, and notice that the changes you made to the dataset were not saved in the database. Later in the chapter we will show how to save changes directly into the database. The grid rows look exactly as they did when you first displayed the dataset. Stop the program again.

Step 9: In the *Design* view, look at the three components placed in the form's component tray by Visual Studio when you added the connection to the *SalesStaff* table:

- `SalesStaffDataSet` is the dataset object that holds the table data in memory and passes the data to the DataGridView control.
- `SalesStaffTableAdapter` is the TableAdapter object that pulls data from the database into your program. It contains a command called an SQL Query that specifies which data is to be selected from the table. By default, all rows and columns are selected.

- `SalesStaffBindingSource` is the BindingSource object that connects your program to the database.

Step 10: Open the form's *Code* window and note the statement in `Form_Load` that tells the table adapter to fill the dataset (the comments were inserted by Visual Studio):

```
Private Sub Form1_Load(ByVal sender As System.Object, _
  ByVal e As System.EventArgs) Handles MyBase.Load

  'TODO: This line of code loads data into the
  'SalesStaffDataSet.SalesStaff' table. You can move,
  'or remove it, as needed.
  Me.SalesStaffTableAdapter.Fill(Me.SalesStaffDataSet.SalesStaff)

End Sub
```

The TableAdapter's `Fill` method opens the database connection, reads the data from the database into the dataset, and closes the connection. The `Me.` qualifier used when naming the `SalesStaffTableAdapter` just indicates that it belongs to the current Form. The argument passed to `Fill` is the *SalesStaff* table inside the `SalesStaffDataSet`. It may seem unnecessary to specify a table name when the dataset contains only one table. But datasets can contain multiple tables, so we must identify which table is to be filled.

This tutorial shows how easy it is to display database data in a Windows form. The DataGridView control is the ideal tool for giving users a quick view of data. In our example, the column names and ordering were taken directly from the database table. As you learn more about the DataGridView, you will be able to rename the columns and change their order.

Checkpoint

10.6 The technique called __________________ links database tables to controls on Visual Basic forms.

10.7 Which component pulls data from one or more database tables and passes it into a dataset?

10.8 When changes are made to a dataset, what happens to the database that filled the dataset?

10.9 Which control displays datasets in a spreadsheet-like format?

10.10 What type of object connects a program to a database?

10.4 Data-Bound Controls

CONCEPT: Some controls can be bound to a dataset. A data-bound control can be used to display and edit the contents of a particular row and column.

In this section, we will show you how to add new data sources to a project. Using a data source, you can bind its fields to individual controls such as text boxes, labels, and list

Data-Bound Controls

boxes. **Data-bound controls** are convenient because they update their contents automatically when you move from one row to the next in a dataset. They can also be used to update the contents of fields. You will learn how to bind a DataGridView to an existing dataset. You will also learn how to use a ListBox control to navigate between different rows of a dataset.

Adding a New Data Source

To add a new data source to an application, open the *Data Sources* window and click the *Add New Data Source* link, as shown in Figure 10-18. The *Data Source Configuration Wizard* window appears (see Figure 10-19), just as it did in Tutorial 10-1. Then you follow the steps to create a connection to a database, as was done in Tutorial 10-1. The data source entry added to the *Data Sources* window is shown in Figure 10-20.

> **TIP:** If you cannot see the *Data Sources* window, select *Show Data Sources* from the *Data* menu.

Figure 10-18 About to add a new data source

Figure 10-19 *Data Source Configuration Wizard*

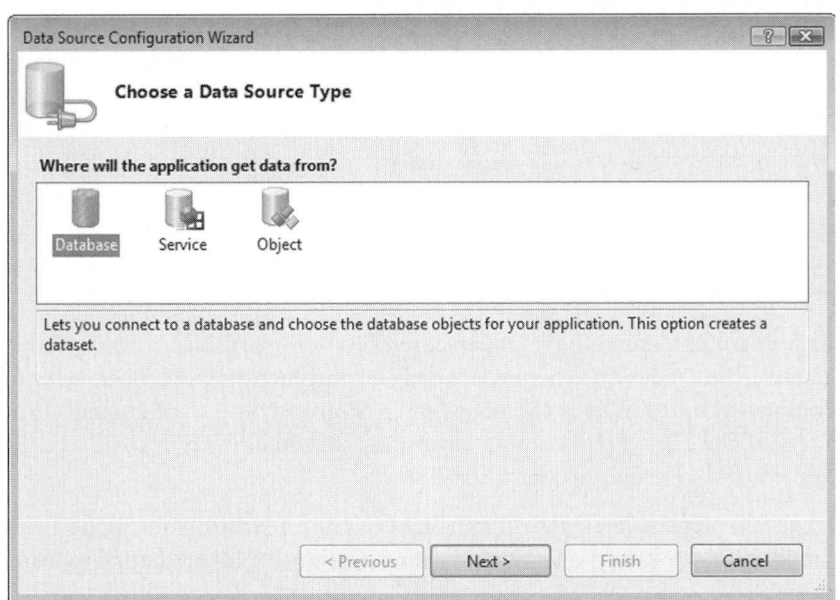

Figure 10-20 *SalesStaff* table in the *Data Sources* window

Deleting a Data Source

Suppose you were to create a data source and then later decide to rename it. Unfortunately, data sources are almost impossible to rename. But you can easily delete a data source and create a new one. To delete an existing data source, select its *XSD file* in the *Solution Explorer* window with the mouse, and then press Delete. A data source named *Employees*, for example, is defined by a file named *Employees.xsd*.

Binding the Data Source to a DataGridView Control

In Tutorial 10-1, you used the *DataGridView Tasks* window to guide you through creating a binding source, table adapter, and dataset. What if you already have a dataset, located in the *Data Sources* window? Then you can bind it to a DataGridView control just by dragging the *SalesStaff* table from the *Data Sources* window to the open area of a form. When you use this technique for data binding, Visual Studio adds a navigation toolbar to the form, as shown in Figure 10-21.

Figure 10-21 After dragging the *SalesStaff* table from the *Data Sources* window onto a form

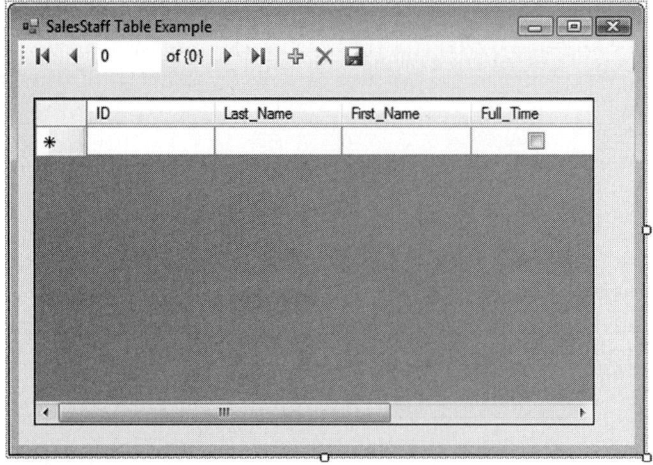

Binding Individual Fields to Controls

If you have an existing dataset in the *Data Sources* window, you can easily create an individual data-bound control for each field by dragging a table from the dataset onto a form that is visible in Design mode. First, click the arrow just to the right of the table name and select *Details* in the drop-down list associated with the table, as shown in Figure 10-22. (The default control type is DataGridView, which we've already used.) Then, when you drag the table name onto a form, a separate control is created for each field. As shown in Figure 10-23, a navigation toolbar is also added to the form. (You may have to wait a few seconds for the controls to appear.)

Although the dataset column names have underscores between words, as in *First_Name*, Visual Studio removes the underscore between words when generating the labels next to the controls. You may want to modify the appearance or properties of the controls. For example, if you want the *Hire_Date* column to display in *mm/dd/yyyy* format, set the `DateTimePicker` control's Format property to *Short*.

By default, varchar and numeric database columns are bound to TextBox controls, bit fields are bound to CheckBox controls, and smalldatetime (and datetime) fields are bound to **DateTimePicker controls**.

Figure 10-22 Selecting a table's binding control, in the *Data Sources* window

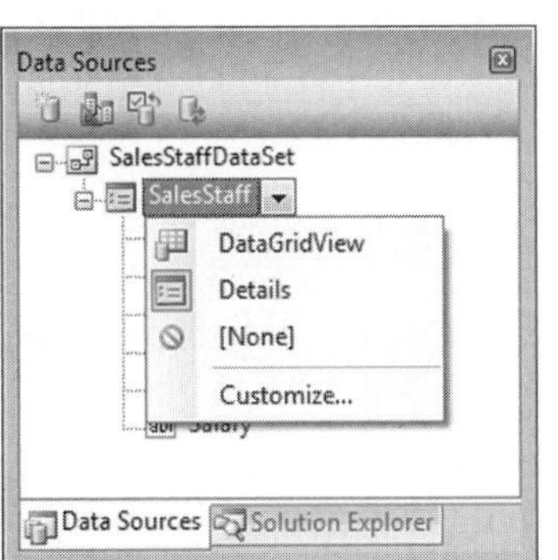

Figure 10-23 After dragging a dataset table onto the form

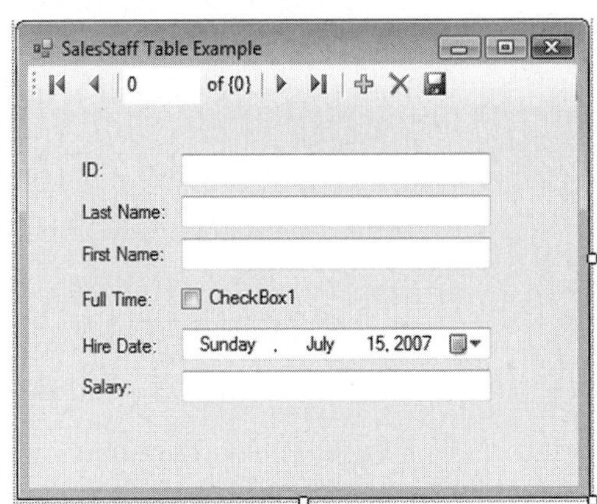

Suppose you would prefer not to let the user modify a protected field such as *ID*; then you can change the binding control type for individual fields in the *Data Sources* window. For example, if we click on the *ID* field in the *SalesStaff* table in the *Data Sources* window, a list of control types appears (see Figure 10-24). If you choose a Label, the user can view the field, but cannot modify its contents.

In Figure 10-25, we show a sample of the same form with a Label control for the *ID* field, and some customizing of the appearance of the other controls. The DateTimePicker control's Format property has four choices: *Long*, *Short*, *Time*, and *Custom*. Changing the format to *Short* causes the dates to be displayed in *mm/dd/yyyy* format, or the equivalent for other world locales.

Figure 10-24 Selecting the control binding type for the *ID* field in the *Data Sources* window

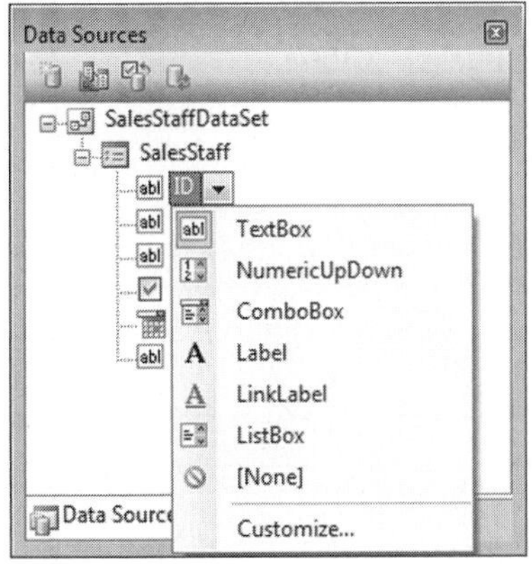

Figure 10-25 Displaying one row of the *SalesStaff* table in bound controls

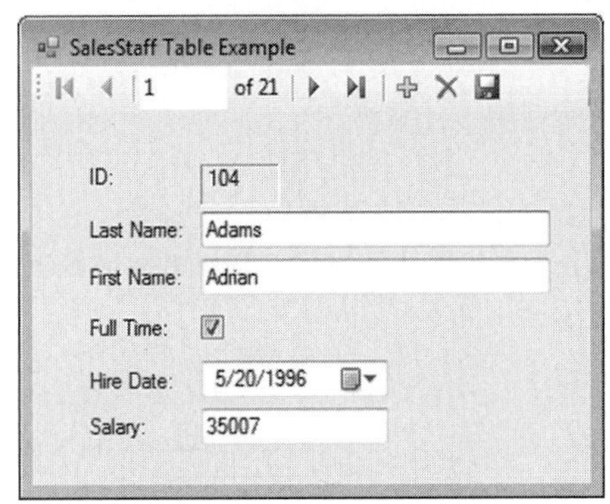

If you want to have only one or two bound controls from a dataset, you can drag individual columns from the *Data Sources* window onto a form. To run and modify this sample program, see the *Binding_Example* program located in the student sample programs folder named *Chap10\Binding_Example*. Tutorial 10-3 shows you how to bind a DataGridView to the *SalesStaff* table.

Tutorial 10-3:
Binding a DataGridView to the *SalesStaff* table

In this tutorial, you will begin by adding a new data source to your application. Then you will bind the data source to a DataGridView control and tell Visual Studio to create a toolstrip with buttons that let the user navigate, insert, delete, and save database rows.

Step 1: Create a new Windows application named *SalesStaff Databound.*

Step 2: Select *Show Data Sources* from the *Data* menu. This will cause the *Data Sources* window to appear.

Step 3: In the *Data Sources* window, click the *Add New Data Source* link.

Step 4: Select the *Company.mdf* database from the Chapter 10 examples folder. This is what you did in Steps 7, 8, and 9 in Tutorial 10-1. When you are asked if the database should be copied to your project folder, answer *Yes.*

Step 5: In the *Data Source Configuration Wizard* window (Figure 10-26), select the *SalesStaff* table and name the dataset *SalesStaffDataSet.* Click the *Finish* button.

Figure 10-26 Data Source Configuration Wizard

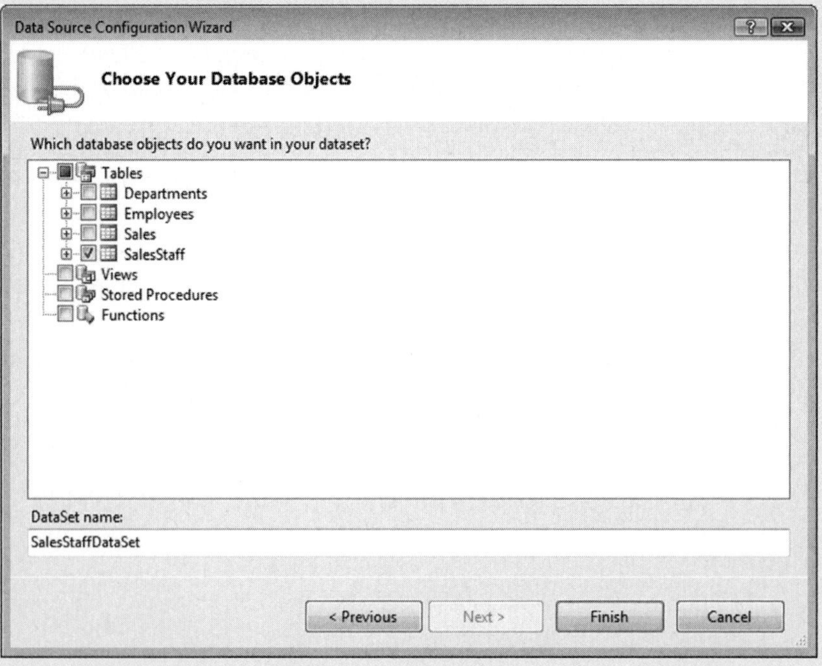

Step 6: Increase the width of the program's form to about 712 pixels and set its Text property to *SalesStaff* table.

Step 7: Drag the *SalesStaff* table name from the *Data Sources* window onto your form. Notice how Visual Studio adds both a DataGridView control and a ToolStrip control to the form. The ToolStrip contains buttons that let the user perform operations on the grid's data. Expand the DataGridView control so it fills the entire form.

Step 8: Set the DataGridView control's Anchor property so it anchors to all sides of the form.

Step 9: Save the project and run the application. You should see output similar to that shown in Figure 10-27.

Step 10: Click the arrow buttons on the Navigation toolbar and notice that the selected row changes. Experiment with the other toolbar buttons to see what they do. Notice how the *Save Data* button permanently saves all changes you make to the database. In design mode, you can double-click this button to examine its Click handler, and find out how changes are saved to the database.

Figure 10-27 Output from the *SalesStaff Databound* application

SalesStaff Table

1 of 21

ID	Last_Name	First_Name	Full_Time	Hire_Date	Salary
104	Adams	Adrian	☑	5/20/1996	35007
114	Franklin	Fay	☑	8/22/1995	56001
115	Franklin	Adiel	☐	4/20/1986	41000
120	Baker	Barbara	☑	4/22/1993	32000
135	Ferriere	Henri	☑	1/1/1990	57000
292	Hasegawa	Danny	☐	5/20/1997	45000
302	Easterbrook	Erin	☐	7/9/1994	22000
305	Kawananakoa	Sam	☑	10/20/1987	42000
396	Zabaleta	Maria	☑	11/1/1985	29000
404	Del Terzo	Daniel	☑	7/9/1994	37500
407	Greenwood	Charles	☐	4/20/1996	23432
426	Locksley	Robert	☐	3/1/1992	18300
565	Smith	Bill	☑	2/5/1999	50009

Step 11: Close the program.

In the next tutorial, you will use data binding to display one row at a time from the *SalesStaff* table in a details view.

In Tutorial 10-4, you will display individual fields from the *SalesStaff* table.

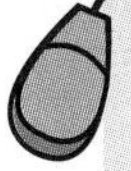

Tutorial 10-4:
Binding individual controls to the *SalesStaff* table

In this tutorial, you will select the *Details* option in the *Data Source* window so you can bind individual controls to fields in the *SalesStaff* table.

Step 1: Create a new Windows application named *SalesStaff Details*.

Step 2: Set the startup form's Text property to *SalesStaff Details*.

Step 3: Select *Show Data Sources* from the *Data* menu. This will cause the *Data Sources* window to appear.

Step 4: In the *Data Sources* window, click the *Add New Data Source* link.

Step 5: Select the *Company.mdf* database from the Chapter 10 examples folder. This is what you did in Tutorial 10-1. When you are asked if the database should be copied to your project folder, answer *Yes*.

Step 6: In the *Data Source Configuration Wizard* window (Figure 10-28), select the *SalesStaff* table and name the dataset *SalesStaffDataSet*. Click the *Finish* button.

Figure 10-28 *Data Source Configuration Wizard*

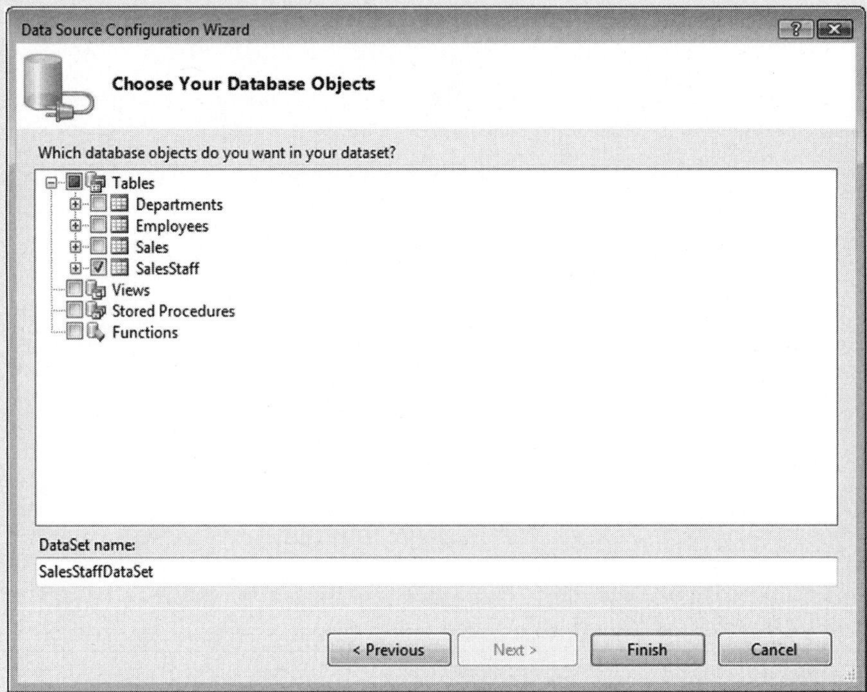

Step 7: In the *Data Sources* window, expand the list of fields under the *SalesStaff* table name.

Step 8: Drag the *Last_Name* field from the *Data Sources* window onto your form. When you do this, you should see a TextBox control appear on the form with a label to its left side. Notice that Visual Studio automatically removes the underscore character between the two words in the field name. You will also see a new ToolStrip control on the form. An example is shown in Figure 10-29.

Figure 10-29 After dragging the *Last_Name* field onto the form

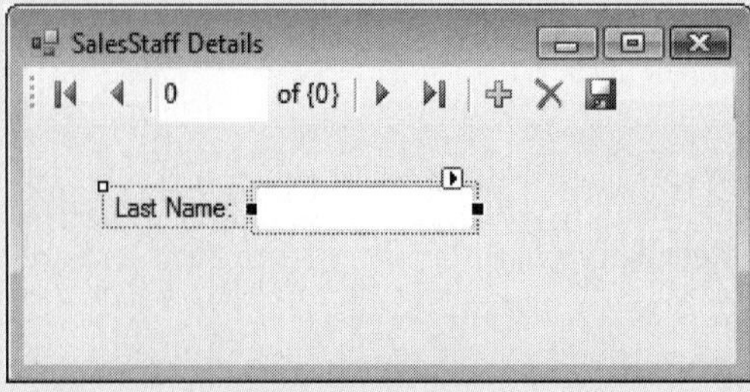

Step 9: Save the project and run the application. Click the navigation buttons in the tool strip and notice how the name changes. Also, the table's row number changes in the tool strip.

Step 10: Stop the application.

Step 11: Drag the remaining columns from the *SalesStaff* table onto the form. You might want to rearrange their order, expand some fields, remove the text from the Full Time checkbox, and change the *Hire_Date* control's Format property to *Short*. An example is shown in Figure 10-30.

Step 12: Save the project and run the application again. Notice how all the fields update at the same time when you click the navigation buttons on the tool strip.

Step 13: Experiment with adding, deleting, and editing individual rows from the table. Changes you make to individual fields will only be saved if you click the *Save Data* button on the tool strip.

Step 14: Close the application.

Figure 10-30 After dragging all *SalesStaff* fields onto the form

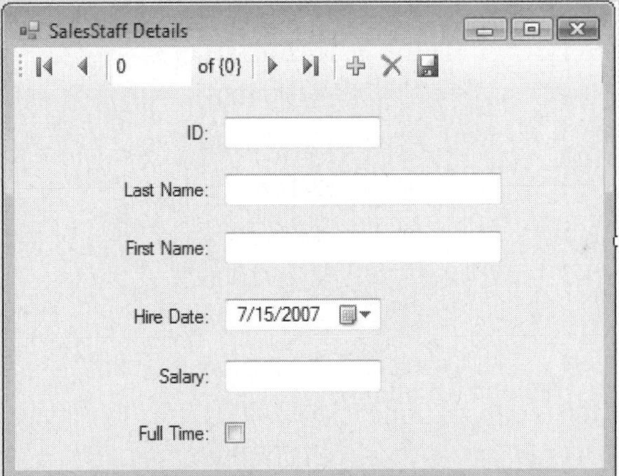

In this tutorial, you have seen how easy it is to work with data-bound tables in Visual Basic. You can display an entire table at once, or you can display each row of a table individually. Editing individual field values, which was a lot of work in previous versions of Visual Basic, has become remarkably easy.

Introducing the *Karate* Database

The database we will use for the next set of examples is called *Karate* (*karate.mdf*), designed around the membership and scheduling of classes for a martial arts school. A table called *Members* contains information about members, such as their first and last names, phone, and so on. It is listed in Table 10-10.

Related to the *Members* table is the *Payments* table, as shown in Table 10-11. It shows recent dues payments by members. Each row in the *Payments* table contains a *Member_Id* value, which identifies the member (from the *Members* table) who made a dues payment. Their relationship is shown by the diagram in Figure 10-31. The line connects the *ID* field in the *Members* table to the *Member_Id* field in the *Payments* table.

Table 10-10 The *Members* table from the *Karate* database

ID	Last_Name	First_Name	Phone	Date_Joined
1	Kahumanu	Keoki	111-2222	2/20/2002
2	Chong	Anne	232-2323	2/20/1995
3	Hasegawa	Elaine	313-3455	2/20/2004
4	Kahane	Brian	646-9387	5/20/1998
5	Gonzalez	Aldo	123-2345	6/6/1999
6	Kousevitzky	Jascha	414-2345	2/20/1992
7	Taliafea	Moses	545-2323	5/20/2005
8	Concepcion	Rafael	602-3312	5/20/2001
9	Taylor	Winifred	333-2222	2/20/1994

Table 10-11 The *Payments* table from the *Karate* database

ID	Member_Id	Payment_Date	Amount
1	1	10/20/2005	$48.00
3	6	11/16/2005	$75.00
2	2	11/20/2005	$80.00
4	4	12/16/2005	$50.00
5	5	1/16/2006	$65.00
6	3	2/16/2006	$75.00
8	8	2/27/2006	$44.00
7	9	3/11/2006	$77.00
9	6	3/11/2006	$77.00
15	1	3/11/2006	$44.00
22	2	3/21/2006	$55.00
17	4	3/27/2006	$44.00
16	3	3/28/2006	$43.00
10	5	4/11/2006	$66.00
11	8	5/11/2006	$77.00
13	6	6/11/2006	$77.00
14	7	7/16/2006	$77.00
19	9	9/20/2006	$44.00

Figure 10-31 Relationship between the *Members* and *Payments* tables

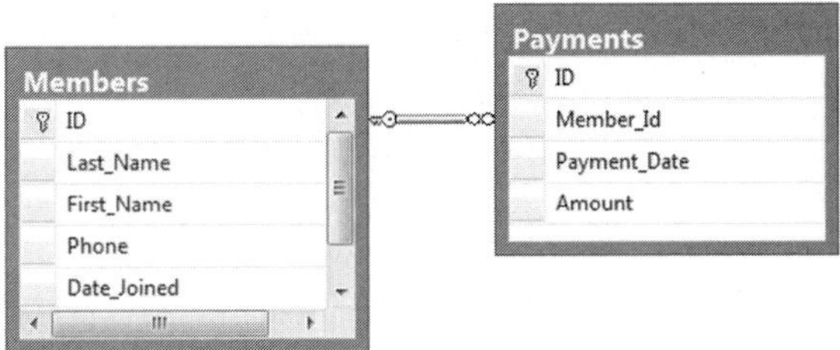

Binding to ListBox and ComboBox Controls

ListBox and ComboBox controls are ideal tools for displaying lists of items and permitting users to select individual items. All you have to do is set the following properties:

- DataSource: The **DataSource property** identifies the table within the dataset that supplies the data.
- DisplayMember: The **DisplayMember property** identifies the column within the table that displays in the list box or combo box.

When you use the mouse to drag a table column from the *Data Sources* window onto a list box or combo box, Visual Studio automatically creates the necessary data components: a dataset, binding source, and table adapter.

Tutorial 10-5 shows you how to display the *Members* table in a list box.

Tutorial 10-5:
Displaying the *Members* table in a list box

In this tutorial, you will use a list box to display the last names of members from the *Members* table in the *Karate* database. When the user clicks a member name, the program will display the date when the member joined.

Step 1: Create a Windows Forms application named *Member_List*. Save the project immediately.

Step 2: Click *Add New Data Source* in the *Data Sources* window. (If you cannot see the *Data Sources* window, select *Show Data Sources* from the *Data* menu.)

Step 3: Follow the steps in the *Data Source Configuration Wizard* to create a connection to the *Members* table in the *Karate.mdf* database, located in the student sample programs folder named *Chap10*. Name the dataset *MembersDataSet*.

Step 4: Set the form's Text property to *Member List*.

Step 5: Add a ListBox control to the form and name it *lstMembers*.

Step 6: Add a Label just above the list box and set its Text property to *Member Names*. Your form should look like the one shown in Figure 10-32.

Step 7: Click the list box's DataSource property. Expand the *Other Data Sources* group, expand *Project Data Sources*, expand *MembersDataSet*, and select *Members* (shown in Figure 10-33). Notice that Visual Studio added three components to the form's component tray: a dataset, a binding source, and a table adapter.

Figure 10-32 *Member List* program with list box

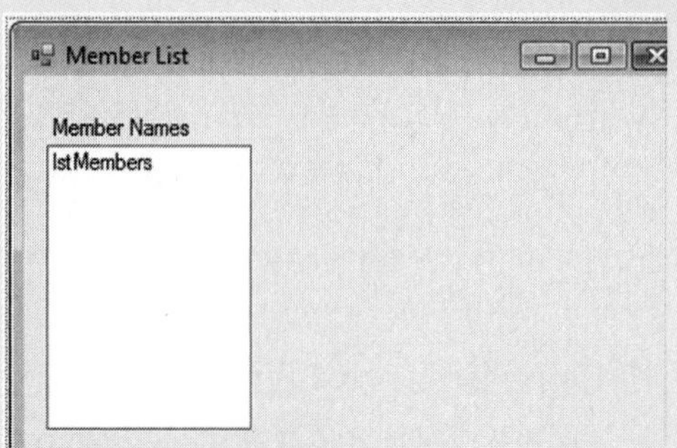

Figure 10-33 Setting the list box's DataSource property

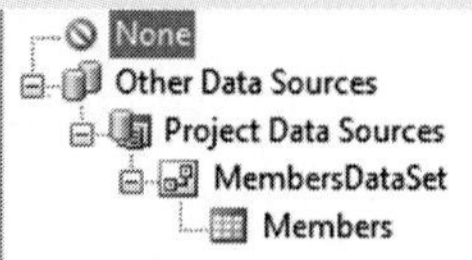

Step 8: Set the list box's DisplayMember property to *Last_Name*.

Step 9: Save and run the application. The list box should contain the last names of members, as shown in Figure 10-34. Close the window and return to *Design* mode.

Figure 10-34 List box filled, at runtime

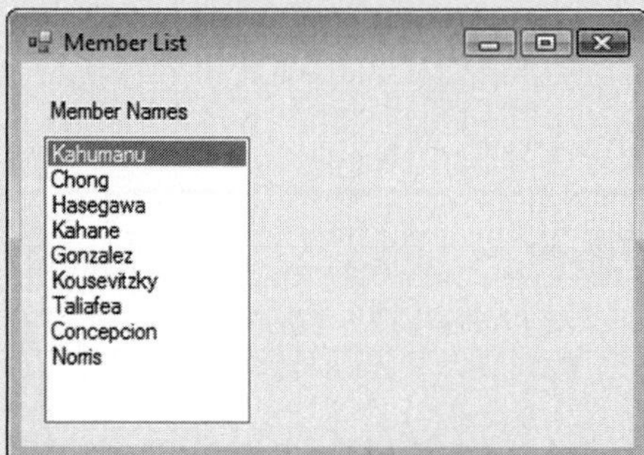

Step 10: Next, you will add a data-bound TextBox control to the form that displays the member's phone number. To do this, click the *Phone* field in the *Data Sources* window, and drag it onto the form.

Step 11: Save and run the program. As you click each member's name, notice how the current phone number is displayed. For a sample, see Figure 10-35.

Figure 10-35 Phone number of selected member displays in a TextBox control

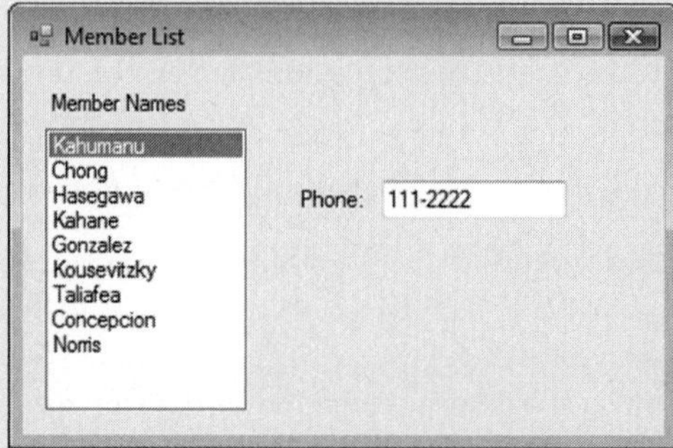

Let's analyze what's happening here. When the user selects a name in the list box, the form's data binding mechanism moves to the dataset row containing the person's name. The Phone TextBox control is data-bound to the same dataset, so it displays the phone number of the person selected in the list box.

Step 12: Add the remaining fields by dragging the field names from the *Data Sources* window onto the form, as shown in Figure 10-36. Choose the Label control type for the *ID* field. In the figure, a DateTimePicker control was used for the *Date_Joined* field. The DateTimePicker control's Format property was set to *Short*. Reposition the controls and resize the form as necessary. The Label control displaying the *ID* field looks best with a BorderStyle property equal to *Fixed 3D*.

Figure 10-36 Displaying the *Members* table in detail controls

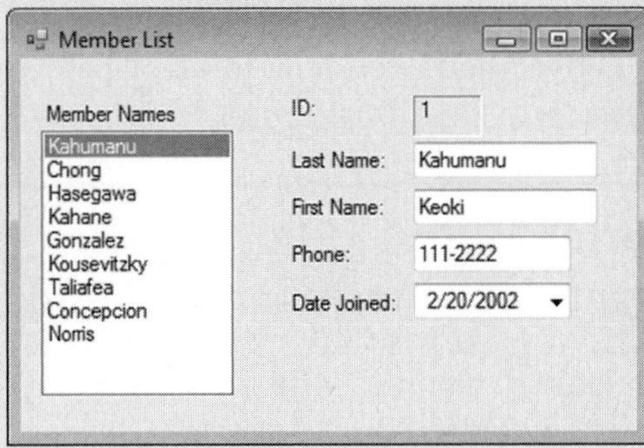

Step 13: Save and rerun the program. Now you have a way to navigate through dataset rows by selecting from a list box!

Step 14: End the program.

Adding Rows to a Database Table

When you add a data source to a project, a special file called a **schema definition file** is created. This is a file with a designer window that displays the names and data types of fields in the table. It has a filename extension of *xsd*. In Tutorial 10-5, for example, the *Members* table was used as a data source and the *Solution Explorer* window contained a file named *MembersDataSet.xsd*. Let's look at the schema definition file, as shown in Figure 10-37. A DataTable named *Members* was created automatically when this data source was added to the project. Associated with every DataTable is a **TableAdapter,** which in this case is named *MembersTableAdapter*.

Figure 10-37 The MembersDataSet schema definition file, containing the *Members* DataTable and the *MembersTableAdapter*

Suppose you would like the code in your application to add a new row to the *Members* table. You can call the TableAdapter's `Insert` method, passing it the column values for the row being added. Here is an example that calls the `Insert` method:

```
MembersTableAdapter.Insert(10, "Hasegawa", "Adrian",
  "305-999-8888",#5/15/2009#)
```

Identity Columns

A database table can have what is called an **identity column.** When new rows are added to the table, the identity column is assigned a new unique integer value. That is the case for the *Payments* table in the *Karate* database. The primary key column, named ID, is also an identity column. Its values are automatically generated in sequence when new rows are added to the table. If we were to call the `Insert` method for the *Payments* table, we would omit the ID column value and just supply the Member_Id, Payment_Date, and Amount values:

```
PaymentsTableAdapter.Insert(5, #5/15/2009#, 50D)
```

Tutorial 10-6 shows you how to insert new rows in the *Payments* table of the *Karate* database.

Tutorial 10-6:
Inserting *Karate* member payments

In this tutorial, you will write a program that adds new rows in the *Payments* table of the *Karate* database.

Step 1: Create a new Windows Forms application named *Insert_Karate_Payments*.

Step 2: In the *Data Sources* window, add a new data source named `PaymentsDataSet`, which uses the *Payments* table from the *Karate.mdf* database.

Step 3: Add three text boxes to the form with appropriate labels. One is named *txtMemberId*, another is named *txtDate*, and the third is named *txtAmount*. Set the form's Text property to *Insert Karate Payments*. Use Figure 10-38 as a guide.

Figure 10-38 The startup form in the *Insert Karate Payments* application

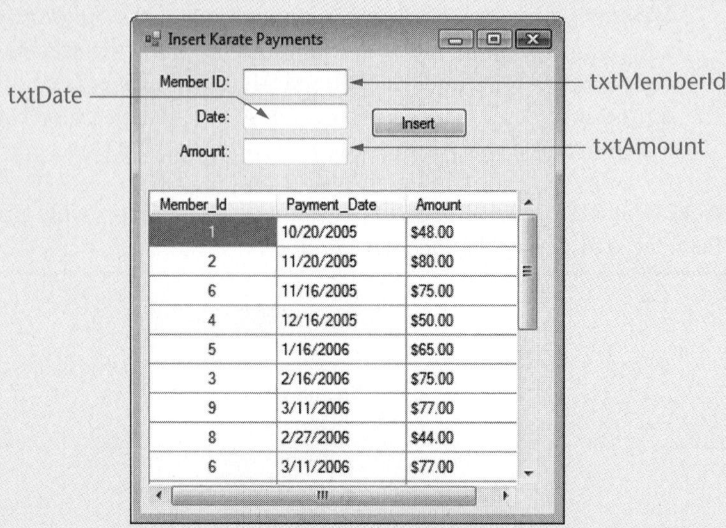

Step 4: Add a button and name it `btnInsert`.

Step 5: Add a DataGridView control and set the following properties: Name = *dgvPayments*; BorderStyle = *None*; BackgroundColor = *Control*; ReadOnly = *True*; RowHeadersVisible = *False*. The ReadOnly property prevents the user from making any changes to the grid's data at runtime.

Step 6: Click the arrow in the grid's upper right corner to display the *DataGridView Tasks* window. Set its data source to the *Payments* table of the `PaymentsDataSet`.

Step 7: Select the grid's Columns property, which opens the *Edit Columns* window and remove the *ID* column. Figure 10-39 shows the Edit Columns window after the ID column was removed.

Figure 10-39 Editing the Columns property of the *dgvPayments* grid

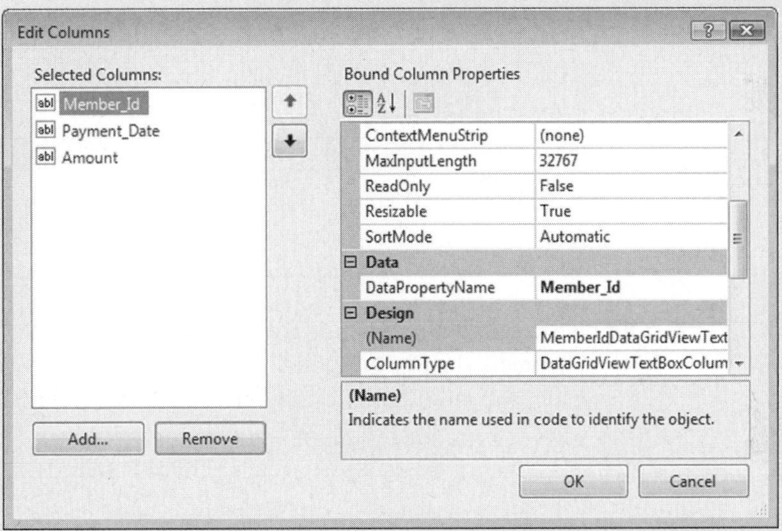

Step 8: Still in the *Edit Columns* window, select the *Member_Id* column, and open the DefaultCellStyle property in the right-hand list box. The *CellStyle Builder* window should appear, as shown in Figure 10-40.

Step 9: In the *CellStyle Builder* window, set the following properties: Alignment = *MiddleCenter*; ForeColor = *Blue*. Click the *OK* button to close the window.

Step 10: In the *Edit Columns* window, select the *Amount* column and open its DefaultCellStyle property.

Step 11: Open its Format property and select *Currency*. Click the *OK* button to close the dialog box.

Step 12: Click the *OK* button to close the *CellStyle Builder* window.

Step 13: Experiment with the three columns, changing colors and formats as you wish. When you finish, click the *OK* button to close the *Edit Columns* window.

Step 14: Save and run the program. You should see a list of payments in the grid. Halt the program.

Figure 10-40 Editing the *Member_Id* column in the *CellStyle Builder* window

CellStyle Builder

⊟ Appearance	
BackColor	
Font	(none)
ForeColor	
SelectionBackColor	
SelectionForeColor	
⊟ Behavior	
Format	
⊟ Data	
NullValue	
⊟ Layout	
Alignment	NotSet
⊞ Padding	0, 0, 0, 0
WrapMode	NotSet

Preview

This preview shows properties from inherited CellStyles (Table, Column, Row)

Normal: #### Selected: ####

OK Cancel

Step 15: Next, you will add code to the Insert button that lets the program save new payments. In *Design* mode, double-click the *Insert* button. Add the following code, shown in bold, to the button's `Click` event handler:

```
Private Sub btnInsert_Click(ByVal sender As System.Object, _
    ByVal e As System.EventArgs) Handles btnInsert.Click

  Try
    Me.PaymentsTableAdapter.Insert(CShort(txtMemberId.Text), _
        CDate(txtDate.Text), CDec(txtAmount.Text))
    Me.PaymentsTableAdapter.Fill(PaymentsDataSet.Payments)
  Catch ex As Exception
    MessageBox.Show(ex.Message, "Data Input Error")
  End Try
End Sub
```

The code you added calls the TableAdapter's `Insert` method, passing to the method the values of the three columns we want to add: *Member_Id*, *Date*, and *Amount*. Each must be converted to a type that matches the appropriate dataset column type. Then, the *Fill* command is called so we can see the new payment in the grid.

TIP: The `Me.` object referred to in Step 15 refers to the current Form object. Its use is optional.

Step 16: Add the following line, marked in bold, to the `Form_Load` event handler. As the comment says, we want the text box to display today's date.

```
Private Sub Form1_Load(ByVal sender As System.Object, _
ByVal e As System.EventArgs) Handles MyBase.Load

  Me.PaymentsTableAdapter.Fill(Me.PaymentsDataSet.Payments)

  ' Set the text box to today's date.
  txtDate.Text = Today().ToString("d")
End Sub
```

Step 17: Save and rerun the program. Add a new payment, using a *Member_Id* value between 1 and 9. Verify that your payment appears in the grid after clicking the *Insert* button. This payment was saved in the database permanently.

Step 18: Add a payment that uses an invalid date format or a nonnumeric value for the amount. When you click the *Insert* button, observe the error message (generated by the `Try-Catch` statement). The message you see was generated by the database and passed to our program via the TableAdapter. Your programs should always recover gracefully when users enter invalid data.

Step 19: End the program.

Using Loops with Datasets

Techniques you've learned about loops and collections in previous chapters apply easily to datasets. You can iterate over the `Rows` collection of a table belonging to a dataset using the `For Each` statement. Usually, it's best to create a strongly typed row that matches the type of rows in the dataset.

The following loop iterates over the `Rows` collection of the *Payments* table of the `PaymentsDataSet` dataset, adding the *Amount* column to a total. The dataset was built from the *Payments* table in the *Karate* database.

```
Dim row As PaymentsDataSet.PaymentsRow
Dim decTotal As Decimal = 0

For Each row In Me.PaymentsDataSet.Payments.Rows
  decTotal += row.Amount
Next
```

Tutorial 10-7 shows how to add a total to the *Karate* student payments.

Tutorial 10-7:
Adding a total to the *Karate* student payments

In this tutorial, you will add statements that calculate the total amount of payments made by students in the Karate School.

Step 1: Open the *Insert_Karate_Payments* program you created in Tutorial 10-6.

Step 2: Add a new button to the form. Set its properties as follows:
Name = `btnTotal`; Text = *Total Payments*.

Step 3: Double-click the new button and insert the following code, shown in bold, to its `Click` event handler. This code uses a loop to get the payment amount value from each row in the dataset and add the value to a total:

```
Private Sub btnTotal_Click(ByVal sender As System.Object, _
    ByVal e As System.EventArgs) Handles btnTotal.Click

  Dim decTotal As Decimal = 0
  Dim row As PaymentsDataSet.PaymentsRow
  For Each row In Me.PaymentsDataSet.Payments.Rows
    decTotal += row.Amount
  Next

  MessageBox.Show("Total payments are equal to " _
      & decTotal.ToString("c"), "Total")
End Sub
```

Step 4: Save and run the program. Click the *Total Payments* button and observe the results. An example is shown in Figure 10-41.

Step 5: End the program.

Figure 10-41 Calculating the total payments

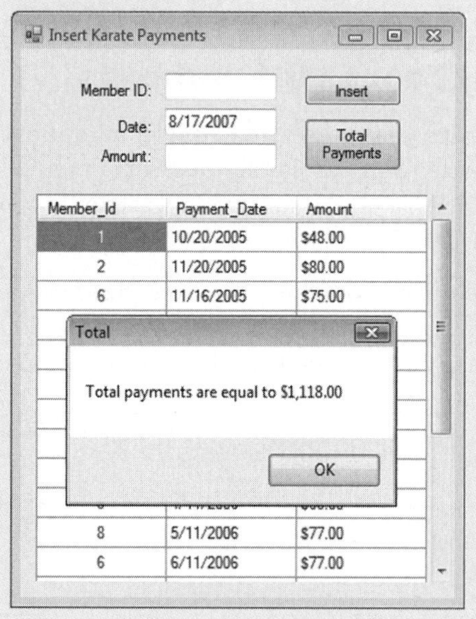

Checkpoint

10.11 Which Visual Studio window displays the list of datasets belonging to a project?

10.12 The ____________ ____________ *Configuration Wizard* is a tool you can use to create a connection to a database and select a database table.

10.13 If a certain data source exists, what is the easiest way to bind it to a DataGridView control?

10.14 How do you bind a single data source column to a text box?

10.15 By default, which control binds to a DateTime field in a data source?

10.16 What is the menu command for adding a new data source to the current project?

10.5 Structured Query Language (SQL)

SQL, which stands for *Structured Query Language*, is a standard language for working with database management systems. SQL has been standardized by the American National Standards Institute (ANSI) and adopted by almost every database software vendor as the language of choice for interacting with their Database Management System (DBMS).

SQL consists of a limited set of keywords. You use the keywords to construct statements, which are also known as **database queries**. These statements are submitted to the DBMS, and in response, the DBMS carries out operations on its data.

> **NOTE:** Although SQL is a language, you don't use it to write applications. It is intended only as a standard means of interacting with a DBMS. You still need a general programming language such as Visual Basic to write database-related applications.

`SELECT` Statement

The **`SELECT` statement** retrieves data from a database. You can use it to select rows, columns, and tables. The most basic format for a single table is as follows:

```
SELECT column-list
FROM table
```

The members of *`column-list`* must be table column names separated by commas. The following statement selects the *ID* and *Salary* columns from the *SalesStaff* table:

```
SELECT ID, Salary
FROM SalesStaff
```

In a Visual Basic program, the dataset produced by this query would have just two columns: *ID* and *Salary*. There is no required formatting or capitalization of SQL statements or field names. The following queries are equivalent:

```
SELECT ID, Salary FROM SalesStaff
select ID, Salary from SalesStaff
Select id, salary from salesstaff
```

As a matter of style and readability, you should try to use consistent capitalization.

If field names contain embedded spaces, they must be surrounded by square brackets, as in the following example:

```
SELECT [Last Name], [First Name]
FROM Employees
```

The `*` character in the column list selects all columns from a table, as shown in the following example:

```
SELECT *
FROM SalesStaff
```

Aliases for Column Names

Column names can be renamed, using the `AS` keyword. The new column name is called an *alias*, as in the following example that renames the `Hire_Date` column to

Date_Hired:

```
SELECT
  Last_Name, Hire_Date AS Date_Hired
FROM
  SalesStaff
```

Renaming columns is useful for two reasons: First, you might want to hide the real column names from users for security purposes. Second, column headings in reports can be made more user friendly if you substitute your own names for the column names used inside the database.

Creating Alias Columns from Other Columns

A query can create a new column (called an alias) from other existing columns. For example, we might want to combine *Last_Name* and *First_Name* from a table named *Members*. We can insert a comma and space between the columns as follows:

```
SELECT Last_Name + ', ' + First_Name AS Full_Name
FROM Members
```

Now the *Full_Name* column can conveniently be inserted into a list box or combo box. In general, when strings occur in queries, they must always be surrounded by apostrophes. The + operator concatenates strings.

Calculated Columns

You can create new columns, whose contents are calculated from existing column values. Suppose a table named *Payroll* contains columns named `employeeId`, `hoursWorked`, and `hourlyRate`. The following statement creates a new column named `payAmount` using `hoursWorked` and `hourlyRate`:

```
SELECT employeeId,
  hoursWorked * hourlyRate AS payAmount
FROM PayRoll
```

Setting the Row Order with ORDER BY

The SQL `SELECT` statement has an **`ORDER BY` clause** that lets you control the display order of the table rows. In other words, you can sort the data on one or more columns. The following is the general form for sorting on a single column:

```
ORDER BY columnName [ASC | DESC]
```

ASC indicates ascending order (the default), and `DESC` indicates descending order. Both are optional, and you can use only one at a time. The following clause orders the *SalesStaff* table in ascending order by last name:

```
ORDER BY Last_Name ASC
```

We can do this more simply, as follows:

```
ORDER BY Last_Name
```

The following sorts the data in descending order by salary:

```
ORDER BY Salary DESC
```

You can sort on multiple columns. The following statement sorts in ascending order first by last name, then within each last name, it sorts in ascending order by first name:

```
ORDER BY Last_Name, First_Name
```

The following SELECT statement returns the first name, last name, and date joined, sorting by last name and first name in the *Members* table of the *Karate* database:

```
SELECT
  First_Name, Last_Name, Date_Joined
FROM
  Members
ORDER BY Last_Name, First_Name
```

Selecting Rows with the WHERE Clause

The SQL SELECT statement has an optional **WHERE clause** that you can use to *filter*, or which rows you want to retrieve from a database table. The simplest form of the WHERE clause is as follows:

```
WHERE columnName = value
```

In this case, *columnName* must be one of the table columns, and *value* must be in a format that is consistent with the column type. The following SELECT statement, for example, specifies that *Last_Name* must be equal to *Gomez*:

```
SELECT First_Name, Last_Name, Salary
FROM SalesStaff
WHERE Last_Name = 'Gomez'
```

Because *Last_Name* is a Text column, it must be compared to a string literal enclosed in apostrophes. If the person's name contains an apostrophe (such as O'Leary), the apostrophe must be repeated. The following is an example:

```
SELECT First_Name, Last_Name, Salary
FROM SalesStaff
WHERE Last_Name = 'O''Leary'
```

Relational Operators

Table 10-12 lists the operators that can be used in WHERE clauses. The following expression matches last names starting with letters B–Z:

```
WHERE Last_Name >= 'B'
```

The following expression matches non-zero salary values:

```
WHERE Salary <> 0
```

Table 10-12 SQL relational operators

Operator	Meaning
=	equal to
<>	not equal to
<	less than
<=	less than or equal to
>	greater than
>=	greater than or equal to

Numeric and Date Values

Numeric literals are not surrounded by quotation marks. The following expression matches all rows in which *Salary* is greater than $30,000. The use of parentheses is optional.

```
WHERE (Salary > 30000)
```

Date literals must be delimited by apostrophes:

```
WHERE (Hire_Date > '12/31/1999')
```

The following expression matches rows containing hire dates falling between (and including) January 1, 1992 and December 31, 1999:

```
WHERE (Hire_Date BETWEEN '1/1/1992' AND '12/31/1999')
```

The following is a complete `SELECT` statement using the `WHERE` clause that selects rows according to *Hire_Date* and sorts by last name:

```
SELECT First_Name, Last_Name, Hire_Date
FROM SalesStaff
WHERE (Hire_Date BETWEEN '1/1/1992' AND '12/31/1999')
ORDER BY Last_Name
```

`LIKE` Operator

The **`LIKE` operator** can be used to create partial matches with varchar column values. When combined with `LIKE`, the underscore character matches a single unknown character. For example, the following expression matches all three-character Account_ID values beginning with `X` and ending with 4:

```
WHERE Account_ID LIKE 'X_4'
```

The % character matches multiple unknown characters. We call % a **wildcard** symbol. For example, the following matches all last names starting with the letter A:

```
WHERE Last_Name LIKE 'A%'
```

Wildcard symbols can be combined. For example, the following matches all *First_Name* values in the table that have 'dr' in the second and third positions:

```
WHERE First_Name LIKE '_dr%'
```

Compound Expressions (`AND`, `OR`, and `NOT`)

SQL uses the `AND`, `OR`, and `NOT` operators to create compound expressions. In most cases, you should use parentheses to clarify the order of operations. The following expression matches rows in which the person was hired after 1/1/1990 and their salary is greater than $40,000.

```
WHERE (Hire_Date > '1/1/1990') AND (Salary > 40000)
```

The following expression matches rows in which the person was hired either before 1992 or after 1999:

```
WHERE (Hire_Date < '1/1/1992') OR (Hire_Date > '12/31/1999')
```

The following expression matches two types of employees: (1) employees hired after 1/1/1990 whose salaries are greater than $40,000; (2) part-time employees:

```
WHERE (Hire_Date > '1/1/1990') AND (Salary > 40000)
OR (Full_Time = 'False')
```

The following expression matches rows in which the hire date does not fall between 1/1/1992 and 12/31/1999:

```
WHERE (Hire_Date NOT BETWEEN '1/1/1992' AND '12/31/1999')
```

The following expression matches rows in which the last name does not begin with the letter A:

```
WHERE (Last_Name NOT LIKE 'A%')
```

Modifying the Query in a Data Source

To modify (edit) a query used by a data source, open its dataset schema file from the *Solution Explorer* window. Suppose an application contains a dataset named *SalesStaffDataSet*. Then the corresponding dataset schema file would be named *SalesStaffDataSet.xsd*. You can open a schema file in *Solution Explorer* by double-clicking its filename. An example is shown in Figure 10-42. The top line shows the database name. The next several lines list the columns in the dataset, identifying the ID column as the primary key. The *SalesStaffTableAdapter* appears next, followed by a list of its database queries. By default, there is one query named *Fill, GetData()* that fills the dataset when the form loads.

Figure 10-42 *SalesStaffDataSet,* in the *Dataset Designer* window

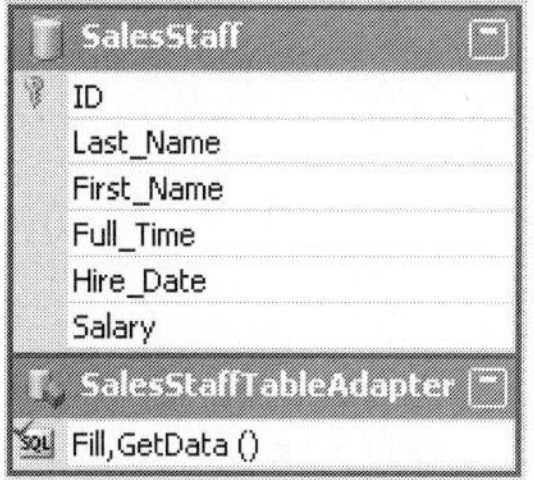

If you right-click the title bar of the *SalesStaffTableAdapter* and select *Configure* from the pop-up menu, you can modify the currently selected query using the *TableAdapter Configuration Wizard*, as shown in Figure 10-43. If the query text is simple enough, you can modify it directly in this window. If the query is more complicated, you may want to use the *Query Builder*, which can be launched by clicking the *Query Builder* button. An example is shown in Figure 10-44.

To close the *Query Builder*, click the *OK* button. Then click the *Finish* button to close the *TableAdapter Configuration Wizard*. Finally, you should save the dataset in the *DataSet Designer* window before closing it. Let's take a closer look at the *Query Builder* tool.

Query Builder

Query Builder is a tool provided by Visual Studio for creating and modifying SQL queries. It consists of four sections, called *panes*, as shown in Figure 10-45.

- The **diagram pane** displays all the tables used in the query, with a check mark next to each field that will be used in the dataset.
- The **grid pane** displays the query in a spreadsheet-like format, which is particularly well suited to choosing a sort order and entering selection criteria.

- The **SQL pane** displays the actual SQL query that corresponds to the tables and fields selected in the diagram and grid panes. Advanced SQL users usually write queries directly into this pane.
- The **results pane** displays the data rows returned by executing the current SQL query. To fill the results pane, right-click in the *Query Builder* window and select *Run* from the *context* menu.

Figure 10-43 Using the *TableAdapter Configuration Wizard*

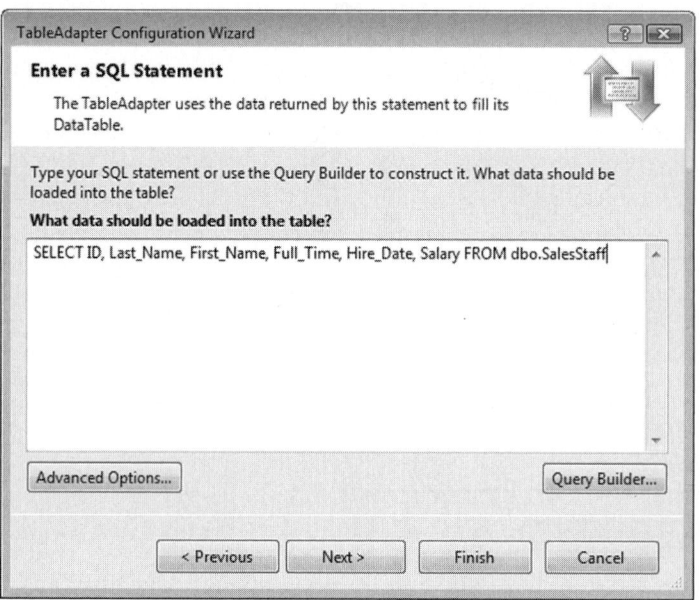

Figure 10-44 Launching the *Query Builder*

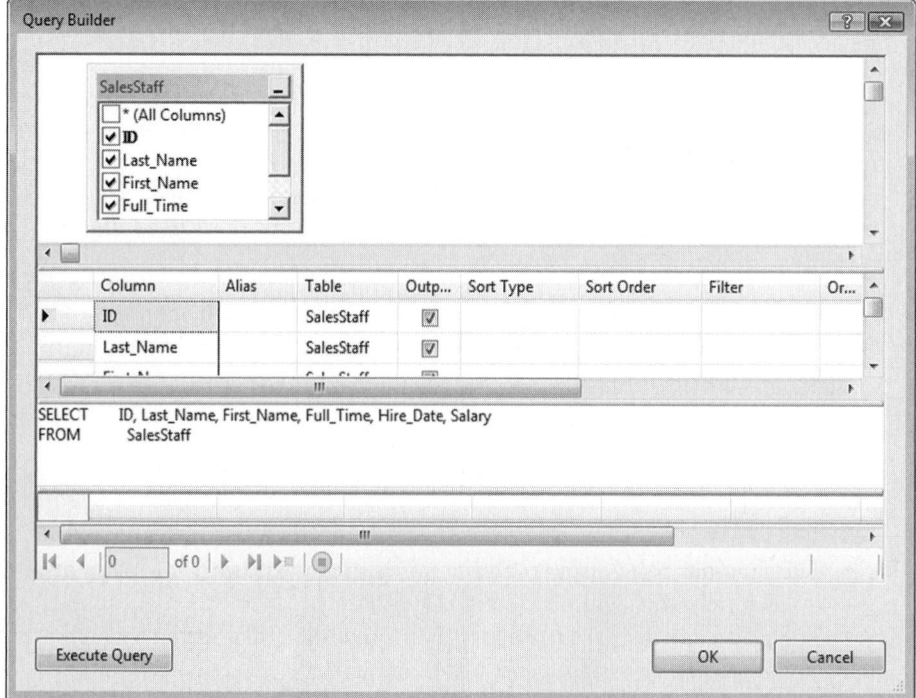

Figure 10-45 Sections of the *Query Builder* window

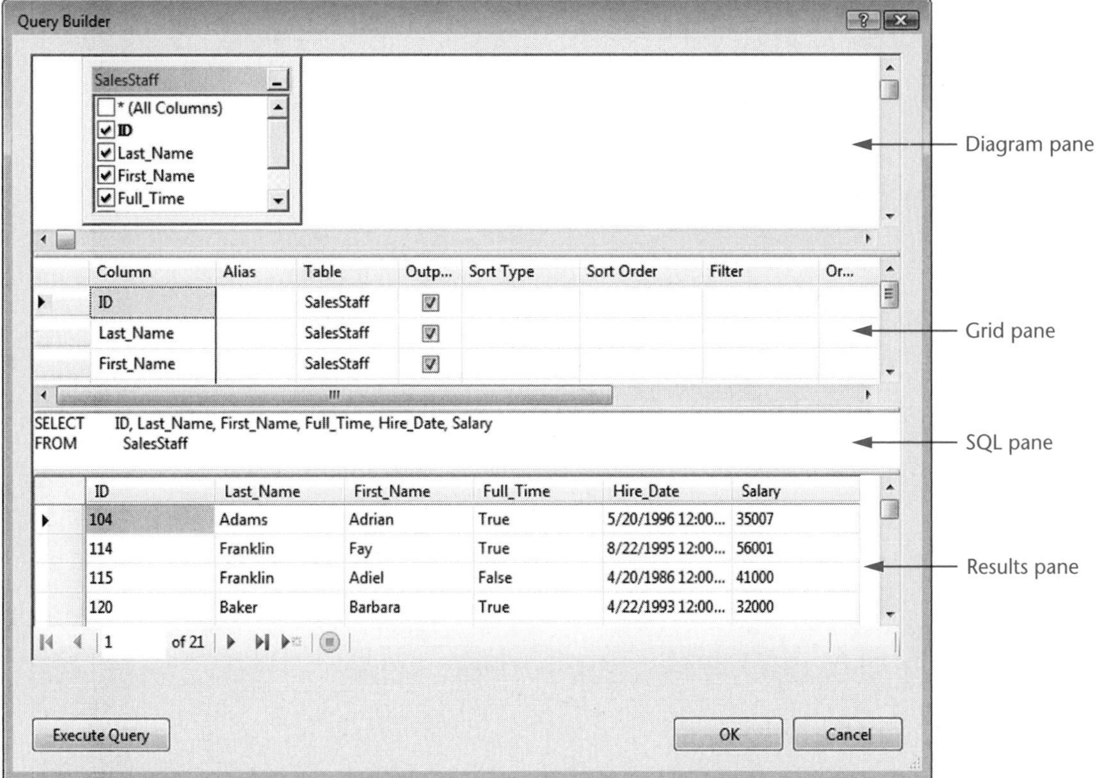

To remove and restore panes, do the following:

- To remove a pane, right-click it and select *Remove Pane* from the pop-up menu.
- To restore a pane that was removed, right-click in the window, select *Show Panes* from the pop-up menu, and select a pane from the list that appears.

To add a new table to the *Query Builder* window, right-click inside the diagram pane and select *Add Table* from the pop-up menu. To close *Query Builder*, click the *OK* button.

Adding a Query to a DataGridView

If you want to add a specific query to a DataGridView control, the easiest way to do it is to use the TableAdapter attached to the grid. Suppose *SalesStaffTableAdapter* is attached to a DataGridView displaying the *SalesStaff* table from the Company database. In the component tray at the bottom of the Form in the Design view, right-click the table adapter icon and select *Add Query*. The *Search Criteria Builder* window appears, as shown in Figure 10-46. Let's modify the query so it looks as follows:

```
SELECT ID, Last_Name, First_Name, Full_Time, Hire_Date, Salary
FROM SalesStaff
WHERE Salary < 45000
```

Figure 10-47 shows what the window looks like after adding a `WHERE` clause to the `SELECT` statement. Notice that you can give a name to the query, which we called *Salary_query*. When you click the *OK* button, a ToolStrip control is added to the form, with a query button, as shown in Figure 10-48. When we run the program and click the *Salary_query* button on the tool strip, the results are as shown in Figure 10-49. Only rows with salaries less than $45,000 are displayed.

Figure 10-46 *Search Criteria Builder* window

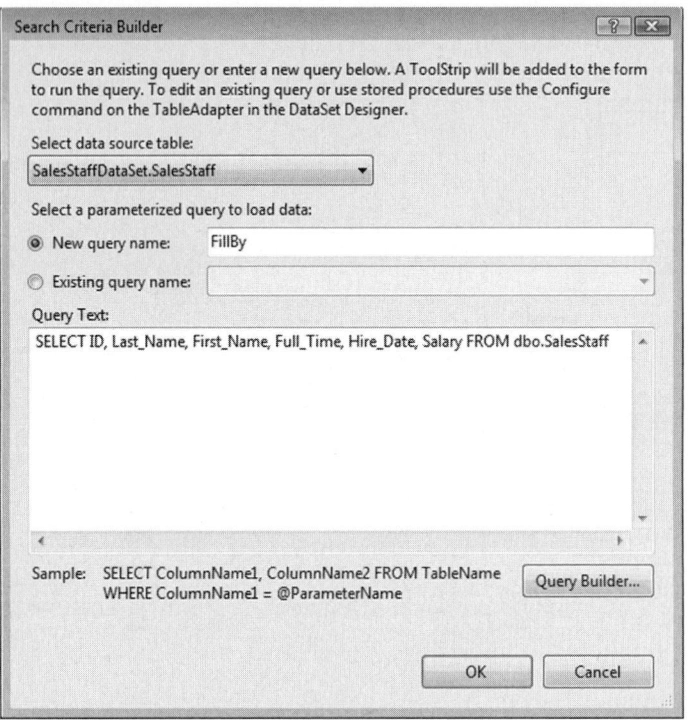

Figure 10-47 Entering a query in the *Search Criteria Builder*

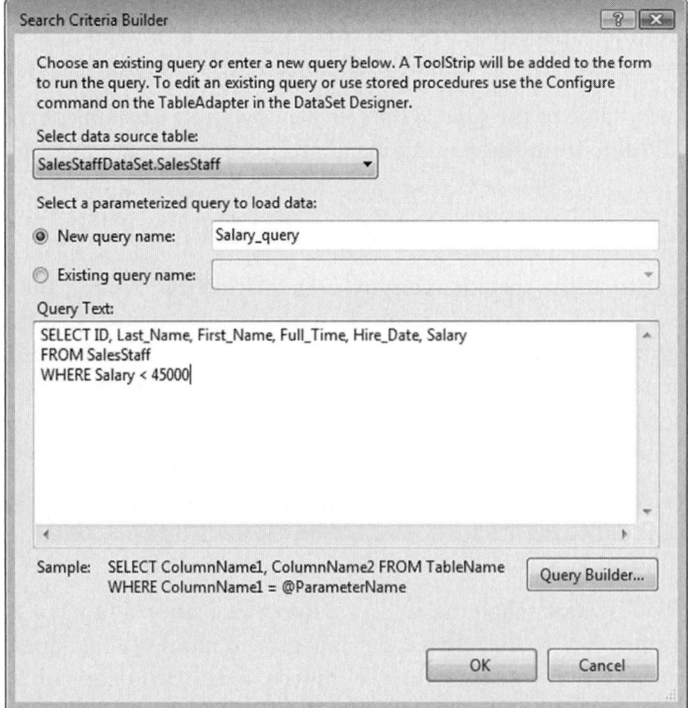

Figure 10-48 Tool strip added to the form, with a query button

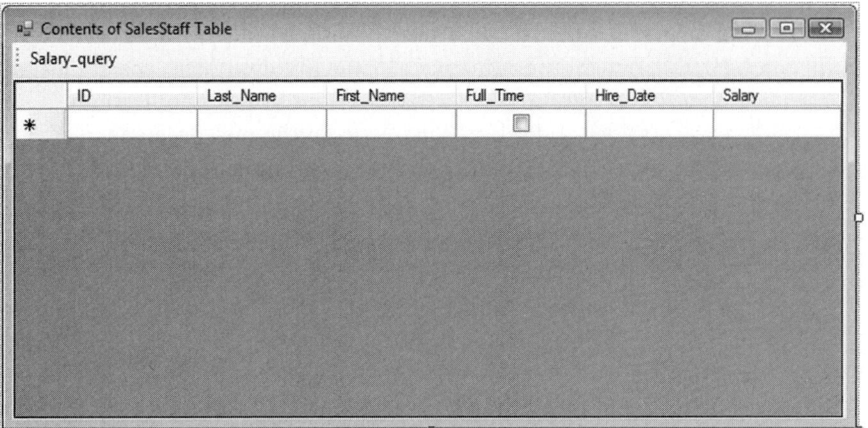

Figure 10-49 Rows filtered by a query named *Salary_query*

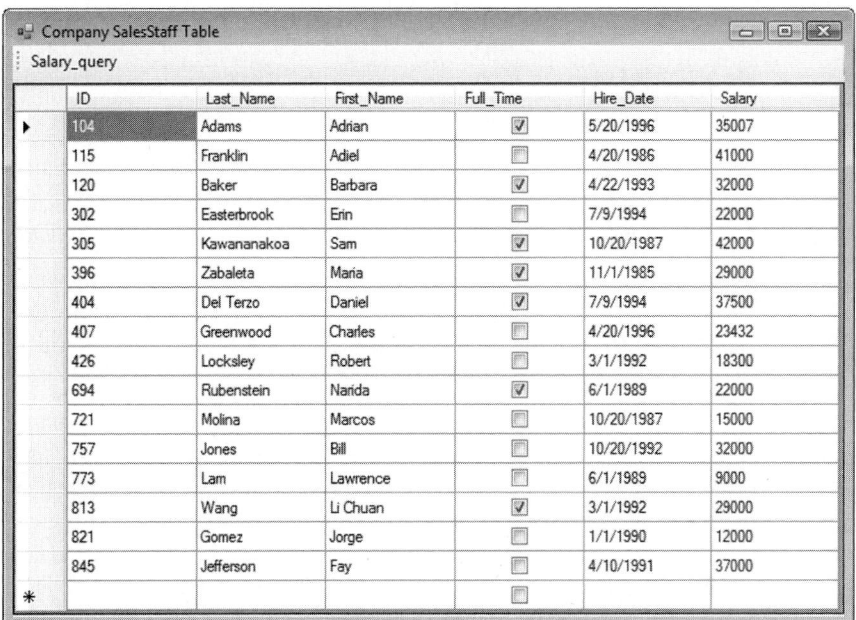

ID	Last_Name	First_Name	Full_Time	Hire_Date	Salary
104	Adams	Adrian	☑	5/20/1996	35007
115	Franklin	Adiel	☐	4/20/1986	41000
120	Baker	Barbara	☑	4/22/1993	32000
302	Easterbrook	Erin	☐	7/9/1994	22000
305	Kawananakoa	Sam	☑	10/20/1987	42000
396	Zabaleta	Maria	☑	11/1/1985	29000
404	Del Terzo	Daniel	☑	7/9/1994	37500
407	Greenwood	Charles	☐	4/20/1996	23432
426	Locksley	Robert	☐	3/1/1992	18300
694	Rubenstein	Narida	☑	6/1/1989	22000
721	Molina	Marcos	☐	10/20/1987	15000
757	Jones	Bill	☐	10/20/1992	32000
773	Lam	Lawrence	☐	6/1/1989	9000
813	Wang	Li Chuan	☑	3/1/1992	29000
821	Gomez	Jorge	☐	1/1/1990	12000
845	Jefferson	Fay	☐	4/10/1991	37000
			☐		

Tutorial 10-8 shows how to filter rows in the *SalesStaff* table.

Tutorial 10-8:
Filtering rows in the *SalesStaff* table

In this tutorial, you will create a query that changes the way *SalesStaff* rows display in a DataGridView control.

Step 1: Copy the *SalesStaff 1* folder you created in Tutorial 10-1 to a new folder named *SalesStaff Queries*.

> **TIP:** To copy a folder in Windows Explorer, right-click its name with the mouse and select *Copy* from the pop-up menu; right-click again and select *Paste* from the pop-up menu. In Windows Vista, the folder will be named *<name> - Copy*, where *<name>* is the original folder name. Right-click the copied folder and select *Rename* from the pop-up menu. Type the new folder name and press Enter. (The same procedure works when copying files.)

Step 2: Open the project from the *SalesStaff Queries* folder (the solution file will still be named *SalesStaff 1.sln*).

Step 3: Right-click the project folder in the *Solution Explorer* window, and choose *Rename*. Rename the folder *SalesStaff Queries*.

Step 4: With `Form1` in the *Design view* window, drag the top edge of the DataGridView control downward about three-quarters of an inch. This will leave room for Visual Studio to insert two ToolStrip controls. Next, right-click the SalesStaffTableAdapter control in the component tray, and select *Add Query* from the pop-up menu.

Step 5: In the *Search Criteria Builder* window, create a new query named *Full_Time*. Set its query text to the following:

```
SELECT ID, Last_Name, First_Name, Full_Time, Hire_Date, Salary
FROM SalesStaff
WHERE (Full_Time = 'True')
```

Step 6: Click the *OK* button to save the query. Save the project and run the application. Click the *Full_Time* tool strip button and observe that only full time employees are displayed. Stop the program and return to *Design* mode.

Step 7: Suppose you have clicked on the *Full_Time* button, but want to return to displaying all rows in the table. You need to add another button to the tool strip. To do so, right-click the SalesStaffTableAdapter control, and select *Add Query*.

Step 8: In the Search *Criteria Builder* window, name the query *All_Rows*, and keep the existing query text. Click *OK* to close the window and create the query. Notice that a second tool strip has been added to the form, as shown in Figure 10-50. The upper part of the DataGridView may have been covered up, so adjust its top border position with the mouse.

Figure 10-50 *SalesStaff* table in a DataGridView, with two query buttons

Company SalesStaff Table

Full_Time

All_Rows

ID	Last_Name	First_Name	Full_Time	Hire_Date	Salary
104	Adams	Adrian	☑	5/20/1996	35007
114	Franklin	Fay	☑	8/22/1995	56001
115	Franklin	Adiel	☐	4/20/1986	41000
120	Baker	Barbara	☑	4/22/1993	32000
135	Ferriere	Henri	☑	1/1/1990	57000
292	Hasegawa	Danny	☐	5/20/1997	45000
302	Easterbrook	Erin	☐	7/9/1994	22000
305	Kawananakoa	Sam	☑	10/20/1987	42000
396	Zabaleta	Maria	☑	11/1/1985	29000
404	Del Terzo	Daniel	☑	7/9/1994	37500
407	Greenwood	Charles	☐	4/20/1996	23432
426	Locksley	Robert	☐	3/1/1992	18300

Step 9: Run the program and click both query buttons. The display should alternate between displaying all rows and only rows for full-time employees.

Step 10: End the program and close the project.

This tutorial has shown you an easy way to create queries that select rows from a database table. Ease of use, however, can mean a lack of flexibility. We must find a way to let the user change the values of queries at runtime. Later in this chapter we will show you how to use query parameters to pass different values to SQL queries.

Checkpoint

10.17 What does the acronym SQL represent, in relation to databases?

10.18 Why will SQL queries work with any database?

10.19 Write an SQL `SELECT` statement that retrieves the *First_Name* and *Last_Name* columns from a table named *Employees*.

10.20 How do you add a query to a TableAdapter in the component tray of a form?

10.21 Write a `WHERE` clause that limits the returned data to rows in which the field named Salary is less than or equal to $85,000.

10.22 Write a `SELECT` statement that retrieves the *pay_rate*, *employee_id*, and *hours_worked* columns from a table named *Payroll*, and sorts the rows in descending order by *hours_worked*.

10.23 Write a `SELECT` statement that creates an alias named *Rate_of_Pay* for the existing column named *pay_rate* in the *Payroll* table.

10.24 Write a `SELECT` statement for the *Payroll* table that creates a new output column named *gross_pay* by multiplying the *pay_rate* column by the *hours_worked* column.

10.25 Write a `SELECT` statement for the *Payroll* table that returns only rows in which the pay rate is greater than 20,000 and less than or equal to 55,000.

10.26 Write a `SELECT` statement for the *Payroll* table that returns only rows in which the *employee_id* column begins with the characters *FT*. The remaining characters in the *employee_id* are unimportant.

10.6 Focus on Problem Solving: *Karate School Management* Application

Suppose you are a black belt in the Kyoshi Karate School and Sensei (the teacher) has asked you to create a management application with the following capabilities:

1. Displays a list of all members. Permits the user to sort on any column, edit individual rows, and delete rows.
2. Adds new students to the *Members* table.
3. Displays members having similar last names.
4. Displays payments by all members. Permits the user to sort on any column.

Techniques for completing most of the tasks have already been demonstrated earlier in this chapter. Other tasks will require some new skills, which we will explain along the way. Before beginning to code the application, you would normally consult with the customer to clarify some user interface details. We will assume Sensei wants the following:

- For Requirement 1, use a DataGridView control. Set options that permit modifying and removing rows. The user will be able to sort by clicking on column headings.
- For Requirement 2, create a data input form with TextBox controls and a DateTimePicker control.
- For Requirement 3, let the user type a partial last name into a text box. Display a grid containing all members whose last names begin with the name entered by the user.
- For Requirement 4, join the *Members* and *Payments* tables and display the results in a DataGridView control.

As much as possible, we will try to avoid duplication of effort, and use existing datasets and DataGridView controls.

General Design Guidelines

Each form will have a *File* menu with a *Close window* option. A startup form will display a menu and a program logo. Each major requirement will be carried out on a separate form to allow for future expansion. When Sensei sees how easy the program is to use, he will surely want to add more capabilities.

Before we start to create the application, let's look at the finished version. Doing so will give you a better idea of how the detailed steps fit into the overall picture. In real life, programmers usually create an incomplete **prototype** or demonstration copy of their program. The prototype stage is where one tries out different versions of the user interface, requiring some reworking, problem-solving, and long discussions with the customer. To save time, we will pretend you designed the program perfectly and never changed your mind.

The startup form, called *frmMain*, displays a program logo and a menu with three major choices, as shown in Figure 10-51.

Figure 10-51 *Karate School Manager* startup form

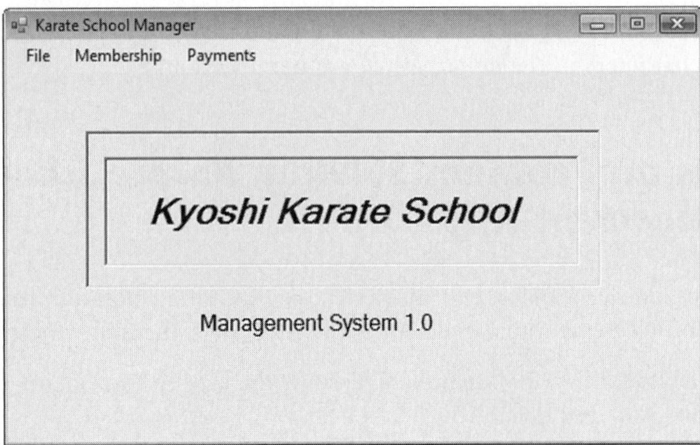

The startup form should be simple, to avoid overwhelming users with details. The menu makes it clear that our system handles two major types of functions: membership and payments. The menu selections are as follows:

```
File
  Exit
Membership
  List all
  Find member
  Add new member
Payments
  All members
```

Membership Forms

Sensei wants to view a list of all members, so we have provided the *All Members* form, as shown in Figure 10-52. The grid allows users to sort on any column, select and delete rows, and modify individual cells within each row. If the user wants to save changes they've made back into the database, they select *Save changes* from the *File* menu.

The *Find Member by Last Name* form, shown in Figure 10-53, lets the user enter all or part of a member's last name. When the user clicks the *Go* button or presses Enter, a list of matching member rows displays in the grid. Sensei has asked that name searches be case insensitive.

Figure 10-52 *All Members* form

All Members

File

ID	First_Name	Last_Name	Phone	Date_Joined
1	Keoki	Kahumanu	111-2222	2/20/2002
2	Anne	Chong	232-2323	2/20/1995
3	Elaine	Hasegawa	313-3455	2/20/2004
4	Brian	Kahane	646-9387	5/20/1998
5	Aldo	Gonzalez	123-2345	6/6/1999
6	Jascha	Kousevitzky	414-2345	2/20/1992
7	Moses	Taliafea	545-2323	5/20/2005
8	Rafael	Concepcion	602-3312	5/20/2001
9	Ben	Norris	333-2222	1/15/1985

Figure 10-53 *Find Member by Last Name* form

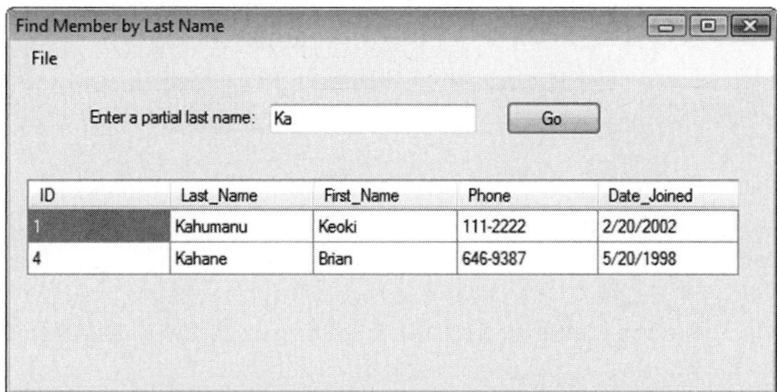

ID	Last_Name	First_Name	Phone	Date_Joined
1	Kahumanu	Keoki	111-2222	2/20/2002
4	Kahane	Brian	646-9387	5/20/1998

The *Add New Member* form, as shown in Figure 10-54, lets the user add a new person to the *Members* table. After entering the fields and choosing a data from the DateTimePicker control, the user selects *Save and close* from the *File* menu. Or, if they want to close the form without saving the data, they select *Close without saving* from the *File* menu.

Figure 10-54 *Add New Member* form

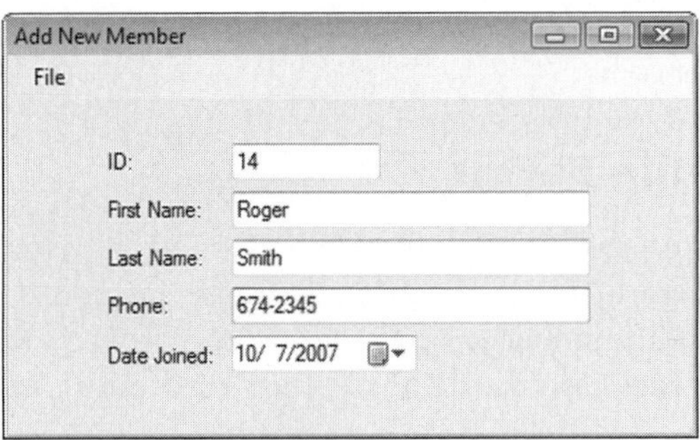

Payment Form

We now turn our attention to the *Payments* subsystem of our application. When the user selects *All Members* from the *Payments* menu on the startup form, the *Payments by All Members* form appears, as shown in Figure 10-55. The rows are initially ordered by last name, but the user can sort on any column by clicking on the column header (once for an ascending sort, and a second time for a descending sort).

Figure 10-55 *Payments by All Members* form

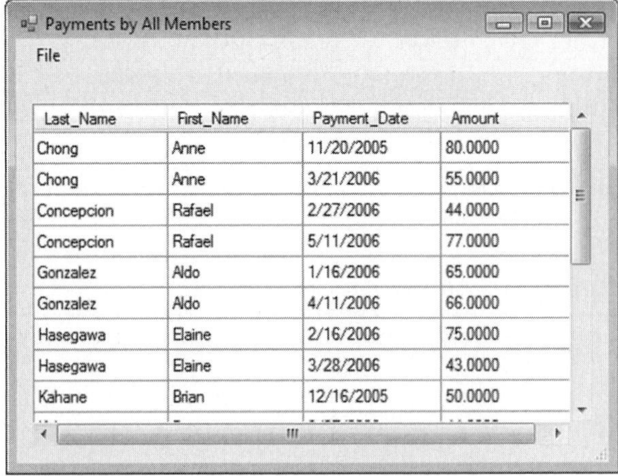

From the user's point of view, the program should be simple. By the time you finish creating it, you will know how to design a simple user interface, open multiple windows, create datasets and connections, search for database rows in various ways, and perform simple configurations of the DataGridView control. Ready? Let's begin.

Tutorial 10-9 creates the *Karate School Manager startup* window.

Tutorial 10-9:
Creating the *Karate School Manager* startup form

In this tutorial, you will create the startup form that first displays when the *Karate School Manager* runs.

Step 1: Create a new Windows Forms application named *Karate School Manager.*

Step 2: Close *Form1* and rename it *frmMain.vb* in the *Solution Explorer* window.

Step 3: Open the form and set its Size.Width property to *530*, and its Size.Height property to *320*. Change its Text property to *Karate School Manager*. Change its StartPosition property to *CenterScreen*. Set its MaximizeBox property to *False*. Set the FormBorderStyle to *FixedSingle*.

Step 4: Insert a Panel control on the form and set its Size.Width and Size.Height properties to *390* and *115*. Insert another Panel control inside the first one, and set its Size property to *360, 80*. Set the BorderStyle property of both panels to *Fixed3D*. Use Figure 10-51 as a guide.

Step 5: Insert a Label control inside the smaller panel and set its Text property to *Kyoshi Karate School*. Set the font to Italic Bold 18 points, so it looks like the text shown in Figure 10-51.

Step 6: Add another Label control near the bottom of the form and set its Text property to *Management System 1.0*. Center the text, and use an 11.25-point font.

Step 7: Add a MenuStrip control to the form containing *File*, *Membership*, and *Payments*. In the *File* submenu, insert *Exit*. In the *Membership* submenu, insert three items: *List all*, *Find member*, and *Add new member*. In the *Payments* menu, insert one item: *All members*. Insert the & character in each menu item according to your preference.

Step 8: Rename the *File/Exit* menu item to `mnuFileExit`. Double-click the item and insert the following statement in its event handler:

```
Me.Close()
```

Step 9: Save the project. When you run the application, verify that the form closes when you click the *File/Exit* menu item.

Tutorial 10-10 focuses on adding the Membership subsystem to the application.

Tutorial 10-10:
Adding the *Membership / List all* function to the *Karate School Manager*

In this tutorial, you will enable the part of the *Karate School Manager* application that lists all members.

Step 1: Open the *Karate School Manager* project, if it is not already open. Open the startup form (`frmMain`) in Design mode.

Step 2: Add a new form to the project named *frmAllMembers.vb*. Resize the form so it looks similar to the one shown in Figure 10-52. Set its Text property to *All Members*.

Step 3: In the *frmMain designer* window, double-click the *Membership / List all* menu item and insert the following code in its event handler:

```
Dim frm As New frmAllMembers
frm.ShowDialog()
```

Step 4: In the *Data Sources* window, select *Add New Data Source*. Create a connection to the *Karate.mdf* database. In the *Choose your database objects* window shown in Figure 10-56, select the *Members* table and name the dataset *AllMembersDataSet*. Click the *Finish* button to save the data source.

Figure 10-56 Creating the `AllMembersDataSet` dataset in the *Data Source Configuration Wizard*

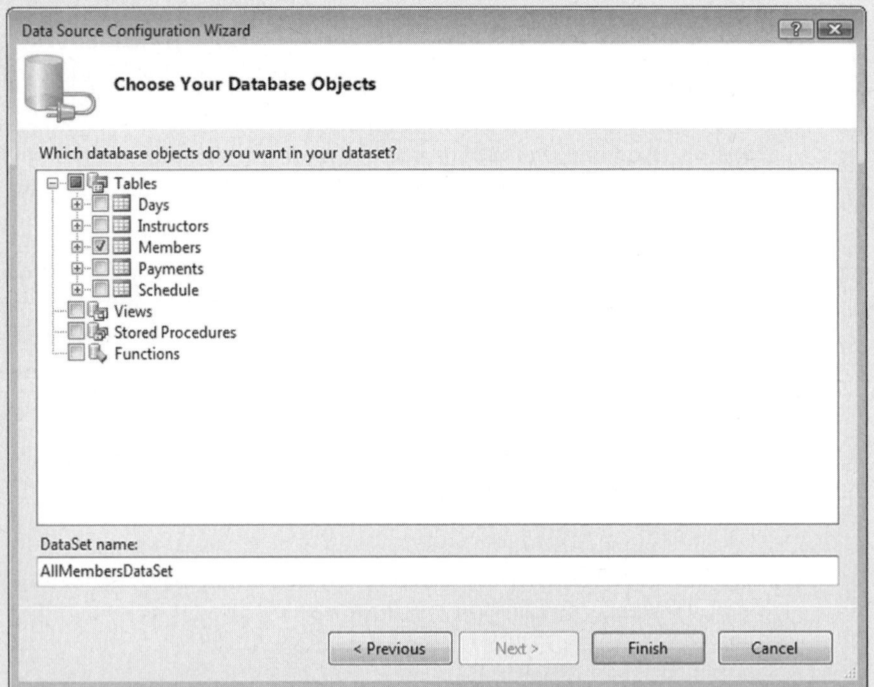

Step 5: Place a DataGridView control on the form and name it *dgvMembers*. Set its Dock property to *Fill*. Set its BackgroundColor property to *Control*. Set its BorderStyle property to *None*.

Step 6: Click the arrow icon in the upper right corner of *dgvMembers*, showing the *DataGridView Tasks* window, as shown in Figure 10-57. In the *ChooseData-Source* drop-down list, select the *Members* table from the `AllMembersDataSet` dataset. Adjust the check boxes in the *Tasks* window so that only *Enable Editing* is checked.

Step 7: If the grid's columns do not appear as shown earlier in Figure 10-52, click the grid's Columns property. Use the arrows next to the column names list to adjust the column order, as shown in Figure 10-58.

Figure 10-57 Tasks for the *dgrMembers* DataGridView control

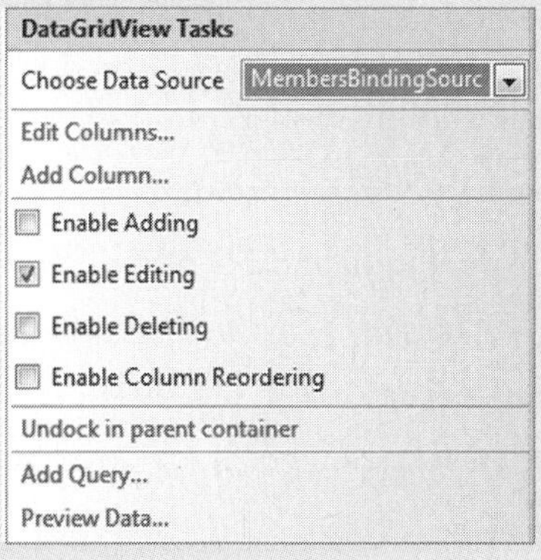

Figure 10-58 Adjusting the column order in the DataGridView control

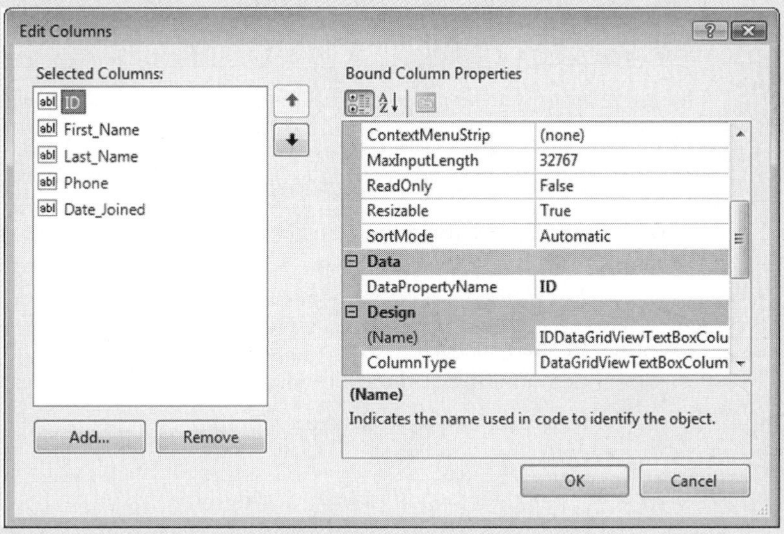

Step 8: Add a *File* menu to the form, with two selections: Save and Close. In the Close menu item's Click handler, insert the Me.Close() statement. Insert the following statement in the Click handler for the *Save* menu item:

```
Me.MembersTableAdapter.Update(Me.AllMembersDataSet.Members)
```

Step 9: Save the project and run the application. From the *startup form* menu, select *Membership / List all.* You should see a list of members similar to that shown earlier in Figure 10-52.

Step 10: Halt the program and return to *Design* mode.

In Tutorial 10-11, you will add the *Membership / Add new member* function to the *Karate School Manager* application.

Using a Binding Source to Add Table Rows

When you bind a data source to controls on a form, Visual Studio automatically adds a BindingSource component to the form. The name of the binding source is based on the dataset name. If a dataset is named `MembersDataSet`, for instance, its binding source will be named `MembersBindingSource`.

A binding source's `AddNew` method adds a blank new row to a dataset. For example:

```
MembersBindingSource.AddNew()
```

The `AddNew` method clears the controls on the form that are bound to the dataset so the user can begin to enter data. The addition does not become permanent until the `EndEdit` method is called as follows:

```
MembersBindingSource.EndEdit()
```

Or, to cancel the operation and not add the new row, call the `CancelEdit` method as follows:

```
MembersBindingSource.CancelEdit()
```

In any case, you have complete control over whether the row is added to the dataset.

Tutorial 10-11: Adding the *Membership / Add new member* function to the *Karate School Manager*

In this tutorial, you will add a form to the *Karate School Manager* program that lets users add new students to the *Members* table.

Step 1: Open the *Karate School Manager* program if it is not already open.

Step 2: Add a new form to the project named `frmAddMember.vb`. Set its Text property to *Add New Member*. Set the following property: FormBorderStyle = *FixedDialog*. Set the form's size to 470 by 300 pixels.

Step 3: In the `frmMain` form, double-click the *Membership / Add new member* menu item and insert the following code in its `Click` event handler:

```
Dim frm As New frmAddMember
frm.ShowDialog()
```

Step 4: Open the *frmAddMember* form in Design view. Then, in the *Data Sources* window, locate the *Members* table under the `AllMembersDataSet` entry. Click next to the *Members* table in the *Data Sources* window and select *Details*. Then drag the table onto the form. This will create a set of data-bound controls. Align the controls as necessary, and move the *First_Name* field above the *Last_Name* field. Use Figure 10-59 as a guide. Set the Format property of the DateTimePicker control to *Short*. Adjust the form's tab stops as necessary.

Figure 10-59 Adding a new member to the *Members* table

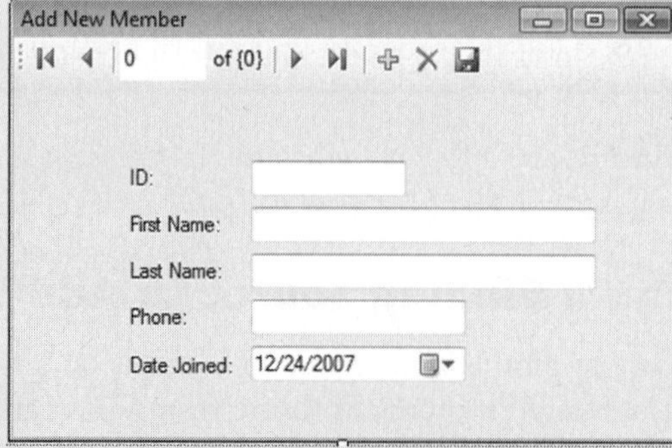

Step 5: Delete the `MembersBindingNavigator` component from the form's component tray. This will cause the ToolStrip (just under the menu) to disappear. You will not need it.

Step 6: Add a *File* menu to the MenuStrip control and insert two items: *Save and close*, and *Close without saving*. Double-click the *Save and close* item and insert the following statements in its event handler:

```
Try
   Me.MembersBindingSource.EndEdit()
   Me.MembersTableAdapter.Update(AllMembersDataSet.Members)
   Me.Close()
Catch ex As Exception
   MessageBox.Show(Me, "Error: " & ex.Message, "Save", _
      MessageBoxButtons.OK, MessageBoxIcon.Warning)
End Try
```

These statements call `EndEdit`, which saves the new row in the dataset. Then the `Update` method call writes the dataset's modifications back to the database.

Step 7: Add the following lines to the end of the `frmAddMember_Load` event handler:

```
Me.MembersBindingSource.AddNew()
Date_JoinedDateTimePicker.Value = Today()
```

The first line puts the dataset into *add new row* mode. The second line initializes the DateTimePicker control to today's date.

Step 8: Double-click the *Close without saving* menu item and insert the following statements in its handler:

```
Me.MembersBindingSource.CancelEdit()
Me.Close()
```

Step 9: Save the project and run the application. Click the *Membership / Add new member* menu selection, and add a new member. Choose a member ID that did not appear when you listed all members in Tutorial 10-10. Or, if you're not sure, display a list of all members first. After you have added the new member, close the dialog (Save and close). Then select *List all* from the *Membership* menu and look for the member you added. For extra practice, try adding a new member who has the same ID number as an existing member. You should see an error message dialog saying: Column ID is constrained to be unique.

Using Query Parameters

When SQL queries search for selected records in database tables, you don't know ahead of time what values the user might want to find. While it is possible to modify an SQL query using program code at runtime, it's not easy because program variables must be concatenated with SQL statements. A **query parameter** is a special variable (preceded by the @ symbol) that is embedded within an SQL query.

We can show why query parameters are useful. Suppose the user had entered a name in the txtLastName control, and you wanted to write a query that would locate all rows in the *Members* table having the same last name. You could write the following statements, but the result is not pretty, and one can easily make a typing mistake:

```
Dim query As String
query = "SELECT ID, Last_Name, First_Name, Phone, Date_Joined " _
  & "FROM Members WHERE Last_Name = '" & txtLastName.Text & "'"
```

Instead, we will insert a query parameter named `@Last_Name` directly into the `SELECT` statement:

```
SELECT ID, Last_Name, First_Name, Phone, Date_Joined
  FROM Members
  WHERE Last_Name = @Last_Name
```

When you call the TableAdapter's `Fill` method, the second argument is assigned to the query's `@Last_Name` parameter as follows:

```
Me.MembersTableAdapter.Fill(Me.FindMemberDataSet.Members, _
  txtLastName.Text)
```

If a query contains more than one parameter, the additional required query parameter values are passed as arguments when calling the `Fill` method. We will use a parameterized query (a query containing a parameter) in Tutorial 10-12.

Tutorial 10-12:
Adding the *Membership / Find member* function to the *Karate School Manager*

In this tutorial, you will add a form that lets users search for members by last name. You will use a partial string match, so if the user does not know the exact spelling of the member name, they can view a list of similar names.

Step 1: Open the *Karate School Manager* project if it is not already open.

Step 2: Add a new form to the project named *frmFindMember.vb*. Set its properties as follows: Text = *Find Member by Last Name*; FormBorderStyle = *FixedDialog*.

Step 3: In the *frmMain* form, double-click the *Membership / Find member* menu item and insert the following code in its event handler:

```
Dim frm As New frmFindMember
frm.ShowDialog()
```

Step 4: Add a MenuStrip control to the *frmFindMember* form and create a *File* menu with one selection: *Close*. In its `Click` handler, insert the `Me.Close()` statement.

Step 5: Add a label, a text box named `txtLastName`, and a button named `btnGo` to the form. Use Figure 10-53, shown earlier, as a guide.

Step 6: From the *Data* menu, select *Add New Data Source*. Create a dataset named `FindMemberDataSet`, which uses the *Members* table. Figure 10-60 shows the *Configuration Wizard* window, in which you name the dataset and select the *Members* table.

Step 7: Next, you will modify `FindMemberNameDataSet` by adding a query parameter that lets the program find members by their last names. In the *Solution Explorer* window, open the *Design* window for *FindMemberDataSet.xsd*. Right-click the entry labeled *Fill, GetData()*, and select *Configure* from the pop-up menu. Change the query text to the following, and click the *Finish* button:

```
SELECT ID, Last_Name, First_Name, Phone, Date_Joined
FROM Members
WHERE (Last_Name LIKE @Last_Name + '%')
```

Step 8: Place a DataGridView control on the form and name it *dgvMembers*. Set its properties as follows: BackgroundColor = *Control*; BorderStyle = *None*; Anchor = *Bottom, Left, Right*; RowHeadersVisible = *False*. Use Figure 10-53, shown earlier, as a guide.

Figure 10-60 Adding the `FindMemberDataSet` dataset to the application

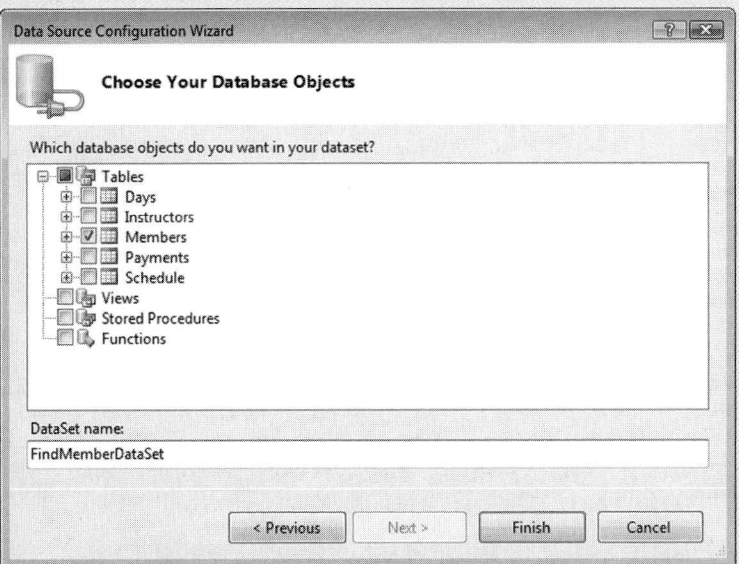

Step 9: Click the smart tag in the grid's upper right corner, displaying the *DataGridView Tasks* window, as shown in Figure 10-61. Bind the grid to the *Members* table of the `FindMemberDataSet` dataset. Disable adding, editing, and deleting of rows.

Figure 10-61 Selecting DataGridView *databinding* options

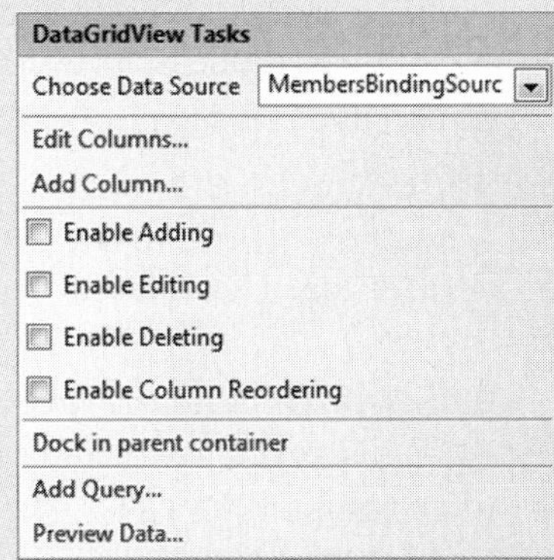

Step 10: Next, you will add a call to the `Fill` method in the event handler for the button that activates the search. Double-click the *Go* button and insert the following code in its event handler:

```
' Perform a wildcard search for last name.
Me.MembersTableAdapter.Fill(Me.FindMemberDataSet.Members, _
  txtLastName.Text)
```

Normally, the `Fill` method has only one parameter, the dataset. But here you pass a second parameter, which is the value to be assigned to the query parameter.

Step 11: Select the form with the mouse and set the Form's AcceptButton property to `btnGo`. This will allow the user to press Enter when activating the search.

Step 12: Remove any statements that might be inside the form's `Load` event handler. (You don't want the grid to fill with data until a member's name has been entered.)

Step 13: Save the project and run the application. From the startup form, click *Membership/Find member* from the menu. When the *Find Member* form appears, enter a partial last name, such as *Ka* and click the *Go* button or press the Enter key. Your output should be similar to that shown in Figure 10-53.

Step 14: Experiment with other partial last names, checking your results against the grid that displays all members.

In Tutorial 10-13, you will add the *Payments / All members* function to the *Karate School Manager*.

Tutorial 10-13:
Adding the *Payments / All members* function to the *Karate School Manager*

In this tutorial, you will create a dataset by joining two tables: *Members* and *Payments*. The dataset will be displayed in a grid.

Step 1: Open the *Karate School Manager* program if it is not already open.

Step 2: Add a new form to the project named *frmPaymentsAll.vb*. Set its properties as follows: Text = *Payments by All Members*. Use Figure 10-55 as a guide.

Step 3: In the `frmMain` form, double-click the *Payments / All members* menu item and insert the following code in its event handler:

```
Dim frm As New frmPaymentsAll
frm.ShowDialog()
```

Step 4: Add a MenuStrip control to the *frmPaymentsAll* form and create a *File* menu with one selection: *Close*. In its `Click` handler, insert the `Me.Close()` statement.

Step 5: Select *Add New Data Source* from the *Data* menu. Add a new data source named *AllPaymentsDataSet*, using the *Payments* table. After the data source has been created, double-click the *AllPaymentsDataSet.xsd* file in the *Solution Explorer* window. Right-click the *Fill, GetData()* entry, and choose *Configure* from the pop-up menu.

Step 6: In the *TableAdapter Configuration Wizard* window that says *Enter a SQL Statement*, click the *Query Builder* button.

Step 7: Add the *Members* table to the upper pane of the *Query Builder* by right-clicking and selecting *Add Table*. After adding the *Members* table, a line should appear between the two tables, as shown in Figure 10-62. This line, with a diamond in the middle, indicates that the ID column in the Payments table is

Figure 10-62 *Query Builder* window, after adding the *Members* table

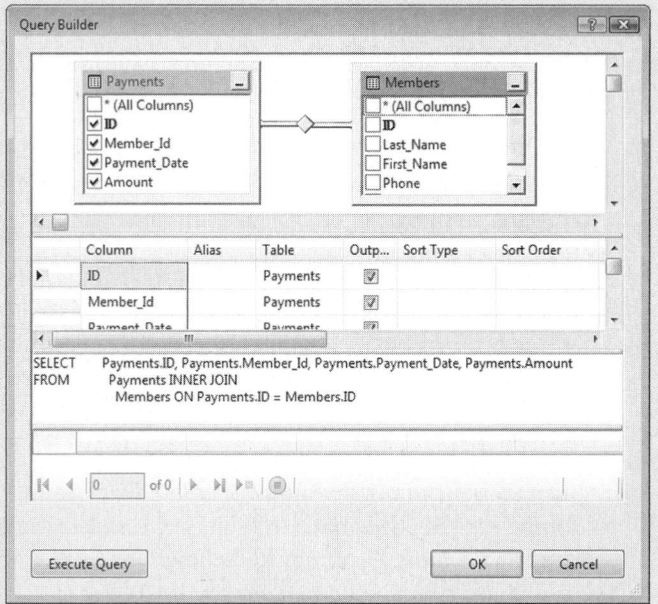

related to the ID column in the Members table. Instead, we want to use the Member_Id column from the Payments table. In the SQL pane of this window, modify the portion of the `SELECT` statement that reads *Payments.ID = Members.ID* so that it now reads: *Payments.Member_Id = Members.ID*. Use Figure 10-63 as a reference.

Figure 10-63 Executing a query containing *Payments* and *Members* tables

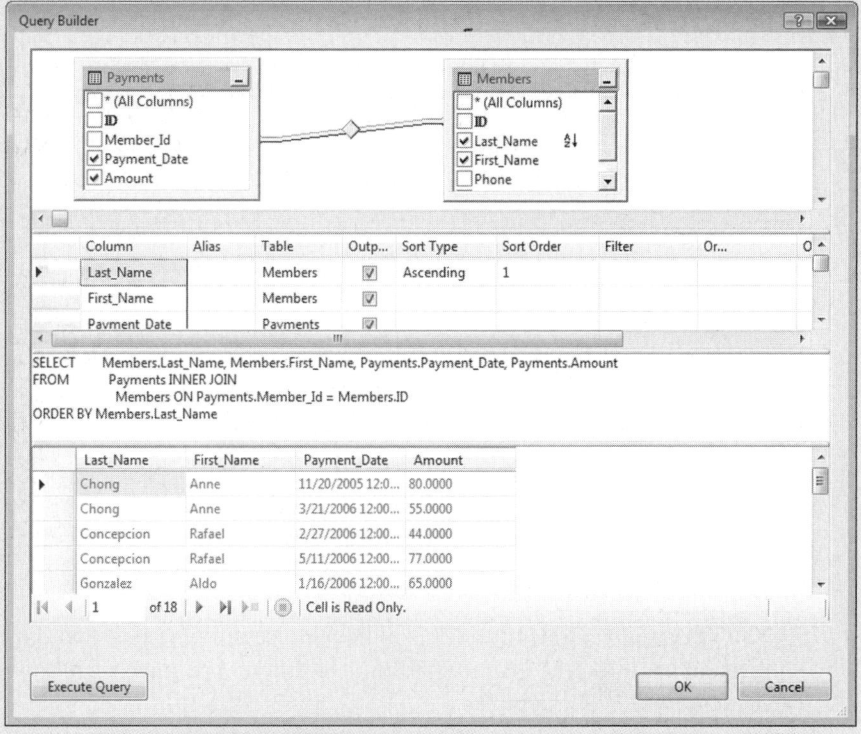

Step 8: Remove all checks from the boxes next to the column names in the upper pane. Then re-check the following fields, in order: *Last_Name*, *First_Name*, *Payment_Date*, and *Amount*.

Step 9: In the *Sort Type* column in the grid pane, select *Ascending* in the *Last_Name* row.

Step 10: Right-click in the window and select *Execute SQL*; a list of names and payments should appear in the bottom pane, as shown in Figure 10-63.

Step 11: Click the *OK* button to close *Query Builder*, and click the *Finish* button to save changes to the dataset. Save your project and close the *Design* window for *AllPaymentsDataSet*.

Step 12: Place a DataGridView control on the form and name it *dgvPayments*. Set its properties as follows: BackgroundColor = *Control*; BorderStyle = *None*; Anchor = *Top, Bottom, Left, Right*; RowHeadersVisible = *False*.

Step 13: Click the small arrow in the upper right corner of *dgvPayments* to open the *DataGridView tasks* window. For the Data Source, choose the *Payments* table of the `AllPaymentsDataSet` dataset. Unselect the *Enable Adding*, *Enable Editing*, and *Enable Deleting* check boxes.

Step 14: Save the project and run the application. Display the *Payments by All members* window. Although the payment information appears, the columns are not in the order we would like. Fortunately, it's easy to modify the column ordering in the DataGridView control.

Step 15: Return to Design mode. Click the Columns property of the *dgvPayments* grid and set the column order to: *Last Name*, *First Name*, *Payment Date*, and *Amount*. Use the arrows next to the Selected Columns list to change the column order. Optionally, you can set the HeaderText property of each column to modify its displayed column heading. You might want to make the column headings look like the ones shown in Figure 10-64.

Figure 10-64 *Payments by All Members* form

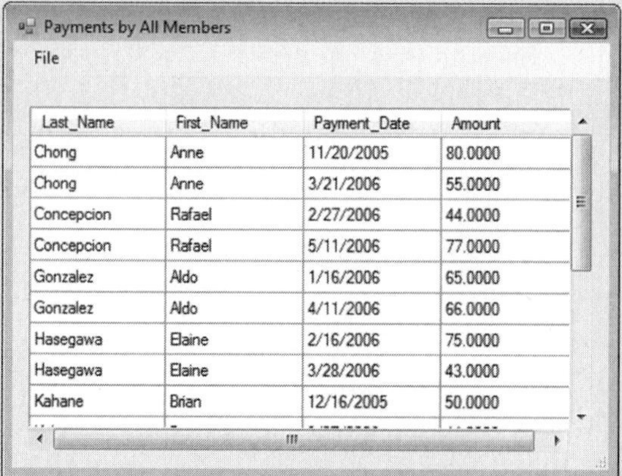

Last_Name	First_Name	Payment_Date	Amount
Chong	Anne	11/20/2005	80.0000
Chong	Anne	3/21/2006	55.0000
Concepcion	Rafael	2/27/2006	44.0000
Concepcion	Rafael	5/11/2006	77.0000
Gonzalez	Aldo	1/16/2006	65.0000
Gonzalez	Aldo	4/11/2006	66.0000
Hasegawa	Elaine	2/16/2006	75.0000
Hasegawa	Elaine	3/28/2006	43.0000
Kahane	Brian	12/16/2005	50.0000

Step 16: Save the project and rerun it.

You've completed this tutorial. You have successfully joined two database tables, using a relation based on the Member_Id table column. You have seen how a dataset can easily contain two database tables.

Complete Source Code

Following is a listing of all the source code in the *Karate School Manager* application. `Option Strict` has been set *On*. Some extraneous comment lines have been removed.

frmMain.vb:

```
Public Class frmMain

    Private Sub mnuFileExit_Click(ByVal sender As System.Object, _
      ByVal e As System.EventArgs) Handles mnuFileExit.Click

        Me.Close()

    End Sub

    Private Sub ListAllToolStripMenuItem_Click(ByVal sender _
      As System.Object, ByVal e As System.EventArgs) _
      Handles ListAllToolStripMenuItem.Click

        Dim frm As New frmAllMembers
        frm.ShowDialog()

    End Sub

    Private Sub AddNewMemberToolStripMenuItem_Click(ByVal _
      sender As System.Object, ByVal e As System.EventArgs) _
      Handles AddNewMemberToolStripMenuItem.Click

        Dim frm As New frmAddMember
        frm.ShowDialog()

    End Sub

    Private Sub FindMemberToolStripMenuItem_Click(ByVal _
      sender As System.Object, ByVal e As System.EventArgs) _
      Handles FindMemberToolStripMenuItem.Click

        Dim frm As New frmFindMember
        frm.ShowDialog()

    End Sub

    Private Sub AllMembersToolStripMenuItem_Click(ByVal _
      sender As System.Object, ByVal e As System.EventArgs) _
      Handles AllMembersToolStripMenuItem.Click

        Dim frm As New frmPaymentsAll
        frm.ShowDialog()

    End Sub

End Class
```

frmAllMembers.vb:

```
Public Class frmAllMembers

    Private Sub frmAllMembers_Load(ByVal sender As System.Object, _
      ByVal e As System.EventArgs) Handles MyBase.Load

        Me.MembersTableAdapter.Fill(Me.AllMembersDataSet.Members)

    End Sub
```

```
        Private Sub CloseToolStripMenuItem_Click(ByVal sender As _
          System.Object, ByVal e As System.EventArgs) _
          Handles CloseToolStripMenuItem.Click

            Me.Close()

        End Sub

        Private Sub SaveToolStripMenuItem_Click(ByVal sender As _
          System.Object, ByVal e As System.EventArgs) _
          Handles SaveToolStripMenuItem.Click

            Me.MembersTableAdapter.Update(Me.AllMembersDataSet.Members)

        End Sub

    End Class
```

frmFindMember.vb:

```
    Public Class frmFindMember

        Private Sub CloseToolStripMenuItem_Click(ByVal sender As _
          System.Object, ByVal e As System.EventArgs) _
          Handles CloseToolStripMenuItem.Click

            Me.Close()

        End Sub

        Private Sub btnGo_Click(ByVal sender As System.Object, _
          ByVal e As System.EventArgs) Handles btnGo.Click

            ' Perform a wildcard search for last name.
            Me.MembersTableAdapter.Fill(Me.FindMemberDataSet.Members, _
               txtLastName.Text)

        End Sub

    End Class
```

frmAddMember.vb:

(This class may contain additional code that was inserted by Visual Studio.)

```
    Public Class frmAddMember

        Private Sub frmAddMember_Load(ByVal sender As System.Object, _
          ByVal e As System.EventArgs) Handles MyBase.Load

            Me.MembersTableAdapter.Fill(Me.AllMembersDataSet.Members)

            Me.MembersBindingSource.AddNew()
            Date_JoinedDateTimePicker.Value = Today()

        End Sub

        Private Sub SaveToolStripMenuItem_Click(ByVal sender As _
          System.Object, ByVal e As System.EventArgs) _
          Handles SaveToolStripMenuItem.Click
```

```
        Try
          Me.MembersBindingSource.EndEdit()
          Me.MembersTableAdapter.Update(Me.AllMembersDataSet.Members)
          Me.Close()
        Catch ex As Exception
          MessageBox.Show(Me, "Error: " & ex.Message, "Save", _
            MessageBoxButtons.OK, MessageBoxIcon.Warning)
        End Try

    End Sub

    Private Sub CloseWithoutSavingToolStripMenuItem_Click(ByVal _
      sender As System.Object, ByVal e As System.EventArgs) _
      Handles CloseWithoutSavingToolStripMenuItem.Click

        Me.MembersBindingSource.CancelEdit()
        Me.Close()

    End Sub

End Class
```

frmPaymentsAll.vb:

```
Public Class frmPaymentsAll

    Private Sub CloseToolStripMenuItem_Click(ByVal sender As _
      System.Object, ByVal e As System.EventArgs) _
      Handles CloseToolStripMenuItem.Click

        Me.Close()

    End Sub

    Private Sub frmPaymentsAll_Load(ByVal sender As System.Object, _
      ByVal e As System.EventArgs) Handles MyBase.Load

      Me.PaymentsTableAdapter.Fill(Me.AllPaymentsDataSet.Payments)

    End Sub

End Class
```

Checkpoint

10.27 In the *Karate* database, which table contains the names and dates when students joined the school?

10.28 In the *frmPaymentsAll* form, which two tables are required when filling the grid?

10.29 Which property of a DataGridView control lets you alter the order in which columns appear?

10.30 What special operator is used in the `WHERE` clause of a query when you want to perform a wildcard comparison?

10.7 Introduction to LINQ (optional)

CONCEPT: LINQ (Language Integrated Query) is a query language that is built into Visual Basic and can be used to query data from many sources other than databases.

In this chapter you've learned about SQL, which allows you to query the data in a database. Visual Studio also provides another querying language named **LINQ** (which stands for Language Integrated Query). Whereas SQL allows you to query the data in a database, LINQ allows you to query many types of data from virtually any source. In this section we will look at how you can use LINQ to query the data in an array. Suppose we have declared the following array of `Integers`:

```
Dim intNumbers() As Integer = {1, 101, 2, 102, 3, 103, 4, 104}
```

If we want to query this array to get all of the values that are greater than 100, we can write the following statement:

```
Dim queryResults = From item In intNumbers _
                   Where item > 100 _
                   Select item
```

Let's take a closer look at the statement. First, notice that the statement begins with `Dim queryResults`. We are declaring an object named `queryResults`, which will hold the results of the LINQ query. Notice that we have not specified a data type. Visual Basic will automatically determine the data type for the object. On the right side of the = operator is the LINQ query. The = operator will assign the results of the LINQ query to the `queryResults` object. The LINQ query reads:

```
From item In intNumbers _
Where item > 100 _
Select item
```

The results of this query will be all the items in the `intNumbers` array that are greater than 100. After the statement executes, we can use a `For Each` loop to examine the values stored in the `queryResults` object. For example, the following code segment shows how we can add the values to a list box named `lstNumbers`.

```
' Create an array of integers.
Dim intNumbers() As Integer = {4, 104, 2, 102, 1, 101, 3, 103}

' Use LINQ to query the array for all numbers
' that are greater than 100.
Dim queryResults = From item In intNumbers _
                   Where item > 100 _
                   Select item

' Add the query results to the list box.
For Each intNum As Integer In queryResults
  lstNumbers.Items.Add(intNum)
Next
```

After this code executes, the values 104, 102, 101, and 103 will be added to the list box, in that order. If you want the results of the LINQ query to be sorted in ascending order, you can use the `Order By` operator as shown here:

```
Dim queryResults = From item In intNumbers _
                   Where item > 100 _
                   Select item _
                   Order By item
```

Adding the `Descending` key word to the `Order By` operator causes the results of the query to be sorted in descending order. Here is an example:

```
Dim queryResults = From item In intNumbers _
                   Where item > 100 _
                   Select item _
                   Order By item Descending
```

As you can see from these examples, LINQ uses operators such as `Where`, `Select`, and `Order By`, that are similar to SQL operators. Unlike the SQL operators, however, the LINQ operators are built into the Visual Basic language. When you write a LINQ query, you write it directly into your Visual Basic program. As a result, the VB compiler checks the syntax of your query and you know immediately if you've made a mistake.

NOTE: In this section we've looked only at how LINQ can be used to query the data in an array. LINQ can be used to query any data that is stored in memory as an object. This includes not only arrays and databases, but many other types of data collections.

Summary

10.1 Database Management Systems

- A database is a collection of one or more tables, each containing data related to a particular topic. A table is a logical grouping of related information. Each row of a table is also called a record. Table columns are also called fields.
- Each table has a design, which specifies each column's name, data type, and range or size. A database schema is the design of tables, columns, and relationships between tables for the database.
- A primary key column uniquely identifies each row of a table. A primary key will sometimes consist of two or more combined columns.
- When you use Visual Basic to read a database table, you must select variable types that match the type of data in the table.
- Most well-designed databases keep redundant data to a minimum. They use key fields to link data stored in multiple tables. This reduces data entry errors and reduces the likelihood of inconsistenet data.
- A relationship is a link that relies on a common field value in the primary and foreign keys to join rows from two different tables. The most common type of relationship is a one-to-many relation.

10.2 Database Concepts

- A data source is usually a database, but can include text files and other sources of data outside a program.
- A binding source keeps track of the database name, location, username, password, and other connection information.
- A table adapter pulls data from one or more database tables and passes it to your program.
- A dataset is an in-memory copy of data pulled from database tables.
- A TableAdapter's `Fill` method opens a database connection, reads data from a database into the dataset, and closes the connection.

10.3 DataGridView Control

- The DataGridView control allows you to display a database table in a grid. The grid can be used at runtime to sort and edit the contents of the table.
- Visual Basic uses a technique called data binding to link database tables to controls.
- A data source is usually a database, but can include text files, Excel spreadsheets, XML data, or Web services.
- A binding source connects data-bound controls to a dataset.
- A table adapter pulls data from one or more database tables and passes it to your program.
- A dataset is an in-memory copy of the data pulled from database tables.
- The DataGridView's smart tag opens the DataGridView Tasks window. In this window, you can choose a data source, edit the grid columns, and enable operations on data such as adding, editing, and deleting.

10.4 Data-Bound Controls

- Using a data source, you can bind its fields to individual controls such as text boxes, labels, and list boxes.
- Data-bound controls update their contents automatically when you move from one row to the next in a dataset.
- You can bind an existing data source to a DataGridView control by dragging a table from the *Data Sources* window to an open area of a form. Similarly, you can individually create data-bound controls such as text boxes and labels by dragging individual fields in the *Data Sources* window onto the open area of a form.

- ListBox and ComboBox controls have two important properties that are required when using data binding: the DataSource property identifies the table within the dataset that supplies the data; the DisplayMember property identifies the column to be displayed.

10.5 Structured Query Language (SQL)

- SQL is a universal language for creating, updating, and retrieving data from databases.
- The SQL `SELECT` statement has an optional `ORDER BY` clause that lets you control the display order of the table rows.
- Applications often need to filter certain rows when retrieving data from data sources. Filtering, or choosing rows to display in a dataset is done by creating a query. In SQL, the `WHERE` statement limits the rows retrieved from a database table.
- The TableAdapter Configuration Wizard and Search Criteria Builder can be used to modify queries.

10.6 Focus on Problem Solving: *Karate School Management* Application

- This section outlines the process of building the *Karate School Management* application, which displays a list of all members; permits the user to sort on any column, edit individual rows, and delete rows; adds new students to the *Members* table; displays members having similar last names; displays payments by all members; and permits the user to sort on any column.

10.7 Introduction to LINQ (optional)

- LINQ, which stands for Language Integrated Query, is a query language that can be used to query many types of data from virtually any source. The LINQ operators are built into Visual Basic, and as a result, LINQ queries are typed as statements in VB programs.

Key Terms

binding source
components
data binding
data source
database
database query
database management system (DBMS)
database schema
data-bound controls
DataGridView control
dataset
DataSource property
DateTimePicker control
design
diagram pane
DisplayMember property
field
foreign key
grid pane
identity column
Language Integrated Query (LINQ)
`LIKE` operator (SQL)
one-to-many relationship
`ORDER BY` clause (SQL)
primary key
prototype
query parameter
relation
relational model
results pane
schema definition file
`SELECT` statement (SQL)
SQL pane
Structured Query Language (SQL)
table
table adapter
`WHERE` clause (SQL)
wildcard
wizard

Review Questions and Exercises

Fill-in-the-Blank

1. A database ____________________ describes the design of tables, columns, and relationships between tables.
2. A ____________________ ____________________ creates a connection to an external data source such as a database.
3. A ____________________ control displays data directly from a dataset, without any programming required.
4. The ____________________ control lets the user select a date using the mouse.
5. Another word for a database table row is a ____________________.

Multiple Choice

1. Which of the following is an in-memory copy of data pulled from one or more database tables?
   a. Table adapter
   b. Table relation
   c. Dataset
   d. Data record
2. Which of the following is not an SQL Server field type?
   a. bit
   b. datetime
   c. largedatetime
   d. float
3. A Visual Basic Double data type corresponds best to which of the following SQL Server column types?
   a. float
   b. currency
   c. integer
   d. real
4. Which of the following is not a property of a ListBox control?
   a. ValueMember
   b. DataSource
   c. DisplayMember
   d. DataMember
5. Which of the following keywords and relational operators is used by SQL when performing wildcard matches?
   a. `EQUAL`
   b. `LIKE`
   c. `MATCH`
   d. `=`

True or False

Indicate whether the following statements are true or false.

1. T F: A TableAdapter's `Fill` method receives a dataset argument.
2. T F: A one-to-many relationship involves connecting a TableAdapter to a dataset.

3. T F: A primary key can only involve a single column of a database table.
4. T F: A data source field such as *Last_Name* can be bound to a TextBox or Label control.
5. T F: The default type of control bound to DateTime fields is the TextBox.
6. T F: The *Karate School Manager* application joins the *Members* table to the *Payments* table when displaying payments by all members.
7. T F: The *Karate School Manager* application requires you to write special event handling code that makes sorting in a DataGridView possible.
8. T F: When the user makes changes to a dataset, the changes are not permanent unless other measures are taken to write the dataset back to a database.
9. T F: In an SQL Server, query parameter names always begin with the @ sign.
10. T F: Query parameters are passed to datasets as arguments when calling a TableAdapter's `Fill` method.

Short Answer

1. Which property of a ListBox control must be set before a program can use the SelectedValue property at runtime?
2. What type of relationship existed between the *Employees* and *Department* tables in Section 10.1?
3. If the *Employees* table contains a foreign key named *dept_id*, is it likely that the values in this field will be unique?
4. What type of component keeps track of the database name, location, username, password, and other connection information?
5. What happens when you drag a table name from the *Data Sources* window onto an open area of a form?
6. Write a statement that uses a TableAdapter named MembersTableAdapter to add a new row to its dataset. The fields to be inserted are MemberID, last name, first name, phone number, and date joined.
7. Which property of a DataGridView control causes the buttons at the beginning of each row to appear?

What Do You Think?

1. When displaying the contents of the *Payments* table in a DataGridView control, the *ID* column displays by default. What would you do to limit the columns to just *Payment_Date* and *Amount*?
2. Suppose you wanted to add a new row to the *Payments* table in the *Karate School Management* application. How would you determine which *Member_id* value to insert in the row?

Algorithm Workbench

1. Suppose a database table named *Address* contains fields named *City* and *State*. Write an SQL `SELECT` statement that combines these fields into a new field named *CityState*.
2. Write statements that create and show an instance of a form named *frmAllMembers*. Be sure the user can only click in the form you have displayed, and not in any other application window.

3. Write an SQL query that retrieves the *ID*, *Title*, *Artist*, and *Price* from a database table named *Albums*. The query should sort the rows in ascending order by *Artist*.
4. Write an SQL query that uses a query parameter to retrieve a row from the *Albums* table that has a particular *ID* value. Retrieve the *ID*, *Title*, *Artist*, and *Price*.
5. Write an SQL query that retrieves columns from the *Payments* table when the *Payment_Date* is earlier than January 1, 2000.
6. Write a statement that fills a table named *Members* in a dataset named *AllMembersDataSet*. The table adapter is named *MembersTableAdapter*.
7. Write an SQL query that retrieves the *ID*, *Last_Name*, and *First_Name* from the *Members* table. You only want rows having a *Date_Joined* value greater than or equal to the value of a query parameter.

Programming Challenges

VideoNote
The Karate Members Grid Problem

1. **Karate Members Grid**

Create an application that uses a DataGridView control to display the *Members* table from the *Karate.mdf* database. Display the Last_Name, First_Name, Phone, and Date_Joined columns. The query you create should order the rows in ascending order by Last_Name. Format the Date_Joined column as *mm/dd/yyyy* (modify the `DefaultCellStyle` property after selecting the grid's `Columns` property.) In the *DataGridView Tasks* window, disable adding, editing, and deleting. A sample of the program's output is shown in Figure 10-65.

Figure 10-65 Displaying the *Karate Members* table in a DataGridView control

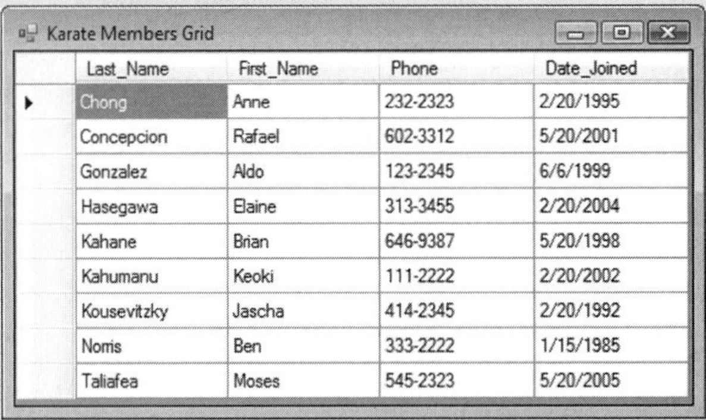

Karate Members Grid

Last_Name	First_Name	Phone	Date_Joined
Chong	Anne	232-2323	2/20/1995
Concepcion	Rafael	602-3312	5/20/2001
Gonzalez	Aldo	123-2345	6/6/1999
Hasegawa	Elaine	313-3455	2/20/2004
Kahane	Brian	646-9387	5/20/1998
Kahumanu	Keoki	111-2222	2/20/2002
Kousevitzky	Jascha	414-2345	2/20/1992
Norris	Ben	333-2222	1/15/1985
Taliafea	Moses	545-2323	5/20/2005

2. **Karate Payments Grid**

Create an application that uses a DataGridView control to display the *Payments* table from the *Karate.mdf* database. Order the rows in ascending order by the Member_Id column. A sample of the program's output is shown in Figure 10-66. Format the column headings, as well as the Payment_Date and Amount columns, as shown in the figure.

Figure 10-66 *Karate Payments* table displayed in a DataGridView control

Karate Payments Grid

Pmt ID	Member ID	Date	Amount Paid
1	1	10/20/2005	$48.00
15	1	3/11/2006	$44.00
2	2	11/20/2005	$80.00
22	2	3/21/2006	$55.00
6	3	2/16/2006	$75.00
16	3	3/28/2006	$43.00
17	4	3/27/2006	$44.00
4	4	12/16/2005	$50.00
5	5	1/16/2006	$65.00
10	5	4/11/2006	$66.00
13	6	6/11/2006	$77.00
3	6	11/16/2005	$75.00

3. **Selecting Sales Staff**

   Create a program that lets the user select rows from the *SalesStaff* table in the *Company mdf* database. Fill a ComboBox control with the full names (last, first). Use a parameterized query (a query containing a parameter) to retrieve the matching table row and display it in data-bound controls. An example is shown in Figure 10-67. You may want to use a DateTimePicker control to display the *Hire Date* field.

Figure 10-67 *Selecting Sales Staff*

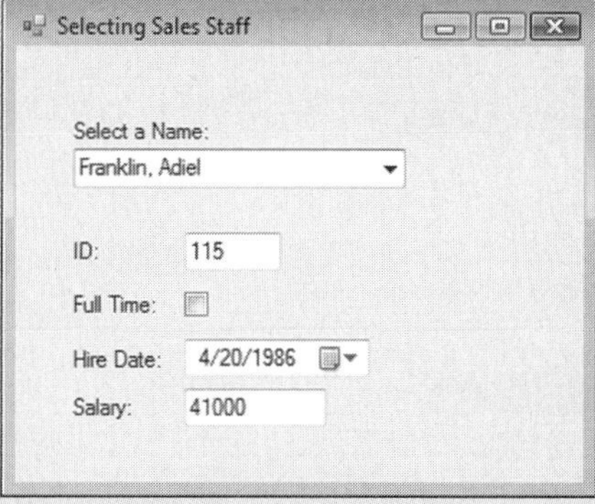

4. **Sales Staff Salaries**

   Using the *SalesStaff* table in the *Company.mdf* database, let the user choose between lists of part-time versus full-time employees. Use radio buttons to make the selection. Display the average salary of the selected group in a label. An example is shown in Figure 10-68. When the program starts, the *Full-time* button is automatically selected.

Figure 10-68 Displaying average salaries of full-time employees

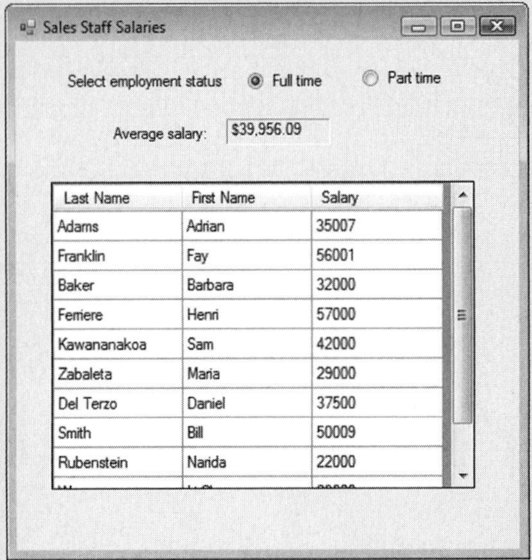

5. **Karate Member Dates**

   Create a program that uses the *Members* table of the *Karate.mdf* database. Let the user select a date from a DateTimePicker control. The program must display the first and last names, the phone numbers, and dates joined of all members who joined before the selected date (see Figure 10-69). Use a parameterized query to retrieve the matching table rows and display them in a DataGridView control.

Figure 10-69 Finding members who joined before a selected date

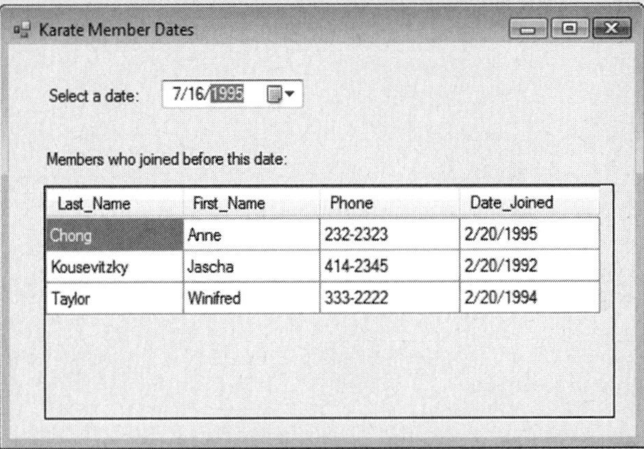

6. **Advanced Karate Member Dates**

   (*Extra challenge project*) Enhance the program you created in Programming Challenge 3 by giving the user a choice between displaying members who have joined before a given date or members who have joined on or after that date. In Figure 10-70, the program shows members who joined before July 16, 1995. In Figure 10-71, a list of members who joined on or after the same date is displayed.

You should create two datasets, one for each type of search. After binding the grid to the first dataset, a component named *MembersBindingSource* is created. If you then bind the grid to the second dataset, a second component named *MembersBindingSource1* is created. At runtime, when the user switches between the radio buttons, their event handlers can assign one of the two binding sources to the DataSource property of the DataGridView control. That would be a good time to call the `Fill` method of the appropriate DataAdapter.

Figure 10-70 Showing members who joined before the chosen date

Figure 10-71 Showing *Karate* members who joined on or after the chosen date

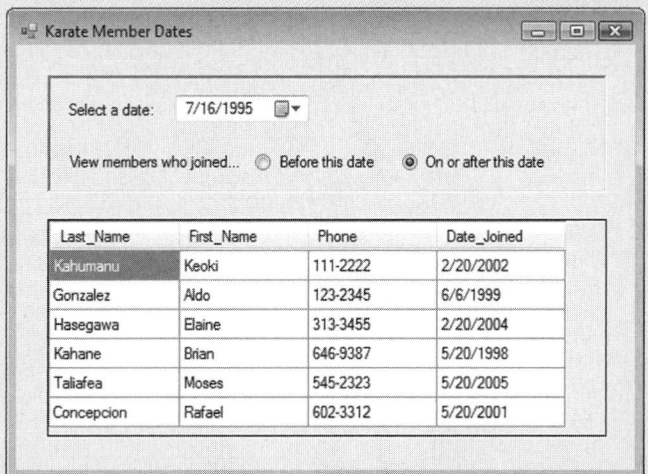

CHAPTER 11 Developing Web Applications

TOPICS

In this chapter, you will learn how to create ASP.NET applications that run under Web Browsers such as Internet Explorer, Netscape, and Mozilla Firefox. Most of the time, we think of running browser-based applications on the Internet, but they can be just as effective on networks limited to a single organization. You will use either Visual Studio 2008 or Visual Web Developer 2008 to create Web applications. Except in cases where we must make a distinction between the two programs, we will refer to both as Visual Studio.

11.1 Programming for the Web

CONCEPT: A Web application runs on a Web server and presents its content to the user across a network, in a Web browser.

HyperText Markup Language

When the Web first became popular, HTML was the only available tool for creating pages with text, graphics buttons, and input forms. HTML, which stands for **HyperText Markup Language**, is a standardized language that describes the appearance of pages. It uses special sequences of characters called tags to embed commands inside the text appearing on a Web page. For example, the following line instructs the browser to display "This text is in bold." in bold type.

```
<b>This text is in bold.</b>This text is normal.
```

The `<b>` tag begins the bold font, and the `</b>` tag ends it. There are a large number of markup tags, explained by many excellent books. Special Web design editors such as

Microsoft Expression Web and Adobe Dreamweaver make editing HTML easy without having to memorize HTML tags.

But what about Web programming? Rather than display static content such as pictures and text, many applications require Web pages to be fully functional programs. Companies like Microsoft and Sun Microsystems decided that Web applications should be written using advanced programming languages. Web-based technologies and tools such as Java Server Pages and Microsoft ASP.NET were created. Scripting languages such as JavaScript and PHP have made Web programming much easier.

ASP.NET

The acronym ASP originally stood for **Active Server Pages**. It was the first server-side Web programming technology introduced by Microsoft. **ASP.NET**, the next generation, is called a **platform** because it provides development tools, code libraries, and visual controls for browser-based applications. ASP.NET provides a way to separate ordinary HTML from object-oriented program code. It also provides many powerful controls, which are similar to Windows Forms controls. ASP.NET lets you transfer a lot of your Visual Basic knowledge to Web applications. Visual Studio checks your Web application's code for errors before running it. Visual Basic code can be stored in a separate file from a page's text and HTML, making it easier for you to code and maintain program logic.

Web applications written for ASP.NET consist of the following parts:

- Content: Web forms, HTML code, Web forms controls, images, and other multimedia
- Program logic, in compiled Visual Basic (or C#) code
- Configuration information

How Web Applications Work

Web applications are designed around a **client-server model**, which means that an entity called a **server** produces data consumed by another entity called a *client*. Put another way, clients make requests satisfied by responses from servers.

When you use a Web browser such as Internet Explorer to access a Web site, your browser is the client. A program called a *Web server* runs on the computer hosting the Web site. Web browsers, such as Internet Explorer, Safari, or Netscape, display data encoded in HTML. Web browsers connect to Web sites, causing HTML data to be sent to the client's computer. The browsers interpret, or render the HTML, displaying the fonts, colors, and images from the pages in the browser windows.

Uniform Resource Locator (URL)

A **URL** (**Uniform Resource Locator**) is the universal way of addressing objects and pages on a network. It always starts with a **protocol**, such as http://, https://, or ftp://. It is followed by a **domain name**, such as microsoft.com, ibm.com, or aw.com. A specially defined domain name for your local computer is called localhost. Then, the URL may end with a specific folder path and/or filename. The following is a complete URL with folder path and filename:

```
http://pearsonhighered.com
```

Displaying a Web Page

What happens when a Web page is displayed by a Web browser? In preparation, a computer must be running a **Web server**. The server waits for connection requests, which occur in two steps:

1. A user running a Web browser connects to the server by opening a network connection and passing a URL to the connection. An example is http://microsoft.com.
2. Using the URL it receives from the user's Web browser, the Web server translates the URL into a physical location within the server computer's file system. The server reads the requested file, now called a **Web page**. The server sends the Web page over the network connection to the user's computer. The user's Web browser renders (interprets) the HTML. Output consists of text, graphics, and sound.

After sending the Web page to the user, the server immediately breaks the connection. It becomes free to handle Web page requests from other users.

After a Web page is displayed, the user may click a **button control** or press [Enter], causing the page contents to be sent back to the Web server. This action, callled a **postback**, occurs when the server processes the page contents and resends the modified page to the browser. The processing might involve updating controls and executing functions in the application's compiled code.

Web Forms

Web applications written in ASP.NET use special Web pages called Web forms. A **Web form**, which can be identified by its *.aspx* filename extension, contains text, **HTML tags**, **HTML controls** (such as buttons and text boxes), and special interactive controls called **Web server controls**. The latter, known also as **ASP.NET Server controls**, are interactive controls such as buttons, list boxes, and text boxes that execute on the server. Though they look like HTML controls, they are more powerful because they have a larger set of properties and they use event handler procedures to carry out actions based on user input. In effect, they behave a lot like Windows Forms controls.

The source code for a Web form is usually stored in a related file called a **code-behind file**, with the filename extension *aspx.vb*. This part of the application is called the **program logic**.

Configuration information can be stored in two files. One file, *Web.config*, contains information about the runtime environment. Another file, *Styles.css*, is a **Cascading Style Sheet** (CSS) file containing HTML styles for customizing the appearance of Web forms.

Web Servers

Web applications must be run using a Web server. You have three choices as follows:

- The **ASP.NET Development Server** is installed automatically with Visual Studio. It is easy to use and requires no special security setup.
- **Internet Information Services (IIS)** is a professional production tool, which is available as an option with various versions of Microsoft Windows. It must be configured carefully to ensure security against hackers.
- A remote Web server is typically available through an Internet Service Provider (ISP) or a corporate Web server. You can copy your application to a remote Web server before running it. You must always have a username and password to publish on a remote server.

HTML Designer

HTML Designer is the tool in Visual Studio that simplifies the design of Web pages and Web forms. The designer generates HTML source code and embeds special codes that identify ASP.NET Web controls. It is possible to create Web forms using a plain text editor, but doing so requires considerable practice. We will use the designer in this book. The designer offers the following views of a Web page:

- ***Design* view:** You can visually edit Web pages, using the mouse to drag controls and table borders. This view most closely resembles Visual Studio's editor for Windows Forms projects.
- ***Source* view:** You use this view to directly edit the HTML source code that makes up a Web form.
- ***Split* view:** This view displays the page's *Design* view and *Source* view in separate panels.

Web Browser Support

Web pages would be easier to create if all end users ran the same Web browser. Unfortunately, browsers have different capabilities and characteristics. To make it easier to adapt to different browsers, the Web server automatically detects the browser type and makes the information available to ASP.NET programs. The programs automatically generate HTML that is appropriate for the user's browser.

TIP: Before publishing your Web applications for end users, test them with browsers other than Internet Explorer (the default). Netscape, Safari, and Firefox are good choices. Netscape can be downloaded from http://browser.netscape.com and Firefox can be downloaded from http://www.mozilla.com.

Types of Controls

When you are designing Web forms, the *Toolbox* window contains Web-related controls placed in the following groups:

- **Standard:** This group contains the most commonly used controls on Web forms. Some are close relatives of Windows forms controls, including Label, Button, ListBox, CheckBox, CheckBoxList, and RadioButton. Others are unique to Web programming, such as the LinkButton and HyperLink controls.
- **Data:** Controls for connecting to data sources; displaying database and XML data in grids and lists.
- **Validation:** Controls for validating user input into controls such as text boxes.
- **Navigation:** Advanced controls for navigating between Web pages.
- **Login:** Controls related to authenticating users when they log into a Web site with usernames and passwords.
- **WebParts:** Controls that let a Web site's users modify the content, appearance, and behavior of Web pages directly from a browser.
- **HTML:** Controls found on HTML Web pages, such as buttons, check boxes, radio buttons, lists, and text boxes. They are compatible with standard HTML, have a limited number of properties, and have no associated classes. Most importantly, they do not generate user events such as `Click` or `SelectedIndexChanged`.

11.1 Describe a Web application in your own words.

11.2 Describe the client-server relationship in a Web application.

11.3 What is a postback?

11.4 Why is ASP.NET called a platform?

11.5 What is meant by *content* in an ASP.NET application?

11.2 Creating ASP.NET Applications

CONCEPT: You can use Visual Studio or Visual Web Developer Express Edition to create Web applications in Visual Basic.

Types of Web Sites

In Visual Studio or Visual Web Developer Express, you select *Open Web Site* from the *File* menu when you want to open an existing Web application. Four types of Web sites are shown in the *Open Web Site* dialog box in Figure 11-1: File System, Local IIS, FTP Site, and Remote Site. ASP.NET applications are also known as Web sites or **Web applications.**

A **File System Web site** runs directly under the *ASP.NET Development Server* supplied with Visual Studio. The application files can be stored in any disk directory you select, or on a network computer. The server is simple to use and does not leave your computer open to security attacks. This type of Web site is best suited to college laboratory environments and non-administrative users (students). We will use File System Web sites in this chapter.

An **HTTP Web site** runs under a Windows operating system utility named Internet Information Services (IIS). It is a professional-quality Web server with powerful security and configuration features, but requires some expertise to set up and maintain. IIS requires you to have administrative rights on the computer running the server in order to test and debug Web applications.

Figure 11-1 The *Open Web Site* dialog box

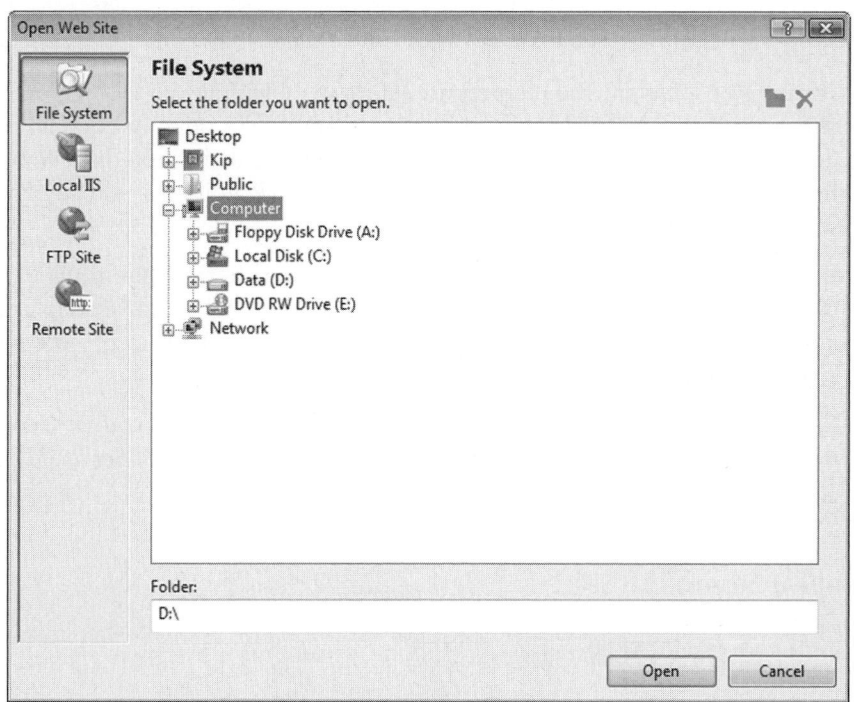

Both **FTP Site** and Remote Site refer to existing ASP.NET Web sites located on remote computers (network or Web). You must supply a username and password to the remote site to upload a copy of your application to the site. Both are useful when you want to publish an application to a public Web site.

VideoNote
Creating a Simple Web Application

Creating a Web Application

In Visual Studio, you create a new Web application (Web site) by choosing *New Web Site* from the *File* menu. The *New Web Site* dialog box provides a list of possible Web sites, as shown in Figure 11-2. We will focus on the most common type: the ASP.NET Web site.

Figure 11-2 *New Web Site* dialog box

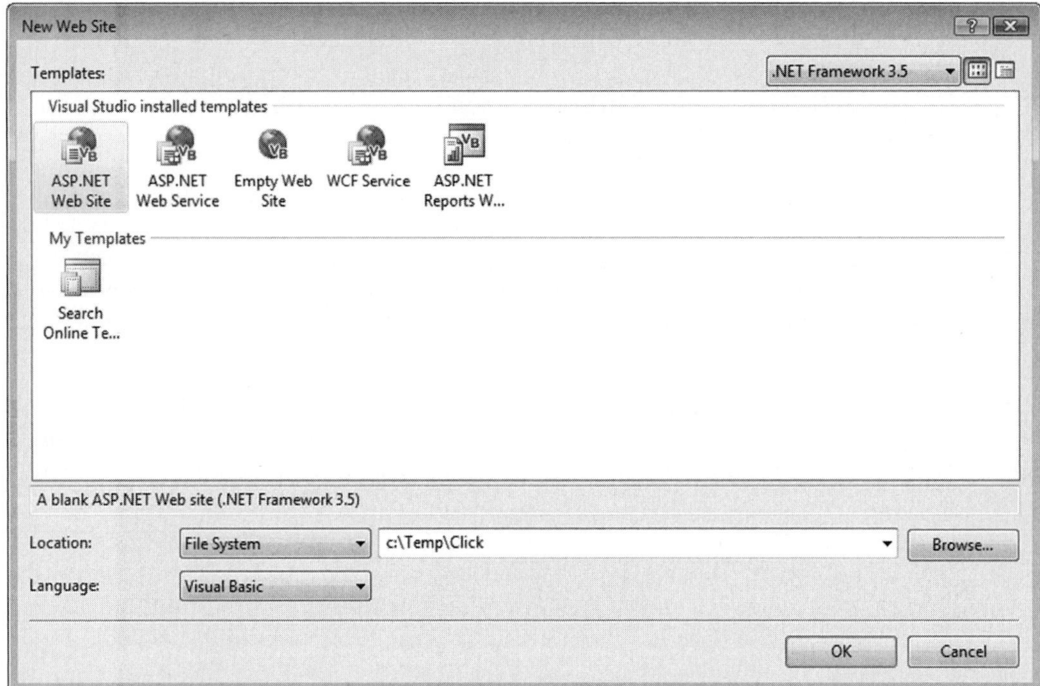

For the Web location, your choices are File System, HTTP, and FTP. If you select File System, your Web application can be located in any folder on your computer or a network drive. If you select HTTP, your Web application will be located on a Web site set up by Internet Information Services (IIS). If you select FTP, you must already have a Web site set up on a remote computer.

If you create a File System Web site, the edit box just to the right of the location lets you choose the path and folder name for your project. Suppose, for example, you create an application named *Click* in the *c:\Temp* folder. Then a project folder named *c:\Temp\Click* is created automatically.

If, on the other hand, you were to create an HTTP Web site, you would choose a location determined by the Internet Information Services (IIS) Web Server. IIS is beyond the scope of this book.

Application Files

When an application is created, a single Web page named *Default.aspx* is automatically included. A second file, called a code-behind file and named *Default.aspx.vb,* is also created. It holds all the Visual Basic code you write for event handlers and program logic. Figure 11-3 shows the *Solution Explorer* window for a sample application named *Click.*

Figure 11-3 Files created for the *Click* application

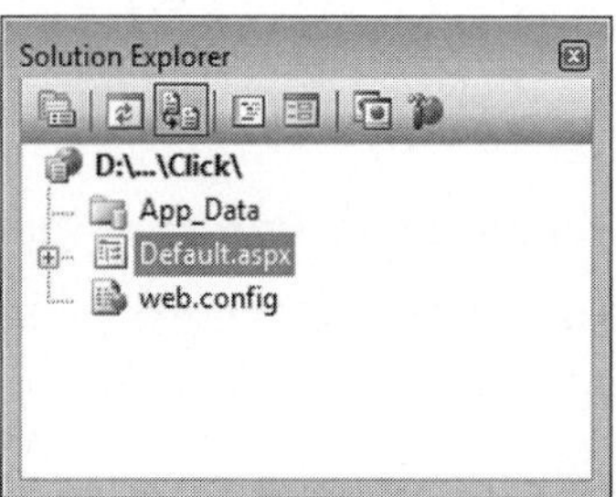

Toolbars

When you create or open a Web project, a toolbar is automatically shown below the menu. In Figure 11-4, the standard toolbar is just below the menu. A second toolbar, called the formatting toolbar (shown only when a form is displayed in Design mode) is next.

Figure 11-4 Menu, standard toolbar, formatting toolbar

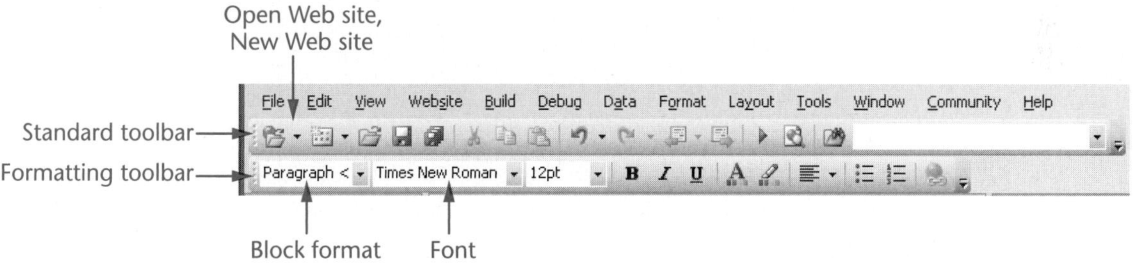

Opening an Existing Web Application

The easiest way to open an existing Web application from Visual Studio is to select a project name from the *Recent Projects* window. In Figure 11-5, if you don't find the name of the project you want to open listed, you can click the *Open: Web Site . . .* link at the bottom of the window. You will be shown an *Open Web Site* dialog box. Navigate to the folder containing the Web site you want to open, and click the *Open* button.

You can also open an existing Web project by selecting *Open Web Site* from the *File* menu.

Figure 11-5 *Recent Projects* window

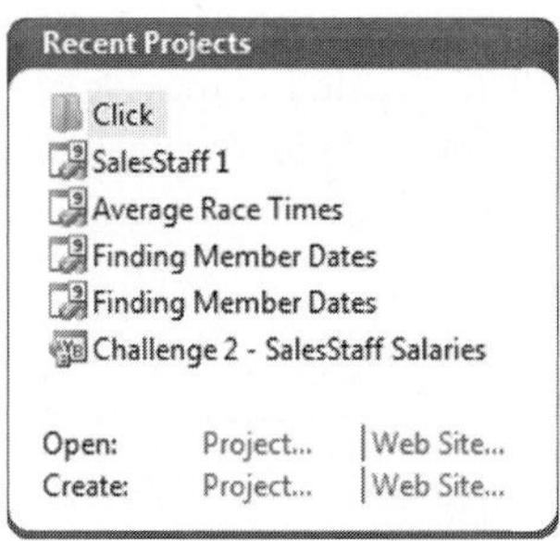

Selecting a Web Browser to Run the Application

When you run a Web application in Visual Studio, a default Web browser will be selected for you. It's a good idea, however, to test programs with more than one browser. To see a list of available browsers, right-click your project name in the *Solution Explorer* window and select *Browse With . . .* from the *pop-up* menu (shown in Figure 11-6).

Figure 11-6 Selecting Internet Explorer to run the application

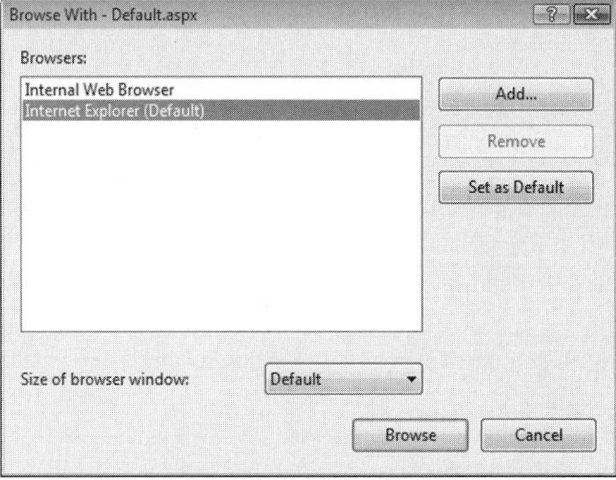

Running a Web Application

To run a Web application, select *Run Without Debugging* from the *Debug* menu. A Web browser such as Internet Explorer will open and display the start page of your application. Visual Studio does not automatically list the *Start Without Debugging* option in the *Debug* menu. You can add it to the toolbar by doing the following: select *Customize* from the *Tools* menu, select the *Commands* tab, click *Debug* in the *Categories* list box, find *Start Without Debugging* in the *Commands* list, and use the mouse to drag it to the *Debug* menu. You can also drag it onto the Visual Studio toolbar.

Static Text

Static text is text you type directly onto a form. Web forms behave like documents, similar to Microsoft Word. In Windows forms, labels are needed for all text displayed on forms; but Web forms do not need labels for that type of text. In Figure 11-7, for example, three lines of text were typed directly onto a Web form in Design mode.

Figure 11-7 Static text typed directly on a form, in *Design* mode

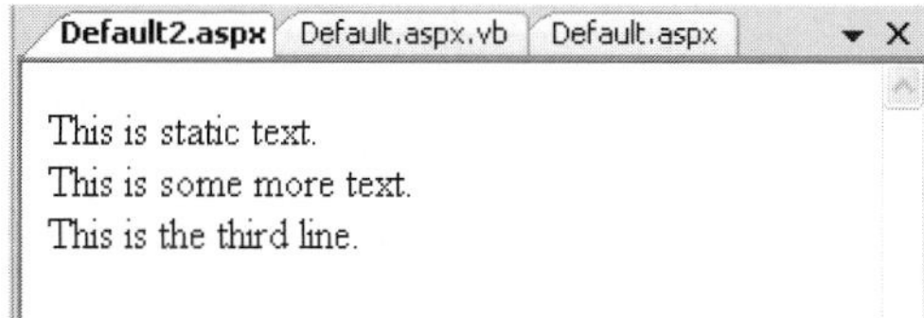

In Tutorial 11-1, you create the *Click* application.

Tutorial 11-1:
Creating the *Click* application

Now you're ready to create your first Web application. Microsoft went to great lengths to make Web development as similar as possible to Windows Forms programming. Your first application will have a short, but elegant name: *Click*.

As a preparation step, decide which directory you will use to save your Web projects. In our examples we will use a directory named *C:\Temp*, but you can choose any name.

Step 1: Start Visual Studio.

Step 2: Select *New Web Site* from the *File* menu. Figure 11-8 shows the *New Web Site* dialog box, which lets you choose the type of Web site, the location, the language, and the application folder name. (Visual Studio users will have one more icon, for *Crystal Reports*.) For the application folder name, enter `Click` (along with the directory you chose to use for Web applications). Click *OK* to close the dialog box.

Figure 11-8 *New Web Site* dialog box

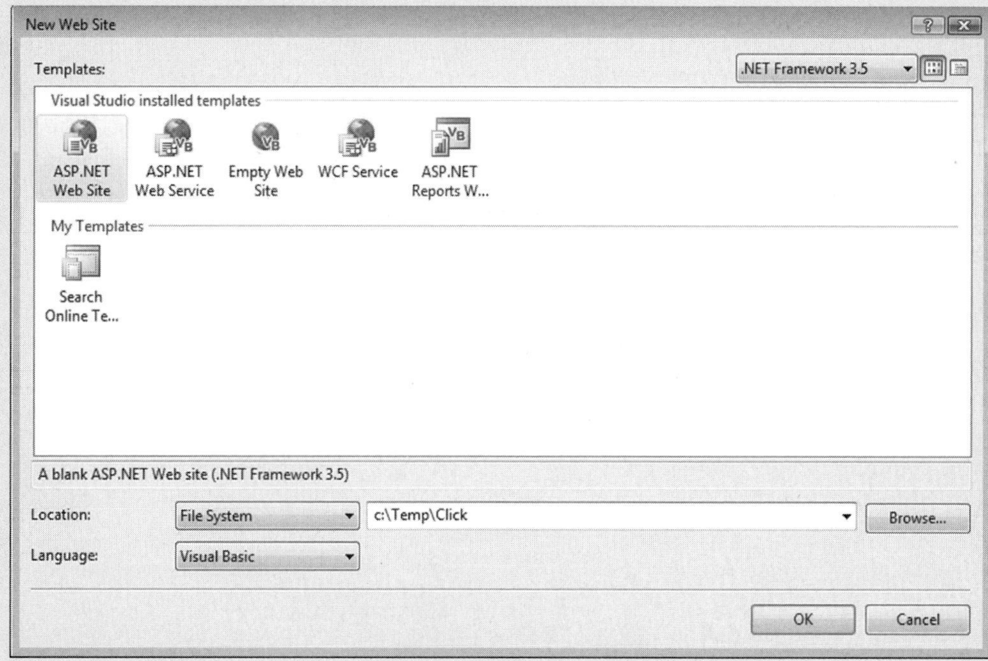

Step 3: If the *Start* page is showing, click its close box ( ) in the upper right corner to close it. Now you should be able to see the *Toolbox* window and the Web application's startup page. An example is shown in Figure 11-9. The three tabs at the bottomof the page let you display the Web page in Design view, Split View (both Design and Source), and Source view (XHTML code).

Figure 11-9 After creating the *Click* application

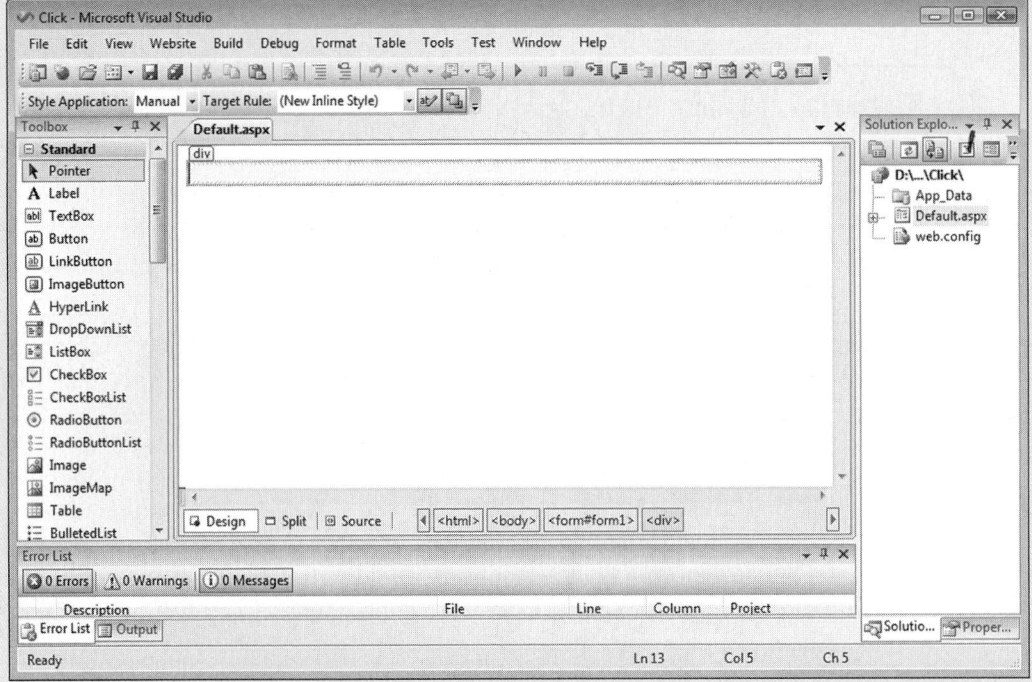

Step 4: Next, you will create a title that displays in the title bar of the Web browser when the application runs. Select *DOCUMENT* from the drop-down list that appears in the *Properties* window and then set the Title property to *Click Application*.

Step 5: Switch to Design view. Then, select *Toolbars* from the *View* menu, and then select *Formatting* (if it is not already selected). The formatting toolbar should appear just below the menu. Look for the *Block Format* drop-down list on the left side of the formatting toolbar just above the *Toolbox* window (see Figure 11-10). Select *Heading 1 <H1>*. This will cause a light blue box to appear on the form in *Design* view, with a small tag labeled *h1* in the upper left corner. The *Block Format* list contains a list of standard HTML formats that affect the font size, color, and other attributes.

Figure 11-10 Block format drop-down list, on formatting toolbar

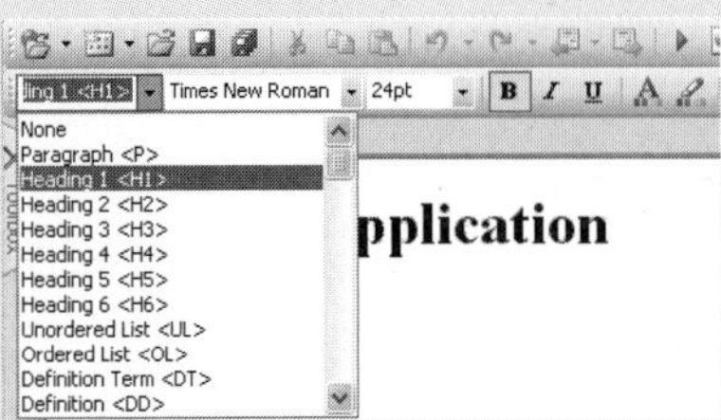

Step 6: Click the mouse inside the blue box labeled *h1* on the Web form and type **`My Click Application`**. Press [Enter] to move to the next line. Figure 11-11 shows a sample of your work so far.

Step 7: Drag a Button control from the *Toolbox* window onto your form. Use the mouse to make it wider. In the *Properties* window, set its Text property to *Click Here*. Set its ID property to `btnClick`.

Step 8: Click the mouse just to the right of the button and press [Enter] to move to the next line. Insert a Label control on the next line. Set its ID property to `lblMessage` and erase its Text property.

Figure 11-11 After typing the program heading in *Heading 1* style

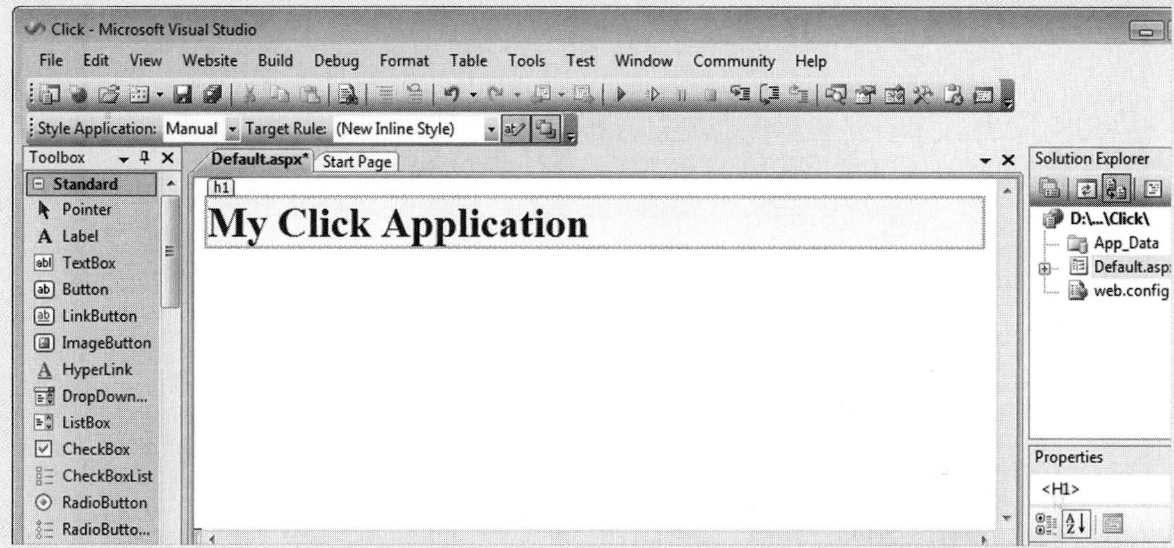

Step 9: Next, you will add code to the button's `Click` event handler that assigns a string to the label. Double-click the Button control and add the following statement (shown in bold) to its event handler:

```
Protected Sub btnClick_Click(ByVal sender As Object, _
    ByVal e As System.EventArgs) Handles btnClick.Click

    lblMessage.Text = "Thank you for clicking the button!"
End Sub
```

You have opened the file named *Default.aspx.vb*, called the code-behind file for this Web form. Code written in this file is by Visual Basic. It can contain classes and objects in the same way as Windows Forms applications.

Step 10: Save and run the project. Run the application by selecting *Start Without Debugging* from the *Start Debug* menu (or press [Ctrl]+[F5]). When the Web browser opens your application, click the *Click Here* button. A message should appear below the button, as shown in Figure 11-12. Our example uses the Internet Explorer Web browser, but your computer may display a different browser, based on its default settings.

Step 11: Close the browser to end the application.

Let's take a final look at the contents of the Web page, which is in many ways like a text document. In the Design view, you can type text directly onto a Web page. Text typed directly on a page is called *static text* because it does not require the use of Label controls. The button on your Web page that says *Click Here* is an ASP.NET server control. The blank Label control named *lblMessage* is also an ASP.NET server control. You may want to try adding more random text, buttons, and labels to the Web page. Experiment with using HTML styles, available in the drop-down list on the left side of the formatting toolbar.

TIP: Another way to run a Web application is to right-click the name of the application's startup page (such as *Default.aspx*) in the *Solution Explorer* window and select *View in browser* from the pop-up menu. Or, you can select from a list of Web browsers by right-clicking and selecting *Browse With....*

Figure 11-12 After clicking the button in the *Click* application

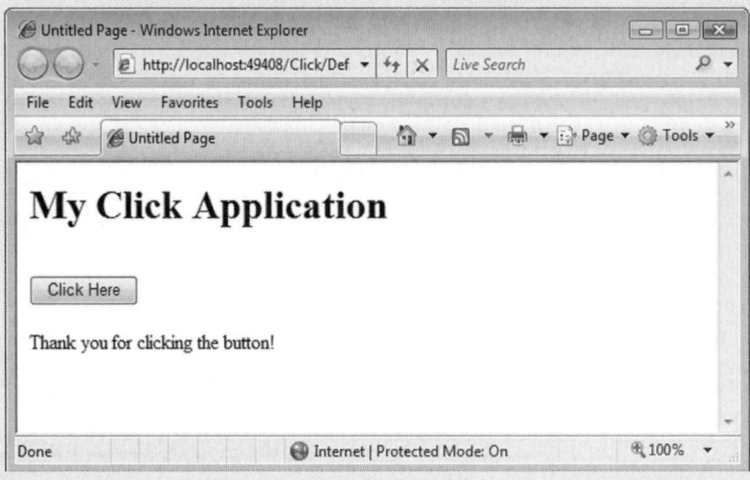

Step 12: Select *Close Project* from the *File* menu.

Running in Debug Mode

You can start a program in Debug mode by selecting *Start Debugging* from the *Debug* menu. The first time you try it, you will see the message box shown in Figure 11-13. When you click the *OK* button, a **Web.config file** is added to your project, containing an option that permits debugging. You can open *Web.config* from the *Solution Explorer* window and see the option that enables debugging.

```
<compilation debug="true"/>
```

Figure 11-13 Debugging an application for the first time

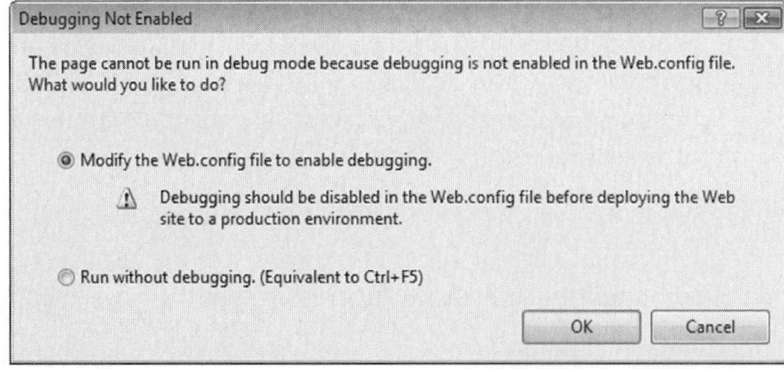

Checkpoint

11.6 Name three types of Web sites you can create with Visual Studio.

11.7 When you create a Web site, which tab must you click to switch from the startup page's Source view to Design view?

11.8 How do you select from a list of Web browsers when running your Web application?

11.9 What is static text, and is it similar to or different from Label controls in Windows forms?

11.10 In the *Click* application, how did you specify the block format named *Heading 1* for the first line of text in the Web form?

11.11 What happens the first time you run a Web application in Debug mode?

11.3 Web Server Controls

CONCEPT: Web Server controls are similar to controls used in Windows applications. You use Web Server controls to make ASP.NET Web applications interactive.

Web server controls make ASP.NET applications dynamic and interactive. The controls are powerful because each is defined by a class with a rich set of properties, methods, and events. The controls look and feel like Windows Forms controls, making them easy for Visual Basic programmers to learn. We often refer to Web server controls simply as *Web controls.*

The following Web controls are the ones you are likely to use often. Except where noted by an asterisk (*), all have counterparts among the controls used on Windows forms.

- Button
- ImageButton
- LinkButton
- Text Box
- Label
- RadioButton
- RadioButtonList*
- CheckBox
- CheckBoxList*
- ListBox
- DropDownList (similar to ComboBox control)
- Image (similar to PictureBox control)
- Calendar (similar to MonthCalendar control)

Web controls have similar properties to their Windows Forms counterparts. Examples of such properties are Text, Enabled, Visible, Font, BorderStyle, ReadOnly, and TabIndex. The following, however, are a few important differences between Web controls and Windows controls:

- The ID property of Web controls is the counterpart to the Name property of Windows controls.
- Web controls have an important new property named AutoPostBack.
- Web controls lose their runtime properties when the user moves away from the current page. Special programming techniques, called *saving state*, are available to overcome this challenge.

How Web Controls Are Processed

Web server controls are unique to ASP.NET. When a user connects to an ASP.NET Web page, a special process takes place, as shown in Figure 11-14. In Step 2, the Web server reads and interprets the Web controls on the page and executes Visual Basic statements in the application's code-behind file. In Step 3, the server creates a modified Web page consisting of standard HTML tags and controls. In Step 4, the modified Web page is sent back to the user and displayed in the Web browser.

Figure 11-14 Connecting to ASP Web pages

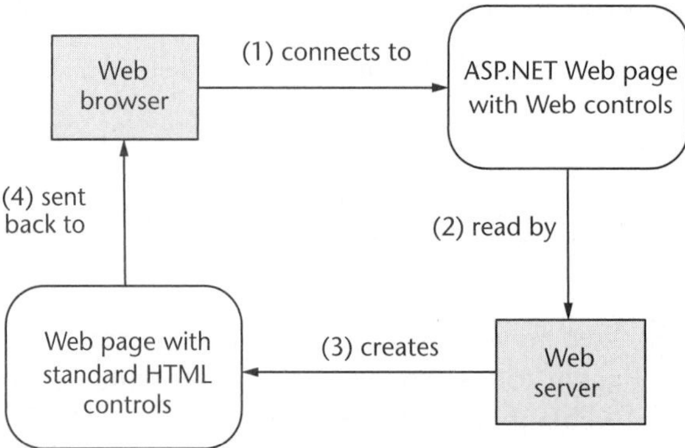

Label Control

The Web **Label control** is almost identical to the Label control on Windows forms. When displaying text, you only need to use a Label if its contents will change at runtime, or if you plan to change its Visible property. Always assign a name to a Label's ID property so you can access it in code. You can create interesting effects by varying the BorderStyle and BorderWidth properties, as shown in Figure 11-15.

Figure 11-15 *BorderStyle* and *BorderWidth* samples for the Label control

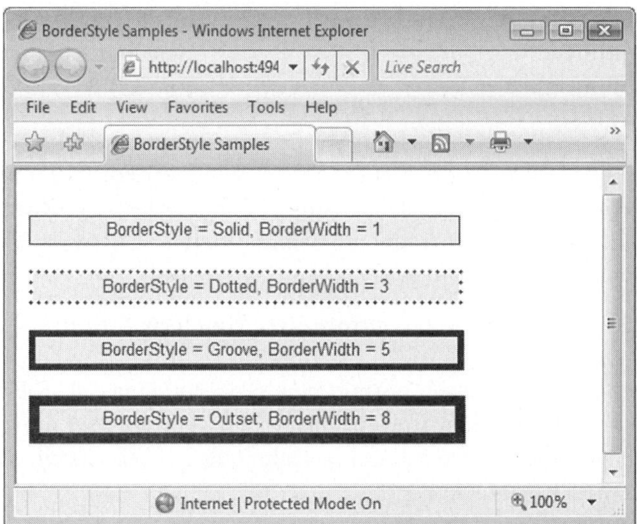

TextBox Control

The Web **TextBox control** is similar in many ways to the TextBox control for Windows forms. The Text property holds text input by the user. The MaxLength property lets you limit the number of characters the user is permitted to type. The TextMode property has the following choices:

- SingleLine: permits the user to enter only a single line of input
- MultiLine: permits the user to enter multiple lines of input
- Password: characters typed by the user appear as asterisks

Internet Explorer and other browsers behave differently when using the TextBox control. To be as compatible as possible with all Web browsers, you should use the Columns property to control the width of the text box. If you want the user to enter multiple lines of input, set the Rows property accordingly.

CheckBox Control

The **CheckBox control** is almost identical to the CheckBox in Windows forms. Use the Text property to set the visible text, and evaluate the Checked property at runtime to determine whether the control has been checked by the user. The TextAlign property lets you position the text to the left or right of the box.

In Tutorial 11-2, you create a Web sign-up for a *Student Picnic* application.

Tutorial 11-2:
Student Picnic application

In this tutorial, you will create a Web sign-up form for a computer department picnic. It will have a title, text boxes for a user to enter their name, a check box, and a button that displays a confirmation message. Figure 11-16 shows the program's output after the *Confirm* button was clicked.

Step 1: Select *New Web Site* from the *File* menu. Set the project folder name to *Picnic*, using the same directory path you used in Tutorial 11-1.

Step 2: Open the *Default.aspx* form in Design view. You can find the filename in the *Solution Explorer* window.

Step 3: Select *DOCUMENT* in the *Properties* window and set its Title property to *Picnic Sign-Up*. This text will appear in the browser's title bar when the application runs.

Step 4: Type the heading **`Computer Department Student Picnic`** directly onto the form and press Enter. Then select the first line of text with the mouse and set its Block format style to *Heading 2 <H2>*. (The Block format tool is located on the left side of the formatting toolbar.)

Step 5: Type **`First Name`** and **`Last Name`** on separate lines.

Step 6: After First Name, leave a space and insert a TextBox control. Set its ID property to *txtFirst*.

Step 7: After Last Name, leave a space and insert a TextBox control. Set its ID property to *txtLast*.

Figure 11-16 The *Student Picnic* application

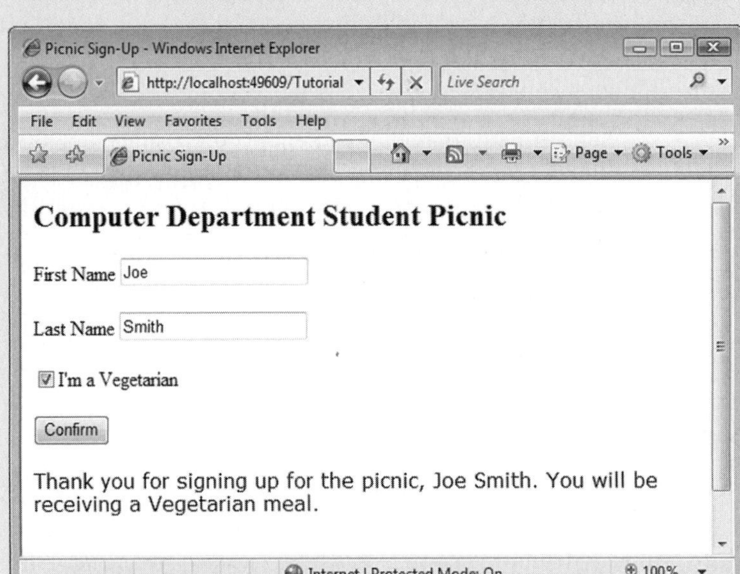

Step 8: On the next line, insert a CheckBox control and set its ID property to *chkVegetarian*. Set its Text property to *I'm a Vegetarian*.

Step 9: Insert a blank line, then on the next line insert a Button control. Set its ID property to *btnConfirm*, and set its Text property to *Confirm*.

Step 10: Insert a blank line, then on the next line insert a Label control. Set its ID property to *lblMessage*. Erase the contents of its Text property. Set its Font.Name property to *Verdana*.

Step 11: Next, you will insert code in the button's `Click` event handler. Double-click the button and add the following statements, shown in bold:

```
Protected Sub btnConfirm_Click(ByVal sender As Object, _
    ByVal e As System.EventArgs) Handles btnConfirm.Click

  lblMessage.Text = "Thank you for signing up for the " _
      & "picnic, " & txtFirst.Text & " " & txtLast.Text & "."

  If chkVegetarian.Checked = True Then
    lblMessage.Text &= " You will be receiving a " _
        & "Vegetarian meal."
  End If
End Sub
```

Step 12: Save the application and press Ctrl+F5 to run it. Enter a person's name, click the check box, and click the *Submit* button. The output should show the name and an additional comment about the meal because the check box was selected.

Event Handling in Web Forms

Events are fired in a different sequence in Web forms than they are in Windows forms. In a Web form, the `Page_Load` event occurs when the page is first loaded into the user's browser, and again every time the page is posted back to the server. The Web form shown in Figure 11-17 inserts a message in the list box every time the `Page_Load` event fires. From the program display, we can see that `Page_Load` fired when the page was first displayed.

Figure 11-17 Loading a Web form

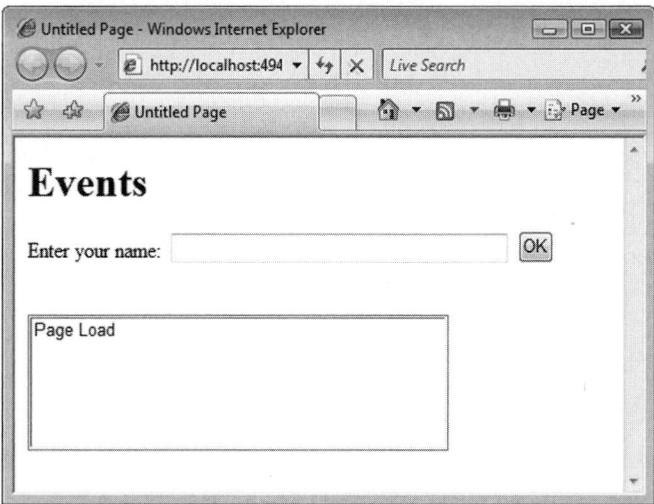

When the user types in a name and clicks the *OK* button, as shown in Figure 11-18, the `Page_Load` event fires again because a postback event occurs. Next, the `TextChanged` event handler executes. This unusual event sequence can be unsettling if you expect the `TextChanged` event to fire immediately, as it does in Windows Forms applications. In particular, you must be careful not to execute any code in the `Page_Load` event handler that changes the states of controls whose event handlers have not yet had a chance to execute.

Figure 11-18 After entering a name and clicking the *OK* button

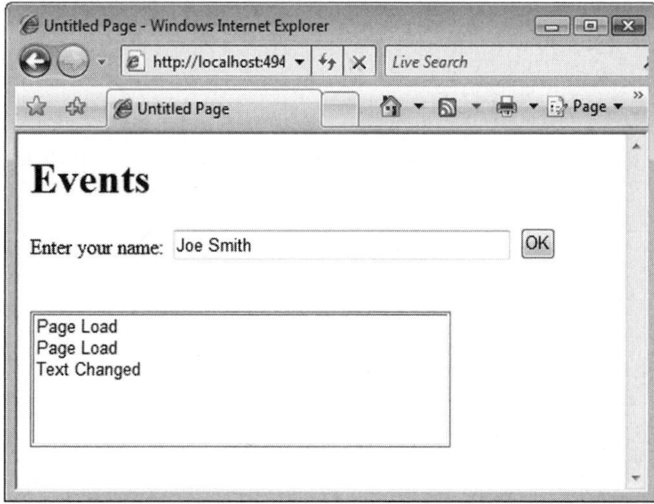

The AutoPostBack Property

When a control's **AutoPostBack property** equals *True*, clicking on the control causes the form to be posted back to the server. You might, for example, want to trigger a database row lookup when the user makes a selection in a list box. The server redisplays the form quickly or slowly, depending on how busy it is at the moment.

AutoPostBack defaults to *False* for the following controls: CheckBox, CheckBoxList, DropDownList, ListBox, ListControl, RadioButton, RadioButtonList, and TextBox. Not all controls have an AutoPostBack property. In particular, the Button, LinkButton, and ImageButton controls automatically post the current page back to the server.

HyperLink, ImageButton, LinkButton, and RadioButtonList

HyperLink Control

The **HyperLink control** provides a simple, easy way to add a link to your page that lets users navigate from the current page to another page. The link appears as underlined text. The HyperLink control does not generate any events, but it has three important properties as follows:

- The Text property contains the text shown to the user at runtime.
- The NavigateURL property contains the location of the Web page you would like the program to display when the user clicks the link. The property editor has a *Browse* button you can use to locate Web pages within your project.
- The Target property controls whether the new page will appear in the current browser window (the default), or in a separate window. To open in a separate browser window, set Target equal to *_blank*.

ImageButton Control

Web pages typically use clickable images as navigation tools. You can create the same effect with the **ImageButton control**. It does not look like or bounce like a typical button—instead, it simply shows an image. When the user hovers the mouse over the image, the mouse cursor changes shape. When the user clicks the image, a `Click` event is generated (which is probably why they call it a button).

You insert the image by placing an image's relative URL (path from the current page to the image file location) in the button's ImageUrl property. Ordinarily, you copy the image file into your project folder. The button generates a `Click` event when the image is clicked by the user. An example of a relative URL is *Images/photo.gif*, where the file named *photo.gif* is located in the *Images* subdirectory.

TIP: If you place the image file in the project's *App_Data* folder, the image does not appear at runtime. Other project folders cause no problem.

LinkButton Control

The **LinkButton control** looks and behaves much like a HyperLink control, with one major difference: it generates a `Click` event. You can write an event handler that executes when the user clicks the button. ImageButton and LinkButton samples are shown in Figure 11-19.

RadioButtonList Control

The **RadioButtonList control** displays a group of radio buttons, as shown in Figure 11-20. You can create individual **RadioButton controls**, but the RadioButtonList is easier to use. Similar to a ListBox, it has a SelectedIndex, SelectedItem, and SelectedValue properties. You can arrange the buttons horizontally or vertically, using the RepeatDirection property. You can set the BorderStyle, BorderWidth, and BorderColor properties to create a frame around the buttons. It has an Items property containing ListItem objects. You can add items using the ListItem collection editor window, as shown in Figure 11-21.

Figure 11-19 Examples of button-type controls

Figure 11-20 *RadioButtonList* example

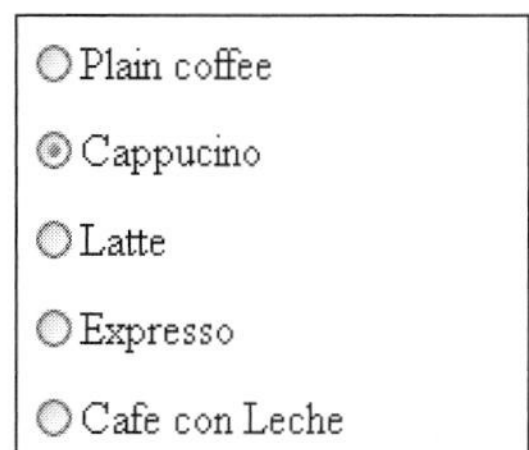

Figure 11-21 *ListItem Collection Editor* window

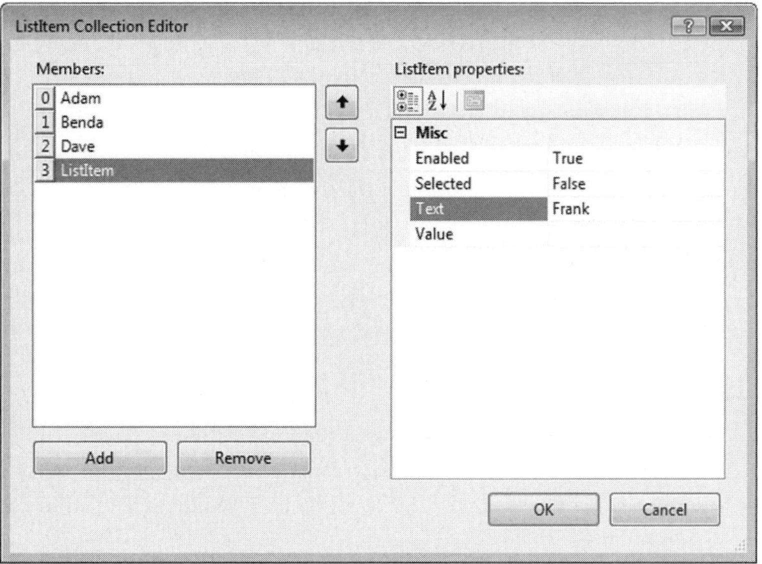

ListBox Control

In many ways, the Web **ListBox control** is similar to the Windows forms ListBox control. It has an Items collection and a `SelectedIndexChanged` event. You can retrieve the following properties at runtime:

- **SelectedIndex:** returns the index of the selected item
- **SelectedItem:** returns the currently selected item, a ListItem object
- **SelectedValue:** returns the contents of the selected item's Value property

In Figure 11-22, the index of the selected item from a list of sales staff members is displayed in a label below the *OK* button.

SelectionMode

You can use the SelectionMode property to determine whether users can select only a single item, or multiple items from a ListBox. The two possible choices are *Single* and *Multiple*. In *Multiple* mode, the user can hold down the Ctrl key to select multiple individual items or hold down the Shift key to select a range of items.

Figure 11-22 Displaying the SelectedIndex of a ListBox control

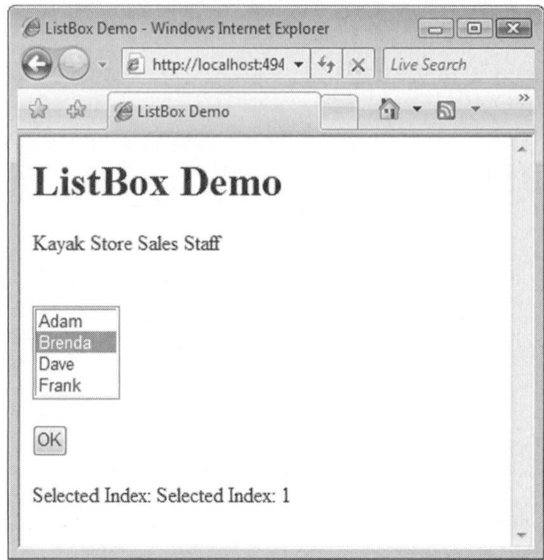

`SelectedIndexChanged` Event

You can use a `SelectedIndexChanged` event handler to respond to selections by the user in any list-type control. There is one important consideration, however: the AutoPostBack property must be set to *True* if you want the user's selection to be detected immediately. Otherwise, the `SelectedIndexChanged` event will not fire until the form is posted back to the server by some other control (such as a button).

When you set AutoPostBack to *True* for a list-type control, users experience a short delay each time they click on the list. Depending on the Web server's response time, the delay could cause performance problems. Most Web applications do not post back to the server every time users select from list-type controls. Instead, the sites use button controls to post all selections on the page back to the server at the same time.

CheckBoxList Control

The **CheckBoxList control** looks like a group of check boxes, but works just like a ListBox. It has SelectedIndex, SelectedItem, and SelectedValue properties. It has an Items collection, and each item has a Selected property (*True* or *False*). Figure 11-23 shows two CheckBoxLists, one with no border, and another with a 1-pixel-wide solid border.

Figure 11-23 CheckBoxList control

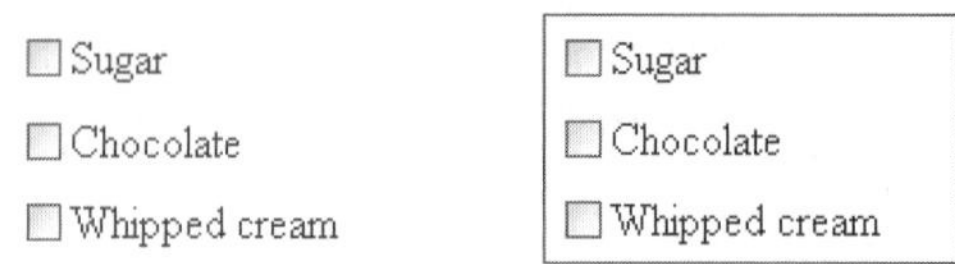

Usually, you will want to iterate over the Items collection to find out which boxes have been checked. The following is a sample:

```
Dim item As ListItem
For Each item In chkAddOns.Items
    If item.Selected Then
        'do something
    End If
Next
```

DropDownList Control

The **DropDownList control** permits the user to select single item from a list. There are two noticeable differences between the DropDownList and its Windows forms counterpart, the ComboBox. First, in a DropDownList, the initial value of SelectedIndex is always 0, causing the first item to display. Second, users cannot enter an arbitrary string into the DropDownList, as they can in a ComboBox.

Figure 11-24 shows a simple example of a list when first displayed on a Web form. We have inserted an initial entry named *(none)* in the first row, located at index position 0.

Figure 11-24 Using the DropDownList control

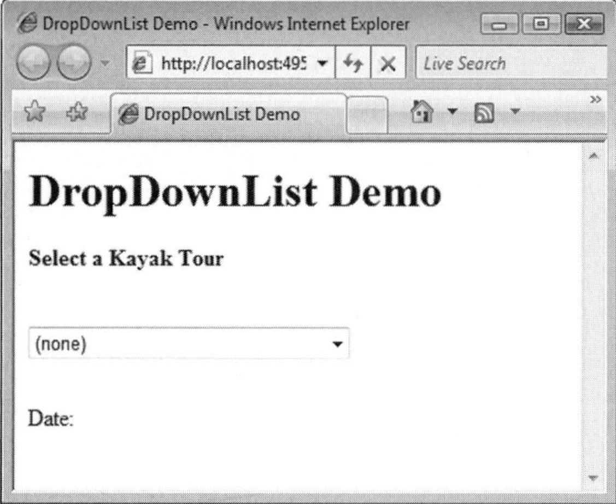

Checkpoint

11.12 Which Web control is the counterpart to the ComboBox in Windows forms?

11.13 Which Web control displays an image and fires a `Click` event?

11.14 Which Web control looks like a hyperlink and fires a `Click` event?

11.15 How can you determine which button in a RadioButtonList control was selected by the user?

11.16 How does setting AutoPostBack to *True* affect a ListBox control?

11.17 Which list-type control automatically initializes its SelectedIndex property to zero?

11.4 Designing Web Forms

CONCEPT: HTML tables can be used to design a Web application's user interface. HTML tables provide a convenient way to align the elements of a Web form.

Using Tables to Align Text and Controls

An **HTML table** is an essential tool for designing the layout of Web forms. You can use it to align text, graphics, and controls in rows and columns. In Figure 11-25, for example, a table contains five rows and three columns. Static text has been placed in column 1, and text boxes have been placed in column 3. The table cells in column 1 are right justified, and the cells in column 3 are left justified. Column 2 is intentionally left blank so it can be used as a spacer between the first and third columns.

Figure 11-25 Aligning text and text boxes with a table

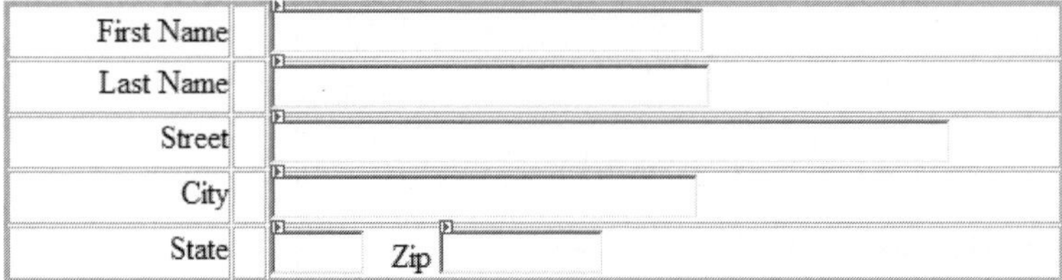

There are two ways to insert a table when viewing a form's design:

- Select *Insert Table* from the *Table* menu. When you do so, the *Insert Table* dialog box appears, letting you set various table layout options (see Figure 11-26).

Figure 11-26 *Insert Table* dialog box

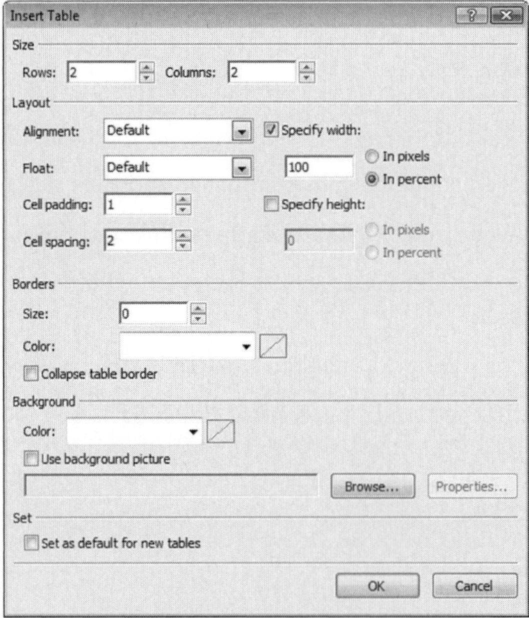

- Select the Table control from the HTML section of the *Toolbox* window. A basic 3 × 3 table is placed on the form, which you can resize by dragging the handles along its right and bottom sides. A sample is shown in Figure 11-27.

Figure 11-27 Empty HTML Table control, in Design view

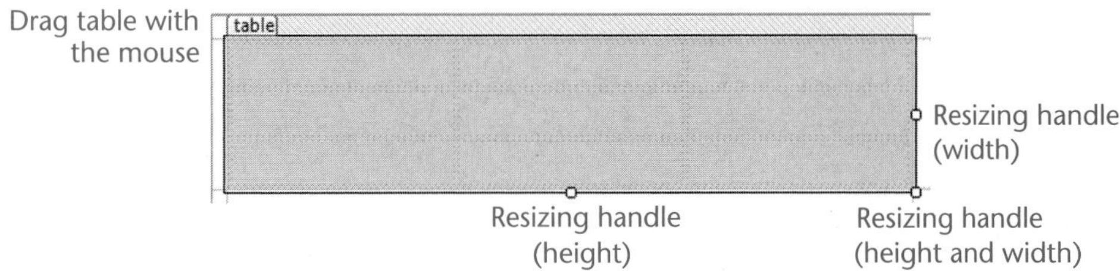

Although the table borders show in Design view, they are invisible at runtime because (by default) the border width equals zero. If you set the Border property to an integer value greater than zero, the table borders appear at runtime. An example is shown in Figure 11-28.

Figure 11-28 Table displayed at runtime with Border = *1* and text in each cell

A	B	C
D	E	F
G	H	I

Adjusting Row Heights and Column Widths

To adjust the width of a column, hover the mouse over the double bar along the column's right border. When the mouse cursor changes to a double vertical bar with arrows pointing left and right, hold down the mouse button and drag the border to its new location. As you do so, the column width (in pixels) displays inside the column. Often, the displayed number gives you a more accurate idea of the column width than the table's visual display.

To adjust the height of a row, hover the mouse over the row's lower border. When the mouse cursor changes to a double horizontal line with arrows pointing up and down, drag the mouse and the border up or down. As you do so, the column height (in pixels) displays inside the column. Often, the displayed number gives you a more accurate idea of the column height than the table's visual display.

Inserting Rows and Columns

The *Table* menu gives you tools to insert new rows and columns, relative to the currently selected cell:

- To insert a row above the current row, select *Insert* from the *Table* menu, and select *Row Above*. Or, press the Ctrl+Alt+↑ keyboard shortcut.
- To insert a row below the current row, select *Insert* from the *Table* menu, and select *Row Below*. Or, press the Ctrl+Alt+↓ keyboard shortcut.

- To insert a column to the left of the current column, select *Insert* from the *Table* menu, and select *Column to the Left*. Or, press the Ctrl+Alt+← keyboard shortcut.
- To insert a column to the right of the current column, select *Insert* from the *Table* menu, and select *Column to the Right*. Or, press the Ctrl+Alt+→ keyboard shortcut.

In each case, the inserted row or column will have the same attributes as the row or column that was selected when you issued the command. Use similar commands in the *Table* menu to delete rows and columns.

Aligning Text Inside Cells

By default, static text typed into table cells is left justified. Each cell's Align property controls the placement of text and graphics in the cell. The possible values are center, left, and right.

Merging Adjacent Cells

Sometimes it is useful to merge, or combine adjacent table cells into a single cell. The cells must be in the same column or row. To do this, drag the mouse over the cells, and select *Merge Cells* from the *Table* menu. Figure 11-29 shows several cells that have been selected by the mouse, prior to being merged.

Figure 11-29 Selecting multiple cells

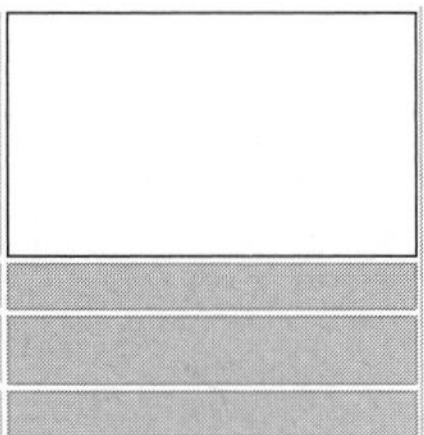

Final Notes

If the height of a row seems to change when you switch from Design mode to Run mode, drag the bottom of the row with the mouse. This causes a specific row height to be encoded in the Style property of each cell in the row.

Start with more columns and rows than you think you need. It's much easier to delete an existing column than to insert a new one without messing up the existing table alignment.

In Design mode, avoid pressing Enter as the last action while editing a cell. Doing so inserts a paragraph tag which is difficult to remove. A paragraph tag can be removed by editing the HTML directly, and removing the `<P>` and `</P>` tags from the cells. In HTML, a table cell is defined by the `<TD>` and `</TD>` tags.

If you're an expert, go ahead and edit the HTML in your forms. However, be careful, because it's easy to introduce errors. If Visual Studio is unable to understand your HTML, it will refuse to load some or all of the controls on your Web form.

In Tutorial 11-3, you write a program that allows users to sign up for a *Kayak Tour*.

Tutorial 11-3:
Signing up for a *Kayak Tour*

In this tutorial, you will write a program that lets the user sign up for kayak tours in Key Largo, Florida. You will use DropDownList, CheckBoxList, ListBox, and Button controls. You will use an HTML table to align the text and controls. You will write short event handlers for the buttons. A sample of the program when running is shown in Figure 11-30.

Figure 11-30 Signing up for a *Kayak Tour*

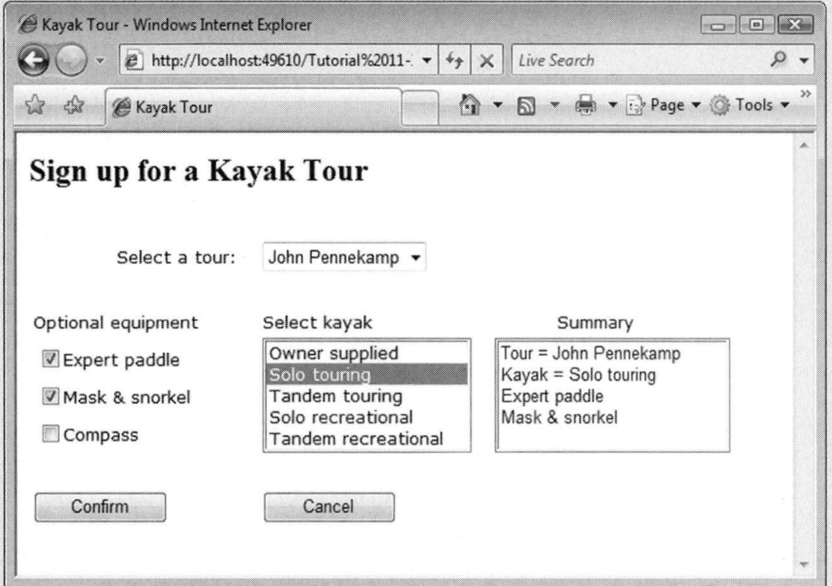

Step 1: Create a new Web site named *Kayak Tour*.

Step 2: Select *DOCUMENT* in the *Properties* window and set its Title property to *Kayak Tour*.

Step 3: Type *Sign up for a Kayak Tour* in the first line of the Web page and set its block format to *Heading 2*. Press Enter at the end of the line.

Step 4: Select *Insert Table* from the *Table* menu and set the size to 6 rows and 5 columns. Click the *OK* button to insert the table.

Step 5: Select the entire table (choose *Select/Table* from the *Table* menu) and modify its Style property. In the *Modify Style* dialog box, shown in Figure 11-31, experiment with various fonts and colors. For our sample, we will use a small Verdana font. Close the *Modify Style* dialog box.

Figure 11-31 Modifying the Style properties for the HTML table

Modify Style
Category:
Font
Block
Background
Border
Box
Position
Layout
List
Table
font-family:
font-size:
font-weight:
font-style:
font-variant:
text-transform:
color:
px
text-decoration:
underline
overline
line-through
blink
none
Preview:
AaBbYyGgLlJj
Description:
width: 158px
OK
Cancel

Step 6: Insert static text and set cell alignments, as shown in Figure 11-32.

Step 7: Using the same figure as a reference, insert a CheckBoxList control in row 4, column 1. Set its ID property to *chkEquipment*.

Step 8: Insert a DropDownList in row 1, column 3, and set its ID property to *ddlTour*.

Step 9: Insert a ListBox in row 4, column 3, and set its ID property to *lstKayak*.

Figure 11-32 The Web form, in Design mode

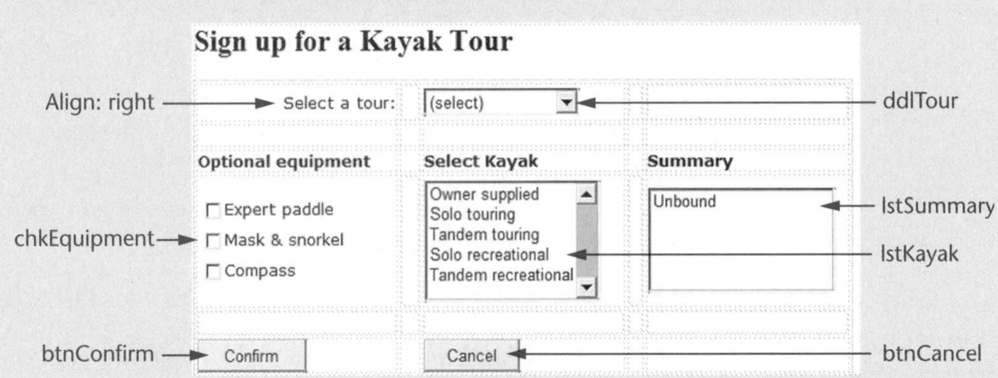

Step 10: Insert a ListBox in row 4, column 5, and set its ID property to `lstSummary`.

Step 11: Insert a Button control in row 6, column 1, and set its ID property to `btnConfirm`. Set the button's Text property to *Confirm*.

Step 12: Insert a Button control in row 6, column 3, and set its ID property to `btnCancel`. Set the button's Text property to *Cancel*.

Step 13: This is a good time to adjust the column widths so they look approximately like those shown in Figure 11-32. Don't try to be too precise, because the column widths will change when you run the program.

Step 14: Insert the following items in `ddlTour`: **`(select)`**, **`Key Largo`**, **`John Pennekamp`**, **`Flamingo Park`**. We made the first entry *(select)* so we can tell when the user has not yet selected a tour.

Step 15: Insert items in `chkEquipment` and `lstKayak` according to the values displayed in Figure 11-32.

Step 16: Double-click the *Confirm* button and insert the following code in its `Click` event handler. The lines you must add are shown in bold.

```
Protected Sub btnConfirm_Click(ByVal sender As Object, _
     ByVal e As System.EventArgs) Handles btnConfirm.Click

   ' This procedure creates a list containing the tour name,
   ' kayak type, and optional equipment. It adds the list to
   ' the lstSummary ListBox.

  With lstSummary
     .Items.Clear()

     If ddlTour.SelectedIndex = 0 Then
       .Items.Add("A tour must be selected")
       Exit Sub
     End If

     If lstKayak.SelectedIndex = -1 Then
       .Items.Add("A kayak type must be selected")
       Exit Sub
     End If

     .Items.Add("Tour = " & ddlTour.Text)
     .Items.Add("Kayak = " & lstKayak.SelectedItem.ToString())

     ' Selected optional equipment (CheckBoxList)
     Dim item As ListItem
     For Each item In chkEquipment.Items
       If item.Selected Then
         .Items.Add(item.Text)
       End If
     Next
  End With
End Sub
```

If the user has not yet selected a tour, `ddlTour`'s selected index will be zero, so we just display a message in `lstSummary` and exit immediately. The same is true if the user forgets to select a kayak type.The CheckBoxList control, which only exists for Web forms, uses the same Items collection as the ListBox control for Windows forms. The DropDownList control uses the same Text property as the ComboBox control for Windows forms.

Step 17: In the *Design* window, double-click the *Cancel* button and insert the following code, shown in bold, in its `Click` event handler:

```
Protected Sub btnCancel_Click(ByVal sender As Object, _
    ByVal e As System.EventArgs) Handles btnCancel.Click

  ddlTour.SelectedIndex = 0
  lstKayak.SelectedIndex = -1

  ' Clear the CheckBoxList
  Dim item As ListItem
  For Each item In chkEquipment.Items
    item.Selected = False
  Next

  lstSummary.Items.Clear()
End Sub
```

Step 18: Save and run the application. Make several selections and compare your form's appearance to Figure 11-30, shown earlier. You can return to Design mode, adjust the table column widths by dragging the borders, and rerun the program. After selecting a tour, click the *Cancel* button to see how it works.

Step 19: When you're done, close the project.

Checkpoint

11.18 How do you merge several cells into a single table cell?

11.19 How do you select a column in a table?

11.20 How do you change a column width?

11.21 How do you set the default font for all cells in a table?

11.22 Which property of a CheckBoxList control contains the individual list items?

11.5 Applications with Multiple Web Pages

CONCEPT: Web applications are not limited to a single Web page. A Web application may have multiple Web forms for displaying data and interacting with the user.

Before long, you will want to create Web applications that have multiple pages. You might collect information on one page, and display a summary on another page. Or, you might display supplementary information on a second page, which the user can select at will. First we will talk about how you add a new page to a project, and then we will show how your program can navigate from one page to another.

Adding New Web Forms to a Project

There are two ways to add a new Web Form to a project:

- Select *Add New Item* from the *Website* menu
- Right-click the name of the project in the *Solution Explorer* window and select *Add New Item*

The *Add New Item* dialog box displays a wide variety of pages, controls, and other objects that can be added to a project. In Figure 11-33, notice that we have selected the *Place code in separate file* option. If you do not select it, your Visual Basic statements (such as event handlers) are embedded in the same file as the Web server controls and HTML. Some programmers prefer it that way, but we do not.

Figure 11-33 Adding a Web form to a project

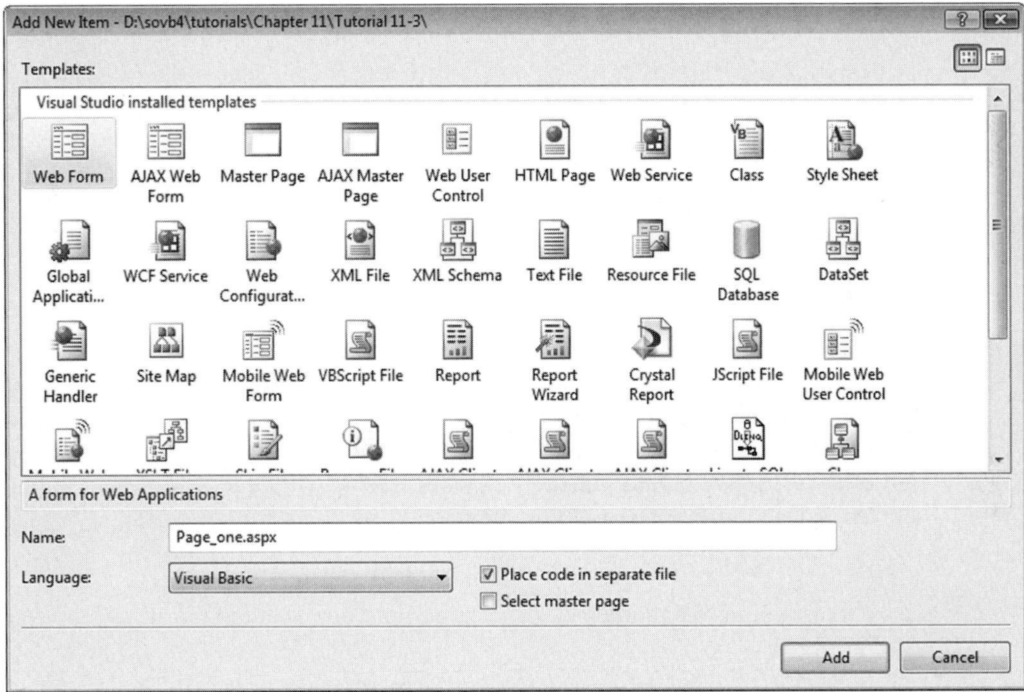

Moving between Pages

There are three common things you can do that will let a program move from a Web page we will call the *source page* to another Web page we will call the *target page*:

- Place the URL of the target page in the NavigateURL property of a HyperLink control. We discussed the HyperLink control in Section 11.3.
- Write code in the `Click` event handler of a Button, ImageButton, or LinkButton control. In a moment, we will show how to call the `Response.Redirect` method.
- Convert a block of static text to a hyperlink. Select a block of text with the mouse, click the *Hyperlink* button on the formatting toolbar (as shown in Figure 11-34), and enter the URL of the target page. Optionally, you can click the *Browse* button to locate a file within your project, as shown in Figure 11-35.

Figure 11-34 Converting a block of text to a hyperlink

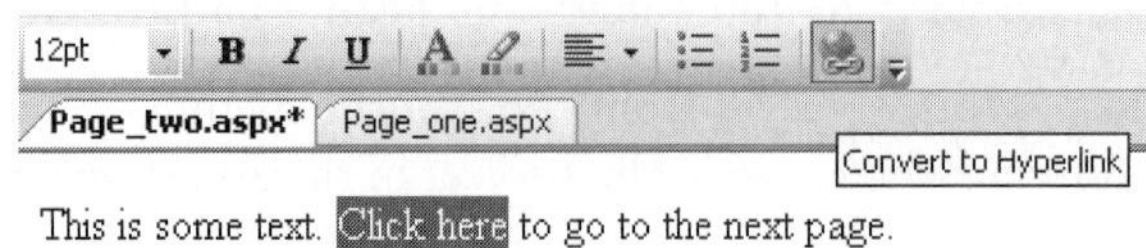

Figure 11-35 Selecting the target page for the hyperlink

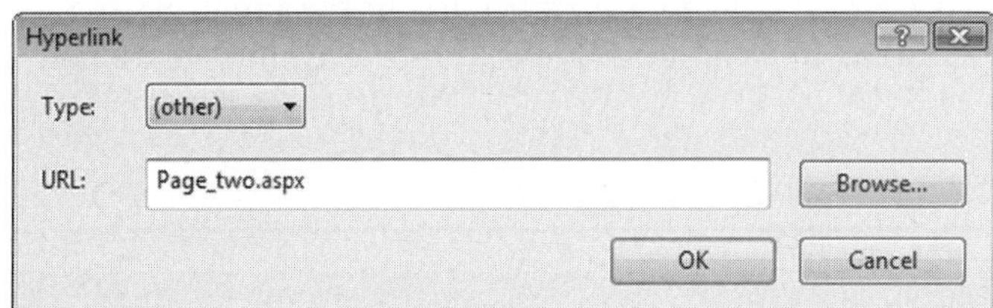

The major difference between these methods is that only one—the call to `Response.Redirect` is initiated by program code. The other two require the user to click a hyperlink.

Calling `Response.Redirect`

In your program code, you can tell the browser to navigate to another page in your application, or any other page on the Web by calling the **`Response.Redirect`** method. A `Response` object automatically exists in every Web page. It is an instance of the `HttpResponse` class. Suppose, for example, a program must transfer to a page named *Page_two.aspx*. We would put the following statement in the `Click` event handler of a Button, ImageButton, or LinkButton control:

```
Response.Redirect("Page_two.aspx")
```

If the target page is on another Web server, we must supply a fully formed URL as follows:

```
Response.Redirect("http://microsoft.com")
```

The following, for example, launches a Google search for the word *horses*:

```
http://www.google.com/search?q=horses
```

In Tutorial 11-4, you add a description form to the *Kayak Tour* application.

Tutorial 11-4:
Adding a description form to the *Kayak Tour* application

In this tutorial, you will extend the *Kayak Tour* program you created in Tutorial 11-3. You will add a Web form that describes the different kayak tours and use a HyperLink control to navigate to the form.

Step 1: Open the *Kayak_Tour* project folder you created in Tutorial 11-3.

Step 2: Add a new Web form named *Tours.aspx*. Type the text shown in Figure 11-36, shortening it if necessary. We used a Verdana font.

Step 3: In the *Default.aspx* form, add a HyperLink control to the cell in row 1, column 5. Set its Text property to *Tour descriptions*. Set its NavigateURL property to *Tours.aspx*. Set its Target property to *_blank*, which will cause the new form to be displayed in a separate browser window.

Figure 11-36 The *Kayak Tour* description Web form

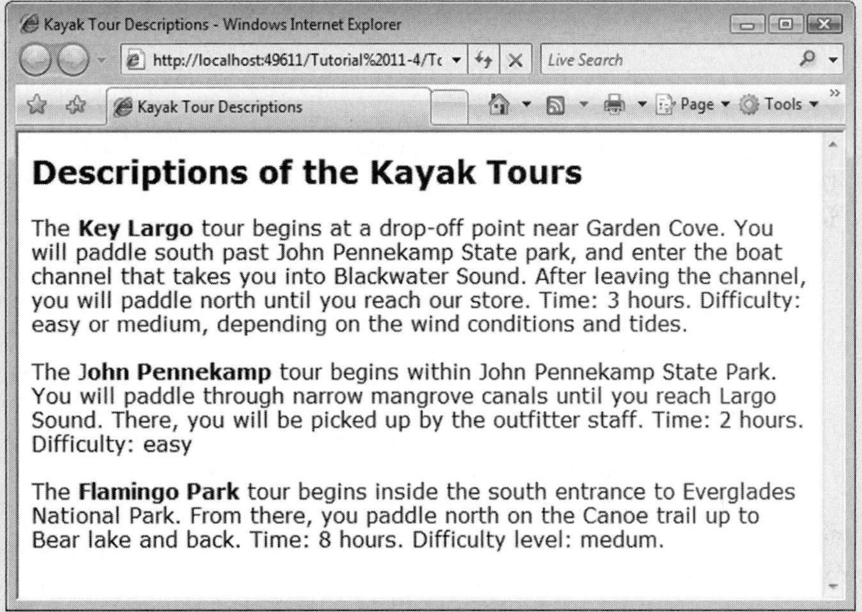

Step 4: Save and run the program. Click the *Tour Descriptions* link, and verify that the *Kayak Tour Descriptions* window opens in a separate browser window. (The user can glance at the descriptions while filling in the *Kayak Tour* form.)

Step 5: Close both browser windows to end the application.

Checkpoint

11.23 Which menu command adds a new Web form to a project?

11.24 How can a HyperLink control be used to navigate between Web pages?

11.25 How do you convert a block of static text to a hyperlink?

11.26 Which method in the Response object navigates to a different Web page?

11.6 Using Databases

CONCEPT: ASP.NET provides several Web controls for displaying and updating a database from a Web application.

You can display and update the contents of database tables very easily in ASP.NET applications. First, we will show how to use the GridView control to display database tables. Then we will show how to use the DetailsView control to display a single row at a time, and how to add a new row to a database table.

Web applications use a different model for accessing databases from Windows Forms applications. Rather than using a dataset, Web forms use a DataSource control. Actually, there are two controls, depending on which type of database you're using. One control is named *AccessDataSource*, for MS Access databases. The other is named *SqlDataSource*, for SQL Server databases. We will use the latter. One important characteristic of the DataSource controls is that they directly update the database, with no separate `Update` method call required.

> **TIP:** In all of our database examples, we will assume that you are connecting to SQL Server database files, rather than a full version of SQL Server. If your college lab uses a database server, please contact your classroom instructor or network administrator for database connection information.

Using a GridView to Display a Table

The **GridView control** offers the ideal way to display a complete table. Similar to the Windows control named DataGridView, it lets you sort on any column, select the column order, and format the data within columns.

Smart Tags

In the Design view, the GridView has a small arrow in its upper right corner called a *smart tag*, as shown in Figure 11-37. When you click on this tag, the *GridView Tasks* menu pops up, as shown in Figure 11-38. You can use it to set various grid properties and connect to a data source.

Figure 11-37 GridView control with smart tag (Design view)

Column0	Column1	Column2
abc	abc	abc
abc	abc	abc
abc	abc	abc
abc	abc	abc
abc	abc	abc

Figure 11-38 The smart tag activates the *GridView Tasks* menu

Column0	Column1	Column2
abc	abc	abc
abc	abc	abc
abc	abc	abc
abc	abc	abc
abc	abc	abc

GridView Tasks
Auto Format...
Choose Data Source: (None)
Edit Columns...
Add New Column...
Edit Templates

Setting Up a Connection

The general steps required to connect your Web form to a database follow. Don't try to do them yet, because we need to provide a few more details during the upcoming tutorial.

1. Copy the database file to the *App_Data* folder inside your project's folder.
2. Select the Data Source type, as shown in Figure 11-39.

Figure 11-39 Choosing a *Data Source Type*

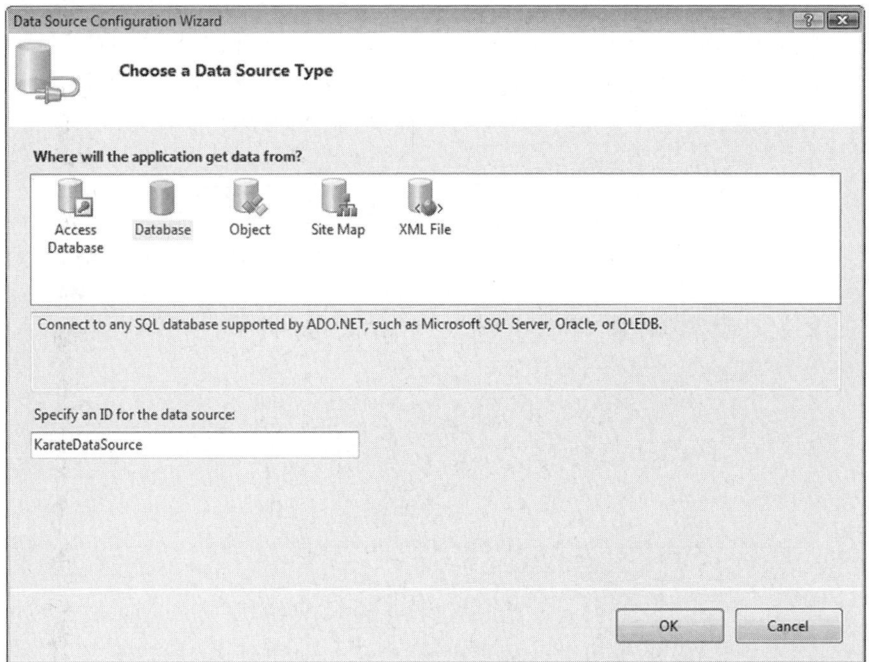

3. Select the database name within the *App_Data* folder, as shown in Figure 11-40.

Figure 11-40 Identifying the *Database* file

4. Configure the `SELECT` statement for the database query, as shown in Figure 11-41. If your query involves more than one table, select the option that says *Specify a custom SQL statement or stored procedure* and click the *Next* button.

Figure 11-41 Configuring the `SELECT` statement

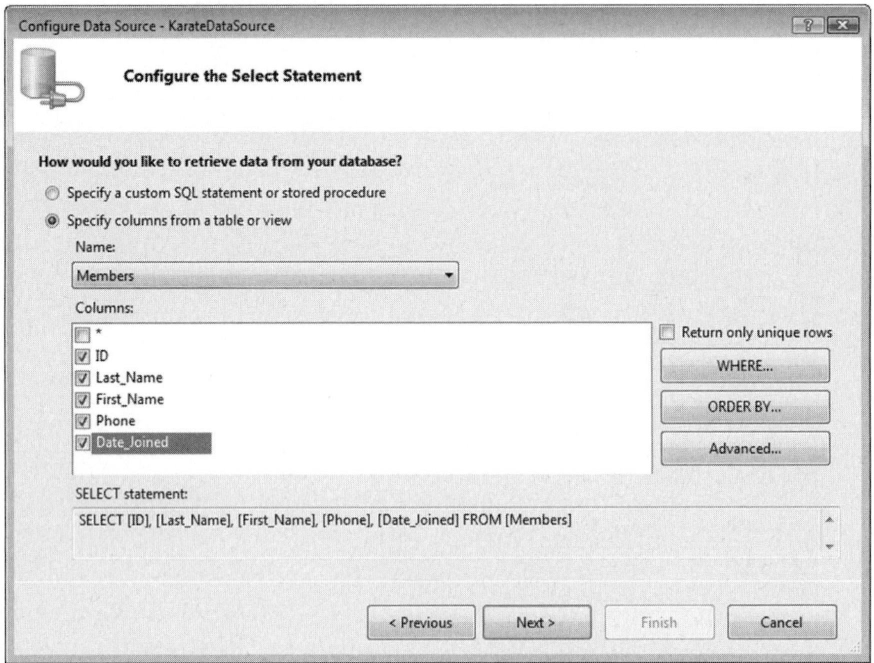

5. If you specified a custom SQL statement in the previous step, Figure 11-42 shows the window in which you can build a query by joining tables. Click the *Query Builder* button.

Figure 11-42 Building a custom SQL statement

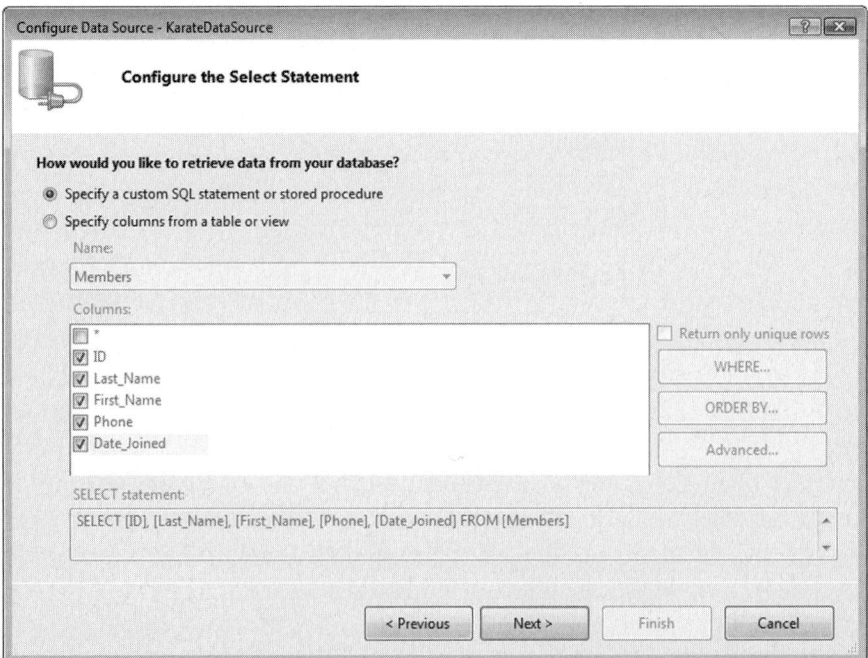

When you're finished, a **DataSource control** (either AccessDataSource or SqlDataSource) is placed on your Web form. The control is only visible at Design mode.

In Tutorial 11-5, you display the *Karate Members* table in a GridView.

Tutorial 11-5:
Displaying the *Karate Members* table in a GridView

In this tutorial, you will create a connection to the *Karate* database, and display the *Members* table in a GridView control. You will perform some basic configuration of the grid's appearance.

Step 1: Create a new Web site named *MemberGrid*.

Step 2: Open a *Windows Explorer* window or *My Computer* window and copy the *Karate.mdf* file from the student sample programs folder named *Chap11* to your project's *App_Data* folder.

Step 3: In the *Solution Explorer* window, right-click the project name and select *Refresh Folder*. Then expand the entry under *App_Data* and look for the *Karate.mdf* filename, as shown in Figure 11-43.

Figure 11-43 Locating the *Karate.mdf* file under *App_Data* in the *Solution Explorer* window

Step 4: In Design view, select *DOCUMENT* in the *Properties* window and set its Title property to *Karate Members*.

Step 5: On the first line of the Web page type **`Members Table, Karate Database`**. Set the block style to *Heading 2*, and press Enter at the end of the line.

Step 6: Place a GridView control on the form. You can find it in the *Data* section of the *Toolbox* window. Drag its right handle until its Width property equals about 638 pixels. Its Height property should equal about 300 pixels.

Step 7: Click the grid's smart tag, opening the *GridView Tasks* dialog box. Select *New Data Source* under the *Choose Data Source* entry.

Step 8: In the *Data Source Configuration Wizard*, select *Database*, change the ID value to *KarateDataSource*, and click the *OK* button.

Step 9: A window that reads *Choose Your Data Connection* will appear. Click the *New Connection* button. When the *Add Connection* window appears, as shown in Figure 11-44, make sure the *Data Source* field is set to *Microsoft SQL Server Database File* (SqlClient). If some other value appears in the field, change it.

Step 10: For the Database file name entry, click the *Browse* button, select the *App_Data* folder, select *Karate.mdf*, and click the *Open* button, then click the *OK* button to close the *Add Connection* dialog. Back in the window that reads *Choose Your Data Connection,* click the *Next* button. When a window appears that reads *Save the Application Connection String to the Application Configuration File*, click the *Next* button.

Step 11: You will be asked to configure the `SELECT` statement (the `SELECT` query) that pulls rows and columns from the database. From the *Name* list, select the *Members* table, as shown in Figure 11-45.

Step 12: Place check marks next to the following columns, in order: *ID*, *Last_Name*, *First_Name*, *Phone*, and *Date_Joined*.

Figure 11-44 Select the *Karate.mdf* database file

Figure 11-45 Configuring the `SELECT` statement

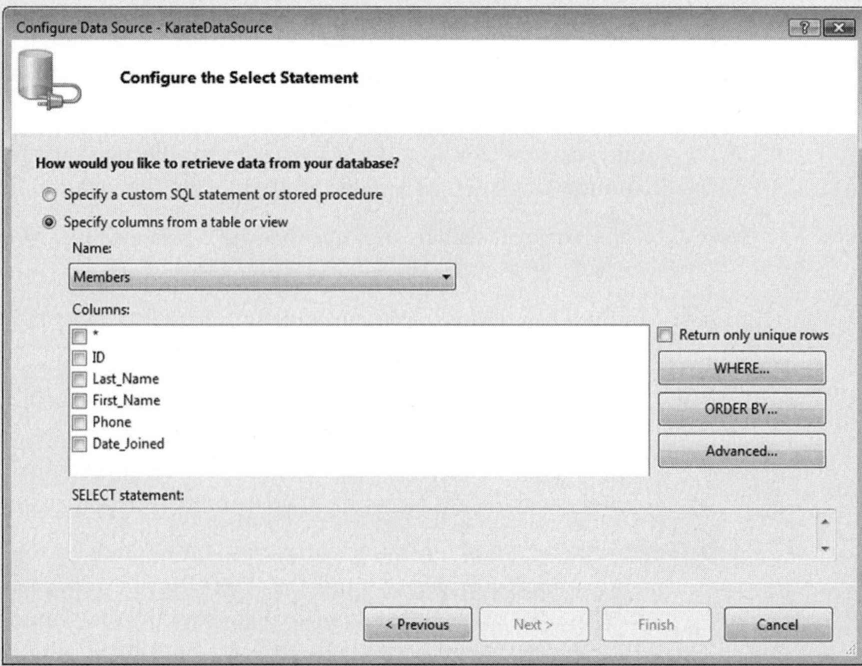

Step 13: Click the *ORDER BY...* button. In the dialog box shown in Figure 11-46, sort by the *Last_Name* column. Click *OK* to close the dialog box.

Step 14: Returning to the *Configure the Select Statement* dialog box, click the *Next* button, which takes you to the *Test Query* dialog box. Click the *Test Query* button. If the displayed columns match those shown in Figure 11-47, click the *Finish* button to close the window.

Figure 11-46 Adding the `ORDER BY` clause

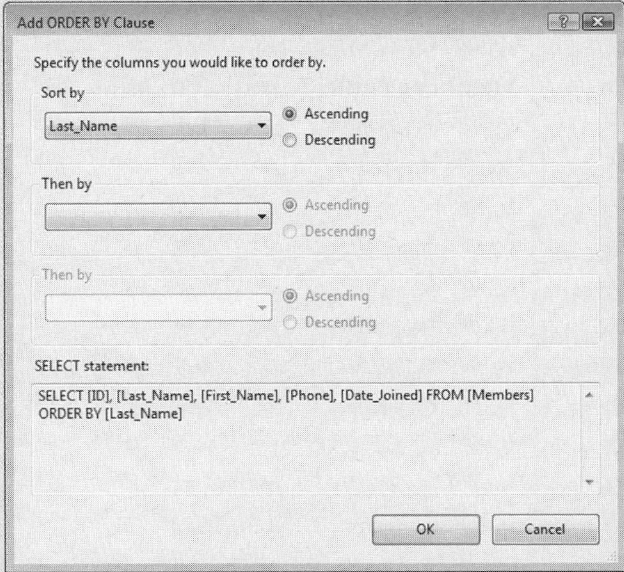

Figure 11-47 Testing the `SELECT` query

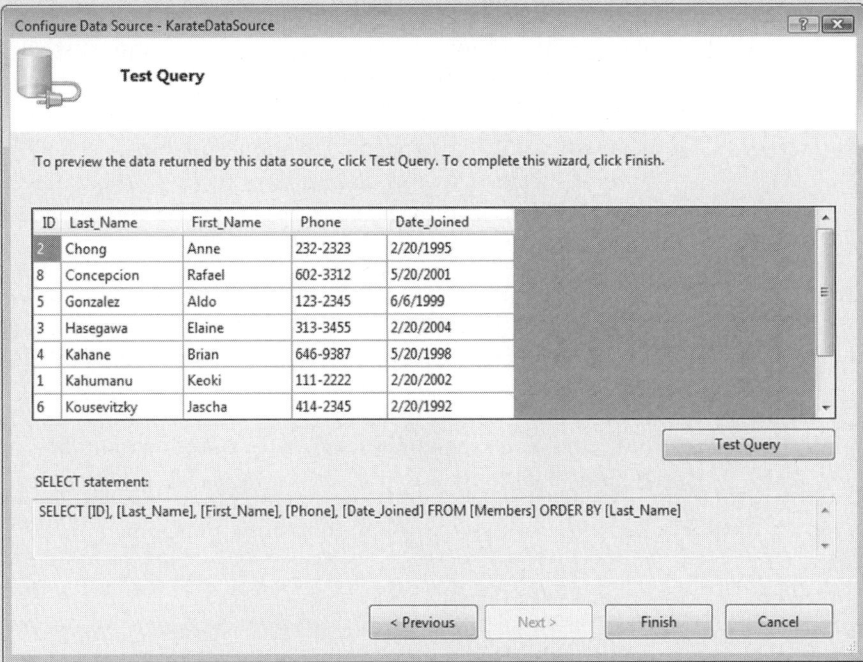

ID	Last_Name	First_Name	Phone	Date_Joined
2	Chong	Anne	232-2323	2/20/1995
8	Concepcion	Rafael	602-3312	5/20/2001
5	Gonzalez	Aldo	123-2345	6/6/1999
3	Hasegawa	Elaine	313-3455	2/20/2004
4	Kahane	Brian	646-9387	5/20/1998
1	Kahumanu	Keoki	111-2222	2/20/2002
6	Kousevitzky	Jascha	414-2345	2/20/1992

Step 15: Click the *GridView*'s smart tag again and check the *Enable Sorting* option.

Step 16: Save and run the Web application. You should see the display shown in Figure 11-48, although some of the data in the rows may be different.

Figure 11-48 Running the Web application

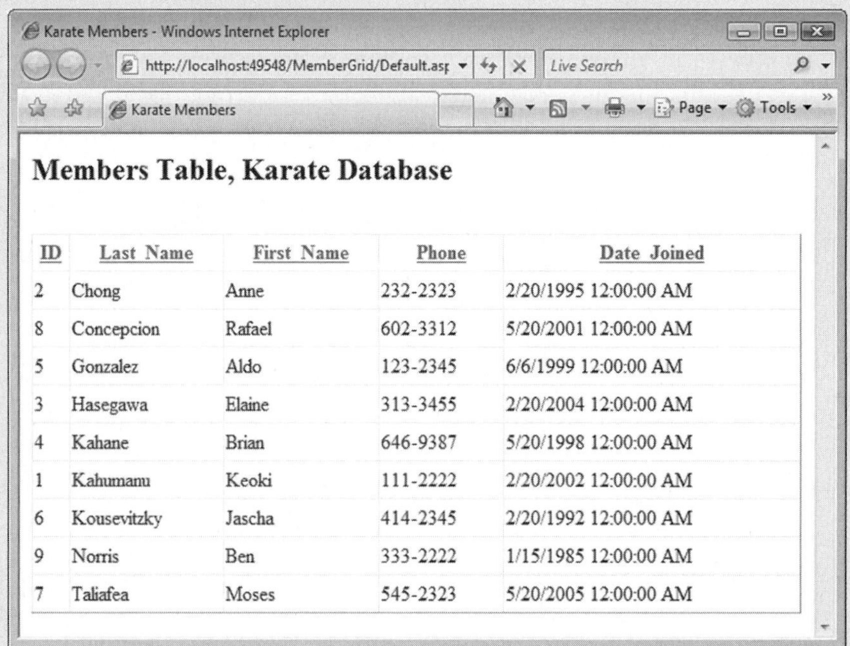

ID	Last Name	First Name	Phone	Date Joined
2	Chong	Anne	232-2323	2/20/1995 12:00:00 AM
8	Concepcion	Rafael	602-3312	5/20/2001 12:00:00 AM
5	Gonzalez	Aldo	123-2345	6/6/1999 12:00:00 AM
3	Hasegawa	Elaine	313-3455	2/20/2004 12:00:00 AM
4	Kahane	Brian	646-9387	5/20/1998 12:00:00 AM
1	Kahumanu	Keoki	111-2222	2/20/2002 12:00:00 AM
6	Kousevitzky	Jascha	414-2345	2/20/1992 12:00:00 AM
9	Norris	Ben	333-2222	1/15/1985 12:00:00 AM
7	Taliafea	Moses	545-2323	5/20/2005 12:00:00 AM

Step 17: Experiment with sorting columns by clicking each of the column headers. If you click the same column twice in a row, it sorts in descending order. Close the browser to end the application.

Step 18: Next, you will format the *Date_Joined* column. Just click the Columns property, which causes the *Fields editor* dialog box to display. In the lower left box, select *Date_Joined*. In the properties list for this column, enter **`{0:d}`** into the DataFormatString property, as shown in Figure 11-49. The *{0:d}* is called a *format specifier*. In this case, it says to use a *short date* format. Format specifiers are described in the Help system under the topic *Formatting overview*.

Step 19: Next, you will set a property that centers the values in the *Date_Joined* column. Expand the entries under the column's ItemStyle property. Change the HorizontalAlign subproperty to *Center*. Finally, set the HtmlEncode property of the *Date_Joined* column to *False*. Click the *OK* button to close the dialog box.

Step 20: Save and rerun the application. Your output should be similar to that shown in Figure 11-50.

Step 21: Close the browser window to end the program.

Figure 11-49 Formatting the *Date_Joined* column

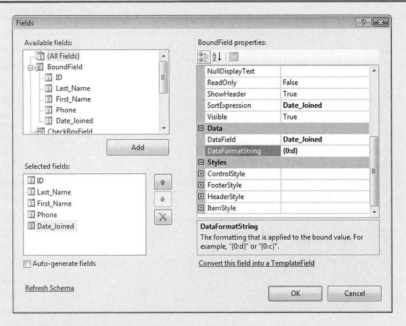

Figure 11-50 After formatting the *Date_Joined* column

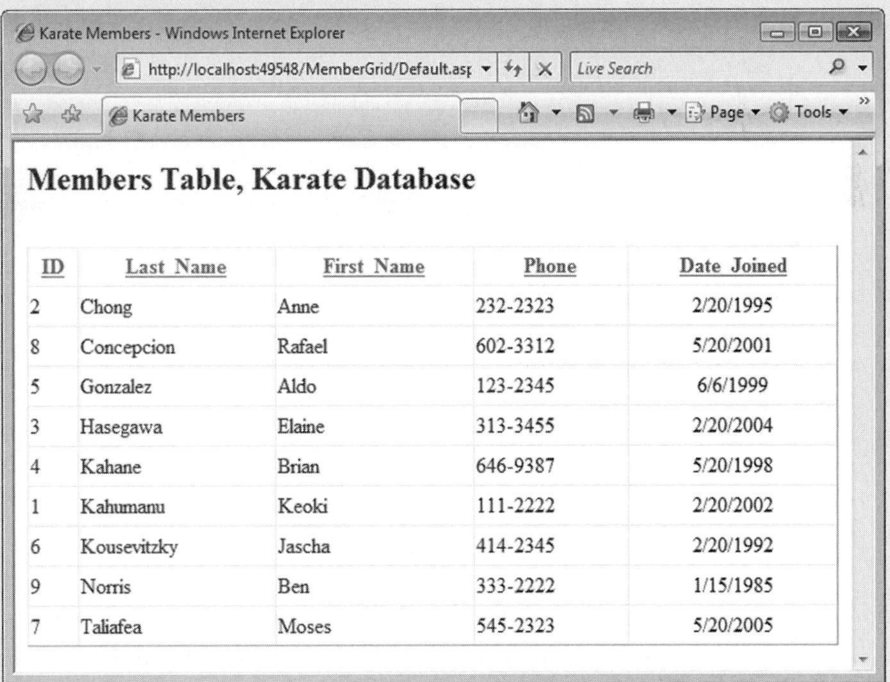

Members Table, Karate Database

ID	Last Name	First Name	Phone	Date Joined
2	Chong	Anne	232-2323	2/20/1995
8	Concepcion	Rafael	602-3312	5/20/2001
5	Gonzalez	Aldo	123-2345	6/6/1999
3	Hasegawa	Elaine	313-3455	2/20/2004
4	Kahane	Brian	646-9387	5/20/1998
1	Kahumanu	Keoki	111-2222	2/20/2002
6	Kousevitzky	Jascha	414-2345	2/20/1992
9	Norris	Ben	333-2222	1/15/1985
7	Taliafea	Moses	545-2323	5/20/2005

As you can see, there are many detailed formatting changes you can make to a GridView control.

Using a DetailsView Control to Modify Table Rows

The **DetailsView control** makes it easy to view, edit, delete, or add rows to a database table. To use it, you must create a data source, as you did in Tutorial 11-5. When you connect the DetailsView to the data source, most of the work is done for you. Microsoft engineers have been working hard to automate as many menial tasks as they can, and database table editing is high on the list of tasks most programmers would prefer *not* to do repeatedly.

The DetailsView control is found in the Data section of the *Toolbox* window. When you place it on a Web form, use its smart tag (upper right-hand corner) to add a database connection and set various options. You did the same for the GridView control in Tutorial 11-5.

In Tutorial 11-6, you will update the *Karate Members* table using a DetailsView control.

Tutorial 11-6:
Updating the *Karate Members* table

In this tutorial, you will write an application that lets the user view, edit, insert, and delete individual rows in the *Members* table in the *Karate* database. You will create an SqlDataSource control and hook it up to a DetailsView control. You will not have to write any program code.

Figure 11-51 shows the finished program right after it starts, with rows sorted by last name. The underlined words *Edit*, *Delete*, and *New* are called *link buttons* (LinkButton controls). They look like HTML links, but function like ordinary button controls.

Figure 11-51 Adding a member at runtime

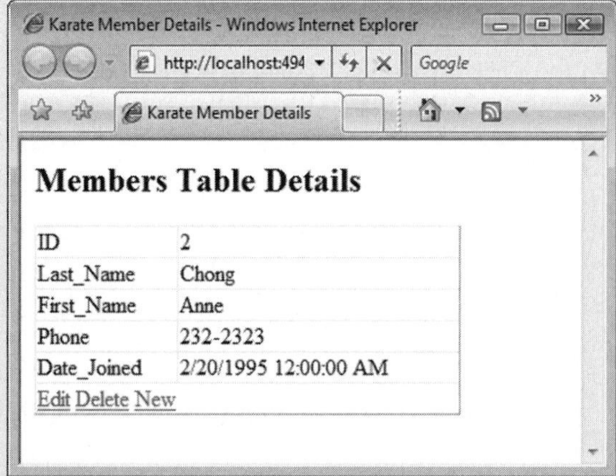

In Figure 11-52, the user has clicked the *New* button and begun to enter data for a new member. The user will soon click the *Insert (link)* button, which will save the new row in the database.

Figure 11-53 shows the same form after the user has clicked the *Insert* button. The new member (Eric Baker) appears in the detail fields.

If the user tries to add a row having an ID number equal to an existing ID in the table, an error page displays, as shown in Figure 11-54. The user can click the browser's *Back* button, enter a different ID, and try again.

Figure 11-52 About to insert a new member

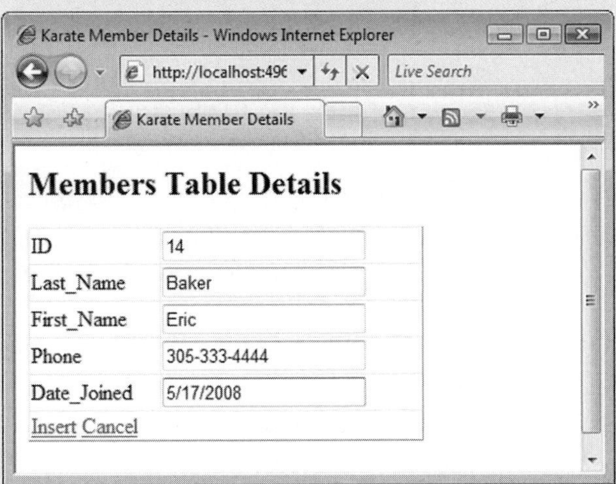

Figure 11-53 After clicking the *Insert* button

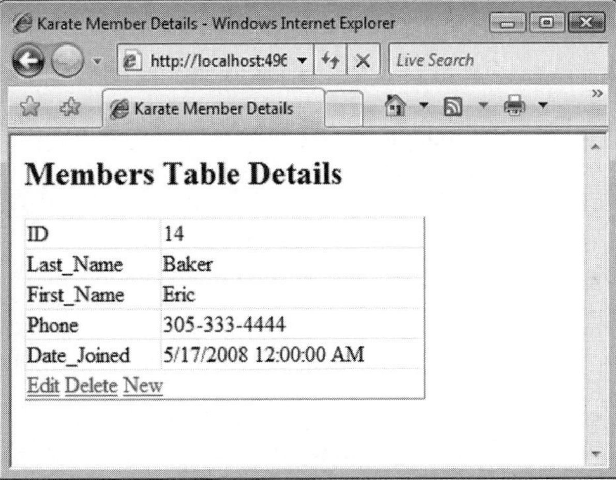

Figure 11-54 Error displayed when the user tries to add a row with a duplicate ID

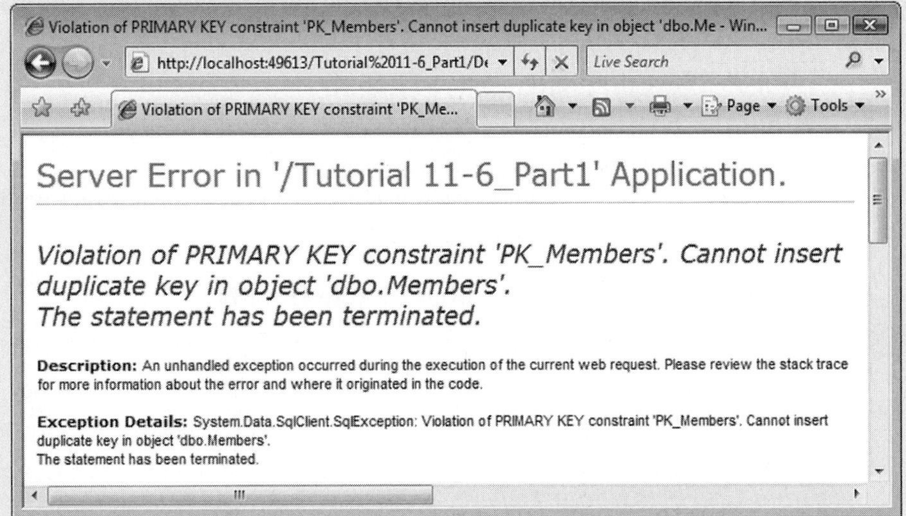

When the user clicks the *Edit* button, he can modify any of the member fields, as shown in Figure 11-55. When the user clicks the *Update* button, changes to the record are saved in the database.

Figure 11-55 After clicking the *Edit* button

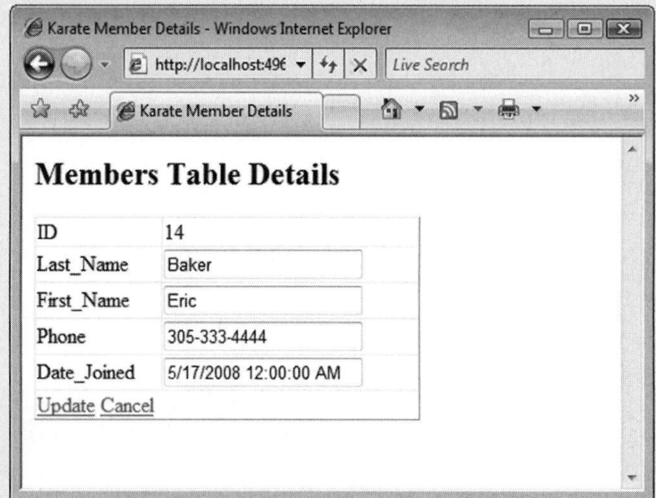

Now let's build the program.

Step 1: Create a new Web site named *Karate_Member_Details*. The underscore characters between words are optional.

Step 2: Copy the *Karate.mdf* database file into your project's *App_Data* folder.

Step 3: Right-click the project in the *Solution Explorer* window and select *Refresh Folder*. Verify that *Karate.mdf* appears under the *App_Data* entry.

Step 4: Select *DOCUMENT* in the *Properties* window and set its Title property to *Members Table Details*.

Step 5: On the first line of the page, insert `Members Table Details`, and give it a *Heading 2* block style.

Step 6: Add a DetailsView control to the page, and set its ID property to *dvwAddMember*. Widen it to about 300 pixels.

Step 7: Save the project. Figure 11-56 shows your work so far.

Figure 11-56 Designing the *Karate Member Details* form

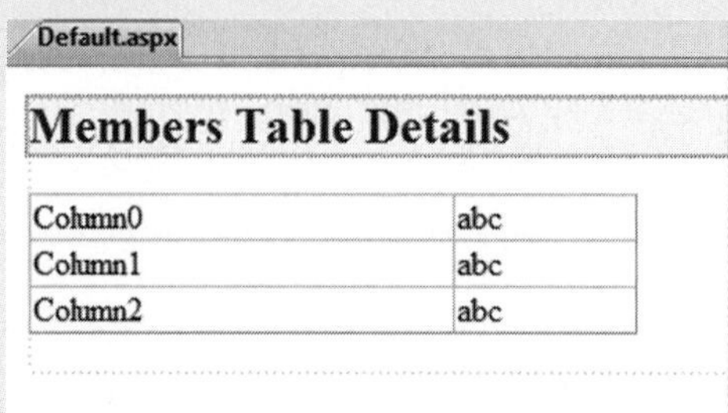

Next, you will add a data source to the project.

Step 8: Select the smart tag in the upper right corner of *dvwAddMember*. Under *Choose Data Source*, select *<New data source>*. Select *Database*, and name the data source **`MembersDataSource`**, as shown in Figure 11-57. Click the *OK* button to continue.

Figure 11-57 Creating the data source

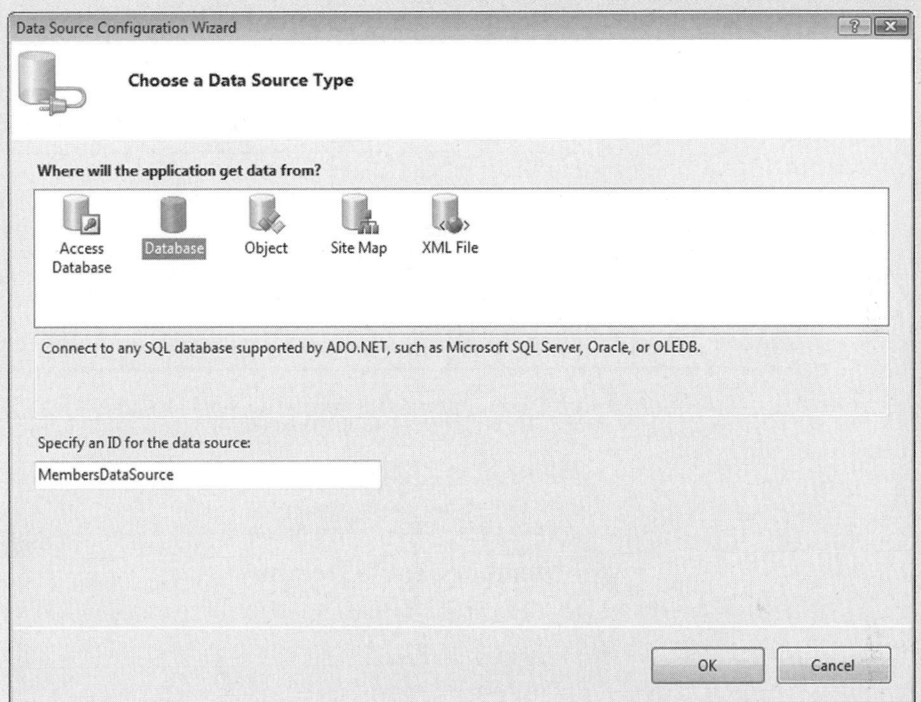

Step 9: As in the previous tutorial, create a connection to the *Karate.mdf* file in the project's *App_Data* folder.

Step 10: When the window entitled *Save the Application Connection String to the Application Configuration File* appears, click the *Next* button.

Step 11: In the next window, select all columns in the *Members* table, and order the rows by *Last_Name* in ascending order. When you return to the window entitled Configure the Select Statement, click the Advanced button.

Step 12: In the *Advanced SQL Generation Options* dialog box, select the *Generate INSERT, UPDATE, and DELETE statements* option, as shown in Figure 11-58. Click the *OK* button, and then click the *Next* button.

Step 13: Click the *Finish* button to close the *Configure Data Source* window. Back in the *Smart Tag* menu for `dvwAddMember`, select the check boxes to enable *Inserting*, *Editing*, and *Deleting*.

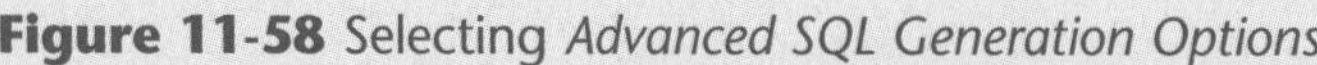

Figure 11-58 Selecting *Advanced SQL Generation Options*

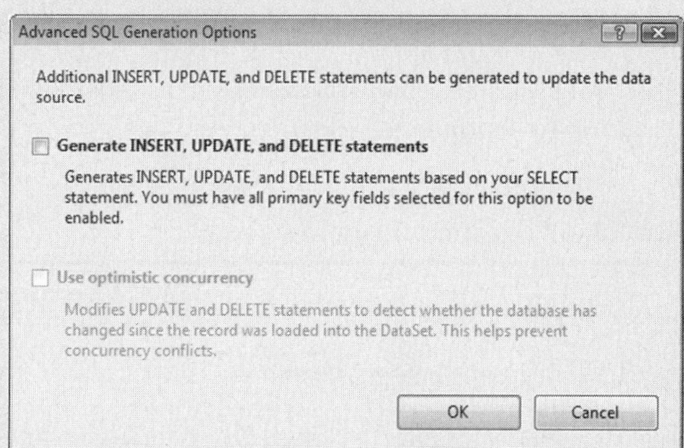

Step 14: Save and run the application. Sample output is shown in Figure 11-59. Click the *Edit* button, change the values of one of the fields (except the ID), and click the *Update* button.

Figure 11-59 Running the *Karate Member Details* application for the first time

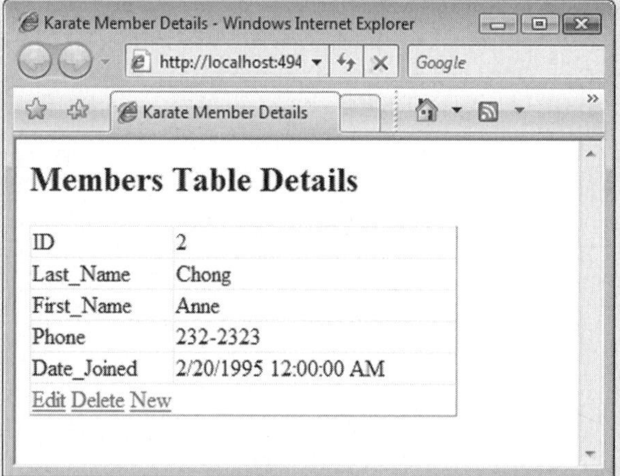

Step 15: Close the browser window and return to Design mode. Let's improve the appearance of the DetailView just a bit. Select it, and set its BorderWidth to *0px* (zero pixels wide). Select its Fields property, causing the *Fields* dialog box to display (see Figure 11-60).

Step 16: In the *Fields* dialog box, select the *Date_Joined* field in the lower left list box. Then in the right-hand list box, set its DataFormatString property to *{0:d}*. You may recall this is the same short date format specifier we used in the GridView control. Also, set the field's HTMLEncode property to *False*. (The format string we inserted would have no effect if we left HTMLEncode set to True.)

Step 17: Next, you will change the field order slightly. Select the *First_Name* field in the lower left list box, and click the arrow pointing upward just to the right side of the box. The *First_Name* field has now moved just above the *Last_Name* field.

Figure 11-60 *Fields* dialog box for the DetailsView control

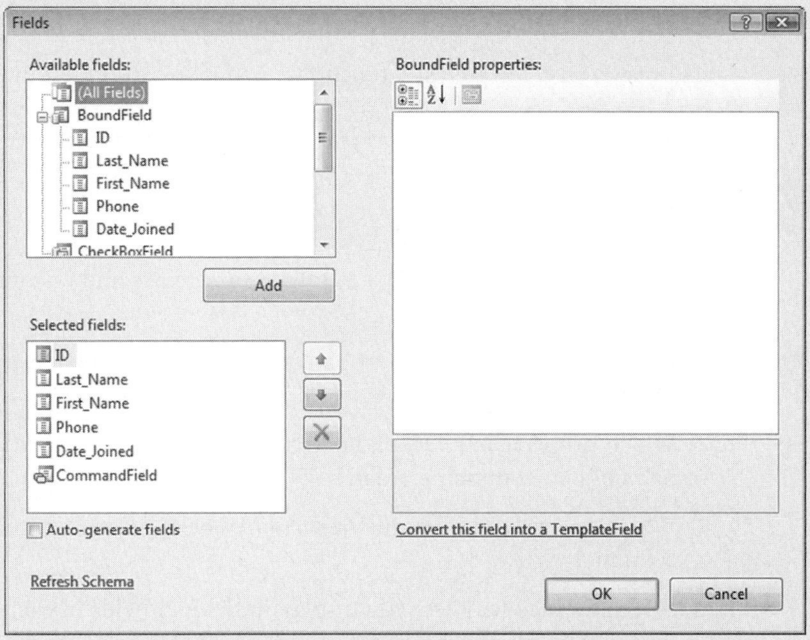

Step 18: Click *OK* to close the *Fields* dialog box. Save and run the program. It should now appear as shown in Figure 11-61.

Figure 11-61 After modifying the field display in the DetailsView control

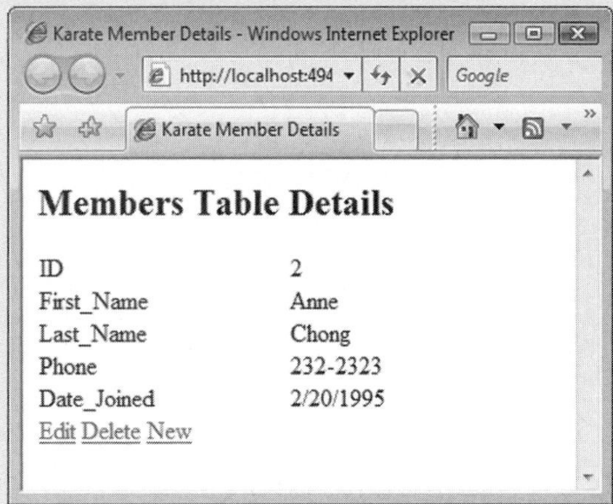

Step 19: When you click the *New* button, the program should clear all the text boxes. Enter the following data: **`14`**, **`Eric`**, **`Baker`**, **`654-3210`**, **`3/1/2008`**. Then click the *Insert* button. The display should now show the record you inserted.

Step 20: Try to insert a new record, using the same ID number. You should see a detailed error message. Click the browser's *Back* button, change the ID to **`15`**, and click the *Insert* button. This time, the insert operation should work.

Step 21: Click the *Delete* button. The record you inserted should disappear, and the first person in the table (probably Anne Chong) should display.

Step 22: Close the Web browser window.

You're done. You created a fully functional update program without writing a single line of code!

Checkpoint

11.27 Which Web control displays database table rows and columns in a grid-like format?

11.28 In a Web form, what type of object provides a connection to an SQL Server database?

11.29 Which property in a DetailsView control permits you to modify the formatting of a column containing a date?

11.30 Which property in a DetailsView control permits you to modify the order of the columns?

11.31 Which Web control lets you display individual fields in each row from a database, using text boxes?

Summary

11.1 Programming for the Web

- Web applications are designed around a client-server model: an entity called a server produces data consumed by another entity called a client. Web applications must be run using a Web server.
- When the Web first became popular, HTML was the only available encoding method for creating Web pages with text, graphics buttons, and input forms.
- Active Server Pages (ASP) was the first server-side Web programming technology introduced by Microsoft. ASP.NET, the current generation, is called a platform because it provides development tools, code libraries, and visual controls for browser-based applications.
- Web applications written for ASP.NET consist of content, in the form of Web forms, HTML code, Web forms controls, images, and other multimedia; program logic, in compiled Visual Basic (or C#) code; and configuration information.
- Visual Studio simplifies the way Web applications are developed.
- A URL (Uniform Resource Locator) provides a universal way of addressing objects and pages on a network.
- Web applications written in ASP.NET use special Web pages called Web forms. A Web form, which can be identified by its *.aspx* file name extension, contains text, HTML tags, HTML controls (such as buttons and text boxes), and Web server controls.

11.2 Creating ASP.NET Applications

- Using Visual Studio, you can create a Web site in the local File System, HTTP (Web server), or FTP site (remote location).
- A File System Web site runs directly under the ASP.NET development server supplied with Visual Studio. An HTTP Web site runs under a Windows operating system utility named Internet Information Services (IIS). An FTP Web site references an existing ASP.NET Web site located on a remote computer (network or Web).
- ASP.NET applications are also known as Web sites or Web applications.
- You can start a program in *Debug* mode by selecting *Start Debugging* from the *Debug* menu. You will be prompted to create a file named *Web.config*, containing an option that permits debugging.

11.3 Web Server Controls

- Web server controls make ASP.NET applications dynamic and interactive. The controls are far more powerful than standard HTML controls because each is defined by a class with a rich set of properties, methods, and events.
- The ID property of Web controls is the counterpart to the Name property of Windows controls. Web controls lose their runtime properties when the user moves away from the current page.
- The Label Web control is almost identical to the Label control on Windows forms. Use a Label only if its contents will change at runtime, or if you plan to change its Visible property.
- The TextBox Web control is similar in many ways to the TextBox control for Windows forms. The Text property holds text input by the user.
- The CheckBox control is almost identical to the CheckBox in Windows forms. Use the Text property to set the visible text and evaluate the Checked property at runtime.
- Events are fired in a different sequence in Web forms than they are in Windows

forms. In a Web form, the `Page_Load` event occurs when the page is first loaded into the user's browser, and again every time the page is posted back to the server.
- When a control's AutoPostBack property equals *True*, clicking on the control causes the form to be posted back to the server.

11.4 Designing Web Forms

- An HTML table is an essential tool for designing the layout of Web forms. Use it to align text, graphics, and controls in rows and columns.
- To insert a table when viewing a form in Design view, select *Insert Table* from the *Table* menu or double-click the HTML Table control from the Toolbox window.
- To adjust the width of a column, hover the mouse over the double bar along the column's right-hand border. To adjust the height of a row, hover the mouse over the row's lower border. After finding the border in this way, hold down the left mouse button and drag the border to change the column or row size.

11.5 Applications with Multiple Web Pages

- Most Web applications have multiple pages. You might collect information on one page, and display a summary on another page. Or, you might display supplementary information on a second page.
- There are two ways to add a new Web page to a project: select *Add New Item* from the *Web site* menu, or right-click in the *Solution Explorer* window and select *Add New Item.*
- To permit your application to navigate from one Web page to another, you can use a HyperLink control, code a call to `Response.Redirect`, or convert a block of static text to a hyperlink.

11.6 Using Databases

- Web applications use a different model for accessing databases than Windows Forms applications. Rather than using a dataset, Web applications often use a DataSource Web server control.
- The GridView control, similar to the Windows control named DataGridView, lets you sort on any column, select the column order, and format the data within columns.
- The DetailsView, like the GridView, connects to a DataSource Web server control.
- Tutorial 11-6 shows how to view, edit, insert, and delete individual rows in the *Members* table of the *Karate* database.

Key Terms

Active Server Pages (ASP)
ASP.NET
ASP.NET Development Server
ASP.NET Server controls
AutoPostBack property
button control
Cascading Style Sheet (CSS)
CheckBox control
CheckBoxList control
client-server model
code-behind file
DataSource control
DetailsView control
domain name
DropDownList control
File System Web site
FTP Site
GridView control

HTML control
HTML Designer
HTML table
HTML tag
HTTP Web site
HyperLink control
HyperText Markup Language (HTML)
ImageButton control
Internet Information Services (IIS)
Label control
LinkButton control
ListBox control
platform
postback
program logic
protocol
RadioButton controls
RadioButtonList control
`Response` object
`Response.Redirect` method
server
static text
TextBox control
Uniform Resource Locator (URL)
Web application
Web.config file
Web form
Web page
Web server
Web server control

Review Questions and Exercises

Fill-in-the-Blank

1. Conventional Web pages contain tags based on the _______________ Markup Language.
2. ASP stands for Active _______________ Pages.
3. URL stands for Uniform _______________ Locator.
4. Web server controls are also known as _______________ server controls.
5. A powerful Web server used by Web developers is named Internet _______________ Services (IIS).
6. The _______________ control displays a sequence of check boxes.
7. The _______________ control displays a hyperlink and has a property named NavigateURL.
8. When creating a new Web site, the choices of location type are _______________, HTTP, and FTP.
9. Debugging configuration information is stored in a file named _______________.
10. The _______________ property of a Label control can be used to make its border solid, dotted, or dashed.
11. The _______________ property of a TextBox control determines whether the box will permit multiple lines of input.
12. When a postback occurs on a Web page, the first event handler to execute is _______________.
13. The _______________ property of an ImageButton control holds the name of the image file.

Multiple Choice

1. Which of the following is the name of the grid-like control that displays database tables?
   a. DataGrid
   b. DataGridView
   c. GridView
   d. TableGrid
2. Which of the following is the standard file name extension for Web forms?
   a. *.aspx*
   b. *.asp*
   c. *.htm*
   d. *.html*
3. Which of the following is not a control category in the *Toolbox* window?
   a. Navigation
   b. Login
   c. WebParts
   d. FileServer
4. Which of the following Web site types requires running Internet Information Services on the local computer?
   a. File system
   b. Local IIS
   c. FTP
   d. Remote Web
5. Which of the following is not a Web server control described in this chapter?
   a. NavigateButton
   b. RadioButtonList
   c. CheckBoxList
   d. LinkButton
6. Which of the following cannot be assigned to the TextMode property of a TextBox control?
   a. MultiLine
   b. Hidden
   c. Password
   d. SingleLine
7. Which of the following properties is (are) found in both the RadioButtonList and ListBox controls?
   a. SelectedIndex
   b. ImageIndex
   c. RepeatDirection
   d. Items
   e. Two of the above are correct

True or False

Indicate whether the following statements are true or false.

1. T F: ASP.NET applications will only work if the user's Web browser is Internet Explorer Version 5.0 or above.

2. T F: The DropDownList control permits the user to type text directly into the first line.
3. T F: The AutoPostBack property does not affect the ListBox control.
4. T F: The ListBox control fires a `SelectedIndexChanged` event.
5. T F: To create Web sites on your local computer, you must be running Internet Information Services (IIS).
6. T F: The default value of SelectedIndex for a DropDownList control is zero.
7. T F: The HyperLink control does not generate a `Click` event.
8. T F: The ImageButton control generates a `Click` event, and does not look like a button.
9. T F: The `Response.NavigateTo` method lets your code transfer control to a different Web page.
10. T F: To fill a GridView control, you must create a data adapter and a dataset.
11. T F: The DetailsView control does not permit deleting a row from a database table.
12. T F: When adding text to a Web form, you can type static text directly onto the form.

Short Answer

1. What are the three basic parts of an ASP.NET application?
2. Which control has a NavigateURL property?
3. How are Web server controls different from HTML controls?
4. What special requirement do remote Web servers have, as opposed to local Web servers?
5. What are the two ways to view a Web form inside Visual Studio?
6. What command lets you select which Web browser will run your Web application?
7. How do you open an existing Web application?
8. What happens the first time you try to run a Web application in Debug mode?
9. How is the DropDownList control different from the ComboBox control?
10. How are the HyperLink and LinkButton controls different?
11. Which Web control property corresponds to the Name property in Windows controls?
12. When the user selects an item from a ListBox and then posts the page back to the server (called a postback), which method executes first: `Page_Load` or `SelectedIndexChanged`?
13. Which property in a ListBox governs whether or not the user's selection is posted back to the server immediately?
14. Which property of a HyperLink control affects whether the target page will display in a new browser window?

What Do You Think?

1. What advantages does a File System Web site have over an HTTP Web site?
2. Why is the HTML Table control useful when designing Web forms?
3. Why should you to test your application with different Web browsers?
4. Why should debugging be disabled when distributing your Web site to the general public?
5. What disadvantage is there to setting AutoPostBack to *True* for a DropDownList control?

Algorithm Workbench

1. Write a code statement that transfers control to a Web page named *PageTwo.aspx*.
2. Write a statement that checks if the first button in a RadioButtonList control named `radButtons` has been selected by the user.
3. Write a statement that removes all items from a ListBox named `lstSummary`.
4. Write a loop that selects all check boxes in a CheckBoxList control named `chkOptions`.

Programming Challenges

VideoNote

The Stadium Seating Problem

1. **Stadium Seating**

   Create an ASP.NET version of the solution program for Programming Challenge 2 in Chapter 3, named *Stadium Seating*.

2. **Room Charge Calculator**

   Implement the *Room Charge Calculator* application from Section 3.7 as a Web application. In place of Group boxes, use Panel Web controls.

3. **Bank Charges**

   Create an ASP.NET version of the solution program for Programming Challenge 6 in Chapter 4, named *Bank Charges*.

4. **Long-Distance Calls**

   Create an ASP.NET version of the solution program for Programming Challenge 10 in Chapter 4, named Long-Distance Calls. Create a hyperlink on the startup form that displays a second browser window containing details about the calling rates.

5. **Karate Payments Grid**

   Write an ASP.NET application that displays the first name, last name, date, and payment amounts of payments made by members in the *Karate.mdf* database. Permit the user to display payments, but not to perform any modifications to the data. Sort the rows by last name. Format the date in short date format, centered. (Don't forget to set the date field's HTMLEncode property to *False*.) For each column except the payment date, left justify the heading by setting the HeaderStyle.HorizontalAlign property to *Left*. Put a blue border around the grid, 1 pixel wide. Use the grid's HeaderStyle property to give the headings white text on a dark blue background. A sample is shown in Figure 11-62.

Figure 11-62 Grid showing *Karate* members names, dates, and payments

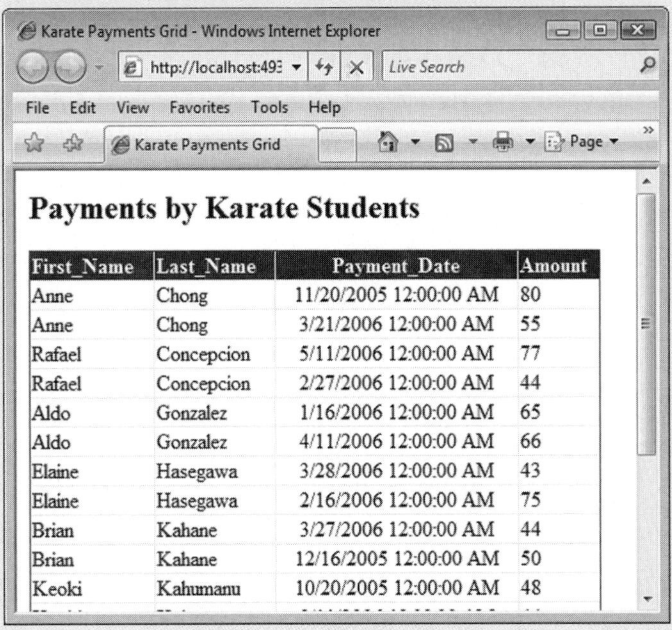

6. **Karate Schedule Details**

   The *Schedule* table in the *Karate.mdf* database contains the following columns: *ID*, *Day*, *Time*, and *Instructor_Id*. The *Day* value is an integer between 0 and 6, where 0 indicates Monday and 6 indicates Sunday. Display the table in a DetailsView control, and permit the user to add, remove, and update records.

CHAPTER 12

Classes, Collections, and Scrollable Controls

TOPICS

This chapter introduces abstract data types and shows you how to create them with classes. The process of analyzing a problem and determining its classes is discussed, and techniques for creating objects, properties, and methods are introduced. Collections, which are structures for holding groups of objects, are also covered. The Object Browser, which allows you to see information about the classes, properties, methods, and events available to your project, is discussed. The chapter shows you how to create scrollable controls, and concludes by introducing inheritance, a way for new classes to be created from existing ones.

12.1 Classes and Objects

CONCEPT: Classes are program structures that define abstract data types and are used to create objects.

One of the most exciting developments in computer software over the last 30 years has been object-oriented programming. **Object-oriented programming** (OOP) is a way of designing and coding applications such that interchangeable software components can be used to build larger programs. Object-oriented programming languages, such as ALGOL, SmallTalk, and C++ first appeared in the early 1980s. The legacy from these languages has been the gradual development of object-like visual tools for building programs. In Visual Basic, for example, forms, buttons, check boxes, list boxes, and other controls are ideal examples of objects. Object-oriented designs help us produce programs that are well suited to ongoing development and expansion.

Abstract Data Types

An **abstract data type** (**ADT**) is a data type created by a programmer. ADTs are very important in computer science and especially significant in object-oriented programming. An **abstraction** is a general model of something—a definition that includes only the general characteristics of an object. For example, the term *dog* is an abstraction. It defines a general type of animal. The term captures the essence of what all dogs are without specifying the detailed characteristics of any particular breed of dog or any individual animal. According to *Webster's New Collegiate Dictionary*, a dog is "a highly variable carnivorous domesticated mammal (*Canis familiaris*) probably descended from the common wolf."

In real life, however, there is no such thing as a mere dog. There are specific dogs, each sharing common characteristics such as paws, fur, whiskers, and a carnivorous diet. For example, Travis owns a rottweiler named Bailey, and Shirley owns a poodle named Snuggles. In this analogy, the abstraction (dog), is like a data type and the specific dogs (Bailey and Snuggles) are instances of the type.

Classes

A **class** is a program structure that defines an abstract data type. You create a class, and then create instances of the class. All class instances share common characteristics. For example, Visual Basic controls and forms are classes. In the Visual Studio Toolbox, each icon represents a class. When you select the *Button* tool from the toolbox and place it on a form, as shown in Figure 12-1, you create an instance of the Button class. An instance is also called an **object**.

Figure 12-1 Instances of the Button class

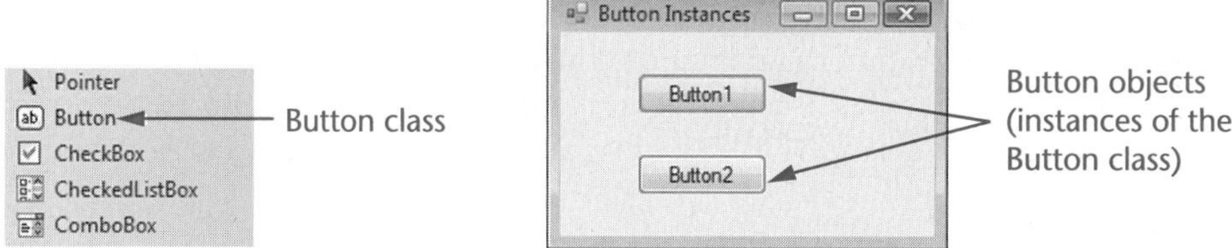

Class Properties, Methods, and Event Procedures

The way a program communicates with each object is determined by the properties and methods defined in the object's class. The Button class, for example, has properties such as Location, Text, and Name. Each Button object contains its own unique set of property values. In the example shown in Figure 12-1, the two buttons have different values in their Location and Text properties.

Methods are shared by all instances of a class. For example, the Button class has a method named `Focus`, which is the same for all Button objects.

Event handlers are also methods, but they are specific to individual objects. For example, a form with several buttons will almost always have different code written in each button's `Click` event procedure.

Object-Oriented Design

Object-oriented programming is not just a matter of randomly dropping classes into a program. The challenge is to design classes in such a way that the resulting objects will effectively cooperate and communicate. The primary goal of object-oriented design is to address the needs of the application or problem being solved. A secondary goal is to design classes that can outlive the current application and possibly be useful in future programs.

The first step, after creating the program specifications, is to analyze the application requirements. **Object-oriented analysis**, as it is called, often starts with a detailed specification of the problem to be solved. A term often applied to this process is **finding the classes.** A famous sculptor once said that inside every block of marble is a work of art waiting to be discovered. So, too, in every problem and every application there are classes waiting to be found. It is the designer's job to discover them.

Finding the Classes

Classes are the fundamental building blocks of object-oriented applications. When designing object-oriented programs, first we select classes that reflect physical entities in the application domain. For example, the user of a record-keeping program for a college might describe some of the application's requirements as follows:

> We need to keep a *list of students* that lets us track the courses they have completed. Each student has a *transcript* that contains all information about his or her completed courses. At the end of each semester, we will calculate the grade point average of each *student.* At times, users will search for a particular *course* taken by a student.

Notice the italicized nouns and noun phrases in this description: list of students, transcript, student, and course. These would ordinarily become classes in the program's design.

Looking for Control Structures

Classes can also be discovered in the description of processing done by an application or in the description of control structures. For example, if the application involved scheduling college classes for students, another description from the program specifications might be:

> We also want to schedule classes for students, using the college's master schedule to determine the times and room numbers for each student's class. When the optimal arrangement of classes for each student has been determined, each student's class schedule will be printed and distributed.

In this description, we anticipate a need for a controlling agent that could be implemented as a class. We might call it `Scheduler`, a class that matches each student's schedule with the college master schedule.

Describing the Classes

The next step, after finding the classes in an application, is to describe the classes in terms of attributes and operations. **Attributes** are characteristics of each object that will be implemented as properties. Attributes describe the properties that all objects of the same class have in common. Classes also have **operations,** which are actions the class objects may perform or messages to which they can respond. Operations are implemented as class methods. Table 12-1 describes some of the important attributes and operations of the record-keeping application that we described earlier.

Table 12-1 Sample attributes and operations

Class	Attributes (properties)	Operations (methods)
`Student`	LastName, FirstName, IdNumber	`Display, Input`
`StudentList`	AllStudents, Count	`Add, Remove, FindStudent`
`Course`	Semester, Name, Grade, Credits	`Display, Input`
`Transcript`	CourseList, Count	`Display, Search, CalcGradeAvg`

The complete set of attributes and operations is often incomplete during the early stages of design because it is difficult to anticipate all the application requirements. As a design develops, the need often arises for additional properties and methods that improve communication between objects. Rather than a weakness, however, this ability to accommodate ongoing modifications is one of the strengths of the object-oriented design process.

Interface and Implementation

The **class interface** is the portion of the class that is visible to the application programmer. The program written to use a class is sometimes called the **client program**, in reference to the client-server relationship between a class and the programs that use it. The class interface provides a way for clients to communicate (send messages) to class objects. In Visual Basic, a class interface is created by declaring public properties, methods, and events.

The **class implementation** is the portion of a class that is hidden from client programs; it is created from private member variables, private properties, and private methods. The hiding of data and procedures inside a class is achieved through a process called **encapsulation**. In this, it might be helpful to visualize the class as a *capsule* around its data and procedures.

Checkpoint

12.1 Give some examples of objects in Visual Basic.

12.2 A text box tool appears in the toolbox and a Textbox control has been placed on a form. Which represents the `TextBox` class and which is an instance of the `TextBox` class?

12.3 When analyzing a problem, how do we select the classes?

12.4 What is an attribute of a class? How are attributes implemented?

12.5 What is an operation of a class? How are operations implemented?

12.6 What is a class interface?

12.7 What is the class implementation?

12.2 Creating a Class

CONCEPT: To create a class in Visual Basic, you create a class declaration. The class declaration specifies the member variables, properties, methods, and events that belong to the class.

VideoNote

Creating a Class

You create a class in Visual Basic by creating a **class declaration**. We will use the following general format when writing class declarations:

```
Public Class ClassName
  MemberDeclarations
End Class
```

`ClassName` is the name of the class. `MemberDeclarations` is one or more declarations of members of the class. Follow these steps to add a class declaration to a Windows application project:

1. Click the *Add New Item* button ( )on the toolbar, or click *Project* on the menu bar, then click *Add Class*. The *Add New Item* dialog box, shown in Figure 12-2, should appear. Make sure that *Class* is selected in the *Templates* pane. Notice that in the figure, the name *Class1.vb* appears in the *Name* text box. In this example, *Class1.vb* is the default name for the file that the class declaration will be stored in, and *Class1* is the default name for the class.

NOTE: The default name may be different, depending on the number of classes already in the project.

Figure 12-2 *Add New Item* dialog box

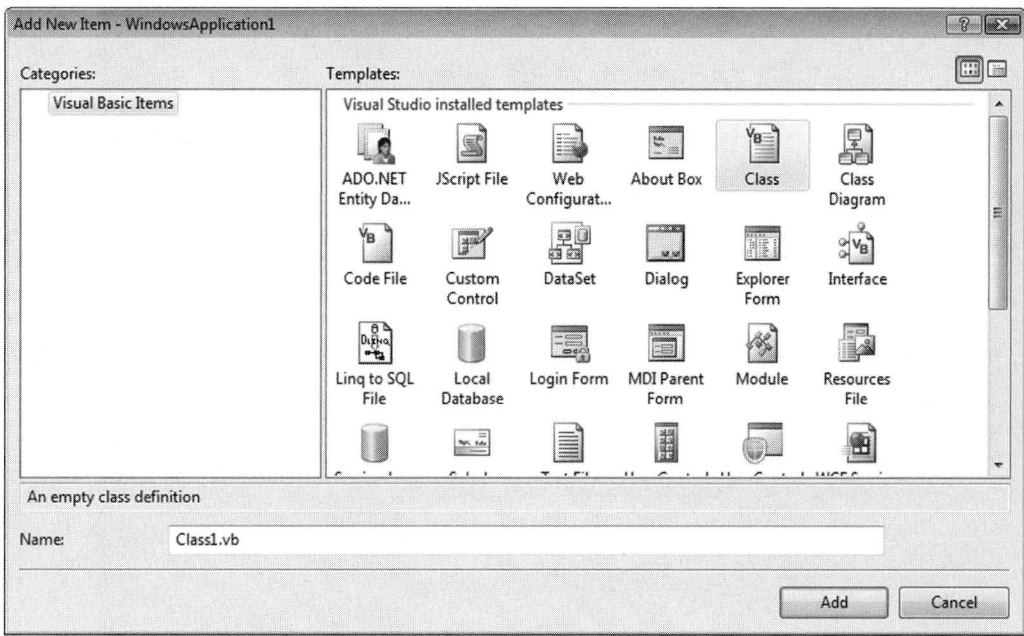

2. Change the default name displayed in the *Name* text box to the name you wish to give the new class file. For example, if you wish to name the new class `Student`, enter *Student.vb* in the *Name* text box.
3. Click the *Add* button.

   A new, empty class declaration will be added to your project. The empty class declaration will be displayed in the *Code* window and an entry for the new class file will appear in the *Solution Explorer* window. The *Solution Explorer* window in Figure 12-3 shows two forms and one class: `frmError`, `frmMain`, and `Student`.

Figure 12-3 *Solution Explorer* window showing two forms and one class

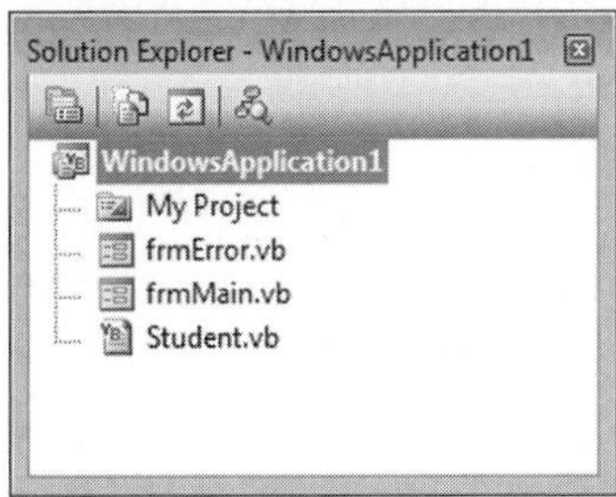

Member Variables

A **member variable** is a variable that is declared inside a class declaration. The variable is a member of the class. A member variable declaration has the following general format:

```
AccessSpecifer VariableName As DataType
```

`AccessSpecifier` determines the accessibility of the variable. Variables declared with the `Public` access specifier may be accessed by statements outside the class, and even outside the same assembly. Roughly speaking, an assembly is a container that holds a collection of classes. Each of the Visual Basic projects you have created so far have been used to create assemblies. Variables declared with the `Private` access specifier may be accessed only by statements inside the class declaration. `VariableName` is the name of the variable and `DataType` is the variable's data type. For example, the following code declares a class named `Student`. The class has three member variables: `strLastName`, `strFirstName`, and `strId`.

```
Public Class Student
  Private strLastName As String           ' Holds last name
  Private strFirstName As String          ' Holds first name
  Private strId As String                 ' Holds ID number
End Class
```

As with structures, a class declaration does not create an instance of the class. It only establishes a blueprint for the class's organization. To actually work with the class, you must create **class objects**, which are instances of the class.

Another access type is called **Friend access**. A class member with Friend access can be used only by other classes inside the same assembly. One Visual Basic program can use classes from another assembly, but it cannot call methods having Friend access specifiers. It can call methods having Public access specifiers.

Creating an Instance of a Class

Creating an instance of a class is a two-step process: You declare an object variable, and then you create an instance of the class in memory and assign its address to the object variable. Although there are only two steps in the process, there are two different techniques for performing these steps. The first method performs both steps in one line of code, as shown in the following example:

```
Dim freshman As New Student
```

This statement creates an object variable named `freshman`. The `New` keyword causes the class instance to be created in memory. The object's address is assigned to `freshman`.

The second method requires two lines of code, as shown in the following example:

```
Dim freshman As Student
freshman = New Student
```

The `Dim` statement in the first line creates an object variable named `freshman`. By default, the object variable is initialized to the value `Nothing`. The second line uses the `New` keyword to create an instance of the `Student` class and assigns its memory address to the `freshman` variable.

When you create instances of a class, each instance has its own copy of the class's member variables.

Accessing Members

Once you have created a class object, you can work with its `Public` members in code. You access the `Public` members of a class object with the dot (`.`) operator. Suppose the `Student` class was declared as follows:

```
Public Class Student
    Public strLastName As String
    Public strFirstName As String
    Public strId As String
End Class
```

In a Windows form, we might create a button `Click` handler procedure that declares `freshman` as a `Student` object. The following statements store values in the object's public member variables:

```
Private Sub btnOk_Click(ByVal sender As System.Object, _
  ByVal e As System.EventArgs) Handles btnOk.Click

  Dim freshman As New Student
  freshman.strFirstName = "Joy"
  freshman.strLastName = "Robinson"
  freshman.strId = "23G794"
End Sub
```

One might think that `strFirstName`, `strLastName`, and `strId` are properties of the `Student` class. But implementing properties as public member variables directly is not a good idea. Doing so allows users of the class to modify the variables directly and prevents the author of the class from including range checking or validating of values assigned to variables. Instead, a much better approach is to implement properties as property procedures.

Property Procedures

A **property procedure** is a function that defines a class property. The general format of a property procedure is as follows:

```
Public Property PropertyName() As DataType
  Get
    Statements
  End Get
  Set(ParameterDeclaration)
    Statements
  End Set
End Property
```

PropertyName is the name of the property procedure, and hence the name of the property that the procedure implements. *DataType* the type of data (such as Integer, String, or Decimal) that can be assigned to the property. Notice that the procedure has two sections: a `Get` section and a `Set` section. The **`Get` section** holds the code that is executed when the property value is retrieved, and the **`Set` section** holds the code that is executed when a value is stored in the property.

TIP: Properties are almost always declared with the Public access specifier so they can be accessed from outside their enclosing class module.

TIP: After you type the first line of a property procedure, Visual Basic will build a code template for the rest of the procedure.

For example, let's add a property to the `Student` class that holds the student's test score average. Because the average test score is a number in the range of 0.0 through 100.0, we want to validate any value stored in the TestAverage property. Therefore, we will include code that checks the size of any value assigned to the property. The modified code for the class follows:

```
Public Class Student
  ' Member variables
  Private strLastName As String          ' Holds last name
  Private strFirstName As String         ' Holds first name
  Private strId As String                ' Holds ID number
  Private sngTestAverage As Single       ' Holds test average

  Public Property TestAverage() As Single
    Get
      Return sngTestAverage
    End Get
    Set(ByVal value As Single)
      If value >= 0.0 And value <= 100.0 Then
        sngTestAverage = value
      Else
        MessageBox.Show("Invalid test average.", "Error")
      End If
    End Set
  End Property
End Class
```

Notice that a private member variable named `sngTestAverage` was added to the class to hold the actual value stored in the TestAverage property. We have declared the variable private to prevent code outside the class from storing values directly in it. To store a test average in an object, the property procedure must be used. This allows us to perform validation on the value before it is stored in an object.

Let's look at the `Get` and `Set` sections of the property procedure. The `Get` section does one thing: It only returns the value stored in the `sngTestAverage` member variable. The code for the `Get` section follows:

```
Get
  Return sngTestAverage
End Get
```

Here is the code for the `Set` section:

```
Set(ByVal value As Single)
  If value >= 0.0 And value <= 100.0 Then
    sngTestAverage = value
```

```
    Else
      MessageBox.Show("Invalid test average.", "Error")
    End If
  End Set
```

The `Set` section has a declaration for a parameter named `value`. When a number is stored in the TestAverage property, the `Set` section is executed and the number being stored in the property is passed into the `value` parameter. The procedure determines whether `value` is within the range of 0.0 through 100.0. If it is, then it is stored in the `sngTestAverage` member variable. If it is not, an error message is displayed.

The following code shows an example of the TestAverage property in use:

```
Dim freshman As Student
freshman = New Student()
freshman.TestAverage = 82.3
```

The last statement stores the value 82.3 in the TestAverage property. Because a value is being stored in the property, this statement causes the `Set` section of the TestAverage property procedure to execute. The number 82.3 is passed into the `value` parameter. Because 82.3 is within the range of 0.0 through 100.0, it is stored in the object's `sngTestAvg` member variable. The following statement would cause an error message to be displayed because the value (107.0) is too large:

```
freshman.TestAverage = 107.0
```

Any statement that retrieves the value in the TestAverage property causes the property procedure's `Get` section to execute. For example, the following code assigns the value in the TestAverage property to the variable `sngAverage`:

```
sngAverage = freshman.TestAverage
```

This statement causes the property's `Get` section to execute, which returns the value stored in the `sngTestAverage` member variable. The following code displays the value in the TestAverage property in a message box:

```
MessageBox.Show(freshman.TestAverage.ToString())
```

Creating Property Procedures for the `Student` Class

Now, let's modify the `Student` class by implementing the following property procedures: `FirstName`, `LastName`, `IdNumber`, and `TestAverage`. The code follows:

```
Public Class Student
  ' Member variables
  Private strLastName As String        ' Holds last name
  Private strFirstName As String       ' Holds first name
  Private strId As String              ' Holds ID number
  Private sngTestAverage As Single     ' Holds test average

  ' LastName property procedure
  Public Property LastName() As String
    Get
      Return strLastName
    End Get
    Set(ByVal value As String)
      strLastName = value
    End Set
  End Property
```

```
    ' FirstName property procedure
    Public Property FirstName() As String
      Get
        Return strFirstName
      End Get
      Set(ByVal value As String)
        strFirstName = value
      End Set
    End Property

    ' IdNumber property procedure
    Public Property IdNumber() As String
      Get
        Return strId
      End Get
      Set(ByVal value As String)
        strId = value
      End Set
    End Property

    ' TestAverage property procedure
    Public Property TestAverage() As Single
      Get
        Return sngTestAverage
      End Get
      Set(ByVal value As Single)
        If value >= 0.0 And value <= 100.0 Then
          sngTestAverage = value
        Else
          MessageBox.Show("Invalid test average.", "Error")
        End If
      End Set
    End Property
  End Class
```

Read-Only Properties

Sometimes it is useful to make a property read-only. Client programs can query a **read-only property** to get its value, but cannot modify it. The general format of a read-only property procedure is as follows:

```
Public ReadOnly Property PropertyName() As DataType
  Get
    Statements
  End Get
End Property
```

The first line of a read-only property procedure contains the `ReadOnly` keyword. Notice that the procedure has no `Set` section. It is only capable of returning a value. For example, the following code demonstrates a read-only TestGrade property that we might add to our `Student` class:

```
' TestGrade property procedure
Public ReadOnly Property TestGrade() As Char
  Get
    If sngTestAverage >= 90
      return "A"c
    ElseIf sngTestAverage >= 80
      return "B"c
```

```
        ElseIf sngTestAverage >= 70
            return "C"c
        ElseIf sngTestAverage >= 60
            return "D"c
        Else
            return "F"c
        End If
    End Get
End Property
```

(You may recall from Chapter 3 that the c suffix identifies single-character constants.) This property returns one of the following character values, depending on the contents of the sngTestAverage member variable: "A", "B", "C", "D", or "F".

A compiler error occurs if a client program attempts to store a value in a read-only property. For example, the following statement would result in an error:

```
freshman.TestGrade = "A"c               ' Error
```

Removing Objects and Garbage Collection

It is a good practice to remove objects that are no longer needed, allowing the application to free memory for other purposes. To remove an object, set all the object variables that reference it to Nothing. For example, the following statement sets the object variable freshman to Nothing:

```
freshman = Nothing
```

After this statement executes, the freshman variable will no longer reference an object. If the object that it previously referenced is no longer referenced by any other variables, it will be removed from memory by the .NET garbage collector. The **garbage collector** is a utility program that removes objects from memory when they are no longer needed.

NOTE: The garbage collector might not remove an object from memory immediately when the last reference to it has been removed. The system uses an algorithm to determine when it should periodically remove unused objects. As the amount of available memory decreases, the garbage collector removes unreferenced objects more often.

Going Out of Scope

Like all variables, an object variable declared inside a procedure is local to that procedure. If an object is referenced only by a procedure's local object variable, it becomes eligible to be removed from memory by the garbage collector after the procedure ends. This is called **going out of scope**. For example, look at the following procedure:

```
Sub CreateStudent()

    Dim sophomore As Student
    sophomore = New Student()
    sophomore.FirstName = "Travis"
    sophomore.LastName = "Barnes"
    sophomore.IdNumber = "17H495"
    sophomore.TestAverage = 94.7

End Sub
```

This procedure declares an object variable named `sophomore`. An instance of the `Student` class is created and referenced by the `sophomore` variable. When this procedure ends, the object referenced by `sophomore` is no longer accessible.

An object is not removed from memory if there are still references to it. For example, assume an application has a global module-level variable named `g_studentVar`. Look at the following code:

```
Sub CreateStudent()

   Dim sophomore As Student
   sophomore = New Student()
   sophomore.FirstName = "Travis"
   sophomore.LastName = "Barnes"
   sophomore.IdNumber = "17H495"
   sophomore.TestAverage = 94.7
   g_studentVar = sophomore

End Sub
```

The last statement in the procedure assigns `g_studentVar` the object referenced by `sophomore`. This means that both `g_studentVar` and `sophomore` reference the same object. When this procedure ends, the object referenced by `sophomore` will not be removed from memory because it is still referenced by the module-level variable `g_studentVar`.

Comparing Object Variables with the `Is` and `IsNot` Operators

Multiple object variables can reference the same object in memory. For example, the following code declares two object variables: `collegeStudent` and `transferStudent`. Both object variables are made to reference the same instance of the `Student` class.

```
Dim collegeStudent As Student
Dim transferStudent As Student
collegeStudent = New Student
transferStudent = collegeStudent
```

After this code executes, both `collegeStudent` and `transferStudent` reference the same object. You cannot use the = operator in an `If` statement to determine whether two object variables reference the same object. Instead, use the **`Is` operator**. For example, the following statement properly determines if `collegeStudent` and `transferStudent` reference the same object:

```
If collegeStudent Is transferStudent Then
   ' Perform some action
End If
```

You can use the **`IsNot` operator** to determine whether two variables do not reference the same object. The following is an example:

```
If collegeStudent IsNot transferStudent Then
   ' Perform some action
End If
```

If you wish to compare an object variable to the special value `Nothing`, use either the `Is` or `IsNot` operator, as shown in the following code:

```
If collegeStudent Is Nothing Then
   ' Perform some action
End If
```

```
If transferStudent IsNot Nothing Then
  ' Perform some action
End If
```

Creating an Array of Objects

You can create an array of object variables, and then create an object for each element of the array to reference. The following code declares `mathStudents` as an array of 10 `Student` objects. Then it uses a loop to assign a `Student` to each element of the array.

```
Dim mathStudents(9) As Student
Dim intCount As Integer
For intCount = 0 To 9
  mathStudents(intCount) = New Student
Next intCount
```

You can use another loop to release the memory used by the array, as shown in the following statements:

```
Dim intCount As Integer

For intCount = 0 To 9
  mathStudents(intCount) = Nothing
Next intCount
```

Writing Sub Procedures and Functions That Work with Objects

Sub procedures and functions can accept object variables as arguments. For example, the following procedure accepts an object variable that references an instance of the `Student` class as its argument and displays the student's grade.

```
Sub DisplayStudentGrade(ByVal s As Student)

  ' Displays a student's grade.
  MessageBox.Show("The grade for " & s.FirstName & _
    " " & s.LastName & " is " & s.TestGrade.ToString())

End Sub
```

The parameter named `s` references a `Student` object. To call the procedure, pass an object variable that references a `Student` object, as shown in the following code:

```
DisplayStudentGrade(freshman)
```

When this statement executes, the `DisplayStudentGrade` procedure is called, and the `freshman` object variable is passed as an argument. Inside the procedure, the variable `s` will reference the same object that `freshman` references.

Passing Objects by Value and by Reference

Object variable parameters may be declared either as `ByVal` or `ByRef`. Be aware, however, that the `ByVal` keyword does not restrict a procedure from accessing and modifying the object the argument references. For example, look at the following `ClearStudent` procedure:

```
Sub ClearStudent(ByVal s As Student)

  s.FirstName = String.Empty
  s.LastName = String.Empty
  s.IdNumber = String.Empty
  s.TestAverage = 0.0

End Sub
```

Let's assume that an object variable referencing a `Student` object is passed to `ClearStudent`. The procedure clears the FirstName, LastName, IdNumber, and TestAverage properties of the object referenced by the argument. For example, look at the following code, which initializes various properties of a `Student` object and then passes the object to the `ClearStudent` procedure:

```
freshman.FirstName = "Joy"
freshman.LastName = "Robinson"
freshman.IdNumber = "23G794"
freshman.TestAverage = 82.3

' Clear the properties of the object.
ClearStudent(freshman)
```

After the `ClearStudent` procedure executes, the properties of the object referenced by the `freshman` variable are cleared.

The `ByVal` keyword guarantees that if you assign a new value to a procedure parameter, the effect will only be temporary. When the procedure ends, the original argument passed to the procedure will be unchanged. For example, the following procedure accepts an object variable as its argument, and then assigns the parameter to another object.

```
Sub ResetStudent(ByVal s As Student)
  ' Try to assign the argument to a new object.

  Dim newStudent As Student
  newStudent = New Student
  newStudent.FirstName = "Bill"
  newStudent.LastName = "Owens"
  newStudent.IdNumber = "56K789"
  newStudent.TestAverage = 84.6

  s = newStudent
End Sub
```

Suppose we call the procedure, as shown in the following code:

```
freshman.FirstName = "Joy"
freshman.LastName = "Robinson"
freshman.IdNumber = "23G794"
freshman.TestAverage = 82.3
ResetStudent(freshman)
```

After the `ResetStudent` procedure executes, the object referenced by the `freshman` variable still contains the data for Joy Robinson. If the parameter named `s` were declared `ByRef`, on the other hand, the variable named `freshman` would contain Bill Owens' information after the procedure call.

Returning an Object from a Function

It is also possible to return an object from a function. For example, the following function prompts the user to enter the data for a `Student` object. The object is then returned to the caller.

```
Function GetStudent() As Student
  ' Get student data and return it as an object.

  Dim s As New Student
  s.FirstName = InputBox("Enter the student's first name.")
  s.LastName = InputBox("Enter the student's last name.")
  s.IdNumber = InputBox("Enter the student's ID number.")
  s.TestAverage = CSng(InputBox("Enter the student's test average."))
```

```
    Return s
End Function
```

The following code assigns the function's return value to the `freshman` object variable:

```
Dim freshman As Student = GetStudent()
```

Methods

A **method** is a Sub procedure or function that is a member of a class. The method performs some operation on the data stored in the class. For example, suppose we wish to add a `Clear` method to the `Student` class, as shown in the following code. To simplify the code listing, the property procedures have been omitted.

```
Public Class Student

  ' Member variables
  Private strLastName As String         ' Holds last name
  Private strFirstName As String        ' Holds first name
  Private strId As String               ' Holds ID number
  Private sngTestAverage As Single      ' Holds test average

  (...Property procedures omitted...)

  ' Clear method
  Public Sub Clear()
    strFirstName = String.Empty
    strLastName = String.Empty
    strId = String.Empty
    sngTestAverage = 0.0
  End Sub

End Class
```

The `Clear` method clears the private member variables that hold the student's first name, last name, ID number, and test average. The following statement calls the method using the object referenced by `freshman`:

```
freshman.Clear()
```

Constructors

A **constructor** is a method that is automatically called when an instance of the class is created. It is helpful to think of constructors as initialization routines. They are useful for initializing member variables or performing other startup operations. To create a constructor, create a method named `New` inside the class. (Alternatively, you can select *New* from the method name drop-down list and a code template is created for you.) Each time an instance of the class is created, the `New` procedure is executed.

For example, let's add a constructor to the `Student` class that initializes the private member variables. The code follows:

```
Public Class Student

  ' Member variables
  Private strLastName As String         ' Holds last name
  Private strFirstName As String        ' Holds first name
  Private strId As String               ' Holds ID number
  Private sngTestAverage As Single      ' Holds test average
```

```
    ' Constructor
    Public Sub New()
      strFirstName = "(unknown)"
      strLastName = "(unknown)"
      strId = "(unknown)"
      sngTestAvg = 0.0
    End Sub

    (The rest of this class is omitted.)

  End Class
```

The following statement creates a `Student` object:

```
Dim freshman As New Student
```

When this statement executes, an instance of the `Student` class is created and its constructor is executed. The result is that `freshman.LastName`, `freshman.FirstName`, and `freshman.IdNumber` will hold the string `"(unknown)"` and `freshman.TestAverage` will hold `0.0`.

Finalizers

A **finalizer** is a class method named `Finalize`, which is automatically called just before an instance of the class is removed from memory. If you wish to execute code immediately before an object is removed, create a `Finalize` method in your class. Because the syntax of `Finalize` is unfamilar, it's easier to let Visual Basic create a code template. When you select `Finalize` in the method name drop-down list, the following code template is created:

```
Protected Overrides Sub Finalize()
  MyBase.Finalize()
End Sub
```

Any code you wish to execute should be placed after the `MyBase.Finalize()` statement. The garbage collector uses an algorithm to determine when it should periodically release all unreferenced objects from memory. Therefore, you cannot predict exactly when the `Finalize` method will be executed.

Displaying Messages in the *Output* Window

Before beginning our class-building tutorial, let's discuss a valuable debugging tool: the *Output* **window**. The *Output* window, shown in Figure 12-4, normally appears at the bottom of the Visual Basic environment while an application is running. If you do not see the *Output* window, you can display it by clicking the *View* menu, then *Other Windows*, then *Output*. Alternatively you can press Ctrl+Alt+O. This window displays various messages while an application is being compiled.

Figure 12-4 *Output* window

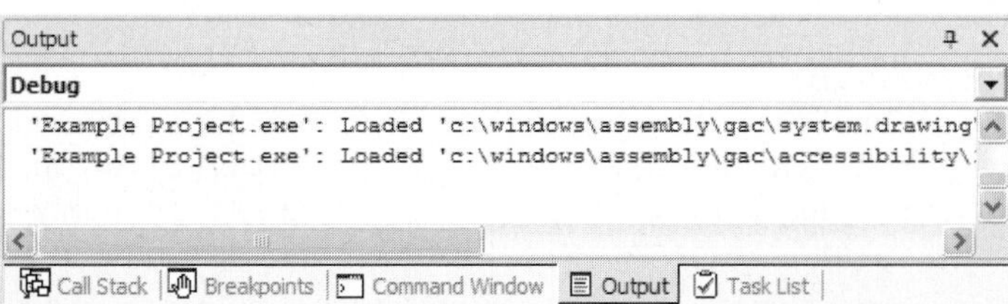

You can display your own messages in the *Output* window with the `Debug.WriteLine` method. The method has the following general format:

```
Debug.WriteLine(Output)
```

`Output` is an expression whose value is to be displayed in the *Output* window. To enable debug messages, insert the following line in your startup form's `Load` event handler:

```
Debug.Listeners.Add(New ConsoleTraceListener())
```

We will use this method in Tutorial 12-1 to display status messages from a class constructor and finalizer. The constructor will be modified as follows:

```
' Constructor
Public Sub New()

  Debug.WriteLine("Student object being created.")
  strFirstName = String.Empty
  strLastName = String.Empty
  strId = String.Empty
  sngTestAverage = 0.0

End Sub
```

The `Debug.WriteLine` method displays a message in the *Output* window each time a `Student` object is created. We can add a similar statement to the `Finalize` method, as follows:

```
Protected Overrides Sub Finalize()

  MyBase.Finalize()
  Debug.WriteLine("Student object destroyed.")
End Sub
```

Each time a `Student` object is removed from memory, the `Debug.Writeline` method will display a message in the *Output* window.

In Tutorial 12-1, you create the `Student` class we have been using as an example, and use it in an application that saves student data to a file.

Tutorial 12-1:
Creating the *Student Data* application

Step 1: Create a new Windows project named *Student Data*.

Step 2: Set up the application's form as shown in Figure 12-5.

Step 3: Perform the following steps to add a new class to the project:

- Click *Project* on the menu bar, and then click *Add Class*.
- In the *Add New Item* dialog box, make sure *Class* is selected in the *Templates* pane. In the *Name* text box, type **`Student.vb`**.
- Click the *Add* button.

A new class file is created and opened in the *Code* window. The contents of the class appear as follows:

```
Public Class Student

End Class
```

Figure 12-5 *Student Data* form

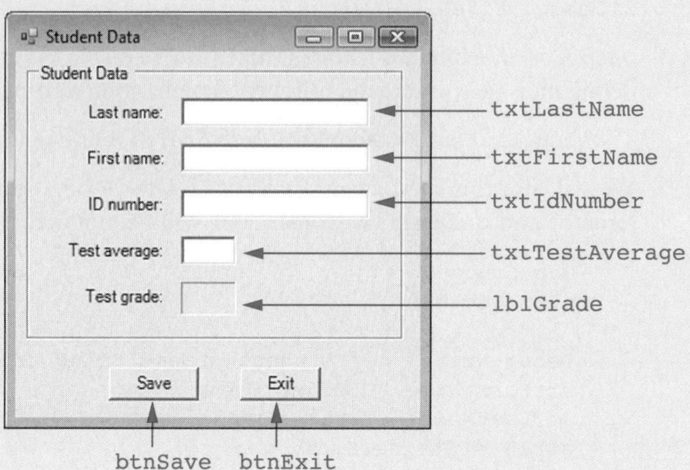

Step 4: Complete the class by entering the following code shown in bold:

```
Public Class Student

  ' Member variables
  Private strLastName As String
  Private strFirstName As String
  Private strId As String
  Private sngTestAverage As Single

  ' Constructor
  Public Sub New()

    Debug.WriteLine("Student object created.")
    strFirstName = String.Empty
    strLastName = String.Empty
    strId = String.Empty
    sngTestAverage = 0.0

  End Sub

  ' LastName property procedure
  Public Property LastName() As String
    Get
      Return strLastName
    End Get
    Set(ByVal value As String)
      strLastName = value
    End Set
  End Property

  ' FirstName property procedure
  Public Property FirstName() As String
    Get
      Return strFirstName
    End Get
    Set(ByVal value As String)
      strFirstName = value
    End Set
  End Property
```

```
    ' IdNumber property procedure
    Public Property IdNumber() As String
      Get
        Return strId
      End Get
      Set(ByVal value As String)
        strId = value
      End Set
    End Property

    ' TestAverage property procedure
    Public Property TestAverage() As Single
      Get
        Return sngTestAverage
      End Get
      Set(ByVal value As Single)
        If value >= 0.0 And value <= 100.0 Then
          sngTestAverage = value
        Else
          Throw New ApplicationException( _
              "Test average must be 0.0 to 100.0")
        End If
      End Set
    End Property

    ' TestGrade property procedure
    Public ReadOnly Property TestGrade() As Char
      Get
        Dim chrGrade As Char
        If sngTestAverage >= 90.0 Then
          chrGrade = "A"c
        ElseIf sngTestAverage >= 80.0 Then
          chrGrade = "B"c
        ElseIf sngTestAverage >= 70.0 Then
          chrGrade = "C"c
        ElseIf sngTestAverage >= 60.0 Then
          chrGrade = "D"c
        Else
          chrGrade = "F"c
        End If
        Return chrGrade
      End Get
    End Property

    End Class
```

When assigning values to the `chrGrade` variable, *Option Strict* requires character literals to be followed by the `c` type identifier. An example is `"A"c`.

Step 5: Now you will add a finalizer that displays a message in the *Output* window. In the method name drop-down list, select `Finalize`. A code template should appear. Complete the template by entering the statement shown in bold in the following code:

```
Protected Overrides Sub Finalize()

  MyBase.Finalize()
  Debug.WriteLine("Student object destroyed.")
End Sub
```

Step 6: Open the application's form in the *Design* window.

Double-click the `btnSave` button to create a code template for its `Click` event procedure. Complete the event procedure by entering the following code, shown in bold:

```
Private Sub btnSave_Click(ByVal sender As System.Object, _
   ByVal e As System.EventArgs) Handles btnSave.Click

  Dim objStudent As Student
  ' Create the Student class instance.
  objStudent = New Student()

  ' Get the data from the form.
  GetData(objStudent)

  ' Display the test grade.
  lblGrade.Text = objStudent.TestGrade

  ' Save the record.
  SaveRecord(objStudent)

  ' Confirm that the record was saved.
  MessageBox.Show("Record saved.", "Confirmation")

  ' Clear the form.
  ClearForm()
End Sub
```

Step 7: Write the following Sub procedures in the same form:

```
Private Sub GetData(ByVal objStudent As Student)

  ' Get the data from the text boxes and store
  ' in the object referenced by the Student.
  Try
    With objStudent
      .LastName = txtLastName.Text
      .FirstName = txtFirstName.Text
      .IdNumber = txtIdNumber.Text
      .TestAverage = CSng(txtTestAverage.Text)
    End With
  Catch ex As Exception
    MessageBox.Show(ex.Message)
  End Try
End Sub

Private Sub SaveRecord(ByVal objStudent As Student)

  ' Append the Student object to the end of a file.
  Dim writer As System.IO.StreamWriter

  Try
    ' Open the file in Append mode.
    writer = System.IO.File.AppendText("students.txt")

    ' Save the properties.
    With objStudent
      writer.WriteLine(.FirstName)
      writer.WriteLine(.LastName)
```

```
            writer.WriteLine(.TestAverage)
            writer.WriteLine(.TestGrade)
          End With

          ' Close the StreamWriter.
          writer.Close()
        Catch ex As Exception
          MessageBox.Show(ex.Message)
        End Try
      End Sub
      Private Sub ClearForm()
        ' Clear the form.
        txtFirstName.Clear()
        txtLastName.Clear()
        txtIdNumber.Clear()
        txtTestAverage.Clear()
        lblGrade.Text = String.Empty

        ' Reset the focus.
        txtLastName.Focus()
      End Sub
```

Step 8: Write the following `Click` event procedure for the *btnExit* button:

```
Private Sub btnExit_Click(ByVal sender As System.Object, _
   ByVal e As System.EventArgs) Handles btnExit.Click

  Me.Close()
End Sub
```

Step 9: Create a `Form_Load` event handler and insert the following line:

```
Debug.Listeners.Add(New ConsoleTraceListener())
```

Step 10: Save the project and run the application. On the application's form, enter the following data:

Last name: **Green**
First name: **Sara**
ID number: **27R8974**
Test average: **92.3**

Click the *Save* button to save the student data to a file. A message box appears indicating that the record was saved. Notice that the message *Student object created* is displayed in the *Output* window. This message was displayed by the `Student` class constructor. Click the *OK* button on the message box.

Step 11: Click the *Exit* button. If the message *Student object destroyed* has not yet been displayed by the class's `Finalize` method, it will be when you click the *Exit* button.

Checkpoint

12.8 How do you add a class module to a project?

12.9 What two steps must you perform when creating an instance of a class?

12.10 How do you remove an object from memory?

12.11 If an object is created inside a procedure, it is automatically removed from memory when the procedure ends, if no variables declared at the class or module level reference it. What is the name of the process that removes the object?

12.12 What are member variables?

12.13 What is a property procedure?

12.14 What does the `Get` section of a property procedure do?

12.15 What does the `Set` section of a property procedure do?

12.16 What is a constructor? What is the `Finalize` method?

12.3 Collections

CONCEPT: A collection holds a group of items. It automatically expands and shrinks in size to accommodate the items added to it. It allows items to be stored with associated key values, which may then be used in searches.

VideoNote
Collections

A **collection** is similar to an array. It is a single unit that contains several items. You can access the individual items in a collection with an index, which is similar to an array subscript. The difference between an array's subscript and a collection's index is that the latter begins at 1. You might recall that an array's subscripts begin at 0.

Another difference between arrays and collections is that collections automatically expand as items are added and shrink as items are removed. Also, the items stored in a collection do not have to be of the same type.

Visual Basic provides a class named `Collection`. When you create a collection in an application you are creating an instance of the `Collection` class. So, creating a collection is identical to creating any other class object. The following statements declare an object variable named `customers`, and then assign a new `Collection` instance to it:

```
Dim customers As Collection
customers = New Collection
```

You can also create a `Collection` instance and assign it to an object variable in one statement as follows:

```
Dim customers As New Collection
```

Adding Items to a Collection

You add items to a collection with the **`Add` method**. We will use the following general format:

```
Object.Add(Item [, Key])
```

`Object` is the name of an object variable that references a collection. The *`Item`* argument is the object, variable, or value that is to be added to the collection. *`Key`* is an optional string expression that is associated with the item and can be used to search for it. (*`Key`* must be unique for each member of a collection.)

Let's define a simple class named `Customer` with two variables and corresponding properties. The properties are abbreviated to save space.

```
Public Class Customer
  Private strName As String
  Private strPhone As String

  Public Property Name As String
    ...
  End Property

  Public Property Phone As String
    ...
  End Property
End Class
```

Suppose we are writing code for a form in our application. At the top of the form, at the class level, we can declare a `Collection` object:

```
Private customers As New Collection
```

Then, in a button's `Click` event handler procedure, we will declare a `Customer` object and assign TextBox values to its properties:

```
Dim myCustomer As New Customer
myCustomer.Name = txtName.Text
myCustomer.Phone = txtPhone.Text
```

Next, we will insert the `Customer` in the `customers` collection:

```
customers.Add(myCustomer)
```

We have not provided a key value, so we probably do not plan to search for customers later on. The collection is simply acting as a convenient container to hold customers.

Suppose, however, that we plan to search for customers at a later time while the application is running. In that case, we can use a different form of the `Add` statement, which allows us to pass a key value as the second argument:

```
customers.Add(myCustomer, myCustomer.Name)
```

This statement adds the `myCustomer` object to the collection, using the `myCustomer.Name` property as a key. Later, we will be able to search the collection for this object by specifying the customer's name.

`Add` Method Exceptions

An `ArgumentException` is thrown if you attempt to add a member with the same `Key` as an existing member. The following code example shows how to handle the exception:

```
Try
  customers.Add(myCustomer, myCustomer.Name)
Catch ex as ArgumentException
  MessageBox.Show(ex.Message)
End Try
```

Accessing Items by their Indexes

You can access an item in a collection by passing an integer to the **`Item` method** as follows:

```
Object.Item(Index)
```

The following statements locate the `Customer` object at index 1 in the collection named customers, assign the object to a `Customer` variable, and then display the customer's name in a message box:

```
Dim cust As Customer = CType(customers.Item(1), Customer)
MessageBox.Show("Customer found: " & cust.Name & ": " &
  cust.Phone)
```

Calling the CType method is necessary because the Item method of a collection returns an Object. We must cast (convert) the Object into a Customer.

Because `Item` is the default method for collections, you can use an abbreviated format such as the following to locate a collection item:

```
Dim cust As Customer = CType(customers(3), Customer)
```

The `IndexOutOfRange` Exception

An exception of the `IndexOutOfRange` type occurs if you use an index that does not match the index of any item in a collection. The following code example shows how to handle the exception:

```
Try
  Dim cust As Customer

  ' Get the collection index from user input
  Dim index As Integer = CInt(txtIndex.Text)

  ' Locate the customer in the collection
  cust = CType(customers.Item(index), Customer)

  ' Display the customer information
  MessageBox.Show("Customer found: " & cust.Name & ": " _
    & cust.Phone)

Catch ex As IndexOutOfRangeException
  MessageBox.Show(ex.Message)
End Try
```

The Count Property

Each collection has a Count property that holds the number of items stored in the collection. Suppose an application has a list box named `lstNames` and a collection named `names`. The following code uses the Count property as the upper limits of the `For Next` loop.

```
Dim intX As Integer
For intX = 1 To names.Count
  lstNames.Items.Add(names(intX).ToString())
Next intX
```

Searching for an Item by Key Value with the `Item` Method

You have already seen how the `Item` method can be used to retrieve an item with a specific index. It can also be used to retrieve an item with a specific key value. When used this way, the general format of the method is as follows:

```
Object.Item(Expression)
```

`Object` is the name of a collection. *`Expression`* can be either a numeric or a string expression. If *`Expression`* is a string, the `Item` method returns the member with the key value that matches the string. If no member exists with an index or key value matching

Expression, an exception of the type `IndexOutOfRangeException` occurs. (If *Expression* is a numeric expression, it is used as an index value and the `Item` method returns the member at the specified index location.)

For example, the following code searches the `studentCollection` collection for an item with the key value 49812:

```
Dim s as Student
s = CType(studentCollection.Item("49812"), Student)
```

After this code executes, if the item is found, the `s` variable will reference the object returned by the `Item` method.

The following code uses the `Item` method to retrieve members by index. It retrieves each member from the collection and displays the value of the LastName property in a message box.

```
Dim intIndex As Integer
Dim aStudent As Student

For intIndex = 1 To studentCollection.Count
  aStudent = CType(studentCollection.Item(intIndex), Student)
  MessageBox.Show(aStudent.LastName)
Next intIndex
```

Using References versus Copies

When an item in a collection is of a fundamental Visual Basic data type, such as Integer or Single, you retrieve a copy of the member only. For example, suppose the following code is used to add integers to a collection named `numbers`:

```
Dim intInput As Integer
intInput = InputBox("Enter an integer value.")
numbers.Add(intInput)
```

Suppose the following code is used to retrieve the integer stored at index 1 and to change its value. Because `intNum` is only a copy of a value in the collection, the item stored at index 1 is unchanged.

```
Dim intNum As Integer
intNum = CType(numbers(1), Integer)
intNum = 0
```

When an item in a collection is a class object, however, you retrieve a reference to it, not a copy. For example, the following code retrieves the member of the `studentCollection` collection with the key value `49812`, and changes the value of its LastName property to *Griffin*.

```
Dim s as Student
s = CType(studentCollection.Item("49812"), Student)
s.LastName = "Griffin"
```

Because a reference to the member is returned, the LastName property of the object in the collection is modified.

Using the `For Each...Next` Loop with a Collection

You may also use the `For Each...Next` loop to access the individual members of a collection, eliminating the need to compare a counter variable against the collection's Count property. For example, the following code prints the LastName property of each member of the `studentCollection` collection.

```
Dim s As Student
For Each s In studentCollection
  MessageBox.Show(s.LastName)
Next
```

Removing Members

Use the **`Remove` method** to remove a member from a collection. The general format is:

```
Object.Remove(Expression)
```

`Object` is the name of a collection. *`Expression`* can be either a numeric or string expression. If it is a numeric expression, it is used as an index value and the member at the specified index location is removed. If *`Expression`* is a string, the member with the key value that matches the string is removed. If an index is provided, and it does not match an index of any item in the collection, an exception of the `IndexOutOfRangeException` type occurs. If a key value is provided, and it does not match the key value of any item in the collection, an exception of the `ArgumentException` type occurs.

For example, the following statement removes the member with the key value `"49812"` from the `studentCollection` collection:

```
studentCollection.Remove("49812")
```

The following statement removes the member at index location 7 from the `studentCollection` collection:

```
studentCollection.Remove(7)
```

To avoid throwing an exception, always check the range of the index you pass to the `Remove` method. The following is an example:

```
Dim intIndex As Integer
' (assign value to intIndex...)

If intIndex > 0 and intIndex <= studentCollection.Count Then
  studentCollection.Remove(intIndex)
End If
```

Similarly, make sure a key value exists before using it to remove an item, as shown here:

```
Dim strKeyToRemove As String
' (assign value to strKeyToRemove...)

If studentCollection.Contains(strKeyToRemove) Then
  studentCollection.Remove(strKeyToRemove))
End If
```

Writing Sub Procedures and Functions That Use Collections

Sub procedures and functions can accept collections as arguments, and functions can return collections. Remember that a collection is an instance of a class, so follow the same guidelines for passing any class object as an argument, or returning a class object from a function.

Relating the Items in Parallel Collections

Sometimes it is useful to store related data in two or more parallel collections. For example, assume a company assigns a unique employee number to each employee. An application that calculates gross pay has the following collections:

```
Dim hoursWorked As New Collection       ' To hold hours worked
Dim payRates As New Collection          ' To hold hourly pay rates
```

The `hoursWorked` collection stores the number of hours each employee has worked, and the `payRates` collection stores each employee's hourly pay rate.

When an item is stored in the `hoursWorked` or `payRates` collections, the employee's number is the key. For instance, let's say James Bourne's ID number is 55678. He has worked 40 hours and his pay rate is $12.50. The following statements add his data to the appropriate collection:

```
hoursWorked.Add(40, "55678")
payRates.Add(12.5, "55678")
```

To calculate his gross pay, we retrieve his data from each collection, using his ID number as the key:

```
sngGrossPay = hoursWorked.Item("55678") * payRate.Item("55678")
```

Employee Collection Program Example

The following code expands this idea. In addition to the `hoursWorked` and `payRates` collection, this code uses a collection to hold the employee names and a collection to hold the employee ID numbers.

```
Dim empNumbers As New Collection        ' Holds employee numbers
Dim employees As New Collection         ' Holds employee names
Dim hoursWorked As New Collection       ' Holds hours worked
Dim payRates As New Collection          ' Holds hourly pay rates

Dim strEmpNumber As String              ' Employee ID number
Dim strEmpName As String                ' Employee name
Dim decGrossPay, decHours, decRate As Decimal
Dim i As Integer                        ' Loop counter

' Add each employee's number to the empNumbers collection.
empNumbers.Add("55678")
empNumbers.Add("78944")
empNumbers.Add("84417")

' Add the employee names to the employees
' collection, with the employee ID number
' as the key.
employees.Add("James Bourne", "55678")
employees.Add("Jill Davis", "78944")
employees.Add("Kevin Franklin", "84417")

' Add each employee's hourly worked to the
' hoursWorked collection, with the employee
' ID number as the key.
hoursWorked.Add(40, "55678")
hoursWorked.Add(35, "78944")
hoursWorked.Add(20, "84417")
```

```
' Add each employee's hours pay rate to the
' payRates collection, with the employee
' ID number as the key.
payRates.Add(12.5, "55678")
payRates.Add(18.75, "78944")
payRates.Add(9.6, "84417")

' Compute and display each employee's
' gross pay.

For intIndex = 1 To employees.Count

   ' Get an employee ID number to use as a key.
   strEmpNumber = empNumbers(intIndex).ToString()

   ' Get this employee's name.
   strEmpName = employees.Item(strEmpNumber).ToString()

   ' Get the hours worked for this employee.
   decHours = CDec(hoursWorked.Item(strEmpNumber))

   ' Get the pay rate for this employee.
   decRate = CDec(payRates.Item(strEmpNumber))

   ' Calculate this employee's gross pay.
   decGrossPay = decHours * decRate

   ' Display the results for this employee.
   lblResult.Text &= "Gross pay for " & strEmpName & _
       " is " & decGrossPay.ToString("c") & vbCrLf
Next
```

Checkpoint

12.17 How do collections differ from arrays?

12.18 How do you add members to a collection?

12.19 How is a key value useful when you are adding an item to a collection?

12.20 How do you search for a specific member of a collection?

12.21 How do you remove a member from a collection?

12.4 Focus on Problem Solving: Creating the *Student Collection* Application

Campus Systems, Inc. is developing software for a university and has hired you as a programmer. Your first assignment is to develop an application that allows the user to select a student's ID number from a list box to view information about the student. The user should also be able to add new student records and delete student records. The application will use the `Student` class and a collection of `Student` class objects. A test application with two forms has already been created for you.

In Tutorial 12-2, you examine the existing forms of the *Student Collection* application.

Tutorial 12-2:
Completing the *Student Collection* application

Step 1: Open the *Student Collection* project from the student sample program folder named *Chap12\Student Collection.*

The project already has two forms, as shown in Figures 12-6 and 12-7. The `frmMain` form has a list box, `lstIdNumbers`, which will display a list of student ID numbers. When a student's ID number is selected from the list box, the data for that student will be displayed in the following Label controls: `lblLastName`, `lblFirstName`, `lblIdNumber`, `lblTestAverage`, and `lblGrade`. The *Add Student* button causes the `frmAdd` form to be displayed. The *Remove* button removes the student whose ID number is currently selected.

Figure 12-6 `frmMain` form

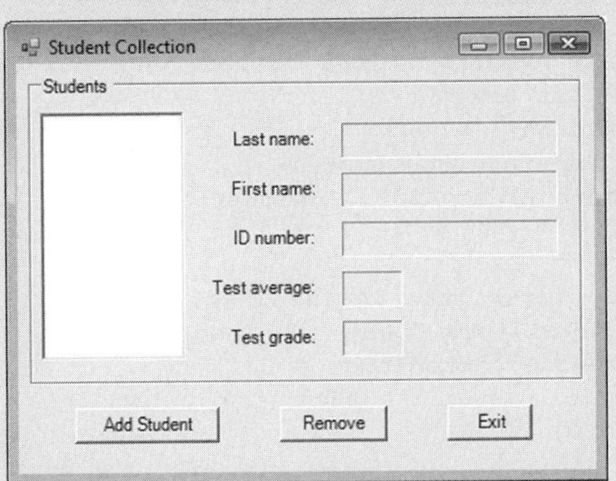

Figure 12-7 `frmAdd` form

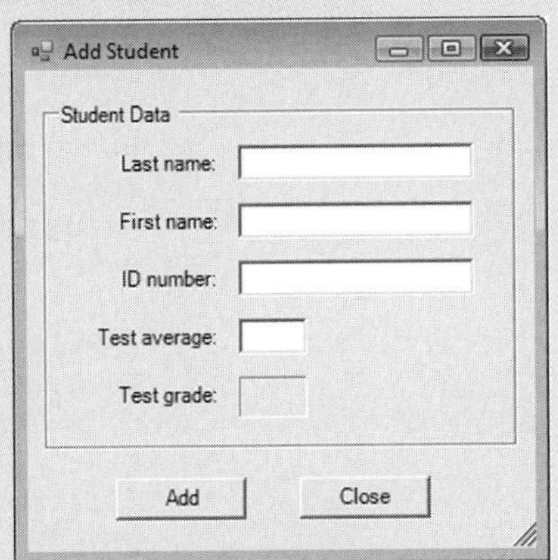

Step 2: Add the `Student` class you created in Tutorial 12-1 to the project. (Click *Project* on the menu bar, and then click *Add Existing Item*. Browse to the folder containing the *Student.vb* file. Select the *Student.vb* file and click the *Add* button.)

Step 3: Add a standard module to the project. Name the module **`StudentCollectionModule.vb`**. Complete the module by entering the following code shown in bold:

```
Module StudentCollectionModule
  Public studentCollection As Collection
End Module
```

This statement declares `studentCollection` as an object variable that will reference a collection. Because it is declared as `Public`, it will be available to all the forms in the project.

Step 4: Double-click on an open area of the `frmMain` form, so the *Code* window displays. Add the following `Load` event procedure to the form:

```
Private Sub frmMain_Load(ByVal sender As System.Object, _
  ByVal e As System.EventArgs) Handles MyBase.Load

  ' Create the collection.
  studentCollection = New Collection
End Sub
```

Step 5: Add the `btnAdd_Click` event handler, `UpdateListBox` Sub procedure, and `ClearForm` Sub procedure as follows:

```
Private Sub btnAdd_Click(ByVal sender As System.Object, _
      ByVal e As System.EventArgs) Handles btnAdd.Click

   ' Display the Add Student form.
   Dim addStudentForm As New frmAdd()

   ' Display the form.
   addStudentForm.ShowDialog()

   ' Update the contents of the list box.
   UpdateListBox()
End Sub

Private Sub UpdateListBox()
   ' Update the list box contents.
   ' Clear the list box.
   lstIdNumbers.Items.Clear()

   ' Load the ID numbers in the collection
   ' into the list box.
   Dim s As Student
   For Each s In studentCollection
      lstIdNumbers.Items.Add(s.IdNumber)
   Next

   ' Select the first item in the list.
   If lstIdNumbers.Items.Count > 0 Then
      lstIdNumbers.SelectedIndex = 0
   Else
      ClearForm()
   End If
End Sub

Private Sub ClearForm()
   ' Clear the form.
   lblFirstName.Text = String.Empty
   lblLastName.Text = String.Empty
   lblIdNumber.Text = String.Empty
   lblTestAverage.Text = String.Empty
   lblGrade.Text = String.Empty
End Sub
```

The `btnAdd_Click` event procedure displays the `frmAdd` form, which allows the user to add a new student object to the collection. After the user closes the `frmAdd` form, the `UpdateListBox` procedure is called. This procedure clears the list box and adds all of the student ID numbers in the `studentCollection` collection to the `lstIdNumbers` list box.

Step 6: Add the `btnRemove_Click` event procedure, as follows:

```
Private Sub btnRemove_Click(ByVal sender As System.Object, _
      ByVal e As System.EventArgs) Handles btnRemove.Click

   ' Exit immediately if no item was selected.
   If lstIdNumbers.SelectedIndex = -1 Then Return
      ' Remove the selected student from the collection.
```

```
   Dim intIndex As Integer

   If lstIdNumbers.SelectedIndex <> -1 Then
     If MessageBox.Show("Are you sure?", "Confirm Deletion", _
         MessageBoxButtons.YesNo) = _
         Windows.Forms.DialogResult.Yes Then
       ' Retrieve the student's data from the collection.
       intIndex = lstIdNumbers.SelectedIndex
       Try
         studentCollection.Remove( _
           lstIdNumbers.SelectedItem.ToString())
         lstIdNumbers.Items.Remove(intIndex)
         UpdateListBox()
       Catch ex As Exception
         MessageBox.Show(ex.Message)
       End Try
     End If
   End If
 End Sub
```

Step 7: Now you will write the `lstNumbers_SelectedIndexChanged` event procedure. This event procedure executes any time the selected item in the list box changes. To create a code template for the procedure, open the form in the *Design* window and then double-click the `lstIdNumbers` list box. The code follows:

```
Private Sub lstIdNumbers_SelectedIndexChanged(ByVal _
    sender As System.Object, ByVal e As System.EventArgs) _
    Handles lstIdNumbers.SelectedIndexChanged

  ' Update the selected student data.
  Dim studentData As Student

  If lstIdNumbers.SelectedIndex <> -1 Then
  ' Retrieve the student's data from the collection.
    Try
      studentData = CType(studentCollection.Item( _
          lstIdNumbers.SelectedItem), Student)
    Catch ex As Exception
      MessageBox.Show(ex.Message)
      studentData = Nothing
    End Try

    ' Display the student data.
    If studentData IsNot Nothing Then
      DisplayData(studentData)
    End If
  End If
End Sub
```

This event procedure displays, in the Label controls, the data for the student whose ID number is selected in the list box.

Step 8: Write the `DisplayData` Sub procedure, as follows:

```
Private Sub DisplayData(ByVal s As Student)

  ' Get the data from the text boxes and store
  ' in the object referenced by s.
  lblLastName.Text = s.LastName
```

```
   lblFirstName.Text = s.FirstName
   lblIdNumber.Text = s.IdNumber
   lblTestAverage.Text = s.TestAverage.ToString()
   lblGrade.Text = s.TestGrade
End Sub
```

This procedure copies the data from a `Student` class object to the Label controls.

Step 9: Write the `btnExit_Click` event procedure, as follows:

```
Private Sub btnExit_Click(ByVal sender As System.Object, _
    ByVal e As System.EventArgs) Handles btnExit.Click

   ' End the application.
   Me.Close()
End Sub
```

Step 10: Now you will write the code for the `frmAdd` form. Add the `btnAdd_Click` event procedure, the `GetData` Sub procedure, the `AddRecord` Sub procedure, and the `ClearForm` Sub procedure, as follows:

```
Private Sub btnAdd_Click(ByVal sender As System.Object, _
    ByVal e As System.EventArgs) Handles btnAdd.Click

   Dim studentRecord As Student

   ' Create the Student class instance.
   studentRecord = New Student()
   ' Get the data from the form.
   GetData(studentRecord)
   ' Display the test grade.
   lblGrade.Text = studentRecord.TestGrade
   ' Save the record.
   AddRecord(studentRecord)
   ' Confirm that the record was saved.
   MessageBox.Show("Record added.", "Confirmation")
   ' Clear the form.
   ClearForm()
End Sub

Private Sub GetData(ByVal s As Student)

   ' Get the data from the text boxes and store
   ' in the object referenced by s.
   s.LastName = txtLastName.Text
   s.FirstName = txtFirstName.Text
   s.IdNumber = txtIdNumber.Text
   s.TestAverage = CSng(txtTestAverage.Text)
End Sub

Private Sub AddRecord(ByVal s As Student)

   ' Add the object referenced by s to the collection.
   ' Use the student ID number as the key.
   Try
      studentCollection.Add(s, s.IdNumber)
   Catch ex As Exception
      MessageBox.Show(ex.Message)
   End Try
End Sub
```

```
Private Sub ClearForm()

   ' Clear the form.
   txtFirstName.Clear()
   txtLastName.Clear()
   txtIdNumber.Clear()
   txtTestAverage.Clear()
   lblGrade.Text = String.Empty

   ' Reset the focus.
   txtLastName.Focus()
End Sub
```

Step 11: Add the `btnClose_Click` event procedure, as follows:

```
Private Sub btnClose_Click(ByVal sender As System.Object, _
        ByVal e As System.EventArgs) Handles btnClose.Click

   ' Close the form.
   Me.Close()
End Sub
```

Step 12: Save the project and run the application. Click the *Add Student* button and add the following students:

Student 1
Last name: **Green**
First name: **Sara**
ID number: **27R8974**
Test average: **92.3**

Student 2
Last name: **Robinson**
First name: **Joy**
ID number: **89G4561**
Test average: **97.3**

Student 3
Last name: **Williams**
First name: **Jon**
ID number: **71A4478**
Test average: **78.6**

Step 13: Close the `frmAdd` form. The main form should now appear as shown in Figure 12-8.

Step 14: Select a student's ID number in the list box. That student's data is displayed in the Label controls.

Step 15: Remove each student by selecting an ID number and then clicking the *Remove* button. Click *Yes* when asked *Are you sure?*

Step 16: Exit the application. Leave the *Student Collection* project loaded for Tutorial 12-3.

Figure 12-8 `frmMain` with students added

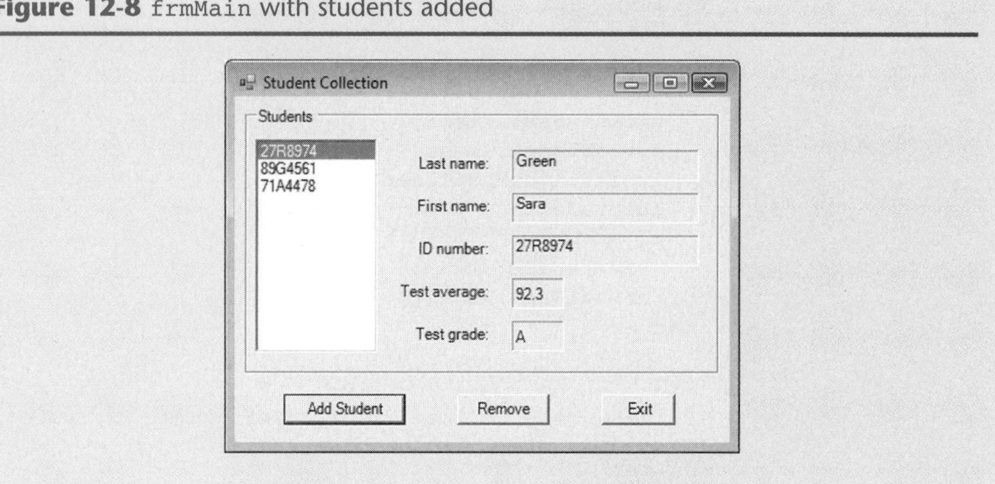

12.5 The Object Browser

CONCEPT: The Object Browser is a dialog box that allows you to browse all classes and components available to your project.

The **Object Browser** is a dialog box that displays information about objects. You can use the Object Browser to examine classes you have created, as well as the namespaces, classes, and other components that Visual Basic makes available to your project. Tutorial 12-3 guides you through the process of using the Object Browser to examine the classes you created in the *Student Collection* project.

Tutorial 12-3:
Using the Object Browser

Step 1: Start Visual Basic and open the *Student Collection* project you created in Tutorial 12-2.

Step 2: Open the Object Browser by performing one of the following actions:

- Click *View* on the menu bar, and then click *Object Browser*.
- Press the F2 key.

The *Object Browser* window, appears as shown in Figure 12-9. The left pane is the *objects* pane, and the right pane is the *members* pane. When you select an item in the *objects* pane on the left, information about that item appears in the *members* pane on the right.

Step 3: Notice in Figure 12-9 that a *Student Collection* entry appears in the *objects* pane. Click the small plus sign that appears to the left of this entry to expand it. The entry *{} Student_Collection* appears. The braces ({}) indicate that *Student_Collection* is a namespace. Visual Basic has created a namespace for this project and named it *Student_Collection*. The contents of the project are stored in this namespace. Click the small plus sign at the left of this entry to expand it. Now entries appear for `frmAdd`, `frmMain`, `Settings`, `Student`, and `StudentCollectionModule`.

Figure 12-9 *Object Browser* window

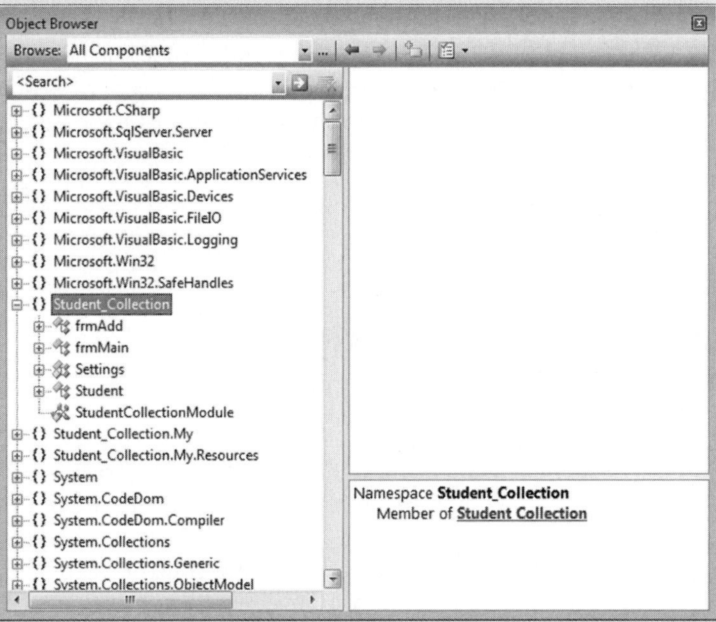

Step 4: Click the entry for `Student`. All members of the `Student` class should be listed in the *members* pane, as shown in Figure 12-10. If you click an entry in the *members* pane, a brief summary of the member is displayed below the pane. If you double-click an entry, the *Code* window appears with the cursor positioned at the selected item's declaration statement.

Figure 12-10 Members of the `Student` class displayed in the *members* pane

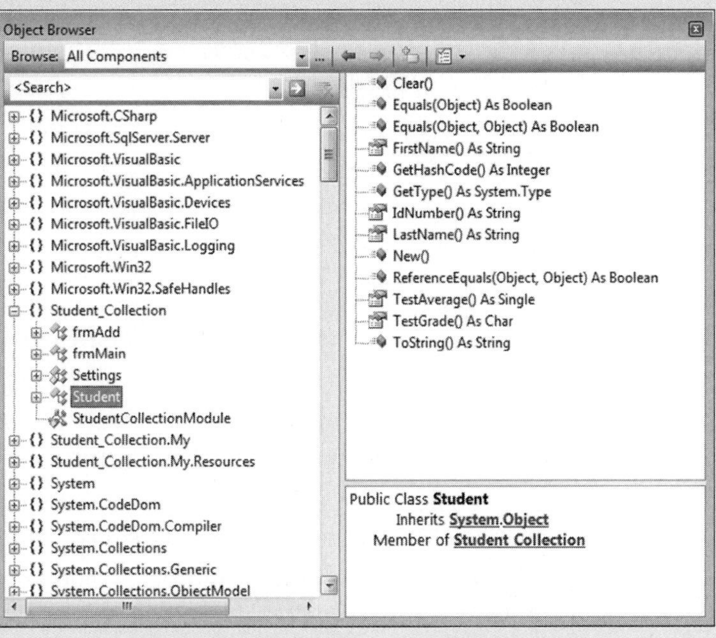

Step 5: Click some other entries under *{} Student_Collection* in the *object* window, such as `frmMain` and `StudentCollectionModule`, to view their members in the *members* window.

Step 6: Because Visual Basic forms and controls are classes, the Object Browser can be used to examine them as well. You can use this tool to quickly find out what methods and properties a control has. For example, type `TextBox` in the Search box and press Enter. The results of the search will appear in the left-hand pane. Double-click the entry for *System.Windows.Forms.TextBox*. The TextBox class should appear selected in the *Objects* pane and the members of the TextBox class should appear in the *members* pane.

Step 7: Close the Object Browser and close the project.

12.6 Focus on GUI Design: Scroll Bars and Track Bars

CONCEPT: The HScrollBar, VScrollBar, and TrackBar controls provide a graphical way to adjust a number within a range of values.

The HScrollBar, VScrollBar, and TrackBar controls allow the user to adjust a value within a range of values. The **HScrollBar control** is used to create a horizontal scroll bar, the **VScrollBar control** is used to create a vertical scroll bar, and the **TrackBar control** is used to create a track bar. Examples of these controls are shown in Figure 12-11. We will refer to these controls as **scrollable controls**.

Figure 12-11 Horizontal and vertical scroll bars and a track bar

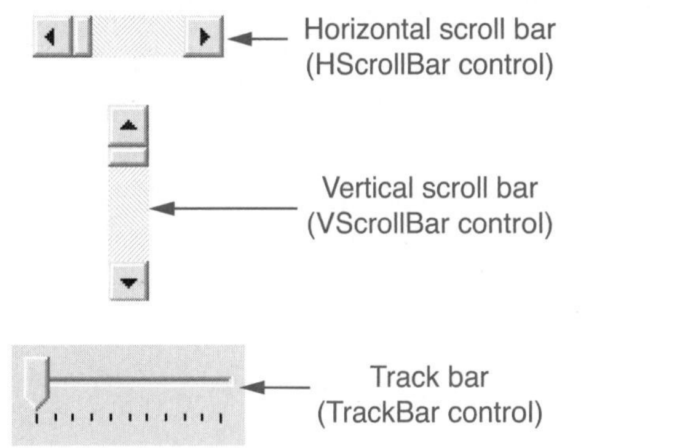

Table 12-2 lists the important properties of scrollable controls.

Scrollable controls hold integers in their **Value property**. The user increases or decreases the Value property by interacting with the scroll bar. The position of a control's slider corresponds with the integer stored in its Value property in the following ways:

- When a horizontal scroll bar or a track bar's slider is moved toward the left, the Value property decreases toward the value stored in the Minimum property.
- When a horizontal scroll bar or a track bar's slider is moved toward the right, the Value property increases toward the value stored in the Maximum property.
- When a vertical scroll bar's slider is moved up, the Value property decreases toward the value stored in the Minimum property.
- When a vertical scroll bar's slider is moved down, the Value property increases toward the value stored in the Maximum property.

Table 12-2 Scrollable control properties

Property	Description
Minimum	The scroll bar or track bar's minimum value
Maximum	The scroll bar or track bar's maximum value
Value	The scroll bar or track bar's current value
LargeChange	The amount by which the Value property changes when the user clicks the scroll bar or track bar area around the slider. Track bars also respond to the Page Up and Page Down keys, which cause the Value property to change by this amount.
SmallChange	The amount by which the Value property changes when the user clicks one of the scroll arrows at either end of a scroll bar. Track bars also respond to the arrow keys, which cause the Value property to change by this amount.
TickFrequency	This is a TrackBar control property only. This property holds the number of units between the tick marks on the control. For example, if Minimum is set to 0 and Maximum is set to 1000, you would set the **TickFrequency property** to 100 to draw ten tick marks.

The **Minimum property** determines the smallest integer the Value property can hold, and the **Maximum property** determines the largest integer the Value property can hold.

The user changes the contents of the Value property by moving the scrollable control's slider. The user may do this by clicking the scroll arrows that appear at either end of a scroll bar, by clicking the area around the slider, or by dragging the slider. TrackBar controls also respond to the Page Up, Page Down, and arrow keys on the keyboard. The following list summarizes the effects of these actions:

- For the HScrollBar and VScrollBar controls, when the user clicks one of the scroll arrows at either end of a scroll bar, the Value property changes by the amount stored in the **SmallChange property**.
- For the TrackBar control, when the user presses any of the arrow keys, the Value property changes by the amount stored in the SmallChange property.
- For all of the scrollable controls, when the user clicks the area around the slider, the Value property changes by the amount stored in the **LargeChange property**.
- For the TrackBar control, when the user presses the Page Up or Page Down key, the Value property changes by the amount stored in the LargeChange property.

NOTE: The Value property cannot reach the number stored in the Maximum property by way of the slider being moved. The largest value that can be reached by moving the slider is Maximum – LargeChange + 1. Similarly, the smallest value that can be reached by moving the slider is Minimum + LargeChange – 1. However, you can store the Maximum or Minimum value in the Value property with an assignment statement.

The scrollable controls trigger a `Scroll` event when the user moves the slider with any of these actions. In order to execute program code each time a scrollable control's slider changes position, you write a `Scroll` event handler.

We will use `hsb` as the prefix for a HScrollBar control name, `vsb` as the prefix for a VScrollBar control name, and `tb` as the prefix for a TrackBar control name. In Tutorial 12-4, you examine an application that uses each of these scrollable controls.

Tutorial 12-4:
Working with scrollable controls

Step 1: Open the *Scrollable Control Demo* project from the student sample programs folder named *Chap12\Scrollable Control Demo*. The application's form is shown in Figure 12-12. This application converts Celsius temperatures to Fahrenheit and meters to feet, and moves a graphic image across the form. The user changes the Celsius temperature with a VScrollBar control named `vsbCent`, changes the distance in meters with an HScrollBar control named `hsbMeters`, and moves the graphic of the sailboat with a TrackBar control named `tbBoat`.

Figure 12-12 *Scrollable Control Demo* form

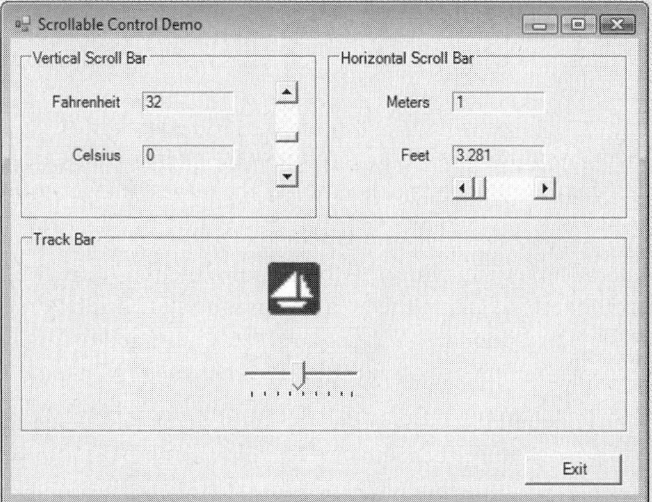

Table 12-3 shows initial property settings for the scroll bar controls.

Table 12-3 Property settings for `vsbCelsius` and `hsbMeters`

Property	`vsbCelsius` setting	`hsbMeters` setting
Minimum	–100	0
Maximum	100	100
LargeChange	20	20
SmallChange	1	1

Step 2: Run the application and experiment with the scroll bars. The application changes the Celsius temperature and converts it to Fahrenheit when you interact with the vertical scroll bar. It changes the meters value and converts it to feet when you interact with the horizontal scroll bar. It also moves the sailboat image when you interact with the track bar.

Step 3: End the application. Open the *Code* window and locate the `vsbCelsius_Scroll` event procedure. The code is as follows:

```
Private Sub vsbCelsius_Scroll(ByVal sender _
    As System.Object, _
    ByVal e As System.Windows.Forms.ScrollEventArgs) _
    Handles vsbCelsius.Scroll
  ' Update the temperatures.
  Dim sngCelsius As Single
  Dim sngFahrenheit As Single

  ' Get the negative of vsbCelsius.Value because
  ' the maximum value is at the bottom of the
  ' scroll bar and the minumum is at the top.
  sngCelsius = -(vsbCelsius.Value)

  ' Calculate fahrenheit temperature.
  sngFahrenheit = CSng((9.0 / 5.0) * sngCelsius + 32)

  ' Display the values.
  lblCelsius.Text = sngCelsius.ToString()
  lblFahrenheit.Text = sngFahrenheit.ToString()
End Sub
```

This procedure uses the number stored in the scroll bar's Value property as a Celsius temperature. It converts the value to Fahrenheit and displays both the Celsius and Fahrenheit temperatures in the Label controls. Note that the negative of the number stored in the Value property is assigned to the `sngCelsius` variable because the VScrollBar control is at its minimum value when the slider is at the top, and is at its maximum value when the slider is at the bottom. This logic seems counterintuitive to this application, so we reverse it by getting the negative of the Value property.

Step 4: Now look at the `hsbMeters_Scroll` event procedure. The code follows:

```
Private Sub hsbMeters_Scroll(ByVal sender As System.Object, _
    ByVal e As System.Windows.Forms.ScrollEventArgs) _
    Handles hsbMeters.Scroll

  ' Update the distances.
  ' 1 meter = 3.281 feet.
  lblMeters.Text = hsbMeters.Value.ToString()
  lblFeet.Text = (hsbMeters.Value * 3.281).ToString()
End Sub
```

This procedure uses the number stored in the scroll bar's Value property as a distance measured in meters. The value is copied to the `lblMeters` control, and then converted to feet. The distance in feet is copied to the `lblFeet` control.

Step 5: Now look at the `tbBoat_Scroll` event procedure. The code follows:

```
Private Sub tbBoat_Scroll(ByVal sender As System.Object, _
    ByVal e As System.EventArgs) Handles tbBoat.Scroll

  ' Move the boat by storing tbBoat's Value
  ' property in picBoat's Left property.
  picBoat.Left = tbBoat.Value
End Sub
```

This procedure stores the number in the track bar's Value property in the picture box's Left property. As the track bar's Value property changes, so does the position of the sailboat image.

Checkpoint

12.22 How do you establish the range of values that may be assigned to a scrollable control's Value property?

12.23 What is the difference between the SmallChange and LargeChange properties?

12.24 When does a scrollable control's `Scroll` event occur?

12.7 Introduction to Inheritance

CONCEPT: Inheritance allows a new class to be based on an existing class. The new class inherits the accessible member variables, methods, and properties of the class on which it is based.

An important aspect of object-oriented programming is inheritance. **Inheritance** allows you to create new classes that inherit, or derive, characteristics of existing classes. For example, you might start with the `Student` class we discussed earlier, which has only general information for all types of students. But special types of students might require the creation of classes such as `GraduateStudent`, `ExchangeStudent`, `StudentEmployee`, and so on. These new classes would share all the characteristics of the `Student` class, and they would each add the new characteristics that make them specialized.

In an inheritance relationship, there is a base class and a derived class. The **base class** is a general-purpose class that other classes may be based on. The **derived class** is based on the base class, and inherits characteristics from it. You can think of the base class as the parent and the derived class as the child.

Let's look at an example. The following `Vehicle` class has two private variables and two property procedures: Passengers and MilesPerGallon. The Passengers property uses the `intPassengers` member variable and the MilesPerGallon property uses the `sngMPG` member variable.

```
Public Class Vehicle
   ' Private member variables
   Private intPassengers As Integer      ' Number of passengers
   Private sngMPG As Single              ' Miles per gallon

   ' Passengers property
   Public Property Passengers() As Integer
      Get
         Return intPassengers
      End Get
      Set(ByVal value As Integer)
         intPassengers = value
      End Set
   End Property

   ' MilesPerGallon property
   Public Property MilesPerGallon() As Single
      Get
         Return sngMPG
      End Get
      Set(ByVal value As Single)
         sngMPG = value
      End Set
   End Property
End Class
```

(The *Vehicle Inheritance* program in the Chapter 12 student sample programs folder contains the code examples shown here.) The `Vehicle` class holds only general data about a vehicle. By using it as a base class, however, we can create other classes that hold more specialized data about specific types of vehicles. For example, look at the following code for a `Truck` class:

```
Public Class Truck
  Inherits Vehicle

  ' Private member variables
  Private sngCargoWeight As Single       ' Maximum cargo weight
  Private blnFourWheelDrive As Boolean   ' Four wheel drive

  ' MaxCargoWeight property
  Public Property MaxCargoWeight() As Single
    Get
      Return sngCargoWeight
    End Get
    Set(ByVal value As Single)
      sngCargoWeight = value
    End Set
  End Property

  ' FourWheelDrive property
  Public Property FourWheelDrive() As Boolean
    Get
      Return blnFourWheelDrive
    End Get
    Set(ByVal value As Boolean)
      blnFourWheelDrive = value
    End Set
  End Property
End Class
```

Notice the second line of this class declaration:

```
Inherits Vehicle
```

This statement indicates that this class is derived from the `Vehicle` class. Because it is derived from the `Vehicle` class, the `Truck` class inherits all the `Vehicle` class member variables, methods, and properties that are not declared as private. In addition to the inherited base class members, the `Truck` class adds two properties of its own: MaxCargoWeight, which hold the maximum cargo weight, and FourWheelDrive, which indicates whether the truck uses four-wheel drive.

In the Form1 form, the following statements create an instance of the `Truck` class:

```
Dim pickUp as Truck
pickUp = New Truck
```

And the following statements store values in all of the object's properties:

```
pickUp.Passengers = 2
pickUp.MilesPerGallon = 18
pickUp.MaxCargoWeight = 2000
pickUp.FourWheelDrive = True
```

Notice that values are stored not only in the MaxCargoWeight and FourWheelDrive properties, but also the Passengers and MilesPerGallon properties. The `Truck` class inherits the Passengers and MilesPerGallon properties from the `Vehicle` class.

Overriding Properties and Methods

Sometimes a property procedure or method in a base class is not appropriate for a derived class. If this is the case, you can **override** the base class property procedure or method by adding one with the same name to the derived class. When an object of the derived class accesses the property or calls the method, the overridden version in the derived class is executed rather than the version in the base class. For example, the `Vehicle` class has the following property procedure:

```
Public Property Passengers() As Integer
  Get
    Return intPassengers
  End Get
  Set(ByVal value As Integer)
    intPassengers = value
  End Set
End Property
```

The `Set` section of this property procedure stores any value passed to it in the `intPassengers` variable. Suppose that in the `Truck` class we want to restrict the number of passengers to either 1 or 2. We can override the Passengers property procedure by writing another version of it in the `Truck` class.

First, we must add the `Overridable` keyword to the property procedure in the `Vehicle` class, as follows:

```
Public Overridable Property Passengers() As Integer
  Get
    Return intPassengers
  End Get
  Set(ByVal value As Integer)
    intPassengers = value
  End Set
End Property
```

The **`Overridable` keyword** indicates that the procedure may be overridden in a derived class. If we do not add this keyword to the declaration, a compiler error will occur when we attempt to override the procedure. The general format of a property procedure with the `Overridable` keyword is as follows:

```
Public Overridable Property PropertyName() As DataType
  Get
    Statements
  End Get
  Set(ParameterDeclaration)
    Statements
  End Set
End Property
```

NOTE: A private property cannot be overridable.

Next, we write the overridden property procedure in the `Truck` class, as follows:

```
' Passengers property
Public Overrides Property Passengers() As Integer
  Get
    Return MyBase.Passengers
  End Get
```

```
    Set(ByVal value As Integer)
      If value >= 1 And value <= 2 Then
        MyBase.Passengers = value
      Else
        MessageBox.Show("Passengers must be 1 or 2.", "Error")
      End If
    End Set
  End Property
```

This procedure uses the **Overrides keyword**, *indicating* that it overrides a procedure in the base class. The general format of a property procedure that overrides a base class property procedure is as follows:

```
Public Overrides Property PropertyName() As DataType
  Get
    Statements
  End Get
  Set(ParameterDeclaration)
    Statements
  End Set
End Property
```

Let's see how the procedure works. The `Get` section has the following statement:

```
Return MyBase.Passengers
```

The **MyBase keyword** refers to the base class. The expression `MyBase.Passengers` refers to the base class's Passengers property. This statement returns the same value returned from the base class's Passengers property.

The `Set` section uses an `If` statement to validate that `value` is 1 or 2. If `value` is 1 or 2, the following statement is executed:

```
MyBase.Passengers = value
```

This statement stores `value` in the base class's Passenger property. If `value` is not 1 or 2, an error message is displayed. So, the following code will cause the error message to appear:

```
Dim pickUp As New Truck
pickUp.Passengers = 5
```

The complete code for the modified `Vehicle` and `Truck` classes follows:

```
Public Class Vehicle
  ' Private member variables
  Private intPassengers As Integer     ' Number of passengers
  Private sngMPG As Single             ' Miles per gallon

  ' Passengers property
  Public Overridable Property Passengers() As Integer
    Get
      Return intPassengers
    End Get
    Set(ByVal value As Integer)
      intPassengers = value
    End Set
  End Property

  ' MilesPerGallon property
  Public Property MilesPerGallon() As Single
```

```
      Get
        Return sngMPG
      End Get
      Set(ByVal value As Single)
        sngMPG = value
      End Set
    End Property

    ' Overriden ToString method
    Public Overrides Function ToString() As String

      ' Return a string representation of a vehicle.
      Dim str As String
      str = "Passengers: " & intPassengers.ToString & _
        " MPG: " & sngMPG.ToString
      Return str
    End Function
  End Class

  Public Class Truck
    Inherits Vehicle

    ' Private member variables
    Private sngCargoWeight As Single      ' Maximum cargo weight
    Private blnFourWheelDrive As Boolean  ' Four wheel drive

    ' MaxCargoWeight property
    Public Property MaxCargoWeight() As Single
      Get
        Return sngCargoWeight
      End Get
      Set(ByVal value As Single)
        sngCargoWeight = value
      End Set
    End Property

    ' FourWheelDrive property
    Public Property FourWheelDrive() As Boolean
      Get
        Return blnFourWheelDrive
      End Get
      Set(ByVal value As Boolean)
        blnFourWheelDrive = value
      End Set
    End Property

    ' Passengers property
    Public Overrides Property Passengers() As Integer
      Get
        Return MyBase.Passengers
      End Get
      Set(ByVal value As Integer)
        If value >= 1 And value <= 2 Then
          MyBase.Passengers = value
        Else
          MessageBox.Show("Passengers must be 1 or 2.", "Error")
        End If
      End Set
    End Property
  End Class
```

Overriding Methods

Class methods may be overridden in the same manner as property procedures. The general format of an overridable base class Sub procedure is as follows:

```
Public Overridable Sub ProcedureName()
  Statements
End Sub
```

The general format of an overridable base class function is as follows:

```
Public Overridable Function FunctionName() As DataType
  Statements
End Function
```

NOTE: A private procedure or function cannot be overridable.

The general format of a Sub procedure that overrides a base class Sub procedure is as follows:

```
AccessSpecifier Overrides Sub ProcedureName()
  Statements
End Sub
```

The general format of a function that overrides a base class function is as follows:

```
AccessSpecifier Overrides Function FunctionName() As DataType
  Statements
End Sub
```

Because a derived class cannot access the private members of its base class, the overridable methods in the base class cannot be declared `Private`. A derived class method that overrides a base class method must keep the same access level (such as `Public`).

Overriding the `ToString` Method

By now you are familiar with the `ToString` method that all Visual Basic data types provide. This method returns a string representation of the data stored in a variable or object.

Every class you create in Visual Basic is automatically derived from a built-in class named `Object`. The **`Object` class** has a method named `ToString` which returns a fully qualified class name (`System.String`), which includes the namespace named *System*. You can override this method so it returns a string representation of the data stored in an object. For example, we can add the following `ToString` method to the `Vehicle` class:

```
' Overriden ToString method
Public Overrides Function ToString() As String
  ' Return a string representation
  ' of a vehicle.
  Dim str As String

  str = "Passengers: " & intPassengers.ToString() & _
      " MPG: " & sngMPG.ToString()
  Return str
End Function
```

Our `ToString` method must be declared `Public` because `ToString` has already been given public visibility in the `Object` class. The `ToString` implementation shown here returns a string showing a vehicle's number of passengers and the miles-per-gallon. When a method is declared with the `Overrides` keyword, it is also implicitly declared as `Overridable`. So, we can override this `ToString` method in the `Truck` class, as follows:

```
Public Overrides Function ToString() As String
  ' Return a string representation
  ' of a truck.
  Dim str As String
  str = MyBase.ToString() & " Max. Cargo: " & _
      sngCargoWeight.ToString() & " 4WD: " & _
      blnFourWheelDrive.ToString()
  Return str
End Function
```

This method calls `MyBase.ToString`, which is the `Vehicle` class's `ToString` method. To that method's return value, it appends string versions of the `sngCargoWeight` and `blnFourWheelDrive` variables. The resulting string is then returned. The following statements, located in a separate class, create a `Truck` object, assign values to its properties, and call the `ToString` method:

```
Dim bigTruck As New Truck
bigTruck.Passengers = 2
bigTruck.MilesPerGallon = 14
bigTruck.MaxCargoWeight = 8000
bigTruck.FourWheelDrive = True
MessageBox.Show(bigTruck.ToString())
```

This code will display the following string in a message box:

```
Passengers: 2 MPG: 14 Max. Cargo: 8000 4WD: True
```

Base Class and Derived Class Constructors

Earlier in this chapter, you learned that a constructor is a special class method named `New`, and the constructor is automatically called when an instance of the class is created. It is possible for both a base class and a derived class to have constructors. For example, look at the following abbreviated versions of the `Vehicle` and `Truck` classes containing constructors:

```
Public Class Vehicle

  Public Sub New()
    MessageBox.Show("This is the base class constructor.")
  End Sub
  ' (other properties and methods...)
End Class

Public Class Truck
  Inherits Vehicle

  Public Sub New()
    MessageBox.Show("This is the derived class constructor.")
  End Sub
  ' (other properties and methods...)
End Class
```

When an instance of the derived class is created, the base class constructor is automatically called first and then the derived class constructor is called. So, creating an instance of the `Truck` class will cause the message *This is the base class constructor* to be displayed, followed by the message *This is the derived class constructor*.

NOTE: The `Overridable` and `Overrrides` keywords are not used with constructors.

Protected Members

In addition to `Private` and `Public`, we will also study the `Protected` access specifier. The **`Protected` access specifier** may be used in the declaration of a base class member, such as the following:

```
Protected decCost As Decimal
```

This statement declares a protected variable named `decCost`. Protected base class members are like private members, except they may be accessed by methods and property procedures in derived classes. To all other classes, however, protected class members are just like private class members.

In Tutorial 12-5, you complete an application that uses inheritance.

Tutorial 12-5:
Completing an application that uses inheritance

In this tutorial, you will complete an application that keeps records about the number of course hours completed by computer science students. You will create a class named `GeneralStudent`, which will have properties to hold the following data: first name, last name, ID number, math hours completed, communications hours completed, humanities hours completed, elective hours completed, and total hours completed. This class will have a method named `UpdateHours` that will calculate the total hours completed when any of the other hours are changed. In addition, the class will override the `ToString` method.

You will also create a class named `CsStudent`, derived from the `GeneralStudent` class. The `CsStudent` class will have a property to hold the number of computer science hours completed. This class will override the `General Student` class's `UpdateHours` method to add the number of computer science hours.

Step 1: Open the Computer Science Student project from the Chapter 12 student sample programs folder. The forms have already been built for you. Figure 12-13 shows the `frmMain` form and Figure 12-14 shows the `frmDisplayStudents` form.

Figure 12-13 `frmMain` form

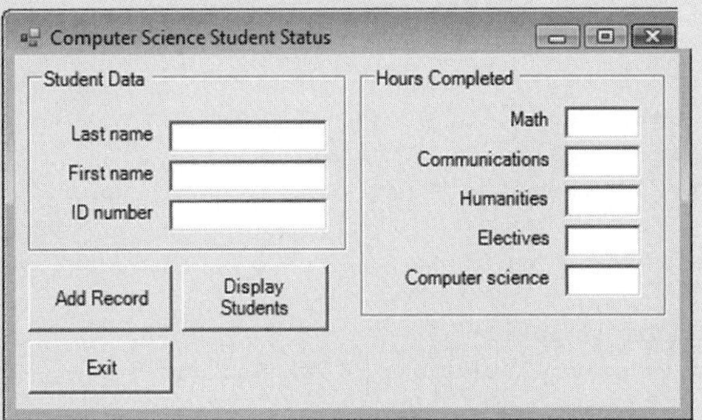

Figure 12-14 `frmDisplayStudents` form

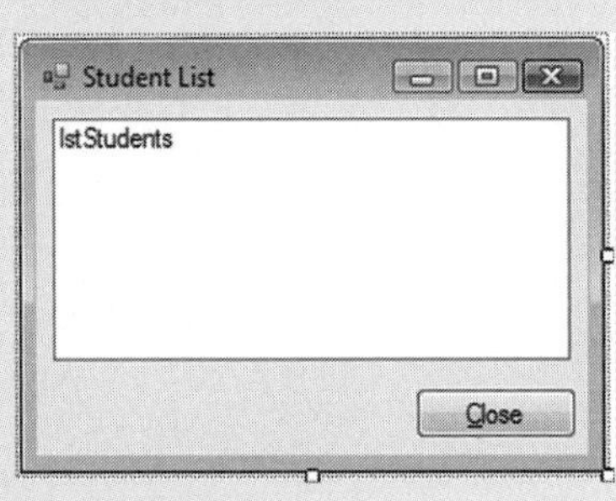

Step 2: Add a new class named `GeneralStudent` to the project. The code for the class follows:

```
Public Class GeneralStudent
  Private strLastName As String
  Private strFirstName As String
  Private strIdNum As String
  Private sngMathHours As Single     ' Math hours completed
  Private sngCommHours As Single     ' Communications hours
                                     ' completed
  Private sngHumHours As Single      ' Humanities hours
                                     ' completed
  Private sngElectHours As Single    ' Elective hours completed
  Protected sngTotalHours As Single  ' Total Hours completed

  Public Sub New()
  ' Initialize the private member variables.
    strLastName = "(Unknown)"
    strFirstName = "(Unknown)"
    strIdNum = "(Unknown)"
    sngMathHours = 0
    sngCommHours = 0
    sngHumHours = 0
    sngElectHours = 0
    sngTotalHours = 0
  End Sub

  Public Overridable Sub UpdateHours()

    ' Update the hours completed.
    sngTotalHours = sngMathHours + sngCommHours _
        + sngHumHours + sngElectHours
  End Sub

  ' Last Name property
  Public Property LastName() As String
    Get
      Return strLastName
    End Get
    Set(ByVal value As String)
      strLastName = value
    End Set
  End Property

  ' First name property
  Public Property FirstName() As String
    Get
      Return strFirstName
    End Get
    Set(ByVal value As String)
      strFirstName = value
    End Set
  End Property

  ' IdNumber property
  Public Property IdNumber() As String
    Get
      Return strIdNum
    End Get
```

```
    Set(ByVal value As String)
      strIdNum = value
    End Set
  End Property

  ' MathHours property
  Public Property MathHours() As Single
    Get
      Return sngMathHours
    End Get
    Set(ByVal value As Single)
      sngMathHours = value
      UpdateHours()
    End Set
  End Property

  ' CommunicationsHours property
  Public Property CommunicationsHours() As Single
    Get
      Return sngCommHours
    End Get
    Set(ByVal value As Single)
      sngCommHours = value
      UpdateHours()
    End Set
  End Property

  ' HumanitiesHours property
  Public Property HumanitiesHours() As Single
    Get
      Return sngHumHours
    End Get
    Set(ByVal value As Single)
      sngHumHours = value
      UpdateHours()
    End Set
  End Property

  ' ElectiveHours property
  Public Property ElectiveHours() As Single
    Get
      Return sngElectHours
    End Get
    Set(ByVal value As Single)
      sngElectHours = value
      UpdateHours()
    End Set
  End Property

  ' HoursCompleted property (read-only)
  Public ReadOnly Property HoursCompleted() As Single
    Get
      Return sngTotalHours
    End Get
  End Property

  ' Overridden ToString method
  Public Overrides Function ToString() As String
```

```
        Dim str As String
        str = "Name: " & strLastName & ", "_
            & strFirstName & " Completed Hours: " _
            & sngTotalHours.ToString()
        Return str
    End Function
End Class
```

Step 3: Add another class named `CsStudent` to the project. This class will be derived from the `GeneralStudent` class. The code for the class follows:

```
Public Class CsStudent
    Inherits GeneralStudent

    ' Private member variables
    Private sngCompSciHours As Single' CS hours completed

    Public Sub New()
        sngCompSciHours = 0
    End Sub

    ' Overridden UpdateHours method
    Public Overrides Sub UpdateHours()
        MyBase.UpdateHours()
        sngTotalHours += sngCompSciHours
    End Sub

    ' CSHours property
    Public Property CompSciHours() As Single
        Get
            Return sngCompSciHours
        End Get
        Set(ByVal value As Single)
            sngCompSciHours = value
            UpdateHours()
        End Set
    End Property
End Class
```

Step 4: Add a standard module named `ComputerScienceStudentModule` to the project. This module will declare a global object variable named `g_csStudentCollection`, which will reference a collection of `CsStudent` objects. The code for the module follows:

```
Module ComputerScienceStudentModule

    ' Module-level declaration
    Public g_csStudentCollection As Collection
End Module
```

Step 5: Now you will write the event procedures and Sub procedures for the `frmMain` form. First, write the form's `Load` event procedure, which creates the collection. The code follows:

```
Private Sub frmMain_Load(ByVal sender As System.Object, _
   ByVal e As System.EventArgs) Handles MyBase.Load

    ' Create the collection.
    g_csStudentCollection = New Collection()
End Sub
```

Step 6: Next, write the `btnAdd_Click` event procedure, the `GetData` method, the `AddStudent` method, and the `ClearForm` method. The code follows:

```
Private Sub btnAdd_Click(ByVal sender As System.Object, _
    ByVal e As System.EventArgs) Handles btnAdd.Click

  ' Add the data entered on the form to the collection.
  ' Perform only minimal error checking, to prevent a
  ' program crash if the user enters invalid data.
  Try
    Dim csData As CsStudent
    csData = New CsStudent()
    GetData(csData)
    AddStudent(csData)
    ClearForm()
    csData = Nothing
    MessageBox.Show("Student record added successfully")
  Catch ex As Exception
    MessageBox.Show(ex.Message, "User Input Error")
  End Try
End Sub

Private Sub GetData(ByVal csData As CsStudent)

  ' Get the data from the form.
  csData.LastName = txtLastName.Text
  csData.FirstName = txtFirstName.Text
  csData.IdNumber = txtIdNumber.Text
  Single.TryParse(txtMath.Text, csData.MathHours)
  Single.TryParse(txtComm.Text, csData.CommunicationsHours)
  Single.TryParse(txtHum.Text, csData.HumanitiesHours)
  Single.TryParse(txtElect.Text, csData.ElectiveHours)
  Single.TryParse(txtCompSci.Text, csData.CompSciHours)
End Sub

Private Sub AddStudent(ByVal csData As CsStudent)
  ' Add a CsStudent object to the collection and use
  ' the IdNumber property as the key.
  Try
    g_csStudentCollection.Add(csData, csData.IdNumber)
  Catch ex As Exception
    MessageBox.Show(ex.Message)
  End Try
End Sub

Private Sub ClearForm()
  ' Clear the form.
  txtLastName.Clear()
  txtFirstName.Clear()
  txtIdNumber.Clear()
  txtMath.Clear()
  txtComm.Clear()
  txtHum.Clear()
  txtElect.Clear()
  txtCompSci.Clear()
  ' Set the focus.
  txtLastName.Focus()
End Sub
```

Step 7: Write the `btnDisplay_Click` and `btnExit_Click` event procedures. The code follows:

```
Private Sub btnDisplay_Click(ByVal sender As System.Object, _
      ByVal e As System.EventArgs) Handles btnDisplay.Click

   ' Display a form showing all the students
   ' in the collection.
   Dim displayForm As New frmDisplayStudents()
   displayForm.ShowDialog()
End Sub

Private Sub btnExit_Click(ByVal sender As System.Object, _
      ByVal e As System.EventArgs) Handles btnExit.Click

   Me.Close()
End Sub
```

Step 8: Next, you will write the code for the `frmDisplayStudents` form. This form has only two event procedures: `frmDisplayStudents_Load`, and `btnClose_Click`. The code follows:

```
Private Sub frmDisplayStudents_Load(ByVal sender As _
      System.Object, ByVal e As System.EventArgs) _
      Handles MyBase.Load
   Dim cs As CsStudent

   For Each cs In g_csStudentCollection
      lstStudents.Items.Add(cs.ToString())
   Next
End Sub

Private Sub btnClose_Click(ByVal sender As System.Object, _
      ByVal e As System.EventArgs) Handles btnClose.Click

   ' Close this form.
   Me.Close()
End Sub
```

Step 9: Save the project and run the application. On the main form, add data for a fictitious student, and then click the *Add Record* button. Repeat this for at least two more students. Click the *Display Students* button to see a list of the students you have added. Figure 12-15 shows an example.

Figure 12-15 *Student List* displayed

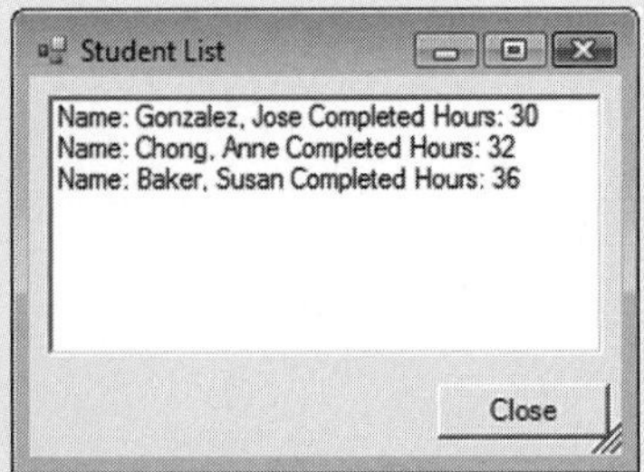

Step 10: Click the *Close* button and end the application.

Checkpoint

12.25 The beginning of a class declaration follows. What is the name of the base class, and what is the name of the derived class?

```
Public Class Fly
  Inherits Insect
```

12.26 What does a derived class inherit from its base class?

12.27 What is overriding, when speaking of class declarations?

12.28 What keyword must you include in the declaration of a property procedure or method in order for it to be overridden in a derived class?

12.29 What keyword must you include in the declaration of a property procedure or method in order for it to override one that exists in the base class?

12.30 When both a base class and its derived class have a constructor, which constructor executes first?

12.31 What is a protected base class member?

Summary

12.1 Classes and Objects

- Object-oriented programming is a way of designing and coding applications that allows interchangeable software components to be used to build larger programs.
- The primary goal of object-oriented design is to address the needs of the application or problem being solved. A secondary goal is to design classes that can outlive the current application and possibly be used in future programs.
- The class interface is the portion that is visible to the application programmer who uses the class. The program written by such a person is also called the client program, in reference to the client-server relationship between a class and the programs that use it.
- The class implementation is the portion of a class that is hidden from client programs; it is created from private member variables, private properties, and private methods.

12.2 Creating a Class

- The steps that must occur when an instance of a class is created are (1) declare an object variable and (2) create an instance of the class in memory and assign its address to the object variable. Each instance of a class has its own unique copy of the class's member variables.
- Members, properties, and methods of a class object are accessed with the dot (.) operator.
- Properties are generally implemented as property procedures. A property procedure is a function that behaves like a property. Property procedures have two sections: `Get` and `Set`. The `Get` section is executed when the value of the property is retrieved. The `Set` section is executed when a value is stored in the property. A read-only property cannot be set by a client program. It is implemented as a property procedure declared with the `ReadOnly` keyword, and does not have a `Set` section.
- To remove an object, set all the object variables that reference it to `Nothing`; it will be removed from memory by the .NET garbage collector.
- An object variable declared inside a procedure is local to that procedure. If an object is referenced only by a procedure's local object variable, the object is automatically removed from memory by the garbage collector after the procedure ends.
- The `Is` and `IsNot` operators compare two object variables to determine if they reference the same object.
- You can create arrays of objects, and you can write Sub procedures and functions that work with arrays of objects.
- A method is a Sub procedure or function that is a member of a class. The method performs some operation on the data stored in the class. You write methods inside the class declaration.
- A constructor is a class method that is automatically called when an instance of the class is created. Constructors are useful for initializing member variables or performing other startup operations. To create a constructor, create a Sub procedure named `New` in the class.
- A finalizer is a class method named `Finalize`, which is automatically called just before an instance of the class is removed from memory.
- Use the *Add Existing Item* dialog box to add an existing class to a project.

12.3 Collections

- A collection is a structure that holds a group of items. It automatically expands and shrinks to accommodate the items added to it, and allows items to be stored with an associated key value, which may be used when searching for collection members.
- The Count property indicates the number of items stored in a collection. The `Add` method stores an item in a collection. The `Item` method finds and returns an object in a collection. The `Remove` method is used to remove an item from a collection.

12.4 Focus on Problem Solving: Creating the *Student Collection* Application

- Tutorial 12-2 develops an application that builds a collection of students and allows the user to select a student's ID number from a list box to view information about the student.

12.5 The Object Browser

- The Object Browser displays information about the classes, properties, methods, and events available to a project.

12.6 Focus on GUI Design: Scroll Bars and Track Bars

- The HScrollBar, VScrollBar, and TrackBar controls provide a graphical way to adjust a number within a range of values.

12.7 Introduction to Inheritance

- Inheritance allows you to create new classes that inherit, or derive, characteristics of existing classes. In an inheritance relationship, there is a base class and a derived class. The base class can be thought of as the parent and the derived class as the child.
- Sometimes a property procedure or method in a base class does not work adequately for a derived class. When this happens, you can override the base class property procedure or method by writing one with the same name in the derived class.
- You must use the `Overridable` keyword in the declaration of a method or property procedure in a base class that is to be overridden. You must use the `Overrides` keyword in the declaration of a method or property procedure in a derived class that overrides another one in the base class.
- Every class that you create in Visual Basic is automatically derived from a built-in class named `Object`. The `Object` class has a method named `ToString` thatreturns a fully qualified class name. You can override this method so it returns a string representation of the data stored in a class.
- It is possible for both a base class and a derived class to have constructors. When an instance of the derived class is created, the base class constructor is called before the derived class constructor.
- Protected base class members are like private members, except they may be accessed by methods and property procedures in derived classes. To all other classes, however, protected class members are just like private class members.

Key Terms

abstract data type (ADT)
abstraction
`Add` method
attributes
base class
class
class declaration
class implementation
class interface
class objects
client program
collection
constructor
derived class
encapsulation
finalizer
finding the classes
Friend access
garbage collector
`Get` section
going out of scope
HScrollBar control
inheritance
`Is` operator
`IsNot` operator
`Item` method
`LargeChange` property
Maximum property
member variable
method
Minimum property
`MyBase` keyword
object
Object Browser
`Object` class
object-oriented analysis
object-oriented programming (OOP)
operations
Output window
`Overridable` keyword
override
`Overrides` keyword
property procedure
`Protected` access specifier
read-only property
`Remove` method
scrollable controls
`Set` section
SmallChange property
TickFrequency property
TrackBar control
Value property
VScrollBar control

Review Questions and Exercises

Fill-in-the-Blank

1. A(n) _______________ is a data type created by a programmer.
2. A(n) _______________ is a program structure that defines an abstract data type.
3. An object is a(n) _______________ of a class.
4. The _______________ is the portion of a class that is visible to the client program that uses the class.
5. The _______________ is the portion of a class that is hidden from client programs.
6. A(n) _______________ procedure is a function that behaves like a class property.
7. The _______________ section of a Property procedure is executed when a client program retrieves the value of a property.
8. The _______________ section of a Property procedure executes when a client program stores a value in a property.
9. A(n) _______________ property cannot be set by a client program.
10. A(n) _______________ is a Sub procedure or function that is a member of the class.

11. A(n) _______________ is a class method that is automatically called when an instance of the class is created.
12. A(n) _______________ is a class method that is automatically called just before an instance of the class is removed from memory.
13. You can display messages for debugging purposes in the _______________ window.
14. A(n) _______________ is a structure that holds a group of items.
15. The _______________ window displays information about the classes, properties, methods, and events available to a project.
16. _______________ is an object-oriented programming feature that allows you to create new classes that derive characteristics of existing classes.
17. A(n) _______________ class is a general-purpose class on which other classes may be based.
18. A(n) _______________ class is based on another class, and inherits characteristics from it.
19. You can _______________ a base class property procedure or method by writing one with the same name in a derived class.
20. _______________ base class members are like private members, except that they may be accessed by methods and property procedures in derived classes.
21. Visual Basic _______________ methods allow you to share data with other Windows applications.

Multiple Choice

1. Which of the following program structures defines an abstract data type?
   a. Variable
   b. Exception
   c. Class
   d. Class object
2. If the variable `status` is declared inside a class, which of the following describes `status`?
   a. Global variable
   b. Constructor
   c. Finalizer
   d. Member variable
3. An object is automatically released when all references to it are set to which of the following?
   a. Nothing
   b. Empty
   c. Clear
   d. Done
4. This section of a property procedure returns the value of the property.
   a. Value
   b. Property
   c. Get
   d. Set

5. This section of a property procedure stores a value of the property.
   a. `Value`
   b. `Property`
   c. `Get`
   d. `Set`
6. A class constructor is a Sub procedure by this name.
   a. `New`
   b. `Constructor`
   c. `Finalizer`
   d. `Main`
7. A class finalizer is a Sub procedure by this name.
   a. `New`
   b. `Finalizer`
   c. `Finalize`
   d. `Main`
8. Which section is missing from a read-only property procedure?
   a. `Get`
   b. `Set`
   c. `Store`
   d. `Save`
9. This process runs periodically to free the memory used by all unreferenced objects.
   a. Garbage collector
   b. Memory collector
   c. Housekeeper
   d. RAM dumper
10. You must use this operator to determine whether two object variables reference the same object.
    a. `=`
    b. `<>`
    c. `Is`
    d. `Equal`
11. Which method is used to store an item in a collection?
    a. `Store`
    b. `Insert`
    c. `Add`
    d. `Collect`
12. Which method is used to search for an item in a collection?
    a. `Find`
    b. `Item`
    c. `Search`
    d. `Member`
13. Which method removes an item from a collection?
    a. `Remove`
    b. `Item`
    c. `Delete`
    d. `Erase`

14. Which property indicates the number of items stored in a collection?
    a. Items
    b. Number
    c. Count
    d. Members
15. Which of the following displays information about the classes, properties, methods, and events available to a project?
    a. Object Browser
    b. Object Navigator
    c. Class Browser
    d. Class Resource List
16. Which property sets the amount by which the Value property changes when the user clicks the scroll bar area around a slider?
    a. LargeChange
    b. SmallChange
    c. UnitChange
    d. ValueChange
17. Which property sets the amount by which the Value property changes when the user clicks one of the scroll arrows at either end of the scroll bar?
    a. LargeChange
    b. SmallChange
    c. UnitChange
    d. ValueChange
18. Which event occurs when a scrollable control's slider changes to a new position?
    a. `Scroll`
    b. `Update`
    c. `Increment`
    d. `Change`
19. In an inheritance relationship, which class is usually a generalized class from which other, more specialized, classes are derived?
    a. Derived
    b. Base
    c. Protected
    d. Public
20. Which type of class member is not visible to derived classes?
    a. Private
    b. Public
    c. Protected
    d. ReadOnly
21. Which keyword indicates that the procedure may be overridden in a derived class?
    a. `Private`
    b. `Overrides`
    c. `Public`
    d. `Overridable`

22. Which keyword indicates that a procedure in a derived class overrides a procedure in the base class?
    a. `Private`
    b. `Overrides`
    c. `Public`
    d. `Overridable`
23. When used in a derived class, which keyword refers to the base class?
    a. `BaseClass`
    b. `Base`
    c. `MyBase`
    d. `Parent`
24. Every class in Visual Basic is derived from a built-in class having which of the following names?
    a. `Object`
    b. `SuperClass`
    c. `Parent`
    d. `System`
25. Class members declared with this access specifier are like private members, except that they may be accessed by methods and property procedures in derived classes.
    a. `Special`
    b. `Secret`
    c. `Public`
    d. `Protected`

True or False

Indicate whether the following statements are true or false.

1. T F: Public properties are part of the class interface.
2. T F: Private member variables are part of the class interface.
3. T F: A class's `New` procedure must be called from a client program.
4. T F: A class method may be either a procedure or a function.
5. T F: A runtime error will occur when you attempt to add a member with the same key to a collection as an existing member.
6. T F: You can use both the `Before` and `After` arguments of a collection's `Add` method at the same time.
7. T F: When retrieving an item from a collection, if the item is of the Integer data type, you can retrieve only a copy of the member.
8. T F: By default, a vertical scroll bar is at its minimum value when the slider is at the bottom and is at its maximum value when the slider is at the top.
9. T F: The Object Browser does not display information about the standard Visual Basic controls.
10. T F: If you attempt to retrieve an item from a collection and specify a nonexistent index, a runtime error is generated.
11. T F: A private property or method cannot be overridden.
12. T F: The `ToString` method cannot be overridden.
13. T F: Protected base class members cannot be accessed by derived classes.

Short Answer

1. How is a class interface created in Visual Basic?
2. What is encapsulation?
3. In the statement `Dim newStudent As Student`, which is the class and which is the object variable?
4. How do you create a read-only property?
5. How is an object different from a class?
6. Do the icons in the Visual Studio Toolbox represent classes or objects?
7. How are properties different from methods?
8. What is the difference between retrieving a collection item that is of a fundamental Visual Basic data type and retrieving one that is a class object?
9. What is encapsulation?
10. What happens to an object created inside a procedure when the procedure finishes?
11. Suppose class A has the following members:

    Private member variable `x`
    Public member variable `y`
    Public property `Data`
    Protected method `UpdateData`

    Suppose also that class B is derived from class A. Which of class A's members are inherited by class B?
12. When a property procedure or method in a base class is not appropriate for a derived class, what can you do?
13. Suppose class B is derived from class A. Class A's `UpdateData` method has been overridden in class B. How can the `UpdateData` method in class B call the `UpdateData` method in class A?

What Do You Think?

1. Suppose that when developing an application, you create a class named `BankAccount` and you declare an object variable of the `BankAccount` type named `checking`. Which is the abstract data type, `BankAccount` or `checking`?
2. Look at the following problem description and identify the potential classes.

    We need to keep a list of customers and record our business transactions with them. Each time a customer purchases a product, an order is filled out. Each order shows a list of items kept in our central warehouse.
3. Does each button on the same form have its own copy of the Visible property?
4. In a student record-keeping program, what attributes might be assigned to a college transcript class?
5. Why are member variables usually declared `Private` in classes?
6. At the end of the following example, how many `Student` objects exist?

```
Dim st1 As New Student
Dim st2 As Student
st2 = st1
```

7. At the end of the following example, how many `Student` objects exist?

```
Dim st1 As New Student
Dim st2 As Student
st2 = st1
st1 = Nothing
```

8. Suppose that an application at an animal hospital uses two classes: `Mammal` and `Dog`. Which do you think is the base class and which is the derived class? Why?
9. Why does it make sense that you cannot use the `Overridable` keyword in a private base class member declaration?

Find the Error

For each of the following questions assume `Customer` is a class. Find the errors.

1.
```
Dim Customer as New customerData
```
2.
```
Dim customerData as Customer
customerData.LastName = "Smith"
```
3.
```
customerData = Nothing
customerData.LastName = "Smith"
```
4.
```
Public Property LastName() As String
    Set
      Return lname
    End Get
    Get(ByVal value As String)
      lname = value
    End Set
End Property
```
5.
```
Dim customerCollection as Collection
customerCollection.Add customerData
```
6. The following code appears in a base class:
```
Private Overridable Function GetData() As Integer
    Statements
End Sub
```
The following code appears in a derived class:
```
' This function overrides the base class function.
Public Function GetData() As Integer
    Statements
End Sub
```

Algorithm Workbench

1. Suppose that an application declares an array of objects with the following statement:
```
Dim employees(9) As Employee
```
Write a loop that creates ten instances of the class and assigns them to the elements of the array.
2. Code a `Dim` statement that declares an object variable of the class type `Transcript`. The statement should not create an instance of the class.
3. Code a statement that creates a `Transcript` object and assigns it to the variable from Question 2.

4. Code a statement that removes the reference used by the object variable used in Questions 2 and 3.

5. Code a single statement that declares an object variable and creates a new instance of the `Transcript` class.

6. Write the property procedures for a property named CustomerNumber that assigns a string value to a member variable named `strCustomerNumber`.

7. Look at the following code for the `Book` class:

```
Public Class Book
  ' Private member variables
  Private strTitle As String
  Private strAuthor As String
  Private strPublisher As String
  Private strIsbn As String

' Constructor
Public Sub New()
  strTitle = String.Empty
  strAuthor = String.Empty
  strPublisher = String.Empty
  strIsbn = String.Empty
End Sub

' Title Property
Public Property Title() As String
  Get
    Return strTitle
  End Get
  Set(ByVal value As String)
    strTitle = value
  End Set
End Property

' Author property
Public Property Author() As String
  Get
    Return strAuthor
  End Get
  Set(ByVal value As String)
    strAuthor = value
  End Set
End Property

' Publisher property
  Public Property Publisher() As String
    Get
      Return strPublisher
    End Get
    Set(ByVal value As String)
      strPublisher = value
    End Set
  End Property
```

```
    ' Isbn property
    Public Property Isbn() As String
      Get
        Return strIsbn
      End Get
      Set(ByVal value As String)
        strIsbn = value
      End Set
    End Property
  End Class
```

Design a class named `TextBook` that is derived from the `Book` class. The `TextBook` class should have the following properties:

- Course (string). This property holds the name of the course that the textbook is used for.
- OrderQuantity (integer). This property holds the number of books to order for the course.

The OrderQuantity property cannot be negative, so provide error checking in the property procedure.

Programming Challenges

1. **E-Mail Address Book**

   Write a program that lets the user display and modify an address book containing names, e-mail addresses, and phone numbers. The program should contain a class named `Address`. The `Address` class should contain the following information about one person: name, e-mail address, phone, and comments. The application should also have a collection named `addressList`, which stores a collection of `Address` objects.

   The main window, shown in Figure 12-16, displays the names from the address book in a list box. The user should be able to input new names and addresses, using a form similar to the one shown in Figure 12-17.

2. **Carpet Price Calculator**

   The Westfield Carpet Company has asked you to write an application that calculates the price of carpeting. To calculate the price of a carpeting, you multiply the

Figure 12-16 *E-mail Address Book* form

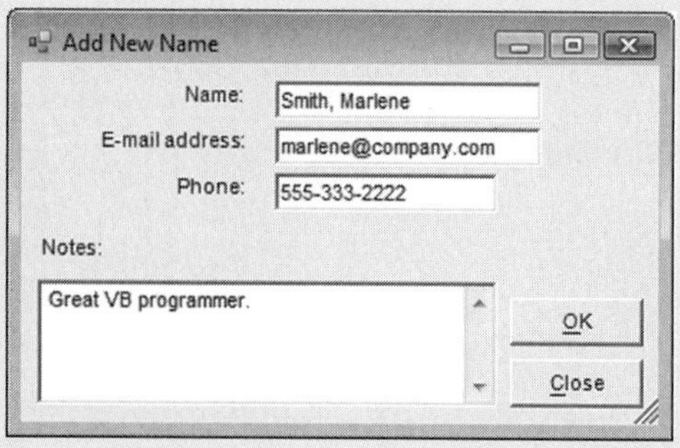

Figure 12-17 *Add New Name* form

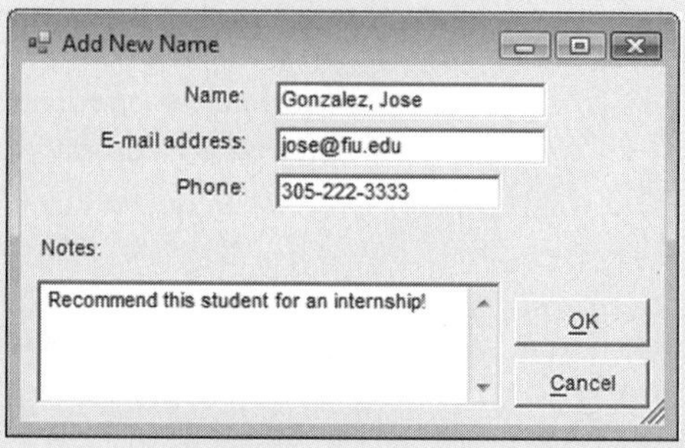

area of the floor (width × length) by the price per square foot of carpet. For example, the area of a floor that is 12 feet long and 10 feet wide is 120 feet. To cover that floor with carpet that costs $8 per square foot would cost $960.

You should create a class named `Rectangle` with the following properties:

Width: A single
Length: A single
Area: A single

The Area property should be read-only. Provide a method named `CalcArea` that calculates width × length and stores the result in the Area property.

Next, create a class named `Carpet` with the following properties:

Color: A string
Style: A string
Price: A decimal

The application should have a form similar to the one shown in Figure 12-18. (The carpet price is the price per square foot.) When the *Calculate* button is clicked, the application should copy the data in the text boxes into the appropriate object properties, and then display the area and price.

Figure 12-18 *Carpet Price Calculator* form

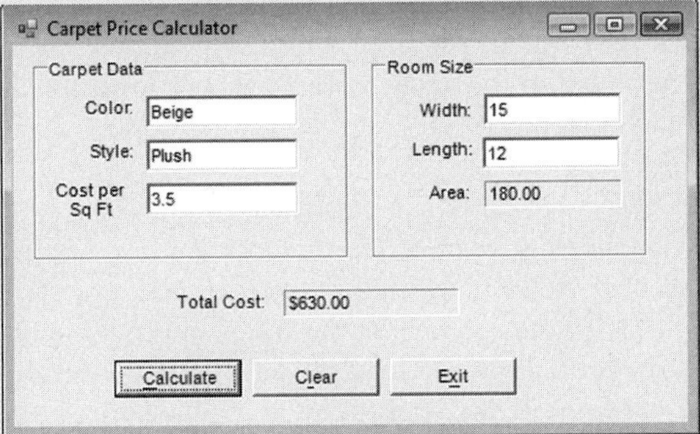

VideoNote The Scrollable Tax Calculator Problem

3. Scrollable Tax Calculator

Create an application that allows you to enter the amount of a purchase, and then displays the amount of sales tax on that purchase. Use a scrollable control such as a scroll bar or a track bar to adjust the tax rate between 0% and 10%. The form should appear similar to the one shown in Figure 12-19.

Figure 12-19 *Scrollable Tax Calculator* form

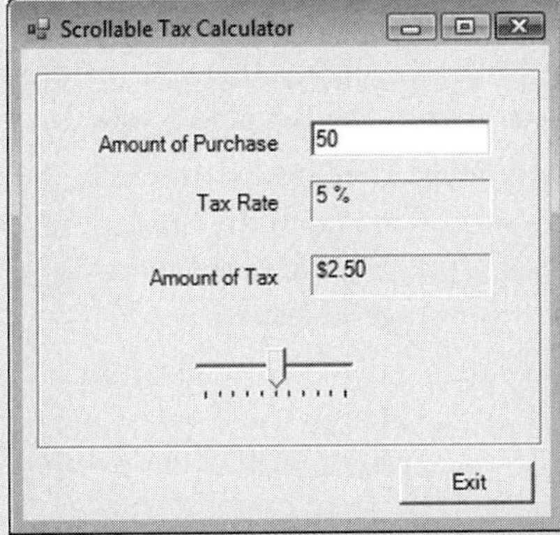

Design Your Own Forms

4. **Saving the Student Collection**

   Modify the student collection application from this chapter so it saves the collection in a file or a database before the program exits. When the program starts up, load the collection from the file or database.

5. **Motor Class**

   Create an application that tracks electric motors in a manufacturing plant. The application should have a Motor class with the following properties:

   - MotorId: Five-digit string, such as `"02340"`
   - Description: String
   - RPM: Single, values in the range 10 to 10000
   - Voltage: Single, values in the range 1 to 500
   - Status: String, three characters.

   The Status values are:

   - ON: Motor is online and running.
   - OFF: Motor is online but not running.
   - MNT: Motor is undergoing maintenance and cleaning.
   - NA: Motor is not available.

   The application should be able to store at least 10 Motor class objects in an array. Create an input form in the application that allows users to input new motor records to be added to the array. Create another form that displays all the motors in the array in a list box.

6. **MotorCollection Class**

   Modify the application you created in Programming Challenge 5 so it uses a collection instead of an array to hold the `Motor` class objects. When the application ends, it should save the contents of the collection to a file or a database. When the application starts up, it should load the data from the file or database into the collection. Be sure to write the appropriate error handlers.

7. **Account Class**

   You are a programmer for the Home Software Company. You have been assigned to develop a class that models the basic workings of a bank account. The class should have the following properties:

   - Balance: Holds the current account balance.
   - IntRate: Holds the interest rate for the period.
   - Interest: Holds the interest earned for the current period.
   - Transactions: Holds the number of transactions for the current period.

   The class should also have the following methods:

   `MakeDeposit` Takes an argument, which is the amount of the deposit. This argument is added to the Balance property.

   `Withdraw` Takes an argument that is the amount of the withdrawal. This value is subtracted from the Balance property, unless the withdrawal amount is greater than the balance. If this happens, an error message is displayed.

   `CalcInterest` This method calculates the amount of interest for the current period, stores this value in the Interest property, and adds it to the Balance property.

Demonstrate the class in an application that performs the following tasks:

- Allows deposits to be made to the account.
- Allows withdrawals to be taken from the account.
- Calculates interest for the period.
- Reports the current account balance at any time.
- Reports the current number of transactions at any time.

8. Inventory Item Class

Create an application that stores inventory records for a retail store. The application should have an `Inventory` class with the following properties:

InvNumber: A string used to hold an inventory number. Each item in the inventory should have a unique inventory number.

Description: A string that holds a brief description of the item.

Cost: A decimal value that holds the amount that the retail store paid for the item.

Retail: A decimal value that holds the retail price for the item.

OnHand: An integer value that holds the number of items on hand. This value cannot be less than 0.

The application should store `Inventory` class objects in a collection. Create an input form in the application that allows users to input new inventory items to be added to the collection. The user should also be able to look up items by their inventory number.

9. Inventory Class Modification

Modify the application you created in Programming Challenge 8 so it saves the contents of the collection to a file or a database. When the application starts up, it should load the data from the file or database into the collection. Be sure to use exception handling.

10. Cash Register

Create an application that serves as a simple cash register for a retail store. Use the `Inventory` class you created in Programming Challenge 8 to store data about the items in the store's inventory. When the application starts up, it should load the entire store's inventory from a file or a database into a collection of `Inventory` objects.

When a purchase is made, the cashier should select an item from a list box. (If an item's OnHand property is set to zero, the item should not be available in the list box.) The item's description, retail price, and number of units on hand should be displayed on the form when selected. The cashier should enter the quantity being purchased, and the application should display the sales tax and the total of the sale. (The quantity being purchased cannot exceed the number of units on hand.) The quantity being purchased should be subtracted from the item's OnHand property. When the application ends, the contents of the collection should be saved to the file or database.

11. Design a Base Class

Begin a new project named *Customer Information*, and design a class named `Person` with the following properties:

- LastName (string)
- FirstName (string)
- Address (string)

- City (string)
- State (string)
- Zip (string)
- Phone (string)

Implement the properties as public property procedures.

Create a form that allows you to store data in each property of a `Person` object.

12. **Design a Derived `Customer` Class**

Open the *Customer Information* project you created in Programming Challenge 2. Design a new class named `Customer`, which is derived from the `Person` class. The `Customer` class should have the following properties:

- CustomerNumber (integer)
- MailingList (Boolean)
- Comments (String)

The CustomerNumber property will be used to hold a unique number for each customer. The Mailing List property will be set to *True* if the customer wishes to be on a mailing list, or *False* if the customer does not wish to be on a mailing list. The comments property holds miscellaneous comments about the customer.

Modify the form so that it allows you to store data in each property of a `Customer` object. To enter the customer comments, use a TextBox control with its Multiline and WordWrap properties set to *True*.

13. **Design a Derived `PreferredCustomer` Class**

A retail store has a preferred customer plan where customers may earn discounts on all their purchases. The amount of a customer's discount is determined by the amount of the customer's cumulative purchases in the store.

- When a preferred customer spends $500, he or she gets a 5% discount on all future purchases.
- When a preferred customer spends $1000, he or she gets a 6% discount on all future purchases.
- When a preferred customer spends $1500, he or she gets a 7% discount on all future purchases.
- When a preferred customer spends $2000 or more, he or she gets a 10% discount on all future purchases.

Open the *Customer Information* project that you modified in Programming Challenge 3. Design a new class named `PreferredCustomer`, which is derived from the `Customer` class. The `PreferredCustomer` class should have the following properties:

- PurchasesAmount (decimal)
- DiscountLevel (single)

Modify the application's form so it allows you to store data in each property of a `PreferredCustomer` object. Add the object to a collection, using the customer number as a key. Allow the user to look up a preferred customer by the customer number, edit the customer data, and remove a customer from the collection.

APPENDIX A

User Interface Design Guidelines

When developing an application, you should carefully plan the design of its user interface. A correctly designed user interface should be simple, self-explanatory, and without distracting features. This appendix covers several important areas of user interface design.

Adhere to Windows Standards

The users of your application are probably experienced with other Windows applications. They will expect your application to provide the features and exhibit the behavior that is common to all Windows applications. The guidelines provided here cover many of the Windows standards. Additionally, you should carefully study applications such as Microsoft Word and Microsoft Excel to observe their forms, menus, controls, and behavior. Microsoft offers an excellent publication called *Windows XP Visual Guidelines*, which you can download at www.microsoft.com.

Provide a Menu System

Avoid using too many buttons on a form. If an application provides many commands or operations for the user to choose from, place them in a menu system. Of course, an application that uses a menu system will have some menus and menu commands that are unique to that application. However, there are many menu commands that are common to most, if not all, applications. Windows applications that use a menu system normally have the following standard menus:

- **File menu commands.** *New*, *Open*, *Close*, *Save*, *Save As*, *Print*, and *Exit*
- **Edit menu commands.** *Copy*, *Cut*, *Paste*, and *Select All*. If an application provides searching capabilities, such as *Find* or *Replace* commands, they are typically found on the *Edit* menu.
- **Help menu commands.** *About*

Color

Use of color should be tailored to your audience. Business applications should use at most one or two colors, preferably subdued. Multimedia applications (such as Windows Media player) tend to be more colorful and use more graphics. In any event, it's a good idea to show your program to potential users and get their feedback. The color combinations that you consider attractive may not be appealing to others. The following are some general color usage guidelines for business applications:

- **Use dark text on a light background.** Combining certain colors for text and background makes the text difficult to read. Use dark colors for the text and light colors for the background. The contrast between dark and light colors makes the text easier to read.
- **Use predefined Windows colors.** Windows uses a predefined set of colors for forms, controls, text, and so on. These colors may be customized by the user. To ensure that your application conforms to a customized color scheme, you should use the predefined system colors. To find the system colors in the *Properties* window, select a color-related property such as *BackColor*. Then click the property's down-arrow button to display a pop-up list of colors. Select the *System* tab to display the system colors.
- **Avoid bright colors.** Bright colors are not recommended in business applications because they can distract the user and make the application appear cluttered and unprofessional. Additionally, many users have color-defective vision and cannot distinguish between certain colors.

Text

The use of nonstandard or multiple fonts can be distracting and makes your forms difficult to read. The following are some suggestions regarding font usage:

- **Use default fonts.** Windows XP uses Tahoma as the default font for text, Trebuchet MS for window title bars, and Franklin Gothic for text larger than 14 points. Avoid using italic and underlined styles, as they are less readable than plain fonts.
- **Use standard type sizes.** For ordinary text, Microsoft recommends 8, 9, or 11 point type. For window title bars, Microsoft recommends 10 point type.
- **Limit your exceptions to these rules.** If you insist on changing the font and/or font size, do so sparingly; do not use more than two fonts and two font sizes on a form.

Define a Logical Tab Order

Recall from Chapter 3 that a control's TabIndex property specifies the control's position in the tab order. The user expects the focus to shift logically when the [Tab] key is pressed. Typically, the control in the upper left corner of the form will be first in the tab order. The control that appears below it or next to it will be next. The tab order will continue in this fashion. If the focus shifts randomly around the form, a user may become confused and frustrated.

Assign Tool Tips

Recall from Chapter 5 that a tool tip is a small box that is displayed when you hold the mouse cursor over a control for a few seconds. The box gives a short description of what the button does. You can define tool tips for a form by creating a ToolTip control.

Provide Keyboard Access

Many users are proficient with the keyboard and can perform operations with it faster than with the mouse. For their convenience, you should develop your applications so they support both mouse and keyboard input. The following are some suggestions:

- **Use keyboard access keys.** Assign keyboard access keys to buttons, option buttons, check boxes, and menu items.
- **Assign a default button.** If a form uses buttons, you should always make the one that is most frequently clicked the default button. Do this by selecting that button as the form's AcceptButton. Recall from Chapter 3 that when a button is selected in a form's AcceptButton property, the button's `Click` event procedure is triggered when the user presses the [Enter] key while the form is active.
- **Assign a cancel button.** If a form has a cancel button, you should select it in the form's CancelButton property. Recall from Chapter 3 that when a button is selected in a form's CancelButton property, the button's `Click` event procedure is triggered when the user presses the [Esc] key while the form is active.

Group Controls

If a form has several controls, try to simplify the form's layout by grouping related controls inside group boxes. This visually divides the form's surface area into separate sections, making it more intuitive for the user.

Form Location

Use the form's Location property, which has two subproperties: X and Y, to position the form in the center of the screen.

Provide a Splash Screen

If your application takes a noticeable amount of time to load, provide a splash screen, which occupies the user's attention and provides reassurance that the application is loading properly.

APPENDIX

B Converting Mathematical Expressions to Programming Statements

In mathematical expressions, it is not always necessary to use an operator for multiplication. For example, the expression $2xy$ is understood to mean "2 times x times y." Visual Basic, however, requires an operator for any mathematical operation. Table B-1 shows some mathematical expressions that perform multiplication and the equivalent Visual Basic expression.

Table B-1 Math expressions in Visual Basic

Mathematical Expression	Operation	Visual Basic Equivalent
$6b$	6 times b	`6 * b`
(3)(12)	3 times 12	`3 * 12`
$4xy$	4 times x times y	`4 * x * y`

When converting mathematical expressions to Visual Basic programming statements, you may have to insert parentheses that do not appear in the mathematical expression. For example, look at the following expression:

$$x = \frac{a + b}{c}$$

To convert this to a Visual Basic statement, $a + b$ will have to be enclosed in parentheses:

```
x = (a + b) / c
```

Table B-2 shows more mathematical expressions and their Visual Basic equivalents.

Table B-2 More math expressions in Visual Basic

Mathematical Expression	Visual Basic Expression
$y = 3\dfrac{x}{2}$	`y = x / 2 * 3`
$z = 3bc + 4$	`z = 3 * b * c + 4`
$a = \dfrac{3x + 2}{4a - 1}$	`a = (3 * x + 2) / (4 * a - 1)`

APPENDIX C Answers to Checkpoints

Chapter 1

1.1 Central Processing Unit (CPU), main memory, secondary storage, input devices, and output devices

1.2 Main memory holds the sequences of instructions in the programs that are running and the data with which those programs are working. RAM is usually a volatile type of memory that is used only for temporary storage.

1.3 Program instructions and data are stored in main memory while the program is operating. Main memory is volatile and loses its content when power is removed from the computer. Secondary storage holds data for long periods of time—even when there is no power to the computer.

1.4 Operating systems and application software

1.5 A set of well-defined steps for performing a task or solving a problem

1.6 To ease the task of programming; programs may be written in a programming language and then converted to machine language

1.7 Procedural and object-oriented

1.8 An application responds to events that occur or actions that take place, such as the clicking of a mouse.

1.9 A property is data stored in an object; a method is an action that an object performs.

1.10 The default name is not descriptive; it does not indicate the purpose of the control.

1.11 A Text Box

1.12 TextBox1

1.13 No; the + symbol is an illegal character for control names.

1.14 The program's purpose, information to be input, the processing to take place, and the desired output

1.15 Planning helps the programmer create a good design and avoid errors that may not otherwise be anticipated.

1.16 To imagine what the computer screen looks like when the program is running; it's the first step in creating an application's forms or windows.

1.17 A diagram that graphically depicts a program's flow

1.18 A cross between human language and a programming language

1.19 A mistake that does not prevent an application from executing, but causes it to produce incorrect results; a mistake in a mathematical formula is a common type of runtime error

1.20 To find and correct runtime errors.

1.21 Testing is a part of each design step. Flowcharts should be tested, code should be desk-checked, and the application should be run with test data to verify that it produces the correct output.

1.22 The *Solution Explorer* window shows a file-oriented view of a project. It allows quick navigation among the project files.

1.23 The *Properties* window shows and allows you to change most of the currently selected object's properties and their values.

1.24 The *Dynamic Help* window displays a list of help topics that changes as operations are performed. The topics that are displayed are relevant to the operation currently being performed.

1.25 The standard toolbar contains buttons that execute frequently used commands.

1.26 You build an application in Design mode. You run an application in Run mode. An application is suspended for debugging purposes in Break mode.

1.27 The toolbar contains buttons that execute frequently used menu commands. The toolbox provides buttons for placing controls.

1.28 A ToolTip is a small box that is displayed when you hold the mouse cursor over a button on the toolbar or in the toolbox for a few seconds. The box gives a short description of what the button does.

Chapter 2

2.1 Text

2.2 With the form selected, double-click the Label control tool in the toolbox.

2.3 To resize the control's bounding box.

2.4 *TopLeft*, *TopCenter*, *TopRight*, *MiddleLeft*, *MiddleCenter*, *MiddleRight*, *BottomLeft*, *BottomCenter*, and *BottomRight*

2.5 Select it and press the Delete key.

2.6 When you resize the PictureBox, the image size adjusts to fit within it.

2.7 Bounding box

2.8 • Click the project name in the *Recent Projects* panel of the *Start* page, as shown in Figure 2-26. The project should open immediately; if not, you may have moved it to a different directory, deleted it, or its files may be corrupt.

- Click the *Open Project* button and browse for the project using the *Open Project* dialog box, as shown in Figure 2-27. Select the solution filename (extension *.sln*) and click the *Open* button.
- Click *File* in the menu bar and click *Open Project* in the *File* menu. Browse for the project using the *Open Project* dialog box, select the solution filename, and then click the *Open* button.

2.9 Alphabetical and categorized. Select alphabetical mode by clicking the *Alphabetical* button. Select categorized mode by clicking the *Categorized* button. When the *Alphabetical* button is clicked, the properties are displayed alphabetically. When the *Categorized* button is clicked, related properties are listed in groups.

2.10 Text is listed under the *Appearance* category. Name is listed under the *Design* category.

2.11 Select it from the list of objects displayed in the object box drop-down list.

2.12 If a control will be accessed in code or will have code associated with it (such as an event procedure), assign it a name. Otherwise, keep the control's default name.

2.13 A property that may only have one of two values: *True* or *False*

2.14 `btnShowName_Click()`

2.15 Nothing. The line is a comment and is ignored.

2.16 A remark, or comment, is a note of explanation that documents something in a program.

2.17 `lblSecretAnswer.Visible = False`

2.18 It closes the application window, causing the application to terminate.

2.19 The F7 key

2.20 Custom, Web, and System

2.21 The background color of the Label's text changes.

2.22 The color of the Label's text changes.

2.23 FormBorderStyle

2.24 You cannot move them until they are unlocked.

2.25 Right-click over an empty spot on the form and select *Lock Controls* from the pop-up menu.

2.26 The same way that you locked the controls: Right-click over an empty spot on the form, and select *Lock Controls* from the pop-up menu.

2.27 `lblTemperature.Text = "48 degrees"`

2.28 When AutoSize is set to *False*, you can set the bounding box of a Label control to be larger than the text it holds. When a label's AutoSize property is set to *True*, the label's bounding box automatically resizes to the length of the text in the label's Text property.

2.29 The BorderStyle property can hold one of the following values: *None*, *FixedSingle*, and *Fixed 3D*. When set to *None*, the label has no border. (This is the default value.) When set to *FixedSingle*, the label is outlined with a border that is a single pixel wide. When set to *Fixed3D*, the label has a recessed 3-dimensional appearance.

2.30
```
lblName.TextAlign = ContentAlignment.TopRight
lblName.TextAlign = ContentAlignment.BottomLeft
lblName.TextAlign = ContentAlignment.TopCenter
```

2.31 Select a control on the form in Design mode, click *Help* on the menu bar, and then click *Dynamic Help*.

2.32 Click the *Index* button on the *Dynamic Help* window, or click *Help* on the menu bar and then click *Index*.

2.33 By selecting *Visual Basic* in the *Language* drop-down list

2.34 A help screen that is displayed for the currently selected item when the F1 key is pressed

2.35 Compile errors and runtime errors

Chapter 3

3.1 Text

3.2 `lblMessage.Text = txtInput.Text`

3.3 Hello Jonathon, how are you?

3.4 It is actually two characters: a space followed by an underscore character. It allows you to break a long programming statement into two or more lines.

3.5 The control is accepting keyboard and/or mouse input from the user.

3.6 `txtLastName.Focus()`

3.7 The order in which controls receive the focus when the user presses the Tab key.

3.8 The TabIndex property, which contains a numeric value, determines the position of a control in the tab order. The control that has the lowest TabIndex value (usually 0) on a form is the first in the tab order. The control with the next highest TabIndex (usually 1) will be the next in the tab order. This sequence continues.

3.9 In the order that controls are created

3.10 That control is skipped in the tab order.

3.11 The `&` character has two effects: It assigns an access key to the button (in this case, the access key is Alt+M because the `&` is in front of the *M*) and it causes the *M* to appear underlined on the button.

3.12 An accept button is a form's button that is clicked when the user presses the Enter key. A cancel button is a form's button that is clicked when the user presses the Esc key. You select accept and cancel buttons with the form's AcceptButton and CancelButton properties.

3.13 A variable is a storage location in the computer's memory; used for holding information while the program is running.

3.14 `Dim intCount As Integer`

3.15 `decInterestRate` is written with the convention used in this book.

3.16 a. `count` Legal
b. `rate*Pay` Illegal; cannot use the * character
c. `deposit.amount` Illegal; cannot use a period
d. `down_payment` Legal, however, the name does not follow the standard convention of using a prefix to indicate its data type

3.17 a. 0
b. 0.0
c. False
d. 0
e. 12:00:00 AM, January 1 of year 1

3.18 `#2/20/2008 5:35 PM`

3.19 Charles Simonyi

3.20 a. 21
b. 2
c. 17
d. 18
e. 3.0
f. 36

3.21 a. 1
b. 2

3.22 `dtmThisTime = TimeOfDay`

3.23 `dtmCurrent = Now`

3.24 Scope defines the area of a program in which a variable or method is visible.

3.25 `dblResult = 4.7`

3.26 `dblResult = 7.0`

3.27 `dblResult = 3.0`

3.28 a. 21
b. 2
c. 17
d. 18

3.29 `dblResult = 28`

3.30 `dblResult = 186478.39`

3.31 An identifier (like a variable) that is given a type and a constant value.

3.32 a. 27
b. 12
c. 58
d. 13

3.33 When the value being assigned cannot be converted to the type of the destination variable.

3.34 CDBl function

3.35 a. 48 (rounds to nearest even integer)
b. 35 (rounds up)
c. 2300
d. ** cannot be converted **

3.36 `dblSalary.ToString("c")`

3.37 a. `"c"`
b. `"e"`
c. `"n"`
d. `"p"`
e. `"f"`

3.38 `ToString("c")`

3.39

Number Value	Format String	`ToString` Value
12.3	n4	12.3000
12.348	n1	12.3
1234567.1	n3	1,234,567.100
123456.0	f1	123456.0
123456.0	e3	1.235E+005
.234	p2	23.40%
–1234567.8	c3	($1,234,567.800)

3.40 `datStart.ToString("T")`

3.41 `datBirth.ToString("D")`

3.42 You can make a form appear more organized by grouping related controls inside group boxes.

3.43 Select the GroupBox with the mouse.

3.44 Copy the control to the clipboard, select the GroupBox with the mouse, and then paste the control from the clipboard into the GroupBox.

3.45 The TabIndex value of the controls inside the GroupBox are relative to the GroupBox control's TabIndex property.

3.46 `Form_Load`

3.47 A compile error (or syntax error), will prevent an application from starting. Examples are misspelled keywords and incorrect use of operators or punctuation. Compiler errors are often reported as soon as you type them. A logic error is a programming mistake that does not prevent an application from starting, but causes the application to produce incorrect results. Examples are incorrect math statements and copying the wrong value to a variable. A logic error may also cause a program to halt sometime during its execution.

3.48 A breakpoint is a line of code that causes a running application to pause execution and enter break mode. While the application is paused, you may perform debugging operations, such as examining variable contents and the values stored in control properties.

3.49 Single-stepping is a useful debugging technique for locating logic errors. In single-stepping, you execute an application's code one line at a time. After each line executes, you can examine variable and property contents. This process allows you to identify the line or lines of code causing the error.

Chapter 4

4.1 a. T
b. T
c. F
d. T
e. T
f. F
g. T

4.2 If the Boolean variable `blnIsInvalid` equals `True`.

4.3 Yes, they both perform the same operation. Only the indentation is different.

4.4 The following statement is preferred because the conditionally executed statement is indented. The indention makes the statement easier to read.

```
If decSales > 10000 Then
  decCommissionRate = 0.15
End If
```

4.5 a. 99
b. 0
c. 99

4.6 Three times

4.7 One time by the `If...Then...ElseIf` statement and four times by the set of `If...Then` statements

4.8

Logical Expression	Result
`True And False`	`False`
`True And True`	`True`
`False And True`	`False`
`False And False`	`False`
`True Or False`	`True`
`True Or True`	`True`
`False Or True`	`True`
`False Or False`	`False`
`True Xor False`	`True`
`True Xor True`	`False`
`Not True`	`False`
`Not False`	`True`

4.9 a. *False*
b. *False*
c. *True*

4.10 f, g, a, b, i, h, e, c, d

4.11 c, a, d, b

4.12 `DialogResult.Abort`

4.13

```
MessageBox.Show("William" & ControlChars.CrLf & _
  "Joseph" & ControlChars.CrLf & "Smith")
```

4.14

```
Select Case intQuantity
  Case 0 To 9
    decDiscount = 0.1
  Case 10 To 19
    decDiscount = 0.2
  Case 20 To 29
    decDiscount = 0.3
  Case Is >= 30
    decDiscount = 0.4
  Case Else
    MessageBox.Show("Invalid Data")
End Select
```

4.15 By examining its Checked property. If the property equals `True`, the radio button is selected. If the property equals `False`, the radio button is not selected.

4.16 Only one

4.17 By examining its Checked property. If the property equals `True`, the check box is selected. If the property equals `False`, the check box is not selected.

4.18 Any or all of them

4.19 By pressing the spacebar

4.20 Local variables are visible only to statements in the same procedure as the variable's declaration. Class-level variables are visible to statements in all the procedures in the form that contains the variable's declaration.

4.21 The declaration of a class-level variable must be outside any procedure, and between the `Class` statement appearing at the top of the file and the `End Class` statement appearing at the bottom. Normally you place the variable declaration for a class-level variable near the top of a form's code, prior to the first procedure.

Chapter 5

5.1 `strInput = InputBox("Enter a number", "Please Respond", CStr(500)`

5.2 `strInput = InputBox("Enter a number", "Please Respond", CStr(500), 100, 300)`

5.3 0

5.4 `Items.Count`

5.5 11

5.6 SelectedItem

5.7 SelectedIndex

5.8 `strSelectedName = lstNames.Items(1).ToString()`

5.9 The loop is an infinite loop because it does not change the value of `intCount`.

5.10 Ten times

5.11 One time

5.12 `intX` is the counter and `intY` is the accumulator.

5.13
```
Dim intCount As Integer = 5

Do While intCount >= 1
  lstOutput.Items.Add(intCount)
  intCount -= 1
Loop
```

5.14
```
Dim intTotal As Integer = 0
Dim intNumber As Integer

Do While intTotal <= 300
  intNumber = CInt(InputBox("Enter a number"))
  intTotal += intNumber
Loop
```

5.15 Posttest

5.16 The loop will execute five times. The message box will display 10.

5.17
```
Dim intCount As Integer

For intCount = 0 To 100 Step 5
  lstOutput.Items.Add(intCount)
Next intCount
```

5.18
```
Dim intCount As Integer
Dim intTotal As Integer
Dim intNum As Integer

intTotal = 0
For intCount = 0 To 7
  intNum = CInt(InputBox("Enter a number"))
  intTotal += intNum
Next intCount
MessageBox.Show("The total is " & intTotal.ToString())
```

5.19 The `For` loop

5.20 The `Do While` loop

5.21 The `Do Until` loop

5.22 1, 1, 2, 2, 1, 2, 3, 1, 2

5.23 600 times

5.24 0

5.25 Items.Count

5.26 SelectedIndex

5.27 A drop-down combo box allows the user to type text into its text area. A drop-down list combo box does not allow the user to type text. The user can only select an item from the list.

5.28 By retrieving the value in the Text property

5.29 A drop-down list combo box

5.30 If CausesValidation equals *True*, the `Validating` event of the control that focus is shifting from will fire.

5.31 A control's `Validating` event is triggered just before the focus shifts to another control whose CausesValidation property is also set to *True*.

5.32 True.

5.33 The `SelectAll` method can be used in code to automatically select the text in a text box.

5.34 `txtSerialNumber.SelectAll()`

5.35 Setting properties of a ListBox, using a `With...End With` block:

```
With lstSample
  .Sorted = True
  .BackColor = Color.Blue
  .ForeColor = Color.Yellow
End With
```

Chapter 6

6.1 If you enter 10, the following will be displayed:

I saw Elba
Able was I

If you enter 5, the following will be displayed:

Able was I
I saw Elba

6.2 Static local variables retain their value between procedure calls. Regular local variables do not.

6.3
```
Sub TimesTen(ByVal intValue As Integer)

  Dim intResult As Integer
    intResult = intValue * 10
    MessageBox.Show(intResult.ToString())
End Sub
```

6.4 `TimesTen(25)`

6.5
```
Sub PrintTotal(ByVal intNum1 As Integer, ByVal intNum2 _
        As Integer, ByVal intNum3 As Integer)

    Dim intTotal As Single
    intTotal = intNum1 + intNum2 + intNum3
    MessageBox.Show(intTotal.ToString())
End Sub
```

6.6 `PrintTotal(intWeight, intCount, intUnits)`

6.7 `ByVal`

6.8 a. `Distance`
b. Two
c. `sngRate` and `sngTime`; they are both Singles
d. Single

6.9
```
Function Days(ByVal intYears As Integer, ByVal intMonths _
    As Integer, ByVal intWeeks As Integer) As Integer
```

6.10 `intNumDays = Days(y, m, w)`

6.11 `Function LightYears(ByVal lngMiles As Long) As Single`

6.12 `sngDistance = LightYears(m)`

6.13
```
Function TimesTwo(intNumber As Integer) As Integer
  Return intNumber * 2
End Function
```

6.14 Step Out; Ctrl+Shift+F8

6.15 Step Into; F8

6.16 Step Over; Shift+F8

Chapter 7

7.1 Make it the startup object.

7.2 `frm`

7.3 To add a new form to a project either: Click the *Add New Item* button on the tool bar, and then select *Windows form,* or select *Add Windows Form* from the *Project* menu. In both cases, the *Add New Item* dialog appears. You can enter a form name and click the *Add* button.

7.4 Visual Studio only: To exclude a form from a project: Right-click the form's entry in the *Solution Explorer* window. On the pop-up menu, click *Exclude From Project.*

7.5 A form file contains a form's code. It has the *.vb* extension.

7.6 When a modal form is displayed, no other form in the application can receive the focus until the modal form is closed. Also, when a statement displays a modal form, no other statements in that procedure will execute until the modal form is closed. A modeless form, however, allows the user to switch focus to another form while it is displayed. When a statement uses a method call to display a modeless form, the statements that follow the method call will continue to execute after the modeless form is displayed.

7.7 `resultsForm.ShowDialog()`

7.8 `resultsForm.Show()`

7.9 In the form's `Activated` event procedure

7.10 `infoForm.lblCustomer.Text = "Jim Jones"`

7.11 The `Me` keyword indicates the currently active form. This can be useful when a form needs to call one of its own methods.

7.12 `Public sngAverage As Single`

7.13 Variable declarations, procedures, and/or functions not associated with a particular form or class

7.14 *.vb*

7.15 (1) Click the *Add New Item* button on the toolbar, or click *Project* on the menu bar, and then click *Add Module*. The *Add New Item* dialog box should appear. (2) Under *Templates,* select *Module.* (3) Change the default name that is displayed in the *Name* text box to the name you wish to give the new module.

7.16 A name that clearly relates it to the *Customers* project, such as CustomersModule

7.17 `Main`

7.18 a. The name of a drop-down menu, which appears on the form's menu bar
b. A command that appears on a drop-down menu, and may be selected by the user
c. A menu item that appears dimmed and cannot be selected by the user
d. A menu item that appears with a check mark to its left
e. A key or combination of keys that causes a menu command to execute
f. Another menu that appears when a command on a drop-down menu is selected
g. A horizontal bar used to separate groups of commands on a menu

7.19 Shortcut keys are different from access keys in that a command's shortcut key may be used at any time the form is active, while a command's access key may only be used while the drop-down menu containing the command is visible.

7.20 `mnu`

7.21 `mnuFileSave`, `mnuFileSaveAs`, `mnuFilePrint`, and `mnuFileExit`

7.22 By placing an ampersand (&) before a character in the Text property.

7.23 The item initially appears as a checked menu item, meaning it appears with a check mark displayed next to it.

7.24 By setting its Enabled property to *False.*

7.25 By testing the value of the menu item's Checked property.

7.26 The ToolStripMenuItem object's `Click` event procedure

7.27 By right-clicking a control

7.28 By setting the control's ContextMenuStrip property to the name of the ContextMenuStrip control.

Chapter 8

8.1 a. `Dim intEmpNums(99) As Integer`
b. `Dim decPayRate(23) As Decimal`
c. `Dim intMiles() As Integer = { 10, 20, 30, 40, 50 }`
d. `Dim strNames(12) As String`

e.
```
Dim strDivisions() As String = { "North", "South", _
      "East", "West" }
```

8.2 The upper boundary (4) cannot appear inside the parentheses when an initialization list is provided.

8.3 a. 101
b. 3
c. 1

8.4 The runtime system throws an exception if a subscript is outside the range of subscripts for an array.

8.5
```
For intCount = 0 To 25
  MessageBox.Show(intPoints(intCount).ToString())
Next intCount
```

8.6
```
Dim intNumber As Integer
For Each intNumber In intPoints
  MessageBox.Show(intNumber.ToString())
Next intNumber
```

8.7 a. 10.00
b. 25.00
c. 32.50
d. 50.00

8.8
```
intTotal = 0                    ' Initialize accumulator.
For intCount = 0 To 99
  intTotal += intValues(intCount)
Next intCount
```

8.9
```
intTotal = 0                    ' Initialize accumulator.
For intCount= 0 To (points.Length – 1)
  intTotal += intPoints(intCount)
Next intCount
dblAverage = intTotal / points.Length
```

8.10
```
Array.Sort(strSerialNumbers)
```

8.11
```
0 18 0
1 4 4
2 27 54
3 52 156
4 100 400
```

8.12
```
ReDim Preserve decSales(49)
```

8.13 (Code example)
```
blnFound = False
intCount = 0
Do While Not blnFound And intCount < intValidNumbers.Length
  If intValidNumbers (intCount) = 247 Then
    blnFound = True
    intPosition = intCount
  End If
  intCount+= 1
Loop
'Was 100 found in the array?
If blnFound Then
  MessageBox.Show("The value was found at position " _
      & intPosition.ToString())
```

```
Else
  MessageBox.Show("The value was not found.")
End If
```

8.14 `Dim intGrades(29, 9) As Integer`

8.15 24 elements (6 rows by 4 columns)

8.16 `decSales(0, 0) = 56893.12`

8.17 `MessageBox.Show(decSales(5, 3).ToString())`

8.18 `Dim intSettings(2, 4) As Integer`

8.19 Four rows and five columns

8.20 `Dim strMovies(49, 9, 24) As String`

8.21
```
If radLifeTimeMember.Checked = True Then
  chkFreePizza.Enabled = True
  chkFreeCola.Enabled = True
End If
```

8.22 500

8.23 By setting the form's TopMost property to *True*.

8.24 It allows you to anchor the control to one or more edges of a form. When a control is anchored to a form's edge, the distance between the control's edge and the form's edge will remain constant, even when the user resizes the form.

8.25 It allows you to dock a control. When a control is docked, it is positioned directly against one of the edges of a form. Additionally, the length or width of a docked control is changed to match the length or width of the form's edge.

8.26 To generate pseudorandom number sequences

8.27 The same sequence is generated each time.

8.28 The system time returned from your computer's clock

8.29 An integer between 0 and 2, 147, 483, 647

8.30 To return a random floating-point number between 0.0 and 1.0.

8.31
```
Dim rand As New Random
intRandomNumber=rand.Next(100)+1;
```

8.32
```
Dim rand As New Random
intRandomNumber=rand.Next(300)+100;
```

Chapter 9

9.1 (1) open the file, (2) write data to the file or read data from the file, and (3) close the file

9.2 `StreamWriter, StreamReader`

9.3 `outputFile = System.IO.File.CreateText("Test.txt")`

9.4 `outputFile.WriteLine(x)`

9.5 `inputFile = System.IO.File.OpenText("Test.txt")`

9.6 `x = inputFile.ReadLine`

9.7 With the `System.IO.File.Exists` method

9.8 With the `Peek` method; when `Peek` returns –1, the end of the file has been reached

9.9 Most Windows users are accustomed to using a dialog box to browse their disk for a file to open, or for a location to save a file.

9.10 Filter: These list boxes display a filter that specifies the type of files that are visible in the dialog box. You store a string in the Filter property that specifies the filter(s) available in the list boxes.

InitialDirectory: You store the path of the directory whose contents are to be initially displayed in the dialog box.

Title: The string stored in this property is displayed in the dialog box's title bar.

Filename: The filename selected or entered by the user is stored in this property.

9.11
```
Text files (*.txt)|*.txt|Word files (*.doc)|*.doc|
All files(*.*)
```

9.12 The ColorDialog control's Color property.

9.13 The FontDialog control's Font property.

9.14 By setting the FontDialog control's ShowColor property to *True* before calling the ShowDialog method.

9.15 in the FontDialog control's Color property.

9.16 By calling the control's `Print` method.

9.17
```
e.Graphics.DrawString("Joe Smith", New Font("MS sans Serif", _
   18, FontStyle.Bold), Brushes.Black, 100, 20)
```

9.18 Header, body, and footer.

9.19 The characters in a proportionally spaced font do not occupy the same amount of horizontal space. All the characters in a monospaced font use the same amount of space.

9.20
```
e.Graphics.DrawString(String.Format("{ 0,12} { 1,8} ", a, b), _
    New Font("Courier", 12, FontStyle.Regular), _
    Brushes.Black, 10, 50)
```

9.21
```
e.Graphics.DrawString(String.Format("{ 0,-12} { 1,8} ", a, b), _
    New Font("Courier", 12, FontStyle.Regular), _
    Brushes.Black, 10, 50)
```

9.22
```
Structure Movie
  strName As String
  strDirector As String
  strProducer As String
  intYear As Integer
End Structure
```

9.23
```
Dim film As Movie
```

9.24 The following statements assume the variable is named `film`:

```
film.strName = "Wheels of Fury"
film.strDirector = "Arlen McGoo"
film.strProducer = "Vincent Van Dough"
film.intYear = 2008
```

9.25 The following statements assume the variable is named `film`:

```
With film
  .strName = "Wheels of Fury"
  .strDirector = "Arlen McGoo"
  .strProducer = "Vincent Van Dough"
  .intYear = 2008
End With
```

Chapter 10

10.1 A database is a container for one or more tables. A table is a set of rows and columns holding logically related data.

10.2 Employee_ID

10.3 Boolean

10.4 There would be too great a chance for misspellings by the data entry person. Also, the department name could change in the future, making maintenance a problem.

10.5 Individual values of a foreign key column can occur multiple times in a table, whereas a primary key can contain values that occur only once. Also, a foreign key links its table with some other table's primary key.

10.6 Data binding

10.7 TableAdapter

10.8 The database is not affected by changes to a dataset unless a special `Update` method is called.

10.9 DataGridView control

10.10 DataConnection object

10.11 Data Sources window

10.12 DataSource

10.13 Click the DataGridView's smart tag (arrow in the upper right corner), and select the data source.

10.14 Select the column in the *Data Sources* window and drag it onto the form.

10.15 DateTimePicker control

10.16 Select *Add New Data Source* from the *Data* menu.

10.17 Structured Query Language

10.18 SQL queries are written using an industry-standard language

10.19 `SELECT First_Name, Last_Name FROM Employees`

10.20 Right-click the table adapter icon in the form's component tray and select *Add Query*.

10.21
```
WHERE Salary <= 85000
If lstKayak.SelectedIndex = -1 Then
  .Items.Add("A kayak type must be selected")
  Exit Sub
End If
```

10.22
```
SELECT pay_rate, employee_id, hours_worked FROM Payroll
   ORDER by hours_worked DESC
```

10.23 `SELECT pay_rate AS Rate_of_Pay FROM Payroll`

10.24
```
SELECT pay_rate, hours_worked, pay_rate * hours_worked
    AS gross_pay FROM Payroll
```

10.25
```
SELECT * FROM Payroll WHERE pay_rate > 20000
    AND pay_rate <= 55000
```

10.26 `SELECT * FROM Payroll WHERE employee_id LIKE "FT%"`

10.27 *Members* table

10.28 *Payments* and *Members* tables

10.29 Columns property

10.30 `LIKE`

Chapter 11

11.1 A Web application is a program running on a Web server that interacts with Web browsers. The connection might be across the Internet, or it might be within a company intranet.

11.2 The Web server generates Web pages, which are consumed by clients (end users) running Web browsers. The clients make requests and the server satisfies the requests.

11.3 A postback occurs when the end user clicks a button or activates a control that sends the contents of the Web page back to the Web server.

11.4 ASP.NET is called a platform because it provides development tools, code libraries, and visual controls for browser-based applications.

11.5 Content is comprised of Web forms, HTML code, Web controls, images, and other multimedia.

11.6 File system, HTTP, and FTP

11.7 Click the *Design* tab.

11.8 Right-click the *Solution Explorer* window and select *Browse with . . . .*

11.9 Static text is text typed directly onto a form in *Design* mode. In can be used in place of Labels (the type used in Windows forms) when you do not need to access it at runtime in program code.

11.10 By selecting the text with the mouse, and then selecting *Heading 1* from the *Block format* pull-down list on the left side of the formatting toolbar

11.11 A dialog window explains that a confirmation option must be set in the *Web.config* file. It creates the file and adds it to the *Solution Explorer* window.

11.12 DropDownList

11.13 ImageButton

11.14 LinkButton

11.15 The SelectedIndex property contains an integer that indicates the selected button.

11.16 As soon as the user makes a ListBox selection, the page is posted back to the server.

11.17 DropDownList

11.18 Drag the mouse over the cells and select *Merge Cells* from the *Layout* menu.

11.19 Click the column select button just above the column along the table border.

11.20 Drag the right-hand border of the column with the mouse.

11.21 From the *Layout* menu, choose *Select*, and then choose *Table*. Open the Style property of the table, and modify the font in the *Style Builder* dialog.

11.22 Items collection

11.23 Select *Add New Item* from the Web site menu.

11.24 Assign the new Web page location to the NavigateURL property.

11.25 Select the block with the mouse and click the *HyperLink* button on the formatting toolbar.

11.26 The `Redirect` method

11.27 GridView control

11.28 SqlDataSource object

11.29 DataFormatString property

11.30 Fields property

11.31 DetailsView control

Chapter 12

12.1 Forms, buttons, check boxes, list boxes, and other controls.

12.2 The TextBox tool represents the class and a specific TextBox control on the form is an instance of the class.

12.3 Select classes by finding the physical entities in the application domain.

12.4 Attributes describe the properties that all objects of the same class have in common. They are implemented as properties.

12.5 Operations are actions the class objects may perform or messages to which they can respond. They are implemented as methods.

12.6 A class interface is the portion that is visible to the application programmer who uses the class.

12.7 A class implementation is the portion of a class that is hidden from client programs.

12.8 (1) Click the *Add New Item* button () on the toolbar, or click *Project* on the menu bar, and then click *Add Class*. The *Add New Item* dialog box should appear. Make sure that *Class* is selected in the *Templates* pane. (2) Change the default class name in the Name text box to the name you wish to give the new class file. (3) Click the *Add* button.

12.9 Declare an object variable, and then create an instance of the class in memory and assign its address to the variable.

12.10 An object is removed by setting all variables that reference it to `Nothing`.

12.11 Garbage collection.

12.12 Variables declared in a class module, but outside of any class methods

12.13 A procedure that behaves like a Class property

12.14 It allows a client program to retrieve the value of a property.

12.15 It allows a client program to set the value of a property.

12.16 A constructor is a class method that is executed automatically when an instance of a class is created. A `Finalize` method is called just before the Garbage Collector removes an object from memory.

12.17 Unlike arrays, which have fixed sizes, collection objects automatically expand as items are added to them, and shrink as items are removed from them. Another difference is this: all elements in an array must be of the same type, but members of collections do not have to be of the same type.

12.18 Use the `Add` method to add members to a collection.

12.19 By adding a key value, you will be more easily able to search for items.

12.20 With the `Item` method

12.21 With the `Remove` method

12.22 By setting the Minimum and Maximum properties

12.23 The SmallChange property sets the amount by which the Value property changes when the user clicks one of the scroll arrows at either end of a scroll bar, or uses the arrow keys to control a track bar. The LargeChange property sets the amount by which the Value property changes when the user clicks the scroll bar area around the slider.

12.24 The Scroll event occurs when the slider changes positions.

12.25 `Insect` is the base class and `Fly` is the derived class.

12.26 All of the base class's members (variables, properties, and methods)

12.27 Overriding is replacing a base Class property procedure or method with one of the same name in the derived class.

12.28 `Overridable`

12.29 `Overrides`

12.30 The base class constructor executes first, followed by the derived class constructor.

12.31 Protected base class members are like private members, except they may be accessed by methods and property procedures in derived classes. To all other code, however, protected class members are just like private class members.

APPENDIX

D Glossary

About box—a dialog box that usually displays brief information about the application

abstract data type (ADT)—a data type created by a programmer

abstraction—a model that includes only the general characteristics of an object

accept button—a button on a form that is clicked when the user presses the Enter key

access key—a key that is pressed in combination with the Alt key; access keys allow the user to access buttons and menu items using the keyboard; also known as a mnemonic

accumulator—the variable used to keep a running total

`Activated` event handler—created in response to an `Activated` event

`Activated` event procedure—a form event procedure that executes each time the user switches to a form from another form or another application

Active Server Pages (ASP)—Microsoft's technology for creating Web-enabled applications

`Add` method—used to add items to a collection

algorithm—a set of well-defined steps for performing a task or solving a problem

Alphabetical button—a button on the *Properties* window that causes properties to be displayed alphabetically

Anchor property—a control property that allows you to anchor the control to one or more edges of a form

`And` operator—a logical operator that combines two expressions into one; both expressions must be true for the overall expression to be true

`AndAlso` operator—uses short-circuit evaluation in compound expressions

append—to write new data immediately following existing data in a file

`AppendText` method—*see* `System.IO.File.AppendText` method

application software—programs that make the computer useful to the user by solving specific problems or performing general operations

arguments—values passed to a Sub procedure or function

array—a group of variables with a single name

array bounds checking—a runtime feature of Visual Basic that does not allow a statement to use a subscript outside the range of subscripts for an array

ascending order—when items are arranged in order, from lowest to highest value

ASP.NET—Microsoft's platform for Web applications; an improvement over Active Server Pages

ASP.NET development server—ASP.NET development software that is automatically installed with Visual Studio and Visual Web Developer Express Edition

ASP.NET Server Controls—interactive controls such as buttons, list boxes, and text boxes that execute on the server

assignment operator—the equal sign (=); it copies the value on its right into the item on its left in an assignment statement

assignment statement—a programming statement that uses the assignment operator to copy a value from one object to another

attributes—the data contained in an object; the characteristics of an object that will be implemented as properties

auto list box—appears while entering programming statements in the *Code* window; displays information that may be used to complete part of the statement

AutoPostBack property—used on Web forms to force the page to be sent to the server when the user clicks on the control

AutoSize property—a Label control property that, when set to *True*, causes the label's size to display all the text in the Text property

Autos window—a debugging window that displays the value and data type of the variables that appear in the current statement, the three statements before, and the three statements after the current statement

BackColor property—establishes the background color for text

base class—the class that a derived class is based on

binary files—files whose contents are not stored as plain text, but as binary data; cannot be read by a text editor

binary number—a number that is a sequence of 1s and 0s

binding source—keeps track of a database name, location, username, password, and other connection information

Boolean property—a value that can be either *True* or *False*

BorderStyle property—a Label control property that determines the type of border, if any, that will appear around the control

bounding box—a transparent rectangular area that defines a control's size on a form

Break mode—the mode in which an application has been suspended for debugging purposes

breakpoint—a line of code that causes a running application to pause execution and enter break mode; while the application is paused, you may examine variable contents and the values stored in certain control properties

buffer—a small holding section of memory that data is first written to; when the buffer is filled, all the information stored there is written to the file

button—a rectangular button-shaped control that performs an action when clicked with the mouse

Button control—when clicked by a user on a Web page, causes the page contents to be sent back to the Web server

`ByRef`—keyword used to declare a parameter variable, causing its argument to be passed by reference

by reference—when passing an argument to a procedure, the procedure has access to the original argument and can make changes to it

`ByVal` keyword— indicates that arguments passed into the variable are passed by value

by value—when passing an argument to a procedure, only a portion of the argument is passed to the procedure

`Call`—a keyword that may be optionally used to call a procedure

cancel button—a button on a form that is clicked when the user presses the Esc key

Cascading Style Sheet (CSS)—file containing HTML styles that affect the appearance of text and graphics on Web pages

Categorized button—a button on the *Properties* window that causes related properties to be displayed in groups

CausesValidation property—a Boolean property; when the focus is shifting from Control A to Control B, and Control B's CausesValidation property is set to *True*, Control A's `Validating` event will fire

central processing unit (CPU)—the part of the computer that fetches instructions, carries out operations commanded by the instructions, and produces some outcome

CheckBox—a box that is checked or unchecked when clicked with the mouse

CheckBox control—allows the user to make yes/no or on/off selections; may appear alone or in groups

CheckBoxList control—looks like a group of check boxes, but works like a list box

`CheckedChanged` event—occurs when the state of a radio button or check box changes

Checked property—A property of radio buttons and check boxes; it is set to *True* when the control is selected and *False* when the control is deselected. Also a MenuItem object property that may be set to *True* or *False*; when set to *True*, the object becomes a checked menu item.

`Chr` function—an intrinsic function that accepts a character code as an argument and returns the character that corresponds to the code

class—a program structure that defines an abstract data type

class declaration—defines a class and member variables, properties, events, and methods

class implementation—the portion of a class that is hidden from client programs

class interface—the portion of a class that is visible to the application programmer who uses the class

class objects—instances of a class

class-level variable—a variable that has class scope

class scope—when you declare a variable inside a class; also known as module scope

client—entity that consumes data and makes requests of a server

client program—a program written to use a class; this term is in reference to the client-server relationship between a class and the programs that use it

client-server model—describes interaction between users of a program (the clients) and the server (as in a Web server)

`Close` method—closes a form and releases its visual par from memory

`Closed` event handler—a form event procedure that executes after a form has closed

`Closing` event handler—a form event procedure that executes as a form is in the process of closing, but before it has closed

codebehind file—stores the source code for a Web form

code template—code that is automatically inserted into an event procedure, consisting of the first and last lines of the procedure; you must add the code that appears between these two lines

code outlining—a Visual Studio tool that lets you expand and collapse sections of code

Code window—a text-editing window in which you write code

collection—an object that is similar to an array; it is a single unit that contains several items and dynamically expands or shrinks in size as items are added or removed

Color dialog box—allows the user to select a color

ColorDialog control—displays a *Color* dialog box

columns—the vertical lists of data in a database table

combined assignment operators—combine an arithmetic operator with an assignment operator

combo boxes—similar to list boxes; display lists of items to the user

ComboBox—a control that is the combination of a ListBox and a TextBox

comments—notes of explanation that document lines or sections in a method; also known as remarks

Common Gateway Interface (CGI)—typically written in languages such as C or Perl; process information collected by HTML controls

compile errors—syntax errors, such as misspelled keywords and incorrect use of operators or punctuation; statements containing compile errors are underlined with a jagged blue line

components—special controls in Visual Basic that provide the linking mechanism in a database

component tray—a resizable region at the bottom of the *Design* window that holds invisible controls

compound operators—*see* combined assignment operators

conditionally-executed—describes statements that are only performed when certain conditions exist

connection object—provides the low-level functionality to interact with a data source

connector symbol—a flowcharting symbol used to connect two flowcharts when a flowchart does not fit on a single sheet of paper or must be divided into sections

constructor—a method that is automatically called when an instance of the class is created

Contents button—on the *Dynamic Help* window; displays a table of contents in which related help topics are organized into groups

context menu—a pop-up menu that is displayed when the user right-clicks a form or control

context-sensitive help—a help screen that is displayed when the F1 key is pressed (for the item that is currently selected)

`ControlChars.CrLf`—a value that can be concatenated with a string to produce multiple line displays

controls—objects, usually used as on-screen elements in a Visual Basic application

Count property—a collection property that holds the number of items in the collection

counter—a variable that is regularly incremented or decremented each time a loop iterates

database—a collection of tables that hold related data

database schema—the design of tables, columns, and relationships between tables for the database

data binding—a Visual Basic technique that links database tables to controls on a program's forms

data-bound controls—update their contents automatically when you move from one row to the next in a dataset

DataGridView control—bound to DateTime fields

dataset—an in-memory cache of records that is separate from the data source but still allows you to work with the data

data source—usually a database, but can include text files, Excel spreadsheets, XML data, or Web services

DataSource control—visible only at design time; for example, AccessDataSource or SqlDataSource

DataSource property—identifies the table within the dataset that supplies the data

data type—the type of information that the variable can hold

DateTimePicker controls—bound to DateTime fields

decision structure—a program structure that allows a program to have more than one path of execution

delimiter—an item that separates other items

derived class—a class that is based on another class

design—in a database table, specifies each column's name, data type, and range or size

Design mode—the mode in which you design and build an application

Design window—contains the application's forms; where one designs the application's user interface by creating forms and placing controls on them

DetailsView control—makes it easy to view, edit, delete, or add rows to a database table

disk drive—stores information by magnetically encoding it onto a circular disk

DisplayMember property—identifies the column within the table that displays in the list box or combo box

DLLs—dynamic-link library files

docked—describes windows that are attached to each other or to one of the edges of the Visual Studio window

Dock property—a control property that allows you to dock a control against a form's edge

domain name—in a URL, the specific designation, such as microsoft.com

`Do Until` loop—a looping structure that causes one or more statements to repeat until its test expression is true

`Do While` loop—a looping structure that causes one or more statements to repeat as long as an expression is true

DropDownList control—permits the user to select a single item from a list

Dynamic Help window—displays a list of help topics that changes as operations are performed; topics displayed are relevant to the operation currently being performed

elements—variables stored within an array

empty string—represented by two quotation marks, with no space between them

Enabled property—a control property that, when set to *False*, disables the control; therefore the control cannot receive the focus, cannot respond to events generated by the user, and appears dimmed or grayed out on the form

encapsulation—the hiding of data and procedures inside a class

event-driven—a type of program that responds to events or actions that occur while the program is running

event handler—a type of method that responds to actions by the user, such as mouse clicks and key presses at the keyboard

event procedure—a procedure that an object executes in response to an event

exception—an event or condition that happens unexpectedly and causes the application to halt

exception handler—in most modern programming languages, a simple mechanism for handling exceptions

execution point—while single-stepping through an application's code, the next line of code that will execute

`Exit Do` statement—stops the execution of a `Do While` or `Do Until` loop

`Exit For` statement—stops the execution of a `For...Next` loop

expression—the input to Visual Basic conversion functions

fields—*see* columns

file—a collection of data stored on a computer's disk

Filename property—a property of the OpenFileDialog and SaveFileDialog controls that holds the name of the file selected or entered by the user with the *Open* and *Save As* dialog boxes

File System Web site—runs directly under the ASP.NET development server supplied with Visual Studio and Visual Web Developer

Filter property—a property of the OpenFileDialog and SaveFileDialog controls used to set filters that control what file types are displayed in the *Open* and *Save As* dialog boxes

finalizer—a class method named `Finalize`; automatically called just before an instance of the class is removed from memory

finding the classes—the object-oriented analysis process of discovering the classes within a problem

flag—a Boolean variable that signals when some condition exists in the program

floating—when windows, such as *Project Explorer*, *Properties*, or *Form Layout* are not docked (attached)

flowchart—a diagram that graphically depicts the flow of a method

focus—the control that has the focus is the one that receives the user's keyboard input or mouse clicks

`Focus` method—gives the focus to a control

Font dialog box—allows the user to select a font, style, and size

Font property—indicates the size and style of a text font

FontDialog control—displays a *Font* dialog box

`For Each...Next` loop—a loop designed specifically to access values from arrays and array-like structures

`For Each` statement—a special loop designed specifically to access values from arrays and array-like structures

foreign key—a column in one table that references a primary key in another table

`For...Next` loop—a loop specifically designed to initialize, test, and increment a counter variable

ForeColor property—establishes the foreground color for text

form—a window, onto which other controls may be placed

formatting—the way a value is printed or displayed

FormBorderStyle property—a property that configures a form's border; allows or prevents resizing, minimizing, or maximizing a window

`FormClosed` event handler—used to execute code immediately after a form has closed

`FormClosing` event handler—used to execute code in response to a form's closing

Friend access—an access type; a class member with Friend access can be used only by other classes inside the same assembly

FTP Web site—references an existing ASP.NET Web site located on a remote computer (network or Web)

function—a specialized routine that performs a specific operation, and then returns or produces information

function procedure—a collection of statements that performs an operation and returns a value

garbage collector——a process that destroys objects when they are no longer needed

`Get` section—in a property procedure; allows a client program to retrieve the value of a property

global scope—the scope of a module-level or class-level variable that is declared with the `Public` access specifier

global variable—a module-level or class-level variable that is declared with the `Public` access specifier

going out of scope—what happens when an object is created inside a procedure, and is automatically removed from memory when the procedure ends

graphical user interface (GUI)—the graphical interface used by modern operating systems

GridView control—displays database tables; allows you to sort on any column, select the column order, and format data within columns

GroupBox—a rectangular border that functions as a container for other controls

GroupBox control—a control that appears as a rectangular border with an optional title that appears in the upper left corner; you group other controls by drawing them inside a GroupBox control

hardware—a computer's physical components

`Hide` method—removes a form or control, but does not remove it from memory

horizontal scroll bar—a horizontal slider bar that, when moved with the mouse, increases or decreases a value

HScrollBar control—used to create a horizontal scroll bar

HTML controls—controls found on most Web pages (not ASP.NET)

HTML Table control—an essential tool for designing the layout of Web forms; used to align text, graphics, and controls in rows and columns

HTML tags—used to design the layout of a Web form

HTTP Web site—runs under a Windows operating system utility named Internet Information Services (IIS)

Hungarian notation—system in which a three-letter prefix is used in variable names to identify their data type

HyperLink control—Web forms control that displays underlined text; when the user clicks on the text, the program navigates to a new Web page

Hypertext Markup Language (HTML)—the notation used when creating ordinary Web pages; determines fonts, images, and positioning of elements

`If...Then`—a statement that can cause other statements to execute under certain conditions

`If...Then...Else`—a statement that will execute one group of statements if a condition is true, or another group of statements if a condition is false

`If...Then...ElseIf`—a statement that is like a chain of `If...Then...ElseIf` statements; they perform their tests, one after the other, until one of them is found to be true

ImageButton control—Web forms control that displays an image on a clickable button

Immediate window—a debugging window used by advanced programmers; allows you to type debugging commands using the keyboard

implicit type conversion—when you assign a value of one data type to a variable of another data type, Visual Basic attempts to convert the value being assigned to the data type of the variable

index—*see* subscript

Index button—a button on the *Dynamic Help* window that displays a searchable alphabetized index of all help topics

`IndexOf` method—searches for a character or a string within a string

infinite loop—a loop that never stops repeating

inheritance—an object-oriented programming feature that allows you to create classes that are based on other classes

InitialDirectory property—a property of the OpenFileDialog and SaveFileDialog controls used to set the path of the directory initially displayed in *Open* and *Save As* dialog boxes

initialization—specifying an initial value for a variable

input—data the computer collects from the outside world

input box—a Windows dialog box that displays a message to the user; it provides a text box for the user to enter input

input device—a device that collects information and sends it to the computer

input file—file from which a program reads data

input validation—the process of inspecting input values and determining whether they are valid

integer division—a division operation performed with the \ operator in which the result is always an integer; if the result has a fractional part, it is discarded

integrated development environment (IDE)—an application that provides the necessary tools for creating, testing, and debugging software

IntelliSense—a feature of Visual Basic that provides help and some automatic code completion while you are developing an application

Internet Information Services (IIS)—Microsoft professional-level Web server

Interval property—a property of the timer control; the value stored in the Interval property is the number of milliseconds that elapse between timer events

intranet—network within a company, usually protected by a firewall

`IPmt` function—returns the required interest payment for a specific period on a loan

`Is` operator—used to compare two object variables to determine whether they reference the same object

`IsNot` operator—used to determine whether two variables do not reference the same object

`IsNumeric` function—an intrinsic function that accepts a string as its argument, and returns `True` if the string contains a number; the function returns `False` if the string's contents cannot be recognized as a number

`Item` method—a collection method that searches for a specific member of the collection and returns a reference to it

Items property—items that are displayed in a list box or combo box are stored as strings in the Items property

`Items.Add` method—a list box and combo box method that adds an item to the end of the control's Item property

Items.Count property—holds the number of items in a list box or combo box

`Items.Insert` method—a list box and combo box method that adds an item at a specific index of the control's Item property

`Items.Remove` method—a list box and combo box method that removes an item from the control's Item property

`Items.RemoveAt` method—a list box and combo box method that removes an item at a specific index of the control's Item property

iteration—one execution of a loop's conditionally-executed statements

JavaScript—scripting language used on Web pages, usually for client-side programming; runs under the control of the browser, not the Web server

keywords—programming language words that have a special meaning; keywords may only be used for their intended purpose

Label—text that cannot be changed or entered by the user; created with a Label control

Label control—used to create labels to display text on a Web form

Language Integrated Query (LINQ)—a query language that can be used to query many types of data from virtually any source.

language syntax—Visual Basic rules that define the correct way to use keywords, operators, and programmer-defined names

leading space—a space that appears at the beginning of a string

`Length` property—a string method that returns the number of characters in the string

lifetime—the time during which the variable exists in memory

`LIKE` operator—used to create partial matches with Text column values

line-continuation character—a space followed by an underscore character; used to break a long programming statement into two or more lines

LinkButton control—used on Web forms; looks like a hyperlink, but generates a `Click` event

LINQ—*see* Language Integrated Query

ListBox—a control that appears as a box containing a list of items

ListBox control—displays a list of items and allows the user to select one or more items from the list

`Load` event procedure—a procedure that is executed each time a form loads into memory

local scope—when variables are declared and used inside a single method or procedure

local variables—variables declared inside a procedure

Locals window—a debugging window that displays the current value and the data type of all the variables in the currently running procedure

logic error—a programming mistake that does not prevent an application from running but causes the application to produce incorrect results

logical operators—operators, such as `And` or `Or`, which connect two or more relational expressions into one, or `Not`, which reverse the logic of an expression

loop—one or more programming statements that repeat

machine language—the language of 1s and 0s, which is the only language the CPU can process

`Main`—a subprocedure that may be designated as the startup object

main memory—also known as random-access memory, or RAM; where the computer stores information while programs are running

Maximum property—a scroll bar or track bar property that holds the control's maximum value

`Me` keyword—may be substituted for the name of the currently active form or object

member variable—declared inside a class declaration; the variable is a member of the class

menu designer—allows you to create a custom menu system for any form in an application

MenuStrip control—consists of ToolStripMenuItem objects; used to construct a menu system on a form

menu system—a collection of commands organized in one or more drop-down menus

MenuItem objects—menu names, menu commands, or separator bars on a menu system

message box—a dialog box that displays a message to the user

`MessageBox.Show` method—displays a Message Box

method—a Sub procedure or function that is a member of a class; performs some operation on the data stored in the class

millisecond—1/1000 of a second

Minimum property—a scroll bar or track bar property that holds the control's minimum value

mnemonic—a key that you press in combination with the Alt key to access a control such as a button quickly; also called an *access key*

`mnu`—standard prefix for menu controls

modal form—when a modal form displayed, no other form in the application can receive the focus until the modal form is closed; no other statements in the procedure that displayed the modal form will execute until the modal form is closed

modeless form—Allows the user to switch focus to another form while it is displayed; statements that follow the modeless `Show` method call will continue to execute after the modeless form is displayed. Visual Basic will not wait until the modeless form is closed to execute these statements.

modularize—to break an application's code into small, manageable procedures

module-level variable—a variable declared inside a module, but not inside a Sub procedure or function

module scope—the scope of a module-level variable declared with the `Dim` keyword or the `Private` access specifier

Multiline property—a TextBox control property that, when set to *True*, allows the text box's text to span multiple lines

`MyBase` keyword—refers to a derived class's base class

Name property—a property that holds the control's name; controls are accessed and manipulated in code by their names

named constant—like a variable whose content is *read-only* and cannot be changed by a programming statement while the program is running

naming conventions—guidelines based on recommendations of professional designers, programmers, and educators narrowing conversion—if you assign a real number to an integer variable, Visual Basic attempts to perform this conversion, which sometimes results in lost data

nested `If` statement—an `If` statement in the conditionally executed code of another `If` statement

nested loop—a loop inside another loop

New Project dialog box—used to indicate the type of application you are starting

newline character—an invisible character that separates text by breaking it into another line when displayed on the screen

`Not` operator—a logical operator that reverses the *truth* of an expression; it makes a true expression false and a false expression true

object—a programming element that contains data and actions

object box—a drop-down list of the objects in the project that appears in the *Properties* window

Object Browser—a dialog box that allows you to browse the many classes and components available to your project

`Object` class—all classes are derived from the built-in `Object` class

object variable—a variable that holds the memory address of an object and allows you to work with the object

object-oriented analysis—during object-oriented design, the process of analyzing application requirements

object-oriented programming (OOP)—a programming technique centered on creating objects; a way of designing and coding applications that has led to using interchangeable software components

one-to-many relationship—when connecting two database tables indicates multiple occurrences of a foreign key

Open dialog box—gives users the capability of browsing their disks for a file to open, instead of typing a long path and filename

OpenFileDialog control—displays an *Open* dialog box

operands—pieces of data, such as numbers, on which operators perform operations

operating system (OS)—a set of programs that manages the computer's hardware devices and controls their processes

operations—actions performed by class objects

operators—perform operations on one or more operands

Options dialog box—accessed from the *Tools* menu; allows you to set various options in the Visual Basic environment

Option Strict—in Visual Basic, a configuration option that determines whether certain implicit conversions are legal

`ORDER BY` clause—In SQL, lets you control the display order of the table rows

`OrElse` operator—uses short-circuit evaluation in compound expressions

`Or` operator—combines two expressions into one; one or both expressions must be true for the overall expression to be true (it is only necessary for one to be true, and it does not matter which one)

output—data a computer sends to the outside world

output device—a device that formats and presents output information

output file—a file into which a program writes data

Output window—displays various messages while an application is being compiled; you may write your own messages with the `Debug.WriteLine` method

`Overridable` keyword—in a procedure declaration, indicates that the procedure may be overridden in a derived class

override—to override a property or method in a base class means to create one of the same name in a derived class; when an object of the derived class accesses the property or procedure, it accesses the one in the derived class instead of the one in the base class

`Overrides` keyword—in a procedure declaration, indicates that the procedure overrides a procedure in the base class

parallel arrays—two or more arrays that hold related data; the related elements in each array are accessed with a common subscript

parameter—a special variable that receives an argument being passed into a method, Sub procedure, or function

Pascal casing—a style of mixing uppercase and lowercase characters in procedure, method, and class names; the first character in the name and the first character of each subsequent word in the name are capitalized and all other characters are lowercase

`Peek` method—a `StreamReader` method that looks ahead in the file, without moving the current read position, and returns the next character that will be read; returns –1 when it reaches the end of the file

PHP—popular server-side scripting language used for many Web applications; major competitor of ASP.NET

PictureBox—displays a graphic image

PictureBox control—a control that can be used to display a graphic image

platform—Operating system + computer hardware; creates a complete environment under which programs can run. May also mean a virtual machine such as JVM (Java Virtual Machine) or CLR (Common Language Runtime).

`Pmt` function—returns the periodic payment amount for a loan

postback—when a Web page is sent back to the Web server for more processing

posttest loop—evaluates its test-expression after each iteration

`PPmt` function—returns the principal payment for a specific period on a loan

precedence—a ranking system that determines which operator works first in an expression where two operators share an operand pretest loop—evaluates its test-expression before each iteration

primary key—a field, or the combination of multiple fields, that uniquely identify each row in a database table

`Print` method—a method of the PrintDocument control that triggers a `PrintPage` event

PrintDocument control—gives an application the ability to print output on a printer

`PrintPage` event procedure (handler)—a PrintDocument control event procedure in which you write code that sends printed output to the printer

`Private` keyword—used to explicitly declare class-level variables private, making the source code more self-documenting

procedural programming—a programming technique centered on creating procedures

procedure—a set of programming language statements that are executed by the computer

procedure call—a statement that calls, or executes, a procedure

program—a sequence of instructions stored in the computer's memory; the instructions enable the computer to solve a problem or perform a task

program code—generally, statements inside methods

program logic—program source code, written in languages such as Visual Basic and C#; in ASP.NET, the program logic is stored in the codebehind file

programmer-defined names—words or names defined by the programmer

programming languages—languages that use words instead of numbers to program the computer

project—a group of files that make up a Visual Basic application

project file—a file ending with the .vbproj extension that contains data describing the Visual Basic project

`Prompt`—a string displayed, typically on a Form or in an Input Box, requesting the user to enter a value

properties—in Visual Basic, an object's attributes

Properties window—shows and allows you to change most of the currently selected object's properties, and those properties' values

property procedure—a function that is a member of a class, and behaves like a property

`Protected` access specifier—Protected base class members are like private members, except they may be accessed by methods and property procedures in derived classes. To all other code, however, protected class members are just like private class members.

protocol—in a URL, the designation http://, https://, or ftp://

prototype—a demonstration copy of a program

pseudocode—statements that are a cross between human language and a programming language

`Public` keyword—used in the declaration of a module level variable or procedure, which makes it available to statements outside the module

queries—SQL statements that retrieve and/or manipulate data in a database

query parameter—when a query contains more than one parameter, these required values are passed as arguments when calling the `Fill` method

RadioButton—a round button that is either selected or deselected when clicked with the mouse

RadioButton control—usually appears in groups and allows the user to select one of several possible options

RadioButtonList control—Web control that displays a grouped list of radio buttons

RadioChecked property—a MenuItem object property that may be set to *True* or *False*; when set to *True* for a checked menu item, the item appears with a radio button instead of a check mark

random access file—a file whose records may be accessed in any order

random-access memory (RAM)—*see* main memory

`Random` class—provides methods and properties that make generating random numbers fairly easy

`Random.Next`— a method that returns the next integer in the series

`Random.NextDouble`—method that returns a random floating point number between 0.0 and 1.0 (not including 1.0)

`Read` method—a `StreamReader` method that reads the next character from a file

read position—the position of the next item to be read from a file

`ReadLine` method—a `StreamReader` method that reads a line of data from a file

Read-only property—a property whose value may be read, but may not be set by a client program

`ReadToEnd` method—a `StreamReader` method that reads and returns the entire contents of a file, beginning at the current read position

record—a complete set of data about a single item, consisting of one or more fields

relation—a link or relationship that relies on a common field value to join rows from two different tables

relational expression—uses a relational operator to compare values

relational model—in databases; relations exist between tables

relational operator—determines if a specific relationship, such as less than or greater than, exists between two values

remarks—also known as comments; notes of explanation that document lines or sections in a method

`Remove` method—a collection method that removes a member

repetition structure—*see* loop

report body—the part of a report that contains the report's data, and is often formatted in columns

report footer—an optional part of a report that contains the sum of one or more columns of data report header—the part of a report that is printed first and usually contains the name of the report, the date and time the report was printed, and other general information about the data in the report

`Response.Redirect` method—transfers control from the current Web form to another Web page or URL on the Internet

`Rnd` function—generates a single precision random number in the range of 0.0 to 1.0

row—*see* record

Run mode—the runtime mode in which you run and test an application

running total—a sum of numbers that accumulates with each iteration of a loop

runtime errors—mistakes that do not prevent an application from executing, but cause it to produce incorrect results

Save As dialog box—gives users the capability of browsing their disks for a location to save a file to, as well as specifying a file's name

SaveFileDialog control—displays a standard Windows *Save As* dialog box

SaveFileDialog property—displays a *Save As* dialog box

scope—the part of the program where the variable is visible, and may be accessed by programming statements

Search button—a button on the *Dynamic Help* window that allows you to search for help topics using keywords

secondary storage—a device, such as a disk drive, that can hold information for long periods of time

seed value—a value used to determine the sequence of random numbers generated by the `Rnd` function

`SelectAll` method—can be used in code to automatically select the text in the text box

`Select Case` statement—a statement in which one of several possible actions is taken, depending on the value of an expression

`Select` statement—the SQL statement used to find records within a database table

SelectedIndex property—holds the index of the selected item in a list box or combo box

SelectedItem property—holds the currently selected item of a list box or combo box

separator bar—a horizontal bar used to separate groups of commands on a menu

sequence structure—a code structure where the statements are executed in sequence, without branching off in another direction

sequential access file—a file whose contents must be read from beginning to end

sequential search—an algorithm that uses a loop to search for a value in an array; it examines the elements in the array, one after the other, starting with the first one

server—entity that produces data consumed by a client

`Set` section—in a property procedure; executes when a client program sets the property to a value

short-circuit evaluation—allows you to skirt the `CheckValue` function; it is the default in languages such as C#, C++, and Java

shortcut key—a key or combination of keys that cause a menu command to execute

ShortcutKeys property—a ToolStripMenuItem object property used to select a shortcut key

`ShowDialog` method—displays a modal form and causes it to receive the focus

`Show` method—displays a modeless form and causes it to receive the focus

ShowShortcut property—a ToolStripMenuItem object property; values may be *True* or *False*; when *True*, the menu item's shortcut key (selected with the ShortcutKeys property) is displayed, when *False*, the shortcut key is not displayed

single dimension array—an array with one subscript, which is useful for storing and working with a single set of data

single-step—a debugging technique where you execute an application's programming statements one at a time; after each statement executes you can examine variable and property contents, which allows you to identify code causing a logic error

SizeMode property—a PictureBox property that determines how the control will position and scale its graphic image

sizing handles—small boxes that appear around a control when it is selected during design mode; used to enlarge or shrink the control

SmallChange property—a scroll bar or track bar property that holds the amount by which the Value property changes when the user clicks one of the scroll arrows at either end of a scroll bar; track bars also respond to the arrow keys, which cause the Value property to change by this amount

software—programs that run on a computer

Solution—a container for holding Visual Basic projects

Solution Explorer window—allows quick navigation among the files in the application

solution file—a file that ends with the .sln extension and contains data describing a solution

splash screen—a form that is displayed while an application is loading

SQL—*see* Structured Query Language

standard module—a file that contains variable declarations, procedures, and functions

standard toolbar—situated below the menu bar; contains buttons that execute frequently used commands

startup object—the object that is initially displayed or executed when an application executes; it may be a form or a Sub procedure named `Main` in a standard module

`Static`—keyword used to declare static local variables

static local variable—variables that are not destroyed when a Sub procedure or function returns; they exist for the lifetime of the application, even though their scope is only the Sub procedure or function in which they are declared and they retain their values between procedure calls

static text—ordinary text typed directly onto a Web form in Design mode

Step Into command—a debugging command that allows you to execute a single programming statement (*see* single-step); if the statement contains a call to a procedure or function, the next execution point that will be displayed is the first line of code in that procedure or function

Step Out command—a debugging command executed while the application is in Break mode; it causes the remainder of the current procedure or function to complete execution without single stepping; after the procedure or function has completed, the line following the procedure or function call is highlighted, and single-stepping may resume

Step Over command—a debugging command executed while the application is in Break mode; it causes the currently highlighted line to execute; if the line contains a procedure or function call, however, the procedure or function is executed and there is no opportunity to single-step through its statements; the entire procedure or function is executed, and the next line in the current procedure is highlighted

step value—the value added to the counter variable at the end of each iteration of a `For...Next` loop

`StreamReader` class—a class that provides methods for reading data to sequential files

`StreamReader` object—an instance of the `Streamreader` class; used to read data to sequential files

`StreamWriter` class—a class that provides methods for writing data to sequential files

`StreamWriter` object—an instance of the `StreamWriter` class, used to write data to sequential files

string concatenation—when one string is appended to another

string literal—a group of characters inside quotation marks

structure—a data type created by the programmer that contains one or more variables, which are known as members

`Structure` statement—used to create a structure

Structured Query Language (SQL)—the standard database language for data storage, retrieval, and (SQL) manipulation

`Sub`—a keyword that precedes the name of a procedure

Sub procedure—a collection of statements that performs a specific task and does not return a value

Sub procedure declaration—the code for declaring a Sub procedure

subscript—a number that identifies a specific element within an array; also known as an index

`Substring` method—returns a substring, or a string within a string

syntax—rules that must be followed when constructing a method; dictate how keywords, operators, and programmer-defined names may be used

syntax error—the incorrect use of a programming language element, such as a keyword, operator, or programmer-defined word

`System.IO.File.AppendText`—a method that opens a text file for data to be written to it; if the file method already exists, data is appended to its current contents

`System.IO.File.CreateText`—a method that opens a text file for data to be written to it; if the file does not exist, it is created

`System.IO.File.Exists`—a method that returns `True` if the specified file exists, or `False` if it does not

`System.IO.File.OpenText`—a method that opens a text file for reading

tab order—the order in which controls receive the focus

tab order selection mode—establishes a tab order when you click controls in the desired sequence

TabIndex property—contains a numeric value, which indicates the control's position in the tab order

table—holds data in a database; organized in rows and columns

table adapter—pulls data from one or more database tables and passes it to the program

TabStop property—when set to *True*, causes a control to be skipped in the tab order

TextAlign property—a property that aligns text within a control

TextBox—a rectangular area on a form in which the user can enter text, or the program can display text

TextBox control—allows you to capture input that the user has typed on the keyboard

text file—contains plain text and may be opened in a text editor

Text property—in Visual Basic, stores the value that becomes the text in a control

TickFrequency property—a TrackBar control property that holds the number of units between the tick marks on the control

Timer control—allows an application to automatically execute code at regular time intervals

Title property—a property of the OpenFileDialog and SaveFileDialog controls used to set the string displayed in the *Open* and *Save As* dialog box title bars

`ToLower` method—a string method that returns a lowercase version of a string

Toolbar, layout—contains buttons for formatting the layout of controls on a form

Toolbar, standard—contains buttons that execute frequently used commands

Toolbox window—contains buttons, or tools, for Visual Basic controls

ToolTip—a small box that pops up when you hover the mouse over a button on the Toolbar on in the

Toolbox; it contains a short description of the button's purpose

ToolTip control—a control that allows you to create ToolTips for the other controls on a form

TopMost property—a form property that, when set to *True*, causes the form to be displayed on top of all the other forms currently displayed

`ToString` method—a method that returns the string representation of a variable

`ToUpper` method—a string method that returns an uppercase version of a string

TrackBar control—used to create a track bar

trailing space—a space that appears at the end of a string

`Trim` method—returns a copy of the string without leading or trailing spaces

`TrimEnd` method—returns a copy of the string without trailing spaces

`TrimStart` method—returns a copy of the string without leading spaces

`Try-Catch` block—a construct used for handling exceptions

twip—1/1440th of an inch; twips are used as a measurement for positioning input boxes on the screen

two-dimensional array—an array of arrays; can be used to hold multiple sets of values

type conversion error—a runtime error that is generated when a nonnumeric value that cannot be automatically converted to a numeric value is assigned to a numeric variable or property

type mismatch error—*see* type conversion error

Unicode—A set of numeric codes that represent all the letters of the alphabet (both lowercase and uppercase), the printable digits 0 through 9, punctuation symbols, and special characters. The Unicode system is extensive enough to encompass all the world's alphabets.

unhandled exception—a way of expressing a runtime error; we say that an exception was thrown and the exception was not handled

URL (Uniform Resource Locator)—universal way of addressing objects and pages on a network

`Validated` event—triggered after the Validating event is triggered and the focus has shifted to another control

`Validating` event—before the focus shifts from Control A to Control B, and Control B's CausesValidation property is set to *True*, Control A's Validating event will fire

Value property—a scroll bar or track bar property that holds the control's current value

variable—a storage location in the computer's memory, used for holding information while the program is running

variable array—a group of variables with a single name

variable declaration—a statement that causes Visual Basic to create a variable in memory

variable scope—the area of a program in which a variable is visible

vertical scroll bar—a vertical slider bar that, when moved with the mouse, increases or decreases a value

Visible property—a Boolean property that causes a control to be visible on the form when set to *True*, or hidden when set to *False*

Visual Web Developer Express—Microsoft product that simplifies the way you develop Web applications

VScrollBar control—used to create a vertical scroll bar

Watch window—a debugging window that allows you to add the names of variables that you want to watch; displays only the variables that you have added

Web applications—applications that run on a network (including the Internet) that use Web browsers as clients

Web.config file—used by ASP.NET applications to save configuration information; we used it to store a debugging option, for example

Web form—a Web page that contains text, HTML tags, HTML controls, and Web server controls

Web server —the program running on a host Web site that processes requests from end users running Web browsers

Web server controls—same as Web forms controls—type of interactive controls used on Web forms that must be decoded and processed by a Web server; generate runtime events such as `Click`, `SelectedIndexChanged`, and `TextChanged`

`WHERE` clause—in SQL, used to filter, or select zero or more rows retrieved from a database table

widening conversion—a conversion in which no data is lost

wildcard—a symbol that matches unknown characters

`With` block—a set of statements enclosed in a `With...End With` statement

`With...End With` statement—allows you to create a `With` block; statements inside a `With` block may perform several operations on the same object without specifying the name of the object each time

wizard—software tool that guides you through the process of linking a control to a database

WordWrap property—a TextBox control property that causes the contents of a multiline text box to word wrap

`Write` method—a `StreamWriter` method that writes data to a file

`WriteLine` method—a `StreamWriter` method used to write a line of data to a file

`Xor` operator—Combines two expressions into one. One expression (not both) must be true for the overall expression to be true. If both expressions are true, or both expressions are false, the overall expression is false.

Index

Symbols

A

B